Readings for Diversity and Social Justice

Second Edition

Readings for Diversity and Social Justice

Second Edition

Edited by

Maurianne Adams, Warren J. Blumenfeld,
Carmelita (Rosie) Castañeda,
Heather W. Hackman, Madeline L. Peters,
and Ximena Zúñiga

Routledge
Taylor & Francis Group

NEW YORK AND LONDON

First edition published 2000 by Routledge
711 Third Avenue, New York, NY 10017

This edition published 2010 by Routledge

711 Third Avenue, New York, NY 10017

Simultaneously published in the UK by Routledge
2 Park Square, Milton Park, Abingdon, Oxon OX14 4RN

Routledge is an imprint of the Taylor & Francis Group, an informa business

© 2000 Routledge

© 2010 Routledge, Taylor and Francis

Typeset in by Sabon and Swiss by Prepress Projects Ltd, Perth, UK

Library of Congress Cataloging in Publication Data

Readings in diversity and social justice / edited by Maurianne Adams...[et al.]. — 2nd ed.
p. cm.
1. Prejudices—United States. 2. Racism—United States. 3. Minorities—United States. 4. Social justice—United States. 5. United States—Race relations. 6. United States—Ethnic relations. I. Adams, Maurianne.
E184.A1R386 2010
305.800973—dc22
2009041584

ISBN 10: 0–415–99139–0 (hbk)
ISBN 10: 0–415–99140–4 (pbk)
ISBN 13: 978–0–415–99139–1 (hbk)
ISBN 13: 978–0–415–99140–7 (pbk)

Contents

Context

Voices

Next Steps

SECTION 10 WORKING FOR SOCIAL JUSTICE: VISIONS AND STRATEGIES FOR CHANGE 587

Context

Table of Intersections

The tables on the following pages will enable readers to see at a glance the multiple issues that are taken up in each one of the selections. This Table of Intersections follows the sequence of the Table of Contents, but it is laid out to show the multiple interconnections discussed in each of the selections. Column indicators are as follows:

R	Racism
Cl	Classism
RO	Religious Oppression
S	Sexism
H	Heterosexism
TG	Transgender Oppression
Ab	Ableism
A&A	Ageism and Adultism
Global Issues	discussion of issues outside of US borders
Language Issues	Non-English or English as second language speakers, or use of American Sign Language rather than vocal speech

Selection number	Author and title	R	CI	RO	S	H	TG	Ab	A&A	Global Issues	Language Issues
	NEXT STEPS										
22	Arminio, "Waking up white"										
23	Ayvazian and Tatum, "Women, race and racism"			X	X	X					
24	Castañeda, "FLEXing cross-cultural communication"										
25	Smith, "The personal is political"		X		X	X				X	
	CLASSISM										
	CONTEXT										
26	Mantsios, "Class in America—2006"	X			X						
27	Collins and Yeskel, "The dangerous consequences of growing inequality"	X									
28	Oliver and Shapiro, "Race, wealth, and equality"	X									
29	Williams, "What has debt got to do with it?"	X									
30	Schmidt, "At the elite colleges"	X									
31	Garcia, Lardner, and Zeldin, "The debt-for-diploma system"										
32	Wolanin, "Students with disabilities: Financial aid . . ."	X									
33	Landesman, "The girls next door"	X			X				X	X	X
34	Dyson, "Unnatural disasters: Race and poverty"	X									
35	Bauer, "Migrant tomato workers face chronic abuse"	X			X				X	X	X
	VOICES										
36	Romero, "Bonds of sisterhood—Bonds of oppression"	X			X						
37	hooks, "White poverty . . . invisibility"	X			X						
38	"Saint," "Why can't everybody fear me like that?"	X							X		
39	Pittleman and Resource Generation, "Classified"	X			X					X	
40	Morgenson, "The debt trap"				X			X			
	NEXT STEPS										
41	Leondar-Wright, "Classism from our mouths" and "Tips from working-class activists"	X			X					X	
42	Pittelman and Resource Generation, "Deep thoughts about class privilege"										

Selection number	Author and title	R	CI	RO	S	H	TG	Ab	A&A	Global Issues	Language Issues
43	Giecek, "Distributing income"							X			
	RELIGIOUS OPPRESSION										
	CONTEXT										
44	Lippy, "Christian nation or pluralistic culture"	X								X	
45	Eck, "Afraid of ourselves" and "Working it out"	X			X					X	
46	Schlosser, "Christian privilege: Breaking a sacred taboo"	X									
47	Blumenfeld, "Christian privilege . . . in public schooling"	X									
48	Joshi, "Religious oppression"	X									
49	Hilberg, "Precedents"	X									
50	Gilbert, "Maps—History of anti-Semitism"	X								X	
51	Eck, "See you in court"	X									
52	Echo-Hawk, "Native American religious liberty"	X									
53	Grinde, "Taking the Indian out of the Indian"	X									
54	Willams, "From Pearl Harbor to 9/11"	X								X	
55	Semple, "A Somali influx unsettles Latino meatpackers"	X	X							X	
	VOICES										
56	Kaye/Kantrowitz, "Jews in the US"	X	X		X	X				X	
57	Ahmad, "Oral history of Adam Fattah"	X			X						X
	Zawam, "Oral history of Hagar Omran"	X			X						
	NEXT STEPS										
58	Nasir and Al-Amin, "Creating identity-safe spaces on college campuses for Muslim students"	X			X						
59	Jeung, "Faith-based multiethnic tenant organizing"	X	X							X	
60	Bernards, "Pioneers in dialogue"	X			X					X	
	SEXISM										
	CONTEXT										
61	Lorber, "Social construction of gender"				X	X	X				
62	Kimmel, "Masculinity as homophobia"				X	X	X				

Selection number	Author and title	R	CI	RO	S	H	TG	Ab	A&A	Global Issues	Language Issues
63	Johnson, "Patriarchy"	X									
64	hooks, "Feminism"	X									
65	Katz, "Violence against women is a men's issue"					X					
66	Heldman, "Out of body image"		X					X			
67	Bernstein, "Women's pay"		X								X
	VOICES										
68	Chernik, "The body politic"							X			
69	Morgan, "Connect: A web of words"		X								
70	Kirk and Okazawa-Rey, "He works, she works"		X								X
71	Fennell, "Girl hate"		X						X		
	NEXT STEPS										
72	Gorski, "The evolution of a pro-feminist"		X						X		
73	Walker, "To stop the violence against women"	X									X
74	National Latina Institute for Reproductive Health, "Statement on healthcare for all"	X								X	
75	Hurdis, "Heartbroken: Women of color feminism"	X	X								
76	Russo and Spatz, "Stop the false race/gender divide"	X	X								
77	LaDuke, "Grassroots: Introduction"	X									
HETEROSEXISM											
	CONTEXT										
78	Blumenfeld, "How homophobia hurts everyone"	X									
79	Deihl and Ochs, "Biphobia"										
80	Gokhale, "The interSEXion: A vision for a queer progressive agenda"	X	X		X		X				
81	Carbado, "Privilege"	X									
82	Griffin, "Sport: Where men are men and women are trespassers"				X		X				
	VOICES										
83	Quindlen, "The Loving decision"	X									
84	Goodman, "Taking the gay insults personally"										

Selection number	Author and title	R	CI	RO	S	H	TG	Ab	A&A	Global Issues	Language Issues
85	Solis y Martinez, "*Mestiza/o* gender"	X			X		X				
	NEXT STEPS										
86	Evans and Washington, "Becoming an ally"	X			X		X				
	TRANSGENDER OPPRESSION										
	CONTEXT										
87	Meyerowitz, "Introduction: How sex changed"	X			X	X					
88	Stryker, "Transgender liberation"	X	X								
89	Spade, "Mutilating gender"		X		X			X	X		
90	Serano, "Trans woman manifesto"				X						
91	Broadus, "The evolution of employment discrimination protections . . ."	X	X		X						
	VOICES										
92	Lie, "Passing realities"										
93	Green, "Look! No, don't! The invisibility dilemma . . ."				X						
94	Bowen, "An entire rainbow of possibilities"	X				X					
	NEXT STEPS										
95	Chess, Kafer, Quizar, and Richardson, "Calling all restroom revolutionaries!"				X			X			
	ABLEISM										
	CONTEXT										
96	Bryan, "Struggle for freedom"	X			X						
97	Cerney, "Historical and cultural influence in deaf education"										X
98	Pliner and Johnson, "Historical, theoretical and foundational principles of UID in higher education"										
99	Wendell, "The social construction of disability"		X		X				X		
100	Davis, "Go to the margins of the class: Disability and hate crimes"	X	X		X	X					
101	Colligan, "Why the intersexed shouldn't be fixed"		X		X	X			X		
102	Grossman, "Mass psychiatric casualties"										

Selection number	Author and title	R	CI	RO	S	H	TG	Ab	A&A	Global Issues	Language Issues
103	Null, "The Gulf War's troubling legacy"										
	VOICES										
104	Erevilles, "Disability in the New World Order"	X	X		X				X	X	
105	Clare, "Gawking, gaping, staring"	X			X	X	X				
106	Jones, "As much love as you can muster"								X		
107	Ashley and Deborah, "How to curse in sign language"			X					X		
108	Kingsley, "What I'd tell that doctor"								X		
109	Pelkey, "In the LD bubble"					X			X		
	NEXT STEPS										
110	Hehir, "Toward ending ableism in education"	X									
111	Oesterreich and Knight, "Facilitating transitions to college for students from culturally, linguistically diverse backgrounds"	X	X							X	X
112	Howland and Gibavic, "Learning disability identity development and social construct"	X			X						
113	The Invisible Disabilities Advocate, "Creating a fragrance-free zone"										
114	Peters, Castañeda, Hopkins, and McCants, "Recognizing ableist beliefs and practices and taking action as an ally"		X								
	AGEISM AND ADULTISM										
	CONTEXT										
115	Bell, "Understanding adultism"	X									
116	Dohrn, "'Look out kid, it's something you did'"	X	X								
117	Durkin, "Police make life hell for youth of color"	X	X								
118	Butler, "Ageism: Another form of bigotry"										
119	Sheets, "Ageing with disabilities: Ageism and more"							X			
120	Center on Aging Studies, University of Missouri—Kansas City, "Black elderly"	X									
	VOICES										
121	Huber, "There is nothing wrong with you: For teens"										
122	Larabee, "Elders' liberation draft policy"										

Selection number	Author and title	R	CI	RO	S	H	TG	Ab	A&A	Global Issues	Language Issues
123	Curry, "People of color over fifty"	X									
	NEXT STEPS										
124	Kivel, "Adultism"	X			X	X					
125	Sazama, "Allies to young people: Tips and guidelines"										
126	Holmes, "Hidden in plain sight"										
127	Markee, "What allies of elders can do"										

WORKING FOR SOCIAL JUSTICE: VISIONS AND STRATEGIES FOR CHANGE

Selection number	Author and title	R	CI	RO	S	H	TG	Ab	A&A	Global Issues	Language Issues
	CONTEXT										
128	Pharr, "Reflection on liberation"	X	X		X	X		X	X		
129	Love, "Developing a liberatory consciousness"	X	X		X				X		
130	Collins, "Toward a new vision: Race, class, and gender"	X	X		X	X		X			
131	Johnson, "What can we do?"	X	X		X	X		X			
	VOICES										
132	Peltier, "Prison writing"	X	X								
133	Anzaldúa, "Allies"	X	X		X	X				X	X
	NEXT STEPS										
134	Smith, "Social struggle"	X	X		X	X				X	
135	Ayvazian, "Interrupting the cycle of oppression"	X	X	X	X						
136	Zúñiga, "Bridging differences through intergroup dialogue"	X			X						
137	Martinez, "Unite and rebel! . . . Building alliances"	X	X	X	X	X		X		X	
138	McClellan and Rizga, "Top 10 youth activism victories"	X	X		X				X	X	

Acknowledgements

The editing team for this volume brings together multiple perspectives on the social justice topics presented in this book—we are male, female, transgender, and gender-queer; gay, lesbian, bisexual, heterosexual, and queer; African American, Latino/a, South Asian, and White; Jewish, Hindu, and Christian; foreign-born, immigrant, and U.S.-born. Some of us have learning disabilities and physical disabilities; are young adults, middle-aged, and elders; were born poor, working class, and middle class; use English as a first language and English as a second language. Our academic specializations include ableism, ageism and adultism, anti-semitism, classism, heterosexism, racism, religious oppression, sexism, and transgender oppression. We include college faculty, current doctoral students, community activists, and Social Justice Education alums who have, cumulatively among the thirteen of us, many decades of experience teaching undergraduate, graduate, professional development and community courses, seminars, and workshops on all of these social justice issues, both as single issues and as intersecting identities.

We have worked together as a collaborative editorial team, valuing the different gifts and perspectives each one of us brings to this work, and moving from dialogue to consensus on the overall scope, organization, and content of this volume. We continue to struggle, as a collegial writing team, with the tendency of libraries, reviewers, and scholars who cite our work to name the first author only. This practice inhibits collaborative work in academe, which metes out rewards to those authors most cited, who are often presumed to be senior or primary. How can we represent the collaborative efforts of a writing team, the synergistic emergence of ideas and sharing of resources, when any line of names, however arranged, suggests a ranking order? The possibility of linking our names in a circle, while intriguing and eye-catching, is perhaps too challenging for typesetters and production teams. We regret that we have not yet found a manageable alternative to the convention of alphabetical order in listing editors and contributors, an ordering that affirms equity if only because it is "merely" alphabetical. As a step in the direction we want to move, however, we place a statement at the beginning of each multiply authored section that honors the nature and value of our collaborative work with a request that people who cite us include the full names of *all* listed authors. We have followed our own preferred practice by including *all* names listed in the works we cite within our sections.

Although working as a collaborative editorial team, we have at the same time delegated specific areas of primary section responsibility. The editors who are named in the Table of Contents and on each section introduction title page have primary responsibility for selecting section content, writing section introductions, and developing section websites, based upon each of our primary areas of knowledge and experience. Decisions and agreement were not always easy—especially as we communicated by email, telephone conference calls, computer-supported conferences, and videoconferences—but this process has only increased our mutual respect and appreciation for the knowledge and insight, the dedication, energy, and goodwill that each of us has brought to this project. For all of us as coeditors, the time and attention we devoted to the process of coordinating our perspectives has been indispensable to the integrity of this volume.

It is especially important for us to acknowledge the contributions of our many generous, knowledgeable, and supportive colleagues, families, friends, and students. We have drawn upon suggestions made by Social Justice Education course instructors and colleagues at the University of Massachusetts, Amherst—Elaine Brigham, Mirangela Buggs, Jen Daigle-Matos, Michael Funk, Eric Hamako, Larissa Hopkins, Molly Keehn, Taj Smith, Rani Varghese, Teeomm Williams, all doctoral students in SJE who teach undergraduate courses dealing with social justice—and feedback from valued colleagues in our home and professional communities, friends, and family, who suggested references, provided logistical support, and encouraged our demanding work during these past two years: Lisa Albrecht, John and Kedhar Bartlett, Micah Bazant, Beth Berila, Kathleen DeVore, Linnea Edstrom, Hanna Eslinger, Diane Fedorchak, Jenifer Fennell, Christopher Hamilton, John A. Hunt, Angela Ibraham, Valerie Jiggetts, Joanna Kent Katz, Michael W. Krupp, Miles Leach, Brenda Lindgren, Betty and David Love, Christopher MacDonald-Dennis, Karen MacGregor, Aquila Ayana McCants, Jane Mildred, Lisa Miller, Susan Raffo, K. Ravishankar, Francesca Rheannon, Shelley Roberts, Taj Smith, Jacoba, Jasmine, and Nico Stauffer, Alina Torres-Zickler, and Riki Wilchins. When you see your names, all of you will understand how much we value and appreciate your many and different generosities and contributions.

We thank Elaine Whitlock for her infinite patience with us as we changed and changed again our minds (and selections) during the past many months. We especially appreciate her resourceful, flexible, and tireless ingenuity in gaining permissions and providing valuable editorial support. And, as we had ten years ago, we once again thank Mary McClintock for her enormous skill, in this instance taking on and solving several especially challenging permission chases.

Ten years ago we were together in Amherst, Massachusetts, preparing the first edition of this book of readings in Maurianne's living room. But this time around we are far-flung, relying for communication on teleconference and videoconference from various points in California, Iowa, Massachusetts, Minnesota, New York, Wyoming, and Santiago, Chile. We thank Christopher Golas, Jeremy Kellem, James Pesta, and Reuben Wagenius for easing our virtual face-to-face conversations and feedback across these enormous distances. We felt as if we were still in the same room—well, almost.

We consider ourselves tremendously fortunate to have worked closely with Catherine Bernard, our editor at Routledge, and her gracious, expert team, Heather Jarrow and Georgette Enriquez. This new edition has benefited immeasurably from Catherine's unwavering commitment, her support and enthusiasm for this project, her careful reading of many iterations of the text, her knowledge of the literature of social justice, her expert and helpful judgment calls on numerous challenges of substance and logistics in preparing this volume, and her tactful but firm guidance in helping us make hard choices.

We appreciate and acknowledge the many ways in which our long-time Social Justice Education colleagues Pat Griffin, Rita Hardiman, Bailey Jackson, Linda Marchesani, Matt Ouellett, Leah Wing, Felice Yeskel—together with generations of social diversity and Social Justice Education course instructors and workshop facilitators from the 1970s through to the present day—have enriched the vision of social justice education that underpins this volume, the range of readings, and each other's instructional practice in the growing community of Social Justice Education students and teachers.

We especially need to thank the many authors of pedagogical designs, activities and resources—some already published in the book text and CD-ROM for *Teaching for Diversity and Social Justice*, second edition—whose work we are drawing upon for this book's website.

Maurianne Adams, Lee Anne Bell,
Warren Blumenfeld, Rosie Castañeda,
Chase Catalano, Keri DeJong,
Heather Hackman, Larissa Hopkins,
Khyati Joshi, Barbara Love, Madeline Peters,
Davey Shlasko, Ximena Zúñiga

May 2009

Readings for Diversity and Social Justice

A General Introduction

OUR APPROACH TO TOPICS AND ISSUES OF SOCIAL JUSTICE

This second edition of *Readings for Diversity and Social Justice* reflects our shared approach to social justice education. This approach links theory with practice. It explores the binaries of privilege and disadvantage rooted in racism, sexism, classism, and other forms of systemic oppression, and notes their historical roots, intergenerational legacies, within-group differences, and local as well as global manifestations. We explore contemporary inequality, social hierarchy, and systemic oppression, and we also note examples of people taking action together for empowerment, equity, liberation, and sustained social change. We pay attention to the ways in which marginalized social groups contest their social inequality by renaming themselves and reframing oppressive binaries in equitable and empowering ways.

The selections in this volume thus offer building blocks for an appreciation of social and cultural differences, and also emphasize the ways in which these social and cultural differences have been used to justify systemic inequalities. *Difference* is generally understood as important in its own right, but it also often serves as the basis for *inequality* when those differences rationalize access to privilege for social groups associated with social "norms"—and when those norms are assumed to be available to everybody, but in practice are not available to marginalized or disadvantaged social groups. The overarching social system that maintains and reproduces these inequities is the system we call *oppression*, and throughout this volume we present different yet compatible explorations of these dynamics, whether focused on personal experience, or analysis of social institutions and the overarching social and cultural system.

Our approach to social difference, social identity, social location, and social inequity calls for appreciation of the multiple, complex, fluid, and cross-cutting aspects of social identities, and awareness that the inequities experienced by any and all disadvantaged groups warrant attention and remedy. The statement that "There is no hierarchy of oppressions" (Audre Lorde 1983) does not mean that different forms of oppression do not affect people in different ways, or vary in their intensity or virulence across different historical periods or various geographies, or that their duration and impact on whole populations does not differ. Despite this caveat, nonetheless, we take a "both/and" approach that acknowledges the obvious differences in experiences of oppression, and at the same time recognizes that all forms of oppression are harmful, that they interact with each other in the lives of individuals and groups in complex ways, and that a fair, equitable, and just society requires an end to all forms of oppression. It is not useful to argue competitive victim status or to ask who has suffered more or longer. It is far more useful to understand all of the dynamics of social oppression as they affect all of us, although in different ways and to different degrees. This point is made in various ways by authors throughout this volume.

DISTINCTIVE FEATURES OF THIS SECOND EDITION

This second edition of *Readings for Diversity and Social Justice* conveys changes that have taken place during the decade since the first edition—new approaches and complexities within our understanding of racism, sexism, or ableism, for example, and new writing on ageism and adultism, immigration, religious oppression, and transgender oppression. As in the first edition, this volume is organized in sections around specific issues of identity and oppression (such as sexuality and heterosexism, or disability and ableism) but it foregrounds the many intersections among these social group identities and their experiences of privilege and disadvantage. We pay attention to the privileges assumed by advantaged social groups but unavailable to disadvantaged social groups, and take the view that systemic oppression is characterized by unequal relationships between those who are privileged or advantaged by the social system and those who are targeted or disadvantaged. We offer instances of resistance to oppression, whether through individual action, coalition, or organized social movements to create lasting change. We root our work in the social movements of the late 1950s through '80s, and the social change and classroom pedagogies that emerged from those transformative movements

We have learned a great deal since the publication of our first edition of readings ten years ago. Our understanding of racism has become more nuanced and contextualized as we learn about the different histories and geographies of U.S. racism (as experienced by Native Americans, Africans, Mexicans, and peoples from throughout the Americas and Asia) and Anglo-based nativism toward immigrant European peoples (Irish, Italians, Jews). The current controversies concerning immigration have helped to reframe our discussions of historical and contemporary racism(s), ethnocentrism, and nationalism. Our analysis of class and classism has focused on global capitalism and global economic interconnectedness, as well as the links between classism and other social oppressions. Our increased attention to global religious oppressions has made it urgent that we focus on the experiences of marginalized, non-Christian communities of faith within the United States. Further, the global historical approach we have taken to anti-semitism within European Christianity led us to focus more clearly on the U.S. Christian domination experienced by Native peoples (outlawed religious practices, forced relocations, forced mission schooling), as well as Hindus, Muslims, Jews, atheists—all who are outside the hegemonic Protestant-Christian U.S. mainstream.

Recent writing on transgender oppression has complicated and enriched our understanding of gender, sexism, and heterosexism by stretching our understanding of the boundaries of gender and of the sex-based gender binaries, and by adding a new perspective on the ways that non-conforming human diversity has been medicalized. Explorations of ageism and adultism have reshaped our approach to all forms of oppression as experienced across the lifespan and suggest a living template for the intersectional experiences of multiple oppressions. We have gained new appreciation for the ways in which various forms of privilege or disadvantage—classed, raced, gendered—intersect and complicate each other in local as well as global settings and life experiences. These new understandings inform this second edition of *Readings for Diversity and Social Justice,* having already reshaped our approach to the second edition of *Teaching for Diversity and Social Justice* (2007).

Readers of our earlier work will be aware that we combine attention to the historically situated experiences of social identity groups with appreciation of the ways in which all peoples have been multiply raced, gendered, classed, able or disabled, with different age statuses. In this new edition, we have selected readings to maximize the interconnections between a "foreground" focus on the subjects of each section with a "background" of intersecting identities and forms of oppression. These intersections are highlighted in a Table of Intersections, located immediately following the more conventional Table of Contents. This Table of Intersections enables readers to identify all selections that treat issues of race, religion, gender, sexuality, disability, class, and age, beyond those in designated topic-based sections.

Not only has our approach to each social justice issue grown more intersectional and less unitary than ten years ago; we have also learned to take a more global, less U.S.-centric approach. The economy is global, as are issues of class and classism, and race, racism, immigration and language, youth and age. Given the multiple zigzag diasporas of peoples crossing oceans and moving across national boundaries, it is no longer useful (if it ever was) to think in terms of domestic as distinct from "foreign" international racial or ethnic identities, especially as communities of color in the United States and elsewhere frame their own racial, ethnic, national self-awareness on current and/or more distant racial, ethnic, national, or religious legacies. Examination of religious oppression in the United States, to offer another example, brings us face-to-face with peoples who may be first-generation U.S. citizens and also the progeny of intergenerational diasporas, so that in this case as well, domestic and international dimensions of religious difference or conflict cannot be neatly separated from each other, or distinguished from class-based or ethnic/race-based group conflicts. The internet creates instantaneous networks and propels social movements across thousands of miles.

We as section editors were faced with significant space constraints as we worked to create a manageable book covering eight distinct manifestations of oppression bookended by conceptual frameworks and steps toward liberation. We do not presume to be exhaustive either in the number of social justice topics we present, or in the depth of our inquiry into each of the social justice topics. We hope that the resources and further thoughts offered on the website will complement the reading selections for those readers seeking greater depth. Section editors worked together to coordinate their approaches to sexism, heterosexism, and transgender oppression, and to clarify the differences as well as the similarities in the experiences of gender role, gender, gender presentation, birth sex, sex presentation, sexual orientation, and transsexual, transgender, and queer identities. These three sections are more closely linked than other sections in the volume, although all editors have collaborated closely in selecting readings that maximize intersections—as with, for example, racism, classism, and religious oppression. The section on racism incorporates the different histories and legacies of racism(s) experienced by Native Americans, African Americans, Mexican Americans and Latinos/as from the diasporas within the Americas, and peoples from Asia, South Asia, and the Middle East. We note the distinctiveness in the experiences of racism by displaced, enslaved, or colonized peoples as well as some of the overarching patterns of similarity in their oppressions. The section on religious oppression brings together the marginalization of several different faith traditions—Hindus, Jews, Muslims, Native Americans—within U.S. Christian hegemony. Given the enormity of the questions taken up in these and other sections, there was no satisfactory way to maintain symmetry among equally pressing but distinctive social justice issues (in keeping with our belief that "There is no hierarchy of oppressions") while also representing and doing justice to the complexity and nuance within each of those "Isms." We use section websites to extend our discussions and provide further resources.

OUR USE OF TERMINOLOGY AND LANGUAGE

We capitalize but do not hyphenate specific ethnicities (African American, Asian American) and capitalize racial designations only when used as proper nouns (Blacks, Latinos/as,

Whites). We note that racial designations such as Black, Latino/a, Native American, Asian/ Pacific Islander, White are not really parallel terms, in that they conflate race, ethnicity, and pan-ethnicity from different historical and geographical legacies. When we move to discussions of global diaspora immigration, race-based or ethnic descriptors become even more problematic. Whenever possible, we use terms that refer to national/geographic origin (people of South Asian descent, for example). We also encourage the use of gender neutral pronouns (hir, ze) as a way of acknowledging identities that have been erased by gender binaries, as pronouns for people who state that they prefer those pronouns. The authors of each section of readings address other considerations of language usage as appropriate to the issues raised in their respective sections.

We want to notice how the terms used to describe the roles people play within the dynamics of oppression can be problematic. We propose terms that signal a focus, not on individual actors so much as on the structured roles and outcomes of an oppressive system. The binary terms "oppressor" and "oppressed," for example, do not reflect the intersections of privilege or disadvantage across different identities and different social locations or positions. We continue to struggle to frame language that doesn't trivialize the power or the damage from the oppressive system we want to expose. We use various terms to emphasize different dimensions of the binaries—terms such as privileged and targeted or marginalized, advantaged and disadvantaged, dominant and subordinate—to convey the relative positions of groups of people within a system of oppression based on social hierarchy. However, not all of the editors or authors of selected readings agree on the same terminology and readers will notice different terms in the section introductions and in reading selections. Our guiding principle is to adopt terms preferred by people from targeted groups who have named themselves "people of color" rather than "non-white"; "gay, lesbian, bisexual" rather than "homosexual"; "people with disabilities" rather than "handicapped." Some of the reading selections will also draw on language used by targeted communities to reclaim previously negative terms such as "queer," "crip," "girl," "tranny" that reframe slurs into terms of pride and ownership. We know that naming is a necessarily fluid and sometimes contradictory and confusing process as people/groups rightly insist on defining themselves rather than acquiescing to names imposed by others. We encourage people to recognize that such terms will continue to evolve and change and to appreciate the significance of the power to name oneself as an important aspect of group identity and resistance.

As already noted in the acknowledgements, we have also struggled over many years—and now in this new edition—to find ways to publicly reflect our own collaboration in a way that does not play into the dynamics of academic power and privilege fostered by the tendency of libraries, reviewers, booksellers, and scholars to cite multiply authored work by the first author "et al." We want to acknowledge our own collaborative work and encourage that of others in ways that do not play into the presumed seniority and power dynamics accorded the first name listed. We have searched for ways of naming all of the authors in our collaborative work in order to contest assumptions of greater or lesser professional power or relative status that follow from the listing of names. We are well aware that our strictly alphabetical approach is also unsatisfactory, in that any line of names, however arranged, suggests a ranking order—and we hope that alphabetizing our names levels the playing field and sends a clear message that we present ourselves and each other as having equivalent authority, expertise, and status. We also place a statement at the beginning of each section honoring the nature and value of our collaborative work with a request that people who cite us *always* include the full names of *all* authors named as responsible for a given section, a practice we also followed in *Teaching for Diversity and Social Justice* (second edition, 2007) where we used the following footnote: "We ask that those who cite this work always acknowledge by name all of the authors listed rather than either only citing the first author or using 'et al.' to indicate coauthors. All authors listed on a chapter collaborated equitably on the conceptualization, development, and writing of this chapter." We have followed our own preferred practice by including all names in the works we cite within our own section introductions and permissions citations. The importance we attach to this challenge to professional practice is clear from the fact that we have already made this point in the Acknowledgements, repeat it here in the General Introduction, and again in the footnotes to all of our multiply authored sections.

SUGGESTIONS ON HOW TO USE THIS BOOK

This volume gathers readings that reflect the new approaches to theory, history, and action that shape social justice education. In our own practice on our own campuses we link the readings in this volume with a social justice practice that is experiential, student-centered, interactive, dialogic, question-probing rather than answer-providing—an approach that is suggested on the website that accompanies this volume, but is more fully described and spelled out in our companion volume *Teaching for Diversity and Social Justice* (second edition, 2007).

Our approach to social diversity and oppression also shapes the overall organization into topical sections that focus on specific manifestations of oppression as experienced by specific social identity groups. We combine a section-by-section focus on specific topics of social diversity and oppression, yet we also call attention to the intersections among social identities and experiences of oppression. Each section introduction highlights these intersections, and the Table of Intersections identifies all of the selections according to topics wherever they may be located in the volume. We urge that all readers use all of the section introductions for key definitions, historical contexts, and current topics for each of the social justice topics, as well as an overview of the goals served by each section's read-ing selections. We encourage course instructors to assign these introductions along with selected readings. We urge readers to use the Table of Intersections to identify readings on topics of interest that may not appear in specific "Ism" sections.

Similarly, all of the sections coordinate examples of the social system that sustains oppres-sion with personal voices that attest to the everyday experience. Each topical section starts with Contexts that offer historical background and overviews of relevant issues, followed by personal descriptions or narratives in the Voices. The Next Steps sections emphasize the extraordinary efforts that individuals and groups of people have made, and continue to make, to challenge privilege and disadvantage in order to create social change. Thus each section concludes with selections that describe pathways for empowerment and change at the individual, institutional, and systemic levels. The many opportunities for change, envisioned in the Next Steps part of each section, lead to a final section on "Visions of Change," which serves as a bookend to the analyses of social diversity and oppression in the opening section "Conceptual Frameworks."

The selections in the final section, "Working for Social Justice: Visions and Strategies for Change," build on the ideas and actions described in the Next Steps part of each section. We want to encourage readers to be hopeful about the prospects of social change and to express that hope through individual and everyday actions, or through community, grassroots, or national coalitions and organizations, all of them smaller or larger steps toward positive social change. As educators, we believe that if we are to present infor-mation about systemic inequities, disadvantage, and oppression—and to expect that we become responsible for these inequities once we know about them—then as educators we must also present pathways of hope by acknowledging the role of social movements in U.S. history and the many contemporary opportunities to participate in social change.

A further innovation in this edition is the website, which provides additional resources, curricula and discussion questions, and ideas for action and application for each of the sections and suggests further avenues for exploring a number of related topics. The website is organized by section and each section website is organized by three subheaders: Further Resources (readings, internet links, films, and videos); Curriculum, Activities, Discussion Questions (materials and handouts to foster an interactive approach to course pedagogy); Action and Next Steps (examples of action projects being taken nationally by coalitions and action groups, internet links to organizations engaged with social action). The section website for "Conceptual Frameworks" provides examples of discussion and review questions and exam rubrics that we can recommend for instructional use. And for instructors, especially, who want to know more about the interactive, experiential, dialogic pedagogies used by the editors of this volume in our classrooms throughout the United States, we recommend *Teaching for Diversity and Social Justice* (second edition, 2007) as a resource. We have incorporated some of the resources and pedagogical activities from this book and its accompanying CD-ROM into a number of the section websites.

The alphabetically organized Permission Acknowledgments at the rear of the book is the only bibliographical citation provided for all of the reading selections. Readers wanting to track citations, notes, and references that were cut from the reading selections because of space constraints will be able to use this to enable them to follow-up on the readings. We did not cut intext page references for direct quotations, although the full citations appear only in the Permission Acknowledgments at the back of the book.

We offer this book for use by different readers in many settings and situations. We use these readings in our own general education and graduate diversity classes and in graduate and undergraduate weekend seminars, in teacher education classes, and in multicultural education classes on our own campuses and communities in California, Iowa, Massachusetts, Minnesota, New Jersey, New York, and Wyoming. We know that the earlier edition has been used in many other settings—in ethnic and women's studies, history, social studies, sociology and psychology courses, in social work and management, and in centers for teaching excellence—wherever there is an interest in the broad range of human experiences that have been shaped by social difference and by privilege or disadvantage. We anticipate that these reading selections will be understood differently, as readers themselves have had similar or dissimilar experiences. Our intention and hope is that they will provide opportunities for personal thought and reflection, empathy, connection, and discussion.

References

Adams, M., Bell, L. A., Griffin, P. (eds) (2007). *Teaching for Diversity and Social Justice*, 2nd edition. New York: Routledge.

Lorde, A. (1983). "There is No Hierarchy of Oppressions." *Interracial Books for Children Bulletin* 14 (3–4), 9.

SECTION 1

CONCEPTUAL FRAMEWORKS

Introduction

Maurianne Adams

Social diversity and *social justice* are often used interchangeably to refer to *social differences* as well as to *social inequality.* These two terms are closely related but not interchangeable. When we refer to *social diversity,* we have in mind differences between social identity groups based on social categories such as race, gender, sexuality, and class. These differences are reflected in a group's traditions, language, style of dress, cultural practices, religious beliefs and rituals, and these are usually termed "differences" from some norm that is privileged. It is difficult to perceive oneself, one's family and group traditions, language, style of dress as part of *diversity*—rather, the norm shapes one's notion of the "differences" of *others*, who are marginalized precisely because they are different. In this sense, it is clear why *diversity* ("difference") profoundly shapes the advantages of some groups (those who are part of the norm) relative to the disadvantages of others (because they are "other") and maintains *social inequalities* that are rationalized on the basis of these differences. We also use terms such as *oppression* and *social justice* to emphasize our focus on inequality as something more than difference.

Thus, although these terms are not interchangeable, they are inextricably linked in everyday discourse in that *diversity* is too often used to provide an excuse or justification for *inequality.* It's much more comfortable to talk about diversity than inequality, although clearly we need to understand both. We need to appreciate and value social and cultural differences, if we are to envision a society that acknowledges and appreciates such differences, by de-centering the norm. At the same time, the appreciation of social diversity is a necessary but not sufficient step to understanding the inequalities experienced by peoples of marginalized social groups. It is necessary to understand injustice if we are ever to dismantle the institutions and policies that maintain injustice and to reconstruct institutions and policies based on fairness, equity, and justice. As Young suggests (in selection 5), our challenge is to appreciate social diversity while working to dismantle social inequality.

Several key assumptions inform our perspective throughout this volume, and we identify them in this section as a cluster of four interrelated conceptual frameworks. Our core assumptions are presented in the General Introduction, and include our awareness that social identity groups occupy unequal social locations or positions relative to each other (that is, one group's privileges are directly related to another group's disadvantages). This awareness leads us to the following four concepts: (1) social group identities (such as racial and gender identities) have been used historically to justify and perpetuate the advantages of privileged groups relative to the disadvantages of marginalized groups; (2) these social identities, together with their relative inequality, have been socially constructed within specific historical conditions, although these social constructions are often rationalized as being derived from the "facts of nature" or sustained by unquestionable religious beliefs; (3) the pervasive historical legacies of inequality require a theory of oppression to account for the complex levels and types of privilege and disadvantage that play out at various levels of human society; and (4) a theory of oppression also calls for frameworks that envision opportunities for empowerment and explain the success of past and present social movements.

(1) SOCIAL IDENTITY IS BASED ON SOCIAL IDENTITY GROUPS IN ADVANTAGED OR DISADVANTAGED SOCIAL LOCATIONS OR POSITIONS

The first conceptual framework presented in this section examines social diversity based on differences in social identity and social location. Tatum (selection 1) defines social identity in a complex, multifaceted way that captures the tensions between dominant and subordinate identities (those privileged or disadvantaged on the basis of social group memberships) and gives examples of the tensions between them in everyday interactions. She explores the development of social identity in the context of identity development more generally and describes the ways in which one's identity comes about through the interaction between one's internal sense of who one is (based upon one's social groupings) and the views of oneself and one's group that are reflected back by others in the broader society.

Kirk and Okazawa-Rey (selection 2) note how social identity combines self-perception with personal reactions to attribution by others, so that different contexts may highlight different dimensions of identity (such as racial identity in one context, gender or sexual or class identity in another). They also consider social identity at different levels of social interaction—at the micro level (between individuals), at the meso level (within communities or social institutions), and at the macro level (the overarching society and culture). Similarly, but without using the same terminology, Harro's "The Cycle of Socialization" (selection 6) walks the reader through specific micro, meso, and macro contexts within which social identities and social roles are learned from early childhood and reinforced during adulthood within trusted and familiar contexts—in families, schools, playgrounds, neighborhoods, the workplace, the media.

Both Tatum, and Kirk and Okazawa-Rey, situate social identity within specific social contexts, in that "social" refers to this individual/societal interaction. Both offer numerous examples of how one's social identity builds upon one's social group expectations of privilege or disadvantage, based upon cumulative, historical legacies of group privilege or disadvantage. The connections between privilege/disadvantage and the experience of social identity are the focus for selection 3, in which Johnson explores a number of everyday examples of historically rooted socially constructed inequalities based on race, gender, sexuality, and disability. His approach, if not his specific examples, is applicable to other forms of oppression treated in this book (such as religious oppression, transgender oppression, or ageism and adultism).

(2) THE SOCIAL CONSTRUCTION OF PRIVILEGE AND OPPRESSION WITHIN SPECIFIC HISTORICAL CONTEXTS

A second conceptual framework involves an explanation of how social group differences are socially constructed in specific historical situations in which their social meanings justify inequality and oppression. In this way, social identities are understood as social creations—and the assumptions of superiority or inferiority, related to privilege and disadvantage, are also understood as social creations. As Johnson explains (selection 3), most of what we experience in personal and social life is itself a social creation—and the social differences we consider so significant, so "natural" or so theologically sanctioned, are in fact based on unexamined cultural constructions and not on essential qualities of groups or persons. The implication of this is momentous, for if we understand how specific historical and cultural conditions have given rise to privilege and to disadvantage, we can also understand that these inequities can be changed. Freire helps us grasp how important it is for people to locate conditions of oppression within history, rather than fatalistically as inevitable—that "humans, in their permanent relations with reality, produce not only material goods . . . but also social institutions, ideas, and concepts . . . create history and become historical-social beings" (1994, 82). He recommends a problem-posing approach to education that takes "the people's historicity as their starting point" (1994, 65).

It can be challenging to discover that skin color, accented speech, perceived gender or sexual orientation, or the presence or absence of a physical or mental disability are useless as indicators of talent, character, intelligence, or morality. Many of the readings in the following sections locate the stereotypes we have been led to believe about "others" within their specific historical and cultural contexts, emphasizing the fact that our assumptions about what it means to be female or male or transgender, gay or straight or queer, white, Latino, or black, young or old, learning disabled or able-bodied, Christian or atheist or Jewish, Hindu, or Muslim have been constructed within historical conditions with cultural presuppositions. Harro points out (selection 6) how we unconsciously absorb stereotypes and prejudices as an unconscious part of our socialization from the people who surround us and whom we trust to know what is right and correct.

The following sections have reading selections that refer explicitly to the historical roots of specific patterns of advantage and disadvantage, and the stereotypes associated with them. Lipsitz (selection 11), and Oliver and Shapiro (selection 28) point to specific moments in history that account for the persistence of racism and classism in the present. Roppolo (selection 10), Hilberg (selection 49), Echo-Hawk (selection 52), Lorber (selection 61), and Cerney (selection 97) demonstrate the value of historical analyses of patriarchy, Christian hegemony in Europe and in the United States, or culturally sanctioned assumptions about age, gender, sexuality, and disability. Understanding that we have inherited these stereotypes as part of our intergenerational legacy helps to demystify them, makes them seem less inevitable and more susceptible to education and change. This historical understanding is important if we are also to learn about social resistance movements in the past that also are our legacy and that inspire us to continue working toward change.

(3) FRAMEWORKS FOR ANALYSIS OF OPPRESSION

Social justice needs a theory of *oppression* in order to make sense of the sources and persistence of social inequality in a pluralistic U.S. society that was founded on concepts of equality of opportunity and fairness in life's rewards. Thus, the third conceptual framework presented in this section involves our moving beyond the individual (or "micro") level of the socialization process, to analyze how oppression is enacted and reproduced at the institutional level ("meso") and the societal/cultural ("macro") level. Even though most of the examples in Tatum (selection 1), Johnson (selection 3), and Harro (selection 6) focus on the individual ("micro") level of privilege and disadvantage, it is clear that our everyday personal experiences take place in larger institutional contexts such as extended families, neighborhoods, schools, places of worship, and that our experiences of privilege or disadvantage in these social institutions are reinforced by the societal and cultural messages we simultaneously pick up from the media and understand to be part of our normative culture.

In selection 4, Bell itemizes the defining features of oppression and presents an inclusive approach to the many different forms of oppression—such as racism, classism, sexism—that also highlights their complex intersections in everyday life. This approach is reinforced and developed by Hardiman, Jackson, and Griffin as the interplay of *levels* of oppression—the individual, the institutional, the societal levels—as well as *types* of oppression—the conscious and the unconscious. They define key terminology and analyze the complex and overlapping ways by which interpersonal, institutional, and societal/cultural dimensions of oppression reinforce each other. They are explicit about several underlying assumptions, namely that there is no hierarchy of oppression, that all forms of oppression are interconnected, and that confronting oppression benefits everyone.

There is more than one way to analyze such a complex societal phenomenon as oppression and this section presents at least three such approaches. The first can be called a *psychological approach* in that it locates the psychological processes of socialization within the institutions and broader culture of a society (for example, Tatum in selection 1, Kirk and Okazawa-Rey in selection 2, and Harro in selection 6). The second can be called a *sociological approach* in that it focuses on the structural and societal dimensions of oppression, and is presented here by Bell, Hardiman, Jackson, and Griffin (selection 4) (Hardiman, Jackson, and Griffin 2007). The third, presented here by Young (selection 5), is located within a *philosophical and political discourse* about theories of social justice, and differentiates *social* justice from *distributive*, *punitive*, or *remedial* theories of justice (Young 1990, 2001). Young analyzes the dynamics of oppression—as do Bell, Griffin, Hardiman, and Jackson—but seen by her as five "faces" or facets that interchangeably describe how oppression is experienced by those who are disadvantaged on the basis of social identity groups—namely through their exploitation, powerlessness, and marginalization by those in dominant social positions, or their experience of cultural imperialism and violence.

These three approaches to the systemic dimension of oppression are compatible and mutually illuminating, while at the same time focusing on different dimensions of complex social phenomena. And they can be used as analytic frameworks for many readings throughout this volume. In selections 47 and 48, for example, Blumenfeld and Joshi explicitly take one or another of these conceptual frameworks to theorize historical and contemporary religious oppression and Christian privilege.

(4) FRAMEWORKS FOR ENVISIONING EMPOWERMENT AND SOCIAL CHANGE

All approaches to oppression have implications for a view of society that might conceivably be characterized instead by fairness and justice. In reading selections 3–5, one can instead imagine what a non-oppressive society might look like, in the absence of each and all five faces of oppression (selection 5), or the reversal of the examples and dynamics of oppression as described in selections 3 and 4. How one might actually describe actions or plan projects toward social change in order to achieve relationships, institutions, and an overarching social system and culture that do not enforce or reproduce oppression is a more challenging question and a challenge that this volume accepts. Each one of the topic sections ends with selections describing Next Steps that people have taken or can imagine taking to transform the specific forms of oppression into empowering relationships and just, equitable social institutions. The volume concludes with a full section describing such steps. So this section on conceptual frameworks, as a prelude to these discussions, presents Harro's "Cycle of Liberation" (selection 7) as a companion piece to her "Cycle of Socialization" (selection 6) in which she describes personal behaviors that anyone can engage in, to challenge and to transform individual behavior at the personal level. Other selections throughout this volume and in the final section add collaborative institutional and societal/cultural change projects to the repertoire of possibilities available for concerted, effective social change.

References

Freire, P. (1994, 1970). *Pedagogy of the Oppression* (new revised edition). New York: Continuum.

Hardiman, R., Jackson, B., Griffin, P. (2007). "Conceptual Foundations for Social Justice Education." In M. Adams, L. A. Bell, P. Griffin (eds), *Teaching for Diversity and Social Justice*, 2nd edition. New York: Routledge. pp. 35–66.

Young, I. M. (1990). "Introduction, Displacing the Distributive Paradigm, Five Faces of Oppression." In *Justice and the Politics of Difference*. Princeton, NJ: Princeton University Press. pp. 3–65.

Young, I. M. (2001). "Equality of Whom? Social Groups and Judgments of Injustice." *Journal of Political Philosophy* 9 (1), 1–18.

1

The Complexity of Identity

"Who Am I?"

Beverly Daniel Tatum

The concept of identity is a complex one, shaped by individual characteristics, family dynamics, historical factors, and social and political contexts. Who am I? The answer depends in large part on who the world around me says I am. Who do my parents say I am? Who do my peers say I am? What message is reflected back to me in the faces and voices of my teachers, my neighbors, store clerks? What do I learn from the media about myself? How am I represented in the cultural images around me? Or am I missing from the picture altogether? . . . What has my social context been? Was I surrounded by people like myself, or was I part of a minority in my community? Did I grow up speaking standard English at home or another language or dialect? Did I live in a rural county, an urban neighborhood, a sprawling suburb, or on a reservation?

Who I am (or say I am) is a product of these and many other factors. Erik Erikson, the psychoanalytic theorist who coined the term *identity crisis*, introduced the notion that the social, cultural, and historical context is the ground in which individual identity is embedded. Acknowledging the complexity of identity as a concept, Erikson writes,

> We deal with a process "located" *in the core of the individual* and yet also *in the core of his communal culture*. . . . In psychological terms, identity formation employs a process of simultaneous reflection and observation, a process taking place on all levels of mental functioning, by which the individual judges himself in the light of what he perceives to be the way in which others judge him in comparison to themselves and to a typology significant to them.

. . .

WHO AM I? MULTIPLE IDENTITIES

Integrating one's past, present, and future into a cohesive, unified sense of self is a complex task that begins in adolescence and continues for a lifetime. . . . The salience of particular aspects of our identity varies at different moments in our lives. The process of integrating the component parts of our self-definition is indeed a lifelong journey.

Which parts of our identity capture our attention first? While there are surely idiosyncratic responses to this question, a classroom exercise I regularly use with my psychology students reveals a telling pattern. I ask my students to complete the sentence, "I am _____," using as many descriptors as they can think of in sixty seconds. All kinds of trait descriptions are used—friendly, shy, assertive, intelligent, honest, and so on—but over the years I have noticed something else. Students of color usually mention their racial or ethnic group: for instance, I am Black, Puerto Rican, Korean American. White students who have grown up in strong ethnic enclaves occasionally mention being Irish or Italian. But in general, White students rarely mention being White. When I use this exercise in coeducational settings, I notice a similar pattern in terms of gender, religion, and sexuality. Women usually mention being female, while men don't usually mention their maleness. Jewish students often say they are Jews, while mainline Protestants rarely mention their religious identification. A student who is comfortable revealing it publicly may mention being gay, lesbian, or bisexual. Though I know most of my students are heterosexual, it is very unusual for anyone to include their heterosexuality on their list.

Common across these examples is that in the areas where a person is a member of the dominant or advantaged social group, the category is usually not mentioned. That element of their identity is so taken for granted by them that it goes without comment. It is taken for granted by them because it is taken for granted by the dominant culture. In Eriksonian terms, their inner experience and outer circumstance are in harmony with one another, and the image reflected by others is similar to the image within. In the absence of dissonance, this dimension of identity escapes conscious attention.

The parts of our identity that *do* capture our attention are those that other people notice, and that reflect back to us. The aspect of identity that is the target of others' attention, and subsequently of our own, often is that which sets us apart as exceptional or "other" in their eyes. In my life I have been perceived as both. A precocious child who began to read at age three, I stood out among my peers because of my reading ability. This "gifted" dimension of my identity was regularly commented upon by teachers and classmates alike, and quickly became part of my self-definition. But I was also distinguished by being the only Black student in the class, an "other," a fact I grew increasingly aware of as I got older.

While there may be countless ways one might be defined as exceptional, there are at least seven categories of "otherness" commonly experienced in U.S. society. People are commonly defined as other on the basis of race or ethnicity, gender, religion, sexual orientation, socioeconomic status, age, and physical or mental ability. Each of these categories has a form of oppression associated with it: racism, sexism, religious oppression/anti-Semitism, heterosexism, classism, ageism, and ableism, respectively. In each case, there is a group considered dominant (systematically advantaged by the society because of group membership) and a group considered subordinate or targeted (systematically disadvantaged). When we think about our multiple identities, most of us will find that we are both dominant and targeted at the same time. But it is the targeted identities that hold our attention and the dominant identities that often go unexamined.

. . .

DOMINATION AND SUBORDINATION

. . .

Dominant groups, by definition, set the parameters within which the subordinates operate. The dominant group holds the power and authority in society relative to the subordinates and determines how that power and authority may be acceptably used. Whether it is reflected in determining who gets the best jobs, whose history will be taught in school, or whose relationships will be validated by society, the dominant group has the greatest influence in determining the structure of the society.

The relationship of the dominants to the subordinates is often one in which the targeted group is labeled as defective or substandard in significant ways. For example, Blacks have historically been characterized as less intelligent than Whites, and women have been viewed as less emotionally stable than men. The dominant group assigns roles to the subordinate that reflect the latter's devalued status, reserving the most highly valued roles in the society for themselves. Subordinates are usually said to be innately incapable of performing the preferred roles. To the extent that those in the target group internalize the images that the dominant group reflects back to them, they may find it difficult to believe in their own ability.

. . .

The dominant group is seen as the norm for humanity. . . . Consequently, it remains perfectly acceptable in many circles to tell jokes that denigrate a particular group, to exclude subordinates from one's neighborhood or work setting, or to oppose initiatives that might change the power balance.

. . .

The truth is that the dominants do not really know what the experience of the subordinates is. In contrast, the subordinates are very well informed about the dominants. Even when firsthand experience is limited by social segregation, the number and variety of images of the dominant group available through television, magazines, books, and newspapers provide subordinates with plenty of information about the dominants. The dominant worldview has saturated the culture for all to learn. Even the Black or Latino child living in a segregated community can enter White homes of many kinds daily via the media. However, dominant access to information about the subordinates is often limited to stereotypical depictions of the "other." For example, there are many images of heterosexual relations on television, but very few images of gay or lesbian domestic partnerships beyond the caricatures of comedy shows. There are many images of White men and women in all forms of media, but relatively few portrayals of people of color.

. . .

In a situation of unequal power, a subordinate group has to focus on survival. It becomes very important for subordinates to become highly attuned to the dominants as a way of protecting themselves. For example, women who have been battered by men often talk about the heightened sensitivity they develop to their partners' moods. Being able to anticipate and avoid the men's rage is important to survival.

Survival sometimes means not responding to oppressive behavior directly. To do so could result in physical harm to oneself, even death. . . .

The use of either strategy, attending very closely to the dominants or not attending at all, is costly to members of the targeted group. "Not-learning" may mean there are needed skills that are not acquired. Attending closely to the dominant group may leave little time or energy to attend to one's self. Worse yet, the negative messages of the dominant group about the subordinates may be internalized, leading to self-doubt or, in its extreme form, self-hate. There are many examples of subordinates attempting to make themselves over in the image of the dominant group—Jewish people who want to change the Semitic look of their noses, Asians who have cosmetic surgery to alter the shapes of their eyes, Blacks who seek to lighten their skin with bleaching creams, women who want to smoke and drink "like a man." Whether one succumbs to the devaluing pressures of the dominant culture or successfully resists them, the fact is that dealing with oppressive systems from the underside, regardless of the strategy, is physically and psychologically taxing.

. . .

The history of subordinate groups is filled with so-called troublemakers, yet their names are often unknown. Preserving the record of those subordinates and their dominant allies who have challenged the status quo is usually of little interest to the dominant culture, but it is of great interest to subordinates who search for an empowering reflection in the societal mirror.

Many of us are both dominant and subordinate. As Audre Lorde said, from her vantage point as a Black lesbian, "There is no hierarchy of oppressions." The thread and threat of violence runs through all of the isms. There is a need to acknowledge each other's pain, even as we attend to our own.

For those readers who are in the dominant racial category, it may sometimes be difficult to take in what is being said by and about those who are targeted by racism. When the perspective of the subordinate is shared directly, an image is reflected to members of the dominant group that is disconcerting. To the extent that one can draw on one's own experience of subordination—as a young person, as a person with a disability, as someone who grew up poor, as a woman—it may be easier to make meaning of another targeted group's experience. For those readers who are targeted by racism and are angered by the obliviousness of Whites, it may be useful to attend to your experience of dominance where you may find it—as a heterosexual, as an able-bodied person, as a Christian, as a man—and consider what systems of privilege you may be overlooking. The task of resisting our own oppression does not relieve us of the responsibility of acknowledging our complicity in the oppression of others.

Our ongoing examination of who we are in our full humanity, embracing all of our identities, creates the possibility of building alliances that may ultimately free us all.

2

Identities and Social Locations

Who Am I? Who Are My People?

Gwyn Kirk and Margo Okazawa-Rey

. . .

Identity formation is the result of a complex interplay among individual decisions and choices, particular life events, community recognition and expectations, and societal categorization, classification, and socialization. It is an ongoing process that involves several key questions:

Who am I? Who do I want to be?
Who do others think I am and want me to be?

Who and what do societal and community institutions, such as schools, religious institutions, the media, and the law, say I am?
Where/what/who are my "home" and "community"?
Which social group(s) do I want to affiliate with?
Who decides the answers to these questions, and on what basis?

Answers to these questions form the core of our existence. . . .

The *American Heritage Dictionary* (1993) defines *identity* as

the collective aspect of the set of characteristics by which a thing is definitely known or recognizable;
a set of behavioral or personal characteristics by which an individual is recognizable as a member of a group;
. . .

The same dictionary defines *to identify* as "to associate or affiliate (oneself) closely with a person or group; to establish an identification with another or others."

These definitions point to the connections between us as individuals and how we are perceived by other people and classified by societal institutions. They also involve a sense of individual agency and choice regarding affiliations with others. Gender, race, ethnicity, class, nationality, sexual orientation, age, religion, disability, and language are all significant social categories by which people are recognized by others. Indeed, on the basis of these categories alone, others often think they know who we are and how we should behave. Personal decisions about our affiliations and loyalties to specific groups are also shaped by these categories. For example, in many communities of color women struggle over the question of race versus gender. Is race a more important factor than gender in shaping their lives? If a Latina speaks out publicly about sexism within the Latino community, is she betraying her people? This separation of categories, mirrored by our segregated social lives, tends to set up false dichotomies in which people often feel that they have to choose one aspect of their identity over another. It also presents difficulties for mixed-race or bisexual people, who do not fit neatly into such narrow categories.
. . .

BEING MYSELF: THE MICRO LEVEL

At the micro level, individuals usually feel the most comfortable as themselves. Here one can say, for example, "I am a woman, heterosexual, middle class, with a movement disability; but I am also much more than those categories." At this level we define ourselves and structure our daily activities according to our own preferences. At the micro level we can best feel and experience the process of identity formation, which includes naming specific forces and events that shape our identities. At this level we also seem to have more control of the process, although there are always interconnections between events and experiences at this level and the other levels.

Critical life events, such as entering kindergarten, losing a parent through death, separation, or divorce, or the onset of puberty, may all serve as catalysts for a shift in how we think about ourselves. A five-year-old Vietnamese American child from a traditional home and community may experience the first challenge to her sense of identity when her kindergarten teacher admonishes her to speak only in English. A White, middle-class professional woman who thinks of herself as "a person" and a "competent attorney" may begin to see the significance of gender and "the glass ceiling" for women when she witnesses younger, less experienced male colleagues in her law office passing her by for promotions. A woman who has been raped who attends her first meeting of a campus group organizing against date rape feels the power of connection with other rape survivors and their allies. An eighty-year-old woman, whose partner of fifty years has just died, must face the reality of having lost her lifetime companion, friend, and lover. Such experiences shape each person's ongoing formulation of self, whether or not the process is conscious, deliberate, reflective, or even voluntary.

Identity formation is a lifelong endeavor that includes discovery of the new; recovery of the old, forgotten, or appropriated; and synthesis of the new and old, as illustrated by several writers in this chapter who reflect on how their sense of identity has developed over the course of their lives. At especially important junctures during the process, individuals mark an identity change in tangible ways. An African American woman may change her name from the anglicized Susan to Aisha, with roots in African culture. A Chinese Vietnamese immigrant woman, on the other hand, may adopt an anglicized name, exchanging Nu Lu for Yvonne Lu as part of becoming a U.S. citizen. Another way of marking and effecting a shift in identity is by altering your physical appearance: changing your wardrobe or makeup; cutting your hair very short, wearing it natural rather than permed or pressed, dyeing it purple, or letting the gray show after years of using hair coloring. . . .

COMMUNITY RECOGNITION, EXPECTATIONS, AND INTERACTIONS: THE MESO LEVEL

It is at the meso level—at school, in the workplace, or on the street—that people most frequently ask "Who are you?" or "Where are you from?" in an attempt to categorize us and determine their relationship to us. Moreover, it is here that people experience the complexities, conflicts, and contradictions of multiple identities, which we consider later.

The single most visible signifier of identity is physical appearance. . . . Questions such as "Where do you come from?" and questioning behaviors, such as feeling the texture of your hair or asking if you speak a particular language, are commonly used to interrogate people whose physical appearances especially, but also behaviors, do not match the characteristics designated as belonging to established categories. At root, we are being asked, "Are you one of us or not?" These questioners usually expect singular and simplistic answers, assuming that everyone will fit existing social categories, which are conceived of as undifferentiated and unambiguous. Among people with disabilities, for example, people wanting to identify each other may expect to hear details of another's disability rather than the fact that the person being questioned also identifies equally strongly as, say, a woman who is White, working class, and bisexual.

Community, like home, may be geographic and emotional, or both, and provides a way for people to express group affiliations. "Where are you from?" is a commonplace question in the United States among strangers, a way to break the ice and start a conversation, expecting answers like "I'm from Tallahassee, Florida," or "I'm from the Bronx." Community might also be an organized group like Alcoholics Anonymous, a religious group, or a political organization like the African American civil rights organization, the National Association for the Advancement of Colored People (NAACP). Community may be something much more abstract, as in "the women's community" or "the queer community," where there is presumed to be an identifiable group. In all of these examples there is an assumption of some kind of shared values, goals, interests, culture, or language.

At the community level, individual identities and needs meet group standards, expectations, obligations, responsibilities, and demands. You compare yourself with others and are subtly compared. Others size up your clothing, accent, personal style, and knowledge of the group's history and culture. You may be challenged directly, "You say you're Latina. How come you don't speak Spanish?" "You say you're working class. What are you doing in a professional job?" These experiences may both affirm our identities and create or highlight inconsistencies, incongruities, and contradictions in who we believe we are, how we are viewed by others, our role and status in the community, and our sense of belonging.

. . .

SOCIAL CATEGORIES, CLASSIFICATIONS, AND STRUCTURAL INEQUALITY: MACRO AND GLOBAL LEVELS

Classifying and labeling human beings, often according to real or assumed physical, biological, or genetic differences, is a way to distinguish who is included and who is excluded from a group, to ascribe particular characteristics, to prescribe social roles, and to assign status, power, and privilege. People are to know their places. Thus social categories such as gender, race, and class are used to establish and maintain a particular kind of social order. The classifications and their specific features, meanings, and significance are socially constructed through history, politics, and culture. The specific meanings and significance were often imputed to justify the conquest, colonization, domination, and exploitation of entire groups of people, and although the specifics may have changed over time, this system of categorizing and classifying remains intact. For example, Native American people were described as brutal, uncivilized, and ungovernable savages in the writings of early colonizers on this continent. This justified the genocide of Native Americans by White settlers and the U.S. military and public officials, as well as the breaking of treaties between the U.S. government and Native American tribes. Today, Native Americans are no longer called savages but are often thought of as a vanishing species, or a non-existent people, already wiped out, thereby rationalizing their neglect by the dominant culture and erasing their long-standing and continuing resistance. . . .

These social categories are at the foundation of the structural inequalities present in our society. In each category there is one group of people deemed superior, legitimate, dominant, and privileged while others are relegated—whether explicitly or implicitly—to the position of inferior, illegitimate, subordinate, and disadvantaged.

Category	Dominant	Subordinate
Gender	Men	Women, transgender people
Race	White	Peoples of color
Class	Middle and upper class	Poor, working class
Nation	U.S./First World	Second, third Worlds
Ethnicity	European	All other ethnicities
Sexual orientation	Heterosexual	Lesbian, gay, bisexual, transgender
Religion	Christian	All other religions
Physical ability	Able-bodied	Persons with disabilities
Age	Youth	Elderly persons
Language	English	All other languages

This hierarchy of advantage and disadvantage has meant that the preponderance of analytical writing about identity has been done by those in subordinate positions: women of color, lesbians, bisexual women, and working-class women. . . . For White people descended from European immigrants to this country, the advantages of being White are not always fully recognized or acknowledged. . . . As a result, White people in the United States tend to think of all identities as equal: "I'm Italian American, you're Polish American. I'm Irish American, you're African American." This assumed equivalence ignores the very big differences between an individualist symbolic identity and a socially enforced and imposed racial identity. . . .

MAINTAINING SYSTEMS OF STRUCTURAL INEQUALITY

Maintaining this system of inequality requires the objectification and dehumanization of subordinated peoples. Appropriating their identities is a particularly effective method of doing this, for it defines who the subordinated group/person is or ought to be. This happens in several ways:

Using the values, characteristics, features of the dominant group as the supposedly neutral standard against which all others should be evaluated. For example, men are generally physically larger and stronger than women. Many of the clinical trials for new pharmaceutical drugs are conducted using men's bodies and activities as the standard. The results, however, are applied equally to both men and women. Women are often prescribed the same dosage of a medication as men are even though their physical makeup is not the same. Thus women, as a distinct group, do not exist in this research.

Using terms that distinguish the subordinate from the dominant group. Terms such as "non-White" and "minority" connote a relationship to another group, White in the former case and majority in the latter. A non-White person is the negative of the White person; a minority person is less than a majority person. Neither has an identity on her or his own terms.

Stereotyping. Stereotyping involves making a simple generalization about a group and claiming that all members of the group conform to this generalization. Stereotypes are behavioral and psychological attributes; they are commonly held beliefs about groups rather than individual beliefs about individuals; and they persist in spite of contradictory evidence. Lesbians hate men. Latinas are dominated by macho Latinos. Women with physical disabilities are asexual. Fat women are good-humored but not healthy. As Andre asserts, "A 'stereotype' is pejorative; there is always something objectionable in the beliefs and images to which the word refers."

Exoticizing and romanticizing. These two forms of appropriation are particularly insidious because on the surface there is an appearance of appreciation. For example, Asian American women are described as personifying the "mysterious orient," Native American women as "earth mothers" and the epitome of spirituality, and Black women as perpetual towers of strength. In all three cases, seemingly positive traits and cultural practices are identified and exalted. This "positive" stereotyping prevents people from seeing the truth and complexity of who these women are.

. . .

Given the significance of identity appropriation as an aspect of oppression, it is not surprising that many liberation struggles have included projects and efforts aimed at changing identities and taking control of the process of positive identity formation and representation. Before liberation struggles, oppressed people often use the same terminology to name themselves as the dominant group uses to label them. One crucial aspect of liberation struggles is to get rid of pejorative labels and use names that express, in their own terms, who people are in all their humanity. Thus the name a group uses for itself gradually takes on more of an insider perspective that fits the evolving consciousness growing out of the political movement.

As with individual identity, naming ourselves collectively is an important act of empowerment. One example of this is the evolution of the names African Americans have used to identify themselves, moving from Colored, to Negro, to Black to Afro-American, and African American. Similarly, Chinese Americans gradually rejected the derogatory label "Chink," preferring to be called Orientals and now Chinese Americans or Asians. These terms are used unevenly, sometimes according to the age and political orientation of the person or the geographic region, where one usage may be more popular than another. Among the very diverse group of people connected historically, culturally, and linguistically to Spain, Portugal, and their former colonies (parts of the United States, Mexico, the Caribbean, and Central and South America), some use more inclusive terms such as Latino or Hispanic; others prefer more specific names such as Chicano, Puerto Rican, Nicaraguan, Cuban, and so on. . . .

COLONIZATION, IMMIGRATION, AND THE U.S. LANDSCAPE OF RACE AND CLASS

Other macro-level factors affecting people's identities include colonization and immigration. . . . This ideology that the United States is "a land of immigrants" obscures several important issues excluded from much mainstream debate about immigration: Not all Americans came to this country voluntarily. Native American peoples and Mexicans were already here on this continent, but the former experienced near-genocide and the latter were made foreigners in their own land. African peoples were captured, enslaved, and forcibly imported to this country to be laborers. All were brutally exploited and violated—physically, psychologically, culturally, and spiritually—to serve the interests of those in power. The relationships between these groups and this nation and their experiences in the United States are fundamentally different from the experiences of those who chose to immigrate here, though this is not to negate the hardships the latter may have faced. These differences profoundly shaped the social, cultural, political, and economic realities faced by these groups throughout history and continue to do so today.

. . . Early in the history of this country, for example, the Naturalization Law of 1790 (which was repealed as recently as 1952) prohibited peoples of color from becoming U.S. citizens, and the Slave Codes restricted every aspect of life for enslaved African peoples. These laws made race into an indelible line that separated "insiders" from "outsiders." White people were designated insiders and granted many privileges while all others were confined to systematic disadvantage. As Mary C. Waters points out, the stories that White Americans learn of how their grandparents and great-grandparents triumphed in the United States "are usually told in terms of their individual efforts." The role of labor unions, community organizations, and political parties, as well as the crucial importance of racism, is usually left out of these accounts, which emphasize individual effort and hard work.

. . .

On coming to the United States, immigrants are drawn into the racial landscape of this country. In media debates and official statistics, this is still dominated by a Black/White polarization in which everyone is assumed to fit into one of these two groups. Demographically, the situation is much more complex and diverse, but people of color, who comprise the more inclusive group, are still set off against White people, the dominant group. Immigrants identify themselves according to nationality—for example, as Cambodian or Guatemalan. Once in the United States they learn the significance of racial divisions in this country and may adopt the term *people of color* as an aspect of their identity here. . . .

This emphasis on race tends to mask differences based on class, another important distinction among immigrant groups. For example, the Chinese and Japanese people who came in the nineteenth century and early twentieth century to work on plantations in Hawai'i, as loggers in Oregon, or building roads and railroads in several western states were poor and from rural areas of China and Japan. The 1965 immigration law made way for "the second wave" of Asian immigration. It set preferences for professionals, highly skilled workers, and members of the middle and upper-middle classes, making this group "the most highly skilled of any immigrant group our country has ever had." The first wave of Vietnamese refugees who immigrated between the mid-1970s and 1980 were from the middle and upper classes, and many were professionals; by contrast, the second wave of immigrants from Vietnam was composed of poor and rural people. The class backgrounds of immigrants affect not only their sense of themselves and their expectations but also how they can succeed as strangers in a foreign land. For example, a poor woman who arrives with no literacy skills in her own language will have a more difficult time learning to become literate in English than one who has several years of formal schooling in her country of origin that may have included basic English.

MULTIPLE IDENTITIES, SOCIAL LOCATION, AND CONTRADICTIONS

The social features of one's identity incorporate individual, community, societal, and global factors, as discussed in the accounts that follow. The point where all the features embodied in a person overlap is called social location. Imagine a diagram made up of overlapping circles, with a circle representing one specific feature of identity such as gender, class, ability, age, and so on. A person's social location is the point at which a part of each circle touches all others—where all elements are present simultaneously. Social location is a way of expressing the core of a person's existence in the social and political world. It places us in particular relationships to others, to the dominant culture of the United States, and to the rest of the world. It determines the kinds of power and privilege we have access to and can exercise, as well as situations in which we have less power and privilege.

Because social location is where all the aspects of one's identity meet, our experience of our own complex identities is sometimes contradictory, conflictual, and paradoxical. We live with multiple identities that can be both enriching and contradictory and that push us to confront questions of loyalty to individuals and groups. . . .

3

The Social Construction of Difference

Allan G. Johnson

The late African American novelist James Baldwin once offered the provocative idea that there is no such thing as whiteness or, for that matter, blackness or, more generally, race. "No one is white before he/she came to America," he wrote. "It took generations and a vast amount of coercion, before this became a white country."

. . .

Baldwin isn't denying the reality that skin pigmentation varies from one person to another. What he is saying is that unless you live in a culture that recognizes such differences as significant, they are socially irrelevant and therefore, in a way, do not exist. A "black woman" in Africa, therefore, who has not experienced white racism, does not *think* of herself as black or experience herself as black, nor do the people around her. African, yes, a woman, yes. But not a *black* woman.

When she comes to the United States, however, where privilege is organized according to race, suddenly she becomes black because people assign her to a social category that bears that name, and they treat her differently as a result. . . .

So Baldwin is telling us that race and all its categories have no significance outside systems of privilege and oppression in which they were created in the first place. This is what sociologists call the "social construction" of reality.

. . .

The same is true with the definition of what is considered "normal." While it may come as a surprise to many who think of themselves as nondisabled, disability and nondisability are socially constructed. This doesn't mean that the difference between having or not having full use of your legs is somehow "made up" without any objective reality. It does mean, however, that how people notice and label and think about such differences and how they treat other people as a result depend entirely on ideas contained in a system's culture.

Human beings, for example, come in a variety of heights, and many of those considered "normal" are unable to reach high places such as kitchen shelves without the assistance of physical aids—chairs and step-stools. In spite of their inability to do this simple task without special aids, they are not defined as disabled. Nor are the roughly 100 million people in the United States who cannot see properly without the aid of eyeglasses. . . .

Disability and nondisability are . . . constructed through the language used to describe people. When someone who cannot see is labeled a "blind person," for example, it creates the impression that not being able to see sums up the entire person. In other words, blind becomes what they *are*. The same thing happens when people are described as "brain damaged" or "crippled" or "retarded" or "deaf"—the person becomes the disability and nothing more. Reducing people to a single dimension of who they are separates and excludes them, marks them as "other," as different from "normal" (white, heterosexual, male, nondisabled) people and therefore as inferior. . . .

There is a world of difference between using a wheelchair and being treated as a normal human being (who happens to use a wheelchair to get around) and using a wheelchair and being treated as invisible, inferior, unintelligent, asexual, frightening, passive, dependent, and nothing more than your disability. And that difference is not a matter of the disability itself but of how it is constructed in society and how we then make use of that construction in our minds to shape how we think about ourselves and other people and how we treat them as a result.

What makes socially constructed reality so powerful is that we rarely if ever experience it as that. We think the way our culture defines something like race or gender is simply the way things are in some objective sense. . . . In the 19th century, for example, U.S. law identified those having *any* African ancestry as black, a standard known as the "one-drop rule," which defined "white" as a state of absolute purity in relation to "black." Native American status, in contrast, required at *least* one-eighth Native American ancestry in order to qualify. Why the different standards? . . . Native Americans could claim financial benefits from the federal government, making it to whites' advantage to make it hard for anyone to be considered Native American. Designating someone as black, however, took *away* power and *denied* the right to make claims against whites, including white families of origin. In both cases, racial classification has had little to do with objective characteristics and everything to do with preserving white power and wealth.

This fact has also been true of the use of race to tag various ethnic groups. When the Chinese were imported as cheap laborers during the 19th century, the California Supreme Court declared them not white. Mexicans, however, many of whom owned large amounts of land in California and did business with whites, were considered white. Today, as Paul Kivel points out, Mexicans are no longer considered white and the Chinese are "conditionally white at times."

. . .

WHAT IS PRIVILEGE?

No matter what privileged group you belong to, if you want to understand the problem of privilege and difference, the first stumbling block is usually the idea of privilege itself. When people hear that they belong to a privileged group or benefit from something like "white privilege" or "male privilege," they don't get it, or they feel angry and defensive about what they do get. *Privilege* has become one of those loaded words we need to reclaim so that we can use it to name and illuminate the truth. . . .

Privilege exists when one group has something of value that is denied to others simply because of the groups they belong to, rather than because of anything they've done or failed to do. If people take me more seriously when I give a speech than they would someone of color saying the same things in the same way, then I'm benefiting from white privilege. That a heterosexual black woman can feel free to talk about her life in ways that reveal the fact that she's married to a man is a form of heterosexual privilege because lesbians and gay men cannot casually reveal their sexual orientation without putting themselves at risk.

. . .

WHAT PRIVILEGE LOOKS LIKE IN EVERYDAY LIFE

. . . Privilege shows up in the daily details of people's lives in almost every social setting. Consider the following examples of race privilege. . . .

- Whites are less likely than blacks to be arrested; once arrested, they are less likely to be convicted and, once convicted, less likely to go to prison, regardless of the crime or circumstances. Whites, for example, constitute 85 percent of those who use illegal drugs, but less than half of those in prison on drug-use charges are white.

. . .

- Whites are more likely than comparable blacks to have loan applications approved and less likely to be given poor information or the runaround during the application process.
- Whites are charged lower prices for new and used cars than are people of color, and residential segregation gives whites access to higher-quality goods of all kinds at cheaper prices.

. . .

- Whites are more likely to control conversations and be allowed to get away with it and to have their ideas and contributions taken seriously, including those that were suggested previously by a person of color and ignored or dismissed.
- Whites can usually assume that national heroes, success models, and other figures held up for general admiration will be of their race.

. . .

- Whites can assume that when they go shopping, they'll be treated as serious customers not as potential shoplifters or people without the money to make a purchase. When they try to cash a check or use a credit card, they can assume they won't be hassled for additional identification and will be given the benefit of the doubt.

. . .

- Most whites are not segregated into communities that isolate them from the best job opportunities, schools, and community services.
- Whites have greater access to quality education and health care.

. . .

- Whites can succeed without other people being surprised.
- Whites don't have to deal with an endless and exhausting stream of attention to their race. They can simply take their race for granted as unremarkable to the extent of experiencing themselves as not even having a race. Unlike some of my African American students, for example, I don't have people coming up to me and treating me as if I were some exotic "other," gushing about how "cool" or different I am, wanting to know where I'm "from," and reaching out to touch my hair.
- Whites don't find themselves slotted into occupations identified with their race, as blacks are often slotted into support positions or Asians into technical jobs.

. . .

- Whites can reasonably expect that if they work hard and "play by the rules," they'll get what they deserve, and they feel justified in complaining if they don't. It is something other racial groups cannot realistically expect.

In the following list for male privilege, note how some items repeat from the list on race but other items do not.

- In most professions and upper-level occupations, men are held to a lower standard than women. It is easier for a "good but not great" male lawyer to make partner than it is for a comparable woman.
- Men are charged lower prices for new and used cars.
- If men do poorly at something or make a mistake or commit a crime, they can generally assume that people won't attribute the failure to their gender. The kids who shoot teachers and schoolmates are almost always boys, but rarely is the fact that all this violence is being done by males raised as an important issue.

. . .

- Men can generally assume that when they go out in public, they won't be sexually harassed or assaulted just because they're male, and if they are victimized, they won't be asked to explain what they were doing there.

- Male representation in government and the ruling circles of corporations and other organizations is disproportionately high.

. . .

- Men are more likely than women are to control conversations and be allowed to get away with it and to have their ideas and contributions taken seriously, even those that were suggested previously by a woman and dismissed or ignored.
- Most men can assume that their gender won't be used to determine whether they'll fit in at work or whether teammates will feel comfortable working with them.
- Men can succeed without other people being surprised.
- Men don't have to deal with an endless and exhausting stream of attention drawn to their gender (for example, to how sexually attractive they are).
- Men don't find themselves slotted into a narrow range of occupations identified with their gender as women are slotted into community relations, human resources, social work, elementary school teaching, librarianship, nursing, and clerical, and secretarial positions.

. . .

- The standards used to evaluate men as *men* are consistent with the standards used to evaluate them in other roles such as occupations. Standards used to evaluate women as women are often different from those used to evaluate them in other roles. For example, a man can be both a "real man" and a successful and aggressive lawyer, while an aggressive woman lawyer may succeed as a lawyer but be judged as not measuring up as a woman.

In the following list regarding sexual orientation, note again items in common with the other two lists and items peculiar to this form of privilege.

- Heterosexuals are free to reveal and live their intimate relationships openly—by referring to their partners by name, recounting experiences, going out in public together, displaying pictures on their desks at work—without being accused of "flaunting" their sexuality or risking discrimination.
- Heterosexuals can marry as a way to commit to long-term relationships that are socially recognized, supported, and legitimated. This fact confers basic rights such as spousal health benefits, the ability to adopt children, inheritance, joint filing of income tax returns, and the power to make decisions for a spouse who is incapacitated in a medical emergency.

. . .

- Heterosexuals can move about in public without fear of being harassed or physically attacked because of their sexual orientation.
- Heterosexuals don't run the risk of being reduced to a single aspect of their lives, as if being heterosexual summed up the kind of person they are. Instead, they can be viewed and treated as complex human beings who happen to be heterosexual.
- Heterosexuals can usually assume that national heroes, success models, and other figures held up for general admiration will be assumed to be heterosexual.
- Most heterosexuals can assume that their sexual orientation won't be used to determine whether they'll fit in at work or whether teammates will feel comfortable working with them.
- Heterosexuals don't have to worry that their sexual orientation will be used as a weapon against them, to undermine their achievements or power.

. . .

- Heterosexuals can live where they want without having to worry about neighbors who disapprove of their sexual orientation.

- Heterosexuals can live in the comfort of knowing that other people's assumptions about their sexual orientation are correct.

In the following list regarding disability status, note again items in common with the other lists and items peculiar to this form of privilege.

- Nondisabled people can choose whether to be conscious of their disability status or to ignore it and regard themselves simply as human beings.
- Nondisabled people can live secure in other people's assumption that they are sexual beings capable of an active sex life, including the potential to have children and be parents.

. . .

- Nondisabled people can assume that they will fit in at work and in other settings without having to worry about being evaluated and judged according to preconceived notions and stereotypes about people with disabilities.

. . .

- Nondisabled people don't have to deal with an endless and exhausting stream of attention to their disability status. They can simply take their disability status for granted as unremarkable to the extent of experiencing themselves as not even having one.
- Nondisabled people can ask for help without having to worry that people will assume they need help with everything.
- Nondisabled people can succeed without people being surprised because of low expectations of their ability to contribute to society.
- Nondisabled people can expect to pay lower prices for cars because they are assumed to be mentally unimpaired and less likely to allow themselves to be misled and exploited.

. . .

- Nondisabled people are more likely to control conversations and be allowed to get away with it and have their ideas and contributions taken seriously, including those that were suggested before by a person with disabilities and then dismissed or ignored.
- Nondisabled people can assume that national heroes, success models, and other figures held up for general admiration will share their disability status.

. . .

- Nondisabled people can generally assume that when they go out in public, they won't be looked at as odd or out of place or not belonging. They can also assume that most buildings and other structures will not be designed in ways that limit their access.
- Nondisabled people can assume that when they need to travel from one place to another, they will have access to buses, trains, airplanes, and other means of transportation.
- Nondisabled people can count on being taken seriously and not treated as children.
- Nondisabled people are less likely to be segregated into living situations—such as nursing homes and special schools and sports programs—that isolate them from job opportunities, schools, community services, and the everyday workings of life in a society.

. . .

Regardless of which group we're talking about, privilege generally allows people to assume a certain level of acceptance, inclusion, and respect in the world, to operate within a relatively wide comfort zone. Privilege increases the odds of having things your own way, of being able to set the agenda in a social situation and determine the rules and standards and how they're applied. Privilege grants the cultural authority to make judgments about others and to have those judgements stick. It allows people to define reality and to have prevailing definitions of reality fit their experience. Privilege means being able to decide who gets taken seriously, who receives attention, who is accountable to whom and for what. And it grants a presumption of superiority and social permission to act on that presumption without having to worry about being challenged.

To have privilege is to be allowed to move through your life without being marked in ways that identify you as an outsider, as exceptional or "other" to be excluded, or to be included but always with conditions. . . .

OPPRESSION: THE FLIP SIDE OF PRIVILEGE

For every social category that is privileged, one or more other categories are oppressed in relation to it. . . . Just as privilege tends to open doors of opportunity, oppression tends to slam them shut.

Like privilege, oppression results from the social relationship between privileged and oppressed categories, which makes it possible for individuals to vary in their personal experience of being oppressed ("I've never been oppressed as a woman"). This also means, however, that in order to have the experience of being oppressed, it is necessary to belong to an oppressed category. In other words, men cannot be oppressed *as men*, just as whites cannot be oppressed as whites or heterosexuals as heterosexuals, because a group can be oppressed only if there exists another group with the power to oppress them.

As we saw earlier, people in privileged categories can certainly feel bad in ways that can feel oppressive. Men, for example, can feel burdened by what they take to be their responsibility to provide for their families. Or they can feel limited and even damaged by the requirement that "real men" must avoid expressing feelings other than anger. But although access to privilege costs them something that may *feel* oppressive, to call it oppression distorts the nature of what is happening to them and why.

. . .

The complexity of systems of privilege makes it possible, of course, for men to experience oppression if they also happen to be of color or gay or disabled or in a lower social class, but not simply because they are male. In the same way, whites can experience oppression for many reasons, but not because they're white.

. . .

Finally, being in a privileged category that has an oppressive relationship with another isn't the same as being an oppressive *person* who behaves in oppressive ways. That males as a social category oppress females as a social category, for example, is a social fact. That doesn't, however, tell us how a particular man thinks or feels about particular women or behaves toward them. This can be a subtle distinction to hang on to, but hang on to it we must if we're going to maintain a clear idea of what oppression is and how it works in defense of privilege.

. . .

4

Theoretical Foundations

Lee Anne Bell

WHAT IS SOCIAL JUSTICE?

We believe that social justice is both a process and a goal. The goal of social justice is full and equal participation of all groups in a society that is mutually shaped to meet their needs. Social justice includes a vision of society in which the distribution of resources is equitable and all members are physically and psychologically safe and secure. We envision a society in which individuals are both self-determining (able to develop their full capacities) and interdependent (capable of interacting democratically with others). Social justice involves social actors who have a sense of their own agency as well as a sense of social responsibility toward and with others, their society, and the broader world in which we live. These are conditions we wish not only for our own society but also for every society in our interdependent global community.

. . .

We realize that developing a social justice process in a society and world steeped in oppression is no simple feat. For this reason, we need clear ways to define and analyze oppression so that we can understand how it operates at individual, cultural, and institutional levels, historically and in the present. Although inevitably an oversimplification of a complex social phenomenon, we believe that the conceptual frameworks presented here can help us make sense of and, hopefully, act more effectively against oppressive circumstances as these arise in our teaching and activism.

WHY SOCIAL JUSTICE EDUCATION NEEDS A THEORY OF OPPRESSION

Practice is always shaped by theory, whether formal or informal, tacit or expressed. How we approach social justice education, the problems we identify as needing remedy, the solutions we entertain as viable, and the methods we choose as appropriate for reaching those solutions are all theoretical as well as practical questions. Theory and practice intertwine as parts of the interactive and historical process that Freire calls "praxis."

DEFINING FEATURES OF OPPRESSION

PERVASIVE

We use the term *oppression* rather than discrimination, bias, prejudice, or bigotry to emphasize the pervasive nature of social inequality woven throughout social institutions as well as embedded within individual consciousness. The term *oppression* encapsulates the fusion of institutional and systemic discrimination, personal bias, bigotry, and social prejudice in a complex web of relationships and structures that shade most aspects of life in our society. . . . Woven together through time and reinforced in the present, these patterns provide an example of the pervasive of oppression.

RESTRICTIVE

On the most general level, oppression denotes structural and material constraints that significantly shape a person's life chances and sense of possibility. Oppression restricts both self-development and self-determination. It delimits who one can imagine becoming and the power to act in support of one's rights and aspirations. A girl-child in the United States in 2006, for example, especially if she is poor or of color, is still unlikely to imagine herself as president since, unlike many other countries, we have yet to elect a woman to this high office. 140 years after the abolition of slavery, African Americans as a group have still not achieved full equality and cannot even rely on their government for basic human treatment and aid in a time of crisis, as in the recent scandalous government desertion of the victims of Hurricane Katrina. Despite rhetoric that anyone can get ahead if they work hard enough, a father's economic status continues to be the best predictor of the status of his offspring, a situation that worsens as economic inequality grows and the possibilities for social mobility steadily decline.

HIERARCHICAL

Oppression signifies a hierarchical relationship in which dominant or privileged groups reap advantage, often in unconscious ways, from the disempowerment of targeted groups. Whites, for example, gain privilege as a dominant group because they benefit from access to social power and privilege, not equally available to people of color. As a group, Whites earn more money and accumulate more assets than other racial groups, hold the majority of positions of power and influence, and command the controlling institutions in society. White-dominated institutions restrict the life expectancy, infant mortality, income, housing, employment, and educational opportunities of people of color.

COMPLEX, MULTIPLE, CROSS-CUTTING RELATIONSHIPS

Power and privilege are relative, however, because individuals hold multiple complex and cross-cutting social group memberships that confer relative privilege or disadvantage differently in different contexts. Identity is not simply additive but multiplicative. An upper-class professional man who is African American, for example (still a very small percentage of African Americans overall), may enjoy economic success and professional status conferred through male, class, and perhaps dominant language and citizenship privilege as an English-speaking native-born citizen, yet face limitations not endured by white, male and female, or foreign national coworkers. Despite economic and professional status and success, he may be threatened by police, be unable to hail a taxi, and endure hateful epithets as he walks down the street. The constellation of identities that shape his consciousness and experience as an African American man, and his varying access to privilege, may fluctuate depending upon whether he is light or dark skinned, Ivy League-educated or a high school dropout, incarcerated, unemployed, or a tourist in South Africa, Brazil, or Europe.

INTERNALIZED

Oppression not only resides in external social institutions and norms but lodges in the human psyche as well. Oppressive beliefs are internalized by victims as well as perpetrators. The idea that poor people somehow deserve and are responsible for poverty, rather than the economic system that structures and requires it, is learned by poor and affluent alike. Homophobia, the deep fear and hatred of homosexuality, is internalized by both straight and gay people. Jews as well as Gentiles absorb antisemitic stereotypes.

. . .

SHARED AND DISTINCTIVE CHARACTERISTICS OF "ISMS"

In grappling with these questions, we have come to believe in the explanatory and political value of identifying both the particular histories and characteristics of specific forms of oppression such as ableism or classism, as well as the patterns that connect and mutually reinforce different oppressions in a system that is inclusive and pervasive. In this book we examine the unique ways in which oppression is manifested through racism, white privilege, and immigrant status; sexism, heterosexism, and transgender experiences; religious oppression and antisemitism; and classism, ableism, and ageism/adultism.

We look at the dimensions of experience that connect these "isms" in an overarching system of domination. For example, we examine the roles of a dominant or advantaged group and (a) subordinated or targeted group(s) in each form of oppression and the differentials of power and privilege that are dynamic features of oppression, whatever its particular form. At the same time, we try to highlight the distinctive qualities and appreciate the historical and social contingencies that distinguish one form of oppression from another. In this model, diversity and the appreciation of differences are inextricably tied to social justice and the unequal ways that power and privilege construct difference in our society.

From our perspective, no one form of oppression is the base for all others, yet all are connected within a system that makes them possible. We align with theorists such as Young who describe distinctive ingredients of oppression without prioritizing one over another. We also share with Young the view that eradicating oppression ultimately requires struggle against all its forms, and that coalitions among diverse people offer the most promising strategies for challenging oppression systematically. Therefore, we highlight theory and practice that demonstrate interconnections among different forms of oppression and suggest common strategies to oppose it collectively.

. . .

CONSTRUCTING AN INCLUSIVE THEORY OF OPPRESSION

We touch on concepts from writing and activism in the Civil Rights, New Left, and women's liberation movements of the 1960s and 1970s, and from more recent movements for equality and social change, to discern lessons about oppression that provide a conceptual framework for understanding its operations. Tracking the history of ideas developed in these movements grounds our theoretical understanding in lived experience and highlights the contradictions and conflicts in different approaches to oppression and social justice as these are lived out in practice over time and place. Here, we highlight broad themes drawn from rich and well-developed academic and social movement traditions to which we are indebted.

RACISM

The social science literature on racism and insights about racism that emerged from the Civil Rights movement of the late 1950s and early 1960s profoundly shaped the way scholars and activists have come to understand oppression and its other manifestations. The Civil Rights movement fired the imagination of millions of Americans, who applied its lessons to an understanding of their particular situations and adapted its analyses and tactics to their own struggles for equality. For example, Native American, Chicano, and Puerto Rican youth styled themselves after the African American youth in the Student Nonviolent Coordinating Committee (SNCC) and Black Panther Party. The predominantly white student antiwar movement drew directly from the experiences of the black freedom struggles to shape their goals and strategies. Early women's liberation groups were spawned within SNCC itself, as black and white women applied the analyses of racial inequality to their own positions as women, as did Latinas within the Puerto Rican Youth. The gay liberation and disability rights movements credit the Civil Rights movement as a model for their organizing and activism, and poor people's and welfare rights movements likewise drew upon this heritage as do immigrant and youth activists today.

Of the many valuable legacies of the Civil Rights movement and the academic traditions focusing on racism, we highlight here two key themes. One is the awareness that racism is a system of oppression that not only stigmatizes and violates the targeted group, but also does psychic and ethical violence to the dominator group as well. The idea that oppression affects, albeit in different ways, both those advantaged and those targeted by oppression has been useful to many other groups as a way to make sense of their experiences of oppression.

The second broad theme is that racism functions not only through overt, conscious prejudice and discrimination but also through the unconscious attitudes and behaviors of a society that presumes an unacknowledged but pervasive white cultural norm. Racial images and ideas are embedded in language and cultural practices promoted as neutral and inclusive. However, the alleged neutrality of social patterns, behaviors, and assumptions in fact define and reinforce a form of cultural imperialism that supports white supremacy. Identifying unmarked and unacknowledged norms that bolster the power position of advantaged groups is an important strategy for examining other forms of oppression as well. Feminists, for example, use the idea to examine practices of male supremacy and patriarchy, and gay and lesbian rights activists use it to analyze heterosexual privilege.

The concept of racial formation has become an important analytic tool. This concept is useful for thinking about the ways in which racism is constructed and reconstructed in different contexts and periods. It works against the tendency to essentialize current social relations as given and encourages ideas about alternative ways to frame and understand human relations against systems of oppression. Critical race theory, Lat Crit theory, and Whiteness studies offer other important tools for analyzing oppression through the use of story to represent how racism operates and to invent alternative scenarios of possibility. . . .

CLASSISM

The New Left movements of the late 1960s and early 1970s espoused ideals of political democracy and personal liberty and applied their political energy to make power socially accountable. New Left critiques of power built on Marxist theory to examine issues of domination and exploitation and to focus on the structural rather than individual factors that maintain oppressive economic and social relations. They also exposed and critiqued normative assumptions that conflate democracy with capitalism and its role in suppressing the exploration of alternative economic and social arrangements.

New Left analyses examine how power operates through normalizing relations of domination and systematizing ideas and practices that are then taken as given. These analyses remind us to continually ask the question "In whose interest do prevailing systems operate?" The question of power and the interests it serves has been a useful analytic tool for examining oppression in all of its multiple forms. Asking who benefits and who pays for prevailing practices helps to expose the hierarchical relationships as well as the hidden advantages and penalties embedded in a purportedly fair and neutral system.

Postcolonial scholars and activists have extended these questions to an analysis of the power dynamics within global relations of transnational capital and their impact on labor, migration, gender and ethnic relations, environmental issues, and national development around the globe. These analyses of how power circulates alert us to the evershifting ways in which power maintains itself in support of the status quo and to the flexibility and persistence necessary to continually challenge its operations.

SEXISM

The women's liberation movement developed important theoretical and analytic tools for a general theory of oppression and liberation. Through consciousness-raising groups, women collectively uncovered and deconstructed the ways that the system of patriarchy is reproduced inside women's consciousness as well as in external social institutions, and challenged conventional assumptions about human nature, sexuality, family life, and gender roles and relations. Consciousness-raising groups developed a process for naming how members of targeted groups can collude in maintaining an unequal system, identifying the psychological as well as social factors that contribute to internalizing oppressive beliefs, and exploring how to raise consciousness to resist and challenge such systems both inside our own consciousness and externally in the world. Feminist practice also sought to create and enact new, more liberated ways of thinking and behaving. Insights from feminist theory and practice have been fruitfully used by other groups to raise consciousness, develop analyses of psychological and social assumptions and practices of their group(s) as these collude in maintaining oppression, and experiment with alternative practices.

MULTIPLE ISSUES

Women of color, lesbians, Jewish feminists, and poor and working-class women brought forth critiques from within the women's movement to critique unitary theories of feminism, stressing the multiple and diverse perspectives, needs, and goals of women from different social groups. These challenges have been used to critique unitary theories of class, race, and gender and to generate a range of analyses and ideas about oppression(s) that take into account both the multiple identities people hold and the range of experiences of oppression lived within any given group. Women of color who are lesbian and poor, for example, experience oppression in multiple and distinctive ways that demand more complex analyses of the mechanisms of oppression in the lives of diverse groups of people. Global feminism and global critical race feminism both critique and add to the strategies and theories developed by previous feminists, highlighting the leadership of women at the margins, building transnational consciousness of shared and distinctive problems women face under postcolonial systems and U.S. imperialism, and developing strategies and solutions locally to address the particularities of their national contexts.

Postcolonial studies and postmodern theories, and ongoing discussions among people in various social movements, continue to challenge binary categorization such as black/white, heterosexual/homosexual, male/female, and notions that essentialize, or treat as innately given, the groupings created within an oppressive social order. The inadequacy of defining the experience of individuals and groups in simplistic binary terms is reflected through challenges within the gay and lesbian movement raised by bisexual, transsexual, and transgender people. The range of experiences of people holding multiple identities and diverse social group memberships poses continuing challenges that theories of oppression account for their experiences.

. . .

4 (CONTINUED)

Conceptual Foundations

Rita Hardiman, Bailey W. Jackson, and Pat Griffin

. . .

CHOICE OF LABELS FOR OPPRESSOR AND OPPRESSED GROUPS

There are currently many terms that are used to describe oppressed and oppressor groups and the individual members of those groups. Oppressed groups are variously referred to as *targets, the targeted, victims, disadvantaged, subordinates*, or *the subordinated*. Oppressor groups are often referred to as *advantaged, dominants, agents*, and *privileged*. The reasons for choosing one term over another vary depending on a number of theoretical, political, pedagogical, and strategic considerations. Indeed, none of these terms is universally accepted. As educators, we must be careful, however, not to trivialize the effects of oppression by the terms that we use in describing this serious social condition and the roles individual people play in the maintenance of this social system. . . .

OPPRESSION OPERATES ON MULTIPLE DIMENSIONS

Oppression is an interlocking, multileveled system that consolidates social power to the benefit of members of privileged groups and is maintained and operationalized on three dimensions: (a) contextual dimension, (b) conscious/unconscious dimension, and (c) applied dimension (see Figure 4.1).

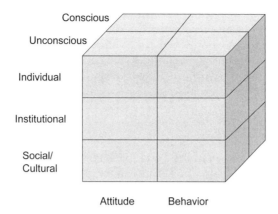

Conscious
Unconscious
Individual
Institutional
Social/
Cultural
Attitude   Behavior

Figure 4.1 Multiple Dimensions of Oppression

The contextual dimension consists of three levels: (a) individual, (b) institutional, and (c) social/cultural. The conscious/unconscious dimension describes how oppression is both intentional and unintentional. The applied dimension describes how oppression is manifested at the individual (attitudes and behaviors), institutional (policies, practices, and norms), and societal/cultural (values, beliefs, and customs) levels. The conscious/unconscious and the applied dimensions will be discussed further within the descriptions of each of the three contextual levels below:

INDIVIDUAL LEVEL

Oppression is maintained at the individual level by attitudes or behaviors of individual persons. These attitudes and behaviors can be conscious or unconscious, but their effects are equally destructive. Examples of individual actions or attitudes include the belief that women are not as capable of making reasonable, rational decisions as men are (conscious attitude); a male employer making unwanted sexual comments to a female employee in the workplace (conscious behavior); a white person automatically taking extra care to protect personal belongings when in the presence of black or Latino people (unconscious attitude); or a temporarily able-bodied person speaking loudly or slowly and using simple terms when addressing a physically disabled person (unconscious behavior).

INSTITUTIONAL LEVEL

Social institutions such as the family, government, business and industry, education, the legal system, and religious organizations are major participants in a system of oppression. Social institutions codify oppression in laws, policies, practices, and norms. As with behaviors and attitudes at the individual level, institutional policies and practices that maintain and enforce oppression are both intentional and unintentional. Examples of the less visible systems include the structural inequality of school funding in the United States, or tax benefits, health care benefits, and similar privileges that are available only to heterosexual couples through the institution of marriage. Other examples of institutional attitudes include the following: lack of an exit interview policy with faculty persons of color who take positions elsewhere to determine how a university can improve its ability to retain faculty of color in a predominantly white university (unconscious institutional norm), a business that decides not to provide bereavement leave to a lesbian employee whose partner dies (conscious institutional policy), and a state legislature that passes a law barring illegal immigrants from accessing public services (conscious institutional law).

Institutions fail to address discrimination and inequality or fail to see the discriminatory consequences of their policies and practices as often as they intentionally act to support, maintain, or advocate social oppression: for example, failing to enforce existing sexual harassment policies or deciding to hold an organizational social event in an inaccessible space without thinking that this decision might preclude the participation of members with mobility impairments.

SOCIETAL/CULTURAL LEVEL

Society's cultural norms and patterns perpetuate implicit and explicit values that bind institutions and individuals. In an oppressive society, the cultural perspective of dominant groups is imposed on institutions by individuals and on individuals by institutions. These cultural norms include philosophies of life, definitions of good and evil, beauty, normal, health, deviance, sickness, and perspectives on time, just to name a few. Cultural norms often serve the primary function of providing individuals and institutions with the justification for social oppression. Examples of these cultural beliefs or norms that influence the perspective of individual and institutional actions and attitudes include the assumption that the definition of a family is a heterosexual nuclear family (can be either conscious or unconscious norm) and the belief that anyone can achieve economic stability in the United States if they are willing to work hard and take personal responsibility for their own achievements (conscious norm).

WE ARE SOCIALIZED TO ACCEPT SYSTEMS OF OPPRESSION AS NORMAL

We are socialized into a system of social oppression through interactions with individuals, institutions, and culture. We learn to accept systems of oppression as normal through interactions with parents, peers, teachers, and other influential individuals in our lives as they, intentionally or unintentionally, pass on to us their beliefs about oppressor and oppressed groups. We also learn to accept oppression as normal through our experiences in schools and religious organizations, and our encounters with health care, criminal justice systems, and other institutions that affect our daily lives. We may not recognize how our embeddedness in particular cultural norms and values affects our views of oppressor and oppressed groups because of the pervasive presence of oppressor ideology. When viewed as a whole, our socialization into acceptance of oppressive systems, through our interactions with individuals, institutions, and cultural norms and values, constitutes a cycle of business as usual until we are able to interrupt it with information or experiences that call into question the truth of what we have learned about the power relationships among different social groups and our own position vis-à-vis these dynamics. At this point, we can choose to interrupt our socialization, to step out of the cycle of socialization with new awareness, information, and action.

THE SYSTEM OF SOCIAL OPPRESSION CO-OPTS THE SOCIAL CATEGORIES USED TO DESCRIBE THE DIFFERENCES AMONG AND BETWEEN SOCIAL GROUPS

. . .

We all have memberships in multiple social identity groups. That is to say, we can be described by our sex, race, sexual orientation, gender, religion, class, age, and ability. Naming our social group memberships/differences serves as a means of naming/describing our social/cultural groupings. They are primarily a way to describe our social group differences. . . . Though we experience our social group memberships as material, tangible identities (for example, woman, Black, heterosexual), we also inherit status associated with these identities in a system of oppression. In this way, oppression co-opts identities by attaching meaning and status to them that support the system of social oppression. The pervasive and systematic nature of oppression normalizes the redefined nature of the differences associated with social identity and transforms them into oppressed and oppressor social group identities at the expense of more neutral or alternative conceptions of identities and status (see Figure 4.2).

Members of oppressed groups are often more acutely aware of their membership because they experience the daily effects of oppression. Members of oppressor groups, on the other hand, are often unaware of themselves as members of a privileged group because the system of oppression enables and encourages them to view the accomplishments and achievements of their group members as deserved, the result of hard work, virtue, or natural superiority. At the same time, members of oppressor groups often blame the struggles, failures, and anger of members of oppressed groups on their inability, deficiency, or refusal to accept things as they are.

We are born into some of our social identities (e.g., race and ethnicity), and others either can be present at birth or can change or be acquired during our lifetime (e.g., age, class, religion, or physical/development ability). For some social group memberships, such as sexual orientation, the debate over whether we are born into or choose our sexual orientation has political consequences for the struggle for gay, lesbian, and bisexual rights. Opponents of gay rights in part base their arguments on the belief that homosexuality and bisexuality are sinful, immoral, and psychologically disturbed behavior choices. Many, but not all, gay rights proponents insist that sexual orientation is not a choice, but a characteristic with which we are born. Similarly, the transgender rights movement has challenged beliefs about the immutability of sex and gender assigned at birth, calling for a more fluid, nonbinary conception of gender and sex.

Most of us have social identities that are disadvantaged by some forms of oppression and privileged by others. Because our membership in oppressor or oppressed groups can change during our lifetime, our relative status in relationship to our multiple identities is not static. For example, a white man who becomes disabled, a Latina with working-class roots who becomes the CEO of a large corporation, or any of us as we grow old and experience changes in our status associated with aging, declining economic status, or disability, experience changes in social status related to group memberships.

Some forms of oppression are closely correlated; thus . . . if one is poor in the United States, whether destitute or among the working poor or chronically unemployed, one is

Examples of Manifestations of Social Oppression	Examples of Oppressor Groups (US-Based)	Examples of Oppressed Groups (US-Based)
Classism	Owning Class, Upper Middle Class, Middle Class	Working Class, Poor
Heterosexism	Heterosexuals	Lesbians, Bisexuals, Gay Men
Ableism	Physical/Developmentally/ Psychologically Able-Bodied People	Physically/Developmentally/ Psychologically Disabled People
Racism	Whites	African American; Asian American; Latina/o; Native American; Multi-Racial People
Religious Oppression	Christians	Jews, Hindus, Buddhists, Muslims, Atheists
Sexism	Men	Women

Figure 4.2. Examples of Multiple Manifestations and Oppressor and Oppressed Groups

more likely to experience illness and impairments that lead to disability due to the lack of access to health care. Similarly, acquiring a disability is closely correlated with being unemployed, being underemployed, or otherwise living on the economic margins of society without adequate access to health care.

The paradigm of "intersectionality," emerging from the fields of sociology, cultural studies, and critical race theory, informs our understanding of the complexities of how people experience privilege and disadvantage based on their social group memberships. Intersectionality suggests that markers of difference do not act independent of one another. Instead, our various social identities interrelate to negate the possibility of a unitary or universal experience of any one manifestation of oppression. An Asian or Latino gay man experiences the privilege of sexism in different ways than a white European heterosexual man because his experience of male privilege is muted by his identity as a man of color in a racist society and a gay man in a homophobic society.

. . .

The list of possible social identities is necessarily incomplete as our understanding of systems of oppression and liberation continues to evolve. Because the list of categories of social groups and the descriptions and types of social group change and expand over time with the heightening of our social consciousness, it is necessary that we acknowledge the limitations of current conceptualizations. For example, sexual orientation (gay, lesbian, bisexual, or heterosexual) was not a distinct identity until the late 19th century. Likewise, transgender and intersex identities as well as many emergent associated identities like "genderqueer" have only entered the lexicon of oppression in the last 15 years.

BORDER IDENTITIES

No attempt to describe the complex dynamics of oppression can be completely all-encompassing of lived experience. Some social identities do not clearly fit into a binary model of oppressed/targeted or oppressor/advantaged. We acknowledge this limitation with the designation *border identities*. Examples of border identities include people of mixed racial backgrounds, and persons who are bicultural by virtue of being born or raised in one country or culture and moving to a new country and cultural milieu. Adopted children of one race who are raised by persons of a different race may also occupy bordered space. Some social identities that could at one time be characterized as targeted identities have, over time, migrated to the advantaged side of the binary or at least moved out of the targeted category as oppressors rename and redefine targeted groups for their own benefit. For example, Roman Catholics were historically subjected to discrimination and violence, but are now integrated into the fabric of mainstream religions in the United States with considerable political power.

Some individuals with border identities may experience both privilege and disadvantage due to their status. For instance a bisexual man who is in a heterosexual marriage is both privileged by having access to rights only enjoyed by heterosexuals, and also potentially targeted by his identity as a bisexual in a binary system of sexual orientation. A transgender or transsexual man may intentionally or unintentionally benefit from male privilege after transitioning yet still be discriminated against by health care, criminal justice, or other social institutions because he is transgender. Similarly, children of color who are adopted by white families may have access to both race or class privilege from their parents, but are also targeted by racism due to their appearance and cultural characteristics.

DISADVANTAGED BY ASSOCIATION

Another group that does not fit within the binary notion of oppressed/advantaged or oppressed/targeted are those who occupy an intermediary or gray space due to their relationship to family members or significant others in their lives. These persons might include parents, spouses/partners, or family members of people with disabilities; parents or siblings of lesbians, gays, bisexual, or transgender people; or white people who are married or partnered to people of color, or have children of color. For example, able-bodied parents of a disabled child may have privilege as nondisabled people, yet their life circumstances are profoundly affected by their relationship to a disabled individual—their child. Their child's targeted status affects the family's income, housing, ability to travel, employment, and social interactions in their community. They may have to deal with the stereotypes or stigma attached to their child or other family member.

Similarly, a white member of a mixed-race couple or a white parent of mixed-race children is affected by racism in a secondary way and has less clear access to systems that advantage Whites in a racist society, due to this relationship. The mixed-race family's ability to find housing, social acceptance, employment, and safety is affected by racism, and this therefore has an impact on the white member of the family as well as the family members who are people of color. People in these situations are "disadvantaged by association" and live a dual existence: having access to privilege and resources in some capacities due to their personal dominant status, but also being a target of discrimination and other manifestations of oppression due to their family status. Individuals who are disadvantaged by association, however, do not automatically become allies. Many individuals in these relationships continue to support or participate in the system of oppression to which their loved one, and indeed they, are subjected by encouraging assimilation or other strategies that collude with oppression.

RELATIONSHIPS AMONG AND BETWEEN OPPRESSOR AND OPPRESSED GROUPS IN A SYSTEM OF OPPRESSION

. . .

INTERNALIZED SUBORDINATION AND DOMINATION

Oppressive systems work most effectively when both advantaged and targeted group members internalize their roles and accept their positions in the hierarchical relationship between them.

Internalized subordination refers to ways in which the oppressed collude with their own oppression. Targeted social groups can live within a system of oppression that injures them or deprives them of certain rights without having the language or consciousness. Freire used the term *conscientization* to name their understanding of their situation as an effect of oppression rather than the natural order of things. Memmi described this process as *psychological colonization* when disadvantaged groups internalize their oppressed condition and collude with the oppressive ideology and social system. Freire refers to this process as oppressed groups playing host to the oppressor.

People who have been socialized in an oppressive environment, and who internalize the dominant group's ideology about their group, have learned to accept a definition of themselves that is hurtful and limiting. They think, feel, and act in ways that demonstrate the devaluation of their group and accept themselves as members of an inferior group. For example, internalized subordination is operating when oppressed group members question the credentials or abilities of members of their own social group without cause, yet unquestioningly accept that members of the oppressor group are qualified, talented, and deserving of their credentials. Internalized subordination also operates when target group members curry favor with dominant group members and distance themselves from their own group.

Conscious collusion occurs when oppressed group members knowingly, but not necessarily voluntarily, go along with their own mistreatment to survive or to maintain some status, livelihood, or other benefit, as when a person of color silently endures racist jokes told by a boss. Such collusion is often seen by the targeted group member as necessary to "live to fight another day." The more insidious form of collusion is unconscious, not knowing that one is collaborating with one's own dehumanization: for example, when a woman blames herself for the actions of her rapist or batterer or when gay and lesbian people, in order to gain acceptance from heterosexuals, exclude members of their community who look or act "too gay."

Internalized domination refers to the behaviors, thoughts, and feelings of oppressor group members who, through their socialization as members of the dominant group, learn to think and act in ways that express internalized notions of entitlement and privilege. Members of oppressor groups are socialized to internalize their dominant status so that it is not seen as privileged, but is experienced as the natural order of things, as rights, rather than as a consequence of systems that provide them with advantages not readily available to other groups.

Examples of internalized domination include men talking over and interrupting women in conversation, while simultaneously labeling women as chatty. Privileged groups learn to expect to be treated well and to be accommodated, as when English-only-speaking people in the United States get irritated when English language learners speak English with an accent. Extreme examples include the "erasure" of targeted group members by failing to acknowledge their existence or importance. For example, historical presentations that Columbus discovered America erase the existence of native peoples who preceded him by several thousand years.

. . .

INDIVIDUAL AND SOCIAL CHANGE

Now that we have described the characteristics of social oppression and the dynamics that serve to maintain oppressive systems, we turn our attention to an equally important topic in our courses: fostering individual and social change. . . . To be able to envision oneself as a change agent, it is necessary to have language that describes this role. We use the terms *ally* for advantaged group members and *empowered targeted group members* to refer to these change agent roles.

ALLIES

Allies are members of the advantaged group who act against the oppression(s) from which they derive power, privilege, and acceptance. Individuals who choose to ally themselves with people who are targeted by oppression may have different motivations for their actions. Some allies may be motivated by an understanding that their privileges come at a cost, and working against oppression can be in one's self-interest. For example, under-standing how eliminating architectural barriers that limit people with disabilities' access to buildings can also benefit temporarily able-bodied people as they themselves age or become disabled. Other allies may be motivated to act by altruistic feelings or by a moral or spiritual belief that oppression is wrong. Another source of motivation may come from one's experience as a person who is "disadvantaged by association" with people who are targeted. For example, having a child who is disabled or having a family member "come out" as lesbian or gay can spur family members to become allies against the oppression that is targeting their loved ones, and themselves by extension. Whatever the motivation for allies, their role as change agents, working with other privileged group members or in coalition with targeted group members to challenge systems of oppression, is an essential aspect of eliminating inequality.

EMPOWERED TARGETED GROUP MEMBERS

Empowered targeted group members reject the inferior status assigned to them in a system of oppression. They work to overcome the internalized aspects of oppression they were socialized to accept. They have pride in their group identity and enjoy a sense of com-munity with others from their social identity group. Feminist conscious-raising groups and gay pride marches are two examples of these efforts. Most importantly, they develop a liberatory consciousness that leads them to become actively involved in efforts to elimi-nate oppression. These efforts include working in coalition with allies or working with other targeted group members. Finally, empowered targeted group members understand the interconnections among different manifestations of oppression and the importance of challenging them all, not only the ones that affect them most directly.

. . .

UNDERLYING ASSUMPTIONS

Several underlying assumptions create a philosophical foundation for our social justice education practice.

IT IS NOT USEFUL TO ARGUE ABOUT A HIERARCHY OF OPPRESSIONS

We believe that little is gained in debating which forms of oppression are more damaging or which one is the root out of which all others grow. Though we acknowledge that some participants believe that there is an urgent need to address one form of oppression over others, we present the perspective that each form of oppression is destructive to the human spirit. We do, however, identify ways in which specific forms of oppression are similar or different, but do not rank the differences identified. Our courses are based on the belief that even if we could eliminate one form of oppression, the continued existence of the others would still affect us all.

ALL FORMS OF OPPRESSION ARE INTERCONNECTED

In addition to our use of an underlying conceptual framework to understand the dynamics of all the forms of oppression, we also recognize that each participant in our courses is a collage of many social identities. Even though a course is focused on sexism, for example, each participant's race, class, religion, sexual orientation, ability, and gender affect how that participant experiences sexism. We encourage participants to explore the intersections of their different social group memberships and also to understand the similarities in the dynamics of different forms of oppression.

CONFRONTING OPPRESSION WILL BENEFIT EVERYONE

Most people can understand how confronting sexism will benefit women or how addressing ableism will benefit people with disabilities. We also believe that men and nondisabled people will benefit from the elimination of sexism and ableism. Unfortunately, some participants react to social justice education as if engaged in a conflict in which one group wins and another loses. However, when people are subjected to oppression whatever their social group membership, their talents and potential achievements are lost and we all suffer from this loss. Moreover, we all have spheres of influence and connections that link us to people who are directly affected by oppression. Even if we are not members of a particular disadvantaged social group, we have friends, coworkers, or family members who are. In addition, we might become members of disadvantaged social groups in the future if, for example, we become disabled or have a change in economic circumstances. Another way we are hurt by oppression is that many people who are members of groups that benefit from oppression live with a burden of guilt, shame, and helplessness and are never sure whether their individual accomplishments are earned or the result of advantages received due to their social group membership. Confronting oppression can free members of all social groups to take action toward social justice. The goal in eliminating oppression is an equitable redistribution of social power and resources among all social groups at all levels (individual, institutional, and societal/cultural). The goal is not to reverse the current power inequity by simply interchanging the groups in power positions.

FIXING BLAME HELPS NO ONE; TAKING RESPONSIBILITY HELPS EVERYONE

We present the perspective that there is little to be gained from fixing blame for our heritage of social injustice. We are each born into a social system in which we are taught to accept things as they are. Nothing is gained by feeling shame about what our ancestors did or what our contemporaries do to different groups of people out of fear, ignorance, or malice. Taking responsibility, in contrast, means acting to address oppression. Rather than becoming lost in a sense of helplessness, our goal is to enable participants to understand how they can choose to take responsibility in their everyday lives for confronting social injustice.

CONFRONTING SOCIAL INJUSTICE IS PAINFUL AND JOYFUL

Most participants do not want to believe that they harbor prejudices about groups of people. Confronting these prejudices in themselves and others is difficult. Participants need to open themselves to the discomfort and uncertainty of questioning what is familiar, comfortable, and unquestioned. Facing the contradictions between what participants have been taught to believe about social justice and the realities of the experiences of different social groups is complex. Participants learn that some of what they were taught is inaccurate. Some necessary information was not part of their education. Participants need to be assisted through this process with hope and care. At the same time, we believe that understanding social oppression and taking action against it can be a joyful and liberating experience. Some participants' lives are changed in exciting and life-affirming ways as a result of their experiences in social justice education courses. They find ways to act on their beliefs and make changes in their personal lives that profoundly affect their personal and professional relationships.

. . .

5

Five Faces of Oppression

Iris Marion Young

. . .

In this chapter I offer some explanation of the concept of oppression as I understand its use by new social movements in the United States since the 1960s. My starting point is reflection on the conditions of the groups said by these movements to be oppressed: among others, women, Blacks, Chicanos, Puerto Ricans and other Spanish-speaking Americans, American Indians, Jews, lesbians and gay men, Arabs, Asians, old people, working-class people, and the physically and mentally disabled. I aim to systematize the meaning of the concept of oppression as used by these diverse political movements, and to provide normative argument to clarify the wrongs the term names.

Obviously the above-named groups are not oppressed to the same extent or in the same ways. In the most general sense, all oppressed people suffer some inhibition of their ability to develop and exercise their capacities and express their needs, thoughts, and feelings. In that abstract sense all oppressed people face a common condition. Beyond that, in any more specific sense, it is not possible to define a single set of criteria that describe the condition of oppression of the above groups. Consequently, attempts by theorists and activists to discover a common description or the essential causes of the oppression of all these groups have frequently led to fruitless disputes about whose oppression is more fundamental or more grave. The contexts in which members of these groups use the term *oppression* to describe the injustices of their situation suggest that oppression names in fact a family of concepts and conditions, which I divide into five categories: exploitation, marginalization, powerlessness, cultural imperialism, and violence.

. . .

OPPRESSION AS A STRUCTURAL CONCEPT

. . . In its traditional usage, oppression means the exercise of tyranny by a ruling group. Oppression also traditionally carries a strong connotation of conquest and colonial domination. The Hebrews were oppressed in Egypt, and many uses of the term oppression in the West invoke this paradigm. . . . New left social movements of the 1960s and 1970s, however, shifted the meaning of the concept of oppression. In its new usage, oppression designates the disadvantage and injustice some people suffer not because a tyrannical power coerces them, but because of the everyday practices of a well-intentioned liberal society. . . .

. . . Oppression in this sense is structural, rather than the result of a few people's choices or policies. Its causes are embedded in unquestioned norms, habits, and symbols, in the assumptions underlying institutional rules and the collective consequences of following those rules. . . . In this extended structural sense, oppression refers to the vast and deep injustices some groups suffer as a consequence of often unconscious assumptions and reactions of well meaning people in ordinary interactions, media and cultural stereotypes, and structural features of bureaucratic hierarchies and market mechanisms—in short, the normal processes of everyday life. . . .

I do not mean to suggest that within a system of oppression individual persons do not intentionally harm others in oppressed groups. The raped woman, the beaten Black youth, the locked-out worker, the gay man harassed on the street, are victims of intentional actions by identifiable agents. I also do not mean to deny that specific groups are beneficiaries of the oppression of other groups, and thus have an interest in their continued oppression. Indeed, for every oppressed group there is a group that is privileged in relation to that group. . . .

Racism, sexism, ageism, homophobia, some social movements asserted, are distinct forms of oppression with their own dynamics apart from those of class, even though they may interact with class oppression. From often heated discussions among socialists, feminists, and antiracism activists in the last ten years, a consensus is emerging that many different groups must be said to be oppressed in our society, and that no single form of oppression can be assigned causal or moral primacy. The same discussion has also led to the recognition that group differences cut across individual lines in a multiplicity of ways that can entail privilege and oppression for the same person in different respects. Only a plural explication of the concept of oppression can adequately capture these insights.

Accordingly, I offer below an explication of five faces of oppression as a useful set of categories and distinctions which I believe is comprehensive in the sense that it covers all the groups said by new left social movements to be oppressed, and all the ways they are oppressed. I derive the five faces of oppression from reflection on the condition of these groups. Because different factors, or combinations of factors, constitute the oppression of different groups, making their oppression irreducible, I believe it is not possible to give one essential definition of oppression. The five categories articulated in this chapter, however, are adequate to describe the oppression of any group, as well as its similarities with and differences from the oppression of other groups. But first we must ask what a "group" is.

THE CONCEPT OF A SOCIAL GROUP

. . . A social group is a collective of persons differentiated from at least one other group by cultural forms, practices, or way of life. Members of a group have a specific affinity with one another because of their similar experience (or way of life), which prompts them to associate with one another more than with those not identified with the group. Groups are an expression of social relations; a group exists only in relation to at least one other group. . . .

A social group is defined not primarily by a set of shared attributes, but by a sense of identity. What defines Black Americans as a social group is not primarily their skin color; some persons whose skin color is fairly light, for example, identify themselves as black. Though sometimes objective attributes are a necessary condition for classifying oneself or others as belonging to a certain social group, it is identification with a certain social status, the common history that social status produces, and self-identification that define the group as a group. . . .

Groups constitute individuals. A person's particular sense of history, affinity, and sep-arateness—even the person's mode of reasoning, evaluating, and expressing feeling—are constituted partly by her or his group affinities. This does not mean that persons have no individual styles, or are unable to transcend or reject a group identity. Nor does it preclude persons from having many aspects that are independent of these group identities. . . .

While I agree that individuals should be free to pursue life plans in their own ways, it is foolish to deny the reality of groups. . . . Even when they belong to oppressed groups, people's group identifications are often important to them, and they often feel a special affinity for others in their group. I believe that group differentiation is both an inevitable and a desirable aspect of modern social processes. Social justice requires not the melting away of differences, but institutions that promote reproduction of and respect for group differences without oppression.

. . .

THE FACES OF OPPRESSION

EXPLOITATION

The central insight expressed in the concept of exploitation is that this oppression occurs through a steady process of the transfer of the results of the labor of one social group to benefit another. The injustice of class division does not consist only in the distributive fact that some people have great wealth while most people have little. Exploitation enacts a structural relation between social groups. Social rules about what work is, who does what for whom, how work is compensated, and the social processes by which the results of work are appropriated operate to enact relations of power and inequality. These relations are produced and reproduced through a systematic process in which the energies of the have-nots are continuously expended to maintain and augment the power, status, and wealth of the haves. . . .

Feminists have had little difficulty showing that women's oppression consists partly in a systematic and unreciprocated transfer of powers from women to men. Women's oppres-sion consists not merely in an inequality of status, power, and wealth resulting from men's excluding them from privileged activities. The freedom, power, status, and self-realization of men is possible precisely because women work for them. Gender exploitation has two aspects: transfer of the fruits of material labor to men, and the transfer of nurturing and sexual energies to men. . . . Thus, for example, in most systems of agriculture production in the world, men take to market the goods women have produced, and more often than not men receive the status and often the entire income from this labor.

. . . Women provide men and children with emotional care and provide men with sexual satisfaction, and as a group receive relatively little of either from men. The gender social-ization of women makes us tend to be more attentive to interactive dynamics than men, and makes women good at providing empathy and support for people's feelings and at smoothing over interactive tensions. Both men and women look to women as nurturers of their personal lives, and women frequently complain that when they look to men for emotional support they do not receive it. The norms of heterosexuality, moreover, are oriented around male pleasure, and consequently, many women receive little satisfaction from their sexual interactions with men.

. . .

Is it possible to conceptualize a form of exploitation that is racially specific on analogy with the gender-specific forms just discussed? I suggest that the category of *menial* labor might supply a means for such conceptualization. In its derivation, "menial" designates the labor of servants. Wherever there is racism, there is the assumption, more or less enforced, that members of the oppressed racial groups are or ought to be servants of those, or some of those, in the privileged group. In most white racist societies this means that many white people have dark- or yellow-skinned domestic servants, and in the United States today there remains significant racial structuring of private household service. But in the United States today much service labor has gone public: anyone who goes to a good hotel or a good restaurant can have servants. Servants often attend the daily—and nightly—activities of business executives, government officials, and other high-status professionals. In our society there remains strong cultural pressure to fill servant jobs—bellhop, porter, chambermaid, busboy, and so on—with Black and Latino workers. These jobs entail a transfer of energies whereby the servers enhance the status of the served.

Menial labor usually refers not only to service, however, but also to any servile, unskilled, low-paying work lacking in autonomy, in which a person is subject to taking orders from many people. Menial work tends to be auxiliary work, instrumental to the work of others, where those others receive primary recognition for doing the job. Laborers on a construction site, for example, are at the beck and call of welders, electricians, carpenters, and other skilled workers, who receive recognition for the job done. In the United States explicit racial discrimination once reserved menial work for Blacks, Chicanos, American Indians, and Chinese, and menial work still tends to be linked to Black and Latino workers. I offer this category of menial labor as a form of racially specific exploitation, as a provisional category in need of exploration. . . .

The injustice of exploitation consists in social processes that bring about a transfer of energies from one group to another to produce unequal distributions, and in the way in which social institutions enable a few to accumulate while they constrain many more. The injustices of exploitation cannot be eliminated by the redistribution of goods, for as long as institutionalized practices and structural relations remain unaltered, the process of transfer will re-create an unequal distribution of benefits. Bringing about justice where there is exploitation requires reorganization of institutions and practices of decision making, alteration of the division of labor, and similar measures of institutional, structural, and cultural change.

MARGINALIZATION

Increasingly in the United States, racial oppression occurs in the form of marginalization rather than exploitation. *Marginals* are people the system of labor cannot or will not use. Not only in Third World capitalist countries, but also in most Western capitalist societies, there is a growing underclass of people permanently confined to lives of social marginality, most of whom are racially marked—Blacks or Indians in Latin America, and Blacks, East Indians, Eastern Europeans, or North Africans in Europe.

Marginalization is by no means the fate only of racially marked groups, however. In the United States a shamefully large proportion of the population is marginal: old people, and increasingly people who are not very old but get laid off from their jobs and cannot find new work; young people, especially Black or Latino, who cannot find first or second jobs; many single mothers and their children; other people involuntarily unemployed; many mentally and physically disabled people; American Indians (especially those on reservations).

Marginalization is perhaps the most dangerous form of oppression. A whole category of people is expelled from useful participation in social life and thus potentially subjected to severe material deprivation and even extermination. The material deprivation marginalization often causes is certainly unjust, especially in a society where others have plenty.

Contemporary advanced capitalist societies have in principle acknowledged the injustice of material deprivation caused by marginalization, and have taken some steps to address it by providing welfare payments and services. The continuance of this welfare state is by no means assured, and in most welfare state societies, especially the United States, welfare redistributions do not eliminate large-scale suffering and deprivation.

Material deprivation, which can be addressed by redistributive social policies, is not, however, the extent of the harm caused by marginalization. Two categories of injustice beyond distribution are associated with marginality in advanced capitalist societies. First, the provision of welfare itself produces new injustice by depriving those dependent on it of rights and freedoms that others have. Second, even when material deprivation is somewhat mitigated by the welfare state, marginalization is unjust because it blocks the opportunity to exercise capacities in socially defined and recognized ways. I shall explicate each of these in turn.

. . .

Today the exclusion of dependent persons from equal citizenship rights is only barely hidden beneath the surface. Because they depend on bureaucratic institutions for support or services, the old, the poor, and the mentally or physically disabled are subject to patronizing, punitive, demeaning, and arbitrary treatment by the policies and people associated with welfare bureaucracies. Being a "dependent" in our society implies being legitimately subject to the often arbitrary and invasive authority of social service providers and other public and private administrators who enforce rules with which the marginal must comply, and otherwise exercise power over the conditions of their lives. In meeting the needs of the marginalized, often with the aid of social scientific disciplines, welfare agencies also construct the needs themselves. Medical and social service professionals know what is good for those they serve, and the marginals and dependents themselves do not have the right to claim to know what is good for them. Dependency in our society thus implies, as it has in all liberal societies, a sufficient warrant to suspend basic rights to privacy, respect, and individual choice.

Although dependency produces conditions of injustice in our society, dependency in itself need not be oppressive. One cannot imagine a society in which some people would not need to be dependent on others at least some of the time: children, sick people, women recovering from childbirth, old people who have become frail, depressed or otherwise emotionally needy persons have the moral right to depend on others for subsistence and support.

An important contribution of feminist moral theory has been to question the deeply held assumption that moral agency and full citizenship require that a person be autonomous and independent. Feminists have exposed this assumption as inappropriately individualistic and derived from a specifically male experience of social relations, which values competition and solitary achievement. Female experience of social relations, arising both from women's typical domestic care responsibilities and from the kinds of paid work that many women do, tends to recognize dependence as a basic human condition. Whereas on the autonomy model a just society would, as much as possible, give people the opportunity to be independent, the feminist model envisions justice as according respect and participation in decision making to those who are dependent as well as to those who are independent. Dependency should not be a reason to be deprived of choice and respect, and much of the oppression many marginals experience would be lessened if a less individualistic model of rights prevailed.

Marginalization does not cease to be oppressive when one has shelter and food. Many old people, for example, have sufficient means to live comfortably but remain oppressed in their marginal status. Even if marginals were provided a comfortable material life within institutions that respected their freedom and dignity, injustices of marginality would remain in the form of uselessness, boredom, and lack of self-respect. Most of our society's productive and recognized activities take place in contexts of organized social cooperation, and social structures and processes that close persons out of such social cooperation are unjust. . . .

POWERLESSNESS

As I have indicated, the Marxist idea of class is important because it helps reveal the structure of exploitation: that some people have their power and wealth because they profit from the labor of others. For this reason I reject the claim some make that a traditional class exploitation model fails to capture the structure of contemporary society. It remains the case that the labor of most people in the society augments the power of relatively few. Despite their differences from nonprofessional workers, most professional workers are still not members of the capitalist class. Professional labor either involves exploitative transfers to capitalists or supplies important conditions for such transfers. Professional workers are in an ambiguous class position, it is true, because they also benefit from the exploitation of nonprofessional workers.

While it is false to claim that a division between capitalist and working classes no longer describes our society, it is also false to say that class relations have remained unaltered since the nineteenth century. An adequate conception of oppression cannot ignore the experience of social division reflected in the colloquial distinction between the "middle class" and the "working class," a division structured by the social division of labor between professionals and nonprofessionals. Professionals are privileged in relation to nonprofessionals by virtue of their position in the division of labor and the status it carries. Nonprofessionals suffer a form of oppression in addition to exploitation, which I call *powerlessness*.

. . . [D]omination in modern society is enacted through the widely dispersed powers of many agents mediating the decisions of others. To that extent many people have some power in relation to others, even though they lack the power to decide policies or results. The powerless are those who lack authority or power even in this mediated sense, those over whom power is exercised without their exercising it; the powerless are situated so that they must take orders and rarely have the right to give them. Powerlessness also designates a position in the division of labor and the concomitant social position that allows persons little opportunity to develop and exercise skills. The powerless have little or no work autonomy; exercise little creativity or judgment in their work; have no technical expertise or authority; express themselves awkwardly, especially in public or bureaucratic settings; and do not command respect. Powerlessness names the oppressive situations Sennett and Cobb describe in their famous study of working-class men.

This powerless status is perhaps best described negatively: the powerless lack the authority, status, and sense of self that professionals tend to have. The status privilege of professionals has three aspects, the lack of which produces oppression for nonprofessionals.

First, acquiring and practicing a profession has an expansive, progressive character. Being professional usually requires a college education and the acquisition of a specialized knowledge that entails working with symbols and concepts. Professionals experience progress first in acquiring the expertise, and then in the course of professional advancement and rise in status. The life of the nonprofessional by comparison is powerless in the sense that it lacks this orientation toward the progressive development of capacities and avenues for recognition.

Second, while many professionals have supervisors and cannot directly influence many decisions or the actions of many people, most nevertheless have considerable day-to-day work autonomy. Professionals usually have some authority over others, moreover—either over workers they supervise, or over auxiliaries or clients. Nonprofessionals, on the other hand, lack autonomy, and in both their working and their consumer/client lives often stand under the authority of professionals.

Though based on a division of labor between "mental" and "manual" work, the distinction between "middle class" and "working class" designates a division not only in working life, but also in nearly all aspects of social life. Professionals and nonprofessionals belong to different cultures in the United States. The two groups tend to live in segregated neighborhoods or even different towns, a process itself mediated by planners, zoning officials, and real estate people. The groups tend to have different tastes in food, decor, clothes, music, and vacations, and often different health and educational needs. Members of each group socialize for the most part with others in the same status group. While there is some intergroup mobility between generations, for the most part the children of professionals become professionals and the children of nonprofessionals do not.

Thus, the privileges of the professional extend beyond the workplace to a whole way of life. I call this way of life *respectability*. To treat people with respect is to be prepared to listen to what they have to say or to do what they request because they have some authority, expertise, or influence. The norms of respectability in our society are associated specifically with professional culture. Professional dress, speech, tastes, demeanor all connote respectability. Generally professionals expect and receive respect from others. In restaurants, banks, hotels, real estate offices, and many other such public places, as well as in the media, professionals typically receive more respectful treatment than nonprofessionals. For this reason nonprofessionals seeking a loan or a job, or to buy a house or a car, will often try to look "professional" and "respectable" in those settings.

The privilege of this professional respectability appears starkly in the dynamics of racism and sexism. In daily interchange, women and men of color must prove their respectability. At first they are often not treated by strangers with respectful distance or deference. Once people discover that this woman or that Puerto Rican man is a college teacher or a business executive, however, they often behave more respectfully toward her or him. . . .

CULTURAL IMPERIALISM

Exploitation, marginalization, and powerlessness all refer to relations of power and oppression that occur by virtue of the social division of labor—who works for whom, who does not work, and how the content of work defines one institutional position relative to others. These three categories refer to structural and institutional relations that delimit people's material lives, including but not restricted to the resources they have access to and the concrete opportunities they have or do not have to develop and exercise their capacities. These kinds of oppression are a matter of concrete power in relation to others—of who benefits from whom, and who is dispensable.

Recent theorists of movements of group liberation, notably feminist and Black liberation theorists, have also given prominence to a rather different form of oppression, which following Lugones and Spelman I shall call *cultural imperialism*. To experience cultural imperialism means to experience how the dominant meanings of a society render the particular perspective of one's own group invisible at the same time as they stereotype one's group and mark it as the Other.

Cultural imperialism involves the universalization of a dominant group's experience and culture, and its establishment as the norm. . . . Often without noticing they do so, dominant groups project their own experience as representative of humanity as such. Cultural products also express the dominant group's perspective on and interpretation of events and elements in the society, including other groups in the society, insofar as they attain cultural status at all.

An encounter with other groups, however, can challenge the dominant group's claim to universality. The dominant group reinforces its position by bringing the other groups under the measure of its dominant norms. Consequently, the difference of women from men, American Indians or Africans from Europeans, Jews from Christians, homosexuals from heterosexuals, workers from professionals becomes reconstructed largely as deviance and inferiority. Since only the dominant group's cultural expressions receive wide dissemination, their cultural expressions become the normal, or the universal, and thereby the unremarkable. Given the normality of its own cultural expressions and identity, the dominant group constructs the differences which some groups exhibit as lack and negation. These groups become marked as Other.

The culturally dominated undergo a paradoxical oppression in that they are both marked out by stereotypes and at the same time rendered invisible. As remarkable, deviant beings, the culturally imperialized are stamped with an essence. The stereotypes confine them to a nature which is often attached in some way to their bodies, and which thus cannot easily be denied. These stereotypes so permeate the society that they are not noticed as contestable. Just as everyone knows that the earth goes around the sun, so everyone knows that gay people are promiscuous, that American Indians are alcoholics, and that women are good with children. White males, on the other hand, insofar as they escape group marking, can be individuals.

Those living under cultural imperialism find themselves defined from the outside, positioned, placed, by a network of dominant meanings they experience as arising from elsewhere, from those with whom they do not identify and who do not identify with them. Consequently, the dominant culture's stereotyped and inferiorized images of the group must be internalized by group members at least to the extent that they are forced to react to the behavior of others influenced by those images. This creates for the culturally oppressed the experience that W. E. B. Du Bois called "double consciousness"—"this sense of always looking at one's self through the eyes of others, of measuring one's soul by the tape of a world that looks on in amused contempt and pity." Double consciousness arises when the oppressed subject refuses to coincide with these devalued, objectified, stereotyped visions of herself or himself. While the subject desires recognition as human—capable of activity, full of hope and possibility—she receives from the dominant culture only the judgment that she is different, marked, or inferior.

The group defined by the dominant culture as deviant, as a stereotyped Other, is culturally different from the dominant group, because the status of Otherness creates specific experiences not shared by the dominant group, and because culturally oppressed groups also are often socially segregated and occupy specific positions in the social division of labor. Members of such groups express their specific group experiences and interpretations of the world to one another, developing and perpetuating their own culture. Double consciousness, then, occurs because one finds one's being defined by two cultures: a dominant and a subordinate culture. Because they can affirm and recognize one another as sharing similar experiences and perspectives on social life, people in culturally imperialized groups can often maintain a sense of positive subjectivity.

Cultural imperialism involves the paradox of experiencing oneself as invisible at the same time that one is marked out as different. The invisibility comes about when dominant groups fail to recognize the perspective embodied in their cultural expressions as a perspective. These dominant cultural expressions often simply have little place for the experience of other groups, at most only mentioning or referring to them in stereotyped or marginalized ways. This, then, is the injustice of cultural imperialism: that the oppressed group's own experience and interpretation of social life finds little expression that touches the dominant culture, while that same culture imposes on the oppressed group its experience and interpretation of social life. . . .

VIOLENCE

Finally, many groups suffer the oppression of systematic violence. Members of some groups live with the knowledge that they must fear random, unprovoked attacks on their persons or property, which have no motive but to damage, humiliate, or destroy the person. In American society women, Blacks, Asians, Arabs, gay men, and lesbians live under such threats of violence, and in at least some regions Jews, Puerto Ricans, Chicanos, and other Spanish-speaking Americans must fear such violence as well. Physical violence against these groups is shockingly frequent. Rape crisis center networks estimate that more than one-third of all American women experience an attempted or successful sexual assault in their lifetimes. Manning Marable catalogs a large number of incidents of racist violence and terror against Blacks in the United States between 1980 and 1982. He cites dozens of incidents of the severe beating, killing, or rape of Blacks by police officers on duty, in which the police involved were acquitted of any wrongdoing. In 1981, moreover, there were at least five hundred documented cases of random white teenage violence against Blacks. Violence against gay men and lesbians is not only common, but has been increasing in the last five years. While the frequency of physical attack on members of these and other racially or sexually marked groups is very disturbing. I also include in this category less severe incidents of harassment, intimidation, or ridicule simply for the purpose of degrading, humiliating, or stigmatizing group members.

. . .

What makes violence a face of oppression is less the particular acts themselves—though these are often utterly horrible—than the social context surrounding them, which makes them possible and even acceptable. What makes violence a phenomenon of social injustice, and not merely an individual moral wrong, is its systemic character, its existence as a social practice.

Violence is systemic because it is directed at members of a group simply because they are members of that group. Any woman, for example, has a reason to fear rape. Regardless of what a Black man has done to escape the oppressions of marginality or powerlessness, he lives knowing he is subject to attack or harassment. The oppression of violence consists not only in direct victimization, but in the daily knowledge shared by all members of oppressed groups that they are *liable* to violation, solely on account of their group identity. Just living under such a threat of attack on oneself or family or friends deprives the oppressed of freedom and dignity, and needlessly expends their energy.

Violence is a social practice. It is a social given that everyone knows happens and will happen again. It is always at the horizon of social imagination, even for those who do not perpetrate it. According to the prevailing social logic, some circumstances make such violence more "called for" than others. The idea of rape will occur to many men who pick up a hitch-hiking woman; the idea of hounding or teasing a gay man on their dorm floor will occur to many straight male college students. Often several persons inflict the violence together, especially in all-male groupings. Sometimes violators set out looking for people to beat up, rape, or taunt. This rule-bound, social, and often premeditated character makes violence against groups a social practice.

Group violence approaches legitimacy, moreover, in the sense that it is tolerated. Often, third parties find it unsurprising because it happens frequently and lies as a constant possibility at the horizon of the social imagination. Even when they are caught, those who perpetrate acts of group-directed violence or harassment often receive light or no punishment. To that extent society renders their acts acceptable.

. . .

[T]he violation of rape, beating, killing, and harassment of women, people of color, gays, and other marked groups is motivated by fear or hatred of those groups. Sometimes the motive may be a simple will to power, to victimize those marked as vulnerable by the very social fact that they are subject to violence. If so, this motive is secondary in the sense that it depends on a social practice of group violence. Violence-causing fear or hatred of the other at least partly involves insecurities on the part of the violators; its irrationality suggests that unconscious processes are at work.

Cultural imperialism, moreover, itself intersects with violence. The culturally imperialized may reject the dominant meanings and attempt to assert their own subjectivity, or the fact of the cultural difference may put the lie to the dominant culture's implicit claim to universality. The dissonance generated by such a challenge to the hegemonic cultural meanings can also be a source of irrational violence.

. . . I have argued that group-directed violence is institutionalized and systemic. To the degree that institutions and social practices encourage, tolerate, or enable the perpetration of violence against members of specific groups, those institutions and practices are unjust and should be reformed. Such reform may require the redistribution of resources or positions, but in large part can come only through a change in cultural images, stereotypes, and the mundane reproduction of relations of dominance and aversion in the gestures of everyday life.

APPLYING THE CRITERIA

. . .

I have arrived at the five faces of oppression—exploitation, marginalization, powerlessness, cultural imperialism, and violence—as the best way to avoid such exclusions and reductions. They function as criteria for determining whether individuals and groups are oppressed, rather than as a full theory of oppression. I believe that these criteria are objective. They provide a means of refuting some people's beliefs that their group is oppressed when it is not, as well as a means of persuading others that a group is oppressed when they doubt it. Each criterion can be operationalized; each can be applied through the assessment of observable behavior, status relationships, distributions, texts, and other cultural artifacts. I have no illusions that such assessments can be value-neutral. But these criteria can nevertheless serve as means of evaluating claims that a group is oppressed, or adjudicating disputes about whether or how a group is oppressed.

The presence of any of these five conditions is sufficient for calling a group oppressed. But different group oppressions exhibit different combinations of these forms, as do different individuals in the groups. Nearly all, if not all, groups said by contemporary social movements to be oppressed suffer cultural imperialism. The other oppressions they experience vary. Working-class people are exploited and powerless, for example, but if employed and white do not experience marginalization and violence. Gay men, on the other hand, are not qua gay exploited or powerless, but they experience severe cultural imperialism and violence. Similarly, Jews and Arabs as groups are victims of cultural imperialism and violence, though many members of these groups also suffer exploitation or powerlessness. Old people are oppressed by marginalization and cultural imperialism, and this is also true of physically and mentally disabled people. As a group, women are subject to gender-based exploitation, powerlessness, cultural imperialism, and violence. Racism in the United States condemns many Blacks, and Latinos to marginalization, and puts many more at risk, even though many members of these groups escape that condition; members of these groups often suffer all five forms of oppression.

Applying these five criteria to the situation of groups makes it possible to compare the oppressions without reducing them to a common essence or claiming that one is more fundamental than another. One can compare the ways in which a particular form of oppression appears in different groups. For example, while the operations of cultural imperialism are often experienced in similar fashion by different groups, there are also important differences. One can compare the combinations of oppressions groups experience, or the intensity of those oppressions. . . .

6

The Cycle of Socialization

Bobbie Harro

INTRODUCTION AND CONTEXT

Often, when people begin to study the phenomenon of oppression, they start with recognizing that human beings are different from each other in many ways based upon gender, ethnicity, skin color, first language, age, ability status, religion, sexual orientation, and economic class. The obvious first leap that people make is the assumption that if we just began to *appreciate differences*, and *treat each other with respect*, then everything would be all right, and there would be no oppression. This view is represented beautifully by the now famous quote from Rodney King in response to the riots following his beating and the release of the police officers who were filmed beating him: "Why can't we all just get along?" It should be that simple, but it isn't.

Instead, we are each born into a specific set of *social identities*, related to the categories of difference mentioned above, and these social identities predispose us to unequal *roles* in the dynamic system of oppression. We are then socialized by powerful sources in our worlds to play the roles prescribed by an inequitable social system. This socialization process is *pervasive* (coming from all sides and sources), *consistent* (patterned and predictable), *circular* (self-supporting), *self-perpetuating* (intradependent) and often *invisible* (unconscious and unnamed). All of these characteristics will be clarified in the description of the *cycle of socialization* that follows.

In struggling to understand what roles we have been socialized to play, how we are affected by issues of oppression in our lives, and how we participate in maintaining them, we must begin by making an inventory of our own social identities with relationship to each issue of oppression. An excellent first learning activity is to make a personal inventory of our various social identities relating to the categories listed above—gender, race, age, sexual orientation, religion, economic class, and ability/disability status. The results of this inventory make up the mosaic of social identities (our *social identity profile*) that shape(s) our socialization.

We get systematic training in "how to be" each of our social identities throughout our lives. The cycle of socialization that follows is one way of representing how the socialization process happens, from what sources it comes, how it affects our lives, and how it perpetuates itself. The "Directions for Change" that conclude this chapter suggest ways for interrupting the cycle of socialization and taking charge of our own lives. For purposes of learning, it is often useful to choose only *one* of our social identities, and trace it through

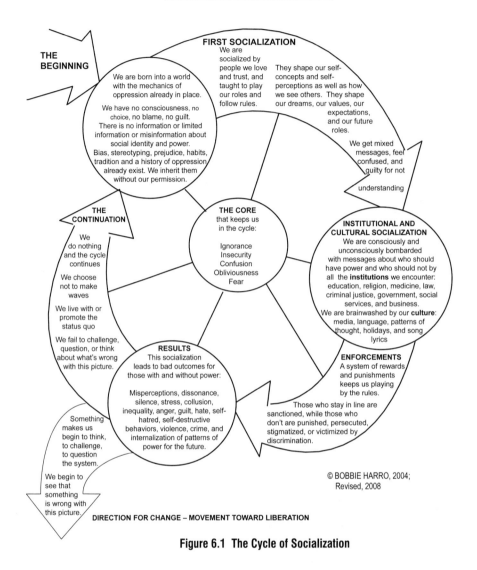

Figure 6.1 The Cycle of Socialization

the cycle of socialization, since it can be quite overwhelming to explore seven identities at once.

THE BEGINNING (CIRCLE NO. 1)

Our socialization begins before we are born, with no choice on our part. No one brings us a survey, in the womb, inquiring into which gender, class, religion, sexual orientation, cultural group, ability status, or age we might want to be born. These identities are ascribed to us at birth through no effort or decision or choice of our own; there is, therefore, no reason to blame each other or hold each other responsible for the identities we have. This first step in the socialization process is outside our control. In addition to having no choice, we also have no initial consciousness about who we are. We don't question our identities at this point. We just *are* who we are.

On top of these givens, we are born into a world where all of the mechanics, assumptions, rules, roles, and structures of oppression are already in place and functioning; we have had nothing to do with constructing them. There is no reason for any of us to feel guilty or responsible for the world into which we are born. We are innocents, falling into an already established system.

The characteristics of this system were built long before we existed, based upon history, habit, tradition, patterns of belief, prejudices, stereotypes, and myths. *Dominant* or *agent* groups are considered the "norm" around which assumptions are built, and these groups receive attention and recognition. Agents have relatively more social power, and can "name" others. They are privileged at birth, and ascribed access to options and opportunities, often without realizing it. We are "lucky" to be born into these groups and rarely question it. Agent groups include men, white people, middle- and upper-class people, abled people, middle-aged people, heterosexuals, and gentiles.

On the other hand, there are many social identity groups about which little or nothing is known because they have not been considered important enough to study. These are referred to as *subordinate* groups or *target* groups. Some target groups are virtually invisible while others are defined by misinformation or very limited information. Targets are disenfranchised, exploited, and victimized by prejudice, discrimination, and other structural obstacles. Target groups include women; racially oppressed groups; gay, lesbian, bisexual and transgendered people; disabled people; Jews; elders; youth; and people living in poverty. We are "unlucky" to be born into target groups and therefore devalued by the existing society. Both groups are dehumanized by being socialized into prescribed roles without consciousness or permission.

FIRST SOCIALIZATION (ARROW NO. 1)

Immediately upon our births we begin to be socialized by the people we love and trust the most, our families or the adults who are raising us. They shape our self-concepts and self-perceptions, the norms and rules we must follow, the roles we are taught to play, our expectations for the future, and our dreams. These people serve as role models for us, and they teach us how to behave. This socialization happens both intrapersonally (how we think about ourselves), and interpersonally (how we relate to others). We are told things like, "Boys don't cry"; "You shouldn't trust white people"; "They're better than we are. Stay in your place"; "Don't worry if you break the toy. We can always buy another one"; "Christianity is the true religion"; "Children should be seen and not heard"; "Don't tell anyone that your aunt is mentally retarded. It's embarrassing"; and "Don't kiss other girls. You're supposed to like boys." These messages are an automatic part of our early socialization, and we don't initially question them. We are too dependent on our parents or those raising us, and we haven't yet developed the ability to think for ourselves, so we unconsciously conform to their views.

It is important to observe that they, too, are not to be blamed. They are doing the best they can to raise us, and they only have their own backgrounds from which to draw. They may not have thought critically about what they are teaching us, and may be unconsciously passing on what was taught to them. Some of us may have been raised by parents who *have* thought critically about the messages that they are giving us, but they are still not in the majority. This could be good or bad, as well, depending on what their views are. A consciously racist parent may intentionally pass on racist beliefs to his children, and a consciously feminist parent may intentionally pass on non-stereotypical roles to her children, so it can go either way.

Regardless of the content of the teaching, we have been exposed, without initial question, to a strong set of rules, roles, and assumptions that cannot help but shape our sense of ourselves and the world. They influence what we take with us when we venture out of our protected family units into the larger world of other institutions.

A powerful way to check out the accuracy of these assertions is to choose one of our social identities and write down at least ten examples of what we learned about being that identity. It's helpful to consider whether we chose an agent or a target identity. We may find that we have thought more about our target identities, and therefore they are easier to inventory. Gender rules are sometimes the easiest, so we might start there. We might also consider doing it for an agent group identity, like males, white people, heterosexuals, gentiles, adults, middle-class people, able-bodied or able-minded people. Most likely, we will find it easier to list learnings for targeted groups than for agent groups.

INSTITUTIONAL AND CULTURAL SOCIALIZATION (CIRCLE NO. 2)

Once we begin to attend school, go to a place of worship, visit a medical facility, play on a sports team, work with a social worker, seek services or products from a business, or learn about laws and the legal system, our socialization sources are rapidly multiplied based on how many institutions with which we have contact. Most of the messages we receive about how to be, whom to "look up to" and "look down on," what rules to follow, what roles to play, what assumptions to make, what to believe, and what to think will probably reinforce or contradict what we have learned at home.

We might learn at school that girls shouldn't be interested in a woodworking shop class, that only white students go out for the tennis team, that kids who learn differently or think independently get put in special education, that it's okay for wealthy kids to miss classes for a family vacation, that it's okay to harass the boy who walks and talks like a girl, that most of the kids who drop out are from the south side of town, that "jocks" don't have to do the same work that "nerds" do to pass, or that kids who belong to another religious group are "weird." We learn who gets preferential treatment and who gets picked on. We are exposed to rules, roles, and assumptions that are not fair to everyone.

If we are members of the groups that benefit from the rules, we may not notice that they aren't fair. If we are members of the groups that are penalized by the rules, we may have a constant feeling of discomfort. We learn that these rules, roles, and assumptions are part of a structure that is larger than just our families. We get consistent similar messages from religion, the family doctor, the social worker, the local store, or the police officer, and so it is hard to not believe what we are learning. We learn that black people are more likely to steal, so store detectives follow them in stores. Boys are expected to fight and use violence, so they are encouraged to learn how. We shouldn't stare at or ask questions about disabled people; it isn't polite. Gay and lesbian people are sick and perverted. Kids who live in certain sections of town are probably on welfare, taking our hard-earned tax dollars. Money talks. White means good; black means bad. Girls are responsible for birth control. It's a man's world. Jews are cheap. Arabs are terrorists. And so on.

We are inundated with unquestioned and stereotypical messages that shape how we think and what we believe about ourselves and others. What makes this "brainwashing" even more insidious is the fact that it is woven into every structural thread of the fabric of our culture. The media (television, the Internet, advertising, newspapers, and radio), our language patterns, the lyrics to songs, our cultural practices and holidays, and the very assumptions on which our society is built all contribute to the reinforcement of the biased messages and stereotypes we receive. Think about Howard Stern, Jerry Springer, *Married with Children*, beer and car advertising, talk radio, *girl* vs. *man*, Christmas vacation, the Rolling Stones' "Under My Thumb," the "old boy's network," and websites that foster hate. We could identify thousands of examples to illustrate the oppressive messages that bombard us daily from various institutions and aspects of our culture, reinforcing our divisions and "justifying" discrimination and prejudice.

ENFORCEMENTS (ARROW NO. 2)

It might seem logical to ask why people don't just begin to think independently if they don't like what they are seeing around them. Why don't we ignore these messages if we are uncomfortable with them, or if they are hurting us? Largely, we don't ignore the messages, rules, roles, structures, and assumptions because there are enforcements in place to maintain them. People who try to contradict the "norm" pay a price for their independent thinking, and people who conform (consciously or unconsciously) minimally receive the benefit of being left alone for not making waves, such as acceptance in their designated roles, being considered normal or "a team player," or being allowed to stay in their places. Maximally, they receive rewards and privileges for maintaining the status quo such as access to higher places; attention and recognition for having "made it" or being the model member of their group; or the privilege that brings them money, connections, or power.

People who go against the grain of conventional societal messages are accused of being troublemakers, of making waves, or of being "the cause of the problem." If they are members of target groups, they are held up as examples of why this group is inferior to the agent group. Examples of this include the significantly higher numbers of people of color who are targeted by the criminal justice system. Although the number of white people who are committing crimes is just as high, those whites are much less likely to be arrested, charged, tried, convicted, or sentenced to jail than are people of color. Do different laws apply depending on a person's skin color? Battering statistics are rising as more women assert their equal rights with men, and the number one suspect for the murder of women in the United States is the husband or boyfriend. Should women who try to be equal with men be killed? The rationale given by some racists for the burning of black churches was that "they were getting too strong." Does religious freedom and the freedom to assemble apply only to white citizens? Two men walking together in a southeastern U.S. city were beaten, and one died, because "they were walking so close, they must be gay." Are two men who refuse to abide by the "keep your distance" rule for men so threatening that they must be attacked and killed? These examples of differential punishment being given to members or *perceived* members of target groups are only half of the picture.

If members of agent groups break the rules, they too are punished. White people who support their colleagues of color may be called "n—— lover." Heterosexual men who take on primary child-care responsibilities, cry easily, or hug their male friends are accused of being dominated by their spouses, of being "sissies," or being gay. Middle-class people who work as advocates on economic issues are accused of being do-gooders or self-righteous liberals. Heterosexuals who work for the rights of gay, lesbian, bisexual, or transgendered people are immediately suspected of being "in the closet" themselves.

RESULTS (CIRCLE NO. 3)

It is not surprising that the results of this systematic learning are devastating to all involved. If we are examining our target identities, we may experience anger, a sense of being silenced, dissonance between what the United States stands for and what we experience, low self-esteem, high levels of stress, a sense of hopelessness and disempowerment that can lead to crime and self-destructive behavior, frustration, mistrust, and dehumanization. By participating in our roles as targets we reinforce stereotypes, collude in our own demise, and perpetuate the system of oppression. This learned helplessness is often called *internalized oppression* because we have learned to become our own oppressors from within.

If we are examining our agent identities, we may experience guilt from unearned privilege or oppressive acts, fear of payback, tendency to collude in the system to be self-protective, high levels of stress, ignorance of and loss of contact with the target groups, a sense of distorted reality about how the world is, fear of rising crime and violence levels, limited worldview, obliviousness to the damage we do, and dehumanization. By participating in our roles as agents, and remaining unconscious of or being unwilling to interrupt the cycle, we perpetuate the system of oppression.

These results are often cited as the problems facing our society today: high drop-out rates, crime, poverty, drugs, and so on. Ironically, the root causes of them are inherent in the very assumptions on which the society is built: dualism, hierarchy, competition, individualism, domination, colonialism, and the scarcity principle. To the extent that we fail to interrupt this cycle we keep the assumptions, the problems, and the oppression alive.

A way that we might personally explore this model is to take one of the societal problems and trace its root causes back through the cycle to the core belief systems or patterns in U.S. society that feed and play host to it. It is not a coincidence that the United States is suffering from these results today; rather, it is a logical outcome of our embracing the status quo, without thinking or challenging.

ACTIONS (ARROW NO. 3)

When we arrive at the results of this terrible cycle, we face the decision of what to do next. It is easiest to do nothing, and simply to allow the perpetuation of the status quo. We may choose not to make waves, to stay in our familiar patterns. We may say, "Oh well, it's been that way for hundreds of years. What can I do to change it? It is a huge phenomenon, and my small efforts won't count for much." Many of us choose to do nothing because it is (for a while) easier to stay with what is familiar. Besides, it is frightening to try to interrupt something so large. "What does it have to do with me, anyway?" say many agents. "This isn't my problem. I am above this." We fail to realize that we have become participants just by doing nothing. This cycle has a life of its own. It doesn't need our active support because it has its own centrifugal force. It goes on, and unless we choose to interrupt it, it will continue to go on. Our silence is consent. Until our discomfort becomes larger than our comfort, we will probably stay in this cycle.

Some of us who are targets have been so beaten down by the relentless messages of the cycle that we have given up and resigned ourselves to survive it or to self-destruct. We are the victims of the cycle, and are playing our roles as victims to keep the cycle alive. We will probably go around a few more times before we die. It hurts too much to fight such a big cycle. We need the help of our brothers and sisters and our agent allies to try for change.

. . .

THE CORE OF THE CYCLE

As we begin to examine this decision, we may ask, "What has kept me in this cycle for so long?" Most answers are related to the themes listed in the core of the cycle: fear, ignorance, confusion, insecurity, power or powerlessness.

Fear—For targets, fear of interrupting the system reminds us of what happens to targets who challenge the existing power structure: being labeled as "trouble-makers," experiencing discrimination, being deported, raped, beaten, institutionalized, imprisoned, or killed. There are far too many examples like these. Some targets may decide not to take the risk.

For agents, the fear of interrupting the system is different. We fear losing our privilege if we interrupt the status quo. Will I be targeted with the targets? Will I have to face my own guilt for the years when I did nothing? Will I experience "pay-back" from targets if I acknowledge my role as an agent? Agent privilege sometimes allows us to avoid action, and the cycle continues.

Ignorance—For both targets and agents, lack of understanding about how oppression and socialization work makes it difficult to initiate change. Agents struggle more from our ignorance because we have not been forced to examine our roles. Because most of us have some agent and some target identities, we may be able to transfer what we learned in our target identities to educate ourselves in our agent identities. For example, a white lesbian may be able to translate her own experiences as a woman and a lesbian to understanding racism. This inability to see the connections may prevent us from interrupting the system.

Targets and agents both struggle with not seeing the big picture, and in our target identities, we may get caught in our own pain to the point that we cannot see the connections to other "isms." For example, a Black man may have experienced so much racism that he cannot identify with gay people or women in the U.S. This may prevent him from interrupting the systems of heterosexism and sexism.

Confusion—Oppression is very complex. It is difficult to know how to interrupt the system. That confusion sometimes prevents both targets and agents from taking action. "What if I use the wrong word when taking a stand on ableism? What if I don't know what to say when someone tells an offensive joke? What if I think I know more than I actually do?" Will I do more harm than good? Targets may know how to deal with their own category of oppression, but not categories in which they are agents. It's easy to make a mistake, and that confusion often prevents action.

Insecurity—Rarely have we been prepared for interrupting oppression, unless we went to a progressive school or worked in a progressive organization that has provided skill-building sessions. Most targets and agents feel somewhat insecure about taking a stand against oppression.

Power or Powerlessness—People with power have gained it through the existing system. It is difficult to risk losing it by challenging that same system. People without power may think they can't make a difference. As long as we are "living" in the Cycle of Socialization with the core themes holding us there, it will be difficult to break out of it, but people do it every day.

CHOOSING THE DIRECTION FOR CHANGE

How do people make the decision to interrupt the cycle and stand up for change? Sometimes the decision is triggered by a critical incident that makes oppression impossible to ignore. Perhaps a loved one is affected by some type of injustice or inequity, and we become motivated to speak out. Heterosexual parents of gay and lesbian children report that they became activists when they saw what their children were experiencing.

Perhaps we have a "last straw" experience, where things have become so intolerable that one last incident pushes us into action. Our discomfort becomes more powerful than our fear or insecurity, and we are compelled to take some action. Women who file sex discrimination suits after years of being overlooked professionally report this example; so do women who leave abusive relationships once and for all.

Sometimes it might be some new awareness or consciousness that we gain. Perhaps a friend from a different identity group shows us a different perspective, or we read a book that makes us think differently, or we enroll in a course that introduces new possibilities. We begin to see the big picture—that groups all over the world are working on these same issues. Change movements are filled with people who made decisions to interrupt the cycle of socialization and the system of oppression. Once you know something, you can't *not* know it anymore, and knowing it eventually translates into action.

These people often share qualities that have developed as a result of uniting for change. They share a sense of hope and optimism that we can dismantle oppression. They share a sense of their own efficacy—that they can make a difference in the world. They empower themselves and they support each other. They share an authentic human connection across their differences rather than fear because of their differences. They are humanized through action; not dehumanized by oppression. They listen to one another. They take one another's perspectives. They learn to love and trust each other. This is how the world changes.

7

The Cycle of Liberation

Bobbie Harro

As people come to a critical level of understanding of the nature of oppression and their roles in this systemic phenomenon, they seek new paths for creating social change and taking themselves toward empowerment or liberation. In my years as a social justice educator, it became increasingly clear that most socially conscious people truly want to "do something about" the injustices that they see and they recognize that simple, personal-level changes are not enough. They want to know how to make system-level change manageable and within their grasp, and they often become frustrated since so little has been written about the process of liberation.

As more students asked, "How do we make a dent in this thing that seems so big?" I began to think about how we might consciously transform the Cycle of Socialization. The cycle "teaches" us how to play our roles in oppression, and how to revere the existing systems that shape our thinking, leading us to blame uncontrollable forces, other people, or ourselves for the existence of oppression. If there is an identifiable pattern of events that repeats itself, becomes self-fulfilling, and leads us to a state of unconsciousness about issues of oppression, then there may be another identifiable pattern of events that leads us toward liberation from that thinking. I began to read about and study efforts to eliminate oppression on a systemic level, and discovered that indeed, some paths were successful at actually creating the kind of lasting change that addressed the root causes of the oppression, and people's roles in it, while other paths were not. These paths were not always the same, and certainly were not linear, but they had in common the same cycle-like traits that characterized the socialization process that teaches us our roles in oppression. There were certain skills and processes, certain ways of thinking and acting in the world, certain seemingly necessary ingredients that were present in every successful liberation effort.

I am defining *liberation* as "critical transformation," in the language and thinking of Paulo Freire. By this I mean that one must "name the problem" in terms of *systemic* assumptions, structures, rules, or roles that are flawed. Significant social change cannot happen until we are thinking on a systemic level. Many people who want to overcome oppression do not start in the critical transforming stage, but as they proceed in their efforts, it becomes necessary for them to move to that level for success.

The following model describes patterns of events common to successful liberation efforts. Its purpose is to organize and name a process that may otherwise be elusive, with the goal of helping people to find their pathway to liberation. It could be characterized as a map of changing terrain where not everyone goes in the same direction or to the same destination or at the same speed, so it should be taken not as a "how to," but rather as a description of what has worked for some.

THE MODEL

The model described in this chapter combines theory, analysis, and practical experience. It describes a cyclical process that seems to occur in most successful social change efforts, leading to some degree of liberation from oppression for those involved, regardless of their roles. It is important to note that one can enter the cycle at any point, through slow evolution or a critical incident, and will repeat or recycle many times in the process. There is no specific beginning or end point, just as one is never "done" working to end oppression. Although there is not a specific sequence of events in the cycle, it is somewhat predictable that all of the levels (intrapersonal, interpersonal and systemic) will occur at some point.

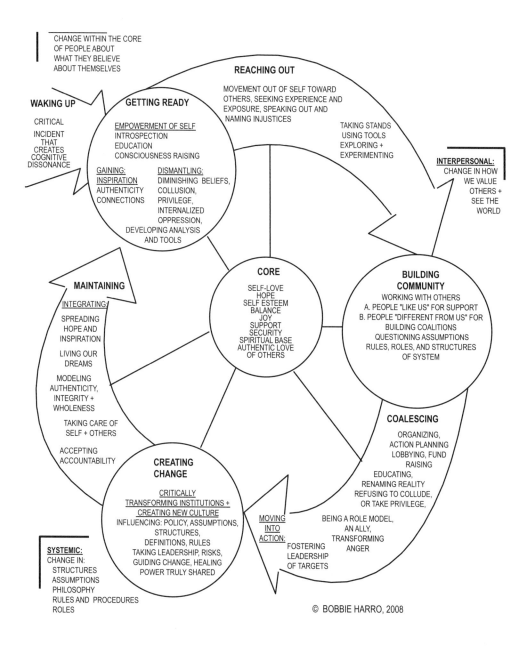

Figure 7.1 The Cycle of Liberation.

WAKING UP

Often liberation begins when a person begins to experience herself differently in the world than s/he has in the past. It is marked by an intrapersonal change: a change in the core of someone about what s/he believes about her/himself. This may be the result of a critical incident or a long slow evolutionary process that shifts our worldviews. I refer to this phase as the *waking up* phase. We may experience some form of cognitive dissonance, where something that used to make sense to us (or that we never questioned), ceases to makes sense. Perhaps a white mother adopts a child who is Puerto Rican and in dealing with her expectations for the child suddenly realizes that she has more deeply based racist attitudes than she thought she did. Perhaps a heterosexual woman who has a gay coworker recognizes that the longer she works with him, the more "ordinary" he becomes to her, and the more she gets angry when people make antigay remarks. Perhaps a welfare recipient begins to get angry that she is often treated with disrespect by service providers and the general public, and begins to see the disrespect as a pattern of how poorer people are treated in the United States. Any of these examples could mark the beginning of the Cycle of Liberation.

GETTING READY

Once we know something, we can't *not* know it anymore. The process may not begin immediately, but odds are that it will begin at some point. Often the first part of the process involves a *getting ready* phase. This involves consciously dismantling and building aspects of ourselves and our worldviews based on our new perspectives. Processes that are central to this first part of liberation are introspection, education, and consciousness raising. We become introspective to identify which aspects of our beliefs, attitudes, and behaviors need to be challenged. We tend to pay attention to and inventory thoughts, language, and actions to see if they are consistent with our newly recognized beliefs, or if they need to be dismantled. We may discover that we need to educate ourselves: read more, talk to people, bounce ideas and views around with others, begin listening to the news with new ears, seek expertise. We may begin to "make sense" of our experiences differently and seek out more chances to explore what we thought we knew, and how it compares to the reality. We may start exercising our questioning and challenging skills to expand our conscious understanding of the world.

This *getting ready* phase is composed of dismantling our wrong or diminishing beliefs (stereotypes, ignorance or misinformation), our discriminatory or privileged attitudes (superiority or inferiority), and behaviors that limit ourselves or others (collusion, oppressive language, or resignation). It also involves developing a consistency among what we believe, how we want to live our lives, and the way we actually do it. We move toward gaining authenticity and coherence between our worldview and how we live. We begin to see connections among all of the aspects of our lives and move toward integrity. Part of this phase also includes developing a coherent analysis of oppression and building a repertoire of skills and tools that will serve us throughout the rest of the process. We begin to take steps to empower ourselves.

The mother of the Puerto Rican child might decide to read about Puerto Rican history and cultures, talk to her Puerto Rican coworker, trace the origins of her assumptions and expectations about her child, or begin to catch herself when she makes excuses for her child's behavior. The heterosexual coworker may take a course on the gay rights movement, or pick up a copy of a gay newspaper, or ask her gay coworker to dinner. The woman on welfare may read a book on welfare rights, or start listening to the economic news, or start to keep a list of examples of "corporate welfare" totaling how much money goes from the federal government to large corporations when they are in financial trouble.

REACHING OUT

Almost inevitably, as we are getting ready, it becomes necessary for us to seek experiences outside ourselves in order to check our reality and to expose ourselves to a wider range of difference than we had before. We need to practice using our skills and tools with others, and experiment with expressing our new views, and speaking out when we disagree, instead of staying silent. This *reaching out* phase provides us with feedback about how our new worldviews will be met by others. We may get pressure from some to stop making waves, and accept the status quo (and this may arrest some people's progress for a while), and we may get encouragement and new friends as a result of taking a stand on something that we were quiet about before.

The adoptive mother may change social workers so she can talk to a Puerto Rican social worker about her child. She may suggest to her partner that they take a class in Spanish, or attend a local Puerto Rican festival. The heterosexual coworker may disclose in a conversation with friends that she supports the domestic partnership clause in their benefit package, or she may have a talk with her kids about not using the term *gay* to mean something bad. She may invite her gay coworker *and his partner* to dinner, or draw comparisons between her primary relationship and his. The woman on welfare may attend her first welfare rights meeting. She may object assertively when she is treated with disdain for using food stamps by the person behind her in the checkout line. She may decide to share her list of examples of corporate welfare with two friends also on welfare. All of these actions mark the transition from intrapersonal to interpersonal liberation.

BUILDING COMMUNITY

The Interpersonal phase of the liberation process is marked by a change in how we value others and interact with them on a regular basis. It is the phase of *building community*, and consists of two steps: dialoguing with *people who are like us* for support (people who have the same social identities as we do, with regard to this issue of oppression), and dialoguing with *people who are different from us* for gaining understanding and building coalitions. This phase is characterized by the creation of an ongoing dialogue, where views are exchanged, people are listened to and valued, and we begin to view each others' points of view as making sense and having integrity, even if they are very different from our own.

In the first step, building community with people who are like us, we seek out people who may have similar experiences to our own, and talk with them to see how they have made sense of their experiences and what we can learn from them. This often begins happening informally, and even sometimes unconsciously: two mothers with adopted children meet in the pediatrician's waiting room and start comparing notes, or two neighbors who both receive welfare benefits talk in the laundry about their frustrations, or two friends going for a hike begin discussing "the gay people" who work with both of them. With increased knowledge and consciousness, these people might start looking for more organized forms of support discussions. These dialogues serve to prove to people that they are not alone in their situation, that there is a bigger "system" operating, that others have faced and are facing similar situations as our own, and that there are more strategies, ideas, and options than we had initially thought. We feel confirmed, and like we are part of a group that wants to change its role with regard to oppression.

A large part of this interpersonal step also involves dialoguing about how we see the "other" group (those with power if we are disempowered, or the disempowered if we possess power and/or privilege), and beginning to identify things that we may mutually have in common. We have moved out of stereotyping the "other" and have discovered those "others" who are more like us than different from us. We may begin to see that the "other" is no more to blame for the oppression than we are—that, in fact, we are both victims of a larger system that pushed us into roles. With this realization, a new level of analysis begins, and it becomes inevitable and necessary to expand our dialogue to include "others."

It's important to note that both privileged groups and targeted groups need to find this support step. We can't change *our* roles only; we must address changing the roles of *everyone* involved, as well as the assumptions and structures of the entire system, and we cannot do that alone. Coalitions are a necessity, and dialoguing across differences is the first step to building coalitions. We will never be able to focus on the real challenge—changing the system—until the barriers and boundaries that divide us are minimized. They will not be eliminated, but they can be significantly diminished in potency and clarified through the dialogue process.

This is not to say that creating dialogues about and across differences is easy. An integral part of this dialogue is exploring our differences, clarifying them, erasing assumptions, and replacing them with firsthand contact and good listening. That means that we must talk about our differences in a civil manner. It is useful, even desirable, to create together some guidelines for how our dialogues across differences will take place, and some principles to guide the process. These are best negotiated by all the parties who will participate.

Our mission is to question and challenge assumptions, structures and rules of the system of oppression, and to clarify our different needs, perceptions, strengths, resources, and skills in the process. Done well, these dialogues result in a deeper and richer repertoire of options and opportunities for changing the system. We are enhanced in many, ways: our energy, our resources, our inspiration, our understanding, our compassion, our empathy, our humanness, and our motivation are all expanded in this process. We discover and are sustained by inspirations that we have not met before. With these new springboards, we move into the coalescing phase.

COALESCING

Having minimized our barriers, joined with allies, and fortified our resolve, we are ready to move into action to interrupt the oppressive system. We may organize, plan actions, lobby, do fund raising, educate and motivate members of the uninvolved public. We coalesce and discover that we have more power as a coalition. This gives us encouragement and confidence. We may find ourselves taking more overt stands, expressing ourselves more assertively, rallying people to support us as we respond to overt oppression. We have begun to "see our reality" differently, and are naming ourselves differently. We are a "we" now, rather than adversaries. We are on the same side as those in our coalition, and that often surprises and confuses the system. We are refusing to "play our roles" and "stay in our places" as we had done before. We are refusing to collude in oppression, and to participate in self-fulfilling prophesies. We are refusing to accept privileges, and we are acting as role models and allies for others. We are interrupting the status quo, by speaking out calmly and with self-confidence. In this process, we have transformed our energy away from anger, frustration, guilt, and mistrust, and toward hope, shared power, trust, and optimism. We begin to see evidence that, working together, and organizing, we can make a difference. This doesn't mean that we will be successful at everything we try, but our likelihood of creating change is greatly enhanced.

CREATING CHANGE

The parameters of this phase of the cycle of liberation include using our critical analysis of the assumptions, structures, rules, and roles of the existing system of oppression, and our coalition power, to begin transforming the system. This means creating anew a culture that reflects our coalition's collective identity: new assumptions, new structures, new roles, and new rules consistent with a more socially just and equitable philosophy. It includes operating from a shifted worldview, where the values of a diverse and united community shape the system. It involves forming partnerships across differences to increase shared power. This manifests in influencing structure, policy, and management of organizations and systems of which we are a part. It involves taking leadership, taking risks, and guiding change. We must continue to heal from past differences by sharing power and by redefining power as collective power, power within, and power created through cooperation. In this phase, the very essence of the system is transformed, and nothing can remain the same after the transformation.

People experience this kind of transformation on a personal level, when, for example they or someone in their family is diagnosed with a terminal illness. Priorities shift, and what is important becomes totally different. With regard to oppression, some examples of critical transformation have occurred when psychiatric facilities began to appoint consumers to their boards of directors, or when community funding agencies began to be run by community constituents rather than elected officials. Critical transformation may take place when an organization decides to use only consensus decision making for all policy decisions, or to use a flat collaborative management structure rather than hierarchical.

Critical transformation in our examples might happen like this. The heterosexual co-worker and the gay coworker might organize a human rights committee in their workplace; conduct dialogues among employees and a public awareness campaign; design a new domestic partners' benefits amendment and a new policy protecting gay, lesbian, bisexual, and transgendered people from discrimination in the workplace. The person receiving welfare benefits might join a welfare rights coalition that lobbies local legislators, speak at a hearing in the state capital, and propose a referendum that for every dollar spent on "corporate welfare" in their state a dollar must also be spent on domestic welfare. The white mother of the Puerto Rican child might join a local Puerto Rican political action committee working to reform curriculum to include relevant Puerto Rican history, literature, famous people, and current events in her child's school. The committee might also be working to reform policies on bilingual education district-wide, so that her child can study and learn in both Spanish and English.

Efforts to critically transform systems are greatly enhanced by a wide range of resources, perspectives and creativity being brought to bear on a commonly defined problem. If good dialogue has taken place and the coalitions are as inclusive of every perspective as possible, systemic change becomes the logical outcome rather than an unlikely or unattainable goal. Making transformation happen is not, however, the last step. Creative new structures, assumptions, rules and roles must be maintained and nurtured.

MAINTAINING

In order to succeed, change needs to be strengthened, monitored, and integrated into the ritual of daily life. Just like anything new, it needs to be taken care of, learned about, "debugged," and modified as needed. It's rare if not impossible that new structures, assumptions, rules and roles are perfect or all-inclusive. It is imperative that a diverse group of "maintainers" work together to keep the change efforts aimed at their goals, and provided with resources. It's also necessary to celebrate successful change efforts. This process says to the larger world, "Look, this can work. You can change things by dialoguing and working together." It spreads hope and inspiration, and provides a model for others.

When a diverse group of people have worked to understand one another, and have created critical transformation together, we teach the lesson of hope and peace. It becomes increasingly possible that we can live our dream of equality and justice for all people. We become more human, more whole, more authentic, more integrated, and by living this way, we increase the likelihood that the human species will survive.

THE CORE OF THE CYCLE OF LIBERATION

At the core of the cycle of liberation is a set of qualities or states of being that hold it together. Some of these are present when people first begin the cycle, and they are nurtured, elaborated on, filled out, and matured as we proceed through the various phases. They exist and operate on both the individual and collective levels throughout the process of liberation. They are made stronger with each phase and with each human connection we make. Liberation is *the practice of love*. It is developing a sense of self that we can love, and learning to love others with their differences from us. Liberation is *finding balance* in our individual lives and in the agendas of our coalitions. Balance keeps us upright and oriented, moving toward our goals. Liberation is the *development of competence*, the ability to make something happen consistent with a goal. It is taking charge of our own destiny and creating the world we want to live in, together with all the others we need to survive. Liberation is the *belief that we can succeed*, a sense of confidence in ourselves and in our collective efforts. Liberation is *joy* at our collective efficacy and at surviving in a world that sometimes tries to kill us. Liberation is the knowledge that *we are not alone*. It is mutual support, encouragement, and trust that others will be there if we fall, and that we need to be there for others. Liberation is *commitment* to the effort of critical transformation, to the people in our community, to the goal of equity and justice, and to love. Liberation is *passion and compassion*, those strong and motivating feelings that we must live by our hearts as well as our minds. Liberation is based in something far bigger than me as an individual, or us as a coalition, or our organization as a community, or any one nation, or any particular world. It's about that force that connects us all to one another as living beings, that force that is defined differently by every spiritual belief system but which binds us by the vision that there can be a better world and we can help to create it.

SECTION 2

RACISM

Introduction

Lee Anne Bell, Carmelita (Rosie) Castañeda, and Ximena Zúñiga[1]

"We the people, in order to form a more perfect union." . . . launched America's improbable experiment in democracy. Farmers and scholars; statesmen and patriots who had crossed an ocean to escape tyranny and persecution finally made real their declaration of independence at a Philadelphia convention that lasted through the spring of 1787.

The document they produced was eventually signed but ultimately unfinished. It was stained by this nation's original sin of slavery, a question that divided the colonies and brought the convention to a stalemate until the founders chose to allow the slave trade to continue for at least twenty more years, and to leave any final resolution to future generations.

Of course, the answer to the slavery question was already embedded within our Constitution—a Constitution that had at its very core the ideal of equal citizenship under the law; a Constitution that promised its people liberty, and justice, and a union that could be and should be perfected over time. And yet words on a parchment would not be enough to deliver slaves from bondage, or provide men and women of every color and creed their full rights and obligations as citizens of the United States. What would be needed were Americans in successive generations who were willing to do their part— through protests and struggle, on the streets and in the courts, through a civil war and civil disobedience and always at great risk—to narrow that gap between the promise of our ideals and the reality of their time.

. . . I believe deeply that we cannot solve the challenges of our time unless we solve them together— unless we perfect our union by understanding that we may have different stories, but we hold common hopes; that we may not look the same and we may not have come from the same place, but we all want to move in the same direction—towards a better future for our children and our grandchildren.

This belief comes from my unyielding faith in the decency and generosity of the American people. But it also comes from my own American story.

—Barack Obama (March 18, 2008)

As we write this introduction, Barack Hussein Obama has become the first person of color to be elected President of the United States. This is no ordinary achievement for a nation whose history reverberates with the colonization, slavery, exploitation, and marginalization of people of color (Native Americans, African Americans, Asian Americans, Arab Americans, Mexican Americans and other Latinos). What does this political moment say about our progress as a nation regarding issues of race and racism? What do the paragraphs quoted above from Obama's speech on racism, made in Philadelphia while he was still a candidate for the presidency, tell us about the obstacles to "a more perfect union" posed by our shared history of racial divisions as well as our shared commitment and optimism that these obstacles can be overcome?

In this section, we challenge commonly held assumptions and set out frameworks and definitions for examining race, racism, and white supremacy in an inclusive and nuanced way. We introduce readers to key concepts in our approach to racism and provide an overview of readings we have selected to illustrate theoretical, conceptual, and personal ways to understand, critically analyze, and challenge contemporary racism in the United States.

RACE AS A SOCIOPOLITICAL CONSTRUCTION

Race is a sociopolitical not a biological construct, one that is created and reinforced by social and institutional norms and practices, as well as individual attitudes and behaviors. Like other constructed social identities addressed in this book, race emerged historically in the United States to justify the dominance peoples defined as "White" (colonists/settlers) held over other peoples defined as "non-White" (first Native Americans and enslaved Africans and later Mexicans, Chinese, Puerto Ricans, and South Asians and others racialized as non-White). Motivated by economic interests and entrenched through law and public policy, we see this process of racialization unfolding historically and continually reinvented to perpetuate economic, political, and social advantage for peoples racialized as White within the United States. We call this process and the system it sustains *white supremacy.*

Racism is the set of institutional, cultural, and interpersonal patterns and practices that create advantages for people legally defined and socially constructed as "White," and the corollary disadvantages for people defined as "non-White" in the United States. While the construction of disadvantage and subordination of different communities of color has been enacted in historically specific ways for differently racialized groups, we call attention to the overarching patterns and practices that illustrate racism across groups, as well as the distinctive ways racism plays out for particular peoples of color at different points in U.S. history. Thus, the frequently unstated assumption that race is a matter of Black/White relationships obscures a far more complex, historically rooted, racial *system* that impacts differently racialized peoples in historically and regionally distinctive ways. Indeed, we talk about *racism(s)* to connote the many different forms racism has taken throughout U.S. history. A critical analysis of racism(s) should thus include how perceived racial phenotype, ethnicity, language, immigration status, and culture impact a people's experience of racism. Further, the analysis of racisms becomes intersectional when we acknowledge that people from all racialized groups—whether advantaged or disadvantaged by racism—are also differently gendered, classed, sexualized, and aged, and that these intersections differentially shape their experiences and the impact of racism on their life chances and opportunities.

We challenge the notion that the United States has become a "post-racial" society in which race no longer matters (because racism is presumed to no longer exist) and argue that this notion reflects the desire to ignore the many ways in which race and racism continue to create and reinforce inequality. As long as patterns of racial inequality persist, we are not a post-racial society. In fact, to value diversity and equality, "transcending race" should not be our goal; rather, we should account for past practices of dominance and marginalization and work assiduously to eradicate racism, devise reparation for its effects in contemporary life, and transform our society into an inclusive and just democracy where differences are respected and valued, and people from all groups are treated justly.

HISTORY OF RACISM: A BRIEF SNAPSHOT

The history of racism in the United States reaches back to before our origins as a nation—through the colonization and attempted extermination of the Native peoples whose land was stolen by conquest, broken treaties, and deception; the enslavement first of Native Americans and then of kidnapped Africans to provide coerced and unpaid labor to develop agricultural and capital wealth for the early European settlers; the displacement of Mexican and Native American people, appropriation of their land and redefining them as "foreign," as borders moved through war and conquest. It continued with the recruitment and then abuse and exploitation of Chinese, Japanese, and Filipino laborers who worked the mines and built the railroads that enabled the expansion of U.S. wealth and power to other parts of the globe (Takaki 1993). Rationalized by Manifest Destiny and a "civilizing" mission, people of European Christian descent determined who could attain citizenship and its corresponding benefits in their new country of residence (Haney-López 1997).

Migrants racialized as "White" expanded and then consolidated advantaged "Whiteness" to eventually include successive waves of immigrants. Some Northern Europeans were absorbed easily while others considered "not quite White" (e.g., Italians, Irish, Jews) took longer but were assimilated as "White" over time (Brodkin Sacks 1994; Gaultieri 2001; Guglielmo 2003; Roediger 1991). In so doing, those who could claim Whiteness reaped the benefits of an economic and political system consolidated under white supremacy. From the attainment of citizenship and incorporation as Whites flowed other advantages, such as property and voting rights that enabled them to further accumulate wealth and to control the political system as well as write a version of history that glorified and normalized their dominance as legitimate and natural. This "colonization of the mind" enabled a writing of history that portrayed Latinos and indigenous peoples as "immigrants" and "foreigners" with no claim to the Americas, while "European Americans were constructed as the natural owners and inheritors of these lands" (Villenas and Deyhle 1999, 421). Non-elite Whites illustrated another form of colonization of the mind—trading the potential of cross-race class alliances against elite Whites in exchange for the benefits of belonging to the "superior" white group, often against their own economic interests.

Nativism, supporting the interests of "native-born" people over "foreign-born" people, combined with racial animus toward (mainly non-Protestant) migrants of color to shape restrictive anti-immigration laws and populist white sentiments (Spikard 2007). Immigration laws of the 1800s restricted immigration as rising nativist sentiments combined racism with the traditional hostility of U.S.-born, white, Anglo-Saxon Protestants toward newer immigrants from Catholic Ireland and Catholic Southern Europe, and East European Jews. Immigration laws tightly restricted immigration from China, Japan, the Philippines, and other parts of the world. Nativism intermingled with race, religion, and class interests to sustain the dominance of white, Anglo-Saxon, Protestant elites while restricting access for other groups. These policies continued to shape political and social life across the United States and to entrench and increase white economic and political advantage until the Immigration Acts of 1965 relaxed barriers to immigration and the Civil Rights Acts of the same era opened up political rights to groups of color. The recent resurgence of anti-immigrant backlash (focused on so-called "illegal aliens") can be seen as a manifestation of this nativism, also evident in "English only" policies.

RACIAL IDENTITIES, RACIAL HIERARCHIES, AND WHITE SUPREMACY

White supremacy and racism rationalize inequality (as natural and given) and homogenize experience by compressing social diversity into binaries and dividing racialized groups into artificial hierarchies. For example, the one-drop rule that defined as "Black" any person with "blood quantum" of a certain percentage (which varied by state and region) exemplifies this binary system. Established during slavery, the one-drop rule ensured that anyone who had a remote relative of African descent, even if this heritage was not visible, could be kept in slavery (and later segregated under Jim Crow laws). This not only protected the interests of a small group of propertied Whites who reaped the benefits of the system but also created a relatively large and growing pool of cheap labor. Conversely, federal standards for who could be considered Native American used blood quantum rules to eliminate most "mixed-bloods" from tribal nationality rolls as a device to decrease Indians' claims for tribal land rights. In both cases, the goal was to perpetuate a system of advantages benefiting White wealth and ownership.

Obviously, the realities of people's lives are far more complex than a racialized binary suggests. We can see this complexity in the widely varying ways that people describe Barack Obama, a man whose ancestry includes Kenyan, Irish, German, and Native American. In his autobiography, he identifies as Black, as do many other dark-skinned people of varying heritages, to acknowledge that they are and have historically been treated as Black by the larger society and to proudly affirm that identity in opposition. Others insist on naming Obama as biracial or multiracial, challenging a black/white binary that renders invisible other ethnic, national, tribal identities, and heritages. That people read Obama's "racial" identity in varying ways illustrates social construction of race in action.

The braided nature of race, class, gender, sexuality, ethnicity, ability, age, and other social categories further complicates social identity. As members of multiple social identity groups, experiences of privilege and oppression are also mediated by cross-cutting issues of status, rank, power, and value linked to class, gender, sexuality, and age. Social identities are not themselves oppressive; in fact, they are often sources of self-understanding, pride, and sustenance. Rather, systemic practices of racism, sexism, classism, ableism, heterosexism, adultism/ageism, transgender and religious oppression create hierarchies that devalue people based on social group membership.

CONTEMPORARY, INTERSECTING MANIFESTATIONS
OF RACISM AND WHITE SUPREMACY

Certainly, there have been periods in the history of the United States when progress on racial issues has seemed to reduce prejudice and discrimination. Many would like to think that institutionalized racism ended with the civil rights movements of the mid-1960s and the laws passed in their wake. Yet, almost 250 years since the abolition of slavery and more than 50 years since the end of legalized segregation in the United States—although important changes have taken place—racist practices endure. The legacies of racism continue through entrenched and persistent economic, political, and social disparities. For instance, racist practices are reproduced through pervasive gaps in wealth and income between Whites as a group and groups of color (see Oliver and Shapiro, selection 28). Racism, sexism, and classism intersect to create huge health disparities for women and their children (see "National Latina Institute for Reproductive Health Statement on Healthcare for All," selection 74). Racism combines with religious oppression to suppress the cultural expression of indigenous groups' religious beliefs and practices (see Echo-Hawk, selection 52, and Grinde, selection 53).

Contemporary manifestations of racism and nativism continue in the actions of U.S. border guards chasing Mexican men and women, often shooting at them indiscriminately (selection 15). Racism is alive in the incarceration without evidence or legal warrant (under the newly passed Patriot Act) of Arab Americans following the terrorist attacks of September 11, 2001. It is at work in the racial profiling of Southeast Asians and fabricated charges of terrorism against them. It abides when undocumented immigrants who have been taxpaying, law-abiding members of their communities are arrested and deported (selection 15). Recognition of the unique and multifaceted ways that individuals encounter racism in combination with gender, class, and other forms of discrimination is necessary for understanding how diverse individuals and groups experience, resist, and organize to dismantle systems of oppression.

While recent advances offer hope, we cannot relax our efforts to push for change in a system that has institutionally embedded racism in all areas of social life, be it immigration, job opportunities, health-care practices, housing, or education. People of color continue to be disproportionately poor, unemployed, underemployed, segregated in decaying communities, on reservations, incarcerated at staggeringly disproportionate rates, and psychologically and physically threatened by stereotyping, bigotry, and hate crimes. Racism impacts the quality of all our lives because it resides within all significant structures of society. Hence, by no measure are we in a post-racial era as many news and political commentators assert.

Historical, economic, political, and social factors continue to shape the experiences with racism of people from diverse racialized groups in both shared and unique ways, as the readings in this section delineate. We hope this introduction and the selected readings that follow will encourage students to develop a sophisticated and complex understanding of race and racism so as to be able to build strong, multiracial coalitions for change. It is up to us to transform historical legacies and current forms of racism and white supremacy in order to create a society with justice for all.

CONTEXTS

The authors in our Context section trace the enduring features of racism and help us consider how racism functions on multiple levels and in different ways for diverse racial groups. As a headnote to this section, we quote an excerpt from (then) Senator Obama's address in Philadelphia on the politics of race, in which he forcefully delineates the chasm between white perceptions and the perceptions of those who bear the onus of our racist history, reminding us that racism is very much alive and demanding our attention and action.

Next, Beverly Daniel Tatum (selection 8) provides a definition of racism as a phenomenon rooted in a system of advantage. Tatum explores how white privilege conveys social influence and power to Whites as a group and corollary disadvantage to people of color, even as it is mediated by socioeconomic status, gender, age, religious affiliation, and mental and physical ability. She also highlights the price we pay for inequality and injustice.

Ronald Takaki (selection 9) reveals the complexity of the racialization process, describing the historical trajectories, similarities, and differences in the experiences of Native Americans, African Americans, Chicanos, and Asian Americans as the American nation developed. He also explores the divergent experiences of immigrants, such as the Irish and Jews, whose assimilation as white over time allowed them entrance into the advantaged white group.

Kimberly Roppolo (selection 10) takes a different slant, focusing on the "dysconcious," symbolic racism toward American Indians that is reflected in the continuing use of Indian mascots. She traces the roots of such stereotypes to a refusal to acknowledge the ongoing psychic and physical violence toward Native peoples and our national legacy of theft, genocide, and dispossession.

George Lipsitz (selection 11) further unpacks the unacknowledged but ever present "possessive investment in whiteness" that shapes public and private life in our society. He explores how white hegemony has been developed and preserved over the course of our history, influenced by the legacies of slavery and segregation, Native American extermination and immigrant restriction, conquest and colonialism. He argues that only an explicitly anti-racist, interethnic movement that acknowledges and challenges the power of white supremacy will be powerful enough to break the hold of the possessive investment in whiteness.

Such a movement requires the kind of sophisticated thinking and analysis offered by Andrea Smith in her piece on the three pillars of white supremacy (selection 12): one based on the logic of slavery; a second on the logic of genocide and colonialism; and a third on the logic of Orientalism and war. Understanding these pillars, Smith argues, helps explain the divergent experiences of African Americans, Native Americans, Asian Americans, Latino Americans, and Arab Americans, all of whom experience racism but not in quite the same ways.

Next, Gloria Anzaldúa (selection 13) develops her concept of "*mestiza* consciousness," one that embraces the complexity of multiple perspectives, learns to tolerate ambiguities, and breaks down dualistic paradigms so as to imagine a new way of thinking about the intersections of race, culture, language, and identity. She argues that *mestiza* consciousness models a way to value the complex racial experiences of our hybrid nation and more creatively address the individual and collective challenges we face.

Maria Root (selection 14) turns to the challenges of naming one's own experience in a society that insists on racial categorizations that perpetuate the status quo. Root shows how racially mixed people can resist and challenge the binaries that fix identity in place.

Finally, the piece by the National Network on Immigrant Rights (selection 15) illustrates how immigration laws work against the rights of immigrants, particularly immigrants of color, in ways that ultimately harm all communities. Taken together, the readings in this section help us think about racism systemically and analytically so as to be prepared for the new forms it may take as white power, as it has in the past, shape-shifts to maintain its hold on society.

VOICES

Our second section recognizes that learning from the personal experiences of people from different groups can be a powerful and often transformative experience. Olivia Chung in "Finding My Eye-dentity" (selection 16) remembers her struggle as an Asian American female, letting go of U.S. societal definitions of attractiveness as she comes to embrace a broader definition of beauty and to see herself as beautiful.

In "Identification Pleas," Eric Gansworth (selection 17), a Native American, describes his experience when the U.S. border patrol, mistakenly assuming he was Latino, rejected his tribal ID card as valid U.S. identification. His story shows how the erasure of individual and group experience through stereotyping deprives people of their humanity. Mona Fayad (selection 18), in "The Arab Woman and I," describes the impact of stereotyping on her life as an Arab woman, showing how misinformation and ignorance lead many Westerners to render her faceless, powerless, passive, and seductive. (Other examples of the experiences of Arab American women can be found in selections 57 and 58.)

Quique Aviles (selection 19) came to Washington, D.C., from El Salvador during a period of political unrest. In "My Tongue is Divided into Two," he describes his journey of learning the English language and using it as a source of empowerment and liberation.

The dangerous notion that race or skin color no longer matters is addressed in the next selection (selection 20). In "The Emperor's New Clothes," Patricia Williams shows how the professed "color blindness" of her son's white teachers led them to ignore the very real victimization he experienced as the only black child on the playground. She shows how "color blindness" can become a rationale for the denial of racism, making it more difficult to come to grips with the ways it pervades our individual lives and institutions.

Finally, Billy Yalowitz (selection 21), a Jewish, white man, chronicles the challenges and celebrations of working for social justice while collaboratively creating a performance piece within a predominately black community. He reflects on his privileged identities as a white, male faculty member attempting to practice anti-racist activism.

NEXT STEPS

In this section, we highlight concrete action steps that challenge the causes and effects of racism and white supremacy and work toward transforming historical legacies through individual actions, dialogues across racial divides, and multiracial coalitions for change. Learning to see whiteness and developing racial consciousness is an important initial step for white people to bridge racial and ethnic divides. For example, in the first selection, Jan Arminio's "Waking up White" (selection 22) describes the process by which white people learn to realize that being White is both a social category and a racial identity. She invites Whites to recognize the historical legacies that shape their social status in society and consciously decide what role they want to play as white individuals in a racist society.

Next, Andrea Ayvazian and Beverly Daniel Tatum (selection 23) illustrate the power of dialogue to validate people's experiences of race and other identities, and to foster deeper understanding and maintain a stronger sense of relational connection even in the midst of conflict.

The Flex Model developed by Carmelita (Rosie) Castañeda (selection 24) supports communication across racial, ethnic, and linguistics groups and provides concrete steps for improving communication in diverse classrooms, cross-racial/ethnic dialogues, and community-based coalitions.

We close with Chip Smith's "The Personal is Political." This selection (selection 25) helps us think about how we each can deepen our engagement in the struggle against white supremacy through becoming aware of privilege and internalized oppression; building intentional relationships based on equality; studying the history of people of color; questioning and challenging the evidence of white supremacy in everyday life; taking inventory of activism in one's community; and examining other aspects of one's community that may lead to increased activism.

Note

1 We ask that those who cite this work always acknowledge by name all of the authors listed rather than only citing the first author or using "et al." to indicate coauthors. All authors listed on a section collaborated equitably on the conceptualization, development, and writing of this section.

References

Brodkin-Sacks, K. (1994). "How Did Jews Become White Folks?" In S. Gregory, R. Sanjek (eds), *Race*. New Brunswick, NJ: Rutgers University Press. pp. 78–102.

Gaultieri, S. (2001). "Becoming 'White': Race, Religion and the Foundations of Syrian/Lebanese Ethnicity in the United States." *Journal of American Ethnic History* 20 (4), 29–59.

Guglielmo, T. A. (2003). "Rethinking Whiteness Historiography: The Case of Italians in Chicago, 1890–1945." In A. W. Doane, E. Bonilla-Silva (eds), *White Out: The Continuing Significance of Racism*. New York: Routledge. pp. 49–61.

Haney López, I. F. (1997). *White by Law*. New York: New York University Press.

Obama, B. (2008). *A More Perfect Union.* Presidential campaign speech delivered on March 18, 2008, at Convention Hall, Philadelphia, PA. Retrieved September 19, 2009, from http://my.barackobama.com/page/content/hisownwords.

Roediger, D. R. (1991). "The Prehistory of the White Worker: Settler Colonialism, Race and Republicanism Before 1800." In *The Wages of Whiteness: Race and the Making of the American Working Class* (revised edition). London: Verso. pp. 19–40.

Spickard, P. (2007). *Almost All Aliens: Immigration, Race and Colonialism in American History and Identity.* New York: Routledge.

Takaki, R. (1993). *A Different Mirror: A History of Multicultural America.* Boston: Little, Brown.

Villenas, S., Deyhle, D. (1999). "Critical Race Theory and Ethnographies Challenging Stereotypes: Latino Families, Schooling, Resilience and Resistance." *Curriculum Inquiry* 29, 413–445.

8

Defining Racism

"Can We Talk?"

Beverly Daniel Tatum

. . .

The impact of racism begins early. Even in our preschool years, we are exposed to misinformation about people different from ourselves. Many of us grew up in neighborhoods where we had limited opportunities to interact with people different from our own families. When I ask my college students, "How many of you grew up in neighborhoods where most of the people were from the same racial group as your own?" almost every hand goes up. There is still a great deal of social segregation in our communities. Consequently, most of the early information we receive about "others"—people racially, religiously, or socioeconomically different from ourselves—does not come as the result of firsthand experience. The secondhand information we do receive has often been distorted, shaped by cultural stereotypes, and left incomplete.

. . .

Sometimes the assumptions we make about others come not from what we have been told or what we have seen on television or in books, but rather from what we have *not* been told. The distortion of historical information about people of color leads young people (and older people, too) to make assumptions that may go unchallenged for a long time. . . .

. . .

Omitted information can have similar effects. For example, another young woman, preparing to be a high school English teacher, expressed her dismay that she had never learned about any Black authors in any of her English courses. How was she to teach about them to her future students when she hadn't learned about them herself? A White male student in the class responded to this discussion with frustration in his response journal, writing "It's not my fault that Blacks don't write books." Had one of his elementary, high school, or college teachers ever told him that there were no Black writers? Probably not. Yet because he had never been exposed to Black authors, he had drawn his own conclusion that there were none.

Stereotypes, omissions, and distortions all contribute to the development of prejudice. *Prejudice* is a preconceived judgment or opinion, usually based on limited information. I assume that we all have prejudices, not because we want them, but simply because we are so continually exposed to misinformation about others. Though I have often heard students or workshop participants describe someone as not having "a prejudiced bone in his body," I usually suggest that they look again. Prejudice is one of the inescapable consequences of living in a racist society. Cultural racism—the cultural images and messages that affirm the assumed superiority of Whites and the assumed inferiority of people of color—is like smog in the air. Sometimes it is so thick it is visible, other times it is less apparent, but always, day in and day out, we are breathing it in. None of us would introduce ourselves as "smog-breathers" (and most of us don't want to be described as prejudiced), but if we live in a smoggy place, how can we avoid breathing the air? If we live in an environment in which we are bombarded with stereotypical images in the media, are frequently exposed to the ethnic jokes of friends and family members, and are rarely informed of the accomplishments of oppressed groups, we will develop the negative categorizations of those groups that form the basis of prejudice.

People of color as well as Whites develop these categorizations. Even a member of the stereotyped group may internalize the stereotypical categories about his or her own group to some degree. In fact, this process happens so frequently that it has a name, *internalized oppression*. . . .

. . .

To say that it is not our fault does not relieve us of responsibility, however. We may not have polluted the air, but we need to take responsibility, along with others, for cleaning it up. Each of us needs to look at our own behavior. Am I perpetuating and reinforcing the negative messages so pervasive in our culture, or am I seeking to challenge them? If I have not been exposed to positive images of marginalized groups, am I seeking them out, expanding my own knowledge base for myself and my children? Am I acknowledging and examining my own prejudices, my own rigid categorizations of others, thereby minimizing the adverse impact they might have on my interactions with those I have categorized? Unless we engage in these and other conscious acts of reflection and reeducation, we easily repeat the process with our children. We teach what we were taught. The unexamined prejudices of the parents are passed on to the children. It is not our fault, but it is our responsibility to interrupt this cycle.

RACISM: A SYSTEM OF ADVANTAGE BASED ON RACE

Many people use the terms *prejudice* and *racism* interchangeably. I do not, and I think it is important to make a distinction. In his book *Portraits of White Racism*, David Wellman argues convincingly that limiting our understanding of racism to prejudice does not offer a sufficient explanation for the persistence of racism. He defines racism as a system of advantage based on race. In illustrating this definition, he provides example after example of how Whites defend their racial advantage—access to better schools, housing, jobs—even when they do not embrace overtly prejudicial thinking. Racism cannot be fully explained as an expression of prejudice alone.

This definition of racism is useful because it allows us to see that racism, like other forms of oppression, is not only a personal ideology based on racial prejudice, but a *system* involving cultural messages and institutional policies and practices as well as the beliefs and actions of individuals. In the context of the United States, this system clearly operates to

C
O
N
T
E
X
T

the advantage of Whites and to the disadvantage of people of color. Another related definition of racism, commonly used by antiracist educators and consultants, is "prejudice plus power." Racial prejudice when combined with social power—access to social, cultural, and economic resources and decision-making—leads to the institutionalization of racist policies and practices. While I think this definition also captures the idea that racism is more than individual beliefs and attitudes, I prefer Wellman's definition because the idea of systematic advantage and disadvantage is critical to an understanding of how racism operates in American society.

. . .

The systematic advantages of being White are often referred to as White privilege. In a now well-known article, "White Privilege: Unpacking the Invisible Knapsack," Peggy McIntosh, a White feminist scholar, identified a long list of societal privileges that she received simply because she was White. She did not ask for them, and it is important to note that she hadn't always noticed that she was receiving them. They included major and minor advantages. Of course she enjoyed greater access to jobs and housing. But she also was able to shop in department stores without being followed by suspicious sales-people and could always find appropriate hair care products and makeup in any drugstore. She could send her child to school confident that the teacher would not discriminate against him on the basis of race. She could also be late for meetings, and talk with her mouth full, fairly confident that these behaviors would not be attributed to the fact that she was White. She could express an opinion in a meeting or in print and not have it labeled the "White" viewpoint. In other words, she was more often than not viewed as an individual, rather than as a member of a racial group.

. . .

Understanding racism as a system of advantage based on race is antithetical to traditional notions of an American meritocracy. For those who have internalized this myth, this definition generates considerable discomfort. It is more comfortable simply to think of racism as a particular form of prejudice. Notions of power or privilege do not have to be addressed when our understanding of racism is constructed in that way.

. . .

RACISM: FOR WHITES ONLY?

. . .

I sometimes visualize the ongoing cycle of racism as a moving walkway at the airport. Active racist behavior is equivalent to walking fast on the conveyor belt. The person engaged in active racist behavior has identified with the ideology of White supremacy and is moving with it. Passive racist behavior is equivalent to standing still on the walkway. No overt effort is being made, but the conveyor belt moves the bystanders along to the same destination as those who are actively walking. Some of the bystanders may feel the motion of the conveyor belt, see the active racists ahead of them, and choose to turn around, unwilling to go to the same destination as the White supremacists. But unless they are walking actively in the opposite direction at a speed faster than the conveyor belt—unless they are actively antiracist—they will find themselves carried along with the others.

. . .

It is important to acknowledge that while all Whites benefit from racism, they do not all benefit equally. Other factors, such as socio-economic status, gender, age, religious affiliation, sexual orientation, mental and physical ability, also play a role in our access to social influence and power. A White woman on welfare is not privileged to the same extent as a wealthy White heterosexual man. In her case, the systematic disadvantages of sexism and classism intersect with her White privilege, but the privilege is still there. This point was brought home to me in a 1994 study conducted by a Mount Holyoke graduate student, Phyllis Wentworth. Wentworth interviewed a group of female college students, who were both older than their peers and were the first members of their families to attend college, about the pathways that led them to college. All of the women interviewed were White, from working-class backgrounds, from families where women were expected to graduate from high school and get married or get a job. Several had experienced abusive relationships and other personal difficulties prior to coming to college. Yet their experiences were punctuated by "good luck" stories of apartments obtained without a deposit, good jobs offered without experience or extensive reference checks, and encouragement provided by willing mentors. While the women acknowledged their good fortune, none of them discussed their Whiteness. They had not considered the possibility that being White had worked in their favor and helped give them the benefit of the doubt at critical junctures. This study clearly showed that even under difficult circumstances, White privilege was still operating.

It is also true that not all people of color are equally targeted by racism. We all have multiple identities that shape our experience. I can describe myself as a light-skinned, well-educated, heterosexual, able-bodied, Christian African American woman raised in a middle-class suburb. As an African American woman, I am systematically disadvantaged by race and by gender, but I systematically receive benefits in the other categories, which then mediate my experience of racism and sexism. When one is targeted by multiple isms—racism, sexism, classism, heterosexism, ableism, anti-Semitism, ageism—in whatever combination, the effect is intensified. The particular combination of racism and classism in many communities of color is life-threatening. Nonetheless, when I, the middle-class Black mother of two sons, read another story about a Black man's unlucky encounter with a White police officer's deadly force, I am reminded that racism by itself can kill.

THE COST OF RACISM

. . . Why should Whites who are advantaged by racism *want* to end that system of advantage? What are the *costs* of that system to them?

A *Money* magazine article called "Race and Money" chronicled the many ways the American economy was hindered by institutional racism. Whether one looks at productivity lowered by racial tensions in the workplace, or real estate equity lost through housing discrimination, or the tax revenue lost in underemployed communities of color, or the high cost of warehousing human talent in prison, the economic costs of racism are real and measurable.

As a psychologist, I often hear about the less easily measured costs. When I ask White men and women how racism hurts them, they frequently talk about their fears of people of color, the social incompetence they feel in racially mixed situations, the alienation they have experienced between parents and children when a child marries into a family of color, and the interracial friendships they had as children that were lost in adolescence or young adulthood without their ever understanding why. White people are paying a significant price for the system of advantage. The cost is not as high for Whites as it is for people of color, but a price is being paid. . . .

The dismantling of racism is in the best interests of everyone.

. . .

9

A Different Mirror

Ronald Takaki

I had flown from San Francisco to Norfolk and was riding in a taxi to my hotel to attend a conference on multiculturalism. Hundreds of educators from across the country were meeting to discuss the need for greater cultural diversity in the curriculum. My driver and I chatted about the weather and the tourists. The sky was cloudy, and Virginia Beach was twenty minutes away. The rearview mirror reflected a white man in his forties. "How long have you been in this country?" he asked. "All my life," I replied, wincing. "I was born in the United States." With a strong southern drawl, he remarked: "I was wondering because your English is excellent!" Then, as I had many times before, I explained: "My grandfather came here from Japan in the 1880s. My family has been here, in America, for over a hundred years." He glanced at me in the mirror. Somehow I did not look "American" to him; my eyes and complexion looked foreign.

. . .

Questions like the one my taxi driver asked me are always jarring, but I can understand why he could not see me as American. He had a narrow but widely shared sense of the past—a history that has viewed American as European in ancestry. "Race," Toni Morrison explained, has functioned as a "metaphor" necessary to the "construction of Americanness": in the creation of our national identity, "American" has been defined as "white."

. . .

But how should "we" be defined? Who are the people "stuck here" in America? One of the lessons of the Los Angeles explosion is the recognition of the fact that we are a multiracial society and that race can no longer be defined in the binary terms of white and black. "We" will have to include Hispanics and Asians. While blacks currently constitute 13 percent of the Los Angeles population, Hispanics represent 40 percent. The 1990 census revealed that South Central Los Angeles, which was predominantly black in 1965 when the Watts rebellion occurred, is now 45 percent Hispanic. A majority of the first 5,438 people arrested were Hispanic, while 37 percent were black. Of the fifty-eight people who died in the riot, more than a third were Hispanic, and about 40 percent of the businesses destroyed were Hispanic-owned. Most of the other shops and stores were Korean-owned. The dreams of many Korean immigrants went up in smoke during the riot: two thousand Korean-owned businesses were damaged or demolished, totaling about $400 million in losses. There is evidence indicating they were targeted. "After all," explained a black gang member, "we didn't burn our community, just *their* stores."

. . .

African Americans have been the central minority throughout our country's history. They were initially brought here on a slave ship in 1619. Actually, these first twenty Africans might not have been slaves; rather, like most of the white laborers, they were probably indentured servants. The transformation of Africans into slaves is the story of the "hidden" origins of slavery. How and when was it decided to institute a system of bonded black labor? What happened, while freighted with racial significance, was actually conditioned by class conflicts within white society. Once established, the "peculiar institution" would have consequences for centuries to come. During the nineteenth century, the political storm over slavery almost destroyed the nation. Since the Civil War and emancipation, race has continued to be largely defined in relation to African Americans—segregation, civil rights, the underclass, and affirmative action. Constituting the largest minority group in our society, they have been at the cutting edge of the Civil Rights Movement. Indeed, their struggle has been a constant reminder of America's moral vision as a country committed to the principle of liberty. Martin Luther King clearly understood this truth when he wrote from a jail cell: "We will reach the goal of freedom in Birmingham and all over the nation, because the goal of America is freedom. Abused and scorned though we may be, our destiny is tied up with America's destiny."

Asian Americans have been here for over one hundred and fifty years, before many European immigrant groups. But as "strangers" coming from a "different shore," they have been stereotyped as "heathen," exotic, and unassimilable. Seeking "Gold Mountain," the Chinese arrived first, and what happened to them influenced the reception of the Japanese, Koreans, Filipinos, and Asian Indians as well as the Southeast Asian refugees like the Vietnamese and the Hmong. The 1882 Chinese Exclusion Act was the first law that prohibited the entry of immigrants on the basis of nationality. The Chinese condemned this restriction as racist and tyrannical. "They call us 'Chink,'" complained a Chinese immigrant, cursing the "white demons." "They think we no good! America cuts us off. No more come now, too bad!" This precedent later provided a basis for the restriction of European immigrant groups such as Italians, Russians, Poles, and Greeks. The Japanese painfully discovered that their accomplishments in America did not lead to acceptance, for during World War II, unlike Italian Americans and German Americans, they were placed in internment camps. Two-thirds of them were citizens by birth. "How could I as a 6-month-old child born in this country," asked Congressman Robert Matsui years later, "be declared by my own Government to be an enemy alien?" Today, Asian Americans represent the fastest-growing ethnic group. They have also become the focus of much mass media attention as "the Model Minority" not only for blacks and Chicanos, but also for whites on welfare and even middle-class whites experiencing economic difficulties.

Chicanos represent the largest group among the Hispanic population, which is projected to outnumber African Americans. They have been in the United States for a long time, initially incorporated by the war against Mexico. The treaty had moved the border between the two countries, and the people of "occupied" Mexico suddenly found themselves "foreigners" in their "native land." As historian Albert Camarillo pointed out, the Chicano past is an integral part of America's westward expansion, also known as "manifest destiny." But while the early Chicanos were a colonized people, most of them today have immigrant roots. Many began the trek to El Norte in the early twentieth century. "As I had heard a lot about the United States," Jesus Garza recalled, "it was my dream to come here." "We came to know families from Chihuahua, Sonora, Jalisco, and Durango," stated Ernesto Galarza. "Like ourselves, our Mexican neighbors had come this far moving step by step, working and waiting, as if they were feeling their way up a ladder." Nevertheless, the Chicano experience has been unique, for most of them have lived close to their homeland—a proximity that has helped reinforce their language, identity, and culture. This migration to El Norte has continued to the present. Los Angeles has more people of Mexican origin than any other city in the world, except Mexico City. A mostly mestizo people of Indian as well as African and Spanish ancestries, Chicanos currently represent the largest minority group in the Southwest, where they have been visibly transforming culture and society.

The Irish came here in greater numbers than most immigrant groups. Their history has been tied to America's past from the very beginning. Ireland represented the earliest English frontier: the conquest of Ireland occurred before the colonization of America, and the Irish were the first group that the English called "savages." In this context, the Irish past foreshadowed the Indian future. During the nineteenth century, the Irish, like the Chinese, were victims of British colonialism. While the Chinese fled from the ravages of the Opium Wars, the Irish were pushed from their homeland by "English tyranny." Here they became construction workers and factory operatives as well as the "maids" of America. Representing a Catholic group seeking to settle in a fiercely Protestant society, the Irish immigrants were targets of American nativist hostility. They were also what historian Lawrence J. McCaffrey called "the pioneers of the American urban ghetto," "previewing" experiences that would later be shared by the Italians, Poles, and other groups from southern and eastern Europe. Furthermore, they offer contrast to the immigrants from Asia. The Irish came about the same time as the Chinese, but they had a distinct advantage: the Naturalization Law of 1790 had reserved citizenship for "whites" only. Their compatible complexion allowed them to assimilate by blending into American society. In making their journey successfully into the mainstream, however, these immigrants from Erin pursued an Irish "ethnic" strategy: they promoted "Irish" solidarity in order to gain political power and also to dominate the skilled blue-collar occupations, often at the expense of the Chinese and blacks.

Fleeing pogroms and religious persecution in Russia, the Jews were driven from what John Cuddihy described as the "Middle Ages into the Anglo-American world of the *goyim* 'beyond the pale.'" To them, America represented the Promised Land. This vision led Jews to struggle not only for themselves but also for other oppressed groups, especially blacks. After the 1917 East St. Louis race riot, the Yiddish *Forward* of New York compared this anti-black violence to a 1903 pogrom in Russia: "Kishinev and St. Louis—the same soil, the same people." Jews cheered when Jackie Robinson broke into the Brooklyn Dodgers in 1947. "He was adopted as the surrogate hero by many of us growing up at the time," recalled Jack Greenberg of the NAACP Legal Defense Fund. "He was the way we saw ourselves triumphing against the forces of bigotry and ignorance." Jews stood shoulder to shoulder with blacks in the Civil Rights Movement: two-thirds of the white volunteers who went south during the 1964 Freedom Summer were Jewish. Today Jews are considered a highly successful "ethnic" group. How did they make such great socioeconomic strides? This question is often reframed by neoconservative intellectuals like Irving Kristol and Nathan Glazer to read: if Jewish immigrants were able to lift themselves from poverty into the mainstream through self-help and education without welfare and affirmative action, why can't blacks? But what this thinking overlooks is the unique history of Jewish immigrants, especially the initial advantages of many of them as literate and skilled. Moreover, it minimizes the virulence of racial prejudice rooted in American slavery.

Indians represent a critical contrast, for theirs was not an immigrant experience. The Wampanoags were on the shore as the first English strangers arrived in what would be called "New England." The encounters between Indians and whites not only shaped the course of race relations, but also influenced the very culture and identity of the general society. The architect of Indian removal, President Andrew Jackson told Congress: "Our conduct toward these people is deeply interesting to the national character." Frederick Jackson Turner understood the meaning of this observation when he identified the frontier as our transforming crucible. At first, the European newcomers had to wear Indian moccasins and shout the war cry. "Little by little," as they subdued the wilderness, the pioneers became "a new product" that was "American." But Indians have had a different view of this entire process. "The white man," Luther Standing Bear of the Sioux explained, "does not understand the Indian for the reason that he does not understand American." Continuing to be "troubled with primitive fears," he has "in his consciousness the perils of this frontier continent. . . . The man from Europe is still a foreigner and an alien. And he still hates the man who questioned his path across the continent." Indians questioned what Jackson and Turner trumpeted as "progress." For them, the frontier had a different "significance": their history was how the West was lost. But their story has also been one of resistance. As Vine Deloria declared, "Custer died for your sins."

By looking at these groups from a multicultural perspective, we can comparatively analyze their experiences in order to develop an understanding of their differences and similarities. Race, we will see, has been a social construction that has historically set apart racial minorities from European immigrant groups. Contrary to the notions of scholars like Nathan Glazer and Thomas Sowell, race in America has not been the same as ethnicity. A broad comparative focus also allows us to see how the varied experiences of different racial and ethnic groups occurred within shared contexts.

During the nineteenth century, for example, the Market Revolution employed Irish immigrant laborers in New England factories as it expanded cotton fields worked by enslaved blacks across Indian lands toward Mexico. Like blacks, the Irish newcomers were stereotyped as "savages," ruled by passions rather than "civilized" virtues such as self-control and hard work. The Irish saw themselves as the "slaves" of British oppressors, and during a visit to Ireland in the 1840s, Frederick Douglass found that the "wailing notes" of the Irish ballads reminded him of the "wild notes" of slave songs. The United States annexation of California, while incorporating Mexicans, led to trade with Asia and the migration of "strangers" from Pacific shores. In 1870, Chinese immigrant laborers were transported to Massachusetts as scabs to break an Irish immigrant strike; in response, the Irish recognized the need for interethnic working-class solidarity and tried to organize a Chinese lodge of the Knights of St. Crispin. After the Civil War, Mississippi planters recruited Chinese immigrants to discipline the newly freed blacks. During the debate over an immigration exclusion bill in 1882, a senator asked: If Indians could be located on reservations, why not the Chinese?

Other instances of our connectedness abound. In 1903, Mexican and Japanese farm laborers went on strike together in California: their union officers had names like Yamaguchi and Lizarras, and strike meetings were conducted in Japanese and Spanish. The Mexican strikers declared that they were standing in solidarity with their "Japanese brothers" because the two groups had toiled together in the fields and were now fighting together for a fair wage. Speaking in impassioned Yiddish during the 1909 "uprising of twenty thousand" strikers in New York, the charismatic Clara Lemlich compared the abuse of Jewish female garment workers to the experience of blacks: "[The bosses] yell at the girls and 'call them down' even worse than I imagine the Negro slaves were in the South." During the 1920s, elite universities like Harvard worried about the increasing numbers of Jewish students, and new admissions criteria were instituted to curb their enrollment. Jewish students were scorned for their studiousness and criticized for their "clannishness." Recently, Asian-American students have been the targets of similar complaints: they have been called "nerds" and told there are "too many" of them on campus.

Indians were already here, while blacks were forcibly transported to America, and Mexicans were initially enclosed by America's expanding border. The other groups came here as immigrants: for them, America represented liminality—a new world where they could pursue extravagant urges and do things they had thought beyond their capabilities. Like the land itself, they found themselves "betwixt and between all fixed points of classification." No longer fastened as fiercely to their old countries, they felt a stirring to become new people in a society still being defined and formed.

. . .

. . . Through their stories, the people who have lived America's history can help all of us, including my taxi driver, understand that Americans originated from many shores, and that all of us are entitled to dignity. "I hope this survey do a lot of good for Chinese people," an immigrant told an interviewer from Stanford University in the 1920s. "Make American people realize that Chinese people are humans. I think very few American people really know anything about Chinese." But the remembering is also for the sake of the children. "This story is dedicated to the descendants of Lazar and Goldie Glauberman," Jewish immigrant Minnie Miller wrote in her autobiography. "My history is bound up in their history and the generations that follow should know where they came from to know better who they are." Similarly, Tomo Shoji, an elderly Nisei woman, urged Asian Americans to learn more about their roots: "We got such good, fantastic stories to tell. All our stories are different." Seeking to know how they fit into America, many young people have become listeners; they are eager to learn about the hardships and humiliations experienced by their parents and grandparents. They want to hear their stories, unwilling to remain ignorant or ashamed of their identity and past.

. . .

Through their narratives about their lives and circumstances, the people of America's diverse groups are able to see themselves and each other in our common past. They celebrate what Ishmael Reed has described as a society "unique" in the world because "the world is here"—a place "where the cultures of the world crisscross." Much of America's past, they point out, has been riddled with racism. At the same time, these people offer hope, affirming the struggle for equality as a central theme in our country's history. At its conception, our nation was dedicated to the proposition of equality. What has given concreteness to this powerful national principle has been our coming together in the creation of a new society. "Stuck here" together, workers of different backgrounds have attempted to get along with each other.

> People harvesting
> Work together unaware
> Of racial problems,

wrote a Japanese immigrant describing a lesson learned by Mexican and Asian farm laborers in California.

. . .

10

Symbolic Racism, History, and Reality

The Real Problem with Indian Mascots

Kimberly Roppolo

The stadium lights starburst above the misty football field. The band blares and pounds out the school's fight song like only a hometown high school band can do. Blond, perky cheerleaders clap as they hop from foot to foot, rousing the fans to a controlled roar. Two of them hold a huge sign, painted painstakingly while sprawled across a dusty, linoleum-lined corridor. The men of the hour prepare to enter the arena of combat. They begin a slow trot, then burst through the paper to shouting cheerleaders—"Kill the Indians!" they scream.

Many people would say I am overreacting to be offended by this scenario. After all, what's more American than high school football? What could be a more wholesome activity for young people in today's age, when so many more dangerous temptations beset them at every side—drugs, alcohol, unprotected sex, and gang activity? I think the danger of this situation is that it is so precisely American. Americans in general see the Indian mascot controversy as "silly," and there are admittedly American Indians who see it the same way. . . . However, I think the danger of this use is more than just its potential to offend. It is representative of an endemic problem: racism against America's First Peoples. Despite the fact that racial problems still exist in our country, for the most part we are in a day and age where racial tolerance and tolerance for all kinds of diversity has increased. But this is not the case with racism against American Indians, largely because racism against American Indians is so ingrained in the American consciousness that it is invisible.

Dr. Cornell Pewewardy of the University of Kansas calls this kind of racism "dysconscious racism," or, in other words, racism that the people themselves who exhibit it are unaware of. The use of American Indian mascots falls under this category. The grossly exaggerated features of the Cleveland Indian, the cartooned vicious savages decorating high school spirit ribbons, the painted, dancing, fake-buckskin-clad white kids running down the sideline doing tomahawk chops, are all unintentionally stereotypical and aren't even perceived by most Americans as negative. They fall in the same category as rock singer Ted Nugent's ridiculous stage antics in a fluorescent mockery of a Plains chief's headdress. They fall under the same category as cigar store Indians topping car dealerships. They fall under the same category as words like "squaw," "papoose," "wagon burner," and "Indian giver." They fall under the same category as Disney's painted bombshell Pocahontas and the 36–24–36 asking-for-it Aztec seductress from *El Dorado* or her grotesquely depicted male counterparts. . . . The average American engages in this behavior without ever being aware of it, much less realizing that it is racism.

Every semester I ask my students what is in the front foyer of Applebee's restaurant. None of them, not even if they work there, are ever able to tell me there is a statue of an Indian man, in nonspecific tribal attire, often with a "special of the day" sign around his neck. Applebee's claims this statue "points to the next nearest Applebee's"; I guarantee that if a major restaurant chain placed a statue of an African American man in supposed tribal dress in the front of each of its restaurants pointing to the next nearest one, people would realize these statues were inappropriate. In the same way, as many others have pointed out, if we had sports teams named the New York Niggers or the Jersey Jigaboos, Americans would know this was wrong. The average American, who would clearly perceive the Louisville Lynched Porch Monkeys as a problematic name for a team doesn't even realize the Washington Redskins emerges from a history of the literal bloody skins of American Indian men, women, and children being worth British Crown bounty money—no one's skin is red. American Indian skin is brown, at least when it is on our bodies and not stripped from us in the name of profit and expansionism. African Americans, thank God, have raised the consciousness of Americans enough through the civil rights movement to keep the more obvious forms of racism usually hidden, though it took publicly armed Black Panthers, the burning of Chicago, and even the riots of Los Angeles to get this point across. American Indians are frankly so used to being literally shot down if we stick our heads up, we aren't nearly as likely to do so. In fact, from our own civil rights movement with AIM, we still have Indians like Leonard Peltier, who stuck their heads up although incarcerated for over twenty years when even the FBI admits its evidence was fabricated.

Racism against American Indians is so intrinsically part of America's political mythology, . . . that without it this country would have to do something it is has never done: face colonial guilt. Everything we see around us was made from stolen American Indian resources, resources raped from this Earth that we consider sacred, an Earth in danger of global disaster from imbalanced greed. We live like no people in the history of the world have ever lived. Our poorest are rich in comparison to the world's average citizen. We all—Indian, Euro American, Asian American, African American, or Chicano—have benefited at least in some material way from the murders of an estimated one hundred million people, crimes that are still going on in this hemisphere, in Mexico, in Argentina, in Oklahoma, in South Dakota, in New Mexico, Arizona, Montana, and more. These acts, along with innumerable rapes, along with untold numbers of sterilizations of women even up to the past few decades, along with the removal of children without cause from their parents' homes, from their cultures, along with the destruction of language, with the outlawing of religious freedom up until 1978, constitute what is defined as genocide under the United Nations Convention on Genocide's definition, a document never signed by the United States, because under it, that very government owes restitution to both American Indians and to African Americans, an estimated forty to sixty million of whom were killed during the slave trade before they ever reached the shores of the "New World."

An estimated six million Jews died in the atrocities committed in Nazi Germany, being treated before and after death in ways the world will never forgive—starved, herded naked like cattle, poisoned to an excruciating death, made into curios—lampshades, little collectibles for the Nazi elite. But this we recognize as inhuman, not the kind of behavior we as people can tolerate. We see the sins of Germany and the sins of Bosnia, where former students report seeing little girls with dolls still in their arms, dead with open eyes in mass graves, for what they are. But unlike the rest of the world, we as Americans cannot see our own. We are not taught in school that Columbus's men smashed babies' heads on rocks in front of their mothers. We are not taught that they sliced people in two for fun, in bets over whose sword was the sharpest. We are not taught they tied men up after slaving in silver mines all day, threw them under their hammocks, and raped their wives above them. We aren't taught that the Pilgrims were called the "cut-throat people" by the Indians, who taught them survival and feasted with them because, at one meal the good Christians invited them to, those very Christians took their knives and slit them from ear to ear. We aren't taught that our "forefathers" roasted Pequot men, women, and children alive in their beds. We aren't taught that Thomas Jefferson promoted miscegenation as a means of eradicating the "Indian problem." We are not taught that American soldiers collected labia and breasts and penises for curios after slaughtering women, children, and old men on what must be considered, when we look at the primary evidence of American history, a routine basis. The list goes on and on. We aren't, indeed, taught a lot of things. And we aren't taught them for a good reason. . . .

American Indian Nations are the only sovereign nations the United States government has ever broken over five hundred treaties with, violations that Russell Means rightly suggests gives these nations the legal justification to issue one huge eviction notice to the United States, the only nations whose citizens are owed . . . billions of dollars in money that was held in "trust" for Indians thought incapable of being responsible for it, billions of dollars that same United States government has lost. Despite this, American Indians serve this country in its military forces in higher numbers per capita than any other ethnic group—and have in every war since the American Revolution. Despite this, American Indians on the whole maintain a huge amount of respect for this country and the flag that flies above it.

The real problem with the kind of dysconscious, symbolic, abstract racism that is perpetuated today by sports mascots and the kind of historical, intentionally inculcated, politically motivated racism that enabled the near total genocide of American Indian peoples is that it enables very real, very concrete, and very conscious acts of violent racism that American Indian people still face in this country and this hemisphere on a daily basis. It is our conceptualization of people that dictates our behavior toward them. Most Americans don't come into contact with Indians on a daily basis because of that very genocide, or when they do, because of the campaign of rape and encouraged miscegenation through intermarriage, they don't realize they do. To most Americans, American Indians themselves are invisible. . . . But for Americans who live near or on reservations or tribally controlled lands and for our neighbors to the south, who very much still realize an Indian presence in "their" countries, . . . and because of the atmosphere of hatred that the dysconsious racism of the rest of the country allows and even promotes, violence abounds.

This is not to say that no other group in America is still subject to prejudice-induced violence. There are occasionally still unspeakable acts against African Americans like the one in Jasper, Texas. There are also unfortunately incidents of violent bigotry against homosexuals, like the one in Laramie, Wyoming, that led to the creation of federal hate-crime legislation. But the fact is that American Indian women are twice as likely as black men to die of homicide. White males commit most of these murders; most involve alcohol sold by white proprietors on reservation borders; many are never prosecuted. Like the murders in the 1970s that instigated the American Indian movement to begin with and the rash of Indian killings that followed it, these murders go largely unnoticed by mainstream America. So do the beatings. So do the rapes. If "real" Indians don't exist in the American mind, then hate crimes against them have no room in the American imagination of possibility. And the media, the same media that descends from that which actively promoted the extermination of Indians through the early 1900s, don't cover that continued extermination now because of their early effectiveness in our erasure.

. . .

Perpetuators of conscious racism in more Indian-populated regions of this country will justify their behavior with accusations that Indians themselves act in such a way that it encourages the negative stereotype—we are all unemployed, government-money-grubbing drunks. Yes, as well as having a higher rate of homicides, American Indians have a higher rate of every cultural malaise that can be imagined—a higher rate of unemployment, a higher rate of high school dropouts, a higher suicide rate, a higher rate of drug abuse, a higher rate of alcoholism, a higher rate of teen pregnancy, a higher rate of infant mortality . . . but one must consider the kind of low self-esteem that both conscious historical racism and dysconscious contemporary racism in the form of things like sports mascots brings about. Not only do Indian people have to deal with the fallout of being "conquered" people, the "survivor guilt" from being alive and suckered in by colonialist capitalism when so many were butchered in its creation, the shame of being men who descended from those unable to protect our women and children in the face of a demonic killing machine we could have never envisioned in our traditional cultures, the shame of being women who descended from those raped and tortured, or those who married or enconcubined themselves to European men as a means of survival. We have to deal with images of ourselves that do not match who we are—human beings. Moreover, Indian people *themselves* sometimes unconsciously internalize the stereotypical images projected on them by mainstream culture—"of course I can't succeed, I'm an Indian. I ought to either be dead or dead drunk." In comparison, the noble-savage ideal promoted by those who claim to be honoring Indians by using mascots based on Native peoples seems complimentary. No wonder some Indians find no problem with racially based mascots. American Indians are *not* all stereotypical unemployed drunks. Most are hardworking struggling, long-suffering individuals who despite the rarity of opportunity for mainstream success fight daily to keep alive what proud cultural and spiritual traditions we have remaining after the near extermination of our peoples, fight daily to minimize the risks of the negative impact of colonization on our children and promote education for them both in our traditional ways and in the mainstream ways that will ensure their success in both of the worlds in which they must live. No, we are not all dead. Neither are our extremely diverse cultures. And far from being the beneficiaries of government welfare, the average American Indian lives far below poverty level—if you have never visited a reservation like the Northern Cheyenne live on in Lame Deer or that Lakota people live on in Pine Ridge or Rosebud, then you have never seen what poverty in this country really is, not even if you have lived in the poorest of poor urban ghettos. . . . [G]overnment "handouts" like commodity cheese, the far-below-standard medical treatment dispensed by the Indian Health Service, or money distributed to the tribe for housing or other needs is dispensed, it falls way short of the government's promises to Indian peoples—that our ancestors and their descendants (us, even those of us with the lowest blood quantums) would be provided for in perpetuity in exchange for our means of providing for ourselves: our lands, the lands that we cultivated for agricultural products, the lands we obtained our game from, the lands our ancestors lived on for centuries and our cultures are tied to, the lands our ancestors rest in. We are more than aware of what we have lost—and cartoonish depictions that make light of both those very losses and us do nothing to encourage mainstream "achievement" among our peoples. And though money from casinos has recently created an influx of capital that some tribes are using to promote economic development, it has by no means enriched the average Indian, and the existence of the casinos themselves, which the tribes as sovereign nations under the United States Constitution have the right to legally create on their own ever-shrinking land bases, is continually under attack from the states, which have no legal jurisdiction over the tribes or their lands.

Sports mascots might indeed seem to be a small issue in light of all of this. And while, admittedly, American Indians have much greater problems to worry about, I would contend that the mascots are both symptomatic of racism and promote it. Some contend that other mascots, like Notre Dame's Fighting Irish, are based on racial identity and that no other group has raised issue with this. However, I would suggest that this is because the creation of "white" as an ethnicity in America's great melting pot has both cooked off cultural identification and a strong sense of heritage for the descendants of late immigrants and early indentured servants and erased colonial guilt for the still-at-the-top-of-the-heap descendants of those who actually engaged in active genocide. The descendants of Irish American immigrants—me included, as some of my ancestors were Irish, along with those who were Cherokee, Choctaw, Creek, German, and Welsh—aren't offended by the Fighting Irish because they don't have a great stake in Irish identity, unlike those who live in Dublin and deal daily with what being Irish, much less Catholic Irish or Protestant Irish, entails. . . .

. . .

After all of the offenses our peoples have suffered throughout the history of Europeans in the Americas and in light of the kind of racism to which American Indians are still subject, it seems a small thing to me that some of us ask that sports mascots that depict American Indians be eliminated. After all, it is not that we are asking for what we will never receive—we aren't asking for a return of our stolen lands or even payment for them, we aren't asking that all of the broken treaties be honored or that the United States pay full restitution to us under the United Nations Convention on Genocide. We aren't even asking for a formal apology by a United States president for the atrocities our ancestors suffered. We are simply asking for the same respect that other ethnic groups receive in this country. We are simply asking to be recognized as people, not as television images, not as cartoons.

11

The Possessive Investment in Whiteness

George Lipsitz

. . .

Whiteness is everywhere in U.S. culture, but it is very hard to see. As Richard Dyer suggests, "[W]hite power secures its dominance by seeming not to be anything in particular." As the unmarked category against which difference is constructed, whiteness never has to speak its name, never has to acknowledge its role as an organizing principle in social and cultural relations. To identify, analyze, and oppose the destructive consequences of whiteness, . . . requires an understanding of the existence and the destructive consequences of the possessive investment in whiteness that surreptitiously shapes so much of our public and private lives.

Race is a cultural construct, but one with sinister structural causes and consequences. Conscious and deliberate actions have institutionalized group identity in the United States, not just through the dissemination of cultural stories, but also through systematic efforts from colonial times to the present to create economic advantages through a possessive investment in whiteness for European Americans. Studies of culture too far removed from studies of social structure leave us with inadequate explanations for understanding racism and inadequate remedies for combating it.

Desire for slave labor encouraged European settlers in North America to view, first, Native Americans and, later, African Americans as racially inferior people suited "by nature" for the humiliating subordination of involuntary servitude. The long history of the possessive investment in whiteness stems in no small measure from the fact that all subsequent immigrants to North America have come to an already racialized society. From the start, European settlers in North America established structures encouraging a possessive investment in whiteness. The colonial and early national legal systems authorized attacks on Native Americans and encouraged the appropriation of their lands. They legitimated racialized chattel slavery, limited naturalized citizenship to "white" immigrants, identified Asian immigrants as expressly unwelcome (through legislation aimed at immigrants from China in 1882, from India in 1917, from Japan in 1924, and from the Philippines in 1934), and provided pretexts for restricting the voting, exploiting the labor, and seizing the property of Asian Americans, Mexican Americans, Native Americans, and African Americans.

The possessive investment in whiteness is not a simple matter of black and white; all racialized minority groups have suffered from it, albeit to different degrees and in different ways. The African slave trade began in earnest only after large-scale Native American slavery proved impractical in North America. The abolition of slavery led to the importation of low-wage labor from Asia. Legislation banning immigration from Asia set the stage for the recruitment of low-wage labor from Mexico. The new racial categories that emerged in each of these eras all revolved around applying racial labels to "nonwhite" groups in order to stigmatize and exploit them while at the same time preserving the value of whiteness.

Although reproduced in new form in every era, the possessive investment in whiteness has always been influenced by its origins in the racialized history of the United States—by its legacy of slavery and segregation, of "Indian" extermination and immigrant restriction, of conquest and colonialism. Although slavery has existed in many countries without any

C
O
N
T
E
X
T

particular racial dimensions to it, the slave system that emerged in North America soon took on distinctly racial forms. Africans enslaved in North America faced a racialized system of power that reserved permanent, hereditary, chattel slavery for black people. White settlers institutionalized a possessive investment in whiteness by making blackness synonymous with slavery and whiteness synonymous with freedom, but also by pitting people of color against one another. Fearful of alliances between Native Americans and African Americans that might challenge the prerogatives of whiteness, white settlers prohibited slaves and free blacks from traveling in "Indian country." European Americans used diplomacy and force to compel Native Americans to return runaway slaves to their white masters. During the Stono Rebellion of 1739, colonial authorities offered Native Americans a bounty for every rebellious slave they captured or killed. At the same time, British settlers recruited black slaves to fight against Native Americans within colonial militias. The power of whiteness depended not only on white hegemony over separate racialized groups, but also on manipulating racial outsiders to fight against one another, to compete with each other for white approval, and to seek the rewards and privileges of whiteness for themselves at the expense of other racialized populations.

. . .

Yet today the possessive investment is not simply the residue of conquest and colonialism, of slavery and segregation, of immigrant exclusion and "Indian" extermination. Contemporary whiteness and its rewards have been created and recreated by policies adopted long after the emancipation of slaves in the 1860s and even after the outlawing of *de jure* segregation in the 1960s. There has always been racism in the United States, but it has not always been the same racism. Political and cultural struggles over power have shaped the contours and dimensions of racism differently in different eras. Antiracist mobilizations during the Civil War and civil rights eras meaningfully curtailed the reach and scope of white supremacy, but in each case reactionary forces engineered a renewal of racism, albeit in new forms, during succeeding decades. Racism has changed over time, taking on different forms and serving different social purposes in each time period.

Contemporary racism has been created anew in many ways over the past five decades, but most dramatically by the putatively race-neutral, liberal, social democratic reforms of the New Deal Era and by the more overtly race-conscious neoconservative reactions against liberalism since the Nixon years. It is a mistake to posit a gradual and inevitable trajectory of evolutionary progress in race relations; on the contrary, our history shows that battles won at one moment can later be lost. Despite hard-fought battles for change that secured important concessions during the 1960s in the form of civil rights legislation, the racialized nature of social policy in the United States since the Great Depression has actually increased the possessive investment in whiteness among European Americans over the past half century.

During the New Deal Era of the 1930s and 1940s, both the Wagner Act and the Social Security Act excluded farm workers and domestics from coverage, effectively denying those disproportionately minority sectors of the work force protections and benefits routinely afforded whites. The Federal Housing Act of 1934 brought home ownership within reach of millions of citizens by placing the credit of the federal government behind private lending to home buyers, but overtly racist categories in the Federal Housing Agency's (FHA) "confidential" city surveys and appraisers' manuals channeled almost all of the loan money toward whites and away from communities of color. In the post-World War II era, trade unions negotiated contract provisions giving private medical insurance, pensions, and job security largely to the white workers who formed the overwhelming majority of the unionized work force in mass production industries, rather than fighting for full employment, medical care, and old-age pensions for all, or even for an end to discriminatory hiring and promotion practices by employers in those industries.

C
O
N
T
E
X
T

Each of these policies widened the gap between the resources available to whites and those available to aggrieved racial communities. Federal housing policy offers an important illustration of the broader principles at work in the possessive investment in whiteness. By channeling loans away from older inner city neighborhoods and toward white home buyers moving into segregated suburbs, the FHA and private lenders after World War II aided and abetted segregation in U.S. residential neighborhoods. . . .

The federal government has played a major role in augmenting the possessive investment in whiteness. For years, the General Services Administration routinely channeled the government's own rental and leasing business to realtors who engaged in racial discrimination, while federally subsidized urban renewal plans reduced the already limited supply of housing for communities of color through "slum clearance" programs. In concert with FHA support for segregation in the suburbs, federal and state tax monies routinely funded the construction of water supplies and sewage facilities for racially exclusive suburban communities in the 1940s and 1950s. . . .

At the same time that FHA loans and federal highway building projects subsidized the growth of segregated suburbs, urban renewal programs in cities throughout the country devastated minority neighborhoods. During the 1950s and 1960s, federally assisted urban renewal projects destroyed 20 percent of the central-city housing units occupied by blacks, as opposed to only 10 percent of those inhabited by whites. More than 60 percent of those displaced by urban renewal were African Americans, Puerto Ricans, Mexican Americans, or members of other minority racial groups. The Federal Housing Administration and the Veterans Administration financed more than $120 billion worth of new housing between 1934 and 1962, but less than 2 percent of this real estate was available to nonwhite families—and most of that small amount was located in segregated areas.

Even in the 1970s, after most major urban renewal programs had been completed, black central-city residents continued to lose housing units at a rate equal to 80 percent of what had been lost in the 1960s. Yet white displacement declined to the relatively low levels of the 1950s. In addition, the refusal first to pass, then to enforce, fair housing laws has enabled realtors, buyers, and sellers to profit from racist collusion against minorities largely without fear of legal retribution. During the decades following World War II, urban renewal helped construct a new "white" identity in the suburbs by helping to destroy ethnically specific European American urban inner-city neighborhoods. Wrecking balls and bulldozers eliminated some of these sites, while others were transformed by an influx of minority residents desperately competing for a declining supply of affordable housing units. As increasing numbers of racial minorities moved into cities, increasing numbers of European American ethnics moved out. Consequently, ethnic differences among whites became a less important dividing line in U.S. culture, while race became more important. The suburbs helped turn Euro-Americans into "whites" who could live near each other and intermarry with relatively little difficulty. But this "white" unity rested on residential segregation, on shared access to housing and life chances largely unavailable to communities of color.

. . .

In 1968, lobbyists for the banking industry helped draft the Housing and Urban Development Act, which allowed private lenders to shift the risks of financing low-income housing to the government, creating a lucrative and thoroughly unregulated market for themselves. One section of the 1968 bill authorized FHA mortgages for inner-city areas that did not meet the usual eligibility criteria, and another section subsidized interest payments by low-income families. If administered wisely, these provisions might have promoted fair housing goals, but FHA administrators deployed them in ways that actually promoted segregation in order to provide banks, brokers, lenders, developers, realtors, and speculators with windfall profits. As a U.S. Commission on Civil Rights investigation

C
O
N
T
E
X
T

later revealed, FHA officials collaborated with blockbusters in financing the flight of low-income whites out of inner city neighborhoods, and then aided unscrupulous realtors and speculators by arranging purchases of substandard housing by minorities desperate to own their own homes. The resulting sales and mortgage foreclosures brought great profits to lenders (almost all of them white), but their actions led to price fixing and a subsequent inflation of housing costs in the inner city by more than 200 percent between 1968 and 1972. Bankers then foreclosed on the mortgages of thousands of these uninspected and substandard homes, ruining many inner-city neighborhoods. In response, the Department of Housing and Urban Development essentially red-lined inner cities, making them ineligible for future loans, a decision that destroyed the value of inner-city housing for generations to come.

Federally funded highways designed to connect suburban commuters with downtown places of employment also destroyed already scarce housing in minority communities and often disrupted neighborhood life as well. Construction of the Harbor Freeway in Los Angeles, the Gulf Freeway in Houston, and the Mark Twain Freeway in St. Louis displaced thousands of residents and bisected neighborhoods, shopping districts, and political precincts. The processes of urban renewal and highway construction set in motion a vicious cycle: population loss led to decreased political power, which made minority neighborhoods more vulnerable to further urban renewal and freeway construction, not to mention more susceptible to the placement of prisons, incinerators, toxic waste dumps, and other projects that further depopulated these areas.

. . .

Minorities are less likely than whites to receive preventive medical care or costly operations from Medicare. Eligible members of minority communities are also less likely than European Americans to apply for food stamps. The labor of migrant farm workers from aggrieved racialized groups plays a vital role in providing adequate nutrition for others, but the farm workers and their children suffer disproportionately from health disorders caused by malnutrition. In her important research on health policy and ethnic diversity, Linda Wray concludes that "the lower life expectancies for many ethnic minority groups and subgroups stem largely from their disproportionately higher rates of poverty, malnutrition, and poor health care."

Just as residential segregation and urban renewal make minority communities disproportionately susceptible to health hazards, their physical and social location gives these communities a different relationship to the criminal justice system. A 1990 study by the National Institute on Drug Abuse revealed that while only 15 percent of the thirteen million habitual drug users in the United States were black and 77 percent were white, African Americans were four times more likely to be arrested on drug charges than whites in the nation as a whole, and seven to nine times more likely in Pennsylvania, Michigan, Illinois, Florida, Massachusetts, and New Jersey. A 1989 study by the Parents' Resource Institute for Drug Education discovered that African American high school students consistently showed lower levels of drug and alcohol use than their European American counterparts, even in high schools populated by residents of low-income housing projects. Yet, while comprising about 12 percent of the U.S. population, blacks accounted for 10 percent of drug arrests in 1984, 40 percent in 1988, and 42 percent in 1990. In addition, white drug defendants receive considerably shorter average prison terms than African Americans convicted of comparable crimes. A U.S. Sentencing Commission study found in 1992 that half of the federal court districts that handled cases involving crack cocaine prosecuted minority defendants *exclusively*. A *Los Angeles Times* article in 1995 revealed that "black and Latino crack dealers are hammered with 10-year mandatory federal sentences while whites prosecuted in state court face a minimum of five years and often receive no more than a year in jail." Alexander Lichtenstein and Michael A. Kroll point out that sentences for African Americans in the federal prison system are 20 percent longer than those given to whites who commit the same crimes. They observe that if blacks received the same sentences as whites for these offenses, the federal prison system would require three thousand fewer prison cells, enough to close completely six of the new five-hundred bed institutions.

Racial animus on the part of police officers, prosecutors, and judges accounts for only a small portion of the distinctive experience that racial minorities have with the criminal justice system. Economic devastation makes the drug trade appealing to some people in the inner city, while the dearth of capital in minority neighborhoods curtails opportunities for other kinds of employment. Deindustrialization, unemployment, and lack of intergenerational transfers of wealth undermine parental and adult authority in many neighborhoods. The complex factors that cause people to turn to drugs are no more prevalent in minority communities than elsewhere, but these communities and their inhabitants face more stress while having fewer opportunities to receive private counseling and treatment for their problems.

The structural weaknesses of minority neighborhoods caused by discrimination in housing, education, and hiring also play a crucial role in relations between inner-city residents and the criminal justice system. Cocaine dealing, which initially skyrocketed among white suburban residents, was driven into the inner city by escalating enforcement pressures in wealthy white communities. Ghettos and barrios became distribution centers for the sale of drugs to white suburbanites. Former New York and Houston police commissioner Lee Brown, head of the federal government's antidrug efforts during the early years of the Clinton presidency and later mayor of Houston, noted, "There are those who bring drugs into the country. That's not the black community. Then you have wholesalers, those who distribute them once they get here, and as a rule that's not the black community. Where you find the blacks is in the street dealing."

You also find blacks and other minorities in prison. Police officers in large cities, pressured to show results in the drive against drugs, lack the resources to effectively enforce the law everywhere (in part because of the social costs of deindustrialization and the tax limitation initiatives designed to shrink the size of government). These officers know that it is easier to make arrests and to secure convictions by confronting drug users in areas that have conspicuous street corner sales, that have more people out on the street with no place to go, and that have residents more likely to plead guilty and less likely to secure the services of attorneys who can get the charges against them dropped, reduced, or wiped off the books with subsequent successful counseling and rehabilitation. In addition, politicians supported by the public relations efforts of neo-conservative foundations often portray themselves to suburban voters as opponents of the "dangerous classes" in the inner cities.

Minority disadvantages craft advantages for others. Urban renewal failed to provide new housing for the poor, but it played an important role in transforming the U.S. urban economy from one that relied on factory production to one driven by producer services. Urban renewal projects subsidized the development of downtown office centers on previously residential land, and they frequently created buffer zones of empty blocks dividing poor neighborhoods from new shopping centers designed for affluent commuters. To help cities compete for corporate investment by making them appealing to high-level executives, federal urban aid favored construction of luxury housing units and cultural centers like symphony halls and art museums over affordable housing for workers. Tax abatements granted to these producer services centers further aggravated the fiscal crisis that cities faced, leading to tax increases on existing industries, businesses, and residences.

. . .

When housing prices increased dramatically during the 1970s, white homeowners who had been able to take advantage of discriminatory FHA financing policies in the past realized increased equity in their homes, while those excluded from the housing market by earlier policies found themselves facing even higher costs of entry into the market in addition to the traditional obstacles presented by the discriminatory practices of sellers, realtors, and lenders. The contrast between European Americans and African Americans is instructive in this regard. Because whites have access to broader housing choices than blacks, whites pay 15 percent less than blacks for similar housing in the same neighborhood. White neighborhoods typically experience housing costs 25 percent lower than would be the case if the residents were black.

. . .

When confronted with evidence of systematic racial bias in home lending, defenders of the possessive investment in whiteness argue that the disproportionate share of loan denials to members of minority groups stems not from discrimination, but from the low net worth of minority applicants, even those who have high incomes. This might seem a reasonable position, but net worth is almost totally determined by past opportunities for asset accumulation, and therefore is the one figure most likely to reflect the history of discrimination. Minorities are told, in essence, "We can't give you a loan today because we've discriminated against members of your race so effectively in the past that you have not been able to accumulate any equity from housing and to pass it down through the generations."

Most white families have acquired their net worth from the appreciation of property that they secured under conditions of special privilege in a discriminatory housing market. In their prize-winning book *Black Wealth/White Wealth*, Melvin Oliver and Thomas Shapiro demonstrate how the history of housing discrimination makes white parents more able to borrow funds for their children's college education or to loan money to their children to enter the housing market. In addition, much discrimination in home lending is not based on considerations of net worth; it stems from decisions made by white banking officials based on their stereotypes about minority communities. The Federal Reserve Bank of Boston study showed that black and Latino mortgage applicants are 60 percent more likely to be turned down for loans than whites, even after controlling for employment, financial, and neighborhood characteristics. . . .

Yet bankers also make money from the ways in which discrimination creates artificial scarcities in the market. Minorities have to pay more for housing because much of the market is off limits to them. Blockbusters profit from exploiting white fears and provoking them into panic selling. Minority home owners denied loans in mainstream banks often turn to exploitative lenders who make "low end" loans at enormously high interest rates. If they fail to pay back these loans, regular banks can acquire the property cheaply and charge someone else exorbitant interest for a loan on the same property.

. . .

The policies of neoconservatives in the Reagan and Bush administrations during the 1980s and 1990s greatly exacerbated the racialized aspects of more than fifty years of these social welfare policies. Regressive policies that cut federal aid to education and refused to challenge segregated education, housing, and hiring, as well as the cynical cultivation of an antiblack consensus through attacks on affirmative action and voting rights legislation clearly reinforced possessive investments in whiteness. In the U.S. economy, where 86 percent of available jobs do not appear in classified ads and where personal connections prove the most important factor in securing employment, attacks on affirmative action guarantee that whites will be rewarded for their historical advantage in the labor market rather than for their individual abilities or efforts.

. . .

Yet even seemingly race-neutral policies supported by both neoconservatives and liberals in the 1980s and 1990s have increased the absolute value of being white. In the 1980s, changes in federal tax laws decreased the value of wage income and increased the value of investment income—a move harmful to minorities, who suffer from a gap between their total wealth and that of whites even greater than the disparity between their income and white income. The failure to raise the minimum wage between 1981 and 1989 and the decline of more than one-third in the value of Aid to Families with Dependent Children (AFDC) payments injured all poor people, but they exacted special costs on nonwhites, who faced even more constricted markets for employment, housing, and education than poor whites.

Similarly, the "tax reforms" of the 1980s made the effective rate of taxation higher on investment in actual goods and services than on profits from speculative enterprises. This change encouraged the flight of capital from industrial production with its many employment opportunities toward investments that can be turned over quickly to allow the greatest possible tax write-offs. Government policies thus discouraged investments that might produce high-paying jobs and encouraged investors to strip companies of their assets to make rapid short-term profits. These policies hurt almost all workers, but they fell particularly heavily on minority workers, who because of employment discrimination in the retail and small business sectors were overrepresented in blue-collar industrial jobs.

. . .

Subsidies to the private sector by government agencies also tend to enhance the rewards of past discrimination. Throughout the country, tax increment financing for redevelopment programs offers tax-free and low-interest loans to developers whose projects use public services, often without having to pay taxes to local school boards or country governments. In St. Louis, for example, tax abatements for wealthy corporations deprive the city's schools (and their majority African American population) of $17 million a year. Even if these redevelopment projects eventually succeed in increasing municipal revenues through sales and earnings taxes, their proceeds go to funds that pay for the increased services these developments demand (fire and police protection, roads, sewers, electricity, lighting, etc.) rather than to school funds, which are dependent upon property tax revenues. Nationwide, industrial development bonds resulted in a $7.4 billion tax loss in 1983, which ordinary taxpayers had to make up through increased payroll taxes. Compared to white Americans, people of color, more likely to be poor or working class, suffer disproportionately from these changes as taxpayers, as workers, and as tenants. A study by the Citizens for Tax Justice found that wealthy Californians spend less than eleven cents in taxes for every dollar earned, while poor residents of the state pay fourteen cents out of every dollar in taxes. As groups overrepresented among the poor, minorities have been forced to subsidize the tax breaks given to the wealthy. While holding property tax assessments for businesses and some home owners to about half of their market value, California's Proposition 13 deprived cities and counties of $13 billion a year in taxes. Businesses alone avoided $3.3 billion to $8.6 billion in taxes per year under this statute.

Because they are ignorant of even the recent history of the possessive investment in whiteness—generated by slavery and segregation, immigrant exclusion and Native American policy, conquest and colonialism, but augmented by liberal and conservative social policies as well—Americans produce largely cultural explanations for structural social problems. The increased possessive investment in whiteness generated by disinvestment in U.S. cities, factories, and schools since the 1970s disguises as *racial* problems the general social problems posed by deindustrialization, economic restructuring, and neoconservative attacks on the welfare state. It fuels a discourse that demonizes people of color for being victimized by these changes, while hiding the privileges of whiteness by attributing the economic advantages enjoyed by whites to their family values, faith in fatherhood, and foresight—rather than to the favoritism they enjoy through their possessive investment in whiteness.

. . .

Yet public opinion polls of white Americans reflect little recognition of these devastating changes. Seventy percent of whites in one poll said that African Americans "have the same opportunities to live a middle-class life as whites," and nearly three-fourths of white respondents to a 1989 poll believed that opportunities for blacks had improved under Reagan. If such optimism about the opportunities available to African Americans does not demonstrate ignorance of the dire conditions facing black communities, it indicates that many whites believe that blacks suffer deservedly, because they do not take advantage of the opportunities offered them. In opinion polls, favorable assessments of black chances for success often accompanied extremely negative judgments about the abilities, work habits, and character of black people. A National Opinion Research Report in 1990 disclosed that more than 50 percent of U.S. whites viewed blacks as innately lazy and less intelligent and less patriotic than whites. More than 60 percent said that they believed that blacks suffer from poor housing and employment opportunities because of their own lack of will power. Some 56.3 percent said that blacks preferred welfare to employment, while 44.6 percent contended that blacks tended toward laziness. Even more important, research by Mary Edsall and Thomas Byrne Edsall indicates that many whites structure nearly all of their decisions about housing, education, and politics in response to their aversions to black people.

. . .

. . . As long as we define social life as the sum total of conscious and deliberative individual activities, we will be able to discern as racist only *individual* manifestations of personal prejudice and hostility. Systemic, collective, and coordinated group behavior consequently drops out of sight. Collective exercises of power that relentlessly channel rewards, resources, and opportunities from one group to another will not appear "racist" from this perspective, because they rarely announce their intention to discriminate against individuals. Yet they nonetheless give racial identities their sinister social meaning by giving people from different races vastly different life chances.

The gap between white perception and minority experience can have explosive consequences. Little more than a year after the 1992 Los Angeles rebellion, a sixteen-year-old high school junior shared her opinions with a reporter from the *Los Angeles Times*. "I don't think white people owe anything to black people," she explained. "We didn't sell them into slavery, it was our ancestors. What they did was wrong, but we've done our best to make up for it." A seventeen-year-old senior echoed those comments, telling the reporter, "I feel we spend more time in my history class talking about what whites owe blacks than just about anything else when the issue of slavery comes up. I often received dirty looks. This seems strange given that I wasn't even alive then. And the few members of my family from that time didn't have the luxury of owning much, let alone slaves. So why, I ask you, am I constantly made to feel guilty?"

More ominously, after pleading guilty to bombing two homes and one car, vandalizing a synagogue, and attempting to start a race war by planning the murder of Rodney King and the bombing of Los Angeles's First African Methodist Episcopal Church, twenty-year-old Christopher David Fisher explained that "sometimes whites were picked on because of the color of their skin. . . . Maybe we're blamed for slavery." Fisher's actions were certainly extreme, but his justification of them drew knowingly and precisely on a broadly shared narrative about the victimization of "innocent" whites by irrational and ungrateful minorities.

The comments and questions raised about the legacy of slavery by these young whites illuminate broader currents in our culture, with enormous implications for understanding the enduring significance of race in our country. These young people associate black grievances solely with slavery, and they express irritation at what they perceive as efforts to make them feel guilty or unduly privileged because of things that happened in the distant past. The claim that one's own family did not own any slaves is frequently voiced in our culture. It is almost never followed with a statement to the effect that of course some people's families did own slaves and we will not rest until we track them down and make them pay reparations. This view never acknowledges how the existence of slavery and the exploitation of black labor after emancipation created opportunities from which immigrants and others benefited, even if they did not personally own slaves. Rather, it seems to hold that, because not all white people owned slaves, no white people can be held accountable or inconvenienced by the legacy of slavery. More important, having dispensed with slavery, they feel no need to address the histories of Jim Crow segregation, racialized social policies, urban renewal, or the revived racism of contemporary neoconservatism. On the contrary, Fisher felt that his discomfort with being "picked on" and "blamed" for slavery gave him good reason to bomb homes, deface synagogues, and plot to kill black people.

Unfortunately for our society, these young whites accurately reflect the logic of the language of liberal individualism and its ideological predispositions in discussions of race. In their apparent ignorance of the disciplined, systemic, and collective *group* activity that has structured white identities in U.S. history, they are in good company. In a 1979 law journal article, future Supreme Court justice Antonin Scalia argued that affirmative action "is based upon concepts of racial indebtedness and racial entitlement rather than individual worth and individual need" and is thus "racist." Yet liberal individualism is not completely color-blind on this issue. As Cheryl I. Harris demonstrates, the legacy of liberal individualism has not prevented the Supreme Court from recognizing and protecting the group interests of *whites* in the Bakke, Croson, and Wygant cases. In each case, the Court nullified affirmative action programs because they judged efforts to help blacks as harmful to whites: to white expectations of entitlement, expectations based on the possessive investment in whiteness they held as members of a group. In the Bakke case, for instance, where the plaintiff argued that medical school affirmative action programs disadvantaged white applicants like himself, neither Bakke nor the Court contested the legitimacy of medical school admissions standards that reserved five seats in each class for children of wealthy donors to the university or that penalized Bakke for being older than most of the other applicants. . . . But they did challenge and reject a policy designed to offset the effects of past and present discrimination when they could construe the medical school admission policies as detrimental to the interests of whites as a group—and as a consequence they applied the "strict scrutiny" standard to protect whites while denying that protection to people of color. In this case, as in so many others, the language of liberal individualism serves as a cover for co-ordinated collective group interests.

   . . .

   . . . But an explicitly antiracist interethnic movement that acknowledges the existence and power of whiteness might make some important changes. Antiracist coalitions also have a long history in the United States—in the political activism of John Brown, Sojourner Truth, and the Magon brothers among others, but also in our rich cultural tradition of interethnic antiracism connected to civil rights activism. . . . These all too infrequent but nonetheless important efforts by whites to fight racism, not out of sympathy for someone else but out of a sense of self-respect and simple justice, have never completely disappeared; they remain available as models for the present.

   . . .

12

Heteropatriarchy and the Three Pillars of White Supremacy

Rethinking Women of Color Organizing

Andrea Smith

Scenario #1

A group of women of color come together to organize. An argument ensues about whether or not Arab women should be included. Some argue that Arab women are "white" since they have been classified as such in the US census. Another argument erupts over whether or not Latinas qualify as "women of color," since some may be classified as "white" in their Latin American countries of origin and/or "pass" as white in the United States.

Scenario #2

In a discussion on racism, some people argue that Native peoples suffer from less racism than other people of color because they generally do not reside in segregated neighborhoods within the United States. In addition, some argue that since tribes now have gaming, Native peoples are no longer "oppressed."

Scenario #3

A multiracial campaign develops involving diverse communities of color in which some participants charge that we must stop the black/white binary, and end Black hegemony over people of color politics to develop a more "multicultural" framework. However, this campaign continues to rely on strategies and cultural motifs developed by the Black Civil Rights struggle in the United States.

These incidents, which happen quite frequently in "women of color" or "people of color" political organizing struggles, are often explained as a consequence of "oppression olympics." . . . In this essay, I want to argue that these incidents are not so much the result of "oppression olympics" but are more about how we have inadequately framed "women of color" or "people of color" politics. . . . [T]he premise behind much "women of color" organizing is that women from communities victimized by white supremacy should unite together around their shared oppression. . . .

This framework has proven to be limited for women of color and people of color organizing. First, it tends to presume that our communities have been impacted by white supremacy in the same way. Consequently, we often assume that all of our communities will share similar strategies for liberation. In fact, however, our strategies often run into conflict. For example, one strategy that many people in US-born communities of color adopt, in order to advance economically out of impoverished communities, is to join the military. We then become complicit in oppressing and colonizing communities from other countries. Meanwhile, people from other countries often adopt the strategy of moving to the United States to advance economically, without considering their complicity in settling on the lands of indigenous peoples that are being colonized by the United States.

Consequently, it may be more helpful to adopt an alternative framework for women of color and people of color organizing. I call one such framework the "Three Pillars of White Supremacy." This framework does not assume that racism and white supremacy is enacted in a singular fashion; rather, white supremacy is constituted by separate and distinct, but still interrelated, logics. . . .

SLAVERY/CAPITALISM

One pillar of white supremacy is the logic of slavery. As Sora Han, Jared Sexton, and Angela P. Harris note, this logic renders Black people as inherently slaveable—as nothing more than property. That is, in this logic of white supremacy Blackness becomes equated with slaveability. The forms of slavery may change—whether it is through the formal system of slavery, sharecropping, or through the current prison-industrial complex—but the logic itself has remained consistent.

This logic is the anchor of capitalism. . . . To keep this capitalist system in place—which ultimately commodifies most people—the logic of slavery applies a racial hierarchy to this system. . . . This helps people who are not Black to accept their lot in life, because they can feel that at least they are not at the very bottom of the racial hierarchy—at least they are not property; at least they are not slaveable.

The logic of slavery can be seen clearly in the current prison industrial complex (PIC). While the PIC generally incarcerates communities of color, it seems to be structured primarily on an anti-Black racism. . . . [P]rior to the Civil War, most people in prison were white. However, after the thirteenth amendment was passed—which banned slavery, except for those in prison—Black people previously enslaved through the slavery system were reenslaved through the prison system. Black people who had been the property of slave owners became state property, through the . . . [convict] leasing system. Thus, we can actually look at the criminalization of Blackness as a logical extension of Blackness as property.

GENOCIDE/COLONIALISM

A second pillar of white supremacy is the logic of genocide. This logic holds that indigenous peoples must disappear. In fact, they must *always* be disappearing, in order to allow non-indigenous peoples rightful claim over this land. Through this logic of genocide, non-Native peoples then become the rightful inheritors of all that was indigenous—land, resources, indigenous spirituality, or culture. As Kare Shanley notes, Native peoples are a permanent "present absence" in the US colonial imagination, an "absence" that reinforces, at every turn, the conviction that Native peoples are indeed vanishing and that the conquest of Native lands is justified. Ella Shoat and Robert Stam describe this absence as "an ambivalently repressive mechanism [which] dispels the anxiety in the face of the Indian, whose very presence is a reminder of the initially precarious grounding of the American nation state itself. . . . In a temporal paradox, living Indians were induced to 'play dead,' as it were, in order to perform a narrative of manifest destiny in which their role, ultimately, was to disappear."

Rayna Green further elaborates . . . "The living performance of 'playing Indian' by non-Indian peoples depends upon the physical and psychological removal, even the death, of real Indians. In that sense, the performance, purportedly often done out of a stated and implicit love for Indians, is really the obverse of another well-known cultural phenom-enon, 'Indian hating,' as most often expressed in another, deadly performance genre called 'genocide'" (Green, 1988). After all, why would non-Native peoples need to play Indian—which often includes acts of spiritual appropriation and land theft—if they thought Indians were still alive and perfectly capable of being Indian themselves? The pillar of genocide serves as the anchor for colonialism—it is what allows non-Native peoples to feel they can rightfully own indigenous peoples' land. It is okay to take land from indigenous peoples, because indigenous peoples have disappeared.

ORIETALISM/WAR

A third pillar of white supremacy is the logic of Orientalism. Orientalism was defined by Edward Said as the process of the West defining itself as a superior civilization by construct-ing itself in opposition to an "exotic" but inferior "Orient." . . . The logic of Orientalism marks certain peoples or nations as inferior and as posing a constant threat to the well-being of empire. These peoples are still seen as "civilizations"—they are not property or "disappeared"—however, they will always be imaged as permanent foreign threats to empire. This logic is evident in the anti-immigration movements within the United States that target immigrants of color. It does not matter how long immigrants of color reside in the United States, they generally become targeted as foreign threats, particularly during war time. Consequently, orientalism serves as the anchor for war, because it allows the United States to justify being in a constant state of war to protect itself from its enemies.

For example, the United States feels entitled to use Orientalist logic to justify racial profiling of Arab Americans so that it can be strong enough to fight the "war on terror." Orientalism also allows the United States to defend the logics of slavery and genocide, as these practices enable the United States to stay "strong enough" to fight these constant wars. . . . For the system of white supremacy to stay in place, the United States must always be at war.

Because we are situated within different logics of white supremacy, we may misunder-stand a racial dynamic if we simplistically try to explain one logic of white supremacy with another logic. For instance, think about the first scenario that opens this essay: if we simply dismiss Latino/as or Arab peoples as "white," we fail to understand how a racial logic of Orientalism is in operation. . . . Latino/as and Arabs are often situated in a racial hierarchy that privileges them over Black people. However, while Orientalist logic may bestow them some racial privilege, they are still cast as inferior yet threatening "civilizations" in the United States. Their privilege is not a signal that they will be assimilated, but that they will be marked as perpetual foreign threats to the US world order.

ORGANIZING IMPLICATIONS

Under the old but still potent and dominant model, people of color organizing was based on the notion of organizing around shared victimhood. In this model, however, we see that we are victims of white supremacy, but complicit in it as well. Our survival strategies and resistance to white supremacy are set by the system of white supremacy itself. What keeps us trapped within our particular pillars of white supremacy is that we are seduced with the prospect of being able to participate in the other pillars. For example, all non-Native peoples are promised the ability to join in the colonial project of settling indigenous lands.

All non-Black peoples are promised that if they comply, they will not be at the bottom of the racial hierarchy. And Black, Native, Latino, and Asian peoples are promised that they will economically and politically advance if they join US wars to spread "democracy." Thus, people of color organizing must be premised on making strategic alliances with each other, based on where we are situated within the larger political economy. . . . [F]or example, Native peoples who are organizing against the colonial and genocidal practices committed by the US government will be more effective in their struggle if they also organize against US militarism, particularly the military recruitment of indigenous peoples to support US imperial wars. If we try to end US colonial practices at home, but support US empire by joining the military, we are strengthening the state's ability to carry out genocidal policies against people of color here and all over the world.

. . . These approaches might help us to develop resistance strategies that do not inadvertently keep the system in place for all of us, and keep all of us accountable. In all of these cases, we would check our aspirations against the aspirations of other communities to ensure that our model of liberation does not become the model of oppression for others.

These practices require us to be more vigilant in how we may have internalized some of these logics in our own organizing practice. For instance, much racial justice organizing within the United States has rested on a civil rights framework that fights for equality under the law. An assumption behind this organizing is that the United States is a democracy with some flaws, but is otherwise admirable. Despite the fact that it rendered slaves three-fifths of a person, the US Constitution is presented as the model document from which to build a flourishing democracy. However, as Luana Ross notes, it has never been against US law to commit genocide against indigenous peoples—in fact, genocide *is* the law of the country. The United States could not exist without it. In the United States, democracy is actually the alibi for genocide—it is the practice that covers up United States colonial control over indigenous lands.

Our organizing can also reflect anti-Black racism. Recently, with the outgrowth of "multiculturalism" there have been calls to "go beyond the black/white binary" and include other communities of color in our analysis, as presented in the third scenario. There are a number of flaws with this analysis. First, it replaces an analysis of white supremacy with a politics of multicultural representation; if we just *include* more people, then our practice will be less racist. Not true. This model does not address the nuanced structure of white supremacy, such as through these distinct logics of slavery, genocide, and Orientalism. Second, it obscures the centrality of the slavery logic in the system of white supremacy, which is *based on a black/white binary*. The black/white binary is not the *only* binary which characterizes white supremacy, but it is still a central one that we cannot "go beyond" in our racial justice organizing efforts.

If we do not look at how the logic of slaveability inflects our society and our thinking, it will be evident in our work as well. For example, other communities of color often appropriate the cultural work and organizing strategies of African American civil rights or Black Power movements without corresponding assumptions that we should also be in solidarity with Black communities. We assume that this work is the common "property" of all oppressed groups, and we can appropriate it without being accountable.

. . .

. . . Simply saying we need to move beyond the black/white binary (or perhaps, the "black/non-black" binary) in US racism obfuscates the racializing logic of slavery, and prevents us from seeing that this binary constitutes Blackness as the bottom of a color hierarchy. However, this is not the *only* binary that fundamentally constitutes white supremacy. There is also an indigenous/settler binary, where Native genocide is central to the logic of white supremacy and other non-indigenous people of color also form "a subsidiary" role. We also face another Orientalist logic that fundamentally constitutes Asians, Arabs, and

Latino/as as foreign threats, requiring the United States to be at permanent war with these peoples. In this construction, Black and Native peoples play subsidiary roles.

Clearly the black/white binary is central to racial and political thought and practice in the United States, and any understanding of white supremacy must take it into consideration. However, if we look at only this binary, we may misread the dynamics of white supremacy in different contexts. . . . [C]ritical race theorist Cheryl Harris's analysis of whiteness as property reveals this weakness. In *Critical Race Theory*, Harris contends that whites have a property interest in the preservation of whiteness, and seek to deprive those who are "tainted" by Black or Indian blood from these same white property interests. Harris simply assumes that the positions of African Americans and American Indians are the same, failing to consider US policies of forced assimilation and forced whiteness on American Indians. These policies have become so entrenched that when Native peoples make political claims, they have been accused of being white. When Andrew Jackson removed the Cherokee along the Trail of Tears, he argued that those who did not want removal were really white. In contemporary times, when I was a non-violent witness for the Chippewa spearfishers in the late 1980s, one of the more frequent slurs whites hurled when the Chippewa attempted to exercise their treaty-protected right to fish was that they had white parents, or they were really white.

Status differences between Blacks and Natives are informed by the different economic positions African Americans and American Indians have in US society. African Americans have been traditionally valued for their labor, hence it is in the interest of the dominant society to have as many people marked "Black," as possible, thereby maintaining a cheap labor pool; by contrast, American Indians have been valued for the land base they occupy, so it is in the interest of dominant society to have as few people marked "Indian" as possible, facilitating access to Native lands. "Whiteness" operates differently under a logic of genocide than it does from a logic of slavery.

Another failure of US-based people of color in organizing is that we often fall back on a "US-centricism," believing that what is happening "over there" is less important than what is happening here. We fail to see how the United States maintains the system of oppression here precisely by tying our allegiances to the interests of US empire "over there."

HETEROPATRIARCHY AND WHITE SUPREMACY

Heteropatriarchy is the building block of US empire. In fact, it is the building block of the nation-state form of governance. . . . Christian Right activist and founder of Prison Fellowship Charles Colson makes the connection between homosexuality and the nation-state in his analysis of the war on terror, explaining that one of the causes of terrorism is same-sex marriage:

> Marriage is the traditional building block of human society, intended both to unite couples and bring children into the world . . . There is a natural moral order for the family . . . the family, led by a married mother and father, is the best available structure for both child-rearing and cultural health. Marriage is not a private institution designed solely for the individual gratification of its participants. If we fail to enact a Federal Marriage Amendment, we can expect not just more family breakdown, but also more criminals behind bars and more chaos in our streets.

Colson is linking the well-being of US empire to the well-being of the heteropatriarchal family. He continues:

When radical Islamists see American women abusing Muslim men, as they did in the Abu Ghraib prison, and when they see news coverage of same-sex couples being "married" in US towns, we make this kind of freedom abhorrent—the kind they see as a blot on Allah's creation. We must preserve traditional marriage in order to protect the United States from those who would use our depravity to destroy us.

As Ann Burlein argues in *Lift High the Cross*, it may be a mistake to argue that the goal of Christian Right politics is to create a theocracy in the United States. Rather, Christian Right politics work through the private family (which is coded as white, patriarchal, and middle class) to create a "Christian America." She notes that the investment in the private family makes it difficult for people to invest in more public forms of social connection. In addition, investment in the suburban private family serves to mask the public disinvestment in urban areas that makes the suburban lifestyle possible. The social decay in urban areas that results from this disinvestment is then construed as the result of deviance from the Christian family ideal rather than as the result of political and economic forces. As former head of the Christian Coalition, Ralph Reed, states: "The only true solution to crime is to restore the family" (Reed, 1990). . . .

As I have argued elsewhere, in order to colonize peoples whose societies are not based on social hierarchy, colonizers must first naturalize hierarchy through instituting patriarchy. In turn, patriarchy rests on a gender binary system in which only two genders exist, one dominating the other. . . . Just as the patriarchs rule the family, the elites of the nation-state rule their citizens. Any liberation struggle that does not challenge heteronormativity cannot substantially challenge colonialism or white supremacy. . . . [S]uch struggles will maintain colonialism based on a politics of secondary marginalization where the most elite class of these groups will further their aspirations on the backs of those most marginalized within the community.

. . . [N]ational liberation politics become less vulnerable to being coopted by the Right when we base them on a model of liberation that fundamentally challenges right-wing conceptions of the nation. We need a model based on community relationships and on mutual respect.

CONCLUSION

Women of color–centered organizing points to the centrality of gender politics within antiracist, anticolonial struggles. Unfortunately, in our efforts to organize against white, Christian America, racial justice struggles often articulate an equally heteropatriarchal racial nationalism. This model of organizing either hopes to assimilate into white America, or to replicate it within an equally hierarchical and oppressive racial nationalism in which the elites of the community rule everyone else. Such struggles often call on the importance of preserving the "Black family" or the "Native family" as the bulwark of this nationalist project, the family being conceived of in capitalist and heteropatriarchal terms. The response is often increased homophobia, with lesbian and gay community members construed as "threats" to the family. . . . Perhaps, instead, we can reconstitute alternative ways of living together in which "families" are not seen as islands on their own. . . .

C
O
N
T
E
X
T

13

La conciencia de la mestiza

Towards a New Consciousness

Gloria Anzaldúa

Por la mujer de mi raza
bablará el espíritu.

José Vasconcelos, Mexican philosopher, envisaged *una raza mestiza, una mezcla de razas afines, una raza de color—la primera raza síntesis del globo*. He called it a cosmic race, *la raza cósmica*, a fifth race embracing the four major races of the world. Opposite to the theory of the pure Aryan, and to the policy of racial purity that white America practices, his theory is one of inclusivity. At the confluence of two or more genetic streams, with chromosomes constantly "crossing over," this mixture of races, rather than resulting in an inferior being, provides hybrid progeny, a mutable, more malleable species with a rich gene pool. From this racial, ideological, cultural and biological cross-pollinization, an "alien" consciousness is presently in the making—a new *mestiza* consciousness, *una conciencia de mujer*. It is a consciousness of the Borderlands.

UNA LUCHA DE FRONTERAS/A STRUGGLE OF BORDERS

Because I, a *mestiza,*
continually walk out of one culture
and into another,
because I am in all cultures at the same time,
alma entre dos mundos, tres, cuatro,
me zumba la cabeza con lo contradictorio.
Estoy norteada por todas las voces que me hablan
simultáneamente.

The ambivalence from the clash of voices results in mental and emotional states of perplexity. Internal strife results in insecurity and indecisiveness. The *mestiza*'s dual or multiple personality is plagued by psychic restlessness.

In a constant state of mental nepantilism, an Aztec word meaning torn between ways, *la mestiza* is a product of the transfer of the cultural and spiritual values of one group to another. Being tricultural, monolingual, bilingual, or multilingual, speaking a patois, and in a state of perpetual transition, the *mestiza* faces the dilemma of the mixed breed: which collectivity does the daughter of a darkskinned mother listen to?

El choque de un alma atrapado entre el mundo del espíritu y el mundo de la técnica a veces la deja entullada. Cradled in one culture, sandwiched between two cultures, straddling all three cultures and their value systems, *la mestiza* undergoes a struggle of flesh, a struggle of borders, an inner war. Like all people, we perceive the version of reality that our culture communicates. Like others having or living in more than one culture, we get multiple, often opposing messages. The coming together of two self-consistent but habitually incompatible frames of reference causes *un choque*, a cultural collision.

Within us and within *la cultura chicana*, commonly held beliefs of the white culture attack commonly held beliefs of the Mexican culture, and both attack commonly held beliefs of the indigenous culture. Subconsciously, we see an attack on ourselves and our beliefs as a threat and we attempt to block with a counterstance.

But it is not enough to stand on the opposite river bank, shouting questions, challenging patriarchal, white conventions. A counterstance locks one into a duel of oppressor and oppressed; locked in mortal combat, like the cop and the criminal, both are reduced to a common denominator of violence. The counterstance refutes the dominant culture's views and beliefs, and, for this, it is proudly defiant. All reaction is limited by, and dependent on, what it is reacting against. Because the counterstance stems from a problem with authority—outer as well as inner—it's a step towards liberation from cultural domination. But it is not a way of life. At some point, on our way to a new consciousness, we will have to leave the opposite bank, the split between the two mortal combatants somehow healed so that we are on both shores at once and, at once, see through serpent and eagle eyes. Or perhaps we will decide to disengage from the dominant culture, write it off altogether as a lost cause, and cross the border into a wholly new and separate territory. Or we might go another route. The possibilities are numerous once we decide to act and not react.

A TOLERANCE FOR AMBIGUITY

These numerous possibilities leave *la mestiza* floundering in uncharted seas. In perceiving conflicting information and points of view, she is subjected to a swamping of her psychological borders. She has discovered that she can't hold concepts or ideas in rigid boundaries. The borders and walls that are supposed to keep the undesirable ideas out are entrenched habits and patterns of behavior; these habits and patterns are the enemy within. Rigidity means death. Only by remaining flexible is she able to stretch the psyche horizontally and vertically. *La mestiza* constantly has to shift out of habitual formations; from convergent thinking, analytical reasoning that tends to use rationality to move toward a single goal (a Western mode), to divergent thinking, characterized by movement away from set patterns and goals and toward a more whole perspective, one that includes rather than excludes.

The new *mestiza* copes by developing a tolerance for contradictions, a tolerance for ambiguity. She learns to be an Indian in Mexican culture, to be Mexican from an Anglo point of view. She learns to juggle cultures. She has a plural personality, she operates in a pluralistic mode—nothing is thrust out, the good the bad and the ugly, nothing rejected, nothing abandoned. Not only does she sustain contradictions, she turns the ambivalence into something else.

She can be jarred out of ambivalence by an intense, and often painful, emotional event which inverts or resolves the ambivalence. I'm not sure exactly how. The work takes place underground—subconsciously. It is work that the soul performs. That focal point or fulcrum, that juncture where the *mestiza* stands, is where phenomena tend to collide. It is where the possibility of uniting all that is separate occurs. This assembly is not one where severed or separated pieces merely come together. Nor is it a balancing of opposing powers. In attempting to work out a synthesis, the self has added a third element which is greater than the sum of its severed parts. That third element is a new consciousness—a *mestiza* consciousness—and though it is a source of intense pain, its energy comes from continual creative motion that keeps breaking down the unitary aspect of each new paradigm.

En unas pocas centurias, the future will belong to the *mestiza*. Because the future depends on the breaking down of paradigms, it depends on the straddling of two or more cultures. By creating a new mythos—that is, a change in the way we perceive reality, the way we see ourselves, and the ways we behave—*la mestiza* creates a new consciousness.

The work of *mestiza* consciousness is to break down the subject-object duality that keeps her a prisoner and to show in the flesh and through the images in her work how duality is transcended. The answer to the problem between the white race and the colored, between males and females, lies in healing the split that originates in the very foundation of our lives, our culture, our languages, our thoughts. A massive uprooting of dualistic thinking in the individual and collective consciousness is the begining of a long struggle, but one that could, in our best hopes, bring us to the end of rape, of violence, of war.

LA ENCRUCIJADA/THE CROSSROADS

A chicken is being sacrificed
    at a crossroads, a simple mound of earth
a mud shrine for *Eshu*,
    Yoruba god of indeterminacy,
who blesses her choice of path.
    She begins her journey.

Su cuerpo es una bocacalle. La mestiza has gone from being the sacrificial goat to becoming the officiating priestess at the crossroads.

As a mestiza I have no country, my homeland cast me out; yet all countries are mine because I am every woman's sister or potential lover. (As a lesbian I have no race, my own people disclaim me; but I am all races because there is the queer of me in all races.) I am cultureless because, as a feminist, I challenge the collective cultural/religious male-derived beliefs of Indo-Hispanics and Anglos; yet I am cultured because I am participating in the creation of yet another culture, a new story to explain the world and our participation in it, a new value system with images and symbols that connect us to each other and to the planet. *Soy un amasamiento*, I am an act of kneading, of uniting and joining that not only has produced both a creature of darkness and a creature of light, but also a creature that questions the definitions of light and dark and gives them new meanings.

We are the people who leap in the dark, we are the people on the knees of the gods. In our very flesh, (r)evolution works out the clash of cultures. It makes us crazy constantly, but if the center holds, we've made some kind of evolutionary step forward. *Nuestra alma el trabajo*, the opus, the great alchemical work; spiritual *mestizaje*, a "morphogenesis," an inevitable unfolding. We have become the quickening serpent movement.

Indigenous like corn, like corn, the *mestiza* is a product of crossbreeding, designed for preservation under a variety of conditions. Like an ear of corn—a female seed-bearing organ—the *mestiza* is tenacious, tightly wrapped in the husks of her culture. Like kernels she clings to the cob; with thick stalks and strong brace roots, she holds tight to the earth—she will survive the crossroads.

Lavando y remojando el maíz en agua de cal, despojando el pellejo. Moliendo, mixteando, amasando, haciendo tortillas de masa. She steeps the corn in lime, it swells, softens. With stone roller on *metate*, she grinds the corn, then grinds again. She kneads and moulds the dough, pats the round balls into *tortillas*.

We are the porous rock in the stone *metate*
squatting on the ground.
We are the rolling pin, *el maíz y agua,*
la masa harina. Somos el amasijo.
Somos lo molido en el metate.
We are the *comal* sizzling hot,
the hot *tortilla*, the hungry mouth.
We are the coarse rock.
We are the grinding motion,
the mixed potion, *somos el molcajete.*
We are the pestle, the *comino, ajo, pimienta,*
We are the *chile colorado,*
the green shoot that cracks the rock.
We will abide.

. . .

SOMOS UNA GENTE

Hay tantísimas fronteras
que dividen a la gente,
pero por cada frontera
existe también un puente.

Gina Valdés

Divided Loyalties. Many women and men of color do not want to have any dealings with white people. It takes too much time and energy to explain to the downwardly mobile, white middle-class women that it's okay for us to want to own "possessions," never having had any nice furniture on our dirt floors or "luxuries" like washing machines. Many feel that whites should help their own people rid themselves of race hatred and fear first. I, for one, choose to use some of my energy to serve as mediator. I think we need to allow whites to be our allies. Through our literature, art, *corridos*, and folktales we must share our history with them so when they set up committees to help Big Mountain Navajos or the Chicano farmworkers or *los Nicaragüenses* they won't turn people away because of their racial fears and ignorances. They will come to see that they are not helping us but following our lead.

Individually, but also as a racial entity, we need to voice our needs. We need to say to white society: We need you to accept the fact that Chicanos are different, to acknowledge your rejection and negation of us. We need you to own the fact that you looked upon us as less than human, that you stole our lands, our personhood, our self-respect. We need you to make public restitution: to say that, to compensate for your own sense of defectiveness, you strive for power over us, you erase our history and our experience because it makes you feel guilty—you'd rather forget your brutish acts. To say you've split yourself from minority groups, that you disown us, that your dual consciousness splits off parts of yourself, transferring the "negative" parts onto us. (Where there is persecution of minorities, there is shadow projection. Where there is violence and war, there is repression

C
O
N
T
E
X
T

of shadow.) To say that you are afraid of us, that to put distance between us, you wear the mask of contempt. Admit that Mexico is your double, that she exists in the shadow of this country, that we are irrevocably tied to her. Gringo, accept the doppelganger in your psyche. By taking back your collective shadow the intra-cultural split will heal. And finally, tell us what you need from us.

. . .

14

50 Experiences of Racially Mixed People

Maria P. P. Root

The 50 questions or comments and experiences evolved from a questionnaire I developed for a study on biracial siblings I conducted from 1996 to 1997. These questions and comments provide an introduction to the way in which race consciousness is brought up directly, sideways, and from all sides for people of mixed heritage. These comments and questions, though not an exhaustive list, provide a window into how this country internalizes assumption about race, belonging, and identity. They socialize the mixed race person to understand as well as question race American style. It is a monoracial system; one race per person. Not everyone experiences these questions or comments similarly. One person might enjoy being asked, "What are you?" whereas their sibling might dread and resent the question. This list provides a launching point for sharing, discussing, laughing, debriefing, and educating.

1. You have been told, "You have to choose; you can't be both."
2. Your ethnicity was mistakenly identified.
3. People assumed your race to be different by phone than in person.
4. You are accused of not acting or wanting to be Latino, Asian, Black . . .
5. You have been told, "Mixed race people are so beautiful or handsome."
6. Strangers looked between you and your parent(s) to figure out if you were related.
7. You have been told, "You don't look Native, Black, Latino . . ."
8. You have been asked, "What are you?"
9. People say things they might not otherwise say if they knew how you identified racially.
10. You have been asked, "Where are you from?"
11. You have repeatedly been the recipient of stares or longer than passing glances from strangers.
12. You have been told, "You look exotic."
13. Your choice of friends has been interpreted as your "selling out" or not being authentic.
14. You have been accused of "acting or wanting to be white."
15. Judgments of your racial authenticity have been based upon your boyfriend's or girlfriend's (partner's) race.
16. Comments are made about your hair or hairstyle, skin color, eye shape etc.

17. You have been subjected to jokes about mixed race people.
18. You have been told, "You think you're too good for your own kind."
19. Grandparent(s) or relatives don't accept you because of your parents' interracial relationship.
20. Your parents or relatives compete to "claim" you for their own racial or ethnic group.
21. You have been told, "You have the best of both worlds."
22. You have been asked about your racial or ethnic heritage as an object of curiosity.
23. Upon meeting you, people seem confused by your last name. They do not think it "matches" you.
24. People assume you are confused about your racial identity or have had a hard time figuring it out.
25. People speak to you in foreign languages because of how they interpret your physical appearance.
26. You have been told, "Society doesn't recognize mixed race."
27. You have been told, "You aren't really Black, Latino, Asian . . ."
28. You have been mistaken for another person of mixed heritage who does not resemble you.
29. You have been told you must be full of self-loathing or hatred because of how you racially identify yourself.
30. You have been told, "You are a mistake."
31. Different people perceive your race differently based upon the company you keep.
32. The race people assign you varies in different parts of the U.S.A.
33. You have difficulty filling out forms asking for a single race.
34. You identify your race differently than others identify you.
35. You are told, "You aren't like other Indians, Asians, Latinos . . ."
36. Your siblings identify their race differently than you do yours.
37. You have been called racial slurs of groups with which you do not share heritage.
38. Friends suggest that you date someone based upon the race or ethnicity with which they think you should identify.
39. Your parents identify your race differently than you identify.
40. You are told, "You aren't Black, Latino, Asian . . . enough"
41. Your mother was assumed to be your nanny or babysitter.
42. A stranger assumes that your father is your "older boyfriend" or your mother is the "older woman."
43. You were treated differently by relatives or your parents than a sibling on the basis of racial features.
44. You were well liked by peers but were not asked for dates.
45. You wish you were darker and try to get as much sun as possible.
46. People assume your father was in the military.
47. You have enrolled in Spanish language classes in order to develop the ability to say "Yes" to the question, "Do you speak the language?" and remove one of the blocks to authenticity.
48. Your otherwise friends become more distant when they think associating with you will make their racial authenticity or popularity questionable.
49. You have been knowingly approached and asked, "Your mother's white (black, Asian), huh?"
50. You have tried to hide one or both parents from view of people who know you but are not your closest friends because you anticipate they will treat you differently.

15

Over-Raided, Under Siege

U.S. Immigration Laws and Enforcement Destroy the Rights of Immigrants

Human Rights Immigrant Community Action Network

A report on human rights violations perpetrated against immigrant and refugee families, workers and communities in the U.S.
From the Human Rights Immigrant Community Action Network
An initiative of the National Network for Immigrant and Refugee Rights
January 2008

EXECUTIVE SUMMARY

Over-Raided, Under Siege: U.S. Immigration Laws and Enforcement Destroy the Rights of Immigrants, the first annual report produced through NNIRR's Human Rights Immigrant Community Action Network (HURRICANE), finds that the Department of Homeland Security is leading a new type of assault on the rights, lives and wellbeing of immigrant families, workers and communities in the United States. The DHS is subjecting immigrant and refugee communities to a deliberate and distinct form of "collective punishment," resulting in widespread violations of basic constitutional and human rights. Over-Raided, Under Siege analyzed over 100 stories of human rights violations and 206 incidents of immigration raids in 2006–2007 and interviewed community leaders and sifted through numerous reports and data to better understand the patterns of recent violations.

Over-Raided, Under Siege demonstrates how the U.S. government continues to build new programs, policies, strategies and laws that systematically violate the human rights of immigrant and refugee members of our communities. Working in tandem with local, county and state governments, law enforcement agencies, employers and private citizen groups, the U.S. government has advanced hundreds of new measures that deny immigrants and refugees due process rights, a living wage, housing, labor protections, and proper health and safety.

The U.S. government's strategies range from justifying immigration enforcement as a national security measure, to directing billions of dollars into private security firms. U.S. immigration services and enforcement policies are shaped by the drive to expand policing, prison building and to criminalize, detect, jail and deport immigrants with impunity.

As a result, U.S. immigration enforcement and border control policies and strategies are fueling a humanitarian crisis that disproportionately impacts immigrant communities. Instead of upholding the rights of immigrants or providing safe and legal means to immigrate, U.S. immigration and border control strategies deliberately force migrants to risk their lives, causing untold suffering and the death and disappearance of hundreds of migrants every year on the U.S.-Mexico border. This crisis follow migrants wherever they go on their journey to interior communities. They face escalating attacks fueled by the

Department of Homeland Security's strategy of almost exclusive reliance on exclusion, detention and removal to "solve" the undocumented problem.

Over the last two years, immigrants have been increasingly marginalized and denied public services in a new way: they are being scapegoated and collectively punished for many of the U.S.'s social and economic ills. Immigrants, especially the undocumented, are blamed for the fiscal crisis. Then, under the guise of immigration control and national security, federal, state, county, and local governments propose and approve policies and ordinances to cut back and privatize public services and gut civil liberties.

With the DHS's ICE, CBP and other law enforcement agencies operating without accountability or effective oversight, immigrants have become especially vulnerable to abuse and violence. Whether they are documented or undocumented, immigrants are now the almost exclusive scapegoat for the faltering economy, the threat of terrorism, the deterioration of services and the social problems afflicting the U.S. In this officially condoned anti-immigrant climate, racial profiling, exploitation in the workplace, hate violence and multiple public policies are being used to deliberately force immigrants to leave or exist in the shadows.

Over-Raided, Under Siege: U.S. Immigration Laws and Enforcement Destroy the Rights of Immigrants concludes that:

1. **The U.S. Department of Homeland Security (DHS) and its Bureau of Immigration and Customs Enforcement (ICE) have broadened its raids strategy and use immigration sweeps as a political response to immigrant rights efforts.**

    ICE deliberately carries out high profile raids in workplaces, stores and other public spaces, in neighborhoods and homes to instill fear in communities and push back on policies and initiatives that protect rights. For example, in New Haven, Connecticut, immigration authorities swept up 31 undocumented immigrants just two days after the city approved a municipal identification card that will allow all city residents, regardless of their citizenship status, to access basic city services.

    These raids are often conducted without warrants or consent, trampling the constitutional rights of entire communities. In collaboration with other law enforcement officials, ICE carried out warrants and deliberately swept up additional people as "collateral" arrests and deportations. ICE raids have become deliberate actions meant to strike fear in families, disrupting workplaces and communities. And as ICE has launched more aggressive raids, an alarming number of children are being left behind without their parents.

    Increasingly, the workplace has become the preferred raid location. ICE agents arrested 4,000 people in workplace raids between October 2006 and September 2007.

2. **Immigrants are being incarcerated at increasing rates, becoming the fastest growing prison population.**

    Detentions have increased 400 percent from 5,532 in 1994 to 27,500 in 2006. In October 2007, ICE was holding 14,764 immigrants in detention facilities throughout the nation. The dramatic growth in immigrant prisons is rooted in the expansion of U.S. policies and strategies criminalizing immigration status and making jail mandatory for all immigrants while their cases are pending.

    The DHS continues building more jail bed space exclusively for immigrants, in public facilities and those contracted out to private prisons corporations, like the Geo Group (formerly Wackenhut) and Halliburton, representing an alarming shift to the privatization of facilities in construction and operation. Furthermore, even government audits have found multiple instances of non-compliance with detention standards related to health care, environmental health and safety, general conditions of confinement, and the reporting of abuse.

3. **DHS is intensifying workplace enforcement by using employers as enforcement agents through Social Security No-Match Letters and other measures, as legislators continue pushing for temporary worker programs reminiscent of failed past initiatives.**

    The Department of Homeland Security's current effort to expand immigration law enforcement in the workplace by using SSA "no-match" letters further criminalizes immigrant workers and undermines labor protections and unions. Immigrant workers are now being charged with "identity theft," a felony crime that allows the DHS to jail them instead of citing them for being out of status, or working without authorization, which is a minor civil offense.

    Simultaneously, DHS Secretary Michael Chertoff supports increasing guest worker programs as part of a program to invest more resources in enforcement as the solution. DHS's proposed expansion of using "no-match" letters as an immigration enforcement tool gives employers power over workers, particularly immigrant workers, who affirm their rights or seek to unionize.

    Employers use the no-match letters, employer sanctions and other official policies and measures to harass and intimidate immigrant workers or indiscriminately fire them when they demand living wages or to stop union organizing.

4. **The humanitarian crisis at the border has reached new heights as migrant deaths hit record numbers and the federal government pours billions of dollars into further militarizing the region.**

    The U.S.-Mexico border has become the epicenter of the humanitarian crisis impacting immigrant and refugee communities, resulting from official immigration services and enforcement policies and strategies.

    To reduce and eventually stop unauthorized migration, in 1993, the U.S. government began implementing a militarization strategy called "prevention through deterrence" at the U.S.-Mexico border. This strategy deliberately forces migrants, who are seeking to reunite with their loved ones or work in the U.S., to risk their lives by crossing into the U.S. through the most dangerous and isolated desert and mountainous regions of the U.S.-Mexico border. Some 5,000 migrant bodies have been recovered since 1994 at the border.

    While various non-partisan and research institutes have declared this strategy a failure at stopping unauthorized migration and to cause more migrant deaths, the U.S. has continued to expand the militarization of the border. In fact, by the end of 2008, DHS aims to increase the number of border patrol agents from 15,000 to 18,300 (this figure represents a doubling of border patrol agents under the Bush administration). DHS also plans to add 370 miles of "fencing," border walls; 300 vehicle barriers, 105 camera and radar towers and three unmanned aerial vehicles.

5. **The dramatic growth in local and state police collaboration with ICE immigration law enforcement severely undermines community safety and further marginalizes immigrants. Local, county and state government collaboration with immigration enforcement further exposes immigrants to abuse at the hands of unscrupulous police, employers, hate groups and others who believe immigrants will not report crimes to avoid detection or deportation.**

    As a result, immigrants, or anyone who "looks or sounds" foreign, are being subjected to new forms of racial, ethnic/nationality and religious profiling and "mapping." For example, on November 9, 2007, the Los Angeles police department announced plans to map the city's Muslim communities in order to identify which might become susceptible to extremism. The LAPD discarded the plan a week later, after Muslim and civil rights groups denounced the measure, arguing it would do the opposite of its intent by making Muslims less willing to work with authorities.

Across the nation, 597 officers in 34 state and local law enforcement agencies have joined the 287(g) program, which allows the Department of Homeland Security to enter into agreements with local law enforcement agencies. Of those 34, 26 joined the program in FY 2007.

KEY RECOMMENDATIONS

In order to prevent further human rights violations against immigrant communities, families and workers, *Over-Raided, Under Siege* **recommends that:**

- The U.S. Bureau of Immigration and Customs Enforcement (ICE) end immigration raids and collaboration with local, county and state police, as well as other government agencies.
- The Department of Homeland Security (DHS) end the practice of jailing persons for immigration status offenses and restore immigrants' full due process rights and access to the courts.
- The Social Security Administration stop sending Social Security no-match letters to employers. To get updated information, simply send letters to employees at their home addresses.
- The federal government ensure that labor laws protecting all workers, regardless of citizenship or immigration status, are enforced.
- DHS end and rollback border militarization policies and strategies that have caused thousands of migrant deaths and countless violations of the human and civil rights of migrants, workers, people of color, youth, communities and Indigenous peoples at the border.

In addition, *Over-Raided, Under Siege* **also recommends that:**

- Congress pass an immigration reform bill to strengthen worker rights, expand civil rights, provide options and access to citizenship and legal permanent residency, clear the visa backlog, reunify families and stop the expansion of guest worker programs.
- The U.S. Bureau of Citizenship and Immigration Services increase options for legal immigration and issue sufficient visas so that migrants can enter safely into the U.S. with full rights protections.
- DHS re-direct and prioritize funding for immigration services to clear the backlog of pending applications for family reunification visas, green cards, citizenship and services for immigrant integration.
- Local law enforcement agencies end collaboration with ICE on enforcement operations.
- DHS, ICE, CBP and other local, county and state law enforcement agencies stop the practice of racial, religious, ethnic and nationality profiling, monitor their progress and end other discriminatory practices.
- Local, county and state governments identify the needs of their immigrant and refugee communities, and implement laws, policies, and procedures to integrate them as full participating members. A human rights framework and adequate budget should be part and parcel of these measures.

. . .

C O N T E X T

THE FIRST VIOLATION IS CALLING PEOPLE ILLEGAL ALIENS

—Excerpt from interview with Ofelia Rivas, O'odham Voice against the Wall, Alijegk (village on U.S. side).

The thought of calling undocumented people "illegal aliens" is the first human rights violation that takes place. The U.S. government has to dehumanize people by calling them aliens. And then it goes on to the treatment they receive as "non-humans." They're packed and transported in small vehicles held in cages until they're sent to a processing center. This is an outright, inexcusable treatment of humans.

And as a O'odham living on the Tohono O'odham nation, I can't condone that type of behavior by my own people. So the organizing of O'odham Voice against the Wall is our first response. They're calling us traditional people, traditionalists. But we're just O'odham, which means people in our language. The O'odham Voice against the Wall was specifically formed to provide safer crossing for the elders and ceremony people.

We didn't consent to this boundary, which we choose to cross on our ancestral routes. We say that this is our right to do so and we continue to cross it, use those routes for gatherings or for visiting our people, our families and also to attend ceremony and make pilgrimages to sacred sites.

The militarization of the border has forever changed our way of life. A lot of people can't even begin to fathom the affect that it will have on our people. Seems like the politicians they only see tomorrow and they don't see 50, 100 years from now that our people will still be here.

All these years that the Border Patrol has been on our lands, in our communities, they still don't know we have ceremonies; they still don't know that we do traditional ceremony hunts, where we hunt for a deer.

Last year a helicopter went right over the hunters and scared the deer. And the hunters weren't able to get a deer for the ceremony. In a different district, the hunters were surrounded by Border Patrol and were disarmed, because they carry rifles to hunt for a deer.

In all the years that they've been here the Border Patrol still have no respect for the land; there's a lot of environmental damage. Three days ago, there was a wind blowing and I could not even see the mountains right in front of me because the dust was so thick, from them driving around and making their own roads.

If you have brown skin and dark hair, the Border Patrol follows you even if you live in the community. They follow me all the time, right to my door, practically, and they always stop me and ask me for documents. And I have to that in my own land, in my own community, in my own yard!

So yes, it's a grave violation of the rights of O'odham people, when our people's language is dying, our children don't speak O'odham any more; health care is dwindling, if any at all. And especially for the people that are in Mexico, it is very limited help at all, from the tribe or from the government at all. It is very damaging.

And so many migrants die on our lands now and the O'odham people are still giving them food and water. It's become criminalized that we give them food and water. You have to give it to them secretly; provide them those things.

. . .

HATE CRIME AGAINST SOUTH ASIAN GOES UNRESOLVED, CONTINUES TO SUFFER

A Bangladeshi immigrant who lives in Los Angeles, CA with his wife and two children was a business owner, running both a Bangladeshi newspaper and a grocery store. On November 11, 2001, two men walked into his grocery store. One asked for cigarettes and the other for change. As the two men walked to the side of the cash register, one man pulled out a gun and the terrified storeowner told them to take all the money. While the first perpetrator pulled cash from the register, the other held a gun to his stomach, berating him the entire time: "Bloody F***ing Arab, I'm going to kill you." On the way out, one of the men yelled "you f***ing stupid Muslims, you make a lot of money and give us nothing. Have more ready the next time when we come back."

The storeowner was emotionally traumatized, and eventually diagnosed with post-traumatic stress syndrome. This prevented him from working and he was forced to sell his grocery store at a significant loss. After selling his grocery business, he did not have the funds to keep his newspaper running and had to shut down production. Eventually, he applied to the State Victim Compensation Board for the losses he suffered as a result of this crime. But instead, he was victimized a second time by this government agency responsible for assisting him. First, the application he submitted to the local office was not forwarded to the State Board until eight months later. While he did receive some compensation, it was about one-tenth of his total income loss. He had to resubmit documents lost by the local Victim Compensation office, and the lack of communication from the State Board caused further delays.

In 2007, more than six years after the robbery and after five years of fighting for his right to compensation, the former business owner was paid the maximum allowed by the state. The crime against him was never categorized as a hate crime and remains unresolved.

. . .

**2005 AND 2007—IMMIGRANTS AND REFUGEES IGNORED
OR HARASSED DURING NATURAL DISASTERS**

A lack of official responsiveness to the impacts of Hurricane Katrina by the federal government left thousands—including immigrants and refugees—abandoned. Like the many African Americans living in areas hit by the storm, the estimated 300,000 immigrants in the area lost their homes, businesses and even family members. In total, more than 1,800 people died in five states—1,577of them in Louisiana.

The federal government failed to respond to the needs of victims on numerous levels. According to an April 2006 report issued by the DHS Inspector General, the Federal Emergency Management Agency (FEMA) was ill-prepared to conduct massive search-and-rescue functions, deliver adequate housing, water and basic supplies, and provide clear communication to evacuees. Two years later, the region continues to suffer from a lack of affordable housing and poverty.

The Asian American Justice Center estimates that the disaster impacted 50,000 Asian Americans living in Louisiana—half of them Vietnamese and 70 percent immigrants. It also devastated Lations, who made up 15.8 percent of the Gulf Coast region.

Two groups that experienced Hurricane Katrina as a recurring nightmare were the 150,000 Hondurans living in Katrina's path that had escaped Hurricane Mitch in 1998 and the Vietnamese that had fled communist-controlled Vietnam after the Vietnam War. Hurricane Katrina transformed them into refugees once again.

While immigrants shared many of the same experiences as other Katrina victims, they also faced special challenges in recovering from the disaster. Undocumented laborers working on farms or in service industry jobs did not seek federal relief after hearing that some undocumented immigrants had been placed into removal proceedings following contact with government authorities. Legal permanent residents, who lost U.S. passports, green cards and other documents certifying their immigration status, were left without proof of their legal status in the U.S.—making it extremely difficult for them to seek government benefits or obtain employment.

Similar problems to those experienced after Katrina arose in October 2007 when wildfires ravaged Southern California. The American Friends Service Committee documented the impact of the firestorms on migrant communities in San Diego. It found immigrant families afraid to seek emergency services at evacuation facilities for fear of deportation. Many heard about the Border Patrol deporting a family that had sought emergency relief at Qualcomm Stadium. Police discovered that 7 of 12 members of the Santiago family were undocumented immigrants, and turned them over to Border Patrol agents, who immediately deported them. According to DHS, the agents were stationed at Qualcomm Stadium to help with emergency relief efforts.

In addition to fear of deportation, a lack of adequate communication posed grave risks to the health and livelihoods of farm workers in the area. Most migrant workers have no formal residence and, as a result, no way of receiving the warnings issued by police through their reverse 911 system. In the dark about the fire hazard, many immigrants continued working in the fields. On October 24, 2007, AFSC documented how workers at the Leslie Farm tomato fields were laboring despite the Air Quality Index registering at 181—a level deemed hazardous to health.

The lack of multi-lingual evacuation information, especially in indigenous languages that predominate in the area, also wreaked havoc on fire victims. Authorities had few resources for communicating with immigrant communities that speak indigenous languages such as Mixteco (bajo and alto) and other languages from the southern areas of Mexico and the northern parts of Central America.

. . .

16

Finding My Eye-dentity

Olivia Chung

I watched the spoken-word group I Was Born With Two Tongues perform and was inspired by their style of reflecting on personal experiences. This piece flowed from my desire for self-expression and hopes of challenging other Asian American girls to question their definition of beauty. I am a second-generation Korean American, born and raised in a loving family in Silver Spring, Maryland. Currently, I'm a sophomore at the University of Pennsylvania, pursuing interests in activism, writing, and hip-hop. My ultimate goal is to keep it real and selflessly live for the Lord.

V O I C E S

Olivia, you wanna get *sang ka pul*?

I'm driving my mother to work, when she randomly brings up the eyelid question. The question that almost every Korean monoeyelidded girl has had to face in her life. The question that could change the future of my naturally noncreased eyelids, making them crease with the cut of a cosmetic surgeon's knife.

You know your aunt? She used to have beany eyes just like you! She used to put on white and black eyeliner every morning to make them look BIG. Then she went to Korea and got the surgery done. Now look! She looks so much better! Don't you want it done? I would do it . . .

I think this is about the 346,983,476th time she has brought this topic up. Using the exact same words. You would look so much more prettier with bigger eyes! she says. *You know, because they look kind of squinty and on top of that you have an underbite, so you look really mean . . .* She explains while narrowing her eyes and jutting out her jaw in emphasis of her point.

A couple of years ago, I would have taken her suggestion seriously. I remember reading a section of *Seventeen* magazine, where the once-did-funky-makeup-for-100-anorexic-white-girls-on-runways beauty expert revealed the secret to applying eye makeup. As a desperate preteen girl seeking beauty advice, I remember it perfectly. Put dark shadow right over the eyelashes, light powder all over, medium shadow over the edge of the crease of your eyelid. That's where I always tripped up. Crease? Umm . . . excuse me? These so-called beauty experts never gave me enough expertise to figure out how to put makeup on my face without looking like a character in a kabuki play. I tried to follow the beauty experts' advice. But I decided it wasn't working when people asked me if I had gotten a black eye.

My friends suggested training my eyelids to fold with tape. *My mother did that and now she has a real crease, one of my friends told me.* I, however, never learned the magic behind that, and always felt too embarrassed to ask. Another friend once excitedly showed me how she had bought a bottle of make-your-own-eye-crease glue from Korea. I let her try it on me too. I could barely open my eyes, thanks to the fierce stinging sensation resulting from the glue that got on my eyeball. And when I finally did take a quick glimpse of myself in the mirror, I saw a stranger with uneven eyelids.

The first time I remember being insulted was when I was little. . . .

In kindergarten, I believe. Oh, it was classic. A little blond kid pulled the edges of his eyes out, yelling, *Ching chong chinaman!* I, being new to this game, could only make a weak comeback. *I'm not Chinese. . . . I'm KOREAN.* I remember feeling a confused hurt, realizing that I looked different and not understanding why being different was bad.

Couldn't we all just get along? I had learned that God loves people as they are, as different as they are. I learned that He looks at the heart, and that it really doesn't matter how a person looks. I think my belief in this, combined with my fear of a sharp object cutting the skin above my eye, kept me away from the *sang ka pul* surgery. Yet, I continued to receive comments on my "chinky" eyes, and I always emerged from these situations feeling confused and angry . . . without ever really knowing why. Why couldn't I be accepted with my so-called chinky eyes? Why in the world were they even called "chinky" eyes? If they meant to insult Chinese, all the Chinese people I knew had huge eyes. With the crease.

As I grew older, the childish "ching chong"s came with less frequency. Still, the magazines continue to give me unhelpful directions on how to apply makeup. Still, I witness my own friends getting the surgery done in an effort to be "more beautiful." Still, my mother continuously confronts me with the dreaded eyelid question. *You wanna get* sang ka pul? I always answer her with an *are-you-crazy?* but simple *no.* All the things I wish I could have told her come flowing on this page with my pen. . . .

Umma, my mother, don't you see that my noncreased eyes are beautiful? Asian eyes are beautiful. Your eyes are beautiful. My eyes are beautiful. Asian is beautiful. After all these years of wanting to open up my eyes with tape and glue and surgery, I have opened up my eyes to a different definition of beauty. A broader definition of beauty, one that embraces differences and includes every girl, who can hold her head up, *sang ka pul*-less and chinky-eyed, because being *Asian is beautiful.*

17

Identification Pleas

Erie Gansworth

So it's the summer of 2002, . . . in the town of Del Rio, Texas, perhaps one of the last places on earth I thought I would be engaged in an identity crisis. . . . I am here with a friend, Donnie, who has a piece of land in this small border town. . . . He asks me if I want to cross the border into Acuña, as it is right there. Though the temperature is over a hundred degrees, we walk across the bridge above the Rio Grande into Mexico. On the exact border, large metal pegs mar the full surface of the pavement, gleam in the heat, and announce the change of country in full-size versions of that dotted line one sees on maps.

Here, trucks pull up, from the United States' end of the bridge, and stop, right on the dotted line. Other trucks meet them on the Mexican side. The drivers descend from their cabs and carry large boxes from the cargo areas of the United States trucks to those of the Mexican trucks. The border guards sit disinterested, watch this transaction under the bright sun, so I take a cue from them that this activity is nothing worth noting, and move on.

. . .

While it was an unpleasantly hot walk across, I see little justification for a bus to make the trip, and again Donnie clarifies that sometimes it is less of a hassle for Mexicans to cross the border if they use the bus instead of walking the bridge.

We leave Mexico a few minutes later, on the bridge's north-bound sidewalk, again stepping on the hot metal pegs, delineating one place from another. Below us, the Rio Grande seems more like the Rio Average, a muddy stream surrounded by dense growth of cane, and above the sidewalk overlooking the river, heavy-gauge steel mesh curves inward on sturdy beams nearly encircling us overhead. This architectural feature is designed to dissuade jumpers from making the five-story leap into the river or thick brush below. Donnie mentions that people have made the attempt and that random surveillance cameras are mounted in the cane—all of this to keep people from entering the United States in inappropriate fashion. . . .

We arrive at the [immigration] office and are both relieved that it is air-conditioned. Donnie shows his license to the officer, who waves him on, and I reach into my pocket, pull out my wallet, and wonder how many minutes it will take for Donnie's truck cab to cool down.

Opening the fold, I am momentarily confused by the version of my face staring back at me from the plastic card in the easiest access slot. I am almost ten years younger, wearing enormous late-eighties glasses, my hair is long, wavy, and pulled back, and behind me the lush foliage of a reservation road fills the rest of the image. It is my tribal identification card, documenting my name, birth date, clan, tribe, reservation address, blood quantum, and the signature of the man on the reservation who officiates on such matters, next to my own signature. Mine is a little more complicated than some, but not unfathomably so. I am a member of the Onondaga Nation, ... The back of the card lists several agreements with the United States, asserting the sovereignty of the Haudenosaunee, the league of six nations to which both the Onondaga and Tuscarora nations belong, known in the United States as "the Iroquois."

The card itself is not confusing to me, of course, but it usually rests in my wallet behind a document I tend to need much more frequently: my driver's license. My license is nowhere to be found within the wallet, and then I suddenly can see the card in my mind, can picture its exact location, and thus can confirm it is not on my body. . . .

Since September 2001, . . . the most consistent change has been nearly relentless requests for my identification from airport personnel. To make things easier on myself and on those asking, I have gotten a "flight wallet" the size of an airline ticket, and in this I keep my boarding pass, frequent flyer card, and, yes, while I am traveling, my driver's license. The flight wallet, at the moment I approach the immigration officer, sits approximately a hundred yards away, in Donnie's truck, across the road, but more important, across the border.

"Identification?" the officer asks, and I hand him my Native American Identification Card. He looks at it, tosses it down, and looks at me, smirking. "Now," he says, ...

"Now," he repeats, snapping the card on his desk this time, perhaps for emphasis, as if he had gotten an ace in a game of solitaire, "do you have any real ID?"

I am what you might call ethnically ambiguous in appearance. Over the years the odd looks, vague frowns, and unasked questions have become the routine. It has been kind of interesting, existing as a walking, breathing Rorschach test for others' perceptions and stereotype templates.

I have been mistaken for Italian, Armenian, Middle Eastern, Hawaiian, Russian, Polish, German, Portuguese, and Jewish, but I am most often wrongly assumed to be Latino. The first time it happened was in a men's room at a concert, when a drunken patron at the next urinal insisted I was a member of Los Lobos, the band whose set had finished about a half hour before. . . . The less glamorous mistake with my ethnicity happens nearly every time I am in the Southwest. This stands to reason, as Mexicans are Indians across the border, in essence, and we are the same in that we had very different, unique cultures before colonialism came along and divided us up with those stainless steel rivets in the bridge.

I was born and raised on a reservation in western New York State, a small place, home to fewer than two thousand people. Many of those people claim full-blood status, though some are blond, some have blue eyes. . . . My complexion is slightly dark, and deepens easily in the summer, so that by the end of June, even with minimal exposure, I usually sport what used to be called "a savage tan." My eyes are dark brown as well, and my hair appears to be black most of the year, but by late summer dark red highlights have burned into it. My body also reveals other telltale signs that prevent me from claiming full-blood status. I have genetic qualities that allow me to grow a beard and a mustache, and I have chosen to cultivate those traits.

. . . My hair was long a fair amount of my childhood and through adolescence—though not the long, straight Lakota hair all Indians are *supposed* to have. It seems many eastern Indians have a rougher textured hair, and mine falls into this category. No matter how much I might brush my hair out every morning, invariably I looked less like any Indians in Edward Curtis photographs and more like Jerry Garcia from the Grateful Dead, ...

On the reservation, as in many other places, hair is a political statement. I learned this reality early. One of my brothers, Lee, . . . began growing his hair long in the late

1960s, before he burned his draft card but after our oldest brother had been shipped out to Vietnam. Lee was suspended from high school a number of times for having his hair too long, until one time my mother grew tired of his forced removals, took him to school herself, grabbed an idle white kid in the hallway whose hair was longer than my brother's, and dragged them both into the office to confront the principal with this discrepancy. My brother was reinstated, but one of his instructors insisted he had missed too much time in his suspensions to graduate, so he went to summer school, but he did it in long hair and graduated in August.

He is not the first member of my family to have an educational institution concern itself with his hair. In the early part of the twentieth century, the Dawes Act was in full swing, and my grandfather's parents were persuaded by government agents to allow their son the great privilege of attending one of the Indian boarding schools. They claimed that he would have a much better chance of surviving in the world if he could learn a trade in the broader culture. He learned to play a western instrument, the piccolo, I believe, and eventually remembered nothing about water drums but was well versed in snare and bass. . . .

Through college I had kept my hair in various stages of long, but it always looked wild, ... In graduate school I got rid of it all and kept a reasonably short style through that period, until I graduated and got past my first set of job interviews. As I began teaching at the college a few miles from the reservation where I grew up, my hair was still fairly short, appropriate for the era, the early 1990s, but as soon as I signed the contract I let it grow back out, and in 1998 my braid was about a foot and a half long, when I decided to get rid of it.

. . .

Other, strangely resonant events occurred in the few months following that, and I finally decided that while I could not stop the perpetuation of this stereotype, I did not have to be a contributing member. Tying off both ends of my braid, I cut it off in 1999, reduced my hair to a flattop, and grew my mustache to join the goatee at the same time. The braid is in my top-right desk drawer, where I keep it to remind me of where I have been.

. . .

Here, at the border, I am suddenly in Los Lobos land again, and my tribal identification is not good enough. National identification papers, it seems, are good enough documentation for the United States from every other nation except those housed within its borders. Haudenosaunee law stipulates we are not citizens of the United States, regardless of any federal laws on Indian citizenship. I am still not sure what the full dynamics are here. Perhaps it is not that our ID cards are not legitimate enough, but instead that braidless and hairy, I am not legitimate enough for my ID. This officer, I see, stares at me, is certain my name is Pedro, Hector, Jesus, and as a result of this perception he wears his illegal alien Polaroid sunglasses. Regardless of what might or might not be in my pocket, he has decided it is all right to treat me with disdain because I have been forward enough to attempt crossing borders without swimming my way in, and am merely getting what I deserve.

. . .

My faculty ID card looks promising. It is contemporary and formal, professionally laminated, and even has a bar code on it . . . . I hand this over and the officer looks at it. He rapid-fires questions at me. Suddenly I am taking a pop quiz on the academic calendar where I teach—when were finals, when was graduation, when does the school year begin, how many courses do I teach, and then it comes: What in Acuña, Mexico could possibly interest a college professor from New York? This question is so odd, so full of his emptiness, that no answer I can give short of "cheap dentistry," "stuffed armadillos," or "controlled substances" would be satisfactory. Back to the wallet.

My driving license convictions card surfaces next. This has my New York State license number on it, and a spotless driving record, I might add, the entire convictions section blank. The officer rejects this offer as well, observing it has no photograph. I suggest he can match the names from this to my other documents, and he merely raises his right eyebrow in a knowing way. . . .

Finally I remember that the attendants at the gym where I work out insist on picture ID, in addition to their own issued membership card, every time I enter. . . . We-solved the dual ID show by photocopying my license and taping it to the gym card. I rifle back through the less-convincing documents in my wallet and find the card, my shoddily photocopied license taped to it, and I am in luck; the numbers are visible, and more important, they match the numbers on my convictions record. I feel like a lotto winner as we compare numbers, the officer and I, and he is satisfied enough to run them through his international-criminal-driver's-license database and see, indeed, that I do live in western New York, or at least that someone who looks remarkably like me does. He gathers my variety pack of ID cards, hands them to me, and tells me, reluctantly, that I am free to go.

My braid is seventeen hundred miles from where I am as I leave the air-conditioned building and head out into the West Texas sun, and the fact that I can now slide my license back into my wallet and become someone I am not—a citizen of New York State, and thus a citizen of the United States of America as well—is no great comfort.

18

The Arab Woman and I

Mona Fayad

I am haunted by a constant companion called The Arab Woman. When I shut myself alone in my home, she steps out of the television screen to taunt me. In the movies, she stares down at me just as I am starting to relax. As I settle in a coffee shop to read the newspaper, she springs out at me and tries to choke me. In the classroom, when I tell my students that I grew up in Syria, she materializes suddenly as the inevitable question comes up: "Did you wear a veil?" That is when she appears in all her glory: the Faceless Veiled Woman, silent, passive, helpless, in need of rescue by the west. But there's also that other version of her, exotic and seductive, that follows me in the form of the Belly Dancer.

As a construct invented by the west, this two-in-one Arab Woman is completely intractable. Her voice drowns mine. It is no use pointing out that in Syria, Arab school girls wear khaki uniforms and are required for school credit to work on urban improvement projects, planting trees and painting walls. Or that Syrian television is constantly running ads for women to join the army. As I try to assert my experience of being an Arab woman, the Arab Woman tries to make me write about *her*. For a brief moment, I give in.

My one personal encounter in Syria with a fully veilled woman happens during my third year at the University of Damascus. I take a bus home. (Yes, we do have buses in the Middle East. We did away with camels as a means of transportation five years ago.) A veiled woman climbs aboard, the only one on the bus. I pay her no attention until she rushes up and embraces me enthusiastically. "Mona, how wonderful to see you!"

I know the voice, but somehow I can't place it. Realizing my predicament, she raises the veil for a minute. It's Mona, a friend of mine from university that I haven't seen recently. A bouncing, energetic person, she is very active socially. I have never seen her veiled. I ask if it's a recent decision.

V
O
I
C
E
S

"Not really. I come from a conservative neighborhood, so I prefer to wear the veil when I arrive there." She shrugs. "My family isn't very concerned, but I prefer to do it this way."

The old souk (market) in downtown Kuwait is one of my favorite places to go. The tradition of bargaining is still in practice. It's a sharp contrast to the cold, impersonal supermarkets that have now almost completely eradicated the social exchanges that have been a part of buying and selling in the Middle East for centuries. In this section of town, many women wear burqas or are completely veiled since they belong to an older genera-tion. Here the real haggling happens, and the high-pitched shouting of women dins the lower and more cracked voices of the men. "What a cheat," the woman announces to whoever is willing to listen. "Can you believe how much he's asking for this worthless piece of cloth?"

In another corner, two women selling men's underwear laugh good-naturedly as they target a young man whose embarrassment is apparent. "How *big* did you say you were?"

These are some veiled Arab women. Neither silent nor passive, they have a place within their culture, like women all across the world. But once again, The Arab Woman has intruded, preventing me from talking about myself, pushing me to feed you what you want to hear.

Part of the reason I obey her is that it's easier to be exotic. To talk about an ordinary Arab woman, one who wears pants or a plain dress or a suit and walks around looking like everyone else is uninteresting, to say the least. I feel pressured to produce something *special*, something different. I try to shut out The Arab Woman who is controlling my thoughts. She is asking me for facts, figures, ways of classifying women so they can be clearly placed in boxes and the doors can be shut on them once and for all. She wants order, a rational explanation, something easy to understand.

After much thinking, it occurs to me that it is you who veil the Arab woman, it is you who make her into a passive victim, it is you who silence her. Arab women get on with our lives. I try to get on with my life, but it is difficult to constantly confront what I am not.

I am not The Arab Woman. And, further, I cannot represent Arab women. Each Arab woman must represent herself, with the range of identities that include Syrian or Saudi Arabian, Berber or Copt, bedouin or society woman from Beirut, Druze or Alawite, vil-lager in the Upper Nile or Minister of Culture from Damascus. We're not an object that can be crushed together and concentrated for Western consumption in a box labelled: Organic Arab Woman.

There's no doubt within *me* that I'm an Arab woman. The problem is whether you will believe me.

19

My Tongue is Divided into Two

Quique Aviles

. . . As far back as I can remember, the promise of English was part of my life.

. . . In 1969, when I was four, my mother borrowed money from her mother to travel to the United States as a tourist. Her real intention was to stay in the States, get a good job, and offer her children a better life. She made a promise to bring us, her four children, one by one—starting with the oldest and ending with the youngest, which was me. . . .

> My tongue is divided into two
> by virtue, coincidence or heaven
> words jumping out of my mouth
> stepping on each other
> enjoying being a voice for the message
> expecting conclusions . . .

I've learned English in three different phases.

PHASE ONE: CURIOSITY AND WONDER

Having a mother who was in the United States meant that my brothers, my sister, and I got American gifts with words in English each time she came home. . . . I would sit with a dictionary and struggle to make out a few words so I could know more about my mother's new world.

In the mid-1970s, the Salvadoran Education Department brought "Televisión Educativa" to schools across the country. With it, came televised English classes . . . .

> my tongue is divided into two
> into heavy accent bits of confusion
> into miracles and accidents
> saying things that hurt the heart
> drowning in a language that lives, jumps, translates . . .

Like most kids anywhere in the world. American music and television were also my English teachers. . . . My family was only the second family in our whole town to own a television. . . . I would watch *Kojak, Mission Impossible*, and *Starsky and Hutch*—swallowing up English, aspiring to be cool, and knowing that my mother had my ticket on layaway.

In late 1978, I had a political awakening. My country was ruled by the military and their martial law against ideas. I was 13 years old and joined the student movement. We demanded books, chalk, better teachers, and cleaner bathrooms. In the revolutionary fervor of those days, the coolness of English was ruined by Marx and Lenin. The language that fed my wonder and curiosity was now, according to my comrades, the language of the enemy of Yankee Imperialism. It was no longer cool. The next thing I knew, I was on a plane to the United States to save me from the death squads.

> My tongue is divided by nature
> by our crazy desire to triumph and conquer
> this tongue is cut up into equal pieces
> one wants to curse and sing out loud
> the other one simply wants to ask for water . . .

PHASE TWO: FRUSTRATION AND NEED (HOW ENGLISH BECAME MY IMPERIAL LIBERATOR)

In the fall of 1980, I started 9th grade at Francis Junior High in Washington, D.C. Kids from Central America were coming into the school in droves every week. We were thrown into English as a Second language (ESL) classes where Mrs. Padrino taught us . . . to say, "Hello, how are you today? I am fine, thank you," in crisp English. On weekends, I went to rallies and protests—ESL classes for leftists. There, I got to repeat "No draft, no war/US out of El Salvador!" . . . .

By this time, I was beginning to understand that English was not just one language. At school, I became friends with Pichi, a chubby white Puerto Rican who . . . spoke three languages: Puerto Rican Spanish (which I barely understood), formal English (which I was beginning to understand), and Black English (which I now understood I needed to learn in order to survive). Pichi became my real ESL teacher:

tongue
English of the funny sounds
tongue
funny sounds in English
tongue
sounds funny in English
tongue
in funny English sounds

It was Pichi who gave me a copy of *Puerto Rican Obituary*, a poetry book by Pedro Pietri, one of the first and most influential of the Nuyorican poets of the 1970s. I had been writing poetry since I was ten years old, mainly rhyming, cheesy love poems. This book changed my life. . . . It introduced me to the possibility of words as a weapon. I started mixing my anger, my Spanish, and my limited English into poetry. . . . But English began to feel good. I began to feel that it was something I could use as revenge.

When it was time for me to start high school, I decided to audition for the Theater Department at the Duke Ellington School of the Arts. With my angry, broken English, I made an impression and got in. My first year was very hard. I was the only Latino in the whole school of more than 400 students. Rosemary Walsh, my acting teacher, would tell me, "You're a good actor, but I can't understand what the fuck you're saying. We're gonna work on you." . . . My second year at Ellington, I was assigned to speech classes. We studied phonetics and the anatomy of our sound-making factory: the mouth, the throat, the vocal chords, and the diaphram. These classes consisted of repetitive speech exercises, such as:

"Theophilus thistle, the unsuccessful thistle sifter, while sifting a sieve of unsifted thistles thrusts three thousand thistles through the thick of his thumb . . ." "Unique New York, Unique New York, Unique New York . . ."

. . .

So, here I was, thinking that I was making so much progress with my English, I could move to New York or L.A. and make it big.

my tongue is divided into two
a border patrol runs through the middle
frisking words
asking for proper identification
checking for pronunciation . . .

By my senior year I had become a punk rocker, a combat-boot wearing rebel. I realized that there were no parts for me in traditional theater, that if I wanted to be an actor, I would have to write my own parts. With that realization, I began a deeper, artistic relationship with the English language. My new teachers became Nikki Giovanni, June Jordan, Lucille Clifton, and Alice Walker—black writers who were using language to say that we are beautiful, that we deserve things. I began to write monologues for characters that came from my life. As I began to develop my own voice, English became my imperial liberator.

PHASE THREE: SUBTLETY AND PAYBACK

I am still learning English. *El inglés.* . . .

Since the mid-1980s I have been writing and performing one-person shows that weave together poetry and monologues in English. Latinos often ask me, "Why don't you do more in Spanish?" I often respond, "Because you all don't pay my rent." But the real answer is: payback. I use English to challenge English speakers to question their assumptions about us Latinos, about each other, and, in these xenophobic times, about immigrants in general. I use it to poke, prod, question, and make people feel uncomfortable. I always read my poems from a music stand (I have very few of them memorized), and whenever I leave my house for a gig, carrying my music stand to the car, I always feel that I am carrying my *machete*. Words are my weapon.

They are also the way I build alliances. I have learned that building trust with someone who is different from you in this country is all about mastering their own version of the English language. Most of my work in D.C. has been with black kids. I go into classrooms and use theater improvisation as a tool for encouraging kids to write about their lives. Most kids want to do improvs about drugs and guns, the thug life. I challenge them by asking, "Does your momma love you? Do you smile? Do you laugh? Are there tender moments in your life?" For the majority of kids, the answer is yes. So I challenge them to create skits about those soft and tender moments and then to write poetry about it. I challenge them not to fulfill society's expectations of poor kids by being drug dealers and thugs. And I always tell them, "Ain't nobody gonna sing our song, so we might as well sing it ourselves."

For me, learning English has been about learning to sing my own song.

> my tongue is divided into two
> my tongue is divided into two
> I like my tongue
> it says what feels right
> I like my tongue
> it says what feels right

20

The Emperor's New Clothes

Patricia J. Williams

My son used to attend a small nursery school. Over the course of one year, three different teachers in his school assured me that he was color-blind. Resigned to this diagnosis, I took my son to an ophthalmologist who tested him and pronounced his vision perfect. I could not figure out what was going on until I began to listen carefully to what he was saying about color.

As it turned out, my son did not misidentify color. He resisted identifying color at all. "I don't know," he would say when asked what color the grass was; or, most peculiarly, "It makes no difference." This latter remark, this assertion of the greenness of grass making no difference, was such a precociously cynical retort, that I began to suspect some social complication in which he was somehow invested.

The long and the short of it is that the well-meaning teachers at his predominantly white school had valiantly and repeatedly assured their charges that color makes no difference. "It doesn't matter," they told the children, "whether you're black or white or red or green or blue." Yet upon further investigation, the very reason that the teachers had felt it necessary to impart this lesson in the first place was that it *did* matter, and in predictably cruel ways: some of the children had been fighting about whether black people could play "good guys."

My son's anxious response was redefined by his teachers as physical deficiency. This anxiety redefined as deficiency suggests to me that it may be illustrative of the way in which the liberal ideal of color-blindness is too often confounded. That is to say, the very notion of blindness about color constitutes an ideological confusion at best, and denial at its very worst. I recognize, certainly, that the teachers were inspired by a desire to make whole a division in the ranks. But much is overlooked in the move to undo that which clearly and unfortunately matters just by labeling it that which "makes no difference." The dismissiveness, however unintentional, leaves those in my son's position pulled between the clarity of their own experience and the often alienating terms in which they must seek social acceptance.

There's a lot of that in the world right now: someone has just announced in no uncertain terms that he or she hates you because you're dark, let's say, or Catholic or a woman or the wrong height, and the panicked authority figures try to patch things up by reassuring you that race or gender or stature or your heartfelt religion doesn't matter; means nothing in the calculation of your humanity; is the most insignificant little puddle of beans in the world.

While I do want to underscore that I embrace color-blindness as a legitimate hope for the future, I worry that we tend to enshrine the notion with a kind of utopianism whose naïveté will ensure its elusiveness. In the material world ranging from playgrounds to politics, our ideals perhaps need more thoughtful, albeit more complicated, guardianship. By this I mean something more than the "I think therefore it is" school of idealism. "I don't think about color, therefore your problems don't exist." If only it were so easy.

But if indeed it's not that easy then the application of such quick fixes becomes not just a shortcut but a short-circuiting of the process of resolution. In the example of my son's experience at school, the collective aversion to confronting the social tensions he faced resulted in their being pathologized as his individual physical limitation. This is a phenomenon that happens all too frequently to children of color in a variety of contexts. In both the United States and the United Kingdom, the disproportionate numbers of black children who end up in special education or who are written off as failures attest to the degree to which this is a profound source of social anxiety.

In addition, the failure to deal straightforwardly with the pervasive practices of exclusion that infect even the very young allowed my son's white schoolmates to indulge in the false luxury of a prematurely imagined community. By this I mean that we can all be lulled rather too easily into a self-congratulatory stance of preached universalism—"We are the world! We are the children!" was the evocative, full-throated harmony of a few years ago. Yet nowhere has that been invoked more passionately than in the face of tidal waves of dissension, and even as "the" children learn that "we" children are not like "those," the benighted creatures on the other side of the pale.

This tension between material conditions and what one is cultured to see or not see—the dilemma of the emperor's new clothes, we might call it—is a tension faced by any society driven by bitter histories of imposed hierarchy. I don't mean to suggest that we need always go about feeling guilty or responsible or perpetually burdened by original sin or notions of political correctness. I do wish, however, to counsel against the facile innocence of those three notorious monkeys, Hear No Evil, See No Evil, and Speak No Evil. Theirs is a purity achieved through ignorance. Ours must be a world in which we know each other better.

To put it another way, it is a dangerous if comprehensible temptation to imagine inclusiveness by imagining away any obstacles. It is in this way that the moral high ground of good intentions knows its limits. We must be careful not to allow our intentions to verge into outright projection by substituting a fantasy of global seamlessness that is blinding rather than just color-blind.

This is a dilemma—being colored, so to speak, in a world of normative whiteness, whiteness being defined as the absence of color. The drive to conform our surroundings to whatever we know as "normal" is a powerful force—convention in many ways is more powerful than reason, and customs in some instances are more powerful than law. While surely most customs and conventions encode the insights of ancient wisdom, the habits of racial thought in Western society just as surely encapsulate some of the greatest mistakes in human history. So how do we rethink this most troubled of divisions, the fault line in our body politic, the fault line in ourselves? The ability to remain true to *one* self, it seems to me, must begin with the ethical project of considering how we can align a sense of ourselves with a sense of the world. This is the essence of integrity, is it not, never having to split into a well-maintained "front" and a closely guarded "inside."

Creating community, in other words, involves this most difficult work of negotiating real divisions, of considering boundaries before we go crashing through, and of pondering our differences before we can ever agree on the terms of our sameness. For the discounted vision of the emperor's new clothes (or a little boy's color) is already the description of corrupted community.

Perhaps one reason that conversations about race are so often doomed to frustration is that the notion of whiteness as "race" is almost never implicated. One of the more difficult legacies of slavery and of colonialism is the degree to which racism's tenacious hold is manifested not merely in the divided demographics of neighborhood or education or class but also in the process of what media expert John Fiske calls the "exnomination" of whiteness as racial identity. Whiteness is unnamed, suppressed, beyond the realm of race. Exnomination permits whites to entertain the notion that race lives "over there" on the other side of the tracks, in black bodies and inner-city neighborhoods, in a dark netherworld where whites are not involved.

At this level, the creation of a sense of community is a lifelong negotiation of endless subtlety. One morning when my son was three, I took him to his preschool. He ran straight

V
O
I
C
E
S

to a pile of Lego and proceeded to work. I crossed the room and put his lunchbox in the refrigerator, where I encountered a little girl sitting at a table, beating a mound of clay into submission with a plastic rolling pin. "I see a Mommy," she said to me cheerfully. "That must mean that your little boy is here somewhere, too." "Yes, he's here," I answered, thinking how sweetly precocious she was. "There, he's over by the Lego."

She strained to see around the bookcases. "Oh yes," she said. "Now I see that black face of his."

I walked away without responding, enraged—how can one be so enraged at an innocent child—yet not knowing what to say just then, rushing to get the jaggedly dangerous broken glass of my emotions out of the room.

I remember being three years old so well. Three was the age when I learned that I was black, the colored kid, monkeychild, different. What made me so angry and wordless in this encounter forty years later was the realization that none of the little white children who taught me to see my blackness as a mark probably ever learned to see themselves as white. In our culture, whiteness is rarely marked in the indicative there! there! sense of my bracketed blackness. And the majoritarian privilege of never noticing themselves was the beginning of an imbalance from which so much, so much else flowed.

But that is hard to talk about, even now, this insight acquired before I had the words to sort it out. Yet it is imperative to think about this phenomenon of closeting race, which I believe is a good deal more widespread than these small examples. In a sense, race matters are resented and repressed in much the same way as matters of sex and scandal: the subject is considered a rude and transgressive one in mixed company, a matter whose observation is sometimes inevitable, but about which, once seen, little should be heard nonetheless. Race thus tends to be treated as though it were an especially delicate category of social infirmity—so-called—like extreme obesity or disfigurement.

Every parent knows a little of this dynamic, if in other contexts: "Why doesn't that lady have any teeth?" comes the child's piping voice. "Why doesn't that gentleman have any hair?" And "Why is that little boy so black?" *Ssshhhh!* comes the anxious parental remonstrance. The poor thing can't help it. We must all pretend that nothing's wrong.

And thus we are coached upon pain of punishment not to see a thing.

Now, to be sure, the parent faces an ethical dilemma in that moment of childish vision unrestrained by social nicety. On the one hand, we rush to place a limit on what can be said to strangers and what must be withheld for fear of imposition or of hurting someone's feelings. As members of a broad society, we respect one another by learning not to inflict every last intimate, prying curiosity we may harbor upon everyone we meet.

That said, there remains the problem of how or whether we ever answer the question, and that is the dimension of this dynamic that is considerably more troubling.

"Why is that man wearing no clothes?" pipes the childish voice once more. And the parent panics at the complication of trying to explain. The naked man may be a nudist or a psychotic or perhaps the emperor of the realm, but the silencing that is passed from parent to child is not only about the teaching of restraint; it is calculated to circumnavigate the question as though it had never been asked. *Stop asking such silly questions.*

A wall begins to grow around the forbidden gaze; for we all know, and children best of all, when someone wants to change the subject, forever. And so the child is left to the monstrous creativity of ignorance and wild imagination.

Again, I do believe that this unfortunate negotiation of social difference has much in common with discussions about race. Race is treated as though it were some sort of genetic leprosy or a biological train wreck. Those who privilege themselves as Un-raced—usually but not always those who are white—are always anxiously maintaining that it doesn't matter, even as they are quite busy feeling pity, no less, and thankful to God for their great good luck in having been spared so intolerable an affliction.

Meanwhile, those marked as Having Race are ground down by the pendular stresses of having to explain what it feels like to be You—why are you black, why are you black, why are you black, over and over again; or, alternatively, placed in a kind of conversational quarantine of muteness in which any mention of racial circumstance reduces all sides to tears, fears, fisticuffs, and other paroxysms of unseemly anguish.

This sad, habitual paralysis in the face of the foreign and the anxiety-producing. It is as though we are all skating across a pond that is not quite thoroughly frozen. Two centuries ago, or perhaps only a few decades ago, the lake was solidly frozen, and if for those skating across the surface things seemed much more secure, it was a much more dismal lot for those whose fates were frozen at the bottom of the pond. Over time, the weather of race relations has warmed somewhat, and a few of those at the bottom have found their way to the surface; we no longer hold our breath, and we have even learned to skate. The noisy, racial chasm still yawns darkly beneath us all, but we few brave souls glide gingerly above, upon a skim of hope, our bodies made light with denial, the black pond so dangerously and thinly iced with the conviction that talking about it will only make things worse.

And so the racial divide is exacerbated further by a welter of little lies that propel us foolishly around the edges of our most demanding social stresses: Black people are a happy people and if they would just stop complaining so much, they would see how happy they are. Black people who say they're unhappy are leftist agitators whose time would be better spent looking for a real job. White people are victims. Poor Bangladeshis are poor because they want to be. Poor white people are poor because rich Indians stole all the jobs under the ruse of affirmative action. There is no racism in the marketplace—"each according to his merit" goes the cant, even as the EEOC has a backlog of 70,000 cases by the most conservative estimates; even as top executives funnel the jobs to school chums and their next of kin, or chief executives at major corporations are captured on tape destroying subpoenaed records of ongoing discriminatory practices. Immigrants are taking over the whole world, but race makes no difference. If sixty percent of young black men are unemployed in the industrialized world, well, let them watch Oprah. If some people are determined to be homeless, well then let them have it, if homelessness is what they like so much . . .

Triage is a word I hear bandied about a lot these days. I have heard it used by many of my friends who are economists; they used it to convey an urgency of limited resources. If there's not enough to go around, then those with the least should be written off first because it will take more to save them anyway. And we don't have more.

This word *triage* originally cropped up in the context of the medical profession. It is a term borrowed from overtaxed hospitals in theaters of war. On body-strewn battlefields, doctors would divide the survivors into three groups. The third, in the worst condition, might be left to die because bandages were better spent wrapped around those more likely to survive.

In the context of today's ghettos, inner cities, and those places doomed to be called the Third World, I hear the word *triage*.

I worry about this image that casts aside so many so easily. It envisions poor and dying populations as separate, distant, severable. I worry that perhaps we have mischosen our metaphors.

I fear triage; I fear that one cannot cut off a third of the world without some awful, life-threatening bleeding in the rest of the body politic. The Malthusian nightmare has never been a simple matter, I think, of letting someone else go hungry, or of letting someone else die. It is a matter of amputation—that's the metaphor I'd rather use. And one can't cut off one's leg and pretend it never belonged.

It is as though we are employing, in our economic analysis of distributive justice, the images of the very earliest days of medical experimentation. *Oh, well, let's see now . . . The soul abides in the liver . . . Therefore we can chop off that troublesome, heretical head and no one will be the less holy for it . . .*

Maybe. But quite a few martyrs have been made that way.

Anthropologist Michael Taussig has written about the phenomenon of public secrets. He writes of a ritual in Tierra del Fuego in which the men come out of the men's hut wearing masks. The women hail them by singing "Here come the spirits!" On some level, everyone must know that these are not spirits but husbands and brothers and fathers and sons, but so powerful is the ritual to the sense of community that it is upon pain of death that the women fail to greet them as spirits.

In our culture, I think that the power of race resembles just such a public secret. I understand the civic ritual that requires us to say in the face of all our differences, We are all one, we are the world. I understand the need for the publicly reiterated faith in public ideals as binding and sustaining community. Such beliefs are the very foundation of institutional legitimacy and no society can hold itself together without them. Yet such binding force comes from a citizenry willing to suspend disbelief for the sake of honoring the spiritual power of our appointed ideals. And where suspicion, cynicism, and betrayal have eaten away at a community to the degree that the folk parading from the men's hut look like just a bunch of muggers wearing masks—or badges, as the case may be—then hailing the spirit will sound like a hollow incantation, empty theater, the weary habit of the dispossessed.

. . .

Such is the legacy of racism in the modern world. Perhaps it is less and less fashionable these days to consider too explicitly the kinds of costs that slavery and colonialism exacted, even as those historical disruptions have continued to scar contemporary social arrangements with the transcendent urgency of their hand-me-down grief.

I realize therefore that it might be considered impertinent to keep raising the ghost of slavery's triangle trade and waving it around; there is a pronounced preference in polite society for just letting bygones be bygones. And I concede that a more optimistic enterprise might be to begin any contemporary analysis of race with the Civil Rights Movement in the United States, or the Notting Hill riots in the United Kingdom. Beginning at those points is a way of focusing one's view and confining one's reference to the legitimately inspiring ideals that coalesced those movements: the aims of color-blindness, the equality of all people, and the possibility of peaceful coexistence.

Yet if that well-chosen temporal slice allows us to be optimistic about the possibility of progress, there are nonetheless limitations to such a frame. First, it is the conceptual prehistory of those movements that explains the toll of racism and its lingering effects. There can be no adequate explanation without reference to it. Second, the diasporic complexity of today's social problems requires an analysis that moves those ideals of the social movements of the 1960s and 1970s beyond themselves, into the present, into the future—to a more complex, practical grappling with such phenomena as the hybridizing of racial stereotypes with the fundamentalisms of gender, class, ethnicity, religion. Third, the problem of race is overlaid with crises in environmental and resource management that have triggered unparalleled migrations from rural to urban locations within national boundaries, and that have impassioned debates about immigration across national boundaries. Finally, not a few aspects of our New Age global economics, much like the commercial profiteering of colonialisms past, threaten to displace not just the very laws to which we persistently make such grand appeal but the nation-state itself. I believe that a genuine, long-term optimism about the future of race relations depends on a thorough excavation of the same.

A memory slips into my mind. I was riding the train from New York to Washington, D.C., some years ago on my way to some lawyers' conference or other; I was accompanied by two black colleagues. An hour into the trip, the train stopped in the city of Philadelphia. A young white woman got on whom my colleagues knew. She was also a lawyer, headed to the same conference. She joined us, sitting among us in a double row of seats that faced each other. A little while later, the conductor came along. The new woman held up her ticket, but the conductor did not seem to see her. He saw four of us seated and only three ticket stubs.

"One of you hasn't paid," he said, staring at me, then at each of my two black friends. I remember pointing to the white woman, and someone else said, "Over there." But the conductor was resolute.

"Which one of you hasn't paid?" he asked again. Two of us kept saying, "Our receipts, see?" and the white woman, speaking *very* clearly said, "Here. I am trying to give you my ticket."

The conductor was scowling. He still did not hear. "I am not moving till one of you pays up."

It was the longest time before the conductor stopped staring in all the wrong directions. It was the longest time before he heard the new woman, pressing her ticket upon him, her voice reaching him finally as though from a great distance, passing through light-years of understanding as if from another universe. The realization that finally lit his face was like the dawning of a great surprise.

How precisely does the issue of color remain so powerfully determinative of everything from life circumstance to manner of death, in a world that is, by and large, officially "colorblind"? What metaphors mask the hierarchies that make racial domination frequently seem so "natural," so invisible, indeed so attractive? How does racism continue to evolve, post-slavery and post-equality legislation, across such geographic, temporal, and political distance?

No, I am not saying that this is the worst of times. But neither will I concede that this is the best of all possible worlds. And what a *good* thing, is it not, to try to imagine how much better we could be . . .

"I had a dream," said my son the other morning. Then he paused. "No," he said, "it was more of a miracle. Do you know what a miracle is?" "Tell me," I said, thunderstruck, and breathless with maternal awe.

"A miracle is when you have a dream and you open your eyes in it. It's when you wake up and your dream is all around you."

It was a pretty good definition, I thought. And even though my son's little miracle had something to do with pirates meeting dinosaurs, I do think that to a very great extent we dream our worlds into being. For better or worse, our customs and laws, our culture and society are sustained by the myths we embrace, the stories we recirculate to explain what we behold. I believe that racism's hardy persistence and immense adaptability are sustained by a habit of human imagination, deflective rhetoric, and hidden license. I believe no less that an optimistic course might be charted, if only we could imagine it. What a world it would be if we could all wake up and see all of ourselves reflected in the world, not merely in a territorial sense but with a kind of nonexclusive entitlement that grants not so much possession as investment. A peculiarly anachronistic notion of investment, I suppose, at once both ancient and futuristic. An investment that envisions each of us in each other.

V
O
I
C
E
S

21

Billy Yalowitz

Billy Yalowitz

The University of Pennsylvania hired me to teach a course about theater and community. I knew I wanted to create a performance like I'd done in other Philadelphia neighborhoods that would be based on oral histories. A faculty member at the university told me about a neighborhood called the Black Bottom that used to be adjacent to the university, just north of the campus. It was a thriving, working-class African American neighborhood, like many neighborhoods in northern cities, that really began to take shape in the 1920s and '30s with the migration from the South. By 1969 the neighborhood was flattened, demolished by urban renewal. Some of my African American friends from the Black Bottom have sardonically called that process "Negro removal."

The Black Bottom is now a community in exile. As a Jew, I know about exile. My background is left wing Jewish from New York City—that's also a community that had, in a sense, gone into exile. The story of my antiracism work begins there. Some of the really important antiracist work in the United States was pioneered by left wing Jews in the 1920s and '30s as part of the labor movement and an early wave of the Civil Rights Movement. I was born in 1959 and grew up with this legacy of antiracism work. I inherited that.

Folks who lived in the Black Bottom now live all over the Philadelphia area and beyond. After thirty or forty years, they're still in close contact with each other, elders now, in their sixties and seventies and eighties. They've wanted their story told for a long time. They're remarkably generous while trying to figure out what restitution might mean for them.

So I decided to create a performance about the Black Bottom. The project is a three-way partnership between the university, the Black Bottom community, and a local high school—University City High School, which was built on the ground where the Black Bottom used to be. The goal has been to give voice to that story and in doing that, to create a vehicle where Penn students could learn about building relationships and listening to people and then creating a performance that's based on the people's stories. This project has transformed the students' lives. It's very clear to me and to them that this has been a very powerful part of their education. . . .

Penn students and faculty and the students and teachers at the high school were for the most part entirely unaware of what happened to the Black Bottom. The Penn students are primarily middle- and owning-class white, some students of color, but they've been actively taught to fear the neighborhood that they live in. The university has acted like many urban universities act, as a kind of colonial power in that neighborhood.

. . .

So here I am. I'm adjunct faculty in the arts at Penn, one of the most marginal characters on the faculty. When I walk over to the University City High School to introduce this project, I'm a Penn professor. I have this "great idea" about the Black Bottom. I've come to work with the African American teachers. They come on board, almost in spite of themselves, because the work is driven by a story that's very familiar to them.

But, boy, I'm this professor "expert," coming in with an agenda instead of coming in to ask, "What do you want to have happen around here? What have you been hoping for? What are some of your ideas?" I don't come in with that at all! I come with a full-blown project that is accurate enough so that I can repair some of the damage that I've already caused, but some of the Black teachers won't even look at me.

What I think I understand now on a deeper level is that we come in with some kind of resource; there has to be an exchange of expertise and knowledge. I know how to get a theater performance up on its feet, and you know firsthand the history of your neighborhood and how institutional racism has made your life so difficult. We have an exchange to make there. At that point, if the agendas are compatible in some way, then it's workable.

In my case, doing antiracism work through the arts has been very effective. It's a cultural resource that I have access to and training in. There I am at Penn, and I can get grant money so that people in the community, without any specialized academic training in theater, can have their voices heard through the arts. I'm interested in a lot of different levels of people who have formal academic or conservatory training working with people who have another kind of training, where there is another kind of virtuosity and aesthetic or skill. For example, in my productions there's often double Dutch or drill team, which are African American street games and dance forms respectively. Or the night before the opening performance of *Black Bottom*, a man who grew up in the Black Bottom and became a city planner gave me a poem he'd written for the performance. He hadn't been involved at all in the performance up until then but told me, "I heard that there's this performance and wrote a poem." It was called "Round the Way." And we included it in the performance that night.

In general, my feeling about working on racism with people of color is that it makes no sense to work directly at it, especially at first. If you can find a project to do together, the issues come up. Race can be talked about very comfortably once you prepare the white people, including myself, to build relationships. I had a seder here, and I invited many of the people from the Black Bottom. That was lovely. They came to my house because they know me. It wasn't, "Let's do a Black-Jewish thing." I don't want to disparage that too much, but finding another way to build the relationship has been much more effective for me.

There are some scary things about doing this as a white male leader. I still don't like having Black people angry at me. At the opening night of the Black Bottom performance, everyone was nervous and really wanted it to go well. I was tense, I wanted it to go well, and people were getting pissed at me. Boy, that was hard. And now I look back on it and say to myself, "That was all right, even though it scared the shit out of me to do that." Any time that you're working hard to produce something like that and when there is something at stake, people are going to have all sorts of feelings come up. You're the leader, and it comes out at you.

I had one high school guy, Darnell [a pseudonym], who had missed the rehearsal and come to the performance late. So we had assigned the understudy role to one of his classmates, who got on stage. The other guy was up there, doing his lines, and Darnell was cursing in the audience, "He's fucking up my lines." So the whole audience is hearing this. So I go over to him, say, "Darnell, we'll get you in tomorrow night, when we have another performance." This is probably the one thing he's cared about in his high school year. So I tried to get him out of the auditorium, put my hand on his back. And he just about swung at me. "Take your hand off my back, Billy." Stanley saw that this was happening, came over to us, and took Darnell outside and talked to him for about forty-five minutes. Darnell came back into the auditorium with Stanley to watch the performance.

Stanley wanted to tell me afterward what had happened. He told me, "You know what I did is I explained to him that you're a good man, that you were not trying to fuck him over. I told him, 'If you blow this thing, the police will come, and you don't want that kind of scene. Or the other thing that's going to happen is if you keep wanting to make this kind of scene here, there's plenty of guys from the Black Bottom neighborhood whose story is being told right now who don't want your little ass interrupting it.' Billy, when you see Darnell tomorrow, I want you to talk with him and put your arms around him." I talked it through with Darnell. The next night, Darnell performed and was pleased with himself.

V
O
I
C
E
S

Where that circles back to is the importance of building relationships, and then something happens that transcends the racial divide. The elder in that case was helping keep that relationship going and helping Darnell understand that I wasn't being this oppressive white guy in this case.

. . .

[Stanley and I have] become friends; it's nothing more than that. I'm part of his crew now. I've listened to him, and I've gained his trust. We have each other's respect. He would do that for anybody. They understand that in his neighborhood. They understand loyalty—that when you go out on a limb, you need people backing you.

I think part of the damage of being white and middle class, and the individualism of your career track, is that you don't stand with other people. You don't have a union and that kind of solidarity with anybody, really. I've crafted this unique career; I've kind of figured out this unique little niche as a director. But it's really led me back into working in communities where I become part of the group and share the resources I have.

That's a lot of what I try to communicate with my students from Penn—that we know very little about humility, the loss of community, and how isolated we are from each other. That's a cost of whiteness and of being middle class, as we construct it—that you're special, that your knowledge separates you. You think you're smarter than other people. What a disability, to think that you're smarter.

I think that for many of us white people, the kind of learning we usually get in school is backward. You theorize and then you try to get out and do something with it. It's not very useful. Maybe it's male, maybe it's white, maybe it's U.S. and middle class. I think it is probably some of all those things. It's a disadvantage. It's a kind of cultural deprivation.

I was lucky. My dad was a working-class Jewish guy. I walked around the streets of New York with him. He would talk with everybody. He talked to the hot dog vendors; he talked to the guys who were pumping gas. I'd ask him, "Do you know that guy?" I think I learned a sense of community from my dad, that you belong to the world.

One of my African American high school students in the performance, Dawn, was doing well. She's very talented. She wanted to be in a scene. And I said, "No!" I don't do that much, but I snapped at her. She had been coming to all the rehearsals. One of my white students, Maggie, who has a nice relationship with Dawn, came up to me afterward and said to me, "You lost Dawn on that one." What I did was, within Maggie's earshot, I went over to Dawn and I said, "Dawn, that was my mistake. I'm sorry; I was worried about getting the work done. There isn't really a reason for you not to be in that scene." Making mistakes and copping to them is really important.

I can get defensive and tense about being correct. But I'm learning that I can have a life where I get to make mistakes, and that's expected, and people will back me. That's a tough one, learning that people will back you if you make mistakes.

Getting criticized when you do this work is inevitable. What equips us to go out and take these risks is that we have a place where we can go and recover from the mistakes we make. I have a support base in Re-evaluation Counseling. I have a network of people who are doing this work all over the world in different ways. So I go to these rehearsals, and I make these mistakes, and I do these things that I'm pleased with. I have a place I can go several times a week and be scared about it, or cry about it, or be very proud about it. As a result, I can actually think better about my work.

In terms of being a white male, having the capacity to notice and be able to heal from when you're terrified, that's a big deal. That's a big deal! I don't think we're going to be able to do this work very well until part of the practice of doing it is to notice how scared we are. Otherwise, I don't think you can make mistakes and really recover from them and learn from them.

. . .

22

Waking Up White

What It Means to Accept Your Legacy, for Better and Worse

Jan Arminio

The realization that I am white actually came only after the birth of my children. Though I recognized since I was young that I had white skin, it was not until recently that I saw my whiteness went beyond my skin. It was a part of my identity—an identity that was socially constructed in part, but my identity nonetheless. It was, it is, who I am.

During high school, college, and early adulthood, I was what could be called a well-intentioned, color-blind white person who believed she treated everyone the same. Though I never yelled racial epithets at anyone, never wrote racial slurs on walls or doors, I did laugh at racist jokes, I never reached out to international students or students of color, and I perpetuated notions of heterosexism. While I was in college, I attended my sister's commencement. The speaker was from a sister institution in Korea. I distinctly remember making fun of her with my friends (who, of course, were all white). We laughed at her accent, her robe, and likely the shape of her eyes, although it truly pains me now to think back on it. I also remember during my first year in college, several African American students lived across the hall. My friends and I said hello to them, but I never invited them to our rooms, never knocked on their door, and never made any attempt to get to know them. I had a number of classes with an African American student who was from a large city. I always wondered why he came to "my" rural institution far from his home, but I never bothered to ask him.

To make a long, unfortunate story short, I did little to improve the world but instead helped to make it an unwelcoming, uncomfortable, and unfriendly place for some. Why? Looking back on this behavior, I can see that it accentuated my membership in my group of friends and my status in society. I can also see I was acting out behavior modeled by others around me. Seeking out social connections that were committed to social justice was foreign. I was simply incapable at that stage in my life of recognizing the hypocrisy of my actions in a country supposedly established on the principle of equality.

But after I graduated, things—and I—began to change. The two most significant changes were that I had children and started in a doctoral program in college student personnel. I credit my children and my doctoral work with helping me to wake up and see who I am and the role I must play as a white person in society.

One of my first memories of this awakening is when my four-year-old son asked me a question that a lot of young children ask when they first learn the terms *white* and *black* to describe people. "Why do we call white people white, when we really are not?" he asked. "We are pink people. We are not white like the clouds on a sunny day. And black people aren't really black, they are brown." I did not know quite how to respond, but I did realize at that instant that someone or a group of someones had chosen to use the words *white* and *black*, thereby emphasizing the contrast. My son had planted a seed that, to grow into genuine understanding, needed accurate information about people, the differences among them, and a critical examination of myself. Through my doctoral work I was able to nurture that understanding. I came to understand who those someones were who came up with the concept of race. They were philosophers, writers, scientists—predominantly white—who developed these categories to serve their own purposes. I came to see that race is not a biological fact but an arbitrary social construction. Still, this fact didn't diminish its social significance. Race, regardless of how it came to be, is a burden of our society.

Another important turning point came at a diversity workshop I was asked to participate in for my doctoral work. I received a handout entitled "White Racial Identity." As soon as I read it, the knowledge hit me that I was a part of this thing called the "white race." I experienced this realization as a jolt in my gut. I had a racial identity. But what did this mean? Why did I not realize this before? What were the implications?

I decided to use the work on my doctoral dissertation to try to better understand my own race and ancestry, my own white identity, and its relationship to the oppression of people of color by conversing with white students about how they made meaning of being white. I bought a transcribing machine to help me in this work. Shortly after that, my children and I were experimenting with my new machine, listening to our voices on the tape recorder. My sons asked if I would pretend that I was interviewing them. I agreed and asked a question that I had prepared to ask my dissertation participants: "What does it mean for you to be white?" Both looked astonished and were speechless. So to warm them up to the topic, I asked, "What is it like being a boy?" They answered quite quickly that boys didn't have to wear pink and play with stupid dolls. Clearly, they had better toys. I then returned to my original question, "What does it mean to be white?" My seven-year-old slowly stated, "It's easier to be lucky if you're white." I was astounded by his ability to capture the subtlety of racism: it's easier to be at the right place at the right time, to have things go your way.

All whites must wake up. This means acknowledging who we were as a group, questioning whether this is still a part of who we are as individuals, and deciding who we want to become. Finding out who we were as a people includes an accurate history of white atrocities and white benevolence rather than the PG-rated version that is more commonplace. The truth demonstrates the best and worst of me that is possible. Knowing who I am means knowing the undesirable tendencies that I must consciously avoid while increasing benevolent behavior. I believe acknowledging my heritage and acquainting myself with my ancestors enhances my ability to accomplish that.

My children have taught me that becoming a just white person means caring for the education of all children. Justness is not about being first in line but, rather, having a place at the table. All of us should be about the task of ensuring that everyone has a place at the table of good education, good housing, safe cities, good medical care, and good jobs. Each of us must ask: What have I done today to accomplish this? Do I reach out to others to better understand differences, or do I cling to the comfort of similarities? Do I accurately view my attitudes and behaviors as both oppressor and oppressed? Do I connect with my experiences of being oppressed in order to work to eliminate those experiences for others or solely to ensure that they will not happen to me? Can I recognize and stop oppressive acts to guarantee that children I bring into this world, live with in my community, and encounter on my campus will not pass on a legacy of oppression?

As my children grow older, the pervasiveness of racism threatens their wisdom. I begin to see other attitudes and behaviors intruding into their lives. My children now seem less able to recognize injustice and condemn it. They seem more willing to blame victims for injustice. I wonder how their painful experiences of being called "faggot" on the school bus have influenced them. Is it leading them to realize that it's less painful to be the perpetrator than the victim? Will their previous sense of justice also become a victim of oppression? The insight my children offered me years ago I must now offer them. I must help them wake up before it's too late for them and other children so they might experience a more just future.

NEXT STEPS

23

Women, Race, and Racism

A Dialogue in Black and White

Andrea Ayvazian and Beverly Daniel Tatum

Beverly Daniel Tatum: . . .

Jean Baker Miller has written eloquently about the constructive power of relational connections and the potentially destructive force of relational disconnections and violations. This theme of connections, disconnections, and violations is certainly central to our thinking about how we can connect across racial lines. What happens when our experience is validated by another in a mutually empathic relationship? We feel a strong sense of connection. But when we have experiences that are not validated, for example, when I as a black woman encounter racism and I am unable to talk about that experience with white colleagues, I may feel a sense of disconnection from them. Or should I choose to share those experiences and in fact find them invalidated by my colleagues, I may question my own perceptions. Without validation from others, I may choose to deny my own perceptions in order to avoid the isolation that comes from disconnection. Repeatedly separating myself from my own experience in order to stay in relationship with others ultimately results in a psychological state of violation. Negotiating the choices involved in maintaining connections across racial lines is a central focus of our dialogue . . . .

Andrea Ayvazian: . . . Beverly and I are venturing into new territory by offering an analysis of our own relationship as a case study of women connecting across racial lines. We want to speak very personally . . . [I]n traveling and doing speaking with Beverly, white women often stop me in hallways and restrooms and at the coffee machine and say, "You two seem so close. How did you create that bond?" . . . We are going to focus on the following three areas, which we call the critical junctures in our relationship: how the relationship was established, the theme of mutuality in our relationship, and difficult periods we have faced. A thread that is also woven into our talk is what we call "common differences," areas where there is sameness between us, where we have similar feelings, viewpoints, even experiences, and yet these similarities are expressed in different ways in our lives. We will close by talking about our friendship as a work in progress. . . .

CRITICAL JUNCTURES

Ayvazian: . . .

In many ways, my kinship with Beverly is *very* easy. Deep affection and admiration flows between us and the friendship is strong, nourishing, and treasured. However, it is also fair to say that nowadays any adult relationship that crosses racial lines is "not easy." If the friends are conscious of the social, political, and economic realities in this country today, their "kinship," . . . will inevitably have times that are "not easy." And we have faced those times.

NEXT STEPS

N
E
X
T

S
T
E
P
S

. . . Beverly and I do not live in the same neighborhood, although we live in the same town, and we do not work in the same place. Our children do not attend the same schools. We were brought together by an agency that does antiracism education, paired up as a biracial team to do some antiracism training at a college in the Boston area. We were brought together initially on a professional basis and immediately had the experience of preparing to work together as a team. . . . Beverly and I call that first professional collaboration, during which our relationship was formed, our "trial by fire." The group of college students with whom we were working proved to be a very challenging group. . . . Yet, this adversarial experience actually pulled us together as a twosome. Going into what turned out to be a hostile environment forced us to really scrutinize the material that we were presenting to the group.

Consequently, Beverly and I had the experience of talking very deeply about painful issues around race and racism very early in our professional/personal relationship. We had potentially difficult conversations analyzing racial inequity because we had to scrutinize the material we were presenting to this challenging group. These conversations in the first days of our relationship, we have discovered, are of the sort that biracial friendships sometimes avoid for months or years. Looking back on it now, we believe that this process was a bonding experience.

We also found that our rides to and from Boston were opportunities to talk not only about our work but about our personal lives. We discovered some common ground as women, as mothers, and as professionals in our community. Early on, Beverly was very helpful to me as I was going through a difficult period with my then 1-year-old son. We forged close personal ties through what was initially a professional connection.

Tatum: . . . As Andrea has told you, we don't live in the same neighborhood, our children don't go to the same school, and we don't worship in the same places; our lives are separate in many ways. Even though we frequently work together and certainly spend leisure time together now that our friendship has developed, our paths would not likely have crossed in other ways. Given the reality of social segregation, work does provide one of the few places where women of color and white women may come together across racial lines. So, it is not an accident that it was our work together that laid the groundwork for a friendship to develop.

. . . [O]ne of the things that has been very important is that at the beginning of our relationship there was an examination of our values as they related to the work that we did. We were forced to talk at a deeper level—not the superficial chitchat that you might engage with someone over the coffee machine—regarding what we thought about a very significant issue, in this case race relations in the United States. The mutuality that evolved in that relationship was very much in keeping with what Jean Baker Miller calls the "five good things." When a relationship is in fact mutually reinforcing, it gives you a feeling of increased zest, a sense of empowerment, greater self-knowledge, increased self-worth, and—most important in the context of a friendship—a desire for more connection (Miller, 1988). . . .

But as in all relationships, conflict arises. There certainly has been some conflict in our relationship, which we want to talk about, too, because it is also an important part of how one negotiates relationships that are going to be genuinely mutual. The most significant conflict, a real test of mutuality in our relationship, occurred when Andrea and I were conducting a workshop in St. Louis about 3 years ago. At that time, we were facilitating a workshop with a group of clergy on racism and, as we often do, we made reference to other "isms," including heterosexism. This topic . . . triggered a rather heated discussion about homosexuality in which a range of religious viewpoints were expressed. As we struggled to deal with this issue . . . Andrea and I became aware of the fact that we had differing strategies for interacting with our participants on this issue. While we were able to deal with that difference productively in the context of the workshop, as we were processing the event on the flight home we had a conversation that led to a real test of the mutuality in our relationship.

As background information for this incident, . . . I had just joined a church, which was a very important and significant step in my personal life, and as we talked about the controversy that had arisen in our workshop, we talked about the positions that our own religious communities had regarding homosexuality and heterosexism in the church. I am a member of a Presbyterian church. At this writing, that denomination is in the midst of a struggle around whether or not to ordain gay men and lesbian women. Andrea is a Quaker and belongs to a Meeting that is openly gay affirming and sanctions and supports same-sex commitment ceremonies. So our two worship communities have very different positions.

Andrea said to me that she didn't understand how I could be a part of a religious community that was exclusionary in the way that the Presbyterian church currently is, and in fact suggested that I should find another church. When she first said it, I was taken aback by the comment but had some trouble figuring out exactly what it was about it that bothered me. In fact, I shared her concern about the heterosexism in my denomination and in my local church. I have raised, and continue to raise, questions about this issue with my pastor and with fellow parishioners. On the other hand, my local congregation is a relatively progressive, predominantly black, Afrocentric congregation that is very affirming of my racial and spiritual identity . . . . I experienced Andrea's suggestion that I should leave this congregation as an affront. . . .

It occurred to me that there was really a lot of white privilege in her statement. As a black woman living in a predominantly white community, there are not many opportunities for me or my children to be part of a community where our African American heritage is explicitly affirmed. Consequently our Sunday worship experience in a congregation that defines itself as "unashamedly black and unapologetically Christian" is extremely valuable to me. I did feel that her statement that I should withdraw from this community was a statement of her white privilege. In fact, she was taking for granted the many churches or worship communities that she can choose from because almost all of them are predominantly white and will affirm her racial identity. . . . Her statement to me was a failure to recognize that privilege.

I felt that I had to say something to her about this. At the same time, I hesitated because this relationship was important to me and I did not want to alienate our friendship. Yet, it was a real juncture in terms of this issue of connections, disconnections and violations, because I could feel myself disconnecting. . . . In order for us to be able to maintain the growth and development of our relationship, certainly being able to talk about my spiritual journey and my worship community was an important point of connection that I needed to be able to maintain. I decided to share my perspective with Andrea, and I am happy to report that she responded in a very validating way. She simply listened to what I had to say and then said, "You're right."

Ayvazian: I want to speak to this because a potentially serious "disconnection" threatened our relationship—a relationship that had developed strong bonds, one that had become mutually important. When Beverly raised her feelings and concerns with me, two things went through my mind—two things that I knew she and I had said specifically to white people many times in the past! One was that when a person of color tells you something you have said or done is racist or reveals your inattention to white privilege, take a deep breath and begin by assuming she/he is correct until proven otherwise. The other point is that as white people strive to be strong white allies, we do not have to hold ourselves to a standard of perfection. It is impossible, given our socialization, our background, the struggle, the sensitivity, and the pain surrounding these issues, that we can be perfect white allies. I try to remember that I am not called to be perfect. I am called to be faithful and

NEXT STEPS

consistent on these issues. Beverly was exactly right. . . . I tried to follow the very advice that I had given to others. . . . That was an important juncture: a disconnection threatened, but we managed to talk it through.

There was another time that a disconnection threatened but was overcome by both of us being aware of what was going on in the relationship. This happened around the time of the Rodney King beating and the Simi Valley verdict in which the four Los Angeles police officers were acquitted. . . . In our shock and grief following the Simi Valley verdict, we essentially separated for a period of time and turned to different communities for comfort and support. Bev talked about her reactions to the events primarily with other African Americans. . . . In my own state of pain, shock, and anger, I found myself talking to two white men who I specifically called and met with, two men who identify as white allies. Meeting with them was the appropriate place for me to take my grief and do some healing and action planning in order to move forward.

. . .

Following the Simi Valley verdict it was appropriate for Beverly and me to separate for a while and immerse ourselves in our own groups to work on these issues. . . . This is an important point because white people can feel a loss, and even a sense of personal rejection, when this happens. . . . Beverly and I see these as normal, necessary, and even predictable after racial trauma. The bridges that have been built may be perfectly strong, but there still may be a need to separate for a time.

Tatum: I want to add just a few comments to what Andrea has said. In fact, the weekend when the events following the Simi Valley verdict were unfolding, I was at a small women's conference, a gathering of about 20 women, to which I had been invited. The only person I knew in the group was the woman who had invited me, and I was the only woman of color there. As we were arriving, everyone was very much aware of the riots that were unfolding in Los Angeles following the acquittal, and what struck me was the reluctance among the group to talk in any serious way about what was going on in Los Angeles. A few people expressed a need to talk about what was happening and what it meant for the country and for their own particular communities, but generally speaking the majority of the participants seemed to disregard these events as someone else's problem, not of concern to us as a group. I felt very alienated by that response, I have to say. Perhaps because I was with white women I didn't know, it did not feel like a safe place for me to completely engage. I was quite concerned about what was happening in communities of color in Los Angeles and in other parts of the country in response to this verdict. Yet I felt that my concern, a part of who I was, a part of my own perspective as an African American woman, could not be safely brought to this meeting. I certainly experienced that as very disconnecting, and in fact I went home early from the conference and declined the invitation to attend the following year.

Ayvazian: . . . White people often say to me, "It sounds like you two work together on issues of racism and talk about them very openly in your friendship, but are you, Andrea, always in the position of learner?" Beverly and I want to take a moment to remind all of us that each individual has multiple social identities. We feel this point is important because there are ways that Beverly and I are, in some areas of systematic oppression, both in the dominant category. We both receive the privilege or advantage, and we support each other in being strong allies. I am not always in the position of being dominant, and Beverly is not always in the position of being targeted. In the area of race inequity and racism—in that form of systematic oppression—I am clearly dominant. I receive the privilege, the unearned advantage and benefit of being white, and Beverly is targeted.

But there are other areas where Beverly and I are both targeted and areas where we are both dominant. We're both targeted as women, and we're both dominant as Christians, as heterosexuals, as able-bodied, as middle class. We felt it was useful to remember that as women we both feel targeted in groups of men where we are negotiating around money, for example. We are both disadvantaged systematically in a society that overvalues male attributes and characteristics. . . . The fact that we are both practicing Christians and women of faith and identify very strongly and publicly in that way means we are both dominant. We are not Jewish or Muslim. We are both able-bodied, both heterosexual, both middle-class women, and we offer each other support in remembering that we have a responsibility to interrupt anti-Semitism, to interrupt homophobia and heterosexism, to interrupt classism, and so on. . . .

. . .

COMMON DIFFERENCES

Ayvanzian: . . .

We are two mothers with school-age children who have many similarities but who have made some different choices, we believe, because of our racial difference. In particular, we have made different choices about the schooling for our sons and the environments we feel they need in order to thrive. My son is in a public school in our town and fits in well in his kindergarten class and in his school. During a parent–teacher conference this past spring, his teacher said to me, "Andrea, your son is just like a thousand other rambunctious, big-for-his-age 6-year-old boys that I have had in my teaching career." And I thought to myself, "I'm sure he is. I'm sure he doesn't stand out in very many ways. He's like a thousand other children that this woman has had in her long career of teaching kindergarten." In our predominantly white community, the same could not be said about Beverly's sons. . . .

Tatum: . . . Like many of the black families I interviewed and wrote about in my book, *Assimilation Blues: Black Families in a White Community* (Tatum, 1987), I have worried about how my children will be responded to by what has been to date an entirely white teaching staff (with the exception of an occasional student teacher of color). Though it may only be an illusion, I believe I have been able to exercise more control over my children's classroom experiences as a result of enrolling them in private schools. There have been times when I have felt that racial issues were present in both peer and teacher interactions, and both my husband and I have been actively involved in negotiating those issues with the school and our children.

The task of raising young African American children, especially boys, in contemporary society is not an easy one. My children are also big for their ages, but unlike for white boys for whom physical maturity is often a social advantage, being black and big for your age places you at some psychological risk: 7-year-old black boys may be thought of as cute; 14-year-old black boys are often perceived as dangerous. The larger you are, the sooner you must learn to deal with other people's negative stereotypes, and you may not yet be cognitively and emotionally mature enough to do so effectively. The smallness of their private school environment, where I can easily make myself known as a parent and where my children may be seen as individuals rather than representatives of a racial group, may offer some small margin of protection for them. They will need all the margin they can get. Though I am a product of public schools myself and I support quality public education, I have not regretted our decision to send our children to private schools.

. . .

CHOOSING THE MARGIN

The last point that we want to talk about as another example of common differences is what Beverly and I have come to call from "margin to center" or from "center to margin." Both of us have been influenced by the works of bell hooks, particularly *Feminist Theory: From Margin to Center* (1984), and Audre Lorde's work, *Sister Outsider*. . . . Beverly and I have remarkably similar political views. We share very similar progressive politics, but again in this area of common differences we have expressed our personal politics in different ways. . . . As a white, middle-class, heterosexual, able-bodied person, I receive considerable privilege in society. (I'm in so many dominant groups.) I start at the center where social, political, and economic power rests. Consequently, bell hooks's book, *Feminist Theory: From Margin to Center*, speaks to me, but in the reverse. I recognize that I start at the center and I feel called to move to the margin.

As I move to the margin, I try to take other progressive people, specifically in my case well-intentioned white people, with me into more progressive politics, living a more progressive agenda, choosing the margin. To accomplish this, I have made decisions like choosing, since 1981, to be a war tax resister, which means I don't pay a portion of my federal income tax every April; I make a public protest, objecting to the priorities reflected in the military portion of our federal budget and our ongoing preparation for and involvement in war. Also in my journey from center to margin, my life partner (who is male) and I have chosen not to sanctify our union and our love of each other in a formal wedding. Instead we had a ceremony of commitment that could be replicated exactly for same-sex couples. We made this decision so that we can advocate as allies to gay, lesbian, and bisexuals as a couple that has chosen in one small way not to accept heterosexual privilege. Because I start with so much privilege—so clearly at the center—these are two ways that I can move to the margin, stir up good trouble, and invite other people like me to question their politics and live their commitments to the principles they hold dear. . . . There are ways that because of my privilege I've had the luxury to step out of the center, to do what is unexpected and in some ways unacceptable. But I have not during the last 5 years suggested that Beverly make the same choices. . . . I recognize that my daily life is more advantaged and more comfortable than hers because of my color. Consequently, I do not advocate that she should choose war tax resistance. She expresses her political convictions in other ways. The same is true around formal marriage and same-sex unions. It has not been an issue for me and it has not been a source of disconnection for us that Beverly has made different choices for her behavior as a strong ally to gay men and lesbians. Her allied behavior is evident in other ways. . . .

Tatum: As Andrea said, this idea, from margin to center, has been important and I'd like to refer to a reading that I found very helpful from Letty M. Russell's book, *Church in the Round: Feminist Interpretation of the Church* (1993). She refers to the work of Audre Lorde and bell hooks, and uses this idea to make the following point. She says, "We make choices about moving from margin toward center or from center toward margin according to where we find ourselves in relation to the center of power and resources and the cultural and linguistic dominance in any particular social structure. Our connection to the margin is always related to where we are standing in regard to social privilege, and from that particular position we have at least three choices, not to choose, to choose the center, or to choose the margins" (p 192).

As Russell points out, our first choice is not to choose. If we make this choice, if we choose not to choose, we are essentially saying that those of us who are marginalized by gender, race, sexual orientation, class, or disability have the possibility of doing nothing. But, as she says, in so doing we internalize the oppression. I think that if we consider not choosing, if we think about internalizing our oppression and allowing ourselves to be defined as marginal, then we have in effect been psychologically violated. . . . because it forces us to disconnect from our own experience, to try to ignore and not name the particular alienation that we are exposed to in our society.

Our second choice . . . is to choose the center. She says, "those on the margin choosing the center do so by emulating the oppressors and doing everything to pass or to be like those who are dominant and be accepted by them" (p. 192). Whenever we make this choice we are choosing disconnection in the sense that we are saying, "Yes I want to be in relationship with you. If I have to deny certain aspects of my experience to do so, then I will. I will disconnect from that part of my experience in order to maintain my connection with you." . . .

Our third choice is for the margin. Here Russell says, "Those on the margin claim the margin by working in solidarity with others from the margin as they move toward the center. They seek a transformed society of justice where they will be empowered to share the center and no one will need to be marginalized" (p. 193). As I reflect on this choice, it seems to me this is the choice of connection. This is the choice of saying, "I will be connected to those who are able to acknowledge and affirm my experience in the world, who are able to stand on the margin with me." . . . Society can be transformed by those on the margin only if we "choose" the margin. Otherwise we collude in our own oppression and the oppression of others.

I choose to stand on the margin as someone who is defined by society as marginal in terms of my race and in terms of my gender. I also recognize that there are places where I am in the center and need to choose the margin because, as Andrea has already pointed out, there are places where I am dominant. But the primary point here is that those of us on the margin—or in the center—claim the margin by working in solidarity with others from the margin as they move toward the center. It is in this context that I can warmly embrace Andrea as my friend, as someone who has chosen to stand on the margin with me. . . .

Ayvazian: . . . We have forged a relationship that is not based on the false goal of color blindness. We recognize the differences in our life experiences and the difference that race makes in a relationship, and we have built a sturdy bridge across that divide.

In closing I want to share with you two lines of a Pat Parker poem called "For the White Person Who Wants to Know How to Be My Friend." The first two lines are as follows: "The first thing you do is forget that I'm black. Second, you must never forget that I'm black." Do I forget that Beverly is black? Sure I do. She is a dear friend with whom I spend time. Love, admiration, and affection flow between us. . . . But do I really forget that Beverly is black? Yes and no. . . . That is who she is in the world, and yes it is forgotten, and no it is not actually ever forgotten. But in the end, I have discovered that the issue . . . for me is, how I have come to understand social, political, and economic power and my unearned advantage and privilege as a white woman in a racist society. . . . It is my understanding of my own whiteness, not my response to her blackness, that allows me to interact with Beverly in a way that continues to foster mutuality, connection, and trust.

. . . Beverly calls us "partners in justice": shoulder to shoulder we move toward our goal. . . .

NEXT STEPS

24

FLEXing Cross-cultural Communication

Carmelita (Rosie) Castañeda

Multicultural competence is a phrase that acknowledges the ability of a person to communicate effectively across cultural boundaries with sensitivity to the cultural differences and preferences involved on both sides of those boundaries. Achieving multicultural competency challenges an individual to know his or her own culture and the cultures of others and to employ that knowledge by engaging people of other cultures in mutually gainful communication. Learning multicultural competency and sustaining its practice in our demographically changing society is imperative in order for people to live, communicate, and remain connected to one another.

Multicultural competence incorporates knowledge and skills that enable people to engage in culturally responsive ways of interacting and functioning in the world (Romney, 2002). It further incorporates the capacity for self-awareness and the ability to model this behavior to others. Cultural responsiveness is determined by many factors, including, but not limited to, people, cultures, situational contexts, environments, and school and work settings (Cheesebro, O'Conner, and Rios, 2006). All these factors impact the ability to communicate with one another from a culturally competent stance.

Writing on cross-cultural communication skills, Clyde W. Ford submits that causing an "us-versus-them" schism by reacting defensively to the speaker's emotional message is counterproductive (1994). However, when we step back from an interaction and reflect on its path, we can change the style of our understanding and response by listening to the speaker's message. Ford advises us to call the following approaches into service as we communicate cross-culturally: "build mutual understanding . . . bridge differences rather than insist on similarity of views . . . seek agreement through synthesis . . . [and] hold the parties you communicate with in the highest positive regard" (1994, 54). Such culturally responsive communication requires stepping back, depersonalizing the emotional content of the interchange, refraining from becoming defensive, and listening to the message by allowing people to express their thoughts freely, whether in a loud or soft voice, in anger or in frustration. It requires, perhaps most importantly, a willingness on the part of the listener to engage in this form of communication.

Accessing the level of cross-communication that authors such as Ford (1994) and Cheesebro, O'Conner, and Rios (2006) describe is a benchmark trait of multiculturally competent people. They are able to recognize that a person's own way of thinking and behaving is not the only way. Because they recognize that there are multiple paths to achieving goals, they are able to think and behave flexibly. Moreover, the sense that our universe is a place inhabited by multiplicity and diversity encourages in multiculturally competent people the ability to be comfortable with differences in others.

The FLEX model below was adapted from a training program developed by M. Arsenault, R. Castañeda and T. Williams (2001) that was used in the Office of Training and Development at the University of Massachusetts Amherst. This model offers suggestions for developing multicultural competence:

Foster interconnectedness
- Understand your own values, beliefs and practices

- Explore commonalities
- Assume the positive
- Recognize humanity

Listen and communicate
- Understand one's frame of reference
- Paraphrase ideas through describing; avoid judgment
- State ideas clearly and constructively

Encourage respect
- Treat others as they would like to be treated
- Consider working with people on their terms
- Preserve dignity

eXplore differences
- Ask questions
- Approach people, ideas, behaviors and actions with curiosity
- Approach ambiguity

This FLEX model provides an introductory tool and constant referent for understanding and practicing multicultural competency.

CONCLUSION

This FLEX model provides more than the upbeat thought processes promoted via its compact phrases. Behind each phrase crouches its behavior-affecting antithesis. For example, if we do not foster interconnectedness and listen and communicate, how can we arrive at an understanding of people of other cultures' values, beliefs, and practices? If we do not encourage respect and explore differences between cultures, how are we to rid our behavior of the anger-invoking insensitivities of communication that distance us from people of other cultures? Utilizing the genuinely effective communication filters, as well as the opportunity for thoughtful introspection and relearned behavior, offered in this FLEX model promotes access to multicultural competency. This tool may spark a motivation to frame words to those from other cultures in ways that engender mutual benefit. When we accomplish that, we inhabit the realm of multiculturally competent communicators.

25

The Personal is Political

Richard (Chip) Smith

Being involved in the struggle against white supremacy is, first, a personal decision. But how to connect one's everyday activities to the large-scale plan of action proposed in this book is not always clear. Doing so is essential, however, to building a movement—person by person, in a widening circle of activity and commitment.

Here are ten ways people can jump into things right where they are—wherever that might be—and, if already involved, how they can deepen that engagement:

1. **Become aware of privilege and internalized oppression.** Peggy McIntosh has a well-regarded exercise, "White Privilege: Unpacking the Invisible Knapsack," which helps European Americans understand how they are privileged by being white. McIntosh points out that people can be aware that others are worse off than they are; but these same people remain unaware—and the culture keeps them unaware—of how this situation translates into their benefiting from privileges themselves.

   "White privilege is like an invisible weightless knapsack of special provisions, maps, passports, codebooks, visas, clothes, tools and blank checks," comments McIntosh. She asks people to take stock of what they have in their own personal knapsacks and offers more than 25 examples—such as, "I can arrange to protect my children most of the time from people who might not like them," or "I am never asked to speak for all the people of my racial group." McIntosh notes that some items everyone in a decent society should be entitled to—things like "the expectation that neighbors will be decent to you, or that your race will not count against you in court." Other privileges confer power, like "My skin color [is] an asset for any move I . . . want to make," or white people are "morally neutral, normative, and average, and also ideal, so that when we work to benefit others, this is seen as work which will allow 'them' to be more like 'us.'"

   A similar exercise can be conducted by men, non-working class people, and heterosexuals to get at the specifics of male, class and hetero privileges. Coming from the opposite side, popular education methods developed by the Brazilian educator Paolo Freire, such as *Pedagogy of the Oppressed*, can help oppressed people gain insights into the social system where they live. Anger at oppressive conditions—which may be deeply internalized or bubbling near the surface—can turn into positive energy to transform society. Regardless of color or nationality, the common objective of these exercises is clarity—an awareness of social reality as it is and one's place in it. Without this kind of clarity, people's attempts to bring about change will likely remain unfocused and only occasionally effective.

2. **Build intentional relationships based on equality . . . .**

   A key element for these relationships to be beneficial for everyone is that they be based on equality. The burden here is on those with privilege to be primarily in a learning mode—being willing to examine the reality of their privilege together with others in the relationship. Ultimately the goal is to turn privilege—be it in education, social access, or material wealth—to everyone's advantage by making it available for use by the social justice movement.

   . . .

   Privilege also affects relationships through the deeply internalized feelings of confidence that people with privilege have—and which other very competent people sometimes lack. Important to building up this sense of confidence is the actual experience of struggle—fighting back, taking leadership—as well as coming to understand the historical and social roots of powerlessness.

3. **Study and discuss the history of peoples of color, as well as of white working class people. . . .** Developing personal relationships is essential; but there is also an obligation to learn other folks' history—and to do it on one's own time, so to speak, and not expect to be spoon-fed by friends.

   All these considerations apply to questions of class and gender as well. One goal . . . has been to approach these varied aspects of people in an intersectional way. . . . The movement is only beginning to create a common history of struggle

N E X T   S T E P S

that people of all nationalities can identify with. Learning each other's histories, and drawing on all our varied experiences, is essential to creating a collective memory appropriate to the emerging society the movement hopes to build.

4. **Question, talk about, and challenge the evidence of white supremacy all around us.** Simply putting into words an observation or a question can help people see more clearly what is going on—the composition of a meeting, people's body language, or who is interrupting whom. Questions are good because they leave the answer open and allow folks to respond freely. At the same time, when someone asks a question back, there is the opportunity to "tell it like it is"—or at least as it appears to you—simply and directly.

Resistance or non-cooperation are options when other people voice a snide comment about a certain part of town, a put-down of a particular class of people, or a color-coded joke. Ted Allen suggested one way to respond in this situation: "Oh, you must think I'm white?" Another is to point to a personal relationship with the targeted group—"Just so you know, my wife is a Chinese immigrant." And however one responds, the goal can be more than just silencing the speaker. Most desirable is being able to turn the conversation into a straightforward discussion of race and its role in society. Tim Wise gives an example from a conversation in a bar, when working to defeat David Duke in his campaign for governor of Louisiana in 1991, and concludes: "There are ways to talk to people" even truly tough cases, and make some headway, break down some defenses, get people to at least begin to question the things they have always taken for granted precisely because they have *never been challenged before* by anyone who looked like them." Finally Noel Ignatiev calls for people to become "race traitors":

. . .

In this spirit, one can be proactive by crossing the color line to hear a speaker, attend a holiday celebration, volunteer one's time, go to church, or take part in a discussion. At the same time, it is important to be sensitive about spaces that people of color reserve for themselves—but not jumping to such a conclusion based on little or no information. Discovering what is possible, and what is not, can feel a little risky, but being willing to step out of one's comfort zone is necessary to break down the social barriers that divide people. Still, the invasion and domination of other people's spaces is a real concern—and verges over into the larger issues of gentrification of neighborhoods and cultural appropriation.

Finally, the direct rejection of privilege can make sense at appropriate times—usually combined with organizing others to do the same. Examples include 1) a group of workers who turn down a raise aimed at undercutting their support for a union contract; or 2) the officers in the Civil War movie *Glory* refusing their pay until black soldiers received the same wages as the white soldiers.

5. **Take a good look at your home.** Paul Kivel, in *Uprooting Racism*, notes that people's homes are their most intimate spaces and they reflect who we are. One useful exercise is to look around and see what our home tell us about ourselves. The pictures on the walls, the books or magazines lying around—or their absence; the sound of conversations, TV shows, or music; the traffic in and out of children, friends, or activists; the smells of food, coffee or farmland—all these aspects of people's homes say something about who we are. There is no pre-judgment implied here, because homes depend in part on how much money folks have, their ages, and whether they live in the city, the suburbs, or the country. The point is, however, that if people profess to be against white supremacy, yet everything in their home reflects a white culture, then there is a disconnect. At the same time, there can be a downside here, too, in collecting—or appropriating as commodities—others' cultures. Consciously altering

the home environment, however, can reflect movement in a new direction—and can reinforce efforts to be consistent in one's values and to identify with a shared history of struggle. As Kivel notes, engaging children in this project can make it a learning experience for the next generation, too.

6. **Challenge white supremacy (sexism, homophobia) in family life.** A lot of emotional energy goes into maintaining the structure of relationships in a family. Raising questions about the internal culture—the humor, the assumptions about peoples of other races, or who does what tasks around the house—can stir up people's defenses. The challenge is to find ways to address these topics while still maintaining a connection with folks. For white people who become anti-racist activists—and in doing so break with their families to varying degrees—facing up to this responsibility is often difficult.

Two women from the South who broke with the white supremacist environment in which they grew up make this point. Mab Segrest, in *Memoirs of a Race Traitor*, tells how she came to accept her obligation to her family at the urging of African American mentors in North Carolina. Anne Braden, in *The Wall Between*, reflects on her own struggles with family members and the slow, almost imperceptible changes she saw in her father's attitudes over decades of loving struggle. Neither woman regrets her rejection of the dominant Southern ways and their values; and each sees her personal transformation as a necessary and liberating step forward. At the same time, by re-engaging with their families, both women were able to understand better the social sources of their parents' prejudices—and, in doing so, come to accept their folks' humanity, while continuing to hold up a mirror to offensive words and practices. Just as the family has a powerful ability to shape and contain a person; so too, once free from its negative influences, one can bring that same power to bear to reshape the family culture. The lessons learned in this most intimate struggle—and the sense of personal wholeness achieved—can radiate outward in relationships with friends, coworkers, and other activists.

7. **Take an inventory of activism in the community.** It can be helpful to look around to see who the grassroots activists are in the community—and then plug into what is going on. By being supportive, putting in the time, and establishing ties on the basis of joint work, people can learn the skills needed to bring about change. Building relationships with folks from different oppressed nationalities helps foster understanding and unity. And if of European descent, orienting oneself in this way helps ground a person's activism—providing a base from which to reach out and organize other white people.

If the community is homogeneous—as is the case with many white people, who overall tend to live in segregated communities—the basic approach can still be the same: seek out those who are active in a progressive way and then link up with them. The problem, however, is that when organizations are racially isolated—as in white suburbia or small-town rural areas—they can drift in directions that end up setting people against other grassroots folks. Efforts to improve suburban schools can pit people against the needs of oppressed nationality children in a nearby city. Or the children of immigrant farmworkers can be viewed as a drain on the state's education resources, rather than the asset they actually are to the community. For white organizers who do not have oppressed nationality people to orient themselves to, the challenge to stay ideologically grounded increases. Under such conditions, seeking out activists and movements of color—even if at some distance from where the person lives—can be important to keeping one's bearings.

8. **Be intentional about building a base for activism at the workplace.** For most people who want to be active, it has to be right where they happen to be at that moment

in their lives. For others, especially students or youth who are not already tied to a job or a community, there can be an element of freedom to shape where they spend their working life. One possibility is to select a workplace based on its potential as an organizing site—by considering the make-up of the workforce, its history of struggle, and the degree to which the workers share connections to a particular town or neighborhood. Then, rather than getting a job, say, as a union staffperson—where the relationships with workers are less direct—one can hire on as a rank-and-file worker for the long haul. On this basis of equality with others, an organizer can then build ties with co-workers over time in a way that fits with the strategic front against white supremacy . . . .

9. **Examine other aspects of life to see if changes would favor increased activism.**

- **Where you live:** perhaps a house or apartment in a different community would enable the building of intentional relationships and a social base for activism.
- **The church, synagogue, sangha, or other religious institution you might attend:** possibilities for increased social engagement might flow from proposing a project or, where necessary, by making a change to a different gathering.
- **The amount of TV watched:** maybe a different pattern of activity would free up some time for activism, for a progressive book club, or for a class at the local community college.
- **One's physical condition:** working out, a basketball league, karate or other activity can help keep a person physically fit and more prepared to take on the challenges of an activist's life. Also, the older a person gets, the more important such activity is so that one can bring all the accumulated wisdom of a lifetime to bear for social change.
- **Where and with whom one socializes:** one of the most segregated spaces in the United States—along with people's religious activities—is where folks relax and enjoy leisure activities. Perhaps other options are available—new places to visit, or new friends to go out with or have over.
- **Learning a new language:** with the increase of immigrants of color in the United States, learning a second language like Spanish, Tagalog, or Haitian Creole is nearly a necessity for anyone who wants to be effective in opposing white supremacy.

Generally, the idea is to look at all the ways one might free up time and develop the ability to be more intentionally engaged with others. Having an overarching political perspective is important, too, since it can help a person see the link between everyday activities and the long-term goal of social transformation. The challenge is for people to take responsibility for their lives, be aware of how they spend their time, and make the best use of whatever freedom—or privilege—they may have.

10. **Finally, what if people are just too busy or overwhelmed by trying to hold everything together?** What if they feel they can't change anything, that they will never be effective as a change agent, or that everyone out there is already doing about what they can anyway? The key here is probably not to "do" anything, but just to be open—to people's history, to really seeing what is going on in one's life, to new relationships, and to new kinds of conversation. This society being the way it is, just about everything a person does is tied in somehow with color, class, and gender. A starting point is to keep one's eyes and ears open—along with one's heart and mind—and see what happens.

NEXT STEPS

CLASSISM

Introduction

Maurianne Adams

As I write this in early May 2009, the global economy remains in deep recession, Chrysler and GE are in bankruptcy, financial markets frozen, and a crisis of confidence has seriously weakened business productivity and undermined international trade. We hear about staggering layoffs with 5.1 million out of work in the past year, 8.5 percent of the workforce with 10 percent unemployment in several states, and 18 percent unemployment for recently discharged military veterans.[1] Millions of U.S. families are today caught in the pernicious cycle of job loss, home foreclosure, and personal bankruptcy.

GLOBAL ECONOMIC CONTEXT: MARKETS AND LABOR

The collapse of financial and credit markets has affected everyone from Main Street(s) to Wall Street(s) in a global context where "Wall Street" also refers to financial networks linking New York and Los Angeles to London, Paris, Berlin, Tokyo, and Shanghai. Similarly, the financial consequences for Main Street extend from Big City and Small Town, USA, to the people of Iceland whose national assets disappeared in the collapse of the high finance bubble. The international and local impacts of venture capitalism have recently become clear in the collapse of global financial markets, economic recession, and unemployment. Other examples of geo-capitalism include the U.S. dependency on international gas and oil supplies, or the geo-economics that "supply" heroin from South Asia and South America, trafficked through international drug refineries, laboratories, and competing drug cartels, and then back to the U.S. "market demand" for drug highs. Global capitalism is deeply implicated in the extremes of global wealth and poverty, as readings in this section will illustrate, for example selection 33 on international sex traffic.

WIDENING U.S. GAP AMONG SOCIAL CLASSES

The Main Street/Wall Street connection is vivid for anyone who is, or knows someone, facing home foreclosure, personal bankruptcy, and unemployment, unable to get a car loan or a line of credit, or afford college tuition. Internet blogs, television, and newspapers report escalating economic shockers—Ponzi schemes (Bernie Madoff and others) and high-flying CEOs requesting bailout money. Public outrage is ignited by the millions of dollars in taxpayer money paid out for bonuses to executives responsible for the arcane financial practices that triggered the economic disaster in the first place (AIG, Goldman Sachs, Freddie and Fannie Mae) when ordinary people are being laid off, unable to get full-time jobs, and losing their health insurance.

These events have brought discussions of class inequity and classism, long an uncomfortable or taboo conversational topic, out into the open. For the purposes of this section we use Leondar-Wright and Yeskel's definition of class as "a relative social ranking based on income, wealth, education, status, and power" (Leondar-Wright and Yeskel 2007, 314). We also use their definition of classism to refer to "The institutional, cultural, and individual set of practices and beliefs that assign differential value to people according to their socioeconomic class; and an economic system that creates excessive inequality and causes basic human needs to go unmet" (Leondar-Wright and Yeskel 2007, Appendix C).

It is less true now than it was one or two years ago, that "people in the United States don't like to talk about class" (selection 26). It is no longer considered subversive or "socialist" to point out the glaring differences of class location or social networks and economic resources, or to notice the dramatic disparities between bailouts for banks contrasted with bankruptcies for ordinary citizens, or policies that consider executive bonus contracts sacrosanct at the same moment that automobile worker union contracts are being stripped and renegotiated.

Persistent inequality on the basis of social and economic class has generally been glaringly visible but difficult to acknowledge in the United States, possibly because of our belief in meritocracy (that hard work and talent will be rewarded), possibly because we equate our democratic system of political equality with a capitalist system based on equality of economic opportunity. Yet the contemporary data, some of it presented through readings in this section, point both to growing economic disparities and to pervasive, historically based inequality of economic opportunities—well before the present recession made them so obvious. The historical record will show that the gap between rich and poor in the United States has more than doubled since 1977; that the historical legacy of racism plays a powerful role in shaping economic success; that the richest fifth accounts for 86 percent of private consumption; and that the Census Bureau is now having to revise downward its poverty threshold in order to accurately reflect current economic realities. In the light of these prospects, it is difficult if not impossible to maintain that poverty can be solved by meritocracy or social mobility alone (that is, the Horatio Alger myth of pulling oneself up by one's bootstraps—as if everyone had boots, let alone boots with straps), or that the poor and unemployed are wholly to blame for their condition.

ECONOMIC, SOCIAL, AND CULTURAL DIMENSIONS OF CLASS: WEALTH AND INCOME, SOCIAL, AND CULTURAL–INTELLECTUAL CAPITAL

Understanding the markers of social economic class is complicated by the different social, intellectual, political, and economic networks for which class privilege provides ready access. For example, the stereotypical superiority of "old money" to "new money" assumes class privilege based on the intergenerational accumulation of wealth as distinct from "self-made millionaires" and looks up to established upper-class status (as distinct from "newcomers"), and to family traditions of elite education, international travel, private clubs, political and corporate leadership, membership on corporate or non-profit Boards of Directors, domestic servants, and professional serving staffs. Thus the indicators of class privilege include *wealth* based on long term investments rather than the uncertainties of *wages* based on labor (this includes the vagaries of high-paid sports or celebrity wages). But the indicators, as in the examples above, also include social and intellectual "capital" that is closely related to economic capital yet distinct from it (and for some "old" or "established" families even entirely separate—as with the loss of economic capital but not the loss of social or intellectual capital).

These distinctive aspects of class privilege are important to notice. By *economic capital,* we generally refer to wealth enhanced by income (as in selections 26 and 28). *Social capital* means access to social resources (elite education, health care, political connections, "white shoe" legal representation) and valuable personal networks that ensure and enhance professional mobility, corporate profits, political leadership. Intellectual and cultural capital refer to a person's knowledge of how to leverage the major social institutions—such as education, the law, the political system, the health-care system—and "who one knows" in order to access these resources for personal benefit. Indicators of intellectual and cultural capital include "proper" accent and speech that indicate sophistication and education (as distinct from regional or ethnic-based accent or speech), an understated but expensive and preferably hand-sewn wardrobe, "good" neighborhood addresses, expensive and tasteful home furnishings.

In this section, "Class in America" (selection 26) presents contrasting class-based portraits that highlight some of the differences in social–cultural capital as well as family wealth and personal income. "At the Elite Colleges" (selection 30) and "The Debt-for-Diploma System" (selection 31) connect social and intellectual–cultural capital as well as economic capital to higher education admissions and affordability. "Race, Wealth and Equality" (selection 28) notes the historical circumstances that have racialized disparities in the accumulation of wealth. In "White Poverty: The Politics of Invisibility" (selection 37), bell hooks portrays the nuanced dynamics of social and cultural capital in her rural southern small town, based on race and complicated by class.

SOCIAL AND PSYCHOLOGICAL DIMENSIONS OF CLASS MYTHS AND STATUS

Another obstacle to our acknowledging the importance of class and classism is the United States is the internalization, by those privileged as well as those disadvantaged by class, of deeply held denials that class exists in the United States—that the building of the United States by (white) European migrants created a classless society (or, perhaps, a middle-class society) that threw off the shackles of class distinctions from the "Old World." (This myth is not widely shared by communities of color in the United States, for many of whom the intersections of racism with class disadvantage is their primary experience.) Most important in the widely-held denial of classism in the United States is a belief in meritocracy and its reverse, the shaming and blaming of those who are economically unsuccessful, seen as failures through no fault but their own. It is not difficult to see how the myth of meritocracy—the belief that it was hard work alone that enabled generations of European immigrants to become middle- and professional class—became ingrained in the U.S. American identity. This myth celebrates the opportunities for success by European colonists and settlers who arrived with economic, racial, and cultural assets and advantage, and it obscures the racial disadvantage for Native American nations confined on reservations, African American descendents of slaves and debt peonage, and Mexican American and Asian victims of wage inequity and unfair labor practices. These points are documented in reading selections by Oliver and Shapiro, Dyson, Bauer, and Romero (selections 28, 34–36)—and to them we add the economic, social, and cultural challenges experienced by people with disabilities (selection 32).

The master narrative still taught in most schools suggests an inevitable, stepwise progress by (white) immigrants into the middle class, and it obscures (or denies) parallel narratives of class revolt and violent suppression of labor organizing and union resistance to inadequate wages, child labor, unpaid overtime, unsafe working conditions—by white working-poor immigrants who worked the mines and the railroads, often Irish and Italian and Eastern European (Loewen 1995; Takaki 1993; Zinn 1995). Most students know nothing of the achievements of the union movement that gave the United States its weekends and outlawed child labor (with the exception of migrant children, see selection 35). This important history cannot be adequately reflected in this section, and resources for further study about the union movement are suggested on the section website.

As with other forms of oppression that play out on the social and cultural levels (as well as institutional and individual levels), the stereotypes that allocate praise for economic success and blame economic failure are so deeply ingrained that they have become internalized by people who are advantaged and disadvantaged alike. The deep shame that accompanies insults such as "white trash" (as described by bell hooks, selection 37) are internal wounds that continue to fester. The consequences of internalized classism are suggested in selections 38, 39, 41, and 42—while the concept of internalized advantage and disadvantage is explained in an earlier section (selection 4).

The meritocratic myth that hard work and talent lead to middle-class status, if not wealth, is also based on a widespread confusion between *democracy* and *capitalism.* The democratic myth that every child (male) can grow up to be President is conflated with the capitalist myth that every child (also male) can become rich by hard work and talent. *Democracy* has characterized the United States since its founding, although limited at its inception to the white, male, propertied, landowning colonial elite. Democracy is a *political* system, characterized by basic freedoms and a representative system (not egalitarian) of decision-making. Struggle has attended each new broadening of representative democracy—to African Americans, to women, to Native Americans, and through changes in the meanings that attach to "whiteness," through naturalization to immigrants (Haney Lopez 1996). But *democracy*, a political system, is not the same as *capitalism*, an economic system characterized by the private ownership of capital (land, buildings, factories, and the labor of others). Early and mid-nineteenth-century American capitalism was built on the displacement of Native Americans, the enslavement of Africans, the peonage of Chinese workers, and the wage exploitation of generations of immigrants from Europe, Asia, and the Americas (Steinberg 1989; Takaki 1993). That democracy and capitalism are thought to be one and the same is another of our myths, and it stifles open, honest discussion about class differences and economic inequities.

INTERSECTIONS OF CLASS WITH OTHER FORMS OF PRIVILEGE AND DISADVANTAGE

It is obvious that every person experiences either privilege or disadvantage on the basis of class position as shaped and complicated by race and racism, gender and sexism, ability or disability and ableism, youth or elder status and ageism or adultism. The ways in which class is shaped by and intersects with other social identities are noted throughout this volume, in readings that show how economic, social, and intellectual–cultural capital (or the lack) are linked to the feminization of poverty and the special vulnerability of women, children, migrants, the disabled, youth, and elders. For example, the connections between classism and racism are clearly delineated in selections 11, 15, 28, 34, and 35; between classism and religious oppression in selections 55 and 56; between classism and sexism in selections 33, 35, 70, and 73; and between classism and ableism in selections 32, 104, and 111. We urge that readers use the Table of Intersections to locate these and other specific reading selections that connect classism with other social justice topics.

One dimension of class—it might be seen as a dimension of social capital—has to do with the powerful role of the medical profession and medical technologies in shaping current understandings and experience of people who define themselves as transgender, people with disabilities, youth, and elders. Selections 88, 89, and 91 show the impact of professional medical terminology and technologies on the choices available to transgender people. Selections 99–101 and 104 extend the analysis of economic, social, and intellectual–cultural capital to the construction of disability and the economic, social, cultural challenges experienced by people with disabilities. Selections 116 and 117 illustrate multiple interconnections between class, ageism and adultism, and racism.

CONTENTS OF THIS SECTION

The reading selections in this section reflect the main issues outlined in this introduction, although not the incredibly rapid pace of economic change at the present moment—a pace of change that affects individuals' and families' economic resources, social status, and social location (see website for updates). The conceptual frameworks presented in section 1 are applicable to many of these selections—most notably the "levels of oppression" (individual, institutional, cultural/societal) and the "five faces of oppression" (presented in section 1, selections 4 and 5). For example, "What has Debt Got to do With it" and "The Debt-for-Diploma System" (selections 29 and 31) illustrate how class aspirations toward upward mobility have been exploited by financial institutions that enrich themselves, but not their customers. Selections 28 and 34 focus on the long-term consequences of institutional and societal classism compounded by racism, and call attention to the marginalization, powerlessness, and violence that result, whether the immediate cause is a "natural" disaster such as Katrina, or the cumulative legacy of historical federal policies. Selections 33 and 35 provide further graphic examples of classism played out through the institutional and cultural "levels" and also through the "faces" of sexual and economic exploitation, political powerlessness, and violence. Selection 38 suggests the emergence of counternarratives of power in the face of economic and social powerlessness.

The first ten selections in this section present Contexts for discussions of class and classism. In selection 26, Mantsios notes the pervasive belief that the United States is classless or, its twin, that everyone is middle class. He shows how this myth is undermined by dramatic differences of class status and opportunity in the United States. He presents composite "portraits" of upper-class and middle-class opportunities contrasted with working-poor constraints. In selection 27, Collins and Yeskel portray the consequences of these disparities, such as the loss of health insurance, rising personal and family debt, job loss, or reduction to part-time work—disparities that have become only more devastating in recent months. They use graphic visual representations to convey the "color" of wealth, how wealth is—and was—concentrated, and top/bottom differences in the ownership of U.S. household wealth. Oliver and Shapiro (selection 28) show how black/white wealth inequality has deep historical roots in generations of structured, race-based economic inequality. It depicts historical moments in which federal policies structured black poverty on the one hand, and white opportunities on the other—for example, the availability of the 1950s GI Bill education grants and Fair Housing Administration suburban housing loans along racial lines, with intergenerational consequences for home ownership and home equity that extend to the present day. Although the emphasis in this selection is on white/black racial patterns in wealth, this kind of historical exploration can serve as a template for identifying the obstacles that held back economic and social mobility for other U.S. communities of color as well.

"What has Debt Got to do With it?" and "The Debt Trap" (selections 29 and 40) present portraits and consequences of the increasing personal debt overload on individuals and families. "What has Debt Got to do With it?" looks at the poverty debt market in which high-interest, debt-generating businesses generate a $5 billion-a-year trade for international chain financial services through the deceptive practices and lush profits of so-called "easy credit" pawnshops, rent-to-own stores, and credit-card vendors. It shows how these poverty-exploiting storefronts advertise "refund anticipation loans," E-Z credit, and check-cashing services while piling on fees and interest rates that are profitable only to the banks and chains that operate them. "The Debt

Trap: Given a Shovel, Americans Dig Deeper into Debt" is part of a series (see resources on the website) which, in this case, zeros in on the personal experience of a white, middle-aged, middle-class woman overwhelmed by divorce, credit card debt, mortgage increases, illness and medical emergencies.

Debt burden is also the theme in selections 30–32, which juxtapose the opportunities with disadvantage, building on the comparisons shown by Mantsios in selection 26 and, taken together, demonstrating how access to higher education has increasingly become "classed," especially as costs skyrocket (122 percent increase in public tuition from 1986–2007), as states decrease their subsidies for public higher education, as federal Pell grants are cut, and as funding of education becomes loan-based, leaving college graduates with huge debts at a time of rising unemployment and underemployment. The financial struggles experienced by college students from low-income families are compounded in the case of students with disabilities (selection 32), who often come from families with low incomes—37 percent, compared with 20 percent of non-disabled peers. Further, students with disabilities struggle with costs for needed professional services—counselors, physical therapists, assistive devices, personal assistants, and a host of other expenses not covered by funding sources.

Some of the readings in Contexts (selections 32–35) highlight the mutually reinforcing negative effects of disability, sexism, and racism intersecting with class and exacerbating its personal destructiveness. Landesman's exposé (selection 33, "The Girls Next Door") of sex trafficking presents an extreme instance of the intersection of gender with class in its horrific account of the sex market for young, uneducated, immigrant women from Eastern Europe and the southern Americas, between 30,000 and 50,000 of whom are sex slaves "hiding in plain sight" in forced captivity in the United States at any given time. Selection 34 revisits the intersection of racism with poverty revealed by Hurricane Katrina, a "natural disaster" that exposed our obliviousness toward and neglect of the endemic, concentrated poverty in the hardest-hit south coastal regions. Selection 35 reports the chronic abuse of female migrant tomato workers in the southeast United States and farm owners' preferences for young male workers (intersecting class with gender), their use of unpaid children working 16–18 hours per week to "help out" their parents as well as discrimination against older workers and women; and the class/race exploitation of non-English-speaking, often non-legal, migrant, seasonal workers whose employers are often their landlords who threaten them with eviction and deportation if they dare stand up for their rights.

Five selections in Voices express both privileged and disadvantaged class position, compounded by racism and sexism. In selection 36, African American and migrant women of color in domestic service are quoted at length about their experiences of exploitation and powerlessness. They vividly describe their domestic isolation, the replay in their workloads of devalued gendered household labor, and their experiences of racial and class insult. In selection 37, bell hooks describes the complex race/class hierarchies of her southern rural childhood apartheid, in which poor Whites cling to their racial advantage and power over Blacks, and in which Whites with class privilege scorn Whites without. "Saint" (selection 38) depicts an inner-city northern childhood in which personal and gang hierarchies are based on gendered violence, fear, and respect. Selection 39 presents snapshots of privilege and wealth based on family advantage, white privilege, cultural capital, social networks, and family legacies derived from a U.S. legacy of land theft, slavery, and exploitation—as well as hard work, monetary investment, education, and good luck. In contrast, selection 40 presents a woman's downward spiral out of marginal middle-class status because of her ballooning credit card and mortgage debt, accelerated by her illness and medical debt in the absence of health insurance.

There are clear implications throughout this section for positive social change, as in the advocacy role taken by the Immigrant Justice Project of the Southern Poverty Law Center (whose testimony is presented in selection 35) or the call for investigation and prosecution of sex traffickers under the Trafficking Victims Protection Act of 2000, or the Protect Act of 2007 (selection 33). Different forms of class exploitation and abuse require remedies at different economic and institutional levels—in the case of the seasonal farmworkers, for example, existing protective legislation (minimal wage, overtime, health and safety, mandatory education) has specific exemptions for farmworkers and those exemptions should be removed at state and federal levels. In addition to legislative changes, strengthened farmworkers unions would be able to negotiate more effectively with agribusinesses, and judicial enforcement of anti-slavery and anti-peonage laws would protect vulnerable, migrant workers. In response to every selection, there are clear steps that can be taken toward legal or institutional remedy, and toward greater equity and empowerment.

The Next Steps selections in this section focus on political, community, and classroom efforts to correct injustice and create greater educational equity. The emphasis in this section on cross-class coalition building points to the importance of class awareness, especially among middle-class people who have thought about class. Selection 41 quotes personal examples of the everyday classism that makes it so difficult for people with assumed privilege to work effectively in cross-class organizations and coalitions, and selection 42 asks questions that will elicit from readers their own examples of internalized class privilege. Selection 43 places participants in advocacy roles for the competing claims at fictional "Sunnyvale Nursing Home" to higher wages for CEOs, doctors, nurses, aides, kitchen workers, security guards, janitors, and gardeners, with all of these wage claims in further competition with subsidies for fixed- and low-income patients or elderly on nursing home waiting lists. Having presented the arguments and advocated for these different roles and positions, participants must then become decision-makers—noting that in a unionized workplace, everyone would vote, and that in a non-union workplace, these would be CEO decisions. This selection illustrates the possibilities for interactive classroom simulations and discussions, as the "participants" described in the activity would presumably be classroom students or workshop colleagues.

Further Next Steps dealing with classism and other social justice issues can be found in other sections of this book, such as selection 59, which describes a faith-based coalition organized on behalf of tenant's rights, and selection 111, which proposes facilitating the transition to college for students without cultural capital. The catastrophic debt triggered by lack of health insurance (selection 40) is addressed by the "National Latina Institute for Reproductive Health's Statement on Healthcare for All" (selection 74).

The final section "Working for Social Justice: Visions and Strategies for Change" has several selections with direct relevance to classism—"What Can We Do?", "Social Struggle," "Unite and Rebel! Challenges and Strategies in Building Alliances," and "Top 10 Youth Activism Victories" (selections 131, 134, 137, 138).

All selections in this section raise questions, challenges, and possibilities for change, that go well beyond the limits of this section. We encourage all readers—instructors and students—to turn to the website for further references and resources, for related discussion questions and classroom activities, and for consideration of some of the challenges and opportunities that could emerge from discussion of the readings in this and other sections.

Notes

1 Abraham, M. R., Wheeler, B., Keohone, E. (March 6, 2009), "Portraits of America's Recession," *ABC News* (http://abcnews.go.com/print?id=7024989); Alvarez, L. (November 18, 2008), "New Veterans Hit Hard by Economic Crisis," *The New York Times* (http://www.nytimes.com/2008/11/18/us); Armour, S. (April 16, 2009), "Foreclosures Take a Big Jump," *USA Today*; Bernard, T. S., Anderson, J. (November 16, 2008), "Bankruptcies by Consumers Climb Sharply," *The New York Times*; Lewis M., Einhorn, D. (January 4, 2009), "The End of the Financial World as We Know It," *The New York Times*.

References

Haney Lopez, I. F. (1996). *White by Law: The Legal Construction of Race.* New York: New York University Press.

Leondar-Wright, B., Yeskel, F. (2007). "Classism Curriculum Design." In M. Adams, L. A. Bell, P. Griffin (eds), *Teaching for Diversity and Social Justice*, 2nd edition. New York: Routledge. pp. 308–333. Appendix C on CD-ROM. (See section website for these materials.)

Loewen, J. W. (1995). "The Land of Opportunity." In *Lies My Teacher Told Me: Everything Your American History Textook Got Wrong.* New York: Simon & Schuster. pp. 200–213.

Steinberg, S. (1989). *The Ethnic Myth: Race, Ethnicity, and Class in America* (updated edition). Boston: Beacon Press.

Takaki, R. (1993). *A Different Mirror: A History of Multicultural America.* Boston: Little, Brown, & Co.

Zinn, H. (1995). *A People's History of the United States* (revised and updated edition). New York: Harper & Row.

26

Class in America—2006

Gregory Mantsios

People in the United States don't like to talk about class. Or so it would seem. We don't speak about class privileges, or class oppression, or the class nature of society. . . . For the most part, avoidance of class-laden vocabulary crosses class boundaries. There are few among the poor who speak of themselves as lower class; instead, they refer to their race, ethnic group, or geographic location. Workers are more likely to identify with their employer, industry, or occupational group than with other workers, or with the working class.

Neither are those at the other end of the economic spectrum likely to use the word "class." In her study of thirty-eight wealthy and socially prominent women, Susan Ostrander asked participants if they considered themselves members of the upper class. One participant responded, "I hate to use the word 'class.' We are responsible, fortunate people, old families, the people who have something." Another said, "I hate [the term] upper class. It is so non-upper class to use it. I just call it 'all of us,' those who are wellborn."

. . .

There are, however, two notable exceptions to this phenomenon. First, it is acceptable in the United States to talk about "the middle class." Interestingly enough, such references appear to be acceptable precisely because they mute class differences. References to the middle class by politicians, for example, are designed to encompass and attract the broadest possible constituency. Not only do references to the middle class gloss over differences, but these references also avoid any suggestion of conflict or injustice.

This leads us to the second exception to the class-avoidance phenomenon. We are, on occasion, presented with glimpses of the upper class and the lower class (the language used in "the wealthy" and "the poor"). In the media, these presentations are designed to satisfy some real or imagined voyeuristic need of "the ordinary person." . .

We are left with one of two possibilities: either talking about class and recognizing class distinctions are not relevant to U.S. society, or we mistakenly hold a set of beliefs that obscure the reality of class differences and their impact on people's lives. Let us look at four common, albeit contradictory, beliefs about the United States.

Myth 1: The United States is fundamentally a classless society. Class distinctions are largely irrelevant today, and whatever differences do exist in economic standing, they are—for the most part—insignificant. Rich or poor, we are all equal in the eyes of the law, and such basic needs as health care and education are provided to all regardless of economic standing.

Myth 2: We are, essentially, a middle-class nation. Despite some variations in economic status, most Americans have achieved relative affluence in what is widely recognized as a consumer society.

Myth 3: We are all getting richer. The American public as a whole is steadily moving up the economic ladder, and each generation propels itself to greater economic well-being. Despite some fluctuations, the U.S. position in the global economy has brought previously unknown prosperity to most, if not all, Americans.

Myth 4: Everyone has an equal chance to succeed. Success in the United States requires no more than hard work, sacrifice, and perseverance: "In America, anyone can become a millionaire; it's just a matter of being in the right place at the right time."

In trying to assess the legitimacy of these beliefs, we want to ask several important questions. Are there significant class differences among Americans? If these differences do exist, are they getting bigger or smaller, and do these differences have a significant impact on the way we live? Finally, does everyone in the United States really have an equal opportunity to succeed?

THE ECONOMIC SPECTRUM

Let's begin by looking at difference. An examination of available data reveals that variations in economic well-being are, in fact, immense. Consider the following:

- The wealthiest 1 percent of the American population holds 34 percent of the total national wealth. That is, they own over one-third of all the consumer durables (such as houses, cars, and stereos) and financial assets (such as stocks, bonds, property, and savings accounts). The richest 20 percent of Americans hold nearly 85 percent of the total household wealth in the country.
- Approximately 183,000 Americans, or approximately three-quarters of 1 percent of the adult population, earn more than $1 million **annually**. There are nearly 400 billionaires in the U.S. today, more than three dozen of them worth more than $10 billion each. It would take the average American (earning $35,672 and spending absolutely nothing at all) a total of 28,033 years (or approximately 400 lifetimes) to earn just $1 billion.

Affluence and prosperity are clearly alive and well in certain segments of the U.S. population. However, this abundance is in contrast to the poverty and despair that is also prevalent in the United States. At the other end of the spectrum:

- Approximately 13 percent of the American population—that is, nearly one of every eight people in this country—live below the official poverty line (calculated in 2004 at $9,645 for an individual and $19,307 for a family of four). An estimated 3.5 million people—of whom nearly 1.4 million are children—experience homelessness in any given year.
- Approximately one out of every five children (4.4 million) in the United States under the age of six lives in poverty.

The contrast between rich and poor is sharp, and with nearly one-third of the American population living at one extreme or the other, it is difficult to argue that we live in a classless society. Big-payoff reality shows, celebrity salaries, and multi-million dollar lotteries notwithstanding, evidence suggests that the level of inequality in the United States is getting higher. Census data show the gap between the rich and the poor to be the widest since the government began collecting information in 1947 and that this gap is continuing to grow. In 2004 alone, the average real income of 99 percent of the U.S. population grew by little more than 1 percent, while . . . the richest 1 percent saw their income rise by 12 percent in the same year.

Nor is such a gap between rich and poor representative of the rest of the industrialized world. In fact, the United States has by far the most unequal distribution of household income. The income gap between rich and poor in the United States (measured as the percentage of total income held by the wealthiest 20 percent of the population versus the poorest 20 percent) is approximately 12 to 1, one of the highest ratios in the industrialized world. The ratio in Japan and Germany, by contrast, is 4 to 1.

Reality 1: There are enormous differences in the economic standing of American citizens. A sizable proportion of the U.S. population occupies opposite ends of the economic spectrum. In the middle range of the economic spectrum:

- Sixty percent of the American population holds less than 6 percent of the nation's wealth.
- While the real income of the top 1 percent of U.S. families skyrocketed by more than 180 percent between 1979 and 2000, the income of the middle fifth of the population grew only slightly (12.4 percent over that same 21-year period) and its share of income (15 percent of the total compared to 48 percent of the total for the wealthiest fifth) actually declined during this period.
- Regressive changes in governmental tax policies and the weakening of labor unions over the last quarter century have led to a significant rise in the level of inequality between the rich and the middle class. Between 1979 and 2000, the gap in household income between the top fifth and middle fifth of the population rose by 31 percent. During the economic boom of the 1990s, the top fifth of the nation's population saw their share of net worth increase (from 59 to 63 percent) while four out of five Americans saw their share of net worth decline. . . .

The level of inequality is sometimes difficult to comprehend fully by looking at dollar figures and percentages. To help his students visualize the distribution of income, the well-known economist Paul Samuelson asked them to picture an income pyramid made of children's blocks, with each layer of blocks representing $1,000. If we were to construct Samuelson's pyramid today, the peak of the pyramid would be much higher than the Eiffel Tower, yet almost all of us would be within six feet of the ground. . . .

Reality 2: The middle class in the United States holds a very small share of the nation's wealth and that share is declining steadily. The gap between rich and poor and between rich and the middle class is larger than it has ever been.

AMERICAN LIFE-STYLES

At last count, nearly 37 million Americans across the nation lived in unrelenting poverty. Yet, as political scientist Michael Harrington once commented, "America has the best dressed poverty the world has ever known." Clothing disguises much of the poverty in the United States, and this may explain, in part, its middle-class image. With increased mass marketing of "designer" clothing and with shifts in the nation's economy from blue-collar (and often better-paying) manufacturing jobs to white-collar and pink-collar jobs in the service sector, it is becoming increasingly difficult to distinguish class differences based on appearance.

Beneath the surface, there is another reality. Let's look at some "typical" and not-so-typical life-styles.

Name: **Harold S. Browning**

Father: manufacturer, industrialist

Mother: prominent social figure in the community

Principal child-rearer: governess

Primary education: an exclusive private school on Manhattan's Upper East Side. . . .

Supplemental tutoring: tutors in French and mathematics

Summer camp: sleep-away camp in northern Connecticut

Secondary education: a prestigious preparatory school in Westchester County

Supplemental education: private SAT tutor. After-school activities: private riding lessons. *Ambition:* "to take over my father's business." *High-school graduation gift:* BMW

Family activities: theater, recitals, museums, summer vacations in Europe, occasional winter trips to the Caribbean.

Higher education: an Ivy League liberal arts college in Massachusetts. *Major:* economics and political science. *After-class activities:* debating club, college newspaper, swim team. *Ambition:* "to become a leader in business"

First full-time job (age 23): assistant manager of operations, Browning Tool and Die, Inc. (family enterprise)

Subsequent employment: 3 years—executive assistant to the president, Browning Tool and Die; responsibilities included: purchasing (materials and equipment), personnel, and distribution networks. 4 years—advertising manager, Lackheed Manufacturing (home appliances). 3 years—director of marketing and sales, Comerex, Inc. (business machines)

Present employment (age 38): executive vice president, SmithBond and Co. (digital instruments). *Typical daily activities:* review financial reports and computer printouts, dictate memoranda, lunch with clients, initiate conference calls, meet with assistants, plan business trips, meet with associates. *Transportation to and from work:* chauffeured company limousine. *Annual salary:* $324,000. *Ambition:* "to become chief executive officer of the firm, or one like it, within the next five to ten years"

Present residence: eighteenth-floor condominium on Manhattan's Upper West Side, eleven rooms, including five spacious bedrooms and terrace overlooking river. . . .

Second residence: farm in northwestern Connecticut, used for weekend retreats and for horse breeding (investment/hobby). . . .

Harold Browning was born into a world of nurses, maids, and governesses. His world today is one of airplanes and limousines, five-star restaurants, and luxurious living accommodations. The life and life-style of Harold Browning is in sharp contrast to that of Bob Farrell.

Name: **Bob Farrell**

Father: machinist

Mother: retail clerk

Principal child-rearer: mother and sitter

Primary education: a medium-size public school in Queens, New York, characterized by large class size, outmoded physical facilities, and an educational philosophy emphasizing basic skills and student discipline. . . .

Supplemental tutoring: none

Summer camp: YMCA day camp. . . .

Secondary education: large regional high school in Queens. . . .

Supplemental education: SAT prep course offered by national chain. *After-school activities:* basketball and handball in school park. *Ambition:* "to make it through college." *High-school graduation gift:* $500 savings bond

Family activities: family gatherings around television set, softball, an occasional trip to the movie theater, summer Sundays at the public beach

Higher education: a two-year community college with a technical orientation. *Major:* electrical technology. *After-school activities:* employed as a part-time bagger in local supermarket. *Ambition:* "to become an electrical engineer"

First full-time job (age 19): service-station attendant. . . .

Subsequent employment: mail clerk at large insurance firm; manager trainee, large retail chain

Present employment (age 38): assistant sales manager, building supply firm. *Typical daily activities:* demonstrate products, write up product orders, handle customer complaints, check inventory. *Transportation to and from work:* city subway

Annual salary: $45,261. *Ambition:* "to open up my own business." *Additional income:* $6,100 in commissions from evening and weekend work as salesman in local men's clothing store

Present residence: the Farrells own their own home in a working-class neighborhood in Queens, New York

Bob Farrell and Harold Browning live very differently: the life-style of one is privileged; that of the other is not so privileged. The differences are class differences, and these differences have a profound impact on the way they live. . . . Yet, as dissimilar as their life-styles are, Harold Browning and Bob Farrell have some things in common; they live in the same city, they work long hours, and they are highly motivated. More important, they are both white males.

Let's look at someone else who works long and hard and is highly motivated. This person, however, is black and female.

Name: **Cheryl Mitchell**

Father: janitor

Mother: waitress

Principal child-rearer: grandmother

Primary education: large public school in Ocean Hill-Brownsville, Brooklyn, New York. . . .

Supplemental tutoring: none

Summer camp: none

Secondary education: large public school in Ocean Hill-Brownsville. . . .

Supplemental education: none. *After-school activities:* domestic chores, part-time employment as babysitter and housekeeper. *Ambition:* "to be a social worker." *High-school graduation gift:* corsage

Family activities: church-sponsored socials

Higher education: one semester of local community college. *Note:* dropped out of school for financial reasons

First full-time job (age 17): counter clerk, local bakery

Subsequent employment: file clerk with temporary-service agency, supermarket checker

Present employment (age 38): nurse's aide at a municipal hospital. *Typical daily activities:* make up hospital beds, clean out bedpans, weigh patients and assist them to the bathroom, take temperature readings, pass out and collect food trays, feed patients who need help, bathe patients, and change dressings. *Annual salary:* $15,820. *Ambition:* "to get out of the ghetto"

Present residence: three-room apartment in the South Bronx, needs painting, has poor ventilation, is in a high-crime area. *Note:* Cheryl Mitchell lives with her four-year-old son and her elderly mother

When we look at the lives of Cheryl Mitchell, Bob Farrell, and Harold Browning, we see life-styles that are very different. We are not looking, however, at economic extremes. Cheryl Mitchell's income as a nurse's aide puts her above the government's official poverty line. Below her on the income pyramid are 37 million poverty-stricken Americans. Far from being poor, Bob Farrell has an annual income as an assistant sales manager that puts him well above the median income level—that is, more than 50 percent of the U.S. population earns less money than Bob Farrell. And while Harold Browning's income puts him in a high-income bracket, he stands only a fraction of the way up [the] income pyramid. Well above him are the 183,000 individuals whose annual salary exceeds $1 million. Yet Harold Browning spends more money on his horses than Cheryl Mitchell earns in a year.

Reality 3: Even ignoring the extreme poles of the economic spectrum, we find enormous class differences in the life-styles among the haves, the have-nots, and the have-littles. Class affects more than life-style and material well-being. It has a significant impact on our physical and mental well-being as well.

. . . In all areas of health, poor people do not share the same life chances as those in the social class above them. Furthermore, lower-class standing is correlated with a lower quality of treatment for illness and disease. The results of poor health and poor treatment are borne out in the life expectancy rates within each class. Researchers have found that the higher your class standing, the higher your life expectancy. Conversely, they have also found that within each age group, the lower one's class standing, the higher the death rate; in some age groups, the figures are as much as two and three times as high.

Reality 4: From cradle to grave, class standing has a significant impact on our chances for survival. The lower one's class standing, the more difficult it is to secure appropriate housing, the more time is spent on the routine tasks of everyday life, the greater is the percentage of income that goes to pay for food and other basic necessities, and the greater is the likelihood of crime victimization. Class can accurately predict chances for both survival and success.

CLASS AND EDUCATIONAL ATTAINMENT

School performance (grades and test scores) and educational attainment (level of schooling completed) also correlate strongly with economic class. Furthermore, despite some efforts to make testing fairer and schooling more accessible, current data suggest that the level of inequity is staying the same or getting worse.

. . .

A little more than thirty years ago, researcher William Sewell showed a positive correlation between class and overall educational achievement. In comparing the top quartile (25 percent) of his sample to the bottom quartile, he found that students from upper-class families were twice as likely to obtain training beyond high school and four times as likely to attain a postgraduate degree. . . .

Reality 5: Class standing has a significant impact on chances for educational achievement.

Class standing, and consequently life chances, are largely determined at birth. Although examples of individuals who have gone from rags to riches abound in the mass media, statistics on class mobility show these leaps to be extremely rare. In fact, dramatic advances in class standing are relatively infrequent. One study showed that fewer than one in five men surpass the economic status of their fathers. For those whose annual income is in six figures, economic success is due in large part to the wealth and privileges bestowed on them at birth. Over 66 percent of the consumer units with incomes of $100,000 or more have inherited assets. Of these units, over 86 percent reported that inheritances constituted a substantial portion of their total assets.

. . .

Reality 6: All Americans do not have an equal opportunity to succeed. Inheritance laws ensure a greater likelihood of success for the offspring of the wealthy.

SPHERES OF POWER AND OPPRESSION

When we look at society and try to determine what it is that keeps most people down— what holds them back from realizing their potential as healthy, creative, productive individuals—we find institutional forces that are largely beyond individual control. Class domination is one of these forces. People do not choose to be poor or working class; instead, they are limited and confined by the opportunities afforded or denied them by a social and economic system. . . . Class divisions arise from the differences between those who own and control corporate enterprise and those who do not.

Racial and gender domination are other forces that hold people down. Although there are significant differences in the way capitalism, racism, and sexism affect our lives, there are also a multitude of parallels. And although class, race, and gender act independently of each other, they are at the same time very much interrelated.

On the one hand, issues of race and gender cut across class lines. Women experience the effects of sexism whether they are well-paid professionals or poorly paid clerks. As women, they are not only subjected to catcalls and stereotyping, but face discrimination and are denied opportunities and privileges that men have. Similarly, a wealthy black man faces racial oppression, is subjected to racial slurs, and is denied opportunities because of his color. . . .

Chances of Being Poor in America					
White Male/ Female	White Female Head[1]	Hispanic Male/ Female	Hispanic Female Head[1]	Black Male/ Female	Black Female Head[1]
1 in 10	1 in 5	1 in 5	1 in 3	1 in 4	1 in 3

1 Persons in families with female householder, no husband present.

Reality 7: Racism and sexism significantly compound the effects of class in society.

None of this makes for a very pretty picture of our country. Despite what we like to think about ourselves as a nation, the truth is that opportunity for success and life itself are highly circumscribed by our race, our gender, and the class we are born into. As individuals, we feel hurt and anger when someone is treating us unfairly; yet as a society we tolerate unconscionable injustice. A more just society will require a radical redistribution of wealth and power. We can start by reversing the current trends that further polarize us as a people and adapt policies and practices that narrow the gaps in income, wealth, and privilege.

27

The Dangerous Consequences of Growing Inequality

Chuck Collins, Felice Yeskel, with United for a Fair Economy and Class Action

. . .

PRESSURES FACING OUR HOUSEHOLDS

Let's start by looking at the impact of the changing economy close to home. There are new pressures and some alarming trends facing a growing number of households in this country. . . .

The decline of leisure time and the breakdown of civil society. One powerful consequence of growing inequality is an erosion in the amount of free time that families have. As individuals and families struggle to stay afloat and remain secure in the changing economy, they are spending more hours at work.

Falling wages in the 1970s and early 1980s were masked by the entry of a second wage earner in many households—usually a woman—into the workforce. Families now have to work longer hours to make up for falling wages. At the same time, temporary and part-time workers generally do not have paid vacations, and their numbers in the workforce are growing. The number of overall hours worked, per household, has increased since 1972. The number of hours worked per person each year has increased 4 percent, from 1,905 in 1980 to 1,966 in 2001. . . .

Technological advances in the workplace, instead of increasing the amount of free time, are having the opposite effect. Productivity has been steadily increasing, but these gains have not translated into higher wages or increased free time. Blue-collar and service workers have experienced a veritable "speed-up" in the workplace as employers squeeze productivity gains into increased profits. Not only are people working longer hours, but in many cases the tempo and scope of their jobs have become more harried and stressful.

. . .

This loss of leisure time has a direct impact on the quality of people's lives. As people have less free time, they have less time available to care for children and elders, less time to be involved in schools and education, and less time to volunteer to help others. This dramatically increases stress, particularly on women, whose unpaid labor is largely performed in this non-monetary "caring economy." Stress leads to increased illness and the unraveling of communities, the breakdown in voluntary mutual-aid systems, and the fragmentation and isolation of people. It leads to "latchkey" children and a lack of support for the next generation, with serious consequences. . . .

Fewer households with health insurance. . . . Between 2000 and 2004, the cost of health care coverage grew by 35.9 percent, while average earnings only grew 12.4 percent. Over the same period, the number of households paying more than one-quarter of their earnings on health care rose by 23 percent, from 11.6 million to 14.3 million. Over 45 million people in the nation lack health insurance, up from 31 million a decade ago. This makes the United States the only industrialized nation that views health care as a privilege, not a basic human right.

Having a job does not guarantee health insurance. The percentage of Americans under the age of 65 covered through employer-sponsored health insurance declined from 70.4 percent in 1999 to 63 percent in 2003. Among low-income Americans, the share of those with employer-sponsored health insurance fell from 40.3 in 1999 to 35.0 percent in 2002. Twenty-four million of those without insurance are employed, 17 percent of whom are in the temporary or contingent workforce. In 2003, 83 percent of part-time employees had no access to health care benefits through their employers.

. . . Thirty-four percent of the nation's 37.4 million Hispanic people have no health insurance, compared to 22 percent of blacks and 12 percent of non-Hispanic whites.

Rising personal debt. Another way families continue to make up for falling wages in order to maintain (or in some cases attain) a certain standard of living is by going deeper into debt. Approximately 60 percent of all American households carry credit card balances, unable to pay their full month bill. In 2004, the credit card industry claimed that the average household consumer debt was approximately $9,000. Yet, when the roughly 40 percent of households that pay their balances each month were taken out of the equation, average household consumer debt was closer to $13,000 and late payments are at a five-year high. Total credit card debt increased from $243 billion in 1990 to $735 billion in 2004. Some of this is rooted in consumerism, but a central reason for growing debt lies in declining or stagnant wages. People are now using credit cards for things like food and medicine—items previously paid for with cash. One downside of growing personal indebtedness is the increasing number of personal bankruptcies, which are now at an all-time high. In 2003, 1.6 million individuals filed for personal bankruptcy, up from 1.4 million in 2002 and almost triple the 661,000 who filed in 1990.

Declining personal savings. The flip side of greater debt is less savings. The savings rate is the percentage of annual income that is actually saved each year. Since 1980, the savings rate has generally fallen. The United States has the lowest savings rate of any industrialized country. In 2003, the U.S. savings rate was 1.4 percent, down from 4.5 percent in 1997 and 10.8 percent in 1984. In contrast, the savings rate in 2003 in Japan was 7 percent and in Germany it was 10.8 percent.

. . . [T]he main reason for the lower savings rate is linked to the rising cost of health care and the increase in other involuntary costs such as day care and bank-service fees.

Diminishing retirement security. Those employees lucky enough to have pensions have ones that are less secure. The percentage of workers in the private labor force in monthly pension plans (where companies bear the risk of falling markets) has declined from 38 percent in 1980 to 25 percent in 1998. These are called "defined-benefit plans," which are better for workers because they are federally insured and provide a guaranteed monthly pension amount. More workers now have "defined-contribution plans," like 401(k) plans, in which the benefit amount depends on how well the underlying investments perform. This growth in private 401(k) pension plans has failed to broaden overall pension coverage. In fact, there is more inequality in 401(k) plans than in defined-benefit plans, as they tend to be held by higher-income workers. The decline in both savings and guaranteed pensions are two concrete indicators of growing insecurity.

Retirement planners suggest that Social Security should be only one leg of the three-legged stool of retirement security. Personal savings and an employer-funded pension fund are the other two legs. But as personal savings plummet and fewer and fewer workers have pension funds, the prospects for a large percentage of people retiring into poverty grows. Worse yet, people will never be able to stop working, even as they go into their seventies.

Growing number of temporary jobs. The greatest percentage of new jobs in the workforce are filled by temporary and part-time workers. Currently about 30 percent of the workforce is what is called "contingent," including temporary, part-time, contract, and day laborers. Some of these workers are voluntarily part-time. But a growing number are involuntarily part-time, often holding two to three jobs to pay their bills. According to the Bureau of Labor Statistics, two-thirds of contingent workers would like traditional permanent jobs. . . . The "temping of America" is part of a larger economic restructuring that is changing the nature of work and contributing to economic inequality.

The growing number of temporary and part-time jobs is a depressing trend for many younger people entering the workforce after high school or college. Only 11 percent of female and 15 percent of male full-time temporary workers have health insurance provided through their employer. In fact, fewer than 30 percent of all contingent workers have health insurance, and only 11 percent have pensions.

Higher education, higher reach. The cost of going to college has risen, while government support to ensure access to higher education has failed to keep pace. Going to college is more of a privilege than it was twenty years ago. Federal college loans have now replaced college grants, rising from 41.4 percent of student financing in 1982 to 58.9 percent in 2001. Student debt between 1991 and 1997 totaled $140 billion—more than the total combined student borrowing for the 1960s, 1970s, and 1980s. Student debt has dramatically increased from an average of $8,200 per student in 1991 to $18,900 in 2003. Many students will still be paying off college loans in their mid-thirties.

The rising cost of college affects who gets to go to college. The country's poorest families are increasingly underrepresented in higher education, particularly at four-year schools. Only 20 percent of all community college students nationally come from families with annual income under $25,000, only 11 percent at public four-year colleges, and just 8 percent at private four-year colleges. In 1995, 83.4 percent of high school students in the top fifth of income-earning households went to college, compared to 56.1 percent of students in the middle three quintiles and 41.3 percent in the bottom quintile. As of 2001, 29 percent of whites had completed four years of college compared to 17 percent of blacks and 11 percent of Hispanics. Higher education is becoming much more class-segregated than it was a decade ago.

. . .

WHAT IS WEALTH AND WHY IS IT IMPORTANT

Income and wages are one index of how prosperity is distributed; the ownership of wealth is another. If income is the stream of money that comes into our lives each year, wealth is our reservoir. From our income stream, we take our bucket and pull out our housing costs, food expenses, and health care costs. At the end of the year, any left over goes into our reservoir, becoming accumulated wealth.

Wealth comprises assets (all the stuff you own) minus liabilities (what you owe). This remainder is called "net worth." If you own a car worth $4,000, but you owe $5,000 in car loans, you are in the red. . . .

Wealth for working-class people is usually in the form of savings, consumer goods like cars, and, if they are fortunate, equity in a home. As people move up the economic ladder, wealth takes the form of greater savings and home value—but also includes second homes, recreational equipment (like boats), shares in corporations (called securities or stocks), bonds, and commercial real estate. It may also include luxury items like high-priced artwork, racehorses, jewelry, and antiques.

Wealth is important because it is what people have to fall back on and pass on to their children. Yet today, about one out of six households in the United States has zero or negative wealth. This means they literally have no financial reserves to fall back on in times of trouble, or, in fact, they owe more than they own. The percentage of households with zero or negative net worth has increased in the last thirty years, from 15.5 percent in 1983 to 17.6 percent in 2001. When factoring in race, the figures increase significantly. The percentage of African American households with zero or negative net worth is disturbingly high, at 30.9 percent or roughly one in three black households.

. . .

It is in the area of wealth and asset accumulation that the legacy of racial discrimination has left its most profound mark. While black and Latino *incomes* have begun to catch up to white earnings, black and Latino *wealth* continues to lag dramatically behind that of white households. Since wealth accumulates over generations, discrimination has taken its toll on wealth accumulation for people of color. Blacks were prohibited from building wealth by slavery and prohibitions against owning property after the Civil War. Bank lending practices have also discriminated against black and Latino households and kept them from home ownership, business development, and other asset-building measures.

In 2001, the median black household had a net worth of just $19,000 (including home equity), compared with $121,000 for whites. Blacks had 16 percent of the median wealth of whites, up from 5 percent in 1989. At this rate, it will take until 2099 to reach parity in median wealth. Blacks were 13 percent of the U.S. population in 2001 but owned 3 percent of the assets. There is obviously a high correlation between income and wealth. Most assetless households are in the bottom fifth of the income ladder. There are people deep in debt all up and down the income spectrum, but in most cases, we can assume that assetlessness correlates with lower income.

THE CONCENTRATION OF WEALTH

In the last twenty years, the overall wealth pie has grown, but virtually all the new growth in wealth has gone to the richest 1 percent of the population.

In 1976, the wealthiest 1 percent of the population owned 20 percent of all the private wealth. The top 10 percent of the population owned about 50 percent of all private wealth. By 2001, the richest 1 percent's share had increased to over 33 percent of all household financial wealth, increasing the top 20 percent's share to 84.4 percent. The top 1 percent of households now has more wealth than the entire bottom 95 percent. As of 2001, to join the top 1 percent club you need at least $5.8 million in net worth.

Financial wealth (net worth minus net equity in owner-occupied housing) is even more concentrated. The top 1 percent of households has nearly half of all stock (44.9 percent) and 39.7 percent of all financial wealth. This is compared to the bottom 90 percent of households, which owns 20.2 percent of all financial wealth.

Between 1962 and 2001, the relative share of wealth owned by the bottom 90 percent of the population declined from 33.1 percent to 28.5 percent. What does this loss of wealth actually mean? It means less savings, growing personal debt, less retirement security, and fewer households having access to home ownership. It means fewer financial reserves to fall back on in the event of a setback or job loss.

THE WEALTH-HOLDERS

. . .

There are three ways in which the very wealthy accumulate money: through slow accumulation over their lifetimes by starting a business and saving; through cornering a critical element of the market and controlling it; or through inheritance.

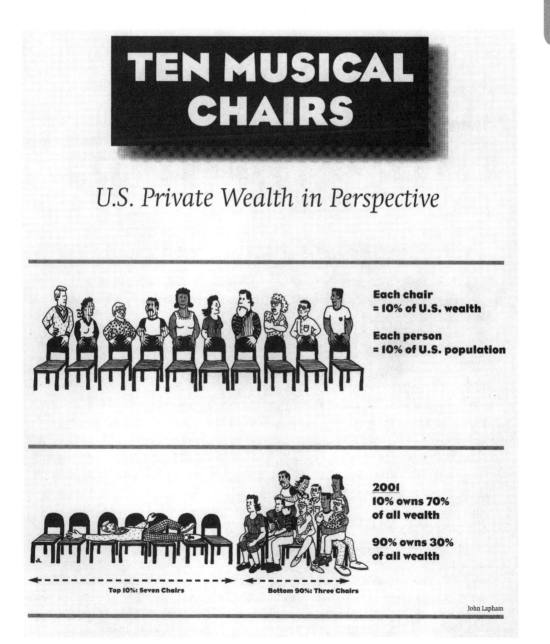

Figure 27.1 Ten Musical Chairs. Source: Arthur B. Kennickel, "A Rolling Tide: Changes in the Distribution of Wealth in the U.S. 1989–2001," Jerome Levy Economics Institute, November 2003.

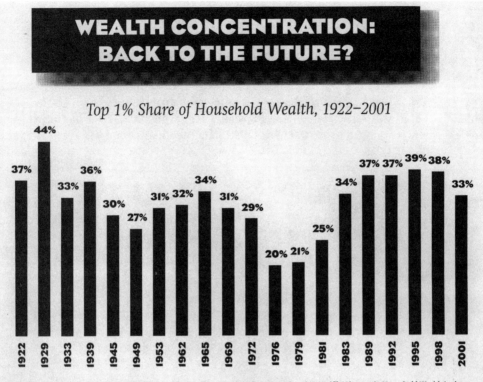

WEALTH CONCENTRATION: BACK TO THE FUTURE?

Top 1% Share of Household Wealth, 1922–2001

Year	%
1922	37%
1929	44%
1933	33%
1939	36%
1945	30%
1949	27%
1953	31%
1962	32%
1965	34%
1969	31%
1972	29%
1976	20%
1979	21%
1981	25%
1983	34%
1989	37%
1992	37%
1995	39%
1998	38%
2001	33%

Sources: 1922–81: Edward N. Wolff, *Top Heavy* (The New Press: 1996). 1983–2001: Edward N. Wolff, "Changes in Household Wealth in the 1980s and 1990s in the U.S.," Jerome Levy Economics Institute, May 2004.

What if workers had been paid for productivity gains?

Between 1973 and 1998, productivity increased 33 percent. What if hourly wages grew at the same rate? What if workers shared in the 1990s productivity gains they helped to create? The average hourly wage in 1998 would have been $18.10, rather than $12.77.[29] That's the difference of $5.33 an hour—more than $11,000 for a full-time, year-round worker. The 30 cents workers gained in their hourly wages between 1997 and 1998 pales by comparison. The cumulative wages lost since 1973 will never be recovered—much less their lost investment potential. This is money working families could have saved, invested, or spent on consumer items rather than going into debt. This is money that could have stimulated markets in low- and moderate-income communities rather than benefiting absentee shareholders who take their investments anywhere on the planet in search of the highest return.

Figure 27.2 Wealth Concentration: Back to the Future?

Most press coverage goes to describing the self-made millionaires, the Horatio Algers of the modern day. In Thomas Stanley and William Danko's best-selling book, *The Millionaire Next Door*, the profile of America's 3.5 million millionaires is not the stereotype of the high-roller with five fancy sports cars and several mansions in desirable zip codes. According to Stanley and Danko, the typical millionaire is white, over fifty-five years old, has a net worth of between $1 and 10 million, and lives in the same house he bought thirty years

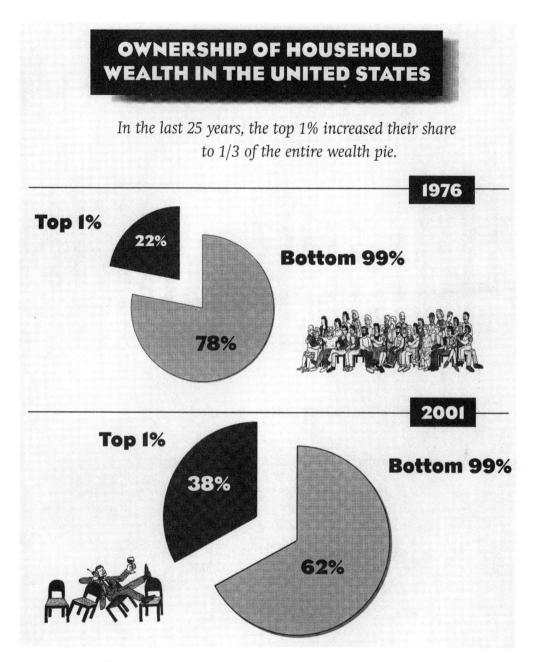

OWNERSHIP OF HOUSEHOLD WEALTH IN THE UNITED STATES

In the last 25 years, the top 1% increased their share to 1/3 of the entire wealth pie.

1976

Top 1% — 22%

Bottom 99% — 78%

2001

Top 1% — 38%

Bottom 99% — 62%

Figure 27.3 Ownership of Household Wealth in the United States. Sources: For 1976: Edward N. Wolff, unpublished data. For 2001: Arthur B. Kennickel, "A Rolling Tide: Changes in the Distribution of Wealth in the U.S. 1989–2001," Jerome Levy Economics Institute, November 2003.

ago. The most common sources of wealth: small-business ownership and steadily rising home value. . . .

But there are many other factors, including timing, luck, and white privilege that are less acknowledged in America's mythology of success. Starting a business in the rapidly expanding economy of the 1950s and 1960s was a very different story than starting a business in today's more competitive global economy. Prior to the 1970s, many domestic small businesses were protected from the full brunt of competition from international producers and national conglomerates. Imagine trying to start a locally owned hardware store or pharmacy today in the same marketplace with Home Depot, Costco, and CVS. Access to credit for the purchase of assets, whether a home in an appreciating neighborhood or a start-up small business, remains a function of education, skill, personal connections, and—despite government antidiscrimination policies—race.

Many of the largest fortunes—those in excess of $10 million—are tied to cornering a part of the market that everyone needs. Indeed, many of the great robber barons of the late 1800s (the Rockefellers, the Carnegies, etc.) dominated some market (usually in natural resources like timber, oil, coal, and steel), or developed a monopoly on a much-needed public service like railroads.

Today, fortunes are made in information-age technology. Bill Gates and Paul Allen, the founders of Microsoft, are good examples. A growing number of the new fortunes on the Forbes 400 annual listing of the richest Americans are built on computers and information technology. Like the railroad barons of the late 1800s, Gates and Allen developed advances in products—computer operating systems and software—that have become central to our lives. Between 1996 and 1999, Bill Gates's personal wealth went from $18 billion to over $85 billion dollars. Thanks to changes in the market and his aggressive charitable giving ($28 billion donated to the Gates Foundation and other charities), Gates's net worth in 2004 was $48 billion, but his personal wealth still exceeds the combined wealth of the bottom 45 percent of the U.S. population.

In spite of the success stories of small entrepreneurs and "dot-com millionaires," the most sure-fire way to get rich remains to be born into a wealthy family. A substantial amount of wealth is passed on from one generation to the next through inheritance. Economist Lester Thurow estimates that between 50 and 70 percent of all wealth is inherited. A 1997 study found that of the 400 individuals and families on the 1997 Forbes 400 list, 42 percent inherited their way onto the list, another 6 percent inherited wealth in excess of $50 million, and another 7 percent started life with at least $1 million. Overall, more than 50 percent started life with at least $1 million. . . .

While it still is possible for a few to make the "rags to riches" transition, it is important to question the underlying belief and value system that dangles this fantasy before our eyes. This national obsession is so compelling that we are willing to accept large-scale poverty in exchange for the prospect of a few lucky folks hitting the big time. We can't possibly *all* invent the next mousetrap or computer operating system. We can't *all* win the lottery. A few folks cornering the market (or hitting the daily number) depends on many others failing. Unfortunately, the classist belief systems we are indoctrinated by are powerful. We are trained to identify up the class spectrum and fantasize about getting there.

28

Race, Wealth, and Equality

Melvin L. Oliver and Thomas M. Shapiro

Over a hundred years after the end of slavery, more than thirty years after the passage of major civil rights legislation, and following a concerted but prematurely curtailed War on Poverty, we harvest today a mixed legacy of racial progress. We celebrate the advancement of many blacks to middle-class status. . . . An official end to "de jure" housing segregation has even opened the door to neighborhoods and suburban residences previously off-limits to black residents. Nonetheless, many blacks have fallen by the wayside in their march toward economic equality. A growing number have not been able to take advantage of the opportunities now open to some. They suffer from educational deficiencies that make finding a foothold in an emerging technological economy near to impossible. Unable to move from deteriorated inner-city and older suburban communities, they entrust their children to school systems that are rarely able to provide them with the educational foundation they need to take the first steps up a racially skewed economic ladder. Trapped in communities of despair, they face increasing economic and social isolation from both their middle-class counterparts and white Americans.

. . .

Disparities in wealth between blacks and whites are not the product of haphazard events, inborn traits, isolated incidents, or solely contemporary individual accomplishments. Rather, wealth inequality has been structured over many generations through the same systemic barriers that have hampered blacks throughout their history in American society: slavery, Jim Crow, so-called de jure discrimination, and institutionalized racism. How these factors have affected the ability of blacks to accumulate wealth, however, has often been ignored or incompletely sketched. By briefly recalling three scenarios in American history that produced structured inequalities, we illustrate the significance of these barriers and their role in creating the wealth gap between blacks and whites.

RECONSTRUCTION: FROM SLAVERY TO FREEDOM WITHOUT A MATERIAL BASE

. . .

The close of the Civil War transformed four million former slaves from chattel to freedmen. Emerging from a legacy of two and a half centuries of legalized oppression, the new freedmen entered Southern society with little or no material assets. . . . The slave's often-cited demand of "forty acres and a mule" fueled great anticipation of a new beginning based on land ownership and a transfer of skills developed under slavery into the new economy of the South. Whereas slave muscle and skills had cleared the wilderness and made the land productive and profitable for plantation owners, the new vision saw the freedmen's hard work and skill generating income and resources for the former slaves themselves. W. E. B. Du Bois, in his *Black Reconstruction in America*, called this prospect America's chance to be a modern democracy.

Initially it appeared that massive land redistribution from the Confederates to the freedmen would indeed become a reality. . . . Real access to land for the freedman had to await the passage of the Southern Homestead Act in 1866, which provided a legal basis and mechanism to promote black landownership. In this legislation public land already designated in the 1862 Homestead Act, which applied only to non-Confederate whites but not blacks, was now opened up to settlement by former slaves in the tradition of homesteading that had helped settle the West. . . .

This social and economic transformation never occurred. . . . First, instead of disqualifying former Confederate supporters as the previous act had done, the 1866 legislation allowed all persons who applied for land to swear that they had not taken up arms against the Union or given aid and comfort to the enemies. This opened the door to massive white applications for land. One estimate suggests that over three-quarters (77.1 percent) of the land applicants under the act were white. In addition, much of the land was poor swampland and it was difficult for black or white applicants to meet the necessary home-steading

CONTEXT

requirements because they could not make a decent living off the land. What is more important, blacks had to face the extra burden of racial prejudice and discrimination along with the charging of illegal fees, expressly discriminatory court challenges and court decisions, and land speculators. . . .

THE SUBURBANIZATION OF AMERICA: THE MAKING OF THE GHETTO

. . .

The suburbanization of America was principally financed and encouraged by actions of the federal government, which supported suburban growth from the 1930s through the 1960s by way of taxation, transportation, and housing policy. . . . As a consequence, employment opportunities steadily rose in the suburban rings of the nation's major metropolitan areas. In addition, transportation policy encouraged freeway construction and subsidized cheap fuel and mass-produced automobiles. These factors made living on the outer edges of cities both affordable and relatively convenient. However, the most important government policies encouraging and subsidizing suburbanization focused on housing. In particular, the incentives that government programs gave for the acquisition of single-family detached housing spurred both the development and financing of the tract home, which became the hallmark of suburban living. While these governmental policies collectively enabled over thirty-five million families between 1933 and 1978 to participate in homeowner equity accumulation, they also had the adverse effect of constraining black Americans' residential opportunities to central-city ghettos of major U.S. metropolitan communities and denying them access to one of the most successful generators of wealth in American history—the suburban tract home.

This story begins with the government's initial entry into home financing. . . . Charged with the task of determining the "useful or productive life of housing" they considered to finance, government agents methodically included in their procedures the evaluation of the racial composition or potential racial composition of the community. Communities that were changing racially or were already black were deemed undesirable and placed in the lowest category. The categories, assigned various colors on a map ranging from green for the most desirable, which included new, all-white housing that was always in demand, to red, which included already racially mixed or all-black, old, and undesirable areas, subsequently were used by Federal Housing Authority (FHA) loan officers who made loans on the basis of these designations.

Established in 1934, the FHA aimed to bolster the economy and increase employment by aiding the ailing construction industry. The FHA ushered in the modern mortgage system that enabled people to buy homes on small down payments and at reasonable interest rates, with lengthy repayment periods and full loan amortization. The FHA's success was remarkable: housing starts jumped from 332,000 in 1936 to 619,000 in 1941. . . .

This growth in access to housing was confined, however, for the most part to suburban areas. The administrative dictates outlined in the original act, while containing no anti-urban bias, functioned in practice to the neglect of central cities. Three reasons can be cited: first, a bias toward the financing of single-family detached homes over multifamily projects favored open areas outside of the central city that had yet to be developed over congested central-city areas; second, a bias toward new purchases over repair of existing homes prompted people to move out of the city rather than upgrade or improve their existing residences; and third, the continued use of the "unbiased professional estimate" that made older homes and communities in which blacks or undesirables were located less likely to receive approval for loans encouraged purchases in communities where race was not an issue.

. . . [T]he FHA . . . provided more precise guidance to its appraisers in its *Underwriting Manual*. The most basic sentiment underlying the FHA's concern was its fear that property values would decline if a rigid black and white segregation was not maintained. The *Underwriting Manual* openly stated that "if a neighborhood is to retain stability, it is necessary that properties shall continue to be occupied by the same social and racial classes" and further recommended that "subdivision regulations and suitable restrictive covenants" are the best way to ensure such neighborhood stability. The FHA's recommended use of restrictive covenants continued until 1949, when, responding to the Supreme Court's outlawing of such covenants in 1948 (*Shelly v. Kraemer*), it announced that "as of February 15, 1950, it would not insure mortgages on real estate subject to covenants."

. . .

The FHA's actions have had a lasting impact on the wealth portfolios of black Americans. Locked out of the greatest mass-based opportunity for wealth accumulation in American history, African Americans who desired and were able to afford home ownership found themselves consigned to central-city communities where their investments were affected by the "self-fulfilling prophecies" of the FHA appraisers: cut off from sources of new investment their homes and communities deteriorated and lost value in comparison to those homes and communities that FHA appraisers deemed desirable. One infamous housing development of the period—Levittown—provides a classic illustration of the way blacks missed out on this asset-accumulating opportunity. Levittown was built on a mass scale, and housing there was eminently affordable, thanks to the FHA's and VHA's accessible financing, yet as late as 1960 "not a single one of the Long Island Levittown's 82,000 residents was black."

CONTEMPORARY INSTITUTIONAL RACISM: ACCESS TO MORTGAGE MONEY AND REDLINING

. . .

In May of 1988 the issue of banking discrimination and redlining exploded onto the front pages of the *Atlanta Journal and Constitution*. This Pulitzer Prize-winning series, "The Color of Money," described the wide disparity in mortgage-lending practices in black and white neighborhoods of Atlanta, finding black applicants rejected at a greater rate than whites, even when economic situations were comparable. . . .

A 1991 Federal Reserve study of 6.4 million home mortgage applications by race and income confirmed suspicions of bias in lending by reporting a widespread and systemic pattern of institutional discrimination in the nation's banking system. This study disclosed that commercial banks rejected black applicants twice as often as whites nationwide. In some cities, like Boston, Philadelphia, Chicago, and Minneapolis, it reported a more pronounced pattern of minority loan rejections, with blacks being rejected three times more often than whites.

The argument that financial considerations—not discrimination—are the reason minorities get fewer loans appears to be totally refuted by the Federal Reserve study. The poorest white applicant, according to this report, was more likely to get a mortgage loan approved than a black in the highest income bracket. In Boston, for example, blacks in the highest income levels faced loan rejections three times more often than whites. . . .

The problem goes beyond redlining. Not only were banks reluctant to lend in minority communities, but the Federal Reserve study indicates that discrimination follows blacks no matter where they want to live and no matter how much they earn. A 1993 *Washington Post* series highlighted banks' reluctance to lend even in the wealthiest black neighborhoods. . . .

These findings gave credence to the allegations of housing and community activists that banks have been strip-mining minority neighborhoods of housing equity through unscrupulous backdoor loans for home repairs. Homes bought during the 1960s and 1970s in low-income areas had acquired some equity but were also in need of repair. Mainstream banks refused to approve such loans at "normal" rates, but finance companies made loans that, according to activists, preyed on minority communities by charging exorbitant, pawn-shop-style interest rates with unfavorable conditions. Rates of 34 percent and huge balloon payments were not uncommon. . . .

In Boston more than one-half of the families who relied on these kinds of high-interest loans lost their homes through foreclosure. One study charted every loan between 1984 and mid-1991 made by two high-interest lenders. Families lost their homes or were facing foreclosure in over three-quarters of the cases. Only 55 of the 406 families still possessed their homes and did not face foreclosure. The study also showed that the maps of redlined areas and high-interest loans overlapped.

. . .

Even briefly recalled, the three historical moments evoked in the pages above illustrate the powerful dynamics generating structured inequality in America. Several common threads link the three scenarios. First, whether it be a question of homesteading, suburbanization, or redlining, we have seen how governmental, institutional, and private-sector discrimination enhances the ability of different segments of the population to accumulate and build on their wealth assets and resources, thereby raising their standard of living and securing a better future for themselves and their children. The use of land grants and mass low-priced sales of government lands created massive and unparalleled opportunities for Americans in the nineteenth century to secure title to land in the westward expansion. Likewise, government backing of millions of low-interest loans to returning soldiers and low-income families enabled American cities to suburbanize and their inhabitants to see tremendous home value growth after World War II. Quite clearly, black Americans for the most part were unable to secure the same degree of benefits from these government programs as whites were. Indeed, in many of these programs the government made explicit efforts to exclude blacks from participating in them, or to limit their participation in ways that deeply affected their ability to gain the maximum benefits. . . .

Second, disparities in access to housing created differential opportunities for blacks and whites to take advantage of new and more lucrative opportunities to secure the good life. White families who were able to secure title to land in the nineteenth century were much more likely to finance education for their children, provide resources for their own or their children's self-employment, or secure their political rights through political lobbies and the electoral process. Blocked from low-interest government-backed loans, redlined out by financial institutions, or barred from home ownership by banks, black families have been denied the benefits of housing inflation and the subsequent vast increase in home equity assets. Black Americans who failed to secure this economic base were much less likely to be able to provide educational access for their children, secure the necessary financial resources for self-employment, or participate effectively in the political process.

. . .

RACIAL INEQUALITY IN CONTEXT

. . .

The most visible advances for blacks since the 1960s have taken place in the political arena. As a result of the civil rights movement, the percentage of Southern blacks registered to vote rose dramatically. The number of black elected officials increased and the black vote became a crucial and courted electoral block. Yet, in 1993, blacks still accounted for less than 2 percent of all elected officials. . . .

Since the 1960s blacks have also made gains in education. By the late 1980s the proportion of blacks and whites graduating from high school was about equal, reversing the late-1950s black disadvantage of two to one. The percentage of blacks and whites attending college in 1977 was virtually identical, again reversing a tremendous black disadvantage. Since 1976, however, black college enrollments and completion rates have declined, threatening to wipe out the gains of the 1960s and 1970s. The trends in the political and education areas indicate qualified improvements for blacks.

Full equality, however, is still far from being achieved. Alongside the evidence of advancement in some areas and the concerted political mobilization for civil rights, the past two decades also saw an economic degeneration for millions of blacks, and this constitutes the crux of a troubling dilemma. Poor education, high joblessness, low incomes, and the subsequent hardships of poverty, family and community instability, and welfare dependency plague many African Americans. Most evident is the continuing large economic gap between blacks and whites. Median income figures show blacks earning only about 55 percent of the amount made by whites. The greatest economic gains for blacks occurred in the 1940s and 1960s. Since the early 1970s, the economic status of blacks compared to that of whites has, on average, stagnated or deteriorated. Black unemployment rates are more than twice those of whites. Black youths also have more than twice the jobless rate as white youths. Nearly one out of three blacks lives in poverty, compared with fewer than one in ten whites. Residential segregation remains a persistent problem today, with blacks being more likely than whites with similar incomes to live in overcrowded and substandard housing. Nearly one in four blacks remains outside private health insurance or Medicaid coverage. Infant mortality rates have dropped steadily since 1940 for all Americans, but the odds of dying shortly after birth are consistently twice as high for blacks as for whites. Close to half (43 percent) of all black children officially lived in poor households in 1986. A majority of black children live in families that include their mother but not their father. . . . A recent major accounting of race relations summarized it like this: "the status of black America today can be characterized as a glass that is half full—if measured by progress since 1939—or a glass that is half empty—if measured by the persisting disparities between black and white Americans."

. . .

DWINDLING ECONOMIC GROWTH AND RISING INEQUALITY

The standard of living of American households is in serious trouble. For two decades the United States has been evolving into an increasingly unequal society. After improving steadily since World War II, the real (adjusted-for-inflation) weekly wage of the average American worker peaked in 1973. During the twenty-seven-year postwar boom the average worker's wages outpaced inflation every year by 2.5 to 3 percent. The standard of living of most Americans improved greatly, as many people bought cars, homes, appliances, televisions, and other big-ticket consumer goods for the first time. The link between growth and mobility was readily apparent. Between the end of World War II and the early to mid-1970s, the economy created a steady stream of jobs that permitted workers and their families to escape poverty and become part of a growing and vibrant middle class. The economy could absorb millions of new workers and a growing part of the population found middle-class life within reach. . . .

Since 1973, however, a far bleaker story has unfolded. Real wages have been falling or stagnating for most families. The 1986 average wage in the United States bought nearly 14 percent less than it had thirteen years earlier. Also beginning in the mid-1970s, after a long period of movement toward greater equality and stability, the distribution of annual wages and salaries became increasingly unequal. . . .

These changes have profoundly affected blacks. Plant closings and deindustrialization more often occur in industries employing large concentrations of blacks, such as the steel, rubber, and automobile sectors. Black men, especially young black men, are more likely than whites to lose their jobs as a result of economic restructuring. One study of deindustrialization in the Great Lakes region found that black male production workers were hardest hit by the industrial slump of the early 1980s. From 1979 to 1984 one-half of black males in durable-goods manufacturing in five Great Lakes cities lost their jobs.

. . .

The underlying weakness of the economy in the 1990s is increasingly apparent. Debt and global competition pose enormous challenges to stable economic growth and vitality. The larger economic context for the analysis of contemporary race relations is dominated by slow or stagnant growth, deindustrialization, a two-tiered job and earning structure, cuts in the social programs that assist those at the bottom, budget deficits, increasing economic inequality, a reconcentration of wealth, a growing gap in incomes between whites and blacks, and a much-diminished American Dream, however one wishes to define or gauge it.

. . .

WHY STUDY WEALTH?

. . .

Although related, income and wealth have different meanings. *Wealth* is the total extent, at a given moment, of an individual's accumulated assets and access to resources, and it refers to the net value of assets (e.g., ownership of stocks, money in the bank, real estate, business ownership, etc.) less debt held at one time. Wealth is anything of economic value bought, sold, stocked for future disposition, or invested to bring an economic return. *Income* refers to a flow of dollars (salaries, wages, and payments periodically received as returns from an occupation, investment, or government transfer, etc.) over a set period, typically one year.

. . .

Most people use income for day-to-day necessities. Substantial wealth, by contrast, often brings income, power, and independence. Significant wealth relieves individuals from dependence on others for an income, freeing them from the authority structures associated with occupational differentiation that constitute an important aspect of the stratification system in the United States. If money derived from wealth is used to purchase significant ownership of the means of production, it can bring authority to the holder of such wealth. Substantial wealth is important also because it is directly transferable from generation to generation, thus assuring that position and opportunity remain in the same families' hands.

Command over resources inevitably anchors a conception of life chances. While resources theoretically imply both income and wealth, the reality for most families is that income supplies the necessities of life, while wealth represents a kind of "surplus" resource available for improving life chances, providing further opportunities, securing prestige, passing status along to one's family, and influencing the political process.

In view of the limitations of relying on income as well as the significance of wealth, a consideration of racially marked wealth disparities should importantly complement existing income data. An investigation of wealth will also help us formulate a more detailed picture of racial differences in well-being. Most studies of economic well-being focus solely on income, but if wealth differences are even greater than those of income, then these studies will seriously underestimate racial inequality, and policies that seek to narrow differences will fail to close the gap.

29

What's Debt Got to Do with It?

Brett Williams

. . .

"THEY WILL GLADLY TAKE A CHECK"

. . . America's Cash Express . . . is a plain, grim storefront, staffed by one woman behind ceiling-high Plexiglas, offering pagers for $80, laser tear gas for $10, and myriad one-stop financial services. Customers can apply for a telephone calling card or a secured credit card for a $25 processing fee and a $300 deposit (to be charged against) in First Deposit National Bank in New Hampshire. The annual fee is $35 and the annual percentage rate is 19.8 percent. You can wire a moneygram to pay a bill (for 10 percent of the total and a 10 percent discount on Greyhound) or "wire money in minutes worldwide" through an American Express moneygram. (In some places American Express charges as much as 24 percent of the amount wired.)

You can file a tax return and receive a refund anticipation loan ("After all . . . it's *your* money!" beams the promotional material). If you want ACE to prepare your return, that costs about $30. You can pay gas, water, telephone, and electric bills; play the lottery ("We've got your ticket!"); and purchase money orders with the cash you receive when you cash your payroll, government, insurance, or tax refund check. Some call these outlets "welfare banks" because of their heavy traffic in public assistance checks, and sometimes the government sends checks and food stamps directly there.

. . . For the most routine checks, the outlet charges 2 percent of the total, but this varies quite a bit depending on the amount and type of the check and whether or not you have ID. It can cost as much as 6 percent to cash a payroll check and 12 percent to cash a personal one. The most outrageous, expensive, and quasi-legal transactions are called "payday loans," advances secured by a postdated personal check. These loans can charge interest from 20 to 35 percent of the amount advanced; a typical transaction would offer the customer $200 for a $260 check. . . .

Despite the shame, expense, and tedium of the process, many residents of this neighborhood conduct all their bankless business at places like America's Cash Express. Citizens in poor urban neighborhoods find it increasingly difficult to get to a bank. Even if there is a local bank, residents often cannot afford its minimum balance requirements, fees for checks, or high bounced-check penalties. They may not have enough money in their account at the end of the month to cash a paycheck to pay their bills. They may need immediate cash to deliver to the phone company in person. Some residents do not have the major credit card that is to serve as a second major ID; some cannot manage a bank's restricted hours. Some cannot open checking or saving accounts because of even minor problems with their credit or immigration histories. . . .

Using check-cashing outlets further impoverishes and disenfranchises residents, leaving them with no records or proof of payment, no ongoing relationship to build up a credit history, and in greater personal danger from carrying cash (itself in jeopardy from fire, theft, or loss). From where they stand, residents may find it hard to connect the storefronts to the larger financial system or to the injustices they endure. . . . Atlanta snack-food salesman Ronald Hayes . . . makes a weekly visit to cash his $400 paycheck and buy a money order to pay a bill per week. The total cost to Hayes is $15 a week. . . . He fails to recognize that he is probably paying ten times more than a bank would charge. Even if some poor residents recognize the cost, others bow to hand-to-mouth demands for immediacy, safety, or convenience. One homeless man, coping successfully with the dangers of carrying cash, purchases a money order made out to himself each month, cashes it repeatedly at a 2 percent rate, and then buys another money order to carry the balance. He carries his money more safely, but at a huge cost. Hudson interviewed two men in Manassas, Virginia, who paid $270 to cash a $4,500 insurance check because they didn't have time to wait for the check to clear. At the Eagle Outlet, where they cashed their check, owner Victor Daigle claimed that his customers "would rather pay a little bit more to us and have their convenience. They go to McDonald's because they want their hamburger right now. . . . They can come to us and get their money right now."

. . .

"THAT'S WHY THEY'RE MY CUSTOMERS"

Another, more venerable fringe bank is the pawnshop, a familiar sight in cities for many years. . . . These have proliferated in Washington, D.C., and throughout the nation, doubling during the 1980s to number 10,091 in 1994 and certainly many more today. They have changed in other ways as well, to become centralized and chain-operated, backed by upscale marketing, ruthless acquisitions, and persistent pressure on local governments to raise usury rates. Like check-cashing outlets, they displace small businesses, family-owned pawnshops, and local chains, offering young residents of urban neighborhoods downscale, minimum-wage, no-benefits financial services jobs.

For example, Cash America, founded in 1983, operates hundreds of shops. One of five chains to be publicly traded, it boasts NYSE: PWN (for "pawn") as its symbol, turns lush profits for investors, and has tried to upgrade the pawnshop image as it eyes markets all over the world. If you multiply its monthly rate by twelve, its average annual percentage rate (APR) hovers at around 200 percent, not unusual in an industry that often charges 240 percent, and it recorded $5 million in net income from lending activities in the last quarter of 2000, up 17 percent from the year before. In Washington, D.C., Famous Pawn has been enormously successful by gobbling up mom-and-pop stores including pawn shops in poor neighborhoods.

. . . The store is stuffed with former collateral for these expensive secured loans: from gold chains, wedding bands, and watches to baseball cards, leather jackets, computers, VCRs, television sets, compact discs, cameras, pianos, guitars, saxophones, power tools, and lawnmowers. . . .

Customers pawn these items for 10 percent interest each month, a relatively low rate set by Maryland and the District. A borrower would receive $100 for a pawned item and redeem it in thirty days for $110. One customer complains: "They don't give you nothin' for it. But when they sell it, that's when they mark it up." If a customer is unable to redeem it after thirty days, the shop will keep it on hold for as long as he or she can pay each month's interest. Often, pawnshops' profits lie in nurturing these long-term relationships with borrowers, who come in to pay their "dues" on the first of each month but eventually give up and let their treasures go. Their misfortune allows Famous Pawn to bulge out of its space, overflowing with pawns, featuring a long line of borrowers every day, and swallowing its neighboring establishments. Secondary buyers cruise through periodically, buying up items in bulk and boosting profits in the retail side of the business, long less profitable than the interest-collecting side.

. . .

[T]he vast majority of borrowers are poor, with incomes between $9,000 and $17,000 a year, according to fringe-bank researcher John Caskey. They are young, in and out of work, and disproportionately of color. Cash America's *Annual Report* describes them this way: "The cash-only individual makes up the backbone of America. He's [*sic*] the hard-working next door neighbor, the guy at the corner service station, or the lady who works as a checker at the local supermarket." Caskey quotes Jack Daugherty of Cash America to somewhat different effect: "I could take my customers and put them on a bus and drive them down to a bank and the bank would laugh at them. That's why they're my customers."

"AND YOU DON'T NEED CREDIT TO GET IT"

. . .

By redefining what they are doing as "renting," rent-to-own stores have emerged to evade usury laws that limit the interest paid by people who buy appliances and furniture on credit. Profits in this $3.7 billion-a-year business stem from astounding markups, as customers often pay five times what they would for retail. By the mid-1990s rent-to-own stores had tripled in number, so that by 1994 there were some seventy-five hundred rent-to-own outlets nationwide. Like check-cashing outlets and pawnshops, they increasingly come in corporate chain sizes.

The Rent-A-Center chain boasts twelve hundred stores, a large share of this market. But another patriotic chain, RentAmerica, dominates the Washington, D.C., area. Mostly located in two poorer suburbs (including Jenkins's) and southeast D.C., RentAmerica is a temple to consumption. To walk in is to discover a lush cornucopia of household consumer goods: florid bedroom furniture; leather couches; brightly colored, blaring television sets; giant, gleaming refrigerators; and shimmering gold jewelry. The store offers impoverished customers a shot at the postwar American dream.

But the American-flag sign that soars from the parking lot, the giddy interior, the slick brochures, and the "convenience" (or urgency?) of instant purchases and free delivery belie RentAmerica's harsh and greedy terms. . . . The terms explain that the baby-bear TV requires seventy-eight weekly payments of $9.99, or $779.22 (plus tax); the twenty-seven-inch TV costs seventy-eight weekly payments of $15.99, or $1,247.22 (plus tax); and the thirty-two-inch TV will not be yours until you have paid in full: 104 weekly payments of $24.99, or $2,598.96 (plus tax). Retail prices are much lower. RentAmerica has the good sense *not* to mention either the alleged or actual prices for gold jewelry, refrigerators,

CONTEXT

freezers, the "bedroom suite," or the "living-room group." The brochure recommends: "Ask for Details!"

. . .

To understand their excesses, it might be helpful to contrast rent-to-own terms and interest rates to the consumer credit available to residents of wealthier neighborhoods, who can receive a 10 percent discount on a purchase up to $300 at Woodward and Lothrop, for example, just by applying for a store card—though if they do not pay on time and in full, they owe 21 percent interest. Or at CompUSA, a computer store in the Maryland/ Virginia suburbs, approved customers can charge a computer and pay no interest for six months; they pay accumulated interest, however, if they do not pay in full at that time. Seeing RentAmerica helps put these admittedly harsh, austere, and misleading terms into perspective.

A FESTIVAL OF DEBT

. . .

Poor neighborhoods in Washington, D.C., are plagued by finance companies peddling loans, to consolidate debt or to make home repairs, to people who are financially desperate or credit starved. These firms target minority, fixed- or low-income, low-wage, and Social Security-dependent households who often hold substantial equity in their homes as their sole resource. Not surprisingly, the finance companies charge high interest: from 36 to 50 percent. They tack on worthless, expensive "credit insurance." They offer shoddy work and pursue ruthless, haranguing collection policies. Sometimes they refinance these loans several times, piling on fees along the way: prepayment penalty fees, more credit insurance, and loan origination fees. They front for some of the country's largest financial institutions: NationsBank (after it acquired ChryslerFirst), Ford Financial Services (whose Associated Services division may keep it afloat), Chemical Bank, ITT, Fleet Financial Services, BankAmerica (through its Security Pacific division), General Motors, General Electric, Westinghouse, and Citicorp. These large lenders front money through lines of credit to finance companies, then buy up and bundle the loans and sell them on Wall Street via secondary securities markets. The customer may be left with shoddy repair work, a huge debt, the threat of foreclosure, and nobody to hold responsible.

. . .

While the poor have developed many creative strategies to provide the essentials of life, such as doubling up, working under the table, managing collective living, and negotiating ongoing exchanges with friends and kin, they are increasingly vulnerable in the current economic climate. When intergenerational network flows, employment, and government assistance fail them, when relatives can no longer provide small loans between checks or the exchange of food stamps for cash, poor people develop strategies to work the fringe banking system: pawning televisions and VCRs when between checks, redeeming them when they can; cashing their checks at America's Cash Express; paying their bills with money orders and moneygrams they purchase at ACE; using the poor person's telephone, the pager; and "renting" their grossly overpriced furniture and appliances for as long as they can.

. . . The same developers who refused to maintain or build low-cost urban housing have gone bust on overpriced condominiums, unnecessary office space, and underutilized shopping centers in the suburbs. The same lenders who disinvested in cities, jobs, workers, and infrastructure squandered their money on junk bonds and takeovers. Now they're back, extending credit to fringe banks for loans of last resort and thus passing on high-cost debt to the poor.

30

At the Elite Colleges

Peter Schmidt

Autumn and a new academic year are upon us, which means that selective colleges are engaged in the annual ritual of singing the praises of their new freshman classes. Surf the websites of such institutions and you will find press releases boasting that they have increased their black and Hispanic enrollments, admitted bumper crops of National Merit scholars or became the destination of choice for hordes of high school valedictorians. Many are bragging about the large share of applicants they rejected, as a way of conveying to the world just how popular and selective they are.

What they almost never say is that many of the applicants who were rejected were far more qualified than those accepted. Moreover, contrary to popular belief, it was not the black and Hispanic beneficiaries of affirmative action, but the rich white kids with cash and connections who elbowed most of the worthier applicants aside.

Researchers with access to closely guarded college admissions data have found that, on the whole, about 15 percent of freshmen enrolled at America's highly selective colleges are white teens who failed to meet their institutions' minimum admissions standards. Five years ago, two researchers working for the Educational Testing Service, Anthony Carnevale and Stephen Rose, took the academic profiles of students admitted into 146 colleges in the top two tiers of Barron's college guide and matched them up against the institutions' advertised requirements in terms of high school grade point average, SAT or ACT scores, letters of recommendation, and records of involvement in extracurricular activities. White students who failed to make the grade on all counts were nearly twice as prevalent on such campuses as black and Hispanic students who received an admissions break based on their ethnicity or race.

Who are these mediocre white students getting into institutions such as Harvard, Wellesley, Notre Dame, Duke, and the University of Virginia? A sizable number are recruited athletes who, research has shown, will perform worse on average than other students with similar academic profiles, mainly as a result of the demands their coaches will place on them. A larger share, however, are students who gained admission through their ties to people the institution wanted to keep happy, with alumni, donors, faculty members, administrators, and politicians topping the list.

Applicants who stood no chance of gaining admission without connections are only the most blatant beneficiaries of such admissions preferences. Except perhaps at the very summit of the applicant pile—that lofty place occupied by young people too brilliant for anyone in their right mind to turn down—colleges routinely favor those who have connections over those who don't. While some applicants gain admission by legitimately beating out their peers, many others get into exclusive colleges the same way people get into trendy night clubs, by knowing the management or flashing cash at the person manning the velvet rope.

Leaders at many selective colleges say they have no choice but to instruct their admissions offices to reward those who financially support their institutions, because keeping donors happy is the only way they can keep the place afloat. They also say that the money they take in through such admissions preferences helps them provide financial aid to students in need. But many of the colleges granting such preferences are already well-financed, with huge endowments. And, in many cases, little of the money they take in goes toward serving the less-advantaged.

A few years ago, *The Chronicle of Higher Education* looked at colleges with more than $500 million in their endowments and found that most served disproportionately few students from families with incomes low enough to qualify for federal Pell Grants. A separate study of flagship state universities conducted by the Education Trust found that those universities' enrollments of Pell Grant recipients had been shrinking, even as the number of students qualifying for such grants had gone up. Just 40 percent of the financial aid money being distributed by public colleges is going to students with documented financial need. Most such money is being used to offer merit-based scholarships or tuition discounts to potential recruits who can enhance a college's reputation, or appear likely to cover the rest of their tuition tab and to donate down the road.

Given such trends, is it any wonder that young people from the wealthiest fourth of society are about 25 times as likely as those from the bottom fourth to enroll in a selective college, or that, over the past two decades, the middle class has been steadily getting squeezed out of such institutions by those with more money?

A degree from a selective college can open many doors for a talented young person from a humble background. But rather than promoting social mobility, our nation's selective colleges appear to be thwarting it, by turning away applicants who have excelled given their circumstances and offering second chances to wealthy and connected young people who have squandered many of the advantages life has offered them.

When social mobility goes away, at least two dangerous things can happen. The privileged class that produces most of our nation's leaders can become complacent enough to foster mediocrity, and less-fortunate segments of our society can become resigned to the notion that hard work will not get them anywhere.

. . .

31

The Debt-for-Diploma System

José Garcia, James Lardner, and Cindy Zeldin

. . .

WHY WORRY?

Student loans have existed in one form or another for half a century. Until the early 1990s, however, they played a small role in the education of a minority of American college students. States kept tuitions at public universities low, with grant aid typically covering about three-quarters of the expense for a low-income student. The average student could earn enough with a summer job to make up the difference. Not anymore. The states have pulled back, grants have shriveled in value, and loans have become the way most students handle most of the cost of college.

. . .

C
O
N
T
E
X
T

The Project on Student Debt, an organization committed to "keeping college within reach," has carved out a place on its Web site for people to tell their student loan stories. Most of them make painful reading. Troy, for example, is a first-generation college graduate. He and his wife finished school seven years ago with about $60,000 in student loan debt each. Today they owe a combined $200,000, as a result of a long period of forbearance when they were unable to make payments but the interest kept accumulating. They pay about $1,200 a month, according to Troy, with "every penny" now going to interest. "I'm in a position that I feel I will never get out of," he says.

Rebecca borrowed $100,000 to pay for pharmacy school. Her husband borrowed $200,000 for medical school. They pay $3,000 a month. Student loans have become "the main driver of all of our life and career decisions," she says. "Our children will be in and out of college before we pay off our own college education in another twenty-five years or so."

. . .

Many students try to hold back the tide of debt by working. Three-quarters of all full-time college students have jobs—on campus or off—with nearly half putting in twenty-five hours or more a week, according to U.S. Department of Education figures. . . . But when students work longer hours at multiple jobs—and when they work off campus as well as on—the formula goes sour. Studying time dwindles (along with time for extracurricular and social activities), grades suffer, and the whole college experience takes on a harsher edge.

In this debt-for-diploma and work-till-you-drop environment, many students get discouraged; fully one-third drop out after the first year. First-generation college students are almost twice as likely as students with college-educated parents to be among the early casualties.

The most common of all cost-reduction strategies—the path followed by more than four hundred thousand college-qualified students from households with incomes of less than $50,000 every year—is to opt for a two-year community college program. The tuition in these programs is significantly lower than it is in four-year programs (though still high enough to produce an average student loan debt of $8,700). But while students often start out with the idea of getting an associate's degree and then transferring to a four-year institution and going for a bachelor's degree, the record shows that only a very small number follow through on that plan.

Community college students are often up against the most complicated situations—full-time jobs, raising children, working by day, taking classes by night. Five years after entering, only about one in five has gotten as far as an associate's degree. Many leave and never return, and many join the ranks of the estimated one out of five student borrowers who may have set out to get an education at a minimum of expense for themselves and their families, but ended up with the worst of all possible results—debt and no diploma.

A POLICY THAT WORKED

For the two-thirds of college students who borrow to foot the tuition bill, signing up for a loan before stepping onto campus has become part of the college-going ritual. But as their parents and grandparents can attest, it wasn't always this way. Deep inside today's jerry-built financial aid system, you can see the remains of a different structure—one that was purposefully crafted to make college affordable and accessible to any graduating high school student with the smarts and the desire to go.

. . . [T]he Servicemen's Readjustment Act of 1944 . . . —subsequently nicknamed the GI bill—helped millions of returning veterans "readjust" to civilian life and provide them with the education, skills, and money to successfully reintegrate into society and the economy. To that end, the GI bill provided grants for tuition, books, and health insurance.

The annual amount available to a veteran in 1948 was $500—enough at the time to pay for all but $25 of a year's tuition at Harvard. On top of that, each veteran got a monthly living-expense stipend of $50—$400 in today's money. As a point of comparison, the average federal grant in 2005 was $2,354—$24,000 short of the tuition and fees at Harvard, and $3,482 short of the public university average.

The GI bill was a spectacular example of what, in a later era, would be called a "big government" program—one enacted, moreover, at a time when the government had already gone deep into debt to pay for the cost of a world war. Yet it produced a reward that few people have ever questioned, paying the country back about $7 for every dollar spent, by some estimates. An estimated 2.3 million veterans took advantage of its higher-education grants; by 1960, the beneficiaries included about half the members of Congress. Through its zero down payment policies and low-interest mortgages, the GI bill helped millions of other veterans and their families buy homes, laying the foundation for the great suburban middle class that symbolized the American dream of widespread prosperity and upward mobility. Not a bad return on a seven-year investment of $91 billion in today's money.

In 1965, the country took another big step forward in its mission of making college affordable for most young people, not just the privileged few. That year, Congress passed the Higher Education Act, extending GI bill-style benefits to nonveterans and creating the grants and loans on which today's system is largely based. The goal, President Lyndon Johnson said when he signed the bill, was to ensure that "a high school senior anywhere in this great land of ours can apply to any college or any university in any of the fifty states and not be turned away because his family is poor."

As a result of this landmark legislation, countless young Americans became the first in their families to attend college; the number of low-income college students nearly doubled between 1965 and 1971. For poor kids, grants were generous enough to cover the cost of going to school. For the middle class, tuition at public universities remained low enough to allow most students to pay the price of admission with a part-time job and some help from Mom and Dad.

In 1972, Congress reaffirmed its commitment to the Higher Education Act—both the goal and the means—by creating what came to be known as Pell grants, in honor of their Senate champion, Claiborne Pell of Rhode Island. Throughout the 1970s, low-income students continued to close in on the enrollment rates of their wealthier contemporaries. . . . Average tuition in the late 1970s for a four-year public college was just over $2,192, in 2006 dollars. Add in room and board, and the total cost was still under $6,900. For those with more substantial means, the tuition at a private college was in the $9,000 neighborhood; the inflation-adjusted total, with room and board included, came to $14,000. To put that into perspective, the cost of attending a private university in 1976 was only slightly higher than the cost of attending a public university today. Borrowing your way through college wasn't the norm, because it wasn't necessary.

TRAGEDY OF NEGLECT

Two-thirds of all financial aid used to come from grants. Now two-thirds comes from loans. What happened? Mainly, it is a story of what did not happen. Over a span of thirty years, elected officials failed to maintain adequate funding for Pell grants, decimating their purchasing power in the wake of rising costs and surging enrollments. . . . In the states, elected officials cut back on funding for public colleges and universities, resulting in steeply rising tuitions. In per-pupil terms, state-level spending on higher education has fallen to a twenty-five-year low, even as government officials and corporate leaders keep pounding out the message of a college degree as the key to a successful future. In one generation, tuition at public universities has risen 122 percent, from $2,628 in 1986–1987 to $5,836 in 2006–2007 (in 2006 dollars). In the last five years alone, tuition and fees at public universities have gone up 40 percent, taking inflation into account. . . .

Just as grant funding was drying up, states were moving resources from need-based to so-called merit-based aid programs. Between 1994 and 2004, spending by the states on need-based scholarships for undergraduates increased by 95 percent, while spending on merit-based aid increased by 350 percent. The proportion of state grants awarded on the basis of merit rather than need rose from 13 percent to 27 percent during this period. . . . In 1995, for example, the average student from a family with an income below $20,000 received $836 in institutional grant aid, while the average student from a family earning $100,000 or more received $239 in grant aid. In 2003, the average award to low-income students had increased 50 percent, to $1,251, while the average award to students from families earning above $100,000 had grown 227 percent, to $781.

. . .

As a result, the gains made during the 1970s in expanding access to college have begun to erode. In fact, the gap in college enrollment between white students, on the one hand, and black and Hispanic students, on the other, has actually widened over the last thirty years, as has the college enrollment gap by socio-economic status. . . .

TODAY'S STUDENTS, TOMORROW'S DEBTORS

Once you're on the hook, there's no easy escape from student loans. The federal government can be a persistent creditor, and it has collection methods all its own—seizing a tax refund, for example, or tapping into a stream of benefit checks.

Bankruptcy? Think again. Student loans, unlike other forms of credit, cannot be discharged that way. There's no statute of limitations, either. About 9 percent of Americans between the ages of fifty-five and sixty-four have student loan debt (the average balance is $17,498). Sandra, at fifty-nine, is one of them. Another contributor to the Project on Student Debt story bank, she writes: "I am not in a high-paying field. I teach at a university and my students are working professionals who work with young children with disabilities." She expects to be making payments until 2012. "I will not fully pay this loan," she says, "until I am almost old enough to receive Social Security."

The average graduate leaves college today with $19,300 in student loan debt (up from $9,250 a little over a decade ago). Despite the hardships, most young adults believe that the personal growth and career opportunities of a college degree make the debt worthwhile. They wish they could have borrowed less, but, by and large, they wouldn't trade their degree for a debt-free existence. Most are doing their best to cope with the payment burden.

. . .

As the level of debt has increased, so has the cost of debt, because of the growing proportion of student loans being issued by private lenders outside the federal rules. Federal loans carry fixed interest rates, currently capped at 6.8 percent. With private loans, interest is unregulated and "risk-based lending" enters the picture, though Congress passed legislation in September 2007 that will gradually reduce the interest rate on new subsidized loans to 3.4 percent in 2011. Several lenders have already come out with loans supposedly designed for students and families with poor credit histories—loans typically carrying interest rates in the 16 to 18 percent neighborhood, according to Bankrate.com. One company, Loan to Learn, has interest rates reaching as high as 16 percent *on top of* a 10 percent up-front fee!

. . .

WHO'S IN CHARGE HERE? ...

. . .

Most of the loans issued under the federal program are the guaranteed kind that the industry thrives on—most, but not all. There is an alternative. It's called direct lending. The William D. Ford Federal Direct Loan program, launched nationally in 1993, was an attempt to find out whether costs could be reduced with the government issuing the loans itself. They were reduced—dramatically. Unlike federally guaranteed student loans, which cost taxpayers 7 cents on every dollar in subsidies to private student lenders, the Direct Loan program costs less than 4 cents per dollar lent.

Proponents in Congress and the Clinton administration originally hoped to switch all federal loans from the guaranteed program to the direct program. By doing so, the Congressional Budget Office has estimated, the federal government could save $12 billion over ten years as a result of lower subsidies and administrative expenses. Because of opposition from Republicans and the student loan industry, however, a compromise was reached. . . . [T]he Direct Loan program would . . . not be allowed to market its loans the way Sallie Mae and other student lenders do. When the Republicans retook control of Congress in 1994, they passed a law prohibiting the Education Department from encouraging or requiring colleges to participate in the Direct Loan program. Thoroughly hamstrung, the program has been losing ground for the past decade; the number of participating schools, never higher than 30 percent, is now down to 25 percent.

. . .

The industry's number one goal for 2007 and 2008, . . . [is] to protect the gravy train of subsidies that lenders receive on federal student loans. If history is any guide, they will protect it well. While Congress finally acted to increase the maximum Pell grant by a few hundred dollars . . . it still isn't enough to allow low-income students to pay for college without going into massive debt, and it certainly isn't enough to shift the center of gravity of the system. Borrowing will continue to be the lifeblood of that system, with lenders reaping profits and young people living in the red.

32

Students with Disabilities

Financial Aid Policy Issues

Thomas R. Wolanin

About nine percent of all undergraduate students in the United States reported having a disability in 2000. This amounts to approximately 1.3 million students. . . . Students with disabilities generally have lower incomes than their peers without disabilities. Thirty-seven percent of students with disabilities in high school came from families with household incomes below $25,000, compared to only 20% of their peers. At the college level, students from the lowest-income quartile have the highest rate of disability, especially independent students. . . .

Low-income students with disabilities, like other low-income students, need financial assistance in order to afford the costs of higher education. However, being disproportionately low-income, students with disabilities have an even greater need for financial assistance than other students. Thus, the financial barriers to higher education opportunities faced by students from low-income families are also even more widespread for students with disabilities . . . .

HAVING A DISABILITY IS EXPENSIVE

In addition to the problems faced by all low-income students, students with disabilities from low-income families face particular financial barriers to higher education not faced by other students. To meet their special needs, persons with disabilities often receive services from a variety of professionals. These may include counselors, doctors, psychologists, and therapists of all kinds, who must be visited in their respective offices, clinics, and hospitals. For persons with disabilities, insurance payments and support from public and private agencies rarely cover the entire cost of the treatments and services they receive. The difference is made up out-of-pocket.

Having a disability also involves incidental costs such as special foods to meet dietary restrictions, cab fares to the doctor, wheelchair maintenance, dog food and veterinary bills for a guide dog, over-the-counter medications, and higher utility bills from running computers and assistive devices. . . . For a low-income student with a disability, in theory at least, all of these additional costs of having a disability can be met through student financial aid sources. . . . Unfortunately, the system does not live up to its ideals, and faces difficulties in practice. . . . Students with disabilities must document to the financial aid administrator the expenses related to their disabilities that are not provided for by another source. This requires self-confidence and self-advocacy skills that often have not been well developed in students with disabilities. These students must undertake the difficult and complex task of cataloging and documenting all of the expenses related to their disabilities and reducing that amount by support received from elsewhere, such as Vocational Rehabilitation

(VR). This is a formidable challenge that would test the skills of anyone and is sometimes unreasonable for students with disabilities.

. . .

Currently, fully meeting the needs of students with disabilities would require diverting resources from other low-income students. This would not be a just or desirable result. The most important policy change required to meet the financial needs of low-income students with disabilities is to expand the amount of financial aid available for all low-income students. Otherwise, the process becomes a matter of rationing and redistributing limited financial aid dollars among various groups of financially needy students, including those with disabilities.

HAVING A DISABILITY IS TIME CONSUMING

Generally, students with disabilities in higher education can attain the same academic levels as their peers without disabilities; however, students with disabilities cannot do it as quickly. Students with disabilities may have conditions that slow them down in general. For example, it takes longer to walk from point A to point B when one's energy and stamina are sapped by chronic illness. A person in a wheelchair or with cerebral palsy needs more time to bathe, dress, shop, and accomplish other self-care tasks. Students with disabilities have multiple demands on their time for the treatments and services required to meet their needs apart from their studies. Trips to doctors, therapists, counselors, and administrators take time. It also takes time to acquire, set up, learn how to use, and maintain auxiliary learning aids such as electronic readers or videotext displays. Software bugs and computer crashes are not just inconveniences for a student with a disability, who must have electronic aids to study—these technical glitches bring a halt to learning.

Further, students with disabilities often take longer to perform academic tasks. Many disabilities, particularly learning disabilities, increase the time needed to process information, which is the central task of most academic work. A student with dyslexia needs more time to read and understand a given amount of written text compared with a student without this disability. The speed at which an aide reads text to a blind student is slower than the reading speed of sighted students. Listening to a lecture over again on tape takes longer than reviewing notes taken in the classroom.

. . .

Given the time demands faced by students with disabilities, it follows that the time to degree completion for students with disabilities is longer than for their peers without disabilities. . . . The longer time that students with disabilities need to complete their studies increases their costs of higher education. Their forgone income is greater than that of their peers without disabilities. Most importantly, even if students with disabilities are taking a reduced or part-time course load, they still have to live full time. They face additional years of room and board costs, semester fees, and the extra costs associated with their disability to make the same academic progress that their peers without disabilities make in a shorter time. They may also be charged more per credit hour or per course if they are taking less than the standard full-time course load.

. . .

In sum, low-income students with disabilities generally have a greater need for financial aid than their peers without disabilities. But, they face additional obstacles in assembling the package of resources to pay for college. A larger burden is placed on students with disabilities who may have less capacity to bear it.

. . .

33

The Girls Next Door

Peter Landesman

The house at 1212 1/2 West Front Street in Plainfield, N.J., is a conventional midcentury home with slate-gray siding, white trim and Victoria lines. . . . American flags fluttered from porches and windows. The neighborhood is a leafy, middle-class Anytown. The house is set back off the street, near two convenience stores and a gift shop. On the door of Superior Supermarket was pasted a sign issued by the Plainfield police: "Safe neighborhoods save lives." The store's manager, who refused to tell me his name, said he never noticed anything unusual about the house, and never heard anything. . . . Cars drove up to the house all day; nice cars, all kinds of cars. Dozens of men came and went. "But no one here knew what was really going on," . . . . And no one ever asked.

On a tip, the Plainfield police raided the house in February 2002, expecting to find illegal aliens working an underground brothel. What the police found were four girls between the ages of 14 and 17. They were all Mexican nationals without documentation. But they weren't prostitutes; they were sex slaves. The distinction is important: these girls weren't working for profit or a paycheck. They were captives to the traffickers and keepers who controlled their every move. . . . The police found a squalid, land-based equivalent of a 19th-century slave ship, with rancid, doorless bathrooms; bare, putrid mattresses; and a stash of penicillin, "morning after" pills and misoprostol, an antiulcer medication that can induce abortion. The girls were pale, exhausted and malnourished.

It turned out that 1212 1/2 West Front Street was one of what law-enforcement officials say are dozens of active stash houses and apartments in the New York metropolitan area—mirroring hundreds more in other major cities like Los Angeles, Atlanta and Chicago—where underage girls and young women from dozens of countries are trafficked and held captive. Most of them—whether they started out in Eastern Europe or Latin America—are taken to the United States through Mexico. Some of them have been baited by promises of legitimate jobs and a better life in America; many have been abducted; others have been bought from or abandoned by their impoverished families.

Because of the porousness of the U.S.-Mexico border and the criminal networks that traverse it, the towns and cities along that border have become the main staging area in an illicit and barbaric industry, whose "products" are women and girls. On both sides of the border, they are rented out for sex for as little as 15 minutes at a time, dozens of times a day. Sometimes they are sold outright to other traffickers and sex rings, victims and experts say. These sex slaves earn no money, there is nothing voluntary about what they do and if they try to escape they are often beaten and sometimes killed.

. . .

[T]he United States has become a major importer of sex slaves. Last year, the C.I.A. estimated that between 18,000 and 20,000 people are trafficked annually into the United States. The government has not studied how many of these are victims of sex traffickers, but Kevin Bales, president of Free the Slaves, America's largest anti-slavery organization, says that the number is at least 10,000 a year. . . . Bales estimates that there are 30,000 to 50,000 sex slaves in captivity in the United States at any given time. Laura Lederer, a senior State Department adviser on trafficking, told me, "We're not finding victims in the United States because we're not looking for them."

ABDUCTION

In Eastern European capitals like Kiev and Moscow, dozens of sex-trafficking rings advertise nanny positions in the United States in local newspapers; others claim to be scouting for models and actresses. In Chisinau, the capital of the former Soviet republic of Moldova—the poorest country in Europe and the one experts say is most heavily culled by traffickers for young women—I saw a billboard with a fresh-faced, smiling young woman beckoning girls to waitress positions in Paris. But of course there are no waitress positions and no "Paris." Some of these young women are actually tricked into paying their own travel expenses—typically around $3,000—as a down payment on what they expect to be bright, prosperous futures, only to find themselves kept prisoner in Mexico before being moved to the United States and sold into sexual bondage there.

. . .

Every day, flights from Paris, London and Amsterdam arrive at Mexico City's international airport carrying groups of these girls, sometimes as many as seven at a time, according to two Mexico City immigration officers I spoke with (and who asked to remain anonymous). One of them told me that officials at the airport—who cooperate with Mexico's federal preventive police (P.F.P.) —work with the traffickers and "direct airlines to park at certain gates. Officials go to the aircraft. They know the seat numbers. While passengers come off, they take the girls to an office, where officials will 'process' them."

. . .

But Mexico is not merely a way station en route to the U.S. for third-country traffickers, like the Eastern European rings. It is also a vast source of even younger and more cheaply acquired girls for sexual servitude in the United States. While European traffickers tend to dupe their victims into boarding one-way flights to Mexico to their own captivity, Mexican traffickers rely on the charm and brute force of "Los Lenones," tightly organized associations of pimps, according to Roberto Caballero, an officer with the P.F.P. Although hundreds of "popcorn traffickers"—individuals who take control of one or two girls—work the margins, Caballero said, at least 15 major trafficking organizations and 120 associated factions tracked by the P.F.P. operate as wholesalers: collecting human merchandise and taking orders from safe houses and brothels in the major sex-trafficking hubs in New York, Los Angeles, Atlanta and Chicago.

. . . Throughout the rural and suburban towns from southern Mexico to the U.S. border, along what traffickers call the Via Lactea, or Milky Way, the agents of Los Lenones troll the bus stations and factories and school dances where under-age girls gather, work and socialize. They first ply the girls like prospective lovers, buying them meals and desserts, promising affection and then marriage. Then the men describe rumors they've heard about America, about the promise of jobs and schools. Sometimes the girls are easy prey. Most of them already dream of El Norte. But the theater often ends as soon as the agent has the girl alone, when he beats her, drugs her or simply forces her into a waiting car.

. . .

[A] U.S. Embassy official told me: "Mexican officials see sex trafficking as a U.S. problem. If there wasn't such a large demand, then people—trafficking victims and migrants alike—wouldn't be going up there."

. . .

BREAKING THE GIRLS IN

. . .

For the Mexican girls abducted by Los Lenones, the process of breaking them in often begins on Calle Santo Tomas, a filthy narrow street in La Merced, a dangerous and raucous ghetto in Mexico City. . . . Most of the girls on Santo Tomas would have sex with 20 to 30 men a day; they would do this seven days a week usually for weeks but sometimes for months before they were "ready" for the United States. If they refused, they would be beaten and sometimes killed. They would be told that if they tried to escape, one of their family members, who usually had no idea where they were, would be beaten or killed. Working at the brutalizing pace of 20 men per day, a girl could earn her captors as much as $2,000 a week. In the U.S., that same girl could bring in perhaps $30,000 per week.

. . .

CROSSING THE BORDER

In November, I followed by helicopter the 12-foot-high sheet-metal fence that represents the U.S.-Mexico boundary from Imperial Beach, Calif., south of San Diego, 14 miles across the gritty warrens and havoc of Tijuana into the barren hills of Tecate. . . . I hovered over the end of the fence with Lester McDaniel, a special agent with Immigration and Customs Enforcement. On the U.S. side, "J-e-s-u-s" was spelled out in rocks 10 feet high across a steep hillside. A 15-foot white wooden cross rose from the peak. It is here that thousands of girls and young women—most of them Mexican and many of them straight from Calle Santo Tomas—are taken every year, mostly between January and August, the dry season. Coyotes—or smugglers—subcontracted exclusively by sex traffickers sometimes trudge the girls up to the cross and let them pray, then herd them into the hills northward.

. . .

"If a girl tries to run, she's killed and becomes just one more woman in the desert," says Marisa B. Ugarte, director of the Bilateral Safety Corridor Coalition, a San Diego organization that coordinates rescue efforts for trafficking victims on both sides of the border. "But if she keeps going north, she reaches the Gates of Hell."

One girl who was trafficked back and forth across that border repeatedly was Andrea. "Andrea" is just one name she was given by her traffickers and clients; she doesn't know her real name. She was born in the United States and sold or abandoned here—at about 4 years old, she says—by a woman who may have been her mother. (She is now in her early to mid-20s; she doesn't know for sure.) She says that she spent approximately the next 12 years as the captive of a sex-trafficking ring that operated on both sides of the Mexican border. Because of the threat of retribution from her former captors, who are believed to be still at large, an organization that rescues and counsels trafficking victims and former prostitutes arranged for me to meet Andrea in October at a secret location in the United States.

. . .

Andrea told me she was transported to Juarez dozens of times. During one visit, when she was about 7 years old, the trafficker took her to the Radisson Casa Grande Hotel, where there was a john waiting in a room. The john was an older American man, and he read Bible passages to her before and after having sex with her. Andrea described other rooms she remembered in other hotels in Mexico: the Howard Johnson in Leon, the Crowne Plaza in Guadalajara. She remembers most of all the ceiling patterns. "When I was taken to Mexico, I knew things were going to be different," she said. The "customers" were American businessmen. "The men who went there had higher positions, had more to lose if they were caught doing these things on the other side of the border. I was told my purpose was to keep these men from abusing their own kids." Later she told me: "The white kids you could beat but you couldn't mark. But with Mexican kids you could do whatever you wanted. They're untraceable. You lose nothing by killing them."

. . .

IN THE UNITED STATES: HIDING IN PLAIN SIGHT

. . .

In the past several months, I have visited a number of addresses where trafficked girls and young women have reportedly ended up: besides the house in Plainfield, N.J., there is a row house on 51st Avenue in the Corona section of Queens, which has been identified to Mexican federal preventive police by escaped trafficking victims. There is the apartment at Barrington Plaza in the tony Westwood section of Los Angeles . . . [a]nd there's a house on Massachusetts Avenue in Vista, Calif., a San Diego suburb, which was pointed out to me by a San Diego sheriff. These places all have at least one thing in common: they are camouflaged by their normal, middle-class surroundings.

"This is not narco-traffic secrecy," says Sharon B. Cohn, director of anti-trafficking operations for the International Justice Mission. "These are not people kidnapped and held for ransom, but women and children sold every single day. If they're hidden, their keepers don't make money."

. . .

But border agents and local policemen usually don't know trafficking when they see it. The operating assumption among American police departments is that women who sell their bodies do so by choice, and undocumented foreign women who sell their bodies are not only prostitutes (that is, voluntary sex workers) but also trespassers on U.S. soil. No Department of Justice attorney or police vice squad officer I spoke with in Los Angeles— one of the country's busiest thoroughfares for forced sex traffic—considers sex trafficking in the U.S. a serious problem, or a priority. A teenage girl arrested on Sunset Strip for solicitation, or a group of Russian sex workers arrested in a brothel raid in the San Fernando Valley, are automatically heaped onto a pile of workaday vice arrests.

. . .

IMPRISONMENT AND SUBMISSION

. . .

All the girls I spoke to said that their captors were both psychologically and physically abusive. Andrea told me that she and the other children she was held with were frequently beaten to keep them off-balance and obedient. . . .

Kevin Bales of Free the Slaves says: "The physical path of a person being trafficked includes stages of degradation of a person's mental state. A victim gets deprived of food, gets hungry, a little dizzy and sleep-deprived. She begins to break down; she can't think for herself. Then take away her travel documents, and you've made her stateless. Then layer on physical violence, and she begins to follow orders. Then add a foreign culture and language, and she's trapped."

Then add one more layer: a sex-trafficking victim's belief that her family is being tracked as collateral for her body. All sex-trafficking operations, whether Mexican, Ukrainian or Thai, are vast criminal underworlds with roots and branches that reach back to the countries, towns and neighborhoods of their victims.

. . .

If anything, the women I talked to said that the sex in the U.S. is even rougher than what the girls face on Calle Santo Tomas. Rosario, a woman I met in Mexico City, who had been trafficked to New York and held captive for a number of years, said: "In America we had 'special jobs.' Oral sex, anal sex, often with many men. Sex is now more adventurous, harder." She said that she believed younger foreign girls were in demand in the U.S. because of an increased appetite for more aggressive, dangerous sex. Traffickers need younger and younger girls, she suggested, simply because they are more pliable. In Eastern Europe, too, the typical age of sex-trafficking victims is plummeting; according to Matei of Reaching Out, while most girls used to be in their late teens and 20s, 13-year-olds are now far from unusual.

Immigration and Customs Enforcement agents at the Cyber Crimes Center in Fairfax, Va., are finding that when it comes to sex, what was once considered abnormal is now the norm. They are tracking a clear spike in the demand for harder-core pornography on the Internet. . . . I had heard of one Web site that supposedly offered sex slaves for purchase to individuals. The I.C.E. agents hadn't heard of it. Special Agent Don Daufenbach, I.C.E.'s manager for undercover operations, brought it up on a screen. A hush came over the room as the agents leaned forward, clearly disturbed. "That sure looks like the real thing," Daufenbach said. There were streams of Web pages of thumbnail images of young women of every ethnicity in obvious distress, bound, gagged, contorted. The agents in the room pointed out probable injuries from torture. Cyberauctions for some of the women were in progress; one had exceeded $300,000. "With new Internet technology," Woo said, "pornography is becoming more pervasive. With Web cams we're seeing more live molestation of children." One of I.C.E.'s recent successes, Operation Hamlet, broke up a ring of adults who traded images and videos of themselves forcing sex on their own young children.

But the supply of cheap girls and young women to feed the global appetite appears to be limitless. And it's possible that the crimes committed against them in the U.S. cut deeper than elsewhere, precisely because so many of them are snared by the glittery promise of an America that turns out to be not their salvation but their place of destruction.

. . .

34

Unnatural Disasters

Race and Poverty

Michael Eric Dyson

The barrage of images in newspapers and on television tested the nation's collective sense of reality. There were men and women wading chest-deep in water—when they weren't floating or drowning in the toxic whirlpool the streets of New Orleans had become. When the waters subsided, there were dead bodies strewn on curbsides and wrapped in blankets by fellow sufferers, who provided the perished their only dignity. There were unseemly collages of people silently dying from hunger and thirst—and of folk writhing in pain, or quickly collapsing under the weight of missed medicine for diabetes, high blood pressure, or heart trouble. Photo snaps and film shots captured legions of men and women huddling in groups or hugging corners, crying in wild-eyed desperation for help, for any help, from somebody, anybody, who would listen to their unanswered pleas. . . .

Men, women, and children tore through deserted streets lined with empty stores, hunting for food and water and clothing for their bodies. They were hurried along by the steadily diminishing prospect of rescue by the government, by *their* government, whose only visible representatives were the police who came after them for looting. There were wailing infants clasping crying mothers who mouthed prayers for someone to please just save their babies. . . . This surely couldn't be the United States of America—and how cruelly that term seemed to mock those poor citizens who felt disunited and disconnected and just plain dissed by their government. This couldn't be the richest and most powerful nation on the globe, leaving behind some of its poorest citizens to fend for themselves.

And yet it was. It was bad enough to witness the government's failure to respond to desperate cries of help scrawled on the tattered roofs of flooded homes. But Hurricane Katrina's violent winds and killing waters swept into the mainstream a stark realization: the poor had been abandoned by society and its institutions, and sometimes by their well-off brothers and sisters, long before the storm. . . .

It's not as if it was news to most folk that poverty exists in the United States. . . . Our being surprised, and disgusted, by the poverty that Katrina revealed is a way of remaining deliberately naive about the poor while dodging the responsibility that knowledge of their lives would entail. We remain blissfully ignorant of their circumstances to avoid the brutal indictment of our consciences. When a disaster like Katrina strikes—a *natural* disaster not directly caused by human failure—it frees us to be aware of, and angered by, the catastrophe. After all, it doesn't directly implicate us; it was an act of God. Even when human hands get involved, our fingerprints are nowhere to be found. We're not responsible for the poor and black being left behind; the local, state, or federal government is at fault.

. . .

There are 37 million people in poverty in our nation, 1.1 million of whom fell below the poverty line in 2004. Some of the poorest folk in the nation, people in the Delta, have been largely ignored, rendered invisible, officially forgotten. FEMA left them dangling precipitously on rooftops and in attics because of bureaucratic bumbling. Homeland Security failed miserably in mobilizing resources to rescue Katrina survivors without food, water, or shelter. . . . But the government and society had been failing to pay attention to the poor since long before one of the worst natural disasters in the nation's history swallowed the poor and spit them back up. The world saw just how much we hadn't seen; it witnessed our negligence up close in frightfully full color.

The hardest-hit regions in the Gulf States had already been drowning in extreme poverty: Mississippi is the poorest state in the nation, with Louisiana just behind it. More than 90,000 people in each of the areas stormed by Katrina in Louisiana, Mississippi, and Alabama made less than $10,000 a year. Black folk in these areas were strapped by incomes that were 40 percent less than those earned by whites. Before the storm, New Orleans, with a 67.9 percent black population, had more than 103,000 poor people. That means the Crescent City had a poverty rate of 23 percent, 76 percent higher than the national average of 13.1 percent. New Orleans's poverty rate ranked it seventh out of 290 large U.S. counties.

Although black folk make up 31.5 percent of Louisiana's population, their offspring account for 69 percent of the children in poverty. Though the national average for elders with disabilities is 39.6 percent, New Orleans hovers near 57 percent. The New Orleans median household income is $31,369, far beneath the national median of $44,684. A full 9 percent of households in New Orleans didn't own or have access to a vehicle. That means that nearly one in four citizens in New Orleans, and one in seven in the greater New Orleans metropolitan area, had no access to a car. . . . And children and elderly folk are even more likely to live in households without access to cars. Children and the elderly made up 38 percent of the population in New Orleans, but they accounted for 48 percent of the households without access to cars in the city. The poor and the near-poor made up the vast majority of those without car access in New Orleans, accounting for nearly 80 percent of the city's car-less population. These facts make it painfully clear just why so many folk could not evacuate before Katrina struck. . . . They simply couldn't muster the resources to escape destruction, and, for many, death.

The most glaring feature of their circumstance suggests that Katrina's survivors lived in concentrated poverty—they lived in poor neighborhoods, attended poor schools, and had poorly paying jobs that reflected and reinforced a distressing pattern of rigid segregation. Nearly 50,000 poor folk in New Orleans lived in areas where the poverty rate approached 40 percent. In fact, among the nation's fifty largest cities with poor black families jammed into extremely poor neighborhoods, New Orleans ranked second. Those households living in concentrated poverty often earn barely more than $20,000 a year. . . .

Concentrated poverty is the product of decades of public policies and political measures that isolate black households in neighborhoods plagued by severe segregation and economic hardship. For instance, the federal government's decision to concentrate public housing in segregated inner-city neighborhoods fueled metropolitan expansion. It also cut the poor off from decent housing and educational and economic opportunities by keeping affordable housing for poor minorities out of surrounding suburbs. . . .

When Katrina swept waves of mostly poor and black folk into global view, it also graphically uncovered their poor health. More than 83,000 citizens, or 18.8 percent of the population in New Orleans, lacked health insurance (the national average is 15.5 percent); the numbers for black women doubled those for white women. Nationally, there are nearly 40 million folk without health insurance, many of them black and poor. They resort to the emergency ward for health maintenance. Their survival is compromised because serious diseases are spotted later than need be. . . .

Concentrated poverty does more than undermine academic success and good health; since there is a strong relationship between education and employment, and quality of life, it keeps the poor from better-paying jobs that might interrupt a vicious cycle of poverty. In New Orleans, severe underemployment and unemployment, and unstable employment, gang up on the black poor. This circumstance is made worse by the densely populated communities and housing in which they live, the sheer social misery of much of post-industrial urban Southern life, and their dreadful infant-mortality and homicide rates—the disenfranchised turn more readily and violently on each other rather than striking against the inequality that puts them at each other's throats.

. . .

But one of the untold stories of Katrina is how the hurricane impacted racial and ethnic minorities other than blacks. For instance, nearly 40,000 Mexican citizens who lived (mostly in trailers) and worked in New Orleans were displaced. Altogether, nearly 145,000 Mexicans in the entire Gulf Coast region were scattered by Katrina. Latinos make up 3 percent of Louisiana's population, 124,222 people of the state's 4,515,770 residents. Many Latinos who live in the South are foreign born and are undocumented laborers on farms or in hotels, restaurants, and other service industry jobs.

The fear that government officials and police would target undocumented immigrants discouraged many Latinos from seeking hurricane relief, despite messages from Mexican president Vicente Fox that the American government had assured him that it wouldn't take such action. In fact, for the first time in more than 150 years, Mexico sent aid to the United States in the form of an army unit of nearly 200 soldiers and 45 vehicles that joined a Mexican Navy crew helping hurricane survivors. It also sent food, medicine, nurses, and doctors to Louisiana, as well as a ship transporting ambulances and trucks. The League of United Latin American Citizens (LULAC) sent translators and established a relief fund, while its Arizona branch sent four container trucks with sleeping bags, water, and food.

Latinos in other areas were affected by the hurricane as well. In Bossier County, Louisiana, many Central Americans were employed in the service industry. And Baldwin County, Alabama, was home to many farm workers who lived in migrant camps. Many of them, and Jamaican immigrants as well, had either lost their documentation or had sought refuge in hotels, and not designated shelter areas, for fear of having their citizenship status scrutinized. That fear outweighed the fact that undocumented immigrants, at least in theory, do have rights to disaster relief.

Thousands of Native Americans on the Gulf Coast were hard hit by the storm as well. According to the National Congress of American Indians (NCAI), several Native American tribes were in harm's way across the damaged region, although early on there was little contact with affected members. In the immediate aftermath of Katrina, there was little information about the death tolls among the six federally recognized Native American tribes in Alabama, Louisiana, and Mississippi, including the Parch Band Creek Indian Tribe in Alabama; the Coushatta Indian Tribe, Jena Band of Choctaw, and Tunica-Biloxi Tribe in Louisiana; and the Chitimacha Tribe and the Choctaw Indians in Mississippi. For one tribe near Chalmette, Louisiana, the local high school served as a tribal morgue, holding the bodies of Native American workers, including shrimpers and other fishermen, who were drowned in the flooding near New Orleans. The Mississippi Band of Choctaw Indians experienced power outages on their reservation and sought shelter at tribal hotels. The NCAI partnered with the National Indian Gaming Association (NIGA) to raise relief funds for Native Americans in the Gulf States.

There were also nearly 50,000 Vietnamese fishermen who labored on the Louisiana coast—while others worked in the service and manufacturing industries—along with a large contingent of Filipino American shrimpers, part of the oldest Filipino community in North America. A community of Vietnamese shrimpers also lived and worked near Mississippi; many of them were displaced, while others died in the horrible pounding of Katrina. There were nearly 30,000 Vietnamese evacuees dispersed to Houston, although many of them were denied entry into the Astrodome, finding shelter instead at Houston's Hong Kong City Mall.

The oversight of Latino, Native American, and Vietnamese and Filipino suffering in the catastrophe not only reinforces for the latter three groups their relative invisibility in

American culture, and for Latinos their relative marginalization in the region. It shows as well that our analysis of minorities must constantly be revised to accommodate a broader view of how race and ethnicity function in the culture. As important as it is, the black-white racial paradigm simply does not exhaust the complex realities and complicated interactions among various minority groups and the broader society.

The black-white racial paradigm was also pressured by an enduring question among social analysts that was revived in the face of Katrina: is it race or class that determines the fate of poor blacks? . . . In this instance, race becomes a marker for class, a proxy, blurring and bending the boundaries that segregate them.

Class certainly loomed large in Katrina's aftermath. Blacks of means escaped the tragedy; blacks without them suffered and died. In reality, it is how race and class interact that made the situation for the poor so horrible on the Gulf Coast. The rigid caste system that punishes poor blacks and other minorities also targets poor whites. Even among the oppressed, however, there are stark differences. Concentrated poverty doesn't victimize poor whites in the same way it does poor blacks. For instance, the racial divide in car ownership discussed earlier partially reflects income, differences between the races. However, as if to prove that not all inequalities are equal, even poor whites are far more likely to have access to cars than are poor blacks. In New Orleans, 53 percent of poor blacks were without cars while just 17 percent of poor whites lacked access to cars. The racial disparity in class effects shows up in education as well. Even poor white children are far less likely to live in, or to attend school in, neighborhoods where poverty is highly concentrated.

Moreover, one must also account for how the privileges of whiteness that transcend class open up opportunities for poor whites that are off limits to the black poor, whether it is a job offer at a restaurant wary of blacks or a schoolroom slot in a largely white, stable community. This is not to deny the vicious caste tensions that separate poor and working class whites from their middle-class and upper-class peers. Such tensions result in a dramatically different quality of life for the well-off and the have-nots. I simply aim to underscore the pull of racial familiarity that is often an unspoken variable, and sometimes the crucial difference, in the lives of the white and non-white poor. It is bad enough to be white and poor; it is worse still to be black, or brown, and female, and young, and poor. Simply said, race makes class hurt more.

. . .

35

Migrant Tomato Workers Face Chronic Abuse

Mary Bauer

. . .

Testimony of Mary Bauer, Director, Immigrant Justice Project, Southern Poverty Law Center, before the Committee on Health, Education, Labor and Pensions, United States Senate, April 15, 2008.

. . .

C
O
N
T
E
X
T

My name is Mary Bauer. I am the Director of the Immigrant Justice Project of the Southern Poverty Law Center. Founded in 1971, the Southern Poverty Law Center is a civil rights organization dedicated to advancing and protecting the rights of minorities, the poor, and victims of injustice in significant civil rights and social justice matters. Our Immigrant Justice Project represents low-income immigrant workers in litigation across the Southeast.

During my legal career, I have represented and spoken with literally thousands of farm-workers in many states. Currently, the Southern Poverty Law Center is representing agricultural workers in at least six class action lawsuits in the South. I have handled dozens of wage and hour cases in many states, and I am familiar with the kinds of routine exploitation that low-wage immigrant workers generally—and farmworkers specifically—experience.

In preparation for this hearing, I interviewed workers and advocates in Immokalee, Florida about their experiences in the field. What they told me is consistent with my own experiences working with farmworkers: Immokalee tomato workers are desperately poor, fearful of retaliation, lack benefits most workers take for granted, and denied access to basic legal protections.

FARMWORKER DEMOGRAPHICS

There are two to three million farmworkers in the United States. Nearly 80% are male, and most are younger than 31 years of age. Most farmworkers are married and/or have children, but most live apart from their immediate family members as a function of their employment.

While the federal government has estimated that the average annual income of farm-workers is a mere $11,000, that estimate is actually quite high because it includes higher paid workers, such as crewleaders. A scholar studying farmworkers has said: "Seasonal farmworkers are the poorest laborers in the United States, earning an average of $6500 per year. Farmworkers who migrate are poorer than settled seasonal laborers, with migrants earning $5,000 per year. The most vulnerable migrant workers, such as those laboring for farm labor contractors in eastern states, earn annual wages as low as $3500."

Piece-rate workers are generally paid by the bucket—in tomatoes, as little as 40 to 45 cents per bucket (a bucket is 32 pounds of tomatoes). At that rate, farmworkers have to pick around two tons of produce (125 buckets) to earn 50 dollars. The piece rate wages paid to tomato workers have not changed significantly in more than twenty years. In addition, workers reported that there is wide uniformity in the wages paid by tomato growers.

Migrant farmworkers are very poor, and they receive very few social benefits. Less than 1% of farmworkers receive general assistance welfare, and only 2% receive Social Security benefits. Farmworkers have long periods of unemployment, and most do not receive any form of pay, including unemployment compensation, during those periods. Crop workers are employed in the U.S. an average of 34½ weeks (66%) of the year.

By the time a migrant farmworker child is 12 years old, he or she may work in the fields between 16–18 hours per week, leaving little time for school work.

FARMWORKER HEALTH AND SAFETY

Agriculture is consistently rated as one of the most dangerous occupations in the United States. Farmworkers suffer from the highest rate of toxic chemical injuries and skin disorders of any workers in the country. The children of migrant farmworkers have higher rates of pesticide exposure, malnutrition, and dental disease than the general population. Children of migrant farmworkers are also less likely to be immunized against disease.

Only 10% of farmworkers report having employer-provided health insurance. None of the Immokalee workers I interviewed reported having any health insurance whatsoever.

C
O
N
T
E
X
T

AGRICULTURAL EXCEPTIONALISM IN THE LAW

Farmworkers were excluded from nearly all major federal labor laws passed during the New Deal. Some laws have been amended since then, but many exemptions remain. The dire situation faced by farmworkers stems from their lack of economic and political power. Because farmworkers have no measurable political influence, there has been little organized opposition to the efforts of agribusiness interests to deny farmworkers most of the legal protections other American workers take for granted. Among other things:

- Farmworkers are not covered by workers' compensation laws in many states.
- Farmworkers are not entitled to overtime pay under federal law.
- On smaller farms and in short harvest seasons, farmworkers are not entitled to the federal minimum wage of $5.85 per hour.
- Child labor laws are riddled with exemptions for farmworkers. Children may legally perform farmwork as young as 10 years of age. By contrast, 16 is the minimum age for most non-agricultural jobs.
- In some states, farmworker children are exempt from the state's compulsory education laws.
- Many state health and safety laws exclude farmworkers.
- Farmworkers are not covered by the National Labor Relations Act and thus have no protection against unfair labor practices when they seek to collectively act for better wages or working conditions, except in the handful of states that have passed statutes extending NRLA-type protections to agricultural workers

. . .

FARMWORKER CONDITIONS IN THE SOUTHEAST ARE THE WORST IN THE NATION

It is not merely coincidental that most of the major documentaries and exposés relating to farmworkers over the past four decades, from the epic "Harvest of Shame" aired in November 1960 to the April 2003 New Yorker article on "American Slaves Today," have focused on conditions in the Southeast. Historically, the worst abuses of migrant farmworkers have occurred in the region. The Southeastern states generally have few laws regulating employment, and those that exist largely exclude farmworkers. The farmworker population in the Southeast has always been composed principally of racial or ethnic minorities and has suffered considerable prejudice as a result. Finally, far more than in any other section of the country, growers in the Southeast have relied on farm labor contractors, or "crewleaders," to recruit, supervise, transport, and pay the harvest workers. Undercapitalized and poorly regulated, farm labor contractors oftentimes abuse or cheat the workers, with the growers avoiding liability by contending that the migrants are employees of the crewleader, rather than the farm.

In Florida, the Coalition of Immokalee Workers has committed to eliminating slavery and other abuses in the agricultural industry. The Coalition has been pivotal in making possible several important slavery and peonage prosecutions. In a recent case brought to court, a federal grand jury indicted six people in Immokalee on January 17, 2008 for their part in what U.S. Attorney Doug Mallow called "slavery, plain and simple." Unfortunately, despite the concerted efforts of the Coalition, slavery and peonage continue in the fields of Florida and the U.S. . . . As United States Judge K. Michael Moore of the Southern District of Florida noted at the sentencing of one defendant found guilty of running a slavery operation in Florida:

> "others at another level in this system of fruit-picking, at a higher level . . . are complicit . . . They rely on migrant workers, and they create a legal fiction or corporation that insulates them between them and the workers themselves so that they can be relieved of any liability for the hiring of illegal immigrants. And yet they stand to benefit the most."

. . .

FARMWORKERS LACK EFFECTIVE LEGAL REMEDIES

Workers face dramatic barriers to obtaining legal redress when their rights are violated.

Migrant farmworkers are disproportionately poor, non-English speaking, geographically isolated immigrants. For many, they are in an unfamiliar country with virtually no money, thousands of miles from home. They do not speak English. They are fearful of retaliation by an employer who is often also their landlord. Farmworkers' very reasonable fear is that the result of their asserting their rights will be not only losing their jobs and their income and being blacklisted from future employment, but also facing eviction and, often, deportation. When their rights are violated, they have few places, if any, to turn.

. . .

There is a particular absence of enforcement against growers, with the majority of enforcement resources devoted to judgment-proof, itinerant farm labor contractors, or "crewleaders," despite the fact that the principal federal farmworker protective law provides that growers are responsible for ensuring farmworkers are properly paid, housed, and transported whenever the growers "employ" the workers.

. . .

Perhaps the greatest shortcoming of reliance on criminal prosecutions to curb farmworker exploitation has been the inability to reach those who benefit economically and have the power to restrain violations of the workers' rights—the farm owners who employ the services of the farm labor contractors.

WOMEN WORKERS FACE SYSTEMIC ABUSE ON THE JOB

It is estimated that there are 70,000 women farmworkers in Florida alone. For some women workers, problems include chronic sexual harassment on the job. The problem has received little public attention but is well-known to farmworker women, many of whom remain silent about sexual exploitation on the job.

According to a study done by Maria Elena Trevino-Lopez, ". . . Ninety % of the farm-worker women, the overwhelming majority of these women being immigrants, reported that sexual harassment is a major problem confronting women farmworkers in the work-place." While investigating harassment of farmworker women in California, the U.S. Equal Employment Opportunity Commission found that hundreds, if not thousands, of farmworker women had to have sex with supervisors to get or keep jobs. In addition, these women put up with a constant barrage of grabbing, touching and propositions for sex by their supervisors.

In one of the few such lawsuits ever brought on behalf of farmworker women in the U.S., the Southern Poverty Law Center represented five Haitian women who were sexually harassed on the job while working in the packing house of Gargiulo, Inc. in Immokalee, Florida. The lawsuit alleged that the women were subjected to repeated, unwelcome sexual advances by their supervisor and then faced retaliation after they complained. The women, who worked as tomato graders, rejected the supervisor's advances and then were suspended without pay, subjected to adverse working conditions and either fired or not rehired for a new packing season.

. . .

In addition to sexual harassment in the workplace, immigrant women face other forms of gender discrimination, including unequal pay for equal work, pregnancy discrimination and disparate treatment.

TOMATO WORKERS IN IMMOKALEE REPORT CHRONIC WORKPLACE ABUSE

I have conducted numerous interviews with tomato workers and their advocates, in Florida and in other states. They report the following chronic difficulties:

- Workers suffer recurring problems with unpaid "waiting time" and other violations of the Fair Labor Standards Act. Workers routinely report that they show up for work and are required to wait, often for hours, until the dew dries and the tomatoes can be picked. Similarly, when it rains, workers are routinely required to wait, and are not paid for that time. As one worker told me: "We are paid only when we pick; we are paid only for the buckets we produce."
- I spoke with Immokalee tomato pickers about claims that workers average over $12 per hour. Every worker and every advocate with whom I spoke disputed that contention. One workers' response summed up the general refrain: "If it were only so!"
- Workers reported to me that their paystubs routinely fail to reflect the actual number of hours worked. Workers report that the hour records on their pay stubs are routinely falsified to show that they have worked substantially fewer hours than they did, in fact, work. Workers report that they are paid only by their production, and the hours are "doctored" to coincide with their production. Thus, workers on identical crews who work identical hours (and who travel to the fields together) will have wildly disparate hours reported on their pay.
- Workers suffer long periods of unemployment and are forced to migrate to obtain other low-paying, short-term jobs. When they do not work—for a day, or a week, or a month—they receive no pay. For low-income families, this is devastating.
- Workers report that government enforcement, particularly as to wage and hour violations, has no practical effect on their own employment situation. Most workers told us that they would not consider calling the Department of Labor under any circumstances. None report having seen or spoken with any government enforcement agents.

C
O
N
T
E
X
T

- Workers report chronic discrimination in hiring, placement, and working conditions. Employers have a strong preference for young men. Men over the age of 35 are considered undesirable. Women, too, are less desirable. All workers reported that sexual harassment of women on the job is a problem.
- Workers report that there are significant difficulties in obtaining safe and decent housing at affordable rates.
- We received numerous reports that children of very young ages work in the field to "help out" the family income. These children typically do not receive their own paystub (a violation of law); their production is simply added onto the pay of their parents.
- Workers report significant problems with uncompensated accidents and illnesses. Because workers are not paid when they do not show up for work (no worker reported having either health insurance or paid vacation or sick time), workers routinely work even when hurt or sick.
- Workers report significant problems with fears of retaliation if they complain or assert their rights. As one worker said: "If you say something, they fire you."
- Workers report significant problems with unsafe and uninsured transportation to and between fields.
- Workers report very significant problems with exposures to pesticides. Many incidents of the overuse of pesticides in the tomato industry, and the effects on workers and their families, have been well-documented. According to the Palm Beach Post, in a recent 10-year period, Florida inspectors found 4609 violations of pesticide regulations, but only 7.6% resulted in fines.
- Some workers are employed through farm labor contractors, rather than directly through the employer. This exacerbates existing abuses, and means that workers have fewer real remedies.

CONCLUSION

The exploitation of migrant farmworkers is one of the major civil rights issue of our time. Laws excluding farmworkers from protection and the restrictions that keep legal services lawyers from effectively representing the most vulnerable workers are morally unacceptable.

. . .

We must all support the efforts made by workers themselves to improve their wages and working conditions. Where workers come together to take courageous actions to enforce their rights—such as the workers who have created the Coalition of Immokalee Workers—those efforts should be supported. The workers who do the backbreaking work to put produce on our table should receive a decent, living wage. Each day we accept the benefits of that labor; we should also accept the concomitant responsibility to ensure that workers are treated fairly.

36

Bonds of Sisterhood—Bonds of Oppression

Mary Romero

. . .

Domestic service reveals the contradiction in a feminism that pushed for women's involvement outside the home, yet failed to make men take responsibility for household labor. Employed middle- and upper-middle class women escaped the double day syndrome by hiring poor women of color to perform housework and child care, and this was characterized as progress. Some feminists defined domestic service as progressive because traditional women's work moved into the labor market and became paid work. However, this definition neglects the inescapable fact that when women hire other women at low wages to do housework, both employees and employers remain women. As employers, women continued to accept responsibility for housework even if they supervised domestics who performed the actual labor. . . .

Although the system of gender domination places the burden of housework on women, middle-class women have financial resources to escape the drudgery of housework by paying someone else to do her work. . . . Thus, middle-class American women aim to "liberate" themselves by exploiting women of color—particularly immigrants—in the underground economy, for long hours at relatively low wages, with no benefits.

. . .

PHYSICAL LABOR

On the surface, the idea of hiring another person to perform the housewife's physical labor appears fairly straightforward. However, it is complicated by the fact that employers hire persons to replace labor at once considered demeaning and closely identified with family roles of mothers and wives. As employers, housewives decide what aspects of their physical labor they no longer want to perform, and in doing so they determine the employee's work. The needs fulfilled through domestics' physical labor structure the work: thus some employers choose to include tasks that they feel are demeaning, others add new tasks and methods of housekeeping that they themselves never engage in, and still others are more interested in having their status affirmed and enhanced than in having their floors scrubbed. . . . The list of physical labor reported by household workers included housecleaning, laundry, sewing, gardening, babysitting, and cooking. . . .

In their efforts to escape the diffuse duties of their housewife roles, employers do not acknowledge work boundaries. Even when the worker's tasks were agreed upon in a verbal contract, employees frequently reported that employers requested additional duties. For instance, household workers commonly complained that employers did not differentiate between housework and child care. In her interviews with women hired to do child care in New York City, Kathy Dobie found that "many of the women are hired as nannies and then asked if they wouldn't mind straightening up a bit. They are asked if they wouldn't clean, then shop, then do the laundry, then, etc." One child care worker told Dobie:

> I give her coffee. I take care of Stephen. I do the laundry. I go out and do the shopping. I buy her birth control tablets. I couldn't believe that. . . . Even the light bulbs in the ceiling, I change. Even her panties, I pick them up when she drops them on the floor.

. . . One of the most common experiences reported by women of color in reference to different standards was the request to scrub floors on their hands and knees rather than simply mopping. Maggie Holmes summed up the feelings of most women of color: "They [white women employers] don't get on their knees, but they don't think nothin' about askin' a black woman." . . .

EMOTIONAL LABOR

. . . Domestics are hired not only for their physical labor but to do emotional labor. . . . One clue to the importance emotional labor has for the employer can be found in accounts showing the lack of concern over the *amount* of housework completed. . . .

> When I went there they told me, "We're not paying you to scrub floors, but paying you just to take care of the woman, be a companion-like"; but I would do it all. If she was sick, I would stay nights. In the summer *we* would rent a summer cottage and I went there for five years with her.

. . .

One Chicana I interviewed explained why she continued working for a seventy-eight-year-old employer who lived a long distance from her, regardless of the low wages: "I guess you can say she needs companionship. I feel sorry for her, you know, she is one of my farthest ones [employers]. I go once a month to her house. I like to go early so I can sit and talk to her."

Domestics almost invariably found themselves counseling and consoling their employers. Mrs. Okamura described the following work situation to Glenn:

> I'd been working for a lady for two hours a week for a long time, but she didn't even give me a chance to work. Upon my arrival, she kept talking and going on and on. For me, housework was much easier because even though I didn't understand English well, I still had to say, "Is that so?" "no" and "yes." . . . They just wanted to complain about their son or their son's wife.

. . .

Gift-giving is domestic workers' almost universal experience and stands as the most obvious symbol of employers' maternalism. Structurally, gift-giving occupies an important place within the underground economy, whereby working-class women are often given presents by middle-class employers in lieu of higher wages and benefits. Chicanas reported that Christmas gifts to them or their children were more common than annual raises. Unlike gift-giving in other work settings, gifts frequently replace higher wages, raises, or other benefits. The following quote from a domestic describes conditions under which the gift occurs: "I'm trying to show you they would do something nice for you when they really felt you needed it. But they wouldn't pay you nothing but these menial wages. Nobody else paid more, and nobody wanted to break the standard." . . .

Employers in domestic service commonly redefine as gifts items that would have gone to the Salvation Army or the trash. Glenn found that old clothes and other discarded items were the most common gifts given to Japanese American domestics. I found a similar case among Chicana domestics. Judith Warner and Helen Henderson reported that sixty percent of the 200 Mexican immigrant women surveyed in Laredo received used clothes from their employers. This practice of giving old clothes within a work setting is unique to domestic service. It is almost inconceivable that the same woman would consider offering her old linen jacket to her secretary.

. . .

PURCHASING STATUS BY HIRING A WOMAN OF COLOR

. . .

Taking an innovative research tack of analyzing family photographs, [one researcher] observed the importance of race and ethnicity in affirming employers' class and racial status in their communities. In her analysis of employers' family albums, she observed that "an attractive, well-dressed black domestic signified the family's membership in 'the better class' in the community." In subsequent interviews with domestics, [she] asked about their inclusion in the employers' family portraits. These African American women confirmed that "whites 'liked to dress blacks up' and sought to show that they had 'good-looking servants.'"

The physical appearances of household workers can be further manipulated to function as visible signs of the hierarchical status distinguishing domestics from employers. . . . White uniforms are used to distinguish the maid from families and friends, particularly when employers fear that others might mistake the reason for her presence. . . . "The maid puts on a uniform when there's company"; otherwise she is allowed to wear jeans. Most private household workers report that employers request a uniform to be worn on particular occasions, such as serving a special dinner or party or when accompanying the family on vacation. Mrs. Nishi expressed her opinion of the employer's request to Glenn: "I had to dress up in the maid's outfit when they had dinner parties. It was all part of it about how phoney these people were that I worked for." . . .

PURCHASING DEFERENCE

Confirmation of the employer's status is not always accomplished by the mere physical presence of women of color or white uniforms; it frequently requires daily practices of deferential behavior that continually affirm and enhance the domestic's inferiority. . . .

> She [employer] would make me feel like I was nothing or like I was doing this [domestic service] because I was so poor or because I was a Mexican. One day she said that Mexican people are all very poor. They weren't educated. And that did it! I dropped what I was doing. I left it there and I said, "here take this and shove it. I don't have to take this abuse from you or from anybody. I'm Mexican, yes, but I'm proud of what I am and I'm working." I says, "Everybody has a job and I have this as my job and if you felt this way, you didn't have to hire me." . . .

Another common and almost universal practice was to address domestics by their first names and employers by their last names. Employer Elinor Birney revealed the significance of the practice to Susan Tucker when she expressed her concern over her daughter's refusal to follow the custom: "The servant calls the woman Mary and Mary calls the servant by her name. Now, I think your employer-employee relationship sometimes could get very sticky if you don't have some separation." West Indian domestics reported that employers in New York used their first names but expected to be addressed formally. Laurino remarked on the irony of the practice because a domestic was in the position of knowing "the personal details of the employer's life, yet will most likely address her as Miss or Mrs.—and in return, she'll be called by her first name."

. . .

Several Chicana domestics similarly reported that employers refused to pronounce their names correctly and eventually Anglicized them. On the basis of the stereotype that all Mexican women are named Maria, white employers in the Southwest frequently refer to all Latina domestics as "Maria."

. . .

Deferential behavior is also constructed through eating arrangements. Rarely did domestics eat in the dining room or in the presence of mistresses' husbands. Mrs. Garcia remembered an employer who told her: "If you brought your lunch you wait out in your car or in the patio or out in the street or where ever." West Indians in New York City employed as live-in workers faced the archetypal situation of the domestic eating alone in the kitchen. As one woman described, "I couldn't eat with them at the table. . . . I have to eat after they finish eating. . . . And then I eat in the kitchen." Aware of the status hierarchy produced from acts of deference, the woman quoted above also commented that "there are people who do that because they want us to know that we are not equal." Another West Indian woman described the purpose of deferential eating arrangements as a way to create symbols of her inferiority: "The first day I got there [the employer] took out a fork and a plate and told me that this was mine to always use. They gave me the impression that I wasn't clean enough."

. . .

Household-labor negotiations frequently occur within the underground economy; they involve few government regulations. Consequently, employers have enormous leeway to determine the working conditions by setting wages, establishing job descriptions, and determining the work structure. . . . Employers decide whether to give raises, and they usually decide whether social security or benefits are obtained. Domestics have little influence over working conditions outside the choice to accept a job or to quit. Given the power that employers exert over working conditions, domestics—more than other workers—feel dependent on and at the mercy of their employers. Since the majority of household workers are not unionized, the struggle to improve working conditions remains an individual struggle.

. . .

The system of gifts and obligations in domestic service tends to shape the personalism in the employee-employer relationship into a strategy of oppression. Redefining work obligations as family or friendship obligations assures employers access to both the emotional and the physical labor of their employees. Personalism camouflages work conditions which become distorted and unintelligible within the context of the interpersonal relationships between domestics and employers. Employers' refusal to relate to domestics' concerns as workers' rights distorts the real conditions of their interaction.

JUST LIKE ONE OF THE FAMILY

Alice Childress testified to the way that personal relationships distort working conditions in her essay on the family analogy in *Like One of the Family: Conversations From a Domestic's Life*. The domestic's view of the employer's attempt to redefine her as "one of the family" rather than as a domestic was presented in an exchange between the two. Mildred, the domestic, overheard the employer tell a friend:

> "We just love her! She's *like* one of the family and she *just adores* our little Carol! We don't know *what* we'd do without her! We don't think of her as a servant!"

Mildred responded later to the employer's characterization by listing the ways her interaction with the family distinguished her as a nonmember, an outsider with inferior status.

> The family eats in the dining room and I eat in the kitchen. Your mama borrows your lace table cloth for her company and your son entertains his friends in your parlor, your daughter takes her afternoon nap on the living room couch and the puppy sleeps on your satin spread . . . and whenever your husband gets tired of something you are talkin' about he says, "Oh, for Pete's sake, forget it. . . ." So you can see I am not *just* like the family.
> . . .

Although the phrase "one of the family" represents "the epitome of the personalized employer-employee association," domestics' use of the family analogy points to aspects of the emotional labor that some workers are willing to accept and those that they reject. On the one hand, this analogy suggests that domestics are engaged in the emotional labor involved in nurturing and caring; on the other hand, it suggests that domestics are treated with respect and are not forced into doing the emotional labor required to create deference.
. . .

THE BUSINESSLIKE RELATIONSHIP

. . .
Establishing and maintaining a businesslike relationship is difficult in many respects. Virtually all contemporary jobs are structured to include breaks. However, regular morning and afternoon breaks are aspects of work culture absent from domestic service. . . .

> One of the biggest problems with household work is that the employers work you too hard. They want you to do everything in one day. They aren't sensitive to you even taking a half hour lunch break.

Structuring breaks and time off is a particularly serious problem for live-in domestics because the hours, tasks and obligations of the job are constantly redefined. Furthermore, live-in workers even find it difficult to guarantee their days off. . . .

> Thursday was my day off. But every Thursday morning, she would get up as she did every other morning and give me something to do. And usually she would say you can

leave after you do so and so. Well, often by the time I finished the task, or giving the children lunch it was usually after 2 o'clock and I had no real day off.

. . .

Like other employers who hire workers in the underground economy, middle-class housewives seldom structure a regular routine for raises. The Chicanas who were interviewed in Denver rarely found employers who offered raises annually or on any regular basis. Domestics generally feel that domestic service is like any other type of job and that employers should thus understand that raises are part of hiring workers. . . .

In their accounts of requesting raises, some domestics expressed a need to force employers to recognize that domestic service is "real work." . . .

So one day I say to her, I say, "Miz Brown," I said, "things is high now." I say, "And what you pay for meat and bread," I say, "that's what I have to pay, too." I say, "I been working here for a long time." I say, "I'd like a raise."

. . .

Wages are the tip of the iceberg. Benefits assumed in other working environments: overtime, vacation, sick pay, a health care plan, and any procedures for redress of grievances, are rarely if ever found in domestic service. At the same time, negative sanctions against employees are common, domestics report that employers expect breakage costs to be borne by the workers. Consider the following account by one of the Chicanas whom I interviewed. After waxing the kitchen floor, Mrs. Tafoya left an open can of floor wax on the dining room table. While she was upstairs vacuuming, her employer opened the sliding doors next to the dining room table to let a breeze in. The curtains flew up, tipped the can, and spilled floor wax onto the table. Mrs. Tafoya was held financially responsible for half of the cost of the repair. . . .

DISCUSSION

Descriptive accounts offered by women of color challenge many perceptions about the function of domestic service in American society today. Even though employers state that they hire domestics to escape the drudgery of housework and to gain freedom to engage in other activities, descriptions of working conditions reveal a more complex set of needs. Interviews with employers and employees alike indicate that domestic service still performs important functions in enhancing the status of middle-class housewives and their families. Moreover, the analysis of the structure of paid housework reveals that the work includes both physical and emotional labor, much of it as shadow work and unpaid labor.

The daily rituals and practices of domestic service reproduce the systems of gender, class, and race domination. All of the gender-specific aspects of unpaid housework—identified in the housewife experience—are also present in domestic service. Even though domestics are paid workers, they do not escape the sexism attached to housework but rather carry the burden for their middle-class women employers. The never-ending job described by housewives is transferred to workers employed by women who treat domestic service as an opportunity to "hire a wife." Employers frequently disregard the contractual or informal labor arrangement made with employees, constantly increasing the work load and incorporating more of their own homemaking duties and obligations. Household workers are faced with tasks that both exceed their job descriptions and are as emotionally and physically burdensome as those completed by housewives. The most common violation of the original labor agreement is the practice of adding child care to general housecleaning instead of keeping the two jobs separate.

. . .

Paid housework that is structured to replicate the unpaid domestic work of the housewife includes practices affirming women's inferiority. The sexist division of labor that exists in employers' homes, assigning mothers and wives the duty of waiting on and serving their husbands and children, is passed on to the domestics. Middle-class women employers who expect women household workers to "pick up" after their husbands and children reproduce the demeaning and sexist aspects of housework. Rejection of such sexist practices is reflected throughout the service sector when workers refuse to "pick up" after others by saying, "I am not your mother." In the same vein, domestics resist practices that structure paid housework to affirm sexist cultural values by requiring the employer to confront her children and husband about leaving their clothes and wet towels on the floor, leaving dishes and glasses throughout the house, and not throwing trash into the garbage. However, many women employers simply perpetuate the sexist division of labor by passing on the most devalued work in their lives to another woman—generally a woman of color. Thus, white middle class women escape the stigma of "women's work" by laying the burden on working-class women of color.

. . .

37

White Poverty: The Politics of Invisibility

bell hooks

In the southern world of racial apartheid I grew up in, no racialized class division was as intense or as fraught with bitter conflict as the one between poor whites and black folks. All black people knew that white skin gave any southern "cracker or peckerwood" (ethnic slurs reserved for the white poor) more power and privilege than even the wealthiest of black folks. However, these slurs were not the product of black vernacular slang, they were the terms white folks with class privilege invented to separate themselves from what they called poor "white trash." On the surface, at least, it made the lives of racist poor white people better to have a group they could lord it over, and the only group they could lord it over were black people. Assailed and assaulted by privileged white folks, they transferred their rage and class hatred onto the bodies of black people.

Unlike the stereotypes projected by the dominant culture about poor black folks, class stereotypes claimed poor whites were supposedly easily spotted by skin ailments, bad dental hygiene, and hair texture. All these things are affected by diet. While poor southern black folks often had no money, they usually had homegrown food to eat. Poor whites often suffered from malnutrition. Living under racial apartheid, black children learned to fear poor whites more than other whites simply because they were known to express their racism by cruel and brutal acts of violence. And even when white folks with class privilege condemned this violence, they could never openly oppose it, for to do so they would have

V
O
I
C
E
S

had to take the word of black folks over those of white folks, thus being disloyal to white supremacy. A white person of privilege opposing violence against blacks perpetuated by poor whites might easily ruin their reputation and risk being seen as a "nigger lover."

When I was a small child we lived in the hills without neighbors nearby. Our closest neighbors were "white trash," as distinct from poor whites. White trash were different because they flaunted their poverty, reveled in it, and were not ashamed. Poor whites, like poor blacks, were committed to trying to find work and lay claim to respectability—they were law abiding and patriotic. White trash saw themselves as above the law and as a consequence they were dangerous. White trash were folks who, as our neighbors were fond of saying, "did not give a good goddamn." They were not afraid to take the Lord's name in vain. Most poor white folks did not want to live anywhere near black folks. White trash lived anywhere. . . .

Our "hillbilly white trash" neighbors lived by their own codes and rules. We did not call them names, because we knew the pain of slurs. Mama made it clear that they were people just like us and were to be shown respect. While they did not bother us and we did not bother them, we feared them. I never felt that they feared us. They were always encouraging us to come over, to play and party with them. To most respectable black people, poor whites and white trash were the lowest of the low. Even when they were nice, black folks felt it was important to keep a distance. I remember being whipped for being overly friendly with poor white neighbors. At that time I did not understand, nor did our parents make it clear, that if anything had happened to us in their homes, as black folks we would just have been seen as in the wrong; that was the nature of Jim Crow justice. While we were encouraged to keep a distance from all white children no matter their class, it was clear that black people pitied and often felt contempt toward the white poor.

Desegregation led to the closing of all black schools. Busing took us out of our all-black neighborhoods into worlds of whiteness we did not know. It was in high school that I first began to understand class separation between whites. Poor white kids kept to themselves. And many of their well-to-do white peers would rather be seen talking to a black person than speaking to the white poor, or worse, to white trash. There was no danger that the black person they were talking to would want to come and hang out at their home or go to a movie. Racial lines were not crossed outside school. There could be no expectation of a reciprocal friendship. A privileged white person might confuse the issue if they showed attention to an underprivileged white peer. Class boundaries had to remain intact so that no one got the wrong idea. Between black and white there was no chance of a wrong idea: the two simply did not meet or mix.

Since some folks saw mama's family as backwoods, as black hillbillies, she was always quick to punish any act of aggression on our part toward an underdog group. We were not allowed to ridicule poor whites—not even if they were taunting us. When we began to ride the bus across town to the white school, it was a shock to my sensibilities to interact with black children who were scornful of the misfortune of others. . . .

To this day I have sad memories of the way Wilma, the white girl who was in my class, was treated by aggressive black children on the bus. Their daily taunts reminded her that she was poor white trash, the lowest of the low, that she smelled bad, that she wore the same dress day after day. In loud mean talk they warned her not to sit next to them. She often stood when there was an empty seat. A big girl with dark hair and unusually fair skin, she endured all the taunts with a knowing smirk. When she was pushed too far she fought back. She knew that with the exception of her ten minutes on that predominately black bus, white power ruled the day. And no matter how poor she was, she would always be white.

. . .

The white poor make up the vast majority of the poor in this society. Whereas mass migration of poor blacks from southern states to northern cities created a huge urban poor population, the white poor continue to live in isolated rural and suburban areas. Now and then they live hidden in the midst of white affluence. From their invention to the present day, the world of trailer park homes has been the territory of the white poor. While marking class boundaries, trailer park communities do not carry the stigma of degradation and deprivation commonly associated with the "ghetto"—a term first used to identify poor white urban immigrant communities. Indeed, in the not so distant past the psychological and economic self-esteem of the white working class and the white poor has been significantly bolstered by the class politics of white supremacy. Currently, we are witnessing a resurgence of white supremacist thinking among disenfranchised classes of white people. These extremist groups respond to misinformation circulated by privileged whites that suggests that black people are getting ahead financially because of government policies like affirmative action, and they are taught to blame black folks for their plight.

While anti-black racism has intensified among whites of all classes in recent years as part of civil rights backlash, overall the white underprivileged are . . . far more likely to see immigrants as the group taking needed jobs. Their racism toward non-white immigrants who are perceived to be taking jobs by virtue of their willingness to work for less mirrors that of black workers who blame immigrants. More and more the white and black poor recognize that ruling class greed ensures their continued exploitation and oppression.

. .

More and more Americans of all colors are entering the ranks of the poor. And that includes white Americans. The evidence is in the numbers. In the essay "Trash-O-Nomics," Doug Henwood states what should be obvious but often is not: "Of course, the average white person is better off than the average non-white person, those of Asian origin excepted, and black people are disproportionally poor. But that sort of formula hides as much as it reveals: most officially poor people are white, and these days, a white household should consider itself lucky if its income is only stagnant rather than in outright decline." It serves white supremacist capitalist patriarchal ruling class interests to mask this reality. Hence, the almost invisibility of the white poor in mass media.

Today, most folks who comment on class acknowledge that poverty is seen as having a black face, but they rarely point to the fact that this representation has been created and sustained by mass media. Concurrently, reports using statistics that show a huge percentage of black folks in the ranks of the poor compared to a small percentage of whites make it seem that blacks are the majority group in the ranks of the poor. Rarely do these reports emphasize that these percentages are based on population size. The reality they mask is that blacks are a small percentage of the population. While black folks disproportionate to our numbers are among the poor, the vast majority of the poor continue to be white. The hidden face of poverty in the United States is the untold stories of millions of poor white people.

Better to have poor and working-class white folks believe white supremacy is still giving them a meaningful edge than to broadcast the reality that the poor of any race no longer have an edge in this society, or that downsizing daily drags previously economically sound white households into the ranks of the poor. . . . Undue media focus on poor nonwhites deflects attention away from the reality of white poverty.

. . .

No doubt ruling class groups will succeed in new efforts to divide and conquer, but the white poor will no longer direct its class rage solely at black people, for the white poor is divided within its ranks. Just as there are many poor whites who are racist, there are a substantial group of poor whites who refuse to buy into white supremacist politics, who understand the economic forces that are crippling the American working class. Progressive white poor and working-class people understand the dynamics of capitalism. All over the United States class unrest is mounting. . . .

Ending welfare will mean that more white women than ever before in our nation's history will enter the ranks of the underclass. Like their black counterparts, many of them will be young. Workfare programs, which pay subsistence wages without the backdrop of free housing, will not enhance their lives. As the future "poorest of the poor" they are far less likely to be duped into believing their enemies are other economically disadvantaged groups than their predecessors. . . .

Given that today's culture is one where the white and black working class and poor have more to say to one another, there is a context for building solidarity that did not exist in the past. That solidarity cannot be expressed solely through shared critique of the privileged. It must be rooted in a politics of resistance that is fundamentally anti-racist, one that recognizes that the experiences of underprivileged white folks are as important as those of people of color. The class segregation that historically divided the white poor from their more privileged counterparts did not exist in predominately black communities. And while generations of white families have historically remained poor, a host of black folks pulled themselves out of poverty into privilege. In solidarity these folks have historically been strong advocates for the black poor even though that too is changing. More often than not they did not encourage solidarity with the white poor because of persistent anti-black racism. Now they must become advocates for the white and black poor, overcoming their anti-white prejudices. Concurrently, the black and white poor must do the work of building solidarity by learning more about one another, about what brings them together and what tears them apart. We need to hear more from all of us who have bridged the gap between white and black poor and working-class experience.

When I left the segregated world of my poor and working-class home environment to attend privileged-class schools, I found I often had more in common with white students who shared a similar class background than with privileged class black students who had no experience of what it might mean to lack the funds to do anything they wanted to do. No matter our color, students from poor and working-class backgrounds had common experiences history had not taught us how to sufficiently name or theoretically articulate. While it was definitely easier for folks from poor white backgrounds to assimilate visually, we all experienced estrangement from our class origin as well as the fear of losing touch with the worlds we had most intimately known. The bonds we forged in solidarity were and are not documented. There is no record of our conversations or how these solidarities shaped our future politics. Many of us used this bonding through class across the boundary of race as a groundwork for a politics of solidarity that has stood the test of time.

While racism remains an integral fact of our culture, it too has changed. Xenophobia more so than racial hatred often characterizes where white citizens stand on race. The utterly segregated black neighborhoods of my upbringing are no more. The white poor in need of shelter move into places where once no white face was ever seen. This contact does not mean an absence of racism. But it does mean that the criteria and the expression of racism has changed. It also means that there is more of a concrete basis for positive interaction between poor black and white folks. When I walk in these communities created by class division, I see grown white and black folks refusing to interact with each other even as I see more interaction than in the past. And I see white and black children freely crossing the boundaries of race to meet at that class juncture which brings them together in a common landscape they call home.

These bonds may mean little given the fact that there are so many more race-segregated white working-class and poor communities. Even in the places where white and black do not meet, there are more diverse opinions about class and race. Nothing is as simple as it was in the past when the needs of the white poor were pitted against the needs of the black poor. Today, poverty is both gendered and racialized. It is impossible to truly understand class in the United States today without understanding the politics of race and gender. Ultimately, more than any previous movement for social justice, the struggle to end poverty could easily become the civil rights issue with the broadest appeal—uniting groups that have never before taken a stand together to support their common hope of living in a more democratic and just world—a world where basic necessities of life are available to everyone, to each according to their need.

38

Why Can't Everybody Fear Me like That?

Saint

V
O
I
C
E
S

All right, my name is Saint. I was born in Brooklyn, Crown Heights. Grew up with my mother and my father my brother my grandfather. All of us lived in the same house for years. I had a pretty good childhood. No problems no stress, basically got everything I want.

I lived in Crown Heights until I was like maybe four or five years old. I can't remember that much because I was young. I used to enjoy it over there because even until now in the same building where we was at, probably still got like eight cousins over there. I've got a lot of family in that same building, in like three different apartments. Ours was like the fourth. It was fun because there's not too many places where you could be five years old and be able to run through a whole building without your parents chasing you 'cause they know there's nothing but your whole family in the building.

. . .

When we moved from there we ended up on Martense on East Flatbush with another set of family, with my mother's uncles and aunts. And it was like the whole building was family because my uncle owned the building. That was my first real house, in Flatbush. It was a nice two-family house with a basement. Me and my brother and my mother and my grandfather had rooms on the top floor. And downstairs was the kitchen the living room, basement. We rented the basement out to some close friends of the family.

My mother and my father used to work for years until recently. My father used to work night shifts and my mother used to work morning shifts. So, one of them was always home because both of them had to work. It was a nice house in a pretty good neighborhood. We had to move out of there because of certain things that I did and police kept coming back and forth to the house and that embarrassed my parents.

. . .

Our block was known for shootouts and a lot of gang activity and stuff like that. So my mother ain't want us outside, so we just had to stay in the house; that's why she moved. She would tell us, "All right, well y'all can't go outside." And as kids, you know we'll always be like, "Aw, we want to go outside." I was about seven, my brother was like nine. We was old enough to realize that yeah, everyday when we sit in our apartment there's always gunshots. Shots probably came through our window before. So we would be mad, but she would never give us a reason like, "Well, people getting shot outside." But we basically knew, we look at it and be like, "All right, we know what time it is."

. . .

It was me, my brother, my mother and my aunt. We was all watching *Leroy The Last Dragon* and we just heard mad gun shots, the gunshots sounded like they were coming from real close. So my mother just told everybody automatically, "Just get on the floor," because we were already used to it. So everybody just got on the floor, we stayed there, and it was like, we're so used to it that I was still watching the movie. I'm on the floor laying down with my head down and all that, and I'm just watching the movie. The gunshots went on for about five or ten minutes. It just kept going and going.

So after a while the movie is done, so I get up and I go and look out the window and I see mad police. So when we go downstairs, there was this drug dealer guy that used to live in the basement right next door to our building. And he was a cool guy because back then, a dollar used to be a lot of money. He used to give kids on the block twenties, like, "Go buy ice cream and keep the change, bring me back a dollar water or something and keep the change for y'all." So all the kids on the block used to love him. A fat Puerto Rican guy named Joe. So we came outside, police just told us that they found him in the basement dead with a lot of drugs on the table. He was down there by himself and people came to rob him. He killed like two of them, but it was like five people and some of them killed him and they said it was a trail of blood leading out. So he must've shot like three or four of them, but he killed two of them down there in the basement and he got killed. And I ain't never forget that because he used to give us money and all that. He was a pretty cool guy; he used to look out for all the young kids on the block. Take us whenever we ran out of money to the arcade. He always used to pass through, look for anybody from the block, and say, "Y'all good? Aight, here, five dollars, go ahead spend it all on video games." So I always remember him even until now.

Once you hear gunshots, and you're in your house, always get on the floor because you don't want a bullet to come through your window and hit you. It happens like that all the time in the hood. So you just start to learn wherever you at, you hear bullets, duck. At least if you in the streets duck. In your house, get on the floor. You can't run because if you run, you might run into a bullet or get hit in your back. That's why it's always good to just get low because it might not be for you.

. . .

Then I went to Walt Whitman Junior High School in Brooklyn; that's in Flatbush too. And that's when everything basically started going downhill. That's when I started smoking weed. I always noticed girls in school, but that's when I really started, because everybody in high school and junior high had a girlfriend. I started cutting school to go by my girlfriend's house and chill. We had hooky parties and stuff like that. That was like '97, '98.

Around them times that's when the gang thing was going on real hard. I kind of stayed away from it a little bit even though we had like our own little crew from our neighborhood that we all stuck up for each other. But we still was getting pressure from other gangs. But we wasn't having it because it was known in the neighborhood, our gang, our hood and the other hood from the other side be the two hoods that we would war. So it don't matter, we war with each other and we war with anyone else. So it was like that for a while. Then I started getting into more fights, because after being around so much of the older people in my neighborhood, it was like a lot of times you see people doing violent things. You like, "Oh that's real violent, but I won't do it." After seeing the same thing every day, you see a kid get stabbed every day, see a kid get shot every day, it's just another part of life. It's nothing for me to do it, so I started getting more violent. I started stabbing people, fighting people for no reason, jumping people.

. . .

The guys that stood up for me were the rough guys from the hood. We looked up to them. "Yeah when I grow up, I want to be like him." Because in the hood it's all about a fear and a respect thing, because once you fear somebody, like really and truly, you respect them. You might fear them, but when I see you fear them, I'll respect them like, "Damn why can't everybody fear me like that?" You could see somebody just walk up to a group of kids about to go in the corner store and just take everybody money. Like damn, I'm walking around with two dollars. This kid came out his crib with nothing, left his house with nothing. And he got fifteen, twenty dollars on him right now. They had all the girls. You know, of course, the girls wanna be with the thugs. So they had all the girls. The rest of the kids—even the thug kids from our hood hung out with the thug kids from them other hoods because like they say, birds of a feather flock together. So they got the perfect crew. Ain't nobody stepping to they crew 'cause everybody in that crew is gangsta. All of us little homies were like, damn, we wanna be like them. They got money and fresh sneakers all the time.

. . .

So I wanted to be just like that. Like when I was younger—the same way when I used to look at the older guys and be like, "Word, I'm gonna grow up and be just like them." Even though you're older, a lot of people think you don't wanna be like nobody. But, really and truly, when you look deep down inside, you're like, "Yeah, I do want to be like him. I want to have the same type of respect he had." So I joined the Crips, thinking that I'm gonna get the same type of respect he had. But I ain't know the type of work that he had to put in to get that respect. I ain't really know what he did to get that respect. I just thought maybe he fought, bust his gun once or twice. Then, when I start hearing stories about what he been through, how he put it down in the hood, then I'm like, "Oh he went through a lot to get the respect that you get." So that's when I'm like, "You know what? I'm gonna go through a lot to get this respect too, because I wanna be just like him." You can't be rolling with a gangsta all day and you a punk. Then they gonna look at you like you a funny-ass n____. How you rolling with this G'ed up n____ and he's a punk ass n____? That's when n____s goin' go up to the G like, "Stop rolling with him, he's soft." So basically, you gotta pull your own weight too, even though you're in a gang and ya'll fight for each other, you got to pull your own weight. So I joined the Crips right after that. Got jumped in. After that you gotta go get high and y'all family, basically.

. . .

My mother, she don't know too much about the gang thing, but she know I'm affiliated. She said that I've been lying to her, 'cause if I tell her, "Yeah, well Mom, I'm Crip," that's gonna stress her out too much. But she already know, basically she's not a stupid woman, she know that I'm gang related. So, it hurts her, she cries, she's like, "You always in and out of jail, you my youngest son, you my baby boy. When you ain't had the GED—you got kicked out of school, you still getting locked up, you went and left the house already, I don't know how you getting money, you twenty years old, you went from a Honda, now you driving a Lexus." My mother's like, "I know you doing something in the streets that's not good." So that hurts her. My mother's a God-fearing woman, go to church every week and all that, so every time I speak to her she like, "You know I pray for you every night." I tell her, "Same thing Ma, you know I pray for you too every night, and I'm good in here, Mom, you ain't gotta worry about nothing." But you know it hurts her a lot, I ain't gonna lie. That's the—the main thing about this, this bid right here that hurts me, is knowing that I hurt my mother so much. I could do this time, it's nothing for me, I've been through this, but just to think about what my mother go through, that hurts me. Sometimes that makes me want to cry, but—you do the crime you gotta do the time, so I never cry, I sit here and do what I gotta do, you feel me? I know—I know it's not easy for my mother. As hard as it is for me, it's probably thirty times harder for my mother, to tell you the truth. Nobody gonna be feeling as much as my mother, as much as my family. But I know my mother feels it the most.

. . .

39

Classified

How To Stop Hiding Your Privilege and Use It For Social Change

Karen Pittelman and Resource Generation

Jaimie: "My parents came from working and middle class families. My dad became a professor of finance and over the course of my life he's steadily been making more money. By the time I was in college my parents had made money on investments and started a business selling study guides for people taking the Chartered Financial Analyst exam. When I was 26 my folks sold the business for many millions of dollars.

There's different ways to look at how they made this money. One is to look at how it had to do with the skin privilege my parents had—I mean my dad's family is Irish and German and my mom's family is Russian Jewish. So the way whiteness has worked and how they've been allowed to be white is part of why my parents had access to a greater range of opportunities.

Another way to look at it is they were really hard-working and they set out to make a lot of money. I have a lot of respect for the work that they did and the way they went from working their way through college to being multi-millionaires.

Then there's another analysis that asks, what were they actually doing? Investing. My dad's analysis about investing is, 'that's the way the free market works.' But there's also the idea that you're loaning money to companies that are raping the earth, destroying people's homelands and paying money to special interest lobby groups that destroy democracy even in our own country.

I feel like what my parents valued was financial security because they wanted to take care of their family, and I don't think that's a bad motivation at all. But I do think that it's sad to see the other kinds of values that get left behind. Having financial security is one way to take care of people, but having community and having a spiritual tradition are also ways to take care of people."

Laurel: "I have an ancestor who was named Edward F. Beale. He's my great great great uncle (or something.) He was the President of the Bureau of Indian Affairs out in California and he was responsible for putting a number of Indians on reservations. He then made millions of dollars off of land back in the 1850s. What I get from that is that he was making millions off of stolen land from Native Americans.

What I would love to do in my family is be able to trace all the different lines of where the money came from. I'd love to gather with other people with wealth and be able to tell our stories with a lot of analysis and make a case for reparations; to be able to really articulate to other people with wealth the ways in which—really literally—the wealth was stolen. To look at how labor was stolen from Chinese people and African American people and how this land was stolen from Native Americans. If we're talking about it from a white wealthy point of view, it might be less threatening to other white wealthy people because we're owning it rather than accusing from the outside.

My mother and my aunt keep saying stuff like, 'He wasn't such a bad guy, Edward F. Beale.' But I guess what I keep trying to articulate—both for them and for myself—is the difference between the institutional and personal. That, for instance, Edward F. Beale was part of a genocidal movement which he profited from, and within that he was an individual person who had relationships and feelings and was blind to what was going on, just like all of us at certain times. The institutional piece doesn't cancel out the personal piece. And the personal doesn't cancel out the institutional."

Noy: "The story of my parents' wealth is not all just about their individual will—so much else played into it. My dad was very poor, but he was extremely fortunate because he got an education at a Wat (a Thai Buddhist temple). He then passed the exams to get into Chulalongkorn, which is like the Harvard of Thailand. That's where he met my mother. My mother's side of the family owned some land, so they were better-off. My parents both became doctors.

They decided to move to the United States in 1971 in part because of all the political turmoil—it was an extremely tumultuous period in Southeast Asian history, and tensions between students and the Thai military were rising. It was only because the U.S. had changed its immigration laws in the 1960s that they were able to go—before that Asian immigration was extremely restricted. It was also easier for them because they were doctors and the law gave preference to professionals, scientists and artists.

My parents set up their own practice and they worked like crazy, so I hardly saw them. Then my dad started getting into the stock market, reading all these books and doing investments. That was how they built up a fairly significant amount of money.

With immigrant families, when one person makes it you get everyone else holding on to you. You get this money and then you are expected to support everyone—filial piety and all. I think it can get a little crazy with the power and the pressure of being in that privileged position. At the same time, there was a real starvation mentality, especially coming from my dad. I remember cutting napkins in half to save money and having really cheap clothes. I think my dad felt like if you act like you have a lot of money then you aren't really Thai anymore."

Katrina: "My father inherited from his father and that money came from a few generations back when his family owned coal mills in western Pennsylvania. But what I'll really inherit will be from money that he earned in his own life as a lawyer.

Then on my mom's side I won't be inheriting money via her branch of the family, but I will be inheriting—similar to on my dad's side—a kind of social elite status and upper class attitude that comes in a pretty direct line from my mom's mom's branch of the family being descended from slave traders. That was back seven generations ago in Rhode Island. At that time, not the guy who I'm descended from, but his sons and their sons, a few of them made a huge fortune in the slave trade. I'm not in a direct line from those huge fortunes, most of which were spent within a few generations. So technically speaking I haven't inherited money directly from the slave trade. However, I have definitely inherited social class status. I think it's important to name that and notice that whether it's the slave trade or any other major financial success in business—even if the money disappears—people typically marry into other families with money. So for us, this 'normal' sense of old-money New England entitlement really settled in.

The process of naming my privilege and the slave trade history has been liberating in the sense that when it was a subconscious thing, the guilt was really strong. It's been a gradual process of saying, 'Okay, since I'm not inherently a bad person, and my people are really good-hearted people nowadays, then I can start to look at this more objectively,' and saying, 'well, this was what the history was and it was totally fucked up and now what am I going to do about it?'"

VOICES

40

The Debt Trap

Given a Shovel, Americans Dig Deeper into Debt

Gretchen Morgenson

The collection agencies call at least 20 times a day. For a little quiet, Diane McLeod stashes her phone in the dishwasher.

But right up until she hit the wall financially, Ms. McLeod was a dream customer for lenders. She juggled not one but two mortgages, both with interest rates that rose over time, and a car loan and high-cost credit card debt. Separated and living with her 20-year-old son, she worked two jobs so she could afford her small, two-bedroom ranch house in suburban Philadelphia, the Kia she drove to work, and the handbags and knickknacks she liked. Then last year, back-to-back medical emergencies helped push her over the edge. She could no longer afford either her home payments or her credit card bills. Then she lost her job. Now her home is in foreclosure and her credit profile in ruins.

. . .

Years of spending more than they earn have left a record number of Americans like Ms. McLeod standing at the financial precipice. They have amassed a mountain of debt that grows ever bigger because of high interest rates and fees. While the circumstances surrounding these downfalls vary, one element is identical: the lucrative lending practices of America's merchants of debt have led millions of Americans—young and old, native and immigrant, affluent and poor—to the brink. More and more, Americans can identify with miners of old: in debt to the company store with little chance of paying up.

It is not just individuals but the entire economy that is now suffering. Practices that produced record profits for many banks have shaken the nation's financial system to its foundation. As a growing number of Americans default, banks are recording hundreds of billions in losses, devastating their shareholders.

. . .

But behind the big increase in consumer debt is a major shift in the way lenders approach their business. In earlier years, actually being repaid by borrowers was crucial to lenders. Now, because so much consumer debt is packaged into securities and sold to investors, repayment of the loans takes on less importance to those lenders than the fees and charges generated when loans are made.

Lenders have found new ways to squeeze more profit from borrowers. Though prevailing interest rates have fallen to the low single digits in recent years, for example, the rates that credit card issuers routinely charge even borrowers with good credit records have risen, to 19.1 percent last year from 17.7 percent in 2005—a difference that adds billions of dollars in interest charges annually to credit card bills. Average late fees rose to $35 in 2007 from less than $13 in 1994, and fees charged when customers exceed their credit limits more than doubled to $26 a month from $11, according to CardWeb, an online publisher of information on payment and credit cards. Mortgage lenders similarly added or raised fees associated with borrowing to buy a home—like $75 e-mail charges, $100 document preparation costs and $70 courier fees—bringing the average to $700 a mortgage, according to the *Department of Housing and Urban Development*. These "junk fees" have risen 50 percent in recent years . . . .

Lenders have been eager to expand their reach. They have honed sophisticated marketing tactics, gathering personal financial data to tailor their pitches. They have spent hundreds of millions of dollars on advertising campaigns that make debt sound desirable and risk-free. The ads are aimed at people who urgently need loans to pay for health care and other necessities.

. . .

Tallying what the lenders have made off Ms. McLeod over the years is revealing. In 2007, when she earned $48,000 before taxes, she was charged more than $20,000 in interest on her various loans. Her first mortgage, originated by the EquiFirst Corporation, charged her $14,136 a year, and her second, held by CitiFinancial, added $4,000. Capital One, a credit card company that charged her 28 percent interest on her balances, billed $1,400 in annual interest. GE Money Bank levied 27 percent on the $1,500 or so that Ms. McLeod owed on an account she had with a local jewelry store, adding more than $400. Olde City Mortgage, the company that arranged one of Ms. McLeod's loans, made $6,000 on a single refinancing, and EquiFirst received $890 in a loan origination fee.

. . .

But with so many borrowers in trouble, some bankruptcy experts and regulators are beginning to focus on the responsibilities of lenders, like requiring them to make loans only if they are suitable to the borrowers applying for them. The *Federal Reserve Board*, for instance, recently put into effect rules barring a lender from making a loan without regard to the borrower's ability to repay it.

. . .

BORROWING TO SHOP

For decades, America's shift from thrift could be summed up in this familiar phrase: When the going gets tough, the tough go shopping. Whether for a car, home, vacation or college degree, the nation's lenders stood ready to assist. Companies offered first and second mortgages and home equity lines, marketed credit cards for teenagers and helped college students to amass upward of $100,000 in debt by graduation. Every age group up to the elderly was the target of sophisticated ad campaigns and direct mail programs. "Live Richly" was a Citibank message. "Life Takes *Visa*," proclaims the nation's largest credit card issuer.

. . .

Mortgage lenders took to cold-calling homeowners to persuade them to refinance. Done to reduce borrowers' monthly payments, serial refinancings allowed lenders to charge thousands of dollars in loan processing fees, including appraisals, credit checks, title searches and document preparation fees.

Not surprisingly, such practices generated dazzling profits for the nation's financial companies. And since 2005, when the bankruptcy law was changed, the credit card industry has increased its earnings 25 percent, according to a new study by Michael Simkovic, a former James M. Olin fellow in Law and Economics at Harvard Law School.

. . .

Among the most profitable companies were Ms. McLeod's creditors. For Capital One, which charges her 28 percent interest on her credit card, net interest income, after provisions for loan losses, has risen a compounded 25 percent a year since 2002. GE Money Bank, which levied a 27 percent rate on Ms. McLeod's debt and is part of the GE Capital Corporation, generated profits of $4.3 billion in 2007, more than double the $2.1 billion it earned in 2003.

. . .

A RISING TIDE OF BILLS

Just two generations ago, America was a nation of mostly thrifty people living within their means, even setting money aside for unforeseen expenses. Today, Americans carry $2.56 trillion in consumer debt, up 22 percent since 2000 alone, according to the Federal Reserve Board. The average household's credit card debt is $8,565, up almost 15 percent from 2000. College debt has more than doubled since 1995. The average student emerges from college carrying $20,000 in educational debt. Household debt, including mortgages and credit cards, represents 19 percent of household assets, according to the Fed, compared with 13 percent in 1980.

Even as this debt was mounting, incomes stagnated for many Americans. As a result, the percentage of disposable income that consumers must set aside to service their debt—a figure that includes monthly credit card payments, car loans, mortgage interest and principal—has risen to 14.5 percent from 11 percent just 15 years ago. By contrast, the nation's savings rate, which exceeded 8 percent of disposable income in 1968, stood at 0.4 percent at the end of the first quarter of this year, according to the Bureau of Economic Analysis.

More ominous, as Americans have dug themselves deeper into debt, the value of their assets has started to fall. Mortgage debt stood at $10.5 trillion at the end of last year, more than double the $4.8 trillion just seven years earlier, but home prices that were rising to support increasing levels of debt, like home equity lines of credit, are now dropping. The combination of increased debt, falling asset prices and stagnant incomes does not threaten just imprudent borrowers. The entire economy has become vulnerable to the spending slowdown that results when consumers like Ms. McLeod hit the wall.

THAT FIRST CREDIT CARD

Growing up in Philadelphia, Diane McLeod never knew financial hardship, she said. Her father owned six pizza shops and her mother was a homemaker. "There was always money for everything, whether it was bills or food shopping or a spur-of-the-moment vacation," Ms. McLeod recalled. "If they worried about money, they never let us know." Hers was a pay-as-you-go family, she said. Although money was not discussed much around the dinner table, credit card debt was not a part of her parents' financial plan, and sometimes personal purchases were put off.

When Ms. McLeod married at 18, she and her husband carried no credit cards. She stayed at home after her son was born, but when she was 27 her husband died. She remarried a few years later and continued as a homemaker until her son turned 13. Between her husband's job laying carpets and her own, money was not exactly tight.

In the mid-'90s, Ms. McLeod got several credit cards. When the marriage began to founder, she said, she shopped to make herself feel better. Earning a livable wage at *Verizon* Yellow Pages, Ms. McLeod finally decided to leave her marriage and buy a home of her own in February 2003. The cost was $135,000, and her mortgage required no down payment because her credit history was good. "I was very proud of myself when I bought the house," Ms. McLeod explained. "I thought I would live here till I died." Adding to her burden, however, was about $25,000 in credit card debt she had brought from her marriage. Because her husband did not have a regular salary, all the cards were in her name.

After she had been in the house for a year, a friend who was a mortgage broker suggested she consolidate her debts into a new home loan. The property had appreciated by about $30,000, and once again she put no money down for the loan. "It was amazing how easy it was," she recalled. "But that's a trap, and I didn't know it then."

Naturally, the refinance had costs. There was an $8,000 penalty to pay off the previous mortgage early as well as roughly $1,500 in closing costs on the new loan. To cover these fees, Ms. McLeod dipped into her retirement account. Only later did she realize that she had to pay an early-withdrawal penalty of $3,000 to the *Internal Revenue Service*. Short on cash, she put it on a credit card.

Soon she had racked up another $19,000 in credit card debt. But because her home had appreciated, she once again refinanced her mortgage. Although she was making $50,000 a year working two jobs, her income was not enough to support the new $165,000 loan. She asked her son to join her on the loan application; with his income, the numbers worked. "Boy, would I regret that," she said. The decision would drive a wedge between mother and son and damage his credit profile as well.

Almost immediately after she refinanced, in late 2005, the department store where she worked her second job, as a jewelry saleswoman at night and on weekends, cut back her hours. She quit altogether, and her son moved out of the house, where he had been helping with the rent, to live with a girlfriend. Ms. McLeod was on her own and paying $1,500 a month on her mortgage. Because the house had been recently appraised at $228,000, she said, she felt sure she could refinance again if she needed to pay off her credit card. "You felt like you had a way out," she said.

But as happens with many debt-laden Americans, an unexpected illness helped push Ms. McLeod over the edge. In January 2006, her doctor told her she needed a hysterectomy. She had health care coverage, but she could no longer work at a second job. She made matters worse during her recovery, while watching home shopping channels. "Eight weeks in bed by yourself is very dangerous when you have a TV and credit card," Ms. McLeod said. "QVC was my friend."

Later that year, Ms. McLeod realized she was in trouble, squeezed by her mortgage and credit card payments, her $350 monthly car bill, rising energy prices and a stagnant salary. She started to sell knickknacks, handbags, clothing and other items on eBay to help cover her heating and food bills. She stopped paying her credit cards so that she could afford her mortgage.

A year ago she was back in the hospital, this time with a burst appendix. Her condition worsened, and she lost the use of one kidney. She spent 19 days in the hospital and six weeks recuperating. Her prescription-drug costs added to her expenses, and by September she could no longer pay her mortgage.

When her father died in early January, she was devastated. About a month later, on Feb. 14, Ms. McLeod was suspended and soon afterward fired from Verizon. Toting up her financial obligations, Ms. McLeod said she owed $237,000 on her home mortgage. Of that, sheriff's costs are $4,350, and "other" fees related to the foreclosure come to $3,000. A house of similar size down the street from Ms. McLeod sold for $153,000 in January. Her credit card debt totals around $34,000, she said. Each month the late fees and over-limit penalties add to her debt. Ms. McLeod said she would probably file for bankruptcy.

Patricia A. Hasson, president of the Credit Counseling Service of Delaware Valley, said Ms. McLeod would probably wind up having to repay 40 percent to 60 percent of her credit card debt. The owner of her mortgages could come after her for the difference between what she owes on her loan and what her house ultimately sells for. The first mortgage was sold to investors; Citigroup declined to say whether it held onto the second mortgage or sold it to investors.

A sheriff's auction of her home on June 12 received no bidders, Ms. McLeod said. The bank will soon evict her. "Oh, I definitely have regrets," Ms. McLeod said. "I regret not dealing with my emotions instead of just shopping. And I regret involving my son in all this because that has affected him and his finances and his self-esteem."

Ms. McLeod says she hopes to be living in an apartment she can afford soon and to get back to paying her bills on time. She does not want another credit card, she said. But even though her credit profile is ruined, she still receives come-ons. Recently an envelope arrived offering a "pre-qualified" Salute Visa Gold card issued by Urban Bank Trust. "We think you deserve more credit!" it said in bold type.

A spokeswoman at Urban Bank said the Salute Visa is part of a program "designed to provide access to credit for folks who would not otherwise qualify for credit." The Salute Visa offered Ms. McLeod a $300 credit line. But a closer look at the fine print showed that $150 of that would go, as annual fees, to Urban Bank.

41

"Classism From Our Mouths" and "Tips From Working-Class Activists"

Betsy Leondar-Wright

We've all learned classist prejudices, and none of us has completely eradicated them from our minds.

. . .

And we all make mistakes. There's not a middle-class person alive who hasn't said dumb, insensitive things that step on working-class toes. Hiding our classist mistakes or defending ourselves ("I didn't mean it that way") doesn't do any good. The only thing to do is to 'fess up, apologize, laugh at ourselves, and commit to learning how do better in the future.

As we talk, working-class people notice how oblivious or how aware of class issues we seem, and make decisions about how much to collaborate with us based on those evaluations, among other factors. The goal of reducing the classism in our speech is not to keep ourselves out of trouble by avoiding angering working-class people, and it's not to reach some kind of perfect non-classist purity. The goal is to make ourselves more trustworthy and to alienate working-class people less so that we can work together for economic justice and other common goals.

TOP THESE!: A FEW CLASSIST THINGS I'VE SAID
(IF I CAN ADMIT MINE, YOU CAN ADMIT YOURS)

- I came back from college and bumped into a working-class guy I'd known in high school. I asked what he was doing. "Bagging groceries at the supermarket." I said, "Oh, is it interesting?" He just looked at me like I was an idiot.
- In college, I was going door-to-door in the dorms signing people up for an Oxfam fast in which we would all skip eating for a day and donate the money for famine relief. One guy said, "No, this isn't for me; I'm working my way through college. This is for people whose parents pay their tuition." I told him, "No, this is for everyone!" I wouldn't take no for an answer. He actually opened a drawer and showed me those little packages of peanut butter crackers he was eating for meals, and still I badgered him to contribute.
- My friend with an Associates degree said, "I am *so* tired of teaching dental hygiene." I said, "Well, why don't you try teaching something else?" She looked at me like I was clueless and said, "Because I don't know anything else."

WHAT'S THE MOST CLASSIST THING YOU'VE HEARD AN ACTIVIST SAY?

Five interviewees' answers to this question – and mine:

Recently I was facilitating a discussion for an organization that was trying to decide how much severance pay to give a staff person leaving because the organization couldn't afford to keep them full-time. Someone said, "Let's give them a huge party and show them we love them, and they'll remember that a lot longer than any money we give them."

—Paul Kivel

Most of the Homeowners Associations wanted in an icky way to "color up" with racial diversity. They were happy to have people of color at the table as long as they were in the minority and didn't get to make any decisions. At one meeting, this one white homeowner was complaining about "why Latinos won't come to our meetings" and she suggested that maybe people should bring their maids! It was too gross!

—Roxana Tynan

Find the Invisible Working-Class People in These Statements

- Women still have to choose between career success and children.
- I bought some land in Vail and built my dream house.
- Everybody got burned in the stock market crash.
- I run an institute at the university.
- When I was a girl, every family had a cook.

—blw

NEXT STEPS

There was a fund-raising event that cost $50 and I heard comments about how "anyone can afford that."

—Pam McMichael

Several times I've heard social welfare professionals say about poor mothers, "We have to speak for them because they can't speak for themselves."

—Theresa Funiciello

There was one guy I worked with, he thought he was the smartest organizer, and he would say things to me like "Can you turn out 500 people for this meeting and then we'll go and do the negotiations for them?" He thought of working-class people as props and their voices as sound bites.

I've heard people patronize, tokenize, and fetishize, like "Let's hear from the welfare recipient now! Isn't she smart?"

—Gilda Haas

A new friend said, "My neighbor wanted to put up a 15-foot fence that would block my view. He's real redneck low-life trailer trash." I told her I was offended by that, and we had a big argument that lasted all day.

—blw

. . .

In many organizations I've been part of, decision-making is hard. Middle-class people with more education are just faster and more articulate. Others are silenced because they can't keep up with the style of arguing.

—Barbara Willer

. . .

N E X T   S T E P S

HANG IN

Low-income folks believe that middle-class folks won't stick around. When the going gets tough, they'll leave. It's a vicious cycle: it happens so much that there's no trust, so middle-class people wonder why they should stick around if they're not trusted. The key is to stick with it even if pushed away. You'll be tested. Like when [civil rights pioneer] Septima Clark sent me as a white person to a black church meeting, and I came back saying they didn't want me there. She asked "What did you expect? Now, next time you go . . ." She kept sending me back to that group until I had built trust.

I really value middle-class activists when they're willing to stick it through hard times—and I say that coming out of an area where doing this work meant Klan harassment and threats.

—Linda Stout

. . .

SUPPORT WORKING-CLASS ISSUES

. . .

Want to be an ally? Honor boycotts, buy union, use union printers, don't cross picket lines, pay a living wage, and give family leave and good benefits.

—Felice Yeskel

In the 1980s in my city, the Nuclear Freeze campaign put a referendum on the ballot, and 60 percent of the voters supported a freeze on nuclear weapons. Then Jobs with Peace proposed a followup referendum calling for more jobs through peace conversion, which had the potential for even more public and labor support. But most of the Freeze people just faded away, uninterested.

I was asked to speak at a statewide Freeze convention, and I made a strong pitch for reaching out to labor and working-class people. Afterwards, in the hallway, a number of working-class people came up to me and said it made a big difference to them; they hadn't had the nerve to raise it themselves.

Sometimes peace activists kind of raise their noses, as if it's more pure to be against war for idealistic reasons, as if it's a bit tawdry to be concerned with jobs and self-interest.

—George Lakey

USE YOUR PRIVILEGE

If you have privilege, have a conversation with low-income leaders about how you could use it strategically. If you have a country house, maybe we could have a retreat there. It's not just your money, it's who you know, what you know, how you talk.

We were organizing a conference on homelessness, and members of our group who were homeless were going to speak. There was a woman who had a lot of classism. She said, "How are you going to find homeless people to ask to speak? Would they know enough? How could you find homeless people who can talk well enough?" I was going to debate someone on the Governor's Council, and she said, "Do you know how to debate? Do you know enough information to debate? Would you be able to keep up with him?" I asked my owning-class coworker to talk with her, and she persuaded her. Now this woman points out classism when it happens. That's the fastest turn-around I've seen. My coworker was able because of her similar background to explain how things sounded. It was a strategic use of privilege.

—Lisa Richards

People with more privilege need to figure out how to equalize things, which doesn't mean to empty out their bank accounts. But it's the responsibility of activists to be generous and to figure out how to support things they care about materially if they possibly can.

—Barbara Smith

NEXT STEPS

I resent people who try to pass as someone like me. I met an upper-middle-class woman who said, "I'm on welfare so I can be a full-time activist with youth." That's not what welfare's there for. I hate it when people hide their privilege and don't acknowledge it.

—Rachel Rybaczuk

If grassroots people have attitudes of racism or antiimmigrant prejudice, a negative approach isn't productive. Nobody likes to be told they are wrong, especially by a more privileged person. Instead, ask questions and help someone learn. Hold fast to principles, but let go of ideology. Equity is a principle, but "only one way to get there" is ideology.

—Barbara Willer

LET GO OF CONTROL

I've seen this pattern over and over. A cross-class alliance is formed to deal with a problem. A group with resources offers to sponsor it. They staff it, they control the funding, they control the information . . . . Next thing you know, we have our own class divide internally. We build power just to give it away, without knowing it's been given away until it's gone.

—Sam Grant

I helped start a community development corporation that created affordable housing. The board was all professionals, and all of us in the houses were neighborhood people. There was so much tension over decision-making and who had the control. We argued over what color paint to use. The middle-class folks didn't get the concerns about power and why the working-class folks were so frustrated. We had no language for it, because everyone was white, so weren't we all the same?

—Barbara Willer

RECOGNIZE WORKING-CLASS PEOPLE'S CONSTRAINTS

I remember going to a national women's group conference. They wanted low-income people and people of color there, so we said sure, Piedmont Peace Project would bring a group of folks in. First, they didn't do a sliding scale, which was shocking enough. But the worst thing was, we came with kids in tow, and we got there and there was no childcare. We had to turn around and go home. We were so used to providing childcare, we assumed there would be childcare.

Some groups have meetings in the middle of the day, and then wonder why no working people come. Ridiculous! We used to plan meetings taking people's work hours into consideration. In farm communities, we'd meet after dark. With millworkers, we'd have meetings in shifts, one in the morning and one at 6 P.M. You've got to know your constituency.

—Linda Stout

42

Deep Thoughts About Class Privilege

Karen Pittelman and Resource Generation

CLASS PRIVILEGE AFFECTS OUR FINANCIAL FUTURE

A job interview is only one of many situations where class privilege affects our financial future. Every time we walk into a bank for a loan, into a real estate broker's office for a home, even into an important meeting at work, being a young person with wealth gives us an unspoken advantage.

Another advantage comes from the fact that class privilege can place us in some very powerful networks. Networks are one of the main ways people find out about things like jobs, housing and business opportunities. Class privilege gives us access to exclusive formal associations like alumni groups and prestigious clubs, as well as informal webs of influential neighbors, family and friends.

These connections don't just tell us about possible opportunities, they can also help us act on them. When someone "in the know" puts in a good word for us, it transforms us from an anonymous name into a friendly face—and that can often make all the difference.

THIS DOESN'T MEAN WE DON'T WORK HARD

Thinking about the impact of class privilege on our lives can be unsettling, especially if we grew up wealthy and don't have any other class experience to compare it to. We want to say that our successes happen because we deserve them—because we worked hard, because we studied and sacrificed, because we were committed to our goals. We want to say that maybe we had that privilege, but we chose not to use it, that we didn't need it, that we could make it on our own merits.

The problem is that privilege isn't something that can be turned on or off. While money can be laid aside unused, privilege is deeply embedded in our lives. It's a part of the experiences that make us who we are, that shape how we see the world and the way the world sees us. Class privilege even becomes a part of our bodies, from straight teeth to a "firm" handshake.

Acknowledging how class privilege impacts our lives doesn't have to mean abandoning pride in ourselves. Our hard work is still hard work. Our fabulousness is still fabulous. It just means that, as young people with wealth, the story of where we are and how we got there is more complicated than a list of our merits. There's a lot more there to uncover.

DEEP THOUGHTS ABOUT CLASS PRIVILEGE

Here are some seriously heavy questions about the impact of class privilege in our lives. Woo hoo! Yeah!

N E X T   S T E P S

Okay, maybe that's a little overzealous. It'd probably be much more fun to watch *MacGyver* reruns and eat Funyuns. But even though it isn't easy, understanding our privilege has the potential to change our lives and our relationships in some amazing ways. Plus, the more we understand, the better we'll be at using our privilege for social change. . . . And, obviously, depending on your background and what's up for you right now in your life, some of these questions will be more or less relevant. Feel free to skip anything that doesn't pertain . . .

BIG DECISIONS

- Think about a big decision you've made recently. Were there ways that having class privilege factored into that decision?
- Has having class privilege ever affected the way you've been able to cope with a difficult or painful time in your life? How so?
- What's one of the biggest risks you've taken—or wish you could have taken—in your life? Were there resources of your own or family resources that you could have fallen back on if it didn't work out? Did that affect your choice to take the risk?

WORK AND SCHOOL

- Has having class privilege affected your education? How so? Has it had an affect on your choices about schools? About what to study?
- Has having class privilege had an affect on your decisions about work? Has it had an impact on your salary, income or level of prestige associated with your work?

WHERE YOU LIVE

- Has having class privilege played a role in your housing decisions? Has it affected where you've lived in the past? Where you live now? The way other people involved, like brokers, realtors and landlords, treated you? Whether you rent or own? If you own, did it impact the way you paid for your home?

DISCRIMINATION

- Are there ways that class privilege *hasn't* made any difference for you in dealing with discrimination? How so?
- Are there ways that class privilege *has* made a difference for you in dealing with discrimination? How so?
- How have your experiences with discrimination impacted the way you understand class privilege?

OTHER KINDS OF PRIVILEGE

- Do you have other kinds of privilege in addition to class privilege? How does that affect the way you look at your experiences with class privilege?
- Has there ever been a time when having privilege made it harder to hear what someone was trying to say to you?

NEXT STEPS

1. polite
12. looks put-together
2. great smile
11. energetic
3. reliable
10. well-rounded
4. high GPA
9. impressive degree
5. confident
8. well spoken
6. impressive résumé
7. great references

N
E
X
T

S
T
E
P
S

If you grew up with wealth . . .

- Were there ways that class privilege had an impact on your daily life? How so?
- Did having class privilege ever affect the way people treated you? How?
- Did having class privilege affect the way you saw your own potential and your role is in the world? How?

If wealth is a more recent thing in your life . . .

- Are there ways that having class privilege has changed your daily life?
- Are there ways that having class privilege has changed the way people treat you?
- Has having class privilege affected your sense of what's possible in your life and your hopes for the future? How so?

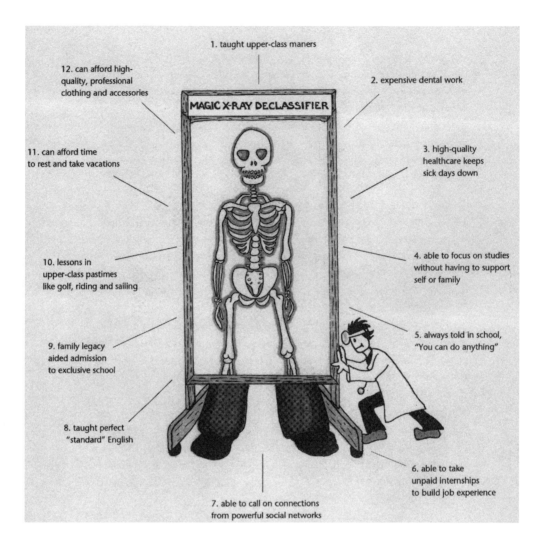

1. taught upper-class maners

2. expensive dental work

3. high-quality healthcare keeps sick days down

4. able to focus on studies without having to support self or family

5. always told in school, "You can do anything"

6. able to take unpaid internships to build job experience

7. able to call on connections from powerful social networks

8. taught perfect "standard" English

9. family legacy aided admission to exclusive school

10. lessons in upper-class pastimes like golf, riding and sailing

11. can afford time to rest and take vacations

12. can afford high-quality, professional clothing and accessories

MAGIC X-RAY DECLASSIFIER

SOCIAL SITUATIONS

- Have you ever been in a situation where you knew the "right" way to act because of your class privilege? Or the "right" way to speak? Or where you got a joke or a reference to something that you understood because you had class privilege?

FINANCIAL STATUS

- Does having class privilege affect your current income and expenses? Do you have loans? Car payments? Mortgage payments? Do you have a financial safety net or family resources you can fall back on?
- Does having class privilege affect the way you are treated at the bank? How?

HEALTH

- Does having class privilege impact the kind of healthcare you receive? The quality of your doctors? Dental work? Therapy?

- If you've had to deal with a major illness or injury, either your own or a family member's, did having class privilege have an impact on your choices about treatments and options?

LEGAL SYSTEM

- If you've had to deal with the police or the legal system, did having class privilege affect your options and the outcome of the experience? How?

"In boarding school, I remember being told, 'You guys are the cream of the cream. The education you are receiving here is preparing you to be leaders in the world.' I realized that the other young people in my class weren't necessarily that special. They were nice, but they weren't so great. It just made me wonder why these people get to be the leaders. Why do I get to be the leader? There's no real reason for that. It's the luck of the draw."

—Christian

43

Distributing Income

You be the Judge

Tamara Sober Giecek with United for a Fair Economy

OBJECTIVES

- Experience the realistic decision making process of determining who should have an increase or decrease in income.
- Explore how most decisions are made in the business world regarding increases and decreases in income.

CONCEPTS AND KEY TERMS

- distribution of income
- how businesses often decide to distribute income
- the merits of belonging to a union

INSTRUCTIONAL TIME

- 55 minutes

PREPARATION

- Five chocolate bars ("$100 Grand" bars if available).
- Seven sets of five sticky notes marked $100,000. Mark one of the seven sets with "B" on the bottom of each $100,000 bill. Hand these to the Bosses when you are handing out the $100,000 sticky note bills.
- Seven 8.5"×11" placards, each displaying one of the job titles in the chart shown below. Put strings through each sign so students can hang them over their necks.
- The following chart made into poster size, and hung at the front of the classroom.

Bosses	$400,000/year
Doctors	$100,000/year
Nurses	$30,000/year
Kitchen Workers and Nurses' Aides	$11,000/year
Gardeners/Security Guards/Janitors	$15–18,000/year
Patients	fixed income, social security
Low-income Elderly on Waiting List	$10,000/year

- Place the profiles below onto seven separate index cards.

You are the **Bosses:** the management of Sunnyvale and of the nursing home chain that owns Sunnyvale.

Possible Arguments:
- Managers here make less money than at other nursing homes. At another chain, managers make $200,000 to $700,000!
- Because of this, turnover is high. There have been three financial managers in five years!
- We deserve a raise! We only received a $5,000 raise last year. We cut costs by reducing the number of nurses and gardeners last year. We should be rewarded for this cost cutting.
- With just three of the $100,000 bills, all five of the top managers could make as much as we would at other nursing homes.

You are the **Doctors** at Sunnyvale.

Possible Arguments:
- If we went into private practice, we'd all make $200,000 a year or more—double the measly amount we make here.
- The patients we treat are getting older and sicker, so our work is getting more complicated.
- We have the longest training and the most advanced skills of anyone here. We deserve to get the biggest raise. Two of the five $100,000 should go to us.

You are the **Nurses** at Sunnyvale.

Possible Arguments:
- There are fewer nurses taking care of more patients than last year. We are working harder and so should get paid more—but we only received a $400 raise last year! For some of us, our rent went up more than that!
- It's ridiculous that we go to four years of specialized school and our pay ceiling is $40,000. It's because most of us are women!
- Just two of the five $100,000 bills would give us raises we think would be fair.

You are the **Janitors, Security Guards, and Gardeners** at Sunnyvale.

Possible Arguments:
- Our work is dirty and sometimes dangerous. We have to work outside in all weather. Two gardeners now do all the work that four gardeners used to do.
- We can hardly support our families on this pay. We can't save money or buy health insurance, or send our kids to college.
- Some of us have worked here since Sunnyvale started 15 years ago, and we've hardly gotten any raises in all that time!
- With two of the $100,000 bills, we could get health insurance and a raise to a living wage.

You are **the Kitchen Workers and Nurses' Aides** at Sunnyvale.

Possible Arguments:
- We can't support our families on the pay here. Many of us don't have cars, phones or health insurance.
- We think it's because we're all women, mostly women of color or recent immigrants, that we're paid less than anyone else here.
- We are the ones who actually care for the patients.
- Our work is dirty and difficult. We change diapers and bathe patients. We stay an average of only five months because we are continually looking elsewhere for higher pay. This high turnover is bad for the patients, who see new faces constantly.
- With two of the $100,000 bills, we could get raises to a wage where we could meet our expenses and pay our monthly bills. With a third one, we could have health insurance.

You are the **Patients** at Sunnyvale.

Possible Arguments:
- The fees for our nursing home are so high that they harm our families. The fees take their money that they need for other things.
- Some nursing homes charge less and have nice facilities that we don't have, like a swimming pool, and activities every day instead of every other day.
- With just two of the $100,000 bills, we could get a cut in the fees we pay AND some new and improved facilities and activities.

You are the **Low-income Elderly People on a Waiting List** to get into one of the 10 government subsidized* slots at Sunnyvale.

Possible Arguments:
- We really need a nursing home. We can't live at home any more, because we can't feed or dress ourselves and we need daily medical care. It might be many months before a Medicaid (subsidized*) slot opens up.
- On our incomes of $10,000 or so, how could we afford the regular $30,000 a year price for Sunnyvale?
- Our families can't afford it either.
- Sunnyvale should spend three of the $100,000 bills subsidizing slots for us, so we can move in now.

* Subsidize: to grant public aid (money) to an individual or a private enterprise (corporation) for public benefits.

N
E
X
T

S
T
E
P
S

CONDUCTING THE LESSON

INCOME DISTRIBUTION ROLE PLAY

1. Tell the class, "We have been talking about how American workers are losing ground. We will now look at "why" this happens by conducting a role-play based on a real life situation where we will look at the fairness in the distribution of incomes."

2. Announce: "Sunnyvale Nursing Home has an extra $500,000. We are going to decide who should get this extra money. These five candy bars represent five $100,000 bills, and at the end of the role-play I will divide the candy up the way the money is allocated in the role-play. Each of you get five $100,000 bills to vote on who you think should get the money. There are seven different groups at Sunnyvale Nursing home, so I need seven volunteers (to sit in the middle of the circle or at the front of the room). You will be given teams and you will be the spokesperson for your team."

3. Divide the rest of the students evenly among the seven volunteers and ask them to sit together as seven separate teams. Give each team's spokesperson their bills (give marked bills to the bosses), index cards, and signs (to hang around their necks).

4. Announce: "Your job is to persuade the other groups that your group should get some of the money. Read and discuss your card with your group, then decide where you think the five $100,000 bills should go. Each spokesperson (and members of their group) will have a turn to state their opinion. You can propose something different than what is on the card; these are just suggestions."

5. After seven people speak in turn, conduct discussion as time allows, then conduct a "vote" by asking the spokesperson from each group to place the $100,000 bills on the chart at the front of the room, allocating the funds as they feel they should be distributed.

6. Announce the tallies of how everyone voted. Then hand out the candy bars according to the bosses' vote (marked on the back of their $100,000 bills). See if people object or offer to share, then hold a discussion. Make the point that in a unionized work-place, workers would be represented in this discussion; at a worker coop, everyone would have a vote; at non-union workplaces, the bosses would decide behind closed doors.

SECTION 4

RELIGIOUS OPPRESSION

Introduction

Maurianne Adams and Khyati Y. Joshi[1]

Ask anyone what the United States stands for and most would include freedom of religion high on their list. One of the most enduring and powerful founding myths is that, in America, all religions can practice freely. A second and equally powerful foundational myth is that the U.S. Constitution requires separation of church and state, protecting religious practice from political interference. These deeply held but generally unexamined assumptions present obstacles to our understanding of the shaping role of Protestant Christianity on the development of political and social institutions in the United States. Deconstructing these myths is essential to understanding the historical role of Christian privilege as well as the religious oppression of non-Christian faith traditions, both of which are central concepts in this section.

This section provides readings that explore Contexts for the ways in which dominant (predominantly Protestant) Christianity in the United States maintained, justified, and continues to reproduce the subordination of non-Christian religions (such as Buddhism, Hinduism, Judaism, Islam, Santeria, Sikhism, Wiccan) as well as non-mainstream Christian sects, through institutional practices such as health care, schooling, and public safety. This section also provides Personal Voices that illustrate the constraints forged by hegemonic Christianity on the religious practices, personal safety, harassment, modes of dress, and everyday lives of different religious minorities. Reading selections in Next Steps show how Christian allies have worked in coalition with marginalized religious communities, and how these coalitions have worked on behalf of anti-oppression and social justice objectives.

CONCEPTUAL APPROACH TO RELIGIOUS OPPRESSION

Deconstructing these two core national myths concerning the role of religion involves exploration of the historical roots of religious and national U.S. identity. It focuses attention to the impact of hegemonic Christianity on governmental and legal policy, and on social institutions such as schools. This section presents multiple examples of how Christianity has been used to maintain cultural and political domination over non-Christian religious groups in the United States. It illustrates how Christianity has become normative in our society, by referring to any important book as a bible, for example, or reckoning time before Christ (B.C.) and anno Domini (A.D.). At the same time, we stress that, while highlighting the historical and social role of (Protestant) Christianity in the United States, we are not questioning the belief systems of Christianity or endorsing non-Christian religious doctrine. Our focus is not on individual dimensions of faith and belief, but on the societal role of religion in justifying and helping to maintain a social system characterized by religious domination and subordination.

When discussing the concept of *religious oppression,* we focus on the social structures, federal and local policies, and cultural practices that maintain *religious hegemony* through "the everyday practices of a well-intentioned liberal society" (Young, selection 5). Readings in this section describe the "five faces of oppression" of Christian privilege (Blumenfeld, selection 47) and the individual, institutional, and societal–cultural levels of oppression (Joshi, selection 48) that have been normalized by (mainly) Protestant U.S. Christianity, as exemplified by efforts to erase Native American Indian religious traditions through federal or state military and legal interventions (Echo-Hawk, selection 52; Grinde, selection 53). Our section title thus draws upon an understanding of *religious oppression* as "structural" and "systemic" (Bell, Hardiman, Jackson, and Griffin, selection 4), operating through society's "unquestioned norms, habits, and symbols," its "normal processes of everyday life," its "assumptions underlying institutional rules and the collective consequences of following those rules" (Young, selection 5).

The terms *Christian hegemony* and *Christian privilege* are critical in deconstructing the two core national myths noted above. The term *Christian hegemony* captures the role of *normative Christianity* in everyday life within U.S. schools, neighborhoods, and workplaces (as in Eck, selection 45). *Hegemony* conveys the unconscious reproduction of oppression carried on as part of everyday life. *Christian hegemony* refers to a society's unacknowledged adherence to a dominant religious world view that in the United States publicly affirms Christian observances, holy days, sacred spaces at the expense of those who are not Christian and within a culture that normalizes Christian values as intrinsic to an explicitly American identity. Christian norms are termed *hegemonic* in that their maintenance depends not on any special effort, but on conducting "business as usual." Examples of hegemonic Christianity include school and workplace holidays keyed to the Christian calendar, political references to the Christian bible, a weekend that supports Christian worship, and the difficulty of refusing Christian proselytizing (see selections 45–48, 55, 57–58). *Christian privilege* refers to the view that Christian beliefs, language, practices do not require any special effort to be recognized, as they are embedded into the U.S. American culture (Schlosser, selection 46).

CORE MYTH 1: FREEDOM OF RELIGION FOR ALL

The founding narrative that dramatizes freedom of religion in the United States derives from the early history of Pilgrims and Puritans, fleeing sectarian religious persecution in England and arriving on American shores to establish a haven of religious freedom for all. More accurately, the Puritans established in the Massachusetts colony a place to practice *their* religion without fear or persecution, but where non-Puritan practice was forbidden and religious heresy rooted out—Puritans hanged four Quakers to make the point. Puritanism was in effect the first of many ethnocentric and parochial "immigrant faiths" planted on U.S. soil in opposition to the Native American religious traditions already practiced in areas colonized by the Puritans, and also in conflict with the Spanish and French Roman Catholic outposts and missions earlier established throughout the Americas. In reality, the colonial period in the Americas was complex, with Quakers, Anabaptists, Catholics, Jews, and others also in search of religious refuge and in economic as well as religious conflict with each other. The mutual ill will and religious competition among different Protestant Christian faith traditions, for example, led the people of New Netherlands to cleanse their colony of Lutherans and Quakers, and to try the same with Jews.

The predominantly Protestant Christian ethos of contemporary U.S. life is rooted in the colonial religious competition over homogeneous religious identity, community control, wealth, and land. This ethos dictated the rules of political life in the colonies (mandatory Church attendance, tax-supported religious institutions) and the assumption of Christian superiority to the oral religious traditions of the Native Americans or enslaved Africans, and, later, to the Buddhist, Hindu, Jewish, and Muslim religious traditions. Similarly, hostility (sometimes violent) was directed against non-Protestant religions such as the Church of Jesus Christ of Latter-Day Saints (the Mormons), the Seventh-Day Adventists, and the Jehovah's Witnesses, each of them critical of Protestant orthodoxy and denominational organization, and resistant to the religious hegemony established by state or federal authorities. Hostility has likewise been directed (and continues to be directed) against Atheists, who are seen as violating a deeply held Christian cultural consensus. To make these points, the historical framework by Lippy (selection 44) examines the conflicts in the United States between a "Christian nation or pluralistic culture" (see section website for further discussion).

CORE MYTH 2: "SEPARATION OF CHURCH AND STATE"

The second myth in need of deconstruction is the belief that the U.S. Constitution requires the separation of church and state. The language about separation is based not in the body of the Constitution (whose only reference to religion is "there shall be no religious test for public office") but in the religion clauses of the First Amendment to the U.S. Constitution (1791). There, the First Amendment stipulates that "Congress shall make no law respecting an establishment of religion, or prohibiting the free exercise thereof" and provides, in effect, a religious mutual assurance pact, agreed upon by the major competing Protestant denominations in the original thirteen colonies, to prevent any one of them from becoming a federally established church supported by federal taxes. (Established state churches were funded by state taxes until the mid-nineteenth century.)

The first part of the religion clause of the First Amendment, known as the *Establishment Clause* ("Congress shall make no law respecting an establishment of religion"), prohibits the federal government from supporting any single religion or religious denomination or sect and is generally known as the *separation of church and state.* This phrase is not derived from the Constitution but instead from an 1802 letter by Thomas Jefferson to the Danbury Baptist Congregation, responding to their worries by assuring them that the Constitution would provide "a wall of separation between Church and State." The second part of the religion clause, known as the *Free Exercise Clause* ("Congress shall make no law . . . prohibiting the free exercise thereof") is understood to assure free religious practice, unencumbered by government. This assurance, however, has been subjected to numerous Supreme Court interpretations, some of which have found against free religious practice for non-Christian groups, especially Native Americans (described by Echo-Hawk in selection 52). (See section website for further detail.)

While successful in preventing the legislative or executive establishment of an officially mandated religion (such as characterized church and state in the early colonies), the Founders were less successful in preventing cultural hegemonic religion, as Jefferson's Christian-centric word "church" (rather than separating "religion and state") illustrates. Similarly, the pervasive cultural assumptions that are rooted in *Christian hegemony* are evident in the state and federal court interpretations directed against non-Christian plaintiffs in cases of free religious practice. For example, courts did not find credible the free religious practice constitutional claims made in the courts by members of marginalized faiths (Eck, selection 51), or efforts by Native American Indians to practice religious rituals in their sacred sites (Echo-Hawk, selection 52). (See section website for further information.)

INTERSECTIONS OF RACE AND RELIGION: THE RACIALIZATION OF U.S. RELIGIONS

During colonial times, the *Christian white* religious communities justified their violence against Native American Indians, and their maintenance of race-based slavery, on the basis of Christian superiority (Native Americans and Africans were considered infidels and heathen) as well as on the emergent ideology of white racial superiority. Settler appropriations of Native American lands, and the brutality and profits of slavery, set in motion an interwoven white *racial* and Christian *religious* national identity that advantaged free, white Christian men as citizens in the new republic. Throughout U.S. history, *Christian, English, free,* and *white* have been juxtaposed to form mutually supporting advantages based on the co-construction of religion, race, and national origins (Fredrickson 2002; Goldschmidt and McAlister 2004; Takaki 1993). Devout colonists perceived Divine purposes behind the malarial and influenza epidemics that wiped out Native Indian populations, and facilitated colonial appropriation of Native American villages and farmlands (Loewen 1995; Mann 2005). The ensuing tribal displacements and cultural genocide were justified by belief in the inevitable victory of Christianity over heathens, and Western civilization over primitive savagery. In later periods of U.S. history, Christian texts rationalized race-based segregation between white and black congregations within the same Protestant denominations (Baptists, Methodists, and Pentecostals) and viewed immigrant Buddhists, Hindus, Muslims, and Sikhs as a barbaric, threatening, racial/religious "Other." Religious profiling, the presumption that religious "others" are terrorists, and the resistance by Christian neighbors to mosques, temples, and *gurdwaras* are detailed in selections by Eck (selections 45 and 51) and Williams (selection 54), and in the Voices selections (selections 56 and 57).

Centuries before the period of European exploration, colonization, and slave trade, European Christian society had traditionally restricted the living conditions of Jews, having pushed Muslims away from its Spanish and East European borders. Jews throughout Christian Europe had been demonized, vilified, expelled, or segregated in ghettos, mainly on religious grounds, although by the eighteenth and nineteenth centuries, as notions of racial superiority or inferiority became part of the culture, Jews in Europe were racialized according to the "pseudo-scientific" view that they constituted an essentially inferior and impure "race" of "Semites." Originally outcast from Christian European society because they did not accept Christ and were blamed for the Crucifixion, Jews had been forcibly converted and absorbed into Christian culture if they converted to Christianity. However, anti-Judaism morphed into racialized anti-semitism, when even the converted Jews came to be seen as "intrinsically and organically evil" (Fredrickson 2002, 19), resulting in expulsions, massacres, and genocide. This essentialized view of inferiority based on racism, and compounded by religion, traveled with European Christian migrants to the "New World" as a template for the racialization of other non-Christian religious groups.

Modern anti-semitism is heir to this centuries-old conflation of religion with racial difference as a way of isolating and delegitimizing the Jew as "Other" (Hilberg, Gilbert, and Kaye/Kantrowitz, selections 49, 50, and 56; further resources on the section website). The Christian domination over the religious "Other" can also be seen in European colonizing projects in Africa, Asia, and the Americas. European colonialism was a worldwide enterprise in which Christian missions to the "natives" were often the forward guard for colonization, economic exploitation, and the spread of white Christianity to the uncultured heathen masses. These religious "others" were increasingly seen through a miasma of entangled religious and racial meanings that justified European domination over peoples whose religions were seen through racial filters (Buddhists, Hindus, African and Asian Muslims, animist religious traditions). In the United States, the extension of *racialization* to Native American Indians, African Blacks, Asians, and Arabs living within white-dominated America continues to exacerbate the exclusion for those communities who identify themselves primarily as *religious* and do not maintain a primary self identity on the basis of race (for example, Native American religions, Muslims, Hindus, and Sikhs).

In the contemporary United States, the racialization of religion continues in a process whereby the religions of brown peoples such as Islam, Hinduism, and Sikhism are identified with their presumed ethnic/racial identity (Arab and South Asian) so that phenotype connotes marginalized religions (Joshi 2006). Thus, *brown skin* has come to connote Muslim, conflating Arabs, South Asians, and Latinos/as into the same identity. The conflation of religious marginalization with ethnocentrism and racism is apparent in selections 48 and 51–58, which illustrate various ways in which religious oppression is experienced as independent yet also connected with racism.

NATIVISM AND ANTI-IMMIGRATION

Before the U.S. Civil War, it is estimated that over half the U.S. population and 85 percent of Protestants were evangelical (Emerson and Smith 2000), and that the total number of immigrants was low (143,000 in 1820s), European and white. Given these early demographics, the linkage between Protestantism and a white American national identity is not surprising. Beginning in the 1840s and continuing into the early twentieth century, European and Asian immigration challenged this homogeneous and racialized, mainly Protestant assumption of American national identity. Starting with Irish Catholics driven by the potato famine of the 1840s, immigration after mid-century consisted mainly of Irish and Italian Catholics and Eastern European Jews in flight from European revolution, poverty, and pogroms, and Chinese and Punjabi laborers seeking employment. By 1920, more than a third of the total population of 105 million Americans included immigrant families (36 million), the majority of them Roman Catholic, Greek Orthodox, and Jewish, with smaller numbers of Buddhists and Sikhs (Daniels 2002)—all of them outside Protestantism and considered ethnically and racially inferior.

These immigrant religious outsiders poked large holes in the already-stretched fabric of Protestant U.S. American national identity. The demographic challenge posed by waves of immigrants to an identity based on religion (Protestantism), culture (Western European heritage), and race (Whiteness) led to violent xenophobic backlash and anti-immigration policies. The first wave of U.S. American "nativism" involved the anti-immigrant backlash by Protestant U.S.-born "Americans" of Northern European ancestry, whose virulent anti-Catholicism was aimed largely at Irish and German Catholics (1830s–1850s). A second wave of nativism was more generally anti-Asian, and led politically to a series of restrictive immigration laws—the Chinese Exclusion Act of 1882 and the Immigration Act of 1917 (known as the "Barred Zone" Act). The nativist backlash culminated with the Johnson–Reed Immigration Act of 1924, which set a cap on immigrants entering the United States at 2 percent of the total of any nation's residents in the United States as of the 1890 census, thus severely limiting Catholic and Jewish immigration. In both the 1917 Asian Barred Zone Act and the 1924 Johnson–Reed Act, while religion was not mentioned in the text of the legislation, a by-product meant the exclusion of non-Protestant faiths. These immigration restrictions, which later restricted refugee Jews fleeing Nazi Europe, for the most part stayed in place until the Immigration Act of 1965.

After World War II the barriers were slowly dismantled for white Ashkenazi Jews and for white Catholics (Italians and Irish), but not for black or brown Catholics or Protestants (African Americans, Puerto Ricans, Chicanos/as and Mexican Americans, South or Central Americans) (see resources on the website). This was a period during which most Jews and Catholics became White or at least "almost" if "not always quite" White (Brodkin Sachs 1998; Guglielmo 2003; Ignatiev 1995; Roediger 1991).

The 1952 McCarran–Walter Act and the 1965 Immigration and Naturalization Act reopened the door to immigration and permanently altered the racial, ethnic, and religious makeup of the United States. By 2000, immigrant and second-generation Americans numbered nearly 55 million people. One outcome is the growing Hindu, Muslim, and Sikh religious, cultural, and ethnic communities in the United States (Eck, selections 45 and 51; Joshi, selection 48; Fattah and Omran, selection 57).

INTERSECTIONS WITH OTHER FORMS OF OPPRESSION

The contemporary conflation of terrorism with Islam makes it especially urgent to disentangle the *religious* dimensions of current domestic and global conflicts and hostilities, from dimensions that are political, ideological, or cultural. We need to understand how religious motives and justifications can inflame cultural, ethnic, racial, and class antagonisms. This point has been captured in the aphorism, "It is not so much that religion has become politicized, but that politics have been religionized" (Juergensmeyer 2003, 2). Religion interacts in important ways with ethnicity, class, gender, and nationalism, and these interacting dimensions of social identity need to be understood in their complex interrelations instead of as either/or forced choices that misinterpret one at the expense of the other.

The complex interrelationship of religion with political, ideological, and cultural forces is important to understand if we are to make sense of current-day conflicts. Religious difference suffuses some of today's most intractable global, regional, ethnic, national, and domestic conflicts, which generate intense partisanship and sectarian solidarity. For example, Christians v. Muslims in the Balkans, Jews v. Muslims in the Middle East, Hindus v. Muslims in South Asia, and Catholics v. Protestants until recently in Northern Ireland illustrate this "co-constitutive relationship" (Goldschmidt and McAlister 2004). Religion links with the other social categories considered elsewhere in this volume—religion *and* race *and* ethnicity *and* economic class—*and* nationalism, this last a phenomenon that has had severe consequences for the religiously-identified "other" and national "outsider" (Marty and Appleby 1997). For example, several reading selections examine the oppression of Native American Indians in the United States as a complex and cumulative interaction of religion (Christian v. heathen), race (White v. Red), culture (civilized v. barbarian), and economic competition over land (Echo-Hawk, selection 52; Grinde, selection 53). Selections by Eck (selections 45 and 51), Joshi (selection 48), Williams (selection 54), and Semple (selection 55) similarly braid religion—Muslim, Hindu, Sikh, Buddhist, Catholic—with race and ethnicity (South Asian Indian, Japanese, Somali, Latino/a). The history of global anti-semitism involves a similarly complex and cumulative braiding of religious hatred, economic resentment, and racial stereotyping.

Contemporary manifestations of Christian hegemony interacting with cultural and political ideology can be seen in divisive instances of "religionized" domestic U.S. politics. They include bitter disputes over competing end-of-life and beginning-of-life issues (such as euthanasia, stem cell research, abortion), competing rights such as "the right to decide" v. "the right to life," the authority of local school boards to substitute Creationism or Intelligent Design for evolution in science curricula. "Religionized" issues also include legal and Constitutional struggles to extend or prohibit gay marriage, controversies concerning school prayer, religious displays at Christmas or Easter, the use of tax-funded vouchers for private religious schools, and the funding of faith-based initiatives as a substitute for increased public services.

STEPS AND CHALLENGES IN ACHIEVING A RELIGIOUS PLURALISM

It is important to also understand Christianity's dramatic historical and contemporary role in contesting oppression and fostering coalitions toward social change. Examples include the role of

Protestant churches in the abolition and civil rights movement. Christian Liberation Theology has contributed to social justice movements worldwide. Jeung (selection 59) provides an example of evangelical Protestants in coalition with Latino/a Catholics and Cambodian Buddhists for equitable housing.

Religion has also been used by oppressed communities as a source of community strength and empowerment. Williams (selection 54) describes the importance of Buddhist solidarity during Japanese internment, and Bernards (selection 60) traces her inspiration from Jewish tradition to build coalitions across communities in religious conflict to foster cooperation and change. Other examples of organized resistance to oppression and maintenance of group solidarity, such as the Black Church, and the role of Hindu temples, Sikh *gurdwaras*, and Muslim mosques to support religious, ethnic, and linguistic-identified communities, are noted in the section website.

While many think we live in a religiously pluralistic democracy, it should be clear we have a long way to go in achieving that goal. Present-day immigration is not only increasing and expanding both the opportunities and the challenges of religious diversity, it is also facilitating the growth of Latino and Asian Catholic and Evangelical congregations whose identity and forms of worship are rooted in culturally and linguistically homogeneous ethnic communities of origin in some cases, and whose congregations are ethnically and culturally pluralistic in others (see section website).

The challenges have already been noted in this section introduction. The opportunities must be noted as well. There are at least two openings in our society that might enable us to strengthen religious pluralism and freedom of religious practice—in our schools and through interfaith organizations.

Schools have tended to avoid education *about religions* (as distinct from *religious education*), whether through fear of violating the Establishment Clause, discomfort when faced with religious differences, or lack of teacher preparedness. The U.S. Supreme Court supports study *about* religions in the nation's public schools, stating that it is both legal and desirable: "It might well be said that one's education is not complete without a study of comparative religions or the history of religion and its relationship to the advancement of civilization . . . [when] presented objectively as part of a secular program of education" (*School District of Abington Township, Pennsylvania,* et al. *v. Schempp* et al.*, 1963*). Similarly, the National Council for Social Studies has urged, "Knowledge about religions is not only a characteristic of an educated person but is absolutely necessary for understanding and living in a world of diversity" (National Council for Social Studies 1998). The section website presents examples of effective K–12 programs that teach *about* religions, with the goal of increasing understanding of all faiths.

There is also a growing tradition of interreligious dialogue and understanding created by peoples motivated by diverse faith and religious traditions to work for social change. Historical examples date back to the abolitionist movement, worker and liberation theology movements, settlement and social reform movements, and the civil rights movement. Today, peace activists and interfaith communities work at the local level to provide support for the needs of different faith communities, members of religious and spiritual communities join forces to safeguard the local and the global environment. Minority religious advocacy organizations work to protect the religious and civil rights for their community members and assist one another (see section website for examples, references, and resources).

Note

1 We ask that those who cite this work always acknowledge by name all of the authors listed rather than only citing the first author or using "et al." to indicate coauthors. All authors listed on a section collaborated equitably on the conceptualization, development, and writing of this section.

References

Brodkin Sachs, K. (1998). *How Jews Became White Folks and What That Says about Race in America*. New Brunswick: Rutgers University Press.

Daniels, R. (2002). *Coming to America: A History of Immigration and Ethnicity in American Life*, 2nd edition. Princeton, NJ: HarperPerennial.

Emerson, M. O., Smith, C. (2000). *Divided by Faith: Evangelical Religion and the Problem of Race in America*. Oxford: Oxford University Press.

Fredrickson, G. M. (2002). *Racism: A Short History*. Princeton, NJ: Princeton University Press.

Goldschmidt, H., McAlister, E. A. (2004). *Race, Nation, and Religion in the Americas*. Oxford, New York: Oxford University Press.

Guglielmo, T. A. (2003). *White on Arrival : Italians, Race, Color, and Power in Chicago, 1890–1945*. New York: Oxford University Press.

Ignatiev, N. (1995). *How the Irish Became White*. New York: Routledge.

Joshi, K. Y. (2006). "The Racialization of Religion in the United States." *Equity and Excellence in Education* 39 (3), 211–226.

Juergensmeyer, M. (November 1, 2004). "Religious Terror and the Secular State." Global and International Studies Program. Paper 22. Retrieved September 4, 2006, from http://repositories.edlib.org/gis/22.

Loewen, J. W. (1995). *Lies My Teacher Told Me: Everything Your American History Textbook Got Wrong*. New York: New Press. Distributed by Norton.

Mann, C. C. (2005). *1491: New Revelations of the Americas before Columbus*, 1st edition. New York: Knopf.

Marty, M. E., Appleby, R. S. (eds) (1997). *Religion, Ethnicity, and Self-Identity: Nations in Turmoil.* Hanover, NH: University Press of New England.

National Council for Social Studies. (1998). "Study about Religions in the Social Studies Curriculum." Retrieved September 26, 2006, from http://www.socialstudies.org/positions/religion/.

Omi, M., Winant, H. (1986). *Racial Formation in the United States: From the 1960s to the 1980s*. New York: Routledge & Kegan Paul.

Roediger, D. R. (1991). *The Wages of Whiteness : Race and the Making of the American Working Class*. London, New York: Verso.

Takaki, R. (1993). *A Different Mirror: A History of Multicultural America*. Boston: Little, Brown and Company.

44

Christian Nation or Pluralistic Culture

Religion in American Life

Charles H. Lippy

. . .

EUROPEANS PLANT CHRISTIANITY IN NORTH AMERICA

. . . Most . . . [colonists] who came from England brought with them a religious consciousness shaped by Protestant Christianity. In southern areas like Virginia, although there were some variations of belief, colonial arrangements included legal establishment of the Church of England. Establishment meant that Church of England parishes and the few

C
O
N
T
E
X
T

clergy serving them were supported by public tax money and that all who lived there would in theory be expected to be part of a parish.

. . .

Before the end of the seventeenth century, however, political changes in Britain mandated in the colonies a broader toleration of variant forms of Protestantism, so long as they did not disrupt public order and peace. Roman Catholics, however, were still not formally recognized, although they had carved a presence for themselves when Maryland was established. . . .

EARLY SIGNS OF DIVERSITY

Even so, patterns of immigration generated a far greater diversity in many parts of the English colonies than was recognized by public policy. From the arrival of the first slave ships in Virginia in 1619, an African tribal substratum made most southern Christian life diverse, since many congregations in time became biracial. White Christians were at first reluctant to share their religion with the slaves, fearing that conversion would automatically bring freedom from the bonds of slavery. When more sustained efforts were made to preach Christianity to African Americans from the middle of the eighteenth century on, the result was a vibrant fusion of African ways with evangelical Protestantism. . . . In addition, some of the first slaves were Muslims, although the conditions of slavery made it impossible for Muslim practice to last very long among the African population.

Ethnicity also contributed to other manifestations of diversity. The Dutch who had originally settled in New York (New Netherlands) brought with them their Calvinistic Reformed faith; even after the English took control, they remained a strong presence. To what became New Jersey, clusters of Scandinavian immigrants brought their Lutheran religion with them. Various communities of German immigrants who came to Pennsylvania carried a variety of religious labels, most still within the orbit of Protestant Christianity. And almost from the inception of the colonies came Jewish immigrants, who remained on the margins of colonial religious life but established synagogues and communities in places such as Charleston, South Carolina; Savannah, Georgia; New York; and Newport, Rhode Island. . . .

English control did not extend to all areas of North America that eventually became part of the United States. The presence of Spanish settlements in areas from Florida through Texas and the Southwest to California adds another layer to the tale of diversity. The last of the Spanish missions, the one in San Francisco, was founded in 1776, the same year that the English colonies proclaimed their independence from Britain. In addition, a Catholicism reflecting the French experience flourished in areas along the Gulf of Mexico from Mobile to New Orleans and along the southern Mississippi River. When these areas became part of the United States, they intensified the story of diversity because of the long history of both Spanish and French Catholicism that had supported adjoining colonial empires.

COMMON THEMES

Presbyterians and Methodists, Lutherans and Dutch Reformed, Congregationalist Puritans and Baptists—all were part of the larger Protestant heritage that had marked European Christianity since the Reformation of the sixteenth century. . . . Even the arrival of thousands of Roman Catholics from Ireland in the 1830s and 1840s did not diminish that influence, for Protestant folk were also the ones who ran the developing businesses and industries and usually the ones elected or appointed to political office. This Protestant Christian character became deeply etched into American culture more subtly as public education began to develop in the 1830s. . . . Hence, even though there were other groups present—Irish Catholics, German Catholics, Jews, and more—this broad evangelical Protestantism influenced every sector of common life, reinforcing the image of the United States as a Christian nation.

The decades between the close of the Civil War and the outbreak of World War I, when immigration from Europe reached its peak, brought challenges to that hegemony. Most of the millions who arrived on American shores in those decades came not from Protestant or even Catholic areas of Northern and Western Europe, but from Southern, Central, and Eastern Europe. The majority were not Protestants, but Roman Catholics, Eastern Orthodox Christians, and Jews. Many Catholic parishes established parochial or parish schools, in part because Protestant assumptions pervaded the public school curriculum and instruction. But some of those in positions of social, economic, and political power recoiled not only at the religious orientation of these immigrants but also at their cultural and ethnic folkways. Calls to Americanize the immigrants, however, were also most often quite clearly calls to Protestantize them, to force them into the dominant religious style and therefore perpetuate the image of the United States as a (Protestant) Christian nation.
. . .

Nonetheless, Protestants from the mainline denominations continued to exert an influence in the business and political affairs of the nation that was increasingly out of proportion to their numbers in the whole population. Hence, after World War I, when Congress enacted the first laws restricting immigration overall, there had already been earlier legislation affecting primarily Chinese and Japanese immigration to California and other areas of the West. The new quotas assured that the bulk of those allowed to enter the United States each year would give at least tacit assent to Protestant Christian belief and thus preserve the image of the U.S. as a Christian nation. . . .

RELIGIOUS FREEDOM AND THE SEPARATION OF CHURCH AND STATE

. . .

In the context of the early Republic, one reason for refraining from having a nationally established religion was pragmatic. If most citizens of the new United States identified with one of the numerous Christian bodies, primarily Protestant ones, no one denomination or sect could count a majority as adherents, much less as members. Already Baptists, Methodists, Presbyterians, Quakers, Lutherans of many ethnic varieties, Episcopalians, and a host of others had learned to live in relative peace and harmony. This diversity, which some later would celebrate as a kind of pluralism, meant that it would be unfair—undemocratic—to single out one group to receive governmental support. Another assumption undergirded this nod to diversity—namely, a conviction that regardless of label, all such groups inculcated the same values and morals that made their followers good citizens. . . .

[T]he danger in having government endorse a particular belief system, no matter how worthy it was, or in giving official status to any one religious group or tradition, no matter how pervasive its influence, was the potential tyranny such a belief or group could exert over others. If a religious community could call on the coercive power of the state to force conformity to its beliefs and practices, it lost its legitimacy. . . .

Even before ratification of the Bill of Rights, the state of Virginia had adopted a statute providing for near-total religious freedom. Inspired by Thomas Jefferson, the Virginia statute became something of a model for other states, since the Constitution restricted only the Congress from establishing a religion. . . . The phrase with which later generations are familiar, *separation of church and state*, is not strictly speaking part of the constitutional or legal heritage of the nation. Rather, it comes from a letter written in 1802 by Thomas Jefferson, while president, to a group of Connecticut Baptists in which he referred to a "wall of separation between church and state." . . .

This legal arrangement did mean that the United States became a nation where extraordinary religious experimentation and diversity prevailed just beneath the surface, even if a broadly evangelical Protestantism centered around a few denominations dominated public life. In the 1830s in upstate New York, for example, Joseph Smith reported having a vision that led to the founding of the Latter-Day Saints, better known as the Mormons. . . . The Saints represent what some historians regard as the first genuinely "new" religion to emerge in the American context. . . . In the 1830s as well, the Shakers, although planted on North American soil by their founder Ann Lee and a handful of adherents just before the American Revolution, also reached their peak. About 6,000 men and women were leading the simple, celibate life in hopes of salvation in nearly two dozen different communities, several of them in upstate New York and New England. . . .

By the end of the nineteenth century, many other groups had emerged, some reflecting the religious styles of the continuing streams of immigrants and others arising from ideas offered by dynamic speakers and writers. Among the better-known immigrant communities are the Amish and their religious cousins, the Mennonites, who sought to live their version of a simple life without involvement in a larger society that they saw as hopelessly corrupted by modernity. . . . These few examples demonstrate some of the diversity and pluralism beginning to color American religious life, a diversity and pluralism made possible in part because of the legal arrangements embedded in the First Amendment. Other factors aided this religious experimentation. The seemingly vast amount of land available in the expanding nation literally meant that there was room for various religious teachers and groups to go about their business without really interrupting or interfering with the lives of those around them. . . .

DIVERSITY, RELIGIOUS FREEDOM, AND THE COURTS

At the same time, some religious groups seemed to many Americans, primarily those identified with Protestant denominations, to push the limits of freedom too far. After all, they were minority groups on the margins of the larger religious culture. If their beliefs and practices were too far out of step with the majority, should they not be restrained or curtailed before they undermined the dominant religious style? In one sense, the basic issues were how much diversity free exercise allowed before it became dangerous and how much control government should wield to protect a presumed majority before it became tyrannical.

. . .

Laws protecting Sabbath observance go back to the colonial period. Among the earliest was a provision in Virginia, part of "Dale's Laws" issued in 1610, that not only required attendance at Christian worship but also prohibited "any gaming" in public or private on Sunday. As the Jewish population of the United States grew, those identified with Orthodox Judaism, with its emphasis on strict observance of the Sabbath from sundown Friday until sundown Saturday, found laws favoring Sunday as the Sabbath discriminatory. However, because the numbers of Jews were small and the Jewish population fairly scattered, there were few challenges to the status quo.

Sunday laws also affected Seventh-Day Adventists, who, as their name indicates, hold to the Hebrew practice of keeping the Sabbath, the seventh day or Saturday, as sacred. Most Christian groups, whether Protestant, Catholic, or Orthodox, that represented the majority of Americans believed that the Christian practice or keeping Sunday, the first day, as a sacred and holy day superseded seventh-day sabbath observance. Well into the twentieth century, many states and local communities legally restricted what kinds of work could be done on Sunday, whether and what goods and products could be sold, and access to certain recreational activities. Popularly known as "blue laws," such regulations aroused little concern when the overwhelming majority of citizens in a town or area accepted the Christian practice for themselves. . . .

The most familiar cases wrestled with whether practices sanctioned by law resulted in a *de facto* establishment of religion, particularly in areas affecting education in public schools. Some of the earliest concerned children who were Jehovah's Witnesses. On religious grounds, Witnesses refuse to salute the flag, insisting that reciting the Pledge of Allegiance places a blasphemous loyalty to the state before their allegiance to God. Most cases brought by Witnesses came decades before the recent controversy over whether the phrase *under God* that was inserted into the Pledge of Allegiance by Congress in 1954 represented unconstitutional support for religion. Until the rights of the Witnesses received legal protection, episodes in several communities resulted in children who were Witnesses being expelled from school and their parents being prosecuted. . . .

As noted above, when public education began to become the norm in the United States in the nineteenth century, a majority of students came from families with ties to mainline Protestant denominations, and curriculum materials often reflected the beliefs and practices of those groups. Christian holidays, such as Christmas and Holy Week before Easter, were times when classes were suspended; Jewish holy days did not as a rule receive such preferential treatment, although Jewish children were not penalized for absences on religious holidays. In some school districts school facilities were used, primarily by Protestant groups, for religious instruction, occasionally held during the regular class day. In 1948, in *McCollum v. Board of Education*, the Supreme Court ruled against using school facilities and class time for instruction in a particular faith tradition, even when participation was voluntary.

. . .

The greatest controversy, however, has revolved around Bible reading and prayer in the public schools and whether such activities represent a tacit establishment or favoring of a particular religious tradition. In local communities there have been other cases, most notably those that challenged prayers at athletic events, such as those included in pregame ceremonies at football games or commencement exercises. . . .

In the early twenty-first century, debates continued over what separation of church and state involved and how to assure the free exercise of religion. Some echoed earlier themes, such as a case involving whether Santeria was a religion and therefore its ritual of sacrificing chickens a protected religious practice. Others touched on dimensions of how religion and education might legally be linked, such as whether states or communities could provide vouchers that citizens could use to defray the cost of parochial or church-sponsored education. Yet others focused on whether creationism was a science and should be included in biology textbooks if theories of evolution were also presented.

In retrospect, it seems that early cases concerned how to protect the rights of religious minorities, but some had come to believe that later cases imposed minority rule on the majority. Regardless, the array of legal cases concerning religion suggested that a deep and abiding diversity marked American life, even if in an earlier epoch a broadly based evangelical Protestantism had exercised dominant influence.

. . .

THE NEW FACES OF PLURALISM

Changes in immigration laws in 1965 have resulted in a dramatic increase in immigrants from both Latin America and Asia, and with them has come a burgeoning interest in the religions indigenous to those areas and fresh awareness of the links between ethnicity and religious style. In the last decade of the twentieth century, the greatest proportional growth in immigration from Latin America, the Near East, and Asia came in the Sun Belt. . . .

In most urban areas across the nation, Roman Catholic parishes have added services in Spanish, recognizing that Hispanic Catholicism brings a rich blend of traditions to Catholic life, many reflecting the cultures of Central and South America. . . . Some Protestant denominations have launched special ministries to Spanish-speaking Americans, while many Pentecostal congregations, like their Roman Catholic counterparts, now provide services and programs designed to reflect the spirituality and concerns of Hispanic followers. Theologically, Hispanic Americans—both Protestant and Catholic—tend to be more traditional and conservative in their thinking, even as their practice reveals considerable syncretism in its expression. Even within the Christian tradition, it has become impossible to look at Anglo-American styles as normative.

Immigration from Asia swelled the ranks of Hindus, Buddhists, and Muslims in the United States. American interest in Asian religious cultures has a long history. In the nineteenth century, Transcendentalist writers such as Ralph Waldo Emerson were drawn to Asian religious philosophy, while thousands devoured reports of seemingly exotic religious practices in Asia through letters from missionaries published in scores of popular religious magazines. But, except for a relatively small number of immigrants from China and Japan on the West Coast, few Americans had first-hand experience with these religions; even fewer were inclined to practice them.

. . .

The 1960s also witnessed a spate of Asian religious figures who sought to gain American converts, particularly from among those who were disenchanted with traditional American religious life and who saw the dominant religious institutions as mired in racism and torn apart over government policy in Vietnam. . . . While some forms of Buddhism, such as that promoted by the Dalai Lama, and some popular forms of Hinduism, like Krishna Consciousness, have attracted primarily American devotees, the majority of American Buddhists, Hindus, and Muslims come from families who are doing what Americans have done for centuries—practicing the religion that the first generation of immigrants brought with them, albeit adapting it to the American context. What is changing the face of pluralism in the first decade of the twenty-first century is the steadily growing presence of immigrants for whom these traditions represent the heritages they bring with them when they come to the United States. . . .

Estimates suggest that the United States was home to only 30,000 Buddhists in 1900, but to two million a century later; to a mere 1,000 Hindus in 1900, but 950,000 at century's end; to just 10,000 Muslims in 1900, but perhaps—and the estimates vary widely here—between two and one-half to four million a century later, not counting those affiliated with the Nation of Islam (U.S. Census Bureau, 2000). The Hindu tradition has never been inclined to proselytize; in other cultural contexts, Buddhists and Muslims have been more active in seeking converts. However, in the U.S. context, there is relatively little

C
O
N
T
E
X
T

association among the various immigrant Buddhist communities and the centers that cater primarily to American converts to the various stands of Buddhism. American Muslims report that they are reticent to proselytize because popular perception links Muslims to international terrorism. Those Americans who have converted to Islam are more likely to be persons of African descent; they join a small but growing number of African immigrants who are also Muslim.

The growth of these groups signals the pluralism that marks American religious life and the impossibility of regarding a single tradition as normative or perhaps even culturally dominant in the twenty-first century.

. . .

45

Afraid of Ourselves

Diana Eck

. . .

After race, the most visible signal of difference is dress, and this is where religious minorities become visible minorities. Many Muslim women wear *hijab*, either a simple head scarf or a full outer garment. A few even wear a face covering called *nikab*. Muslim men may wear a beard, and Sikh men may wear not only a beard but also a turban wrapped around their uncut hair. Jewish men may wear a yarmulke, or skullcap. Buddhist monks may wear saffron, maroon, black, brown, or gray robes, depending upon their culture of origin. In all these cases looking different may sometimes trigger uneasiness and even fear—the fear that we do not know who "they" are or perhaps that we do not know who "we" are. As Americans, we are literally afraid of ourselves.

Our visible differences are on the rise, not just in the building of mosques and temples, but in the visible presence of people of many religious traditions. And this religious difference often has consequences. Just ask the young Sikh man I sat next to at the *langar* meal in the Fremont gurdwara in California. "You can't show up at a job interview wearing a turban and beard," he said. He was clean-shaven and had a short haircut, but this was the result of having spent five years in the U.S. and having experienced discrimination because of his looks. To some Americans, turbaned Sikhs look like what they imagine snake charmers or genies to be, he said. Others associate the turbaned look with militancy and even terrorism. He found he had no choice but to cut his hair. For observant Sikh women, the visibility of not cutting their hair can also be a burden, as a young woman named Kimpreet recalled when we interviewed her. Kimpreet had grown up in New Jersey, and hers was the only Sikh family in town. She told us, "I was the 'other.' I was the girl with the really, really super long hair who couldn't cut it because of her religion." The thread worn by young Zoroastrians after their *navjote* initiation also elicits this sense of the "other." A Zoroastrian friend confided, "It's very common when young people are in gym class and changing their clothes, someone will come up and say, 'What's that?' If they say, 'This is part of my Zoroastrian custom,' the next line usually is 'Zoro-what?' They want to know what kind of cult is that?"

. . .

Perhaps the most prominent icons of our new visible religious differences are the Muslim women wearing the head scarf. They are now visible almost everywhere, and every one of them has a story to tell. My friend Mary Lahaj is about my age, and our grandparents came to this country at about the same time, only hers came from Lebanon, whereas mine came from Sweden. Mary and I are both religious and both scholars as well. I am a Methodist and Mary a Muslim. But as third-generation Americans, our experience has been quite different in one respect. I have never experienced the discrimination that Mary has experienced just by being who she is, wearing a head scarf outside the home as part of her faith. Mary describes one incident when she experienced herself as the object of raw fear. She told us, "I was wearing my *hijab* in the toy store Child World, and I was buying some toy guns for my son and his two friends. As I turned the corner this young man about fourteen almost bumped into me. And when he saw me, he just got this awful expression on his face, like he was scared to death. You know, there was just this image of me with my head cover and these toy rifles in my arms, and he looked simply terrified." The guns, of course, fit right into the prejudicial image of Muslims that this fourteen-year-old had already encountered, and then there she was—my friend Mary, the terrorist.

About the time Mary and I met in 1994, an article in the *Minneapolis Star Tribune* told of a woman in full Islamic dress, including a partial face covering, being arrested in the Mall of America for wearing a disguise, which was banned by local ordinance. The police asked her to remove it, but she refused, arguing for the freedom of religious practice. Eventually a settlement was reached, but the issue of the *hijab* persists. A schoolgirl has her scarf pulled off by a classmate, for example, or a white American woman wearing a head scarf in Tukwila, Washington, near Seattle, is accosted and chased through a parking lot by a group of young people yelling, "You Muslim! Go home!" These are stories of harassment and incivility, and at the other end of the scale are stories of civil rights abuses and discrimination, especially in the workplace.

. . .

Couple a deep negativity toward religious difference with a deep ignorance of other religious traditions, and we have a recipe for prejudice. For example, in 1990 a small item in the *New York Times* caught my eye under the headline "Yoga and the Devil: Issue for Georgia Town." The dateline was Toccoa, Georgia, and apparently officials barred a town-sponsored yoga class "because the relaxation of yoga exercises would open practitioners to the influence of the devil. 'The people who are signed up for the class are just walking into it like cattle to a slaughter,' said a leader of a local group comprised of Baptists, Lutherans, and other Christians." Defenders of the class insisted that the class was only for stretching and relaxing not for promoting religion. Clearly what to many Americans has been a spiritual practice is perceived as threat in what must be a fairly homogeneous town. The small town of Winter, Wisconsin, was the scene of another such incident. A high school student found the computers of the school district blocked, preventing her from access to information on Wicca, and a member of the school board accused her of being a "devil worshiper" for seeking such information. The district had installed a computer filter system to restrict Internet access to subjects deemed controversial. The student complained, "I tried to look up Buddhism and it was blocked. Then, I tried to look up Wicca and it was blocked. Then, I looked up Christian churches and you could find anything you want." The case attracted nationwide attention, and eventually the school district changed the system before the case reached the courts. But at the civic level, it is yet another example of the potent mixture of fear and ignorance that sparks so many incidents of outright discrimination.

In New Jersey in the late 1980s, the dot, or *bindi*, on the forehead worn by many Hindu women stood for the strangeness of the whole Indian immigrant community in the eyes of a racist group calling themselves the Dot Busters. The attacks had nothing to do with

Hinduism as a religion but were directed at all South Asian immigrants. In 1987 in Jersey City, a climate of constant low-level harassment turned to violence. A thirty-year-old Indian immigrant, Navroze Mody, was beaten to death by a gang chanting "Hindu, Hindu!" They conflated race, religion, and culture in one naked cry of hatred.

At that time, the Indian immigrant community was about fifteen thousand strong in Jersey City, and it was part of a much larger Indian community in northern New Jersey. Before the attack in the summer of 1987, a local newspaper had called attention to the rising number of incidents of harassment against South Asians. In response, it received a venomous letter signed by the "Jersey City Dot Busters":

> I hate [Indian people], if you had to live near them you would also. We are an organization called dot busters. We have been around for 2 years. We will go to any extreme to get Indians to move out of Jersey City. If I'm walking down the street and I see a Hindu and the setting is right, I will hit him or her. We plan some of our most extreme attacks such as breaking windows, breaking car windows, and crashing family parties. We use the phone books and look up the name Patel. Have you seen how many of them there are? . . . You said that they will have to start protecting themselves because the police cannot always be there. They will never do anything. They are a week race physically and mentally. We are going to continue our way. We will never be stopped.

The letter was published a month before the death of Navroze Mody. Then, a few weeks later, a young resident in medicine, Dr. Sharan, was assaulted by three young men with baseball bats as he walked home late one night in Jersey City. He was beaten severely and left unconscious with a fractured skull. Sharan was in a coma for a week and suffered severe neurological damage. He recalled that one of the young people yelled, "There's a dothead! Let's get him!" as they set out after him with their bats.

These incidents were a severe blow to the Indian immigrant community and jarred the community into taking political action seriously. A group called Indian Youth Against Racism (IYAR) was formed with a base at Columbia University. The group helped in getting a bill passed in the New Jersey legislature in 1990 that raised the mandatory penalties for "bias crimes." It documented instances of violence against Indians in New Jersey, and it helped implement a series of educational programs on South Asian cultures for students and faculty at a Jersey City high school. But the attacks have not ceased. In 1991 there were fifty-eight cases of hate crimes against Indians in New Jersey. In 1992 an Indian physician was hit on the head and sprayed with Mace, and an Indian businessman was struck on the head with a bat. In 1998 an Indo-Caribbean man was beaten on the streets of Queens. The Asian American Legal Defense and Education Fund has started tracking incidents and organizing community awareness.

America's Muslims are also targeted solely on the basis of their religion. The image of the violent Muslim was called into play almost immediately when the Murrah Federal Building in Oklahoma City was bombed on April 19, 1995. Muslim families in Oklahoma and all over America felt a backlash of harassment because of the mistaken assumption, broadcast only for a few minutes, that the bombing was linked to "Middle Eastern-looking" men. Across the country, Islamic centers became the targets of drive-by shootings and telephoned bomb threats. Muslim students were assaulted on campus, a fake bomb was thrown at a Muslim day care facility, and individual Muslims reported a great increase in harassment by co-workers and in public. Muslim parents feared for their children's safety and in some cases kept them home from school. On May 19, 1995, the Council on American-Islamic Relations (CAIR), a newly formed Muslim watchdog organization, released a report detailing more than two hundred incidents of anti-Muslim threats, harassment, and property damage reported in the aftermath of the bombing.

What the media failed to report was that in Oklahoma City, Muslim firemen were involved in rescue efforts in the Murrah Building, Muslim doctors worked in the city's emergency rooms, and Muslim organizations donated money and time to the relief effort. Yet a nationally televised memorial service at which President Clinton and Rev. Billy Graham spoke included Catholic and Jewish words of consolation, but nothing from the Muslim community of Oklahoma. This was despite the fact that Muslims had specifically asked to participate because they had been so visibly affected as the focus of blame for the tragedy. Oklahoma City has become a turning point in Muslim consciousness of their vulnerability here in America. It is hard to lay to rest the stereotypes generated over years of negative imaging.

. . .

45 (CONTINUED)

Working it Out

Diana Eck

One of the places we most commonly encounter religious difference in America today is the workplace. What religious attire may one wear? A cross? Yarmulke? Head scarf? Turban? Where and when is it appropriate to pray? What facilities do employers need to provide, and what policies do they need to implement? Religious difference is a question not just for theological schools and religious institutions but increasingly for businesses and corporations, offices and factories. These are the places where "we the people" most frequently meet, and how we manage our encounters here might be far more important than how we cope with imaginary encounters in the realm of theologies and beliefs.

The most common workplace issues have traditionally concerned working on the Sabbath, which is Saturday for Jews and Seventh-Day Adventists. Consider the case of a computer operator at a hospital in Fort Smith, Arkansas. Although he is a Seventh-Day Adventist and asked not to work on Saturdays, he was placed on call on Saturdays. When he refused to make himself available on his Sabbath, the hospital fired him. Title VII of the Civil Rights Act of 1964 prohibits discrimination on the basis of race, color, religion, national origin, or sex. In interpreting the act in relation to the religious practices of work-ers, the employer must try to make "reasonable accommodation" of religious practice, at least as long as it does not impose an "undue hardship" on the employer. In this case, the court ruled that the hospital was in violation of the Civil Rights Act. But just what constitutes "reasonable accommodation" and "undue hardship" is the thorny issue as each case comes forward.

In the past ten years the Equal Employment Opportunity Commission (EEOC), which considers workplace complaints that may violate the Civil Rights Act, has reported a 31 percent rise in complaints of religious discrimination in the workplace. This is not surpris-ing given the number of new immigrants in the workforce and the range of questions their attire, their holidays, and their religious life bring to the workplace environment. We have already looked at the incivility and prejudice Muslim women wearing the *hijab* may encounter. But sometimes incivility slides up the scale toward discrimination. For example, in 1996 Rose Hamid, a twelve-year veteran flight attendant with U.S. Air, became increasingly serious about her faith in the wake of some health problems and made the decision to wear a head scarf. Her first day at work, she was ordered to take it off because it was not part of the uniform of a flight attendant, and when she refused she was put on unpaid leave. Rose filed a complaint with the Equal Employment Opportunity Commission. What is reasonable accommodation in Rose's case? Rose had modeled different ways in which the colors of her uniform would be duplicated in her scarf, and some would argue that reasonable accommodation would mean allowing some flexibility in the uniform as long as it was readily recognizable. But U.S. Air moved Rose to a job that did not require a uniform and hence put her out of public visibility. . . .

Hair and beards have also raised workplace issues. In 1987 a Sikh immigrant, Prabhjot Kohli, who had managed a pharmaceutical company in India before coming to the U.S., was turned down for a job at Domino's Pizza in Baltimore because of his religiously mandated beard. "Domino's wants clean-shaven people," he recalls being told, "and you've got a beard." In this case, wearing the baseball cap was not enough. For Domino's it was a business decision: people prefer to be served pizza by clean-shaven employees. The case went to the Maryland Human Relations Commission and was resolved only after a twelve-year lawsuit. In January 2000 the pizza chain dropped its no-beard policy. In California, Manjit Singh Bhatia, a machinist, was removed from his job at Chevron company because new safety requirements mandated the shaving of facial hair. His beard might prevent him from having an airtight seal when he wore a respirator. Chevron moved him to a different job that did not require a respirator and promised to reinstall him as a machinist if a respirator were developed that he could safely use. For the courts, this was "reasonable accommodation."

Some Muslim men, though not all, choose to keep a neatly trimmed beard, considering it part of their customary religious observance. A discrimination case went to court in New Jersey where members of the Newark police force sued for the right to wear a beard for religious reasons. In a 1999 ruling (*Fraternal Order of Police v. City of Newark*) the U.S. Court of Appeals upheld the right of Muslim members of the Newark police force to wear beards on the job. As we have seen from the Sikh experience however, workplace decisions on beards have varied. And so too with Muslim men. A bus driver for a New York transit company can now wear a beard, but an employee of one of the major airlines cannot.

Prayer in the workplace is another issue that has gained complexity with the new immigration. A Christian group might gather at 7:15 to pray together before work. A Buddhist meditation group might spend part of its lunch hour in sitting practice. In the spring of 1998 I received a CAIR bulletin with information on three similar cases of workplace prayer accommodation in manufacturing plants around Nashville. Whirlpool Corporation reportedly had refused to allow Muslim employees to offer obligatory prayers on the job. One Muslim employee quit, and the others continued to perform their obligatory midday prayer secretly during bathroom breaks. When CAIR intervened, contacted the managers, and began a dialogue, together they envisioned a solution: the Muslim employees could perhaps customize their coffee breaks so that they could fit an Islamic prayer schedule. Today, Muslim organizations, including CAIR, are taking the initiative in providing the kind of information that might head off the endless round of discrimination cases. They have published a booklet called *An Employer's Guide to Islamic Religious Practices*, detailing what employers might need to know about the obligations of Muslim workers.

Employers today are encountering workplace issues most of us have never even thought about. For example, where do Muslim cab drivers who work the airport routes pray during the long days in line at the airport? In Minneapolis, at last word, they stand outside in a lot, according to Salina Khan of *USA Today*. She wrote, on June 25, 1999,

Taxi driver Farhad Nezami rolls out his prayer rug, removes his shoes and raises his hands to begin the early afternoon prayer. Nezami's not worshipping in a mosque. He's standing in a lot near the Minneapolis-St. Paul International Airport that about 300 Muslim cab drivers turn into a makeshift prayer hall several times a day. They pray there in rain, snow and sleet because the Metropolitan Airports Commission has repeatedly denied their request for a room for four years.

The case is not clear-cut, and it probably falls more in the realm of civility than legality. But Denver handled a similar case differently. A hundred Muslim cab drivers there put the question to the Denver Airport authority and received a positive response. Jillian Lloyd of the *Christian Science Monitor* reported, "When the city of Denver moved a glass shelter to its international airport this winter, giving Muslim cabbies a warm place to pray to Allah, it did not merely show government goodwill toward a religious minority. The move highlighted the growing willingness of American employers to provide for their workers' religious needs."

At the federal level, the White House has addressed the complexity that our new religious texture has brought to the workplace. In 1997 it released *Guidelines on Religious Exercise and Religious Expression in the Federal Workplace*. They provide a pathway through some of the issues, generally following one principle: "Agencies shall not restrict personal religious expression by employees in the Federal workplace except where the employee's interest in expression is outweighed by the government's interest in the efficient provision of public services or where the expression intrudes upon the legitimate rights of other employees or creates the appearance, to a reasonable observer, of an official endorsement of religion." For example, employees can keep a Bible or Koran in their desk and read it during breaks. Employees can speak about religion with other employees, just as they may speak about sports or politics. Employees may display religious messages on items of clothing to the same extent as they are permitted to display other messages. A supervisor can post an announcement about an Easter musical service on a bulletin board or can invite co-workers to a daughter's bat mitzvah as long as there is no indication of expectation that the employee will attend. There is a veritable thicket of examples in this nine-page document. It is the first herald of a new day in the workplace.

. . .

46

Christian Privilege

Breaking a Sacred Taboo

Lewis Z. Schlosser

. . .

A BEGINNING LIST OF CHRISTIAN PRIVILEGES

1. I can be sure to hear music on the radio and watch specials on television that celebrate the holidays of my religion.
2. I can be sure that my holy day (Sunday) is taken into account when states pass laws (e.g., the sale of liquor) and when retail stores decide their hours (e.g., on Saturdays, they are open about 12 hours; on Sundays, they are closed or open for only a few hours).
3. I can assume that I will not have to work or go to school on my significant religious holidays.
4. I can be financially successful and not have people attribute that to the greed of my religious group.
5. I can be sure that when told about the history of civilization, I am shown people of my religion who made it what it is.
. . .
6. I can worry about religious privilege without being seen as self-interested or self-seeking.
7. I can be sure that when my children make holiday crafts, they will bring home artistic symbols of the Christian religion (e.g., Easter bunny, Christmas tree).
8. I am never asked to speak for all the people of my religious group.
9. I can, if I wish, arrange to be in the company of people of my religion most of the time.
10. I can do well in a challenging situation without being called a "credit to my religion" or being singled out as being different from other members of my religious group.
. . .
11. I can be sure that my children will be given curricular materials that testify to the existence and importance of the Christian religion.
. . .
12. I can have a "Jesus is Lord" bumper sticker or Icthus (Christian fish) on my car and not worry about someone vandalizing my car because of it.
13. I can buy foods (e.g., in grocery store, at restaurants) that fall within the scope of the rules of my religious group.
14. I can travel and be sure to find a comparable place of worship when away from my home community.
. . .

15.. I can be sure when I hear someone in the media talking about g-d that they are talking about my (the Christian) g-d.

. . .

16. I can be sure that people are knowledgeable about the holidays in my religion and will greet me with the appropriate holiday greeting (e.g., Merry Christmas).

17. I can remain oblivious to the language and customs of other religious groups without feeling any penalty for such a lack of interest and/or knowledge.

18. I can display a Christmas tree and/or hang holly leaves in my home without worrying about my home being vandalized because of my religious identification.

. . .

47

Christian Privilege and the Promotion of "Secular" and Not-So "Secular" Mainline Christianity in Public Schooling and in the Larger Society

Warren J. Blumenfeld

. . .

THE "FACES" OF [RELIGIOUS] OPPRESSION

Many overt forms of oppression are obvious when a dominant religious group tyrannizes a subordinated group, as in the mass slaughter of Jews and other stigmatized minorities in Nazi Germany, and the merciless killing of Jews and Muslims during the Christian "Crusades." Other forms of religious oppression are not as apparent, especially to members of dominant groups. Oppression in its fullest sense also refers to structural/systemic constraints imposed on groups even within constitutional democracies, and "[i]ts causes are embedded in unquestioned norms, habits, and symbols, in the assumptions underlying institutional rules and the collective consequences of following those rules." Young places these forms of oppression and privilege under five overarching categories or "faces" of powerlessness, exploitation, marginalization, cultural imperialism, and violence. The following sections adapt Young's taxonomy to investigate the concept of Christian privilege and religious oppression in the United States (Young 1990).

POWERLESSNESS

Subordinated groups have less access to social power than members of dominant groups to engage in the decision-making processes that affect the course of their lives or that name the terms of their existence. "[T]he powerless are situated so that they must take orders and rarely have the right to give them . . . and they rarely command respect" (Young 1990, 43).

Historical foundations of religious powerlessness in the colonial period. The spiritual beliefs and identity that were foundational to the Native peoples originally inhabiting the vast territories now known as the United States were violently confronted with the advent of Christian European expansionism to North America. The Pilgrims, for example, who left England for Massachusetts in 1620 believed that they were a divinely chosen people, and soon established "a biblical commonwealth" considered superior to "heathen," "infidel" Native peoples. Massachusetts Puritans crafted their own form of Christianity in which "the church and the state were to support and protect each other."

Over the decades after the Puritans first landed on the shores of North America, other Christian, primarily Protestant "settlers" from Europe included Presbyterians, Methodists, Lutherans, Dutch Reformed, Congregationalist Puritans, and Baptists. In their attempts to assure religious freedom for themselves, under the leadership of William Penn, Quakers founded the colony of Pennsylvania, and Roman Catholics founded Maryland in the 1640s. In the following decades, however, Protestants established political power in Maryland, and in 1704, Protestant legislators passed anti-Catholic legislation unequivocally titled "An Act to Prevent the Growth of Popery within This Province" banishing Jesuits from the territory.

The pattern of Protestant domination and powerless subordinated religious groups continued from the colonial period throughout U.S history. As recently as the middle-20th century, shortly after the U.S.'s entry into World War II, the government, in a mass relocation effort, interned over 112,000 Japanese Americans, many of them Buddhist, in concentration camps located far from their homes. Many of these incarcerated Japanese were U.S. citizens, born and living in this country for years. Officials used government policy to confiscate the homes, stores, and other property of the politically powerless Japanese Buddhists and to suspend their rights.

EXPLOITATION

Young views the "face" of exploitation as "a steady process of the transfer of the results of the labor of one social group to benefit another" . . . .

Religious justifications for exploitation. In colonial America, as private farms grew larger and farmers needed more cheap laborers to cultivate the land and tend the crops, many white landowners turned increasingly to the slave trade for their labor. Race and religion were intertwined as justifications for slavery in the Americas where "heathen" black Africans were stolen from their homelands and forced into slavery for the remainder of their lives. They were carried by slave ships, some of which were named the "Jesus," the "Grace of God," the "Angel," the "Liberty," and the "Justice," many with Christian ministers on board to help oversee the passage. In fact, Protestant churches offered scriptural justifications for slavery.

Conflicts between biblical justifications for slavery and biblical arguments for abolition split many Protestant congregations. The issue of slavery became a lightening rod in the 1840s among members of The Baptist General Convention, to organize a separate Southern Baptist Convention on a pro-slavery plank. One-hundred and fifty years later, the Southern Baptist Convention officially apologized to African Americans for its support and collusion with the institution of slavery, and also apologized for its rejection of civil rights initiatives of the 1950s and 1960s.

The expansion of the republic and movement west was in part justified by "Manifest Destiny": the belief that God intended the U.S. to extend its holdings and power across North America over native Indian tribes from east to west. The doctrine of "Manifest

Destiny" also assumed Anglo-Saxon superiority. "This continent," a congressman declared, "was intended by Providence as a vast theatre on which to work out the grand experiment of Republican government, under the auspices of the Anglo-Saxon race" (Takaki 1993, 176).

During the early years of the new republic, with its increasing population and desire for land, political leaders, such as George Washington and Thomas Jefferson, advocated that Indian lands be obtained through treaties and purchase. President Jefferson in 1803 wrote a letter to then Tennessee political leader, Andrew Jackson, advising him to convince Indians to sell their "useless" forests to the U.S. government and become farmers. Jefferson and other government leaders overlooked the fact that this style of individualized farming was contrary to Indian communitarian spiritual/cultural traditions.

MARGINALIZATION

Marginalization is the "face" of oppression whereby entire categories of people—in the following examples, non-Protestant Christians—are restricted from meaningful involvement in the social life of the community and nation, and thus subjected to acute economic deprivation and even annihilation. Young defines *marginals* as "people the system of labor cannot or will not use" (1990, 44).

Marginalization in the schools and society. The media constitute a major societal and institutional means of transmitting religious norms and beliefs, while maintaining the marginalization of the "other." Beaman describes the marginalization of new religious movements, "cults," Muslims, and indigenous Native peoples (2003, 315):

> New religious movements attract media attention for apocalyptic views and actions, and remain "cults" in public discourse. Muslims are the subject of biased media reports that seem to result in attacks on mosques and anti-Muslim sentiment. Aboriginals, for whom daily life and the physical world are inseparable from spirituality, are constructed as "problematic" because of their demands for equality and restitution.

Schools are another institutional means by which social norms are maintained and reproduced. Norms of Christian privilege and marginalization of members of other faith communities and non-believers in the schools are conveyed by curricular materials (curricular *hegemony*), which focus upon heroes, holidays, traditions, accomplishments, and importance of a European-heritage, Christian experience. Students who are Hindu, Muslim, Sikh, Jewish, and of other faiths, and non-believers, for example, see few, if any, people who look like them, who believe as they believe, or who adhere to the cultural expressions that they adhere to introduced and discussed in their classroom lessons.

In addition, the school calendar is organized to meet the needs of Christian faith communities, while marginalizing others. Examples include Jewish students who are compelled to request an excuse from school to attend religious services for their "High Holy Days" on and between Rosh Hashanah and Yom Kipper, which usually fall during the beginning of the academic year. In addition, Jehovah's Witnesses, who do not celebrate holidays—religious or otherwise—must also seek permission to be excused from the observance of holidays in school. (Jehovah's Witnesses, while a Christian denomination, are often marginalized within Christianity, and not accorded the same degree of Christian privilege as members of other so-called "mainstream" Christian faith communities.)

Muslim students, faculty, and staff often are not accorded the opportunity to have a safe prayer space on campus to perform the *salat* (prayer), as required by the Five Pillars of Islam. A case in point involved a 17-year-old high school junior in Ohio who was barred by school administrators from praying in an empty classroom at lunch and before and after class hours. Though a 1963 U.S. Supreme Court case ruled unconstitutional any *mandatory* prayers or Bible readings at public schools, subsequent rulings declared the constitutionality of many forms of personal religious expression on school campuses. In this case, the Council on American-Islamic Relations (CAIR) stepped in on the student's behalf, and convinced the school district to reverse its policy.

CULTURAL IMPERIALISM

Young states that "[c]ultural imperialism involves the universalization of a dominant group's experiences and culture, and its establishment as the norm" (1990, 45).

Christian cultural imperialism and privilege. The manifestations of Christian privilege as cultural imperialism are numerous. First, the federal and school calendars are scheduled around Christian holidays and celebrations. In fact, the Christian holiday of Christmas has been declared a *national* holiday in which most businesses and government offices are closed and services suspended.

Society marks time through a Christian lens. Even the language we use in reference to the mainstream calendar reflects Christian assumptions. Not long ago we heard and read of the coming of the "21ˢᵗ Century," and the dawning of "*The* new millennium." Let us not forget, however, that the year 2000 is calculated with reference to the birth of Jesus, and it is, therefore, the beginning of the next *Christian* millennium. In fact, the dictionary definition of "millennium" notes "the thousand years mentioned in Revelation 20 during which holiness is to prevail and Christ is to reign on earth." This fact is apparent when someone mentions the date followed by "in the year of our Lord, Jesus Christ." The century markers B.C. (before Christ) and A.D. (*anno Domini*) are clearly Christian in origin. Therefore, the year 2000 is *one* important milepost, though, for many religious traditions, it also marks a heightening of their invisibility. Even recent attempts to decenter Christian hegemony in the marking of time by replacing B.C. with B.C.E. (before the common era) and A.D. with C.E. (common era), do not in actuality affect the marking of time before and after a "common" (Christian) era.

The workweek is structured to allow Christians the opportunity to worship on Sundays without conflicting with their Monday to Friday work schedules. For most of our history, state and local "Blue Laws" restrict sales, business operations, recreational activities, and governmental services on Sunday, the Sabbath for most Christian denominations. "Blue Laws" date back to colonial times when Sunday church attendance was mandatory. In 1816, a Jewish man named Abraham Wolf was convicted in Pennsylvania of the "crime" of "having done and performed worldly employment on the Lord's day" (Sunday). He appealed his sentence but lost.

In the schools, children or their parents or caretakers of other faiths must take responsibility to request accommodations from school officials either to be excused from ongoing school activities or to be absent to practice their religious traditions. For example, a Muslim elementary school student in central Iowa requested permission to attend the school library or to remain in her classroom for the duration of her lunch period during the Muslim holy month of Ramadan in which it was her practice to fast from sunrise to sunset. The school, however, had a *written* policy mandating that students must be present in the cafeteria during their lunch breaks. After repeated discussions with the school principal, the mother of the student convinced him to allow her daughter to go to an alternate space during the month of Ramadan while the student's classmates were at lunch.

Other examples of Christian cultural imperialism are numerous: the promotion of music, especially Christmas, by radio stations, and Christmas specials played on TV throughout November and December each year; Christmas decorations (often hung at taxpayer expense) in the public square throughout the United States; and the widespread availability of Christian holiday decorations, greeting cards, food, and other items during Christian (and Easter) holiday seasons.

Further examples of Christian cultural imperialism include the phrase "under God" in the Pledge of Allegiance or "In God We Trust" on U.S. currency and *Annuit Coeptis* (He [God] (or Providence) has favored our undertakings) on the Great Seal of the United States and printed on the back of the one-dollar bill, or the teaching of "Intelligent Design." The phrase "under God" was added to the school Pledge of Allegiance in 1954 during the Cold War in reaction to what many saw as a godless Soviet Union attempting to impose its economic and political system throughout the world. The phrase "In God We Trust" was added to U.S. coins during the American Civil War by Abraham Lincoln, and to paper currency in the 1950s during the Cold War.

Deculturalization and schooling of native peoples. In an attempt to add further dimensions and elaborations of Young's concept of cultural imperialism, I employ Spring's discussions of "cultural genocide" defined as "the attempt to destroy other cultures" through forced acquiescence and assimilation to majority rule and Christian cultural and religious standards. This cultural genocide works through the process of "deculturalization," which Spring describes as "the educational process of destroying a people's culture and replacing it with a new culture" (2004, 3).

An example of "cultural genocide" and "deculturalization" can be seen in the case of Christian European American domination over Native American Indians, whom European Americans viewed as "uncivilized," "godless heathens," "barbarians," and "devil worshipers."

White Christian European Americans deculturalized indigenous peoples through many means: confiscation of land, forced relocation, undermining of their languages, cultures, and identities, forced conversion to Christianity, and forced removal of Native children to Christian day schools and off-reservation boarding schools far away from their people.

The first of many off-reservation Indian boarding schools was established in Carlisle, Pennsylvania in 1879 and run primarily by white Christian teachers, administered by Richard Pratt, a former cavalry commander in the Indian Territories. At the school, Indian children were stripped of their culture: the males' hair was cut short, they were forced to wear Western-style clothing, they were prohibited from conversing in their native languages and English was compulsory, all their cultural and spiritual symbols were destroyed, and Christianity was imposed.

"Civilizing" Indians became a euphemism for Christian conversion. Christian missionaries throughout the United States worked vigorously to convert Indians. A mid-19th century missionary wrote: "As tribes and nationals the Indians must perish and live only as men, [and should] fall in with Christian civilization that is destined to cover the earth."

VIOLENCE

A number of groups live with the constant fear of random and unprovoked systematic violence directed against them simply on account of their social identities. The intent of this xenophobic (fear and hatred of anyone or anything seeming "foreign") violence is to harm, humiliate, and destroy the "other."

During colonial times, religious dissension was violently repressed. For example, the Pilgrims "warned out of town" a Sephardic Jewish merchant, and banished Quaker missionaries. Later, as Quakers kept coming, the Puritans enacted harsher penalties, for example, cutting off their ears, or using hot irons to bore holes through their tongues. Then between 1659 to 1661, Puritans executed four Quakers on the gallows on Boston Common.

Recent examples of religious violence. Violence against Muslims, Sikhs, Hindus, and Jews has escalated in the United States since September 11, 2001. The Council on American Islamic Relations (CAIR), an American Muslim civil and human rights organization, in their 2005 annual report listed a total of 1,522 civil rights violations against American Muslims, 114 of which were violent hate crimes. This was a 49% increase in total incidents from just one year before. The report included incidents of violence, as well as harassment and discriminatory treatment, including "unreasonable arrests, detentions, searches/seizures, and detentions." The CAIR report included an incident in which a Muslim woman wearing a *hijab* (the garment many Muslim women wear in public) was taking her baby for a walk in a stroller, and a man driving a truck nearly ran them over. The woman cried out that, "You almost killed my baby!," and the man responded, "It wouldn't have been a big loss."

Nearly one-quarter of all reported civil rights violations against American Muslims involve unwarranted arrests and searches. Law enforcement agencies routinely "profile" Muslims of apparent Middle Eastern heritage in airports or simply while driving in their cars for interrogation and invasive and aggressive searches. In addition, governmental agencies, such as the IRS and FBI, continue to enter individuals' homes and mosques and make unreasonable arrests and detentions. Anti-Muslim hate crimes also occur on college and university campuses across the United States.

Sikhs have been the targets of increasing numbers of hate crimes as well. Since 2002, the Sikh Coalition organization listed 62 hate crimes directed against Sikh citizens of the United States. Many of the attacks committed against Sikhs are classified under the category of "personal attacks" or assaults as well as vandalism and arson. One incident involved a Sikh student at the University of North Carolina who was assaulted by three local teenagers. National attention focused on the severe beating of Rajinder Singh Shalsa in New York City, and the fatal shooting of Sikh gas station owner Balbir Singh Sodhi in Mesa, Arizona. It is widely assumed that Sikhs are targeted because they wear turbans, which the public imagination equates with terrorism.

Hindus have likewise been targeted. In June 2003, for example, Saurabh Bhalerao, a 24-year-old Indian graduate student studying in Massachusetts, was robbed, burned with cigarettes, beaten, stuffed in a truck, and twice stabbed before his assailants dumped him along the road. The attackers allegedly misidentified this Hindu student for a Muslim because during the assault, the perpetrators yelled at him, "Go back to Iraq."

Each year the Anti-Defamation League, a Jewish social advocacy organization, documents incidents of anti-Jewish hate crimes. They reported over 1500 such incidents in 2004 alone, including verbal and physical assault, harassment, vandalism, property damage, and other acts of hate. These included the burning of a Holocaust museum in Indiana, and the spray-painting of swastikas and epithets on the walls and driveway of a Jewish community center near Phoenix, Arizona. This latter incident occurred on my campus, Iowa State University, in 2005. Among the swastikas, the vandals also spray-painted anti-Muslim, racist, misogynist, and homophobic epithets.

"MULTI-FACETED" PRIVILEGE AND OPPRESSION: IMMIGRATION BATTLES

The history of the 19th-century anti-immigration battles illustrates the intersections and interactions among Young's five faces of powerlessness, exploitation, marginalization, cultural imperialism, and violence, by which non-Christian religious status interacted with subordinated racial(ized) status. Throughout the 19th and into the 20th centuries, nativist exclusionist movements gained momentum within the United States. "Nativist" refers to an anti-immigrant ideology by US-born, European-heritage Protestants, directed especially against non-Protestants such as Italian or Irish Catholics, Eastern European Jews, Asian Hindus, Muslims, Sikhs, and Buddhists. In some cases, non-white, non-Protestant ethnic and religious groups were *socially constructed* as lower "racial" forms by the mainline

Protestant power structure as a justification for exclusion, exploitation, marginalization, cultural imperialism, and violence. Subsequently, religion was itself "racialized."

Strong "nativist" currents against Asian Muslim, Sikh, and Buddhist immigrants led the United States Congress to bar Chinese immigrants in 1882, and also made it illegal for Chinese to marry white or black Americans. The exclusionist sentiment regarding the Chinese held by many U.S. citizens was summarized by the editor of the newspaper in Butte, Montana: "The Chinaman's life is not our life, *his religion is not our religion.* . . . He belongs not in Butte." The Immigration Act of 1917 further prohibited immigration from Asian countries from the "barred zone," including parts of China, India, Siam, Burma, Asiatic Russian, Polynesian Islands, and parts of Afghanistan.

This "nativist" anti-immigration fever culminated in 1924 with the National Origins Act, which set restrictive quotas of immigrants from *Eastern* and *Southern* Europe, that is, mainly on Catholics and Jews (the latter referred to as members of the so-called "Hebrew race"). The law, however, permitted large allocations of immigrants from Great Britain and Germany in order to "protect our values . . . [as] a Western Christian civilization." Jews were considered racial as well as religious undesirables by the 19th century scientific community as a lower "racial" type, with essential immutable biological characteristics— a trend that increased markedly into the early 20th century CE. Once seen as largely a religious, ethnic, or political group, Jews were viewed by "nativists," who valued American racial and religious "purity," as a "mixed race" (a so-called "mongrel" or "bastard race"), a people who had crossed racial barriers by interbreeding with black Africans during the Jewish Diaspora.

These restrictions on immigration based on "national origins" were not lifted until The Immigration and Nationality Act of 1965. This legislation resulted in dramatic increases in immigration from both Asian and Latin American countries of many religious backgrounds including Islamic, Hindu, Buddhist, Jain, Sikh, Zoroastrian, varying forms of Catholicism, and African, and Afro-Caribbean religious traditions. The 1965 law allowed for 170,000 immigrants from the Eastern Hemisphere and 120,000 from the Western Hemisphere with 20,000 immigrants per Eastern Hemisphere country. Partly as a result of the removal of restrictions on immigration that were specifically race-based and implicitly religion-based reflecting between 1882 until the 1960s—an effort to create an U.S.-American culture that was Protestant as well as northern European—the United States today stands as the most religiously diverse country in the world. This diversity poses great challenges as well as opportunities. To quote Eck: "[T]he presumption that America is foundationally Christian is being challenged, really for the first time. There is no going back. As we say in Montana, the horses are already out of the barn" (2001, 46).

48

Religious Oppression of Indian Americans in the Contemporary United States

Khyati Y. Joshi

In the United States, we have a Constitutionally guaranteed "freedom of religion," the right to choose and practice the faith we hold dear; the Constitution prohibits the state from sponsoring a religion and from restricting people's exercise of their religious beliefs. But having free choice is not the same as to have one's choice accepted and supported by the institutions and culture of one's country, rather than ignored, marginalized, exoticized or demonized. In this section, I discuss the concepts of religious oppression and Christian privilege and then apply them to the contemporary experiences of Indian American Hindus, Muslims and Sikhs. The dynamics of religious oppression and Christian privilege are complicated by the fact that these populations are religious minorities as well as members of visible racial and ethnic minority groups. While followers of these faiths have been present in the U.S. since the early 1800s, it was not until the passage of the Immigration Act of 1965 that the United States saw the arrival of substantial numbers of immigrant families—families that established homes, built ethnoreligious communities, and sent their children into the U.S. school system in substantial numbers.

RELIGIOUS OPPRESSION

Religious discrimination is not a post 9/11 phenomenon. Indeed, it is not even a 21st century phenomenon, nor has it been limited to non-Christian faiths. The United States has a history of religious intolerance from its beginnings. Native Americans, Catholics, Quakers, Mennonites, and Eastern Orthodox Christians faced religious persecution in 17th, 18th and 19th century America. Here, I use the term *religious oppression* to refer to the historic and systemic pattern of domination and subordination of religious minorities at cultural, institutional, and interpersonal levels—and focus my attention here on the experiences of Hindus, Muslims, and Sikhs within the dominant U.S. Christian milieu. This subordination is a product of the unequal power relationships among religious groups within American society and is supported by the actions of individuals, and by institutional structures (*religious discrimination*), as well as by cultural norms (*religious prejudice*) and societal practices. Through religious oppression, Christianity is used to marginalize, exclude, and deny the members and institutions of non-Christian religious groups in society the privileges and access that accompany a Christian affiliation. Using the term *religious oppression* to refer to a social system operating at these three levels—individual, institutional, and cultural/societal—recognizes that the disadvantages of non-Christianity exist not merely at the one on one level but also at a societal and institutional level where individuals are socialized, punished, rewarded and guided in ways that maintain and perpetuate oppressive structures.

In the context of America's racial schema, religious oppression sets up a dichotomy between the privilege and normativity associated with Whiteness and Christianity, and the othering of dark skin and non-Christian-ness. For Indian American Hindus, Muslims and

Sikhs, who are not white and not Christian, religious discrimination may be exacerbated by racial discrimination. This privileging and othering takes place at the overarching level of society and culture, where norms are perpetuated implicitly and explicitly. By comparison with these hegemonic (or assumed and every-day) norms, these non-Christian "other" religions come to be seen as evil, wrongful, deviant and/or sick. In the act of defining Hinduism, Islam and Sikhism as exotic and illegitimate, and thereby excluding them from society, American white Christians are able to represent themselves as good, normal, and righteous. Moreover, because systemic racialization of religion reinforces this pattern of religious exclusion and inferiority, that same discourse serves to reinforce the inclusion and superiority of white Christianity.

Societal norms are reproduced through written laws and policies as well as inscribed in the daily behaviors of the populace. Christian holidays—"holy days"—are endorsed institutionally through a calendar that serves the convenience and priorities of Christians, as in a Monday–Friday workweek and Sunday worship, or official days off for Christmas. Government sanction reinforces the dominant status of Christianity and the implied illegitimacy of other faiths. The mindset of rightness and privilege is manifested in the treatment of religious minorities by members of the majority—whether that treatment is meant to harm and threaten members of the target religion (as does the assumption that Muslims or Sikhs are terrorists), or "save" them (by Christian proselytizing). These attitudes and behaviors, whether conscious or not, maintain systemic religious oppression.

Let me be clear. I am not saying Christianity, as a faith or a belief system, is to be held accountable for religious oppression, or that all Christians consciously or purposely harbor prejudice toward non-Christians or approve of institutional religious discrimination. But I am saying that Christianity and Christian identity in the U.S. functions as a tool of oppression in the largely unconscious privileging of Christians through a hegemonic culture and social system. The issue at hand here is not one of intention, but one of consequences, of noticing the effects on religious minorities of the many instances of marginalization and disadvantage, despite our pluralistic society.

In the case of Hindus, Muslims, and Sikhs, the phenomenon of religious oppression in the U.S. exists and is perpetuated by and through a specific combination of facts and acts, each building upon its precedent. These include: (1) in the sociocultural and historical context of the United States, Christians have the power to define normalcy; (2) because Christianity has been normalized, the belief systems of Hinduism, Islam, and Sikhism are misrepresented and/or discounted; (3) the normalization of Christianity within social institutions leads to harassment, discrimination, and other forms of unequal treatment towards non-Christians; (4) religious oppression justifies violence or the threat of violence.

1. CHRISTIAN GROUPS HAVE THE POWER TO DEFINE NORMALCY

To be nominally Christian requires no conscious thought or effort on the part of Christian Americans. "Business as usual" follows their schedule and reflects their theological understandings. Social norms and rituals, language, and institutional rules and rewards all presume the existence of a Christian sociopolitical history and sociocultural norms of dress, behavior, and worship. America's vocabulary of faith, practice, prayer, belief, sites of worship and religious history largely ignore the existence of other religions, some of which are older than Christianity (for example, Buddhism, Hinduism, Judaism, and Native American spiritual practices).

We can observe Christianity's normative nature at three levels of society: institutional, societal/cultural, and individual. At the institutional and societal levels, there are examples in federal and state law and policy. Clearly, the First Amendment requires that the state allow and accommodate individual religious practices, and forbids the government to show hostility toward any particular religion. While acknowledging that this is nominally true, we must look at which religion is accommodated and which religions are not. The United States Senate and House of Representatives each employ Chaplains whose salaries are paid for by all U.S. taxpayers; both are Christian. An image of Moses with the Ten Commandments, along with other "law-givers," is etched in stone on the wall of the Supreme Court of the United States of America. The vacation schedules of most public schools are structured around Christian holidays, particularly Christmas and Easter. "Spring Break," for example, often coincides with the week between Palm Sunday and Easter. Policies like these permit Christian children to accompany their parents to worship and participate in the festivities leading up to each holiday without missing school or having to make up work.

Christian hegemony at the cultural and societal level is maintained in American society via the exercise of Christian privilege. In the United States, Christian privilege, like white privilege, exists through the cultural power norms that are largely invisible and thus unquestioned. Some examples of the norms underlying Christian privilege are:

- WORSHIP. The idea that it is something that occurs in a church, led by a member of the clergy. Here, the church represents both a place outside the home to go and pray, and the idea that prayer, properly performed, is done in groups and led by a person imbued by an institution with special theological authority.
- IMAGES of God, derived from western (i.e., Christian) art and literature. This god is anthropomorphized in a particular manner: singular, male, white, often elderly, and usually bearded, with two arms and two legs.
- ARCHITECTURE. The norms for houses of worship in which, for example, a steeple is "normal" but a minaret is something foreign.
- PRAYER. The Western image involves an act of worship performed in a seated or kneeling position, in silence, and with crossed hands.
- SACRED STORIES. In American society, Biblical stories, however fantastical, are treated as credible. . . . Stories based in the Christian tradition, such as the Virgin birth, are believed to be credible and true, whereas stories based in the Muslim tradition, such as Mohammed's midnight flight to heaven, or the Hindu tradition, such as Vishnu's periodic visitation upon earth in different incarnations, are not believed and considered to be incredible and fantastical.
- HOLIDAYS. State and federal holidays, including the position of the "weekend" on Saturday and Sunday, are structured around the Christian calendar.
- SAFETY. Most Christians are able to pray publicly and visibly in safety, without fear of violence or mockery. Also, Christian congregations can build their houses of worship without opposition from neighbors and local authorities.

Christian privilege benefits not only people who identify with Christianity or consider themselves "religious," but also those born Christian who are no longer observant. Christian privilege involves a legacy of public acceptance from which Christians benefit whether they want to or not, and whether they know it or not. It is an unearned perquisite of their identity as Christians. They can live their lives unaware of the daily exclusions, insults, and assaults endured by Hindus, Muslims, and Sikhs.

Contrariwise, non-Christians find themselves forced to explain their religions not in their own terms but by reference to a Christian vocabulary: "What is your church like? What is your Bible? When is your Christmas?" The conveniences of life as a Christian are lost to the Hindu who must leave work to observe a Hindu New Year, the Sikh who must cut his hair in order to join the military, or the Muslim student who must participate in gym class while fasting for Ramadan.

2. THE BELIEF SYSTEMS OF HINDUISM, ISLAM, AND SIKHISM, ALONG WITH THEIR RESPECTIVE HISTORIES AND CULTURES ARE DELEGITIMIZED, MISREPRESENTED AND/OR DISCOUNTED

By exacerbating the "otherness" of Indian American Hindus, Muslims, and Sikhs, the racialization of religion contributes to the delegitimization of these three faiths in a number of ways. First, in everyday interactions the Christian norm is applied, and Hinduism, Islam and Sikhism are compared to this norm. Second, differences, real or imagined, from the Christian norm are highlighted, such as the Christian posture of "prayer" (kneeling, with the fingers of both hands interlaced) compared to Muslim bowing eastward or to Hindu *aarti* (fire offering). In terms of belief, the power of the norm is found at the line between what the western mind views as "credible" and what it considers "incredible." Consider these three stories: A Jewish virgin gives birth to the child of God, after an angel visits her at night and tells her what to name the child. A prophet rides a flying horse to Heaven, accompanied by an angel. God comes to earth in the form of a dwarf and saves the world from a demon king. The first of these stories is the Biblical story of the Annunciation and the birth of Jesus to the Virgin Mary. What makes it more credible or "believable" an idea than Mohammed's midnight flight from Jerusalem, or Vishnu's periodic visitation of the Earth in different incarnations? Yet in the United States, it is. Biblical stories, however fantastical, are treated as fact, or at least as "faith." The beliefs of other religions are viewed as silly (at best) or heretical (at worst); they are branded with the more dismissive terminology of "myth" or "superstition."

Christian norms are reinforced by the Christian majority who assume these norms, and also assume without question the illegitimacy of other different faith traditions by comparison. The perception of illegitimacy grows out of ignorance, contempt, and mischaracterization of Hinduism, Islam, and Sikhism by the mass media as well as social and political institutions and individuals. Its negative effect is felt most dramatically by children and adolescents from marginalized faith traditions, whose home belief systems are invalidated and even actively contested by educators, other adults, and peers, and whose invisibility is manifested in the absence of news coverage or the congratulatory public service announcements aired around Christmas, Easter, and other "recognized" holidays. Disrespect is shown by the co-opt of holy images and prayers to sell candles, perfume, and other commercial goods.

3. HARASSMENT, DISCRIMINATION, AND OTHER FORMS OF DIFFERENTIAL TREATMENT ARE INSTITUTIONAL AND UNCHALLENGED

Another dimension of Christian privilege appears in the non-acceptance, disrespect, and invisibility of minority religious traditions, despite the Constitutional guarantee of the free exercise of religion. Christian privilege in this case involves both legal "freedom" (which is shared, at least in theory, by members of other religions) and social sanction, which is not available to marginalized faith traditions. As Christians are made to be confident, comfortable, and oblivious to their privilege because of the omnipresence of Christianity in the American culture and social system, other religious groups are made unsure, uncomfortable and alienated. Being Christian protects one from many kinds of hostility, distress, and violence, which—even when subtle—are part of daily experience for people of Hindu, Sikh, Muslim, and other non-western religious backgrounds. While society's endorsement may be tacit, and even invisible to the Christian eye, it's absence is conspicuous and visible to these religious minorities.

4. VIOLENCE AND THE THREAT OF VIOLENCE

Many South Asian and Arab Americans and other "double minorities"—non-White and non-Christian—experience verbal attacks and physical threats and attacks from people who are both White and Christian. Students in the k-12 school setting are threatened because of their religious identity (often signified by turban or hijab) and racialized phenotype. While hate crimes and threats of violence against these populations did in fact increase during the weeks and months after September 11, 2001, they were not confined to this "9/11 backlash" and in fact have occurred both before and since that time.

Indian American Hindus, Muslims and Sikhs are part of immigrant communities, and for these communities, although experiencing racism, the experience of religion is paramount. The communities are built on the edifice of religion, and while they also encounter racism, the experience of religious oppression is critical and must not be ignored. The impact of racial oppression takes on *religious* dimensions, arising from the belief in religion as something especially profound and "never changing." Religious oppression results in Indian American Sikhs, Muslims and Hindus identifying more closely with their home religion, magnifying religion's role in one's life and increasing the likelihood the individual will identify as "religious" and engage in worship, ritual, and religious study in adulthood.

49

Precedents

The Destruction of the European Jews

Raul Hilberg

. . .

Anti-Jewish policies and actions did not have their beginning in 1933. For many centuries, and in many countries, the Jews had been victims of destructive action. . . . The first anti-Jewish policy started in the fourth century after Christ in Rome. Early in the fourth century, during the reign of Constantine, the Christian Church gained power in Rome, and Christianity became the state religion. From this period, the state carried out Church policy. For the next twelve centuries, the Catholic Church prescribed the measures that were to be taken with respect to the Jews. Unlike the pre-Christian Romans, who claimed no monopoly on religion and faith, the Christian Church insisted on acceptance of Christian doctrine.

For an understanding of Christian policy toward Jewry, it is essential to realize that the Church pursued conversion not so much for the sake of aggrandizing its power (the Jews have always been few in number), but because of the conviction that it was the duty of true believers to save unbelievers from the doom of eternal hellfire. Zealousness in the pursuit of conversion was an indication of the depth of faith. The Christian religion was not one of many religions, but the true religion, the only one. Those who were not in its fold were either ignorant or in error. The Jews could not accept Christianity.

In the very early stages of the Christian faith, many Jews regarded Christians as members of a Jewish sect. The first Christians, after all, still observed the Jewish law. They had merely added a few nonessential practices, such as baptism, to their religious life. But their view was changed abruptly when Christ was elevated to Godhood. The Jews have only one God. This God is indivisible. He is a jealous God and admits of no other gods. He is not Christ, and Christ is not He. Christianity and Judaism have since been irreconcilable. An acceptance of Christianity has since signified an abandonment of Judaism.

In antiquity and in the Middle Ages, Jews did not abandon Judaism lightly. With patience and persistence the Church attempted *to convert* obstinate Jewry, and for twelve hundred years the theological argument was fought without interruption. The Jews were not convinced. Gradually the Church began to back its words with force. . . . Step by step, but with ever widening effect, the Church adopted "defensive" measures against its passive victims. Christians were "protected" from the "harmful" consequences of intercourse with Jews by rigid laws against intermarriage, by prohibitions of discussions about religious issues, by laws against domicile in common abodes. The Church "protected" its Christians from the "harmful" Jewish teachings by burning the Talmud and by barring Jews from public office.

. . .

Expulsion is the second anti-Jewish policy in history. In its origin, this policy presented itself only as an alternative—moreover, as an alternative that was left to the Jews. But long after the separation of church and state, long after the state had ceased to carry out church policy, expulsion and exclusion remained the goal of anti-Jewish activity.

. . .

The expulsion and exclusion policy was adopted by the Nazis and remained the goal of all anti-Jewish activity until 1941. That year marks a turning point in anti-Jewish history. In 1941 the Nazis found themselves in the midst of a total war. Several million Jews were incarcerated in ghettos. Emigration was impossible. A last-minute project to ship the Jews to the African island of Madagascar had fallen through. The "Jewish problem" had to be "solved" in some other way. At this crucial time, the idea of a "territorial solution" emerged in Nazi minds. The "territorial solution," or "the final solution of the Jewish question in Europe," as it became known, envisaged the *death* of European Jewry. The European Jews were to be killed. This was the third anti-Jewish policy in history.

To summarize. Since the fourth century after Christ there have been three anti-Jewish policies: *conversion, expulsion,* and *annihilation.* The second appeared as an alternative to the first, and the third emerged as an alternative to the second.

The destruction of the European Jews between 1933 and 1945 appears to us now as an unprecedented event in history. Indeed, in its dimensions and total configuration, nothing like it had ever happened before. As a result of an organized undertaking, five million people were killed in the short space of a few years. The operation was over before anyone could grasp its enormity, let alone its implications for the future.

Yet, if we analyze this singularly massive upheaval, we discover that most of what happened in those twelve years had already happened before. The Nazi destruction process did not come out of a void; it was the culmination of a cyclical trend. One may observe

Table 49.1 Canonical and Nazi Anti-Jewish Measures

Canonical Law	Nazi Measure
Prohibition of intermarriage and of sexual intercourse between Christians and Jews, Synod of Elvira, 306	Law for the Protection of German Blood and Honor, September 15, 1935
Jews and Christians not permitted to eat together, Synod of Elvira, 306	Jews barred from dining cars (Transport Minister to Interior Minister, December 30, 1939)
Jews not allowed to hold public office, Synod of Clermont, 535 . . .	Law for the Re-establishment of the Professional Civil Service, April 7, 1933 . . .
Jews not permitted to show themselves in the streets during Passion Week, 3d Synod of Orléans, 538	Decree authorizing local authorities to bar Jews from the streets on certain days (i.e., Nazi holidays), December 3, 1938
Burning of the Talmud and other books, 12th Synod of Toledo, 681 . . .	Book burnings in Nazi Germany . . .
Jews obliged to pay taxes for support of the Church to the same extent as Christians, Synod of Gerona, 1078 . . .	The "Sozialausgleichsabgabe" which provided that Jews pay a special income tax in lieu of donations for Party purposes imposed on Nazis, December 24, 1940
Jews not permitted to be plaintiffs, or witnesses against Christians in the Courts, 3d Lateran Council, 1179, Canon 26 . . .	Proposal by the Party Chancellery that Jews not be permitted to institute civil suits, September 9, 1942 (Bormann to Justice Ministry, September 9, 1942) . . .
The marking of Jewish clothes with a badge, 4th Lateran Council, 1215, Canon 68 (Copied from the legislation by Caliph Omar II [634–644], who had decreed that Christians wear blue belts and Jews, yellow belts)	Decree of September 1, 1941 (Jews must [wear the] yellow star of David)
Construction of new synagogues prohibited, Council of Oxford, 1222	Destruction of synagogues in entire Reich, November 10, 1938 (Heydrich to Göring, November 11, 1938)
Christians not permitted to attend Jewish ceremonies, Synod of Vienna, 1267 . . .	Friendly relations with Jews prohibited, October 24, 1941 (Gestapo directive)
Compulsory ghettos, Synod of Breslau, 1267	[Compulsory ghettos] by order by Heydrich, September 21, 1939
Christians not permitted to sell or rent real estate to Jews, Synod of Ofen, 1279 . . .	Decree providing for compulsory sale of Jewish real estate, December 3, 1938 . . .
Jews not permitted to act as agents in the conclusion of contracts, especially marriage contracts, between Christians, Council of Basel, 1434, Sessio XIX	Decree of July 6, 1938, providing for liquidation of Jewish real estate agencies, brokerage agencies, and marriage agencies catering to non-Jews
Jews not permitted to obtain academic degrees, Council of Basel, 1434, Sessio XIX	Law against Overcrowding of German Schools and Universities, April 25, 1933

. . .

the trend in the three successive goals of anti-Jewish administrators. The missionaries of Christianity had said in effect: *You have no right to live among us as Jews.* The secular rulers who followed had proclaimed: *You have no right to live among us.* The German Nazis at last decreed: *You have no right to live.*

These progressively more drastic goals brought in their wake a slow and steady growth of anti-Jewish action and anti-Jewish thinking. The process began with the attempt to drive the Jews into Christianity. The development was continued in order to force the victims into exile. It was finished when the Jews were driven to their deaths. The German Nazis, then, did not discard the past; they built upon it. . . .

The significance of the historical precedents will most easily be understood in the administrative sphere. The destruction of the Jews was an administrative process, and the annihilation of Jewry required the implementation of systematic administrative measures in successive steps. There are not many ways in which a modern society can, in short order, kill a large number of people living in its midst. This is an efficiency problem of the greatest dimensions, one which poses uncounted difficulties and innumerable obstacles. Yet, in reviewing the documentary record of the destruction of the Jews, one is almost immediately impressed with the fact that the German administration knew what it was doing. With an unfailing sense of direction and with an uncanny path-finding ability, the German bureaucracy found the shortest road to the final goal. . . . Necessity is said to be the mother of invention, but if precedents have already been formed, if a guide has already been constructed, invention is no longer a necessity. The German bureaucracy could draw upon such precedents and follow such a guide, for the German bureaucrats could dip into a vast reservoir of administrative experience, a reservoir that church and state had filled in fifteen hundred years of destructive activity.

In the course of its attempt to convert the Jews, the Catholic Church had taken many measures against the Jewish population. These measures were designed to "protect" the Christian community from Jewish teachings and, not incidentally, to weaken the Jews in their "obstinacy." It is characteristic that as soon as Christianity became the state religion of Rome, in the fourth century A.D., Jewish equality of citizenship was ended. "The Church and the Christian state, concilium decisions and imperial laws, henceforth worked hand in hand to persecute the Jews." Although most of these enactments did not cover all of Catholic Europe from the moment of their conception, they became precedents for the Nazi era. Table 49.1 compares the basic anti-Jewish measures of the Catholic Church and the modern counterparts enacted by the Nazi regime.

50

Maps—History of Anti-Semitism

Sir Martin Gilbert

The maps are shown on the following pages.

TWO THOUSAND YEARS OF JEWISH LIFE IN EUROPE

This map shows the age of the principal European Jewish communities in 1939. It was the Jewish communities shown here - their culture, their customs, and their deep local roots - which the Nazis sought utterly to destroy in the second world war.

0   miles   200
0   km   200

NORWAY 88 YEARS

ESTONIA 600 YEARS

LATVIA 400 YEARS

North Sea

DENMARK 317 YEARS

LITHUANIA 600 YEARS

HOLLAND 800 YEARS

WHITE RUSSIA 550 YEARS

BELGIUM 700 YEARS

GERMANY 1,618 YEARS

POLAND 850 YEARS

UKRAINE 822 YEARS

LUXEMBOURG 653 YEARS

CZECHOSLOVAKIA 1,000 YEARS

CRIMEA 1,900 YEARS

FRANCE 1,936 YEARS

HUNGARY 1,900 YEARS

RUMANIA 1,800 YEARS

AUSTRIA 1,030 YEARS

Adriatic Sea

YUGOSLAVIA 1,000 YEARS

Black Sea

ITALY 2,100 YEARS

GREECE 2,239 YEARS

Most of the Jewish communities of Europe had come into existence hundreds of years *before* the founding of the States of which they were to become a part. Others had subsequently been destroyed by expulsion and persecution in the middle ages - but had then been refounded a second, a third, and even a fourth time. The Jews of Germany had already been living continuously in different parts of Germany for more than 1,500 years when the German Empire was established in 1870, the year of German unity under Bismarck.

The age, by 1939, of the Jewish communities of Europe.

—·—· The European frontiers of 1937.

© Martin Gilbert 1978

SOME EARLY RECORDS OF JEWISH TOWN LIFE IN EUROPE BEFORE 1600

Jewish settlements throughout Europe flourished from Roman times. Early local records show different aspects of Jewish town life, from trade and prosperity to persecution and expulsion. This map gives 19 examples of contemporary records mentioning Jews *before* 1600. By 1937 there were more than 35,000 European towns and villages with Jewish communities. This map shows the European frontiers of that year. The Nazis made it one of their first aims to drive the Jews from their long-established homes, including from each of the towns shown here.

1561. Tallin. Jews, who had lived in the town for at least 200 years, expelled. They were not allowed to return until the town was annexed by Russia in 1710.

1489. Minsk. Jews obtain the lease of all customs dues

1173. Wroclawek. Local coins discovered with Hebrew inscriptions.

1367. Przemysl. Local records mention a Jewish community in the town.

1117. Jewish houses attacked during a local rebellion.

960 AD. Worms The local Jews send a letter to Palestine asking for verification of a rumour that the Messiah had come.

321 AD. An Imperial Decree mentions the Jewish citizens.

1074 Permission granted to the Jews to trade without having to pay customs dues.

1310. A Jewish scribe completes a fine illuminated manuscript.

576 AD. A local document records that the five hundred Jewish citizens in the town and neighbourhood were forced to chose between baptism and expulsion.

839 AD. Local records reveal a Jewish family owning land outside the city walls, and being protected by special order of the Emperor Louis the Pious.

1229. Munich A Jew appears in court as a witness during a trial.

1188. Strasbourg. Jews flee the town to avoid persecution from the crusaders, but return soon afterwards.

388 AD. Bishop Ambrose comments on the destruction of the synagogue "by act of God". It was soon rebuilt.

1090. Prague. A Christian scribe mentions Jewish citizens.

1204. Vienna. The existence of a synagogue is recorded.

81 AD. A Greek inscription refers to the Jewish community, and to the liberation of a Jewish slave.

140 BC. A Greek inscription records the arrival of Jews from Egypt.

142 BC. Rhodes. A Roman decree announces the renewal of a pact of friendship between the Roman Senate and the Jewish nation.

Tallin
Minsk
Wroclawek
Przemysl
Kiev
Cologne
Brussels
Frankfurt
Worms
Prague
Strasbourg
Munich
Vienna
Clermont-Ferrand
Milan
Carcassonne
Kerch
Salonica
Rhodes

Adriatic Sea
Black Sea

PERSECUTION, EXPULSION AND REFUGE, 1050 AD - 1650

In the six hundred years between 1050 AD and 1650 the Jews were frequently uprooted from their homes, and driven out of the lands in which they had lived and traded for many generations, even for centuries. This map shows some of the expulsions, and a few of the towns in which the Jews rebuilt their lives and livelihood. In these same towns, four hundred years later, their descendants were to be uprooted again, when the Nazis sought their total elimination from European life and culture

■ Some of the areas from which the Jews were expelled, often with great violence and cruelty, between 1050 AD and 1650

⊙ Some of the towns in which Jews found refuge from persecution; towns in which they were to grow and flourish, but from which, in the Nazi era, they were deported to death camps, or murdered in mass-execution sites

0   miles   150

0   km   200

North Sea

ESTONIA

LITHUANIA

Polotsk

Vitebsk

1495

Vilna

Minsk

Grodno

Gomel

FROM SPAIN 1492

Hamburg

1096-1192

Bialystok

Pinsk

Chernigov

Amsterdam

Posen

1495

Kalisz

Lodz

Lublin

Kiev

Antwerp

1182

THE GERMAN STATES

1159

Lvov

Zhitomir

BOHEMIA   SILESIA

CRACOVIA

Tarnopol

1306

Strasbourg

1348

UKRAINE

FRANCE

AUSTRIA

1349

HUNGARY

1421

1271

1349

1648

Kishinev

1322

Milan

THE CRIMEA

Venice

Trieste

PROVENCE

Genoa

Belgrade

1349-1360

Livorno

Niš

Black Sea

1498

Skopje

Rome

Salonica

FROM SPAIN FOLLOWING THE EXPULSION OF JEWS IN 1492

Corfu

Aegean Sea

Adriatic Sea

CRETE

Mediterranean Sea

© Martin Gilbert 1978

THE PERSECUTION OF THE JEWS OF GERMANY IN THE FIRST FIVE YEARS OF NAZI RULE 1933 - 1938

9 March 1933. First anti-Jewish riots in Berlin.
1 April 1933. All Jewish shops in Berlin boycotted.
10 May 1933. In Berlin the Nazis hold a public burning of books written by Jewish and other authors.
October 1933. All hospitals in Berlin declared "free" of Jewish doctors. These doctors could find no other hospital work.

30 January 1933. Hitler becomes the Chancellor of Germany. Many Jews arrested, ill-treated, and tortured.
15 September 1935. The Nuremberg Laws make the Jews second class citizens, and lead to their being driven from public and professional life.
9 November 1938. 191 synagogues set on fire throughout Germany. Over 2,000 Jews murdered in the camps.
15 November 1938. All German schools closed to German Jewish children.

North Sea

Baltic Sea

Esterwegen

Sachsenhausen

1933 - 1939. Of Germany's 525,000 Jews in 1933, over 280,000 emigrated or escaped by 1939.

Berlin
Columbia Haus

13 March 1933. All Jewish lawyers and judges expelled from the law courts.

Braunschweig

Buchenwald

THURINGIA

Breslau

Nuremberg

FRANCONIA

1933. The first Province to eliminate Jews from all official and professional positions.

13 March 1933. Jewish owned shops ransacked and destroyed.

Dachau

Munich

10 August 1938. The synagogue destroyed.

1935. 100,000 German children swear "eternal enmity" to the Jews.

9 June 1938. Synagogue destroyed.

—·— The borders of Germany, 1919 - 1937.

······· Other European borders.

From 1933, "Jews not wanted" signs were put up throughout Germany on shops, cafes, sports stadiums, and on roads leading into towns and villages. In some towns, all Jewish names were scratched off war memorials of the first world war. The savage anti-Jewish propaganda of the "Stürmer" magazine was in public display cases, and within six years, the 2,000 year old Jewish community was turned into a community of outlaws who could expect nothing but harassment and persecution.
Concentration camps set up on German soil by 1938.

Among the many indignities forced upon the Jews was a revival of the medieval practice of making all Jews wear a yellow "Star of David" on their clothing.

© Martin Gilbert 1978

C
O
N
T
E
X
T

GERMAN OFFICIAL PLANS FOR THE "FINAL SOLUTION", 20 JANUARY 1942

The number of Jews mentioned at the Wannsee Conference, country by country and area by area, for eventual deportation, and subsequent death. More than 14 million people were thus marked out for death.

One of the macabre features of the numerical list of the Jews submitted to the Wannsee Conference was the fact that no figure was given for the Jews of Estonia, merely a brief note that Estonia was 'Free of Jews'. This was true; the 1,000 Estonian Jews who had come under German rule in October 1941 had all been murdered during the three months before the Wannsee Conference.

ESTONIA
"Free of Jews"

USSR
5 million

NORWAY
1,300

LATVIA
3,500

DENMARK
5,600

LITHUANIA
34,000

HOLLAND
160,800

BIALYSTOK DISTRICT
400,000

WHITE RUSSIA
446,484

BELGIUM
43,000

Wannsee
GERMANY
131,800
Berlin

Chelmno

GENERAL GOVERNM.
2,284,000

EASTERN TERRITORIES
420,000

FRANCE OCCUPIED ZONE
165,000

BOHEMIA AND MORAVIA
74,200

88,000

UKRAINE
2,994,684

SLOVAKIA

AUSTRIA

HUNGARY
742,800

FRANCE UNOCCUPIED ZONE
700,000

43,700

CROATIA
40,000

10,000

SERBIA

RUMANIA
342,000

ITALY
58,000

BULGARIA

ALBANIA
200

0 miles 200
0 km 300

48,000

GREECE
69,600

In December 1941, a month *before* the Wannsee Conference, the first Nazi extermination camp had already come into operation, at Chelmno, responsible for the mass-murder of Jews, Gypsies, and Soviet prisoners-of-war. After passing through corridors marked 'To the showers' and 'To the doctor', the victims were forced into a large truck which was in fact a gas-chamber, where they were killed within a few minutes. By the end of 1944 more than 360,000 Jews had been murdered in Chelmno alone.

The Wannsee Conference also specified the number of Jews in *unconquered* countries for eventual destruction, including 330,000 from Britain, 18,000 from Switzerland, 6,000 from Spain and 4,000 from Ireland.

© Martin Gilbert 1978

THE CONCENTRATION CAMPS

Between 1939 and 1945, six million unarmed and innocent Jewish civilians - men, women, children and babies - were murdered in Nazi-controlled Europe, as part of a deliberate policy to destroy all traces of Jewish life and culture. As many as two million of these were killed in their own towns and villages, some confined in ghettoes where death by slow starvation was a deliberate Nazi policy, others taken to be shot at mass-murder sites near where they lived. The remaining four million Jews were forced from their homes and taken by train to distant concentration camps, where they were murdered by being worked to death, starved to death, beaten to death, shot, or gassed.

Among the hundreds of thousands of *non*-Jews sent by the Nazis to concentration camps were anti-Nazis, Jehovah's Witnesses, homosexuals, the mentally ill, and the chronically sick. In addition, more than 250,000 Gypsies were murdered, in a Nazi attempt to eliminate Gypsies as well as Jews from the map of Europe.

Auschwitz concentration camp in which more than 2 *million* people were murdered between 1941 and 1944, including Jews, Gypsies, and Soviet prisoners-of-war.

■ Camps set up solely for the murder of Jews.

卐 Other camps in which Jews and non-Jews were put to forced labour, starved, tortured, and murdered in conditions of the worst imaginable cruelty. Most of these camps had "satellite" labour camps nearby.

In many of the camps shown here so-called "medical" experiments were carried out, without anaesthetics, solely to satisfy the curiosity and sadism of the doctors. Hundreds of otherwise healthy "patients" were tortured and murdered during these experiments.

North Sea

Baltic Sea

Vaivara

卐 Klooga
ESTONIA

LATVIA

LITHUANIA

USSR

卐 Stutthof

Neuengamme 卐

卐 Ravensbrück

Chelmno

Treblinka

Bergen-Belsen 卐

Sachsenhausen

POLAND

Sobibor

Mittelbau Dora 卐

Gross Rosen

Auschwitz 卐 Maidanek

Buchenwald 卐

GERMANY

卐 Plaszow

Belzec

Flossenberg 卐

CZECHOSLOVAKIA

Natzweiler 卐

FRANCE

Dachau 卐

Mauthausen 卐

AUSTRIA

HUNGARY

RUMANIA

Gospič 卐 Jasenovac

YUGOSLAVIA

卐 Sajmište

Adriatic Sea

ITALY

0   100 miles
0   100 km

© Martin Gilbert 1978

NON-JEWISH VICTIMS OF NAZI RULE

In all occupied lands, the Nazis carried out large-scale reprisals against completely innocent and unarmed civilians, whenever a single German soldier was killed by partisans, or even when German property was attacked. In mass-murder actions against non-**Jews**, they also massacred 4 *million* unarmed Soviet prisoners-of-war, 1 *million* Soviet civilians, more than 1 *million* Polish civilians, and 1½ *million* Yugoslav civilians. In May 1940, at two villages near Dunkirk, a total of 170 *disarmed* British prisoners-of-war were murdered in cold blood. In June 1944, at three villages near Caen, 70 *disarmed* Canadian prisoners-of-war were likewise murdered, by German S.S. troops.

■ Twenty-six of many thousands of Nazi reprisal and murder actions against unarmed *non*-**Jews**, with the approximate number murdered in each massacre.

▨ Countries in each of which more than a *million* non-**Jewish** civilians died as a result of deliberate Nazi brutality.

Burashevo 350
Jeglava 700
Mikulino 275
Baranowicze 1,000
Zinyany 484
Gorodets 434
Prague 860
Holland 7 March 1945 400
POLAND
Borow 300
Ala 1,758
Zamosc 200
Lidice 250
Studenets 402
Dunkirk 170
Caen 70
Brno 395
Oradour-sur-Glane 642
Belgrade 4,750
Kragujevac 7,253
Kraljevo 1,700
Rome 335
Distomon 270
Kalvrithia 50
Athens 200
Klissura 233
Kastelli 200

North Sea
English Channel
Baltic Sea
GERMANY
CZECHOSLOVAKIA
AUSTRIA
HUNGARY
RUMANIA
FRANCE
ITALY
Adriatic Sea
YUGOSLAVIA
BULGARIA
Black Sea
GREECE
CRETE
Mediterranean Sea
U.S.S.R.

0 miles 200
0 km 150

In each of the actions shown here, unarmed men, women and children, almost all non-**Jews**, were chosen as the victims of Nazi hatred and vengeance. Many of those killed were beaten to death by blows of rifle butts, burned to death after petrol had been poured over them and ignited *while they were still alive*, or stripped naked and then shot. Those murdered at Klissura included 50 children under ten years of age. At Mikulino, all those killed were women patients in a mental hospital. In the Ardeatine caves in Rome, 253 Catholics and 70 **Jews** were murdered, among them many shopkeepers, students, lawyers and peddlers.

An estimated 32,000 German civilians were executed between 1933 and 1945 for so-called "political" offences. Those killed included Conservatives, Socialists, Communists, Catholics, Protestants, writers, journalists and teachers. All over Europe, non-**Jews** who were discovered sheltering Jews were also shot.

© Martin Gilbert 1978

THE DEPORTATION OF JEWS FROM HOLLAND, BELGIUM, FRANCE, ITALY AND GREECE

Driven from their homes and deprived of their possessions, more than four million of the six million Jews of Europe who were murdered by the Nazis were sent in cattle trucks to Nazi death camps in the east. Up to a thousand people were forced into each train, deprived of food or water, and shunted eastwards. Many died during the journey. On arrival at the death camps, the majority, weakened, sick and bewildered, were sent straight to the gas-chambers.

⊙ Some of the principal towns from which Jews were deported from the countries shown here.

卐 Some of the deportation centres, in which Jews were confined before deportation.

⤢ Main deportation routes, mostly operating between July 1942 and August 1944.

卐 Death camps.

This map shows some of the longest of the deportation journeys, from western Europe and the Balkans. As a result of the journeys shown here more than **320,000** Jews perished.

— · — · — European frontiers of 1937.

© Martin Gilbert 1978

CONTEXT

JEWISH REVOLTS 1942–1945

Despite the overwhelming military strength of the German forces, many Jews, while weakened by hunger and terrorised by Nazi brutality, nevertheless rose in revolt against their fate, not only in many of the Ghettoes in which they were forcibly confined, but even in the concentration camps themselves, snatching from the very gates of death the slender possibility of survival.

✡ Ghettoes in which Jews rose up in revolt against the Germans, with dates. Many of those who revolted were able to escape to the woods, and to join Jewish, Polish or Soviet partisan groups.

卐 Death camps in which the Jews revolted, with date of the revolt. In almost every instance, those who revolted were later caught and murdered.

This map shows twenty of the Ghettoes and five of the death camps in which Jews joined together and sought, often almost unarmed, to strike back at their tormentors. These twenty-five uprisings are among the most noble and courageous episodes not only of Jewish, but of world history.

PONARY
19 MAY 1944

Vilna
1 SEPTEMBER 1943

River Neimen

Mir
9 AUGUST 1942

Nieswiesz
22 JULY 1942

Kuldichvo
25 MARCH 1943

Kletsk
21 JULY 1943

0 miles 50
0 km 80

Bialystok
16 AUGUST 1943

River Vistula

TREBLINKA
2 AUGUST 1943

Lakhva
3 SEPTEMBER 1942

Warsaw
19 APRIL 1943

Minsk Mazowiecki
10 JANUARY 1943

CHELMNO
17 JANUARY 1945

Krushin
17 DECEMBER 1942

SOBIBOR
14 OCTOBER 1943

River Bug

Lutsk
12 OCTOBER 1942

Lublin
3 NOVEMBER 1943

Chenstochov
25 OCTOBER 1943

Tuchin
3 SEPTEMBER 1942

Bedzin
3 AUGUST 1943

Vistula

River

Tarnow
1 SEPTEMBER 1943

Brody
17 MAY 1943

Kremenetz
9 SEPTEMBER 1942

AUSCHWITZ
7 OCTOBER 1944

Lvov
1 JUNE 1943

River Dniester

Stryj
28 APRIL 1943

C Z E C H O S L O V A K I A

HUNGARY

© Martin Gilbert 1978

CONTEXT

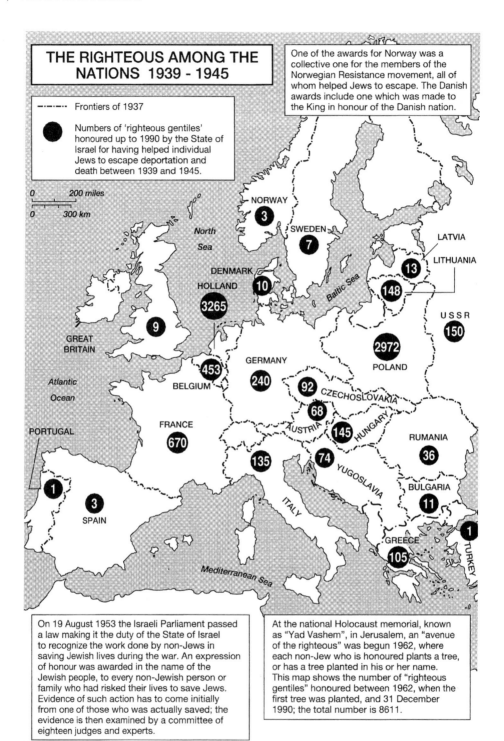

THE RIGHTEOUS AMONG THE NATIONS 1939 - 1945

One of the awards for Norway was a collective one for the members of the Norwegian Resistance movement, all of whom helped Jews to escape. The Danish awards include one which was made to the King in honour of the Danish nation.

--·--·-- Frontiers of 1937

● Numbers of 'righteous gentiles' honoured up to 1990 by the State of Israel for having helped individual Jews to escape deportation and death between 1939 and 1945.

0   200 miles
0   300 km

NORWAY **3**

North Sea

SWEDEN **7**

Baltic Sea

LATVIA
LITHUANIA **13**

DENMARK
HOLLAND **10**

148

USSR **150**

GREAT BRITAIN **9**

GERMANY **2972**

POLAND

Atlantic Ocean

453
BELGIUM

240

92 CZECHOSLOVAKIA

68
AUSTRIA

145 HUNGARY

RUMANIA **36**

PORTUGAL

FRANCE **670**

135

74 YUGOSLAVIA

BULGARIA **11**

1
3
SPAIN

ITALY

GREECE **105**

TURKEY **1**

Mediterranean Sea

On 19 August 1953 the Israeli Parliament passed a law making it the duty of the State of Israel to recognize the work done by non-Jews in saving Jewish lives during the war. An expression of honour was awarded in the name of the Jewish people, to every non-Jewish person or family who had risked their lives to save Jews. Evidence of such action has to come initially from one of those who was actually saved; the evidence is then examined by a committee of eighteen judges and experts.

At the national Holocaust memorial, known as "Yad Vashem", in Jerusalem, an "avenue of the righteous" was begun 1962, where each non-Jew who is honoured plants a tree, or has a tree planted in his or her name. This map shows the number of "righteous gentiles" honoured between 1962, when the first tree was planted, and 31 December 1990; the total number is 8611.

© Martin Gilbert 1978

THE JEWISH DEATH-TOLL
1939–1945

This map shows the number of Jews murdered in Nazi-dominated Europe between 1939 and 1945. All the figures are approximate, but most of them are probably *underestimates*. In all, more than **5,950,000** deaths are shown even with these minimum figures.

NORWAY 868

ESTONIA 1,000

North Sea

DENMARK 120

LATVIA

HOLLAND 106,000

LITHUANIA

BELGIUM 24,000

4,565,000

GERMANY 125,000

POLAND

WESTERN USSR

LUXEMBOURG 700

CZECHOSLOVAKIA 277,000

FRANCE 83,000

HUNGARY 300,000

RUMANIA 264,000

AUSTRIA 70,000

YUGOSLAVIA 60,000

ITALY 7,500

Adriatic Sea

Black Sea

FURTHEST ADVANCE OF THE GERMAN ARMY 1942

GREECE 65,000

Approximate Jewish death-toll, country-by-country.

European frontiers of 1937.

Mediterranean Sea

© Martin Gilbert 1978

51

See You in Court

Diana Eck

The American Constitution guarantees that there will be "no establishment" of religion and that the "free exercise" of religion will be protected. As we have seen, these twin principles have guided church-state relations in the United States for the past two hundred years. But the issues have become increasingly complex in a multireligious America, where the church in question may now be the mosque, the Buddhist temple, the Hindu temple, or the Sikh gurdwara. Every religious tradition has its own questions. Can a Muslim schoolteacher wear her head covering on the job as a public school teacher? Can a Sikh student wear the *kirpan*, the symbolic knife required of all initiated Sikhs, to school, or a Sikh worker wear a turban on a hard-hat job, in apparent violation of safety regulations? Should a crèche be displayed in the Christmas season on public property? Can the sanctity of Native lands be protected from road building? Should the taking of peyote by Native Americans be protected as the free exercise of religion? Can a city council pass an ordinance prohibiting the sacrifice of animals by the adherents of the Santería faith?

These difficult questions make clear that one vital arena of America's new pluralism is the courts. Since about 1960, church-state issues in America have been increasingly on court agendas. Just as the "church" is not a single entity in multireligious America, the "state" is multiple too, with zoning boards, city councils, state governments, and the federal government. At all levels, courts hear disputes and offer interpretations of laws and regulations and the constitutional principles that undergird them.

The First Amendment principles of nonestablishment of religion and the free exercise of religion sometimes almost seem to be in tension: the free exercise of religion calling for the protection of religious groups, while the nonestablishment of religion prohibiting any such special treatment. On the "no establishment" side, a landmark Supreme Court decision was made in the case of *Everson v. Board of Education* (1947) in which a school busing program in New Jersey was ruled to be accessible to students going to parochial schools. The Supreme Court's decision was clearly and narrowly defined: the busing program was a "generally available benefit" that should not be denied to children simply because their destination was a religious school. While the court has consistently ruled against state support of private religious schools, in this case, the benefit in question was not to the schools, but to the children. Justice Black wrote, "[T]he First Amendment requires the state to be neutral in its relations with groups of religious believers and non-believers; it does not require the state to be their adversary. State power is no more to be used so as to handicap religions than it is to favor them." The extended logic of this decision was that religious communities should have "equal access" to those benefits that are available to nonreligious communities. In other words, if a high school gymnasium in Bethesda, Maryland, can be used by the Girl Scouts or the Garden Club, its use cannot be denied to a Hindu temple community for its annual fall Diwali festival.

In "free exercise" cases, the *Sherbert v. Verner* decision in 1963 set a precedent that guided religious liberty cases for thirty years. In South Carolina, Adell Sherbert, a Seventh-Day Adventist, was fired from her job because she refused to accept a schedule requiring her to work on Saturday, her Sabbath, and was then refused state unemployment compensation. In her case, the Supreme Court articulated three questions to guide its decision: Has the religious freedom of a person been infringed or burdened by some government action?

If so, is there a "compelling state interest" that would nonetheless justify the government action? Finally, is there any other way the government interest can be satisfied without restricting religious liberty? In sum, religious liberty is the rule; any exception to the rule can be justified only by a "compelling state interest." This form of reasoning came to be called the "balancing test"—balancing state interest against the religious freedom of the individual.

In the Sherbert case, the court ruled that there was no state interest compelling enough to warrant the burden placed upon Sherbert's religious freedom. Similarly, when an Amish community in Wisconsin insisted on withdrawing its children from public schools after the eighth grade and the State of Wisconsin insisted the children comply with compulsory education laws, the Supreme Court applied the three-pronged test and ruled that the religious freedom of the Amish outweighed the state's interest in four years' more compulsory education (*Wisconsin v. Yoder*, 1972).

Beginning in the 1980s, however, a series of Supreme Court rulings gradually weakened the force of the Sherbert balancing test and, in the view of many, weakened the constitutional guarantee of the free exercise of religion. These rulings began to raise disturbing questions about the religious rights of minorities. In the case of *Lyng v. The Northwest Indian Cemetery Protective Association* (1988), the issue was whether the Native Americans' right to preserve intact their sacred sites outweighed the government's right to build roads through Forest Service land. The Yurok, Karok, and Tolowa Indians argued that building a logging road through the land would have "devastating effects" on their religious ways. A lower court acted to prevent the Forest Service from building the road, but the Forest Service appealed to the Supreme Court. In this case, the Supreme Court supported the Forest Service, saying,

> Incidental effects of government programs which may make it more difficult to practice certain religions, but which have no tendency to coerce individuals into acting contrary to their religious beliefs [do not] require government to bring forward a compelling justification for its otherwise lawful actions. . . However much we might wish that it were otherwise, government simply could not operate if it were required to satisfy every citizen's religious needs and desires. . . . Whatever rights the Indians may have to the use of the area, however, those rights do not divest the government of its right to use what is, after all, its land.

Here, the balance tipped precipitously in favor of the government, whose policies, just incidentally, compromised Native religious practice.

For the Indians, one of the issues in this and other cases is whether the government recognizes the deeply held religious importance of preserving particular sacred sites undisturbed. A Hopi and Navajo case (*Wilson v. Block*, 1983) questioned whether a ski area could be built on a sacred mountain. The court ruled that the Forest Service had not infringed the religious rights of the Indians because it had not denied them access to the mountain. But the Navajo and Hopi argued that the mountain, the home of the Kachinas—divine messengers—would be desecrated by its commercial development. The court seemed to give little weight to the fact that the Native peoples considered the mountain to be inherently sacred, the very locus of the Divine, and not simply the place where they pray to the Divine. Here, the very nature of Native religious claims for the sanctity of the land seemed to be undermined, or perhaps not even understood, by the court's reasoning.

These and other cases led many to see an increasingly restrictive interpretation of the scope of religious freedom by the Supreme Court. In each case, the government did not have to demonstrate a "compelling interest" in order to restrict religious freedom. And in each case, the government did not have to alter its basic procedures to accommodate a specific religious claim. For example, an Abnaki Indian asked that his daughter, Little Bird of the Snow, be exempt from having to have a Social Security number in order to receive the benefits from the Aid to Families with Dependent Children program (*Bowen v. Roy*, 1986). The father insisted that to assign a number to his daughter would "rob her of her spirit" and interfere with her spiritual growth by making her a number, regulated by the federal government. The court ruled that the First Amendment could not be interpreted to require the government to alter its procedures in this way. Little Bird of the Snow would have to have a Social Security number.

Altering government procedures to accommodate various religious practices was also at stake in the case of *Goldman v. Weinberger* (1986). Dr. Goldman, an Orthodox Jewish psychiatrist serving in the U.S. Air Force, insisted on his right to wear his yarmulke on duty in the hospital, even though Air Force regulations prohibited a uniformed officer from wearing a head covering inside. The Air Force insisted that its code of military discipline requires that it not be continually making exceptions. The court said it would defer to the Air Force's judgment in this matter, which was to say: no yarmulkes.

Friday prayer for a Muslim prisoner was decided along similar lines in the case of *O'Lone v. Estate of Shabazz* (1987). Here, a Muslim prison inmate wanted to return from the work gang at noon for Friday prayers with other Muslims. He was turned down because officials insisted that it would require extra prison security at the work site and the gate in order to bring him back, and the court upheld the prison system's refusal to alter prison practices. In making this ruling, the court also said that a restrictive institution like the prison system had security needs and regulations that would necessarily mean that constitutional rights would not be as broad as those of ordinary citizens.

These increasingly restrictive interpretations of the guarantees of the First Amendment culminated in the controversial 1990 Supreme Court decision about peyote use. In this case (*Employment Division, Department of Human Resources of Oregon v. Smith*, 1990) two members of the Native American church ingested peyote, as is common in the ceremonial life of the church, and were subsequently fired from their jobs for "misconduct." The state of Oregon denied them unemployment compensation because they had been dismissed for the use of peyote, which was classified as an illegal drug. The Supreme Court upheld Oregon's decision, arguing that the state had a "generally applicable" law against drug use. The law did not specifically target the Native American church or any other group, and carving out exceptions to such laws would be impracticable, according to the 5–4 majority of the court. Justice Antonin Scalia argued that to require the government to demonstrate a "compelling state interest" in enforcing generally applicable laws would be "courting anarchy."

The Smith decision thus reversed many years of court precedent, which presumed that religious freedom would be the rule, with any infringement requiring the demonstration of a compelling state interest. Many critics insisted that for the court to refuse to apply the balancing test to "generally applicable laws" would seriously damage the first-amendment protection of religious freedom. The Smith decision, critics argued, would be especially hard on minority religions, since generally applicable laws are passed by the majority. Freedom of religion, on the other hand is not subject to majority rule. The purpose of the Bill of Rights was precisely to limit the power of the majority in areas of fundamental rights, such as the freedom of conscience and speech.

The Santería Church of the Lukumi Babalu Aye in Hialeah, Florida, was a minority group in danger of losing its freedom of religious practice due to its unpopular and widely misunderstood practice of animal sacrifice. An estimated fifty thousand practitioners of the Afro-Caribbean Santería religion now live in South Florida, and their ceremonial life includes the sacrifice of chickens, pigeons, or other small animals to the *orisha*, their gods. The case that came to the Supreme Court (*Church of the Lukumi Babalu Aye v. City of*

Hialeah, 1993) began in 1987 when Ernesto Pichardo, a priest of the Santería religion, purchased a building and a former used car lot to open a place of worship. The city council of Hialeah met to consider the matter, and many voices hostile to Santería were raised. The council passed three ordinances that effectively prohibited animal sacrifice within the city limits. As the city attorney explained, "This community will not tolerate religious practices which are abhorrent to its citizens."

Ernesto Pichardo and his community protested, insisting that the ordinances specifically targeted Santería, as they did not prohibit the killing of animals within city limits for secular reasons but only for religious ones and only, seemingly, for those of the Santería religion. Indeed, the ordinances specifically excluded Jewish kosher slaughter practices. Animals could be killed in butcher shops and restaurants but not in the religious context of Santería. Many quipped that the Church of Lukumi Babalu Aye was being persecuted for killing a few chickens with a prayer, while Frank Perdue and Colonel Sanders kill tens of thousands without one. The question before the Supreme Court was whether the three ordinances passed by the city council were constitutional or whether they violated the constitutional rights of the practitioners of Santería by specifically legislating against their religious practices. The judges unanimously struck down the ordinances, stating that they were not generally applicable laws at all but specifically aimed at the Santería religion. As Justice Anthony M. Kennedy wrote, "Although the practice of animal sacrifice may seem abhorrent to some, 'religious beliefs need not be acceptable, logical, consistent, or comprehensible to others in order to merit First Amendment protection.'"

The Santería case was an easy one, resting on the principle that "government may not enact laws that suppress religious belief or practice." However, many people, including Justice David Souter, were still disquieted about the merits and the precedent of the Smith decision. By this time, legislation called the Religious Freedom Restoration Act had been introduced in Congress precisely to restore the religious freedom many people in public life felt had been eroded with the Smith decision. This act, passed in 1995, stated simply, "The government cannot burden a person's free exercise of religion, even if the burden results from a rule of general applicability, unless the burden is essential to further a compelling governmental interest and is the least restrictive means of furthering that interest." In effect, it reinstituted the balancing test of the Sherbert case, this time in law. The legislation was eventually ruled unconstitutional by the Supreme Court in 1997, in part because it was a legislative maneuver to reestablish a form of judicial reasoning. This, the court believed, was the prerogative of the judiciary.

Questions of religious freedom lie at the heart of some of America's most hotly contested cases. The courts are one site of the encounter and disputation that are endemic to America's new pluralism. They represent the difficult places where we the people do not seem to be able to resolve our differences on our own. Cases involving America's newer religious communities have gradually made their way into the court system and into case law. The willingness to take advantage of access to the courts is itself a signal of the Americanization process.

In California's Livingstone School District, for instance, the schools and the Sikh community arrived at a stand-off on the question of whether three young Khalsa-initiated students would be permitted to attend school wearing the symbolic *kirpan*, a ceremonial dagger that is one of the five sacred symbols of the Sikh faith and is worn by all initiated Sikhs. In 1994 classmates of an eleven-year-old Sikh youngster had spotted his *kirpan* when his shirt slid up on the playground and reported this to the teacher. From the standpoint of the school, policy prohibited carrying weapons, including knives, on the school premises. From the standpoint of the Sikh youngster and his two siblings, the *kirpan* was part of their religious life, a symbol of their historic willingness to stand up for justice, and being required to take it off amounted to an infringement of their religious freedom.

The U.S. District court barred the three youngsters from wearing the *kirpan*, and their parents kept them home from school. But when the case came to the Ninth U.S. Circuit Court of Appeals, the court overturned the ruling and required the Livingstone School District to make "all reasonable efforts" to accommodate the religious beliefs and practices of the three Sikh youngsters. According to the ruling, as long as the *kirpans* are small, sewn in the sheath, and not a threat to the safety of other students, the Sikh students must be allowed to wear them to school. Here, the courts were an avenue for working out a genuine dilemma that schools had not before encountered.

In New Jersey the Indo-American Cultural Society also found the court system necessary in order to resolve a community dispute having to do with its annual festival of Navaratri, the "Nine Nights" of the Goddess, observed on a series of weekend nights on the grounds of the Raritan Convention Center in Edison. This fall festival attracted as many as twelve thousand celebrants, and though it was arguably well out of earshot of residential areas, a group of citizens tried to block the festival. A 1995 meeting with the Township Council of Edison revealed a level of overt prejudice that was shocking to the representatives of the Indo-American Cultural Society. The chair of the society wrote to the township council following the meeting,

> We wonder if there is any awareness in Edison of freedoms of assembly and religion. We are immigrants to a democracy that provided the model for the constitution India adopted less than fifty years ago. We wonder how the folk who inspired our struggle against colonialism can arbitrarily dismiss our rights.

The council passed an ordinance aimed at restricting the hours of the festival, permits for the festival were delayed, and the Indo-American Cultural Society responded by seeking an injunction against what it considered the township's unfair ordinance. Eventually, in July of 1996, a district judge upheld the rights of the Indo-American Cultural Society. But all this required the willingness of the Hindus to use the court system. Reflecting on the whole affair, Vivodh Z. J. Anand, a New Jersey human rights advocate, wrote,

> As a New Jersey State Civil Rights Commissioner, I have, since my immigration in 1963 at the height of the American Civil Rights movement, personally struggled for equity. I can report that the courts seem to be the only venue available to resolve vexing communal conflicts. While advocacy groups for a wide spectrum of social issues exist, the onus of resolving issues of religious freedom and rights, and in this case the more complex conflation of religious and racial "otherness," seems to rest only on those who are wronged and whose rights have been compromised.

Anand went on to report that during the entire struggle of the Indian community in New Jersey not a single religious group or community leader reached out to support the Indo-American Cultural Society in its well-publicized case. "In our democracy there is a paucity of institutions to study, educate, arbitrate, and promote the credence of the religious 'other.' Yet for a democracy to flourish, it is imperative that both individuals and groups be enabled to recognize that their own stories may be found in the stories and lives of fellow citizens who may appear dissimilar to themselves."

52

Native American Religious Liberty

Five Hundred Years After Columbus

Walter R. Echo-Hawk

. . .

HISTORICAL SUPPRESSION OF NATIVE RELIGION

Christopher Columbus's baggage included Europe's long heritage of religious intolerance. In 1492 Spain—fresh from centuries of religious crusades against the infidels for possession of holy places in the Middle East— . . . the Spanish Inquisition was in full force and effect. The King expelled the Jews from Spain on August 2, and, on January 4, military unification as a Christian nation was achieved with the Moorish defeat, which led to the expulsion of the Moslems.

. . .

On 12 October 1492, Columbus wrote this about the native inhabitants he encountered on his arrival in the Western Hemisphere:

> They ought to be good servants and of good intelligence . . . . I believe that they would easily be made Christians because it seemed to me that they had no religion. Our Lord pleasing, I will carry off six of them at my departure to Your Highnesses, in order that they may learn to speak.

. . .

Old World attitudes of religious intolerance became ingrained in the United States government's Indian policies from the very inception of this nation. . . . A basic goal of federal Indian policy was to convert the "savage" Indians into Christian citizens and separate them from their traditional ways of life. President Jackson's Indian removal policy was justified in the name of converting and civilizing the Indians. During this removal period, Supreme Court decisions that upheld the government's taking of Indian lands and the reduction of tribal sovereignty from independent nation to "domestic dependent nation" status under discovery and conquest principles of international law referred to Indians as "heathen" savages.

Christian missionaries, hired as government Indian agents, were an integral part of federal Indian policy for over one hundred years. The government placed entire reservations and Indian nations under the administrative control of different denominations to convert the Indians and separate them from their traditions. A number of federal laws, still on the books today, authorize the secretary of the interior to give Indian lands to missionary religious groups for "religious or educational work among the Indians," 25 U.S.C. 348. In *Quick Bear v. Leupp*, 210 U.S. 50, 81–82 (1908), the Supreme Court upheld the use of federal funds to establish a Catholic school on the Rosebud Indian Reservation despite a claim that this government support of religion violated the Establishment Clause of the First Amendment.

. . .

Despite the government's goal to supplant tribal culture with Christianity, many Indians clung to their beliefs and practices even after they were confined on reservations. Chief Walking Buffalo's remarks show defiant native resistance to government-enforced proselytization:

> You whites assumed we were savages. You didn't understand our prayers. You didn't try to understand. When we sang our praises to the sun or moon or wind, you said we were worshipping idols. Without understanding, you condemned us as lost souls just because our form of worship was different than yours.
>
> We saw the Great Spirit's work in almost everything: sun, moon, trees, wind, and mountains. Sometimes we approached him through these things. Was that so bad? I think we have a true belief in the supreme being, a stronger faith than that of most of the whites who have called us pagans . . . . Indians living close to nature and nature's ruler are not living in darkness.

Consequently, in the 1890s, federal authorities become more belligerent toward Indian religion. In that decade. United States troops were called in to quell the Ghost Dance, a widely practiced tribal religion that impeded government assimilation policies. In 1890, more than one hundred Lakota Ghost Dance worshipers were massacred at Wounded Knee, South Dakota. In 1892, Pawnee Ghost Dance leaders were arrested in Oklahoma. In the same year, the BIA [Bureau of Indian Affairs] outlawed the Sun Dance religion and banned other ceremonies that were declared "Indian offenses" and made punishable by withholding of rations or thirty days' imprisonment. Facing the threat of military intervention, arrest, and starvation, many Indians stopped practicing the Ghost Dance and took other rituals underground.

Formal government rules suppressing tribal religions continued well into the 1900s. In 1904, the BIA promulgated regulations for its Court of Indian Offenses, including "offenses" that banned Indian religious leaders and ceremonies:

> . . . The "sun dance," and all other similar dances and so-called religious ceremonies, shall be considered "Indian offenses," and any Indian found guilty of being a participant in any one or more of these offenses shall . . . be punished . . . .

> The usual practices of so-called "medicine men" shall be considered "Indian offenses" . . . and whenever it shall be proven . . . he shall be adjudged guilty of an Indian offense, and upon conviction . . . shall be confined in the agency guardhouse . . . .

Even though this ban was lifted in 1934, serious government infringements on native religious freedom continued into the 1970s. Tribes witnessed governmental suppression of their religious practices in numerous ways: arrests of traditional Indians for possession of tribal sacred objects such as eagle feathers; criminal prosecutions for the religious use of peyote; denial of access to sacred sites located on federal lands; actual destruction of sacred sites; and interference with religious ceremonies at sacred sites. . . .

The treatment of native worship by the Supreme Court in the recent *Lyng* and *Smith* decisions, analyzed below, is especially troubling when considered in the context of the above history. Given the long history of government suppression of tribal religions, it is highly doubtful that these unique and irreplaceable indigenous religions can continue to survive without any American legal protection.

THE LYNG DECISION: NEED FOR FEDERAL SACRED SITES LEGISLATION

. . .

Worship at sacred sites is a basic attribute of religion itself. Since the inception of the major world religions, control over holy places in the Middle East has always been of deep international concern. Beginning around A.D. 1000, the Christian world engaged in a number of military/religious crusades, spanning several centuries, to wrest control of its holy places from the non-Christian world. Following the Crusades, Christian nations resorted to numerous treaties with countries in control of the Holy Land to preserve sacred sites and protect freedom of worship there. The Crimean War between France and Russia was fought over control of Christian holy places.

However, when most Americans think of holy places, they think only of well-known Middle Eastern sites familiar to the Judeo-Christian tradition, such as the Church of the Holy Sepulchcr (Grave of Christ) and Basilica of the Nativity in Jerusalem and Bethlehem; Mecca; the Wailing Wall; or Mount Sinai. . . .

Traditional Native American religious sites—some of which rank among the most beautiful and breathtaking natural wonders left in America—serve a variety of important roles in tribal religion, which should be readily understandable to most people. However, in truly understanding and protecting Native American holy places, society may have to confront and modify basic values first implanted in this hemisphere by Columbus, because native sacred sites arc natural, not man-made, sites. . . . It is undoubtedly difficult for a culture with an inherent fear of "wilderness" and a fundamental belief in the "religious domination" of humans over animals to envision that certain aspects of nature can be sacred. . . .

[H]owever, federal agencies such as the Forest Service and the National Park Service have repeatedly destroyed irreplaceable native sacred sites. The courts have consistently been unwilling to find any protections for Indians under the First Amendment or any statute. The struggle in the courts culminated in 1988, when the Supreme Court ruled in *Lyng* that Indians stand outside the purview of the First Amendment entirely when it comes to protecting tribal religious areas on federal lands for worship purposes.

In *Lyng*, a sharply divided Court denied First Amendment protection to tribal worship at a sacred site in northern California that would admittedly be destroyed by a proposed Forest Service logging road. The frightening aspect of the Court's refusal to protect worship at this ancient holy area was that the Court withheld protection, knowing that "the threat to the efficacy of at least some religious practices is extremely grave." . . .

In short, government may destroy an entire Indian religion under *Lyng* with constitutional impunity, unless it also goes further and punishes the Indians or forces them to violate their religion. The Court reached this result by an unprecedented narrow construction of the Free Exercise Clause. It held that Free Exercise protections arise *only* in those rare instances when government *punishes* a person for practicing religion or *coerces* one into violating his religion. Because it is hard to imagine rare instances in which that will happen, the Court's narrow interpretation renders the Free Exercise Clause a virtual nullity. This crabbed reading of the Bill of Rights is one that should deeply concern all citizens who cherish religious freedom principles, because, under *Lyng*, United States law guarantees less religious freedom than most other democracies and some nondemocratic nations.

As to the Indians in *Lyng*, the Court disclaimed judicial responsibility to safeguard religious freedom from government infringement, stating that any protection for them "is for the legislatures and other institutions." Former Justice Brennan's dissent noted the "cruelly surreal result" produced by the majority decision:

[G]overnmental action that will virtually destroy a religion is nevertheless deemed not to "burden" that religion.

. . .

As a result of *Lyng*, there are no legal safeguards for native worship at sacred sites under the United States Constitution and laws, laying bare a basic attribute of religion itself. This legal anomaly has frightening implications for remaining tribal religions struggling to survive. . . .

From a policy standpoint, no religious group should be stripped of First Amendment protections in a democratic society so that its ability to worship is made wholly dependent on administrative whim. This is especially true for unpopular or despised minority religious groups, such as American Indians, who have suffered a long history of government religious suppression.

The failure of American law to protect holy places illustrates a larger failure of law to incorporate indigenous needs into a legal system otherwise intended to protect all citizens. Certainly, if this country contained holy ground considered important to the Judeo-Christian tradition, American law and social policy would undoubtedly accord stringent protections. Because important Judeo-Christian sites are located in other nations, it is understandable that, as American law developed in the United States, it never addressed this aspect of religious freedom. Thus, when native religious practitioners—who are the only ones with religious ties to holy ground located in this country—petitioned the courts, they found that the law was ill equipped to protect their religious liberty. However, if the purpose of law is to fairly protect all fundamental interests of our diverse and pluralistic society, then it must someday address indigenous needs, so that all basic human rights are fairly and equally protected.

. . .

53

Taking the Indian Out of the Indian

U.S. Policies of Ethnocide through Education

Donald A. Grinde Jr.

As the genocidal policies to eliminate Native American populations in North America began to lose momentum at the end of the nineteenth century (the Native American population in the United States had been reduced to 500,000 by 1890), American Indians faced a new U.S. colonial policy that aimed to obliterate American Indian culture through education. This "civilizing" policy had three cornerstones: Christianization, education, and the instilling of private property (usually in that order). . . . These policies were erroneously based on the assumption that Native Americans had no educational structures, no sense of property, and an inferior brand of spirituality. In fact, Native Americans had educational systems long before 1492, with Native teachers and scholars imparting knowledge to children and adults on a day-to-day basis both before and after white contact. Elders as well as people knowledgeable about specific ideas and techniques instructed members of their societies about a broad range of topics including history, religion, arts and crafts, literature, geography, zoology, botany, medicine, law, political science, astronomy, soil science, and theater. Since American Indian models of instruction centered on oral tradition, Europeans often typified Native American education as "primitive," defective, or nonexistent. . . .

In the nineteenth century, white Americans took these assumptions one step further and declared that American Indians had no government, education, or spirituality. Although such observations of Native American cultures meant little to the soldiers who were sent to conquer Native peoples, these ideas and policies were important to the reformers, educators, and missionaries who wanted to convert Native peoples to the civilization of white Christian capitalism. . . .

In the late nineteenth century, the chief advocate for the "civilization" policy was Captain Richard Henry Pratt, a veteran of Indian wars and the Civil War. In 1879, Pratt petitioned the federal government for the army barracks at Carlisle, Pennsylvania, and turned it into an off-reservation boarding school for American Indian children. . . . By the early twentieth century, American Indian boarding schools could be grouped into four categories:

1   Agency reservation boarding schools established and conducted by the federal government. The schools were built, furnished, and funded by the U.S. government, and all employees were appointed by the commissioner of Indian affairs upon nomination by the Indian agent.
2   Reservation boarding schools established by religious groups under contract to educate at a specific per capita rate.
3   Independent reservation boarding schools established by the government but made independent of supervision by Indian agents because they were located too far from government agencies.
4   Mission reservation boarding schools established by religious associations with their own paid employees. . . .

In government boarding schools, posters were given to American Indian schoolchildren well into the twentieth century that exhorted white Christian values:

1   Let Jesus save you.
2   Come out of your blanket, cut your hair, and dress like a white man.
3   Have a Christian family with one wife for life.
    . . .
4   Go to church often and regularly.
5   Do not go to Indian dances or to medicine men.

    . . .

Thus, education was presented to American Indians as a value system to be substituted for their traditions and as a mechanism to destroy traditional Native American ways. American Indian students attending government boarding schools were immersed in a totally different culture; students' clothes, habits, and appearance changed. . . . Just like the white man's religion, the white man's education demanded a cleansing process. The option of adding the white man's learning to Native cultures was not allowed. Instead, the American Indian was required to rid himself of his traditional knowledge if he wished to acquire a civilized education. . . .

By the early twentieth century, this militant cultural war against American Indians began to change. In 1904, Pratt left Carlisle after publicly calling for the abolition of the Bureau of Indian Affairs. . . . Thus, this new educational philosophy offered some cultural preservation and respect but promised little in the way of equality for Native Americans. . . .

In conclusion, it was clear by the 1920s that coercive educational policies had not only failed but also actually continued the genocidal practices that marked the U.S. government's relationship with Native peoples from the outset. The overall American Indian population had dropped from about 500,000 in the 1880s to 250,000 in 1934 when these policies were formally abandoned under the Indian New Deal. The Indian New Deal was created and controlled by white academics who usurped the power of missionaries in the Bureau of Indian Affairs when Franklin D. Roosevelt became president in 1933. While these social scientists did not grant American Indian people much self-determination during and after Roosevelt's Indian New Deal, they did abandon the coercive aspects of the "civilization" policies, stating that Native Americans should have a choice between "assimilating" into the dominant society and retaining traditional ways. Throughout much of the last half of the twentieth century, the tensions in American Indian affairs have focused on more empowerment for Native communities. But there is still little power for American Indian nations when it comes to the allocation of their resources: ethnocide (the systematic destruction of a people's ways) was finally abandoned in the 1930s, but economic exploitation of Native American resources still continues largely unabated into the twenty-first century.

54

From Pearl Harbor to 9/11

Lessons from the Internment of Japanese American Buddhists

Duncan Ryûken Williams

Buddhist priests, classified by the Federal Bureau of Investigation (FBI) as potentially the most dangerous Japanese aliens, were among the first groups arrested by government officials following the bombing of Pearl Harbor on December 7, 1941. . . . Unlike Japanese American Christian priests and ministers, Buddhist priests were closely associated with Japan and thus with potentially subversive activity. . . . This perception that Buddhists (in contrast to Christians) were more Japanese than American was held not only by the FBI and the Wartime Relocation Authority (WRA) but also by the public at large, including some members of the Japanese American community. The history of Japanese American Buddhism during World War II, in fact, centers on this question of identity, both ethnic and religious.

. . .

The first Japanese Buddhist priests arrived in Hawaii and the U.S. mainland in the 1890s to minister to the first-generation issei. Most issei were Buddhists who had initially immigrated to Hawaii to work on plantations and to the mainland as contract laborers for railroad, lumber, mining, and cannery companies as well as on farms. In 1900, the Japanese immigrant population had risen to 24,326, most of them transient men. In 1930, however, the Japanese American population had grown to 138,834 and increasingly was composed of families with stable jobs and even small businesses. By the eve of the war,

Buddhist temples functioned as both religious and community centers in all areas where Japanese Americans were concentrated, especially in California. . . . The FBI's decision to target Buddhist priests can be traced primarily to the conflation of Buddhism with state Shinto, which emphasized worship of the emperor as a deity and loyalty to the Japanese imperial empire. Not until the postwar period would Americans see Japanese Buddhism as a distinct tradition.

Newspaper editors and members of Congress accused all Japanese, including Japanese American children, of being loyal to the Japanese government and called for their removal from the West Coast. After their priests were taken away to "enemy alien" camps, the remaining members of Buddhist temples tried their best to continue religious services as well as community affairs. For example, the wives of priests and nonordained temple leaders took on duties that priests previously had performed exclusively.

By February 1942, the U.S. government set in motion the large-scale incarceration of the broader Japanese American community. On February 19, 1942, President Roosevelt issued Executive Order 9066, which ultimately led to the designation of restricted military zones on the West Coast and the subsequent removal of all persons of Japanese ancestry from those areas. In the ensuing months, the atmosphere in the community was one of anxiety, uncertainty, and fear. . . .

During this period of war hysteria, some Buddhists converted to Christianity, while others burned Japanese-language books and other personal Japanese cultural artifacts in an attempt to destroy, literally and symbolically, their Japaneseness while simultaneously demonstrating their Americanness. Mary Nagatomi, for example, remembers her parents telling her to go to the wood stove used for the family bath to burn everything in the household with "Made in Japan" on it, including her favorite traditional Japanese doll set. The one item the family members could not bring themselves to burn was a set of Buddhist sutras, which the father buried after wrapping the scriptures in kimono cloth, placing them in a metal rice-cracker box, and using a backhoe to dig a hole for them on the family farm. These sacred texts remain buried somewhere in central California, a silent testimony to the enduring Buddhist identity of one family, testimony that could not be completely obliterated despite the seeming necessity of doing so.

. . .

Japanese American Buddhists faced a crisis of identity and faith as they endured a harsh journey to the internment camps and the realities of the desert heat, coupled with the knowledge that they were prisoners in their own land. Within the camps, surrounded by barbed wire and armed guards, arose the question of what it means to be simultaneously American and Buddhist. What is an American Buddhist?

Buddhist life in the camps revolved around the barrack "churches," which held religious services and education classes (in some cases in mess halls and recreation buildings), especially on Sundays. According to the Reverend Arthur Takemoto, a young man during the internment period, Buddhist teachings such as those on suffering and patience helped alleviate the pain and confusion that many residents faced: "Understanding the basic tenets of Buddhism orients people to understand the reality of life, that things don't go the way we want them to go. This becomes *dukkha*, suffering and pain. To be able to accept a situation as it is means we could tolerate it more."

. . .

In this way, Buddhism not only provided a spiritual refuge for internees but also served the social function of maintaining family and communal cohesion through ancestral and life-cycle rituals and traditional Japanese festivals and ceremonies.

While Buddhism was, in this sense, a repository of Japanese traditions, it was also forced to operate in the context of an Americanization program promoted by the WRA. This program was organized to assimilate the Japanese and allow them to demonstrate loyalty to the United States. According to the *Investigation of Un-American Propaganda Activities in the United States* (1943) prepared by the Subcommittee of the U.S. House of Representatives Special Committee on Un-American Activities, camp administrators should promote recreational activities such as baseball and basketball as well as encourage internees to join groups such as the Boy and Girl Scouts and the YMCA/YWCA. Being Buddhist obviously was not listed as a method of demonstrating loyalty, but Buddhist groups made their own attempts at Americanization.

In May 1944, the name of the largest Buddhist organization in the Topaz Camp was changed from the Buddhist Mission of North America (BMNA) to the Buddhist Churches of America (BCA) to give the organization a more Christian-sounding name. The camp experience, however, only accelerated an assimilation process that had already begun prior to the war. The swastika symbol, often used on Buddhist temple stationery or on temple equipment prior to the internment, disappeared and was replaced almost universally by the dharma wheel. . . . By singing *gathas* as hymns, including Dorothy Hunt's "Onward Buddhist Soldiers" . . . Buddhists within the camp created a new medium for Americanizing Buddhism. They did so, however, in a way that honored their Buddhist traditions while simultaneously demonstrating loyalty to the United States. The young members of the community, having studied the Buddhist "Junior Catechism," for example, used a Christian medium to maintain Buddhist identity. Many of these elements constitute what might be called the Protestantization of Buddhism. . . .

As Buddhists attempted to find a place in mainstream American society, the English-speaking nisei also worked to gain a place for American Buddhism in the public sphere. They organized two closely related campaigns to remember the lives and sacrifices made by the many nisei servicemen who had served in the 100th/442nd in Europe or as translators and intelligence gatherers in the Pacific Theater's Military Intelligence Service. A war veteran and devout Buddhist, Tad Hirota, led a *B* for Buddhism campaign to have the army officially recognize Buddhists in the armed services by creating a *B* designation on dog tags. (During World War II, the military had only three official preferences: *P* for Protestant, *C* for Catholic, and *H* for Hebrew.) . . . After some deliberation, a compromise was reached in 1949 that designated *X* to be used on dog tags for anyone not of the existing three religious preferences. Furthermore, an additional dog tag could be supplied by the soldier's church or temple that would positively identify his religion. The National Young Buddhist Coordinating Council subsequently campaigned for a Buddhist symbol to be placed on the headstones of Buddhist veterans at national cemeteries. After petitions were sent to Secretary of Defense, Louis Johnson, the army agreed late in 1949 to inscribe the "Buddhist emblem" for American soldiers of the Buddhist faith. These two campaigns represent an important legacy of the camps, testing both Japanese American Buddhist loyalty to America and America's loyalty to its Buddhist citizens.

. . .

While the long history of the Japanese American Buddhist experience obviously holds lessons for more recent Asian American immigrant Buddhist groups, one wonders if the war and incarceration experience cannot also inform and illuminate the recent unfolding of a "new religious America," as Diana Eck puts it. In particular, one wonders whether the targeting and harassment of Muslim Americans, Arab Americans, and those who may look like those who were responsible for the 9/11 attacks (such as Sikhs and other south Asians) parallels the Japanese American experience following Pearl Harbor.

According to the Council on American-Islamic Relations, which was tracking anti-Muslim incidents long before 9/11, cases of discrimination and attacks have soared since that event. Ethnic and religious profiling at airports and workplaces as well as physical violence (including the shooting of Balbir Singh Sodhi, a Sikh gas station owner in Mesa, Arizona) recall the hate crimes and discrimination faced by Japanese Americans after

Pearl Harbor. Just as Japanese American Buddhist temples were vandalized and ancient Buddhist symbols, such as the swastikas (manji) that hung at temple doors, were riddled with shotgun fire by angry white neighbors, one saw an angry mob of three hundred people chanting "U.S.A., U.S.A." and marching on a mosque in Bridgeview, Illinois, right after 9/11. Whether it was the vandalizing of a Muslim bookstore in Alexandria, Virginia, on September 12, or someone shooting into a Dallas-area mosque, the Islamic Center of Irving, Islamic symbols quickly became targets for those caught up in war hysteria. "Visible religion," whether in dress or looks, combined with ethnic profiling has once again proved to be a factor in how American religious pluralism and tolerance are defined.

Just as hundreds of Buddhist priests were picked up by the FBI and hysterical claims were made that Buddhist bells were going to send Morse code message to the Japanese navy, the post-9/11 period has seen its share of indiscriminate arrests of thousands of young Muslim "enemy aliens" as well as the targeting of Muslim charitable organizations accused of having terrorist links. Many have developed the same kind of loyalty strategies as Japanese Americans did following Pearl Harbor: calls by organizations such as the American Muslim Council to cooperate with the FBI and support the president or drives to donate blood for the victims of the World Trade Center. While the rush to conversion, a strategy followed by some Japanese American Buddhists, is not an option for many Muslims, not only Muslims but also Sikhs and Hindus have sought ways of demonstrating loyalty to America, such as flying American flags or toning down religious or ethnic differences.

. . .

In the sixty years since Pearl Harbor, America has changed dramatically for Japanese Americans. In a June 2000 White House ceremony, President Bill Clinton bestowed the military's highest award, the Medal of Honor, on twenty-two Asian American war veterans. Japanese American veterans of the 442nd Regimental Combat Unit and the 100th Battalion, such as Senator Daniel Inoue (D-Hawaii), were honored for their valor in war. This action clearly signaled that Japanese Americans are no longer seen as foreigners. . . . Japanese American and Buddhist occupation of such high-profile public positions demonstrates a significant shift in America's religious, social, and political life. . . .

While the camp experience appears to have accelerated these types of post-war assimilationist tendencies—wanting to belong and to appear loyal—a lingering suspicion of mass incarceration and the denial of civil liberties for Muslim Americans remains strong among Japanese Americans, especially after the FBI brought in five thousand men, primarily of Arab and south Asian descent, for questioning in the domestic "war on terror." Within two and a half weeks of 9/11, two *New York Times* articles, "War on Terrorism Stirs Memory of Internment" and "Recalling Internment and Saying 'Never Again,'" chronicled what many Japanese Americans felt was a special responsibility to guard against ethnic scapegoating. Proclaiming that "we need to do everything that we wish good Americans had done 59 years ago," the executive director of the San Francisco Japanese American Cultural and Community Center, Paul Osaki, was one of many community leaders speaking out against violence and discrimination against Muslim Americans. On September 19, Japanese American leaders coordinated an unprecedented gathering of ethnic and religious leaders, including those from the American-Arab Anti-Discrimination Committee, the American Muslim Council, and the Council on American-Islamic Relations, to meet at the National Japanese American Memorial in Washington, D.C., and call for law enforcement officers and others to adequately address hate violence against religious and ethnic minorities.

. . .

Many Japanese Americans took on the conflicted identity of being a Japanese American Buddhist in the crucible of war. One wonders if 9/11 will also turn out to be similarly significant for Muslim Americans as they struggle with Americanization and resistance to it in their ethnic and religious identity formation.

55

A Somali Influx Unsettles Latino Meatpackers

Kirk Semple

Grand Island, Neb.—Like many workers at the meatpacking plant here, Raul A. Garcia, a Mexican-American, has watched with some discomfort as hundreds of Somali immigrants have moved to town in the past couple of years, many of them to fill jobs once held by Latino workers taken away in *immigration* raids.

Mr. Garcia has been particularly troubled by the Somalis' demand that they be allowed special breaks for prayers that are obligatory for devout Muslims. The breaks, he said, would inconvenience everyone else. "The Latino is very humble," said Mr. Garcia, 73, who has worked at the plant, owned by JBS U.S.A. Inc., since 1994. "But they are arrogant," he said of the Somali workers. "They act like the United States owes them."

Mr. Garcia was among more than 1,000 Latino and other workers who protested a decision last month by the plant's management to cut their work day—and their pay—by 15 minutes to give scores of Somali workers time for evening prayers. After several days of strikes and disruptions, the plant's management abandoned the plan. But the dispute peeled back a layer of civility in this southern Nebraska city of 47,000, revealing slow-burning racial and ethnic tensions that have been an unexpected aftermath of the enforcement raids at workplaces by federal immigration authorities.

Grand Island is among a half dozen or so cities where discord has arisen with the arrival of Somali workers, many of whom were recruited by employers from elsewhere in the United States after immigration raids sharply reduced their Latino work forces. The Somalis are by and large in this country legally as political refugees and therefore are not singled out by immigration authorities.

In some of these places, including Grand Island, this newest wave of immigrant workers has had the effect of unifying the other ethnic populations against the Somalis and has also diverted some of the longstanding hostility toward Latino immigrants among some native-born residents. "Every wave of immigrants has had to struggle to get assimilated," said Margaret Hornady, the mayor of Grand Island and a longtime resident of Nebraska. "Right now, it's so volatile."

The federal immigration crackdown has hit meat- and poultry-packing plants particularly hard, with more than 2,000 immigrant workers in at least nine places detained since 2006 in major raids, most on immigration violations. Struggling to fill the grueling low-wage jobs that attract few American workers, the plants have placed advertisements in immigrant newspapers and circulated fliers in immigrant neighborhoods.

Some companies, like Swift & Company, which owned the plant in Grand Island until being bought up by the Brazilian conglomerate JBS last year, have made a particular pitch for Somalis because of their legal status. Tens of thousands of Somali refugees fleeing civil war have settled in the United States since the 1990s, with the largest concentration in Minnesota. But the companies are learning that in trying to solve one problem they have created another.

Early last month, about 220 Somali Muslims walked off the job at a JBS meatpacking plant in Greeley, Colo., saying the company had prevented them from observing their prayer schedule. (More than 100 of the workers were later fired.) Days later, a poultry company in Minnesota agreed to allow Muslim workers prayer breaks and the right to refuse handling pork products, settling a lawsuit filed by nine Somali workers. In August, the management of a Tyson chicken plant in Shelbyville, Tenn., designated a Muslim holy day as a paid holiday, acceding to a demand by Somali workers. The plant had originally agreed to substitute the Muslim holy day for *Labor Day*, but reinstated Labor Day after a barrage of criticism from non-Muslims.

. . .

Nationwide, employment discrimination complaints by Muslim workers have more than doubled in the past decade, to 607 in the 2007 fiscal year, from 285 in the 1998 fiscal year, according to the federal *Equal Employment Opportunity Commission*, which has sent representatives to Grand Island to interview Somali workers. The Civil Rights Act of 1964 forbids employers to discriminate based on religion and says that employers must "reasonably accommodate" religious practices. But the act offers some exceptions, including instances when adjustments would cause "undue hardship" on the company's business interests.

The new tensions here extend well beyond the walls of the plant. Scratch beneath Grand Island's surface and there is resentment, discomfort and mistrust everywhere, some residents say—between the white community and the various immigrant communities; between the older immigrant communities, like the Latinos, and the newer ones, namely the Somalis and the Sudanese, another refugee community that has grown here in recent years; and between the Somalis, who are largely Muslim, and the Sudanese, who are largely Christian.

In dozens of interviews here, white, Latino and other residents seemed mostly bewildered, if not downright suspicious, of the Somalis, very few of whom speak English. "I kind of admire all the effort they make to follow that religion, but sometimes you have to adapt to the workplace," said Fidencio Sandoval, a plant worker born in Mexico who has become an American citizen. "A new culture comes in with their demands and says, 'This is what we want.' This is kind of new for me."

. . .

For their part, the Somalis say they feel aggrieved and not particularly welcome. "A lot of people look at you weird—they judge you," said Abdisamad Jama, 22, a Somali who moved to Grand Island two years ago to work as an interpreter at the plant and now freelances. "Or sometimes they will say, 'Go back to your country.'"

Founded in the mid-19th century by German immigrants, Grand Island gradually became more diverse in the mid- and late-20th century with the arrival of Latino workers, mainly Mexicans. The Latinos came at first to work in the agricultural fields; later arrivals found employment in the meatpacking plant. Refugees from Laos and, in the past few years, Sudan followed, and many of them also found work in the plant, which is now the city's largest employer, with about 2,700 workers.

In December 2006, in an event that would deeply affect the city and alter its uneasy balance of ethnicities, immigration authorities raided the plant and took away more than 200 illegal Latino workers. Another 200 or so workers quit soon afterward. The raid was one of six sweeps by federal agents at plants owned by Swift, gutting the company of about 1,200 workers in one day and forcing the plants to slow their operations.

Many of the Somalis who eventually arrived to fill those jobs were practicing Muslims and their faith obliges them to pray at five fixed times every day. In Grand Island, the workers would grab prayer time whenever they could, during scheduled rest periods or on restroom breaks. But during the holy month of *Ramadan*, Muslims fast in daylight hours and break their fast in a ritualistic ceremony at sundown. A more formal accommodation of their needs was necessary, the Somali workers said.

Last year, the Somalis here demanded time off for the Ramadan ceremony. The company refused, saying it could not afford to let so many workers step away from the production line at one time. Dozens of Somalis quit, though they eventually returned to work. The situation repeated itself last month. Dennis Sydow, the plant's vice president and general manager, said a delegation of Somali workers approached him on Sept. 10 about allowing them to take their dinner break at 7:30 p.m., near sundown, rather than at the normal time of 8 to 8:30.

Mr. Sydow rejected the request, saying the production line would slow to a crawl and the Somalis' co-workers would unfairly have to take up the slack. The Somalis said their co-workers did not offer a lot of support. "Latinos were sometimes saying, 'Don't pray, don't pray,'" said Abdifatah Warsame, 21.

After the Somalis went out on strike on Sept. 15, the plant's management and the union brokered a deal the next day that would have shifted the dinner break to 7:45 p.m., close enough to sundown to satisfy the Somalis. Because of the plant's complex scheduling rules, the new dinner break would have also required an earlier end to the shift, potentially cutting the work day by 15 minutes.

In a counterprotest on Sept. 17, more than 1,000 Latino and Sudanese workers lined up alongside white workers in opposition to the concessions to the Somalis. . . . The union and the plant management backed down, reverting to the original dinner schedule. More than 70 Somalis, including Mr. Warsame, stormed out of the plant and did not return; they either quit or were fired.

Since then, Ramadan has ended and work has returned to normal at the plant, but most everyone—management, the union and the employees—says the root causes of the disturbances have not been fully addressed. A sizeable Somali contingent remains employed at the factory—Somali leaders say the number is about 100; the union puts the figure at more than 300, making similar disruptions possible next year.

. . .

Xawa Ahmed, 48, a Somali, moved to Grand Island from Minnesota last month to help organize the Somali community. A big part of her work, Ms. Ahmed said, will be to help demystify the Somalis who remain. "We're trying to make people understand why we do these things, why we practice this religion, why we live in America," she said. "There's a lot of misunderstanding."

56

Jews in the U.S.

The Rising Costs of Whiteness

Melanie Kaye/Kantrowitz

BEFORE AMERICA NO ONE WAS WHITE

In 1990 I had returned to New York City to do antiracist work with other Jews, when a friend sent me an essay by James Baldwin. "No one was white before he/she came to America," Baldwin had written:

It took generations, and a vast amount of coercion, before this became a white country. . . . It is probable that it is the Jewish community—or more accurately, perhaps, its remnants—that in America has paid the highest and most extraordinary price for becoming white. For the Jews came here from countries where they were not white, and they came here in part because they were not white, and incontestably—in the eyes of the Black American (and not only in those eyes) American Jews have opted to become white. . . .

Everything I think about Jews, whiteness, racism, and contemporary U.S. society begins with this passage. What does it mean: *Jews opted to become white.* Did we opt? Did it work? Was it an illusion? Could we have opted otherwise? Can we still?

Rachel Rubin, a college student who's been interning at Jews for Racial and Economic Justice, where I'm the director, casually mentions: when she was eight, a cross was burned on her lawn in Athens, Georgia. I remember the house I moved into Down East Maine in 1979. On the bedroom door someone had painted a swastika in what looked like blood. I think about any cross-country drive I've ever taken, radio droning hymn after Christian hymn, 2000 miles of heartland.

On the other hand, I remember the last time I was stopped by cops. It was in San Francisco. I was getting a ride home after a conference on Jews and multiculturalism. In the car with me were two other white Jews. My heart flew into my throat, as always, but they took a quick look at the three of us and waved us on—*We're looking for a car like this, sorry.* I remember all the stories I've heard from friends, people of color, in which a quick look is not followed by a friendly wave and an apology. Some of these stories are about life and death.

Liberals and even progressives kneejerk to simplistic racial—black/white—terms, evade the continuing significance of race, and confound it with class. Race becomes an increasingly complex muddle. Growing numbers of bi- and multiracial children. *Hispanic*—not a racial identity, but a cultural/linguistic category conflating Spain with its former colonies. No one was *Asian* before they came to America, either; the term masks cultures diverse and polychromatic as anything Europe has to offer; yet *Asian American* has emerged as a critical and powerful identity. In the academy, obligatory nods to issues of race/class/gender result in language so specialized it's incomprehensible to most people, including those most pressured by these biases, and students tell me, "When Jews are mentioned in class, there's an awkward silence."

Where is *Jewish* in the race/class/gender grid? Does it belong? Is it irrelevant? Where do those crosses and swastikas fit in?

RACE OR RELIGION?

"Race or religion?" is how the question is usually posed, as though this doublet exhausts the possibilities. Christians—religiously observant or not—usually operate from the common self-definition of Christianity, a religion any individual can embrace through belief, detached from race, peoplehood, and culture.

But I have come to understand this detachment as false. Do white Christians feel kinship with African-American Christians? White slaveowners, for example, with their slaves? White Klansmen with their black neighbors? Do white Christians feel akin to Christians converted by colonialists all over the globe? Doesn't Christianity really, for most white Christians, imply *white*? And for those white Christians, does *white* really include *Jewish*? Think of the massive Christian evasion of a simple fact: Jesus Christ was not, was never, a

Christian. He was a Jew. What did he look like, Jesus of Nazareth, 2000 years ago? Blond, blue-eyed?

Of course Jewish is not a race, for Jews come in all races. Though white-identified Jews may skirt the issue, Jews are a multiracial people. There are Ethiopian, Indian, Chinese Jews. And there are people of every race who choose Judaism, or were adopted or born into it from mixed parents. The dominant conception of Jewish—European, Yiddish-speaking—is in fact a subset. Ashkenazi. Estimated at 85–97 percent of Jews in the U.S. today, Ashkenazi Jews are those whose religious practice and diaspora path can be traced through Germany. The huge wave of Jewish immigration from Eastern Europe was Ashkenazi (as was the earlier, much smaller, highly assimilated community of German Jews, who looked with dread upon the arrival of—from their perspective—an impoverished, Yiddish-babbling, superstitious horde). Ashkenazi Jews also migrated to the far points of the globe—to South America, Australia, Africa, Asia. They may be very fair or very dark.

Sephardic Jews are those whose mother tongue is/was Ladino (Judeo-Español) and whose religious practice and diaspora path can be traced at some point through the Iberian Peninsula (Spain and Portugal), where they flourished, unghettoized, contributing along with Muslims to Spanish culture, until the Inquisition (read: *torture*) forced conversion or expulsion from Spain of all non-Christians. Sephardim migrated to—and lived for generations and even centuries—in Holland, Germany, Italy, France, Greece, the Middle East, and the Americas. The first Jews in the New World were Sephardim: 1492 marks not only Columbus's voyage but also the expulsion of the Jews from Spain. Some Sephardim consider themselves the aristocrats of the Jews, and look with contempt upon the Ashkenazi history of ghettoization and persecution. They may also be quite fair or quite dark.

Mizrachi Jews are those who lived in the Arab world and Turkey (basically, what was once the Ottoman Empire), as minorities in Muslim rather than Christian culture. Their mother tongue often is/was Judeo-Arabic. *Mizrachi* means "Eastern," commonly translated as "Oriental," and is used by and about Israelis, often interchangeably with *Sephardim*. The Spanish Sephardim sometimes resent the blurring of distinctions between themselves and the Mizrachim, reacting with pride in their history and with Eurocentric bias against non-Europeans, referring to themselves as "true" or "pure" Sephardim. The confusion between the categories is only partly due to Ashkenazi ignorance/arrogance, lumping all non-Ashkenazi together. Partly, it's the result of Jewish history: some Jews never left the Middle East, and some returned after expulsion from Spain, including to Palestine. Some kept Ladino, some did not. I imagine there was intermarriage. Mizrachim, though they may also range from fair to dark, are usually defined as "people of color."

The point is, categories of white and color don't correspond neatly to Jewish reality. (What does correspond is Ashkenazi cultural hegemony—in the U.S., where they are dominant by numbers, and in Israel, where Sephardi/Mizrachi Jews make up about two-thirds of the Jewish population and strongly contest this hegemony.) Jewish wanderings have created a people whose experience eludes conventional categories of race, nationality, ethnicity, geography, language—even religion. Cataclysm and assimilation have depleted our store of common knowledge.

No, Jews are not a single race. Yet there is confusion here, and subtext. Confusion because we have so often been racialized, hated *as if* we were a race. Ethnic studies scholars have labored to document the process of racialization, the fact that race is not biological, but a sociohistorically specific phenomenon. Observing Jewish history, Nancy Ordover has noted, offers an opportunity to break down this process of racialization, because by leaving Europe, Jews changed our "race," even as our skin pigment remained the same.

For the Jews came here from countries where they were not white, and they came here in part because they were not white. . . .

Confusion, too, because to say someone *looks Jewish* is to say something both absurd (Jews look a million different ways) and commonsense communicative.

When I was growing up in Flatbush, Brooklyn, every girl with a certain kind of nose—sometimes named explicitly as a Jewish nose, sometimes only as "too big"—wanted a nose job, and if her parents could pay for it, often she got one. I want to be graphic about the euphemism *nose job*. A nose job breaks the nose, bruises the face and eye area like a grotesque beating. It hurts. It takes weeks to heal.

What was wrong with the original nose, the Jewish one? Noses were discussed ardently in Flatbush, this or that friend looking forward to her day of transformation. My aunts lavished on me the following exquisite praise: *Look at her—a nose like a shiksa* (gentile woman). This hurt my feelings. Before I knew what a *shiksa* was, I knew I wasn't it, and, with that fabulous integrity of children, I wanted to look like who I was. But later I learned my nose's value, and would tell gentiles this story so they'd notice my nose.

A Jewish nose, I conclude, identifies its owner as a Jew. Nose jobs are performed so that a Jewish woman does not look like a Jew.

Tell me again Jewish is just a religion.

Yet Nazi racial definitions have an "only a religion" response. Even earlier, the lure of emancipation (in Europe) and assimilation (in the U.S.) led Jews to define Judaism as narrowly as possible, as religion only: "a Jew at home, a man in the streets," a private matter, taken care of behind closed doors, like bathing.

Judaism, the religion, does provide continuity and connection to Jews around the globe. There is something powerful even for atheists about entering a synagogue across the continent or the ocean, and hearing the familiar service.

But to be a Jew one need not follow religious practice; one need not believe in god—not even to become a rabbi (an element of Judaism of which I am especially fond). Religion is only one strand of being Jewish. It is ironic that it is precisely this century's depletion of Jews and of Jewish identity, with profound linguistic and cultural losses—continuing as Yiddish and Ladino speakers age and die—that makes imaginable a Jewishness that is *only a religion*—only now, when so much else has been lost. But to reduce *Jewishness* to *Judaism* is to forget the complex indivisible swirl of religion, culture, language, history that *was* Jewishness until, in the eighteenth century, Emancipation began to offer some Jews the possibility of escaping from a linguistically/culturally/economically isolated ghetto into the European "Enlightenment." To equate Jewishness with religion is to forget how even the contemporary, often attenuated version of this Jewish cultural swirl is passed down *in the family*, almost like genetic code.

Confusion and subtext. *Jewish* is often trivialized as something you choose, a preference, like tea over coffee. In contrast with visible racial identity, presumptions of choice—as with gayness—are seen as minimizing one's claim to attention, sympathy, and remedy. As a counter to bigotry, *I was born like this* strategically asserts a kind of victim-status, modeled on race, gender, and disability: If you can't help yourself, maybe you're entitled to some help from others. . . .

What happens if, instead, I assert my right to choose and not suffer for it. To say, *I choose*—my lesbianism and my Jewishness. Choose to come out, be visible, embrace both. I could live loveless or sexless or in the closet. I could have kept the name *Kaye*, and never once at Christmas—in response to the interminable "What are you doing for . . . ? Have you finished your shopping?"—answer, "I don't celebrate Christmas. I'm a Jew." I could lie about my lover's gender. I could wear skirts uncomfortably. I could bleach my hair again, as I did when I was fifteen. I could monitor my speech, weeding out the offensive accent, as I was taught at City College, along with all the other first and second generation immigrants' children in the four speech classes required for graduation, to teach us not to sound like ourselves. I could remain silent when queer or anti-Semitic jokes are told, or when someone says, "You know how *they* are." I could endure the pain in the gut, the hot shame. I could scrunch up much, much smaller.

In the U.S., *Christian*, like *white*, is an unmarked category in need of marking. Christianness, a majority, dominant culture, is not about religious practice and belief, any more than Jewishness is. As *racism* names the system that normalizes, honors, and rewards whiteness, we need a word for what normalizes, honors and rewards Christianity. Jews designate the assumption of Christianity-as-norm, the erasure of Jews, as *anti-Semitic*. In fact, the erasure and marginalization of non-Christians is not just denigrating to Jews. We need a catchier term than *Christian hegemony* to help make visible the cultural war against all non-Christians.

Christianism? Awkward, stark, and kind of crude—maybe a sign that something's being pushed; *sexism* once sounded stark and kind of crude. Such a term would help contextualize Jewish experience as an experience of marginality shared with other non-Christians. Especially in this time of rising Christian fundamentalism, as school prayer attracts support from "moderates," this contextualization is critical for progressive Jews, compelling us to seek allies among Muslims and other religious minorities.

I also want to contextualize Jews in a theoretical framework outside the usual bipolar frame of black/white—to go beyond dualism; to distinguish race from class, and both from culture; to understand whiteness as the gleaming conferral of normality, success, even survival; to acknowledge who owns what, and in whose neighborhood; to witness how money does and does not "whiten."

> *For in the eyes of the Black American (and not only in those eyes) American Jews have opted to become white. . . .*

To begin to break out of a polarity that has no place for Jews, I survey the range of color in the United States. People of color, a unity sought and sometimes forged, include a vast diversity of culture and history, forms of oppression and persecution. Contemporary white supremacists hate them all, but define some as shrewd, evil, inscrutable, sexually exotic, and perverse, and others as intellectually inferior, immoral, bestial, violent, and sexually rapacious. If it is possible to generalize, we can say that the peoples defined as shrewd and evil tend to be better off economically—or at least *perceived* as better off economically— than those defined as inferior and violent, who tend to remain in large numbers stuck at the bottom of the economic ladder (and are assumed by the dominant culture to be stuck there), denied access to decent jobs and opportunities, systematically disadvantaged and excluded by the educational system.

In other words, among the creeping fearsome dark ones are, on the one hand, those who exploit, cheat, and hoard money they don't deserve, and, on the other, those (usually darker) who, not having money, threaten to rob and pillage hard-working tax-paying white Christians. In this construct, welfare fits as a form of robbery, the women's form; the men are busy mugging. Immigrant bashing—whether street violence or political movements like "English-only" and California's overwhelming passage of Proposition 187—becomes a "natural" response to "robbery."

It is easier now to see where Jews fit: we are so good with money. Our "darkness" may not show, and this ability to pass confers protection and a host of privileges. But we are the model money-grubbing money-hoarding scapegoats for an increasingly punitive economic system. Jews, Japanese, Koreans, Arabs, Indians, and Pakistanis—let's face it: *interlopers*—are blamed for economic disaster; for controlling the economy or making money on the backs of the poor; for raising the price of oil; for stealing or eliminating jobs by importing goods or exporting production.

At the same time, those defined as inferior and violent are blamed for urban crime and chaos, for drugs, for the skyrocketing costs and failures of social programs. This blame then justifies the oppression and impoverishment of those brought here in chains and the peoples indigenous to this continent. Add in the darker, poorer immigrants from Latin America and the Caribbean, and recent immigrants from China and Southeast Asia. Media codes like "inner-city crime" and "teen gangs" distort and condense a vast canvas of poverty, vulnerability, and exploitation into an echoing story of some young men's violent response to these conditions. Thus those who are significantly endangered come to be defined as inherently dangerous.

That is, one group is blamed for capitalism's crimes; the other for capitalism's fallout. Do I need to point out who escapes all blame?

When a community is scapegoated, members of that community are most conscious of how they feel humiliated, alienated, and endangered. But the other function of scapegoating is at least as pernicious. It is to protect the problem which scapegoats are drafted to conceal: the vicious system of profit and exploitation, of plenty and scarcity existing side by side.

THE COST OF WHITENESS

Aryan ideology aside, Jews are often defined as white, though this wipes out the many Jews who are by anyone's definition people of color, and neglects the role of context: many Jews who look white in New York City look quite the opposite in the South and Midwest. Radicals often exclude the category *Jewish* from discussion, or subsume us into *white*, unless we are by *their* definition also people of color, in which case they subsume us as *people of color*.

The truth is, Jews complicate things. *Jewish* is both a distinct category and an overlapping one. Just as homophobia is distinct from sexism yet has everything to do with sexism, anti-Semitism in this country is distinct from racism yet has everything to do with racism. It's not that a Jew like myself should "count" as a person of color, though I think sometimes Jews do argue this because the alternative seems to be erasure. But that means we need another alternative. The problem is a polarization of white and color that excludes us. We need a more complex vision of the structure of racism, one that attends to the sick logic of white supremacists. We need a more complex understanding of the process of "whitening."

57

Oral History of Adam Fattah

Amna Ahmad

I used to wear a little charm around my neck that said *Allah* in Arabic, so naturally people in my school would identify me as Muslim. The Muslim population at my school is also definitely significant, so it's not very difficult to point us out.

. . .

I had a government teacher who used to talk about religion in my class. He used to speak about how all religions—though he focused mainly on talking about Judaism, Islam, and Christianity—can be considered very similar. He used to put the words "Judaism," "Islam," and "Christianity" on the board and write all the characteristics they had in common, such as prayer and the concept of fasting. He actually made sense in the way he approached the idea of likening one religion to another and definitely inspired an interest in me in the topic. . . .

While many of my teachers seem to approach the topic of Islam respectfully, as was the case with my government class teacher, the administration at my high school has made it inconvenient for me to practice my religion. Unfortunately they don't allow students a place to pray during school. Once I had actually gone to my guidance counselor to set up my schedule for the following term and asked her to switch my last period class, which was gym, with my lunch period so that I would have been able to leave school early enough to go to the mosque and pray. My guidance counselor simply would not allow that. As a result of her obvious indifference, I missed an entire term of going to the mosque on Fridays for Jummah prayer. I viewed myself as being at a huge disadvantage and was really upset about the situation. . . .

Sometimes, it seems as though Islamic practices are barely tolerable for administrators. Every so often I feel like I'm being penalized for putting religion before education. This year especially, I'm taking very difficult classes and to take off for three days because of the Eid is hard because I have to miss three days of very difficult work. I can usually only take off for one day of those three because otherwise I would miss more work than I could possibly make up. I often spend entire weekends just focusing on making up the work that I miss. That puts me very far behind. The Islamic holiday season becomes very stressful, and stress is something I really don't need in my life right now. Every time I have to take off for a Muslim holiday I end up having to explain to a teacher or fight with a teacher who argues, "There's no NYC Board of Ed law recognizing it as a holiday. You can't take off on Muslim holidays." . . .

Every so often, I feel as though it is more difficult to be the parent of a Muslim child than a Muslim student when dealing with the complications of the world of academia. A few years ago, my mother went to a parent-teacher conference for my brother, Muhamad. . . . I remember my mother's facial expression when she got home and I was immediately affected by the clear discontentment she expressed following the brief visit. My mother took the seat in front of Muhammad's math teacher when her turn had come. The math teacher was being very condescending and she looked down on my mother because she was wearing the veil, which is a key aspect of Islamic culture. She assumed right away that my mother didn't speak very good English. She spoke to her in language that was choppy, with a face that was uninviting to someone who was meeting her for the first time. With little concern for making a good first impression on a parent, she seemed to presume that my mother wasn't very well educated. When my mother started speaking to her after keeping silent for the first few minutes, it because clear to the teacher that she had been wrong. The math teacher was surprised by the fact that my mother was very well educated and spoke perfect English once she was given a chance. My mother has a bachelor's degree and two master's degrees. She herself is a teacher and was so affected by this feeling of being belittled by a stranger. She knew that she would never approach a parent in a way that communicates such degradation and disrespect. I don't think I would have thought the teacher's approach was motivated by prejudice had I not seen it in the red of my mother's eyes when she returned home to tell the story.

I would never have put too much consideration into connecting my Muslim identity with the more adverse experiences I have had in my life had I not seen it in the eyes of the woman who was prevented from attending school by immigrant parents who didn't know better; the woman who went back to college after raising three boys into maturity.

57 (CONTINUED)

Oral History of Hagar Omran

Hoda Zawam

I identify myself as an Arab American. That's what I am because I was born here. I'm an American, but I'm not like every other American. I spice up the average American by being an Arab American because I have merged both cultures together. It's just like adding rainbow sprinkles on vanilla ice cream.

I am Egyptian and so are both of my parents. Even though I was born and raised here, my parents really stick to Egyptian culture. We eat a lot of Egyptian food. We listen to Arabic music and are very family oriented. . . .

I started wearing the hijab when I was a 6th grader. It wasn't hard for me because it doesn't really matter how I look—I'm still the same person from the inside. . . . My friends were cool and they all wore hijab and they made hijab look good, fun, and easy. Hijab makes me feel proud and it makes me stand out because everyone knows that I'm Muslim. Hijab is not a burden on me, rather it's a pleasure.

I'm an 11th grader in high school. My school is nice and it's pretty cool. But it's not fair that our holidays are not considered government holidays and we don't get time off, just like the Christians get off for Christmas, and the Jews get off for Hanukah. Now that we're a big population in America and we are not a minority anymore, we should get our rights. Another problem is the absence of halal food in schools. So, I don't feel that Muslims are treated equally in this country. . . .

I will never forget the day after September 11th when I went back to school. All of my friends said, "It couldn't be you guys. You guys are really good." My friends reacted this way because they know me, my personality and my family.

But then it was different with strangers after September 11th. We got stereotyped, like when this one guy that came up to me and said, "You immigrant! Go back to your country. You freakin' Arab terrorist!" I was in shock. The first thing I said to him was, "This is my country. I was born and raised here. I'm not an immigrant and neither am I a terrorist!" He was stupefied that I was able to speak such good English and at the fact that I am an American. His reaction was a result of ignorance because he automatically assumed that if you're wearing the hijab that you're an immigrant and you can't speak English. I really don't understand why when one person does something wrong, the whole Muslim community and religion gets blamed for it.

I hate when people assume things about me and believe all the stereotypes that they hear. They believe stereotypes like all Arabs are terrorists and all the girls that wear the hijab are oppressed and forced to wear it. I think all these stereotypes are wrong and they come from ignorance. If you inform the public about these wrong assumptions they'll change their minds about the Muslim community on the whole. I think that Muslims are not depicted correctly here in America, especially through the media.

V
O
I
C
E
S

One story I experienced dealing with stereotypes was with one of my teachers who brought in a cartoon called "The Veil." He then asked the class, "What do you guys think about that?" All the responses were around the same line: oppression, suppression, no women's rights, Taliban, sexism, forced, and sympathy. Since I was the only hijabi in my class my teacher asked me, "What do you think about this cartoon?" I responded by explaining that what everyone thinks are stereotypes, and that none of it was true. I told them how the veil is supposed to protect women, keep them modest, keep them focused, help them respect themselves and others, and keep them pure of heart and soul. Islam values women and it treats them as jewels to be protected. I explained to them that the hijab brings out your personality not your looks. Women are not supposed to be talked to because of their looks or how big their boobs are or their butt or something. It's supposed to be about your personality. When you wear the hijab, it's not like a guy is going to check you out, look you up and down. He's going to talk to you because of your personality, not the way you look. Hijab makes me proud that I'm Muslim and it makes me respect my own body, myself, and it also makes other people respect me.

So as you can see I'm not weird and bizarre, even if I'm not the norm. I am different and unique. I can do fun things like going to beaches, pools, ice skating, skiing, paintballing, biking, and rollerblading. And, I do swim, believe or not, with my hijab. I have fun because I am a normal human being like you are, but I can do it all while I'm fully covered. I also have a life, a family that loves me, a God that cares for me, and a God that I pray to five times a day. I mean what more can you want from life when you are loved, know where your right path is? I want to finish school, get a good education, and get a good career. I want to represent the Muslim community as intelligent, educated, and civilized. I want to take part in raising the standards of the Muslim Ummah and benefiting them.

58

Creating Identity-Safe Spaces on College Campuses for Muslim Students

Na'ilah Suad Nasir and Jasiyah Al-Amin

. . .

The current national political context has brought Islam (as both a practice and an identity) into the media forefront. The events of 9/11 and the resulting war in Iraq have sparked renewed interest in the religion of Islam and the life of Muslims. One only has to visit any chain bookstore to notice an explosion of books on Islam, terrorism, and Islamic extremists. Unfortunately, this attention has been largely negative, and Muslim communities across the nation are increasingly fearful of discrimination and even violence. This context has made the discussion that we undertake in this article of the issues faced by Muslim college students at once more difficult and more important.

In this brief commentary, we explore some issues that arise for Muslim students on college campuses, drawing on both our own personal experiences and discussions and interviews with Muslim students from a wide range of college campuses. . . .

We begin with the stories of two students from different backgrounds and with very different experiences on their respective campuses.

N E X T   S T E P S

RASHID

Rashid is a tall, African-American young man with a ready smile and playful eyes, who carries himself with dignity and humility. In our interview he wore an indigo-blue African-style long dashiki and loose pants. He grew up in a medium-sized Northern California city in a family that has struggled through economic and other woes. He won a full basketball scholarship to a well-know institution in another (but still liberal) state. Like many students, college was his first experience living out of the state, and the transition, while exciting, was a bit unsettling. But he adjusted to his new environment well and enjoyed a central role on the basketball team and a good relationship with his coach and teammates. Although he was raised a Christian, he started reading about Islam his freshman year and converted during his sophomore year. He describes this as the turning point in his life on campus.

Rashid's conversion shifted, first and foremost, his relationship with his coach, who was suspicious of Islam. He accused Rashid of becoming a black nationalist, of hating whites, and of being racist. After his junior year, he asked Rashid not to return to the team. Rashid then became active in the largely international Muslim student group on campus and declared Islamic studies as a second major. Here he encountered another obstacle—a non-Muslim Islamic-studies professor who was openly hostile to him and derogatory about Islam.

FATIMA

Fatima is a soft-spoken (almost shy) young woman, with a bit of hesitancy in her voice that lessens as she gets more passionate about her topic. At our interview she wore jeans and a college sweatshirt with a white scarf over her hair, pinned under her chin. Although her father is from Pakistan, Fatima grew up in the same state where she attends college, but in a different region. She says the Muslim community wasn't her first priority in choosing a college, although she knew it was important, partly because her oldest brother (who was already in college and active in the Muslim Student Association in another state when she was choosing a college) told her so.

Her experience as a Muslim on her liberal college campus has been a positive one. She reported no instances of prejudice, and she said she feels involved with both the Muslim community and the broader community on campus. About a month before we spoke with her, Fatima had made a decision, which for her was a step in the practice of her faith—to wear *hijab*. Her biggest problem on campus was finding a place to pray and make *wudu* (a special way of washing up for prayer). She expressed concern about how she is perceived and about stereotypes of "oppressed" foreign Muslim women.

These two stories illustrate some of the variation in Muslim students' experiences on college campuses, which have to do both with characteristics of the student (including class, race, gender, and types of support needed) and characteristics of the campuses and their surrounding communities (including how "liberal" the campus is, the presence of Islamic student groups on campus, and the existence and constitution of the Islamic studies faculty). However, there are also important convergences in their accounts. Below we consider several core issues that these stories illustrate (and that others' experiences corroborate).

N
E
X
T

S
T
E
P
S

THE BURDEN OF MANAGING A POTENTIALLY "RISKY" IDENTITY

All of the students we talked to described (in one way or another) the burden of constantly feeling that others were judging them in terms of negative stereotypes about Islam, such as "Muslim terrorist" or "oppressed Muslim woman." Interestingly, this fear has much more to do with a perception of potential threat than any actual acts of prejudice or discrimination. . . .

For the students we interviewed, this threat became particularly salient in moments of practicing Islam (such as praying while on campus), where they felt vulnerable and highly visible. Since Muslim students need to pray five times a day, they constantly have to search out places to do so, such as an empty classroom. One student noted, "You have to find a place to pray, so you look like you are sneaking, then you find a room, and people are thinking, what is she doing in there?" This student revealed her anxiety that others may judge her as sneaky or strange.

. . .

AN IDENTITY-THREATENING ENVIRONMENT AND
LOWERED ACADEMIC ACHIEVEMENT

This anxiety about the stereotypes that the Muslim identity might trigger also affects students' academic performance. . . . While our sample was not systematic or representative, we did observe that students who reported more discrimination and contention tended to perform more poorly academically. For instance, while Fatima, a biology major, is in excellent academic standing, Rashid left his university several units short of graduating, returning several years later to complete his degree. Most students we talked to had not been actively denigrated, but they felt taxed by the need to constantly manage others' impressions of them. This identity-management process required energy and time that could have been devoted to their studies.

A hostile environment also made students want to distance themselves emotionally, and such distancing sometimes resulted in a disconnection not just from that particular campus community but from school in general. In some cases, Muslim students reported that the experience of prejudice (at worst) and lack of understanding (at best) on the part of their professors affected their academic performance more directly. For example, Rashid's contentious relationship with the Islamic-studies professor resulted in his refusal to do some of the readings for the course (because he felt that they misrepresented the Muslim experience) and contributed to his low grades in the several courses with that professor that he needed to take for his second major.

AN IDENTITY-SAFE ENVIRONMENT AND WELL-BEING

While academic performance is certainly an important effect of a welcoming campus environment, students' feelings of well-being are perhaps equally significant. That is, students should feel positive about life and grow as people during their college years. They should feel whole and healthy. Our conversations made it clear that students who found their university environment supportive of their practice of Islam, who felt that they were accepted as Muslims and as students and who didn't feel penalized or ostracized, were able to grow in the practice of their faith at their own pace and with full confidence.

For instance, two of the female students we interviewed (both of whom were raised Muslim) spoke of deciding during their college careers to begin wearing *hijab* on campus. They reported the relief and acceptance they felt at receiving compliments on how they looked with the scarf on from both Muslims and non-Muslims. The first day Fatima wore *hijab* on campus, one of her professors told her that she looked beautiful. This remark made her feel good about this step in her faith.

. . .

CONFLUENCE OF GENDER, RACE, RELIGION, AND CLASS

Our two stories illustrate another important point about negotiating Islam on college campuses: Islamic identity interacts with other identities to color both how a student is perceived by others and how he responds to such perceptions. It is significant that Rashid is Muslim, male, African-American, and physically imposing (he is tall and muscular), as he noted in our conversation with him. It may also be significant that he is a first-generation college student from a working-class family, since his resources for surviving college are fewer than those of more affluent or system-savvy students. We might note that the response of the basketball coach to his becoming Muslim was a largely racialized response—the coach objected to what he judged as a black-nationalist political philosophy and feared that Islam would make Rashid too radical regarding race and politics.

We see in Rashid's story that negative reactions to him were compounded by the fact that he belongs to multiple stigmatized groups. He not only has to negotiate being Muslim on a largely non-Muslim campus but also being African-American on a largely white campus, as well as a student athlete (which makes him highly visible and subject to scrutiny). He was explicitly told that he couldn't be both a black male athlete and a serious student activist, but that he had to choose between the two. Then, once his identity as a Muslim caused him to be released from the basketball team and he turned to his school work more seriously, he encountered resistance from others as he attempted to take up a "serious-student" identity.

In other work we have named these sets of identities "identity constellations" to capture the idea that people have not just one but multiple, sometimes conflicting, identities. The opportunity to reorganize these sets is more or less available in different contexts. Indeed in some environments, students are asked to choose among the various identities within these constellations, as Rashid's story shows. He (and other African-American students) talked about the feeling that they must decide whether to affiliate with the Muslim or the African-American campus community. A female student joked that before she began wearing *hijab*, the Muslims on campus didn't speak to her, but once she began covering, the African-American students stopped speaking to her. Such forced choices make students feel as though they have to privilege one aspect of their identities to the detriment of other equally important parts of themselves.

SMALL COMFORTS AND ACTS OF KINDNESS

Our final point is a brief one, but it is critically important. When we asked students about what made their experiences as Muslims positive, they invariably mentioned incidents that

NEXT STEPS

seemed to us quite trivial—for instance, professors who acknowledged Ramadan or who complimented them on wearing *hijab*. One student noted with great fondness the special dinner and breakfast packets the dining hall provided during Ramadan. These small acts of kindness were highly valued by students and made a huge difference to their sense that both they and the practice of their religion belonged on campus.

Other things that make campuses more identity-safe for Muslim students include:

- A strong, diverse, and supportive Muslim student group on campus;
- Professors who are knowledgeable about Islam and positive towards it (this especially includes the Islamic-studies professors, since this program is where students often go in order to learn about themselves and to feel connected and supported);
- The presence of a broader student community that is accepting of Islam and its practices;
- Access to physical spaces that facilitate the practice of Islam without ridicule or judgment (for instance, having a private place to pray and wash up for prayer);
- Access to *halal* meals (foods that don't contain pork and for which meats are slaughtered in a particular way) and the accommodation of the special meal times (before sunrise and after sundown) during the month of Ramadan.

CONCLUDING THOUGHTS

While this article has focused on Muslim students, we'd like to conclude with a more global perspective on the important work of supporting all students' religious practices and identities (as well as other dimensions of difference) on college campuses. . . . The idea that it benefits the larger organization to encourage the development of individuals in their respective communities is reflected in the experience of the students whose stories appear here. . . .

NEXT STEPS

59

Faith-Based, Multiethnic Tenant Organizing

The Oak Park Story

Russell Jeung

On a bright San Francisco morning in the fall of 2000, an unlikely group emerged laughing from an ornate skyscraper. Among the three dozen assembled were undocumented residents from Mexico, a European American minister, Cambodian refugees, and a Taiwanese American city planner. They had just won almost one million dollars from their landlord in one of the largest legal settlements of its kind . In addition to winning monetary damages for forty-four households, the group's victory transformed the complex into brand new apartments that are held permanently at affordable rents. Overcoming obstacles of race and class, the Oak Park Tenants Association is a model of faith-based, multiethnic community organizing.

This housing victory was unlikely because it involved primarily Latinos, some of whom avoid the government for documentation reasons, and Cambodians, who had been tortured by their government. Linguistic isolation prevented them from understanding the American legal system or fully integrating into this society. And because the tenants were on public assistance or worked as day laborers, they could not afford other housing if they were to be forced out. Despite these fears and structural barriers, the tenants organized against substandard living conditions that threatened their health and safety. Remarkably, these two ethnic groups joined together as a tenants association and remained united throughout the three-year struggle. . . .

THEORIES OF SOCIAL CAPITAL AND COMMUNITY ORGANIZING

Both social movement research and community organizing literature assert that social capital is a necessary factor for group mobilization. . . . This capital may be "bridging" and encompass people across social cleavages, or it may be "bonding" and reinforce exclusive identities. For example, religious institutions may bridge Latinos and Asians as they attend a Catholic church and connect them to job opportunities offered by other parishioners. On the other hand, a Buddhist temple may merely bond those who are Thai because of the language and rituals employed. . . .

Faith-based organizers . . . can draw upon networks established within congregations. . . . Networks of faith-based organizations offer space where multiethnic groups can cooperate and participate in politics. Organizers in these faith-based, immigrant networks have utilized four key principles that they have found to be successful. First, they apply the "Iron Rule" that organizers should not do for others what they can do for themselves. Instead they aim to develop local leadership and organizational capacity so that groups themselves can voice and lobby for their concerns. Second, immigrants organize around issues of self-interest that tend to be broad based. . . . Third, faith-based organizers recognize that ethnic faith-based institutions offer great networking opportunities. . . . Lastly, organizing immigrants requires an understanding of the group's history and traditions, as well as their community strengths. . . . This case study of Oak Park involves immigrants coming from Buddhist, Catholic, and evangelical Protestant backgrounds. . . .

OAK PARK APARTMENTS: HISTORY AND DEMOGRAPHICS

Oak Park Apartments originally was a fifty-six-unit apartment complex in the San Antonio/Fruitvale district of Oakland, California. The one-bedroom apartments all faced a central courtyard, which filled with scores of children after school. With an average family size of more than six persons, Oak Park children had to sleep in the living rooms. In fact, the complex was well known for being an over-crowded tenement for recently arrived refugees.

Oak Park's neighborhood is an exemplar of an impoverished, underclass barrio. According to the 2000 U.S. Census, the community was 52 percent Hispanic, 25 percent Asian, 16 percent African American, 3 percent white, and 1 percent Native American or

NEXT STEPS

Pacific Islander. . . . One-third of the families in the neighborhood were below the poverty level and 62 percent had not completed high school.

Those living at Oak Park were even worse off than their neighbors. The Cambodians, who arrived in the mid-1980s, had gone through the genocidal killing fields of the Pol Pot regime and still suffer greatly from posttraumatic stress syndrome. . . . The ravages of war and the refugee experience created such dislocation that few could concentrate to learn English and gain meaningful employment. . . . By the mid-1990s, 45 percent of Oak Park households were Cambodian, 45 percent were Latino . . .

Another group came to Oak Park in the 1990s, but religious faith connected them rather than ethnic bonds. In the late 1980s, a nonprofit organization, Harbor House, began offering English as a Second Language (ESL) tutoring at Oak Park as part of its Christian ministry to refugees. . . . I moved to Oak Park in 1992 to do participant observation research with Southeast Asian youth. As we got to know our neighbors, they began to ask for assistance, so . . . [we] began a tutoring program, ESL classes, and a mentorship group for boys. Other college graduates interested in doing urban ministry came to volunteer, and by 1997 evangelical Christians rented five Oak Park units. Soon independent from Harbor House and loosely organized as Oak Park Ministries (OPM), this collection of whites, Latinos, and Chinese Americans brought in other volunteers to run the programs. . . .

OAK PARK'S HOUSING CONDITIONS

. . .

In the winter of 1997–98, El Nino rains flooded the Oak Park courtyard, backed up the sewers, and leaked through the roof. Gabrielle Alvarez, wife of Francisco Martinez, remembers how sewage ruined their entire apartment: "Around 1998 all the filth started coming out of the bathroom. We went to do the wash and when we returned, the whole hallway, everything was full of water! At that time I didn't have the money to just go somewhere else to sleep with my kids. And it was worse when it dried. A smell lingered that no one could stomach. It took two days to clean up, but the smell lasted more than a week." . . . Trash littered the building, the complex lacked fire extinguishers, and extermination service was a rarity. Mice and roaches overran the complex. . . . Although the tenants complained about the lack of security at Oak Park and about the housing conditions, the management did not respond.

Inside apartments, mold blackened entire walls as the rains brought about damp conditions. The environmental conditions created by the mold and roaches led to extremely high asthma rates at Oak Park. That year, at least eight households had to make emergency room visits because of asthma attacks. Later, when we tested six children from three different households, all had mold spores found in their bloodstream. Unfortunately, because of their lack of income, the families had to endure these conditions as their children became sick.

OPM members living at Oak Park suffered through the same conditions. A three-by-five-foot piece of the ceiling, under the weight of gallons of rainwater, fell onto one woman's bed. During a shower, another tenant's hand went through the rotted bathroom wall when he tried to brace himself against it. By the end of 1997, OPM members began to take more decisive actions.

NEXT STEPS

BONDS OF TENANT SOLIDARITY: BUILDING UPON ETHNIC SOCIAL CAPITAL

To organize their fellow tenants at Oak Park, OPM members drew upon the respective ethnic bonds of the Cambodians and Latinos. Along with calling upon the trust and respect that they had earned from their neighbors, they were able to form the Oak Park Tenants Association to take a collective stand. By helping tenants recognize their common concerns, they helped establish the group identity of the tenants association.

As stated earlier, both the ethnic communities possessed extended familial networks within Oak Park. Francisco Martinez and Gabrielle Alvarez vocally supported the lawsuit and facilitated organizing through their relationships with others at Oak Park. Gabrielle Alvarez was close to her next-door neighbors, who would cook and sell tamales together. Francisco Martinez developed friendships with men of other Spanish-speaking households and assisted them in getting work. These personal ties later would provide the trust necessary to work together in suing the landlord.

In addition, the ESL classes encouraged further face-to-face interaction and group activity, especially among the Cambodian tenants. At the twice-a-week ESL classes, mothers would share stories of their past and their daily concerns. The year following the stabbing of the Mexican tenant, these Cambodians decided to continue their New Year festivities but invited Latino participation in a community potluck. Over three hundred persons celebrated together that year. Salsa music followed tunes of traditional Khmer folkdances, with the Macarena being played every third song. . . .

Because the tenants were accustomed to meeting in the apartments of OPM members for party planning, ESL classes, or potlucks, they did not hesitate to attend meetings regarding Oak Park's living conditions. In the first tenants' meeting with Oak Park management in December 1997, representatives identified their most serious issues: leaking roofs, sewage problems, security, and infestation. The management claimed that plans were under way to renovate the buildings, but the meeting devolved into a shouting match, and even greater mistrust of the landlord resulted. . . . OPM then met with each household individually, asking them about the damages caused by rain and mold and informing them of their housing rights. . . .

Once a few other tenants agreed to sue, OPM called larger group meetings. These group meetings especially capitalized on the close ties of the ethnic groups. For Khmer translation, we obtained the free services of Suon In, a leader at the Cambodian Buddhist Temple and staff person for Asian Community Mental Health Services. His involvement at the temple made a recognized and trusted partner in the organizing effort. Carlos Flores, one of the OPM members, worked as a community organizer for another nonprofit and used his language skills to facilitate the Spanish-speaking meeting. He explained his approach toward organizing: "People have a desire to make things better for themselves, to make things that are unjust just. But a lot of times, people don't know how to do so even though they see something is really wrong. Organizing brings a broader perspective of the wider, systemic injustices. God really wants justice to happen, so organizing people for justice on earth brings hope to people and a wider perspective. And that's related to my faith in the gospel."

. . .

The personal relationships that OPM organizers had formed with their fellow tenants were another form of bonding social capital. Having attended their marriages and funerals, tutored their children, and acted as their English teachers, OPM members built particularly strong ties with the Cambodians. We traded on this earned respect to gather the tenants to group meetings and secure a hearing. . . .

NEXT STEPS

The family ties and close interactions promoted ethnic social capital, but they also led to ethnic divisions. To overcome mistrust and segregation, OPM attempted to forge a group identity as tenants. Large trilingual group meetings, held in our cramped living room, brought the ethnic groups together. In these sessions, Martinez recognized that the tenants shared the same issues: "For my part, when we joined the lawsuit nobody knew if we were going to win or not. What helped us was when we all got together. You know the saying; 'There is strength in numbers'? In these apartments there are many tenants. If we all have the same problems, like with the electricity coming and going, and we come together, we can do anything."

. . .

With high amounts of trust and reciprocity, forty-four of the fifty-six house-holds at Oak Park joined the lawsuit by February 1998, much to the surprise of the attorney. In total, we had 197 plaintiffs in our case, almost all of whom were noncitizen, limited English-speaking, and low-income immigrants.

SUSTAINING THE LAWSUIT: BRIDGING SOCIAL CAPITAL

. . .

In June 1999 the landlords claimed corporate bankruptcy and the building went into federal receivership. The tenants association discussed mass relocation to other sites as a likely event. More vacant units became boarded so that Oak Park looked increasingly like an abandoned slum. In October 1999, Section 8 officials gave thirty-day notices to the grandmothers Pheng and Chen because Oak Park failed to pass their inspections.

These events would have broken the tenants association if not for continued media attention. In October 1999, reporters gathered again at Oak Park to hear that De La Fuente's Decent Housing Task Force had named it as one of the city's seven worst slums. The press, both mainstream and ethnic, helped the tenants feel that they were not alone in their cause. Sarah Prum stated: "News about the lawsuit with Oak Park was even on the news in Long Beach. People I know there called and asked me what was going on and asked me what I was doing on the news." This attention further strengthened the tenants' ethnic social capital in that they felt they became celebrities in their own communities. Gabrielle Alvarez exclaimed: "I went to Mexico, and a cousin of mine said, 'I know that woman!' She saw me here in Oakland on TV. The same with my mom, she said she saw me on the news. We became famous because of our situation, to try to better it."

Fortunately, in July 2000 the City Attorney's Office developed a creditors' plan in which the City of Oakland, Fannie Mae, and the tenants would jointly take over Oak Park through bankruptcy proceedings. This concerted strategy brought the landlord back to the negotiating table. The tenants agreed to settle their case only on the condition that Oak Park be sold, be brought up to code, and made permanent, affordable housing. Finally, almost four years after the initial organizing efforts, the Oak Park Tenants Association achieved their housing victory. We received $950,000 in damages and gained permanent, affordable housing. The tenants learned invaluable lessons about their rights and their abilities to effect change. . . .

The bridging social capital that the OPM members brought to the Oak Park Tenants Association was invaluable. Because of their own religious faith, they remained committed to loving their neighbors and to seeking social justice. Their networks with attorneys, government officials, media, and nonprofit organizations proved significant in each step of the organizing process. Not only did they bridge the Oak Park Tenants Association to outside resources, but they also facilitated communication between Cambodian and

Latino families. Since the lawsuit, Oak Park families continue to join together to do youth organizing, intergenerational family events, and, of course, for parties.

. . .

60

Pioneers in Dialogue

Jews Building Bridges

Reena Bernards

At every family seder when I was young, along with my grandmother who made the gefilte fish and horseradish with her own hands, and my father at the head of the table in a big chair fluffed with pillows, there were always some Gentiles. I remember being surprised that a Lutheran minister could sing along in Hebrew, which he was required to learn in seminary. And I remember the five-year-old daughter of one minister who enthusiastically took a big bite out of a fresh piece of horseradish, only to turn beet red and gag when she learned what this bitter herb was all about. These were not ordinary Christians. They were ministers, priests, nuns, educators, and theologians who had dedicated themselves to understanding Jews. They came to our seder year after year because my father was one of the pioneers in Christian–Jewish dialogue.

In the 1960s *dialogue* meant Jews and Christians studying together to understand the differences and similarities of their beliefs. It meant explaining to Christians that, in the eyes of Jews, Christianity did not supersede Judaism and that the religion of the Jews remains a unique and philosophically distinct monotheistic faith. It meant exploring with Christians the religious roots of anti-Semitism, helping them reexamine their contemporary texts to remove references to Jews as killers of Jesus or doomed souls because of a lack of belief in Christ. For Jews such as my father, dialogue was a natural response to living as a minority in a Christian-dominated society. It was a way to make oneself understood, and to help create a safer environment for other Jews.

The historic course of Jewish involvement in cross-cultural dialogue changed dramatically after the Six-Day War in 1967. The day after the war began my father frantically tried to gather signatures from his Gentile friends for a newspaper ad in support of Israel, to no avail. He was particularly pained by the lack of support from Black leaders. Along with other rabbis he had marched in Selma, Alabama, during the civil rights battles and assumed that the Black-Jewish alliance was strong and in the interest of both communities.

By the late 1960s that alliance could no longer be taken for granted. The painful rift brought yet another phase of dialogue into Jewish life during the 1970s and 1980s, this time between Blacks and Jews seeking to establish an alliance based on a more in-depth understanding of each other. No longer could issues such as Israel, the Palestinians, South Africa, and, most important, the economic disparity between Jews and Blacks be avoided. Many Black-Jewish groups also moved to the personal level, as participants told and compared their stories of growing up as members of a minority community.

My own work in dialogue began well into this stage in the history of Jewish engagement in cross-cultural communication. I founded the Dialogue Project between American Jewish and Palestinian Women in 1989, after the outbreak of the Palestinian intifada. My goal was to build an understanding between mainstream women leaders from both communities. Although it now seems obvious, it wasn't until years later that I realized the connection between my work and my father's. Both come from a commitment to breaking Jews' historic isolation from other peoples. This isolation is certainly a result of anti-Semitism, and it serves to reinforce it.

My father and I came to the process of dialogue from very different directions. He was a leader in the Jewish community (as National Director of Inter-religious Cooperation for the Anti-Defamation League); I was a community organizer active in grassroots efforts to bring together low-income Whites and Blacks on issues of housing, neighborhood development, and community empowerment. I left community organizing to work for Middle East peace because it was an issue that deeply affected me personally. Before I knew it I was promoting dialogue as a means of bridging the tremendous ideological and political gaps between American Jews and Arabs, as earlier Jewish leaders in the United States had used dialogue to bridge gaps between American Jews and Christians.

THE ROLE OF DIALOGUE

This work in Arab-Jewish relations led me to consider the role of dialogue in our increasingly multiethnic society, and I began to teach the practice of cross-cultural dialogue to diverse groups of community leaders in the United States. Other communities, such as African Americans and Asian Americans, are using dialogue as a method of bridging understanding between communities that are often pitted against one another. One such group, the Afro-Asian Relations Counsel, was founded in Washington, D.C., after Korean grocery store owners came in conflict with their Black customers. They discovered that through intensive discussions they were able to separate the cultural issues from the political ones. Whereas they had previously seen the other community as committed to their downfall and in collusion with the racism they faced in the broader society, through the process of dialogue they were able to stop seeing the other as their enemy. Blacks came to understand that immigrant Koreans were able to succeed in opening businesses because they pool capital and help one another overcome economic obstacles. Koreans came to understand that their ways of showing respect to a stranger are seen as distancing and actually disrespectful in the more outwardly expressive African American community.

Such lessons are important, but they do not go far enough in their impact. In order for dialogue to affect significantly the nature of race relations in our country, it must lead to deeper alliances and actions. For example, one potential project that came out of an African-Asian dialogue suggested that Black and Korean college students do internships in the businesses in each other's community, leading to an exchange of skills and knowledge as well as a sense of joint purpose. A Black-Jewish dialogue group in Washington, D.C., decided to focus on the issue of gun control, holding weekly vigils outside the headquarters of the National Rifle Association as well as lobbying for local legislation.

The ultimate purpose of dialogue is to create new relationships that work to change society. While the process may seem slow to many activists, the underlying thrust is radical. By forging alliances among minority groups where differences have kept them apart, the dialogue process breaks down the ability of the ruling establishment to divide and conquer. If members of minority communities do not allow themselves to be polarized, stronger movements for change can emerge. The point is not to recreate the civil rights alliance as

NEXT STEPS

it was, but to come together with a new understanding and create new movements that are stronger and have a heightened awareness of the richness of diversity.

. . .

The purpose of dialogue is not to obliterate legitimate conflict between groups. Dialogue participants are often aware that the people to whom they are talking are their opponents in a political battle. Each side maintains its right to continue to wage the political fight at every level; participation in a dialogue is not a truce. Yet dialogue enables groups to search for new options and possibilities and to create win-win solutions that were not considered before.

JEWISH PARTICIPATION IN DIALOGUE

In many ways dialogue comes naturally to Jews. Several years ago I attended a workshop for Jews, Christians, and Muslims in Louisiana, led by the renowned Rev. Scott Peck. The purpose was ambitious: to build community with each other. Each group responded differently to the task. The Christians spoke in soft, conciliatory tones. The Muslims were guarded as they rationally explained Islam to the group. The Jews jumped in and bared our chests. We spoke about our own personal dilemmas, argued with fellow Jews, revealed our psychological pain, and challenged the other groups on basic assumptions—all without stopping to catch our breath.

We were at home in that process: this is the water we swim in. Dialogue fits Jewish notions of how you make change in the world: you talk, you study, you discuss, you argue. The Talmud itself is the record of an internal dialogue between rabbis as they tried to figure out the controversial issues of their day. Perhaps, it is no surprise that Sigmund Freud, the father of psychotherapy, was a Jew. What could be more Jewish than having a dialogue with the different parts of yourself?

. . .

Yet I have also noticed that the comfort Jews have with dialogue can lead to some serious problems between ourselves and the other groups we wish to engage. First, we sometimes have a need to control the agenda and are often fearful of giving up this control to the will of the group. Perhaps this comes from our fear of being used, which we have in common with other oppressed groups. Our history makes us mistrustful of those who have not already shown their allegiances to us. But because we Jews are often the initiators of dialogue, we need to remember that for the effort to be successful we have to overcome our fears and allow the power and control to be shared.

Second, Jews are often more willing to talk than to take concrete political action. To many Jews sitting and talking until agreements are hammered out is a natural part of the dialogue process. We believe that our very survival depends on being understood. Our yardstick of success is often whether we think learning is taking place on both sides. In addition, while early Christian-Jewish dialogue was often motivated by Jewish concerns for our own safety, dialogue with African American or American Arab partners requires a commitment to their security needs as well. At this point in history they often feel more urgent about their political and economic situation than we do as Jews. We therefore need to note that, to others, "just talking" is often seen as useless and a dialogue is successful only if it leads to concrete political action.

Because of these different expectations and tendencies, it is important to carefully craft the dialogue experience. Every group should pay attention to the steps involved in creating a dialogue, and should build the experience according to the particular needs of their group. What follows are some suggestions.

N
E
X
T

S
T
E
P
S

SETTING UP A DIALOGUE

One important principle applies to all successful dialogues: *all sides must feel empowered by the process*. This means that they should feel that their needs are being considered in the development of the dialogue group. This principle needs to be followed in making decisions on such issues as sponsorship, leadership, place, participant list, development of the agenda, and funding.

There are many other issues to consider over the life of a dialogue group that relate to this sense of empowerment. Should the group be public or confidential, short-term or long-term, discussion-only or action-oriented? Answers to these questions often reveal the important differences between participating communities. Resolving them collectively could be the most important test of the success of a dialogue experience.

I like to talk of a *leadership partnership* as an important ingredient in dialogue. When I started the dialogue between American Jewish and Palestinian women, I put a great deal of energy into building a relationship with my counterpart in the Palestinian community, Najat Arafat Khelil, president of the Arab Women's Council. Najat and I have spent many hours together, building both our friendship and our work relationship. We have lived through political crises together, including the intifada and the Gulf War, working to understand each other's perspective. It hasn't always been easy, and there were times when we shouted at each other or went for days without talking. We always knew, however, that we would work through it because we have a deep commitment to each other and to the success of our group. I believe that this was the glue that held our project together. Najat and I modeled that it is possible to work through issues and to bridge the ideological, religious, and political gaps.

Due to the sensitive nature of the dialogue experience, it is important to use a consultatory leadership style in order to involve other people in the decision-making process. I recommend that early on leaders set up a steering committee with an equal number of members from the different communities. This committee can help decide all structural issues for the group, setting up the agenda for meetings and deciding on joint projects. . . .

All parties in the dialogue need to be involved in the fundraising efforts, even if the dollar amounts they are able to raise are different. Some groups make the mistake of allowing one community to raise the funds, with the understanding that the other community will take on other pieces of the work. This can lead to a power imbalance and a difference in the sense of ownership of the project. A more equitable solution is to engage each community in raising what it can in the manner that it is most accustomed. In addition, the two communities can meet together with foundation boards or donors, helping expand and share access to funding sources.

AGREEING ON GOALS AND EXPECTATIONS

There are five potential goals for a dialogue group:

1. *Building community and celebrating differences*. Members of an organization or community come together to learn about each other's culture. The sharing of music, dance, food, and life stories is used as a means of building a sense of camaraderie.
2. *Healing pain and building understanding*. Participants are given an opportunity to voice their unique feelings and perspectives on a given problem or experience. This

kind of open dialogue can be used after a traumatic event occurs in a community, or as a means of hearing from diverse people within a common institution.

3. *Problem solving about areas of conflict.* A more in-depth discussion occurs to find new solutions to intercommunal conflicts. Participants move from seeing the problem as a conflict between them, to seeing it as a common dilemma, engaging in joint problem solving.

4. *Modeling a different relationship.* Community leaders make a conscious commitment to demonstrate to the broader community that a more positive type of relationship is possible between members of their groups. They show by example that a relationship of mutual respect can lead to alternative ways of interacting.

5. *Action toward political change.* Dialogue participants embark on a joint political campaign, organizing their communities to change the conditions that lead to separation between groups. Groups sign a joint statement, hold press conferences, organize rallies, support candidates, and engage in other visible activities designed to build coalitions on issues where there is common ground.

The most important criterion for a successful dialogue is that the goals and expectations be clear from the beginning. It is legitimate to say that you just want to celebrate differences, and to accomplish those goals you organize a potluck dinner or a cultural event. It is also all right to build a dialogue around problem solving without going to the next stage of action, *as long as this is clear from the beginning.* But most leaders and community activists will want to be engaged in dialogue for the purpose of ultimately taking action. Be aware of differences in expectations that need to be acknowledged and managed along the way.

In addition, dialogue organizers need to be persistent and at the same time pay close attention to timing. Does your group want to attract publicity or remain confidential? Sometimes agreeing on stages of public exposure is helpful. For example, members may choose to first write or speak about a dialogue only within their own communities. As the project proceeds, the group can then decide to more fully go public. . . .

Using an experienced facilitation team will often enable a group to handle difficult conflicts more successfully. This special team can include members of each community (such as the organizers), who can understand what the participants are going through and detect any unexpressed emotions. You may also want to add a third member of the team from outside both communities who is able to provide support to both groups. In addition, the facilitation team can help the group reexamine its guidelines for dialogue. These guidelines should be periodically reviewed by the group, so that any necessary changes can be made. For example, a group may decide to add to its original guidelines that certain words not be used if they are found to be inflammatory to one of the parties. These suggestions help ensure safety even when the issues feel scary.

Another important ingredient for safety is to allow for separate caucuses. Caucusing means that there are times when the members of each community will go into separate meetings to check in with members of their own group. For example, if you as a Jewish participant have a strong reaction to what a member of the other group has said, before getting angry you can discuss your feelings with your fellow Jews, ask for their advice, and hear their perspectives. Then, if you decide to confront the issue in the dialogue, you will feel on stronger footing and will have had a chance to work out some of your own emotions first. . . .

NEXT STEPS

EXPECTING CRISIS

Every dialogue group can expect to go through at least one major crisis. In fact, every dialogue meeting will have its own "mini-crisis"; that is the time when the group is experiencing some chaos as it faces unresolved issues. This is the nature of group interaction, but it is also endemic to the dialogue process. If you expect a crisis then you will not be overwhelmed when it happens, nor will you experience the crisis as a failure. Instead, the crisis becomes an opportunity for each group to go deeper and to further understand the nature of its relationship to others.

When the Dialogue Project was on its joint trip to the Middle East, our major crisis involved visiting Yad Vashem, the Holocaust memorial museum. We had agreed ahead of time that each community could show the other community its homeland in any way it chose. The Jewish women decided a visit to the museum should be on the agenda. Palestinians, however, were reluctant to go. They already knew about the Holocaust and felt that its memory had been used politically against their community despite the fact that they were not responsible for its occurrence. The tensions this caused the group were resolved only after a visit to a refugee camp in Gaza. The Palestinian women could see that the Jews were deeply affected by the visit, and they were moved by the Jewish women's recognition of their pain. They then told the Jewish women that they would go to Yad Vashem, because they understood the need to witness each community's pain together. In this case, the group came through this crisis stronger and more assured of everyone's commitment to peace.

THE LIMITS OF DIALOGUE

The process of dialogue has its critics. Jonathan Kuttab, a West Bank human rights lawyer who was one of the first Palestinians to meet with Israeli Jews after the 1967 war, speaks of the pitfalls of a "false dialogue." A false dialogue is one in which participants are more interested in getting along than in delving into the depths of the conflict. Kuttab warns that dialogue groups may abandon moral positions in the name of compromise. Because of the desire to succeed there may be a tendency to underplay political differences and to focus on more comfortable issues such as mutual stereotypes, which downplay the nature of the oppressive situation. Dialogue participants can be tempted to ignore the realities in their own societies as they attempt to build a bridge to the other side.

Kuttab claims that a key pitfall in dialogue is the assumption of a false symmetry between groups where there is actually a large power imbalance. The basic condition of oppressor and oppressed is ignored, and members of the group are subtly pressured into an acceptance of the status quo. In this sense participants in dialogue can be coopted or misused. Finally, Kuttab charges that dialogue should never be a substitute for action.

Yet Kuttab himself speaks of a dialogue in service of "peace, justice, and reconciliation." By setting up a process that empowers both sides, an honest and open exchange can occur. Potentially through the process of exploring the dynamics of conflict, each community and individual will find new sources of power to effect political change.

CONCLUSION

. . .

In a world where interethnic, interreligious, and intercommunal conflicts threaten global security, conflict resolution methods are needed more than ever. Here in the United States, as our country becomes more multicultural, building an understanding among groups is essential for our cohesion as a nation. The experience that Jews bring is a vital resource. The more we as Jews can hone our skills, improve in problem areas, and become conscious about what makes dialogue work, the more we will be able to make a valuable contribution to a multicultural society. Dialogue is the wave of the future.

NEXT STEPS

SEXISM

Introduction

Heather Hackman

"Question gender!" is one of my favorite bumper stickers for a number of reasons. First, it challenges a presupposed notion made by most of U.S. society today that gender is fixed and unchangeable. Second, it represents a fundamental entry point for understanding how sexism operates in this society. And third, it is a call to action that is direct, unapologetic, and long-ranging in its potential to free everyone from the tyranny of rote gender roles and the seemingly intractable hold sexism and patriarchy have on this society.

At first glance it may not be obvious why I would start a section about *sexism* (the systematic oppression of women on institutional, cultural, and individual levels) and *patriarchy* (the ideology of male supremacy that justifies male dominance and the subordination of women in all aspects of society) with a discussion about gender. A closer examination of sexual harassment, for example, answers this question by demonstrating how this form of sexism is connected to this society's objectification of women, which can then be traced to this society's view of what a woman should look, act, and essentially be like, which can then be linked to this society's core ideas about gender. Therefore, this section's approach of examining gender before discussing specific examples of sexism serves to expose how socially constructed gender roles are an essential root of sexism in this society.

This approach is not new, of course—twenty years of activism has thankfully moved the fields of women's studies, queer studies, and gender studies to a more critical stance regarding gender as a core organizer for these forms of oppression. But there are still many people for whom the idea of fundamentally questioning gender is both new and suspect. The importance of interrogating gender when studying sexism becomes clear, however, when we realize how the structures of sexism in this society feed into and are nourished by the maintenance of hierarchies of power based on gender.

Leslie Feinberg, in the 1996 book *Transgender Warriors,* raises the provocative question: "Are you a guy or a girl?" I pose a similar question in the college classes I teach and receive quizzical or comedic looks as students wonder why I would ask what they perceive as a ridiculously obvious question. "Can't you *tell*? Just look at us," they seem to say. But what I can "tell" may or may not be their true gender identity. It is certainly what they are presenting as their gender at that moment in time, but I cannot tell whether what I see is the expression of the socially constructed gender roles they have been forced, sometimes violently, to adhere to, or if it is truly their deeply felt sense of self with respect to gender—their gender identity. In truth, one cannot know the full story about another's gender without a little more information. Lorber and Kimmel (selections 61 and 62) clarify this point by differentiating between socially constructed *gender roles* (meaning what society says a woman and a man are supposed to be) and a person's *gender identity* (meaning one's self-identification of their gender irrespective of what society says). These two readings explain that mainstream U.S. notions of gender are not "real," so much as constructed and accepted roles and ways of being that are assigned to us all by the dominant power structure.

GENDER ROLES, GENDER SOCIALIZATION, AND GENDER IDENTITY

Understanding how gender supports sexism requires the explanation of a few key concepts and terms such as gender roles, gender socialization, and gender identity. *Gender roles* are the rigid categories (and there are only two) that characterize what it means to be "feminine" and "masculine" in this society. They are clearly articulated, ruthlessly enforced, and inflexible in their expression. Men do not cry, women should always look beautiful (for men), men never ask for directions, women are "natural" caretakers, men are tough, women are emotional, men are studs, women are domestic, and so on. These roles are taught to us by a process of *gender socialization* (see Harro, selection 6) whereby the messages of what it means to be a man or woman are conveyed to us by every possible socializing structure in society—our families tell us how to behave, our schools tell us what we can achieve, and our media tells us what we need to look like. And because people who identify as women make up over half of the U.S. population, this socialization begins before birth to insure the highest level of compliance from women as well as men.

There are three characteristics of gender roles that support the overarching systems of sexism, heterosexism, and transgender oppression, and the intersections between them. The first is that, although in reality these gender roles are *social constructions* (something we learn through the socialization processes in our society), we are taught to believe that masculinity and femininity are biological not social, "natural" not cultural, inherent to being a man or a woman instead of learned behaviors. One particular tool used to socialize people into this thinking is the "essentialist" argument, which asserts that these gender roles are inextricably tied to one's biological sex and are therefore real, inherent, and "natural," even though there is not a direct or causal relationship between one's biological sex and one's gender identity. But because our society shapes us into gender roles from the moment we are born (and punishes us if we do not adhere to them), it *appears* as if there is a causal relationship between biological sex and gender, implying that we are marked with gender roles from birth and they cannot be changed. As a result, the sexist dynamics inherent in these gender roles (e.g. women are naturally domestic and therefore should not work outside of the home) are also labeled as "natural" and unchangeable. And ultimately, anyone who does not fit into or who intentionally contests this rigid gender binary is therefore labeled as "unnatural" or sick and patriarchy and gender oppression remain unchallenged.

Fortunately, the work by the intersex community has disproven the assumption that biology determines gender and has thus freed us from the idea that gender is "natural" (see website for further resources). In addition, if gender roles were "natural" they would manifest similarly in societies all over the world, but a global analysis reveals a rather diverse understanding and expression of gender across societies (Nanda 2000). Similarly, if these roles were set and unchangeable they would be consistent throughout history, and yet within U.S. history alone the notion of what it means to be a man or woman has changed over time due to political, economic, and social influence. As such, what is perceived as "real" regarding gender roles is actually a manifestation of certain rules and expectations put on all of us by the macro gendered power structure.

A second core characteristic of gender roles is that *they are based on heteronormativity*, which refers to the normalizing of heterosexuality and the pathologizing of being lesbian, gay, or bisexual. In my classes I often conduct an exercise where we divide into groups and develop lists of what it means to "act like a 'man'" or "act like a 'lady.'" For the sixteen years I have been doing this exercise, every element of what it has meant to "act like a 'lady'" has been connected to the heterosexual male gaze. Looking pretty, acting feminine, knowing how to cook, wanting children and the like, of and by themselves, are not at all problematic, but when analyzed through a lens of gender critique it is apparent that they are consistently tied to heterosexual relationships and the need for women to appeal to heterosexual men. The connection between heterosexuality and what it means to be a real woman implies that lesbian and bisexual women are not actually women, are a threat to these gender roles for their lack of compliance, and therefore should be met with contempt and even violence. Suzanne Pharr (1988) suggests that homophobia is a weapon of sexism precisely because of the relationship between gender role conformity and what she termed "compulsory heterosexuality." This issue is discussed in more detail by Blumenfeld (selection 78 and introduction to section 6).

A third important characteristic of gender roles is that *masculine and feminine roles are diametrically opposed, as opposites in a binary, and also hierarchically positioned, as superior or inferior*. For every characteristic that students defined as "masculine," for example being tough and superior, they defined "feminine" as the exact opposite, weak and inferior. Looking even further, all human attributes labeled as feminine are consistently devalued in this society and used to insult or harass men, thus speaking volumes about the true status of women in this society. As evidence, the two worst things a man can be called are a "fag" (tied into the heteronormativity discussed above) and a "woman," and the worst thing a man can do is to "throw like a girl" or "cry like a sissy." Of course, while most people transgress gender roles on a daily basis, the existence of these roles and the rules that shape them are well known by all as demonstrated by the fact that it never takes students more than 10 minutes to generate multiple examples.

Thankfully, *gender identity* can be thought of in ways that are more flexible than gender roles. *Gender identity* arises from an inner, self-reflective location and manifests a person's more authentic gendered self as a woman, man, or transgendered person. While gender roles exist in relation to each other within a binary, gender identity exists along a continuum and has a range of expressions. The section on transgender oppression (section 7) more thoroughly explains the concept of gender identity and its range of expressions and is a critical companion section for fully understanding sexism in this society. Gender roles and identity are experienced by others through their "expression" or "presentation." A person's expression or presentation of a gender role is based on the dichotomous categories of how "man" and "woman" should look, act, and feel like, whereas the expression or presentation of a person's gender identity exists within a broader and more fluid context that more accords with the complexity of gender. To present or express one's gender on the basis of accepted gender roles usually garners acceptance and approval from individuals and institutions. On the other hand, gender expression that does not conform to the dominant power structure's ideals often results in disapproval, marginalization, and violence.

SEXISM AND FEMINISM

So, if gender roles are based on social constructions and not on nature, why does society create this dichotomy and respond so violently to those who do not adhere to it? The answer is quite simply that oppression itself requires binaries. It is much easier to maintain an unequal status quo when two social identity groups (within the same axis of identity) are positioned as diametrically opposed to each other (see selections 4 and 5). As such, these roles form the structural and ideological basis for the oppression of women, or *sexism*, in our society. In this reader's companion book, *Teaching for Diversity and Social Justice* (second edition), Botkin, Jones, and Kachwaha define sexism as, "a system of advantages that serves to privilege men, subordinate women, denigrate women-identified values and practices, enforce male dominance and control, and reinforce norms of masculinity that are dehumanizing and damaging to men" (2007, 174). Allan Johnson (selections 3 and 63) furthers advances our understanding of sexism by describing *patriarchy* as the system and ideology that supports the dominance of men and the oppression of women on all levels of society.

The bell hooks reading (selection 64) offers a different take on understanding sexism by explaining what *feminism* is. In the words of another bumper sticker, "feminism is the radical notion that women are people." Contrary to popular backlash rhetoric, feminism is not about hating men, but it does unapologetically require an end to the domination of women by men. While feminism certainly has a range of theoretical underpinnings from liberal to Marxist to environmental, a common element among them is the need to dismantle the patriarchal power structures that serve to subordinate women and transgender folks and unfairly advantage men in every aspect of society. Because of the connections noted among sexism, heterosexism, and transgender oppression, feminism also seeks an end to gender binaries and heteronormative societal structures.

With a foundation comprised of gender binaries and the exercising of patriarchal power on individual, cultural, and institutional levels, the day-to-day mechanisms used to keep sexism in place take many forms. For example, if gender roles state that women are to be "feminine" and look attractive to men, then the creation of limiting and dehumanizing notions of "ideal female beauty" for women is an effective tool for keeping women powerless, especially in the public domain. Caroline Heldman's article on body image (selection 66) aptly describes the societal impact of these fabricated images of beauty on women and how they conspire to disempower women economically, psychologically, and politically. The Chernik reading (selection 68) adds to this discussion by demonstrating the deadly effects of this imagery on women in the form of eating disorders and the illusory power that the cult of thinness (Nagy Hesse-Biber 2007) creates in this society. Other aspects of sexism such as the wage gap discussed in Aaron Bernstein's piece (selection 67), violence against women discussed in the Katz article (selection 65), reproductive freedom as seen in the Fennell piece (selection 71), or the use of language as seen in both the Morgan and Kirk and Okazawa-Rey pieces (selections 69 and 70) all represent both products of and tools to maintain sexism in our society.

HISTORY OF RESISTANCE AND MOVEMENTS FOR CHANGE

Acquiring a basic understanding of the dynamics of sexism in society begs the question of what to do about it. When teaching this to undergraduates in my classes, students will often say that sexism has been around "forever" and, even though it is wrong, they say there is nothing you can do about it. I am sure that there are a range of reasons for their thinking here, but one that warrants highlighting is the often complete lack of historical knowledge about the history of individual women's resistance to these constraints and the women's social change movements in this country. While complicated and often problematic, the history of the women's movements in the United States demonstrates powerful and effective ways to challenge both the manifestations of sexism and the foundations that give rise to it. From the first "women's rights convention" in Seneca Falls, NY, in 1848 to the presidential election of 2008, we have seen examples of women making history through their challenges to the limiting gender roles and power structures that marginalize them. At its best, this history demonstrates the need for a broad-based platform addressing women's rights, the power of consciousness-raising groups, the transformational power of claiming voice, and the necessity for cross-issue organizing. There were also a range of mistakes made along the way and in particular the first and second waves' inaccurate, simplifying assumptions concerning a single, uniform, universal woman's experience. In the first wave, although the agenda called for "women's rights," the needs of women of color, poor and working-class women were marginalized in favor of the eventual limited agenda of suffrage. In the second wave, these same groups as well as lesbian and bisexual women, women with disabilities, and women who were not Christian were also pushed to the side in favor of the white, middle-class agenda for "equal rights."

Because of space limitations, this section cannot discuss the many important lessons gleaned from these movements and the value of knowing this history (see section website for resources). It does, however, take these lessons seriously and highlights how we can actualize them in this current moment of fighting for women's rights—the "third wave." The Next Steps part of this section begins with Paul Gorski's explanation of why, as a man, he has a personal investment in feminism and an end to sexism (selection 72). This selection illustrates the importance of men taking action to end sexism. To be clear, if sexism is to be dismantled, a key lesson learned from our history is the need to educate men about the ways that sexism and patriarchy ravage their humanity as well as the lives of the women they care about and engage them, as men, in the struggle for change. It is crucial that men as well as women acknowledge that no form of oppression can be eradicated until the advantaged group can see how their core values are compromised by the existence of that oppression.

This is followed by the work of Alice Walker (selection 73), which addresses another lesson from a long history of women's activism—the impact of internalized oppression. Her article calls this out in simple but powerful ways, and, although it does not blame women for sexism, it does demand that women take responsibility for the internalization of negative messages and transform these debilitating ideas into sources of power. Another lesson learned from the history of the women and men working to end sexism is the need for a broad and deep agenda for change instead of assuming that what works for white, middle-class women works for all women. The inclusion of the brief statement from the National Latina Institute for Reproductive Health and their position regarding health care for all is a small step in redressing this historic mistake (selection 74). The lessons of the first two waves can be reflected in the willingness of contemporary feminist activists to broaden the "women's health" agenda so that it encompasses root causes as well as corollary manifestations of sexism in health care.

As stated above, one of the most egregious mistakes of both waves of the women's movement was the racist lack of attention to the needs and voices of women of color. The Hurdis reading (selection 75) discusses the critical importance of including the voices of women of color in today's third-wave feminism, while the Russo and Spatz reading (selection 76) helps white women remember not to be seduced by the apparent political expediency of white privilege and class privilege to advance their own agenda at the expense of women of color and working-class women. At the end of the section Winona LaDuke (selection 77) offers lasting insight into the overall mindset that is necessary to end the oppression of women and create social change from the ground up.

All of the readings in this section share one common element—they acknowledge the real-life complexity of addressing the oppression of women. It is vital to understand that if there is to be an effective and sustained movement to end the sexist oppression of women, it cannot be done without examining intersecting issues of racism, classism, heterosexism, and transgender oppression, to name a few. As such, to more deeply understand the issues presented in this section it is important to read selections from other sections in this book. For example, the Landesman, Bauer, Romero, and Morgenson selections (33, 35, 36, and 40) located in the classism section discuss sex trafficking, immigration, sex discrimination in the work place (whether agricultural or domestic), and burdensome debt. In the section on racism, the Chung, Fayad, Castañeda, and Smith readings (selections 16, 18, 24, and 25) highlight the role of heteropatriarchy in the maintenance of racism, the connections between sexism and racism, and ways to cross-culturally communicate about issues of race. Similarly, in the section on ableism the Colligan reading (selection 101) explains why the intersexed should not be "fixed" and is key to understanding that biological sex exists on a continuum and thus supports the deconstruction of the "essentialist" position regarding gender. And, of course, the readings of the sections on heterosexism and transgender oppression are vital for fully understanding the overlapping complexity and mutually reinforcing structures of oppression among these three forms of oppression.

SUMMARY

In conclusion I would like to underscore that this section offers only a sampling of issues and ideas for readers to begin to understand the very complex and multifaceted issue of the oppression of women. As mentioned above, there is no single voice for "women's issues" and therefore I strongly encourage the use of the supplemental materials from the section website to gain a more comprehensive view of sexism in the United States. References for additional books or articles, specific articles themselves (e.g. the well-known and often used, "The 'Rape' of Mr. Smith"), references for films and videos, links to websites and to current sources of discussion and action, and activities that can be used in the classroom or training settings to further explore sexism in U.S. society can all be found on the section website for this book.

In moving forward with this information I would like to emphasize the importance of actually using it to create change, however subtle it may be, in this society regarding the oppression of women. In an era where for the first time a woman has made a strong and convincing run for the White House, where increasing numbers of women are in professional positions of power, and women are represented in more equal numbers in college admissions, it is tempting to say that sexism is over. However, when we dig a little deeper we can see that sexism and patriarchy are both firmly intact and the need for broad-based, consistent action has never been greater. Now is the time and it will require the work of all of us to end sexism and transform our society into one in which all women feel safe and free and able to fully achieve any dream they have.

References

Botkin, S., Jones, J., Kachwaha, T. (2007). "Sexism Curriculum Design." In M. Adams, L. A. Bell, P. Griffin (eds), *Teaching for Diversity and Social Justice*, 2nd edition. New York: Routledge. pp. 173–194.

Feinberg, L. (1996). *Transgender Warriors*. Boston: Beacon Press.

Nagy Hesse-Biber, S. (2007). *The Cult of Thinness*. New York: Oxford University Press.

Nanda, S. (2000). *Gender Diversity: Crosscultural Variations*. Long Grove, IL: Waveland Press.

Pharr, Suzanne. (1988). *Homophobia as a Weapon of Sexism*. Little Rock, AR: Chardon Press.

61

"Night to His Day"

The Social Construction of Gender

Judith Lorber

Talking about gender for most people is the equivalent of fish talking about water. Gender is so much the routine ground of everyday activities that questioning its taken-for-granted assumptions and presuppositions is like thinking about whether the sun will come up. Gender is so pervasive that in our society we assume it is bred into our genes. Most people find it hard to believe that gender is constantly created and re-created out of human inter-action, out of social life, and is the texture and order of that social life. Yet gender, like culture, is a human production that depends on everyone constantly "doing gender."

And everyone "does gender" without thinking about it. Today, on the subway, I saw a well-dressed man with a year-old child in a stroller. Yesterday, on a bus, I saw a man with a tiny baby in a carrier on his chest. Seeing men taking care of small children in public is increasingly common—at least in New York City. But both men were quite obviously stared at—and smiled at, approvingly. Everyone was doing gender—the men who were changing the role of fathers and the other passengers, who were applauding them silently. But there was more gendering going on that probably fewer people noticed. The baby was wearing a white crocheted cap and white clothes. You couldn't tell if it was a boy or a girl. The child in the stroller was wearing a dark blue T-shirt and dark print pants. As they started to leave the train, the father put a Yankee baseball cap on the child's head. Ah, a boy, I thought. Then I noticed the gleam of tiny earrings in the child's ears, and as they got off, I saw the little flowered sneakers and lace-trimmed socks. Not a boy after all. Gender done.

Gender is such a familiar part of daily life that it usually takes a deliberate disruption of our expectations of how women and men are supposed to act to pay attention to how it is produced. Gender signs and signals are so ubiquitous that we usually fail to note them—unless they are missing or ambiguous. Then we are uncomfortable until we have success-fully placed the other person in a gender status; otherwise, we feel socially dislocated. . . .

For the individual, gender construction starts with assignment to a sex category on the basis of what the genitalia look like at birth. Then babies are dressed or adorned in a way that displays the category because parents don't want to be constantly asked whether their baby is a girl or a boy. A sex category becomes a gender status through naming, dress, and the use of other gender markers. Once a child's gender is evident, others treat those in one gender differently from those in the other, and the children respond to the different treatment by feeling different and behaving differently. As soon as they can talk, they start to refer to themselves as members of their gender. Sex doesn't come into play again until puberty, but by that time, sexual feelings and desires and practices have been shaped by gendered norms and expectations. Adolescent boys and girls approach and avoid each other in an elaborately scripted and gendered mating dance. Parenting is gendered, with different expectations for mothers and for fathers, and people of different genders work at different kinds of jobs. The work adults do as mothers and fathers and as low-level workers and high-level bosses, shapes women's and men's life experiences, and these experiences produce different feelings, consciousness, relationships, skills—ways of being that we call feminine or masculine. All of these processes constitute the social construction of gender.

Gendered roles change—today fathers are taking care of little children, girls and boys are wearing unisex clothing and getting the same education, women and men are working at the same jobs. Although many traditional social groups are quite strict about maintaining gender differences, in other social groups they seem to be blurring. Then why the one-year-old's earrings? Why is it still so important to mark a child as a girl or a boy, to make sure she is not taken for a boy or he for a girl? What would happen if they were? They would, quite literally, have changed places in their social world.

To explain why gendering is done from birth, constantly and by everyone, we have to look not only at the way individuals experience gender but at gender as a social institution. As a social institution, gender is one of the major ways that human beings organize their lives. Human society depends on a predictable division of labor, a designated allocation of scarce goods, assigned responsibility for children and others who cannot care for themselves, common values and their systematic transmission to new members, legitimate leadership, music, art, stories, games, and other symbolic productions. One way of choosing people for the different tasks of society is on the basis of their talents, motivations, and competence—their demonstrated achievements. The other way is on the basis of gender, race, ethnicity—ascribed membership in a category of people. . . .

Western society's values legitimate gendering by claiming that it all comes from physiology—female and male procreative differences. But gender and sex are not equivalent, and gender as a social construction does not flow automatically from genitalia and reproductive organs, the main physiological differences of females and males. In the construction of ascribed social statuses, physiological differences such as sex, stage of development, color of skin, and size are crude markers. They are not the source of the social statuses of gender, age grade, and race. Social statuses are carefully constructed through prescribed processes of teaching, learning, emulation, and enforcement. Whatever genes, hormones, and biological evolution contribute to human social institutions is materially as well as qualitatively transformed by social practices. . . . Thus, . . . gender cannot be equated with biological and physiological differences between human females and males. The building blocks of gender are *socially constructed statuses*. . . .

FOR INDIVIDUALS, GENDER MEANS SAMENESS

Although the possible combinations of genitalia, body shapes, clothing, mannerisms, sexuality, and roles could produce infinite varieties in human beings, the social institution of gender depends on the production and maintenance of a limited number of gender statuses and of making the members of these statuses similar to each other. Individuals are born sexed but not gendered, and they have to be taught to be masculine or feminine. As Simone de Beauvoir said: "One is not born, but rather becomes, a woman . . . ; it is civilization as a whole that produces this creature . . . which is described as feminine."

. . .

Many cultures go beyond clothing, gestures, and demeanor in gendering children. They inscribe gender directly into bodies. . . . In Western societies, women augment their breast size with silicone and reconstruct their faces with cosmetic surgery to conform to cultural ideals of feminine beauty. Hanna Papanek notes that these practices reinforce the sense of superiority or inferiority in the adults who carry them out as well as in the children on whom they are done. . . .

Sandra Bem argues that because gender is a powerful "schema" that orders the cognitive world, one must wage a constant, active battle for a child not to fall into typical gendered attitudes and behavior. In 1972, *Ms. Magazine* published Lois Gould's fantasy of how to raise a child free of gender-typing. The experiment calls for hiding the child's anatomy from all eyes except the parents' and treating the child as neither a girl nor a boy. The child, called X, gets to do all the things boys *and* girls do. The experiment is so successful that all the children in X's class at school want to look and behave like X. At the end of the story, the creators of the experiment are asked what will happen when X grows up. The scientists' answer is that by then it will be quite clear what X is, implying that its hormones will kick in and it will be revealed as a female or male. That ambiguous, and somewhat contradictory, ending lets Gould off the hook; neither she nor we have any idea what someone brought up totally androgynously would be like sexually or socially as an adult. The hormonal input will not create gender or sexuality but will only establish secondary sex characteristics; breasts, beards, and menstruation alone do not produce social manhood or womanhood. Indeed, it is at puberty, when sex characteristics become evident, that most societies put pubescent children through their most important rites of passage, the rituals that officially mark them as fully gendered—that is, ready to marry and become adults.

Most parents create a gendered world for their newborn by naming, birth announcements, and dress. Children's relationships with same-gendered and different-gendered caretakers structure their self-identifications and personalities. Through cognitive development, children extract and apply to their own actions the appropriate behavior for those who belong in their own gender, as well as race, religion, ethnic group, and social class, rejecting what is not appropriate. If their social categories are highly valued, they value themselves highly; if their social categories are low status, they lose self-esteem. Many feminist parents who want to raise androgynous children soon lose their children to the pull of gendered norms. My son attended a carefully nonsexist elementary school, which didn't even have girls' and boys' bathrooms. When he was seven or eight years old, I attended a class play about "squares" and "circles" and their need for each other and noticed that all the girl squares and circles wore makeup, but none of the boy squares and circles did. I asked the teacher about it after the play, and she said, "Bobby said he was not going to wear makeup, and he is a powerful child, so none of the boys would either." In a long discussion about conformity, my son confronted me with the question of who the conformists were, the boys who followed their leader or the girls who listened to the woman teacher. In actuality, they both were, because they both followed same-gender leaders and acted in gender-appropriate ways. (Actors may wear makeup, but real boys don't.)

For human beings there is no essential femaleness or maleness, femininity or masculinity, womanhood or manhood, but once gender is ascribed, the social order constructs and holds individuals to strongly gendered norms and expectations. Individuals may vary on many of the components of gender and may shift genders temporarily or permanently, but they must fit into the limited number of gender statuses their society recognizes. In the process, they re-create their society's version of women and men: "If we do gender appropriately, we simultaneously sustain, reproduce, and render legitimate the institutional arrangements. . . . If we fail to do gender appropriately, we as individuals—not the institutional arrangements—may be called to account (for our character, motives, and predispositions)" (West and Zimmerman 1987).

The gendered practices of everyday life reproduce a society's view of how women and men should act. Gendered social arrangements are justified by religion and cultural productions and backed by law, but the most powerful means of sustaining the moral hegemony of the dominant gender ideology is that the process is made invisible; any possible alternatives are virtually unthinkable.

FOR SOCIETY, GENDER MEANS DIFFERENCE

The pervasiveness of gender as a way of structuring social life demands that gender statuses be clearly differentiated. Varied talents, sexual preferences, identities, personalities, interests, and ways of interacting fragment the individual's bodily and social experiences. Nonetheless, these are organized in Western cultures into two and only two socially and legally recognized gender statuses, "man" and "woman." In the social construction of gender, it does not matter what men and women actually do; it does not even matter if they do exactly the same thing. The social institution of gender insists only that what they do is *perceived* as different.

If men and women are doing the same tasks, they are usually spatially segregated to maintain gender separation, and often the tasks are given different job titles as well, such as executive secretary and administrative assistant. If the differences between women and men begin to blur, society's "sameness taboo" goes into action. At a rock and roll dance at West Point in 1976, the year women were admitted to the prestigious military academy for the first time, the school's administrators "were reportedly perturbed by the sight of mirror-image couples dancing in short hair and dress gray trousers," and a rule was established that women cadets could dance at these events only if they wore skirts. Women recruits in the U.S. Marine Corps are required to wear makeup—at a minimum, lipstick and eye shadow—and they have to take classes in makeup, hair care, poise, and etiquette. This feminization is part of a deliberate policy of making them clearly distinguishable from men Marines. Christine Williams quotes a twenty-five-year-old woman drill instructor as saying: "A lot of the recruits who come here don't wear makeup; they're tomboyish or athletic. A lot of them have the preconceived idea that going into the military means they can still be a tomboy. They don't realize that you are a *Woman* Marine" (1989).

If gender differences were genetic, physiological, or hormonal, gender bending and gender ambiguity would occur only in . . . [those] who are born with chromosomes and genitalia that are not clearly female or male. Since gender differences are socially constructed, all men and all women can enact the behavior of the other, because they know the other's social script: "'Man' and 'woman' are at once empty and overflowing categories. Empty because they have no ultimate, transcendental meaning. Overflowing because even when they appear to be fixed, they still contain within them alternative, denied, or suppressed definitions" (J.W. Scott 1988). Nonetheless, though individuals may be able to shift gender statuses, the gender boundaries have to hold, or the whole gendered social order will come crashing down.

. . .

GENDER AS PROCESS, STRATIFICATION, AND STRUCTURE

As a social institution, gender is a process of creating distinguishable social statuses for the assignment of rights and responsibilities. As part of a stratification system that ranks these statuses unequally, gender is a major building block in the social structures built on these unequal statuses.

As a *process*, gender creates the social differences that define "woman" and "man." In social interaction throughout their lives, individuals learn what is expected, see what is expected, act and react in expected ways, and thus simultaneously construct and maintain the gender order: "The very injunction to be a given gender takes place through discursive routes: to be a good mother, to be a heterosexually desirable object, to be a fit worker, in sum, to signify a multiplicity of guarantees in response to a variety of different demands all at once" (J. Butler 1990). Members of a social group neither make up gender as they go along nor exactly replicate in rote fashion what was done before. In almost every encounter, human beings produce gender, behaving in the ways they learned were appropriate for their gender status, or resisting or rebelling against these norms. Resistance and rebellion have altered gender norms, but so far they have rarely eroded the statuses.

Gendered patterns of interaction acquire additional layers of gendered sexuality, parenting, and work behaviors in childhood, adolescence, and adulthood. Gendered norms and expectations are enforced through informal sanctions of gender-inappropriate behavior by peers and by formal punishment or threat of punishment by those in authority should behavior deviate too far from socially imposed standards for women and men.

Everyday gendered interactions build gender into the family, the work process, and other organizations and institutions, which in turn reinforce gender expectations for individuals. Because gender is a process, there is room not only for modification and variation by individuals and small groups but also for institutionalized change.

As part of a *stratification* system, gender ranks men above women of the same race and class. Women and men could be different but equal. In practice, the process of creating difference depends to a great extent on differential evaluation. As Nancy Jay (1981) says: "That which is defined, separated out, isolated from all else is A and pure. Not-A is necessarily impure, a random catchall, to which nothing is external except A and the principle of order that separates it from Not-A." From the individual's point of view, whichever gender is A, the other is Not-A; gender boundaries tell the individual who is like him or her and all the rest are unlike. From society's point of view, however, one gender is usually the touchstone, the normal, the dominant, and the other is different, deviant, and subordinate. In Western society, "man" is A, "wo-man" is Not-A. (Consider what a society would be like where woman was A and man Not-A.) . . . The dominant categories are the hegemonic ideals, taken so for granted as the way things should be that, . . . [t]he characteristics of these categories define the Other as that which lacks the valuable qualities the dominants exhibit.

. . .

Societies vary in the extent of the inequality in social status of their women and men members, but where there is inequality, the status "woman" (and its attendant behavior and role allocations) is usually held in lesser esteem than the status "man." Since gender is also intertwined with a society's other constructed statuses of differential evaluation—race, religion, occupation, class, country of origin, and so on—men and women members of the favored groups command more power, more prestige, and more property than the members of the disfavored groups. Within many social groups, however, men are advantaged over women. The more economic resources, such as education and job opportunities, are available to a group, the more they tend to be monopolized by men. In poorer groups that have few resources (such as working-class African Americans in the United States), women and men are more nearly equal, and the women may even outstrip the men in education and occupational status.

As a *structure*, gender divides work in the home and in economic production, legitimates those in authority, and organizes sexuality and emotional life. As primary parents, women significantly influence children's psychological development and emotional attachments, in the process reproducing gender. Emergent sexuality is shaped by heterosexual, homosexual, bisexual, and sadomasochistic patterns that are gendered—different for girls and boys, and for women and men—so that sexual statuses reflect gender statuses.

When gender is a major component of structured inequality, the devalued genders have less power, prestige, and economic rewards than the valued genders. In countries that discourage gender discrimination, many major roles are still gendered; women still do most of the domestic labor and child rearing, even while doing full-time paid work; women and men are segregated on the job and each does work considered "appropriate"; women's work is usually paid less than men's work. Men dominate the positions of authority and leadership in government, the military, and the law; cultural productions, religions, and sports reflect men's interests. . . .

Gender inequality—the devaluation of "women" and the social domination of "men"— has social functions and a social history. It is not the result of sex, procreation, physiology, anatomy, hormones, or genetic predispositions. It is produced and maintained by identifiable social processes and built into the general social structure and individual identities deliberately and purposefully. The social order as we know it in Western societies is organized around racial, ethnic, class, and gender inequality. I contend, therefore, that the continuing purpose of gender as a modern social institution is to construct women as a group to be the subordinates of men as a group. The life of everyone placed in the status "woman" is "night to his day—that has forever been the fantasy. Black to his white. Shut out of his system's space, she is the repressed that ensures the system's functioning."

. . .

There is no core or bedrock human nature below these endlessly looping processes of the social production of sex and gender, self and other, identity and psyche, each of which is a "complex cultural construction." *For humans, the social is the natural.* Therefore, "in its feminist senses, gender cannot mean simply the cultural appropriation of biological sexual difference. Sexual difference is itself a fundamental—and scientifically contested— construction. Both 'sex' and 'gender' are woven of multiple, asymmetrical strands of difference, charged with multifaceted dramatic narratives of domination and struggle" (Haraway 1990).

62

Masculinity as Homophobia

Fear, Shame, and Silence in the Construction of Gender Identity

Michael S. Kimmel

We think of manhood as eternal, a timeless essence that resides deep in the heart of every man. We think of manhood as a thing, a quality that one either has or doesn't have. We think of manhood as innate, residing in the particular biological composition of the human male, the result of androgens or the possession of a penis. We think of manhood as a transcendent tangible property that each man must manifest in the world, the reward presented with great ceremony to a young novice by his elders for having successfully completed an arduous initiation ritual. . . .

I view masculinity as a constantly changing collection of meanings that we construct through our relationships with ourselves, with each other, and with our world. Manhood is neither static nor timeless; it is historical. Manhood is not the manifestation of an inner essence; it is socially constructed. Manhood does not bubble up to consciousness from our biological makeup; it is created in culture. Manhood means different things at different times to different people. We come to know what it means to be a man in our culture by setting our definitions in opposition to a set of "others"— racial minorities, sexual minorities, and, above all, women.

. . .

This idea that manhood is socially constructed and historically shifting should not be understood as a loss, that something is being taken away from men. In fact, it gives us something extraordinarily valuable—agency, the capacity to act. It gives us a sense of historical possibilities to replace the despondent resignation that invariably attends timeless, ahistorical essentialisms. Our behaviors are not simply "just human nature," because "boys will be boys." From the materials we find around us in our culture—other people, ideas, objects—we actively create our worlds, our identities. Men, both individually and collectively, can change.

MASCULINITY AS A HOMOSOCIAL ENACTMENT

Other men: We are under the constant careful scrutiny of other men. Other men watch us, rank us, grant our acceptance into the realm of manhood. Manhood is demonstrated for other men's approval. It is other men who evaluate the performance. Literary critic David Leverenz argues that "ideologies of manhood have functioned primarily in relation to the gaze of male peers and male authority." Think of how men boast to one another of their accomplishments—from their latest sexual conquest to the size of the fish they caught—and how we constantly parade the markers of manhood—wealth, power, status, sexy women—in front of other men, desperate for their approval.

That men prove their manhood in the eyes of other men is both a consequence of sexism and one of its chief props. "Women have, in men's minds, such a low place on the social ladder of this country that it's useless to define yourself in terms of a woman," noted playwright David Mamet. "What men need is men's approval." Women become a kind of currency that men use to improve their ranking on the masculine social scale. (Even those moments of heroic conquest of women carry, I believe, a current of homosocial evaluation.) Masculinity is a *homosocial* enactment. We test ourselves, perform heroic feats, take enormous risks, all because we want other men to grant us our manhood.

Masculinity as a homosocial enactment is fraught with danger, with the risk of failure, and with intense relentless competition. "Every man you meet has a rating or an estimate of himself which he never loses or forgets," wrote Kenneth Wayne in his popular turn-of-the-century advice book. "A man has his own rating, and instantly he lays it alongside of the other man." Almost a century later, another man remarked to psychologist Sam Osherson that "[b]y the time you're an adult, it's easy to think you're always in competition with men, for the attention of women, in sports, at work."

MASCULINITY AS HOMOPHOBIA

. . .

Homophobia is a central organizing principle of our cultural definition of manhood. Homophobia is more than the irrational fear of gay men, more than the fear that we might be perceived as gay. "The word 'faggot' has nothing to do with homosexual experience or even with fears of homosexuals," writes David Leverenz. "It comes out of the depths of manhood: a label of ultimate contempt for anyone who seems sissy, untough, uncool." Homophobia is the fear that other men will unmask us, emasculate us, reveal to us and the world that we do not measure up, that we are not real men. We are afraid to let other men see that fear. Fear makes us ashamed, because the recognition of fear in ourselves is proof to ourselves that we are not as manly as we pretend, that we are, like the young man in a poem by Yeats, "one that ruffles in a manly pose for all his timid heart." Our fear is the fear of humiliation. We are ashamed to be afraid.

Shame leads to silence—the silences that keep other people believing that we actually approve of the things that are done to women, to minorities, to gays and lesbians in our culture. The frightened silence as we scurry past a woman being hassled by men on the street. That furtive silence when men make sexist or racist jokes in a bar. That clammy-handed silence when guys in the office make gay-bashing jokes. Our fears are the sources of our silences, and men's silence is what keeps the system running. This might help to explain why women often complain that their male friends or partners are often so understanding when they are alone and yet laugh at sexist jokes or even make those jokes themselves when they are out with a group.

The fear of being seen as a sissy dominates the cultural definitions of manhood. It starts so early. "Boys among boys are ashamed to be unmanly," wrote one educator in 1871. I have a standing bet with a friend that I can walk onto any playground in America where 6-year-old boys are happily playing and by asking one question, I can provoke a fight. That question is simple: "Who's a sissy around here?" Once posed, the challenge is made. One of two things is likely to happen. One boy will accuse another of being a sissy, to which that boy will respond that he is not a sissy, that the first boy is. They may have to fight it out to see who's lying. Or a whole group of boys will surround one boy and all shout "He is! He is!" That boy will either burst into tears and run home crying, disgraced, or he will have to take on several boys at once, to prove that he's not a sissy. (And what will his father or older brothers tell him if he chooses to run home crying?) It will be some time before he regains any sense of self-respect.

Violence is often the single most evident marker of manhood. Rather it is the willingness to fight, the desire to fight. The origin of our expression that one has a chip on one's shoulder lies in the practice of an adolescent boy in the country or small town at the turn of the century, who would literally walk around with a chip of wood balanced on his shoulder—a signal of his readiness to fight with anyone who would take the initiative of knocking the chip off.

As adolescents, we learn that our peers are a kind of gender police, constantly threatening to unmask us as feminine, as sissies. One of the favorite tricks when I was an adolescent was to ask a boy to look at his fingernails. If he held his palm toward his face and curled his fingers back to see them, he passed the test. He'd looked at his nails "like a man." But if he held the back of his hand away from his face, and looked at his fingernails with arm outstretched, he was immediately ridiculed as a sissy.

As young men we are constantly riding those gender boundaries, checking the fences we have constructed on the perimeter, making sure that nothing even remotely feminine might show through. The possibilities of being unmasked are everywhere. Even the most seemingly insignificant thing can pose a threat or activate that haunting terror. On the day the students in my course "Sociology of Men and Masculinities" were scheduled to discuss homophobia and male-male friendships, one student provided a touching illustration. Noting that it was a beautiful day, the first day of spring after a brutal northeast winter, he decided to wear shorts to class. "I had this really nice pair of new Madras shorts," he commented. "But then I thought to myself, these shorts have lavender and pink in them. Today's class topic is homophobia. Maybe today is not the best day to wear these shorts."

Our efforts to maintain a manly front cover everything we do. What we wear. How we talk. How we walk. What we eat. Every mannerism, every movement contains a coded gender language. Think, for example, of how you would answer the question: How do you "know" if a man is homosexual? When I ask this question in classes or workshops, respondents invariably provide a pretty standard list of stereotypically effeminate behaviors. He walks a certain way, talks a certain way, acts a certain way. He's very emotional; he shows his feelings. One woman commented that she "knows" a man is gay if he really cares about her; another said she knows he's gay if he shows no interest in her, if he leaves her alone.

Now alter the question and imagine what heterosexual men do to make sure no one could possibly get the "wrong idea" about them. Responses typically refer to the original stereotypes, this time as a set of negative rules about behavior. Never dress that way. Never talk or walk that way. Never show your feelings or get emotional. Always be prepared to demonstrate sexual interest in women that you meet, so it is impossible for any woman to get the wrong idea about you. In this sense, homophobia, the fear of being perceived as gay, as not a real man, keeps men exaggerating all the traditional rules of masculinity, including sexual predation with women. Homophobia and sexism go hand in hand.

The stakes of perceived sissydom are enormous—sometimes matters of life and death. We take enormous risks to prove our manhood, exposing ourselves disproportionately to health risks, workplace hazards, and stress-related illnesses. Men commit suicide three times as often as women. . . .

In one survey, women and men were asked what they were most afraid of. Women responded that they were most afraid of being raped and murdered. Men responded that they were most afraid of being laughed at.

HOMOPHOBIA AS A CAUSE OF SEXISM, HETEROSEXISM, AND RACISM

Homophobia is intimately interwoven with both sexism and racism. The fear—sometimes conscious, sometimes not—that others might perceive us as homosexual propels men to enact all manner of exaggerated masculine behaviors and attitudes to make sure that no one could possibly get the wrong idea about us. One of the centerpieces of that exaggerated masculinity is putting women down, both by excluding them from the public sphere and by the quotidian put-downs in speech and behaviors that organize the daily life of the American man. Women and gay men become the "other" against which heterosexual men project their identities, against whom they stack the decks so as to compete in a situation in which they will always win, so that by suppressing them, men can stake a claim for their own manhood. Women threaten emasculation by representing the home, workplace, and familial responsibility, the negation of fun. Gay men have historically played the role of the consummate sissy in the American popular mind because homosexuality is seen as an inversion of normal gender development. There have been other "others." Through American history, various groups have represented the sissy, the non-men against whom American men played out their definitions of manhood, often with vicious results. In fact, these changing groups provide an interesting lesson in American historical development.

At the turn of the 19th century, it was Europeans and children who provided the contrast for American men. The "true American was vigorous, manly, and direct, not effete and corrupt like the supposed Europeans," writes Rupert Wilkinson. . . . By the middle of the century, black slaves had replaced the effete nobleman. Slaves were seen as dependent, helpless men, incapable of defending their women and children, and therefore less than manly. Native Americans were cast as foolish and naive children, so they could be infantalized as the "Red Children of the Great White Father" and therefore excluded from full manhood.

By the end of the century, new European immigrants were also added to the list of the unreal men, especially the Irish and Italians, who were seen as too passionate and emotionally volatile to remain controlled sturdy oaks, and Jews, who were seen as too bookishly effete and too physically puny to truly measure up. In the mid-20th century, it was also Asians—first the Japanese during the Second World War, and more recently, the Vietnamese during the Vietnam War—who have served as unmanly templates against which American men have hurled their gendered rage. Asian men were seen as small, soft, and effeminate—hardly men at all.

Such a list of "hyphenated" Americans . . . composes the majority of American men. So manhood is only possible for a distinct minority, and the definition has been constructed to prevent the others from achieving it. Interestingly, this emasculation of one's enemies has a flip side—and one that is equally gendered. These very groups that have historically been cast as less than manly were also, often simultaneously, cast as hypermasculine, as sexually aggressive, violent rapacious beasts, against whom "civilized" men must take a decisive stand and thereby rescue civilization. . . . But whether one saw these groups as effeminate sissies or as brutal uncivilized savages, the terms with which they were perceived were gendered. These groups become the "others," the screens against which traditional conceptions of manhood were developed.

Being seen as unmanly is a fear that propels American men to deny manhood to others, as a way of proving the unprovable—that one is fully manly. Masculinity becomes a defense against the perceived threat of humiliation in the eyes of other men, enacted through a "sequence of postures"—things we might say, or do, or even think, that, if we thought carefully about them, would make us ashamed of ourselves. After all, how many of us have made homophobic or sexist remarks, or told racist jokes, or made lewd comments to women on the street? How many of us have translated those ideas and those words into actions, by physically attacking gay men, or forcing or cajoling a woman to have sex even though she didn't really want to because it was important to score?

POWER AND POWERLESSNESS IN THE LIVES OF MEN

I have argued that homophobia, men's fear of other men, is the animating condition of the dominant definition of masculinity in America, that the reigning definition of masculinity is a defensive effort to prevent being emasculated. In our efforts to suppress or overcome those fears, the dominant culture exacts a tremendous price from those deemed less than fully manly: women, gay men, nonnative-born men, men of color. This perspective may help clarify a paradox in men's lives, a paradox in which men have virtually all the power and yet do not feel powerful.

Manhood is equated with power—over women, over other men. Everywhere we look, we see the institutional expression of that power—in state and national legislatures, on the boards of directors of every major U.S. corporation or law firm, and in every school and hospital administration. Women have long understood this, and feminist women have spent the past three decades challenging both the public and the private expressions of men's power and acknowledging their fear of men. Feminism as a set of theories both explains women's fear of men and empowers women to confront it both publicly and privately. Feminist women have theorized that masculinity is about the drive for domination, the drive for power, for conquest.

This feminist definition of masculinity as the drive for power is theorized from women's point of view. It is how women experience masculinity. But it assumes a symmetry between the public and the private that does not conform to men's experiences. Feminists observe that women, as a group, do not hold power in our society. They also observe that individually, they, as women, do not feel powerful. They feel afraid, vulnerable. Their observation of the social reality and their individual experiences are therefore symmetrical. Feminism also observes that men, as a group, *are* in power. Thus, with the same symmetry, feminism has tended to assume that individually men must feel powerful.

This is why the feminist critique of masculinity often falls on deaf ears with men. When confronted with the analysis that men have all the power, many men react incredulously. "What do you mean, men have all the power?" they ask. "What are you talking about? My wife bosses me around. My kids boss me around. My boss bosses me around. I have no power at all! I'm completely powerless!"

Men's feelings are not the feelings of the powerful, but of those who see themselves as powerless. These are the feelings that come inevitably from the discontinuity between the social and the psychological, between the aggregate analysis that reveals how men are in power as a group and the psychological fact that they do not feel powerful as individuals. They are the feelings of men who were raised to believe themselves entitled to feel that power, but do not feel it. No wonder many men are frustrated and angry.

. . .

The dimension of power is now reinserted into men's experience not only as the product of individual experience but also as the product of relations with other men. In this sense, men's experience of powerlessness is *real*—the men actually feel it and certainly act on it—but it is not *true*, that is, it does not accurately describe their condition. In contrast to women's lives, men's lives are structured around relationships of power and men's differential access to power, as well as the differential access to that power of men as a group. Our imperfect analysis of our own situation leads us to believe that we men need *more* power, rather than leading us to support feminists' efforts to rearrange power relationships along more equitable lines.

. . .

Why, then, do American men feel so powerless? Part of the answer is because we've constructed the rules of manhood so that only the tiniest fraction of men come to believe that they are the biggest of wheels, the sturdiest of oaks, the most virulent repudiators of femininity, the most daring and aggressive. We've managed to disempower the overwhelming majority of American men by other means—such as discriminating on the basis of race, class, ethnicity, age, or sexual preference.

. . .

Others still rehearse the politics of exclusion, as if by clearing away the playing field of secure gender identity of any that we deem less than manly—women, gay men, nonnative-born men, men of color—middle-class, straight, white men can reground their sense of themselves without those haunting fears and that deep shame that they are unmanly and will be exposed by other men. This is the manhood of racism, of sexism, of homophobia. It is the manhood that is so chronically insecure that it trembles at the idea of lifting the ban on gays in the military, that is so threatened by women in the workplace that women become the targets of sexual harassment, that is so deeply frightened of equality that it must ensure that the playing field of male competition remains stacked against all newcomers to the game.

Exclusion and escape have been the dominant methods American men have used to keep their fears of humiliation at bay. The fear of emasculation by other men, of being humiliated, of being seen as a sissy, is the leitmotif in my reading of the history of American manhood. Masculinity has become a relentless test by which we prove to other men, to women, and ultimately to ourselves, that we have successfully mastered the part. The restlessness that men feel today is nothing new in American history; we have been anxious and restless for almost two centuries. Neither exclusion nor escape has ever brought us the relief we've sought, and there is no reason to think that either will solve our problems now. Peace of mind, relief from gender struggle, will come only from a politics of inclusion, not exclusion, from standing up for equality and justice, and not by running away.

63

Patriarchy, the System

An It, Not a He, a Them, Or An Us

Allan G. Johnson

"When you say patriarchy," a man complained from the rear of the audience, "I know what you *really* mean—me!" A lot of people hear "men" whenever someone says "patriarchy," so that criticism of gender oppression is taken to mean that all men—each and every one of them—are oppressive people. Not surprisingly, many men take it personally if someone merely mentions patriarchy or the oppression of women, bristling at what they often see as a way to make them feel guilty. And some women feel free to blame individual men for patriarchy simply because they're men. Some of the time, men feel defensive because they identify with patriarchy and its values and don't want to face the consequences these produce or the prospect of giving up male privilege. But defensiveness more often reflects a common confusion about the difference between patriarchy as a kind of society and the people who participate in it. If we're ever going to work toward real change, it's a confusion we'll have to clear up.

To do this, we have to realize that we're stuck in a model of social life that views everything as beginning and ending with individuals. Looking at things in this way, we tend to think that if evil exists in the world, it's only because there are evil people who have entered into an evil conspiracy. Racism exists, for example, simply because white people are racist bigots who hate members of racial and ethnic minorities and want to do them harm. There is gender oppression because men want and like to dominate women and act out hostility toward them. There is poverty and class oppression because people in the upper classes are greedy, heartless, and cruel. The flip side of this individualistic model of guilt and blame is that race, gender, and class oppression are actually not oppression at all, but merely the sum of individual failings on the part of blacks, women, and the poor, who lack the right stuff to compete successfully with whites, men, and others who know how to make something of themselves.

What this kind of thinking ignores is that we are all participating in something larger than ourselves or any collection of us. On some level, most people are familiar with the idea that social life involves us in something larger than ourselves, but few seem to know what to do with that idea. . . . How, for example, do we participate in patriarchy, and how does that link us to the consequences it produces? How is what we think of as "normal" life related to male dominance, women's oppression, and the hierarchical, control-obsessed world in which they, and our lives, are embedded?

Without asking such questions we can't understand gender fully and we avoid taking responsibility either for ourselves or for patriarchy. Instead, "the system" serves as a vague, unarticulated catch-all, a dumping ground for social problems, a scapegoat that can never be held to account and that, for all the power we think it has, can't talk back or actually *do* anything. . . .

If we see patriarchy as nothing more than men's and women's individual personalities, motivations, and behavior, for example, then it probably won't even occur to us to ask about larger contexts—such as institutions like the family, religion, and the economy—and how people's lives are shaped in relation to them. From this kind of individualistic perspective, we might ask why a particular man raped, harassed, or beat a woman. We wouldn't ask, however, what kind of society would promote persistent *patterns* of such behavior in everyday life, from wife-beating jokes to the routine inclusion of sexual coercion and violence in mainstream movies. . . .

If the goal is to change the world, this won't help us. We need to see and deal with the social roots that generate and nurture the social problems that are reflected in the behavior of individuals. We can't do this without realizing that we all participate in something larger than ourselves, something we didn't create but that we have the power to affect through the choices we make about *how* to participate.

That something larger is patriarchy, which is more than a collection of individuals (such as "men"). It is a system, which means it can't be reduced to the people who participate in it. . . .

[P]atriarchy [is] a kind of society that is more than a collection of women and men and can't be understood simply by understanding them. *We are not patriarchy*, no more than people who believe in Allah *are* Islam or Canadians *are* Canada. Patriarchy is a kind of society organized around certain kinds of social relationships and ideas. As individuals, we participate in it. Paradoxically, our participation both shapes our lives and gives us the opportunity to be part of changing or perpetuating it. But *we are not it*, which means that patriarchy can exist without men having "oppressive personalities" or actively conspiring with one another to defend male privilege. To demonstrate that gender oppression exists, we don't have to show that men are villains, that women are good-hearted victims, that women don't participate in their own oppression, or that men never oppose it. If a society is oppressive, then people who grow up and live in it will tend to accept, identify with, and participate in it as "normal" and unremarkable life. That's the path of least resistance in any system. It's hard not to follow it, given how we depend on society and its rewards and punishments that hinge on going along with the status quo. When oppression is woven into the fabric of everyday life, we don't need to go out of our way to be overly oppressive in order for an oppressive system to produce oppressive consequences. As the saying goes, what evil requires is simply that ordinary people do nothing.

. . .

The crucial thing to understand about patriarchy or any other kind of social system is that it's something people participate in. It's an arrangement of shared understandings and relationships that connect people to one another and something larger than themselves. . . .

PATRIARCHY

The key to understanding any system is to identify its various parts and how they're arranged to form a whole. . . . Patriarchy's defining elements are its male-dominated, male-identified, and male-centered character, but this is just the beginning. At its core, patriarchy is a set of symbols and ideas that make up a culture embodied by everything from the content of everyday conversation to literature and film. Patriarchal culture includes ideas about the nature of things, including men, women, and humanity, with manhood and masculinity most closely associated with being human and womanhood and femininity relegated to the marginal position of "other." It's about how social life is and how it's supposed to be; about what's expected of people and about how they feel. It's about standards of feminine beauty and masculine toughness, images of feminine vulnerability and masculine protectiveness, of older men coupled with young women, of elderly women alone. It's about defining women and men as opposites, about the "naturalness" of male aggression, competition, and dominance and of female caring, cooperation, and subordination. It's about the valuing of masculinity and maleness and the devaluing of femininity and femaleness. It's about the primary importance of a husband's career and the secondary status of a wife's, about child care as a priority in women's lives and its secondary importance in men's. It's about the social acceptability of anger, rage, and toughness in men but not in women, and of caring, tenderness, and vulnerability in women but not in men.

Above all, patriarchal culture is about the core value of control and domination in almost every area of human existence. From the expression of emotion to economics to the natural environment, gaining and exercising control is a continuing goal of great importance. Because of this, the concept of power takes on a narrow definition in terms of "power over"—the ability to control others, events, resources, or oneself in spite of resistance—rather than alternatives such as the ability to cooperate with others, to give freely of oneself, or to feel and act in harmony with nature. To have power over and to be prepared to use it are defined culturally as good and desirable (and characteristically "masculine"), and to lack such power or to be reluctant to use it is seen as weak if not contemptible (and characteristically "feminine").

. . .

Going deeper into patriarchal culture, we find a complex web of ideas that define reality and what's considered good and desirable. To see the world through patriarchal eyes is to believe that women and men are profoundly different in their basic natures, that hierarchy is the only alternative to chaos, and that men were made in the image of a masculine God with whom they enjoy a special relationship. It is to take as obvious the idea that there are two and only two distinct genders; that patriarchal heterosexuality is "natural" and same-sex attraction is not; that because men neither bear nor breast-feed children, they cannot feel a compelling bodily connection to them; that on some level every woman, whether heterosexual or lesbian, wants a "real man" who knows how to "take charge of things," including her; that females can't be trusted, especially when they're menstruating or accusing men of sexual misconduct. To embrace patriarchy is to believe that mothers should stay home and that fathers should work out of the home, regardless of men's and women's actual abilities or needs. It is to buy into the notion that women are weak and men are strong, that women and children need men to support and protect them, all in spite of the fact that in many ways men are not the physically stronger sex, that women perform a huge share of hard physical labor in many societies (often larger than men's), that women's physical endurance tends to be greater than men's over the long haul, that women tend to be more capable of enduring pain and emotional stress. And yet such evidence means little in the face of a patriarchal culture that dictates how things *ought* to be . . . .

To live in a patriarchal culture is to learn what's expected of us as men and women, the rules that regulate punishment and reward based on how we behave and appear. These rules range from laws that require men to fight in wars not of their own choosing to customary expectations that mothers will provide child care, or that when a woman shows sexual interest in a man or merely smiles or acts friendly, she gives up her right to say no and control her own body. And to live under patriarchy is to take into ourselves shared ways of feeling—the hostile contempt for femaleness that forms the core of misogyny and presumptions of male superiority, the ridicule men direct at other men who show signs of vulnerability or weakness, or the fear and insecurity that every woman must deal with when she exercises the right to move freely in the world, especially at night and by herself. Such ideas make up the symbolic sea we swim in and the air we breathe. They are the primary well from which springs how we think about ourselves, other people, and the world. As such, they provide a taken-for-granted everyday reality, the setting for our interactions with other people that continually fashion and refashion a shared sense of what the world is about and who we are in relation to it. This doesn't mean that the ideas underlying patriarchy determine what we think, feel, and do, but it does mean they define what we'll have to *deal with* as we participate in it.

The prominent place of misogyny in patriarchal culture, for example, doesn't mean that every man and woman consciously hates all things female. But it does mean that to the extent that we don't feel such hatred, it's *in spite of* paths of least resistance contained in our culture. Complete freedom from such feelings and judgments is all but impossible. It is certainly possible for heterosexual men to love women without mentally fragmenting them into breasts, buttocks, genitals, and other variously desirable parts. It is possible for women to feel good about their bodies, to not judge themselves as being too fat, to not abuse themselves to one degree or another in pursuit of impossible male-identified standards of beauty and sexual attractiveness. All of this is possible; but to live in patriarchy is to breathe in misogynist images of women as objectified sexual property valued primarily for their usefulness to men. This finds its way into everyone who grows up breathing and swimming in it, and once inside us it remains, however unaware of it we may be. So, when we hear or express sexist jokes and other forms of misogyny we may not recognize it, and even if we do, say nothing rather than risk other people thinking we're "too sensitive" or, especially in the case of men, "not one of the guys." In either case, we are involved, if only by our silence.

The symbols and ideas that make up patriarchal culture are important to understand because they have such powerful effects on the structure of social life. By "structure," I mean the ways that gender privilege and oppression are organized through social relationships and unequal distributions of rewards, opportunities, and resources. This appears in countless patterns of everyday life in family and work, religion and politics, community and education. It is found in family divisions of labor that exempt fathers from most domestic work even when both parents work outside the home, and in the concentration of women in lower-level pink-collar jobs and male predominance almost everywhere else. It is in the unequal distribution of income and all that goes with it, from access to health care to the availability of leisure time. It is in patterns of male violence and harassment that can turn a simple walk in the park or a typical day at work or a lovers' quarrel into a life-threatening nightmare. More than anything, the structure of patriarchy is found in the unequal distribution of power that makes oppression possible, in patterns of male dominance in every facet of human life, from everyday conversation to global politics. By its nature, patriarchy puts issues of power, dominance, and control at the center of human existence, not only in relationships between men and women, but among men as they compete and struggle to gain status, maintain control, and protect themselves from what other men might do to them.

. . .

THE SYSTEM IN US IN THE SYSTEM

One of the most difficult things to accept about patriarchy is that we're involved in it, which means we're also involved in its consequences. This is especially hard for men who refuse to believe they benefit from women's oppression, because they can't see how this could happen without their being personally oppressive in their intentions, feelings, and behavior. For many men, being told they're *involved* in oppression can only mean they *are* oppressive.

A common defense against this is to attribute everything to "society" as something external and autonomous, with wants, needs, interests, and the power to control people by making them into one sort of person or another. . . .

Societies don't exist without people participating in them, which means that we can't understand patriarchy unless we also ask how people are connected to it and how this connection varies, depending on social characteristics such as race, gender, ethnicity, age, and class. . . .

From this perspective, *who* we and other people think we are has a lot to do with *where* we are in relation to social systems and all the positions that people occupy. We wouldn't exist as social beings if it weren't for our participation in one social system or another. It's hard to imagine just who we'd be and what our existence would consist of if we took away all of our connections to the symbols, ideas, and relationships that make up social systems. . . .

In this sense, like all social systems, patriarchy exists only through people's lives. Through this, patriarchy's various aspects are there for us to see over and over again. This has two important implications for how we understand patriarchy. First, to some extent people experience patriarchy as external to them; but this doesn't mean that it's a distinct and separate thing, like a house in which we live. Instead, by participating in patriarchy we are *of* patriarchy and it is *of* us. Both exist *through* the other and neither can exist without the other. Second, patriarchy isn't static; it's an ongoing *process* that's continuously shaped and reshaped. Since the thing we're participating in is patriarchal, we tend to behave in ways that create a patriarchal world from one moment to the next. But we have some freedom to break the rules and construct everyday life in different ways, which means that the paths we choose to follow can do as much to change patriarchy as they can to perpetuate it.

We're involved in patriarchy and its consequences because we occupy social positions in it, which is all it takes. Since gender oppression is, by definition, a system of inequality organized around gender categories, we can no more avoid being involved in it than we can avoid being female or male. *All* men and *all* women are therefore involved in this oppressive system, and none us can control *whether* we participate, only *how*. . . .

Because privilege is conferred by social systems, people don't have to feel privileged in order to *be* privileged. When I do public presentations, for example, I usually come away feeling pretty good about what happened and, therefore, about myself. If anyone were to ask me to explain why things went so well, I'd probably mention my abilities, my years of experience in public speaking, the quality of my ideas, and so on, as well as the interest and contributions of the audience. The last thing that would occur to me, however, would be that my success was aided by my gender, that if I'd performed in exactly the same way but happened to be a woman, research shows quite clearly that I'd have been taken less seriously, been evaluated less positively, and attributed less of my success to my own efforts and ability. The difference between the two outcomes is a measure of my gender privilege, and there is little I can do to get rid of it, because its authority doesn't rest in me but in society itself, especially in cultural images of gender. The audience doesn't know it's conferring gender privilege on me, and I may not be aware that I'm receiving it. But the privilege is there, nonetheless, whether we intend or want it. That all this may feel "natural" and nonprivileged only deepens the system's hold on all who are involved in it.

Since we're born into patriarchy, and since participating in social life is what makes us who we are, we can't escape growing up sexist to some degree. This means that the question we have to ask ourselves isn't whether sexism is part of who we are, but how broadly and deeply it is ingrained in us, how it appears in our experience and behavior, and what we can do about it. No one wants to think of themselves as involved in social oppression, but being involved doesn't mean we're bad or to blame for oppression, for people can and do participate in systems that produce horrible, immoral consequences without being horrible and immoral people. None of us is responsible or to blame for the world we were born into or the inevitable way in which we took it into ourselves. But—and this "but" is crucial—the ongoing reconstruction of that society is shaped by how people like us choose to participate in it once we're here. We are involved; we are part of the problem; the question is whether we'll choose to also be part of the solution.

64

Feminism

A Movement to End Sexist Oppression

bell hooks

A central problem within feminist discourse has been our inability to either arrive at a consensus of opinion about what feminism is or accept definition(s) that could serve as points of unification. Without agreed upon definition(s), we lack a sound foundation on which to construct theory or engage in overall meaningful praxis. Expressing her frustrations with the absence of clear definitions in a recent essay, "Towards A Revolutionary Ethics," Carmen Vasquez comments:

> We can't even agree on what a "Feminist" is, never mind what she would believe in and how she defines the principles that constitute honor among us. In key with the American capitalist obsession for individualism and anything goes so long as it gets you what you want. Feminism in American has come to mean anything you like, honey. There are as many definitions of Feminism as there are feminists, some of my sisters say, with a chuckle. I don't think it's funny.

It is not funny. It indicates a growing disinterest in feminism as a radical political movement. It is a despairing gesture expressive of the belief that solidarity between women is not possible. It is a sign that the political naïveté which has traditionally characterized woman's lot in male-dominated culture abounds.

Most people in the United States think of feminism or the more commonly used term "women's lib" as a movement that aims to make women the social equals of men. This broad definition, popularized by the media and mainstream segments of the movement, raises problematic questions. Since men are not equals in white supremacist, capitalist, patriarchal class structure, which men do women want to be equal to? Do women share a common vision of what equality means? Implicit in this simplistic definition of women's liberation is a dismissal of race and class as factors that, in conjunction with sexism, determine the extent to which an individual will be discriminated against, exploited, or oppressed. Bourgeois white women interested in women's rights issues have been satisfied with simple definitions for obvious reasons. Rhetorically placing themselves in the same social category as oppressed women, they were not anxious to call attention to race and class privilege.

Women in lower class and poor groups, particularly those who are non-white, would not have defined women's liberation as women gaining social equality with men since they are continually reminded in their everyday lives that all women do not share a common social status. Concurrently, they know that many males in their social groups are exploited and oppressed. Knowing that men in their groups do not have social, political, and economic power, they would not deem it liberatory to share their social status. While they are aware that sexism enables men in their respective groups to have privileges denied them, they are more likely to see exaggerated expressions of male chauvinism among their peers as stemming from the male's sense of himself as powerless and ineffectual in relation to ruling male groups, rather than an expression of an overall privileged social status. From the very onset of the women's liberation movement, these women were suspicious of feminism precisely because they recognized the limitations inherent in its definition. They recognized the possibility that feminism defined as social equality with men might easily become a movement that would primarily affect the social standing of white women in middle and upper class groups while affecting only in a very marginal way the social status of working class and poor women.

. . .

In a recent article in a San Francisco newspaper, "Sisters—Under the Skin," columnist Bob Greene commented on the aversion many women apparently have to the term feminism. Greene finds it curious that many women "who obviously believe in everything that proud feminists believe in dismiss the term "feminist" as something unpleasant; something with which they do not wish to be associated." Even though such women often acknowledge that they have benefited from feminist-generated reform measures which have improved the social status of specific groups of women, they do not wish to be seen as participants in feminist movement:

> There is no getting around it. After all this time, the term "feminist" makes many bright, ambitious, intelligent women embarrassed and uncomfortable. They simply don't want to be associated with it.
>
> It's as if it has an unpleasant connotation that they want no connection with. Chances are if you were to present them with every mainstream feminist belief, they would go along with the beliefs to the letter—and even if they consider themselves feminists, they hasten to say no.

Many women are reluctant to advocate feminism because they are uncertain about the meaning of the term. Other women from exploited and oppressed ethnic groups dismiss the term because they do not wish to be perceived as supporting a racist movement; feminism is often equated with white women's rights effort. Large numbers of women see feminism as synonymous with lesbianism; their homophobia leads them to reject association with any group identified as pro-lesbian. Some women fear the word "feminism" because they shun identification with any political movement, especially one perceived as radical. Of course there are women who do not wish to be associated with women's rights movement in any form so they reject and oppose feminist movement. Most women are more familiar with negative perspectives on "women's lib" than the positive significations of feminism. It is this term's positive political significance and power that we must now struggle to recover and maintain.

Currently feminism seems to be a term without any clear significance. The "anything goes" approach to the definition of the word has rendered it practically meaningless. What is meant by "anything goes" is usually that any woman who wants social equality with men regardless of her political perspective (she can be a conservative right-winger or a nationalist communist) can label herself feminist. Most attempts at defining feminism reflect the class nature of the movement. Definitions are usually liberal in origin and focus on the individual woman's right to freedom and self-determination. . . .

This definition of feminism is almost apolitical in tone; yet it is the type of definition many liberal women find appealing. It evokes a very romantic notion of personal freedom which is more acceptable than a definition that emphasizes radical political action.

. . . Feminism is a struggle to end sexist oppression. Therefore, it is necessarily a struggle to eradicate the ideology of domination that permeates Western culture on various levels as well as a commitment to reorganizing society so that the self-development of people can take precedence over imperialism, economic expansion, and material desires. Defined in this way, it is unlikely that women would join feminist movement simply because we are biologically the same. A commitment to feminism so defined would demand that each individual participant acquire a critical political consciousness based on ideas and beliefs.

. . .

Feminism defined in political terms that stress collective as well as individual experience challenges women to enter a new domain—to leave behind the apolitical stance sexism decrees is our lot and develop political consciousness. . . . By repudiating the popular notion that the focus of feminist movement should be social equality of the sexes and emphasizing eradicating the cultural basis of group oppression, our own analysis would require an exploration of all aspects of women's political reality. This would mean that race and class oppression would be recognized as feminist issues with as much relevance as sexism.

When feminism is defined in such a way that it calls attention to the diversity of women's social and political reality, it centralizes the experiences of all women, especially the women whose social conditions have been least written about, studied, or changed by political movements. When we cease to focus on the simplistic stance "men are the enemy," we are compelled to examine systems of domination and our role in their maintenance and perpetuation. . . .

Feminism is the struggle to end sexist oppression. Its aim is not to benefit solely any specific group of women, any particular race or class of women. It does not privilege women over men. It has the power to transform in a meaningful way all our lives. . . .

Feminism as a movement to end sexist oppression directs our attention to systems of domination and the inter-relatedness of sex, race, and class oppression. Therefore, it compels us to centralize the experiences and the social predicaments of women who bear the brunt of sexist oppression as a way to understand the collective social status of women in the United States. Defining feminism as a movement to end sexist oppression is crucial for the development of theory because it is a starting point indicating the direction of exploration and analysis.

The foundation of future feminist struggle must be solidly based on a recognition of the need to eradicate the underlying cultural basis and causes of sexism and other forms of group oppression. Without challenging and changing these philosophical structures, no feminist reforms will have a long range impact. Consequently, it is now necessary for advocates of feminism to collectively acknowledge that our struggle cannot be defined as a movement to gain social equality with men; that terms like "liberal feminist" and "bourgeois feminist" represent contradictions that must be resolved so that feminism will not be continually co-opted to serve the opportunistic ends of special interest groups.

C O N T E X T

65

Violence against Women Is a Men's Issue

Jackson Katz

Most people think violence against women is a women's issue. And why wouldn't they? Just about every woman in this society thinks about it every day. If they are not getting harassed on the street, living in an abusive relationship, recovering from a rape, or in therapy to deal with the sexual abuse they suffered as children, they are ordering their daily lives around the *threat* of men's violence.

But it is a mistake to call *men's* violence a *women's* issue. Take the subject of rape. Many people reflexively consider rape to be a women's issue. But let's take a closer look. What percentage of rape is committed by women? Is it 10 percent, 5 percent? No. *Less than 1 percent of rape is committed by women.* Let's state this another way: over 99 percent of rape is perpetrated by men. Whether the victims are female or male, men are overwhelmingly the perpetrators. But we call it a women's issue? Shouldn't that tell us something?

A major premise of . . . [my work] is that the long-running American tragedy of sexual and domestic violence—including rape, battering, sexual harassment, and the sexual exploitation of women and girls—is arguably more revealing about *men* than it is about women. Men, after all, are the ones committing the vast majority of the violence. Men are the ones doing most of the battering and almost all of the raping. Men are the ones paying the prostitutes (and killing them in video games), going to strip clubs, renting sexually degrading pornography, writing and performing misogynistic music.

When men's role in gender violence is discussed—in newspaper articles, sensational TV news coverage, or everyday conversation—the focus is typically on men as perpetrators or potential perpetrators. These days, you don't have to look far to see evidence of the pain and suffering these men cause. But it is rare to find any in-depth discussion about the culture that's producing these violent men. It's almost like the perpetrators are strange aliens who landed here from another planet. It is rarer still to hear thoughtful discussions about the ways that our culture defines "manhood," and how that definition might be linked to the endless string of stories about husbands killing wives, or groups of young men raping girls (and sometimes videotaping the rape) that we hear about on a regular basis.

Why isn't there more conversation about the underlying social factors that contribute to the pandemic of violence against women? Why aren't men's attitudes and behaviors toward women the focus of more critical scrutiny and coordinated action? These days, the 24/7 news cycle brings us a steady stream of gender-violence tragedies: serial killers on the loose, men abducting young girls, domestic-violence homicides, periodic sexual abuse scandals in powerful institutions like the Catholic Church and the Air Force Academy. You can barely turn on the news these days without coming across another gruesome sex crime—whether it's a group of boys gang-raping a girl in a middle school bathroom or a young pregnant woman who turns up missing, and whose husband emerges a few days later as the primary suspect.

Isn't it about time we had a national conversation about the male causes of this violence, instead of endlessly lingering on its consequences in the lives of women? Thanks to the battered women's and rape crisis movements in the U.S., it is no longer taboo to discuss women's experiences of sexual and domestic violence. This is a significant achievement. To an unprecedented extent, American women today expect to be supported—not condemned—when they disclose what men have done to them (unless the man is popular, wealthy, or well-connected, in which case all bets are off.)

This is all for the good. Victims of violence and abuse—whether they're women or men—should be heard and respected. Their needs come first. But let's not mistake concern for victims with the political will to change the conditions that led to their victimization in the first place. . . . It is one thing to focus on the "against women" part of the phrase; but someone's responsible for doing it, and (almost) everyone knows that it's overwhelmingly men. Why aren't people talking about this? Is it realistic to talk about preventing violence against women if no one even wants to say out loud who's responsible for it?

For the past two decades, I've been part of a growing movement of men, in North America and around the world, whose aim is to reduce violence against women by focusing on those aspects of male culture—especially male-peer culture—that provide active or tacit support for some men's abusive behavior. This movement is racially and ethnically diverse, and it brings together men from both privileged and poor communities, and everyone in between. This is challenging work on many levels, and no one should expect rapid results. For example, there is no way to gloss over some of the race, class, and sexual orientation divisions between and among us men. It is also true that it takes time to change social norms that are so deeply rooted in structures of gender and power. Even so, there is room for optimism. We've had our successes: there are arguably more men today who are actively confronting violence against women than at any time in human history.

Make no mistake. Women blazed the trail that we are riding down. Men are in the position to do this work precisely because of the great leadership of women. The battered women's and rape crisis movements and their allies in local, state, and federal government have accomplished a phenomenal amount over the past generation. Public awareness about violence against women is at an all-time high. The level of services available today for female victims and survivors of men's violence is—while not yet adequate—nonetheless historically unprecedented.

. . .

[I propose] that we adopt a much more ambitious approach. If we are going to bring down dramatically the rates of violence against women—not just at the margins—we will need a far-reaching cultural revolution. At its heart, this revolution must be about changing the sexist social norms in male culture, from the elementary school playground to the common room in retirement communities—and every locker room, pool hall, and board-room in between. For us to have any hope of achieving historic reductions in incidents of violence against women, at a minimum we will need to dream big and act boldly. It almost goes without saying that we will need the help of a lot more men—at all levels of power and influence—than are currently involved. Obviously we have our work cut out for us. As a measure of just how far we have to go, consider that in spite of the misogyny and sexist brutality all around us, millions of non-violent men today fail to see gender violence as their issue. "I'm a good guy," they will say. "This isn't my problem."

For years, women of every conceivable ethnic, racial, and religious background have been trying to get men around them—and men in power—to do more about violence against women. . . . On both a micro and a macro level, women in this era have success-fully broken through the historical silence about violence against women and found their voice—here in the U.S. and around the world.

Yet even with all of these achievements, women continue to face an uphill struggle in trying to make meaningful inroads into male culture. Their goal has not been simply to get men to listen to women's stories and truly hear them—although that is a critical first step. The truly vexing challenge has been getting men to actually go out and *do* something about the problem, in the form of educating and organizing *other men* in numbers great enough to prompt a real cultural shift. Some activist women—even those who have had great faith

C
O
N
T
E
X
T

in men as allies—have been beating their heads against the wall for a long time, and are frankly burned out on the effort. I know this because I have been working with many of these women for a long time. They are my colleagues and friends.

My work is dedicated to getting more men to take on the issue of violence against women, and thus to build on what women have achieved. The area that I focus on is not law enforcement or offender treatment, but the *prevention* of sexual and domestic violence and all their related social pathologies—including violence against children. To do this, I and other men here and around the world have been trying to get our fellow men to see that this problem is not just personal for a small number of men who happen to have been touched by the issue. We try to show them that it is personal for them, too. *For all of us*. We talk about men not only as perpetrators but as victims. We try to show them that violence by men against each other—from simple assaults to gay-bashing—*is* linked to the same structures of gender and power that produce so much men's violence against women.

We also make it clear that these issues are not just personal, to be dealt with as private family matters. They are political as well, with repercussions that reverberate throughout our lives and communities in all sorts of meaningful and disturbing ways. For example, according to a 2003 report by the U.S. Conference of Mayors, domestic violence was a primary cause of homelessness in almost half of the twenty-five cities surveyed. And worldwide, sexual coercion and other abusive behavior by men plays an important role in the transmission of HIV/AIDS.

Nonetheless, convincing other men to make gender violence issues a priority is not an easy sell . . . [and, t]here is no point in being naïve about why women have had such a difficult time convincing men to make violence against women a men's issue. In spite of significant social change in recent decades, men continue to grow up with, and are socialized into, a deeply misogynistic, male-dominated culture, where violence against women—from the subtle to the homicidal—is disturbingly common. It's *normal*. And precisely because the mistreatment of women is such a pervasive characteristic of our patriarchal culture, most men, to a greater or lesser extent, have played a role in its perpetuation. This gives us a strong incentive to avert our eyes.

Women, of course, have also been socialized into this misogynistic culture. Some of them resist and fight back. In fact, women's ongoing resistance to their subordinate status is one of the most momentous developments in human civilization over the past two centuries. Just the same, plenty of women show little appetite for delving deeply into the cultural roots of sexist violence. It's much less daunting simply to blame "sick" individuals for the problem. You hear women explaining away men's bad behavior as the result of individual pathology all the time: "Oh, he just had a bad childhood," or "He's an angry drunk. The booze gets to him. He's never been able to handle it."

But regardless of how difficult it can be to show some women that violence against women is a social problem that runs deeper than the abusive behavior of individual men, it is still much easier to convince women that dramatic change is in their best interest than it is to convince men. In fact, many people would argue that, since men are the dominant sex and violence serves to reinforce this dominance, it is not in men's best interests to reduce violence against women, and that the very attempt to enlist a critical mass of men in this effort amounts to a fool's errand.

For those of us who reject this line of reasoning, the big question then is how do we reach men? We know we're not going to transform, overnight or over many decades, certain structures of male power and privilege that have developed over thousands of years. Nevertheless, how are we going to bring more men—many more men—into a conversation about sexism and violence against women? And how are we going to do this without turning them off, without berating them, without blaming them for centuries of sexist oppression? Moreover, how are we going to move beyond talk and get substantial numbers of men to partner *with* women in reducing men's violence, instead of working *against* them in some sort of fruitless and counterproductive gender struggle?

. . .

I understand the skepticism of women who for years have been frustrated by men's complacency about something as basic as a woman's right to live free from the threat of violence. But I am convinced that men who are active in gender-violence prevention today speak for a much larger number of men. I would not go so far as to say that a silent majority of men supports everything that gender-violence prevention activists stand for, but an awful lot of men privately cheer us on. I have long felt this way, but now there is a growing body of research—in social norms theory—that confirms it empirically.

Social norms theory begins with the premise that people often misperceive the extent to which their peers hold certain attitudes or participate in certain behaviors. In the absence of accurate knowledge, they are more likely to be influenced by what they *think* people think and do, rather than what they *actually* think and do. . . .

There have been a number of studies in the past several years that demonstrate that significant numbers of men are uncomfortable with the way some of their male peers talk about and treat women. But since few men in our society have dared to talk publicly about such matters, many men think they are the only ones who feel uncomfortable. Because they feel isolated and alone in their discomfort, they do not say anything. Their silence, in turn, simply reinforces the false perception that few men are uncomfortable with sexist attitudes and behaviors. It is a vicious cycle that keeps a lot of caring men silent.

I meet men all the time who thank me—or my fellow activists and colleagues—for publicly taking on the subject of men's violence. I frequently meet men who are receptive to the paradigm-shifting idea that men's violence against women has to be understood as a men's issue, as their issue. These men come from every demographic and geographic category. They include thousands of men who would not fit neatly into simplistic stereotypes about the kind of man who would be involved in "that touchy-feely stuff."

Still, it is an uphill fight. Truly lasting change is only going to happen as new generations of women come of age and demand equal treatment with men in every realm, and new generations of men work with them to reject the sexist attitudes and behaviors of their predecessors. This will take decades, and the outcome is hardly predetermined. But along with tens of thousands of activist women and men who continue to fight the good fight, I believe that it is possible to achieve something much closer to gender equality, and a dramatic reduction in the level of men's violence against women, both here and around the world. And there is a lot at stake. If sexism and violence against women do not subside considerably in the twenty-first century, it will not just be bad news for women. It will also say something truly ugly and tragic about the future of our species.

. . .

66

Out-of-Body Image

Caroline Heldman

On a typical day, you might see ads featuring a naked woman's body tempting viewers to buy an electronic organizer, partially exposed women's breasts being used to sell fishing line, or a woman's rear—wearing only a thong—being used to pitch a new running shoe. Meanwhile, on every newsstand, impossibly slim (and digitally airbrushed) cover "girls" adorn a slew of magazines. With each image, you're hit with a simple, subliminal message: Girls' and women's bodies are objects for others to visually consume.

If such images seem more ubiquitous than ever, it's because U.S. residents are now exposed to anywhere from 3,000 to 5,000 advertisements a day—up from 500 to 2,000 a day in the 1970s. The Internet accounts for much of this growth, and young people are particularly exposed to advertising: 70 percent of 15- to 34-year-olds use social networking technologies such as MySpace and Facebook, which allow advertisers to infiltrate previously private communication space.

Although mass media has always objectified women, it has become increasingly provocative. More and more, female bodies are shown as outright objects (think Rose McGowan's machine-gun leg in the recent horror movie *Grindhouse*), are literally broken into parts (the disembodied woman's torso in advertisements for TV's *The Sarah Connor Chronicles*) or are linked with sexualized violence (simulated crime scenes on *America's Next Top Model* featuring seemingly dead women).

A steady diet of exploitative, sexually provocative depictions of women feeds a poisonous trend in women's and girls' perceptions of their bodies, one that has recently been recognized by social scientists as self-objectification—viewing one's body as a sex object to be consumed by the male gaze. Like W.E.B. DuBois' famous description of the experience of black Americans, self-objectification is a state of "double consciousness . . . a sense of always looking at one's self through the eyes of others."

Women who self-objectify are desperate for outside validation of their appearance and present their bodies in ways that draw attention. A study I did of 71 randomly selected female students from a liberal arts college in Los Angeles, for example, found that 70 percent were medium or high self-objectifiers, meaning that they have internalized the male gaze and chronically monitor their physical appearance. Boys and men experience self-objectification as well, but at a much lower rate—probably because, unlike women, they rarely get the message that their bodies are the primary determination of their worth.

Researchers have learned a lot about self-objectification since the term was coined in 1997 by University of Michigan psychology professor Barbara Fredrickson and Colorado College psychology professor Tomi-Ann Roberts. Numerous studies since then have shown that girls and women who self-objectify are more prone to depression and low self-esteem and have less faith in their own capabilities; which can lead to diminished success in life. They are more likely to engage in "habitual body monitoring"—constantly thinking about how their bodies appear to the outside world—which puts them at higher risk for eating disorders such as anorexia and bulimia. And they are prone to embarrassment about bodily functions such as menstruation, as well as general feelings of disgust and shame about their bodies.

Self-objectification has also been repeatedly shown to sap cognitive functioning, because of all the attention devoted to body monitoring. For instance, a 1998 study asked two groups of women to take a math exam—one group in swimsuits, the other in sweaters. The swimsuit-wearers, distracted by body concerns, performed significantly worse than their peers in sweaters.

Several of my own surveys of college students indicate that this impaired concentration by self-objectifiers may hurt their academic performance. Those with low self-objectification reported an average GPA of 3.5, whereas those with high self-objectification reported a 3.1. While this gap may appear small, in graduate-school admissions it represents the difference between being competitive and being out of the running for the top schools.

Another worrisome effect of self-objectification is that it diminishes political efficacy—a person's belief that she can have an impact through the political process. In another survey of mine, 33 percent of high self-objectifiers felt low political efficacy, compared to 13 percent of low self-objectifiers. Since political efficacy leads to participation in politics, having less of it means that self-objectifiers may be less likely to vote or run for office.

The effects of self-objectification on young girls are of such growing concern that the American Psychological Association published an investigative report on it last year. The APA found that girls as young as 7 years old are exposed to clothing, toys, music, magazines and television programs that encourage them to be sexy or "hot"—teaching them to think of themselves as sex objects before their own sexual maturity. Even thong underwear is being sold in sizes for 7- to 10-year-olds. The consequence, wrote Kenyon College psychology professor Sarah Murnen in the journal *Sex Roles*, is that girls "are taught to view their bodies as 'projects' that need work before they can attract others, whereas boys are likely to learn to view their bodies as tools to use to master the environment."

Fredrickson, along with Michigan communications professor Kristen Harrison (both work within the university's Institute for Research on Women and Gender), recently discovered that self-objectification actually impairs girls' motor skills. Their study of 202 girls, ages 10 to 17, found that self-objectification impeded girls' ability to throw a softball, even after differences in age and prior experience were factored out. Self-objectification forced girls to split their attention between how their bodies looked and what they wanted them to do, resulting in less forceful throws and worse aim.

One of the more stunning effects of self-objectification is its impact on sex. Nudity can cause great anxiety among self-objectifiers, who then become preoccupied with how their bodies look in sexual positions. One young woman I interviewed described sex as being an "out of body" experience during which she viewed herself through the eyes of her lover, and, sometimes, through the imaginary lens of a camera shooting a porn film. As a constant critic of her body, she couldn't focus on her own sexual pleasure.

Self-objectification can likely explain some other things that researchers are just starting to study. For instance, leading anti-sexist male activist and author Jackson Katz observes, "Many young women now engage in sex acts with men that prioritize the man's pleasure, with little or no expectation of reciprocity." Could this be another result of women seeing themselves as sexual objects, not agents?

Disturbingly, some girls and women celebrate their object status as a form of empowerment. This is evident in a booming industry of T-shirts for women that proclaim their object status, such as one on which "Fuck Foreplay" is written across a half-used tube of KY Jelly, suggesting that the wearer is ready for penetration at a moment's notice. (This shirt also propagates the notion that men do not enjoy foreplay.) Other shirts make light of rape, with words such as "Violate Me" or "No Means Eat Me Out First."

It would be encouraging if these choices reflected the sexual agency for women that feminists have fought so hard for, but they do not. The notion of objectification as empowering is illogical, since objects are acted upon, rather than taking action themselves. The real power in such arrangements lies with boys and men, who come to feel entitled to consume women as objects—first in media, then in real life.

At the root of this normalization of self-objectification may lie new consumer values in the U.S. Unlike the "producer citizen" of yesteryear—invoked in the 1960s by John F. Kennedy's request to "ask not what your country can do for you, ask what you can do for your country"—the more common "consumer citizen" of today asks what the country, and everyone else, can do for him or her. Consumer citizens increasingly think of relationships with others as transactions in which they receive something, making them more comfortable consuming other human beings, visually or otherwise.

Self-objectification isn't going anywhere anytime soon. So what can we do about it? First, we can recognize how our everyday actions feed the larger beast, and realize that we are not powerless. Mass media, the primary peddler of female bodies, can be assailed with millions of little consumer swords. We can boycott companies and engage in other forms of consumer activism, such as socially conscious investments and shareholder actions. We can also contact companies directly to voice our concerns (see *Ms.'* backpage No Comment section, for example) and refuse to patronize businesses that overtly depict women as sex objects.

An example of women's spending power, and the limits of our tolerance for objectification, can be found in the 12-percent dip in profits of clothing company Victoria's Secret this year—due, according to the company's CEO, to its image becoming "too sexy." Victoria's Secret was not the target of an organized boycott; rather, its increasingly risqué "bra and panty show" seems to have begun alienating women, who perhaps no longer want to simply be shown as highly sexualized window dressing.

Another strategy to counter one's own tendency to self-objectify is to make a point of buying products, watching programs and reading publications that promote more authentic women's empowerment. This can be difficult, of course, in a media climate in which companies are rarely wholeheartedly body-positive. For instance, Dove beauty products launched a much-lauded advertising campaign that used "real women" (i.e., not super-skinny ones) instead of models, but then Dove's parent company, Unilever, put out hypersexual ads for Axe men's body spray that showed the fragrance driving scantily clad women into orgiastic states.

Locating unadulterated television and film programming is also tough. Even Lifetime and Oxygen, TV networks created specifically for women, often portray us as weak victims or sex objects and present a narrow version of thin, white "beauty." Action films that promise strong female protagonists (think of the women of *X-Men*, or Lara Croft from *Tomb Raider*) usually deliver these characters in skintight clothes, serving the visual pleasure of men.

Feminist media criticism, at least, is plentiful. *Ms., Bitch* and others, along with publications for young girls such as *New Moon Magazine*, provide thoughtful analyses of media from various feminist perspectives. NOW's Love Your Body website (http://loveyourbody. nowfoundation.org) critiques offensive ads and praises body-positive ones. Blogs, both well-known and lesser-known, provide a platform for women and girls to vent about how the media depicts them. And there's some evidence that criticizing media helps defuse its effects: Murnen's study found that grade-school girls who had negative reactions to pictures of objectified women reported higher self-esteem.

A more radical, personal solution is to actively avoid media that compels us to self-objectify—which, unfortunately, is the vast majority of movies, television programs and women's magazines. My research with college-age women indicates that the less women consume media, the less they self-objectify, particularly if they avoid fashion magazines. By shutting out media, girls and women can create mental and emotional space for true self-exploration.

What would our lives look like if we viewed our bodies as tools to master our environment, instead of projects to be constantly worked on? What if our sexual expressions were based on our own pleasure as opposed to a narrow, consumerist idea of male sexual pleasure? What would disappear from our lives if we stopped seeing ourselves as objects? Painful high heels? Body hatred? Constant dieting? Liposuction? Unreciprocated oral sex?

It's hard to know. Perhaps the most striking outcome of self-objectification is the difficulty women have in imagining identities and sexualities truly our own. In solidarity, we can start on this path, however confusing and difficult it may be.

67

Women's Pay

Why the Gap Remains a Chasm

Aaron Bernstein

During the heyday of the women's movement more than 30 years ago, "59¢ on the dollar" was an oft-heard rallying cry, referring to how little women earned compared with men. Those concerns seem outdated today, when it's easy to find female doctors, lawyers, pop stars, even Presidential advisers. The progress toward equality in the workplace also shows up in government data on wages, which pegs women's average pay at 77% of men's compensation today.

But there's new evidence that women's advances may not be quite so robust after all. When you look at how much the typical woman actually earns over much of her career, the true figure is more like 44% of what the average man makes. That's the conclusion of a new study by Stephen J. Rose, an economist at Macro International Inc., a consulting firm, and Heidi I. Hartmann, President of the Institute for Women's Policy Research in Washington.

Why the big discrepancy? The Bureau of Labor Statistics (BLS) numbers, published every year, are accurate as far as they go. But they only measure the earnings of those who work full-time for an entire year. Only one-quarter of women, though, achieve this level of participation consistently throughout their working lives. So Rose and Hartmann looked at the pay of all men and women over 15 years, including those who worked part-time and dipped in and out of the labor force to care for children or elderly parents. This long-term perspective still shows an arc of progress: The 44%, based on average earnings between 1983 and 1998, jumped from 29% in the prior 15 years. But the more comprehensive view gives a less rosy picture of women's position in the work world.

Outright discrimination against women probably accounts for only about 10 percentage points of the pay gap, according to numerous studies. The bulk of the problem, then, lies with the conflicting needs and norms of society and employers. A majority of men and women still work in largely sex-segregated occupations, Rose and Hartmann's study shows, leaving many women stuck in lower-paying jobs such as cashiers and maids.

Family responsibilities, too, typically still fall more heavily on women, and neither society nor employers have found good ways to mesh those with job demands. Rose and

Hartmann's data show that women can get equal treatment today—but mostly when they behave like traditional men and leave the primary family responsibilities at home. For the majority who can't or won't do that, the work world remains much less accommodating. Of course, many women choose to take time off or to work part-time to be with their children rather than stay on the job. Yet that choice itself is constrained by the widespread lack of day care and flexible job options, Hartmann argues. "The 44% gap we found shows that there are still tremendous differences in how the labor market treats men and women," she says.

Hartmann and Rose came to their results by examining long-term earnings trends. The 77% figure comes from the BLS's 2002 earnings survey and looks at how much full-time, year-round workers make in a given year. By contrast, Rose and Hartmann used a University of Michigan survey that has tracked a sample of randomly chosen people and their children since 1968. They looked at how much each person made between 1983 and 1998 in every year from age 26 to 59 (to exclude students and retirees).

One surprise was just how many women work most of their adult lives. Fully 96% of these prime-age women worked at least one of those 15 years, and they clocked an average of 12 years on the job. In other words, few women these days drop out altogether once they have kids.

But those few years out of the labor market carry a stiff penalty. More than half of all women spent at least a year out of the labor force, the study found, and they earned an average of $21,363 a year over the years they worked, after inflation adjustments, vs. nearly $30,000 for women who stuck with it for all 15 years. Indeed, anyone who drops out risks derailing their career and permanently slashing their pay. Just one year off cuts a woman's total earnings over 15 years by 32%, while two years slice it by 46% and three by 56%, according to Hartmann and Rose. The work world penalizes men nearly as much; their average pay drops by 25% if they take off a year. Fewer than 8% of men did so, however. "Our economic system is still based on a family division of labor, and women pay the price," says Rose.

Women also take a big hit for going part-time. On average, they work a lot less than men: 1,498 hours a year, vs. 2,219 worked by the typical man. The fewer hours women work account for about half of the total pay gap between the sexes, Rose and Hartmann concluded. Some women have turned to self-employment as a way to fit work and family together. But they often must accept lower pay in the process. Brita Bergland, a Windsor (Vt.) resident, found it difficult to manage her sales job at a printing company while she also cared for her aging mother and her daughter. So she struck out on her own six years ago and has managed the worklife balance much better ever since. The cost: about a $15,000 cut in annual earnings, down from the $55,000 to $60,000 she made as an employee. "These are the choices women make because society doesn't help them to support children and parents," says Bergland, who's now 50.

And while many women have made great strides in some highly visible professions such as law and medicine, historical patterns of sex segregation remain strong across much of the economy. Overall, just 15% of women work in jobs typically held by men, such as engineer, stockbroker, and judge, while fewer than 8% of men hold female-dominated jobs such as nurse, teacher, or sales clerk. These findings were reiterated in a detailed BLS analysis released on June 2 that uses the 2000 Census to look at the jobs men and women hold.

Such a sex-segregated economy leaves women with some startling disadvantages. Overall, they earn less than men with the same education at all levels. Incredibly, male dropouts pulled down an average of $36,000 a year between 1983 and 1998, after inflation adjustments, while women with a bachelor's degree made $35,000. Women with a graduate degree averaged $42,000, but men got nearly $77,000.

The good news is that the pay gap continues to narrow no matter how it's measured. That's likely to continue; female college graduation rates surpass those of men, and they're catching up in grad school, too, so they're likely to gain from an economy that rewards skill. Women also should benefit from the ongoing shift to services, where they're more likely to work, and lose less than men from the decline of factory jobs.

Still, speedier progress probably won't happen without more employers making work sites family-friendly and revamping jobs to accommodate women and men as they seek to balance work and family demands. "The workplace needs to change to match the work-force," says Ellen Bravo, national director of 9 to 5, National Association of Working Women. Until that happens, a woman's labor will continue to be worth a fraction of a man's.

68

The Body Politic

Abra Fortune Chernik

My body possesses solidness and curve, like the ocean. My weight mingles with Earth's pull, drawing me onto the sand. I have not always sent waves into the world. I flew off once, for five years, and swirled madly like a cracking brown leaf in the salty autumn wind. I wafted, dried out, apathetic.

I had no weight in the world during my years of anorexia. Curled up inside my thinness, a refugee in a cocoon of hunger, I lost the capacity to care about myself or others. I starved my body and twitched in place as those around me danced in the energy of shared existence and progressed in their lives. When I graduated from college crowned with academic honors, professors praised my potential. I wanted only to vanish.

It took three months of hospitalization and two years of outpatient psychotherapy for me to learn to nourish myself and to live in a body that expresses strength and honesty in its shape. I accepted my right and my obligation to take up room with my figure, voice and spirit. I remembered how to tumble forward and touch the world that holds me. I chose the ocean as my guide.

Who disputes the ocean's fullness?

Growing up in New York City, I did not care about the feminist movement. Although I attended an all-girls high school, we read mostly male authors and studied the history of men. Embracing mainstream culture without question, I learned about womanhood from fashion magazines, Madison Avenue and Hollywood. I dismissed feminist alternatives as foreign and offensive, swathed as they were in stereotypes that threatened my adolescent need for conformity.

Puberty hit late; I did not complain. I enjoyed living in the lanky body of a tall child and insisted on the title of "girl." If anyone referred to me as a "young woman," I would cry out, horrified, "Do not call me the W word!" But at sixteen years old, I could no longer deny my fate. My stomach and breasts rounded. Curly black hair sprouted in the most embarrassing places. Hips swelled from a once-flat plane. Interpreting maturation as an unacceptable lapse into fleshiness, I resolved to eradicate the physical symptoms of my impending womanhood.

Magazine articles, television commercials, lunchroom conversation, gymnastics coaches and write-ups on models had saturated me with diet savvy. Once I decided to lose weight, I quickly turned expert. I dropped hot chocolate from my regular breakfast order at the Skyline Diner. I replaced lunches of peanut butter and Marshmallow Fluff sandwiches with small platters of cottage cheese and cantaloupe. I eliminated dinner altogether and blunted my appetite with Tab, Camel Lights, and Carefree bubble gum. When furious craving overwhelmed my resolve and I swallowed an extra something, I would flee to the nearest bathroom to purge my mistake.

Within three months, I had returned my body to its preadolescent proportions and had manipulated my monthly period into drying up. Over the next five years, I devoted my life to losing my weight. I came to resent the body in which I lived, the body that threatened to develop, the body whose hunger I despised but could not extinguish. If I neglected a workout or added a pound or ate a bite too many, I would stare in the mirror and drown myself in a tidal wave of criticism. Hatred of my body generalized to hatred of myself as a person, and self-referential labels such as "pig," "failure" and "glutton" allowed me to believe that I deserved punishment. My self-hatred became fuel for the self-mutilating behaviors of the eating disorder.

As my body shrank, so did my world. I starved away my power and vision, my energy and inclinations. Obsessed with dieting, I allowed relationships, passions and identity to wither. I pulled back from the world, off of the beach, out of the sand. The waves of my existence ceased to roll beyond the inside of my skin.

And society applauded my shrinking. Pound after pound the applause continued, like the pounding ocean outside the door of my beach house.

. . .

By the time I entered the hospital, a mess of protruding bones defined my body, and the bones of my emaciated life rattled me crazy. I carried a pillow around because it hurt to sit down, and I shivered with cold in sultry July. Clumps of brittle hair clogged the drain when I showered, and blackened eyes appeared to sink into my head. My vision of reality wrinkled and my disposition turned mercurial as I slipped into starvation psychosis, a condition associated with severe malnutrition. People told me that I resembled a concentration camp prisoner, a chemotherapy patient, a famine victim or a fashion model.

In the hospital I examined my eating disorder under the lenses of various therapies. I dissected my childhood, my family structure, my intimate relationships, my belief systems. I participated in experiential therapies of movement, art and psychodrama. I learned to use words instead of eating patterns to communicate my feelings. And still I refused to gain more than a minimal amount of weight.

I felt powerful as an anorexic. Controlling my body yielded an illusion of control over my life; I received incessant praise for my figure despite my sickly mien, and my frailty manipulated family and friends into protecting me from conflict. I had reduced my world to a plate of steamed carrots, and over this tiny kingdom I proudly crowned myself queen.

. . .

I spent my remaining month in the hospital supplementing psychotherapy with an independent examination of eating disorders from a social and political point of view. I needed to understand why society would reward my starvation and encourage my vanishing. In the bathroom, a mirror on the open door behind me reflected my backside in a mirror over the sink. Vertebrae poked at my skin, ribs hung like wings over chiseled hip bones, the two sides of my buttocks did not touch. I had not seen this view of myself before.

In writing, I recorded instances in which my eating disorder had tangled the progress of my life and thwarted my relationships. I filled three and a half Mead marble notebooks. Five years' worth of: *I wouldn't sit with Daddy when he was alone in the hospital because I needed to go jogging; I told Derek not to visit me because I couldn't throw up when he was there; I almost failed my comprehensive exams because I was so hungry; I spent my year at Oxford with my head in the toilet bowl; I wouldn't eat the dinner my friends cooked me for my nineteenth birthday because I knew they had used oil in the recipe; I told my family not to come to my college graduation because I didn't want to miss a day at the gym or have to eat a restaurant meal.* And on and on for hundreds of pages.

This honest account of my life dissolved the illusion of anorexic power. I saw myself naked in the truth of my pain, my loneliness, my obsessions, my craziness, my selfishness, my defeat. I also recognized the social and political implications of consuming myself with the trivialities of calories and weight. At college, I had watched as classmates involved themselves in extracurricular clubs, volunteer work, politics and applications for jobs and graduate schools. Obsessed with exercising and exhausted by starvation. I did not even consider joining in such pursuits. Despite my love of writing and painting and literature, despite ranking at the top of my class, I wanted only to teach aerobics. Despite my adolescent days as a loud-mouthed, rambunctious class leader, I had grown into a silent, hungry young woman.

And society preferred me this way: hungry, fragile, crazy. *Winner! Healthy! Fantastic!* I began reading feminist literature to further understand the disempowerment of women in our culture. I digested the connection between a nation of starving, self-obsessed women and the continued success of the patriarchy. I also cultivated an awareness of alternative models of womanhood. In the stillness of the hospital library, new voices in my life rose from printed pages to echo my rage and provide the conception of my feminist consciousness.

I had been willing to accept self-sabotage, but now I refused to sacrifice myself to a society that profited from my pain. I finally understood that my eating disorder symbolized more than "personal psychodynamic trauma." Gazing in the mirror at my emaciated body, I observed a woman held up by her culture as the physical ideal because she was starving, self-obsessed and powerless, a woman called beautiful because she threatened no one except herself. Despite my intelligence, my education, and my supposed Manhattan sophistication, I had believed all of the lies; I had almost given my life in order to achieve the sickly impotence that this culture aggressively links with female happiness, love and success. And everything I had to offer to the world, every tumbling wave, every thought and every passion, nearly died inside me.

As long as society resists female power, fashion will call healthy women physically flawed. As long as society accepts the physical, sexual and economic abuse of women, popular culture will prefer women who resemble little girls. Sitting in the hospital the summer after my college graduation, I grasped the absurdity of a nation of adult women dying to grow small.

Armed with this insight, I loosened the grip of the starvation disease on my body. I determined to recreate myself based on an image of a woman warrior. I remembered my ocean, and I took my first bite.

Gaining weight and getting my head out of the toilet bowl was the most political act I have ever committed.

. . .

Eating disorders affect us all on both a personal and a political level. The majority of my peers—including my feminist peers—still measure their beauty against anorexic ideals. Even among feminists, body hatred and chronic dieting continue to consume lives. Friends of anorexics beg them to please start eating; then these friends go home and continue their own diets. Who can deny that the millions of young women caught in the net of disordered eating will frustrate the potential of the next wave of feminism?

. . .

As young feminists, we must place unconditional acceptance of our bodies at the top of our political agenda. We must claim our bodies as our own to love and honor in their infinite shapes and sizes. Fat, thin, soft, hard, puckered, smooth, our bodies are our homes. By nourishing our bodies, we care for and love ourselves on the most basic level. When we deny ourselves physical food, we go hungry emotionally, psychologically, spiritually and politically. We must challenge ourselves to eat and digest, and allow society to call us too big. We will understand their message to mean too powerful.

Time goes by quickly. One day we will blink and open our eyes as old women. If we spend all our energy keeping our bodies small, what will we have to show for our lives when we reach the end? I hope we have more than a group of fashionably skinny figures.

69

Connect

A Web of Words

Robin Morgan

• Threat • Shout • Bellow • Hit • Slap • Smack • Strike • Beat • Bash • Batter • Pummel • Punch • Slash • Stamp • Pound • Maul • Hammer • Bludgeon • Fist • Belt • Knife • Gun • Punish • Control • Mutilate • *Blood* • Ambulance • Sorry • Drunk • Welt • Swollen • Scar • *Lies* • Made Me Do It • Deserved It • Her Own Fault • Taught a Lesson • *Shame* • Neighbors • Secret • Whimper • *Fear* • Skulk • Shuffle • Wince • Tremble • Shudder • Shake • Cower • Cringe • Flinch • Crawl • Listen • Wait • Whisper • Bruise • Bandage • *Guilt* • Bumped into a Door • He Didn't Mean • Shatter • Wound • Fracture • Rupture • Harassment • Provoked It • Stalking • Invited It • Restraining Order • Funeral • *Scream* • Stranger Rape • Acquaintance Rape • Date Rape • Marital Rape • Child Rape • Asked for It • Wanted It • *Entitlement* • Masculine • *Selflessness* • Feminine • Disgust • Bitch • Cunt • Slit • 'Ho • Witch • Hag • Illiteracy • Purdah • Suttee • Clitoridectomy • Infibulation • Stoning • *Terror* • Burka • Chador • Forced Shrouding • Pornography • Forced Exposure • Sex Traffick • *Hunger* • Child Bride • Kidnapped Bride • Mail-order Bride • Bride Burnings • Harem • Forced Marriage • Child Marriage • Slavery • *Humiliation* • Tears • Begging • Prostitution • *Poverty* • Hooker • Pimp • John • Brothel • *Loneliness* • Hemorrhage • *Lovelessness* • Dread • *Exhaustion* • Hide • Run • Where • Duty • Family • Minister • Priest • Rabbi • Mullah • Trapped • *Again* • Stupid • Ugly • Fat • Old • Face-lift • Backstreet Abortion • Maternal Mortality • Female Infanticide • Suicide • *No* • Femicide • Gynocide • Genocide • Silence • *No* • Weep • Howl • *Blood* • Gasp • Wail • Grief • Mourning • Secrets • Lies • Propaganda • Torture • Waterboard • Electrodes • Lash • Cane • Whip • Burn • *Starve* • Boy Next Door • Serial Killer • Gang • Sect • Nation • Empire • Molotov Cocktail • IED • Patriot Missile • Peacekeeper Missile • "Big Boy" A-bomb • "Nuclear Hardness" • "Deep Penetration Capacity Bomb" • "Potent Kill Capability" • "Rigid, Hardened Silo • Erector Launchers" • "Thrust Ratios" • "Soft Targets" • Toy Gun • Toy Tank • Toy Missile • *No* • How • *Planet* • *Why* • Madness • *Rage* • Shrill • Strident • *Yes* • Crazy • *Hope* • Bread • Shelter • You *Too?* • Recognition • *Truth* • Strength • Dignity • Yes • *Transformation* • Human • *Together* • Yes •

70

He Works, She Works, but What Different Impressions They Make

Gwyn Kirk and Margo Okazawa-Rey

Have you ever found yourself up against the old double standard at work? Then you know how annoying it can be and how alone you can feel. Supervisors and coworkers still judge us by old stereotypes that say women are emotional, disorganized, and inefficient. Here are some of the most glaring examples of the typical office double standard.

The family picture is on HIS desk: Ah, a solid, responsible family man	The family picture is on HER desk: Hmm, her family will come before her career
HIS desk is cluttered: He's obviously a hard worker and busy man	HER desk is cluttered: She's obviously a disorganized scatterbrain
HE'S talking with coworkers: He must be discussing the latest deal	SHE'S talking with coworkers: She must be gossiping
HE'S not at his desk: He must be at a meeting	SHE'S not at her desk: She must be in the ladies' room
HE'S having lunch with the boss: He's on his way up	SHE'S having lunch with the boss: They must be having an affair
HE'S getting married. He'll get more settled	SHE'S getting married: She'll get pregnant and leave
HE'S having a baby: He'll need a raise	SHE'S having a baby: She'll cost the company money in maternity benefits
HE'S leaving for a better job: HE recognizes a good opportunity	SHE'S leaving for a better job: Women are undependable
HE'S aggressive	SHE'S pushy
HE'S careful	SHE'S picky
HE loses his temper	SHE'S bitchy
HE'S depressed	SHE'S moody
HE follows through	SHE doesn't know when to quit
HE'S firm	SHE'S stubborn
HE makes wise judgments	SHE reveals her prejudices
HE is a man of the world	SHE'S been around
HE isn't afraid to say what he thinks	SHE'S opinionated
HE exercises authority	SHE'S tyrannical
HE'S discreet	SHE'S secretive
HE'S a stern taskmaster	SHE'S difficult to work for

71

Girl Hate

Jenifer Fennell

In 1976, I had an abortion. I was 14 and pregnant by a boy who had, a couple months earlier, written a vicious letter to me with help from another boy who was our mutual friend. The letter accused me of being a "slut" and talked about the "puppies" I'd one day give birth to. I had spent the previous evening driving around with another group of boys and I could only guess that this behavior was what I was being punished for. My new boyfriend, Al, and our friend, Kenny, dropped the letter in my mailbox. I was on my way to meet the school bus when I found it, and I was so excited. "A love letter," I thought. "My first!" I didn't make it to my bus. Crying and throwing up, I ran home to find my mother.

Here's the context: at 14, I had spent three years living with relatives and family friends before entering the foster care system. My mother was widowed, bi-polar and dying of cancer, so my 13-year-old brother, Stan, and I lived with anyone who'd have us. At the time of the abortion, Stan and I were briefly living with our mother again. It would be the last time before she died.

Like so many girls who find themselves pregnant at a young age, I lacked safety nets. Scared and insecure because my life was so unpredictable, I tried to create family connections that might prove stable. But what tools did I have to work with? According to the culture I lived in, not a whole lot more than what boys thought of my looks. Though I was a child, I'd been fending for myself in basic ways for years. I'd long since learned I couldn't depend on adults. So, losing my family, I tried desperately to create one of my own. I thought sex might bind a boy to me. When that didn't work, I got pregnant again. Three months after I turned 17 and 18 months after my mother died, my daughter, Naomi, was born.

When Naomi was 16 and a boy said something truly hateful to her, I was astonished and grateful to see her cut ties with him immediately. At 14, I had fought like crazy to reestablish a connection with the boy who hurt me. Instead of challenging his behavior, I explained and apologized for my own. Decades later I can name my reaction to that girl-hating letter and can trace the links between my own overriding fear of abandonment and my willingness to accept any fault in that budding relationship as mine. His letter laid the blame for his fear and jealousy at my feet, where, because I believed I was worthless, I thought it belonged. And since I was blameworthy, I reasoned, I was lucky that he would forgive me and later have sex with me.

My mother arranged for me to have the abortion, a two-day process that began with a pelvic exam that was anything but routine for me. Some years earlier, I was at summer camp with girls who called me a boy when they saw my naked body in the dormitory shower. I still have no idea what they thought they saw, but on that day I decided that I must be deformed, and, with a young child's circular logic and limited information, figured that I must have gotten that way by masturbating. Like so many other girls, I had absorbed the idea that touching my body was deathly wrong. That day in the doctor's office, I was sure the doctor would look at me and know what I'd been doing. I was panicked and literally sick with humiliation. The nurse never left my side. She stroked my sweaty hand and murmured as tears rolled down my face.

Naturally, the aging male doctor did not comment on any deformity as there was none. Instead, at the end of the exam he leaned around the sheet draped over my knees and said, "You know, you can do something for the smell. Just dab a little perfume in your pubic hair."

In a piece on the necessity of reproductive freedom, why tell this sad but ordinary story of a confused, lonely, pregnant teenager? Because pregnancy and the decision to raise a child or have an abortion happen to real people and real people are never as simple as statistics. Because this sort of everyday misogyny is the national backdrop for any conversation about abortion. Because girl-hating figures so prominently in this story and without girl-hatred, this pregnancy and this abortion never would have happened. For those who anguish over the unborn, the never-to-be-born, if you want to prevent abortion, start by working to create a world where girls feel valued. Valuing girls means raising them to feel so good about themselves, their bodies, their sexuality, and the futures awaiting them that they recognize abuse for what it reveals about the abuser, not for what they secretly think it means about them. Equally importantly, valuing girls means countering the messages no one actually says, but that get communicated anyway, like the one I got about masturbation. This layered message alienated me from my body and from the pleasure I got from it, adding to my sense that my body was something for others to use and keep or discard. *Tell* girls what you want them to know. Say, "You're brilliant and capable and beautiful exactly as you are. Your body is yours and there's nothing wrong with feeling good." And if you've swallowed the poison, tell yourself these things, too.

If you're a woman, ask yourself this: how many implicit and explicit messages have you gotten over the years that tell you nothing matters more than how you look? Maybe you got them from your mother, who was always on a diet, or from friends who commented on your outfit or from TV or the covers of magazines or from boys and men who paid more attention to your cleavage than your words. Repeatedly told their worth lies in their sexual attractiveness, how can it be surprising when young girls who want attention or love try to get it by having sex?

If you've grown up with abstinence-only "sex education," you've been told that your worth lies nestled between your legs and you better guard it with your life, save it for the boy who will marry you. On the surface, this message seems to encourage girls to assert themselves, to give them the right to say "No." But the underlying message depends on the same self-negating logic: you've got only one asset, and you better protect it.

At the heart of the controversy over reproductive freedom is the issue of who has the right to control *your* body. Keeping abortion safe and legal is just one of the ways we can, as a culture, ensure that girls have the absolute right to define and control their lives. Providing access to safe and effective birth control and clear, non-judgmental information about how to use it tells girls that we trust them to decide when and with whom to start having sex. And informative, sex-positive sex education teaches girls to say yes because *they* want to, and to otherwise feel absolutely free to say no.

At 14, I felt no freedom to say no. I was scared, lonely, and largely on my own. Fortunately for me, before she died my mother told me over and over again how smart I was. She said I could do anything I wanted. It took me a while, but in the end I believed her.

72

The Evolution of a Pro-Feminist

Paul C. Gorski

1. QUICKENING

Grandma sat in the dark of her house, donning a pink pressed nurse's uniform. Motionless, she stared into the silence, fingers caressing the worn armrests of her recliner.

I lay, just eight years old, on the fold-out couch, close enough to hear the rhythm of her breathing. Pretending to sleep, I stared at Grandma, studying her.

Just eight years old, and already I had been conditioned by family lore. Grandma's husband—my Grandfather—was the family hero. Grandfather, the WWII Prisoner of War. Grandfather, the career military officer. Grandfather, the abusive father and husband. Grandfather, the philanderer. Grandfather, from whom Grandma spent thirty years protecting my Mom and her siblings.

Grandfather was the hero and Grandma was Grandma. Grandma, who volunteered at hospitals for two decades. Grandma, who, against Grandfather's wishes, started nursing school the year she turned 50. Grandma, who, refusing financial support from Grandfather or his pension, paid her tuition by working at a bait shop. Grandma, the matriarch of a vast extended family.

So there I was, just eight years old, watching Grandma. I watched and wondered why my mother's mother, just two years into her first "career," chose the midnight shift.

And in that moment Grandma eclipsed family lore, becoming herself before me. The wrinkles in her face: sweet signs of overcoming. The slight distance in her eyes: a celebration of persevering. Her stillness: a calm confidence, a meditation before bursting out.

If she spoke just then she'd have said *This is the me I always intended to be. This is the me . . .* Then Grandma lifted herself from her recliner, gently smoothing the front of her uniform.

"Time to go," she whispered. *Time to go*, my conscience echoed. And as Grandma stepped out of the dark of her house I felt as though my pulse assumed the rhythm of her footsteps.

Grandma chose the midnight shift.

Grandma *CHOSE* the midnight shift.

And who shouldn't choose?

And who shouldn't choose?

And who shouldn't—

Time to go.

2. PRO-FEMINISM

I refer to myself as "pro-feminist" rather than "feminist." I understand feminism as a movement founded by and fomented through the labor of women to secure their liberation from male dominance (or "patriarchy") and sexism. One of the ways I witness patriarchy, even among men who identify with the feminist movement, is in our willingness to battle sex and gender oppression so long as we control the process for doing so. So, as a pro-feminist, I *act* in support of feminism and *work* to eliminate the injustices women experience. But I also acknowledge that, despite these efforts, I benefit from patriarchy, at least in the economic sense. I acknowledge, as well, that it is one thing to fight oppression, but it is something else altogether to fight oppression *while I am experiencing the oppression I'm attempting to fight.* Failure on my part to make this distinction is, in essence, a symptom of patriarchy, an example of male privilege. So by identifying as pro-feminist, I remind myself that among the most fundamental human rights is the right for oppressed people to decide for themselves how to win their liberation. It is my role, then, to *serve* rather than *lead* toward these ends.

3. WHY I AM A PRO-FEMINIST

i. I believe that violence against women in all its forms—sexual harassment, rape, domestic violence, and so on—is a form of terrorism. And I, as a citizen, never can be spiritually whole if I know this violence exists and choose to do nothing about it.

ii. I believe that the hyper-masculinity of the Western world contributes to other forms of violence, such as unjust military intervention. And I, as a human being, never can be spiritually whole if I comply with such devastating social conditions.

iii. I believe that patriarchal sex and gender roles limit my ability to live and contribute to society fully. This is an important distinction: I do not believe that I am *oppressed* due to my sex or gender identity. Rather, I believe that I have been socialized to *repress* the parts of me that do not fit snugly into the masculine "box." And I, as a teacher and activist, never can be spiritually whole without climbing out of that box.

iv. As a working class man in a capitalist society, I believe that the male privilege—dangling perpetually like a carrot before me—that grants me greater economic access than women (higher pay, more opportunity for job advancement) is also meant to entice me into seeing women (regardless of socioeconomic status) as my competition. I believe I am socialized to perpetuate a system that provides me with some economic advantage, even though this advantage is miniscule compared with the economic advantage wealthy elite (white) men secure for themselves by using me as a protective buffer for patriarchy. Doing so requires me to alienate myself from women (as well as people of color) within my own socioeconomic stratus while diverting my attention from the systems and structures that hurt all working class (and low-income) people. And I, as a brother and son, never can be spiritually whole if I am willing to oppress anyone—including those, such as working class women, within my own community—out of economic greed.

v. Grandma.

NEXT STEPS

73

To Stop the Violence against Woman

Alice Walker

WOMAN

TO STOP THE VIOLENCE
AGAINST
WOMAN
WOMAN
MUST STOP THE VIOLENCE
AGAINST
HERSELF.

WE CAN BEGIN TO DO THIS
NOW, NOW THAT WE SEE
A SKY
AND NOT A ROCK
A STICK
OR A FIST
ABOVE ALL
OUR HEADS.

WOMAN

TO STOP THE VIOLENCE
AGAINST WOMAN,
STOP THE VIOLENCE
THAT YOU
PERPETUATE
AGAINST
YOUR OWN
SISTER
WHO IS
A WOMAN, YOUR OWN
DAUGHTER
WHO IS
A WOMAN,
YOUR OWN
DAUGHTER-IN-LAW
WHO IS
A WOMAN,
YOUR OWN
MOTHER
WHO IS
A WOMAN.

WOMAN

TO STOP THE VIOLENCE
AGAINST WOMAN,
STOP THE VIOLENCE
THAT LIVES
IN OPPOSITION
TO YOUR LIFE,
DEEP IN YOUR
OWN TERRORIZED AND
UNCHERISHED
HEART.

WOMAN

REMEMBER WHO WE ARE:
NOT "GUYS"
BUT
THE MOTHER
OF ALL
LIVING.
WE CREATE OUT OF OUR OWN BLOOD
AND MILK
THE CREATURES
WHO OPPRESS
US;
WHETHER THEY ARE MEN
OR
OURSELVES.

WOMAN

AWAKE!
ARISE!
STAND UP!

WOMAN

TO STOP THE VIOLENCE
AGAINST
WOMAN,
GET UP
ON YOUR PERFECTLY
UNBOUND
FEET!
WE HAVE LOST THE EARTH
LIVING ON OUR KNEES.

74

National Latina Institute for Reproductive Health (NLIRH) Statement on Healthcare for All

National Latina Institute for Reproductive Health

The National Latina Institute for Reproductive Health (NLIRH) supports healthcare reform that will move our current system toward one that will improve the health, and well-being of all Latinas, their families and communities. NLIRH embraces a human rights approach to health care, ensuring that all health services are accessible, available, affordable, and of good quality for everyone. These services should be provided on an equitable basis, free from discrimination or coercion. Healthcare reform can take many paths, and it is important that the needs of all Latinas, including immigrant women, women of color and low-income women, are front and center.

NLIRH supports a system that includes all people, regardless of income, immigration status, or any other limiting factor. The current healthcare system leaves many Latinas falling through the cracks; 38% of Latinas are uninsured, the highest rate amongst all groups of women. Some Latinas may have an income too high to qualify for Medicaid, yet too low to afford private insurance. Many Latinas who would qualify based on income are not eligible. Among the ineligible are undocumented Latinas and legal permanent residents who have been in the United States for less than five years. This lack of access to healthcare contributes heavily to the health disparities that Latinas face, in turn affecting many other aspects of Latinas' quality of life.

It is important that such a system includes a full and comprehensive range of services, including coverage for family planning, abortions, prenatal care and preventive services. Currently Latinas—especially low-income, uninsured and immigrant Latinas—face numerous obstacles to obtaining these services, including cost and lack of access. Under the Hyde Amendment, no federal funds can be used for abortion services, meaning that many women on Medicaid are unable to access a full range of options when facing an unintended pregnancy, and may turn to unsafe terminations if they do not wish to carry the pregnancy to term. This and other obstacles create a disproportionate burden of morbidity and mortality on Latinas.

Moreover, NLIRH supports a system that is not only inclusive of all people and offers a comprehensive range of services, but is also one that emphasizes culturally competent and linguistically appropriate services. Comprehensive care is meaningless unless it is provided in a language with which patients are comfortable and accompanied by physicians and other clinicians that understand the needs of Latinas, immigrant women, and low-income women. Unless Latinas feel free of judgment, coercion and discrimination at our doctors' offices, health disparities will continue regardless of availability and access. Supporting health care reform that incorporates a human rights framework would ensure a holistic approach to the care needed for all Latinas to advance *salud, dignidad y justicia*!

NEXT STEPS

75

Heartbroken

Women of Color Feminism and the Third Wave

Rebecca Hurdis

This essay isn't just about an adopted, woman of color feminist; rather, it is a story about how I came to believe that I was worthy of all of these identities. It isn't just a story about feminism or solely about adoption. It is an exploration of where the mind stops and the heart follows. . . . The struggle is not to find one place where I can exist, but to find it within myself to exist in all of these places, uncompromisingly. To live a life of multiplicity is as difficult as it is to write about it.

. . .

Growing up in a transracial adopted family, I was often confused by the images of the "normal, nuclear families." We didn't look like any other family I saw. I couldn't comprehend how I could love my family, feel accepted by them and believe that I belonged to them as much as my phenotypically white brothers. Yet every time I looked in the mirror, my reflection haunted me, because the face that stared back was not the same color as my family's This awareness was reinforced by the sometimes brutal questions of others. I constantly had to explain that I really was my brother's sister. He was not my husband but truly my brother. I was not the foreign exchange student that just never left. Embarrassed by the attention, I tried to ignore the differences. I took the negativity and dissociation I felt and began to internalize the feelings. I fooled myself into thinking and acting the role of a "good little Asian saved from her fallen country and brought to the land of salvation." I began to believe the messages about being an Asian girl and about being adopted. This compliance was one of the only ways I learned to gain acceptance and validation as a child. I realized that my identity was being created *for* me not *by* me.

. . .

When I would talk to my friends about it, they wouldn't and couldn't understand. I was told that I was making too big a deal out of being Asian and besides I *was* just like everyone else. They thought that I just worried too much. My friends went so far as to convince me by telling me that "I wasn't really Asian, I was white." But the truth couldn't be denied, just as the color of my skin couldn't either. . . .

I came across feminism as a first-year student at Ohio State University. I was extremely depressed at the time. Everything—my created identity, the world of whiteness that I knew, the denial of my race—that I had worked so hard at repressing and ignoring throughout my life was finally surfacing and emerging. I no longer had the validation of whiteness to protect my false identity. The world that I had understood was changing, and I was confronted with defining myself without the associations of my family and friends. I was forced to step outside of my white world, shedding my blinders to find that I wasn't white and that I had never really been so. The only illusion was the one that I had created for myself, the one that had found acceptance. But I was beginning to realize the cost of this facade.

. . .

My first women's studies course focused on the history of the women's movement, the social context and the contemporary issues facing feminism today. We looked at issues ranging from violence to sexual orientation to women-centered spirituality to representation in music and film to body image. I began to recognize my extensive history of sexual, mental and physical abuse with boyfriends, and I started to comprehend the cycle of abuse and forgiveness. I was able to begin to stop blaming myself and shift the responsibility back to those who had inflicted the abuse. Initially I had disconnected the abuse from racism, even though it was heavily intertwined and simultaneous. It was just too large for me to understand, and it was still too early for me to grapple with race. I still was thinking that I just needed to become the "right" kind of Asian American and then everything would make sense.

I know that for a lot of women of color, feminism is perceived as being a white woman's movement that has little space or acknowledgment for women of color. I understand how that is true, but back then this class became a catalyst for change and healing. It was a major turning point in my life, where I was able to break my silence and find empowerment within myself and for myself. Women's studies offered me a place where there was validation and reason. I was uncovering and understanding how my own internalization was tied to ideologies of racism and sexism. Although the analysis of racism was somewhat limited in these courses, it served as a lead for future interests. Women's studies and feminism was a steppingstone toward striving for a holistic understanding of myself.

. . .

But I left college feeling as though there was something missing to this feminism. Professors would talk about Black feminism or women of color feminism, but merely as another mark on their feminist timeline. Little time was dedicated to really examining the intersection of race and gender. Back home I went to my local new-age store (which also doubled as the feminist bookstore) and stumbled on *This Bridge Called My Back: Writings by Radical Women of Color* (edited by Cherré Moraga and Gloria Anzaldúa). It was the first time I had found a book that had the words "women of color" as part of the title. It was as if I had found the pot of gold at the end of the feminist rainbow. Even though I didn't find myself completely represented in the book, specifically because none of the contributors had been an adopted child, I did find my thoughts, anger and pain represented through the eloquent voices of other women of color. Their writings incorporated race and sexuality.

Reading this anthology, I realized I was entitled to feeling something other than apologetic. I could be angry. I could be aggressive. I could be the opposite of this little china doll that everyone expected me to be. Given my background, this book was life-changing. It represented one of the first moments where I could claim something that was mine; something different from my parents, my friends, my community; something other than whiteness. I remember sitting at the town beach on a hot and humid August day, flipping through the book, my mind exploding and expanding. As I sat there frantically reading, I recall looking up at the sun, closing my eyes and thanking the goddess that I had found this work. Through this discovery I had found that I was not alone. Not only was I feminist, but I was a woman of color feminist.

What makes my relationship to women of color feminism different from most other women of color is how and why I entered the conversation. I began looking at race through gender, where most have the reverse experience. This idea of entry point is crucial. I call myself a woman of color before I call myself an Asian American. It reflects how I have come to see myself and how I understand my own identity. The term "women of color" seems broadly inviting and inclusive while "Asian American" feels rigid and exclusive. Women of color feminism took me from being a victim to being a warrior.

I am now in an ethnic studies graduate program trying to explore if women of color are within feminism's third wave, and if so, where. I began this project as an undergraduate but I had hit a wall. It was difficult locating voices that represented generation X or third wave women of color feminism. Not much had been written, as our voices were just beginning to emerge. I found women of color feminists in alternative places such as zines, anthologies, magazines and pop culture. I felt frustrated that our voices were deemed not "accredited" enough to be represented in the mainstream.

I held a certain expectation for Jennifer Baumgardner and Amy Richard's book, *Manifesta: Young Women, Feminism, and the Future*. This book markets itself as being *the* text for the third wave of feminism, and I had high hopes that it would address issues of race, gender and class sexuality. Instead, I found the specific history of white (privileged) women. . . .

I found it astounding that there is no extensive discussion of women of color feminism. This indicates that Baumgardner and Richards feel as though this is a separate issue, a different kind of feminism. It is as if their work is the master narrative of feminism, with women of color feminism as an appendage. I had hoped that they would have considered such books as *This Bridge Called My Back* and Audre Lorde's *Sister Outsider* as ground-breaking, as they are deemed by most generation X women of color. These books were life-changing to me not only because their critiques have historical value, but also because what these writers were saying in the 1980s was still relevant in the 1990s. *Manifesta* is successful in creating momentum for young white women's activism through the attempt to move feminism out of academia and back into a social and political movement. But the book's greatest contribution was that it raised a need for creating a lineage for women of color feminism.

. . .

What is it about the word "feminism" that has encouraged women of color to stand apart from it? Feminism has been indoctrinated into the academy through the discipline of women's studies. It has moved out of the social and political spaces from where it emerged. Women's studies have collapsed the diversity that was part of the feminist movement into a discipline that has become a homogenous generality. For women in the third wave then, one needs to have the academic training of women's studies to be an "accredited feminist." Once race is added to the complexity, many women of color feel as though the compromise or negotiation is just too high a price to pay to be called a feminist. Women of color's participation in women's studies and feminism still causes splintering in our identities.

Many women believe that there is a certain required persona to be a feminist. In the ethnic studies course "Women of Color in the U.S." at Berkeley, for example, students expressed feeling that they didn't have enough knowledge or background to be able to call themselves feminists. The students' comments reflect how many women of color find difficulty in accessing feminism. Often the response is that "feminism is a white woman's thing." Whiteness in feminism comes to represent privilege, power and opportunity. It rarely positions women of color as being as legitimate as the identities of white women. Women's studies has been accurately accused of treating race as a secondary oppression through offering courses about race that are separate from the central curriculum, while ethnic studies feels more comfortable as a place to discuss race and gender. But even in ethnic studies, women's experiences and histories still remain on the margins. Like women's studies, they too have had problems integrating gender into the analysis of race.

. . .

Although I am a self-proclaimed woman of color feminist, I struggle with being an "authentic" woman of color feminist. Even though I realize it is self-defeating, I worry that other women of color will look at my feminism and judge it as being socialized whiteness and an effect of adoption. The roots of my feminism are connected to my adopted mother, although I am uncertain whether she would identify as a feminist. She was a woman who wouldn't let us watch the *Flintstones* or the *Jetsons* because of their negative portrayal of women, yet she unquestionably had dinner on the table every night for her husband, sons

NEXT STEPS

and daughter. Most important, she raised me to believe I could be whoever I wanted to be and in that a strong woman. If feminism has been bestowed onto me from my adopted mother, then I choose not to look at it as another indicator of whiteness or of being whitewashed. Rather, I see it as a gift that has shown me not the limitations of mainstream feminism but the possibilities of women of color feminism. People sometimes question my attachment to feminism. Despite the criticisms, it has served as a compass that navigates me away from paralysis into limitless potential.

. . .

Women of color feminism has currently been reduced to a general abstraction that has flattened out difference and diversity, causing tension between women of color. Instead of collectively forming alliances against whiteness, women of color now challenge the opposing identities that exist under the umbrella term "women of color." It raises questions about entitlement and authenticity. It tries to suppress the heterogeneous composition of women of color feminism by trying to create a unifying term. Yet the differences of class, racialization and sexuality have arisen and persisted, challenging assumptions that all women of color are in solidarity with each other. We all come with backgrounds and histories that differ from one another and despite knowing this, we still maintain this ideal and creation of the authentic "women of color." The one that is the right class, the right race, the right sexuality. We must refuse being reduced to an abstraction. We must address the conflicts that have begun to fester paralysis instead of fostering change. But that also means that we need to revitalize women of color feminism so that those actions can begin to take place.

It is crucial to explore and expose the problems of women of color feminism, but we also need to be weary of what we are willing to sacrifice. I think a new, third space is being created in women of color feminism. Those of us who are not easily recognized and acknowledged as women of color are coming to feminism as a place to discuss the implications of invisibility. We are pushing, expanding and exploding ideologies of multiplicity and intersectionality. We come as transracial adoptees, women of mixed race, bisexuals, refugees and hundreds of other combinations. For us, women of color feminism continues to be a living theory and a way to survive.

NEXT STEPS

76

Stop the False Race/Gender Divide

A Call to Action

Ann Russo and Melissa Spatz

Where do feminists stand on issues of race and racism? The 2007–2008 democratic primary struggle between Hillary Clinton and Barack Obama brought out significant divides among feminists around gender and race. A small constituency of feminists garnered national attention by arguing that sexism trumped racism and that gender, not race, was the most enduring inequality. They argued that feminists must support Hillary Clinton because she is a woman who faced misogyny in her presidential campaign. Mainstream media took these ideas as if they represented most feminists and used them to fan the flames of a race/gender divide, harkening back to the divisive politics around suffrage in the late 19th and early 20th century. In the summer of 2008, we wrote this statement addressed primarily to white progressive and feminist activists to refuse such divisive and racist rhetoric and commit to coalitional feminist politics.

WE REFUSE . . .

We refuse a feminism that assumes that "women" are a homogeneous group. Women identify along a spectrum of identities, and gender is not always the most prominent one. Multiple systems of oppression and privilege, including racism, white supremacy, class hierarchy, religious intolerance, xenophobia, anti-immigrant policies, heterosexism, ableism and ageism shape women's lives and experiences.

We refuse a feminism that pits sexism against racism, that claims that sexism is more entrenched than racism, and that the existence of sexism means that racism no longer exists. Sexism, racism, and other forms of oppression are interconnected. The misogynist spectacle against Hillary Clinton is tied to her white, middle-class heterosexuality, and differs from attacks on women who are not. We are dismayed that when media pundits frame Michelle Obama as an angry black woman, or as unpatriotic, or suggest that she should be the target of a "lynching party," there has been no similar outcry by white feminists.

We refuse a feminism that claims to speak for all women, while denying and minimizing the ongoing legacy of white supremacy and racism in this country. This legacy includes the ways that women's movements are embedded in white supremacist structures, ideas, and practices. We refuse to participate in ʳ   zations that demand allegiance to women without accountability for privilege ɑ   ɔmplicity in racism, class exploitation, homophobia, transphobia, imperialism, ableism, ageism, etc.

We refuse a feminism that marginalizes and undermines young women's voices and perspectives. We reject the adultism of older activists who dismiss the views of young women as naïve, unrealistic, sexist, and based in sexual fantasy. We reject the presumption that if younger women do not agree with older women, it is because they are less radical.

We refuse a feminism that mobilizes white folks by cultivating solidarity on the basis of whiteness. We reject any attempt to play divide and conquer by cultivating the racism of white middle class professional women and white working class women and men against people of color. We reject the reframing of racism as "racial resentment."

We refuse a feminism that blames people of color for focusing attention on racism as if that focus was the cause of sexism and misogyny. We refuse this zero sum game politics, and we refuse to undermine efforts to dismantle white supremacy in order to bolster attention to sexism. We reject attempts by some white feminists to silence people of color and to cultivate white racist bonding with claims of "reverse racism."

We refuse a feminism that confuses a campaign with a movement. We reject the idea that as feminists, we must agree on a candidate. We must engage all candidates around their positions on issues and use campaigns as opportunities to push candidates to address our issues and visions for social change.

NEXT STEPS

AND WE COMMIT . . .

We commit to consistently challenge ourselves to be self-reflective. We do not claim to have all of the answers. We are firmly committed to building our awareness of, and accountability for, our own participation in systems of power and privilege.

We commit to critically engaging our communities about this historic moment in U.S. feminism and progressive politics. We will take an active role in creating community dialogues and town hall forums that re-center feminist and women's activism based in coalitional politics.

We commit to holding all politicians accountable for their politics, rather than their identities. We believe that identity does matter in terms of who is represented in the government, and yet, we believe that candidates must be evaluated based on their commitments and actions.

We commit to challenging misogyny, racism and other forms of oppression in media coverage. We will challenge all discourses that make women of color invisible, by assuming that gender = white women, and race = men of color. We will disrupt the media's promotion of divisions between gender-based and race-based agendas, between racial and ethnic groups, and between political movements.

We commit to speaking publicly against white supremacy as it operates in our movement and in the upcoming election. It is the responsibility of progressive white women and feminists to consistently dialogue, challenge, disrupt, and transform white supremacist thinking, ideas, and practices.

We commit to challenging feminist media activists and organizations to use an anti-oppression approach. We commit to look at interconnected forms of oppression in media coverage, and we challenge other activists to do the same. We call on NOW's "Media Hall of Shame" to include all forms of oppression shaping women's representations, including racism, white supremacy, heterosexism, ableism, classism, adultism, xenophobia.

We commit to creating intergenerational dialogues between women of all ages. Older women need to check adultism. It is important to learn from young women, particularly young women of color and those facing multiple oppressions, who do not enter the social justice movement with a race versus gender versus sexuality divide. All of us, old and young, must create intergenerational dialogues that honor our different knowledge, experiences, and frames of reference.

We commit to building a broad-based movement for social justice by working in solidarity across differences. We commit to being accountable for our own privilege and complicity in systems of oppression. This accountability is a necessary starting point to creating collaborations, coalitions, and alliances across identities and issues.

NEXT STEPS

77

Grassroots

Introduction

Winona LaDuke

I have spent my entire adult life as what you might call a political activist. I have testified at hearings, demonstrated at countless protests, and been involved in litigation. I've worked in a number of Native communities across the continent, and founded the White Earth Land Recovery Project (WELRP) on my home reservation. With our work here, we've been able to recover more than seventeen hundred acres of our land and create a land trust, while we work toward recovery of more of our own birthright. We also continue to work to protect our wild rice from genetic modification and ecosystems from contamination by pesticides, and to stop clear cuts of the forest. From inside my own house, we roast fair-trade and organic coffee. I have written books about the environment, run for vice president twice (as Ralph Nader's Green Party running mate in 1996 and 2000), and been arrested because I don't think that a thousand-year-old tree should become a phone book.

The perception of me, or of any well-known activist, is probably far from reality. Activists, the thinking goes, must be organized, focused, always working on the next strategy. My real life, the one in which I conduct all of my activism, is, of course, messy. If you came over, you might find my five children, ages four to sixteen, three dogs, fifteen horses, a few cats, several interns from around the country, and many friends who double as coworkers helping with WELRP's work. The 2000 veep campaign was conducted with me breastfeeding my newborn son before and after each stump speech and during many an interview. I still coordinate the sustainable food projects central to the White Earth Land Recovery Project literally from my kitchen table at the same time as I figure out meals for my kids, take coffee orders for Muskrat coffee company, and pop in videos for my youngest to watch on TV. I talk to Native community leaders from across the country as I cook meals and clean up (sort of an endless job). I write books at the same table where I make rawhide ornaments for sale as part of WELRP and help with maple syruping in the spring season, and my house is filled with labels that spell out the Ojibwe words for "bed," "book," "cupboard," and "table" as part of my ongoing commitment to indigenous language and culture preservation. My activism is simply in my life—it has to be, or it couldn't get done.

My own life as an identified activist has made me wonder at the term itself. What separates simple "responsibility" in life—motherhood, for example—from the fine line that one crosses to become an "activist"? I have been surprised and moved by encountering so many other mothers in my years as an activist: mothers in Chiapas breastfeeding their babies like anyone else, but who mask their faces as they speak with me because they can't afford to have their identifies known; Mohawk and Ojibwe mothers who face down General Motors and Potlach Corporation, knowing that if they don't, their kids won't ever know clean water, and generations ahead will have contaminated breast milk.

I have developed longstanding friendships with women who are engaged in struggles of responsibility—for their land, their own community health, and the water their children drink. Are these women feminists? That depends on who defines the term. Many of these women, including myself, are committed to the process of self-determination and believe

NEXT STEPS

in our inherent rights, as bestowed by the Creator, to live with dignity, peace, clean air and water, and our duty to pass on this legacy to our children and the generations to follow.

At the United Nations Conference on the Status of Women in Beijing, China, in 1995, I asked women from small countries around the world why they came all this way to participate in what was, in essence, a meeting. "I came because the World Bank is here," explained Victoria Tauli-Corpuz, an Igarok woman from the Philippines whose village is targeted for a Word Bank-funded dam. "I believe that those people at the World Bank and the IMF, those who make the decisions which will transform my life, should see my face." That sentiment applies whether you are an Igarok woman from the Philippines or Sherry Honkala from the Kensington Welfare Rights Union, challenging federal budget cuts to aid for dependent families or tending to the needs of homeless families. The message of self-determining women is the same for all people: *We want control over our lives, and we will challenge those who impose laws on our bodies, our communities, and our future.*

I believe that women move to activism out of sheer necessity. As a group, we are not of privilege—budget cuts devastated our household, the military wreaks havoc on our bodies and our homelands. The National Priorities Project reports that $152.6 billion spent on military aid in 2003 could have provided Head Start for an additional 20,211,205 children, health coverage for an additional 89,780,249 children, affordable housing vouchers for an additional 22,894,974 families, or salaries for 2,673,864 new elementary school teachers. Feminist activism, then, doesn't begin or end with my uterus: this is about my whole body, my life, and the lives of my children. We are women who redefine "Women's Issues," and say all issues are women's issues. I say: *We are the mothers of our nations, and anything that concerns our nations is of concern to us as women.* Those choices and necessities move us to speak out and to be active.

I happen to come from a line of these women who speak out, and I continue this work—our work. Women's work. My grandmother Helen Peskin, a Jewish woman from the Ukraine, recently passed into the Spirit World. Her early years were formed by the reality of war, first the Cossacks who overran her village and then the Nazis. With her life came a sheer determination to not be a victim, to speak for peace, to make a better life, and to demand dignity. Of her ninety years on this earth a good forty were spent as a seamstress: a purse maker, a member of the Pocket Book Makers Union in the garment district in New York, a folk dancer, and a peace activist. *A woman's work is about economic justice, and about quality of life.* My mother, Betty LaDuke, made her own path as a muralist and art professor, one of the first women on the faculty of her college, and like other women, she had to do it better than any man around because it took that much to get recognized. She has done this work in a way that celebrates life, and celebrates the work of other women. And she has done this work by linking with women in Eritrea, Nigeria, and Peru. *A women's work is about creating and celebrating life.* Our parents' struggles become our own, in our own time. We can't escape from that history, nor can we escape from our time in it.

In the lives of women in my family, it was never about just our own selves, it was about the collective dignity and *everyone's* health and rights. This is counter, in many ways, to Americanism. Americanism teaches individualism. My family, and indeed movements for social transformation, are not about anything as limited as the better job or the better advantage for the individual woman. Even the tragic deaths of three of my closest friends, activists all, are lessons in the urgency of change on a broader scale. Marsha Gomez, a gifted artist, was killed by her own son, who lacked the psychiatric medical attention he so desperately needed; Nilak Butler passed from ovarian cancer because she did not have adequate health coverage; and Ingrid Washinawatok El-Issa was assassinated by the FARC, Revolutionary Armed Forces of Colombia, with a gun and a bullet that came from my tax dollars in the second most highly financed recipient of U.S. military aid in the world.

NEXT STEPS

The compelling reason behind activism is that our most personal lives—even the intimacy of death—are actually embroidered in the reality of public policy, foreign policy, military aid, and economics. Each day, then, I, like the women in my family before me, and like so many other women in the world, recommit to continue this struggle for life, and to celebrate its beauty in the process. That struggle and that celebration are who we are as women, as we take responsibility for our destinies.

. . .

NEXT STEPS

HETEROSEXISM

Introduction

Warren J. Blumenfeld

Oppression directed against all females, lesbians, gay males, bisexuals, transgender people, and intersexuals[1] goes by many names and definitions. What connects them is the socially constructed and enforced binary systems that divide people into either/or gender or sexual categories based upon societal norms of self-presentation. The socially constructed notions of "sex," "gender," and "sexuality" are organized and maintained through oppositional binary frames with their attendant meanings, social roles, values, stereotypes, behavioral and attitudinal imperatives, expressions, and expectations. These features serve to maintain power and privilege for those who accord with these norms, while marginalizing and disempowering groups and individuals who violate them. This structure is established and enforced on the societal, institutional, and individual/interpersonal levels (see selection 4 for elaboration of this framework). The most extreme and overt forms of oppression are directed against those who most directly challenge, confound, or contest these binary frames.

This section should be read in the context of the preceding section on sexism and the following section on transgender oppression. These three sections, taken together, present a comprehensive view of the ways in which societal privileges and disadvantages follow socially constructed understandings of the roles and expressions that attach to sex, gender, and sexuality. The section website provides further resources to explore and understand these three interrelated yet distinctive components of sex, gender, and sexuality.

HETEROSEXISM DEFINED

I define *heterosexism* as the overarching system of advantages bestowed on heterosexuals, based on the institutionalization of heterosexual norms or standards that privilege heterosexuals and heterosexuality, and exclude the needs, concerns, cultures, and life experiences of lesbians, gay males, and bisexuals. Often overt, though at times subtle, heterosexism is oppression by neglect, omission, erasure, and distortion. A related concept is *heteronormativity* (Warner 1991) and *compulsory heterosexuality* (Rich 1986), which emphasizes the normalization and privileging of heterosexuality on the personal/interpersonal, institutional, and societal levels.

Examples of heterosexism include parents who automatically expect their children to marry a person of the other sex; media portrayals of only heterosexuals in positive and satisfying relationships; teachers presuming that all of their students are heterosexual, and teaching only about the contributions of heterosexuals. Heterosexism also takes the form of pity toward lesbian, gay, and bisexual (LGB) people as unfortunate human beings who "can't help being the way they are."

Heterosexism's more active and visible component, called *homophobia,* is oppression by intent, purpose, and design. Derived from the Greek terms *homos,* meaning "same," and *phobikos,* meaning "having a fear of and/or an aversion toward," *homophobia* refers to the fear and hatred of those who love or are attracted emotionally and sexually to people of the same sex. Homophobia includes prejudice, discrimination, harassment, and acts of violence brought on by that fear and hatred. Related concepts include *lesbophobia* or *lesbiphobia*, which can be defined as the fear, hatred, discrimination, and acts of violence directed against women who love women, and *biphobia*, which is fear, hatred, and oppression directed against bisexuals: people who love and are emotionally and sexually attracted to people of other sexes. For the purposes of this section, *heterosexism* is a more inclusive and expansive term than terms based on a "phobia" meaning a fear that is "irrational" or "unreasonable." This section takes the view that some fears and hatreds (and forms of prejudice) are *taught* as a normalized process of socialization (see selection 6) and thus exist within the realm of *learned* responses. Therefore, for purposes of discussion throughout this book and this section, though we sometimes use the terms "homophobia" and "biphobia," we are also employing the term "heterosexism" in its expanded and inclusive form.

Heterosexism forces LGB people to struggle constantly against their own invisibility, and makes it much more difficult for them to integrate a positive identity. LGB people themselves often find it difficult not to internalize society's negative notions of homosexuality and bisexuality. Internalized oppression, in this instance heterosexism, can be defined as the internalization, consciously or unconsciously, of external attitudes, myths, and stereotypes of inferiority, inadequacy, self-hatred, and sense of "otherness" by the targets of systematic oppression, here lesbians, gay males, and bisexuals. Internalizing these external negative societal messages is not our fault, for we too have been socialized within the systemic framework of heterosexism. There are, however, steps we can take to reduce, or even eliminate, internalized oppression, though working to end internalized oppression can be an extensive process.

OPPRESSION AND LIBERATION FRAMEWORKS

The history of homosexuality and bisexuality includes incredible pain and enormous pride, overwhelming repression and victorious rejoicing, stifling invisibility and dazzling illumination. Throughout the ages, homosexuality and bisexuality have been called many things: from "sin," "sickness," and "crime," to "orientation," "identity," and even "a gift from God." Though same-sex behavior has probably always existed in human and most non-human species, the concept of "homosexuality," "bisexuality," and "heterosexuality," in fact sexual orientation in general, is a relatively modern Western concept. Because the notion of sexual orientation is relatively new, the construction of an identity and sense of community based on these identities is also relatively recent.

RELIGIOUS ENDORSEMENTS FOR HETEROSEXUALITY

Many people cite religious texts to support the social norms of heterosexuality, even though there is no monolithic theological endorsement for heterosexuality. Instead, religious scholars from various faith traditions and denominations within those traditions interpret religious textual passages related to same-sex sexuality, same-sex relationships, and transgressive expressions of gender very differently (see section website for further resources on this issue).

Though many religious denominations throughout the years have worked vigorously to end oppression toward a number of groups, including those who transgress heterosexual norms, religious textual passages have been referenced throughout the ages to justify and rationalize the practices that marginalize, harass, deny rights, persecute, and oppress entire groups of people based on their non-conforming sexual or other identities. During various historical periods, people within different faith traditions have applied specific religious texts to establish and maintain hierarchical positions of power, domination, and privilege over individuals and groups targeted by these texts. For example, individuals, organizations, and entire nations have quoted specific textual passages to justify the construction and maintenance of the institution of slavery, the persecution and murder of Jews, male domination over and denial of rights of women, adult domination and persecution of young people, and demonization, marginalization, denial of rights, and extreme forms of oppression against LGB people, considering them anywhere from being creations of the Devil, to sinners and immoral, to being the embodiment of evil in the world, which, left unchecked, would result in the destruction of peoples and nations.

History has shown a symbiotic relationship between religious teachings concerning homosexuality and bisexuality, and the secular, legal, and political policies against homosexuality and bisexuality, whereby the religious justifies the secular, legal, and political. Religious, philosophical, social, and political attitudes set the groundwork for restrictive laws enacted toward the latter stages of imperial Roman civilization, and on, throughout the Middle Ages (enforced by Catholic Church practices and policies in medieval Europe), to the punitive civil laws of the nineteenth and twentieth century and into the present day. Laws doling out punishments, such as denial of marriage and child custody benefits, restrictions on engaging in military service, constraints in gaining employment, housing, insurance, health benefits, and public accommodations, flogging, banishment, bodily mutilation, incarceration, and death of the accused, have existed at various times in most countries. When we come to the contemporary United States, we must ask whether a society, founded on the guiding principle of the separation of religion from government, has the right to formulate and pass legislation based on religious tenets, which are not accepted by all—a question of great significance, given the continuing religious sanctions supporting heterosexuality.

"MEDICAL MODEL" SUPPORTS FOR HETEROSEXUALITY

One important rationale for heterosexuality is based upon the biological and psychological pathologizing of sexually transgressive people. From the so-called "Eugenics Movement" of the mid-nineteenth century though the twentieth century and beyond, medical and psychological professions have often proposed and addressed, in starkly medical language, the alleged "deficiencies" of, for example, gay, lesbian, bisexual, and transgender people, as well as people who are differently-abled, youth, people of color, and elders (see sections 8 and 9).

Some members of the scientific community view LGB people as constituting a distinct biological type, characterized medically as a pathology. Rather than considering homosexuality and bisexuality merely as a manifestation of emotional and physical attractions along a broad sprectrum of emotional and sexual possibilities, some sectors of the medical and psychological communities continue to pathologize homosexuality in medical and psychological terms. This has resulted in LGB people (often against their will) being hospitalized, committed to mental institutions, jailed, lobotomized, electroshocked, castrated, sterilized, and subjected to "aversion therapy," "reparative therapy," "Christian counseling," and genetic counseling.

By deploying the "medical model" to investigate and pathologize the "other," heteronormativity is perceived as unremarkable, an unquestioned, hegemonic norm against which all others are judged. Heterosexual norms justify and explain away the otherwise unacceptable persecution and oppression of non-conforming sexual identity groups, while avoiding issues of domination, privilege, subordination, and marginalization. This "medicalization" of homosexuality and bisexuality only serves to strengthen oppression and heterosexual privilege through its relative invisibility. Given this invisibility, issues of oppression and privilege are neither analyzed nor scrutinized, neither interrogated nor confronted.

We take the position that any problems with homosexuality and bisexuality are not with the sexual identity *per se*, not with who we are, but rather with the ways we are socially constructed and treated. Rather than projecting ourselves through the "medical model" as deficient, defective, diseased, disabled, criminal, inadequate, immature, functionally limited, troubled, many of us choose to project homosexuality and bisexuality though a "wellness model." This approach fosters a positive social identity with a strong sense of culture and community, and envisions the LGB experience as one of difference in the spectrum of human intimacy, relationships, emotions, and sexuality, and a difference to be cherished, nurtured, and supported.

SOCIAL JUSTICE MODEL OF LIBERATION

Since the early to mid-nineteenth century, a linear history of homosexuality and bisexuality, predominately in the West, begins with the formation of a homosexual "identity" and a sense of community brought about by the growth of industrialization, competitive capitalism and wage labor, and the rise of modern science, which provided people with more social and personal options outside the home (D'Emilio 1983). It is only within the last 150 or so years that there has been an organized and sustained political effort to protect the rights of people with same-sex and both-sex attractions, and those who cross traditional constructions of gender expression. During this time, many individuals and organizations have rejected the medical and religious rationales for homosexuality and bisexuality, while embracing a social justice model, which investigates and attempts to address the ways in which social structures promote and maintain issues of domination and subordination.

A brief chronology of the movements toward societal liberation in this arena follows. The "Homosexual Emancipation Movement" began in Germany in the 1860s when Karl Heinrich Ulrichs, a lawyer from Hanover, wrote on the topic of same-sex love. Karoly Maria Benkert (also known as Karl Maria Kertbeny) coined the terms "homosexual" and "heterosexual" in 1869 to convince the religious, legal, and scientific communities that same-sex attractions, though not the norm, were widespread and therefore should not be legally penalized. Literary tradition in England in the nineteenth century c.e. celebrated same-sex relationships. The first homosexual rights group in the United States formed in 1924 in Chicago—called the Society for Human Rights, it was founded by Henry Gerber, a German U.S.–American who had been influenced by the emancipation movement in Germany. The "Homophile Movement" in the United States began with such groups as the Mattachine Society and Daughters of Bilitis (see section website for resources describing this history). Many historians and activists place the beginning of the modern movement for lesbian, gay, bisexual, and transgender equality at the Stonewall Inn, a small bar frequented by young people including drag queens, lesbians, bisexuals, gay males, street people, students, and others located in New York City's Greenwich Village. In the early morning of June 28, 1969, when New York City police officers conducted a routine raid on the bar, the occupants fought back with bottles, rocks, bricks, trash cans, and parking meters used at battering rams in a pitched battle lasting five days.

Out of the ashes of the Stonewall Inn, a number of groups formed, for example the Gay Liberation Front, Gay Activists Alliance, Radical Lesbians, and others. The Christopher Street Liberation Day Umbrella Committee formed in New York City to plan activities and a march on Sunday June 28, 1970, up Sixth Avenue. From that first march grew others throughout the world. June each year is now reserved for local "Gay, Lesbian, Bisexual, and Transgender Pride" activities.

Bisexuals, who had (since the beginning) been alongside gay and lesbian activists, began to organize for the rights of bisexuals in the mid- to late 1970s. For a number of reasons neither the gay and lesbian rights movement nor mainstream political movements initially responded to the needs of bisexuals. At first, bisexual women organized themselves in same-sex groups for support and consciousness-raising; bisexual men later followed this example.

By 1972, parents and friends were organizing support groups for themselves and their loved ones. Today, a national network of local chapters of the organization Parents, Families, and Friends of Lesbians and Gays (or PFLAG) offers support and is on the front lines in helping to defeat heterosexism.

Founded to fight governmental and societal inaction, in 1986, the intergenerational direct-action group ACT UP (AIDS Coalition to Unleash Power) formed in New York City. A network of local chapters quickly grew in over 120 cities throughout the world under the theme "Silence = Death" beneath an inverted pink triangle. In addition, the youth-oriented group Queer Nation formed in 1990 with independent chapters soon appearing in local communities around the country. Chanting, "We're here. We're queer. We're fabulous. Get used to it," Queer Nation members stressed "queer visibility" and an end to heterosexual privilege and heterosexism.

And on the cutting edge of the movement for equality and pride are transgender people who are coming out of another closet in large numbers and making the links in our understanding of transgender oppression, heterosexism, and sexism (see section 7). Young people are "coming out of the closet" with pride earlier than ever before and organizing school and community-based groups (such as Gay/Straight Alliances) in middle schools and high schools, colleges, and communities throughout the country and around the world. A growing number of LGB people are raising children, proving that love is what it takes to make a family. Some activists are pushing for the right for same-sex couples to marry, others are working to lift the ban against LGB from openly serving in the military, while the opposition is trying to prevent these from happening. Others are working tirelessly to eliminate the harassment, bullying, and violence directed against anyone who appears "different" that continues to plague our schools and society, which harms and literally kills so many each year.

Originally meaning "different" or "outside the norm," the term *queer* has often been used as a derogatory term. Some lesbian, gay, bisexual, and transgender people, however, have turned the term around by using it in an inclusive way and as a term of empowerment. First, young people adopted the term as a non-label to deconstruct sexual and gender categories as a form of resistance. It is used now at times to denote a person who is not heterosexual or not gender-normative. Following the lead of young people, what has come to be referred to as "Queer Theory" and "Queer Studies," with such notable writers as Michel Foucault, Judith Butler, and Eve Kosovsky Sedgwick, among many others, is now having enormous impact on college and university campuses as a bona fide academic discipline (see website for further resources).

READING SELECTIONS IN THIS SECTION

This section begins with a number of essays conveying key historical and social contexts of heterosexism. "How Homophobia Hurts Everyone" (selection 78) provides a conceptual framework by discussing what homophobia is and how it affects everyone regardless of their actual or perceived sexual identity. Marcia Deihl and Robyn Ochs (selection 79) define biphobia and investigate myths about bisexual people.. "The InterSEXion: A Vision for a Queer Progressive Agenda" (selection 80) by Deepali Gokhale cuts to the core of heterosexism by looking at the economic systems that support oppression. Devon W. Carbado (selection 81) provides an expanded and nuanced investigation of the concept of dominant group privilege. Pat Griffin (selection 82) addresses issues of heterosexism and, specifically, anti-female oppression in organized sports.

We begin the Voices section with "The Loving Decision" (selection 83), which connects the cause for the legalization of same-sex marriage with past battles for interracial marriage. Ellen Goodman (selection 84) forcefully argues for the right of adoption of children by same-sex couples. Daniel E. Solís y Martínez (selection 85) crosses cultural, gender, and sexuality borders to negotiate a personal vision of identity.

In the concluding Next Steps section, Nancy J. Evans and Jamie Washington (selection 86) provide both a theoretical and a practical foundation on the ways in which heterosexually identified people can become allies to lesbian, gay, bisexual, and transgender people.

This section represents heterosexism from multiple perspectives, and emphasizes the more overt forms of this type of oppression. Other selections that convey the joyful and day-to-day lived experiences and illustrate the diverse and multifaceted historical and cultural aspects of LGB people in Western and non-Western perspectives appear among the Further Resources/ Reading Selections on the heterosexism section website.

Note

1 A percentage of the population (approximately 1 in 2000) is born with male and female sexual organs to various degrees, or indeterminate genitalia. They are neither male nor female but, rather, comprise another birth sex. So, in actuality, there are more than two sexes.

References

D'Emilio, J. (1983). "Capitalism and Gay Identity." In A. Snitow, C. Stansell, S. Thompson (eds), *Powers of Desire: The Politics of Sexuality*. New York: Monthly Review Press. pp. 100–113.

Rich, A. C. (1986). *Compulsory Heterosexuality and Lesbian Existence. Blood, Bread, and Poetry: Selected Prose, 1979–1985*. New York: Norton.

Warner, M. (1991). "Introduction: Fear of a Queer Planet." *Social Text* 9 (4), 3–17.

78

How Homophobia Hurts Everyone

Warren J. Blumenfeld

It is often said that, in the midst of misfortune, something unexpectedly valuable arises, and this has indeed been my experience. While traveling alone through Scandinavia one summer, I began to lose the vision in both my eyes. When I reached Denmark. I went to a hospital for an evaluation, and, after a number of tests, a physician notified me that my retinas had detached, probably because of a congenital defect. She advised immediate surgery to prevent further deterioration, and I was admitted to the Community Hospital in Copenhagen.

The next day, my sister, Susan, flew to Copenhagen to be with me for what turned out to be nearly two months.

That summer in this distant northern land, fearing the permanent loss of my vision, I lay in a narrow hospital bed longing for friends and relatives back home. But as Susan sat with me day after day, giving her love, her courage, her humor (and spectacular Danish pastries), something remarkable happened. Amid the bells of a distant church tolling away the passing hours, Susan and I genuinely got to know one another for the first time.

Although we inhabited the same house for over seventeen years, there was always some unspoken tension between us, some wall keeping us apart. Having only eighteen months separating us in age, we attended the same schools and had similar peer groups. For the first few years of our lives, we seemed to get along fine. We had a few friends in common, and we usually found time to play together most days. Our closeness, however, was soon to come to an end.

By the time I reached the age of seven or eight, I was increasingly becoming the target of harassment and attack by my peers, who perceived me as someone who was different. Names like *queer, sissy, little girl*, and *fag* were thrown at me like the large red ball the children hurled on the school yard in dodge ball games. During subsequent years, the situation only got worse. I tried to avoid other children and increasingly kept to myself. Susan and I grew apart. Only when we were both in our early twenties, about the time I went to Denmark, were we beginning to rediscover one another and to share the details of our lives.

While in college, I began to sort out how I had suffered as a gay male under the force of homophobia, but until my hospitalization I had very little idea how it had also affected Susan growing up as my heterosexually oriented younger sister. Smart, attractive, outgoing, she appeared to have, at least from my vantage point, plenty of friends and seemed to fit in. In Denmark, however, she confided to me that, throughout our school years, she was continually teased for having a "faggot" brother. On one occasion, she recalled some of the older boys laughing at her, asking if she were "like her brother." When she witnessed other students harassing me, peer pressure, coupled with her own fear of becoming a target, compelled her to distance herself from me by adding her voice to the chorus of insults. I felt betrayed, and at the time despised her for it.

Our time together in my hospital room permitted us the needed chance to define the basis of our past estrangement. Through the tears, the apologies, the rage at having been raised in an oppressive environment, and the regrets over losing so much precious time, we began the process of healing our relationship. As it turned out, my vision was not the only thing restored to me that summer.

This essay represents the growth of a seed planted in my mind back in Denmark. It centers around one primary premise: within each of the numerous forms of oppression, members of the target group (sometimes called "minority") are oppressed while on some level members of the dominant or agent group are hurt. Although the effects of oppression differ qualitatively for specific target and agent groups, in the end everyone loses.

Most of us hold simultaneous membership in a number of groups based, for example, on our personal and physical characteristics, on our abilities and class backgrounds, and on our cultural, racial, or religious identifications. We may find ourselves both in groups targeted for oppression and in those dominant groups granted relatively higher degrees of power and prestige. By examining how we are disadvantaged as well as looking at the privileges we have, we can develop empathy for individuals different from ourselves and create a basis for alliances.

This essay, therefore, is really about alliances: support for the maintenance and strengthening of alliances where they currently exist and assistance in forging new ones where

C
O
N
T
E
X
T

none has existed before—specifically, alliances between and among lesbians, gay males, bisexuals, transgender people, and heterosexuals.

HOW ARE LGBT PEOPLE OPPRESSED BY HOMOPHOBIA?

Lesbians, gay males, bisexuals, and transgender (LGBT) people are among the most despised groups in the United States today. Perhaps paradoxically, for many in our society, love of sameness (i.e., *homo*-sexuality) makes people different, whereas love of difference (i.e., *hetero*-sexuality) makes people the same.

Much has been written about the ways homophobia in many Western cultures targets LGBT people, ranging from negative beliefs about these groups (which may or may not be expressed), to exclusion, denial of civil and legal protections, and, in, some cases, overt acts of violence. Negative attitudes internalized by members of these groups often damage the spirit and stifle emotional growth.

Homophobia operates on four distinct but interrelated levels: the *personal*, the *interpersonal*, the *institutional*, and the *cultural* (also called the collective or societal).

Personal homophobia refers to a personal belief system (a prejudice) that LGBT people either deserve to be pitied as unfortunate beings who are powerless to control their desires or should be hated, that they are psychologically disturbed, genetically defective, unfortunate misfits, that their existence contradicts the "laws" of nature, that they are spiritually immoral, infected pariahs, disgusting—to put it quite simply, that they are generally inferior to heterosexuals.

Interpersonal homophobia is manifest when a personal bias or prejudice affects relations among individuals, transforming prejudice into its active component—discrimination. Examples of interpersonal homophobia are name calling or "joke" telling intended to insult or defame individuals or groups; verbal and physical harassment and intimidation as well as more extreme forms of violence; the withholding of support, rejection, or abandonment by friends and other peers, coworkers, and family members: refusal of landlords to rent apartments, shop owners to provide services, insurance companies to extend coverage, and employers to hire on the basis of actual or perceived sexual identity. And the list goes on.

A study by the National Gay and Lesbian Task Force (NGLTF) found that more than 90 percent of the respondents had experienced some form of victimization based on their sexual identity and that over 33 percent had been threatened directly with violence. Approximately one-third of the respondents were assaulted verbally, while more than one in fifteen were physically abused by members of their own families.

Reports of violence directed against lesbians, gay males, bisexuals, and transgender people have increased each year since the NGLTF has been keeping records, and such incidents are only the tip of the iceberg. By no means are they isolated to certain locales; rather, they are widespread, occurring throughout the country.

In 2009, the United States Congress passed the Matthew Shepard and James Byrd Jr. Hate Crimes Prevention Act, which for the first time made it a federal crime to assault or attack a person based on sexual orientation or gender identity.

Institutional homophobia refers to the ways in which governments, businesses, and educational, religious, and professional organizations systematically discriminate on the basis of sexual orientation or identity. Sometimes laws, codes, or policies actually enforce such discrimination. Few institutions have policies supportive of LGBT people, and many actively work against not only those minorities but also heterosexuals who support them.

Consider, for example, the "Briggs" Initiative in the late 1970s: had it passed, it would have required the dismissal of California teachers who support gay, lesbian, and bisexual rights regardless of those teachers' actual sexual identification. The U.S. military has a long-standing policy excluding lesbians, gays, and bisexuals from service. In most instances, rights gained through marriage, including spousal benefits and child custody consider-ations, do not extend to LGBT people. Homosexual acts were outlawed in a number of states until 2003. And although a number of municipalities and some states have extended equal protection in the areas of employment, housing, insurance, credit, and public accom-modations, no such statute exists on the national level.

Although agreement concerning same-sex relationships and sexuality does not exist across the various religious communities, and while some denominations are rethinking their negative stands on homosexuality and bisexuality, others preach against such behav-iors, and as a matter of policy exclude people from many aspects of religious life simply on the basis of sexual identity.

Until 1973, established psychiatric associations considered homosexuality a disordered condition. People were often institutionalized against their will, made to undergo danger-ous and humiliating "aversion therapy," and even, at times, lobotomized to alter their sexual desires. Same-sex lovers and friends are often still denied access to loved ones in hospital intensive-care units because of hospital policy allowing only blood relatives or a legal spouse visitation rights.

Today, although a number of practitioners within both the psychiatric and the medical professions hold genuinely enlightened attitudes regarding the realities of homosexuality, bisexuality, and transgenderism, some, unfortunately, remain entrenched in their negative perceptions of same-sex attractions and gender expression, and these perceptions often affect the manner in which they respond to their clients.

Cultural homophobia (sometimes called *collective* or *societal* homophobia) refers to the social norms or codes of behavior that, although not expressly written into law or policy, nonetheless work within a society to legitimize oppression. It results in attempts either to exclude images of lesbians, gays, bisexuals, and transgender people from the media or from history or to represent these groups in negative stereotypical terms. The theologian James S. Tinney suggests seven overlapping categories by which cultural homophobia is manifested.

1, 2 *Conspiracy to silence* and *denial of culture*. These first two categories are closely aligned. Although not expressly written into law, societies informally attempt to prevent large numbers of individuals of a particular minority (or target) group from congregating in any one place (e.g., in bars and other social centers), deny them space to hold social or political functions, deny them access to materials, attempt to restrict representation in any given educational institution or employment in any business, and inhibit frank, open, and honest discussion of topics of interest to or concerning these groups.

3 *Denial of popular strength*. Many studies have found that a significant percentage of the population experiences same-sex desires, and that these individuals often define their identity in terms of these desires. The cultural assumption exists, however, that one is heterosexual until "proven guilty." According to Tinney, "Society refuses to believe how many blacks there are in this country 'passing' for white and how many lesbians and gays [and bisexuals] are out there passing as heterosexuals" (Tinney, 1985, 5).

4 *Fear of overvisibility*. A form of homophobia is manifested each time LGBT people are told that they should not define themselves in terms of their sexuality or gender identity or when they are accused of being "blatant" by expressing signs of affection in public, behaviors that heterosexual couples routinely take for granted. They are given the message that there is something inherently wrong with same-sex desire and that individuals so inclined should keep such desire well hidden and to themselves.

5 *Creation of defined public spaces.* Society tends to force disenfranchised individuals and groups into ghettos, where there is little possibility of integration into the general life of the community. Neighborhoods, business establishments, and even professions are thus set aside for LGBT people as they are for other target groups. Individuals enter these areas hoping to find temporary respite from the outside world's homophobia.

6 *Denial of self-labeling.* Epithets and other derogatory labels are directed at every target group. LGBT people have chosen terms of self-definition (e.g., gay, lesbian, bisexual, transgender, for example) to portray the positive aspects of their lives and loves more adequately. Recently, increasing numbers of lesbians, gays, bisexuals, and transgender people have reappropriated such terms as *queer, faggot*, and *dyke* in order to transform these venomous symbols of hurt and bigotry into tools of empowerment.

7 *Negative symbolism* (stereotyping). Stereotyping groups of people is used as a means of control and a further hindrance to understanding and to meaningful social change. Stereotypes about LGBT people abound, ranging from their alleged predatory appetites, to their physical appearance, to the possible "causes" of their desires.

In addition to Tinney's categories of cultural homophobia, psychologist Dorothy Riddle suggests that the concepts of *tolerance* and *acceptance* should also be included: tolerance because it can, in actuality, be a mask for an underlying fear or even hatred (one is tolerant, e.g., of a baby crying on an airplane while simultaneously wishing it would stop or go away), and acceptance because it assumes that there is indeed something to accept.

HOW HOMOPHOBIA HURTS EVERYONE

It cannot be denied that homophobia, like other forms of oppression, serves the dominant group by establishing and maintaining power and mastery over those who are marginalized or disenfranchised. Individuals maintain oppressive behaviors to gain certain rewards or to avoid punishment, to protect their self-esteem against psychological doubts or conflicts, to enhance their value systems, or to categorize others in an attempt to comprehend a complex world. By excluding entire groups of people, those in positions of power obtain economic, political, ideological, and other privileges. In many ways, though, oppression, in this instance homophobia, ultimately limits heterosexuals.

Homophobia inhibits the ability of heterosexuals to form close, intimate relationships with members of their own sex.

Young people often form close same-sex attachments during their childhood years. But once they reach a certain age (usually around the time of puberty), their elders encourage them to distance themselves from these friends, with the implication that if they do not, their sexuality will be called into question. This means—especially for males—no more sleeping over at each other's houses, no more sharing intimate secrets, no more spending as much time together. Ultimately, this situation tends to hinder the ability of heterosexual adults to get as close to a same-sex friend as they once did when they were very young.

Homophobia locks all people into rigid gender-based roles that inhibit creativity and self-expression.

Much has been written about gender roles and how they constrain both females and males. In Western culture, concepts of masculinity and femininity promote the domination of males over females and reinforce the identification of maleness with power. Males are encouraged to be independent, competitive, goal oriented, and unemotional, to value physical courage and toughness. Females, on the other hand, are taught to be nurturing, emotional, sensitive, expressive, to be caretakers of others while disregarding their own needs.

Gender roles maintain the sexist structure of society, and homophobia reinforces those roles—for example, by casting such epithets as *faggot, dyke,* and *homo* at people who step outside designated gender roles. This pervasive social conditioning based on anatomical sex effectively generates great disparities between males and females. For evidence of this inequality one need only look at the preponderance of men over women in upper management positions and other positions of prestige, or at the fact that women still do not earn equal pay for equal work. There is also evidence, in a classic 1935 anthropological study of three cultures by Margaret Mead, that there is an increased incidence of violence against women in male-dominated societies.

Homophobic conditioning (and indeed all forms of oppression) compromises the integrity of heterosexual people by pressuring them into treating others badly, actions contrary to their basic humanity.

By way of analogy. Frederick Douglass, the famous nineteenth-century abolitionist who escaped slavery, described what he called "the dehumanizing effects" of slavery not on slaves alone, but also on white slave owners, whose position to slavery corrupted their humanity. Describing his experiences with Mrs. Sophia Auld, mistress of the Baltimore household in which Douglass lived and worked during the 1820s, Douglass wrote,

> My new mistress proved to be a woman of the kindest heart and finest feelings. But, alas, this kind heart had but a short time to remain such. The fatal poison of irresponsible power was already in her hands, and soon commenced its infernal work. Slavery soon proved its ability to divest her of (her) heavenly qualities. Under its influence, the tender heart became stone, and the lamblike disposition gave way to one of tigerlike fierceness.
>
> (Douglass 1845, 77–78)

Homophobia can be used to stigmatize, silence, and, on occasion, target people who are perceived or defined by others as gay, lesbian, or bisexual but who are in actuality heterosexual.

For more than two millennia in the West, antihomosexual laws and decrees have been enacted by religious denominations and governments carrying punishments ranging from ridicule to death of the "accused." These decrees have been used to justify harsh treatment of those discovered or believed to have engaged in same-sex activity. But what is often forgotten or overlooked is the fact that these same laws have, on occasion, been used by individuals and governments to silence opponents, regardless of whether they have engaged in same-sex activity.

In 1871, Paragraph 175 of the German Penal Code banned homosexuality. It was later used by the Nazi regime to incarcerate and ultimately to send great numbers of men suspected of being homosexual to their death, and was also at time employed to incarcerate Catholic clergy, many of whom were heterosexual, as well as non-Catholic heterosexuals who opposed state authority. In addition, "sodomy" laws remained on the books until 2003 in many states in the U.S. Although designed chiefly to harass persons engaging in same-sex activity, they have also been used to prosecute heterosexuals.

The Lambda Legal Defense and Education Fund—a New York-based gay, lesbian, bisexual, and transgender-oriented legal organization—defended a twenty-six-year-old heterosexual man who was denied health insurance because he was unmarried, living in New York City with a male roommate, and therefore presumed to be gay and stereotypically assumed to be at increased risk for HIV/AIDS. Heterosexual male hairdressers and female gym teachers and other heterosexuals working in professions widely perceived to be "gay," along with single people living in red-lined "gay" zip codes, are also vulnerable to victimization by similar homophobia-based discrimination.

Violent "queer-bashing" is not infrequently directed against heterosexuals who are also perceived to be gay or lesbian. The clear implication here is that all people are at risk for attack, irrespective of their actual sexual identity, so long as any group remains the target of violent hate-motivated assaults.

Homophobia generally restricts communication with a significant portion of the population and, more specifically, limits family relationships.

No matter how they are constituted, families will continue to produce lesbian, gay, bisexual, and transgender offspring. The political and theocratic Right argues loudly that homosexuality poses a direct threat to "traditional family values." In actuality, however, it is homophobia that strains family relationships by restricting communication among family members, loosening the very ties that bind. Children, fearing negative reactions from parents, hold back important information about their lives. Parents, often not wanting to hear about their child's sexual or gender identity, never truly get to know their children. Even when parents and children reside in the same house, secret upon secret adds up to polite estrangement and sometimes to a total break.

When LGBT people finally do "come out" to their relatives and friends, the heterosexual relatives and friends sometime go into a "closet" as their homophobia and/or that of those around them leads them to withhold the truth from friends and neighbors. Indeed, family members sometime become targets of stigmatization when the truth about an LGBT relative becomes known. In any case, the emotional toll can be great.

Homophobia ultimately undermines the process of parenting in all families. It harms not only those in the more obvious cases where there are LGBT children, or LGBT parents, but it also imposes great impediments to "mainstream" heterosexual families with heterosexual children.

Societal homophobia prevents some lesbian, gay, bisexual, and transgender people from developing an authentic self-identity, and adds to the pressure to marry, which in turn places undue stress and oftentimes trauma on themselves as well as their heterosexual spouses and their children.

The suppression of information about the gay, lesbian, bisexual, and transgender experience reinforces the heterosexist assumption that everyone is or should be heterosexual and should conform to standard conceptualizations of gender expression. This assumption, coupled with the frequently very real penalties for not conforming to heterosexual norms, has pressured many people either to hide their true sexual and/or gender identity or has restricted their self-realization. Some have married in an attempt to "fit in" or "pass," or in hopes of "being cured" of their same-sex attractions and/or their gender expressions.

Homophobia is one cause of premature sexual involvement that increases the chances of teen pregnancy and the spread of sexually transmitted diseases (STDs).

Young people, of all sexual identities, are often pressured to become *heterosexually* active to prove to themselves and others that they are "normal." If homophobia were reduced in the schools and society at large, in all likelihood, fewer young people would act out *heterosexually* during adolescence.

Homophobia combined with sexphobia (fear and revulsion of sex) results in the elimination of any discussion of the lives and sexuality of sexual minorities as part of school-based sex education, keeping vital information from all students. Such a lack of information can kill people in the age of AIDS.

Some religious and community leaders, educators, and parents actively work to prevent honest and nonjudgmental information concerning homosexuality, bisexuality, and transgenderism—indeed, sexuality and gender in general—from reaching young people. Students of all sexual and gender identities need this information to make informed decisions about their sexual activity. Without it, they are placed at greater risk for unwanted pregnancy, STDs, and HIV infection.

Homophobia (along with racism, sexism, classism, sexphobia, and others) inhibits a unified and effective governmental and societal response to AIDS.

It can be reasonably argued that if the majority of people with AIDS had initially been middle-class, white, suburban heterosexual males, rather than gay and bisexual men, people of color, working-class people, sex workers (prostitutes), and drug users, then governmental and societal institutions would have mobilized immediately to defeat the epidemic.

Because of the lack of wide-scale early attention, AIDS has spread to pandemic proportions. The government and society, at least initially, did not make a true commitment to education, research, and treatment. Funding remained insufficient for as many years as AIDS retained its erroneous reputation of a disease of outcast sexual and social minorities. The result was, and in some sectors continues to be, that many heterosexuals have a false sense that they will not be affected, and take no precautions.

Homophobia prevents heterosexuals from accepting the benefits and gifts offered by the lesbian, gay, bisexual, and transgendered communities: theoretical insights, spiritual visions and options, contributions in the arts and culture, to religion, to family life, indeed to all facets of society.

In cultures where homophobia is present, there have been active attempts to falsify historical accounts of same-sex love—through censorship, deletion, half-truths, and altering pronouns signifying gender—making accurate reconstruction extremely difficult. This effectively distorts society's collective memory (i.e., history), clouding our sense of identity as individuals and as social beings. Everyone loses from this suppression of the truth.

John Boswell cites an example of this censorship in a manuscript of *The Art of Love* by the Roman author Ovid. A phrase that originally read, "A boy's love appealed to me less" (*Hoc est quod pueri tanger amore minus*) was altered by a Medieval moralist to read, "A boy's love appealed to me not at all" (*Hoc est quod pueri tanger amore nihil*), and an editor's note that appeared in the margin informed the reader. "Thus you may be sure that Ovid was not a sodomite" (*Ex hoc nota quod Ovidius nonfreit Sodomita*).

Boswell also cites a Renaissance example of homophobic censorship in which Michelangelo's grand-nephew changed the sex of the subject of his uncle's sonnets to make them more acceptable to the public.

Closer to our time, government-sponsored censorship of art deemed "homoerotic" by the National Endowment for the Arts ultimately restricted creativity and freedom of expression of the entire artistic community.

In addition, traditional religious teachings on homosexuality keep lesbians, gays, bisexuals, and transgender people from entering religious life or from being true to themselves. These teachings also inhibit the ability of many congregations to value and celebrate human diversity and, most importantly, impedes spiritual growth.

Homophobia saps energy from more constructive endeavors.

Like all forms of oppression, homophobia inhibits our ability to understand the nature and scope of truly serious and far-reaching social problems (e.g., poverty, illiteracy, war, disease, environmental decay, crime, and drug addiction). Oppression results in the scapegoating and distancing of people from one another, diminishing our capacity to address these problems and thereby degrading the quality of life for all of us. By reducing the various forms of oppression, we quite literally make our society more socially efficient, increasing our ability to find solutions to the social and ecological challenges that threaten our collective future.

Homophobia inhibits appreciation of other types of diversity, making it unsafe for everyone because each person has unique traits not considered mainstream or dominant. Therefore, we are all diminished when any one of us is demeaned.

As Reverend Martin Niemoeller wrote during World War II,

> In Germany they came first for the Communists, and I didn't speak up because I wasn't a Communist. Then they came for the Jews, and I didn't speak up because I wasn't a Jew. Then they came for the trade unionists, and I didn't speak up because I wasn't a trade unionist. Then they came for the Catholics, and I didn't speak up because I was a Protestant. Then they came for me, and by that time no one was left to speak up.
>
> (in Bartlett, 1980, 824)

The meaning is quite clear. When any particular group of people is scapegoated, it is ultimately everyone's concern. For today, gay, lesbian, bisexual, and transgender people are targeted. Tomorrow, they may come for you. Therefore, it is in everyone's self-interest to work actively to dismantle all the many forms of oppression, including homophobia.

CONCLUSION

In truth, homophobia is pervasive throughout the society and each of us, irrespective of sexual or gender identity, is at risk of its harmful effects. Within the schools, homophobia compromises the entire educational environment. Though homophobia did not originate with us and we are not to blame, we are all responsible for its elimination and, therefore, all can gain by a closer examination of the issues.

Lesbians, bisexuals, gay males, and transgender people have been, and continue to be, on the front lines in fighting against homophobia, and standing by our sides are supportive heterosexual allies—people who have worked and continue to work through their own homophobic conditioning, who are secure with their own sexual identities, who have joined us and have not cared when others called their sexuality into question.

We are *all* born into a great pollution called homophobia (one among many forms of oppression) that falls upon us like acid rain. For some people, spirits are tarnished to the core; others are marred on the surface, but no one is completely protected. Yet neither are we to blame. We had no control over the formulation of this pollution, nor did we direct it to pour down upon us. On the other hand, we all have a responsibility, indeed an opportunity, to join together to construct protective shelters from the corrosive effect of oppression while working to clean up the homophobic environment in which we live. Once sufficient steps are taken to reduce this pollution, we will all breathe a lot easier.

CONTEXT

References

Bartlett, J. (1980). *Bartlett's Familiar Quotations*. Boston: Little, Brown and Company.
Douglass, F. (1982[1845]). *Narrative of the Life of Frederick Douglass, an American Slave, Written by Himself*. H.A. Baker, Jr. (ed.). New York: Penguin.
Tinney, J.S. (1983). "Interconnections." *Interracial Books for Children Bulletin* 14(3–4),4–6.

79

Biphobia

Marcia Deihl and Robyn Ochs

I was in a feminist bookstore. As the woman rang up my purchase, she asked me if a "lesbian discount" was appropriate. I was somewhat taken aback, but I said (half in jest), "Well, I'm bisexual, so how about half?" She didn't smile and I didn't get a discount.

My friend had been active in her lesbian community for several years. Then she fell in love with a man. When her lesbian "friends" found out, they ostracized her and held a "funeral" for her.

I came out to my brother several years ago and he seems on many levels to accept my bisexual identity. However, about a year ago I was visiting him and he took special care to request that I not discuss my bisexuality in the presence of his friends.

I told a heterosexual male friend that I was bisexual. His response was to make repeated attempts to sexualize our relationship. He made the false assumption that since I was bi-SEX-ual, I was attracted to everybody.

STORIES AND STEREOTYPES

These are all stories that have happened to bisexuals. Some of these mirror homophobia, others heterophobia, and still others are specifically "biphobic." All of them oppress bisexuals.

Biphobia: What is it? It is fear of the other and fear of the space between categories. Our identity categories are founded on the illusion that there are two separate and mutually exclusive sexual identities—female and male—and that there are two separate and mutually exclusive sexual orientations—homosexual and heterosexual. You are either one or the other and are attracted to one or the other. Those who are not like you are very different—opposite, in fact—and you needn't worry about becoming like them. There is no space for fluidity. Biphobia, like homophobia, is prejudice based on negative stereotypes. It is often born of ignorance.

Everybody knows about bisexuals. They're going through a stage before settling into their "mature" gay or straight identity ("She's really a lesbian, but she can't admit it yet." "He's just experimenting. He'll go back to his wife in the end." "She's a BUG: Bisexual Until Graduation."). Or, they're afraid of the other sex and find the same sex less threatening. Or, they're sex maniacs and swingers who can't commit.

C
O
N
T
E
X
T

In April of 1983, an "April Fools" cartoon appeared in Boston's *Gay Community News*. It showed a jilted lesbian who had been left by her bisexual lover for a man. After that, she was prepared with "bisexuality insurance." The BiVocals, a newly formed bisexual support group, angrily responded, "Sometimes we do leave women for men. We also leave men for women, women for women, and men for men. But we don't leave our lovers any more cruelly or frequently than any other group . . . And sometimes we are assholes, just like some lesbians" (BiVocals 1983, 4).

FEAR FROM HETEROSEXUAL PEOPLE

Homophobic heterosexual men and women alike react to bisexuality as they react to homosexuality. But with bisexuality, there is the added dimension of identification with the perceived "straight half" of a bisexual person. They may be even more threatened, because they see that the "other" is not different enough, turning fantasy into a very real possibility.

Sigmund Freud and Alfred Kinsey agree that there is a spectrum of sexuality from exclusively heterosexual to exclusively homosexual. This view is shared by a number of current researchers. For example biologist Joan E. Roughgarden of Stanford University says, "We should be calling humans bisexual because this idea of exclusive homosexuality is not accurate of people. Homosexuality is mixed in with heterosexuality across cultures and history" (quoted in Driscoll 2008, para 26). Somerset Maugham once said, "I tried to persuade myself that I was three-quarters normal and that only a quarter of me was queer . . . whereas it was the other way round" (Rutledge 1988, 46).

Heterosexually-identified people resisting their own same-sex fantasies due to internalized homophobia will probably be threatened by bisexuality in others. ("I don't deserve what I want." "It's sinful.") Those who respond heterosexually for positive, clear, inner-directed reasons are less likely to be threatened.

We can't "convert" anyone. We don't have the right to come out for anyone else or to insist that someone is "really bisexual." We don't have the right to judge another's reasons for pursuing or avoiding intimacy with a given sex. We simply want it to be known that there are more than two options, and a wide range of variations. Some of our best allies are secure heterosexual people.

Heterosexual men and women will react slightly differently to bisexual men and bisexual women than they might react to gay men and lesbians. A homophobic straight man may respond similarly to a bisexual man as he does to a gay man (e.g., "Sissy!"). This sentiment may mask the outrage that men feel about other men renouncing their patriarchal prerogative of superiority to women. We have seen documentaries in which the Marines refer to recruits in basic training as "ladies" and "girls" in a derogatory sense. These names are considered the worst possible put-down for men who aren't being "masculine" enough. Another typical homophobic reaction is "I just know he's going to make a pass at me." In this imagined situation, a heterosexual man sees himself in the position of potential "prey." Terrified and outraged, he fears being overpowered, a situation familiar to most women.

Heterosexual women cannot write off bisexual men as "just friends" with no potential sexual undercurrents, as they might do with gay men. But they cannot assume that these men are attracted to them either. Heterosexual women may see bisexual women as better "initiation" experiences than lesbians, or they may assume that bisexual women are after them.

Bisexuality defies old categories and evokes new responses. Many heterosexuals and homosexuals alike deny the existence of bisexuality. A great deal of this ignorance is rooted in our invisibility. We range from being dismissed as a politicized identity group ("Oh, everyone's a little bit bisexual!") to being seen as a point of contention in a film or television plot. In this instance, bisexuality becomes visible when a character who was previously assumed to be heterosexual or homosexual leaves someone for someone else, engages in a triangulated relationship, or "cheats," and is then re-cast as bisexual.

Furthermore, some bisexuals are more invisible than others. Although there are notable exceptions, bisexuals who are not middle or upper class, conventionally "beautiful," able-bodied, or white are rarely represented. And bisexuals who lead unremarkable lives are usually seen by others—depending upon the sex of their partners—as gay or as straight. By and large, the only bisexual people who are recognized *as bisexuals* are those with multiple male and female partners, or those who leave one lover for another, lending fuel to the perception that these are common bisexual behaviors.

FEAR FROM LESBIAN AND GAY PEOPLE

The early homophile (1950s and 1960s), gay liberation (1970s), and later equality movements have fought for the right of gay men and lesbians to exist, to love, and to be treated with dignity. Therefore, any perceived "regression" by gay people "converting" back to heterosexuality is considered a threat. This feeling is understandable. The gay and lesbian communities are under siege, especially in the so-called "culture wars" being waged by the political and theocratic right, and people under constant siege usually respond by banding together to form a united front. Thus, formerly gay and lesbian people who "turn bi" are often met with feelings of betrayal and anger. But these reactions belie the truth of the situation.

Why are bisexuals perceived as such a threat to so many gay men and lesbians? We see a combination of society's homophobia and internalized biphobia at work here. A recurring theme in Robyn's previous same-sex relationships was her lovers' fear that Robyn would leave her for a man. After all, so much of our society is structured to encourage and support heterosexual relationships. Though this has finally begun to change, families, the media, and institutions such as marriage and health insurance "family plans" are largely based on the configuration of the married heterosexual couple. These lovers may have felt that they could not possibly compete with the odds so stacked against them.

There is no denying that the encouragement of heterosexuality and the discouragement of homosexuality are real. But Robyn also felt that there was a certain amount of internalized biphobia at work there, too: the feeling that whatever she had to offer, and whatever they had together couldn't possibly outweigh the external benefits of heterosexual privilege. This view contains an underlying assumption that anyone who has the choice would ultimately choose heterosexuality, and that lesbians and gay men choose homosexual relationships because they are unable to be heterosexual. The number of bisexuals in committed same-sex relationships shows that this isn't necessarily so.

Some say that bisexuals are only half oppressed. Yet we are not put on half-time when we are fired by a homophobic boss; we do not lose only half of our children when we lose a custody battle; we cannot say to a gay-basher, "But I'm bisexual. Please only beat me up on only one side of my body!"

After Marcia was asked if she warranted the "lesbian discount," she thought seriously about it. "I respected the woman's right to run her store the way she wanted. I loved the idea that there was such a thing as a lesbian discount—a rare opportunity for lesbians to be rewarded, not made invisible or degraded. But, then I thought of my many years of gay and lesbian pride marches and my six years of playing in a feminist band that performed 25 to 50 percent lesbian material. During that time, I identified first as straight, then as lesbian, and finally as bisexual. I think I *did* deserve at least half of the discount! They based their decision on my label, not my *labor*."

Bisexuals should not automatically be categorized along with heterosexuals and end up being excluded from gay and lesbian communities. Yet, it is generally only famous bisexual people—reclassified as "gay" or "lesbian" people—like Virginia Woolf, Sappho, Christopher Isherwood, James Baldwin, Vita Sackville-West, Kate Millet, and Bessie Smith, who are embraced by lesbians and gay men. Modern-day bisexuals working common jobs and bearing ordinary names are not.

We won't accept it both ways. Lesbian and gay communities cannot have it both ways; either bisexuals are in or we're out. The feminist bookstore offering a lesbian discount was a store for *all* women, but lesbians got a discount; heterosexual and bisexual women did not. It seemed in this instance we were *out* of the community. We want to be in, but we are called divisive when we then name ourselves as a distinct category. Such attitudes often keep us away and only reinforce the impression that we have "deserted the ranks."

Like heterosexual people who may be ignoring their homosexual inner signals, some gay men and lesbians may be repressing their bisexuality. If they act on these desires, they may fear the loss of their gay identity, their community, their culture, and their closest friends, as we noted in the case of the "funeral" story above. Others, who have chosen positively to be gay or lesbian, tend to be supportive of bisexuality in others. Those who are threatened or unsure of themselves are less so.

A clear example of biphobia is the exclusion of some bisexuals from lesbian and gay communities. This is ironic when one considers that the lesbian and gay liberation movement in the United States is united around the right to love whomever we please, and to have our relationships validated and recognized, even when they do not conform to society's norms. Bisexuals are often pushed into a closet *within* a closet.

THE BISEXUAL ARTIST/CITIZEN TODAY: OUTSTANDING IN OUR FIELD

Can you spot a bisexual when you meet one? Perhaps, but not necessarily. We come in every conceivable outer package—just like all other groups. What is important is what is inside. Our psyches are not split down the middle. We do not get up every day and think, "Should I be straight or gay today?" We are, every day, in all situations, bisexual.

In sum, we are not defined by our behavior, but by our essence. If we walk down the street holding hands with a woman, people will assume we are lesbians. If we walk down the street holding hands with a man, people will assume we are heterosexual. But we aren't shifting; others' perceptions are.

As public television's Mr. Rogers told very young children, each of us is unique, with our own gifts and limitations. We are all artists, we are all queers; we are all "oddists." And lesbian, gay, bisexual, and transgender people have been forced to be creative. We experience a conflict between inner experience and outer demands that requires that we invent ourselves and think on our feet at every moment. Perhaps this is why we have contributed more than our share to the arts. As Fran Leibowitz quipped, "If you removed all of the homosexuals and homosexual influence from what is generally regarded as American culture, you would pretty much be left with *Let's Make a Deal*" (Rutledge 1988, 93). We would do well to join some Native American Indian cultures in considering differences in sexuality and gender expression as special, honored gifts, not as threatening deviations.

Being bisexual and naming ourselves makes us special. But that's just the first step. We have our cultural work cut out for us. We need to create what wasn't there before—our own lives, music, theater, writing, and art—just as some of us did with women's culture. We need art that reflects, analyzes, reinvents, and inspires our daily lives. We must not simply react to biphopia, we must come together with others like ourselves to create new realities in art and in life.

Though we are unique, we are also like everyone else: we are citizens of this planet. We need to work in coalitions because we want to help clear up the many problems that face us and our children and grandchildren today. Problems of poverty, global warming, unjust wars, and violence affect us all. In order to solve these problems, action must be taken against heterosexism, sexism, racism, and class privilege. And since we are all minorities, we must work together on common causes in order to be effective. As connecting links at the intersection between gay and straight, bisexuals can play a unique role in this work.

Bisexuals are not fence-sitters: there is no fence. Sexuality is a giant field in which lesbian and gay people are clustered mostly on one side and heterosexually-identified people are clustered mostly on the other. We are not locked in place. Sometimes we travel toward one end, sometimes toward the other, and we can do this in a day or in a lifetime. We hereby declare a field day.

References

BiVocals. (1983, April 23). "Gay-Identified Bisexuals." Letter to the Editor in *Gay Community News*, 4.

Driscoll, E.V. (2008). "Bisexual Species: Unorthodox Sex in the Animal Kingdom: Homosexual Behavior is Common in Nature, and It Plays an Important Role in Survival." *Scientific American*, August 10. <http://richarddawkins.net/article,2850,Bisexual-Species-Unorthodox-Sex-in-the-Animal-Kingdom,Scientific-American>

Rutledge, L. (1988). *Unnatural Quotations*. Boston: Alyson Publications.

80

The interSEXion

A Vision for a Queer Progressive Agenda

Deepali Gokhale

This vision is based on the fact that the queer community is a microcosm of humanity, intersecting through the common experiences of the oppression of gender identity and sexual identity, the observation that oppression is rooted in greed and perpetuated by the fear of scarcity, the assertion that no oppression can end without removing the systems that perpetuate it, the recognition that oppression and exploitation are the bases on which current power structures and economies rely, and the observation that because queer liberation requires the end of all forms of oppression and exploitation, the liberation of queer people can be seen as the key to the liberation of humanity itself.

THE ROOT OF QUEER OPPRESSION

Heterosexism is the belief that there are only two genders, and that a sexual relationship between a man and a woman is compulsory for full acceptance into society. It would seem that the root of queer oppression is heterosexism, and so queer folks should work against heterosexism. In order to get into any sort of depth in this work, we would need to know why heterosexism exists in the first place, and we would find that the reason for heterosexism is because it enforces patriarchy, which could lead us to join forces with the women's movement and oppose patriarchy. That venture would expose the fact that the reason patriarchy needs enforcement is because it is essential to capitalism, and that capitalism at its essence relies on greed. Therefore, the root of queer oppression, and in fact, the root of all systemic oppression as it exists in the world today, is unbridled greed.

Capitalism is based in greed, and as it exists today, cannot exist without exploiting labor. One person cannot make a disproportionately large share of profits unless somewhere in the process, another person is making a disproportionately small one. The most basic example of this is in the patriarchal nuclear family, where the man makes profits at the expense of a woman's (and children's) free labor. The people who most benefit from this unbridled greed are the ones who came up with capitalism to begin with: wealthy white men. This is true worldwide; every oppression that is in place exists to ultimately support white male power, and the United States is the clear leader and greatest benefactor of this system.

The main tools used to make an oppressive system work are a defined norm, economic power, and violence. In her book entitled *Homophobia: A Weapon of Sexism*, Suzanne Pharr explains it this way:

> To understand the connection among the oppressions, we must examine their common elements. The first is a defined norm, a standard of rightness and often righteousness wherein all others are judged in relation to it. This norm must be backed up with institutional power, economic power, and both institutional and individual violence . . . . In the United States, that norm is male, white, heterosexual, Christian, temporarily able-bodied, youthful, and has access to wealth and resources . . . .
>
> In order for these institutions to be controlled by a single group of people, there must be economic power . . . . Once economic control is in the hands of the few, all others can be controlled through limiting access to resources, limiting mobility, limiting employment options. People are pitted against one another through the perpetuation of the myth of scarcity which suggests that our resources are limited and blames the poor for using up too much of what little there is to go around . . . . The maintenance of societal and individual power and control requires the use of violence and the threat of violence. Institutional violence is sanctioned through the criminal justice system and the threat of the military—for quelling individual or group uprisings.

(1988, 53–56)

The patriarchal nuclear family, living in a single-family house in the suburbs, serves as the building block for capitalism. As the arbitrarily defined norm, it provides the perfect conditions for the oppression of women. Since men earn wage labor, they can easily control women's access to resources, and can easily accuse women of "spending too much" of "their" hard-earned money. By isolating women from each other, the nuclear family provides a safe haven for men to be violent towards women and thus enforce their power.

In relation to institutional power, the isolated nuclear family unit makes it easy for mass media to be the only source of information citizens receive, since people are no longer talking to their neighbors, and ideally, by isolating the male in the household as the only breadwinner, the nuclear family can easily be moved around for the convenience of those who need wage labor. Because each family needs a house, a car, and their own household items, the nuclear family also promotes the wasteful unending consumerism and environmental exploitation required for "economic progress." Irrespective of whether the nuclear family is actually the "norm," as long as this belief is widespread, other types of families can be judged by whether they conform to that structure.

Everyone strives to conform to the nuclear family model, and a false sense of pride and righteousness is evident in those who "make it." That many poor people, people of color, and immigrants do not fit into that kind of family is considered "their fault," and not the result of those in power limiting access to the resources it takes to sustain a nuclear family. When this shame and blame is internalized, those who don't fit the norm fight amongst themselves about why another oppressed group is the "problem with society."

It is not just gender oppression that keeps capitalism in place. It requires the exploitation of the labor of anyone outside the "norm": the white, wealthy, young, temporarily-abled, English-speaking Christian American male citizen. Racism exists to exploit the work of people of color, sexism exists to exploit women's work, xenophobia exists to exploit the "third world," and ageism/ableism devalues those who are assumed "less productive." Many of us experience more than one of these oppressions. In addition to the myth of the nuclear family, patriotism, the illusion of a meritocracy, and religious oppression are the tools used to brainwash one group to look down on another and trust that the system is working for the "believers." The illusion of scarcity and fear of our neighbors keeps us isolated from and fighting with each other. Divide and conquer is the rule. Meanwhile, those in power continue to reap the rewards.

A VISION FOR LIBERATION: THE INTER*SEX*ION

It is because the queer community categorically rejects this setup, simply by being who we are, that we are such a threat to those in power. When they call gay marriage a threat to human civilization as we know it, they are referring to the fact that gender oppression in the form of heterosexism is the weapon that keeps them in power, and if those gender "norms" weren't considered essential, there would be no way to enforce that oppression. It is precisely because we live outside the basic unit of the very nuclear family structure that would otherwise permit capitalism to continue unchallenged, and because our community experiences not only queer oppression but all oppressions, that we are most capable of creating an alternative culture outside of the culture of exploitation, resolving it for ourselves so that it can be expanded for those outside of our community.

A defining characteristic of the queer community is that within it is reflected all of the oppressions and privileges in our surrounding geography, and that these oppressions and privileges play out in similar proportions and methods. It is the intersection of every oppression and privilege, and the wholeness of the queer community is its power. There is no better place to understand the intersection of oppressions and figure out how to achieve liberation for all forms of life. Because we are an intersection based on gender identity and sexual identity, we can call ourselves the "interSEXion."

We can start by building a real sense of wholeness within the queer community. While our oppressors would like us to remain separate and at odds with each other, we can use our queer oppression to bind us into making connections and understanding the nature of oppression itself. We can begin by socializing with each other. We can each individually learn about our own oppressions so that we know what we need. We can also learn about our privileges, and use them to end the oppression of others. We can end racism, classism, sexism, and any other oppression within our community. We can create a safety net for ourselves so that we are not reliant on the systems of oppression used against us for our basic needs. We can pass the values of liberation that we create from one generation to the next, without the sense of ownership that is inherited with blood relations, and instead allowing each generation to use its own experience and creativity in the struggle. In this way, we will keep intact within our community what is being used to divide and conquer us elsewhere.

Once we have this safer community, non-reliant on the systems of oppression that keep us divided, we can break the systems of oppression for everyone else. We can use our wholeness as an advantage outside the queer community. As whole people with multiple identities, we can use our non-queer identities as bridges to other oppressed communities. Although it may be true that any oppressed community can build bridges, the queer community is particularly fortunate to have representatives from the actual communities surrounding it. Because the queer identity can many times be made invisible, queer people can have access to those communities in ways that no other oppressed community can.

Currently, the progressive community seems to operate in isolated spaces, divided by our issues and oppressions, with no one group to bind it together. We could use our wholeness and reflection of our geography to ensure our policy would most likely be beneficial for all progressive communities around us, and we can be the glue that binds it together and moves it forward. In many cases, we are leading those "other" progressive movements anyway.

The queer community could have a central "policy group" that would be informed by and be informative to any number of affinity groups. The responsibility of the policy group would be to take in the information from the affinity groups, get resources and create infrastructure to support the groups, and to create an overall policy/strategy/direction for achieving our goal of ending exploitation and oppression. This policy group would be accountable not only to the affinity groups, but also to individuals in the community, and we can hold community forums to keep a dialogue going with those individuals who may not belong to any group.

Our affinity groups could organize by whatever affinity they chose (geography, race, ethnicity, religion, class, gender, sexuality, age, campaign, cause, . . .), they could be groups that already exist (like AIDS Survival Project, ZAMI, Trikone Atlanta), and they could dissolve if/when they were no longer necessary, like if they were organized around a campaign. The groups could provide safe spaces for people to talk about particular oppressions or issues. People could belong to as many affinity groups as they wanted. The goals for each group for now could be: figuring out the most important issues for a particular affinity group, building a coalition to support the group, and figuring out a proactive strategy to address the group's issues in order to inform the policy group.

If the affinity groups and the queer community make up an "inner circle" around our interSEXion, our allies could form a second circle around the first. Issue or campaign-based affinity groups can access our allies to form coalitions when needed. Our allies would benefit because through the interSEXion, we could be the quickest connection between allies that would form a coalition. Our allies could create connections even further outside our intersection, and reach people who would never associate themselves with a queer agenda, but would work on a particular issue or campaign through our allies.

Positioning our queer community as the interSEXion would not only ensure that we remain at the center of our own liberation, but it would also require us to leave no one behind. Being the interSEXion implies our community's wholeness, and it requires us to be no less than a full human rights movement. It requires us to honor and celebrate the wholeness of each individual in it, and restricts some of us from achieving our goal of liberation unless everyone in our community is free from oppression. It requires us to identify which parts of our community are underrepresented and to nurture those who are most wounded. It means we cannot even start towards a path of liberation until we are on equal footing within our own community. It requires us to walk our talk and liberate ourselves in order to liberate the world around us, and it is the reason why our interSEXion may be the key to the end of exploitation.

Reference

Pharr, S. (1988). *Homophobia: A Weapon of Sexism*. Little Rock: Chardon Press.

81

Privilege

Devon W. Carbado

. . . This essay is part of a larger intellectual project to encourage a shift in—or at least a broadening of—our conceptualization of discrimination. My aim is to expand our notion of what it means to be a perpetrator of discrimination. Typically, we define a perpetrator of discrimination as someone who acts intentionally to bring about some discriminatory result. This is a narrow and politically palatable conception; it applies to very few of us. In this essay I suggest that those of us who unquestionably accept the racial, gender, and heterosexual privileges we have—those of us who fail to acknowledge our victimless status with respect to racism, sexism, and homophobia—are also perpetrators of discrimination.

Informing this privileged-centered understanding of discrimination is the notion that taking identity privileges for granted helps to legitimize problematic assumptions about identity and entitlement, assumptions that make it difficult for us to challenge the starting points of many of our most controversial conversations about equality. We simply assume, for example, that men should be able to fight for their country (the question is whether women should be entitled to this privilege); that heterosexuals should be able to get married (the question is whether the privilege should be extended to gays and lesbians); that white men should be able to compete for all the slots in a university's entering class (the question is whether people of color should be entitled to the privilege of "preferential treatment").

While a privileged-centered conception of discrimination usefully reveals the bi-directional effects of discrimination—namely, that discrimination allocates both burdens and benefits—the conception may prove entirely too much. After all, all of us enjoy some degree of privilege. Are all of us perpetrators of discrimination? The answer may depend on what we do with, and to, the privileges we have. Each of us makes personal and private choices with our privileges that entrench a variety of social practices, institutional arrangements, and laws that disadvantage other(ed) people.

For example, many of us get married and/or attend weddings, while lesbian and gay marriages are, in most parts of the United States (and the world), not legally recognized. Others of us have racially monolithic social encounters, live in de facto white only (or predominantly white) neighborhoods, or send our kids to white only (or predominantly white) schools. Still others of us have "straight only" associations—that is, our friends are all heterosexuals and our children's friends all have mommies and daddies. These choices are not just personal; they are political. And their cumulative effect is to entrench the very social practices—racism, sexism, classism, and homophobia—we profess to abhor.

In other words, there is a link between identity privileges, and our negotiation of them, on the one hand, and discrimination, on the other. Our identities are reflective and constitutive of systems of oppression. Racism requires white privilege. Sexism requires male privilege. Homophobia requires heterosexual privilege. The very intelligibility of our identities is their association, or lack thereof, with privilege. This creates an obligation on the part of those of us with privileged identities to expose and to challenge them.

Significantly, this obligation exists not only as a matter of morality and responsibility. The obligation exists for a pragmatic reason as well. We cannot change the macro-effects of discrimination without ameliorating the power effects of our identities. Nor can our political commitments have traction unless we apply them to the seemingly "just personal" privileged aspects of our lives. Resistance to identity privileges may be futile, we cannot know for sure. However, to the extent that we do nothing, this much is clear: we perpetuate the systems of discrimination out of which our identities are forged.

But precisely what constitutes an identity privilege? Further, how do we identify them? And, finally, what acts are necessary to deprivilege our identities and to disrupt their association with power. These questions drive this essay. . . .

HETEROSEXUAL PRIVILEGES

Like maleness, heterosexuality should be critically examined. Like maleness, heterosexuality operates as an identity norm, the "what is" or "what is supposed to be" of sexuality. This is illustrated, for example, by the nature versus nurture debate. The question about the cause of sexuality is almost always formulated in terms of whether homosexuality is or is not biologically determined rather than whether sexual orientation, which includes heterosexuality, is or is not biologically determined. Scientists are searching for a gay, not a heterosexual or sexual orientation, gene. Like female identity, then, homosexuality signifies "difference"—more specifically, sexual identity distinctiveness. The normativity of heterosexuality requires that homosexuality be specified, pointed out. Heterosexuality is always already presumed.

Heterosexuals should challenge the normativity and normalization of heterosexuality. They should challenge the heterosexual presumption. But heterosexuals might be reluctant to do so to the extent that they perceive such challenges to call into question their (hetero)sexual orientation. As Lee Edelman observes in a related context, there "is a deeply rooted concern on the part of . . . heterosexual males about the possible meanings of [men subverting gender roles]" (1990, 50). According to Edelman, heterosexual men consider certain gender role inversions to be potentially dangerous because they portend not only a "[male] feminization that would destabilize or question gender" but also a "feminization that would challenge one's (hetero)sexuality" (1990, 50). Edelman's observations suggest that straight men may want to preserve what I am calling the "heterosexual presumption." Their investment in this presumption is less a function of what heterosexuality signifies in a positive sense and more a function of what it signifies in the negative—*not* being homosexual.

And there are racial dimensions to male investment in heterosexuality. For example, straight black male strategies to avoid homosexual suspicion could relate to the racial aspects of male privileges: heterosexual privilege is one of the few privileges that some black men have. These black men may want to take comfort in the fact that whatever else is going on in their lives, they are not, finally, "sissies," "punks," "faggots." By this I do not mean to suggest that black male heterosexuality has the normative standing of white male heterosexuality. It does not. Straight black men continue to be perceived as heterosexually deviant (overly sexual; potential rapists) and heterosexually irresponsible (jobless fathers of children out of wedlock). Still, black male heterosexuality is closer to white male heterosexual normalcy and normativity than is black gay sexuality. Consequently, some straight (or closeted) black men will want to avoid the "black gay [male] . . . triple negation" to which Marlon Riggs refers in the following quote: "Because of my sexuality I cannot be Black. A strong, proud, 'Afrocentric' black man is resolutely heterosexual, not even bisexual. . . . Hence I remain a sissy, punk, faggot. I cannot be a black gay man because, by the tenets of black macho, a black gay man is a triple negation" (1999, 307) . . .

Keith Boykin, former director of the Black Gay and Lesbian Leadership Forum, maintains that "heterosexual sexual orientation has become so ingrained in our social custom, so destigmatized of our fears about sex, that we often fail to make any connection between heterosexuality and sex" (1997). Boykin is only half right. The socially constructed normalcy of heterosexuality is not due solely to the desexualization of heterosexuality in mainstream political and popular culture. It is due also to the sexualization of heterosexuality as normative and to the gender-norm presumptions about heterosexuality—that it is the normal way sexually to express one's gender.

Moreover, it is not simply that homosexuality is sexed that motivates or stimulates homophobic fears about gay and lesbian relationships. These fears also relate to the fact that homosexuality is stigmatized and is perceived to be an abnormal way sexually to express one's gender. The disparate social meanings that attach to gay and lesbian identities on the one hand and straight identities on the other make individual acts of heterosexual signification a cause for concern.

Recently, I participated in a workshop where one of the presenters "came out" as a heterosexual in the context of giving his talk. This sexual identity disclosure engendered a certain amount of whispering in the back row. Up until that moment, I think many people had assumed the presenter was gay. After all, he was sitting on a panel discussing sexual orientation and had participated in the Gay and Lesbian section of the American Association of Law Schools. There were three other heterosexuals on the panel, but everyone knew they were not gay because everyone *knew* them; they had all been in teaching for a while, two were very senior, and everyone knew of their spouses or partners. Everyone also knew that there was a lesbian on the panel. She, too, had been in teaching for some time and had been out for many years. Apparently, few of the workshop participants knew very much about the presenter who "came out." Because "there is a widespread assumption in both gay and straight communities that any man who says something supportive about issues of concern to lesbian or gay communities must be gay himself," there was, at the very least, a question about his sexuality. Whatever his intentions were for "coming out," whatever his motivations, his assertion of heterosexuality removed the question. . . .

I became sensitized to the politics of heterosexuals "coming out" in the context of reading about James Baldwin. Try to find a piece written about Baldwin and count the number of lines before the author comes out as heterosexual. Usually, it is not more than a couple of paragraphs, so the game ends fast. The following introduction from a 1994 essay about Baldwin is one example of what I am talking about: "The last time I saw James Baldwin was late autumn of 1985, when my wife and I attended a sumptuous book party" (Forrest 1994, 267). In this case, the game ends immediately. Independent of any question of intentionality on the author's part, the mention of the wife functions as an identity signifier to subtextually "out" his heterosexuality. We *read* "wife," we *think* heterosexual.

C
O
N
T
E
X
T

My point here is not to suggest that the essay's overall tone is heterosexually defensive; I simply find it suspicious when heterosexuals speak of their spouses so quickly (in this case the very first sentence of the essay) when a subject (a topic or a personality—here, James Baldwin) implicates homosexuality. . . . The author engages in what I call "the politics of the 3Ds"—disassociation, disidentification, and differentiation. The author is "different" from Baldwin (the author sleeps with women), and this difference, based as it is on sexual identity, compels the author to disassociate himself from and disidentify with that which makes Baldwin "different" (Baldwin sleeps with men).

Heterosexual significations need not always reflect the politics of the 3Ds. In other words, the possibility exists for heterosexuals to point out their heterosexuality without reauthenticating heterosexuality. Consider, for example, the heterosexual privilege list that I give below. While each item on the list explicitly names—outs—heterosexuality, in none of the items does heterosexuality remain unproblematically normative.

As a prelude to the list, I should be clear that the list is incomplete. Nor do the privileges reflected in it represent the experiences of all heterosexuals. As Bruce Ryder observes: "Male heterosexual privilege has different effects on men of, for example, different races and classes. . . . In our society, the dominant or 'hegemonic' form of masculinity to which other masculinities are subordinated is white, middleclass, and heterosexual. This means that the heterosexual privilege of, say, straight black men takes a very different shape in their lives than it does for straight white men" (1991, 292). My goal in presenting this list, then, is not to represent every heterosexual man. Instead, the purpose is to intervene in the normalization of heterosexual privileges. With this intervention, I hope to challenge the pervasive tendency of heterosexuals to see homophobia as something that puts others at a disadvantage and not something that actually advantages them.

HETEROSEXUAL PRIVILEGES: A LIST

1. Whether on television or in the movies, (white) heterosexuality is always affirmed as healthy and/or normal (black heterosexuality and family arrangements are still, to some degree, perceived to be deviant).
2. Without making a special effort, heterosexuals are surrounded by other heterosexuals every day.
3. A husband and wife can comfortably express affection in any social setting, even a predominantly gay one.
4. The children of a heterosexual couple will not have to explain why their parents have different genders—that is, why they have a mummy and a daddy.
5. (White) heterosexuals are not blamed for creating and spreading the AIDS virus (though Africans—as a collective group—are blamed).
6. Heterosexuals do not have to worry about people trying to "cure" their sexual orientation (though black people have to worry about people trying to "cure" black "racial pathologies").
7. Black heterosexual males did not have to worry about whether they would be accepted at the Million Man March.
8. Rarely, if ever, will a doctor, on learning that her patient is heterosexual, inquire as to whether the patient has ever taken an AIDS test and if so, how recently.
9. Medical service will never be denied to heterosexuals because they are heterosexuals (though medical services may not be recommended to black people because they are black).
10. Friends of heterosexuals generally do not refer to heterosexuals as their "straight friends" (though nonblack people often to refer to black people as their "black friends").

11. A heterosexual couple can enter a restaurant on their anniversary and be fairly confident that staff and fellow diners will warmly congratulate them if an announcement is made (though the extent of the congratulation and the nature of the welcome might depend on the racial identities of the couple).

12. White heterosexuals do not have to worry about whether a fictional film villain who is heterosexual will reflect negatively on their heterosexuality (though blacks may always have to worry about their racial representation in films).

13. Heterosexuals are entitled to legal recognition of their marriages throughout the United States and the world.

14. Within the black community, black male heterosexuality does not engender comments like "what a waste," "there goes another good black man," or "if they're not in jail, they're faggots."

15. Heterosexuals can take jobs with most companies without worrying about whether their spouses will be included in the benefits package.

16. Child molestation by heterosexuals does not confirm the deviance of heterosexuality (though if the alleged molester is black, the alleged molestation becomes evidence of the deviance of black [hetero]sexuality).

17. Black rap artists do not make songs suggesting that heterosexuals should be shot or beaten up because they are heterosexuals.

18. Black male heterosexuality does not undermine a black heterosexual male's ability to be a role model for black boys.

19. Heterosexuals can join the military without concealing their sexual identity.

20. Children will be taught in school, explicitly or implicitly, about the naturalness of heterosexuality (they will also be taught to internalize the notion of white normativity).

21. Conversations on black liberation will always include concerns about heterosexual men.

22. Heterosexuals can adopt children without being perceived as selfish and without anyone questioning their motives.

23. Heterosexuals are not denied custody or visitation rights of their children because they are heterosexuals.

24. Heterosexual men are welcomed as leaders of Boy Scout troops.

25. Heterosexuals can visit their parents and family as who they are, and take their spouses, partners, or dates with them to family functions.

26. Heterosexuals can talk matter-of-factly about their relationships with their partners without people commenting that they are "flaunting" their sexuality.

27. A black heterosexual couple would be welcomed as members of any black church.

28. Heterosexual couples do not have to worry about whether kissing each other in public or holding hands in public will render them vulnerable to violence.

29. Heterosexuals do not have to struggle with "coming out" or worry about being "outed."

30. The parents of heterosexuals do not love them "in spite of" their sexual orientation, and parents do not blame themselves for their children's heterosexuality.

31. Heterosexuality is affirmed in most religious traditions.

32. Heterosexuals can introduce their spouses to colleagues and not worry about whether the decision will have a detrimental impact on their careers.

33. A black heterosexual male does not have to choose between being black and being heterosexual.

34. Heterosexuals can prominently display their spouses' photographs at work without causing office gossip or hostility.

35. (White) heterosexuals do not have to worry about "positively" representing heterosexuality.

36. Few will take pity on a heterosexual on hearing that she is straight, or feel the need to say, "That's okay" (though it is not uncommon for a black person to hear, "It's okay that you're black" or "We don't care that you're black" or "When we look at you, we don't see a black person").

37. (Male) heterosexuality is not considered to be symptomatic of the "pathology" of the black family.

38. Heterosexuality is never mistaken as the only aspect of one's lifestyle, but is perceived instead as merely one more component of one's personal identity.

39. (White) heterosexuals do not have to worry over the impact their sexuality will have personally on their children's lives, particularly as it relates to their social lives (though black families of all identity configurations do have to worry about how race and racism will affect their children's well-being).

40. Heterosexuals do not have to worry about being "bashed" after leaving a social event with other heterosexuals (though black people of all sexual orientations do have to worry about being "racially bashed" on any given day).

41. Every day is (white) "Heterosexual Pride Day."

CONCLUSION: RESISTING PRIVILEGES

I have argued that one of the ways to contest gender and sexual orientation hierarchy is for heterosexual men to detail their social experiences on the privileged side of gender and sexual orientation. In advancing this argument, I do not mean to suggest that the role of these men is to legitimize "untrustworthy" and "self-interested" victim-centered accounts of discrimination. There is a tendency on the part of dominant groups (e.g., males and heterosexuals) to discount the experiences of subordinate groups (e.g., straight women, lesbians, and gays) unless those experiences are authenticated or legitimized by a member of the dominant group. For example, it is one thing for me, a black man, to say I experienced discrimination in a particular social setting; it is quite another for my white male colleague to say he witnessed that discrimination. My telling of the story is suspect because I am black (racially interested). My white colleague's telling of the story is not suspect because he is white (racially disinterested). The racial transparency of whiteness—its "perspectivelessness"—renders my colleague's account "objective." . . .

Assuming that the identification/listing of privileges methodology I have described avoids the problem of authentication, one still might wonder whether the project is sufficiently radical to dismantle gender and sexual orientation hierarchies. Certainly the lists I have presented do not go far enough. They represent the very early stages in a more complicated process to end gender and sexual orientation discrimination.

The lists, nevertheless, are politically valuable. . . .

None of this is to say that awareness and acknowledgement of privilege is enough. Resistance is needed as well. But how does one resist? And what counts as resistance? With respect to marriage, for example, does resistance to heterosexual privilege require heterosexuals to refrain from getting married and/or attending weddings? It might mean both of those things. At the very least, resistance to identity privilege would seem to require "critical acquiescence": criticizing, if not rejecting, aspects of our life that are directly linked to our privilege. A heterosexual who gets married and/or attends weddings but who also openly challenges the idea that marriage is a heterosexual entitlement is engaging in critical acquiescence.

In the end, critical acquiescence might not go far enough. It might even be a cop out. Still, it is a useful and politically manageable place to begin.

References

Boykin, K. (1997). *One More River to Cross: Black and Gay in America*. New York: Doubleday.

Edelman, L. (1990). "Redeeming the Phallus: Wallace Stevens, Frank Lentricchia, and the Politics of (Hetero)sexuality." In J.A. Boone and M. Cadden (eds.), *Engendering Men: The Question of Male Feminist Criticism*. New York: Routledge.

Forrest, L. (1994). "Evidences of Jimmy Baldwin." In L. Forrest (ed.), *Relocations of the Spirit*. Emeryville, CA: Asphodel Press/Moyer Ball.

Riggs, M.T. (1999). "Black Macho Revisited: Reflections of a SNAP! Queen." In D.W. Carbado (ed.), *Black Men on Race, Gender, and Sexuality: A Critical Reader*. New York: New York University Press.

Ryder, B. (1991). "Straight Talk: Male Heterosexual Privelege." *Queen's Law Journal*, 16, 287–303.

82

Sport

Where Men Are Men and Women Are Trespassers

Pat Griffin

. . . Sport is more than games. As an institution, sport serves important social functions in supporting conventional social values. In particular, sport is a training ground where boys learn what it means to be men. Masculinity does not come naturally; it must be carefully taught. Specific rewards and punishments provide clear messages about acceptable and unacceptable behavior for boys. Boys who show an interest in "girl" activities, such as playing with dolls, dancing, or cooking, are teased by peers. Young boys learn at an early age that participation in athletics is an important, if not required, part of developing a masculine identity and gaining acceptance among peers.

Every Saturday morning in the fall little boys stagger up and down fields under the weight of full football drag, imitating the swagger and ritual they see in their professional sports heroes. Many fathers worry if their sons do not exhibit an interest in sports. They teach their sons to throw, catch, swing bats, shoot hoops. Adults comment on the size of young boys by predicting in which sports they will excel. Participation on school athletic teams, especially the big four (football, basketball, baseball, and ice hockey) ensure popularity and prestige among classmates and in the larger community. Young boys idolize professional and college team-sport athletes and coaches because of their physical size, strength, toughness, and competitiveness. Young boys and adult men wear caps, T-shirts, and jackets with their favorite professional or collegiate team mascot and colors.

Men's athletic events, especially the big four team sports, draw huge numbers of spectators. Men of all colors and social classes study team statistics and participate in intense postcontest analyses of strategy and performance. Cities spend millions of dollars building sports arenas with tax subsidies to woo men's professional teams to town or prevent them from moving to another city. The athletic equipment and clothing industries are multibillion-dollar enterprises that depend on the large number of boys and men who buy their increasingly sophisticated and specialized products.

The importance of sport in socializing men into traditional masculine gender roles also defines the sport experience for women. Because sport is identified with men and masculinity, women in sport become trespassers on male territory, and their access is limited or blocked entirely. Despite huge increases in women's sport participation, there is still tremendous resistance to an equitable distribution of resources between men's and women's athletics. *USA Today* reported that on the 25th anniversary of the passage of Title IX, the federal law prohibiting sex discrimination in education, 80 percent of college and university athletic programs in the United States are still not in compliance with the law.

Sometimes resistance to women's sport participation is more personal. In the spring of 1997 Melissa Raglin, 12, was the starting catcher for a Boca Raton Babe Ruth baseball team. During a game the plate umpire asked Melissa if she was wearing a protective cup. Melissa removed her helmet and catcher's mask and told him she was a girl. However, the Babe Ruth rules state that all players (assumed to be male) must wear a cup to protect their genitals. When Melissa, who had been playing in the Babe Ruth league for over two seasons, refused to comply with the rule, she was prohibited from playing catcher. She was allowed to play again only when she ordered a special cup designed for women, even though most doctors agree that there is no medical reason why a girl should wear a protective cup. This example shows the absurd lengths to which some men will go to try to humiliate a young girl to make sure she knows that she is trespassing on male turf. Male league officials' insistence that Melissa wear a cup, even at the risk of ridicule in news stories, demonstrates the seriousness and importance of protecting sport from female encroachment.

Women's presence in sport as serious participants dilutes the importance and exclusivity of sport as a training ground for learning about and accepting traditional male gender roles and the privileges that their adoption confers on (white, heterosexual) men. As a result, women's sport performance is trivialized and marginalized as an inferior version of the "real thing." These arguments ignore the overlap in sport performances among men and women in all sports and the growing interest among young girls in sport participation.

Sexism as a system of male privilege and female subordination is based on the acceptance of particular definitions of gender (what constitutes a man or a woman) and gender roles (what qualities, talents, and characteristics women and men are supposed to have). Women's serious participation in sport brings into question the "natural" and mutually exclusive nature of gender and gender roles. If women in sport can be tough minded, competitive, and muscular too, then sport loses its special place in the development of masculinity for men. If women can so easily develop these so-called masculine qualities, then what are the meanings of femininity and masculinity? What does it mean to be a man or a woman? These challenges threaten an acceptance of the traditional gender order in which men are privileged and women are subordinate. Thus, they account for much of the strong resistance to gender equity in sport and the need to marginalize and control the growth of women's athletics.

THE POWER OF THE LESBIAN LABEL

One of the most effective means of controlling women in sport is to challenge the femininity and heterosexuality of women athletes. When a woman is called "masculine," "unfeminine," or "dyke," she knows she has crossed a gender boundary or challenged male privilege. In this way, homophobia serves as glue that holds traditional gender role expectations in place. Because most women are afraid to be called lesbian or to have their femininity called into question, their sport experience can be controlled by using the lesbian label to intimidate them. The purpose of calling a woman a lesbian is to limit her sport experience and make her feel defensive about her athleticism.

Though lesbians are the direct targets of these insinuations, antilesbian bias affects the experience of all women. Using the lesbian label to discourage the bonding that occurs among women in athletics is an effective way to keep women from discovering their own power. Consequently, stigmatizing lesbian identity serves the interests of those who want to maintain the imbalance of opportunity and power in athletics based on gender. As long as women's sports are associated with lesbians and lesbians are stigmatized as sexual and social deviants, the lesbian label serves an important social-control function in sport, ensuring that only men have access to the benefits of sport participation and the physical and psychological empowerment available in sport.

The preservation of athletics as a male-only activity is essential in maintaining a gender order in which men and women adopt separate and unequal gender roles. The interconnections of sexism, homophobia, and heterosexism are powerful forces that ensure that male privilege and dominance endure.

SPORT AND THE MAINTENANCE OF MASCULINITY

Sport for men serves five social functions that ensure that the gender order supporting presumed male superiority and female subordination is maintained. These functions are (1) defining and reinforcing traditional conceptions of masculinity, (2) providing an acceptable and safe context for male bonding and intimacy, (3) reinforcing male privilege and female subordination, (4) establishing status among other males, and (5) reinforcing heterosexuality.

DEFINING AND REINFORCING TRADITIONAL CONCEPTIONS OF MASCULINITY

Team sports in particular teach boys masculinity skills. They learn to be competitive and tough. They learn to deny feelings of compassion or other feelings that coaches teach them to associate with weakness. Boys learn to value physical strength and size, aggressiveness, and a will to dominate. Young boys learn to accept the necessity of establishing hierarchical relationships among competitors and teammates based on athletic performance. None of these qualities or values are innate, but young boys learn that they are essential and natural components of a masculine identity. Boys who are perceived to be weak or soft or who do not have an interest in developing these traditional masculine qualities are shunned, harassed, and ridiculed by peers. Adult men who were labeled "sissy" in elementary school or "faggot" and "pussy" in later grades can tell painful stories of abuse that attest to the intensity of this socialization process.

Much of this harassment takes place on athletic teams and in physical education classes. Male coaches and physical educators are important teachers of masculinity. Lessons learned on the athletic field reinforce the importance of learning to "be a man." "Proving one's manhood," facing challenge "like a man," and dominating opponents represent a hard strength and stoicism especially prized in team sports.

Not all men in sport can easily meet the standards of masculinity set in athletics. Gay men, men of color, and poor and working-class men represent what Connell calls *competing masculinities*. Their experiences of masculinity are mediated by their race, sexual identity, and class status. Because their social group memberships deviate from the white, heterosexual, and middle-class norm, these men have less access to privilege even though they might excel in sport. A gay male athlete must hide his identity. An African-American male athlete is stereotyped by racist expectations and disadvantaged by institutional racism. These competing masculinities also enable these men to create a different approach to the development of masculinity, as in the ironic stance of the gay male athlete described by Pronger.

PROVIDING A CONTEXT FOR ACCEPTABLE AND SAFE MALE BONDING AND INTIMACY

Athletics is one of the few social contexts in which men can openly express physical affection and love for other men. Team members spend an enormous amount of time together during the course of a season, practicing and competing, traveling to games, spending nights in hotels, and socializing. The emotional intensity of competition and sharing the highs and lows of winning and losing encourage strong bonds among teammates. . . .

In addition to this emotional bond, athletics involves physical intimacy as well. Participating in team sports in particular requires physical contact with both teammates and opponents. In addition, athletes spend a lot of time together in hotel rooms, locker rooms, showers, and whirlpool baths—all places that suggest a high degree of physical closeness or nudity. During victory celebrations men can, without fear of ridicule, hug and kiss each other. Men can also cry without shame about losing a big game. Fanny slaps and chest bumps are commonplace in men's athletics, especially in team sports. It is not a coincidence that expressions of male-to-male physical affection and love are acceptable in few other contexts. In athletics men can admire other men's bodies and their physical accomplishments openly without arousing suspicions about their heterosexuality. The bond among male teammates is an important lesson in male solidarity around their masculine identities. . . .

REINFORCING MALE PRIVILEGE AND FEMALE INFERIORITY

Defining masculinity is as much about rejecting so-called feminine qualities as it is about embracing so-called masculine ones. Male coaches send strong messages about women and about the need for men to avoid being like women when they compare a poor performance by a male athlete to that of a girl (for example, throwing like a girl). Many coaches know they can inspire male athletes to perform better by calling them demeaning names intended for women (pussies) or hybrids like wussy (wimp and pussy). Being called a woman, compared to a woman, or—the worst insult—being beaten by a woman in any sport contest provokes anger and shame in many men and boys. . . .

As Mariah Burton Nelson points out in her insightful book *The Stronger Women Get, The More Men Love Football*, many men need to establish the "fact" that no matter what gains women make in sport, they could never play football. They believe that football is the epitome of athletic excellence and legitimacy. In New Jersey a female member of a high school football team was physically assaulted by her male team-mates who were trying to dissuade her from playing. Elizabeth Balsley was punched, hit with blocking dummies, and spat upon as she walked toward the practice field. Three of her male teammates were charged with assault, suspended from classes for two to four days, and barred from playing in one football game. . . . As this incident illustrates, young women who dare to challenge the notion that football is too tough for women must be taught a lesson.

This need to establish male superiority extends beyond comparing the performance merits of male and female athletes. Studies of talk in men's locker rooms describe consistent patterns of antiwoman and antigay interactions. Many men talk about women as sexual possessions or receptacles, not as equals or even as human beings. In this climate male athletes learn to despise qualities within themselves that they perceive to be feminine and to accept female inferiority in sport as fact. They develop a sense of entitlement and superiority in relationship to women on and off the athletic field. . . .

A study by Crosset, Benedict, and McDonald indicates that there is a higher incidence of violence against women by male athletes than by other men on college campuses. Athletic team participation in gang rapes or the development of a scoring system to rank sexual conquests are disturbing examples of how bonding among male athletes based on contempt for women can lead to antisocial criminal behaviors. . . .

ESTABLISHING STATUS AMONG OTHER MALES

Sport is the single most important element of the peer-status system for U.S. adolescent males. Moreover, athletics is a rehearsal for the status many white, middle-class boys hope to achieve later through work, education, and economic accumulation. Poor, working-class men of all colors often view success as a professional athlete as the only route, no matter how unrealistic, to economic success and social status. As a result, athletics takes on a special status in the culture of boys and young men. Messner describes how boys learn that acceptance by and status with peers, fathers, and coaches is achieved by winning in sports. According to Messner, boys learn that just participating in sports is not enough. To achieve the kind of attention and connections they seek, it is necessary to be better than other boys, to beat them in sports. In high school and college, male athletes, particularly team-sport athletes, are often treated as high-status members of the community by peers, teachers, and other community members. As such, they often receive special treatment and recognition not given to other boys. . . . Being judged acceptable in this public sport-performance hierarchy is an important ritual in establishing self-worth among boys and young men. Sport for boys is serious business, and girls have no place in it.

REINFORCING HETEROSEXUALITY

For many people the male team-sports hero is the epitome of masculinity: strong, tough, handsome, competitive, dating or married to the most desirable woman. An accepted perquisite of professional athletic fame for men is a rich and varied sex life with many willing young female groupies. Many people believe that the terms *gay man* and *athlete* used together are an oxymoron. A gay male athlete violates both the image of male athletes as strong, virile, and heterosexual and the image of gay men as swishy and effeminate. Just as it is important to keep women out of sport or marginalized in sport, it is essential to keep gay men in sport invisible. If gay men can be strong, tough, competitive, and part of a male bonding experience in the locker room with straight men, how can straight men confidently differentiate themselves from gay men? Just as young men in athletics learn that women are inferior, they also learn that gay men are contemptible. Being called a "faggot" or "pansy" is an insult of the highest order to one's sense of masculinity. The incidence of antigay talk in locker rooms and the participation of male athletes in gay bashing reflect this attitude.

Maintaining the myths that all male athletes are heterosexual and that sexual attraction among male athletes does not occur allow men to enjoy the physical and emotional intimacy of the athletic team experience. They do not need to worry that teammates might think they are gay. These myths also protect male athletes from confronting the possibility that someone else in that locker room might be gay. Many heterosexual men are extremely uncomfortable with the possibility of being the object of another man's sexual interest. By displaying contempt for gays through antigay name-calling, jokes, harassment, or violence, men reassure themselves and teammates that everyone in the locker room is heterosexual in an intimate all-male context. If this illusion is threatened by the presence of openly gay men, the complex feelings of love and intimacy, physical contact, and communal nudity could not be enjoyed without fear and suspicion. The fear of being perceived as gay or being the object of gay sexual desire is a powerful social control that keeps men in athletics safely within the bounds of traditional masculinity.

This need to believe that there are no gay men present in the locker room or on the playing field makes the male athletic environment extremely hostile for openly gay athletes and coaches. . . . A closeted gay athlete can participate without suspicion, as long as he is willing to keep his identity a secret. Being an athlete is so consistent with traditional masculine and heterosexual expectations for men that gay athletes can pass if they are willing to. While women athletes must constantly prove their heterosexuality, most people assume that male athletes are heterosexual unless they provide evidence that they are not. . . .

Defenders of a sexist and heterosexist status quo are right to fear the potential that sport has for the empowerment of women. Sport can be a catalyst for empowering women to become the center of their own experience, whether demanding equal access to resources; making connections among sexism, racism, and heterosexism; developing and reveling in their own strength and physical competence; or falling in love with a teammate. When women take sport participation seriously, it is, as Mariah Burton Nelson asserts, a feminist activity: "All of us collectively, are a threat—not to men exactly, but to male privilege and to masculinity as defined through manly sport." . . .

83

The Loving Decision

Anna Quinlan

Same-sex marriage was beaten back at the ballot box. Now here's a history lesson on why victory is inevitable in the long run.

One of my favorite Supreme Court cases is *Loving v. Virginia*, and not just because it has a name that would delight any novelist. It's because it reminds me, when I'm downhearted, of the truth of the sentiment at the end of "Angels in America," Tony Kusher's brilliant play: "The world only spins forward."

Here are the facts of the case, and if they leave you breathless with disbelief and rage it only proves Kushner's point, and mine: Mildred Jeter and Richard Loving got married in Washington, D.C. They went home to Virginia, there to be rousted out of their bed one night by police and charged with a felony. The felony was that Mildred was black and Richard was white and they were therefore guilty of miscegenation, which is a $10 word for bigotry. Virginia, like a number of other states, considered cross-racial matrimony a crime at the time. It turned out that it wasn't just the state that hated the idea of black people marrying white people. God was onboard, too, according to the trial judge, who wrote, "The fact that He separated the races shows that he did not intend for the races to mix." But the Supreme Court, which eventually heard the case, passed over the Almighty for the Constitution, which luckily has an equal-protection clause. "Marriage is one of the basic civil rights of man," the unanimous opinion striking down the couple's conviction said, "fundamental to our very existence and survival." That was in 1967.

Fast-forward to Election Day 2008, and a flurry of state ballot propositions to outlaw gay marriage, all of which were successful. This is the latest wedge issue of the good-old-days crowd, supplanting abortion and immigration. They really put their backs into it this time around, galvanized by court decisions in three states ruling that it is discriminatory not to extend the right to marry to gay men and lesbians.

The most high-profile of those rulings, and the most high-profile ballot proposal, came in California. A state court gave its imprimatur to same-sex marriage in June [2008]; the electorate reversed that decision on Nov. 4 with the passage of Proposition 8, which defines marriage as only between a man and a woman. The opponents of gay marriage will tell you that the people have spoken. It's truer to say that money talks. The Mormons donated millions to the anti effort; the Knights of Columbus did, too. Like the judge who ruled in the *Loving* case, they said they were doing God's bidding. When I was a small child I always used to picture God on a cloud, with a beard. Now I picture God saying, "Why does all the worst stuff get done in my name?"

Just informationally, this is how things are going to go from here on in: two steps forward, one step back. Courts will continue to rule in some jurisdictions that there is no good reason to forbid same-sex couples from marrying. Legislatures in two states, New York and New Jersey, could pass a measure guaranteeing the right to matrimony to all, and both states have governors who have said they would sign such legislation.

Opponents will scream that the issue should be put to the people, as it was in Arizona, Florida and California. (Arkansas had a different sort of measure, forbidding unmarried couples from adopting or serving as foster parents. This will undoubtedly have the effect of leaving more kids without stable homes. For shame.) Of course if the issue in *Loving* had been put to the people, there is no doubt that many would have been delighted to make racial intermarriage a crime. That's why God invented courts.

The world only spins forward.

"I think the day will come when the lesbian and gay community will have its own *Loving v. Virginia*," says David Buckel, the Marriage Project director for Lambda Legal.

Yes, and then the past will seem as preposterous and mean-spirited as the events leading up to the *Loving* decision do today. After all, this is about one of the most powerful forces for good on earth, the determination of two human beings to tether their lives forever. The pitch of the opposition this year spoke to how far we have already come—the states in which civil unions and domestic partnerships are recognized, the families in which gay partners are welcome and beloved.

The antis argued that churches could be forced to perform same-sex unions, when any divorced Roman Catholic can tell you that the clergy refuse to officiate whenever they see fit. They argued that the purpose of same-sex marriage was the indoctrination of children, a popular talking point that has no basis in reality. As Ellen DeGeneres, who was married several months ago to the lovely Portia de Rossi (great dress, girl), said about being shaped by the orientation of those around you, "I was raised by two heterosexuals. I was surrounded by heterosexuals. Just everywhere I looked: heterosexuals. They did not influence me." As for the notion that allowing gay men and lesbians to marry will destroy conventional marriage, I have found heterosexuals perfectly willing to do that themselves.

The last word here goes to an authority on battling connubial bigotry. On the anniversary of the *Loving* decision last year, the bride wore tolerance. Mildred Loving, mother and grandmother, who once had cops burst into her bedroom because she was sleeping with her own husband, was quoted in a rare public statement saying she believed all Americans, "no matter their race, no matter their sex, no matter their sexual orientation, should have that same freedom to marry." She concluded, "That's what *Loving*, and loving, are all about."

84

Taking the Gay Insults Personally

Ellen Goodman

In my business, it's only fair to acknowledge a bias. My bias is named Ruthie. Ruthie is the youngest cousin in a bumper crop of babies that have extended our family over the last few years. When she was adopted, we didn't pass out cigars, we passed out Baby Ruth bars. So maybe it's our fault that she's now in the sugar-rush stage of toddlerhood, leaving her parents joyously breathless and regularly transforming her grandmother's house into Early Childproof Decor.

Did I mention that Ruthie has two daddies, something her toddler cousins take for granted? Did I mention that Ruthie's birth mother chose this couple to raise her, picking these two men from all the dossiers at the adoption agency?

Ruthie is why I take it personally when the Vatican calls gay adoptions "gravely immoral" or says that such adoptions "mean doing violence to these children." Ruthie is why I grimace when Russell Johnson, chairman of the Ohio Restoration Project, says, "experimenting on children through gay adoption is a problem." Ruthie and her parents are not an experiment. They are a family. Part of my family.

Once again, we are back to the subject of gay adoption. This month, Catholic Charities in Boston was called on the Vatican carpet. For years the agency had operated a kind of "don't ask, don't tell" policy. Over the course of two decades, Catholic social workers had placed 13 children with gay parents, saving most from the revolving door of foster care.

But Roman Catholic law forbids gay adoption, and Massachusetts state law forbids discrimination. Faced with a conflict, the bishops overrode the board of Catholic Charities and ended its long and cherished role in adoption.

Now this issue is rolling out across the country, all the way to San Francisco. There, the new archbishop appears to be on a similar collision course with Catholic Charities and secular laws. In Massachusetts, Governor Mitt Romney, nodding madly to conservatives in his bid for a presidential run, has filed a bill to grant a religious exemption to discrimination laws. But if you give one church permission to discriminate against gays, what's next? Permission to discriminate against blacks or Jews who want to adopt? Isn't that where we came from?

It seems that many see gay adoption as another issue to rally the right in the culture wars. There are now efforts underway in 16 states for laws to ban gay adoptions. These would add to a crazy quilt of state laws ranging from Florida, which bans gay adoptions but allows gay foster parents, to Mississippi, which bans adoption by gay couples but not gay singles, to Utah, which prohibits all unmarried couples from adoption.

But let's put my Ruthie bias aside for the moment. Let's even put aside the studies that support my bias: A comprehensive review of them coming out next week from the Evan B. Donaldson Adoption Institute shows *again* that children of gay parents do fine.

If some still insist that it is "gravely immoral" to raise children in gay households, what exactly do those wedge drivers propose to do?

We have always had gay parents. Most had children the old-fashioned way, hiding their sexuality as long as they could. Now they can also do it the new-fashioned way with every reproductive aid from sperm bank to surrogate.

A researcher analyzing the 2000 Census estimated 250,000 kids being raised by same-sex couples. If gay parenting is harmful, do we take children away from their biological gay parents? Do we make it unlawful for gays to use fertility technologies? How? If there are states that allow gay adoption, would we ban interstate travel for that? And what do we say to a birth mother who picks a gay couple? No?

Today 60 percent of agencies accept applications and 40 percent knowingly place children with gay parents. Social workers, whether at religious, state, or private agencies, want only one thing: to find safe, good homes in a country with 500,000 children adrift.

"The effect of all this opposition is not to prevent gay people from becoming parents," says Adam Pertman of the Donaldson Adoption Institute. "All it can do is diminish the pool of mothers and fathers for children who need homes."

We all talk about "the best interest of the child." What makes up that interest? On my list are attention, love, security, humor, and a besotted family racing to keep one step ahead of a toddler. Of course, a little bias on that child's behalf never hurts.

85

Mestiza/o Gender

Notes towards a Transformative Masculinity

Daniel E. Solís y Martínez

. . . On December 9, 1531, on the sacred hill of Tepeyacac, just outside the recently-conquered city of Tenochitlan, an indigenous man who is now known only as Juan Diego combined the traditional Mexica goddess Tonantzín with the Spaniards' Virgin Mary to create the Virgin of Guadalupe. Juan Diego, a recent convert to Catholicism, was visited on Tepeyacac by an unusually brown-skinned Virgin Mary. This seemingly indigenous Virgin Mary told Juan Diego to visit the Spanish Bishop in Mexico City and to ask him to build a church dedicated to her at Tepeyacac. Juan Diego did as she asked; but the Bishop refused to believe the lowly *indigena* (indigenous person) Juan Diego and demanded proof of this miraculous apparition of the Mother of God. Juan Diego returned to the sacred hill in search of proof and found the Virgin Mary waiting for him. The Virgin Mary instructed him to ascend to the mountaintop of Tepeyacac where he would find a bounty of beautiful flowers miraculously growing out of season that would serve as his proof. Juan Diego gathered the flowers into his cloak and then descended the holy mountain to return to the disbelieving Bishop.

Once again, Juan Diego repeated the Virgin Mary's request for the construction of a church at Tepeyacac. The Bishop again demanded proof. Juan Diego simply replied by unfurling his cloak and dropping the flowers at thc feet of the Bishop, immediately filling the room with a tremendous fragrance. It was at that moment that the Bishop saw the divine imprint of the brown-skinned Virgin Mary on Juan Diego's cloak. Being humbled by both the choice of the indigenous Juan Diego as the Virgin Mary's messenger and the brown skin of the Virgin herself, the Bishop agreed to build the church at Tepeyacac.

The acceptance of the brown-skinned Virgin Mary on Juan Diego's cloak by the Spanish Bishop was the beginning of the officially-sanctioned cult of the Virgin of Guadalupe in the Americas. Within the racially-mixed form of the Virgin of Guadalupe, indigenous people like Juan Diego were able to merge their traditional religions with the Catholicism imposed on them by the colonizing Spanish, so as to produce a truly new form of cultural and religious expression. Given their inability to directly confront the more powerful Spanish, the indigenous peoples of Mexico and Central America used the Virgin of Guadalupe to create within the dominance of the Spanish a space of their own. Utilizing the legitimization that the Spanish Catholic Church conferred on the Virgin of Guadalupe, *indigenas* such as Juan Diego forged religious customs that were neither Catholic nor the traditional practices of the Mexica, but that mixed elements from both. The birth of the brown-skinned Virgin of Guadalupe was a powerful event that signaled the beginning, first in Mexico and Central America and then in the United States, of a process of cultural mixing that has given rise to new ethnic and national identities.

The story of Juan Diego, with its unequal marriage of conflicted ideas and practices in the face of powerful forces, is a compelling metaphor for my own life as a Latino gay man attempting to create a way of being queer that is ethical, freeing and true to myself. Like Juan Diego's merging of the repressed indigenous goddess Tonantzín into the ascendant European Virgin Mary, I endeavor to create my own gayness through a blending of two distinct systems of homosexuality: that which my parents brought with them from El Salvador and that which I grew into in the United States. Growing up, my queerness was contained by my family within the traditional homosexuality of El Salvador. In that system, homosexuality is a matter of gender difference that is expressed by both sexual behavior and deviant gender practices. In El Salvador and much of Latin America, homosexual men and boys like me are seen not as women or men but instead occupy an ambiguous place in between. Under this particular system of homosexuality, my parents raised me quite differently from my brothers: I am the only one who was taught by my mother and grandmother how to cook, clean, sew, and even now am responsible for organizing family events such as birthdays, holidays and dinners. As a child, I was allowed to socialize with girls and women, all without my gayness being explicitly named. Within my home, my budding gayness was silently accepted and integrated into the larger fabric of my family so long as it did not threaten the heterosexual status quo. . . .

Throughout Latin America and in El Salvador, homosexuality is understood primarily as a matter of gender. Homosexual behavior—particularly the act of penetration—determines to a large degree whether one is or isn't a man. *Maricónes, culeros*, and *putos* are all words that name the non-maleness of the homosexual in the traditional Latin American conceptualization of homosexuality. Mexican anthropologist Héctor Carrillo describes the traditional operation of this gender-sexuality system in Mexico as creating men through non-men. . . . Carrillo notes the distinction between, ". . . masculine men were *hombres* or *machos,*" and ". . . their counterparts were the effeminate men, the *maricones*, who were perceived as having forfeited their manhood altogether" (Carrillo 2003, 352). Carrillo further explains that *maricones* served to legitimize the masculinity of the *hombres*. As such, normative masculinity in the Latin American context was not possible without *maricones*. . . .

In the traditional understanding of homosexuality in Latin America, homosexual male-bodied individuals are not men at all. Instead, they are seen as another type of gender category altogether, existing in a shifting location between women's femininity and men's bodies. Carrillo's observations of Mexican homosexuality hold true for much of Latin America. In fact, many names for male homosexuals throughout Latin America speak to this in-between gendered status. In most of its Latin American articulations, homosexuality is a matter of gender, not sexual identity.

This in-between homosexual gender is centered on the matter of penetration: he who is penetrated is a homosexual. By being the receptive partner in anal intercourse, Latin American *homosexuales* give up their claim to masculinity. Instead they enter into a gender space that borrows and claims much from femininity but that is decidedly different from woman-ness. This articulation of homosexuality as a different gender, which essentializes it into a biological trait, creates spaces for Latin American *homosexuales* within Latin American societies and families. These spaces are often created not by the overt presence of homophobic discourses, but instead by their silent operation. Queer Puerto Rican sociologist Manolo Guzmán describes ". . . this absence of speech [as] no longer talking about things like marriage, represents a suspension of the assumption of heterosexuality" (Guzmán 2006, 88). It is in those spaces of absent speech in which Latin American homosexuality rests. My own parents' response to my budding gender deviance and homosexuality was shaped by this system of homosexual gender. My family's acceptance of my queer impulses was predicated on its safe containment in the traditional queer gender space of the Latin American family structure. So long as my homosexuality was not explicitly named it did not threaten the traditional supremacy of my father over our family. . . .

My childhood experiences in the vast stretches of Los Angeles were defined by a constant shift between two separate worlds firmly divided by a border made up of language, class, and race. The Salvadoreño culture of my home and neighborhood in the eastern San Fernando Valley was an island in the surrounding sea of Americanness. Moving from the Spanish of my family to the English of my teachers and school forced me from an early age to be constantly aware of the need to shift my way of being depending on where I was. Who I was depended on where I was, who I was with and what language I was speaking. Like many budding homo boys, the need to constantly move back and forth between worlds made me a talented performer from an early age. I quickly became a skilled border-crosser.

At the very core of my role switching was a fundamental clash between the migrant gender-sexuality worldview of my family and the "native" system of the United States. My parents were locked in a battle—internally and externally—to craft a family that was the best of the values and cultural forms they had been raised with, but that at the same time recognized the sheer reality that they were not in El Salvador anymore. This battle was never explicitly named by my parents as the source of their discomfort with my brothers' and my own rapid Americanization, but it quietly informed every action they took. . . . My parents' struggle was centered in our home. Patriarchy was the central axis around which my parents constructed our family. My father worked an inhuman amount of hours as a machine-shop operator to support my family, but his salary was simply not enough to make ends meet. In the rapidly de-industrializing Los Angeles of the 1980s, machine-shop work was on the decline. My father's lack of an American education and legal status exacerbated the dwindling supply of work, resulting in a continuous cycle of migration from one job to the next. This instability finally forced my father to allow my mother's entrance into the working world. Like my grandmother and aunt, she too became a domestic worker for the rich and white of the West San Fernando Valley.

The emergence of my mother as our family's co-supporter led to fierce fights for dominance and power within our home. Quite simply, my mother's departure from her traditional role as homemaker undermined my father's masculinity. The assault on my father's manhood was twofold. Since he couldn't fully provide for all of our family's financial needs, he was failing at his manly obligations. This was compounded by the loss of mental and physical control over my mother. It was perhaps the loss of total control over my mother that most undermined my father's masculine power. With work, my mother gained independence as she learned how to drive and for the first time had money of her own to spend. Implicit in my father's frustration was the fear that her daily sojourns to the outside world would corrupt my mother and render her unfit as both mother and wife. My

V
O
I
C
E
S

father's fears would explode in dramatic and often violent outbursts aimed particularly at my mother, but also at my brothers and me. These poverty-driven gendered struggles set the stage for the emergence of my queerness within my family.

As is the case for many homo boys, from an early age my mother was my world. The bond between us was one of sameness; in my mind I was just like her. My mother is fond of reminding me of how as a baby she alone had the power to stop my tears. To this day, she is still one of the few people that can get me to shut up. Given the close affinity between my mother and me, when my parents would fight I would stand at her side ready to battle my father, and often my older brother as well. It wouldn't matter who was wrong or right, but simply that my mother was threatened. Since I saw my mother as not only my role model but as the source from which I had sprung, when she was threatened I was threatened.

Often the fights between my parents were about the bond of affinity between my mother and me. My father accused her of spoiling me, which in our working class home had strong undertones of feminization and emasculation. In claiming that my mother was spoiling me, my father was really saying that she was turning me into a non-boy. His accusations were further complicated by his patronizing of my older brother as his Chosen Son. Subtly undermining my mother's authority over him, my father drew my older brother into his orbit as an ally. As time wore on, those battle lines became entrenched gender lines dividing us into two opposing camps: my father and older brother as the men and my mother and I as the women. It was in those moments of anger, of a family divided along lines of what I can only call queer genders that my own unique place in my family began to emerge.

My queer gender developed out of those fights within my family. While never openly named by either of my parents, they had tacitly agreed that I was to be raised differently from my clearly male-gendered brothers. I was to be the *culerito*. As a child, I was the son taught to cook, clean, listen and nurture. At the never-ending string of quinceañeras, birthday parties, and baptismal celebrations, I was always with the women. I would sit among my mother, grandmother, aunt, godmother, and a host of their friends, listening to them gossip about one another, or lovingly (yet critically) pick at their husbands, their sons, and their daughters. Meanwhile, my brothers would play with other boy-children. My inclusion in these circles of women was never questioned, at least while I was present. If whispered conversations of concern about my affiliation with women happened between my mother and her women friends, I was not aware. . . .

The relative acceptance of my family was matched by the unease I felt towards the world "*out there.*" I don't really remember an exact moment when I became conscious of the fact that my love for girl-child toys and women superheroes was a *private* matter—a matter of the home and family. Somehow I just understood that it was not okay for me to take my dolls out of the home. Whenever I played with the other children in my apartment complex, I never mentioned that my favorite G.I JOE was Scarlett, the red haired counter-terrorist vixen of the team, and I certainly never dared to bring her out with me to play. Like my constant transitions from English and Spanish between school and home, I also switched my gender performance from home to the outside. The queer child I was inside my home butched it up whenever I crossed the threshold of our door. . . .

My family's tolerance of my gayness was markedly different from the clearly defined homosexuality of the United States that I found first on the playgrounds and in the class-rooms of my elementary school, and later on in the queer identity groups I joined as a teenager. The homosexuality I found outside of my family was one of a clearly defined gayness that was accessed through personal identification. In what I call the American system of homosexuality, a person was gay either because they called themselves gay or because others labeled them that way. As I grew older, I discovered communities of queer people in the United States built around a shared sense of identity and personal experience. At the core of these communities was the idea of "coming out"—or publicly naming one's queerness to others. This explicitly named gayness was quite different from the unnamed ambiguous position I held within my family. After I came out, my position in my family changed as I sought to force them to accept American gayness as the basis for how they understood me and my queerness. My efforts led to great conflicts between myself and most of my family members. As I grew increasingly isolated from my family, I realized that American gayness with its emphasis on the individual wasn't sufficient for me or my particular situation. I began to seek a way to construct an empowering queerness that challenged heterosexism but that also didn't isolate me from the people I love so much.

Constructing my queerness solely out of either Latin American homosexuality or American gayness presents great obstacles to the type of queerness I want to embody. Like Juan Diego, my options are seemingly limited. Do I choose the gendered homosexuality I grew up with in my family or the individualistic gayness of the country I was born in? Given the overwhelming power of both types of homosexuality to resist challenges to their oppressive elements, I find myself moving within and between both systems to create the queerness I seek. . . .

At the core of both my journey and this essay is a creative process of reclamation. Rather than simply giving up on both of these homosexualities, I seek to work within them by taking elements from both and combining them together in a new way that can challenge the oppressive components within each. Queer theorist José Esteban Muñoz, in studying the oppositional and creative use of mainstream heterosexual and queer cultures by queer performance artists of color, has articulated a process similar to the one I wish to engage in. Muñoz calls this process disidentification. He describes this as,

> . . . the third mode of dealing with dominant ideology, one that neither opts to assimilate within such a structure nor strictly opposes it; rather, disidentification is a strategy that works on and against dominant ideology . . . this 'working on and against' is a strategy that tries to transform a cultural logic from within, always laboring to enact permanent structural change while at the same time valuing the importance of local or everyday struggles of resistance.
>
> (1999, 11–12)

Moving beyond the binary idea that in the face of oppressive forces one can either purely resist or assimilate, Muñoz instead sees disidentification as a means to creatively engage with structures of injustice. Disidentification allows marginalized individuals to take the tools of oppression used against them and use them in new ways that alter their meaning so as to challenge the very oppression from which they are drawn. Muñoz values disidentification because it presents a means to escape the binary of assimilation and counteridentification which both serve to reinforce the dominance of oppressive systems. It is what Muñoz calls 'working on and against' that makes disidentification a powerful means of altering the harmful elements of both Latin American homosexuality and American gayness.

I utilize disidentification to blend the two forms of homosexuality so as to construct a third path of queerness that can escape the limitations of both. Through disidentification, I can work against the totalizing power of Latin American homosexuality to trap queers in the gender system of man/woman. A third queerness can also work against a gayness in the United States that is increasingly becoming nothing more than a colorful and non-threatening alternative to heterosexuality. As gayness in the United States becomes more mainstream, it is not only leaving unchallenged dominant ideals of consumerism as citizenship, but in fact it is using those same ideals as the definition of social justice for queers. Since both forms of homosexuality are limiting and perpetuate violent forms of oppression, I must create a queerness through my daily practices that draws from the most transformative in both while challenging the most repressive in each. . . .

With the *mestiza/o gender* I am creating, my queerness moves beyond a matter of sexual identity and becomes an encompassing gender location. I embrace the ambiguous position of the Latin American *puto* and realize that pursuing masculinity is not only futile but it is harmful both to me and others. The *mestiza/o* politics of ambiguity show me that to be a gay man in a unified and stable sense isn't possible. The acts of exclusion that are required in creating a stable identity of gay masculinity, through the *mestiza/o* lens, are exposed as immoral and highly suspect. By buying into the binary gender system, queer men support the oppression of women, transpeople, and other gender deviants. The space that Latin American homosexuals occupy in the gender system can provide queer men with a means to construct identities that alter patriarchy and create coalitions of change with others. The gendered basis of Latin American homosexuality, however, must be tempered by the protection of the individual that American gayness so heavily emphasizes. By ensuring that individuals are allowed to develop and creatively construct their own identities, the gendered articulation of homosexuality in Latin America can become truly emancipatory. This *mestiza/o* combination is what I seek to create by living it everyday.

I recognize the potential dangers of engaging in the selective extraction and mixing of elements from diverse cultures, but I believe that the need for new forms of homosexualities justifies taking those risks. A politics of *mestizaje* can produce an impure queerness that is less about how each individual identifies, but instead focuses on how individuals relate to one another in the pursuit of justice. Claiming common cause with others, that is building a coalitional community of change, is an uneven process that must center not on the identities people wear and own, but instead on the act of relating. Who we relate to and how we relate to them is what should define us as queer. Thinking about queerness as a set of relations moves it from the realm of individual sexual identity towards a way of being. This shift sets queerness in the realm of gender, an all-encompassing script that defines who and what we are. *Mestizaje* opens up the category of gender, which is rightfully seen as a limiting force, into a means to structure the conflicting mixture of privilege and oppression that defines many queer men's masculinities. . . . Like the race mixing that *mestiza/o* has traditionally referred to, I am interested in creating a gayness that is a mixture—imperfect, always in process of becoming, yet resisting with all of its might. It is towards that end, that I write these notes, themselves imperfect and in process of articulation. . . .

References

Carrillo, H. (2003). "Neither Machos nor Maricones: Masculinity and Emerging Male Homosexual Identities in Mexico." In M.C. Gutmann (ed.), *Changing Men and Masculinities in Latin America*. Durham, NC: Duke University Press.

Guzmán, M. (2006). *Gay Hegemony/Latino Homosexualities*. New York: Routledge.

Muñoz, J.E. (1999). *Disidentifications: Queers of Color and the Performance of Politics*. Minneapolis: University of Minnesota Press.

86

Becoming An Ally

A New Examination

Nancy J. Evans and Jamie Washington

What does it mean to be an ally? Students in a graduate program that prepares student affairs professionals in higher education responded to this question with the following reflections:

- Being an ally is being supportive of other people who are different than you. . . . This support should be flexible and elastic so that it does not define a person but rather the person defines the needed support. (gay male)
- Being an ally is being open to learning. It is essential to be open to admitting your ignorance in order to grow. Being an ally also requires a commitment. . . . Being an ally requires an examination of our own privilege. In order to be an ally we have to be able to recognize how our privilege might play a role in the oppression of the very group/ identity we want to be an ally to. Being an ally is using your powers for good. (lesbian)
- Being an ally is being aware of your own identities, advocating for the rights of others, supporting a cause, and challenging the oppression that particular populations face. It can mean lending a supportive hand to a peer. Being an ally is recognizing the inequality and inequity that exists in society, persistence, learning and teaching. (heterosexual woman)
- Being an ally is listening to other views and ideas without judgment; putting yourself in someone else's shoes; respecting people for who they are; advocating for resources, respect, equal treatment, laws; challenging your previous personal beliefs and ideas; working with underrepresented populations to better understand them and their unique needs; wanting to learn how to help, even in the little things; using non-discriminating language; [it is] important to the campus climate and overall student development; [it is] difficult and can have backlash. [An ally] must be committed and ready. (heterosexual male)
- An ally looks different to everyone. Sometimes an ally is a listening ear and a shoulder to cry on. Sometimes an ally is a fighter, fighting the powers to see justice done. (heterosexual woman)
- Being an ally is confusion, hard, being yelled at, learning, acceptance, fighting to change, and learning you don't have to be right. . . . An ally can be the scapegoat in the room. Being an ally is knowing that you have privilege and oppressions and you can use both. Sometimes it is being called out and trying to realize you can learn from that. Learning when you can tell a story and learning when you can't explain no matter what and to just shut up. (questioning woman)

As these students suggest, being an ally is a difficult and complex role that can take on many meanings and require a wide variety of actions, many of which are challenging. What it means to be an ally often depends on who one asks and the particular situation and context in which one is involved. In this essay, we examine various definitions of *ally*, explore factors associated with becoming an ally of LGBT individuals, including the

N
E
X
T

S
T
E
P
S

importance of recognizing heterosexual privilege, motivations for becoming an ally, the practice of advocacy, what an ally should know, and positive and negative consequences of advocacy. This essay is a revised and updated version of a chapter that appeared in the book, *Beyond Tolerance: Gays, Lesbians and Bisexuals on Campus*.

DEFINITIONS

As most writers and scholars in the area of oppression and multicultural education will concur, our language is imperfect and inherently "ism"-laden or oppressive. Therefore, clarifying the meaning of the term, "ally," is important. According to Webster's New World Dictionary of the American Language, an ally is "someone joined with another for a common purpose." This definition serves as a starting point for developing a working definition of *ally* as this term relates to issues of oppression. In our earlier work, we defined ally as "a person who is a member of the 'dominant' or 'majority' group who works to end oppression in his or her personal and professional life through support of, and as an advocate with and for, the oppressed population." More recently, Broido defined allies as "members of dominant social groups (e.g., men, Whites, heterosexuals) who are working to end the system of oppression that gives them greater privilege and power based on their social group membership" (2000). While similar to our earlier definition, Broido highlighted that allies must work at the systemic level, as well as the individual level, and more clearly defined what it means to be a member of a dominant group in terms of access to privilege and power.

Both definitions stress that although an oppressed person can certainly be a supporter and advocate for his or her own group, the impact and effect of such activity are different for the dominant group, and are often more powerful when the supporter is not a member of the oppressed population. Understanding this notion is an important first step toward becoming an ally for any "targeted" or oppressed group. Members of the LGBT community will sometimes argue that they can be allies for other members of the community, since "the community" is an umbrella group that includes many different subgroups, e.g., lesbians, gay males, bisexuals, transgendered individuals, and other populations that might choose to identify with the LGBT community (pansexual, questioning, etc.). We certainly acknowledge that with regard to dimensions of identity *other than* sexual identity, members of oppressed groups can be allies to other oppressed groups. For example, a gay man can be an ally to a lesbian woman with regard to *gender* oppression. With regard to *sexual* identity, however, both are oppressed. Given the definitions noted above, only heterosexual individuals can serve as allies of lesbian, gay, and bisexual people.

HETEROSEXUAL PRIVILEGE

The individual who decides to undertake the ally role must recognize and understand the power and privileges that one receives, accepts, and experiences as a heterosexual person. According to Johnson, who drew on the work of Peggy McIntosh, "privilege exists when one group has something of value that is denied to others simply because of the groups they belong to, rather than because of anything they've done or failed to do" (2006, 21). McIntosh noted that privilege comes in two forms: "unearned advantages and conferred dominance," with the former being things of value freely given to members of one group but arbitrarily denied to another group, and the latter referring to power given to one group over another. Developing awareness of one's privilege is often the most painful part of the process of becoming an ally.

Some of the powers and privileges heterosexuals generally have that gay and lesbian, and in some cases bisexual and transgender, persons do *not* have include:

- Family memberships to health clubs, pools, and other recreational facilities
- The right to legalized marriage
- The ability to purchase property as a couple
- The option to file joint income tax returns
- The ability to adopt children as a couple
- Health insurance for one's life partner
- The right to make decisions on health-related issues as they relate to one's life partner
- The assumption that one is psychologically healthy

In addition to such tangible privileges of the heterosexual population, there are a great many other, not so tangible, privileges. One important intangible privilege is living one's life without fear that people will find out that who one falls in love with, dreams about, or makes love to is someone of the same sex or that they were not always the gender with which they now identify. These fears affect the lives of gay, lesbian, bisexual, and transgender persons from the day they first begin to have "those funny feelings" until the day they die. Although many LGBT persons overcome these fears and turn the fear into a positive component of their lives, they have still been affected, and those wounds, even after healed, can be easily reopened.

Coming to terms with the very fact that "as a heterosexual I do not experience the world in the same way as LBGT people do" is an important step in becoming an ally. This awareness begins to move the heterosexual from being a caring, liberal person who feels that we are all created equal and should be treated as such, toward being an ally who begins to realize that although equality and equity are goals that have not yet been achieved, they can have a role in helping to make these goals realities.

Mohr introduced a model of heterosexual identity development, a process that he saw as related to the development of LGBT-affirmative attitudes. This model focuses on the development of awareness of heterosexual privilege. Mohr suggested that four "working models of sexual orientation" exist. Similar to Helms's contact status of white racial identity development in which individuals see themselves as color-blind, in the first working model proposed by Mohr, *democratic heterosexuality*, heterosexuals "tend to view people of all sexual orientations as essentially the same" (2002, 540–541). Individuals using this model rarely think about sexual identity issues and consider them unimportant. *Compulsory heterosexuality*, the second working model, is underscored by a belief that heterosexuality is the only acceptable form of sexual identity and that individuals who identify as LGBT are sick, perverted, and deserve to be oppressed. Individuals who base their beliefs on the third working model, *politicized heterosexuality*, recognize the privilege associated with heterosexuality and experience the emotions of guilt, sadness, and shame noted earlier that come with this awareness. They may also idealize LGBT people rather than seeing them as individuals who lead complex lives that are not solely centered around their sexual and gender identities. In the fourth working model, *integrative heterosexuality*, individuals are cognizant of the system of oppression that exists related to gender and sexual identity and the ways in which this system affects all people, regardless of their specific identity.

When heterosexual persons first learn that their lesbian, gay, bisexual, or transgender friends are truly mistreated on the basis of sexual or gender identity, they often feel anger toward heterosexuals and guilt toward themselves for being members of the same group.

NEXT STEPS

This process can only happen, however, if individuals have progressed at least to Mohr's third working model, when persons have an understanding of sexual and gender identity and do not see it as grounds for discrimination, violence, or abuse. These feeling do not occur when the person still believes that lesbian, gay, bisexual, or transgender persons are sick sinners who either need to have a good sexual relationship with a person of the other sex or see a psychologist or a spiritual leader so that they can be cured. Such persons, who might be classified as being in Mohr's second working model, are not yet ready to start down the ally road.

MOTIVATIONS FOR BECOMING AN ADVOCATE

What motivates heterosexuals to become LGBT rights advocates? There are certainly more popular and less controversial causes with which one can become involved. Goodman noted that support of social justice in general is related to empathy, moral and spiritual values, and self-interest. Since involvement in LGBT rights advocacy is often deemed a moral issue, moral development theory suggests some possible underlying reasons for such activity. Lawrence Kohlberg hypothesized that moral reasoning develops through three levels: preconventional, conventional, and postconventional. At the preconventional level, moral decisions are based on what is good for the individual. Persons functioning at this level may choose to be involved in gay rights issues to protect their own interests or to get something out of such involvement (e.g., if this issue is particularly important to a supervisor whose approval is sought). At the conventional level, Kohlberg indicated that decisions are made that conform to the norms of one's group or society. Individuals at this level may work for LGBT rights if they wish to support friends who are gay, lesbian, bisexual, or transgender or to uphold an existing institutional policy of nondiscrimination. Kohlberg's third level of reasoning involves decision making based on principles of justice. At this level the individual takes an active role to create policies that assure that all people are treated fairly and becomes involved in LGBT rights advocacy because it is the right thing to do.

While Kohlberg focused on justice as the basis of moral decision making, Carol Gilligan used the principle of care as the basis of her model of moral reasoning. Her three levels of reasoning are (1) taking care of oneself, (2) taking care of others, and (3) supporting positions that take into consideration the impact *both* on self and others. Using this model, individuals at the first level become advocates to make themselves look good to others or to protect themselves from criticism for not getting involved. At the second level, individuals reason that they should "take care of" LGBT people. The final perspective leads individuals to believe that equality and respect for differences create a better world for everyone, and that these are worthwhile goals.

One could argue that the latter position in each scheme is the enlightened perspective that any advocate needs to espouse. We should, however, be aware that not every person is functioning at a postconventional level of moral reasoning, and that arguments designed to encourage people to commit themselves to LGBT rights advocacy need to be targeted to the level that the individual can understand and accept. Kohlberg indicated that active involvement in addressing moral issues is an important factor in facilitating moral development along his stages. We can, therefore, expect that as people become involved in LGBT rights issues, their levels of reasoning may move toward a postconventional level.

In some ways paralleling our analysis of the moral reasoning that may be involved in advocacy, Edwards introduced a conceptual model of ally identity development. He suggested that self-interest, altruism, and a desire for social justice can all motivate potential allies. *Aspiring allies for self-interest* would take action when an LGBT person they care about is in danger of being hurt. They act on behalf of specific individuals to stop specific actions that are harmful or discriminatory and do not understand or care about the larger system of oppression that affects LGBT people as a group. Edwards noted that aspiring allies for self-interest often thrive on the feelings of power that come with "rescuing" their friend and being seen as a hero, thus perpetuating the system of oppression that creates the problem in the first place.

Edwards suggested that as individuals become aware of the privilege they experience, they can become motivated to be allies to assuage the guilt they feel. While *aspiring allies for altruism* would see the issues that confront LGBT individuals as a group, they would be likely to place the blame for oppression on other heterosexual individuals rather than seeing that they also benefit from an oppressive system. They would be likely to exhibit a paternalistic attitude as they seek to come to the aid of the oppressed LGBT population and, consciously or unconsciously, expect recognition and praise for the work they do on behalf of this group.

The final type of allies that Edwards discussed is *allies for social justice*. These allies "work *with* those from the oppressed group in collaboration and partnership to end the system of oppression" (2006, 51). They would be aware that acting to end oppression of LGBT people in the end benefits heterosexuals as well. Thus, their goal in working to address the issue of oppression would be to achieve a just society rather than to gain recognition for their efforts.

Edwards acknowledged that individuals may experience each of these motivations for ally work depending on the specific situation in which they find themselves. He also stated that "the Ally for Social Justice status is an aspirational identity one must continuously work towards" (53). He argued that understanding each motivation can lead to the development of more consistent and effective ally behaviors.

ADVOCACY IN ACTION

Advocacy can take a number of different forms and target various audiences. Heterosexual supporters may focus some of their energy toward LGBT individuals themselves. At other times the target may be other heterosexuals, and often strategies developed for college and university campuses are focused on the campus community as a whole.

Advocacy with LGBT people involves acceptance, support, and inclusiveness. Examples of acceptance include listening in a nonjudgmental way and valuing the unique qualities of each individual. Support includes such behaviors as championing the hiring of LGBT staff; providing an atmosphere in which LGBT issues can be discussed in training or programming; or attending events sponsored by LGBT student organizations. Inclusiveness involves activities such as the use of nonexclusionary language; publications, fliers, and handbooks that take into account sexual and gender identity differences; and sensitivity to the possibility that not everyone in a student organization or work setting is heterosexual.

Being an advocate among other heterosexuals is often challenging. Such a position involves modeling advocacy, support, and confronting inappropriate behavior. In this context, heterosexual supporters model nonheterosexist behaviors such as being equally physical with men and women, avoiding joking or teasing someone for nontraditional gender behaviors, and avoiding making a point of being heterosexual. Allies are spokespersons for addressing LGBT issues proactively in program and policy development. Confronting such behaviors as heterosexist joke telling; the exclusion of LGBT people either intentionally or by using language that assumes heterosexuality; discriminatory hiring practices; or the

N E X T

S T E P S

evaluation of staff based on factors related to their sexual or gender identities is also part of the role of the advocate.

Advocacy in the institution involves making sure that issues facing LGBT students and staff are acknowledged and addressed. This goal is accomplished by developing and promoting educational efforts that raise the awareness level and increase the sensitivity of heterosexual students, staff, and faculty on campus. Such activities include inviting speakers to address topics relevant to the LGBT community; developing panel discussions on issues related to sexual and gender identities; including LGBT issues as a topic in resident advisor training programs; promoting plays and movies featuring LGBT themes; and advocating for curricular inclusion across the academic disciplines focusing on LGBT-related issues and themes.

Encouraging LGBT student and staff organizations is also part of institutional advocacy. Such groups need to have access to the same campus resources, funding, and sponsorship as other student and staff organizations. Developing and supporting pro-LGBT policies are also necessary aspects of advocacy. Anti-harassment policies, anti-discriminatory hiring policies, and provisions for gay and lesbian couples to live together in campus housing are arenas that deserve attention.

STEPS TOWARD BECOMING AN ALLY

When dealing with issues of oppression, there are four basic levels of ally involvement. The following examples relate specifically to being an ally to LGBT persons.

- *Awareness* is the first level. It is important to become more aware of who you are and how you are different from and similar to LGBT people. Such awareness can be gained through conversations with LGBT individuals, attending awareness-building workshops, reading about LGBT life, and self-examination.
- *Knowledge/education* is the second level. You must begin to acquire knowledge about sexual and gender identities and the experiences of LGBT people. This step includes learning about laws, policies, and practices and how they affect LGBT people, in addition to educating yourself about LGBT culture and the norms of this community. Contacting local and national LGBT organizations for information can be very helpful.
- *Skills* make up the third level. This area is the one in which people often fall short because of fear, or lack of resources or supports. You must develop skills in communicating the knowledge that you have learned. These skills can be acquired by attending workshops, role-playing certain situations with friends, developing support connections, or practicing interventions or awareness raising in safe settings—for example, a restaurant or hotel out of your hometown.
- *Action* is the last, but most important, level and is the most frightening step. There are many challenges and liabilities for heterosexuals in taking actions to end the oppression of LGBT people. Some are addressed later in this essay in our discussion of factors that discourage advocacy. Nonetheless, action is, without doubt, the only way that we can effect change in the society as a whole; for if we keep our awareness, knowledge, and skill to ourselves, we deprive the rest of the world of what we have learned, thus keeping them from having the fullest possible life.

In addition to the four levels of ally involvement, there are six additional points to keep in mind:

1. Defining yourself as an ally is somewhat presumptuous. Whether your actions would qualify as those of an ally can best be determined by members of the LGBT population. Certainly, a person can advocate for equity and social justice for LGBT people without the permission of the LGBT community but declaring oneself to be an ally and demanding recognition as such can be off-putting to many LGBT people. Referring again to Edwards's model, such behavior seems more indicative of someone who is motivated by self-interest or altruism rather than by social justice.

2. Have a good understanding of sexual and gender identities and be aware of and comfortable with your own. If you are a person who chooses not to identify with a particular sexual or gender identity, be comfortable with that decision, but recognize that others, particularly LGBT people, may see your stance as a cop-out.

3. Talk with LGBT people and read about the coming-out process. This is a process and experience that is unique to this oppressed group. Few other populations of oppressed persons need to disclose so much to family and close friends in the same way. Because of its uniqueness, this process brings challenges that are often not understood.

4. As any other oppressed group, the LGBT population gets the same messages about homosexuality, bisexuality, and gender expression as everyone else. As such, there is a great deal of internalized heterosexism, homophobia, and transgender oppression. There are LBGT people who believe that what they do in bed is nobody's business, and that being an "out" lesbian, gay, bisexual, or transgender person to them would mean forcing their sexual practices on the general society, something they feel should not be done. It is, therefore, very important not only to be supportive, recognizing that you do not share the same level of personal risk as a lesbian, gay, bisexual, or transgender person, but also to challenge some of the internalized oppressive notions, thus helping to develop a different, more positive, perspective.

5. As with most oppressed groups, there is diversity within the LGBT community. Heterosexism is an area of oppression that cuts across, but is not limited to, race, ethnicity, gender, class, religion, culture, age, and level of physical or mental ability. For all of these categories, there are different challenges. Certainly, LGBT individuals as members of these diverse populations share some common joys and concerns; however, issues often manifest themselves in very different ways in different groups, thus calling for different strategies and interventions.

6. It is difficult to enter into a discussion about heterosexism and homophobia without the topic of AIDS/HIV infection arising. Knowing at least basic information about the illness is necessary for two reasons: (1) to address myths and misinformation related to AIDS and the LGBT community, and (2) to be supportive of the members of the community affected by this disease. Although we recognize that AIDS is a health issue that has and will continue to affect our entire world, the persons who live in the most fear of this disease and have lost the most members of their community are LGBT individuals. Accepting that reality helps an ally to understand the intense emotions that surround this issue within the community.

These six points and the previously discussed levels of ally involvement provide some guidelines for becoming an effective ally. Although we recognize that these concepts seem fairly reasonable, there are some real challenges or factors that can discourage a potential ally from taking these steps.

NEXT STEPS

FACTORS THAT DISCOURAGE ADVOCACY

Involvement in LGBT rights advocacy can be a scary and unpopular activity. Individuals who wish to take on such a role must be aware of and reconcile themselves to several potentially unpleasant outcomes. Some of these problems involve reactions from other heterosexuals, and some come from members of the LGBT community.

An assumption often is automatically made within the heterosexual community that anyone supporting LGBT rights is automatically gay, lesbian, bisexual, or transgender. Although such an identity is not negative, such labeling can create problems, especially for unmarried heterosexuals who might wish to become involved in a heterosexual romantic relationship. Heterosexuals also often experience derisive comments from other heterosexuals concerning involvement in a cause that is viewed as unimportant, unacceptable, or unpopular. Friends and colleagues who are uncomfortable with the topic may become alienated from the heterosexual supporter of LGBT rights, or may noticeably distance themselves from the individual. Difficulty may arise in social situations if the heterosexual ally is seen in the company of LGBT individuals. Discrimination, either overt or subtle, may also result from getting involved in controversial causes. Such discrimination may take the form of poor evaluations, failure to be appointed to important committees, or encouragement to seek a position at a school "more supportive of your ideas."

The LGBT community may also have trouble accepting the heterosexual ally. Often an assumption is made that such persons are really gay, lesbian, bisexual, or transgender but not yet accepting of their identity. Subtle or not-so-subtle pressure is placed on such people to come out or at least to consider the possibility of a nonheterosexual identity.

The LGBT community is one that has its own language and culture. Heterosexual supporters can feel out of place and awkward in settings populated exclusively or mainly by gay males, lesbians, bisexuals, and transgender people. LGBT people may be exclusionary in their conversations and activities, leaving the heterosexual ally out of the picture.

Since most LGBT people have had mainly negative experiences with heterosexuals in the past, the motives of heterosexuals involved in LGBT rights activities are often questioned. These experiences make it difficult for LGBT people to accept that individuals will involve themselves in a controversial and unpopular cause just because it is "right." Many LGBT individuals also believe that persons who are not members of their community cannot truly understand the issues they face and should therefore leave it to LGBT people to educate and advocate for their own rights. They can become angry and resentful of heterosexuals' involvement in programs, spaces, and activities they believe should be exclusively theirs.

THE BENEFITS OF BEING AN ALLY

Although the factors that discourage individuals from being an ally are very real, there are many benefits of being an ally, including:

1. You open yourself up to the possibility of close relationships with an additional percentage of the world.
2. You become less locked into sex role stereotypes
3. You increase your ability to have close and loving relationships with same-sex friends.
4. You have opportunities to learn from, teach, and have an impact on a population with whom you might not otherwise interact.

5. You may be the reason a family member, coworker, or community member finally decides that life is worth something and that dependence on chemicals or other substances might not be the answer.

6. You may make the difference in the lives of adolescents who hear you confront anti-LGBT epithets that make them feel as if they want to drop out of junior high, high school, or college. As a result of your action, they will know they have a friend to turn to.

7. Lastly, you can get invited to some of the most fun parties, have some of the best foods, play some of the best sports, have some of the best intellectual discussions, and experience some of the best music in the world, because everyone knows that LGBT people are good at all these things.

Although the last factor is meant as a joke, there is a great deal of truth concerning the positive experiences to which persons open themselves when they allow themselves to be a part of and include another segment of the population in their world. Imagine what it could be like to have had such close friends as Tennessee Williams, Cole Porter, Bessie Smith, Walt Whitman, Gertrude Stein, Alice Walker, James Baldwin, Virginia Woolf, Joan of Arc (trans). Imagine the world without their contributions. It is possible for gay, lesbian, bisexual, and transgender people, as well as heterosexuals, to make a difference in the way the world is, but we must start by realizing equity in our humanness and life experiences.

References

Broido, E.M. (2000) "The Development of Social Justice Allies during College: A Phenomenological Investigation." *Journal of College Student Development*, 41, 3–18.

Edwards, K.E. (2006). "Aspiring Social Justice Ally Identity Development: A Conceptual Model. *NASPA Journal*, 43 (2), 39–60.

Johnson, A.G. (2006). *Privelege, Power, and Difference* (second edition). Boston: McGraw-Hill.

Mohr, J.J. (2002). "Heterosexual Identity and the Heterosexual Therapist: An Identity Perspective on Sexual Orientation Dynamics in Psychotherapy. *Counseling Psychologist*, 30, 532–566.

NEXT STEPS

SECTION 7

TRANSGENDER OPPRESSION

Introduction

Chase Catalano and Davey Shlasko[1]

Transgender issues are receiving increasing attention in both academia and popular culture in recent years. Recent publication of *The Transgender Studies Reader* (Stryker and Whittle 2007) and the *Transgender Rights Anthology* (Currah, Juang, and Minter 2006) demonstrates the emergence of an academic discourse about social justice issues for transgender communities. Students at the University of Vermont, University of Massachusetts Amherst, University of Michigan, and University of California (Berkeley, Santa Barbara, San Diego, and Santa Cruz), along with many other state and private colleges, have begun organizing for transgender inclusion in residence halls, bathrooms, health insurance coverage, and non-discrimination policies.

In the pop culture realm, transgender characters have been depicted on mainstream television shows, such as *ER, Grey's Anatomy, Eli Stone, Law & Order: SVU,* and *Crime Scene Investigation* (*CSI*), even occasionally played by trans actors. Unfortunately, these mainstream media depictions of trans people and trans characters almost always portray white trans people, which is an unrealistic representation of the diversity within transgender communities. Further, these representations tend to showcase trans people either as victims or as medical anomalies, and not as complex people with lives and interests beyond their gender.

At the same time, violence and discrimination against transgender people are of pandemic proportions. As of this writing, gender identity and expression are not included in federal hate crimes legislation, so federal law enforcement agencies are not required to track or report crimes based on gender identity and expression, as they do with hate crimes based on federally protected classes, such as race, religion, and sex (Currah and Spade 2007). For this reason it is very difficult to state with any certainty the number of bias-motivated crimes against transgender and gender non-conforming people. However, members of the trans community try to keep track of publicized incidents, and memorialize each year at the Transgender Day of Remembrance transgender and gender non-conforming people who have been murdered.[2] According to these community groups' estimates, at least 245 people were murdered in anti-transgender hate crimes between 1998 and 2008. This is definitely a drastic underestimate, as it only counts people whose transgender identities were known, and as police departments in most jurisdictions have no obligation and indeed no way to report these murders as hate crimes.

Currently, thirteen states plus Washington, D.C., include gender identity and expression in non-discrimination laws, policies, or judicial findings (National Center for Transgender Equality [NCTE] 2007). Together with local statutes, this means that only 37 percent of the U.S. population is legally protected against such discrimination based on gender identity and expression (NCTE 2007). Further legislation is pending federally and in several states.

Because non-discrimination laws do not protect most transgender people in the United States, we may be denied housing, employment, and public benefits with little if any legal recourse. For example, in a 2008 survey of transgender people in California, 70 percent reported experiencing workplace discrimination based on their gender identity or gender expression—despite the fact that transgender Californians had been protected by comprehensive non-discrimination laws since 2004. Additionally, survey respondents were twice as likely as the general population to be receiving unemployment benefits (14 percent v. 7 percent) and to be living below the federal poverty level of $10,400 (23 percent v. 11.7 percent). Fewer than half were employed full time, and 20 percent had been homeless since their transition (Transgender Law Center 2009). Trans people also are arrested and imprisoned disproportionately to the general population, due both to economic marginalization and to stereotyping by police officers, and once in prison they are extremely vulnerable to sexual assault, medical neglect, and other abuses (Sylvia Rivera Law Project 2007).[3]

The reality represented by these discouraging statistics leads us to identify the oppression of transgender people as a problem worthy of study and action within a multi-issue social justice liberation movement.

DEFINITIONS

Transgender oppression is closely related to sexism and to heterosexism, and there are also important differences (see Griffin 2007, 167–173, reprinted on this section's website). In order to distinguish them, we need to define some terminology. Many people understand gender to be synonymous with sex, referring to the categories of male and female. In fact, *sex* and *gender* are not the same things, and both are more complicated than a male/female binary. In this section (as in the preceding two sections on sexism and heterosexism), we use *sex* to describe biological factors, such as chromosomes, genitals, and hormone levels, that are used to categorize people as male or female. In reality, more possibilities exist; many people have some aspect of their biology that would challenge simple categorization of their body as male or female (Fausto-Sterling 2000; Kessler 2002). Individuals whose physical bodies are not easily categorized as male or female are called *intersex*.[4]

Gender refers to a wide range of social/cultural meanings that are ascribed to biological sex. We like to think of gender as composed of both *gender identity* and *gender expression*. *Gender identity* refers to a person's internal self-concept with regard to gender categories like man and woman. *Gender expression* refers to behaviors, such as attire, demeanor, and language, through which we intentionally or unintentionally communicate gender. As Hackman describes (in the introduction to the section on sexism), *gender roles* are specific sets of expectations for gender expression, which characterize what men and women are "supposed to" be in a particular society. The dominant assumption is that an individual's sex, gender identity, and gender expression always line up—for example, that all female-bodied people identify as women and express themselves through femininity—and further that there are two and only two sexes, and two and only two genders (where identity and expression are conflated). This faulty assumption, often referred to as the *sex/gender binary*, is the foundation of our analysis of transgender oppression.

It is also common to confuse gender identity and expression with *sexual orientation* (i.e., the gender/s one is emotionally, romantically, or sexually attracted to), and, thus, to confuse transgender oppression with heterosexism. In fact, one's gender identity and expression are not necessarily related to one's sexual orientation. Transgender people, like all people, have a variety of sexual orientations including heterosexual, gay, lesbian, pansexual, and queer.[5] For further discussion of gender, sexuality, and terminology, we refer readers to the sections on heterosexism and sexism, as well as to Pat Griffin's discussion included on this section's website.

Based on these definitions, we use the term *transgender* broadly to describe people whose gender identity and/or gender expression do not match societal expectations (Catalano, McCarthy, and Shlasko 2007) and for whom this fact is central to their identity and/or important in determining their life circumstances. Transgender is also a term of self-identity that is claimed by some, but not all, people who fit in our broad definition. People who fall under the transgender umbrella may or may not identify as transgender, and may also identify with others terms such as male-to-female (MtF), butch, female-to-male (FtM), genderqueer, gender non-conforming, femme, androgynous, or two-spirit. We fully support the right of all people to name and define their own identity and experiences, because empowerment for marginalized peoples requires this kind of self-determination. Terms of self-identity are important tools that help people to survive with, in, and/or in resistance to the gender binary. At the same time, we define transgender broadly so that we can discuss social phenomena that affect people in this category, across many variations in how people understand and describe themselves.

We define *transgender oppression* as the system of oppression that targets and marginalizes people who are transgender in the broadest sense. The system privileges non-transgender people, also called *cisgender*[6] people, whose gender identity and expression conform with relative ease to societal expectations. Like other forms of oppression, transgender oppression is harmful and limiting to everyone, including those who occupy a privileged position. It has particular impact on those who transition from living entirely or primarily in one of the two socially sanctioned genders (man or woman) to living entirely or primarily in the other, or who live between or outside these categories. Often, this is the group that people are referring to when they say transgender. Although we use transgender more broadly, many of the phenomena we focus on as examples of transgender oppression are particularly evident for this group.

Because many people view gender as a presumed-natural binary, those of us whose experience does not match this assumption are often viewed as unnatural. The medical system reinforces this view, especially with regard to those of us who choose to change our bodies, in the *Diagnostic and Statistical Manual-IV* (American Psychiatric Association 2000), which classifies the desire to change the sex of one's body (through hormones, surgeries, or other options) as evidence of a mental illness called gender identity disorder. This diagnosis forms the basis of the "*medical model*" of transgender identity, which positions transgender identity as an illness with biomedical transition as the cure, thereby establishing medical authority to "diagnose" gender identity and to supervise gender transition.

One central assumption of the medical model is that all trans people experience extreme distress about being trans. This can lead well-meaning allies to feel pity or sympathy for transgender people. Some trans people do experience internal struggles about their gender, and many trans people also find joy and pride in our gender identity and expression. The medical model ignores this aspect of trans experience.

It is difficult to overestimate the historical and current impact of the medical model on transgender lives, communities, and movements. Much of how we understand transgender has been shaped by the medical model. Transgender people inevitably end up having to navigate the medical system's assumptions about us, whether because we choose to participate in the system in order to seek medical transition or because medical providers pass judgment on our non-conformity and create barriers to accessing even basic primary health care. Dean Spade's piece in this section (selection 89) addresses some of the complexities of trans communities' relationships to the medical model.

Like all forms of oppression, transgender oppression can be internalized. At the most basic level, *internalized transgender oppression* is internalization of the sex/gender binary. The binary asserts that only two categories of people exist: masculine, man-identified males and feminine, woman-identified females. For some trans people, the internalization of this belief system may lead us to doubt whether we can be a "real" man or a "real" woman, or even whether we are "real" at all. For others, the internalization of the gender binary may lead us to enact hyperfemininity or hypermasculinity in attempts to "prove" our identity. Internalized oppression can lead to depression and suicidality; in some studies 35 percent of transgender participants report having thought seriously about suicide, and 16–32 percent report having attempted suicide (Clements-Nolle, Marx, Guzman, and Katz 2001; Xavier 2000).

Another aspect of internalized transgender oppression is internalization of the medical model. Many trans people disagree with some aspects of the medical model and prefer to see trans identity not as pathology but rather as a natural expression of human variation. Yet the influence of the medical model is so pervasive that we may accidentally accept some of its assumptions even if we do not believe in them (such as the assumption that all trans people experience a certain kind of discomfort in their bodies).

When we are able to come together as a community, we can mitigate some of the brutal effects of internalized oppression and create space for trans people to have more agency in defining and making choices about our lives. The recent emergence of numerous trans memoirs, biographies, and documentaries, as well as trans advocacy organizations around the world, are further examples of resistance by trans people who refuse to buy into the messages of shame and isolation. We hope more will be published about the complexities of internalized transgender oppression and the ways in which individuals and communities are working toward liberation.

SEXISM, HETEROSEXISM, AND TRANSGENDER OPPRESSION

There are various ways to understand the relationships among sexism, heterosexism, and transgender oppression. The way we think of it is that these three systems, along with the oppression of intersex people, are conceptually distinct but overlapping systems. They have in common an overarching system of norms and expectations related to bodies, gender, sexuality, and family relationships that dictate which identities are considered normal, which are deviant, and in some cases which identities are acknowledged to exist at all.

In addition, there are many specific manifestations of oppression that play out similarly. For example, lesbian, gay, and bisexual (LGB) and transgender (T) people may be labeled as mentally ill when we are not and may be discouraged from interacting with children because of irrational fears that we will influence the children to become LGB or T. Both women and trans people are often targeted for sexual assault and are encouraged to entrust our bodies to doctors while dissociating from our own knowledge of what our bodies need and want. In addition, sexism, heterosexism, and transgender oppression often occur in tandem. When a gay man with a feminine gender expression is targeted for violence based on his femininity, gender nonconformity, and presumed sexual orientation, all three systems are at play. With the constant evolution of terminology and philosophy around transgender issues, we look forward to seeing the new ways we will conceive and describe these relationships.

The history of trans communities and movements has often been intertwined with LGB activism and with feminism. Many LGB organizations now include transgender issues in their mission and extend the acronym to LGBT. The inclusion of transgender within LGB movements and organizations acknowledges the historical connections of the communities and has created space for the concerns of trans people to be addressed as part of broader LGBT liberation efforts. However, it is not always a natural fit, and often these organizations struggle with how to enact their intention of being trans-inclusive. The lumping in of T with LGB has also reinforced confusion about the meaning of transgender, which many people misunderstand as being a sexual orientation.

In some ways, transgender liberation movements should be a natural fit with feminist movements, as they share a fundamental goal of eliminating oppression based on gender. However, ideological conflicts between trans and non-trans feminists have surfaced on many fronts.[7] In order to work together to overcome the overlapping systems that target all women (whether or not they are trans) and all trans people (whether or not they are women), trans and feminist movements need to seek a mutually beneficial definition of feminism that would "dismantle the structures that prop up gender as a system of oppression, but [. . .] without passing moral judgment on people who feel the need to change their birth-assigned gender" (Stryker 2008, 3).

Even with the tension around trans issues in feminist and LGBT movements, trans people have always been part of LGBT and feminist organizing. Trans people's participation in these and other social movements has been omitted from many accounts, sometimes out of carelessness and sometimes out of intentional reframing of the historical facts (Namaste 2000; Nestle, Howell, and Wilchins 2002; Stryker 2008), leading to widespread ignorance about trans people's history and, indeed, our very existence.

By setting aside space for discussion about transgender oppression, we acknowledge and honor the experiences of those who transgress the gender binary, without taking away from other equally important issues. The first-time inclusion of this section in a general book of readings on diversity and social justice is an important step forward for transgender studies and activism. Students, teachers, and staff now have access to information about transgender issues as part of a broader social justice curriculum. Some trans students and teachers will have a chance to see themselves reflected in the pages of a reading assignment for the first time. As with any anthology, this section is only a sampling of what is available. We hope that it will encourage readers to seek out more information and to find your own voices about this issue.

INTRODUCTION TO THE READINGS

The pieces in this section provide a basic framework for understanding the context, acknowledging some voices, and exploring next steps about transgender experience and transgender oppression. In selecting pieces, we considered what resources would be most relevant and appealing to today's undergraduate students, some of whom are thinking about transgender issues for the first time. With this in mind, our focus is mostly on contemporary transgender communities and the mainstream of transgender political organizing.

We also wanted to emphasize the interconnections among transgender oppression and other forms of oppression, especially racism and classism. One of the criticisms we often hear when attempting to include transgender issues in college curricula or student life programming is that the transgender movement is a white, upper-class movement and, thus, transgender oppression is a white, upper-class problem. Indeed it is true that much—though certainly not all—of transgender theorizing that has been published is from a perspective of race and class privilege. That should not be surprising, as most published academic theory on many topics tends to come from that perspective. In fact, gender transgression exists in all cultures, and transgender communities in the United States are as diverse racially as the nation as a whole. As far as class, the economic survey data cited above suggest that transgender people are disproportionately likely to become working class and poor, even if they were raised with class privilege. We have attempted to include readings that speak to the diversity of trans experiences, and to the complex interplay among systems of oppression as they impact trans lives.

Joanne Meyerowitz's excerpt from her book *How Sex Changed: A History of Transsexuality in the United States* (selection 87) outlines the historical evolution of transgender identities and definitions in the United States, using the iconic 1950s case of Christine Jorgensen to show how science has affected this evolution. Susan Stryker's piece (selection 88) outlines the Compton's Cafeteria Riots of the 1960s, an early example of the transgender social justice activism in U.S. history. Dean Spade (selection 89) describes some of the complexities of and problems with the medical model, including how class and gender non-conformity can limit access to medical care. Julia Serano (selection 90) discusses the rejection of trans women's issues from the feminist movement and explores some links between misogyny and transgender oppression. Finally, Kylar Broadus (selection 91) reviews some of the prominent court cases related to employment protections for transgender workers and analyzes the arguments used on both sides of these cases.

For our Voices section, in "Passing Realities," Allie Lie (selection 92) gives a compelling account of her daily experience, including her desire to be recognized and her complex relationships with family and strangers. Jamison Green's "Look! No, Don't!" (selection 93) discusses his experience of passing and invisibility after biomedical transition. In "An Entire Rainbow of Possibilities," Gary Bowen (selection 94) describes his understanding of his gender based on his Native American heritage and gives voice to some of the intersections of race, ability, and transgender experience.

In our Next Steps section, "Calling All Restroom Revolutionaries" (selection 95) reports on an organization of college students who advocate for inclusive restrooms, which benefit not only trans students but also people with disabilities and parents of young children. For more information on next steps and resources for allies, please go to this section's website.

FURTHER RESOURCES

This section provides an introduction to transgender history, voices, and issues and the system of transgender oppression. There is far more that could and should be explored about the range of gender transgression in the United States and globally, both historically and currently, and the variety of ways in which trans-ness has been understood by gender transgressors and those who have observed and studied their transgression. Even though this section is U.S.-focused, there are conversations going on around the world about transgender issues in culture, law, and policy. We encourage readers who would like more international perspective, as well as many further U.S.-related resources, to go to the section website.

Notes

1 We ask that those who cite this work always acknowledge by name all of the authors listed rather than only citing the first author or using "et al." to indicate coauthors. All authors listed on a section collaborated equitably on the conceptualization, development, and writing of this section.
2 For more information see http://www.transgenderdor.org and http://www.rememberingourdead.org.
3 Unfortunately very little research has been conducted about trans populations at a national or international level. As additional statistical data about trans populations become available, we will provide updated links on the section website.
4 For more information on intersex issues, we refer readers to the Intersex Society of North America (http://www.isna.org), and to Sumi Colligan's piece in the ableism section of this anthology.
5 Some transgender people also identify as bisexual, but many trans people reject this category because the word itself reinforces the gender binary, and instead use pansexual or queer.
6 *Cisgender* means non-trans, from the etymology of *cis* meaning "on the same side," whereas *trans* means "across or crossing."
7 For more discussion on transgender inclusion in feminist movements see Califia (2003); Prosser (1998); Raymond (1979); Stone (1991); Stryker (2008).

References

American Psychiatric Association. (2000). *Diagnostic and Statistical Manual of Mental Disorders: DSM-IV-TR*. Washington, DC: American Psychiatric Association.
Califia, P. (2003). *Sex Changes: Transgender Politics*, 2nd edition. San Francisco, CA: Cleis Press.

Catalano, C., McCarthy, L., Shlasko, D. (2007). "Transgender Oppression Curriculum Design." In M. Adams, L. A. Bell, P. Griffin (eds), *Teaching for Diversity and Social Justice*, 2nd edition. New York: Routledge. pp. 210–246.

Clements-Nolle, K., Marx, R., Guzman, R., Katz, M. (2001). "HIV Prevalence, Risk Behaviors, Health Care Use, and Mental Health Status of Transgender Persons: Implications for Public Health Intervention." *American Journal of Public Health* 91, 915–921.

Currah, P., Juang, R., Minter, S. (2006). *Transgender Rights Anthology*. Minneapolis: University of Minnesota Press.

Currah, P., Spade, D. (2007). "Introduction to Special Issue: The State We're in: Locations of Coercion and Resistance in Trans Policy, Part I." *Sexuality Research and Social Policy: Journal of NSRC* 4 (4), 1–6.

Fausto-Sterling, A. (2000). *Sexing the Body: Gender Politics and the Construction of Sexuality*. New York: Basic Books.

Griffin, P. (2007). "Overview: Sexism, Heterosexism, and Transgender Oppression." In M. Adams, L. A. Bell, P. Griffin (eds), *Teaching for Diversity and Social Justice*, 2nd edition. New York: Routledge. pp. 167–172.

Kessler, S. J. (2002). *Lessons from the Intersexed*. New Brunswick, NJ: Rutgers University Press.

Meyerowitz, J. (2002). *How Sex Changed: A History of Transsexuality in the United States*. Cambridge, MA: Harvard University Press.

Namaste, V. K. (2000). *Invisible Lives: The Erasure of Transsexual and Transgendered People*. Chicago: University of Chicago Press.

National Center for Transgender Equality. (2007). *Discrimination*. Retrieved April 26, 2009, from http://nctequality.org/Issues/Discrimination.html.

Nestle, J., Howell, C., Wilchins, R. (eds) (2002). *Genderqueer: Voices from beyond the Sexual Binary*. Los Angeles: Alyson Books.

Prosser, J. (1998). *Second Skins: The Body Narratives of Transsexuality*. New York: Columbia University Press.

Raymond, J. (1979). *The Transsexual Empire: The Making of the She-Male*. London: The Women's Press.

Stone, S. (1991). "The Empire Strikes Back: A Posttranssexual Manifesto." In J. Epstein, K. Strauss (eds), *In Body Guards: The Cultural Politics of Gender Ambiguity*. New York: Routledge. pp. 280–304.

Stryker, S. (2008). *Transgender History*. Berkeley, CA: Seal Press.

Stryker, S., Whittle, S. (2007). *The Transgender Studies Reader*. New York: Routledge.

Sylvia Rivera Law Project. (2007). "'It's War in Here': A Report on the Treatment of Transgender and Intersex People in New York State Men's Prisons." Retrieved April 26, 2009, from http://srlp.org/files/warinhere.pdf.

Transgender Law Center. (March, 2009). "The State of Transgender California: Key Findings from the 2008 California Transgender Economic Health Survey." Keynote Presentation at the Transgender Leadership Summit, San Diego, CA.

Xavier, J. M. (2000). "The Washington Transgender Needs Assessment Survey." Retrieved April 4, 2009, from http://www.glaa.org/archive/2000/tgneedsassessment1112.shtml.

87

Introduction—How Sex Changed

A History of Transsexuality in the United States

Joanne Meyerowitz

On December 1, 1952, the *New York Daily News* announced the "sex change" surgery of Christine Jorgensen. The front-page headline read: "Ex-GI Becomes Blonde Beauty: Operations Transform Bronx Youth," and the story told how Jorgensen had traveled to Denmark for "a rare and complicated treatment." For years, Jorgensen, born and reared as a boy, had struggled with what she later described as an ineffable, inexorable, and increasingly unbearable yearning to live her life as a woman. In 1950 she sailed to Europe in search of a doctor who would alter her bodily sex. Within months she found an endocrinologist who agreed to administer hormones if she would in return cooperate with his research. Over the next two years she took massive doses of estrogen and underwent two major surgeries to transform her genitals. At the end of 1952 the *New York Daily News* transformed her obscure personal triumph into mass media sensation.

. . .

Jorgensen was more than a media sensation, a stage act, or a cult figure. Her story opened debate on the visibility and mutability of sex. It raised questions that resonated with force in the 1950s and engage us still today. How do we determine who is male and who is female, and why do we care? Can humans actually change sex? Is sex less apparent than it seems? As a narrative of boundary transgression, the Jorgensen story fascinated readers and elicited their surprise, and as an unusual variant on a familiar tale of striving and success, it inspired them. It opened possibilities for those who questioned their own sex and offered an exoticized travelogue for armchair tourists who had never imagined that one could take a journey across the sex divide. In the post-World War II era, with heightened concerns about science and sex, the Jorgensen story compelled some readers to spell out their own versions of the boundaries of sex, and it convinced others to reconsider the categories they thought they already knew. In response, American doctors and scientists began to explore the process of defining sex.

. . .

At the start of the twenty-first century, we routinely distinguish sex, gender, and sexuality, but we cannot, it seems, seal off the borders. Scientists, their popularizers, and their critics still debate whether sex-linked genes or prenatal sex hormones or specific sites of the brain determine the behaviors associated with masculinity and femininity and with hetero- and homosexuality. In much of the popular culture, sex still seems to dictate particular forms of gender, which in turn dictates particular forms of sexuality. In this default logic, a female is naturally and normally a feminine person who desires men; a male is naturally and normally a masculine person who desires women. All other permutations of sex, gender, and sexuality still appear, if they appear at all, as pathologically anomalous or socially strange. . . . [T]he categories of sex, gender, and sexuality—now analytically distinct—remain insistently intertwined in American science and culture.

Jorgensen was not the first transsexual, nor was the publicity accorded her the first media coverage of sex-change surgery. Cross-gender identification, the sense of being the other sex, and the desire to live as the other sex all existed in various forms in earlier centuries and other cultures. The historical record includes countless examples of males who dressed or lived as women and females who dressed or lived as men. Transsexuality, the quest to transform the bodily characteristics of sex via hormones and surgery, originated in the early twentieth century. By the 1910s European scientists had begun to publicize their attempts to transform the sex of animals, and by the 1920s a few doctors, mostly in Germany, had agreed to alter the bodies of a few patients who longed to change their sex.

. . .

The sex-change experiments in Europe reached the United States through the popular culture. From the 1930s on, American newspapers and magazines—and later radio, television, and film—broadcast stories on sex change. . . .

Only after World War II did American doctors and scientists seriously address the issue of sex change. . . . From the start, the doctors and scientists fought among themselves about the explanatory powers of biology and psychology, the use and abuse of medical technology, and the merits of sex-change operations.

In the point and counterpoint of debate, the doctors and scientists gradually shifted their focus from concepts of biological sex to concepts of what they came to call gender. When they tried to explain the desire to change sex, they less often referred to conditions of mixed bodily sex and more frequently wrote of "psychological sex," and later "gender identity," a sense of the sexed self that was both separate from the sex of the body and, some claimed, harder to change than the body itself. The sex of the body, they now asserted, had multiple components—hormones, chromosomes, genitals, and more—some of which could be altered. A few of them began to emphasize the immutability of adult gender identity and to acknowledge the despair of those patients who wanted the sex of their bodies to match their unshakable sense of self. This new understanding of gender was forged and refined in the discourse on transsexuality. With it, more American doctors gradually began to endorse and perform "sex reassignment surgery."

From the doctors' and scientists' point of view, medical examinations and psychological tests could determine a person's sex and verify a person's gender identity. From the point of view of their patients, sex and gender were usually matters of self-knowledge. They had studied themselves, and sometimes they had also read widely in the medical literature. Like the doctors, many of them distinguished between the sex of the visible body and the firm sense of sex that came from an inner sense of self. They had determined for themselves what they were and what they wanted to become. After Christine Jorgensen made the news, hundreds of them approached doctors in order to convince them to recommend or perform surgery. But they ran into constant conflicts with doctors who insisted on their own authority to define sex and gender, diagnose the condition, and recommend the treatment.

. . . After Jorgensen made the news, American doctors and scientists took up the taxonomic process of sorting out a tangled thicket of varied conditions of sex, gender, and sexuality. On the ground, those who identified as transsexuals, transvestites, lesbians, and gay men sorted themselves out in a parallel social process. Amidst a multiplicity of variations, some of them came to define their conditions not only in contradistinction to the mainstream norm—the heterosexual masculine male or heterosexual feminine female—but also with regard to others on the margins. In everyday life, especially in the cities, they gravitated toward each other, schooled each other in the customs and language of particular subcultures, and developed their own vernacular that delineated finer gradations of gender variance than the language used by doctors.

In the 1960s the complicated process of redefining sex took place within a culture increasingly preoccupied by a "sexual revolution," by more liberal attitudes toward individual choice, and by revitalized human rights movements that insisted on social change in the name of justice. In this climate the doctors and scientists who studied transsexuality began to organize programs, clinics, conferences, and associations to promote study of and treatment for transsexuals, and self-identified transsexuals began to organize to demand their own rights.

. . .

[T]he birth of a new identity evolved socially and politically into the birth of a new minority. Self-identified transsexuals distinguished themselves from other "deviants" and saw themselves as members of a distinct social group. In the late 1960s and early 1970s a few transsexuals began to challenge the doctors' authority and to reject the medical model that cast them primarily as patients. They observed and sometimes joined the 1960s movements for civil rights, feminism, and gay liberation, and they began to organize collectively and demand the right to quality medical care and also the right to live, free from harassment, with whatever presentation of gender they chose to express. By the century's end the push for transsexual rights had blossomed into a vocal social movement with local, national, and international organizations and with a new scholarship that sought again to clarify the contested meanings of sex.

. . .

As this thumbnail sketch suggests, the history of transsexuality engages a number of key trends of the twentieth century. It demonstrates the growing authority of science and medicine, and it points to the impact of sensational journalism. It illustrates the rise of a new concept of the modern self that placed a heightened value on self-expression, self-improvement, and self-transformation. It highlights the proliferation of sexual identities, and it offers a new angle of vision into the breakdown of traditional norms of gender. In the 1970s and 1980s the women's and gay liberation movements eclipsed transsexuality as the sites of public debate over sex, gender, and sexuality. But the history of transsexuality had already laid the definitional groundwork and helps explain the peculiar configuration that sex, gender, and sexuality had already assumed in American popular culture, medicine, and law.

. . .

88

Transgender Liberation

Susan Stryker

. . .

THE COMPTON'S CAFETERIA RIOT OF 1966

By the middle of the 1960s life in the United States was being transformed by several large-scale social movements. . . . The most militant phase of the transgender movement for social change, from 1966 to 1969, was part of this massive social upheaval.

The 1966 Compton's Cafeteria Riot in San Francisco's seedy Tenderloin neighborhood was similar to earlier incidents at Cooper's [in Los Angeles in 1959] and Dewey's [in Philadelphia in 1965]. For the first time, however, direct action in the streets by transgender people resulted in lasting institutional change. One weekend night in August—the precise date is unknown—Compton's, a twenty-four-hour cafeteria at the corner of Turk and Taylor streets, was buzzing with its usual late-night crowd of drag queens, hustlers, slummers, cruisers, runaway teens, and down-and-out neighborhood regulars. The restaurant's management became annoyed by a noisy young crowd of queens at one table who seemed be spending a lot of time without spending a lot of money, and it called in the police to roust them—as it had been doing with increasing frequency throughout the summer. A surly police officer, accustomed to manhandling Compton's clientele with impunity, grabbed the arm of one of the queens and tried to drag her away. She unexpectedly threw her coffee in his face, however, and a melee erupted: Plates, trays, cups, and silverware flew through the air at the startled police officers, who ran outside and called for backup. Compton's customers turned over the tables and smashed the plateglass windows and then poured out of the restaurant and into the streets. The paddy wagons arrived, and street fighting broke out in Compton's vicinity, all around the corner of Turk and Taylor. Drag queens beat the police with their heavy purses and kicked them with their high-heeled shoes. A police car was vandalized, a newspaper stand was burned to the ground, and—in the words of the best available source on what happened that night, a retrospective account by gay liberation activist Reverend Raymond Broshears, published in the program of San Francisco's first Gay Pride march in 1972—"general havoc was raised in the Tenderloin." The small restaurant had been packed when the fighting broke out, so the riot probably involved fifty or sixty patrons, plus police officers and any neighborhood residents or late-night passersby who jumped into the fray.

CONTEXTUALIZING COMPTON'S

Although the exact date of the riot remains a mystery . . . its underlying causes are reasonably clear. Understanding why the riot happened where and when it did reveals a great deal about the issues that have historically motivated the transgender social justice struggle and helps us understand similar dynamics at work today.

The location of the riot was by no means random. San Francisco's downtown Tenderloin neighborhood had been a sex-work district since the early 1900s. . . .

Much of the so-called vice trade in the neighborhood was supported by nonresidents of one sort or another. . . . But the neighborhood's resident population tended to be those who could least afford to live elsewhere, or who were prevented from doing so: released convicts and parolees, old-timers on small pensions, recent immigrants, pimps, prostitutes, drug addicts, alcoholics—and transgender women.

Housing and employment discrimination against transgender people are still legal in most places in the United States, and this discrimination was even more common in the past than it is now. In the 1960s, more so than today, a person who looked transgendered would be less likely to be rented to and would have a great deal of trouble finding work. As a result, a great many transgender women lived in the Tenderloin in cheap residential hotels, many of them along Turk Street near Compton's. To meet their basic survival needs they often worked as prostitutes or as maids in the hotels and bars where their friends sold sex. While most people who participated in the Tenderloin's illicit economy of sex, drugs, and after-hours entertainment were free to come and go, the neighborhood functioned as more of an involuntary containment zone for transgender women. Police actually helped concentrate a population of transgender women in the Tenderloin by directing them to go there when they were picked up in other parts of the city.

The police could be especially vicious to "street queens," whom they considered bottom-of-the-barrel sex workers, and who were the least able to complain about mistreatment. Transgender women working the streets were often arrested on suspicion of prostitution even if they were just going to the corner store or talking with friends; they might be driven around in squad cars for hours, forced to perform oral sex, strip-searched, or, after arriving at the jail, humiliated in front of other prisoners. Transgender women in jail often would have their heads forcibly shaved, or if they resisted, be placed in solitary confinement in "the hole." And because they were legally men (with male genitalia in spite of their social lives as women, and often in spite of having breasts and no facial hair) they would be placed in the men's jail, where their femininity made them especially vulnerable to sexual assault, rape, and murder.

This chronically bad situation became even worse in the mid-1960s, when U.S. involvement in the war in Vietnam escalated. Wartime is typically a time of heightened surveillance of commercial sexual activity in cities where large numbers of troops are being mobilized for deployment. . . . There were wartime crackdowns on prostitution in San Francisco during the Spanish-American War in the Philippines in the 1890s, during World War II in the 1940s, and during the Korean conflict in the 1950s. Among the hardest-hit establishments in San Francisco during the crackdown associated with the 1964–66 escalation of U.S. troops in Vietnam were the gay and drag bars, which even then catered to the "Don't ask, don't tell" military crowd.

Yet another factor that changed an already grim situation from bad to worse for transgender women in the Tenderloin was the effect of urban renewal and redevelopment. Their increasingly serious plight was directly related to very broad-scale social and economic changes. . . .

In response to the massive social dislocations of urban renewal and redevelopment. Tenderloin residents launched a grassroots campaign for economic justice in 1965. . . . Their immediate goal was to establish needed social services by qualifying the neighborhood for federal antipoverty funding. . . . The Tenderloin organizers not only had to document economic need in their neighborhood; they also had to persuade poor communities of color that adding an additional antipoverty target zone predominately populated by white people would be the right thing to do, even if that meant the already existing zones got a smaller slice of a fixed amount of money. Compounding matters even further, most of the white people were queer, and most of the people of color were straight. The eventual establishment of the Central City Anti-Poverty Program thus represented a singular accomplishment in the history of U.S. progressive politics: the first successful multiracial gay/straight alliance for economic justice.

Tenderloin activists involved in the antipoverty organizing campaign were striving to create conditions in which people could truly participate in structuring the society they lived in instead of just reacting to changes created by others. One unexpected consequence of neighborhood mobilization was the formation of Vanguard, an organization made up mostly of young gay hustlers and transgender people. Vanguard, which formed in the summer of 1966, is the earliest known queer youth organization in the United States. . . .

Vanguard described itself as "an organization of, by, and for the kids on the streets." Its goals were to promote a sense of self-worth among its members, to offer mutual support and companionship, to bring youth issues to the attention of older people, and to assert its presence in the neighborhood. One of the group's early flyers urged people to think past racial divisions and focus instead on shared living conditions: "You've heard about Black Power and White Power," the flyer said, before telling its readers to "get ready for Street Power." . . . Vanguard's first major political action . . . was to confront the management of Compton's Cafeteria over its poor treatment of transgender women. Compton's Cafeteria functioned as a chill-out lounge for the whole neighborhood; for young people who often had no homes, families, or legal employment, who were marginalized by their gender or sexuality, it provided an especially vital resource.

Vanguard held its meetings at Compton's, and during the course of the summer of 1966, tensions there had been on the rise. As the restaurant's customers increasingly claimed its turf as their own, the management asserted its property rights and business interests more and more strongly. It instituted a "service charge" for each customer to make up for income lost to tables of young people "camping out" and not buying any food, but it applied the charge in a discriminatory manner. It hired security guards to harass the street kids and shoo them outside, particularly the transgender youth. And with greater and greater frequency, it called the cops. In July, Vanguard worked with ministers from Glide [Glide Memorial United Methodist Church] and with older members of San Francisco's homophile organizations to set up a picket line protesting the mistreatment of its members, much as the customers and gay activists in Philadelphia had done at Dewey's. In San Francisco, however, the restaurant's management turned a deaf ear to the complaints.

Soon after the picket failed to produce any results, frustration boiled over into militant resistance.

. . .

Looking back, it's easy to see how the Compton's Cafeteria riot in 1966 was related to very large-scale political, social, and economic developments and was not just an isolated little incident unrelated to other things that were going on in the world. The circumstances that created the conditions for the riot in the first place continue to be relevant in the transgender movement today: discriminatory policing practices in minority communities, harmful urban land-use policies, the unsettling domestic consequences of U.S. foreign wars, access to healthcare, civil rights activism aiming to expand individual liberties and social tolerance on matters of sexuality and gender, and political coalition building around the structural injustices that affect many different communities. The violent resistance to the oppression of transgender people at Compton's Cafeteria did not solve the problems that transgender people in the Tenderloin faced daily. It did, however, create a space in which it became possible for the city of San Francisco to begin relating differently to its transgender citizens—to begin treating them, in fact, as citizens with legitimate needs instead of simply as a problem to get rid of. That shift in awareness was a crucial step for the contemporary transgender social justice movement—the beginning of a new relationship to state power and social legitimacy. It would not have happened the way that it did without direct action in the streets on the part of transgender women who were fighting for their own survival.

. . .

89

Mutilating Gender

Dean Spade

. . .

This essay examines the relationship between individuals seeking sex reassignment surgery (SRS) and the medical establishments with which they must contend in order to fulfill their goals. . . .

Throughout this essay, I draw on my own experience of attempting to find low-cost or free counseling in order to begin the process of getting a double mastectomy. The choice to use personal narrative in this piece comes from a belief that just such a combination of theoretical work about the relationships of trans people to medical establishments and gender norms and the experience of trans people is too rarely found. Riki Anne Wilchins describes how trans experience has been used by psychiatrists, cultural feminists, anthropologists, and sociologists "travel[ling] through our lives and problems like tourists . . . [p]icnicking on our identities . . . select[ing] the tastiest tidbits with which to illustrate a theory or push a book." In most writing about trans people, our gender performance is put under a microscope to prove theories or build "expertise" while the gender performances of the authors remain unexamined and naturalized. I want to avoid even the appearance of participation in such a tradition, just as I want to use my own experience to illustrate how the requirements for diagnosis and treatment play out on individual bodies. The recent proliferation of academic and activist work on trans issues has created the impression in many people (mostly non-trans) that problems with access to services for trans people are being alleviated, and that the education of many specialists who provide services to trans people has made available sensitive therapeutic environments for trans people living in large metropolitan areas who can avail themselves of such services. My unsuccessful year-long quest for basic low-cost respectful counseling services in Los Angeles, which included seeking services at the Los Angeles Gender Center, the Los Angeles Gay and Lesbian Services Center, and Children's Hospital Los Angeles is a testament to the problems that still remain. This failure suggests the larger problems with the production of the "transsexual" in medical practice, and with the diagnostic and treatment criteria that made it impossible for the professionals from whom I sought care to respectfully engage my request for gender-related body alteration.

I hope that the use of my experience in this paper will provide a grounding illustration of the regulatory effects of the current diagnosis-treatment scheme for GID and resist the traditional framing of transsexual experience which posits trans people as victims or villains, insane or fascinating. Instead, I hope to be part of a project already taken up by Riki Anne Wilchins, Kate Bornstein, Leslie Feinberg, and many others which opens a position for trans people as self-critical, feminist, intellectual subjects of knowledge rather than simply case studies.

I. GOVERNANCE: PASSING AS A TRANSSEXUAL

Here's what I'm after: a surgically constructed male-appearing chest, no hormones (for now—maybe forever), no first-name change, any pronouns (except "it") are okay, although when it comes to gendered generics I happen to really like "Uncle" better than "Aunt," and definitely "Mr. Spade." Hausman writes, "transsexuals must seek and obtain medical treatment in order to be recognized as transsexuals. Their subject position depends upon a necessary relation to the medical establishment and its discourses." I've quickly learned that the converse is also true, in order to obtain the medical intervention I am seeking, I need to prove my membership in the category "transsexual"—prove that I have GID—to the proper authorities. Unfortunately, stating my true objectives is not convincing them.

   . . .

II. THE TRANSSEXUAL CHILDHOOD

"When did you first know you were different?" the counselor at the L.A. Free Clinic asked. "Well," I said, "I knew I was poor and on welfare, and that was different from lots of kids at school, and I had a single mom, which was really uncommon there, and we weren't Christian, which is terribly noticeable in the South. Then later I knew I was a foster child, and in high school, I knew I was a feminist and that caused me all kinds of trouble, so I guess I always knew I was different." His facial expression tells me this isn't what he wanted to hear, but why should I engage this idea that my gender performance has been my most important difference in my life? It hasn't, and I can't separate it from the class, race, and parentage variables through which it was mediated. Does this mean I'm not real enough for surgery?

I've worked hard to not engage the gay childhood narrative—I never talk about tomboy-ish behavior as an antecedent to my lesbian identity, I don't tell stories about cross-dressing or crushes on girls, and I intentionally fuck with the assumption of it by telling people how I used to be straight and have sex with boys like any sweet trashy rural girl and some of it was fun. I see these narratives as strategic, and I've always rejected the strategy that adopts some theory of innate sexuality and forecloses the possibility that anyone, gender-troubled childhood or not, could transgress sexual and gender norms at any time. I don't want to participate in an idea that only some people have to engage a struggle of learning gender norms in childhood either. So now, faced with these questions, how do I decide whether to look back on my life through the tranny childhood lens, tell the stories about being a boy for Halloween, not playing with dolls: What is the cost of participation in this selective recitation? What is the cost of not participating?

Symptoms of GID in the Diagnostic and Statistical Manual (DSM-IV) describe at length the symptom of childhood participation in stereotypically gender inappropriate behavior. Boys with GID "particularly enjoy playing house, drawing pictures of beautiful girls and princesses, and watching television or videos of their favorite female characters. . . . They avoid rough-and-tumble play and competitive sports and have little interest in cars and trucks." Girls with GID do not want to wear dresses, "prefer boys' clothing and short hair," are interested in "contact sports, [and] rough-and-tumble play." Despite the disclaimer in the diagnosis description that this is not to be confused with normal gender non-conformity found in tomboys and sissies, no real line is drawn between "normal" gender non-conformity and gender non-conformity which constitutes GID. The effect is two-fold. First, normative childhood gender is produced—normal kids do the opposite of what kids with GID are doing. Non-GID kids can be expected to: play with children of the own sex, play with gender appropriate toys (trucks for boys, dolls for girls), enjoy fictional characters of their own sex (girls, specifically, might have GID if they like Batman or Superman), play gender appropriate characters in games of "house," etc. Secondly, a regulatory mechanism is put into place. Because gender nonconformity is established as a basis for illness, parents now have a "mill of speech," speculation and diagnosis to feed their children's gender through should it cross the line. As Foucault describes, the invention of a category of deviation, the description of the "ill" behavior that need be resisted or cured, creates not a prohibitive silence about such behavior but an opportunity for increased surveillance and speculation, what he would call "informal-governance."

The Diagnostic Criteria for Gender Identity Disorder names, as a general category of symptom, "[a] strong and persistent cross-gender identification (not merely a desire for any perceived cultural advantages of being the other sex)." This criterion suggests the possibility of a gender categorization not read through the cultural gender hierarchy. This requires an imagination of a child wanting to be a gender different from the one assigned to hir without having that desire stem from a cultural understanding of gender difference defined by the "advantaging" of certain gender behavior and identities over others. To use an illustrative example from the description of childhood GID symptoms, if a child assigned "female" wants to wear pants and hates dresses, and has been told that this is inappropriate for girls, is that decision free from a recognition of cultural advantages associated with gender? Since a diagnosis of GID does not require a child to state the desire to change genders, and the primary indicators are gender inappropriate tastes and behaviors, how can this be separated from cultural understandings of what constitutes gender difference and gender appropriateness? If we start from an understanding that gender behavior is learned, and that children are not born with some innate sense that girls should wear dresses and boys shouldn't like Barbie or anything pink, then how can a desire to transgress an assigned gender category be read outside of cultural meaning? Such a standard does, as Billings and Urban argue, privatize and depoliticize gender role distress. It creates a fictional transsexual who just knows in hir gut what man is and what woman is, and knows that sie is trapped in the wrong body. It produces a naturalized, innate gender difference outside power, a fictional binary that does not privilege one term.

The diagnostic criteria for GID produces a fiction of natural gender, in which normal, non-transsexual people grow up with minimal to no gender trouble or exploration, do not crossdress as children, do not play with the wrong-gendered kids, and do not like the wrong kinds of toys or characters. This story isn't believable, but because medicine produces it not through a description of the norm, but through a generalized account of the transgression, and instructs the doctor/parent/teacher to focus on the transgressive behavior, it establishes a surveillance and regulation effective for keeping both non-transsexuals and transsexuals in adherence to their roles. In order to get authorization for body alteration, this childhood must be produced, and the GID diagnosis accepted, maintaining an idea of two discrete gender categories that normally contain everyone but occasionally are wrongly assigned, requiring correction to reestablish the norm.

It's always been fun to reject the gay childhood story, to tell people I "chose" lesbianism, or to over articulate a straight childhood narrative to suggest that lesbianism could happen to anyone. But not engaging a trans childhood narrative is terrifying—what if it means I'm not "real"? Even though I don't believe in real, it matters if other people see me as real—if not I'm a mutilator, an imitator, and worst of all, I can't access surgery.

Transsexual writer Claudine Griggs' book takes for granted that transsexuality is an illness, an unfortunate predicament, something fortunate, normal people don't have to go through. . . .

This is precisely the approach I want to avoid as I reject the narrative of a gender troubled childhood. My project would be to promote sex reassignment, gender alteration, temporary gender adventure, and the mutilation of gender categories, via surgery, hormones, clothing, political lobbying, civil disobedience, or any other means available. But that political commitment itself, if revealed to the gatekeepers of my surgery, disqualifies me. One therapist said to me, "You're really intellectualizing this, we need to get to the root of why you feel you should get your breasts removed, how long have you felt this way?" Does realness reside in the length of time a desire exists? Are women who seek breast enhancement required to answer these questions? Am I supposed to be able to separate my political convictions about gender, my knowledge of the violence of gender rigidity that has been a part of my life and the lives of everyone I care about, from my real "feelings" about what it means to occupy my gendered body? How could I begin to think about my chest without thinking about cultural advantage?

III. CHOOSING PERSPECTIVE: PASSING "FULL-TIME"

From what I've gathered in my various counseling sessions, in order to be deemed real I need to want to pass as male all the time, and not feel ambivalent about this. I need to be willing to make the commitment to "full-time" maleness, or they can't be sure that I won't regret my surgery. The fact that I don't want to change my first name, that I haven't sought out the use of the pronoun "he," that I don't think that "lesbian" is the wrong word for me, or, worse yet, that I recognize that the use of any word for myself—lesbian, transperson, transgender butch, boy, mister, FTM fag, butch—has always been/will always be strategic is my undoing in their eyes. They are waiting for a better justification of my desire for surgery—something less intellectual, more real.

I'm supposed to be wholly joyous when I get called "sir" or "boy." How could I ever have such an uncomplicated relationship to that moment? Each time I'm sirred I know both that my look is doing what I want it to do, and that the reason people can assign male gender to me easily is because they don't believe women have short hair, and because, as Garber has asserted, the existence of maleness as the generic means that fewer visual clues of maleness are required to achieve male gender attribution. This "therapeutic" process demands of me that I toss out all my feminist misgivings about the ways that gender rigidity informs people's perception of me.

. . .

Perhaps the most overt requirement for transsexual diagnosis is the ability to inhabit and perform "successfully" the new gender category. Through my own interactions with medical professionals, accounts of other trans people, and medical scholarship on transsexuality, I have gathered that the favored indication of such "success" seems to be the gender attribution of non-trans people. Because the ability to be perceived by non-trans people as a non-trans person is valorized, normative expressions of gender within a singular category are mandated.

. . .

IV. MAYBE I'M NOT A TRANSSEXUAL

The counselor at the L.A. Free Clinic decided I wasn't transsexual during the first (and only) session. When I told him what I wanted, and how I was starting counseling because I was trying to get some letter that I could give to a surgeon so that they would alter my chest, he said, "You should just go get breast reduction." Of course, he didn't know that most cosmetic surgeons won't reduce breasts below a C-cup (I wouldn't even qualify for reduction), and that breast reduction is a different procedure than the construction of a male-looking chest. I also suppose that he wasn't thinking about what happens to gender deviants when they end up in the hands of medical professionals who don't have experience with trans people.

> *Some surgeons have strong reactions to transsexual patients, and often, if the surgery is done in a teaching hospital, the surgeon turns out to be a resident or staff member who is offended by the procedure. "In one case, with which I am familiar," writes a doctor, "the patient's massive scars were probably the result of the surgeon's unconscious sadism and wish to scar the patient for 'going against nature.'"*

To this counselor, my failure to conform to the transsexuality he was expecting required my immediate expulsion from that world of meaning at any cost. My desire couldn't be for SRS because I wasn't a transsexual, so it must be for cosmetic surgery, something normal people get.

All my attempts at counseling, and all those experiences of being eyed suspiciously when I suggested that I was trans, or told outright I was not by non-trans counselors, made me expect that I would get a similar reception from trans people in activist or support contexts. This has not been the case. I've found that in trans contexts, a much broader conception of trans experience exists. The trans people I've met have, shockingly, believed what I say about my gender. Some have a self-narrative resembling the medical model of transsexuality, some do not. However, the people I've met share with me what my counselors do not: a commitment to gender self-determination and respect for all expressions of gender. Certainly not all trans people would identify with this principle, but I think it makes better sense as a basis for identity than the ability to pass "full-time" or the amount of cross-dressing one did as a child. Wilchins posits an idea of identity as "an effect of political activism instead of a cause." I see this notion reflected in trans activism, writing, and discussion, despite its absence in the medical institutions through which trans people must negotiate our identities.

Feinberg writes:

> Once I figured out that "transgendered" was someone who transcended traditional stereotypes of "man" and "woman," I saw that I was such a person. I then began a quest for finding words that described myself, and discovered that while psychiatric jargon dominated the discourse, there were many other words, both older and newer, that addressed these issues. While I accepted the label of "transsexual" in order to obtain access to the hormones and chest surgery necessary to manifest my spirit in the material world, I have always had a profound disagreement with the definition of transsexualism as a psychiatric condition and transsexuals as disordered people.

V. TELLING STORIES: STRATEGIC DEPLOYMENT OF THE TRANSSEXUAL NARRATIVE

. . .

After attending only three discussion group meetings with other trans people, I am struck by the naiveté with which I approached the search for counseling to get my surgery-authorizing letters. No one at these groups seems to see therapy as the place where they voice their doubts about their transition, where they wrestle with the political implications of their changes, where they speak about fears of losing membership in various communities or in their families. No one trusts the doctors as the place to work things out. When I mention the places I've gone for help, places that are supposed to support queer and trans people, everyone nods knowingly, having heard countless stories like mine about these very places before. Some have suggestions of therapists who are better, but none cost less than $50/hr. Mostly, though, people suggest different ways to get around the requirements. I get names of surgeons who do not always ask for the letters. Someone suggests that since I won't be on hormones, I can go in and pretend I'm a woman with a history of breast cancer in my family and that I want a double mastectomy to prevent it. I have these great, sad, conversations with these people who know all about what it means to lie and cheat their way through the medical roadblocks to get the opportunity to occupy their bodies in the way they want. I understand, now, that the place that is safe to talk about this is in here, with other people who understand the slipperiness of gender and the politics of transition, and who believe me without question when I say what I think I am and how that needs to look.

. . .

VII. CONCLUSION

Personal narrative is always strategically employed. It is always mediated through cultural understandings, through ideology. It is always a function of selective memory and narration. Have I learned that I should lie to obtain surgery, as others have before me? Does that lesson require an acceptance that cannot successfully advocate on behalf of a different approach to my desire for transformation?

An examination of how medicine governs gender variant bodies through the regulation of body alteration by means of the invention of the illness of transsexuality brings up the question of whether illness is the appropriate interpretive model for gender variance. The benefits of such an understanding for trans people are noteworthy. As long as SRS remains a treatment for an illness, the possibility Medicaid coverage for it remains viable. Similarly, courts examining the question of what qualified a transsexual to have legal membership in the new gender category have relied heavily on the medical model of transsexuality when they have decided favorably for transsexuals. A model premised on a disability- or disease-based understanding of deviant behavior is believed by many to be the best strategy for achieving tolerance by norm-adherent people for those not adhering to norms. Such arguments are present in the realm of illicit drug use and in the quest for biological origins of homosexuality just as they are in the portrayal of transsexuality as an illness or disability.

However, it is vital that the costs of such an approach also be considered. First, the medical approach to gender variance, and the creation of transsexuality, has resulted in a governance of trans bodies that restricts our ability to make gender transitions which do not yield membership in a normative gender role. The self-determination of trans people in crafting our gender expression is compromised by the rigidity of the diagnostic and treatment criteria. At the same time, this criteria and the version of transsexuality that it posits produce and reify a fiction of normal, healthy gender that works as a regulatory measure for the gender expression of all people. To adopt the medical understanding of transsexuality is to agree that SRS is the unfortunate treatment of an unfortunate condition, to accept that gender norm adherence is fortunate and healthy, and to undermine the threat to a dichotomous gender system which trans experience can pose. The reification of the violence of compulsory gender norm adherence, and the submission of trans bodies to a norm-producing medical discipline, is too high a price for a small hope of conditional tolerance.

90

Trans Woman Manifesto

Julia Serano

This manifesto calls for the end of the scapegoating, deriding, and dehumanizing of trans women everywhere. For the purposes of this manifesto, *trans woman* is defined as any person who was assigned a male sex at birth, but who identifies as and/or lives as a woman. No qualifications should be placed on the term "trans woman" based on a person's ability to "pass" as female, her hormone levels, or the state of her genitals—after all, it is downright sexist to reduce any woman (trans or otherwise) down to her mere body parts or to require her to live up to certain societally dictated ideals regarding appearance.

Perhaps no sexual minority is more maligned or misunderstood than trans women. As a group, we have been systematically pathologized by the medical and psychological establishment, sensationalized and ridiculed by the media, marginalized by mainstream lesbian and gay organizations, dismissed by certain segments of the feminist community, and, in too many instances, been made the victims of violence at the hands of men who feel that we somehow threaten their masculinity and heterosexuality. Rather than being given the opportunity to speak for ourselves on the very issues that affect our own lives, trans women are instead treated more like research subjects: Others place us under their microscopes, dissect our lives, and assign motivations and desires to us that validate their own theories and agendas regarding gender and sexuality.

Trans women are so ridiculed and despised because we are uniquely positioned at the intersection of multiple binary gender-based forms of prejudice: transphobia, cissexism, and misogyny.

Transphobia is an irrational fear of, aversion to, or discrimination against people whose gendered identities, appearances, or behaviors deviate from societal norms. In much the same way that homophobic people are often driven by their own repressed homosexual tendencies, transphobia is first and foremost an expression of one's own insecurity about having to live up to cultural gender ideals. The fact that transphobia is so rampant in our society reflects the reality that we place an extraordinary amount of pressure on individuals to conform to all of the expectations, restrictions, assumptions, and privileges associated with the sex they were assigned at birth.

While all transgender people experience transphobia, transsexuals additionally experience a related (albeit distinct) form of prejudice: *cissexism*, which is the belief that transsexuals' identified genders are inferior to, or less authentic than, those of *cissexuals* (i.e., people who are not transsexual and who have only ever experienced their subconscious and physical sexes as being aligned). The most common expression of cissexism occurs when people attempt to deny the transsexual the basic privileges that are associated with the trans person's self-identified gender. Common examples include purposeful misuse of pronouns or insisting that the trans person use a different public restroom. The justification for this denial is generally founded on the assumption that the trans person's gender is not authentic because it does not correlate with the sex they were assigned at birth. In making this assumption, cissexists attempt to create an artificial hierarchy. By insisting that the trans person's gender is "fake," they attempt to validate their own gender as "real" or "natural." This sort of thinking is extraordinarily naive, as it denies a basic truth: We make assumptions every day about other people's genders without ever seeing their birth certificates, their chromosomes, their genitals, their reproductive systems, their childhood socialization, or their legal sex. There is no such thing as a "real" gender—there is only the gender we experience ourselves as and the gender we perceive others to be.

While often different in practice, cissexism, transphobia, and homophobia are all rooted in *oppositional sexism,* which is the belief that female and male are rigid, mutually exclusive categories, each possessing a unique and nonoverlapping set of attributes, aptitudes, abilities, and desires. Oppositional sexists attempt to punish or dismiss those of us who fall outside of gender or sexual norms because our existence threatens the idea that women and men are "opposite" sexes. . . .

In addition to the rigid, mutually exclusive gender categories established by oppositional sexism, the other requirement for maintaining a male-centered gender hierarchy is to enforce *traditional sexism*—the belief that maleness and masculinity are superior to femaleness and femininity. Traditional and oppositional sexism work hand in hand to ensure that those who are masculine have power over those who are feminine, and that only those born male will be seen as authentically masculine. For the purposes of this manifesto, the word *misogyny* will be used to describe this tendency to dismiss and deride femaleness and femininity.

Just as all transgender people experience transphobia and cissexism to differing extents (depending on how often, obvious, or out we are as transgender), we experience misogyny to differing extents too. This is most evident in the fact that, while there are many different types of transgender people, our society tends to single out trans women and others on the male-to-female (MTF) spectrum for attention and ridicule. This is not merely because we transgress binary gender norms per se, but because we, by necessity, embrace our own femaleness and femininity. Indeed, more often than not it is our expressions of femininity and our desire to be female that become sensationalized, sexualized, and trivialized by others. While trans people on the female-to-male (FTM) spectrum face discrimination for breaking gender norms (i.e., oppositional sexism), their expressions of maleness or masculinity themselves are not targeted for ridicule—to do so would require one to question masculinity itself.

When a trans person is ridiculed or dismissed not merely for failing to live up to gender norms, but for their expressions of femaleness or femininity, they become the victims of a specific form of discrimination: *trans-misogyny*. When the majority of jokes made at the expense of trans people center on "men wearing dresses" or "men who want their penises cut off," that is not transphobia—it is trans-misogyny. When the majority of violence and sexual assaults committed against trans people is directed at trans women, that is not transphobia—it is trans-misogyny. When it's okay for women to wear "men's" clothing, but when men who wear "women's" clothing can be diagnosed with the psychological disorder transvestic fetishism, that is not transphobia—it is trans-misogyny? When women's or lesbian organizations and events open their doors to trans men but not trans women, that is not transphobia—it is trans-misogyny.

In a male-centered gender hierarchy, where it is assumed that men are better than women and that masculinity is superior to femininity, there is no greater perceived threat than the existence of trans women, who despite being born male and inheriting male privilege "choose" to be female instead. By embracing our own femaleness and femininity, we, in a sense, cast a shadow of doubt over the supposed supremacy of maleness and masculinity. In order to lessen the threat we pose to the male-centered gender hierarchy, our culture (primarily via the media) uses every tactic in its arsenal of traditional sexism to dismiss us:

1 The media hyperfeminizes us by accompanying stories about trans women with pictures of us putting on makeup, dresses, and high-heeled shoes in an attempt to highlight the supposed "frivolous" nature of our femaleness, or by portraying trans women as having derogatory feminine-associated character traits such as being weak, confused, passive, or mousy.

2 The media hypersexualizes us by creating the impression that most trans women are sex workers or sexual deceivers, and by asserting that we transition for primarily sexual reasons (e.g., to prey on innocent straight men or to fulfill some kind of bizarre sex fantasy). Such depictions not only belittle trans women's motives for transitioning, but implicitly suggest that women as a whole have no worth beyond their ability to be sexualized.

3 The media objectifies our bodies by sensationalizing sex reassignment surgery and openly discussing our "man-made vaginas" without any of the discretion that normally accompanies discussions about genitals. Further, those of us who have not had surgery are constantly being reduced to our body parts, whether by the creators of tranny porn who overemphasize and exaggerate our penises (thus distorting trans women into "she-males" and "chicks with dicks") or by other people who have been so brainwashed by phallocentrism that they believe that the mere presence of a penis can trump the femaleness of our identities, our personalities, and the rest of our bodies.

Because anti-trans discrimination is steeped in traditional sexism, it is not simply enough for trans activists to challenge binary gender norms (i.e., oppositional sexism)—we must also challenge the idea that femininity is inferior to masculinity and that femaleness is inferior to maleness. In other words, by necessity, trans activism must be at its core a feminist movement.

. . .

It is no longer enough for feminism to fight solely for the rights of those born female. That strategy has furthered the prospects of many women over the years, but now it bumps up against a glass ceiling that is partly of its own making. Though the movement worked hard to encourage women to enter previously male-dominated areas of life, many feminists have been ambivalent at best, and resistant at worst, to the idea of men expressing or exhibiting feminine traits and moving into certain traditionally female realms. And while we credit previous feminist movements for helping to create a society where most sensible people would agree with the statement "women and men are equals," we lament the fact that we remain light-years away from being able to say that most people believe that femininity is masculinity's equal.

. . .

But it is not enough for us to empower femaleness and femininity. We must also stop pretending that there are essential differences between women and men. This begins with the acknowledgment that there are exceptions to every gender rule and stereotype, and this simply stated fact disproves all gender theories that purport that female and male are mutually exclusive categories. We must move away from pretending that women and men are "opposite" sexes, because when we buy into that myth it establishes a dangerous precedent. For if men are big, then women must be small; and if men are strong then women must be weak. And if being butch is to make yourself rock-solid, then being femme becomes allowing yourself to be malleable; and if being a man means taking control of your own situation, then being a woman becomes living up to other people's expectations. When we buy into the idea that female and male are "opposites," it becomes impossible for us to empower women without either ridiculing men or pulling the rug out from under ourselves.

It is only when we move away from the idea that there are "opposite" sexes, and let go of the culturally derived values that are assigned to expressions of femininity and masculinity, that we may finally approach gender equity. By challenging both oppositional and traditional sexism simultaneously, we can make the world safe for those of us who are queer, those of us who are feminine, and those of us who are female, thus empowering people of all sexualities and genders.

91

The Evolution of Employment Discrimination Protections for Transgender People

Kylar W. Broadus

Employment discrimination is a pressing issue for transgender people. In a recent survey, the Transgender Law Center found that nearly one of every two respondents had experienced gender identity discrimination on the job. A 1999 study by the San Francisco Department of Public Health reached a similar result, finding that 46 percent of transgender people reported workplace discrimination. The circumstances under which transgender people encounter discrimination at work are varied. Many transgender people are fired when they transition on the job. A transgender candidate may not be hired because the gender reflected in the person's documents or work history may differ from the person's current gender. A transgender employee may be terminated if an employer or coworker becomes aware of the person's transgender status. Finally, many transgender people have lost jobs because of prejudice and irrational fears about bathroom access. Just as was true for many other marginalized groups in the past, some employers and coworkers do not wish to share a bathroom with a transgender person.

While workplace discrimination against transgender people is common, transgender people increasingly are receiving support and assistance during their on-job transition. . . . [A]ccording to the Human Rights Campaign, more than two hundred employers have adopted nondiscrimination policies that protect transgender workers. Documenting these success stories is important, both as a source of hope for other transgender people and as evidence that, with a little support and guidance, employers can behave in a non-discriminatory manner toward their transgender employees. Nonetheless, the brutal reality is that many transgender people still will face unemployment or severe underemployment solely because they are transgender. . . .

As an African American FTM (female-to-male transsexual) who lost my career after transitioning on the job at a private company in Missouri, I have experienced this reality firsthand. Like many other transsexual people, I repressed my transgender identity and struggled to live in my birth sex for many years. For me, that meant trying to live as a masculine-appearing black woman. Despite the challenges I faced in that identity, I was able to build a successful career as a claims adjustor for State Farm Insurance, where I worked for eight years, from 1989 to 1997. During that time, I was promoted on several occasions and eventually worked as a claims specialist—not a glamorous job, but one that I enjoyed and at which I excelled.

In 1995, at the age of thirty-two, I came out to my employer as transsexual. As part of my medically supervised transition, I began to dress and live as a man, including at my job. From that point forward, I faced a constant barrage of criticism about my appearance, dress, demeanor, and performance. While my superiors could tolerate a somewhat masculine-appearing black woman, they were not prepared to deal with my transition to being a black man. With growing despair, I watched my professional connections, support, and goodwill evaporate, along with my prospects for remaining employed. Before fully accepting that reality, however, I tried everything possible to save the career I had worked so many years to build, including filing a lawsuit alleging sex discrimination against State Farm in federal court. Like the vast majority of other transsexual plaintiffs in that era, I lost.

Had I brought my case today, it is possible, though far from certain, that the outcome would have been different. In the past few years, transgender plaintiffs have been successful in sex discrimination cases in a growing number of jurisdictions and courts. The following is an overview of how the legal landscape for transgender plaintiffs alleging workplace sex discrimination has begun to change.

The first reported cases in which transsexual plaintiffs sought protection under sex discrimination statutes date to 1975. In that year, two different federal district courts in California and New Jersey held that Title VII, a federal law prohibiting sex discrimination in employment, does not protect transsexual employees. In *Voyles v. Ralph K. Davies Medical Center*, a hemodialysis technician was fired shortly after she informed her supervisor that she was transsexual and intended to undergo sex reassignment from male to female. The employee filed a lawsuit under Title VII, alleging that the hospital had discriminated against her on the basis of sex. The court dismissed her case, holding that

Congress had enacted Title VII to protect women, not transsexuals, and that nothing in the legislative history of Title VII indicated any congressional intent "to embrace 'transsexual' discrimination, or any permutation or combination thereof."

Similarly, in *Grossman v. Bernards Township Bd. of Educ.*, a teacher who was fired after she underwent sex reassignment surgery filed a lawsuit alleging that the school had violated Title VII. Like the court in *Voyles*, the court dismissed her case, concluding that she was fired "not because of her status as a female, but rather because of her change in sex from the male to the female gender." Also as in *Voyles*, the court noted "the absence of any legislative history indicating a congressional intent to include transsexuals within the language of Title VII," concluding that the term "sex" must be given "its plain meaning."

In the decades following *Voyles* and *Grossman*, most courts adopted the reasoning in those early decisions. With few exceptions, courts dismissed claims by transgender people on the grounds that (1) sex discrimination laws were not intended to protect transgender people; and (2) the "plain" or "traditional" meaning of the term *sex* refers only to a person's biological identity as male or female, not to change of sex. . . .

Over time, however, these two rationales have become increasingly anachronistic and difficult to reconcile with the increasingly expansive interpretation of sex discrimination laws in cases involving nontransgender plaintiffs. In 1989, for example, the U.S. Supreme Court [in *Price Waterhouse v. Hopkins*] expressly rejected the notion that the term *sex* in Title VII refers only to a person's biological status as male or female, holding that it also includes stereotypical assumptions and preconceptions about how men and women are supposed to behave, dress, and appear. Ann Hopkins, the plaintiff in the case, was denied a partnership in an accounting firm, in part because her demeanor, appearance, and personality were deemed insufficiently "feminine." To improve her chances for partnership, Hopkins was told that she should "walk more femininely, talk more femininely, dress more femininely, wear make-up, have her hair styled, and wear jewelry." The Supreme Court rejected the employer's argument that Title VII should be applied to prohibit only discrimination against women for being women or against men for being men, as opposed to prohibiting employers from enforcing stereotypical assumptions based on gender. "As for the legal relevance of sex stereotyping, we are beyond the day when an employer could evaluate employees by assuming or insisting that they matched the stereotype associated with their group, for '[i]n forbidding employers to discriminate against individuals because of their sex, Congress intended to strike at the entire spectrum of disparate treatment of men and women resulting from sex stereotypes.'"

After *Price Waterhouse*, courts increasingly have been hard-pressed to explain why the reasoning in that decision would not apply equally to a transgender person. Logically, if Title VII prohibits an employer from discriminating against an employee because of her allegedly "unfeminine" personality or appearance, then must it not also prohibit an employer from discriminating against a transsexual person, either for retaining some characteristics of his or her birth sex or for assuming a masculine or feminine identity? In either case, the employer has discriminated on the basis of sex by "assuming or insisting that employees match the stereotypes associated with their group." . . .

Most recently, in a case decided in 2004, the Sixth Circuit held that Title VII protected a transsexual police officer who was fired for being insufficiently "masculine," after more than twenty years of service on the force. In the past, as described above, most courts dismissed such claims out-of-hand, despite the precedent of *Price Waterhouse*, based on the notion that simply by definition, a transgender person is not entitled to protection. In *Smith*, the court rejected this categorical exclusion of transgender people as unprincipled, holding: "Sex stereotyping based on a person's gender non-conforming behavior is impermissible discrimination, irrespective of the cause of that behavior; a label, such as 'transsexual,' is not fatal to a sex discrimination claim where the victim has suffered discrimination because of his or her gender non-conformity."

In addition to these groundbreaking federal precedents, state courts also have become more receptive to sex discrimination claims brought by transgender plaintiffs under state sex discrimination laws. In New Jersey, for example, an appellate court held that transgender people are protected under a New Jersey law prohibiting sex discrimination in employment. . . . Holding that "sex" is "broader than anatomical sex" and "comprises more than a person's genitalia at birth," the court concluded that the New Jersey statute protected the plaintiff "from gender stereotyping and discrimination for transforming herself from a man to a woman."

Similarly, in 2000 the Connecticut Human Rights Commission held that transsexual people are protected under a Connecticut law prohibiting sex discrimination in employment. . . . Other states with positive administrative or court decisions on this issue include Massachusetts and New York. The European Court of Justice and courts in other countries also have reached similar results.

These recent positive decisions may be the harbinger of a new trend. As we enter the twenty-first century, it is possible that federal and state courts generally will be more receptive to transgender plaintiffs and more willing to construe sex discrimination statutes to include them. From a purely legal perspective, it is perhaps too soon to tell, and we would do well to remember that a single negative U.S. Supreme Court decision on this issue could bring these recent positive developments to a screeching halt, at least in the federal courts. From a broader perspective, however, there can be no doubt that this judicial shift is an indicator of a much broader and more important change than any mere evolution in legal doctrine. . . . Rather than seeing transgender people as lurid oddities, both the public and the courts have begun to view transgender people as a legitimate minority and to see us as human beings who are entitled to equal dignity and equal protection under the law.

As a former litigant in a transgender discrimination case, I am keenly aware of the law's tremendous power to reflect and shape larger societal messages of acceptance or rejection. When I lost my case, I was devastated not only by the loss of my job and my career but, even more profoundly, by the terrible message that loss conveyed—that as a transgender person, I was not worthy of legal protection or recognition. . . .

Rights both empower transgender people to contest discrimination and allow us to envision ourselves, and to be seen by others, as fully human. As lawyers and litigants continue to struggle to win individual cases and to set precedents that will benefit the community as a whole, we must not lose sight of this fundamental dimension of legal advocacy.

92

Passing Realities

Allie Lie

CAMBRIDGE—SUMMER 1998

We leave the café on Massachusetts Avenue, my young sons, "J" and "A," and I. It's seasonably hot and humid. I wear flip-flops, khaki shorts, a sleeveless T-shirt, and a wide-brimmed straw hat. I am not "presenting." I've promised the boys I won't embarrass them. (Children are defenseless against attacks aimed at nonconformity. Adults—their mother, for instance—just have to deal with it.)

As we cross Mass Ave., we come to a small park-cum-island in the middle of the intersection. Two men sit on one of the benches, and their small dog, tethered to a red nylon leash, sits beneath the bench. A, my oldest, who has a fondness for animals that way surpasses any he'd have for humans, goes up and asks if he can pet the dog. J and I have walked past them and are on the other side of the park. I hear the man saying, "Sure"—I see him nod in my direction—"but you'd better ask your mother first."

After work she stops at a grocery store a block from her apartment. She has been here many times, both *en femme* and not. Today, as with every working day, she is *en femme*. She goes to the freezer section, pulls out a frozen yogurt and takes it up to the checkout counter. The middle-aged man behind the counter is not particularly friendly. No one who works at the store is. Once she pays for the yogurt, she asks the checkout man where she can find a plastic spoon. He gestures over his shoulder with a thumb, "Over there . . . pal."

She finds the spoons, then walks over to one of the luncheon tables in the front of the store and sits. She begins slowly eating the yogurt, carving out small, hard-frozen spoonfuls from the top layer, working around the edges first. She holds the spoon upside down, puts it in her mouth, and sucks on it meditatively. As she does this, she overhears the sotto voce reprimand of the store manager behind her. Words like harassment, trouble, careful . . .

I am with the boys again, this time buying ice cream. The line at the counter has unwound itself into an amorphous crowd. No one seems to know who's next or who's helping whom. Someone has been summoned from the back of the store. A man appears and begins scanning the crowd. Our eyes meet. "Ma'am, what would you like?" J and A and I squeeze up to the counter. J takes my hand. "Dad, he called you . . ." "Shush, I know."

I order two vanilla cones for J and myself. As usual, A takes more time deciding. J gets his cone, then I get mine. The cashier motions to A (who wears his hair long because he's terrified of change and, despite his adolescent male misogyny, appears enviably androgynous). "What kind of cone would she like?" A looks at the floor.

"He'll have a sugar cone, please."

At a different grocery store . . .
"I'd like to write a check. How much over the amount can I write it for?"
Shrug. "Do you have a card?" "Yes."
Shrug again. "Fifty . . .?"

She writes the check and hands it to the cashier. The cash register jams—seems not to like what it's been told. The cashier looks at her apologetically, then summons help. A manager appears.

"Her total came to——." "And she wrote a check?" "Yes. But he wrote it for $30 over the amount." "Does he have a card?" "Yes, she does." "Well, she can only write it for 25 over the amount . . ." "That's no problem," she says. "I'll just write another check."

The cashier is again apologetic. "Do you mind?" "No," she says. "Not at all."

I am in the men's room of a restaurant. I have just washed my hands and looked in the mirror. This mirror is particularly unforgiving—thus I trust it. I am seldom happy with what I see. Reflective surfaces are to be avoided at all costs. The disparity between what I want to see and what actually greets me is too great. What I want to see: someone who could be Michelle Pfeiffer's female second cousin. What I see: longish, thinning hair; age lines (a.k.a. nasal labial folds); the faint, plucked remnants of beard; the wrong cheeks; the wrong lips. At times like this I think the course my life has taken is evidence of a delusional personality. I'm reminded of Nabokov's *Despair*, the story of a man who imagines that a stranger who looks not even remotely like him is his virtual twin.

This is why I am surprised when I turn to leave the restroom and see another man entering, noticing me, halting, then looking back to double-check the sign on the door.

CAMBRIDGE—LATE FALL 1998

She leaves the elevator at the sixth floor and heads for the door marked "The Ass. of Tedium, Drudgery, and Objectified Labor." She is here for a job interview—a job she already knows she doesn't want, but after three months of uncompensated unemployment, a job that she needs like nobody's business. She is dressed in her only polyester power suit, in burgundy with matching jacket and skirt. She opens the door and walks to the receptionist's desk. "I'm here to see Mrs. Z." "Take a seat, she'll be right with you."

She's had to pee for the last half hour. "Excuse me, may I please use the restroom first?"

The receptionist takes a key from her desk drawer and hands it to her. "Down at the end of the hall." She thanks the receptionist, exits the office and hurries to the room marked "W." She tries the lock. The door doesn't budge. She tries again. Still no success. The key ring is attached to a plastic badge. She turns the badge over and reads the words written in black indelible marking pen: "Men's Room."

CAMBRIDGE—WINTER 1998–99

E and I have been separated for more than six months now. We'd been through couples counseling eight months before the separation. Eight months slogging through the muck of my midlife journey back and forth across the gender boundaries; eight months of soul searching (for both of us); dredging up all our fears, our needs; establishing who we are and what we are about. I volunteered everything I knew about myself and about the *condition* mental health practitioners choose to call *gender identity disorder*. I offered texts, testimonials, contacts for spouse and significant other support groups. She heard, but chose not to listen. The work failed. It was finally determined that (1) I couldn't live unless I established permanent residence in the land of the feminine, and (2) she couldn't live with me if I did.

Shortly after our separation, I transitioned to three-quarter time living as Allie. Very shortly after that I was fired from my job. I assured E that I'd continue to support her and the boys in any way I could; I borrowed money from my family and engaged in exhausting legal battles for unemployment benefits and for financial damages as the result of my unlawful firing. Through all this I remained committed to my newly found state of mental health, determined that I could face anything as Allie. I was also amply aware of the irony that, as hormones inexorably reduced Robert's potency, shrinking his gonads to the size of unripe May apples, Allie had more *balls* than Robert ever did.

Soon there were many people who knew me only as Allie, people who had never seen the vestiges of my past. The boys were introduced to her: J actually liked her; A would take some time. E, whenever we met, appeared as if she'd seen a ghost.

So now E and I are standing in her kitchen (formerly known as "ours"). We are discussing logistics: She will be going through a routine exam at a local hospital—nothing serious, but it will leave her groggy and in need of transportation home. Would I mind picking her up from the hospital? No, of course not. I want to do anything to help. Good. E wants to say something else . . . What . . . ? When you pick me up . . . ? Yes . . . ? Will you be wearing women's clothes?

The snow leaves only a small path on the sidewalk. I am heading back to my apartment after visiting the boys. I'm wearing clogs and a big wool hat but still not technically "presenting." I'm right behind a family of out-of-town parents and their college-age kids. The father is holding up the rear of the caravan. He senses me walking up behind him. The caravan is moving slowly, a herd of contented cows. The father turns to look at me, smiles, then moves to the side of the walkway. He yells to the others in front of him, "Wait, let this woman pass."

WESTERN PENNSYLVANIA—CIRCA WINTER 1961:
ONE PASSING RETROGRADE FANTASY

"My daughter would like to play basketball."
"Sorry, the team isn't coed."
"Excuse me?"
"No girls. Only boys."
"My daughter is a boy."
   A look of confusion . . .
   "Go ahead, dear, show the man your penis."
   "Well, ah . . . yes . . . But he can't play looking the way he does."
   "How do you mean?"
   "His hair. The pigtails. He can't play like that."
   "Why not?"
   "It'll affect his playing."
   "Go ahead, dear, show the man . . ."
She dribbles the basketball a few times, then shoots from mid court. The ball whooshes through the net.
   "That's fine . . . but . . . she still looks like a girl."
   "Well, naturally . . . . He *is* a girl."

93

Look! No, Don't! The Invisibility Dilemma for Transsexual Men

Jamison Green

. . .

Walking down the street in San Francisco or New York City, Boston, Atlanta, Portland, Seattle, London, Paris, Rome, no one seems to take any special interest in me. I am just another man, invisible, no one special. I remember what it was first like to feel that anonymity as testosterone gradually obliterated the androgyny that for most of my life made others uncomfortable in my presence. It was a great relief . . .

Now . . . people are quite comfortable with my male presentation. My psyche seems to fit nicely into male packaging: I feel better; people around me are less confused, and so am I. So why tell anyone about my past? Why not just live the life of a normal man? Perhaps I could if I were a normal man, but I am not. I am a man, and I am a man who lived for 40 years in a female body. But I was not a woman. I am not a woman who became a man. I am not a woman who lives as a man. I am not, nor was I ever a woman, though I lived in a female body, and certainly tried, whenever I felt up to it, to be a woman. But it was never in me to be a woman. Likewise, I am not a man in the same sense as my younger brother is a man, having been treated as such all his life. I was treated as other than a man most of the time, as a man part of the time, and as a woman only rarely. Certainly I was treated as a little girl when I was young, but even then people occasionally assumed I was a little boy. I always felt like something "other." Can I be just a man now, or must I always be "other"?

. . .

Seeking acceptance within the system of "normal" and denying our transsexual status is an acquiescence to the prevailing binary gender paradigm that will never let us fit in, and will never accept us as equal members of society. Our transsexual status will always be used to threaten and shame us. We will always wear a scarlet T that marks us for treatment as a pretender, as other, as not normal, as trans. But wearing that T proudly—owning the label and carrying it with dignity—can twist that paradigm and free us from our subordinate prison. By using our own bodies and experience as references for our standards, rather than the bodies and experience of non-transsexuals (and non-transgendered people), we can grant our own legitimacy, as have all other groups that have been oppressed because of personal characteristics.

Transgendered people who choose transsexual treatment, who allow themselves to be medicalized, depend on a system of approval that grants them access to treatment. That approval may be seen as relieving them of their responsibility—or guilt—for being outside the norm. They then become either the justification for the treatment by embodying the successful application of "normal" standards; or they become the victims of the treatment when they realize they are still very different in form and substance from non-transsexual people, and they still suffer from the oppression they wished to escape by looking to doctors to make them "normal." By standing up and claiming our identity as men (or women) who are also transpeople, by asserting that our different bodies are just as normal for us as anyone else's is for them, by insisting that our right to modify our bodies and shape our own identities is as inalienable as our right to choose our religion (though not nearly as inexpensive or painless), we claim our humanity and our right to be treated equally under law and within the purviews of morality and culture.

. . .

Look! No, don't! Transsexual men are men. Transsexual men are men who have lived in female bodies. Transsexual men may appear feminine, androgynous or masculine. Any man may appear feminine, androgynous, or masculine. Look! What makes a man a man? His penis? His beard? His receding hairline? His lack of breasts? His sense of himself as a man? Some men have no beard, some have no penis, some never lose their hair, some have breasts. All have a sense of themselves as men.

. . . Look! No, don't! What is true, what is false? What is a "real" man?

I am real; I am an authentic and reliable man. I am also a transsexual man. I am a man who lived for 40 years in the body of a woman, so I have had access to knowledge that most men do not have. Invisibility has been a major issue in my life. Throughout my childhood and young adulthood I—my identity—was, for the most part, invisible. I was always defined by others, categorized either by my lack of femininity, or by my female body, or by the disquieting combination of both. The opportunity to escape the punishing inadequacy imposed on me by self-styled adjudicators of sex role performance was one I could not ignore. I simply will not accept a similar judgement of my masculinity. And I have yet to meet someone who could look me in the face, who could spend any time at all in conversation with me, who would deny my masculinity now the way they would dismiss it before as "just a phase" or "inappropriate behaviour for a girl."

. . . One of the most difficult things for me to reconcile about my own transition was my movement out of a place in lesbian culture and into a white heterosexual embodiment. Let me emphasize: Not all transsexual men have lesbian histories, and not all transsexual men are heterosexual. Nonetheless, my personal politics are quite closely aligned with queer culture, so I am again a different sort of heterosexual man. I am not afraid of homosexuality, though I do not practice it. Many gendered and heterosexist social constructs collapse like cardboard sea-walls against the ocean of my transsexual reality.

. . .

Look! No, don't! It all comes down to attitude. If you accept me—if you can acknowledge that I am a man, even a transsexual man—then you can accept that life has variation, life is rich, you don't control it, you experience it. You can still analyse concepts, you can still have opinions, you can even disagree with me. And if you don't accept me, well, then you don't. But as you go through life categorizing and qualifying, judging and evaluating, remember that there are human beings on the other end of the stick you're shaking, and they might have ideas and feelings and experiences that are different from your own. Maybe they look different from you, maybe they are tall women with large hands, maybe they are men who have given birth to their own children, maybe the categories you've delineated won't work in all cases. Look! No, don't! Transsexual men want to disappear because we are tired of being forced into categories, because we are beyond defending ourselves.

Look! No, don't! Transsexual men are entering the dialogue from more perspectives, more angles, than were ever theorized as being possible for them. Maybe if we are ignored we will go away. Maybe if we are continually not permitted to speak, not allowed to define ourselves, not given any corner of the platform from which to present our realities, then we will disappear and refrain from further complicating all the neat, orderly theories about gender and sex. Maybe if no one looks at us we will be safe.

At first I thought my transition was about not being looked at any longer, about my relief from scrutiny; now I know it is about scrutiny itself, about self-examination, and about losing my own fear of being looked at, not because I can disappear, but because I am able to claim my unique difference at last. What good is safety if the price is shame and fear of discovery? So, go ahead: Look!

94

An Entire Rainbow of Possibilities

Gary Bowen

I'm a gay transman of Apache and Scotch-Irish descent, left-handed, differently abled, the parent of two young children—one of whom is also differently abled—of an old Cracker frontier family from Texas, a person who values his Native heritage very deeply, and who is doing his best to live in accordance with the Spirit, and who keeps learning more about his heritage all the time. . . . I am also a gay author and editor, with several books in print, as well as numerous short stories.

Arriving at this current place has been a journey not only of self-discovery, but of discovery about my family and my culture. Coming out transgendered was easy; grappling with racism, classism and ableism and other barriers is much harder. Once I figured out that "transgendered" was someone who transcended traditional stereotypes of "man" and "woman," I saw that I was such a person. I then began a quest for finding words that described myself, and discovered that while psychiatric jargon dominated the discourse, there were many other words, both older and newer, that addressed these issues. While I accepted the label of "transsexual" in order to obtain access to the hormones and chest surgery necessary to manifest my spirit in the material world, I have always had a profound disagreement with the definition of transsexualism as a psychiatric condition and transsexuals as disordered people.

My own transgendered state is a sacred calling given to me by Spirit, not a neurosis discovered by white medicine. Further, the battles that rage in feminist circles and elsewhere about the legitimacy and nature of the transgendered identity smack of racism to me, centered as they are upon white experience and white authors to the exclusion of minority voices and viewpoints, many of which contradict some of the conventional wisdom about what transsexualism is and what it means. It is extremely important to remember that "transsexual" and "transgendered" are terms that have arisen out of the dominant culture's experience with gender, and are not necessarily reflective of a wide variety of people, cultures, beliefs, and practices relating to gender.

As a person of Native descent I look to my ancestors for guidance in these matters. But the record is broken; trying to learn about the sacred people is like trying to reassemble a million pieces of pottery with only a few hundred potshards as clues. This then is the thing I know: that Spirit gives to each of us Visions of who we are which we must manifest in the material world to the best of our ability. Transgendered people, combining elements of male and female, are at the interstice of the material and spiritual worlds and are thus able to act as mediators for the benefit of our communities. We earn honor for our wisdom and strength, measured by our hard work on behalf of our families and communities. For this reason the sacred people are an integral part of our communities, not alienated or shameful, but often hidden to protect them from the ravages of the dominant culture. And, where white culture has triumphed, they have been almost entirely lost to the contemporary Native world—which means that there are many Native people today who do not know about or who do not value our sacred people.

It is important for Native people to reclaim our sacred people who have been murdered, burned, beaten, hanged, imprisoned, flogged, stripped, humiliated, and otherwise forced into compliance with the dominant standards of gender and sexuality or exterminated when they resisted. It is common for white people to refer to these people as "berdache"

V
O
I
C
E
S

if they have male genitalia, and as "amazons" if they have female genitalia, but these terms are offensive, being foreign terms that depend upon white standards of reference and which ignore Native traditions. I prefer to use the Sioux word "winkte" for those people who are described in English as "m2f" (male to female) and "kurami" (from the Yuma kwe'rhame) for people who are "f2m" (female to male). However, while these Native terms overlap in meaning with terminology used by the dominant society, they are not identical because Native concepts of gender and identity differ in significant ways from the dominant culture.

I don't use the term "two-spirit" to describe myself; where I grew up it was a pejorative term for a person of mixed blood. Further, there is no consensus of opinion as to just who is meant by the term "two-spirit," and not only that, if translated into Native tongues it acquires unfortunate meanings; among my people it means "ghost-haunted"—a powerful concept and important in many Native spiritual systems, but having nothing to do with gender or orientation.

In my understanding of Spirit, Spirit is not divided in itself, but is an integrated whole. It is not a thing in balance, as implied by dichotomies of male/female, gay/straight, and black/white so prevalent in the white way of thinking; but a complete and complex thing which includes an entire rainbow of possibilities—not just the opposite ends of a spectrum. That is why there are seven cardinal directions: east, west, north, south, up, down, and center, as the Native viewpoint embraces dimensions not normally noticed by the dominant culture; so too does Spirit embrace dimensions of humanity not normally accepted by the dominant culture. There are many names for sexual minorities among Native Americans; two-spirits are a particular community that have elected that term to describe themselves, but I am not one of them.

There are many "magpies" who are drawn to latch onto the bright, shiny aspects of Native culture, who misappropriate Native culture, customs, and artifacts in the belief that they are "honoring" Native people by imitating them without understanding them. It is better for non-Native people to follow our example by looking to their own ancestors and reclaiming their own transgendered spirituality. European cultures from the Vikings to the Greeks had and honored transgendered people; even the Christian Church recognized saints that lived as members of the opposite sex or engaged in same sex unions. No European culture lacks a transgendered tradition; white people need to reclaim their own sacred people instead of appropriating ours.

The process of reclamation is an extraordinarily difficult one in which the seeker must come face to face with the atrocities of the past, grieve for what has been lost, and carefully sift through the destruction to recover the little that remains. This is true whether the seeker is examining Native American or Euro-American history. History is not ancient and irrelevant; history is the reason why things are the way they are now.

95

Calling All Restroom Revolutionaries!

*Simone Chess, Alison Kafer, Jessi Quizar,
and Mattie Udora Richardson*

Everyone needs to use bathrooms, but only some of us have to enter into complicated political and architectural negotiations in order to use them. The fact is, bathrooms are easier to access for some of us than for others, and the people who never think about where and how they can pee have a lot of control over how using restrooms feels for the rest of us. What do we need from bathrooms? What elements are necessary to make a bathroom functional for everyone? To make it safe? To make it a private and respectful space? Whose bodies are excluded from the typical restroom? More important, what kind of bodies are assumed in the design of these bathrooms? Who has the privilege (we call it pee-privilege) of never needing to think about these issues, of always knowing that any given bathroom will meet one's needs? Everyone needs to use the bathroom. But not all of us can.

And that's where People in Search of Safe and Accessible Restrooms (PISSAR) comes in. PISSAR, a coalition of UC-Santa Barbara undergrads, grad students, staff, and community members, recognizes that bathrooms are not always accessible for people with disabilities, or safe for people who transgress gender norms. PISSAR was formed at the 2003 University of California Student of Color Conference, held at UC-Santa Barbara. During the lunch break on the second day of the conference, meetings for the disability caucus and the transgender caucus were scheduled in adjacent rooms. When only a few people showed up for both meetings, we decided to hold a joint session. One of the members of the disability caucus mentioned plans to assess bathroom accessibility on the campus, wondering if there was a similar interest in mapping gender-neutral bathrooms. Everyone in the room suddenly began talking about the possibilities of a genderqueer/disability coalition, and PISSAR was born.

For those of us whose appearance or identity does not quite match the "man" or "woman" signs on the door, bathrooms can be the sites of violence and harassment, making it very difficult for us to use them safely or comfortably. Similarly, PISSAR acknowledges that, although most buildings are required by the Americans with Disabilities Act to provide accessible bathrooms, some restrooms are more compliant than others and accessible bathrooms can often be hard to find. PISSAR's mission, then, is threefold: 1) to raise awareness about what safe and accessible bathrooms are and why they are necessary; 2) to map and verify existing accessible and/or gender-neutral bathrooms on the campus; and 3) to advocate for additional bathrooms. We eventually hope to have both web-based and printed maps of all the bathrooms on campus, with each facility coded as to its accessibility and gender-safety. Beyond this initial campaign, PISSAR plans to advocate for the construction or conversion of additional safe and accessible bathrooms on campus. To that end, one of our long-term goals is to push for more gender-neutral bathrooms and showers in the dormitories, and to investigate the feasibility of multistall gender-neutral bathrooms across the campus as a whole.

As it turned out, we weren't the only restroom revolutionaries on campus. We soon joined forces with a student-run initiative to stock all campus tampon and pad machines, a group called, appropriately enough, Aunt Flo and the Plug Patrol. Aunt Flo's goal is to use funds garnered from the sale of tampons and pads in campus bathroom dispensers (blood

N
E
X
T

S
T
E
P
S

money, if you will) to support student organizations in a time of tremendous budget cuts. We liked their no-euphemism approach to the bathroom and the body and joined their effort to make the campus not only a safer and more accessible place to pee but also to bleed. We also expanded our focus to include issues of childcare, inspired in part by one of our members' experiences as a young mom on campus. PISSAR decided to examine whether campus bathrooms featured changing tables, a move that increased our intersectional analysis of bathroom access and politics.

By specifically including the work of Aunt Flo and concerns about childcare access, PISSAR challenges many of the assumptions that are made about genderqueer and disabled bodies. Why shouldn't every gender-neutral restroom have a tampon/pad machine? Putting tampon/pad machines only in women's rooms, and mounting them high on the wall, restricts the right to menstruate conveniently to those with certain bodies. It suggests that the right to tampons and pads is reserved for people who use gender-specific women's rooms and can reach a lever hanging five feet from the ground. This practice reinscribes ideas about disabled bodies being somehow dysfunctional and asexual (as in, "People in wheelchairs get their periods too?") and perpetuates the idea that genderqueer folks are inherently unbodied (as in, "Only real women need tampons, and you don't look like a real woman").

. . .

From the information garnered in the PISSAR patrols, we are in the process of making a map that will assess the safety and accessibility of all the bathrooms on campus. The map is vital to our project because it offers genderqueer and disabled people a survey of all the restrooms on campus so that they can find what they need without the stigma and frustration of telling a possibly uninformed administrator the details of their peeing needs. For people who have never had to think about bathrooms, the map's detailed information suggests the ways in which our everyday bathrooms are restrictive and dangerous. Thus the map also functions as a consciousness-raising tool, educating users about the need for safe and accessible restrooms.

PISSAR patrols aren't simply about getting information. They're also a way to keep our bodies involved in our project. PISSAR is, after all, a project about bodies: about bodily needs, about the size and shape of our bodies, and about our bodily presentation. The very nature of our bathroom needs necessitates this attention to the body. So it makes sense that when we tried to theorize about what a safe, respectful restroom might look like, we realized we needed to meet in the bathroom. Because the bathroom is our site, and the body in search of a bathroom is our motivation, we recognized early on the need to be concerned with body and theory together. PISSAR's work is an attempt at embodying theory, at theorizing from the body.

. . .

Our concern with body/theory is also evident in our insistence that bathroom accessibility is an important issue for a lot of different people. Everyone should be able to find a bathroom that conforms to the needs of their body. Everyone should be able to use a restroom without being accused of being in the "wrong" place. Everyone should have access to tampon dispensers and facilities for changing diapers, regardless of gender or ability. Homeless folks should have access to clean restrooms free of harassment. Bathroom activism is, from the outset, a multi-identity endeavor. It has the potential to bring together feminists, transfolks, people with disabilities, single parents, and a variety of other people whose bathroom needs frequently go unmet. It creates a much needed space for those of us whose identities are more complicated than can be encompassed in a single-issue movement. Viewed in this light, restroom activism is an ideal platform from which to launch broader coalition work. In PISSAR, we tend to think about "queerness" as encompassing more than just sexual orientation; it includes queer bodies, queer politics, and queer coalitions.

ABLEISM

Introduction

Carmelita (Rosie) Castañeda, Larissa E. Hopkins, and Madeline L. Peters[1]

WHAT IS A DISABILITY?

The Americans with Disabilities Act (ADA) (U.S. Dept. of Justice 1999) considers a person disabled if she or he has a significant impairment that interferes with a major life function, such as walking, seeing, hearing, learning, speaking, breathing, care of one's self, sitting, standing, or lifting. The ADA covers both physical and mental impairments, such as mental retardation, hearing impairments, visual impairments, speech or language impairments, emotional disabilities, orthopedic impairments, autism, traumatic brain injury, attention deficit disorders, learning disabilities, depression, mental illness (such as bipolar disorder or schizophrenia), and chronic illnesses, such as diabetes, HIV/AIDS, cancer, epilepsy, multiple disabilities. The Individuals with Disabilities Education Act (P.L. 101–476) is a federal law that requires schools to provide free and appropriate education in the least restrictive environment. Disabilities are wide-ranging and impact the lives of many people worldwide. We must understand the broadest sense of the word *disability* and expand beyond the image of someone in a wheelchair or a person with a visual or hearing impairment, in order to recognize that disability is a vast category that includes an infinite number of possible experiences. Well over 74 percent of all Americans live with invisible disabilities (The Invisible Disabilities Advocate 1997).

ABLEISM AND DISABILITY OPPRESSION

Ableism or disability oppression is the term used to describe the all-encompassing system of discrimination and exclusion of people who live with developmental, medical, neurological, physical, and psychological disabilities. Similar to other forms of oppression discussed in this book, ableism functions on individual, institutional, and cultural levels to advantage people who are temporarily able-bodied and disadvantage people with disabilities (Griffin, Peters, and Smith 2007; see selection 4). We use the term *temporarily able-bodied* to raise consciousness that people who do not have disabilities may become disabled by illness, the process of growing older, accidents, and war, for example. Disability oppression theory also addresses how we value productivity. Economic productivity is a highly valued standard in the United States and this emphasis contributes to our undervaluing other social and material contributions, and stereotypes of dependence or independence follow from this emphasis on economic productivity.

HISTORICAL TREATMENT OF PEOPLE WITH DISABILITIES

Before the eighteenth century, disability was perceived through a religious lens and considered an unchangeable condition that resulted from sin (Covey 1998). Infants with disabilities were dropped off balconies to their death; children with disabilities were abandoned and left to live on the streets. This family and social abandonment left people with disabilities no choice but to beg for food and money to survive and the term *handicapped* emerged from people with disabilities who used their cap in hand to plead for help. Many people with disabilities were placed in jails or asylums where they endured inhumane treatment. By the early eighteenth century, people with disabilities were seen as freaks, monsters, and less than human. Societal curiosity about people with severe disabilities made "freak shows" very popular. Paradoxically, "freak shows" became one of the few viable ways for people with disabilities to earn a living.

As scientific and medical fields became more professionally powerful, scientific and medical guidelines shaped the ways in which disability was perceived and understood. Early medical textbooks classified people with disabilities as genetically defective. The medicalization of disability fostered the belief that people with disabilities needed to be monitored and controlled by licensed physicians and medical specialists with authoritarian power over people with disabilities. The medical goal was to cure the disability, get rid of a deformity, fix the body, and/or numb the existing pain of the person who was described as the patient. This thinking and methodology resulted in solutions that were invasive, usually by surgery or drugs, and which required submission from the person with a disability. The view that disabilities are deficiencies that require medical treatment and repair remains pervasive today.

During the 1880s and 1890s, people with mental retardation, as well as people who spoke English as a second language, were considered disabled or defective. For example, "medical imbecility" was attributed to people with mental retardation, as well as to paupers, prostitutes, immigrants, and others unable to express themselves in English (Longmore and Umanski 2001). The power of the early-nineteenth-century eugenics movement spurred policies to segregate and sterilize people considered to be hopelessly unredeemable because of their disabilities. Eugenics at its most extreme became the "scientific" rationale for Germany's genocidal policies during World War II in which thousands of people with mental or physical disabilities were gassed or starved to death (Gallagher 1995).

Veterans returning with disabilities from World War II spurred the medical field to focus on rehabilitation and the development of devices to help soldiers return to work and live productive lives, rather than be restricted to hospitals or asylums. Although a new focus on rehabilitation emerged, many people with disabilities continued to be segregated and treated as patients who needed supervision and care from others who knew best. In the 1960s and 1970s, a social movement among people with disabilities and allies began to emerge leading to the Independent Living Movement. On the heels of other civil rights and justice movements, disability activists organized and powerfully fought for their civil rights. This struggle resulted in the passage of Section 504 of the Rehabilitation Act of 1973 and the ADA in 1990, both significant feats protecting the rights of people with disabilities.

As of September 25, 2008, the ADA was amended, thereby expanding the basic definition of disability. The significant change is the expansion of protection for people with disabilities. The new regulation better defines the term "substantially limits" and expands the definition of "major life activities." For example, learning, reading, concentrating, thinking, communicating, and working are now recognized as major life activities. Also added to the law are major bodily functions, such as functions of the immune system. The amended ADA further states that conditions that are episodic or in remission may be labeled as disabilities when the active impairment can substantially limit a major life activity. The amendment serves to broaden the definition of disability so that more types of disability are recognized.

CURRENT ISSUES IN DISABILITY DISCOURSE

Current issues regarding disability have existed for decades but have not received the attention or debate regarding diagnosis and treatment to the extent that we are presently seeing. These issues include, but are not limited to, attention deficit hyperactivity disorder (ADHD) diagnosis and treatment for children and adults; traumatic brain injury (TBI) and post-traumatic stress disorder (PTSD) diagnosis and treatment for our veterans of war; the disproportionality and overdiagnosis of learning disabilities among students of color; and new developments in the cause and treatment of autism and Asperger's syndrome.

ADHD is categorized by the *Diagnostic and Statistical Manual of Mental Disorders-IV* (American Psychiatric Association 1994) by a constellation of symptoms, such as inattentiveness, impulsivity, and hyperactivity with evidence of a clear clinically significant impairment in social, academic, or occupational function. It has been presumed that adults diagnosed with ADHD would outgrow or learn to compensate for the hyperactivity component of the disorder, whether they are treated or not treated. However, there is no conclusive empirical evidence to support this claim. There is growing concern both for the overdiagnosis and overmedication of children, as well as the underdiagnosis and testing of specific groups of people who may have the disability.

Discussions regarding PTSD and TBI are increasingly being brought to our attention as significant numbers of veterans of war are returning with PTSD and mild-to-severe TBI. TBI can result from any type of injury to the brain that causes it to swell, such as artillery fire, car crashes, explosions, and any non-war-related incidents, such as sporting activities. The manifestations of TBI include impaired cognition, sensory processing, communication, and mental health, and/or personality changes (National Institute of Neurological Disorders and Stroke 2009). Although the incidence of TBI among veterans is on the rise, the actual statistics are still unknown.

During World War I, veterans returning from the war were diagnosed with "shell shock," uncontrollable shaking, reoccurring nightmares, and imagined re-enactments of the horrific events. Today, these symptoms along with others are categorized as PTSD. Well over 1.5 million service personnel have been deployed to Iraq and Afghanistan since 2002 (Karney, Ramchand, Osilla, Caldarone, and Burns 2008), and PTSD is currently one of the enduring and invisible effects. It is possible to see those who have lost a limb, or are stooped with back pain; however, veterans with PTSD are among the undetectable wounded. Veteran's Hospitals and medical facilities around the nation are encountering staggering numbers of veterans who cannot get the full treatment that they need to navigate the changed world that they face. With a single trauma, PTSD generally lasts from three to five years (Kessler, Sonnega, Bromet, Hughes, and Nelson 1995), although many experience multiple traumas in life, and a typical person with PTSD may experience symptoms that last more than twenty years (Breslau, Kessler, Chilcoat, Schultz, Davis, and Andreski 1998; Kessler 2000).

Another pressing issue within disability discourse brings our attention to the overrepresentation of students of color in special education. As early as 1968, a disproportionate representation of students of color, particularly African Americans, in special education raised concern as to the legitimacy of such placement (Dunn 1968). What we have witnessed since 1968 is a much higher percentage of African Americans in special education. The National Research Council (2002) was addressing whether the overrepresentation of African Americans in special education was a perceived or real problem and if the impact of poverty played a role in the placement of these students. According to research conducted by the National Academy of Sciences, African Americans are the most likely to be labeled as having a disability. In 2002 Donovan and Cross noted that 14.28 percent of African Americans were found to have a disability in comparison to 11.34 percent of white students. Students of color are labeled as mentally retarded, learning disabled, and emotionally or behaviorally dysfunctional, resulting in referrals to psychologists and intervention teams (Harry and Klingner 2006). According to the U.S. Department of Education, in the late 1990s only 25.5 percent of students with disabilities graduated with a standard diploma and only 22 percent graduated who were labeled with emotional issues (U.S. Department of Education 2000). Rendering a solution requires education reform that will include overhauling educational processes and organizational structures, and stressing effective teacher preparation and professional development in multicultural education.

An additional matter in the arena of disability issues is that of autism and Asperger's syndrome. Autism or autism spectrum disorders (ASD) has seen an increase in reportage since the 1980s, to six in one thousand people, with boys being diagnosed four times more than girls (http://www.emedtv.com 2009). This increase may be due to changing diagnostic evaluations. ASD is a developmental disorder of the brain that affects communication and social skills and may result in repetitive actions. It has been observed that children reaching adulthood generally do not live independently, although there are ranges of vocational success among this population, and this success may be attributed to the existing range of cognitive developments from retardation to extremely high functioning persons.

UNIVERSAL ARCHITECTURAL AND INSTRUCTIONAL DESIGN

Advocates for people with disabilities have called for an adaptation of architectural design, as well as instructional changes to curriculum and pedagogy, that will allow access for all people (Pliner and Johnson in selection 98). Universal Architectural Design (UAD) incorporates ramps, Braille signage, wider hallways and doorways, lower/adjustable desks and fixtures, and easy access door openers. The same principle of access for everyone is applied in Universal Instructional Design (UID). Both UAD and UID benefit all people with and without disabilities.

GLOBAL ISSUES

The global population of people with disabilities is growing because of aging, ethnic and sectarian violence, war, poverty, and the contamination of the environment (Harrison 2004). It is estimated that there are 600 million people with disabilities in today's world. Many countries are passing laws that recognize the rights of people with disabilities. Great Britain and Austria adopted the Disability Discrimination Act of 1995, while countries such as South Africa, Malawi, Uganda, the Philippines, Finland, Brazil, Austria, and Germany have adopted statutes that prohibit discrimination against people with disabilities (Harrison 2004).

ABLEISM INTERSECTIONS

The complex social identities people occupy and the social context we live in largely shape how people with disabilities are treated and how one's disability is personally experienced. As people with disabilities represent various races, classes, genders, sexual orientations, ages, and religious backgrounds, people often simultaneously experience intersections with racism, classism, heterosexism, ageism, transgender oppression, religious oppression, and sexism.

The intersection between one's disability and classism is a glaringly important example of how the issues may be intertwined. Low-income people with disabilities face many barriers as the costs of health care, computers, software applications, assistive technology, and digital hearing aids (to name a few) are expensive, resulting in some receiving inadequate health care, limited employment opportunities, and significant learning disadvantages while attending school. On the contrary, people with disabilities who are born into families with greater financial means gain significant access to expensive medical treatment and diagnostic testing, assistive technology, personal care attendants, and other necessary resources.

Likewise, the intersection between disability and sexism further demonstrates how our complex identities and societal manifestations of oppression are overlapping. Unlike the current attention focusing on veterans returning from war with PTSD, there continues to be little consideration given to the reality that one out of nine women is diagnosed with PTSD symptoms, most often as a result of experiencing rape, sexual assault, domestic abuse, and/or violence (http://www.emedicinehealth.com 2009). Sexual assault, for example, has wide-reaching effects on women, including an impact on physical and mental health, functionality, issues regarding basic needs, and difficulty reading social cues. With PTSD, a raised hand, a half-open door, a pointed object, or phraseology in a conversation can unconsciously set in motion intense reactions and the re-creation of the original traumatic incident. The continued cultural and institutional silencing of women being disproportionately and violently targeted perpetuates a cycle of abuse against women that is significantly tied to numbers of women being diagnosed with particular disabilities.

READINGS IN THIS SECTION

In this section, we have attempted to create a better understanding of the complexities of disability by including a representation of issues, ideas, and experiences of people with disabilities across multiple social identities. The section in no way represents every aspect of disability history, reform, treatment, and social, educational, or international issues and experiences. Rather, we present an overview of the issues that individuals, instructors, students, and others can refer to in their search for and journey to more insight and strategies regarding disabilities.

The articles in this section are as varied as the issues regarding disability. We begin our section with Willie Bryan's overview of the disability rights movement (selection 96) as a way of contextualizing the historical issues that were faced and the types of efforts that were led by people with disabilities. Another article that highlights historical developments is Janet Cerney's (selection 97) recounting of historical figures, events, and cultural shifts that have strongly shaped deaf education.

Focusing on global issues, we have included two articles that address war and a third on neocolonialism and disabilities. By examining the number of medical disabilities experienced by veterans who participated in the Gulf War, Gary Null (selection 103), provides an introductory overview of the consequences of war on the participants, while David Grossman's piece (selection 102) shares stunningly important information about the effects of war on the human body and the significant number of soldiers who become psychiatric casualties. On another global front, Nirmala Erevelles' article (selection 104) gives us more insight into how transnational capitalism and (neo)colonial institutions and policies have influenced the social construction of disability in Third World contexts and have particularly impacted the lives of Third World women.

Discussions on disability and hate crimes are often omitted by the media and Lennard Davis (selection 100) draws our attention to this omission. Davis uses the lack of news coverage of a hate crime in which the murdered victim, James Byrd, is described only by his race, ignoring the fact that he was also a person with a disability. Davis asks that we deconstruct hierarchies of oppression by acknowledging intersections and the multiple identities that are targeted by oppression. Further, drawing upon intersections, Sumi Colligan's article (selection 101) explores the parallels between the cultural representations and everyday struggles of intersexed persons and people with disabilities with a particular focus on the medicalization of intersexed/disabled bodies and the construction of asexuality.

The personal narratives included in this section provide a glimpse into the many ways that people with disabilities, who live across multiple social identities, experience issues of oppression and liberation. Eli Clare's personal narrative (selection 105) about society's dehumanizing actions and reactions toward people with disabilities elicits the urgent need for better role models, heroes, and allies. As a genderqueer person with a physical disability, Clare describes the common use of demeaning language and belittling stares that play a significant role in the perpetuation of ableism and transgender oppression. Lesley Jones (selection 106) describes her thoughts, feelings, and experiences living with Asperger's syndrome as a child speaking to adults. The narrative tells the reader about emotionally hurtful events that happened at school. Throughout her story she reflects on her experiences and offers counsel to adults to support children living with Asperger's syndrome.

Another account of a child growing up with a disability is provided by Ashley and Deborah's story (selection 107) in "How to Curse in Sign Language." The article describes a mother and daughter's struggle for educational rights in the public school system, and acceptance within a religious institution and society in general. Jason Kingsley (selection 108) reflects on what he would tell parents and doctors about being born with Down syndrome. He reminds them not to set limitations on people with Down syndrome and their ability to learn, have relationships, and participate in all kinds of life activities. In "The LD Bubble," Lynn Pelkey (selection 109) shares her elementary and secondary public school experience in special education classrooms for students with learning disabilities. Her narrative describes her feelings of isolation and the hurtful effects this had on her self-esteem and her connection to her peers. Her message is one of overcoming institutionalized ableism and making progress in the college context.

The final section offers multiple ways to address the prejudice and discrimination toward people with disabilities on the individual, cultural, and institutional levels. Thomas Hehir (selection 110) opens this section by offering four suggestions to address ableist practices. Hehir asserts that we must challenge ableist assumptions in education that contribute to lower levels of success in educational pursuits and gainful employment. Also in this section is an article by Heather Oesterreich and Michelle Knight (selection 111) that examines how the intersections of race, class, language, and disability inform the responsibilities of special educators to help students with disabilities. The overrepresentation of working-class students of African, Latino/Latina, and Native American heritages in special education have been a long-standing part of special education reform. Oesterreich and Knight provide "Teacher Tips" to educators in order to increase the social and cultural capital of students with disabilities to support their prospective college-going and vocational identities. The authors are proponents of Universal Instructional Design, including use of assistive technology to meet the needs of particular students. Susan Pliner and Julia Johnson's article (selection 98) outlines the core principles and concepts of Universal Instructional Design necessary for achieving accessibility and inclusion in institutions of higher education. Critical for understanding how social conditions affect disability, Susan Wendell's article (selection 99) explores the physical, social, and cultural environments that cause disability.

Cheryl Howland and Eva Gibavic's article (selection 112) presents a learning disability identity development model that incorporates a discussion of several influential variables from dual diagnosis to support systems. Overall, this model helps individuals come to a greater understanding of the complex stages people with learning disabilities might encounter. Also included are additional influences of other identity development models, such as gender, race, and moral identity development. In "Creating a Fragrance-Free Zone" (selection 113), the Invisibilities Disabilities Advocate alerts us to the growing environmental illness identified as multiple chemical sensitivity. This article provides concrete practices that can be incorporated individually and institutionally to create safe and comfortable environments for all people. Finally, Madeline Peters, Carmelita (Rosie) Casteñeda, Larissa Hopkins, and Aquila McCants (selection 114) provide examples of beliefs and practices that are ableist on individual, cultural, and institutional levels, followed by the actions people can take to eliminate these discriminatory practices and act as unified allies. For additional information on disabilities please refer to our section website.

Note

1 We ask that those who cite this work always acknowledge by name all of the authors listed rather than only citing the first author or using "et al." to indicate coauthors. All authors listed on a section collaborated equitably on the conceptualization, development, and writing of this section.

References

Americans with Disabilities Act of 1990 (ADA), PL 101–336, (July 26, 1990). Title 42, U.S.C. §§ 12101 et seq: U.S Statutes at Large. 104, 327–78.

American Psychiatric Association. (1994). *Diagnostic and Statistical Manual of Mental Disorders (DSM-IV)*. Washington, D.C.: American Psychiatric Association.

Breslau, N., Kessler, R. C., Chilcoat, H. D., Schultz, L. R., Davis, G. C., Andreski, P. (1998). "Trauma and Post-Tramatic Stress Disorder on the Community. The 1996 Detroit Area Survey of Trauma." *Archives of General Psychiatry* 55, 626–632.

Covey, H. (1998). *Social Perceptions of People with Disabilities in History*. Springfield, IL: Charles Thomas.

Donovan, S. Cross, C. (2002). *Minority Students in Special and Gifted Education*. Washington, DC: National Academy Press.

Dunn, L. M. (1968). "Special Education for the Mildly Retarded: Is Much of it Justifiable?" *Exceptional Children* 35, 5–32.

emedicinehealth.com (2009). "Post Traumatic Stress Disorder." Retrieved May 1, 2009, from http://www.emedicinehealth.com/post-traumatic_stress_disorder_ptsd/article_em.htm.

emedtv.com (2009). "Autism." Retrieved May 1, 2009, from http://www.autism.emedtv.com.

Gallagher, H.(1995). *By Trust Betrayed: Patients, Physicians, and the License to Kill in the Third Reich*. Arlington, VA: Vandamere.

Griffin, P., Peters, M. L., Smith, R. M. (2007). "Ableism Curriculum Design." In M. Adams, L. A. Bell, P. Griffin (eds), *Teaching for Diversity and Social Justice*, 2nd edition. New York: Routledge. pp. 335–358.

Harry, B., Klingner, J. (2006). *Why Are So Many Minority Students in Special Education. Understanding Race and Disability in Schools*. New York: Teachers College Press.

Harrison, O. (2004). "As Disability is Emerging Globally, So Is Advocacy for Full Participation for People with Disabilities." *Access New England* 9 (1), 1. Retrieved June 25, 2006, from http://www.adaptenv.org/newsletter/pdf/Access_Fall_2004.pdf.

Karney, B., Ramchand, R., Osilla, K., Caldarone, L., Burns, R. (2008). *Predicting the Immediate and Long-Term Consequences of Post-Traumatic Stress Disorder, Depression, and Traumatic Brain Injury in Veterans of Operation Enduring Freedom and Operation Iraqi Freedom*. Santa Monica, CA: RAND Center for Military Health Policy Research.

Kessler, R. C., (2000). "Posttraumatic Stress Disorder: The Burden to the Individual and to Society." *Journal of Clinical Psychiatry* 61 (Suppl. 5), 4–12.

Kessler, R.C., Sonnega, A., Bromet, E., Hughes, M., Nelson, C.B. (1995). "Posttraumatic Stress Disorder in the National Comorbidity Survey." *Archives of General Psychiatry* 52, 1048–1060.

Longmore, P., Umanski, L. (eds) (2001). *The New Disability History: American Perspectives*. New York: New York University Press.

National Institute of Neurological Disorders and Stroke. (2009). Retrieved May 1, 2009, from http://www.ninds.nih.gov.

National Research Council. (2002). *Addressing Overrepresentation of African American Students in Special Education: The Prereferral Intervention Process*. Arlington, VA: National Council for Exceptional Children.

The Invisible Disabilities Advocate. (1997). "Invisible Disabilities: What Does That Mean?" Retrieved from http://www.invisibledisabilities.org/ids.htm.

United States Department of Education. (2000). *The Longitudinal Evaluation of School Change and Performance in Title I Schools: Final Report*. Washington, D.C.: Planning and Evaluation Service, United States Department of Education.

United States Department of Justice. (1999). ADA Legal Documents: Public Law 101–336. U.S. Department of Justice home page http://usdoj.gov/crt/ada/pubs/ada.txt.

96

Struggle for Freedom

Disability Rights Movements

Willie V. Bryan

. . .

LACK OF CONCERN

Since World War II, there has been an increasing emphasis on human and civil rights in the United States. Minorities and women have spoken out on their own behalf attempting to gain the privileges, freedoms, and rights guaranteed for all Americans by the Constitution. While legal and social ground has been won and lost throughout the years, many minorities and women now enjoy a somewhat more equal existence in the United States than some fifty years ago. Still, the battle for equality is far from victorious. While other groups continue their struggle, individuals with disabilities have joined forces to end discrimination in their lives and claim a life of equality in the United States.

The Civil Rights movement of the sixties resulted in legislation designed to bar discrimination based on sex, race, and national origin; however, prohibition of discrimination based on physical and/or mental disabilities was not included. As Thomas D. Schneid reminds us, a bill introduced in Congress in 1971 to amend Title VI of the Civil Rights Act of 1964 to prohibit discrimination based on physical or mental disability died in committee. Similarly, in 1972, another bill introduced in Congress, this time to amend Title VII of the Civil Rights Act to bar discrimination in employment based upon physical or mental disabilities, also died in committee. This may be seen as somewhat of a barometer of the level of concern lawmakers and many other nondisabled Americans had with regard to the civil rights of persons with disabilities.

Perhaps the lack of concern demonstrated by these actions of Congress is more of a reflection of ignorance of the needs and capabilities of persons with disabilities rather than a blatant desire to deny the civil rights of a group of people. At the time, the thought was that employers should not be forced to hire persons who could not adequately perform the required tasks. Persons with disabilities and their friends certainly were not advocating employment of nonqualified persons; they were simply asking that employers be required to look beyond a person's limitation to see abilities and attempt to match them with the required job. Employers also had a number of misconceptions with regard to employing persons with disabilities, such as they would not be able to secure insurance for the person and the company's insurance premiums would increase. Another major misconception was the belief that persons with disabilities were unsafe employees. This erroneous belief was held despite safety records indicating that persons with disabilities had fewer accidents than nondisabled employees. Many employers were aware that by making modifications to the work site and/or its environment, a significant number of jobs could be made accessible to persons with disabilities; however, these same employers harbored the belief that making these accommodations would be too expensive. Again, this belief was held even though the DuPont Company had demonstrated that many changes to a work site could be done inexpensively.

These and other misconceptions were firmly held by employers because persons with disabilities and their advocates did not vigorously dispute them. The lack of opposition to discrimination against persons with disabilities with respect to employment allowed long-held stereotypes and prejudices to continue unchallenged. Activism would be necessary to dramatize the extent of the lack of concern for the rights of persons with disabilities and cause action to be taken to correct the neglect that had become an accepted method of treatment of persons with disabilities.

MINORITY STATUS

The political wheels of American progress appear to turn best when pressure is applied. For example, protests by minorities, particularly African Americans, led to the Civil Rights Act of 1964. Similarly, women's organizations engaged in various activities that placed pressure on state and federal government leaders to enact legislation that required equality of rights for women. One may assume that in a free and open democracy which most of us enjoy in America, there would be available on an equal basis to all citizens, the right to vote, to live wherever one can afford, the right to eat wherever one desires, and the right to be educated at the maximum level of one's abilities. However, it was precisely the denial of these basic rights, rights upon which this country was founded, rights for which thousands of Americans have paid the supreme price, that led multitudes of Americans into the streets to practice civil disobedience, until these and other basic rights were granted.

In the process of securing these rights, the minority groups learned that their minority status was not shameful. In fact, they learned that they were a very important cog in the wheel of American life and by withholding their labor and being selective as to how and where they spent their hard earned money, they could considerably slow down the democratic wheel of progress. These groups also learned that by networking they added strength to their demands.

Until recently, persons with disabilities were not widely considered a minority group. In fact, it was not until the Rehabilitation Act of 1973 that they were considered a "class" of people. Persons with disabilities are members of other groups of people, they are male or female, and they have an ethnic identity; their rights and privileges are associated with whatever cultural and/or gender group they belong. It is ironic that with regard to human rights their disabilities were secondary to their cultural and/or gender identity, but with regard to their rights as citizens, their disabilities were primary, overshadowing gender and/or cultural identity. Since disability groups were not considered a culture at the time, the person with a disability was viewed as a "disabled member of another class." To be more specific, they were considered to be a disabled female or a disabled American Indian female. Hopefully, the point has been made. It is in part because of this dual and sometimes triple classification that the disability label was not considered a class unto itself.

Another reason for the lack of class status is that there are large numbers of disabilities and each one is considered a separate condition within its own group identity. For example, there are persons who have disabilities resulting from polio, arthritis, visual impairments, hearing impairments, lupus, mental illness, mental retardation, amputations, and paralysis, to mention only a few. In most cases, there was and continues to be associations or foundations which are considered the official representative for all who have a particular condition. This has the effect of segregating disabilities into distinct disease groups, thus causing each disabling condition to stand alone and not be part of a larger whole. This internal segregation combined with society's segregation of persons with disabilities has been devastating to efforts of persons with disabilities to unite and demand their constitutional rights.

Although it would not be until the passage of the Rehabilitation Act of 1973 that persons with disabilities would obtain the classification of minority status and be officially viewed as a class of people, several years before the passage of the act they began to think of themselves as a minority. And more importantly, they began to view their life conditions as having been deprived of their basic human rights similar to other minority groups. They also began to think of themselves as being oppressed and disenfranchised. With this realization, they began to unite and to speak openly about the manner in which they were being excluded from full participation in society's activities. Thinking of themselves as oppressed minorities, they also thought of the manner in which other minority groups had placed their agenda before the American people; thus a "grassroots disability rights movement" began which has resulted in the passage of the ADA in 1990.

GRASSROOTS MOVEMENT

. . .

Despite the concern exhibited by charitable organizations and Congress, the one aspect often missing was the involvement of persons with disabilities. For example, much of the legislation prior to the Rehabilitation Act of 1973 had been developed with little, if any, input from persons with disabilities. Charitable organizations established telethons to raise funds for research and/or provide services without giving much thought to the negative images being projected. This was "business as usual" or stated another way, it was the continuation of the paternalistic attitude that has existed in America for many decades. Perhaps without meaning harm to persons with disabilities, nondisabled persons have treated them as though they are incapable of determining and expressing how they would like to live their lives. Regardless of how well-intended the motivation of a non-oppressed person there are some things he/she will either overlook or not understand with regard to the effects of being oppressed. Therefore it is imperative that those effected must be involved in determining the best methods for eliminating the problems created by oppression.

There are undoubtedly many reasons why it took persons with disabilities approximately two centuries before they organized and began to speak out on their own behalf. With "sit-ins," marches, and attempts to integrate previously segregated southern schools, the fifties served as the "staging" years of the Civil Rights movement; then in the sixties the final "assault" years were launched which culminated in victory with the passage of the Civil Rights Act of 1964. Similarly for the Disability Rights Movement, the sixties served as the "staging" years with emphasis on consumerism, self-help, and demedication demands as well as demands for self-care rights and deinstitutionalism. Perhaps then the seventies can be considered the "watershed" years of the movement. The sixties was the decade when persons with disabilities began to view themselves as oppressed minorities and demanded their constitutional rights. Similar to the Civil Rights Movement which culminated in the Civil Rights Act of 1964, the Disability Rights Movement led to what has been called the Civil Rights Act for persons with disabilities: The American's With Disabilities Act of 1990.

. . .

Activism: . . . In the early seventies, rehabilitation leaders backed by disability rights groups began to push for changes in the legislation to advocate a broader nonvocational role for rehabilitation programs. In 1972, such legislation was passed by Congress and Verville informs us that President Nixon vetoed the legislation because it "strayed too far from the essential vocational objective of the program."

This Act had provisions for Independent Living Centers. It would take six more years before this important concept would become a reality. The veto of the 1972 Rehabilitation Act is a classic example of not involving those most effected. Perhaps the veto served a useful purpose in that it became an issue around which the grassroots movement could unite. While attempting to get the Independent Living Centers provisions included in future legislation, the disability rights organizations gained considerable experience in politics, coalition building, and lobbying, as well as the act of compromising, thus gaining the respect of lawmakers and the admiration of millions of persons both with and without disabilities.

In the interim, additional legislation was passed with provisions to issue directives that persons with disabilities were not to be discriminated against nor treated as second-class citizens. One such piece of legislation was the Rehabilitation Act of 1973. Included in this legislation was Section 504 which forbade any United States institution that received federal financial assistance in the amount of $2,500 or more and all federal and state agencies from discriminating against persons with disabilities in employment. . . .

INDEPENDENT LIVING MOVEMENT

. . .

The quest for independence by most Americans does not occur by accident, but is a quality that is taught and reinforced to every American youth, both by formal teaching and by example. American history is replete with both fictional and factual persons accomplishing or attempting to accomplish extraordinary deeds to establish or maintain their independence.

Independence is therefore highly valued in American society; it is considered an essential building block in constructing and maintaining a democracy. Freedom, to an extent, is reliant upon its citizens having the independence to build better lives for themselves and in the process of accomplishing their dreams, they lift freedom and democracy to new levels. Conversely, being dependent is devalued in American society and those that are considered so are often assigned lower positions on the social totem pole. To many, the word "dependent" denotes lack of initiative, laziness, and a burden upon society. Although public and private social welfare agencies and organizations including hospitals, clinics, and rehabilitation centers, to mention a few, have been developed to assist persons who by virtue of illness, accident, or birth defects must rely upon assistive services, the recipients are often viewed in a negative light and at best given sympathy instead of empathy and understanding.

Illness or disability often places the individual, and sometimes the family, in a state of dependency. For some it is a permanent situation, but for the majority it is temporary. The degree to which a person becomes dependent is obviously effected by several things, not the least of which are attitudes. [A]ttitudes of family, friends, medical and rehabilitation personnel as well as employers have an impact on the level of dependency of the person with a disability.

Given the value placed on independence by American society, no one should be amazed that persons with disabilities began to recognize and resent the limited role society drafted for them. They correctly perceived that society equated disability with dependency. They also recognized that this perception created a very low ceiling and an almost insurmountable wall around their abilities to function and achieve.

. . .

In the early seventies, persons with disabilities began to realize that to be truly free they must take and maintain control of their lives. This train of thought resulted in the development of Independent Living Centers (ILCs). Dejong provides a brief history of the genesis of Independent Living Centers as he reveals that a small group of persons with disabilities at the University of Illinois and at the University of California at Berkeley moved out of their residential hospital setting into the community and organized their own system for delivery of survival services. The centers established by these students became the blueprint by which future centers would be established. As might be expected, since the inception of these centers, the scope of services has expanded. Even so, the idea of persons with disabilities taking greater control of their lives remains the same. Perhaps Dejong best summarizes the independent living philosophy when he said the dignity of risk is what the independent movement is all about. Without the possibility of failure, a person with a disability is said to lack true independence and the mark of one's humanity: the right to choose for good or evil.

When one considers that the independent living movement was initiated by persons with disabilities, many of whom were persons with severe disabilities such as spinal cord injuries, it became quite apparent that these individuals exhibited courage of the highest magnitude. Although prior to the movement they lived in conditions that made them almost totally dependent upon others, it was however a safe environment; therefore, moving from this safe environment to face the many uncertainties created by a society with many barriers and obstacles certainly qualifies the founding members as pioneers.

. . . Laurie also contributes to our understanding of the goal of independent living centers with these comments:

> Independent living is freedom of choice, to live where and how one chooses and can afford. It is living alone or with a roommate of one's choice. It is deciding one's own pattern of life: scheduling food, entertaining, vices, virtues, leisure and friends. It is freedom to take risks and freedom to make mistakes.

Frieden and Cole define the independent living concept as control over one's life based on the choice of acceptable options that minimize reliance on others in making decisions and in performing everyday activities. This may include managing one's affairs, participating in day-to-day life in the community, fulfilling a range of social roles, and making decisions that lead to self-determination and the minimizing of physical or psychological dependence upon others.

Frieden, Richards, Cole, and Bailey tell us that the independent living movement was based on the premise that with reasonable support services, adults with disabilities could manage their own affairs, and participate as full members of the community in all respects. They continue by speaking to the philosophy of the movement as full participation in community life and point out that the movement also was an advocate for a set of services that would meet the long-term support needs of citizens with disabilities. . . .

MORE THAN WORK

Work is so much a central part of most Americans' lives that it, in part, defines who we are. It is common for Americans to describe someone by identifying their occupation. For example, we may identify someone as Mary Smith the attorney, or John Smith the teacher. Work has been the defining feature in American lives for many years. The Puritan work ethic is a standard by which Americans often judge each other. While we no longer subscribe to the theory of hard work for all, we most certainly subscribe to the idea of work for all. Work provides us with economic power to purchase goods and services which in part by virtue of the amount and types of goods we accumulate determines our social standing in America. Social condemnation is the reward for those that are able to work but do not. Work not only is a means by which we develop, maintain or improve our societal standing in American society, it also is patriotic. In a capitalist society, it is through the production of products that our nation develops its standing in the world as compared to other nations.

Obviously, work has many important meanings to Americans and American society. Considering the position work holds in American life, it is easy to understand why virtually all rehabilitation legislation prior to the 1972 Rehabilitation Act emphasized "vocational rehabilitation." In fact, when we speak of rehabilitating a person with a disability we think the ultimate goal of the rehabilitation process is to make the person ready for a job. There is one thing wrong with this approach: what about the person who is unable to work because of the severity or perhaps type of disability? Unless they and/or their families have sufficient financial resources, they have to rely upon sympathy and charity of others as well as some social welfare assistance from the federal government. Because of the social stigma of not working and receiving charity, these persons' independence, self-dignity, and ability to participate as full American citizens are in jeopardy.

Perhaps these reasons, as well as others, caused the disability rights movement leaders to lobby Congress to deemphasize "vocational" in the Rehabilitation Act of 1972. It is unfortunate that the Nixon Administration did not comprehend what persons with disabilities were saying as they lobbied for removal of "vocational" from the rehabilitation act. In part, what they were saying, and perhaps today we are just beginning to hear, is that a person's worth, self-respect, and dignity should not be measured by employment and moreover measured by whether employed in a job, especially if that person is unable to work. The leaders were wise to note that no person with a disability would be totally free until all persons with disabilities had opportunities to more fully participate in American life. Again it was this type of thinking that led them to push for independent living centers, and the abolishment of the segregation of persons with disabilities so they could not only become more involved in American society, but also make decisions that would effect the quality of their lives. In short, they recognized that to be free, life for a person with a disability meant more than being able to work.

. . .

C
O
N
T
E
X
T

97

Historical and Cultural Influences in Deaf Education

Janet Cerney

HISTORICAL AND CULTURAL CONTEXT IN THE EDUCATION OF DEAF STUDENTS

Conceptualizing the issues surrounding the education of deaf students involves understanding the historical context of deaf education, the political platforms that have developed, and the current forces that are impacting deaf education today. The subject of deaf education is highly charged both emotionally and politically. The answers are neither perfect nor simple.

For centuries the education of deaf children has been polarized into two main camps, the manualists (those who sign) and the oralists (those who rely on speech and speech-reading). A third camp has more recently been added—supporters of cued speech (those who use a sound-based visual communication system). But the clash between manualists and oralists reaches deep into history and deep into the emotions and experiences of those who have been educated under their slogans. So that we can gain sensitivity toward the plight of deaf students and not repeat the mistakes of our past, it seems important that educators, parents, and administrators understand the history behind the controversy and recognize the juncture between feelings and facts.

A GLIMPSE INTO HISTORY

On April 15, 1817, a motley group of twelve deaf students entered the Connecticut Asylum for the Education and Instruction of Deaf and Dumb Persons. They ranged in age from 12 to 51 years old. Some students were from prominent New England families, while others came from the unrestrained and spirited deaf community at Martha's Vineyard. Their walk through the open doors signified the beginning of formal deaf education in America, a history that has sparked one of the most radical and controversial educational wars of all time.

This bold beginning to American deaf education was laid by the friendship and camaraderie of two men: Thomas Hopkins Gallaudet, a hearing minister, and his chosen counterpart Laurent Clerc, a deaf Frenchman. It was through their joined effort that the school thrived. Culturally, the school was deaf friendly, embracing the visual language of its students. . . .

The prompt and spectacular success of the Connecticut Asylum brought enthusiasm to the burgeoning field of deaf education. By 1820, plans to educate deaf Americans were being made around the country. As new residential schools for the deaf began to spring up, many deaf students discovered language and a new cultural family after living for years in communicative isolation within hearing communities. Within the walls of these schools, the older deaf children would pass down to younger generations of children the cultural attribute that made deaf Americans a distinct subculture within America—sign language.

This early academic culture was marked by a prevalent respect for deaf people as teachers and school leaders. Hearing administrators tended to approach the students from a loving but paternalistic viewpoint, consistent with other educational institutions of that time. Sign language flourished, and the brightest deaf students were later recruited as teachers. By 1858, deaf teachers accounted for a full 40.8% of the total teaching force in schools for the deaf.

. . .

Frederick Knapp also attempted inclusion in 1877, when he admitted deaf pupils to his private school in Baltimore. However, his perspective was far more condescending, as he believed that "the more deaf students socialized with hearing students, the less they would notice their defect." In Knapp's school, hearing children were forbidden to sign to deaf children, in an attempt to keep them from reminding deaf students of their affliction. If a hearing or deaf child were caught signing, he or she was forced to wear gloves to signify "punishment and stupidity."

Although American Sign Language enjoyed widespread support through the first half of the nineteenth century, by mid-century, a new method of teaching deaf children, oralism, began to emerge. This method emphasized lipreading and speech and prohibited the use of signs. It gained international support during a meeting of administrators and teachers in Milan, Italy, in 1880. Though this deaf educators' conference drew participants from France, Italy, America, and various other European countries, it was dominated by the oral teachers from France and Italy. The American delegation included Thomas Hopkins Gallaudet's two sons, Edward Miner Gallaudet (the president of Gallaudet College) and Thomas Gallaudet, who both spoke strongly in support of sign language. The oralist agenda dominated, though, and in the end a motion passed to pledge full support to this "method of articulation"—giving international approval to the idea that deaf children should be forced to communicate without signs. . . .

The highly vocal Alexander Graham Bell led the charge to abolish sign language, becoming the "most feared enemy of the American Deaf." He firmly believed that deaf people were "a defective race of human beings" and a "great calamity to the world." Ironically, both his mother and wife were deaf, and Bell himself was a fluent signer. In 1883, he presented a paper to the National Academy of Science in New Haven, Connecticut, "Upon the Formation of a Deaf Variety of the Human Race." His presentation supposed that since we can modify breeds of animals by careful selection, it should be possible similarly to modify the varieties of the human race. Based on his assumption that deaf marriages lead to deaf children, he found deaf residential schools, deaf community events, socializations, and the hiring of deaf teachers disturbing and intolerable in nature because they could lead to intermarriage.

Initially, the residential schools were skeptical of Bell's efforts. Though many teachers, including Edward Miner Gallaudet, found value in teaching some speech techniques to hard of hearing students, they were mostly interested in teaching content to students through signs instead of wasting endless hours on speechreading drills. Bell and other oralists realized that in order to have a significant effect on these institutions, they would have to organize. Bell used his influence to enlist the National Education Association in his struggle against sign language. Ultimately, he was able to use their lobbying powers to win the hearts of politicians and public school teachers for the oralist movement. By 1920, despite deaf students' need to use signs to communicate and build a knowledge of the world, 80% of deaf students were educated without using any signs.

The effect on deaf education and the deaf community was devastating. The ban on sign language had a great impact on the deaf teachers, who had once been welcomed. As oralism spread, deaf teachers were removed from their positions, some without any compensation, and were quickly replaced by hearing teachers who did not know sign but were well versed on the drills of speech training. The ranks of deaf teachers shrank rapidly, as most administrators would not risk their positions by hiring a deaf teacher. By the time pure oralism was at its height, the number of deaf teachers had shrunk from 40% to only 14% of the total deaf education work force. This viable career option for deaf adults was removed, leaving them to search for less desirable work.

In enforcing the oralist teaching framework, children were subjected to sitting on their hands, having their hands tied behind their backs, and receiving other hideous forms of punishment to deter them from signing. Even now, our older deaf population remembers vividly the variety of punishments enacted for breaking the stringent rules of oralism.

. . .

The pendulum swing toward oralism also brought with it a movement of deaf students from residential schools to day schools and integrated classroom settings. The roots of this movement seem to have begun in Bell's strong conviction that deaf people should not associate with each other, for fear that this association would encourage deaf marriages and the continuation of deaf culture. Though vehemently opposed by most deaf people, many other people, including doctors, hearing parents, and their professional organizations, once again led the charge for a forced assimilation of the deaf student population. Perhaps the most serious threat came in the form of a seemingly well-meaning initiative, the Education for All Handicapped Children Act of 1975. This law mandated that all children should receive a "free, appropriate public education" in the "least restrictive environment." Many parents of disabled children welcomed the opportunity to have their children live at home and to enroll them in public schools. Regardless of its good intentions, the law strikes at the heart of the residential schools, where generations of deaf students have found their community, their language, and a shared culture. A related by-product of this law has been a shifting away of funds from the residential schools and shrinking enrollments. For some residential schools, it has meant a slow death, the painful closing of an institution that is dearly loved and valued.

Today, many deaf community members believe that "the dark world of oralism," in which educators tried to eliminate signing, has given way to an uncertain world of inclusion, where deaf children face "a different kind of isolation." The deaf community's insistence on its status as a unique and culturally viable minority group seems at odds with the educational system of assimilation. A language-rich learning environment, where deaf students have full access to direct communication with everyone in their environment, is not even remotely possible in most current integrated settings. Given this situation, what can be done to ensure that deaf students have full access to the educational system? Are the cultural elements of the residential schools able to be adapted to the inclusion setting? What is a communicative, rich learning environment for deaf students, and how can one be nurtured and maintained? Is the essence of hearing/deaf peer relationships anemic in comparison to deaf/deaf relationships, or do they provide sufficient foundations on which to build solid friendships? How do the issues of isolation and alienation impact student learning? As we explore the answers to these questions, it is imperative that we listen to the stories of deaf students and the professionals who serve them. It is through their eyes that we can truly understand the complexity of issues that frustrate those children we serve.

CULTURAL COMPETENCY: SALIENT VALUES OF THE DEAF COMMUNITY

Imagine—deafness not as a defect, but as a source of connection! Imagine yourself deaf, growing up with a beautiful language, visual literature, humor, and theater.

Imagine taking pride in your identity without any desire to become a member of the majority culture.

The critical juncture of communication and relationship building is culture. Many agree that educators can best serve deaf children by understanding the salient features of deaf culture in order to create culturally competent learning environments for deaf students. While it certainly seems true that a rudimentary understanding of the cultural heritage of deaf students would give educators greater insight into the world of being deaf, this knowledge should be coupled with inquiry into the level of ownership that deaf students hold to this heritage.

The salient values of deaf culture are tied to language, and the sites of cultural transmission, namely residential schools. In the deaf community, initial conversations usually begin by asking where you are from. A deaf person often responds by naming the residential school attended, rather than their hometown. Due to the fact that the majority of hearing parents do not learn to sign, depriving their child of meaningful family relationships, deaf friendships become extremely important to deaf people. Friendships from their residential school days often last a lifetime.

For deaf people, sign language is often an "embodiment of their personal and cultural identity." As with other languages, signed conversations have a certain etiquette that serves as both an exclusive and inclusive gate into the culture and community of deaf people. For new signers, this etiquette, or lack thereof, gives the person away. But as Edward Miner Gallaudet himself wrote, the greatest value of sign language to the deaf is to be found in "the facility it affords for free and unconstrained social intercourse"—which in fullness of expression is in "no respect inferior, and is in many respects superior, to articulated speech as a means of communicating ideas." "Speech and hearing thinking is negatively valued in deaf culture," while mastery of ASL and ASL storytelling are highly valued. It is sometimes assumed that ASL does not have literature, since it is not written down. However, there is a wealth of ASL literature—stories woven around themes of how deaf people see their own lives, their world within the deaf community, and the outside world, namely, the hearing community. Deaf literature often surfaces and flourishes at deaf events and informal gatherings—including vibrant ASL jokes, naming rituals, sign play, plays, fables, tall tales, stories, historical accounts, legends, anecdotes, poetry, and much more. Much of the literature of deaf culture is related directly, or indirectly to issues of power, control and domination between the hearing and deaf world.

· · ·

Members of the deaf community highly value their deaf identity, as well as the collective value of deaf children. The shared experience of deafness generally overrides other dividing factors such as socioeconomic status or ethnicity. Fierce loyalty, hugs, and long goodbyes, are common markers of deaf culture, as is intermarriage. As many as 9 out of 10 deaf people marry other deaf in America. Deaf adults feel strongly about the need for deaf role models in the lives of deaf children and go out of their way to nurture these children with exposure to aspects of their culture. Deaf children who have had no exposure to deaf adults sometimes believe that they will grow up hearing, because they have never met a deaf adult. Many stories in deaf literature expand on this experience and serve as subtle reminders for the deaf adult population to be active in the lives of young deaf children. These cultural values that drive the deaf community are passed on from generation to generation as deaf children become deaf adults.

· · ·

98

Historical, Theoretical, and Foundational Principles of Universal Instructional Design in Higher Education

Susan M. Pliner and Julia R. Johnson

> To educate as the practice of freedom is a way of teaching that anyone can learn. . . . To teach in a manner that respects and cares for the souls of our students is essential if we are to provide the necessary conditions where learning can most deeply and intimately begin.

Although institutes of higher education serve an increasingly diverse student body, they have traditionally been resistant to change, especially in accommodating the needs of students marked as "minorities" because of race, class, ethnicity, gender, disability, religion, nationality, or sexual identification or orientation. After 150 years of status quo preservation, the creation of higher education environments that are accepting and supportive of students with diverse needs is a formidable task that requires a major cultural transformation. In order to create inclusive environments for diverse student populations, the system of higher education must be totally reconfigured, which will require shifts in our educational practices that range from how we admit students, to the curriculum we teach, to pedagogical practices, to career placement, and so forth. These changes not only are desirable from an ethic of inclusion, they also are necessary because our higher education institutions cannot operate in a cultural vacuum: Educational institutions must engage in the same inexorable challenges for inclusion that our total society is facing, that is, full integration and nothing less.

The concept of universality provides an important starting point for educational and social transformation. Activists such as Russell note the preliminary steps needed to achieve "universal social justice" and "the possibility for a common humanity . . . for human emancipation." One primary step toward full integration is accessibility or access to programs and physical structures. Universal Instructional Design offers a range of options and strategies to achieve this first step of accessibility and inclusion.

. . .

CORE PRINCIPLES AND CONCEPTS OF UNIVERSAL INSTRUCTIONAL DESIGN

The goal of Universal Design for Learning (UDL) (Center for Applied Special Technology; CAST 2001) or Universal Instructional Design (UID) (Silver, Bourke, and Strehorn 1998) is to expand institutional teaching methodologies so that students with disabilities and all students with diverse learning needs have equal access to classroom teaching and learning. When classroom teaching practices are inclusive of diverse learning styles and needs from their inception, it is not necessary for students to rely as heavily on support systems that are secondary to primary instructional programs. Furthermore, the established bureaucracy that students must navigate in order to receive accommodations are alleviated by a UID approach. Aune and Kroeger note that "barrier-free environments that are naturally inclusive and that require minimal amounts of adaptation would alleviate much of the tension that results when 'disability interacts with institutions, systems, space and culture.'"

The development of UID as a concept draws from many different fields, but the term itself is borrowed directly from the architectural concept of Universal Design. Universal Design, introduced by Ronald Mace, is designed to make physical spaces accessible and usable by all people, including persons with physical disabilities. The Center for Universal Design at North Carolina State University defines Universal Design as "the design of products and environments to be usable by all people, to the greatest extent possible, without the need for adaptation or specialized design." The Center for Universal Design developed the following guiding principles for implementing Universal Design so that all persons would have access to physical space. These concepts include:(1) equitable use; (2) flexibility in use; (3) simple and intuitive use; (4) perceptible information; (5) tolerance for error; (6) low physical effort; and (7) size and space for approach and use. One commonly understood implementation of these principles is to provide ramps so that wheelchair users, as well as parents pushing strollers, can gain access to buildings (equitable use, flexibility in use, size and space for approach and use). Providing Braille lettering in elevators, the presence of electric door openers, accessible and marked parking, and bathroom stalls large enough to accommodate wheelchairs are additional examples with which most are familiar.

Universal Design in architecture is meant to accommodate the range of potential users in a physical environment. Similarly, Universal Instructional Design or Universal Design for Learning (UDL) accommodates a range of diverse learners in a learning environment. The principles of Universal Design have been applied to instruction, materials, and technology. CAST has led the field in applying UID to the use of technology in teaching and learning. CAST defines UDL as "a new paradigm for teaching, learning, and assessment, drawing on new brain research and new media technologies to respond to individual learner differences." This new paradigm requires a shift in thinking about how faculty design courses to include

> alternatives to make it accessible and appropriate for individuals with different backgrounds, learning styles, abilities, and disabilities in widely varied learning contexts. The "universal" in universal design does not imply one optimal solution for everyone. Rather, it reflects an awareness of the unique nature of each learner and the need to accommodate differences, creating learning experiences that suit the learner and maximize his or her ability to progress

CAST emphasizes the need for flexibility and encourages faculty to consider a framework for designing courses that provide for flexible means of representation, expression, and engagement.

At present, disability studies and education scholars who focus on issues of access have adapted the core principles of Universal Design in architecture to learning and instruction, resulting in the development of UID. The most current list is provided by Scott, Mc Guire, and Shaw, and includes nine primary principles for implementing UID:

1. Equitable use—making classroom material accessible to diverse learning needs and styles
2. Flexibility in use—the practice of using a variety of instructional methods
3. Simple and intuitive—teaching "in a straightforward and predictable manner"
4. Perceptible information—ensuring that course material is accessible to students regardless of their "sensory abilities"

5. Tolerance for error—building diversity of learning "pace and prerequisite skills" into course process
6. Low physical effort—designing instruction "to minimize . . . physical effort" so that students can attend to essential learning
7. Size and space for approach and use—engaging the classroom space in ways that addresses diverse student needs based on "body size, posture, mobility, and communication"
8. A community of learners—teaching and learning environment supports and encourages "interaction and communication among students and between students and faculty"
9. Instructional climate—all students are encouraged to meet "high expectations" as they are "welcomed" to participate in the course.

These principles highlight the need for a varied and flexible approach to teaching because no single method supports or challenges all students. Multiple methods and materials provide a sufficiently broad base that enables all students to learn. In our overview of the remaining articles in this volume, we explain how specific examples of UID principles can be implemented.

At its core, UID calls for equity and inclusiveness in education. UID engages faculty in thinking more broadly about the following: what they teach; why and how they teach it; and, why and how they assess student learning. UID calls for innovative teaching techniques and materials that are suitable for general use, and that are particularly helpful to students with identified or unidentified disabilities, students learning in a second (or third or fourth) language, or students who need additional academic support. Examples of such techniques include:

1. Routine placement of syllabi and reading lists on computer disks or the Web (so that text can be formatted by individual students according to needs)
2. Variable options for assignment and assessment of all students (multiple exam formats, flexibility in time and location, flexibility in presentation of ideas)
3. Provision of supplemental materials in multiple formats, such as oral lectures with overhead projection of "key point" outlines, study guides, or prepared notes.

Students do not have to be disabled to benefit from greater access to teaching materials. Furthermore, UID also allows faculty the freedom to be more flexible in achieving course goals and expectations. Too often, faculty assume that their methods of delivery are synonymous with the student's achievement of course goals. On the contrary, student learning goals are often more easily achieved when the possibilities of diverse learning styles and methods are explored.

The application of UID principles enables all students to have access to a greater range of teaching materials and this access to teaching materials, in turn, is one way to transform educational structures and create more equitable and socially just learning environments. Quite simply, UID is about social justice and transforming oppressive social relationships. As such, it is consistent with the missions of multicultural education and social justice education.

. . .

99

The Social Construction of Disability

Susan Wendell

. . .

I see disability as socially constructed in ways ranging from social conditions that straightforwardly create illnesses, injuries, and poor physical functioning, to subtle cultural factors that determine standards of normality and exclude those who do not meet them from full participation in their societies. I could not possibly discuss all the factors that enter into the social construction of disability here, and I feel sure that I am not aware of them all, but I will try to explain and illustrate the social construction of disability by discussing what I hope is a representative sample from a range of factors.

SOCIAL FACTORS THAT CONSTRUCT DISABILITY

First, it is easy to recognize that social conditions affect people's bodies by creating or failing to prevent sickness and injury. Although, since disability is relative to a person's physical, social, and cultural environment, none of the resulting physical conditions is necessarily disabling, many do in fact cause disability given the demands and lack of support in the environments of the people affected. In this direct sense of damaging people's bodies in ways that are disabling in their environments, much disability is created by the violence of invasions, wars, civil wars, and terrorism, which cause disabilities not only through direct injuries to combatants and noncombatants, but also through the spread of disease and the deprivations of basic needs that result from the chaos they create. In addition, although we more often hear about them when they cause death, violent crimes such as shootings, knifings, beatings, and rape all cause disabilities, so that a society's success or failure in protecting its citizens from injurious crimes has a significant effect on its rates of disability.

The availability and distribution of basic resources such as water, food, clothing, and shelter have major effects on disability, since much disabling physical damage results directly from malnutrition and indirectly from diseases that attack and do more lasting harm to the malnourished and those weakened by exposure. Disabling diseases are also contracted from contaminated water when clean water is not available. Here too, we usually learn more about the deaths caused by lack of basic resources than the (often life-long) disabilities of survivors.

Many other social factors can damage people's bodies in ways that are disabling in their environments, including (to mention just a few) tolerance of high-risk working conditions, abuse and neglect of children, low public safety standards, the degradation of the environment by contamination of air, water, and food, and the overwork, stress, and daily grinding deprivations of poverty. The social factors that can damage people's bodies almost always affect some groups in a society more than others because of racism, sexism, heterosexism, ageism, and advantages of class background, wealth, and education.

Medical care and practices, traditional and Western-scientific, play an important role in both preventing and creating disabling physical damage. . . . Lack of good prenatal care and dangerous or inadequate obstetrical practices cause disabilities in babies and in the women giving birth to them. Inoculations against diseases such as polio and measles prevent quite a lot of disability. Inadequate medical care of those who are already ill or injured results in unnecessary disablement. On the other hand, the rate of disability in a society increases with improved medical capacity to save the lives of people who are dangerously ill or injured in the absence of the capacity to prevent or cure all the physical damage they have incurred. Moreover, public health and sanitation measures that increase the average lifespan also increase the number of old people with disabilities in a society, since more people live long enough to become disabled.

The pace of life is a factor in the social construction of disability that particularly interests me, because it is usually taken for granted by non-disabled people, while many people with disabilities are acutely aware of how it marginalizes or threatens to marginalize us. I suspect that increases in the pace of life are important social causes of damage to people's bodies through rates of accident, drug and alcohol abuse, and illnesses that result from people's neglecting their needs for rest and good nutrition. But the pace of life also affects disability as a second form of social construction, the social construction of disability through expectations of performance.

When the pace of life in a society increases, there is a tendency for more people to become disabled, not only because of physically damaging consequences of efforts to go faster, but also because fewer people can meet expectations of 'normal' performance; the physical (and mental) limitations of those who cannot meet the new pace become conspicuous and disabling, even though the same limitations were inconspicuous and irrelevant to full participation in the slower-paced society. Increases in the pace of life can be counterbalanced for some people by improvements in accessibility, such as better transportation and easier communication, but for those who must move or think slowly, and for those whose energy is severely limited, expectations of pace can make work, recreational, community, and social activities inaccessible.

. . .

Pace is a major aspect of expectations of performance; non-disabled people often take pace so much for granted that they feel and express impatience with the slower pace at which some people with disabilities need to operate, and accommodations of pace are often crucial to making an activity accessible to people with a wide range of physical and mental abilities. . . .

Much of the public world is also structured as though everyone were physically strong, as though all bodies were shaped the same, as though everyone could walk, hear, and see well, as though everyone could work and play at a pace that is not compatible with any kind of illness or pain, as though no one were ever dizzy or incontinent or simply needed to sit or lie down. (For instance, where could you rest for a few minutes in a supermarket if you needed to?) Not only the architecture, but the entire physical and social organization of life tends to assume that we are either strong and healthy and able to do what the average young, non-disabled man can do or that we are completely unable to participate in public life.

A great deal of disability is caused by this physical structure and social organization of society. For instance, poor architectural planning creates physical obstacles for people who use wheelchairs, but also for people who can walk but cannot walk far or cannot climb stairs, for people who cannot open doors, and for people who can do all of these things but only at the cost of pain or an expenditure of energy they can ill afford. Some of the same architectural flaws cause problems for pregnant women, parents with strollers, and young children. This is no coincidence. Much architecture has been planned with a young adult, non-disabled male paradigm of humanity in mind. In addition, aspects of social organization that take for granted the social expectations of performance and productivity, such as inadequate public transportation (which I believe assumes that no one who is needed in the public world needs public transportation), communications systems that are inaccessible to people with visual or hearing impairments, and inflexible work arrangements that exclude part-time work or rest periods, create much disability.

When public and private worlds are split, women (and children) have often been relegated to the private, and so have the disabled, the sick, and the old. The public world is the world of strength, the positive (valued) body, performance and production, the non-disabled, and young adults. Weakness, illness, rest and recovery, pain, death, and the negative (devalued) body are private, generally hidden, and often neglected. Coming into the public world with illness, pain, or a devalued body, people encounter resistance to mixing the two worlds; the split is vividly revealed. Much of the experience of disability and illness goes underground, because there is no socially acceptable way of expressing it and having the physical and psychological experience acknowledged. Yet acknowledgement of this experience is exactly what is required for creating accessibility in the public world. The more a society regards disability as a private matter, and people with disabilities as belonging in the private sphere, the more disability it creates by failing to make the public sphere accessible to a wide range of people.

Disability is also socially constructed by the failure to give people the amount and kind of help they need to participate fully in all major aspects of life in the society, including making a significant contribution in the form of work. Two things are important to remember about the help that people with disabilities may need. One is that most industrialized societies give non-disabled people (in different degrees and kinds, depending on class, race, gender, and other factors) a lot of help in the form of education, training, social support, public communication and transportation facilities, public recreation, and other services. The help that non-disabled people receive tends to be taken for granted and not considered help but entitlement, because it is offered to citizens who fit the social paradigms, who by definition are not considered dependent on social help. It is only when people need a different kind or amount of help than that given to 'paradigm' citizens that it is considered help at all, and they are considered socially dependent. Second, much, though not all, of the help that people with disabilities need is required because their bodies were damaged by social conditions, or because they cannot meet social expectations of performance, or because the narrowly-conceived physical structure and social organization of society have placed them at a disadvantage; in other words, it is needed to overcome problems that were created socially.

Thus disability is socially constructed through the failure or unwillingness to create ability among people who do not fit the physical and mental profile of "paradigm" citizens. Failures of social support for people with disabilities result in inadequate rehabilitation, unemployment, poverty, inadequate personal and medical care, poor communication services, inadequate training and education, poor protection from physical, sexual, and emotional abuse, minimal opportunities for social learning and interaction, and many other disabling situations that hurt people with disabilities and exclude them from participation in major aspects of life in their societies.

For example, Jongbloed and Crichton point out that, in Canada and the United States, the belief that social assistance benefits should be less than can be earned in the work force, in order to provide an incentive for people to find and keep employment, has contributed to poverty among people with disabilities. Although it was recognized in the 1950s that they should receive disability pensions, these were set, as were other forms of direct economic help, at socially minimal levels. Thus, even though unemployed people with disabilities have been viewed by both governments as surplus labour since at least the 1970s (because of persistently high general rates of unemployment), and efforts to increase their employment opportunities have been minimal, they are kept at poverty level incomes based on the 'incentive' principle. Poverty is the single most disabling social circumstance for people with disabilities, since it means that they can barely afford the things that are necessities for non-disabled people, much less the personal care, medicines, and technological aids they may need to live decent lives outside institutions, or the training or education or transportation or clothing that might enable them to work or to participate more fully in public life.

Failure or unwillingness to provide help often takes the form of irrational rules governing insurance benefits and social assistance, long bureaucratic delays, and a pervasive attitude among those administering programs for people with disabilities that their 'clients' are trying to get more than they deserve. . . .

I do not want to claim or imply that social factors alone cause all disability. I do want to claim that the social response to and treatment of biological difference constructs disability from biological reality, determining both the nature and the severity of disability. I recognize that many disabled people's relationships to their bodies involve elements of struggle that perhaps cannot be eliminated, perhaps not even mitigated, by social arrangements. But many of the struggles of people with disabilities, and much of what is disabling, are the consequences of having those physical conditions under social arrangements that could, but do not, either compensate for their physical conditions, or accommodate them so that they can participate fully, or support their struggles and integrate those struggles into the cultural concept of life as it is ordinarily lived.

CULTURAL CONSTRUCTION OF DISABILITY

Culture makes major contributions to disability. These contributions include not only the omission of experiences of disability from cultural representations of life in a society, but also the cultural stereotyping of people with disabilities, the selective stigmatization of physical and mental limitations and other differences (selective because not all limitations and differences are stigmatized, and different limitations and differences are stigmatized in different societies), the numerous cultural meanings attached to various kinds of disability and illness, and the exclusion of people with disabilities from the cultural meanings of activities they cannot perform or are expected not to perform.

The lack of realistic cultural representations of experiences of disability not only contributes to the 'Otherness' of people with disabilities by encouraging the assumption that their lives are inconceivable to non-disabled people but also increases non-disabled people's fear of disability by suppressing knowledge of how people live with disabilities. Stereotypes of disabled people as dependent, morally depraved, superhumanly heroic, asexual, and/or pitiful are still the most common cultural portrayals of people with disabilities. Stereotypes repeatedly get in the way of full participation in work and social life. For example, Francine Arsenault, whose leg was damaged by childhood polio and later by gangrene, describes the following incident at her wedding:

> When I got married, one of my best friends came to the wedding with her parents. I had known her parents all the time I was growing up; we visited in each other's homes and I thought that they knew my situation quite well.
>
> But as the father went down the reception line and shook hands with my husband, he said, "You know, I used to think that Francine was intelligent, but to put herself on you as a burden like this shows that I was wrong all along."

Here the stereotype of a woman with a disability as a helpless, dependent burden blots out, in the friend's father's consciousness, both the reality that Francine simply has one damaged leg and the probability that her new husband wants her for her other qualities. Moreover, the man seems to take for granted that the new husband sees Francine in the same stereotyped way (or else he risks incomprehension or rejection), perhaps because he counts on the cultural assumptions about people with disabilities. I think both the stigma of physical 'imperfection' (and possibly the additional stigma of having been damaged by disease) and the cultural meanings attached to the disability contribute to the power of the stereotype in situations like this. Physical 'imperfection' is more likely to be thought to 'spoil' a woman than a man by rendering her unattractive in a culture where her physical appearance is a large component of a woman's value; having a damaged leg probably evokes the metaphorical meanings of being 'crippled,' which include helplessness, dependency, and pitifulness. Stigma, stereotypes, and cultural meanings are all related and interactive in the cultural construction of disability. . . .

100

Go to the Margins of the Class

Disability and Hate Crimes

Lennard J. Davis

With great ceremony, the press reported the February 1999 conviction of white supremacist John William King for the kidnapping and murder of James Byrd, Jr., who had been chained to a truck in Jasper, Texas, dragged two miles, and dismembered. Likewise, the conviction of coconspirator Lawrence Russell Brewer in September 1999 seemed to imply that justice had been done. If justice in a broader sense is to be served, however, another fact of the case deserves attention. Byrd was not only black and the victim of race hatred; he was also disabled. The press has noted this so casually that few people realize it; those who do, including myself, found out that Byrd was severely arthritic and subject to seizures. This information was ferreted out only after extensive searches of news reports.

Indeed, I myself was uncertain that Byrd was a person with disabilities. I recalled reading, on the day the crime was first reported, that a disabled African American had been brutally murdered. Since I was interested in disability, the article caught my eye. Yet when the story reappeared days, weeks, and months later, Byrd was simply referred to as African American. Almost all the news stories contained this simplification. Indeed, when I decided to write a piece on the subject for *The Nation*, I at first thought I might have made an error in thinking that Byrd was a person with disabilities. When I went to the library to look up the articles on microfilm, I found that the *New York Times* mentioned only twice, in the first two reports, that Byrd was a person with disabilities. Any newspaper story I checked tended to follow that pattern.

. . .

Initially, I wanted to write this story as an op-ed piece for the *New York Times*. An acquaintance who is on the editorial board of the paper read my initial article and responded in a somewhat condescending and negative way. He asked me if I seriously thought that race could be equated with disability, whether the history of lynching and slavery could be meaningfully equated with occasional violence against people with disabilities. The editors for both these progressive journals saw race as the primary category and disability as a poor third cousin of race. Their assumption was that violence toward a person of color with disabilities is primarily the result of the color and much less the result of the disability.

But disability is hardly a minor category. Approximately 16 percent of Americans have a disability and, as such, they comprise a significant minority group with an inordinately high rate of abuse. According to the Center for Women's Policy Studies, disabled women are raped and abused at a rate more than twice that of nondisabled women. The risk of physical assault, robbery, and rape, according to researcher Dick Sobsey, is at least four times as great for adults with disabilities as for the general population. In February 1999, for example, a mentally retarded man in Keansburg, New Jersey, was abducted by a group of young people who tortured, humiliated, and assaulted him. In March 1999, advocates for another mentally retarded man filed a lawsuit against a group of Nassau County, New York, police officers who beat him while he was in custody.

People with disabilities and deaf people report that they are routinely harassed verbally, physically, and sexually in public places. In private institutions or group homes, they are often the prime victims of violence and sexual abuse; in their own homes, they are subjected to sexual abuse, domestic violence, and incest, preyed upon by family members, family "friends," and "caretakers." So the question remains, why is American society largely unaware of or indifferent to the plight of people with disabilities? Is it because as an ableist society, we do not really believe that disability constitutes a serious category of oppression? Whenever race and disability come together, as in the King case, ethnicity tends to be considered so much the "stronger" category that disability disappears altogether.

As a society, we have long been confronted by the existence of discrimination against people of color. Students pour over the subject of race in their textbooks and read the work of multicultural writers in high school and college. Martin Luther King Day and Kwanzaa raise our consciousness, and the heroic tales of people like Rosa Parks inspire us.

But while we may acknowledge we are racist, we barely know we are ableist. Our schools, our textbooks, our media utterly ignore the history of disability; the dominant culture renders invisible the works of disabled and deaf poets, writers, and performance artists. The closest we have come to a national media engagement is the 1998 six-part NPR radio series *Beyond Affliction* and a few references to deafness in the TV series ER. Motion pictures still largely romanticize or pathologize disability; there is not much else to make the experience of 16 percent of the population come alive realistically and politically.

Yet 72 percent of people with disabilities are unemployed, and their income is half the national average. Among working-age adults with disabilities, the poverty rate is three times that of those without impairments. One-third of all disabled children live in poverty; and despite the Americans with Disabilities Act, a judicial backlash has been under way ever since its passage in 1990. From 90 to 98 percent of discrimination cases brought under the ADA by people with disabilities have been lost in court. . . .

Anita Silvers notes this fact when she writes: "the courts tend to implement prohibitions against discrimination so as to favor paradigmatic members of the protected class. In doing so, they propel individuals whose experiences diverge from those of the class's prototypes, but who are equally at risk, to the class's margins." Thus when disability meets race, disability is propelled to the margins of the class.

From a legal perspective, one wants to make sure that members of a historically unprotected class receive proper justice and consideration under the law. Thus in America, women and minorities have been the focus of antidiscrimination law. There has been much cultural work done to make it acceptable at the end of the millennium for such groups to have public respect and sympathy. Countless novels, movies, and plays have accomplished this goal over the course of the twentieth century. It is unimaginable that a film could be made now that would present African Americans, Native Americans, or women as members of a deservedly subordinate, disenfranchised group. Thus the courts will, in the most obvious cases, uphold the right of members of such groups to redress wrongs in housing, employment, discrimination, and so on.

However, disability occupies a different place in the culture at this moment. Although considerable effort has been expended on the part of activists, legislators, and scholars, disability is still a largely ignored and marginalized area. Every week, films and television programs are made containing the most egregious stereotypes of people with disabilities, and hardly anyone notices. Legal decisions filled with ableist language and attitudes are handed down without anyone batting an eyelid. . . . Newspapers and magazines barely notice the existence of disability and largely use ableist language and metaphors in their articles. In other words, disability may be the last significant area of discrimination that has not yet been resolved, at least on the judicial, cultural, and ethical levels, in the twentieth and twenty-first centuries. . . .

So when it comes to violence against people with disabilities, several factors intervene. Although many states have statutes that describe disability in a list of categories that are protected under hate crime legislation, the actual enforcement of such policies may be muted by the intersectionality I have been describing. The Violent Crime Control and Law Enforcement Act of 1994 defines a hate crime as one "in which the defendant intentionally selects a victim, or in the case of a property crime, the property that is the object of the crime, because of the actual or perceived race, color, religion, national origin, ethnicity, gender, disability or sexual orientation of any person." . . .

Tellingly, though, a distinction is often made in this legislation. For example, previously under California's hate crime law, a murder committed because of the victim's race, color, religion, ancestry, or national origin could bring the death penalty or life in prison without parole. However, the maximum penalty for a murder based on gender, sexual orientation, or disability was twenty-five years to life in prison. A new bill signed in September 1999 increases the maximum in those latter categories to life in prison without parole. Federal efforts to prevent hate crimes, however, are now restricted to race, color, religion, and national origin.

Several U.S. senators have sponsored legislation to extend protections to gender, disability, and sexual orientation. But this idea ultimately did not pass into law and, even if it had, hate crimes based on disability are unlikely to carry as stringent a penalty as crimes based on hate for race, color, religion, or national origin. . . .

But how do we determine, in any philosophical sense, that one kind of identity is more important than another? Historically, although the United States was founded on a separation of church and state, religion has been seen as a "holy" category certainly higher in status than, for example, one's sexual orientation; race, so embroiled in the nation's history, must be more important than something like disability; and so on—the arguments are based more on ad hoc judgments about the viciousness of different kinds of prejudice than on any principle one can articulate. This seems to be the same unreflective influence that gives priority to race over gender or disability in the intersectionality argument.

We can see this contradiction in another arena. The FBI is required to keep track of hate crimes. It has produced a report that found that of the 8,049 incidents of hate crime reported to police in 1997, 12 were motivated by bias based on disability; of these, 9 were based on the victim's physical condition and 3 were based on the victim's mental condition. These numbers seem shockingly low when compared to other studies such as Dick Sobsey's tabulations. Sobsey also notes that when a person with disabilities is a victim of crime, it tends to be a violent crime rather than a property crime.

. . .

Indeed, I am sure that when it comes time for the FBI to list the report on Byrd, they will file it under racial hate crime rather than a disability-related crime. Also, many of the crimes against people with disabilities will simply be seen as ordinary rather than hate crimes. So the rape or murder of a mentally ill resident of a sheltered facility will be seen as a rape or murder, not as one motivated by the status of the person involved. Indeed, one of the arguments used by opponents of hate crime legislation, particularly as it applies to gender or disability, is that crimes such as rapes will have to be investigated by the FBI, putting an undue burden on that organization. Since such crimes are daily occurrences, and since it could be argued that rape itself is a hate crime against women, the FBI will be taxed to the utmost in trying to detail all these acts of violence.

Intersectionality argues that individuals who fall into the intersection of two categories of oppression will, because of their membership in the weaker class, be sent to the margins of the stronger class. What these statistics suggest is that the category of disability, while a weak one to judges or legislators, is a powerful one to those who seek to victimize. Rather than minimizing an identity, victimizers are drawn to the double or triple categories of race, gender, and disability. Each of these categories enhances the opportunity for hate and the likelihood that the crime will go unnoticed, unreported, or disbelieved. For example, the Center for Women's Policy Studies reports that virtually half of the perpetrators of sexual abuse against women with disabilities gained access to their victims through disability services, and that caregivers commit at least 25 percent of all crimes against women with disabilities. In other words, the dependency of such women, compounded by their lower economic status, ethnicity, and diminished mobility or ability to communicate to authorities, is an enticement to victimizers.

. . .

The point here is that the general climate of ableism makes it comfortable for us to regard systematic violence against people with disabilities as accidental. Could one claim that the university's policy of negligence toward students with disabilities, especially after being forewarned, was a willed act of violence? The consciousness of the general public and the legal system would have to undergo a dramatic change for the truth of such a claim to be obvious.

Likewise, the definition of "hate" has to change as well. One of the reasons there is resistance to calling attacks against people with disabilities "hate" crimes is because the general ideology toward people with disabilities rules out hate as a viable emotion. In our culture, it is permissible to "pity" or even "resent" people with disabilities. . . . Thus the idea that crimes against people with disabilities might be a result of "hate" seems to most people somehow wrong. Who would act violently toward a person using a wheelchair merely because that person could not walk? . . . someone cannot see a clearly posted sign, cannot walk up unblocked stairs, needs special assistance above what other "normal" citizens need[?] This kind of hatred is one that abhors the possibility that all bodies are not configured the same, that weakness and impairment are the legacy of a cult of perfection and able embodiment. When the law begins to catch on to this level of hatred, justice will be served.

. . .

101

Why the Intersexed Shouldn't Be Fixed

Insights from Queer Theory and Disability Studies

Sumi Colligan

The initiatives the Intersex Society of North America (ISNA) promoted to prevent "corrective" surgery for genitals not clearly identifiable as male or female have recently come to my attention. This discovery has stimulated my own reflections on the parallels between American cultural representations and the everyday struggles of the intersexed and those of people with disabilities. Both groups are subjected to anomalous classification, medical management, silencing, and shame; both groups titillate the projected, and often repressed, fantasies of outsiders; and both intersexed and disabled individuals and organizations are challenging the assumptions that underlie these negative images to reclaim their own impassioned, desirable, and desirous bodies. These activists seek to assert the value of their own presence in the world and to raise questions about a system of cultural ordering that renders them symbolically, if not literally, neutered or "fixed."

David Mitchell and Sharon Snyder point out that while there is an abundance of critical theory on the body, disability remains largely untheorized, often appearing as a natural backdrop for the exploration of already established social issues and themes. They explain: "Within this common critical methodology physical difference exemplifies the evidence of social deviance even as the constructed nature of physicality itself fades from view." Yet opportunities to explore the cultural construction of physicality and its intersections with race, class, gender, and sexuality are abundant, appearing both within the realms of popular and medical culture. These references are often quite explicit and should not require the sensitized lens of disability studies for quick detection. For example, apropos of disability and the trans and/or nebulously gendered, talk show host Jerry Springer is quoted as saying:

> When you think of all the things that could go wrong at birth or at least not be as they ought to be, from blindness to mental retardation to cystic fibrosis to, indeed, the entire litany of possible birth defects, why do we assume that the one thing that can never be out of sync is our gender identity? And yet, while we are quick to heap our love and compassion and charity on any of these disabilities, if it has something to do with sex suddenly we don't want to hear about it. . . . And so with the same compassion that we are offering to those who are trying to fix other parts of their body that perhaps aren't working as they should, why not a word of understanding to those whose gender seems to be out of whack?

A number of issues here go unquestioned: Why are charity and compassion considered to be a desirable and automatic response to certain kinds of physical variation? Why is there an assumption that disability has nothing to do with sex? Why do genitals and gender identity have to match? Why is being fixed a moral imperative?

It is instructive to begin to explore these intersections and parallels by interrogating the meaning of *fixed*. The dictionary definition of the verb indicates "to set in order," "to repair," "to attach or fasten immovably"; even the noun, *fix*, is defined as "an embarrassing or uncomfortable position." Through the lens of *fixed*, I consider how and why Western cultures have come to disable the intersexed and neuter the disabled, subjecting them to similar disciplines of normalization. . . .

MEDICALIZING INTERSEXED/DISABLED BODIES: RETROFITTING AND REFORM

Michel Foucault has documented the forces that have converged in the last two centuries in Western Europe and the United States that contribute to the medical scrutiny of the flesh and its moral attributes. For example, in *The Birth of a Clinic*, Foucault describes processes by which the bodies of individuals undergoing medical treatment came to be viewed as discrete and docile entities whose hidden recesses contained the secrets to their ailments. Likewise, in *The History of Sexuality*, he addresses a range of professions (demography, pedagogy, medicine, and psychiatry among them) that emerged during this period to shape the contours of modernity. These fields used their professional powers to name, locate, regulate, punish, and remold individuals associated with aberrant corporealities. Foucault referred to these approaches as "bio-power," as they are "techniques that make possible a special alliance between specialized knowledge and institutionalized power in the state's management of life."

However, whereas Foucault draws out the implications of the deployment of these forms of power/knowledge to define and contain illness, madness, and sexuality, historian Henri-Jacques Stiker notes that disability is lacking from Foucault's analysis. I contend that such an analysis should be broadened to include the role that the development of statistics played in turning disability into deviance, a process that included upholding a statistical norm against which all else was rendered abnormal. Moreover, the analysis should consider the manner in which the growth of the rehabilitation industry was catalyzed by a drive to remove the "lack" and restore the disabled body to its "assumed, prior normal state." As we shall see, all these powers collided and collaborated to refashion, retrofit, and reform intersexed and disabled bodies to eradicate their "abnormalities" from our social presence and/or to render them invisible.

In Foucault's introduction to *Herculine Barbin: Being the Recently Discovered Diary of a Nineteenth Century French Hermaphrodite*, he states that by the mid-1800s, medical doctors had concluded that everyone had a "true" sex, which even when masked, could be discerned by the penetrating eye of science. This conviction was also corroborated by Alice Dreger, a researcher of French and British physicians between 1860 and 1915, who remarks that "the history of hermaphroditism is largely the history of struggles over the 'realities' of sex—the nature of 'true' sex, the proper role of the sexes, the question of what sex can, should, or must mean." The medical examination of hermaphrodites rested on the assumption of sexual dimorphism such that one's true sex could only be read as male or female. The sorting out of the sexes was conducted by navigating one's way through "genital geography," deciphering anatomical excesses and deficiencies, and distinguishing "veritable" from "pseudo vulvas." If anatomy alone wasn't quick to release its secrets, doctors would also seek clues in behaviors and aptitudes because of an assumed linear correlation between genitals and gendered attractions and performances (ergo, testicles and ovaries are us). Additionally, parents were interrogated for recollections of maternal impressions and "hereditary antecedents," physical indicators of past parental transgressions. Overall, if bodies and actions didn't conform to medical expectations and social conventions, they were forced to comply to nature's imagined calling by medical declaration and legal protocol.

In the past fifty years, surgery and hormonal therapy have become routine, technical solutions for individuals whose genitals are deemed medically problematic. That normative physicality is being constructed here should be readily apparent and is captured humorously by intersex ("intersex" is in common use now because it doesn't carry the mythical connotations of "hermaphrodite") writer Raphael Carter who defines ambiguous genitalia as "genitalia that refuse to declare their sex to doctors—no doubt on the principle that under interrogation by the enemy you should give only name, rank and serial number." This queering of medical authority serves to underscore the invasive consequences of accepted medical definitions and procedures. Intersex reporter Martha Coventry reveals that according to scientific standards, "girls, if they perceive themselves, or want to be perceived as fully 'feminine,' should have clitorises no longer than $3/8$ inch at birth. Boys, if they hope to grow up 'masculine,' should have penises that are about one inch in stretched length at birth. Girls should have vaginas fit for future intercourse, and boys should have urethra openings at the tip of the penis in order to be able to urinate standing up."

Of course, the irony here is that self-identity has nothing to do with this medical intervention because surgeons now generally perform these reconstructive feats on the intersexed in infancy. Biologist Anne Fausto-Sterling argues that the intersexed excite discomfort in medical professionals because "they possess the irritating ability to live sometimes as one sex and sometimes as the other, and they raise the specter of homosexuality." It is clear, then, that intersexed babies are being fixed, at least in part, as a form of rehabilitation that facilitates their bodily deployment into society according to heteronormative measures. In keeping with the body's truth, doctors, however, contend that their medical tampering is simply a means of restoring the infants to their naturally gendered state, denying the role that culture plays in enforcing this imperative.

In parallel fashion, in the last several centuries, people with disabilities have been subjected to pacification through the medical gaze's fixation on essentialized and internalized bodily truths and to reform through the disciplined practices of sheltered workshops, special education, and physical rehabilitation. The benevolence and charity that have been extended to these individuals rest on their willingness, through medical treatment, physical retraining, and mental acquiescence, to strive to achieve normative standards of bodily appearance and physical, linguistic, and cognitive use. By means of these institutional practices, "the disabled are to be 'raised up,' restored." Indeed, historian Stiker concludes: "rehabilitation marks the appearance of a culture that attempts to complete the act of identification, of making identical."

Alternatively, for those who can't be medically disappeared as with the intersexed, there remains the role of desexualized, childlike, dependents who are destined to institutionalization as they await the promise of cure. As historian Paul Longmore notes, these individuals are extended the benevolent hand of charity because, particularly in the United States, their images help reaffirm the virtue and moral fitness of its nondisabled citizens. Stiker asserts that cure suggests removal and that rehabilitation suggests assimilation. Regardless of an emphasis on cure or rehabilitation, "compassion tends to be channeled into normalizing." And either way, intersexed and disabled persons, viewed as destabilizing physical, sexual, gendered, and classificatory presences, have clearly been the targets of coercive regimes of routinization which have nearly, but not so successfully, extinguished their bodily knowledge and their desires.

FIXING BODIES, EXTINGUISHING DESIRES: CONSTRUCTING ASEXUALITY

. . . Both intersexed and disabled bodies have been construed as threatening, with their imagined excesses and deficiencies. Consequently, these bodies have been stripped of their ability to pleasure and be pleasured through the mechanism of denial, the social erasure of sexuality. From this standpoint, both intersexed and disabled bodies are lurking in the social margins, fluctuating between the overly intrusive and the wispy. In this vein, James Porter notes:

> viewed in itself (an essentializing perspective—but that is part of the point), a disabled body seems somehow too much a body, too real, too corporeal: it is a body that, so to speak, stands in its own way. From another angle, which is no less reductive, a disabled body seems to be lacking something essential, something to make it identifiable and something to identify with; a body that is deficiently itself, not quite a body in the full sense of the word, not real enough.

And as Foucault has aptly demonstrated, societal regulatory regimes have been deployed not only to survey these excesses and deficiencies but to contain them as well.

Medicalization of the intersexed and disabled has profoundly shaped their cultural representations and interpersonal relationships, as well as their phenomenological experiences of and with their own bodies. Whereas historically, the intersexed conjured up erotic associations, more recently, repeated medical diagnosis and intervention and medical jargon bantered about in exclusionary or hushed tones have contributed to shrouding disabled/intersexed bodies with an aura of taboo, secrecy, and shame. Overall, medical and cultural assumptions about sex being reserved for heterosexed, symmetrical, and genitally specific bodies tend to promote the expectation that sex and sexuality are privileges awarded to the "normate" only.

The rigid molding of bodies to conform to conventional standards and allowances clearly exacts a toll in conceiving of alternative means of desiring. For the intersexed, "to grow up in a world in which there is no name, at least no spoken name, for what you are" is frightening and confusing. Fear of rejection undermines sexual choices. For instance, Morgan Holmes, an intersexed bisexual, explains: "I learned then that my desire wasn't necessarily linked to my physical difference. However, even that knowledge could not assuage the fear that my lovers of whatever sex, but particularly female, would know I had a fake 'cunt' and would abandon me." In this way, the expectation that our bodies should be strictly products of nature and not culture (as if any human body occupies space outside of culture), awards sexual gratification and relationships to those whose bodies pass the test of normative authenticity.

The story of a person called Toby who was brought up as a girl, then lived as a boy, eventually adopted the label of neuter, and in 1987, endeavored to form a self-help group for others who similarly self-identified, further illustrates the psychic cost of growing up with a body that the surrounding culture denies is possible. "As Toby conceived it, the group's purpose was to provide a forum for people who think of themselves as neuter and/or asexual to make (nonsexual) connections with others." Toby's hope was that such a group would provide " 'a setting free of pressure to define ourselves in terms of maleness or femaleness.' " While asexuality should be respected as a chosen identity and practice, the fact that abstinence is the only acceptable alternative in our society for the unmarried, disabled, or nonheteronormative leaves me wondering why neuter was the one option to fill the interspace. Is this yet one more instance of a presence concealed as an absence because Western binary categories disallow more creative possibilities?

C
O
N
T
E
X
T

What is perhaps most remarkable in the testimonies of intersex though, particularly those individuals whose bodies have escaped medical tampering, is the sense of contentedness with their own bodies. In the video ISNA produced, "Hermaphrodites Speak," Angela Moreno describes the delight she received from her large clitoris at the age of twelve before doctors insisted on performing a "clitoral reduction" as "time in the pleasure garden before the fall." She asserts that what has been most profoundly removed from the intersexed through medical intervention is a uniquely "hermaphroditic eroticism."

Unfortunately, the idea that our bodies harbor our deepest truths tends to obscure the part that our culture and its naturalizing agents play in imposing these so-called truths upon us. Instead we are cast in the role of deceivers if we don't wear our bodies on our sleeves, for we are said to deprive others of their ability to manage us, anchor us, and fix our meaning. Joshua Gamson suggests that on television talk shows, for example, "any dissonance between genital status and genital identity [is taken] as a sign of inauthenticity." Foucault would, in fact, argue that this compulsion to speak incessantly of our sexualities is a manifestation of modern surveillance techniques rather than an expression of our innermost thoughts. This point would indicate that, as much as discourse may attempt to contain the truth of our bodies, there will inevitably be discontinuities between the stories we tell and our bodies themselves. From this vantage point, there can never be a complete correlation between our genital status and our gender identities, no matter who we are. Moreover, David Halperin further complicates this issue of truth telling by stating that "coming out" has the advantage of "claiming back . . . a certain interpretive authority," but never effectively eliminates the "superior and knowing gaze" of the outside viewer.

On the other hand, those of us who have visible disabilities are often neutralized by external fixations that rob us of the opportunity to speak our own pleasures and desires. Part of the problem is that the larger society simply assumes that sexuality and disability are so antithetical to one another that there is no discussion to be had. Certain British disability theorists assert: "In modern Western societies, sexual agency (that is, potential or actual independent sexual activity) is considered the essential element of full adult personhood, replacing the role formerly taken by paid work: because disabled people are infantalized, and denied the status of active subjects, so consequently their sexuality is undermined." Eli Clare argues further that, because disabled bodies are equated so thoroughly with medical pathology, they are generally denied even the distorted and magnified sexuality attributed to many marginalized people.

The tendency to deny any recognition to the sexuality of people with disabilities also contributes to a blurring of their gender identification such that they share a gender ambiguity not so dissimilar from the intersexed. Disability and queer writer Eli Clare explains: "The construction of gender depends not only on the male and female body, but also on the nondisabled body." This refusal to read disabled bodies correctly may even pose a problem for entry and acceptance into gay, lesbian, bisexual, and transgender subcultures as they, too, rely upon visible markers to signify group membership. Attention to the more culturally loaded, but misunderstood qualities of disabled bodies may cause "their less visible identity to be neglected." More generally, visuality and visibility produce complex and contradictory effects for those whose bodies are deemed unnatural because the impulse to stabilize our identities and to mold us into singular subjects is there regardless of the source of our visibility (i.e., by our appearance, our actions, and/or our words). The fact that all of us, in some way, participate in this dynamic suggests that these misreadings are powerful cultural scripts to resist and transform.

. . .

102

Mass Psychiatric Casualties

Dave Grossman

In every war in which American soldiers have fought in this [twentieth] century, the chances of becoming a psychiatric casualty—of being debilitated for some period of time as a consequence of the stresses of military life—were greater than the chances of being killed by enemy fire. The only exception was the Vietnam War, in which the chances were almost equal.

—Richard Gabriel, *No More Heroes*

Are the warriors of today any better than those who fought in the trenches of World War I? Are today's warriors tougher than those who landed on the beaches of Normandy or Iwo Jima in World War II? Are they better than the ones who fought their way out of the frozen Chosen or the Puson Perimeter in Korea? No. Today we are no better than those heroes. And we are no worse. We are the same warriors. We might be better equipped, better trained and better prepared, but we are the same basic, biological organisms as those who have gone before us.

Richard Gabriel, in his excellent book, *No More Heroes*, tells us that in the great battles of World War I, World War II and Korea, there were more men pulled off the front lines because of psychiatric wounds than were killed in combat. There was a study written on this phenomenon in World War II entitled "Lost Divisions," which concluded that American forces lost 504,000 men from psychiatric collapse. A number sufficient to man 50 combat divisions!

On any given day in World War II, thousands of psychiatric casualties were in camps close to the front lines. A procedure called "Immediacy, Expectancy, and Proximity" was applied, meaning they were kept in proximity of the front lines with a sense of immediacy and expectancy that they would go back into battle. Even with that in place, as well as the normal cycles where men rotated out of combat after a reasonable time, more soldiers were lost from psychiatric casualties than all of the physical casualties combined.

Very few people know about this. While everyone knows about the valiant dead, most people, even professional warriors, do not know about the greater number of individuals who were quietly taken out of the front lines because they were psychiatric casualties. This is another aspect of combat that has been hidden from us, and it is something we must understand.

Worst of all were those rare situations in which soldiers were trapped in continuous combat for 60 to 90 days. In those cases, 98 percent became psychiatric casualties. Fighting all day and all night for months on end is a twentieth century phenomenon. The Battle of Gettysburg in 1863 lasted three days, and they took the nights off. This has been the case throughout history. When the sun went down, the fighting stopped, and the men gathered around the campfire to debrief the day's fight.

It was not until the twentieth century, beginning with World War I, that battles went day and night, for weeks and months without end. This resulted in a huge increase in psychiatric casualties and it got vastly worse when soldiers were unable to rotate out of the battle. On the beaches of Normandy in World War II, for example, there were no rear lines, and for two months there was no way to escape the horror of continuous fighting, of continuous death. It was learned then that after 60 days and nights of constant combat, 98 percent of all soldiers became psychiatric casualties.

. . .

Consider the six-month-long Battle of Stalingrad, the decisive World War II Soviet victory that stopped the German southern advance and turned the tide of the war. Some Russian reports say that their veterans of that great battle died around age 40, while other Russian males not involved lived into their 60s and 70s. The difference? The war veterans had been exposed to continual stress 24 hours a day for six, long, grueling months.

To fully comprehend the intensity of mental stress from combat, we must keep other environmental stressors in mind, while at the same time understanding the body's physiological response as the sympathetic nervous system is mobilized. In addition, we must understand the impact of the parasympathetic nervous system's "backlash" that occurs as a result of overwhelming demands placed upon it.

If we agree that we are basically no different creatures than the warriors of World War I, World War II and Korea, then we must admit that the same thing could happen to us. . . .

103

The Gulf War's Troubling Legacy

Gary Null

With only 148 Americans officially killed in action and only 467 wounded, ours seemed to be a shining victory in the Gulf. But this victory has lost its glow somewhat, now that we know that tens of thousands of our Gulf service people have become sick from a debilitating and sometimes deadly syndrome. According to H. Lindsey Arison III, aide to the undersecretary of the U.S. Air Force, there are now 50,000 veterans suffering from Gulf War syndrome, including about 11,000 on active duty.

Arison outlines the causes of Gulf vets' health problems. First, they were exposed to nonlethal levels of chemical and biological agents released primarily by direct Iraqi attack via missiles, rockets, artillery, or aircraft munitions and by fallout from allied bombings of Iraqi chemical warfare munitions facilities during the thirty-eight-day 1991 war.

Exposure to chemical and biological agents alone is one thing. But the effects of these were exacerbated by a whole gamut of other factors to which vets were exposed. Arison enumerates them: nerve agent pretreatment pills that our service people were ordered to take; investigational botulinum toxoid vaccines; anthrax vaccines; and depleted uranium, used in armor-piercing munitions. Other factors enter into the synergistic mix including oil fire contamination and pesticides, and some people believe that an artificially engineered bacterium/virus cross called a mycoplasma, and, separately, that a vaccine ingredient, the adjuvant squalene, were significant factors, too.

Arison emphasizes the point that since different people were exposed to different hazards at different levels, a whole variety of symptomatologies have arisen in Gulf War vets. This variability of symptoms is sometimes taken to mean that Gulf War syndrome is a "mystery illness" or that people are imagining things, when in fact it just shows that the syndrome is a multifactorial problem.

SYMPTOMS

Gulf War syndrome (GWS) is manifested in many ways. Chronic fatigue immune dysfunction syndrome (CFIDS) affects over half of the victims, according to Dr. Garth Nicolson, who, with his wife, molecular biophysicist and University of Texas professor Dr. Nancy Nicolson, has examined and evaluated many syndrome patients. Public health expert Dr. Leonard Horwitz estimates that 80 to 90 percent of syndrome patients are plagued with severe aches and pains in their joints. Others commonly experience dizziness, nausea, stomach pains, light sensitivity, intense anxiety, breathing difficulty, muscle spasms, diarrhea, blurred vision, inexplicable skin rashes, bleeding gums, eye redness, night sweats, and acute migraine-like headaches. Sexual and urination disorders plague numerous victims, and 25 percent have acquired multiple chemical sensitivities, which means they have become allergic to a wide variety of chemical substances and can consequently have severe reactions to even the most common household items.

According to Drs. Garth and Nancy Nicolson, the CFIDS characteristic of sick Gulf vets is induced by an unusual microorganism that seems to be the product of weaponization, that is, human manipulation of germs for the purposes of warfare. The Nicolsons report that the organism present in each of the CFIDS patients is an odd variant of a typical mycoplasma. Ordinarily, a mycoplasma is a cross between a bacterium and a virus, and can be effectively combated with antibiotics. But in this case, the organism contains human immunodeficiency virus (HIV-1) and anthrax genes. Since it is not possible for the typical mycoplasma to naturally mutate into a modified form of anthrax and the alleged AIDS virus, this seems to be an engineered organism. The Nicolsons contend that the U.S. military created this mycoplasma and sold it to Iraq, which subsequently used it against U.S. troops.

. . .

104

Disability in the New World Order

Nirmala Erevelles

. . .

In this chapter, I speak from the critical vantage point of two theoretical perspectives: Third World feminism(s) and disability studies. By deploying the term Third World feminism(s), I am referring to the political constituency of women of African, Caribbean, Asian, and Latin American descent, as well as Native peoples of the United States who constitute an oppositional alliance against the sexist, racist, imperialist, neocolonial structures that shape our lives. When defining Disability Studies, I refer particularly to the social, political, and economic conditions within the category of "disability" which is constituted as "deviant" difference, and the ideological effects that such constructions of "disability" have on the reproduction of racial, gendered, and class oppression. At the same time, my discussion will address the actual conditions and experiences of Third World people's lives when mediated via the oppressive and often violent social relations of race, class, caste, gender, and disability.

The dialectical relationship between poverty and disability has been recognized for some time. Living with a disability adds to the risks of living in poverty, while at the same time, conditions of poverty increase the possibility of becoming disabled. In this essay, I will elaborate on this relationship between poverty and disability in Third World contexts—with a special focus on India—in the wake of sweeping economic reforms implemented by state governments in deference to structural adjustment policies (SAPs) which have been recommended by the World Bank and the IMF. . . .

ENGENDERING ECONOMIC REFORM: IMPLICATIONS FOR DISABILITY

Third World feminists have documented how the effects of (neo)colonial institutions and policies have transformed indigenous patriarchies and consolidated hegemonic middle-class cultures in metropolitan and colonized areas in support of oppressive patriarchal structures, albeit in new forms. This has been especially true in the context of the SAPs, where women and children have become the most vulnerable populations. Critics of the World Bank and the IMF have pointed out that SAPs were instituted to prioritize the efficient management of debt, rather than to transform the abject conditions of poverty in contexts where women and children represent the disproportionate percentage of the world's poor. Programs instituted by the World Bank and the IMF also supposedly sought to include women as active participants in wage labor markets to enable their emancipation from patriarchal oppression.

However, most of the labor activities offered to Third World women are for low-wage work, because these women are considered "cheap" and "pliable" labor in both factory production and the service industry. As a result, this new gendered labor shift has forced men out of jobs, and, as a result, poor Third World women are forced to balance wage labor along with subsistence and domestic production. Because of the sharp fall in the purchasing power of their incomes, Third World women, many of whom are single heads of households, are faced with the sole responsibility of meeting household reproduction costs. In the desperation for employment, poor women are forced to take jobs in the informal and other low-wage sectors while, at the same time, their unpaid labor escalates because they must stretch limited funds to cover the subsistence of their households. Additionally, their health is also affected because of reduced food consumption, stress, and domestic violence—experiences that affect fertility, infant mortality, and disabling conditions in both their children and themselves.

It is this economic context that sets the stage for the social construction of disability. According to Elwan, UNICEF's list of major causes of disability among children in Third World countries includes inadequate nutrition of mothers and children, vitamin deficiencies, abnormal prenatal or perinatal events, infectious diseases, accidents, and various other factors including environmental pollution and lack of adequate sanitation—all of which occur as a result of poverty conditions. Notwithstanding the World Bank's claims that the SAPs would eventually lead to a reduction in poverty, according to UNICEF, there has been a drop of 10% to 25% in average incomes, a 25% reduction in spending per capita on health, and a 50% reduction in spending per capita on education in the poorest countries in the world. Though officials argue that they advise sound macroeconomic policies and strategies that favor investment in basic human capital—primary health care and universal primary education—the implementation of the SAP's belie this claim. Abbasi points out that even though World Bank lending for health services has increased over the years, low-income countries are unable to meet and maintain health service costs and at the same time pay their debts, and have therefore begun to levy a small fee also called a "user charge" to all clients using public health services. In already destitute communities, these user charges have resulted in a decline in access to health services with disastrous consequences to these populations. As a result, according to Andrew Creese, a health economist at the World Health Organization (WHO), increases in maternal mortality and the incidence of communicable diseases such as diphtheria and tuberculosis have been attributed to such policies.

India offers a good case study of these practices. Forced to implement the structural adjustment programs (SAPs) in the early 1990s to meet the deficit in its balance of payments, the Indian state was encouraged to liberalize its economy, which required that it perform three main functions: protect and sustain the functioning of markets; use all policy instruments available to entice foreign capital investment; and undertake certain minimal expenditures so as to ameliorate the excesses perpetrated by the market. The implementation of the SAPs has only exacerbated the relationship between poverty and disability in India. Thus, for example, nearly fifteen thousand children in India under the age of five go blind because of a vitamin A deficiency caused by malnutrition. Additionally, limited access to clean water supplies as well as overcrowding in inadequate and unsanitary living conditions are responsible for the spread of intestinal, infectious, and vector-carrying diseases that also contribute to the onset of disability.

Even health policies actively supported by the international organizations barely address the crux of the problem. For example, the Indian state's investment in "Health for All by 2000," based on the Alma Ata Declaration of 1978, fostered only two major programs— oral rehydration therapy and immunization—instead of providing general health care for everyone. While such programs produced good statistics that claimed a lower rate of infant mortality, malnutrition and morbidity rates increased. And in the current context, as SAPs have mandated the increased privatization of health care and user financed health services, the transfer of resources from its poor clients to the wealthy investors of health care is the main outcome.

Additionally, even the rehabilitation projects, such as community based rehabilitation (CBR) programs (which are actively supported by the World Bank and other international organizations, such as ActionAid), also have served to accentuate inequalities along the axes of gender, class, caste, and disability. The dominant representation of the philosophy of CBR has been to integrate disabled people into the social mainstream. In a context where the resources allocated to rehabilitation programs are low and where there is a shortage of trained personnel to provide these services, CBR has become one of the most cost-efficient means to save on mounting staff costs, waste of labor, and the low efficiency of services. Thus, in an attempt to ensure maximum cost-efficiency, policy makers assume that the primary support for these programs will come from the community, where parents and workers, supervised by health volunteers (a village rehabilitation worker, or VRW, and a multipurpose rehabilitation worker, or MRW), will provide more specialized services to disabled members of the community.

However, the very concept of inclusion becomes exploitative in such contexts. Like the health programs supported by SAPs, CBR only serves to transfer the costs of services to the community. Thus, for example, even one of its advocates, Maya Thomas, director of the disability division ActionAid International-India has admitted that "the trend of progressive impoverishment of rural dwellings and the growing abandonment of extended family systems leave little economic and manpower resources in families that continue to look after the needs of their disabled members." Further, in patriarchal contexts, the provision of rehabilitation services by the family predominantly implies the woman, and so this becomes another burden in the life of the rural housewife caught up in her struggle for day-to-day economic survival. At the same time, most of the rehabilitation aides, who are low down in the occupational hierarchy and who receive pitiably low wages, are once again predominantly poor women from the community. Therefore, what has happened is that these state-initiated policies that have been celebrated for their cost-effectiveness are actually geared to "[mobilize] people's resources for government programs," where the additional costs of these services continue to be absorbed by both the paid and unpaid labor of women.

. . .

105

Gawking, Gaping, Staring

Eli Clare

Gawking, gaping, staring: I can't say when it first happened. When first a pair of eyes caught me, held me in their vice grip, tore skin from muscle, muscle from bone. Those eyes always shouted, "Freak, retard, cripple," demanding an answer for tremoring hands, a tomboy's bold and unsteady gait I never grew out of. It started young, anywhere I encountered humans. Gawking, gaping, staring seeped into my bones, became the marrow. I spent thirty years shutting it out, slamming the door.

The gawkers never get it right, but what I want to know is this: will you? When my smile finds you across the room, will you notice the odd angle of my wrists cocked and decide I am a pane of glass to glance right through? Or will you smile back?

Thirty years, and now I am looking for lovers and teachers who will hold all my complexities and contradictions gently, honestly, appreciatively. Looking for heroes and role models who will accompany me through the world. Looking for friends and allies who will counter the gawking, gaping, staring.

I come from peoples who have long histories of being on stage—freaks and drag queens, court jesters and scientific experiments. Sometimes we work for money and are proud. Other times we're just desperate. We've posed for anthropologists and cringed in front of doctors, jumped through hoops and answered the same questions over and over, performed the greatest spectacles and thumbed our noses at that shadow they call normal.

William Johnson—African American and cognitively disabled in the mid-1800s—worked the freak-show stage. He donned an ape costume and shaved his head, save for a tuft of hair at the very top, and became the monkey man, the missing link, the bridge between "brute" and "man." P.T. Barnum, showman extraordinaire and shaper of the institution of the freak show, named William's exhibit "What-Is-It?" People paid to gawk, and William died a well-off man. The folks who performed alongside William affectionately called him the "dean of freaks." Today that question—what is it?—still lingers, still haunts us, only now the gawkers get in for free.

Billy Tipton worked the jazz stage with his piano, saxophone, and comedy routines. Billy lived for fifty years as a female-bodied man. He married five times and adopted three sons. He turned down major, high-profile music gigs. He died of a bleeding ulcer rather than seeking out medical care. He was much admired by the men he played music with. This we know about Billy, but there is also much we don't know: how he thought of himself, his gender; what prompted him to make the move from woman to man; what went through his head as he lay dying in his son's arms. But really, the questions I want to ask aren't about his gender but rather about his life as a musician. *Billy, what did your body feel like as your fingers raced into a familiar song, playing in front of great throngs of people?* The gawking started after his death as the headlines roared, "Jazz Musician Spent Life Concealing Fantastic Secret."

I listen to the histories and everywhere hear the words *cripple, queer, gimp, freak*: those words hurled at me, those words used with pride. When I walk through the world, the bashers see a fag, the dykes see a butch, and I myself don't have many words. I often leave it at genderqueer or transgender butch. The gawkers never get it right. They think I'm deaf or "mentally retarded." They think I'm a twenty-one-year-old guy or a middle-aged dyke. They can't make up their minds, start with sir, end with ma'am, waver in the middle. They think I am that pane of glass.

Cripples, queers, gimps, freaks: we are looking for lovers and teachers—teachers to stand with us against the gawking; lovers to reach beneath our clothing, beneath the words that attempt to name us, beneath our shame and armor, their eyes and hands helping return us to grace, beauty, passion. *He cradles my right hand against his body and says, "Your tremors feel so good." And says, "I can't get enough of your shaky touch." And says, "I love your cerebral palsy." This man who is my lover. Shame and disbelief flood my body, drowning his words. How do I begin to learn his lustful gaze?*

Believing him takes more than trust. I spent so many years shutting the staring out, slamming the door. Friends would ask, "Did you see that person gaping at you?" and I'd answer, "What person?" It's a great survival strategy but not very selective. In truth the door slammed hard, and I lost it all, all the appreciation, flirtation, solidarity that can be wrapped into a gaze. These days I practice gawking at the gawkers and flirting as hard as I know how. The first is an act of resistance; the second, an act of pride. I am looking for teachers.

If I had a time machine, I'd travel back to the freak show. Sneak in after hours, after all the folks who worked long days selling themselves as armless wonders and wild savages had stepped off their platforms, out of their geek pits, from behind their curtains. I'd walk among them—the fat women, the short-statured men commonly called dwarves and midgets, the folks without legs, the supposed half-men/half-women, the conjoined twins, the bearded women, the snake charmers and sword swallowers—as they took off their costumes, washed their faces, sat down to dinner. I'd gather their words, their laughter, their scorn at the customers—the rubes—who bought their trinkets and believed half their lies. I'd breathe their fierceness into me.

I am looking for teachers and heroes to show me the way toward new pride, new understanding, new strength, a bigger sense of self. Often it is history I turn to, history I grasp and mold in my search. I am not alone in this endeavor. I think of a kid we've come to know as Brandon Teena: twenty-one years old, living as a guy in rural Nebraska, revealed as female-bodied, raped, and murdered by so-called friends. In trans community, we've chosen him. Claimed him as an FTM (a female-to-male trans person) based on how his life makes sense to us without listening to his confusion. Named him Brandon Teena without paying attention to the dozen other names he used. We have made him hero, martyr, symbol of transphobic violence. I think again of Billy Tipton. In the lesbian community, many have taken Billy to be an emblem of the sexism in the jazz world of the mid-1900s. They shape his life as a man into a simple survival strategy that allowed him to play music. I myself read the life of William Johnson and find someone who turned a set of oppressive material and social conditions to his benefit and gained a measure of success and community. That reading strengthens me. But in truth William might have been a lonely, frightened man, coerced, bullied, trapped by freak-show owners and managers. We use and reshape history, and in the process it sometimes gets misshapen.

At the same time, we all need teachers and heroes: folks to say, "You're not alone. I too was here. This is what I did and what I learned. Maybe it'll help." My best heroes and teachers don't live on pedestals. They lead complex, messy lives, offering me reflections of myself and standing with me against the gawkers.

The gawkers who never get it right. They've turned away from me, laughed, thrown rocks, pointed their fingers, quoted Bible verses, called me immoral and depraved, tried to heal me, swamped me in pity. Their hatred snarls into me, and often I can't separate the homophobia from the ableism from the transphobia.

The gawkers never get it right, but what I want to know is this: will you? If I touch you with tremoring hands, will you wince away, thinking cripple, thinking ugly? Or will you unfold to my body, let my trembling shimmer beneath your skin?

These days, I practice overt resistance and unabashed pride, gawking at the gawkers and flirting as hard as I know how. The two go together. On the Castro, I check out the bears, those big burly men with full beards and open shirts. One of them catches my eyes. I hold his gaze for a single moment too long, watch as it slips down my body. He asks, "Are you a boy or a girl?" not taunting but curious. I don't answer. What could I possibly say? I walk away smiling, my skin warm.

In another world at another time, I would have grown up neither boy nor girl, but something entirely different. In English there are no good words, no easy words. All the language we have created—transgender, transsexual, drag queen, drag king, stone butch, high femme, nellie, fairy, bulldyke, he-she, FTM, MTF (a male-to-female trans person)— places us in relationship to masculine or feminine, between the two, combining the two, moving from one to the other. I'm hungry for an image to describe my gendered self, something more than the shadowland of neither man nor woman, more than a suspension bridge tethered between negatives. I want a solid ground with bedrock of its own, a language to take me to a brand new place neither masculine nor feminine, day nor night, mortise nor tenon. What could I possibly say to the bears cruising me at 3 P.M. as sunlight streams over concrete?

Without language to name myself. I am in particular need of role models. I think many of us are. Who do we shape our masculinities, our femininities, after? Who shows us how to be a drag queen, a butch, a trannyfag (a gay FTM) who used to be a straight married woman and now cruises the boys hot and heavy, a multigendered femme boy/girl who walks the dividing line? I keep looking for disabled men to nurture my queer masculinity, crip style. Looking for bodies a bit off-center, a bit off-balance. Looking for guys who walk with a tremble; speak with a slur; who use wheelchairs, crutches, ventilators, braces; whose disabilities shape, but don't contradict, their masculinities.

And in truth I am finding those role models. There is a freak show photo: Hiram and Barney Davis offstage—small, wiry men, white, cognitively disabled, raised in Ohio. They wear goatees, hair falling past their shoulders. They look mildly and directly into the camera. Onstage, Hiram and Barney played "Waino and Plutano, the Wild Men of Borneo." They snapped, snarted, growled, shook their chains at the audience. People flocked to the "Wild Men," handing over good money to gape. I hope just once Hiram and Barney stopped mid-performance, up there on the sideshow platform, and stared back, turning their mild and direct gaze to the rubes, gawking at the gawkers.

It usually takes only one long glance at the gawkers—kids on their way home from school, old women with their grocery bags, young professionals dressed for work. Just once I want someone to tell me what they're staring at. My tremoring hands? My buzzed hair? My broad, off-center stance, shoulders well-muscled and lopsided? My slurred speech?

Just once. But typically one long, steely glance, and they're gone. I am taking Hiram and Barney as my teachers.

The gawkers never get it right, and what I want to know is this: will you? When I walk through the world, will you simply scramble for the correct pronoun, failing whichever one you choose, he not all the way right, she not all the way wrong? Or will you imagine a river at dusk, its skin smooth and unbroken, sun no longer braided into sparkles? Cliff divers hurl their bodies from thirty, forty, fifty feet, bodies neither flying nor earth-bound, three somersaults and a half turn, entering the water free-fall without a ripple. Will you get it right?

I am looking for friends and allies, for communities where the staring, gaping, gawking finally turns to something else, something true to the bone. Places where strength gets to be softened and tempered, love honed and stretched. Where gender is known as more than a simple binary. Where we are encouraged to swish and swagger, limp and roll, and learn the language of pride. Places where our bodies begin to become home. Gawking, gaping, staring: I can't say when it first happened.

106

As Much Love as You Can Muster

Lesley A. Jones

Thanks to undiagnosed Asperger's syndrome (AS), I grew up in "Backwards Land." I walked funny and couldn't play sports well. I was chastised for, and embarrassed by, my strange gestures and habits. I was bullied by other children—and sometimes even by teachers! I couldn't write properly (dysgraphia); I often misunderstood what people were saying to me (central auditory processing disorder); and I sometimes had a hard time recognizing people (mild prosopagnosia). I was often criticized for choosing to spend my time with books rather than my peers. I was a bright child, but I couldn't get the help I needed—because I was bright. I floundered because, until I was an adult, I wasn't able to get the diagnosis that marked the beginning of my true self-understanding.

Today, life has really improved for the child with AS. But I still hear parents talk about many problems with their children, their children's teachers, and their children's peers. While I can't go back and change my childhood, by taking you on a tour of Backwards Land as I experienced it, maybe I can help you to understand more about your priceless child and how to help her or him navigate the often frustrating paths of Backwards Land with a little more grace.

As you well know, your child has a unique perspective on the world. You have a child who can see that the emperor has no clothes and doesn't hesitate to tell everyone. There are difficulties and hardships involved with raising (or being!) a child who really does march to the beat of a different drummer—a child with a neurology so different he sometimes seems to come from another planet, yet so similar to those around him that people are frequently puzzled when you tell them your child has special needs. But you know all too well that even though your child is amazingly skilled in certain areas, there are those gaps, those empty places—those disabilities that you and your child wrestle with every day.

I can't tell you how to raise your child. Even if I could, my answer would just be, "with as much love as you can muster." But I can tell you some of the things I would change about my own childhood. Hopefully, my insights will shine some light on your child's world. If I could turn back the clock and make some changes, here are things I'd try to make different.

I'd get a proper diagnosis. The pain you felt when your child was diagnosed with AS may have blinded you to the true gift of that diagnosis. Most parents are very upset to learn that their child has AS. But, stop to think about the difficulties of my labelless childhood and be grateful that someone has identified your child's problem and provided the means to help people understand and respect your child's needs. With the verification provided by an official label, you can fight to secure the proper individualized education plan (IEP) for your child and feel wholly justified in that battle. Everyone knows that a child with a disability needs accommodations! When you count your blessings, don't forget to count an accurate diagnosis for your child.

If I could change my childhood, adults would have focused more on the things I could do and spent less time punishing me for the things I couldn't do. I often hear parents say, "we refuse to use AS as an excuse," and I think that's good. However, expecting a child with AS to think, feel, and act like a child without AS is too much of a burden. Children need permission to be angry—as long as they learn not to lash out at others. Children need permission to find things difficult—as long as they never give up the fight to learn new things. Each child needs permission to be the child she or he is—not the child everyone wishes her or him to be.

Being lectured to and chastised all the time made me alternate between rage and withdrawal. I think it's easy to get caught up in a desire to help a child succeed and a frustration with their limitations—and end up pushing them too hard. I appreciate that my parents didn't give up on trying to help me succeed, but I wish they could have spent more time letting me know that they were proud of the things that I could do. I was a very sensitive child, and I wasn't very good at understanding that my parents loved me just by looking at their actions. I needed to hear the words, too. Your child can't guess that you love her or him—tell them, and do it often!

If I could go back in time and change things, the adults in my life would realize that I wasn't learning new social skills just by being exposed to lots of children every day. Children with AS don't "absorb" social rules the way other children do. I used to beg to be home-schooled instead of being thrown back in the "shark tank" of school. I understand now that my parents didn't have the time or resources to home-school me. But with a proper diagnosis, there should have been other options that would have exposed me to less peer abuse and more opportunities for personal and social growth. If your child complains of bullying, please take her or him seriously and do whatever you can to change the situation!

If I could change my past, I would have been allowed to use a typewriter for my school-work when I asked for it (third grade) instead of being pushed to complete mountains of schoolwork with insufficient motor skills. I wish I'd been tutored in handwriting by a therapist, but allowed to type my class work so that it would be legible. I would have had a much better chance of keeping up with my classmates and not had to suffer the dual insult of being punished for poor handwriting and, then, being punished for poor performance caused by my poor handwriting.

If I could rewrite my history, I would have been placed in gentler gym classes, designed to help less coordinated students, where I wouldn't have to suffer through kickball, basketball, or (shudder) dodgeball. I understand that sports are supposed to help children learn team spirit. But how much team spirit can a child learn who is constantly insulted for poor performance? After the team captains had chosen everyone for their teams except me, they would sometimes ask if they could just play with a team short one player—instead of having to take me on their team. That's no environment for a child to learn how to become a team player!

For sports, I wish I'd been placed with children with other mild physical disabilities. I could have learned more about accommodating others and caring about others' special needs. Because all players would have been more evenly matched in skills, no one would have batted an eye at my terrible clumsiness and inability to kick, throw, or catch a ball. If your child is treated like less than a person when it comes to sports, look for new options. You probably can't change the attitudes of those children your child has been playing with, but you may be able to get your child placed in a more appropriate group of children who are more willing to accept your child as she or he is.

Most important of all, I would have been frequently reminded that I was unique and talented instead of only being told, at school, that I was lazy, willful, and not living up to my potential—and being told, at home, that I was a disappointment and embarrassment to the family. I'm sure that my parents really did love me, but in their frustration and disappointment, they forgot to tell me about their love. I wouldn't be surprised to learn that my teachers were impressed with some of my special skills, but I never heard their praise, only their lectures about my shortcomings.

As a child with AS, I needed acceptance and affirmation most of all. I needed to work from a base of high self-esteem about all the good in me, not struggle to dig myself out of a pit of despair caused by focusing only on all my failings.

Every child with AS needs to know she or he is loved and accepted for who she or he is. Now, as an adult, I'm able to love and accept myself. But, the struggle to come to this place of self-esteem would not have been so monumental if a positive self-image had been nurtured in me from an early age. I can't stress how vital it is to help children with AS believe in themselves and their inherent goodness and worth.

107

How to Curse in Sign Language

Ashley and Deborah

. . .

When I arrived at Starbucks, I saw Deborah, sitting alone, not drinking any coffee. She appeared to be in her midforties and was wearing tapered jeans and white shoes. She looked like a nurse who was exhausted after working the night shift. Raising a child like Ashley, I thought, she must feel fatigued all the time. She sat in her chair like someone who had been standing for years.

I sat down and introduced myself. There was no small talk. Deborah started right in with her story. She had grown up in a rural setting, in Virginia Beach, in a middle-class Catholic home. The household income was just enough to meet the family's needs. Deborah had a twin brother, and their extended family was large. Family gatherings often included more than seventy-five people, "nudging and talking over each other," she told me. "I loved it."

. . .

The problems continued even after the birth of their son, Chip. Finally, after months of drama and upheaval, Deborah—with the support of an Episcopal minister—filed for divorce, went to court, and eventually got custody of her son.

Ashley came into Deborah's life through an announcement posted at a local United Methodist church not long after she and her young son had moved to Richmond. Deborah was trying to rebuild her life. She was working in computers, a career she had set in motion when she was still a cop, and completed her bachelor's degree in computer science while working full-time. She was also taking an exercise class at the aforementioned church. One day, she arrived early, thirty minutes before her class began. To kill time, she stood around reading various postings on the church bulletin board. The tip of a yellow piece of paper, burled under the rest, caught her eye, and she uncovered an announcement from the United Methodist Family Services. This organization was holding an adoption information program for people who might consider "challenging" adoptions. She decided to attend the session just to "see what the group had to say."

. . .

After the meeting, Deborah signed up for a nine-week training session followed by what is known as a "home study." This training was a prerequisite for going any further in the adoption process. According to Deborah, "the leaders of the training didn't pull any punches and shared the very difficult things involved in the adoption of special-needs or older children." Many of these children would need lifelong care. Many would require advanced medical supervision at home. Many would have emotional problems. But after each session, Deborah "felt even more strongly about adoption as an option." Most people who have gone through the adoption process consider the home study to be the most difficult. It requires the prospective parent to undergo multiple background checks, physical exams, and a financial audit; to obtain three letters of recommendation; to write an autobiography; and to submit to three unannounced home inspections by a social worker. Deborah passed the home study with an almost perfect score, and then, in her words, "the search began."

It lasted over a year and a half. Deborah was looking for a child with physical disabilities, not a child with emotional challenges. Here and there were children who could be a good match, but they always went to another family. "I began to wonder," Deborah said, "if I had read my 'leading' incorrectly." She was on the verge of giving up when she got a call from her social worker about Ashley. Deborah was one of two finalists vetted from a field of eighty-five. "Don't expect much," the social worker said. "Ashley looks different. She is not the cutest baby around."

Ashley had been born to an alcoholic, anorexic mother fourteen weeks prematurely. She weighed just over one and a half pounds, and her medical birth records state that she smelled of alcohol when she was delivered. A liver biopsy was performed right after her birth, and it showed that a tumor was present. She also had a "brain bleed." Even more threatening to Ashley's health was a rare condition she had, called Juvenile Xanthogranulomas, which cause tumors to form all over the body. These tumors, according to Deborah, "formed on Ashley's skin, under her skin, on her eyes and ears, on other vital organs, and on her brain."

Deborah and her social worker drove to Ashley's foster mother's apartment. Deborah was warned again about Ashley's condition. At that point, Ashley was about eighteen months old and had just been through surgery to have her first brain tumor removed. She was a "failure to thrive" baby, which meant she ate nothing and only drank a little milk. The apartment was nice enough, Deborah remembers, but had a hushed feeling.

After the introduction and pleasantries, the foster mother pointed to a crib. The three women walked over together, and Deborah peered down at the baby she was told was not quite normal. But that is not what she saw. "I thought she was beautiful," Deborah recalled. "Her left eye, because of glaucoma, was about twice the size of her right eye. And although that skewed the symmetry of her face, she had a smile that lit up the room! She was not the least bit intimidated by having three extra people in her small space and was quite friendly with everyone. She let everyone hold her, and as we all talked and cooed to her, she explored everyone's face with her hands."

Deborah walked away from the crib and pulled the social worker aside. "I love that baby," she said. "I would very much like her to be a part of my family." . . .

Ashley's early struggle for life was far from over. She had a second brain tumor removed just before she turned two years old. Soon, she also had her gallbladder removed because of a tumor, and there was another one forming between her ears and brain. Ashley also had a seizure disorder. On top of all that, she was deaf and blind. Most of us would have seen Ashley's life as either not worth living or pitiful. Deborah saw something different. Deborah saw her as nothing exceptional, as just a little baby.

. . .

After coffee, I followed Deborah to her house in the burbs. It was a typical suburban house with a slight difference. Out front was a large street sign that said *deaf-blind child area*. Once inside, Deborah gave me the obligatory tour, the dining room, the kids' rooms, and the kitchen, with its linoleum floor and faux wood cabinets. I noted that Deborah had a peaceful, quiet way about her when she wasn't talking about Ashley's struggles. Anger did not have a place in her world. Faith played a huge role in Deborah's life. As we walked through her house she told me that finding a church that was welcoming to Ashley had been nearly impossible. The world—even churches, it seemed—shared my fear of people like Ashley and all of its subtle manifestations.

"When I have tried to take her into the service with me," Deborah said, "I am constantly asked to take her out because of the noises she makes and her overall restless nature. It is always the same old story—Ashley appears and acts different from others in the church. It really saddens me." This actually wasn't surprising. Most of the major religions of the world have a long history of associating disability with sin, evil, or the devil. The Church has often been one of the leading institutions to dehumanize people on the wrong side of normal.

. . .

Ashley had had terrible experiences at her regular public school. Referring to Ashley's school trouble, Deborah said, "You know, they are often afraid of Ashley, some of the kids and the teachers. They treat her sometimes as if she is contagious." I nodded my head, feeling ashamed for understanding their feelings. "They *stare*."

These gazes, according to Deborah, were some of the most painful things that she and her daughter endured together. "Surgeries or any medical procedures are things that hurt, but only for a short while," Deborah continued. "The pain of rejection, the pain of being thought of as somehow a 'broken' or inferior person, the pain of ridicule or derision doesn't go away." These experiences "were ten times as painful as her surgeries."

At the time of my visit, Ashley was attending a wonderful school called the Starling Child Care and Learning Complex. . . .

This institution was also committed to a policy of inclusion. As we walked through the halls, I saw many students with disabilities. Ashley was in a fully inclusive, mixed-age classroom. When Deborah and I arrived, the class was having lunch. "There is my little girl," Deborah said, pointing across the small kids' desks, her face illuminated with the first smile I saw all day. I followed the trajectory of Deborah's outstretched hand and saw a little girl who struck me as strong, not sickly at all. She had a body that looked at least twelve years old. "She's a good eater," Deborah said. "Isn't she beautiful?"

I didn't answer the question. Not because I disagreed with Deborah, but because I really had no way to make sense out of Ashley. I didn't see Ashley as a whole. It was as if all I could take in were parts of her. She was wearing a red dress, and her hair was short and black. Her right eye was smaller than its counterpart and was glassy and colorless. She walked around the lunch table like a spinning top that had lost its centrifugal force. She made strange noises, which ranged in pitch from a low hum to an ear-piercing scream. Ashley heard nothing but felt vibrations.

I hoped Deborah didn't notice, but I was staring at Ashley. Not a genial get-to-know-you kind of glance, but a deeply dehumanizing stare, the kind of look that Deborah had talked about earlier. This is the type of stare that people with physical disabilities are very familiar with. But I didn't know how to stop. I didn't know how to make sense out of Ashley. I am ashamed to write this, but a part of me wondered if Ashley and I belonged to the same species.

Ashley confronted me with my own deep prejudices about what it means to be a valuable human being. I didn't know if I could truly value a body that was so damaged. Ashley also challenged some of my ideas about intelligence. If Ashley couldn't hear, speak, or see, how could she learn? And if Ashley couldn't learn, was she a fully functioning member of the human race?

Unfortunately, my reaction to Ashley is not without historical precedent. The history of the deaf, blind, and the deaf/blind is a story of being seen as less than human. . . .

It was Aristotle's contention that, of all the senses, hearing contributed most to intelligence and knowledge. This led Aristotle to characterize deaf individuals as senseless and incapable of reason. Much of the early marginalization of the deaf had to do with religious mythology. The ability to speak was considered a gift from the breath of God. Without speech, the deaf were denied moral status. Even during the Enlightenment, a period defined by questioning religious beliefs, the deaf were denied full humanity. . . .

As we waited for Ashley, Deborah talked about how her daughter was treated. "My experience has been that people will try to avoid that which they do not understand. So many people look at Ashley, see the physical differences in her, and assume that everything else about her is different, *and inferior*. What they don't see is the warmth and compassion inside her, her ability to forgive and forget all the slights from other people, her drive to experience everything she possibly can, her love of nature, and her gentleness around babies and young children."

. . .

At this point in our day, it was time for Ashley's language instruction, a mix of American Sign Language (ASL), touch sign, and speech therapy. Later, I asked Deborah about sign language and about whether Ashley's blindness prevented her from using it. Deborah reminded me that while Ashley has no vision at all in her left eye, the vision in her right eye is 20/2000. This means she can focus at about one to two inches from her face. Deborah elaborated: "She does her signing directly in front of her body, and if she perceives the person to whom she is signing is not paying attention, she will gently put her hands on both sides of their face and move their face to look at her."

Ashley's language instructor came right up to me and introduced herself. "I'm Theresa," she said as she shook my hand. Theresa was in her late thirties and was a large, joyful woman. She seemed like a natural educator, and had a son with a learning disability who struggled with learning to read and write.

"I think that helps me when I work with Ashley," she said. "You know, a struggle with language is a struggle with language whether you're deaf-blind or not. "Theresa then turned her attention to her student, signing something to Ashley who signed back. But because I don't know ASL, I had no idea what was being communicated. "I asked her if she was ready to work," Theresa translated. "What did she say?" I asked. "What would any kid say? No, of course," Theresa reported.

I spent the next twenty minutes watching Theresa, trying to understand what she could see, but I could not. Deborah pointed out that the first thing Theresa did when she saw Ashley was smile. I didn't smile when I first saw Ashley, thinking that Ashley couldn't see my expression. Deborah laughed when I mentioned this to her. "To Ashley, your body can't lie." Ashley could feel a smile even if she couldn't see it. After Theresa smiled at Ashley, she touched her on her arm and then got down close to Ashley's stronger eye. She spoke and signed, "Good afternoon." Then she asked, "How are you?"

Theresa was vigilant about letting Ashley know what was going on in her environment. She signed and told Ashley what was on the floor, what chairs had been moved, what time the bell would ring. According to Deborah, this is essential. "One of the biggest potential sources for stress and frustration for Ashley is not being aware of something, especially something that would impact her. She needs access to the environment."

. . .

But like many deaf children, Ashley has had, at best, limited access to signing class-rooms. When Ashley started school at the age of two and a half, she was in a classroom led by a teacher who signed with the other signing children. According to Deborah, after one year the school district abolished all signing classes and reassigned the teachers to classes for children with cochlear implants, which are a huge issue in the deaf community. The National Institutes of Health describes a cochlear implant as "a small electronic device that can help to provide a sense of sound to a person who is profoundly deaf or severely hard-of-hearing. The implant consists of an external portion that sits behind the ear and a second portion that is surgically placed under the skin." Many in the deaf community believe, however, that cochlear implants are a nefarious form of cultural genocide for the deaf. The essence of deaf culture is its language—sign language. Implants threaten to suck the life out of ASL.

Teachers are now told to emphasize speech and not to sign. Lipreading was also actively discouraged or prevented. "Classroom teachers were instructed to cover their mouths when they spoke so the children would not be able to read their lips," Deborah said. "The entire emphasis was on getting the children to adjust to their implants and learn to 'hear' and speak." Children without implants, which are initially painful and not always effective, were moved into segregated classrooms with children who had a myriad of other dis-abilities. Without signing support, according to Deborah, "the education of those children like Ashley suffered greatly. Many formative years were lost, and I'm not sure they will ever be made up."

. . .

What is the cost of teaching speech versus developing Ashley's mind and communication skills through ASL? Research is unequivocal: Deaf and deaf-blind children who acquire signing early have the best educational outcomes. Without signing, education becomes limited. "The school would like to pigeonhole Ashley as incapable of doing academic work," Deborah said, "Rather, they do things like learning to cook, community trips, and learning to clean up." A policy of emphasizing speech for these children is really a policy of forced assimilation of a unique minority group.

"It has been my experience," said Deborah, "that the school staff expects the children to change and is determined to help 'fix' them. The sad thing in my mind is that these children are not 'broken' and do not need fixing." . . .

Before the end of the language lesson Deborah tapped my shoulder and pointed to Ashley. "Do you see that?" she asked me. I didn't know what she was talking about, so I just shrugged my shoulders. "She's laughing. Take a close look."

I looked to the other side of the room. I watched Ashley's face, not her awkward gait or her colorless eye, but her whole face. Her face looked like a Picasso, a face held together with its own inherently savage beauty. Deborah was right; Ashley was laughing. And so was Theresa. I looked back at Deborah, and she was laughing too. Everyone was in on the joke except me. "What's so funny," I asked. "Oh nothing," Deborah said. I pressed her again. "Well, I don't want you to think less of Ashley, but Ashley just cursed us all out in sign language," said her mother. "She has a problem with that; we're working on it." . . .

I ended my day with Deborah and Ashley back at their home. The plan was to have dinner with the family: Ashley; her brother, Chip; and Deborah. Deborah had invited me to dinner at the beginning of the day, when we sat talking at Starbucks, and I had lied, saying I had somewhere I needed to be. But now I wouldn't have missed a dinner with this family for the world. Deborah and I had some time to kill before the rest of the family got home. So before dinner we sat around and talked about Ashley's experiences, the power of language, and the importance of inclusion. When we got onto the latter topic, Deborah told me a story that she had already shared with me over e-mail and in a phone conversation. In fact, she had already shared this story with me during our day together. It was as if this story was somehow the essence of her and Ashley's struggle.

It was the Christmas season, December 2002. That night, Deborah and the kids piled into their car and headed to the elementary school for the big holiday show. Ashley had been given a part. This was huge. Ashley was educated in a fully segregated special educational room, but on this night she would be on the stage with the rest of the kids. She was given a tiny baby rattle that she was supposed to shake at various times during the performance with the prompting of her aide. That's all the teachers thought she was capable of, but Deborah went along with the plan. At least Ashley would be on the stage.

Deborah and Chip sat in the makeshift auditorium, on steel-blue chairs. She had her camera in hand, just like all the other parents. When the lights went out, Ashley walked on the stage with the rest of the kids. She wobbled a little, but she found her spot. These things matter, Deborah thought. These small moments of inclusion. Sure, it's just a first-grade holiday program. But if Ashley can't be here, what's next? Who gets to draw these lines, and where would they stop? No, this night, this act of inclusion mattered, Deborah thought. She poised her camera and sat on the edge of her seat.

Then it happened. Before the program began, Ashley was placed three feet to the side of the group. Her aide stood next to her, holding her hand. The aide did not know touch sign or American Sign Language, Ashley's primary forms of communication. The only way Ashley would have to communicate would be to grip the aide's hand harder.

The first song was "Frosty the Snowman." Ashley waited for her cue, a slight touch on the hand, to shake the rattle. As the kids sang, she swayed. The aide seemed nervous, but when the time for Ashley's part came, she shook the rattle with force. Deborah was filled with a sense of pride. When the first song was over, there were more songs to come, but not for Ashley. The aide led her off the stage. Deborah wondered why. What was going on? Why was she leaving? Ashley was supposed to stay on stage for the whole night. That had been the plan all along, but someone didn't want Ashley on the stage for the whole performance. As they escorted Ashley off the stage and out of the auditorium, a parent in a fancy coat stopped the aide and, looking right past Ashley, said, "Good job." To the aide.

. . .

Ashley lived in a world without sight or sound, but she had heightened senses of smell, of taste, of touch. As Deborah explained to me, "If Ashley doesn't recognize a particular food on her plate, she smells it first. If she is looking for new clothes, she runs her hands down the fabric first to see if it is something that feels like she wants it to feel." We should not underestimate the power of touch. The philosopher Jean-Jacques Rousseau believed that touch was the essence of an ethical life; touch defined our humanity.

. . .

Before I said my good-byes I asked Deborah if she had anything she could give me to help me remember our day. She left the room and came back holding a photograph of Ashley sitting on the beach. "I just love this picture," she said as she handed it to me. "This is my beautiful little girl. Feeling everything."

That picture was taken in the late summer of 2002 at Virginia Beach. It was a few days before school started. Deborah, who had fond memories of the beach, had saved a little money for a vacation. She got her family a hotel room right on the ocean, so the kids could see the sun rise. On the last day of their holiday, they went out on the beach at sunset. Deborah's twin brother, a photographer, was there. Ashley had been to other bodies of water before—lakes, rivers—but she had never been to the ocean. She stepped onto the sand, wobbled a little, as everyone does on the beach, and started walking toward the ocean. But fifty feet or so from the water, she stopped and put her hands out. Other kids were running around in the sand, whining about the cold, asking to go home and eat ice cream, but not Ashley. She stood there in a world of vibration and taste and touch, "relishing every sensory experience."

After a while, Ashley walked up to the line where the ocean meets the sand and sat down. The reaching palms of the surf touched the tips of her toes and she lifted her hands to feel the wind and salt spray. She sat like that for five minutes on the edge of the world, the sea, a shifting line, its edges never anywhere for long. Ashley pressed her hands out like she was feeling someone's face. When a wave washed up on shore, the spray lifted off the water and the ocean came to her toes and then her shins. She laughed in a pitch somewhere between a scream and a song.

108

What I'd Tell That Doctor

Jason Kingsley

I am Jason Kingsley. I am now almost twenty-nine years old. Ten years ago I wrote an article for *Count Us In: Growing Up with Down Syndrome*, a book that Mitchell Levitz and I wrote. That article is about a confrontation I would have had with the obstetrician—if I had met him—about what he said years ago to my parents when I was born.

What I would say to the obstetrician is the same as what I would say to the parents of any newborn child who is born with a disability and who is born with Down syndrome.

The things I said ten years ago are true now and even more so.

When I wrote that article, I was still in school. But now I am on my own. I live in a house with two other roommates. We have very little supervision. We do our own cooking; we do our own shopping and cleaning. We do take public transportation. And above all else, our house is accessible to the community and to our work.

All three of us work in the community. I happen to work in the White Plains (New York) Public Library. My roommate Raymond works at PETCO, a pet store, and has been there for six years. And Yaniv works at an Armonk (New York) law firm.

In conclusion, I hope you will look at this article that I wrote ten years ago. Then get *Count Us In: Growing Up with Down Syndrome* and read the whole thing. You will find it very essential, inspiring, and helpful.

Here is my article:

When I was born, the obstetrician said that I cannot learn, never see my mom and dad and never learn anything and send me to an institution. Which I think it was wrong.

Today we were talking about if I could see my obstetrician and talk to him, here are things I would say . . .

I would say, "People with disabilities *can learn*!"

Then I would tell the obstetrician how smart I am. Like learning new languages, going to other foreign nations, going to teen groups and teen parties, going to cast parties, becoming independent, being . . . a lighting board operator, an actor, the backstage crew. I would talk about history, math, English, algebra, business math, global studies. One thing I forgot to tell the obstetrician is I plan to get a academic diploma when I pass my RCTs . . .

I performed in "The Fall Guy" and even wrote this book! He never imagined how I could write a book! I will send him a copy . . . so he'll know.

I will tell him that I play the violin, that I make relationships with other people, I make oil paintings, I play the piano, I can sing, I am competing in sports, in the drama group, that I have many friends, and I have a full life.

So I want the obstetrician will never say that to any parent to have a baby with a disability any more. If you send a baby with a disability to an institution, the baby will miss all the opportunities to grow and to learn . . . and also to receive a diploma. The baby will miss relationships and love and independent living skills. Give a baby with a disability a chance to grow a full life. To experience a half-full glass instead of the half-empty glass. And think of your abilities not your disability.

109

In the LD Bubble

Lynn Pelkey

. . .

As much as I want to find the perfect words to express what it is like to be dyslexic, I cannot. I can no more make you understand what it is like to be dyslexic than you can make me understand what it is like not to be. I can only guess and imagine. For years, I have looked out, wanting to be normal, to shed the skin that limits me, that holds me back. All the while, others have looked upon me, as well. There were those who have pitied me and those who have just given up on me, those who stood by, supporting me and believing in me, and those who looked at me as if I were an exhibit at the zoo. But, in general, people have shown a desire to understand what dyslexia is and how to teach those afflicted with it. Each side, it seems, longs to understand the other.

My dyslexia is like a bubble. I am enclosed in an invisible sheath that allows me to come excitingly close to being "normal" but never completely there. It is flexible yet confining. I can move within it but never outside of it. You cannot see it, but I can feel it. It has thick walls that are impossible to break free from. Sometimes, I hardly know it is there at all, and other times I have felt as if it were suffocating me, killing me.

I invite you into my world for two reasons. One is the hope that you will gain some insight, understanding, compassion, or even strength. I also write for myself in the hope that this process will help me to love myself for who I am and all that I can be. For, you see, I believe I was taught to hate myself.

"Dyslexia" is a label and only a label, but it carries so much negative weight. Had I been described as "gifted and talented," this, too, would have meant dealing with a label, but a positive one. Why must LD categories be classified around negative attributes? Can we not focus on strengths or positive attributes? As a child, my foundation for hating myself grew out of my much noted shortcomings and a lack of any abilities deemed positive.

I cannot remember my infancy, but I doubt very much that I hated myself then. My memories of my early years of childhood are happy. I was loved, and I felt loved. It was during my elementary school years that I started to feel different from the other children. It was discovered that reading and writing were difficult for me. I began some special programs designed to assist in my learning process. On the playground, in gym and art classes, or playing games, I was the same as any other child, but academically I could not achieve what other children could. As academics took on a more important role in my daily life, being with my playmates became less than pleasurable. We were no longer equal. At times, I was physically separated from my classmates. During these times, I was brought to the "special" room where I would receive help with my school work in hopes of bringing me "up to my class level." No one ever said this to me directly; it was what I overheard: "She is not doing as well as the other children," "She is having difficulty," "Scoring low," "Not trying," "Lazy." I knew the latter two were not true, but they certainly did not make me feel good about myself. It was in these ways that I became *less than*.

. . .

At first, the gap between me and my classmates was small. However, it was not long before I was ashamed of myself. I would compare myself to those around me. My performance was always less, the lowest, the bottom of the class. As the years passed, the gap grew, and the shame turned to deep-rooted self-hate. The gap, the shame, and the self-hate were not just my doing. Others, too, perceived me as "less than," and they taught me to accept their perceptions. Other students did not have any trouble telling me what was wrong with me, "Stupid," "Mental," "Idiot." I had to go to the "Retard Room" for a lot of my classes. This classroom was different from all the other classrooms. The doors were metal, and they had a long, thin window, which made it difficult to see in or out of the room. This had some advantages, because once you were inside, people in the hallways could not see you. The trick was getting into the room. I would usually hang out across the hall, by the entrance to the library, until after the second bell, waiting for a chance when the coast was clear. Then, quick as a dart, I would run into the room. In an arc printed across the top of the door in big black letters was "Remedial Reading." RR. The Retard Room.

The normal class had neat little rows of wooden-topped desks with metal blue legs facing the front of the classroom. The teacher's desk and the blackboard looked back at them. Above the blackboards were rolled up maps of far-off places that would snap up like the shades in my bedroom. The rooms were quiet in color. I always wanted to be in one of those rooms.

The RR was different. We had one large room about the size of two normal rectangular tables. Our tables did not face the front of the room but were randomly placed throughout the room. Our blackboard was on wheels, and it was mostly used as a partition to separate us from each other. We did not have any maps; I guess they felt there was not a need to teach us that kind of stuff because we wouldn't need it for the types of lives that we would lead. It was during a humiliating episode with my cousin that I learned that Massachusetts was a state and not a country. The RR was cheerfully decorated, the bulletin boards were covered with construction paper in bright and happy colors. The decorations and colors would change to correspond with the seasons. The curtain that divided the room had been embroidered with a sort of spring scene. It was all very cute, like kindergarten. This room only fortified my feelings that I was dumb. Something was very wrong. All the other kids my age were growing up, but I was still in kindergarten. I felt humiliated going in and out of that room.

. . .

During junior high, I did have a few regular classes such as science, art, and gym, but the rest of my time was spent in the Retard Room. I do not recall exactly the first day that I entered the remedial reading room at the junior high school, but I do remember an assortment of feelings associated with being there: fear, anxiety, uncertainty, and many more. I did not have one positive feeling about going into that room. Just me and the guys. What a group! Maybe about ten of us, ranging in types and degrees of disabilities. One girl (me) and the rest boys. That's right, I was the only girl in the whole school that was stupid, and it remained that way until I graduated.

. . .

Being LD must be similar to how some gay people feel. You spend so much time and energy trying to hide who you really are. You are ashamed of what you are, and at times you long to be like others, but you are who you are, and so you lead this double life. Some know you as LD, and others know you as one of them, but you are not one of them. You are just pretending. You hate yourself for being LD, and you hate yourself for being a fake. And in the end, who are you? It is all very confusing. All the while you really just want to be you, without any fears. We LDs live a life of deceit—pretending to be like others—and shame—not wanting to be who we are.

My self-efficacy, my belief about my competence, fell into the category of failure-accepting. I expected to fail, so I set no goals, believing my ability was set (I had none). Thus, I learned helplessness. Everything was black and white, with no grey areas. There was good and evil, positive and negative, and, of course, smart and dumb. As I grew, I started to believe the negative stereotypes associated with my academic abilities. I was stupid! I couldn't do it! I accepted these stereotypes and let them define me. I erased myself. I hid who I was out of shame. I also had a growing fear of the unknown. What was really wrong with me? There had to be a reason and an explanation for why I was the way I was. Would it get worse as I got older? Was this it? Was I retarded? I was not sure that I wanted the answers to these questions. Eventually, I turned my back on academics.

. . .

Not long ago, it became very clear to me that I would have to come face-to-face with my feelings about being stupid if I was going to find peace within myself. Four years ago, my mother encouraged me to go with her to an open house at a local community college, the same college that I had flunked out of ten years earlier. I agreed to go, but I had no intention to sign up. I went just to satisfy her, to say that I went. I started to talk to a woman about my diagnosis, and she guaranteed me that if I wanted to learn, they could and would teach me. The next thing I knew, I was agreeing to give college another try. I can still remember sitting in class the first day and thinking to myself, "How long are you going to carry on this charade?" I was certain that I would last only about a week or two. But, I kept hanging in there. I was facing the monsters of my past. I was no longer going to be held back. I had to admit what I was. I heard myself saying out loud to my professors that I had dyslexia. It's not that it all came easy to me, because it didn't. Saying it made it very real. All the promises that were made to me on that open house day didn't quite pan out. I was supposed to have my books on tape, have extra time to do assignments, and be given untimed tests. This all sounded good, but it took a lot of work and persistence to get the things that I needed. I really learned to become an advocate for myself. I no longer fell into the role of helplessness; I knew that if I did, I wouldn't make it. As the semester went on, I realized that I wanted this. Not only did I want to succeed, but I wanted to be one of the best. I had a goal.

No longer were my classrooms "special." They were real. I was with real students. At first, I did not say anything, because I was sure that they must be so much smarter than me. After all, this was college, someplace I thought I would never be. As time passed, I realized that I wasn't the dummy in the class. The professor would ask a question, I would have an answer in my head, and most of the time someone would say what I was thinking. I wasn't so different after all. In time, I began to ask questions or respond to those asked. And I was learning, right along with the normal students. The gap that was once about the size of the Grand Canyon was beginning to close. I couldn't believe it when my fellow students asked me for help. This sounds very childish, but it was an experience that I had missed out on as a child, and it was a wonderful feeling. I was not worthless, and my opinion mattered. My success at that college was a milestone for me. Not only did I graduate with an Associate's Degree, but I did so with honors.

My success at the community college gave me the strength to believe in myself enough to continue my education. So here I am, a junior at a four-year college with a goal. Being LD has become less important to me. There are arrangements that I make due to my disability so that I am able to learn, but no one is giving me the answers. I certainly don't get a free ride. I don't have a tattoo on my forehead saying that I am dyslexic, but I don't hide it either.

In junior high school, being LD was a big part of my life. At that time, the universe revolved around me. I was my biggest concern. I was self-centered. My world consisted of very little, and so being LD was a big part of who I was. But as I became older, I grew out of the self-centered mode and into a more complex way of being. As my life evolved, being LD became a smaller piece of the whole.

Above all, I thank my parents for their unconditional love and support. I am fortunate to have had parents who emphasized my attributes rather than my shortcomings. They always saw in me what others could not, and they taught me to love myself for what I could do. It is from their encouragement that I found the strength to face my fears and become who I am. While my disability will last my lifetime, it no longer has to limit me.

I now strive to see myself as my parents see me.

110

Toward Ending Ableism in Education

Thomas Hehir

There is much that educators, parents, and advocates can do toward ending ableism in education. As is the case with racism and sexism, progress toward equity is dependent first and foremost on the acknowledgment that ableism exists in schools. The examples given here have centered around three disability groups: the deaf, the blind and visually impaired, and the learning disabled. However, I believe that deconstructing dominant educational practices applied to other disability groups can yield similar results. Ableist assumptions and practices are deeply embedded in schooling. Further, the absence of discussion and dearth of scholarly inquiry within mainstream educational circles concerning the effects of ableism is stunning.

Though the lack of attention to ableism in schooling is unfortunate, activists within the disability community have long recognized its impact. Therefore, as more adults with disabilities take on more powerful roles in society and seek to influence schooling, the attention to these issues will hopefully increase. In addition to this political force, the lack of acceptable educational outcomes for large numbers of children with disabilities in an era of standards-based reform should force a reexamination of current practices. Fortunately, there is a foundation in both research and practice upon which to build a better future. Schools can take action now. I offer the following suggestions:

Include disability as part of schools' overall diversity efforts. Schools are increasingly recognizing the need to explicitly address diversity issues as the country becomes more racially and ethnically diverse. Some schools are expanding diversity efforts to include disability. Recently, a local high school student with Down's syndrome, whom I had met at a school assembly devoted to issues of disability rights, addressed one of my classes. She stated, "There are all kinds of kids at my school: Black kids, Puerto Rican kids, gay and lesbian kids. Meagan uses a wheel chair. Matt's deaf, and I have Down's syndrome. It's all diversity." Her high school has done a great job of including disabled kids and has incorporated discussions about disability in its efforts to address diversity issues. Adults with disabilities address student groups and disability is presented in a natural way. Students learn about people with disabilities who have achieved great things as well as those who live ordinary lives. People with disabilities are not presented in a patronizing or stereotypical manner. Deaf people are not "hearing challenged" nor are people with mental retardation "very special." Ableism is not the norm; disability is dealt with in a straightforward manner. In schools like this, students with disabilities learn about their disabilities and learn how to be self-advocates.

Encourage disabled students to develop and use skills and modes of expression that are most effective and efficient for them. This article has sought to demonstrate that the strong preference within society, reflected in school practice, to have disabled students perform in the same way that nondisabled children perform can ultimately be handicapping for some students. This is not to say that it is not desirable for disabled kids to be able to perform in the way nondisabled kids perform. For instance, deaf students who can read lips have a competitive advantage in a hearing world. However, assuming that most deaf children can develop elaborate language through oral methods has been proven false, and employing these methods without allowing for the natural development of language almost assures poor language development. What may appear to be a paradox to some is that a deaf child who has well-developed language through learning ASL from birth may actually have a higher likelihood of reading lips because he simply has a larger vocabulary. The problem is not, therefore, in the natural desire of parents and educators to have children be able to perform in a typical manner, but rather the missed educational opportunities many disabled kids experience because of a lack of regard for what are often disability-specific modes of learning and expression.

. . .

Move away from the current obsession with placement toward an obsession with results. The movement to include greater numbers of students with disabilities, particularly those with significant cognitive disabilities, in regular education classes has had a profound effect on the education of students with disabilities. Over the past decade, more and more students with disabilities are educated for more of the day in regular education classrooms.

The inclusion movement in education has supported the overall disability movement's goal of promoting societal integration, using integration in schooling as a means to achieve this result. In 1977, disability activists took over federal offices in San Francisco for twenty-five days, demanding that regulations for implementing Section 504 of the Rehabilitation Act, the first federal act to broadly ban discrimination based on disability, be released. Of particular concern to the protesters were leaked draft regulations that provided for separate segregated education for disabled students. Judy Heumann, one of these protesters, stated, "We will accept no more segregation." The final rules were revised to encourage integration in schooling, and the newly passed PL 94–142 (later renamed IDEA) incorporated the current requirement that children be educated in the least restrictive environment (i.e., in regular classes as much as is appropriate for the child).

The strong legal preference for placement in regular classes, coupled with the political movement of disability activists and parents, has resulted in significant positive change for students with disabilities, who are moving on to jobs and accessing higher education at unprecedented levels. Virtually every school has had to confront the issue of inclusion as parents seek integration for their children with disabilities. However, like all change movements, inclusion has encountered opposition. Some opposition has reflected deeply held negative attitudes toward people with disabilities similar to that experienced by Joe and Penny Ford when he sought enrollment in first grade. I can recall a principal challenging me in a large public meeting concerning our efforts to promote inclusion in Chicago: "You don't really mean kids who drool in regular classes?" The reaction against the integration of students with significant disabilities into regular schools and classrooms has been so strong that TASH, an advocacy group promoting integration, adopted the slogan, "All means all," which reflects the group's efforts to clarify its goal to promote integration for students with significant disabilities.

Another source of criticism has come from within the disability community. Deaf advocates have expressed concerns over the lack of language development and communication access many deaf children experience in regular classes. Supported by some of the research cited above, advocates for the learning disabled have questioned the ability of regular education classrooms to provide the intensive help these students need for skill development. These criticisms receive support from research. The NLTS documented that many students integrated into regular education classrooms did not receive much in the way of accommodation or support, and that many who were integrated into regular classes failed, thus increasing their likelihood of dropping out. The issue is so controversial within the community that virtually every disability group has developed a position. A review of websites reveals, for example, TASH's strong support for full inclusion and deep reservation on the part of the Learning Disabilities Association of America (see www.tash.org and www.ldanatl.org).

The controversy over inclusion within the disability community is ultimately dysfunctional and allows those who would limit the rights of students with disabilities to use this as a wedge issue. Fortunately, the community united during the reauthorization of IDEA in 1997 to help prevent a weakening of the act. However, threats to IDEA's fundamental protections remain. In 2001, Congress considered amendments to the Elementary and Secondary Education Act that would enable schools to fully exclude some students with disabilities. In order to fight these regressive provisions, the community must be united.

I believe the lens of ableism provides a useful perspective through which the inclusion issue can be resolved within the disability community. First, there needs to be a recognition that education plays a central role in the integration of disabled people in all aspects of society both by giving children the education they need to compete and by demonstrating to nondisabled children that disability is a natural aspect of life. Central to this role is the need for students with disabilities to have access to the same curriculum provided to nondisabled children. Further, education plays a vital role in building communities in which disabled children should be included. Therefore, for most children with disabilities, integration into regular classes with appropriate accommodations and support should be the norm.

However, the lens of ableism should lead to the recognition that for some students certain disability-related skills might need attention outside the regular classroom. Learning Braille or ASL or how to use a communication device are typically not in the curriculum and might be more efficiently taught outside the mainstream classroom. The dyslexic high school student who needs intensive help in reading may feel deeply self-conscious if such instruction is conducted in front of his nondisabled friends. The 19-year-old student with a significant cognitive disability may need to spend a good deal of time learning to take public transportation, a skill that will ultimately increase her ability to integrate into the community as an adult. Nondisabled students do not spend time in school learning this skill because they learn this easily on their own. The nature of mental retardation is such that this type of learning does not typically happen incidentally; it must be taught over time and within the context in which the skill will be used. Uniting around the goal of societal integration and recognizing that the difference inherent in disability is a positive one that at times gives rise to disability-specific educational needs may help advocates move away from the fight over placement to one that focuses on educational results.

Promote high standards, not high stakes. An important point to reiterate here is that the most damaging ableist assumption is the belief that disabled people are incapable. Therefore, the movement to include students with disabilities in standards-based reforms holds promise. However, high-stakes testing that prevents students from being promoted or from receiving a diploma based on performance on standardized tests is problematic, given the concerns previously cited about basic access to the curricula and those surrounding the construct validity of the tests. In a very real sense, some students with disabilities will have to become nondisabled in order to be promoted or graduate. This is ableism in the extreme. Thus, a promising movement, standards-based reform, may ultimately reinforce current inequities if performance on high-stakes tests becomes the only means by which disabled students can demonstrate what they know and are able to do. As such, disability advocates should oppose high-stakes testing. It is important to note that disabled students are not the only group for whom high-stakes testing is being questioned. Other groups that have been poorly served by our educational systems, such as children from high-poverty backgrounds and children with limited English proficiency, may be equally harmed by these policies.

. . .

NEXT STEPS

111

Facilitating Transitions to College for Students with Disabilities from Culturally and Linguistically Diverse Backgrounds

Heather A. Oesterreich and Michelle G. Knight

The overrepresentation of working-class African American, Latino/Latina, and Native American students in special education has been well documented and the implications that are raised for identification and intake of students with disabilities has been the focus of special education reform for many years. Even as schools have worked to change how students are identified for special education, special educators continue to see a disproportionate number of working-class African American, Latino/Latina, and Native American students in their caseloads. Disproportionate representation is not a problem because something is inherently wrong with special education; however, placement in special education is linked to a number of negative issues including poor graduation rates, high drop-out rates, and limited access to postsecondary education opportunities. Specifically, the overrepresentation of working-class culturally and linguistically diverse students with disabilities in special education is coupled with an underrepresentation in college attendance. Recent research suggests that disability in combination with other characteristics (e.g., race and class) has a much more powerful effect on educational attainment than any one of these characteristics alone. This article examines how the intersection of race, class, and disability informs the responsibilities of special educators. A diverse set of practices needs to be used with working-class African American, Latino/Latina, and Native American students with disabilities to increase their social and cultural capital and support their prospective college-going identities.

THE LAY OF THE LANDS

Increasing opportunities for educational access to college for underserved populations, including students who are first-generation, working-class, and underrepresented culturally and linguistically diverse students labeled with a disability, is a priority of K–16 educational systems. Frequently, however, the hectic pace and large caseloads for special education teachers require them to focus on the immediacy of high school completion for their students. Recently, demographic shifts in the college freshman population highlight the growing numbers of students with disabilities entering college. In 2000, 6% of full-time, first-time freshmen who were enrolled in 4-year public and private institutions had disabilities. Although this statistic represents an increase of postsecondary students reporting a disability, it obscures the link between the race and class of students with disabilities in high school and their transition to college. The increase in students with disabilities who attend college is most notable in students labeled with a learning disability (LD). They have increased from 16.1% to 40.4% of college students with disabilities in the past 12 years. Notably, this increase represents a Caucasian, upper-middle class increase in postsecondary attendance and attainment.

This race and class divide leads to a differentiation in the academic college preparation that many affluent, Caucasian students with LD receive, as opposed to that provided to poor, culturally and linguistically diverse students. These students often are labeled with more stigmatizing disabilities within special education. They also are underrepresented as a result of their disability in college preparation courses, including advanced placement courses. In addition, they cannot afford and do not have access to private tutoring and other out-of-school services (e.g., SAT preparation). These discrepancies in access to quality education limit culturally and linguistically diverse students' acquisition of social and cultural capital to assist them in developing college-going identities.

BUILDING SOCIAL AND CULTURAL CAPITAL FOR COLLEGE

Students' social and cultural capital creates differences in college-going identities. Social capital for students with disabilities in relation to college includes the availability of information-sharing networks about college. Cultural capital is the value placed on obtaining a college education and the information available about acquiring one. Special educators' ability to influence working-class African American, Latino/Latina, and Native American students with disabilities' college-going identities and their subsequent success in college is directly related to nurturing social and cultural capital in relation to college. This includes addressing social and economic stratification that exists in society in relation to race, class, and disability; understanding the law; and facilitating the selection of a college with resources and demographics that match students' social, economic, and emotional needs.

ADDRESSING SOCIAL AND ECONOMIC STRATIFICATION

In a society where inequities in college access still reflect racism, classism, and ableism, it is useful to assist students in understanding the economic and social stratification that affects college admittance and completion. Helping students to understand that their life possibility may be situated in structures of oppression while at the same time helping them to challenge the belief of society that they are deficient, disinterested, with confused priorities, and responsible for their own failure to enter college provides youth with disabilities a place to understand the lives that they are living. With facilitation by the special education teacher, students can not only critique social structures but can also be encouraged to become active agents in fighting the social structures by viewing themselves as college material.

UNDERSTANDING THE LAW

Special education teachers must provide the cultural capital about the differences in services provided in K–12 and postsecondary schools. Under Section 504 of the Rehabilitation Act of 1973 and the Americans With Disabilities Act (ADA) of 1990, at the postsecondary level, students must self-identify with the ADA office on a college campus. In addition, they are responsible for the documentation verifying their need for accommodation, making specific requests for accommodations, and meeting the same academic requirements of all other students. This differs dramatically from the K–12 setting, where it is the responsibility of the institution to reach out and identify students in need of special education, pay for the documentation to evaluate these students, and provide specialized programming. If special education teachers do not work with students, particularly working-class, African American, Latino/Latina, and Native American students with disabilities, who are more likely to be first-generation college students, in identifying these fundamental differences between postsecondary and K–12 services, the transition between the two systems can leave students frustrated and isolated without the accommodations that they require to meet the academic standards of postsecondary education.

Becoming advocates. In this legal context, students must advocate in relation to their disabilities. Special education teachers need to work with students to be able to name their disability, understand the nature of their learning difficulties, and know strategies that allow them to negotiate their learning difficulties. Students who learn early on how to state their accommodation needs in functional, real-world terms will be able to help postsecondary institutions effectively accommodate their needs.

College visits. In addition to teaching students about the shift in laws between K–12 and postsecondary institutions, when dealing with first-generation college students, part of fortifying their social and cultural capital lies in the necessity and structure of on-campus visits. These visits must include planned meetings at the ADA office and a presentation by the personnel there to create a sense of accessibility.

Community connections. Providing mentors, role models, community leaders, and speakers to motivate students can raise their social capital and sense of advocacy in making the shift between disability laws. Specifically, these adults should reflect the race, class, and

NEXT STEPS

Table 111.1 Teacher Tips for Increasing Social and Cultural Capital for Post-Secondary Education

Social and Cultural Capital	Questions to Ask	Teacher Tips
Admissions requirements		
These include requirements such as GPA scores, short essays, and minimum standardized test scores that depend on the institution. Students with disabilities may have nontraditional testing materials as well as documentation that could be essential when they apply	Does the school have a separate admission policy for students with disabilities? Do admission requirements include the recognition of certificates of attendance, GEDs, or high school diplomas? Can other documentation be included to support the student beyond academic achievement?	Review the admissions requirements of the institution(s) with the student Create checklists of admission requirements and follow through with the students to make sure they are taking the right steps to meet those requirements Assist students with applications and study sessions for required admissions tests
Cost		
Tuition costs can be daunting to students and their families. Financial aid is often available for students, but aid alone does not always cover all the costs especially the "hidden" costs of books, living expenses, and accommodations and extra educational supports	Are the cost and opportunities for financial aid consistent with the need of the student? What forms are required for financial aid? How far in advance do students need to start applying for financial aid? Do they have specific disability assistance? Are grants available explicitly for students with disabilities?	Create spreadsheets that compare costs of tuition as well as "hidden" costs that will be important to consider (i.e., additional testing materials to document their disabilities, tutoring, technology, transportation needs) Host a family Free Application for Federal Student Aid (FAFSA) night to assist students and their families with forms. Information for the FAFSA is available at http://www.fafsa.ed.gov Assist students with research of specific financial aid resources for students with disabilities, available in Creating Options: Financial Aid for Individuals with Disabilities at http://www.heath.gwu.edu
Demographics		
Demographics include race/ethnicity, language, gender, and disabilities of the full-time, part-time, nontraditional students, faculty, and staff that create the higher institution environment	What is the representation of students and faculty/staff who are African American, Latino/Latina, or Native American on the campus? How many students and faculty/staff with disabilities does the college serve? Are their academic/social groups in any of these areas? Are there institutionally supported mentor programs in these areas?	Create math assignments in which students chart the racial and disability demographics of institutions they are interested in attending Have students develop an interview protocol to ask students with disabilities about their experiences and any advice they might offer Contact the admissions offices for student/faculty/staff names for students to interview. The interviews can be conducted via phone, Internet (i.e., e-mail, instant messaging), or in person

Social and Cultural Capital	Questions to Ask	Teacher Tips
Disability office/resources		
Institutions of higher education have offices for student services for students with disabilities, but often students are unfamiliar with these offices and the specific services they provide. This is a particularly important resource because these offices represent advocates for the students and their rights	Do they offer the services (e.g., books on tape, text-to-speech software) that the student requires and is familiar with? What other academic support systems are available? Is there are a free writing center on campus or a study skills course offered? What about accessible and free tutoring labs?	Assist students with naming their disabilities, knowing specific tests that are required to verify disabilities, and having lists of accommodations
Use books such as *Peterson's Colleges With Programs for Students With Learning Disabilities or Attention Deficit Disorders* to help students research schools that match their needs
Compile a specific contact list with e-mails and phone numbers of individuals in the student services office
Location		
Students with disabilities should consider the campus that will best suit them and their specific needs when looking at institutions of higher education	Do students need to live at home to defer costs? Is being close to their family for gatherings a necessity for the student? Does the stimulation of a city or the confines of a small town better appeal to the student?	Coordinate students interested in visiting the same schools together or in small groups for support and to cut on costs of transportation
Assist students in critically analyzing the pros and cons of campuses for their specific needs
Size		
One size does not fit all in education. Most students coming from the secondary education setting can be thrown off by the 300-person lecture halls they may experience in higher education. Students with disabilities need to know how their classes will be able to accommodate their specific needs regarding attention, identity, and participation in the classroom environment	How large is the university? What is the average class size? What types of interactions with faculty are promoted institutionally? What is the standard format/size of general education courses? What is the student-to-teacher ratio in the college in which the student will be studying? Do the classes get smaller, population-wise, as the course of study continues?	Arrange for students to shadow a freshman on a college campus to experience different types of courses
Acknowledge and discuss with students that some classes may be in a format with which they are not familiar and help them plan accommodations such as tutoring, extra time on tests, and making regular visits to the professor's office

disability status of the students. They can help working-class, culturally and linguistically diverse students with disabilities realize that their college attendance is part of a larger community pattern and that they have been preceded by earlier college graduates and will be followed by others following their example.

Addressing economic limitations. Although connecting to campuses and people is important for working-class culturally and linguistically diverse students with disabilities, the economic realities associated with college tuition, student fees, and cost of living are only compounded by economic burdens implicit within the necessary documentation of a disability. Section 504 of the Rehabilitation Act of 1973 and the ADA Act of 1990 places the burden on the student to provide and pay for appropriate testing and evaluation to document disability. Each postsecondary institution has specific requirements for what constitutes viable documentation, but the minimum standards require the certified qualifications of the evaluator, the types of testing, and other background documents that must be provided. In addition, the evaluation must have been conducted within the last 3 to 5 years. This type of testing can cost from $300 to $3,500.

To help defray the costs of the burden of proof of disability, special education teachers should ensure that their working-class students graduate with a complete, up-to-date battery of tests verifying their disabilities so that these tests can be used by the students in their freshman year of college—and perhaps beyond—as verification of the necessity to them of services from the ADA on campus.

SELECTING A COLLEGE

Selecting a college to apply to and attend is important for any student, but it takes on added significance for working-class, African American, Latino/Latina, or Native American students with a disability. Several resources exist to assist teachers, counselors, students, and families in the college selection process, and much has been written about college selection for low-income, culturally and linguistically diverse youth. Rarely, however, is the information combined. Table 111.1 includes questions and strategies that special education teachers should use to help their working-class, culturally and linguistically diverse students with disabilities research their decisions for postsecondary attendance.

SUMMARY

A critical challenge facing special educators over time has been the overrepresentation of working-class African American, Latino/Latina, and Native American students in their programs. Although much has been done to curtail this overrepresentation, educators have a long way to go now in terms of making sure that those students who are currently overrepresented in special education have the social and cultural capital to envision possibilities for themselves beyond high school. Special educators can be at the forefront of bridging the racial, economic, and ability gaps in college admittance, retention, and graduation by engaging in professional practices that confront the discrimination and bias that may have placed many of those students in special education classrooms. Their intentionality and attention to thinking and promoting college in the future of their students can change the landscape of postsecondary attainment for working-class African American, Latino/Latina, and Native American students with disabilities.

NEXT STEPS

112

Learning Disability Identity Development and Social Construct

A Two-Tiered Approach

Cheryl L. Howland and Eva Gibavic

INTRODUCTION: THE LD WALL

Most of the time people with a learning disability (LD) look, act and perform like everyone else. However, when they encounter an experience that puts them face to face with their disability it is very much like hitting a wall at full speed. The LD Wall is usually invisible to everyone else, yet when a person with a learning disability hits this "wall" s/he can have a powerful and painful reaction.

So here we have a student with LD having just hit the LD wall. Our student is unable to perform as required, and s/he is also having a reaction to the impact. In addition, all around him/her are family, teachers, and friends who did *not* hit this wall and who cannot perceive that there is a wall. These non-learning-disabled individuals often cannot see or understand that our student is severely impacted by his/her experience and, while our student may have a real desire and need to perform in the prescribed manner, s/he cannot.

In the moment when individuals face their hidden disability, having been impacted by their learning disability "wall," they have to deal with the following: 1. They cannot perform in the prescribed manner. 2. They are hurting from the impact. 3. Their experience is denied and questioned by well meaning parents, peers, teachers and others who do not understand. 4. They MUST perform somehow. 5. If you were that person, how would you react?

RESISTANCE TO ASSISTANCE

Why do some students with learning disabilities resist when teachers and other professionals try to help them? Why are some willing and eager for accommodations one day and reluctant the next? What is at the core of their refusals? Why do some teachers still see some students with learning disabilities as "willful non-learners"?

These questions are ones that are often raised in our consulting work by college students, parents, grade school teachers, college professors, and disability advocates. Even with the best of intentions and most current knowledge, teachers and parents can become frustrated with a student's resistance. Even with the best of intentions, students can feel that there is a failure on the part of many helpers to "get it," to truly walk in their LD shoes. This can lead to a functional collapse in the teaching/learning contract and an inability to positively address the issues faced by people with learning disabilities.

THE HOWLAND/GIBAVIC MODEL OF IDENTITY DEVELOPMENT
IN PERSONS WITH LEARNING DISABILITIES

The kernel of our identity development model was formed by the basic premise that neurodevelopmental differences plus life circumstances impact our sense of who we are, in other words, our identity. Who we become in life begins with our inherent make up and evolves and changes over our life as a result of our experiences. Our goal was to propose a model that would assist helpers, learners, parents and teachers understand the developmental processes that can impact individuals with a learning disability. As these experiences are multi-faceted, we propose a complex, two-tiered model of identity development. The model is based in the stage theory of development, well grounded in the works of Erikson, Vgotsky, Kohlberg and Gilligan, and Jackson and Hardiman.

At the time we began our work, an extensive literature search revealed no models of identity development for individuals with learning disabilities, but as our work continued two models were published at the University of Massachusetts by Rodis and Pliner. While very helpful, we found the models to be limited in their respective abilities to address the complex yet powerful effects of social influences, the widely varying impacts of different types of learning disabilities, and the ongoing life challenges that routinely occur when the expectations of self and others collide with an individual's learning disabilities. These ongoing collisions with the "LD wall," which can result in grief, relief, and resistance periodically over the course of a lifetime, is central to the recycling and re-adjusting of individual identity. In essence, while adjustment and integration can occur with each run-in with the wall, there is typically another "wall" around the corner. The "walls" associated with learning disabilities present themselves through life's various experiences as does a continuation of identity integration. For a model to provide assistance in understanding the experience of an individual with a learning disability, it needs to have a level of complexity, complexity that is not typically explicit in identity development models. Our two-tiered model speaks to these considerations.

TIER ONE: INFLUENTIAL VARIABLES: SOCIAL SYSTEMS AND TIMING

Support Systems: How a person receives and perceives support from their family, community, and teachers represents perhaps the most significant variable in the development of a positive sense of identity related to a learning disability. Children who receive positive support from their family, school and surrounding community develop a positive self-identity more often than a child who is perceived as deficient and or defective by their family, peers, educators and culture. Families and school structures with less knowledge, resources, and social support can contribute to a negative identity development by labeling and stereotyping the child as stupid or lazy or ill-behaved.

Timing: The timing of when a person becomes aware that they have a learning disability and the particular life stage they are in can have a significant impact on the development of their self-identity. Some children in elementary school receive a sufficient amount of remediation and support so that as they grow up they see their LD as only a small part of their learning portfolio. Conversely, children with poor school services and a lack of support can experience the shame of having an LD that shapes their entire school experience. Children who receive their diagnosis in high school have spent a significant part of their learning experience without an understanding of their learning needs. This can result in an inaccurate series of labels and poor self-beliefs. Individuals who receive diagnosis in college or in later adult years may have developed a number of compensation techniques that have assisted them in living and learning while lacking remediation and accommodation and may have developed a significant and largely inaccurate belief system and defensiveness about their learning. This can often be seen as strong negative resistance to help from helping professionals when it may be a positive coping skill developed by the individual struggling to maintain positive self-worth.

Social Receptivity/Acceptance: In 1994 and 1999, the Emily Hall Tremaine Foundation funded two Roper Starch national opinion surveys looking at the social perception of individuals with learning disabilities. The results of these surveys showed that an "alarming 48% of parents think that in the long run being labeled as learning disabled causes children and adults more trouble than if they struggle privately with their learning problems." Some individuals such as Tri-athlete Bruce Jenner (dyslexia) are spared this stigma due to success in other areas, such as sports.

Dual Diagnosis: Having another diagnosis in addition to a learning disability is not unusual for people with learning disabilities. Co-morbidity rates are high, with many people struggling with emotional/behavioral difficulties, ADHD, as well as mental health and other medical issues. The interplay among these multiple diagnoses can complicate and intensify the self-identity process.

Cause of the Disability: While most often the cause of a learning disability is unclear, if the cause of a specific learning disability can be ascertained it can be a powerful variable in terms of self-understanding.

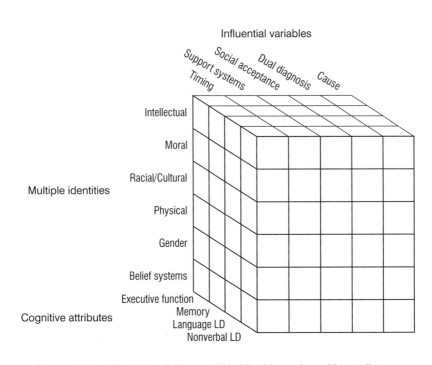

Figure 112.1 Influential variables, multiple identities and cognitive attributes.

NEXT STEPS

Multiple Identity Development

Multiple Intelligences: Gardner's theory of Multiple Intelligences posits the existence of eight different forms of intelligence: linguistic, logical mathematical, musical, visual spatial, interpersonal, intrapersonal, natural, and bodily kinesthetic. People with learning disabilities struggle to understand and experience the development of their gifts as positive identities ("I succeed") that are separate from their disability identities ("I struggle"). Those who are able to see themselves from multiple capability perspectives are better able to integrate disability identities than those who are not.

Moral Identity Development: Identity development theory is founded upon theories of moral reasoning and development. Most recognize that children begin with a self-centered approach to the world and, through experiences, develop into beings that interrelate to others in an interdependent, socially-conscious manner. The stages of moral development can influence passage through the stages of learning disability identity development and affect how an individual will respond to his/her learning issues.

Racial/Cultural Identity: In societies where one racial group is unfairly advantaged, people from marginalized cultures and races are impacted by racial oppression, which further influences their racial/cultural identity development. As a student of color struggles to achieve a positive self-identity, the addition of a learning disability and the concurrent stereotyping can further complicate integration, growth, and resolution of one's identity. The interplay between racism and ableism can be seen in the much higher percentages of students of color who are being placed in special education classes (Harry and Klingner 2006).

Gender Identity: Gender oppression continues to be a significant factor influencing how individuals are treated in our society and plays a role in learning disability assessment and intellectual expectations. Boys are diagnosed with an LD more often than are girls. It has been suggested that this is . . . [because boys tend to act out in the classroom more than girls and, as a result, are subjected to more disciplinary action.]

Physical Identity: Physical identity can be experienced positively for some and negatively for others. Peers, as mentioned above, may give an outstanding athlete respect that s/he does not receive academically. Physical attractiveness may have a socially positive effect, whereas individuals with physical challenges or medical co-morbidities may experience negative social reinforcement.

Belief Systems: Individual beliefs can have a profound influence on learning disability identity development and integration. For example, a student of ours was told by a teacher in middle school that individuals with dyslexia have limited brain space and that perhaps her brain was full. She approached all of her learning challenges from that foundation of belief and perspective. The belief acted as a powerful disincentive to achievement.

Cognitive Attributes

Learning Disabilities: Learning disabilities are defined in various ways, but for simplicity in this model we have chosen to delineate four areas, those involved with the auditory/language area, the nonverbal/visual-perceptual area, memory issues and those related to organizational/executive functioning.

Auditory/Language Processing: Included in this would be central auditory processing, receptive and expressive language, including syntax and word retrieval, written language, and phonologically based dyslexia. Also under this broad category we recognize that some math disabilities are verbally based, having to do with math vocabulary and syntax specific to mathematical reasoning.

Nonverbal/Visual-Spatial Processing: Nonverbal communication is believed to represent 60% of all human communication. Individuals who struggle with nonverbal communication

NEXT STEPS

fail to accurately perceive and/or express those many and varied nonverbal signals which most of us take for granted. When this happens, they are often socially isolated due to poor social skills development. In addition these people can struggle academically with nonverbal forms of analysis, synthesis and reasoning.

Memory Difficulties: Students who struggle with various memory issues can have their learning impacted by short and long term deficits in verbal, auditory, visual, and/or working memory. Working memory allows the individual to hold the various parts of a problem actively in mind or 'on-line.'

Executive Functioning: The executive realm involves the ability to initiate tasks, focus and sustain attention for the task, inhibit behaviors unrelated to the task and inhibit preponderant responses, as well as develop appropriate strategies and shift strategies as required to complete the task.

TIER TWO: STAGES OF IDENTITY DEVELOPMENT

Tier Two of our model addresses the following Stages of Identity Development: Problem with the Wrong Name, Diagnosis, Grief and/or Relief, Resistance and/or Alienation, Passing, Redefinition, and Ongoing Resolution Process

Problem with the Wrong Name: In this stage, the individual and the family has an understanding that there is something different, perhaps something wrong in the learning process, whether it be a problem with behavior, a slower reading rate, an inability to comprehend reading material, and/or difficulty in mathematics, but there is no actual diagnosis. This lack of clarity can often lead to mislabeling, with individuals being called "dumb," "stupid," "lazy," "slacker," or "willful non-learner."

Diagnosis: With diagnosis of a learning disability, a greater understanding of the individual's learning strengths and weaknesses is developed. The individual, if a child, may or may not be told about the diagnosis and what it means. Many college students come to school with a poor understanding of their learning strengths and struggles.

Grief and/or Relief: Diagnosis typically brings change. These changes may be seen by the individual as positive, leading to a sense of relief, such as an individual who appreciates specialized help. There can also be a sense of grief. Grief may come in the recognition of one's differences and/or due to changes that may be seen as unwanted and negative. A great deal depends on the reaction of the individual's family and teachers, and the nature of the changes.

Resistance and or Alienation: In this stage, the individual may resent the learning disability itself, resent the consequences of the label, and/or resent the remediation that s/he has received due to the LD. This often co-occurs with the "Passing" stage: the individual may be resistant in classes, while at the same time trying to pass socially.

Passing: The individual downplays the LD, denying it when possible and trying to be like peers. This is a very common stage/place for a student to be in because our society does not easily accept differences and who really wants the disability label?

Redefinition: The individual realizes that passing and resistance doesn't make the LD go away and doesn't make life easier. This re-evaluation may result from some sort of crisis or may grow out of recognition of the value of the individual's strengths as well as different learning needs.

Ongoing Resolution Process: This stage is perhaps the most important to understand. This stage offers the understanding that the whole model is not static, but rather an ever changing launching point as an individual goes through life. It is here that the above-mentioned influences, variables and the actual disability take on a fluidity that forces a person living with a learning disability to re-cycle through an ongoing process.

NEXT STEPS

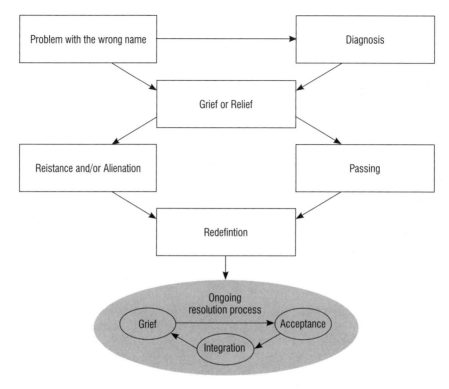

Figure 112.2 Stages.

USING THE MODEL

Using these components, including stages and the factors, should guide us to a better understanding of an individual and, therefore, how best to address a variety of issues, including personal, educational and clinical.

CASE STUDY

"David" was a student diagnosed with a significant language-based learning/reading disability with some indication of ADD but with a solid IQ. In the past, he had refused to register with Disability Services. He was seeking readmission to school after failing out two previous times. The admitting Dean required David to sign a contract agreeing to register with Disability Services, meet with me weekly, and achieve a solid 2.0 or better for the semester.

For our first meeting, he was angry, defensive, and independent-minded. He held little hope that anyone including me could or would help him. He came from a working class background where he was the first person in his family to attend college. He'd received little or no help for his disability in high school and (he told me later) expected me to be just another adult who was a harsh judge of his motivation and performance.

David was stuck in the 'resistance and alienation' stage of learning disability development and was only willing to attempt school out of love and respect for his mother who was ill. He wanted very much to please her and she had asked him for one Christmas present—a "C" average. He was particularly angry with one professor who had failed him several times and who was unwilling to budge on his grade. Most professionals and adults in David's life saw his struggle as a failure of his character. His anger and resistance reinforced their misunderstanding of David and what he truly wanted and felt about his situation.

In order for us to be helpful to David, we had to allow him to be safe in his resistance and alienation while simultaneously encouraging the part of him that wanted to succeed. Additionally, we had to really help him succeed academically. He was assigned to an Academic Assistant who would work jointly with both of us to help him develop learning strategies that worked for him. We set him up with a schedule that respected his need for physical fun and relaxation but that also made study time more automatic and routine. He met with us every week and soon his resistance faded in the face of his burgeoning academic success. He did not, however, wish anyone including his roommate to know that he was meeting with us and protected his privacy fiercely. He had moved from resistance and alienation to passing. Over the course of our two-year relationship David moved in and out of resistance and alienation, passing, and into the ongoing resolution process. He would sometimes hit his "LD Wall" and find himself angry and resistant all over again. But we were able to show that while his learning disability and the frustration associated with it was likely a permanent part of his life, he could and would develop coping skills that would allow him to live a good and successful life. David was able to give his mother her Christmas present that year and for two more Christmases afterward. Most importantly, he took our help and understanding and made it his own. He graduated with a 3.2 GPA.

The Howland/Gibavic model of LD Identity Development allows for a greater understanding of the nature and complex struggles associated with developing a positive LD self-identity, while providing a template that shows the way for individuals and professionals alike to relate and work positively and effectively with themselves and others with learning disabilities.

NEXT STEPS

113

Creating a Fragrance-Free Zone

A Friendlier Atmosphere for People Living with Environmental Illness

Invisible Disabilities Advocate

Did you know there is a growing number of people who can become ill from simply running an errand in a store, going to work or attending a gathering? Simple tasks that most of us take for granted can cause this group to have mild to severe medical reactions. Even their own homes and work environments can lash out at them.

Why is this happening? "Approximately 12.6% of the population suffers from multiple chemical sensitivity (MCS), a condition in which they experience reactions from exposure to low concentrations of common chemicals . . ."

MCS (also known as Environmental Illness or Toxic Injury) is " . . . marked by *multiple symptoms* in *multiple organ systems* (usually the neurological, immune, respiratory, skin, 'GI,' and/or musculoskeletal) that recur chronically in response to *multiple chemical exposures*. MCS Symptoms commonly include difficulty breathing, sleeping and/or concentrating, memory loss, migraines, nausea, abdominal pain, chronic fatigue, aching joints and muscles, and irritated eyes, nose, ears, throat and/or skin. In addition, some with MCS show impaired balance and increased sensitivity not just to odors but also to loud noises, bright lights, touch, extremes of heat and cold, and electromagnetic fields."

The numbers of Americans battling MCS seem to be rising quickly. Most with MCS tell a story of once being healthy and not effected by fragrances. "MCS usually starts with either an acute or chronic toxic exposure, after which this initial sensitivity broadens to include many other chemicals and common irritants . . ." Many experts have found that once a person becomes reactive to a chemical or toxin, their intolerance is rarely reversible.

Furthermore, "In 1998, it was estimated that 26.3 million Americans have been diagnosed with asthma." Asthma is a serious respiratory disorder that can constrict and cause swelling of the airways. "The Institute of Medicine placed fragrance in the same category as second hand smoke in triggering asthma in adults and school age children." What's more, "Up to 72% of asthmatics report their asthma is triggered by fragrance. Asthmatics and others that are negatively impacted by fragrance often have difficulties working, obtaining medical care, and going about activities of daily living because of others' use of scented products."

For those living with asthma and/or MCS, just going to work, a meeting or an activity may expose them to chemicals that could make them ill. These reactions can be very serious and have changed the lives of millions. Because they have to avoid public situations and even having people in their own homes, they can also experience isolation, loneliness, lose their jobs and may even become homebound.

WHAT CHEMICALS?

Most of us are aware that such things as pollution and car exhaust fumes are not good for us. We even realize that sometimes a work environment, like a lab or factory can be hazardous. However, most do not even think twice when entering a building, automobile or even a home that may contain new paint, car smell, carpet or mold, glue, stain, vinyl upholstery, plastic, rubber, smoke, household cleaners, etc.

Moreover, the culprits most of us will never even give a thought to being bothersome are our sweet smelling perfumes, colognes and fragranced products. But aren't these made from natural ingredients like flowers and herbs? Actually, "Perfume formulations changed sometime around the late 70s and early 80s. Today, they are approximately 95–100% synthetic (man-made)." Even seemingly harmless fragrances in our favorite soap, deodorant, lotion, powder, candles, air freshener and laundry products can cause reactions for many.

For the average person, short term exposures to these environmental, everyday household products and perfumes may only seem "bothersome" on occasion. Nevertheless, many people claim they never believed they had an issue until they suddenly or gradually developed their sensitivity or intolerance after normal use of these items.

Author Connie Pitts explained why, "Perfumes, colognes, and many other *scented* products contain an abundance of harmful chemicals, many of which are listed on the EPA's

Hazardous Waste List. They also include numerous carcinogenic chemicals, neurotoxins, respiratory irritants, solvents, aldehydes, hundreds of untested and unregulated petrochemicals, phthalates (which can act as hormone disrupters), narcotics, and much more."

WHAT CAN WE DO?

Because many with asthma, MCS and immune disorders risk becoming ill when they go to work, to run errands, to a doctor's office or when attending a gathering, we can all do our part to help.

1) For our own well-being and for the sake of others, we can discontinue the use of products containing VOCs, synthetic fragrances and harmful chemicals.
2) Make meetings and events Fragrance-Free for all to enjoy. This can be done simply by posting this information along with the notices for the event in bulletins, emails, websites and flyers.
3) Office or building management can ask the cleaning crew to start using natural cleaning products like baking soda, vinegar, hydrogen peroxide or environmentally safe products. Moreover, they should not use "air fresheners" in the building or bathrooms. Instead, exhaust fans and air purifiers can do the job.
4) Office or building management can create a list of people who are sensitive to chemicals and fragrances. They would then call people on the list when someone paints the walls, shampoos the carpet, replaces the carpet, gets new furniture or uses glues, insecticides, stains, polishes, etc. In addition, signs should be placed on the doors to notify all employees and customers of the use of these products.
5) Before visiting someone in their home or inviting them to ours, we should ask those living with asthma, chronic illness, immune issues, MCS and/or allergies what fragrances, lotions, soaps, deodorants, candles, air fresheners, detergents, cleaning products, etc. they can and cannot tolerate.
6) For added protection, a Fragrance-Free Zone can be implemented.

CREATING A FRAGRANCE-FREE ZONE:

A Fragrance-Free Zone is a smoke, fragrance and chemical free area, designed for those who report mild to serious reactions to these items. Adding a Fragrance-Free Zone can help many in our community work and frequent your establishment in comfort.

At first glance, we may think there are not enough people who struggle with these issues to justify the hassle of providing a Fragrance-Free Zone. However, for every 100 people in America, there is an average of 10 with asthma, 20 with an autoimmune disorder and/or 12.5 with MCS.

Here are basically 3 types of Fragrance-Free Zones that can be implemented in the office or store:

Fragrance-Free Zone #1: Building, Office or Store Policy. Establish a policy of no perfumes or fragrances worn by employees inside the building. In addition, the use of nontoxic cleaning supplies, natural pesticides, etc. can be included. This concept is becoming more and more popular among businesses, doctor's offices and churches, because it makes

N
E
X
T

S
T
E
P
S

it possible for many to work in or visit your building. Many medical facilities and religious organizations are also asking patients and congregations not to wear fragrances.

Fragrance-Free Zone #2: Separate Room in Workplace. This is a separate room or floor of a building for employees that provides extra protection from fragrances, as well as paints, glues, formaldehyde, mold, smoke and chemical cleaners. It is sealed off with walls, a door to a direct entrance and exit. It also contains a Fragrance-Free bathroom and a break-room (if space permits).

Fragrance-Free Zone #3: Section in Office. This is a simple and quick way to set up a section in the office. Designate several rows of desks just for those with chemical sensitivities. You can post signs to signify that this section is a perfume, cologne, fragrance and smoke free zone. Put this section in an area where they can have easy access to an outside entrance and away from high traffic areas.

Please note that just creating a "section" within a room is not always a viable answer. Perfumes and fragrances can permeate the air and waft through the area, as well as linger in the hallway, lobby and bathrooms. "Scented products are volatile substances and get into the air quickly. Once in the air, containment to a defined space is impossible. Further, scented products are designed to diffuse into the air and linger."

Finally, "According to the AARDA, approximately 50 million Americans [or] 20 percent of the population . . . suffer from some 80 autoimmune diseases." Thus, for the benefit of all around us, particularly those with immune disorders, when we are sick with a cold or a virus, maybe we should consider staying home. After all, we could infect several more people, who in turn infect several more people—causing them to miss work, activities and maybe even be hospitalized. Consequently, even when we are just "coming down with" a virus or we are "getting over" something, we can still be contagious. If we cannot stay home from work, we should at least steer clear of other people, especially those with immune issues.

Thank you for your cooperation in providing a safer environment, so that millions of people can live better lives, with fewer boundaries! Without everyone's help, going to work or entering a building can put many at risk of having mild to severe reactions that may last several hours or even several weeks. With it, many can live their lives with less risk of exposure.

NEXT STEPS

114

Recognizing Ableist Beliefs and Practices and Taking Action as An Ally

*Madeline Peters, Carmelita (Rosie) Castañeda,
Larissa Hopkins, and Aquila McCants*

Ableism is a pervasive form of oppression that tends to be minimally examined and understood by mainstream society. From a young age we learn powerful messages about groups of people, especially those who are perceived to be different than us. These consistent messages are translated into strongly rooted beliefs, stereotypes, and behaviors directed towards other human beings. Our internalization of negative thoughts and subsequent actions has systematically, generation-by-generation, supported the dehumanization and denigration of people with disabilities.

It is vitally important that we begin to question the historical and contemporary patterns and practices that reproduce the discrimination and exclusion of people with intellectual, emotional, and physical disabilities. Challenging ableism truly requires that we recognize how this oppression is manifested on the individual, institutional, and cultural levels of engagement. It is with this recognition that we will be able to replace our harmful language and behaviors with empowering words and actions, and our marginalizing institutional practices with supportive and inclusive practices. By reevaluating our perceptions and stereotypical responses, we can learn to build respectful, dynamic and fulfilling relationships with people living with disabilities. A significant factor necessary for challenging manifestations of oppression is the formation of allies.

An ally is typically a member of advantaged social groups who uses their social power to take a stand against social injustice directed at targeted groups. For example, White people who speak out against racism, men who speak out against sexism, and heterosexual people who challenge heterosexism and homophobia. An ally works to be an agent of social change rather than an agent of oppression. While there are many important characteristics of an effective ally, there are a few that we would like to highlight. We believe an ally takes responsibility for learning about his/her own and targeted group heritage, culture and experience, and how oppression works in everyday life. Allies listen to and respect the perspectives and experiences of targeted group members. They acknowledge unearned privileges and work to eliminate or change privileges into rights that targeted group members also enjoy. Allies recognize that unlearning oppressive beliefs and actions is a lifelong process, and welcome each learning opportunity. They are willing to take risks, try new behaviors, and act in spite of their own fear and resistance from other advantaged group members. Allies believe they can make a difference by acting and speaking out against social injustice.

The chart below is designed to provide people with information needed in becoming a stronger, more supportive, and aware ally to people living with disabilities. The left side of the chart organizes perceptions, language, and behaviors about the limiting factors at three levels of engagement: individual, institutional, and societal/cultural levels. The right side of the chart responds to the limiting factors by providing people with examples of supportive ally behaviors and actions. The need for each of us to act as an ally by fostering supportive practices is imperative for the well-being of all people.

N
E
X
T

S
T
E
P
S

Recognizing Ableist Beliefs and Practices and Taking Action as an Ally

Limiting Factors for People with Disabilities	Supportive Practices for People with Disabilities
Individual	
Denying people with disabilities equal opportunities and seeing him/her as second class citizens. Behaving as if people with disabilities are invisible, a nuisance, disgusting, and should be institutionalized	Recognize the full potential and humanity of people with disabilities in relationships, employment, and cultural, political, social and physical activities in our multicultural world
Assuming that people with disabilities are unaware and unable to make decisions regarding their daily needs. Limiting and/or interfering with their ability to make their own decisions	Accept that a person is more than their disability. They are complex human beings with the ability to make decisions about their daily needs with varying degrees of success and failure like the rest of the population
Not acknowledging people with disabilities: i.e., ignoring, not speaking to, avoiding eye contact, and behaving as if people with disabilities do not exist	Be aware of your body language and avoid staring at people with disabilities. Refrain from talking about the person with a disability in front of them. Establish eye contact and speak directly to the person with a disability
Imposing "help" thereby taking control away from the person: i.e., grabbing the arm of a person who is blind to assist them across the street without asking	Ask the person with a disability if they need assistance, allowing them to have control of the situation. Stay within the boundaries of the stated request for assistance
Not treating people with disabilities as you would treat others: i.e., being afraid to give feedback or advice to person with a disability by being overly concerned about how the person will react to criticism	State ideas and concerns clearly and constructively. Recognize that constructive feedback is meant to help a person grow and learn
Establishing lower expectations for people with disabilities: i.e., a teacher setting lower standards for a student who is deaf or a teacher who inflates the grade of a person with a disability not based on the person's ability but based on the teacher's pity	Lowered expectations are demeaning and a disservice to the person with a disability and only reflect ableist assumptions. Recognize that inflating grades does not benefit people with disabilities. Understand that accommodations can be put in place to allow students to successfully participate and excel in the classroom
Not encouraging people with disabilities to take risks	Encourage people with disabilities to reach their full potential. Encouragement includes praise when one has met a goal and an inquiry about the next goal to be set, suggesting that higher goals are attainable
Discounting the opinions of people with disabilities, except on issues of disabilities	Seek the opinions of people with disabilities for their perspectives on any issue. They may have valuable opinions and may have experience on a breadth of issues
Institutional	
Employing people with disabilities in low-paying occupations or guiding people with disabilities to solely work in jobs geared towards disability services and/or other related specialized fields: i.e., instilling in people with disabilities that the only work available to them is menial tasks	Recognize that people with disabilities can perform essential functions of various jobs. People with disabilities can and do work in every field of employment, from entertainment, science, and technology to philosophy and mathematics, and have strong qualities and attributes like other employees and deserve to earn a livable wage
Assuming all people with disabilities require the same services thereby establishing a uniform system of accommodations	Recognize and provide services on a case by case basis, because all disabilities are manifested differently in each individual
Scheduling only special activities for accessibility, rather than making all activities accessible or placing people with disabilities in segregated environments, without the goal and practice of inclusive integration: i.e., all students with special needs are required to meet together in the basement of the school	Schedule all activities with accessibility in mind: i.e., space should be wheelchair accessible, bathrooms should be conveniently located; be conscientious of how lighting impacts individuals with disabilities; advocate for a chemically free/fragrance free environment. Mainstream people with disabilities so that they are afforded similar social, cultural and academic experiences. Make inclusive integration the norm (i.e., use multiple teaching methods, make sure all handouts are also printed in Braille and/or on MP3 auditory format; verbally describe all visual aids; welcome sign language interpretation; and provide frequent breaks)

N
E
X
T

S
T
E
P
S

Recognizing Ableist Beliefs and Practices and Taking Action as an Ally

Limiting Factors for People with Disabilities	Supportive Practices for People with Disabilities
Depictions of people with disabilities in mainstream media as different, grotesque, evil, villains, monsters, an alien: i.e., Beauty and the Beast, The Hunchback of Notre Dame, and The Hulk	Recognize that the media has used people with disabilities to incite fear of difference. Be acquainted with positive portrayals of people with disabilities in the media, such as "My Left Foot," etc. Seek out media that portrays people with disabilities as human beings who are living their everyday lives
Maintaining a "hidden" and/or separate set of policies that require people with disabilities to jump through additional hoops in order to prove they need a particular type of service/accommodation	Institutions need to implement policies that are inclusive of the needs of all people with consideration to the individual needs of people with disabilities. Separate is not equal

Cultural

Assuming that the lives of people with disabilities (i.e., daily living, relationships, choices, passions, emotions, work and lack of work, housing, education, abilities, and civic rights) revolve solely around their disability (ies)	Assume that the lives of people with disabilities are full, diverse and complex. People with disabilities make daily decisions, have plans for the future, and enjoy relationships, work and leisure. They also have passions, hobbies, families and friends. The disability is not the essence of who they are in the world
Assuming that people with disabilities do not want a career and prefer to live off of government assistance	Government assistance has never been more than subsistence living. Most people with or without a disability would rather make a meaningful contribution to society than be subject to the stigma of being "lazy" and receiving "a handout." Although many are entitled to disability assistance, they also are searching (despite barriers) to find something more meaningful in their lives, such as good employment, decent shelter, and stimulating recreation
Using limiting language or language with negative connotations to describe people with disabilities: i.e., associating them with terms such as "sick," "bad," "disabled," "broken," "mental," "scary," "stupid," and "sped." For example, "Sam is in Sped, where all the stupid children are"	Recognize that language is a reflection of how people see one another. Use words that locate people with disabilities in a positive and nondestructive manner. Refer to people with disabilities as people first. For example, "Sam is in room 224"
A belief system that people with the same disabilities are the same or share the same experience, not taking their individuality into account	Understand that all people with disabilities are individuals and all individuals have unique qualities. Some wheelchair users are able to walk brief distances, some individuals who are legally blind may be able to see and experience certain sights, and people with learning disabilities may have an Intelligence Quotient in the gifted-to-genius range
Societal belief that people with disabilities are helpless and/or unable to accomplish daily living tasks, thus taking individual power away from the person: i.e., in a restaurant the wait staff asking friends to order for a person with a disability	To think of people as helpless is yet another way of disempowering a group or an individual. All individuals and groups with disabilities lead their daily lives with the same dreams and aspirations as everyone else. There may be accommodations to help them meet their daily goals, but they are not helpless. Helplessness is a learned behavior that can be countered by empowering people to advocate for and do things for themselves as much as is possible
During certain holiday seasons, the gathering of families, the cluttering of aisles, the overcrowded nature of shopping centers, and the added daily responsibilities may result in one's disability becoming more prominent: i.e., increase anxiety, depression, and post traumatic stress syndrome (PTSD)	The holiday seasons are important times to raise one's awareness of the needs of people with disabilities. It is important to be aware of accessibility in your home, and in public spaces, and to be attentive to those who may be left alone. Be supportive and reassuring of the individual's situations
Society's standards of beauty leave people with disabilities invisible: i.e., popular magazines, catalogs, and advertisements do not feature photographs of people with visible disabilities	Society's standards of beauty need to be inclusive of all people from diverse backgrounds, and thus need to include people with disabilities. Recognize that traditional standards of beauty have limited our society's perception of beauty. Standards of beauty are based on the eye of the beholder. Recognize that people with disabilities are beautiful

NEXT STEPS

SECTION 9

AGEISM AND ADULTISM

Introduction

Keri DeJong and Barbara J. Love[1]

Like sundown laws of the old South requiring black people to leave town before dark, youth escort laws requiring young people to be accompanied by an adult over the age of twenty-one years or to depart malls before 7 p.m. aim to regulate the presence of members of the subordinate group to suit the needs and preferences of members of the dominant group. These laws determine when and under what circumstances youth, the target group, can be in the presence of adults, the dominant group, reinforcing and highlighting adult power and the powerlessness of youth. Rooted in the adage of a not-so-long-gone era, "Children are to be seen and not heard," youth escort laws reflect absolute adult power over young people along with societal attitudes of disdain and lack of respect for youth.

In this section we provide examples of the treatment of youth as criminals or potential criminals and undesirables whose behavior must be watched, controlled, and regulated—as well as examples of the ways in which elders are targeted for exclusion, marginalization, and invisibility. Baggy pants laws provide one example of laws that criminalize behavior displayed by young people. House Bill 1626 ("Baggy Pants Bill") states: "It shall be unlawful for any person to appear in public wearing his pants below his waist and thereby exposing his skin or intimate clothing" (Thomas 2004). These laws do not target the exposed expanse of buttocks and cracks displayed by white, middle-aged, large-bellied white men who don't pull their pants over their extended stomachs. Though these working-class white men may be stigmatized for this display, nevertheless, they are not the legal targets of baggy pants laws. Nor are young white women who wear low-slung jeans exposing their bare midriffs. Instead, baggy pants laws are clearly aimed at black youth and other youth of color as well as white youth who identify with youth of color by adopting a hip-hop style of dress. One lawmaker declared, "If we have kids going around wearing pants below their butts, it's not nice, not decent . . . I see how senior citizens respond to these kids. They're afraid" (Parker 2007, 3). Societal prohibitions against and contempt for growing older are equally pernicious. The advertisements and newslines that regularly "pop-up" on computer screens urging us to fight back against aging is an indicator of the negative societal attitude toward growing old. Predatory lending practices and the disproportionate targeting of elders for reverse equity and other mortgage schemes designed to prey on elders with fixed incomes result in elders being forced from their homes, often with devastating results (references to examples and resources are on our section website). Mandatory retirement age and scandalous nursing home conditions, coupled with the prevalence of stereotypes and disparaging humor, all signal loss of power and mistreatment of people who are old in current society.

In this section, we are concerned with the oppression of young people and elders and the ways in which access to participation in society and relationships of domination and subordination are organized on the basis of age. Chronological age is a physical reality. What is deemed appropriate for people of any age group is societally constructed. The roles, behaviors, and expectations that society has deemed appropriate for any given age group vary across societies and within societies across time, corresponding to the economic and technological developments within that society. We acknowledge the physical and biological realities of youth and elders as age-based, social identity groups, and that some social relationships, such as the caretaking of the very young and of elders, are rooted in biological determinants. As discussed in the section on conceptual frameworks (selections 3–5), we contend that decisions about power, voice, and decision-making are socially determined rather than based on biological differences. In other words, young people and elders are socially constructed identities with attendant stereotypes and misinformation. Our presentation of ageism and adultism as issues of social justice acknowledges that, like all other forms of oppression, the oppression of young people and elders exists independently of our ability to observe and acknowledge it.

DEFINITIONS AND MANIFESTATIONS OF AGEISM AND ADULTISM

One of the first writers on ageism, Robert Butler (1975, 12), defines ageism as "A process of systematic stereotyping of and discrimination against people because they are old. . . . Old people are categorized as senile, rigid in thought and manner, old fashioned in morality and skills" (35). John Bell (selection 115) defines adultism as "behaviors and attitudes based on the assumption that adults are better than young people, and entitled to act upon young people without their agreement. This mistreatment is reinforced by social institutions, laws, customs, and attitudes." To these definitions we add a social justice framework that includes an examination of the loss of power, loss of voice, and loss or limited access to participation in society from a basis of equity. This includes the legal, societal, and institutional norms and practices that marginalize and exclude elders and young people and give adults the power to act on and for young people and elders without their agreement. Thus, while elders may be revered for their presumed wisdom, they are nevertheless legally excluded from the workplace. While young people may be appreciated for their vigor, energy, and enthusiasm, their participation is likewise restricted.

Although adultism and ageism are both forms of oppression sharing the identity marker of age, we distinguish between the two, specifically naming *adultism* as the oppression of young people by adults and elders, and *ageism* as the oppression of elders by youth and adults. Some writers use the term "ageism" to refer interchangeably to the oppression of elders and young people. Rather than using the same term to refer to both types of oppression, we find it important to distinguish between the two given the distinctive ways in which these two age-related forms of oppression play out in everyday life.

Our focus in this section is limited to illustrating the ways in which the mistreatment of young people and elders meets our theoretical framework for understanding oppression and providing examples of everyday manifestations of the oppression of young people and elders—that is, examples that are normalized by the culture, rather than dramatic or horrific. The litany of critical issues in the everyday lives of young people and elders illustrates the long-term consequences of the loss and/or absences of power among members of these two groups. Our focus is on creating the framework for understanding how these experiences illustrate not only mistreatment but oppression as well.

The elements of oppression described in the section on conceptual frameworks (selections 4 and 5) are underlying conceptual tools for the analysis of the experiences of both young people and elders. For example, it is useful to think about the way that schools have become more like prisons. The presence of metal detectors, police or security guards in classrooms, and building design that emphasizes surveillance indicate that society has accepted a view of young people as a criminal threat. Similarly, in an effort to ensure that they continue to receive the income of elder residents, nursing homes have been charged with illegally forcing elders to remain in the institution rather than choosing where they wish to live. A federal lawsuit filed on behalf of 8,500 institutionalized Floridians claims that nursing homes pressured politicians to pass legislation making it more difficult for elders to qualify for community care (*AOL News* 2008). These examples illustrate powerlessness, which Young describes as an element of oppression (selection 5).

Recognition of the oppression of young people and elders is hampered by the normalization of mistreatment, which renders it invisible. A variety of laws and institutional arrangements make age the sole criteria for determining when an individual can leave school, drive a car, drink alcohol, get married, or join the armed services. Mandatory retirement ages and age-based health-care allocations clearly indicate the denial of power and privilege on the basis of age. Similar to the suggestion of a former Harvard University president that biological difference accounted for the limited participation of women in math and science, there will be those who assume that biological and developmental differences justify the differential treatment of young people and elders. As the scientific community was quick to condemn the assertions of that university president, our goal is to increase the consciousness about the oppression of young people and elders so that objection to this oppression can be as clear and unequivocal (Bombardieri 2005).

INTERNALIZED AGEISM AND ADULTISM

The designation of young people and elders as social identities is so widespread that people of every culture, language, religion, and nationality are sure that their ways of responding to these identities are rooted in the rationality of laws, policies, and principles dictated by biology. Across many societies, people are sure that the control of members of these two groups, by those with more power, more resources, more strength, and more size, is justified by that size, strength, power, and possession of those resources. This assumption of the rightness of those with more power and more resources to make decisions about the lives of those with less power and fewer resources is shared not only by those of the dominant group but by those of the target group as well. Both young people and elders have internalized the belief that decisions regarding their lives are appropriately made by members of the dominant group (middle-aged adults). Bonnichsen (2003) contends,

> Very few young people actually feel solidarity with young people as a group . . . [Many young people] spend their entire childhood identifying with the perspective of adults . . . [and] feel that . . . other young people . . . actually deserve to be treated with disrespect. . . . [Youth employ a variety of strategies] to dissociate themselves from other young people, trying to shed the negative status of childhood. (2)

Young people are encouraged and rewarded for practicing adultism toward other young people. Similar to the practice among some black people who provide greater respect and deference to other black people who look and act more like white people, young people sometimes accord respect on an age-based scale and act out the oppression on anyone younger, weaker, with fewer resources, and smaller than themselves. They learn quickly (from their own experience) the prevailing conditions under which humans can behave in an oppressive way toward other humans.

"I'm having a senior moment" is a common expression among elders who have accepted the idea that forgetfulness is a condition of aging. The stereotypes, prejudices, and forms of discrimination against elders, discussed by Butler (selection 118), are practiced not only by middle-aged adults and younger people; they are also practiced and reinforced by elders with each other.

This enforcement of the oppression of elders by elders constitutes internalized ageism. The depression sometimes associated with isolation, feeling unwanted, and fear of senility can be a manifestation of internalized ageism. As elders internalize feelings of loss of value, being a bother, worthlessness, feeling that they are unworthy of the caretaking of others, and living with the fear of one day being unable to take care of themselves, they are, in effect, internalizing ageism. For both young people and elders, it is the acceptance of these negative stereotypes about themselves that makes it difficult to name their mistreatment as a form of oppression and to effectively organize to change it.

As in the case of elders, the internalization of the oppression by young people has many negative and dysfunctional consequences. One consequence is the enforcement of adultism by young people on other young people. A second major consequence of internalizing adultism is that young people learn the roles of target and agent of oppression to be played out in other manifestations of oppression (racism, sexism, classism, and the like). In this way, adultism intersects with all other forms of oppression in its preparation of young people for the roles required to secure their participation in the maintenance of the oppressive system. Young people are taught to perform the role of subordinant[2] and concomitantly learn to desire the role of dominant. Concern about learning appropriate behavior in order to be safe is often the guise under which this socialization takes place. Young people (as subordinants) are taught that adults (as dominants) are entitled to speak for them and to make decisions for them. In turn, they learn not to trust their own thinking, decisions, or feelings. The internalization of the idea that dominants know best what is appropriate for subordinants and are entitled to make decisions for them is replayed in every other manifestation of oppression where young people will eventually be required to play the role of dominant and subordinant.

INTERCONNECTION BETWEEN AGEISM, ADULTISM, AND OTHER FORMS OF OPPRESSION

Other forms of oppression converge with ageism and adultism to produce differential results for members of particular intersecting social identity groups. The interaction between age-based oppression and racism, for instance, means that elders of color are more likely to have lower income than white elders, or that young people of color are more likely to attend underfunded schools with limited curricular offerings, police in hallways, and metal detectors at the door. Youth of color are less likely to complete high school or college, are more likely to be placed in foster-care settings, and are five to ten times more likely to be imprisoned than white youth (Fulbright-Anderson, Lawrence, Sutton, Susi, and Kubisch, 2005). African American youth, and in some cases Latino/a youth, receive fewer primary care, mental health, and asthma services than white youth even when family income and health insurance are taken into account. Schools spend, on average, nearly $9,000 less per pupil on youth of color than on white youth.

Ageism intersects with classism and sexism to produce differences in the distribution of retirement resources for the elderly. Women of all ethnic groups live longer than men and generally have fewer economic or health-care resources than men in their old age. Women, poor and working-class people, and people of color often make less contributions to Social Security and hence have fewer benefits (O'Rand, cited by Calasanti and Slevin 2001). Middle- and upper-class elders are more likely to have pensions from discretionary funds that were invested for retirement. Ageism intersects with heterosexism so that same-sex partners cannot collect survivor benefits that are restricted to "spouses."

When a boy plays dress-up with his sisters and is ridiculed or told that his behavior is inappropriate, messages of adultism, sexism, heterosexism, and transgender oppression are conveyed simultaneously. Because the boy in this example could potentially experience name calling, social isolation, or even violence for dressing, acting like, or simply aligning himself with girls, he is forced to perform a prescribed version of masculinity that clearly distinguishes his gender apart from that of his sisters' and simultaneously conveys the ideas that it is shameful to be or act "like a girl." Ridicule and shame are often used to teach the role of dominant and subordinant to young people and are justified to be "for their own good." In their efforts to keep young people safe from the violence, adults' "that's-just-the-way-it-is" attitude conveys a sense of powerless-ness to youth who, as other forms of oppression are experienced, are thereby trained to accept them without questioning, challenging, or fighting back.

Infantilization is an idelological tool of adultism and functions on both the micro and macro levels. At both levels, infantilization involves judging the attitudes, beliefs, and behaviors of some person, or members of social groups, as infantile or immature, and judging others to be adult or mature. It then uses this judgment of a person's or group's "being childlike" to justify the consolidation of resources, power, voice, and decision-making into the hands of those who are understood to be more "adult" or "mature."

On the micro level, talking to an elder in the tone used to address young people is an example of infantilizing an elder. On the macro level, judging elders as "childlike" is used to justify the exercise of power and decision-making over them and [to erase] their thinking and voice from decisions about their own lives. Judging Native American peoples as "childlike" was used to justify removal from their lands and erasing their religion and culture. Judging African people as "childlike" was used to justify taking their land and resources, removing them from their African homes, and selling them into unpaid servitude for life. Judging elders and people with disabilities as "childlike" is used to justify the exercise of power and decision-making over them and to erase their thinking and voice from decisions about their own lives.

The language of "developing nations and economies" presents a more global example of infantilization on the macro level. Those nations that consider themselves "developed" judge other nations, based on judgments about culture, religion, political institutions, and economies, to be "underdeveloped" and that judgment justifies their treatment of those nations as youth in need of adult supervision and direction. This infantilization justifies the actions of global imperial powers, conceived of as adult, mature cultures, political systems, and economies, to require that "developing" nations enact economic, social, and political policies deemed in the direction of "development" and which coincidentally benefit imperial powers, even when detrimental to the needs of the people in those "developing" nations.

GLOBAL DIFFERENCES IN THE TREATMENT OF YOUNG PEOPLE AND ELDERS

The treatment of young people and old people varies from one society to another, and within different cultural groups in a given society. For instance, research shows differences between Western and non-Western and between post-industrial and less-industrialized societies in the treatment of both young people and elders (Rogoff 2003, 9). Although the focus in this section is on the experiences of young people and elders in U.S. society, it is important to recognize the variations among and within cultural and socioeconomic groups globally as well as within the United States.

Different treatment does not connote oppression or the lack of oppression. In many societ-ies, for instance, elders are revered based on the assumption that with age comes increased wisdom. At the same time, there is an assumption in many of those same cultures that age brings inevitable senility and decline. We recognize that both the revering of elders and youth and the oppression of elders and youth can exist within the same racial/cultural/familial context. Our research shows that this simultaneous revering and enforcement of oppression occurs across societies in Africa, Asia, and Latin America, as well as Europe and North America. In addition, it is not limited to rural, urban, industrialized, agrarian, or post-technological contexts.

LIBERATION: ELIMINATING AGEISM AND ADULTISM
AND THE TRANSFORMATION OF SOCIETY

Age-based identities are shared by all humans, across race, gender, class, nationality, sexuality, language, religion, ability, culture, ethnicity, or any other identity, whether target or agent—although their specific meanings will differ in various cultures. Every single human is or has been young. Every human who lives long enough will become an elder. Age-based oppression affects all humans, and so it is in the interest of all humans to work for the elimination of ageism and adultism. Our purpose in seeking a deeper understanding of oppression is to facilitate liberation, that is, the transformation of society through the elimination of age and adult oppression. Here and there, we see bits and parts of models and theory that contribute to our unfolding vision of a liberatory society.

There are alternative ways to think about how to treat young people and elders. Rogoff's (2003) discussion of child-rearing practices among certain groups in Uganda provides one image of how young people can thrive when treated with complete care and respect. Holt's (1967) warning against dual standards for the treatment of young people and adults could provide the first principle of a "bill of rights" for young people. Finally, Freire (1994) encourages our movement toward change, contending that our ontological vocation is to become more fully human by engaging the world in an effort to transform it.

In many parts of the world, young people, elders, and their allies are engaged in research and model building that result in societal transformation and lead to the creation of a liberatory society. They are developing relationships, organizations, programs, and policies that enable young people and elders to participate in society from a position of equity. As we broaden our understanding of these manifestations of oppression and work toward the elimination of ageism and adultism, young people and elders can increasingly anticipate living empowered lives with complete dignity and respect. This is a benefit for every single human.

THE SELECTIONS

The selections in the Context section address definitions of ageism and adultism and individual, institutional, societal, and cultural manifestations of ageism and adultism. Robert Butler's article (selection 118) defines ageism on the basis of attitudes, stereotypes, and behavior patterns that embody the mistreatment and oppression of elders, and it discusses institutional manifestations of ageism. John Bell's article (selection 115) defines adultism and describes common occurrences of adultism. His discussion provides a method for examining individual behavior to determine the extent to which it perpetuates adultism. Sheets (selection 119) discusses the experiences of elders with disabilities, while the selection on "Black Elderly" (selection 120) describes specific difficulties encountered by elders who are black. Paul Kivel's discussion in "Adultism" (selection 124) offers a grounding framework for understanding manifestations of adultism.

The selections in Voices, by Huber (selection 121), Larabee, (selection 122), and Curry (selection 123), describe young people and elders' experiences of ageism and adultism. We note that it was challenging to find descriptions of the experience of adultism written by young people, as was locating the voices of elders. Most descriptions of the experiences of young people and elders that we found were, more often than not, written by middle-aged adults. We think that this reflects the reality of the oppression and the internalization of powerlessness (but see some recent resources on the section website).

The selections in Next Steps offer strategies to eliminate ageism and adultism and to impel liberation. They include specific suggestions for what allies can do. John Bell (selection 115), Jenny Sazama with Boston Area Youth (selection 125), and Paul Kivel (selection 124) each describe strategies to learn about adultism, interrupt adultism, and support the empowerment of young people. They provide suggestions to stimulate thinking about both individual and systemic and institutional changes that can help in the elimination of adultism. Holmes (selection 126) provides curricular ideas for dealing with ageism in schools and Markee (selection 127) provides a helpful discussion of specific things that allies of elders can do. We include Marge Larabee's "Elder Liberation Draft Policy Statement" (selection 122) because it provides a good model for examining the oppression of elders from a position of empowerment and with a view toward liberation. In addition to a description of conditions for elders, this statement discusses both how elders can work on ending internalized oppression and what they can do to promote their own liberation, as well as what allies can do to support elders to have good lives.

Notes

1 We ask that those who cite this work always acknowledge by name all of the authors listed rather than only citing the first author or using "et al." to indicate coauthors. All authors listed on a section collaborated equitably on the conceptualization, development, and writing of this section.

2 We prefer the spelling *subordinant* because it parallels the term used to refer to dominants. We do not use the term *dominate* to refer to those in the dominant role. The use of the term *subordinate*, which is a modifying adjective, seems to contribute to the reduction and objectification of members of the group to which this term is applied.

References

AOL News. (September 20, 2008). "For Some, Nursing Homes Are a Prison." Retrieved April 8, 2009, from http://www.tilrc.org/assests/news/0908comm20.html.

Bombardieri, M. (January 17, 2005). "Summers' Remarks on Women Draw Fire." *The Boston Globe.* Retrieved April 8, 2009, from http://www.boston.com/news/local/articles/2005/01/17/summers_remarks_on_women_draw_fire/.

Bonnichsen, S. (2003). "Objections to Calling Adultism an Oppression." Retrieved December 13, 2008, from http://www.youthlib.com/notepad/archives/2003/12/objections_to_c.html.

Butler, R. N. (1975). *Why Survive? Being Old in America.* New York: Harper and Row.

Calasanti, T. M., Slevin, K. F. (2001). *Gender, Social Inequalities and Ageing.* Walnut Creek, CA: AltaMira Press.

Freire, P. (1994). *Pedagogy of the Oppressed.* New York: Continuum.

Fulbright-Anderson, K., Lawrence, K., Sutton, S., Susi, G., Kubisch, A. (2005). *Structural Racism and Youth Development: Issues, Challenges, and Implications.* Aspen Institute Roundtable on Community Change. Washington, D.C.: Aspen Institute.

Holt, J. (1967). *How Children Learn*. New York: Putnam.

Parker, L. (October 14, 2007). "Several U.S. Cities Snapping over Baggy Pants." *USA Today.* Retrieved March 10, 2009, from http://www.usatoday.com/news/nation/2007-10-14-Baggy_N.htm.

Rogoff, B. (2003). *The Cultural Nature of Human Development.* New York: Oxford University Press.

Thomas, B. (May 13, 2004). "Memo to Britney: Lose the Low-Slungs." MSNBC, US News. Retrieved April 29, 2009, from http://www.msnbc.msn.com/.

115

Understanding Adultism

A Key to Developing Positive Youth-Adult Relationships

John Bell

Most of us are youth workers because we care about young people. Personally we want to both be effective and have good relationships with young people. . . .

To be successful in our work with young people, we must understand a particular condition of youth: that young people are often mistreated and disrespected simply because they are young. The word *adultism* refers to behaviors and attitudes based on the assumption that adults are better than young people, and entitled to act upon young people without their agreement. This mistreatment is reinforced by social institutions, laws, customs, and attitudes.

. . . [E]xcept for prisoners and a few other institutionalized groups, young people are more controlled than any other group in society. . . . [M]ost young people are told what to eat, what to wear, when to go to bed, when they can talk, that they will go to school, which friends are okay, and when they are to be in the house. . . . [T]he opinions of most young people are not valued; they are punished at the will or whim of adults; their emotions are considered "immature." In addition, adults reserve the right to punish, threaten, hit, take away "privileges," and ostracize young people when such actions are deemed to be instrumental in controlling or disciplining them.

If this were a description of the way a group of adults was treated, we would all agree that their oppression was almost total. However, for the most part, the adult world considers this treatment of young people as acceptable because we were treated in much the same way, and internalized the idea that "that's the way you treat kids." . . .

THE HEART OF IT

. . .

Adults have enormous importance in the lives of almost every young person. This fact may make it difficult to understand what I am calling *adultism*. Not everything the adult world does in relation to young people is *adultist*. It is certainly true that children and young people need love, guidance, rules, discipline, teaching, role modeling, nurturance, protection. Childhood and adolescence are a steady series of developmental stages, each of which has a different set of needs, issues, and difficulties. For example, a three year old needs a different amount of sleep than a 15 year old; or, what works to physically restrain a seven year old will not work with an 18 year old; or, how you explain conception and birth to an inquisitive toddler will be quite different from how you explain these to a sexually active teenager.

Differing cultural, ethnic, gender, class, or religious approaches to these developmental stages can further complicate the identification of *adultism*. For example, what is considered "weak" in one gender, may be considered "strong" in another; or, belching may be considered rude in one culture and an expression of appreciation in another; or, childhood sex play may be condoned in one culture and condemned in another.

The point is that no one act or policy or custom or belief is in itself necessarily *adultist*. Something can be labeled *adultist* if it involves a *consistent* pattern of disrespect and mistreatment that has any or all of the following affects on young people:

- an undermining of self-confidence and self-esteem;
- an increasing sense of worthlessness;
- an increasing feeling of powerlessness;
- a consistent experience of not being taken seriously;
- a diminishing ability to function well in the world;
- a growing negative self-concept;
- increasing destructive acting out;
- increasing self-destructive acting "in" (getting sick frequently, developing health conditions, attempting suicide, depression, etc.);
- feeling unloved or unwanted.

Certainly these serious conditions do not entirely stem from *adultism*. Other factors like sexism, racism, poverty, physical or mental disability, and so on, may also contribute to these results. But systematic disrespect and mistreatment over years simply because of being young are major sources of trouble.

EVIDENCE THAT ADULTISM EXISTS

Other "isms" like racism and sexism are well established and accepted as realities. They each have a huge body of literature and research documenting the effects and history of the oppression. There are novels, movies, media presentations, political organizations, and social movements devoted to illuminating and or eliminating the existence of the "ism."

The concept of *adultism*, the systematic mistreatment and disrespect of young people, is relatively new and has not been widely accepted as a reality. There is certainly much research and literature on children and youth, but very little that concludes that young people are an oppressed group in our society, with parallels to other such groups. Part of my effort in this article is to draw forth enough examples, primarily from the United States, to point to the reality of *adultism*.

COMMON STATEMENTS

Consider how the following comments are essentially disrespectful. What are the assumptions behind each of them? Do you remember having heard any of these as a younger person?

- "You're so smart for fifteen!"
- "When are you going to grow up?"
- "Don't touch that, you'll break it!"
- "As long as you are in my house, you'll do it!
- "You're being childish."

C
O
N
T
E
X
T

- "You're so stupid (or clumsy, inconsiderate, etc.)!"
- "Go to your room!"
- "Don't ever yell at your mother like that!" (yelling)
- "She doesn't understand anything." (about a baby)
- "You are too old for that!" or "You're not old enough!"
- "Oh, it's only puppy love."
- "What do you know? You haven't experienced anything!"
- "It's just a stage. You'll outgrow it."

COMMON OCCURRENCES

PHYSICAL AND SEXUAL ABUSE

There are numerous examples of disrespect toward young people. Of course, there is the obvious oppressive treatment: physical and sexual abuse of young people. Official reports of child abuse reached 2.7 million in 1993.

OTHER PUNISHMENT AND THREATS

There is also a whole range of nonphysical punishments or threats: being routinely criticized, yelled at, invalidated, insulted, intimidated, or made to feel guilty with the effect of undermining a child's self-respect; being arbitrarily or unfairly "grounded" or denied "privileges." If young people protest against their mistreatment, they are often subjected to more punishment.

DENIED CONTROL

Young people are denied control and often even influence over most of the decisions that affect their bodies, their space, and their possessions. For example, most adults seem to think they can pick up little children or kiss them or pull their cheeks or touch their hair without asking or without its being mutual. Adults can often be seen grabbing things out of children's hands without asking.

VERBAL INTERACTIONS

Most young people know that in a disagreement with an adult, their word will not be taken over the adult's. Most adults talk down to children, as if children could not understand them. Adults often talk about a young person with the young person present as if he or she were not there. Many adults give young people orders to do things or lay down rules with no explanation. Adults, in general, do not really listen to young people, do not take the concerns of a young person as seriously as they would an adult's, and have a hard time hearing the thinking of young people as worthy of adult respect, let alone on a par with the quality of adult thinking. Yet young people are expected to listen to adults all the time.

COMMUNITY INCIDENTS

Adolescent young people are frequently followed by security guards in stores, passed over by clerks who serve adults in line behind them, chased from parks or gathering places for no good reason by police, assumed by passing adults to "be up to no good." The media often promote negative images and stereotypes of them, especially of urban youth and black youth.

SCHOOL EXAMPLES

Schools subject students to incredible control through the use of hall passes, detention, suspension, expulsion, and other penalties. Any community certainly needs rules to live by, but the rules in most school communities are *imposed* on young people and enforced by the adult staff.

Consider these examples:

- Teachers sometimes yell at students with impunity, but students are disciplined if they yell back at teachers.
- Young people are sometimes punished unfairly because adults feel frustrated.
- Students are forced to accept their "grades" that, over time, cause students to eventually internalize a lifelong view of themselves as "smart" or "average" or "dumb"—with profound impact on many aspects of their lives. However, students do not get to officially "grade" teachers. If a student receives an "F," it is assumed the student failed, not the teacher.
- Young people have no real power in the important decisions that affect their lives in school.

SOCIETAL ADULTISM

LAWS

There is a different set of laws for young people. They do not have the same rights as adults. Of course, some laws specifically protect young people from mistreatment but other laws unduly restrict the life and freedom of young people. Curfew ordinances that exist in many communities apply to young people but not to adults. In divorce cases, until a recent landmark custody case, young people were not even permitted to have a voice in deciding which parent, if either, they wished to live with.

CHILD DEVELOPMENT LITERATURE AND EDUCATION

An institutional example of *adultism* can be found in the literature of child development, which is full of misinformation and unfounded claims about young people that severely underestimates what young people are capable of. For example, in one classic textbook used by many students of child development, *The Magic Years* by Selma Freiberg, the author states that the only reason an infant before six months of age cries is because of physical pain. An infant has no emotional pain before this age, she says, because "an infant's intelligence has not yet developed the cognitive apparatus that gives rise to emotional responses." Many parents, including myself, in observing their own infants closely, know that this is not true. Yet, young child development professionals, often without children, are taught a distorted view of infant functioning as if it were gospel.

THE EFFECT OF CULTURAL PRACTICES: AN INTERESTING EXAMPLE

Generations of young people in western culture have grown up with their development limited by vast cultural biases that consistently underestimate human potential or misunderstand human development. For example, Joseph Chilton Pierce, in his *Crack in the Cosmic Egg*, found that in certain Ugandan cultures, infants reach the milestones of sitting, walking, and talking in half the time it takes for children in the United States. This seems to challenge accepted western norms. Researchers hypothesized two reasons for such seemingly accelerated development:

- From the moment of birth until well into the toddler stage, infants spend most of their time strapped skin to skin next to their mothers. From this vantage point the infants intimately experience the rhythms of body movement and speech, the cues in the environment that their mothers paid attention to, and constant tactile closeness.
- When not being carried, infants and toddlers were given loving massages for long periods every day by their mothers and other women in the community.

Researchers concluded that the combinations of these two practices stimulate complex neurological, motor, and hormonal systems of the infants to speed sitting, walking, and talking compared to what is considered "normal" in the West. The mere existence of such huge differences in the rate of development raises large questions about our assumptions about what is normal.

(The interesting back end of the Ugandan example is that at age five, after this extremely intimate early childhood experience, the children go through a rite of passage that includes being sent alone into the forest for several days, then being forced to leave their mother's home and sent to live with another relative. This shock appears to arrest the earlier rapid development, and maturation slows way down.)

GENERAL ADULT ATTITUDES

Many of us have heard older people say to us or other young people something like, "Growing up is giving up. You'd better get used to it." It is the accumulation of disappointments, losses, smashed dreams, unaccepted love, and other such painful experiences that lead adults to say things like that. This crippling attitude is gradually forced upon young people. It is like a contagion, a virus about aging.

INSTITUTIONAL EXAMPLES

Young people in this country are forced to go to school for 12 years, whether school is an effective learning environment for them or not. They are forced by law and by parents (with the exception of those who exercise the demanding option of home schooling). If their spirit, energy, or learning style does not dovetail with the prevailing teacher, school, or educational philosophy, they begin to "fail," have "special needs," are "tracked," and may eventually be labeled as a "dropout." Throughout the 12 years, students have no voice, no power, no decision-making avenues to make significant changes. A critique of our educational system is beyond the scope of this article. Suffice to say here that while society's motivation of providing education for all its young people is laudable, the school system as an institution perpetuates *adultism*.

Another institutional example is the absence of socially responsible, productive, and connected roles for young people in most societies. Certainly in the United States, young people find few jobs, no real policy-making roles, no positions of political power, and no high expectations of young people's contributions to society.

On the other hand, the youth market is exploited for profit as the manufacturing and entertainment industries manipulate styles, fads, popularity, and all other aspects of mass culture.

A MIRROR

A handy mirror for reflecting what may be *adultist* behavior is to ask oneself questions like the following:

- "Would I treat an adult this way?"
- "Would I talk to an adult in this tone of voice?"
- "Would I grab this out of an adult's hand?"
- "Would I make this decision for an adult?"
- "Would I have this expectation for an adult?"
- "Would I limit an adult's behavior this way?"
- "Would I listen to an adult friend's problem in this same way?"

Sometimes the answer may be "no" for good reason, depending on the circumstance. For example, I insist that my six year old son hold my hand when crossing the street, but not my 18 year old daughter. However, many times there is no justifiable reason for treating a younger person differently except habit and attitude. If your "no" sounds a little hollow, it might be worth re-examining your reasons for doing it.

THE EMOTIONAL LEGACY

I hope this short list of examples begins to put our work with young people in a larger context. Most of the examples I used have been reported to me by young people. They consistently report that the main message they get from the adult world is that they are not as important as adults; they do not feel that they are taken seriously; they have little or no power.

They say that the emotional legacy of years of this kind of treatment is a heavy load, which can include any or all of the following: anger, feelings of powerlessness, insecurity, depression, lack of self-confidence, lack of self-respect, hopelessness, feeling unloved and unwanted.

What are some possible results of such feelings on their behavior, especially as they get into adolescence and early adulthood?

- Some act "out" by bullying, being prone to violence, rebelling against the "norm," leaving home early, and so on.

- Some act "in" by becoming self-destructive: suicide, alcohol and drug abuse, depression, etc.
- Some gain a sense of belonging or safety by joining a gang, a clique, a club, teams
- Some isolate themselves, being lonely, not asking for help, not having any close relationships, not trusting.

Again, *adultism* is not the only source of such behaviors, but it surely plays a major role.

A LINK TO OTHER FORMS OF OPPRESSION

There is another important reason for understanding and challenging *adultism*. The various ways we were disrespected and mistreated have, over time, robbed us of huge amounts of our human power, access to our feelings, confidence in our thinking and ability to act, and enjoyment of living. The pain we experience as young people helps condition us to play one of two roles as we get older: to accept further mistreatment as women, as people of color, as workers, etc., or to flip to the other side of the relationship and act in oppressive ways toward others who are in relatively less powerful positions than ours.

A simple illustration might help make this clear. Picture this: a sixth grader is humiliated by the teacher in front of the class for not doing the math problem at the board correctly. The recess bell rings. He is fuming. He feels disrespected. He goes outside and picks on someone to get his feelings out. Whom does he pick on? Someone smaller and often someone younger. And so it goes: the 6th grader picks on the 5th grader. The 5th grader turns and knocks down the 3rd grader. The 3rd grader hits the 1st grader. The 1st grader goes home and picks on his little sister. The little sister turns and kicks the cat.

We can observe among a group of children the mistreatment being passed down among them. It is being passed down the line of physical power, bigger to smaller, and often older to younger.

The significance of this early experience becomes clearer when it is generalized to other forms of the abuse of power. Men, for example, who were routinely beaten as little boys, grow up to be wife beaters. This is a clinical truism. Similarly, white people, disrespected as children, turn the same attitude, embellished with misinformation, on people of color.

This is one of the pervasive and lasting effects of the mistreatment of young people. Bullies have been bullied. Abusers have been abused. People who have been put down put others down. If a person had not been disrespected and mistreated over and over again as a child and young person, that person would not willingly accept being treated that way as he got older, nor would he willingly heap disrespect on others.

Adultism, racism, sexism, and other "isms" all reinforce each other. The particular ways young people are treated or mistreated are inseparable from their class, gender, or ethnic background. However, the phenomena of being disrespected simply because of being young holds true across diverse backgrounds.

. . .

116

"Look Out, Kid, It's Something You Did"

The Criminalization of Children

Bernadine Dohrn

A seismic change has taken place. Youngsters are to be feared. Our worst enemy is among us. Children must be punished, held accountable, expelled. We have developed zero-tolerance for children.

The tragedy at Columbine further escalated the decade-long process of criminalizing the behavior of children, recasting an additional icon to accompany the fearful, racially coded language describing *some* youth in trouble with the law as "superpredators." The newly sensationalized school shootings of 1997–1999 involved suburban or small-town religious White boys with guns, killing their fellow students, spawning a White, upper-middle-class discourse of violent youth based on alienation and isolation. School shootings have become a trope—an inspiration for politicians, funding streams, educational pandemonium, and law enforcement expansion. Yet perhaps more significantly, beneath the rarely occurring but dominant focus on youth homicides, normal youth behavior and misbehavior became further criminalized, all in the name of safety. Children bore the brunt of the national soul-searching into the conditions of childhood in America at the end of the twentieth century.

No one can ignore the shocking fact that in the decade of 1985–1994, 25,000 children were murdered in the United States. In fact, there is the equivalent of a Columbine virtually every day in America. The proliferation of lethal handguns in the possession of children that resulted in children killing children (83% of victims aged 12–18 were killed by handguns); the syndication of youth gangs into illegal-drug cartels; the flourishing of youth violence reported on local TV news stations; the resulting public fear and pandering of politicians and law enforcement officials; and the popularization of youth demonization by noted academics—these are the tangled elements that reinforce and strengthen one another, spiraling into an overlapping system of causes and consequences and qualitative changes in how society perceives, and even thinks about, its adolescents.

Today, behaviors that were once punished or sanctioned by the school vice-principal, family members, a neighbor, or a coach are more likely to lead to an adolescent being arrested, referred to juvenile or criminal court, formally adjudicated, incarcerated in a detention center, waived or transferred to adult criminal court for trial, sentenced under mandatory sentencing guidelines, and incarcerated with adults. The increase in discretion ceded to prosecutors and police has transformed the decision of what to charge for a given offense: Yesterday's battery may be inflated into assault, simple assault into aggravated assault, a schoolyard fight into multiple felony charges. The arrest of multiple juvenile defendants for each incident further escalates youth crime statistics.

This massive shift toward criminalizing youngsters is evident in the increasing numbers of court cases, detained and incarcerated youth in overcrowded facilities, and legislative crackdowns on juvenile crime. In the past decade, the number of formally processed delinquency cases increased 78%.

Within this climate, a less visible, less sensational shift has quietly been executed. This change profoundly impacts millions of children, their classmates and families, and our common future.

This decade of relentless reconditioning of how citizens think about children—on the part of law enforcement, legislators, professionals, academics, the media, and frightened neighborhood residents—has shifted the paradigm. Through the catalyst of changes in criminal and juvenile law, much of adolescent behavior has been criminalized and youngsters themselves demonized. Casting children as frightening makes full use of racial, ethnic, and gender stereotyping, resulting in both disproportionate impact as well as generalizations impacting all youth. This transformation in how we think about ourselves thinking about children has taken an incalculable toll on adults and children alike. The daily discourse about children has shifted from innocence to guilt, from possibility to punishment, from protection to fear. This sinister criminalization of childhood now permeates basic life: the schools, the parks and neighborhoods, child protection, and health care.

In the 1990s, fiscal priorities shifted from education, child protection, and scholarships to prison construction, law enforcement growth, and expanded mechanisms for the social control and exile of sectors of youth. Correctional spending nationally now exceeds $40 billion per year, to pay for a 500% rise in the prison population since 1972. In two short decades, budgets for prisons grew twice as fast as for education; prison spending increased 823% between 1988 and 1995, while education expenditures grew only 374%. More sobering, the vast majority of the states now spend at least one and a half times as much on prisons as they do on education.

In the past decade, New York State spent more than $700 million on prisons, while slashing the state and city college budgets by $600 million, with one result being that the number of people of color enrolled in New York's state colleges and universities is substantially lower than the number currently incarcerated there. Not only are more children currently seeing the inside of prison walls rather than classrooms, there is a new movement to place more, and younger, children into the adult criminal system.

One hundred years ago in Chicago, the world's first juvenile court for children was premised on the removal of children from adult jails and adult poorhouses. At the centennial of the juvenile court, children are being reincarcerated with adults, tried as adults in adult criminal court, and subject to imputation of adult *mens rea* with mandatory-sentencing statutes that reject rehabilitation as a goal.

. . .

CRIMINALIZING YOUTH BEHAVIORS

A major consequence of the tidal wave of fear, violence, and terror associated with children has been adult legislative and policy decisions to criminalize vast sectors of youth behavior. In part, this tendency is fueled by an organized drive on the part of certain political forces to "get tough on youth violence"; in part the changes have resulted from an accumulation of legislative reactions to a particular sensationalized case, the hackneyed mantra to "do something."

The sum total of a decade's *legal* responses is the transformation of the social landscape that children inhabit. Schools have become military fortresses. Hanging out becomes illegal. Fewer systems want to work with adolescents in need. Youngsters who have themselves been neglected or abused by adults pose too many challenges and have too many problems to be addressed. Health care and mental health services are rarely organized for adolescents. Schools want to get rid of the troublemakers and the kids who bring down the test scores. Minor offenses are no longer dealt with by retail stores, school disciplinarians, parents, or youth workers, but rather the police are called, arrests are made, petitions are filed.

Six of seven juvenile arrests are for a nonviolent offense. Of the 2.7 million arrests of young people under 18 years of age, property offenses (particularly larceny/theft), drug offenses, disorderly conduct, runaways, curfew and loitering, and liquor law violations account for the vast majority of the arrests. Ironically, if all male children aged 10–18 were incarcerated until their 25th birthday, eliminating youth crime tomorrow, there would still be 90% of violent crime: the adult offenders. The intense focus on a youth crime epidemic thus is a social choice rather than a strategic response to the facts about crime and public safety.

The criminalizing of adolescent behavior takes place in multiple ways. Major social institutions for youth have constricted eligibility and eased methods for expulsion. Schools, child welfare systems, probation, and health services have all made it easier to violate, terminate, exclude, and expel youngsters. Where these youth go for survival, help, socialization development, care, and attention is unclear. One door that always remains open is the gateway to juvenile and criminal justice. Overcrowded juvenile correctional institutions, deficient youth facilities, and disproportionate minority confinement are among the consequences.

POLICING THE SCHOOLS

> I would there were no age between ten and three- and twenty, or that youth would sleep out the rest; for there is nothing in the between but getting wenches with child, wronging the ancientry, stealing, fighting.
> —Shakespeare, *The Winter's Tale*, act III, scene III. ll. 61–66

Schools have become a major feeder of children into juvenile and adult criminal courts; simultaneously, schools themselves are becoming more prisonlike. Closed campuses, locker searches, contraband, interrogations and informers, heavily armed tactical police patrols, uniforms (M. M. Harrigan, personal communication, 1998)—these are elements of public and even private high school life today. It is paradoxical but fundamental that a handful of high-profile school shootings masks a broader and deeper criminalization of school life, accompanied by the policing of schools, which has transformed public schools across America into a principal referral source for juvenile-justice prosecution.

Two policies contribute to this dramatic new role for schools: first, the increased policing of schools, leading to a significant increase in school-based arrests and the simultaneous abdication of educators; and second, the substantial increase in school exclusions, including suspensions/expulsions of students, propelled initially by the legislative green light that mandated "zero-tolerance" policies for gun possession as a condition of federal funding. That limited definition of zero-tolerance rapidly exploded, in practice, to include misdeeds of all sorts, both in school and outside of school. Rather than insisting on the teaching potential in adolescent misbehavior for both the miscreant and the other students, rather than seizing the "teachable moment," rather than keeping an educational perspective on sanctioning and social accountability, principals and teachers—admittedly under pressure from frightened parents—have ceded their authority to law enforcement personnel, particularly to police and prosecutors, and willingly participated in excluding troublemakers, difficult kids, disabled youth, and children in trouble from the very education that is their primary hope. These so-called zero-tolerance and security policies were escalating before the high-profile school shootings of 1997–98 and the 1999 Columbine High School tragedy. Since then, the policies, the dollars, and the hardware for policing and militarizing schools have mushroomed, and the trend is likely to continue into the next decade.

School-Based Arrests. How grave is the school crime problem? In 1997, there were more than 180,000 school fights leading to arrests, almost 120,000 thefts in schools leading to arrests, nearly 110,000 incidents of school vandalism leading to arrests, and fewer than 20,000 violent crimes. Serious violent crime is extremely rare within schools and constitutes a small percentage of the total amount of school offending. Ninety percent of principals surveyed reported no major serious, violent crime in their schools. In fact, victim self-reports indicate that actual school crime numbers have not changed significantly during the past 20 years.

The first three categories (some 400,000 arrests) are noteworthy. Most school crime is theft, some 62%. School-based incidents such as fighting, theft, and vandalism have traditionally been handled within a school disciplinary system. Forty years ago, an offender would be sent to the office of the vice-principal, a parent might be called, detention hall (remaining for an hour after school) might be mandated, a letter of apology might be required. It would have been difficult to imagine police being called, arrests and handcuffs employed, court filings and incarceration being options.

In today's Chicago public schools, and increasingly in suburban and rural school districts, police are routinely employed by schools. Some schools employ police officers in their teacher salary lines, and encourage police in uniforms, armed, tactical-unit police, and plainclothes police to patrol their schools. Police officers may make half again their salary by moonlighting with the public schools outside their regular duty hours. School-assigned police may be evaluated based on their numbers of arrests. Police may be under no obligation to consult with the school principal about how to respond to a particular youth's misbehavior or to a particular incident. In certain locations, police fail to inform principals or school officials that a student has been arrested during school hours, on school grounds. One authority has replaced another.

At Paul Robeson High School in Chicago, for example, local police precinct data indicate that 158 students were arrested at Robeson in 1996–97. The breakdown of those arrest charges, from a major urban high school, is revealing: 61 arrests for pager possession, 21 for disorderly conduct, 14 for mob action, 16 for (nonfirearms) weapon possession. In 1998, after the school adopted a strategy of small-school reform—breaking the massive high school into smaller units where no youth slips through the cracks—arrests plummeted to 28, 22 of those for pager violations!

Massive locker searches began in 1994–95 in Chicago schools, resulting in numerous student arrests during a single day's lockdown: 40 students at Westinghouse High School, 46 at Kenwood High School, 50 at Roosevelt High School, and 57 at Lincoln High School. In each case, the substantial majority of teens were charged with possession of beepers. Possession of pagers appears to be an offense that is both a status offense (for which adults would not be arrested) and an expansion of drug laws by labeling pagers as "drug para-phernalia" or contraband: transforming a technological convenience into a crime. School-based arrests for possession of pagers is a classic example of the criminalization of youth.

Additional school-based arrests include offense charges such as disorderly conduct or mob action, discretionary decisions that could be based on incidents involving significant disruptions or merely minor occurrences. Decisions to call a shouting match, a no-harm tussle, or locker graffiti a crime, to arrest rather than see a teachable moment, to prosecute rather than resolve disputes—these practices are turning schools into policed territory. Researchers suggest that the expectation of school crime in fact creates it.

This pattern of accelerating school incidents into delinquency offenses or criminal acts further heightens disproportionate minority arrests and confinement in juvenile justice. To date, it is the large, public, urban high schools that have become sites of substantial police presence, that are under pressure to control youth misbehavior, and that are without influential parents with resources to buffer their children from the juvenile justice system. Since Jonesboro and Littleton, suburban and rural high schools are also becoming fortresses, and arrests and mandatory expulsions are escalating. This bleeding of urban responses into middle-class life has its own dynamic and momentum, focusing more, perhaps, on drugs, tobacco, dress, and behavior toward authority, with more private institutionalization of youth as a consequence.

The increasing regimentation of school time results in few breaks, little time for lunch, less physical education, an attrition of music, art, and humanities classes, and closed campuses in high schools. Closed campuses result from neighborhood residents' and parents' complaints about the mobile presence of children during the school day. Teachers monitor student lunch periods and move their own lunch time to the end of the day, shortening the school day. In fact, schools are increasingly simulating prisons, as if preparing their students for a likely future: locked in, regimented, searched, uniformed, pressured to become informers, and observed with suspicion.

Search and seizure of student lockers, backpacks, and persons is legitimized. A culture of informing on fellow students is encouraged and mandated by school officials, without exploration of ethical considerations and conflicting values involved. The blurring of school discipline and delinquency accelerates.

When school sanctioning is handed over to law enforcement *in the first instance* for the vast majority of minor school infractions, not only do the offender and the victim fail to learn from the incident, and not only is the consequence more likely to be crushing rather than illuminating, but the entire community fails to take hold of the problem as a school-community matter.

The failure to place serious reliance on peer juries, teen courts, or community-justice alternatives and to rely instead on armed police for school safety has startling and profound consequences. It is an abdication of adult responsibility and engagement with youngsters. It creates a juvenile delinquency record for vast numbers of youth who might otherwise not be in trouble with the law. Having any delinquency or criminal record has increasing consequences for scholarships, higher education, job eligibility, and escalated sanctions if there is a subsequent police investigation or arrest.

School Exclusion: Suspensions and Expulsions. Suspensions and expulsions from schools have simultaneously exploded as a new national trend, exemplified by the struggle over the expulsion of six Decatur, Illinois, high school students and their subsequent arrest. Fueled by federal legislation in 1994 mandating a one-year "exclusion" for possession of a firearm on school property (Gun Free Schools Act, 1994), new legislation was passed in every state within a 5-month period to maintain federal-funding eligibility. One year later, the Safe School Act (1994) revised and expanded the prohibition to "dangerous weapon" rather than "firearm"; and "dangerous weapon" was defined, in the amended language, as "a weapon, device, instrument, material, or substance, animate or inanimate, that is used for, *or is readily capable of,* causing death or serious bodily injury." This opened the door for a stampede—and for wide discretionary expansion of the new exclusion policy by school personnel that is applied disproportionately to African American and Latino students. In Decatur, for example, 82% of all expulsions of students for over 3 years involved African American youth, although they constitute only 46% of school enrollment. These youth are frequently left with dubious alternative education, leading to dropping out or incarceration, or with no educational resources or supports.

In Massachusetts, for example, the number of school expulsions or exclusions under state law rose to more than 1,500 in 1996–97, with a disproportionate racial impact. Statewide, although African American students made up 8.4% of the school population, in 1996–97 they suffered 23% of the expulsions; Latinos, who were 10% of the school population, constituted 33.8% of the expelled students. This pattern is doubly troubling in states such as Massachusetts where there is no mandatory alternative education. Further, it is rare to find students with legal representation at the administrative expulsion hearings. In Chicago, approximately 20 hearings per day are scheduled on expulsion of Chicago public school students. All but a handful of students are expelled, according to the law students who sit as administrative hearing officers.

This synergistic relationship of police and principals goes further in Chicago, where law permits schools to suspend or expel students who have been charged or convicted of violating the law, even when the alleged delinquent or criminal behavior did not occur on school property or during school hours. These laws and regulations presume that principals will find out about non-school-based felony arrests and convictions of students from their closer relationship with police and prosecutors. This embrace is codified in a series of laws recently passed by the Illinois legislature that facilitate even greater exchange of information between law enforcement personnel, schools, and child welfare personnel.

The Illinois School Records Act (105 ILCS 10/6, 1999) permits state's attorneys and police officers unrestricted access to student records and further requires the school to make law enforcement requests part of the child's permanent record; other provisions (705 ILCS 405/5–325) require school officials to provide to the State's Attorney, upon request, information or a written report relating to the alleged commission of an offense; and Illinois Public Aid Code (305 ILCS 5.11–9, 1999) permits law enforcement access to certain public aid records without subpoena or notice requirements. The U.S. House of Representatives seeks to offer incentives to states to accommodate even greater exchange of information between schools and law enforcement by including in a proposed juvenile justice bill a provision that gives states additional funds if they make juvenile records available to schools (Juvenile Justice and Delinquency Prevention Act, 1999).

This wholesale relaxation of confidentiality protections for youth, protections that were a fundamental principle of the original Juvenile Court Act founders in Chicago in 1899, has further increased the incidence of suspensions/expulsions and of school-based arrests. Schools are routinely notified of a student's non-school-site arrests, probation, or detention. The knowledge that a student is in trouble or is a troublemaker may be a factor in a student being more intensely scrutinized or being seen as a "bad kid."

It is worth noting that the school front door, as well as the exit door, has been transformed. School principals and administrators have wider discretion to refuse to enroll a student, even a public school student who resides in the appropriate district. This constricted eligibility for school registration is evident to those working with special education students, youth being released from juvenile detention or corrections, or youngsters in crisis who may manifest behavior problems. School enrollment and registration, once assumed to be a right, has become an arena of vast discretion and terrain for further educational exclusion.

Jane Addams and the other Hull House women, a century ago, were proponents of compulsory education, the abolition of child labor, and the creation of a separate court for children. These innovations were interrelated, for the primary goal was education and opportunity for children, not the exploitation of hazardous labor or incarceration with adults in prisons or adult poorhouses. Grace Abbott and her colleagues continued to document school attendance for decades as a bellwether for the well-being of children. What irony that 100 years after the establishment of the world's first juvenile court, schools and courts have again partnered, but this time to exclude, arrest, expel, and suspend children *from* school and to punish, prosecute, and imprison them in the criminal justice system.

. . .

Loitering, Curfew, and Association Offenses. Local municipalities, frequently authorized by state legislatures, have rushed to enact new curfew ordinances, some 1,000 since 1990. Curfew laws, directed at youth to prevent youth crime in the late evening, fail to address the peak juvenile crime times, between 2 P.M. and 5 p.m. during the school year. Gang offending is similarly concentrated in mid to late afternoon.

In 1992, the Chicago City Council enacted the Gang Congregation Ordinance, which prohibits criminal street gang members from loitering with one another or with others in any public place (*City of Chicago v. Morales*, 1999). The ordinance created a criminal offense punishable by a fine of up to $500, imprisonment for not more than 6 months, and a requirement to perform up to 120 hours of community service. During the 3 years of its enforcement, police made more than 42,000 arrests and issued more than 89,000 dispersal orders. The ordinance was overturned by an appellate court, the Illinois Supreme Court, and the U.S. Supreme Court as unconstitutionally vague and failing to provide notice to the public about what conduct was illegal.

Curfew ordinances are notorious for being subject to racial and ethnic disparities in enforcement. Furthermore, arrests of girls for curfew violations increased by 155.2% between 1987 and 1996. Curfew violations have vastly widened the net of criminal involvement for youth, particularly youth of color and young women.

YOUNG WOMEN IN JUVENILE JUSTICE

Each year, girls account for one in four arrests of youth in America, yet their presence in the juvenile justice system remains largely invisible. Young women have traditionally been arrested and incarcerated in large numbers for status offenses: arrests and prosecutions of young women declined after the JJDP of 1974 mandate to deinstitutionalize and divert youth charged with status offenses into programs providing alternatives to legal adjudication. But the past decade of criminalizing youth has resulted in increasing arrests of girls, once again, for status offenses or other minor violations of law.

Fully one quarter of all female delinquency arrests are for status offenses (as compared with less than 10% for boys), while another quarter of girls arrested are charged with larceny theft (basically, shoplifting)! Girls arrested for running away from home increased by 20.7%, and as noted above, curfew arrests of girls mushroomed an astonishing 155.2%. Although media reports suggest that girls, as well as male delinquents, have become violent predators, the facts again belie this characterization of violence.

Arrests of girls for violent crime index offenses during the decade 1987–1996 did skyrocket, up 118.1%. Female delinquency charges for "other assault" increased 142.6% in the same period. Assault charges can range from conduct involving simple verbal aggression and threats, to minor school conflicts, nonserious disputes, and harmless fights; increasingly girls have been arrested for simple assault. Analysis suggests that much of the "tyranny of small numbers" (this phrase is attributed to Barry Krisberg, 1994) results from relabeling or bootstrapping—the practice by police, prosecutors, or judges that transforms a nondelinquency, noncriminal offense into an offense subject to incarceration. Girls, for example, are more likely to be arrested for noninjury assaults or as bystanders or companions to males involved in fighting. Virtually every person-to-person offense among girls in the Maryland juvenile justice system (97.9%) involved assault, and half of those were a fight with a family member, generally a parent. This form of escalated charging is most pronounced against African American girls.

Legislative erosion and organized opposition to the JJDP mandate against incarcerating children charged with status offenses has taken multiple forms, resulting in greater reincarceration of young women. In 1980, the definition of status offender in the federal law was amended to exclude children "who violated a court order." Girls in foster care placements or group homes, for example, who run away, can be classified as delinquents and incarcerated, rather than characterized as status offenders who could be diverted away from court adjudication into specified programs for youth. This subversion of the original intent and purpose of JJDP falls most heavily on female delinquents, where the gender double standard results in judges sentencing girls to detention for contempt citations (violations of court orders) in far greater numbers than boys—apparently attempting to control and contain young women to protect them from themselves, in a manner that would not occur with young men. The 4.3% likelihood of incarceration for girls in juvenile justice accelerates to 29.9% when they are held in contempt.

One consequence of the combination of traditional and contemporary juvenile justice pressures on young women is a racial, two-track system of justice, where White girls are institutionalized in private facilities and young women of color are detained in public facilities.

The numbers of girls held in private institutions has dramatically increased; 62% of incarcerated girls are being held in private facilities, and 85% of those are detained for "nondelinquent" offenses (such as violations of court orders, or status offenses). The number of young women detained in public detention facilities has remained steady. Translated bluntly, this means that White girls are recommended for "treatment" whereas African American and Latina girls are detained.

Pending federal legislation would encourage the uses of contempt violations as a path to detention and once again would permit the holding of children in adult jails. It is girls, frequently held in rural and small-town jails for minor infractions, who become most subject to violent abuse and suicide in such confinement.

Women have become the fastest growing sector of people in prison in the past decade; similarly, detentions of girls increased 23% between 1989 and 1993. Girls remain in detention longer awaiting placement in private facilities or correctional institutions and are generally disliked by those working in the overwhelmingly male system of juvenile justice. The failure to take into account past or current physical or sexual abuse and the lack of appropriate gender and cultural programming to address the needs of young women delinquents is pervasive.

Transgressions by girls have historically been treated differently from male misbehavior. It is profoundly disturbing that the combined invisibility and double standard paternalism/harshness against young females result in increasing loss of freedom for young women and inequality of response in programming. The women of Hull House would be dismayed and enraged by this backtracking on fundamental justice for children.

. . .

CHILDREN IN ADULT CRIMINAL COURTS

Crucial questions are going unasked as children are increasingly appearing in adult criminal courts. Criminal courts operate on guilty pleas, and informed, competent decisions to plead guilty may not be possible for many children. Adult courts fail to acknowledge the youth of the child, to take into account the child's age, developmental capacity, or experience when assessing culpability. Adult courts impose adult sentences, which differ from delinquency sentences in two critical ways: they are determinate, and they are significantly longer. Determinate sentences result in extended incarceration of children, beyond a time when they may be rehabilitated. Longer sentences mean that a child will ultimately be incarcerated in an adult prison, where they may be subject to physical abuse, suicide, and an education from adult offenders, rather than rehabilitation for a future productive life. Youth sent to the adult criminal system are essentially cut off from educational and counseling programs, from juvenile probation officers, and from appropriate medical and mental health services. Sending children to prison encourages more sophisticated criminal behavior. There is ample evidence that children respond better to positive prevention programs than they do to punitive legislative measures.

THE EROSION OF CIVIC RESPONSIBILITY FOR CHILDREN

Addressing the needs of both public safety and positive youth development requires an active and participating public. If the only popular cry is for short-term fixes—"get them out of the neighborhood," "lock them up and throw away the key," and "something must be done"—society will continue on its current course of escalating punishment for children and increasing adult abdication of responsibility. If schools are not for learning from mistakes, if child welfare is not for protecting children who have been harmed, if health systems are not geared to healing youth—further reliance on exclusion, punishment, and prison becomes the likely option. Tens of thousands of productive adults who passed through the juvenile justice system in their youth are witness to the healing and redemptive effect of getting a second chance: the program, the judge, the probation officer who made a difference and allowed them to turn their life around.

The real adult problem is masked by our social focus on the "youth problem." In scapegoating kids, we reveal that as a society, we don't like adolescents very much. Youth, being the intelligent people they are, are vividly aware of the angry popular and policy backlash directed against them. They are keenly alert to issues of fairness (which are at the heart of justice); they observe the adult world around them with a laserlike ability to identify hypocrisy. They see that their voices, their opinions, and their interests are largely ignored, as are their rights as future citizens.

The use of the law to enforce a legal-educational-political system that harms the aspirations and best intentions of youth cannot be good for society. Holding children accountable for protracted social failures reeks of expediency and runs counter to developing international human rights standards for children around the world. Adult citizens are engaged in the social neglect and abuse of children, both in public fiscal policy and in the absence of the commitment of our own precious time and imagination.

Criminalizing youth behaviors, policing schools, punishing children by depriving them of an education, constricting social protections for abused and neglected youth, and subjecting youth to law enforcement as a "social service"—these trends smack of social injustice, racial inequity, dehumanization, and fear-filled demonization of youngsters, who are our prospective hope. At stake here is the civic will to invest in our common future by seeing other people's children as our own.

117

Police Make Life Hell for Youth of Color

Kathy Durkin

Going to the grocery store, visiting a friend and walking home from work or school are all ordinary, everyday occurrences. But not so for hundreds of thousands of people, mostly from African-American and Latina communities, who are stopped, questioned, asked for their I.D., searched and often arrested here in New York—and around the country. It happens to many youth and even to children.

At a time when more white people appear to be rejecting racism at the polls, racial profiling by police departments and other state agencies is on the rise. It is systemic and deeply entrenched in the "criminal justice system" nationwide.

Statistics given in new studies and reports starkly bear this out. But the statistics cannot convey the intimidation, anxiety and anger that so many people, especially Black and Latin@ youth, must live with on a daily basis, nor the effect this can have throughout their lives on them and their families.

In the first quarter of this year, New York City police, by their own report, stopped, questioned and/or searched 145,098 people, more than half of them African Americans. At this alarming rate, a record 600,000 people will be stopped this year.

In the last two years, nearly 1 million New Yorkers were harassed by police in this manner—90 percent of them people of color. That's 1,300 a day. And it's legally allowed.

These operations, just in the past two years, have put more than 1 million innocent people, mostly African-American and Latin@, into the huge police database; they are subject to future criminal investigations merely by their inclusion there.

The New York Civil Liberties Union (NYCLU) is challenging the legality of these potentially discriminatory practices and demanding information on the database kept by the NYPD—which the department refuses to turn over. It contains personal information on everyone stopped by police, though the vast majority—90 percent—have not been charged with any crimes.

The NYCLU is also demanding full disclosure from the NYPD about police shootings in this city. The full story of this horror is not known. In addition to the terrible, tragic and totally unjustified killings of unarmed individuals like Sean Bell, Amadou Diallo, Ousmane Zongo and Patrick Dorismund, countless other people of color have been shot. Yet the NYPD refuses to reveal what proportion of those shot over the last 10 years have been members of oppressed nationalities. In the two years prior to that, it was 90 percent (nyclu. org).

Another aspect of the NYPD's racial profiling scheme is the campaign of terror targeting youth for possessing miniscule amounts of marijuana. This, too, usually happens in communities of color, even though social studies show a higher rate of marijuana use among white youth (nyclu.org). In 2007 alone, police arrested more than 100 people per day, or 39,700 in total, for this so-called crime.

The NYCLU has just issued a report entitled, "The Marijuana Arrest Crusade in New York City: Racial Bias in Police Policy 1997–2007," by Prof. Harry G. Levin and Deborah Peterson Small. It describes the NYPD's campaign against oppressed youth. Of the nearly 400,000 people arrested in that 10-year period, 205,000 were African Americans and 122,000 were Latin@s. This represented a tenfold increase over the previous 10-year period.

Since decriminalization in 1977, the possession of a small amount of marijuana has not constituted a "crime" in New York City—as long as it is not shown in public. Possession since then has been merely a "violation," such as speeding and other traffic infractions.

However, the police frequently stop Black and Latin@ youth and then arrest them on the charge of misdemeanor possession—when, most of the time, this is not the case. High school students are kept in jail overnight until they go to court. Then they are pressured into a plea bargain, usually with an overworked, court-appointed attorney representing them.

In a city where police can gun down a young man like Sean Bell just hours before his wedding and get off with not even a slap on the wrist, youth stopped by cops never know what might happen to them.

These youth are then labeled with criminal records, which will follow them for the rest of their lives and can create future obstacles for them in higher education, employment and housing. They're also driven into the "criminal justice" system—their fingerprints and photographs go into the NYPD database—when they've done nothing wrong.

It is well known that there is serious drug abuse in many high-pressure professions in this city, yet the police don't occupy financial centers or carry out random searches in wealthy neighborhoods.

Rafael Mutis, coordinator of 7 Neighborhood Action Partnership Network, which works to repeal the draconian New York State Rockefeller drug laws, explains that "drug use" has become a pretext for stop-and-frisk searches in low-income neighborhoods. "They don't go after people on Wall Street," he said, "where there's a daily snowstorm" of cocaine use (highbridgehorizon.com).

It is no coincidence that police repression has increased even as billionaire Mayor Michael Bloomberg and his Wall Street cronies are trying to make New York City a haven for the super-rich, and the real-estate tycoons are gentrifying working-class neighborhoods as fast as they can. "Law-enforcement" agencies are helping them out by stepping up the intimidation of low-income and oppressed people to suppress opposition and try to drive them further out of the city.

All people need to show solidarity with the oppressed communities, especially the youth, in this struggle against police repression.

118

Ageism

Another Form of Bigotry

Robert N. Butler

Just as racism and sexism are based on ethnicity and gender, ageism is a form of systematic stereotyping and discrimination against people simply because they are old. As a group, older people are categorized as rigid in thought and manner, old-fashioned in morality and skills. They are boring, stingy, cranky, demanding, avaricious, bossy, ugly, dirty, and useless.

An ageist younger generation sees older people as different from itself; it subtly ceases to identify with its elders as human beings. Old men become geezers, old goats, gaffers, fogies, coots, gerries, fossils, and codgers, and old women are gophers and geese. A crone, hag, or witch is a withered old woman.

Ageism takes shape in stereotypes and myths, outright disdain and dislike, sarcasm and scorn, subtle avoidance, and discriminatory practices in housing, employment, pension arrangements, health care, and other services. Older persons are subject to physical, emotional, social, sexual, and financial abuse. They are the focus of prejudice regarding their capacity for work and sexual intimacy, which Freud described as the two most important human activities. Taking away the validation of work or purposeful activities and demeaning the capacity for love are surely the most profound forms of age prejudice.

Historically, older persons have been venerated in most societies and cultures *in word*, although not always in deed. In fact, to be old or disabled was always a liability for practical reasons. Nomadic groups from North Africa to Alaska abandoned their old when the welfare of the entire tribe or group was at stake.

The term *ageism*, which I introduced in 1968, is now part of the English language. It is identical to any other prejudice in its consequences. The older person feels ignored or is not taken seriously and is patronized. Anthropologist Barbara Myerhoff speaks about "death by invisibility" when she describes an older woman who, "unseen," was "accidentally" killed by a bicyclist.

This invisibility extends to emergencies, such as the tragic case of September 11, 2001, in New York City. Animal activists evacuated dogs and cats within twenty-four hours after the World Trade Center was attacked, while disabled or older persons were abandoned in their apartments for up to seven days before ad hoc medical teams arrived to rescue them. Older persons were also invisible in the devastation caused by Hurricane Katrina in New Orleans.

Reminiscent of the great social scientist George Mead's concept of the "looking glass self," older persons may turn ageist prejudice inward, absorbing, accepting, and identifying with the discrimination. Some examples:

- Simone De Beauvoir, author of *The Coming of Age*, described her disgust at growing old, although she wrote lovingly of her own mother's aging in *A Very Easy Death*.
- Comedian George Burns noted the unfortunate tendency of old people to conform to their stereotype—what he called the old person's "act"—by learning to shuffle about and decondition in a kind of identification and collaboration with the ageist society that demeans them.
- Yale psychologist Becca R. Levy reports that constant bombardment of negative stereotypes increases blood pressure. *Ageism can make an older person sick.*

Advertisements and greeting cards depict older persons as forgetful, dependent, childlike, and—perhaps the ultimate insult in our society—sexless. Conversely, older people who continue to have sexual desires are dirty old men and ridiculous old women.

Wrinkles, crow's feet, liver spots, and dull skin are disparaged in our youth-dominated culture and exploited by the cosmetics industry and plastic surgeons. Women who have relied upon their appearance for self-definition and men and women who have depended upon a youthful appearance in their work are up against overwhelming odds. The clock does not stop. When does one cease to be beautiful and start on the journey to being over-the-hill? How many women past fifty can look like model Lauren Hutton or Susan Sarandon? How many men and women can overcome disability with elegance and style?

A study conducted by the American Academy of Facial, Plastic and Reconstructive Surgery revealed that baby boomers have received nearly a quarter of a million face-lifts and other cosmetic surgeries. Most of these patients were over fifty. The Associated Press has quoted Karen Seccombe, a University of Florida sociologist, who said, "The thought of saggy breasts, hair loss or wrinkles doesn't sit well with people who have grown up emphasizing fitness and youth."

The film and television industries help to perpetuate ageism.

- Less than 2 percent of prime-time television characters are sixty-five or older, although this group is 12.7 percent of the population.
- 11 percent of male characters between fifty and sixty-four are categorized as old versus 22 percent of female characters.
- 75 percent of male characters sixty-five and older are characterized as old versus 83 percent of female characters of the same age.

- Only one-third of older characters are women.
- Middle-aged and older white males have joined women and minorities on the sidelines, as white men under forty get most of the jobs writing for television and film. Employment and earning prospects for older writers have declined relative to those for younger writers.
- According to one study, approximately 70 percent of older men and more than 80 percent of older women seen on television are portrayed disrespectfully, treated with little if any courtesy, and often looked at as "bad."
- Although Americans who are forty and over are 42 percent of the American population, more than twice as many roles are cast with actors who are under forty.

But there is some good news, too. By the 1990s, soap operas such as *The Guiding Light* were presenting older characters having more love affairs and not just worrying about their children. In 1994 *New York Magazine* put Paul Newman on the cover, calling him "The Sexiest (70 year old) Man Alive," and *More* magazine offered women over forty an alternative to those that cater to women in their twenties. Older models began to make their appearance in general women's magazines, too. One widely circulated magazine advertisement in 1994 described "Betty Mettler, age 101, Noxzema user since 1925."

OUR CULTURE'S FEAR OF GROWING OLD

As Tolstoy noted, *"Old age is the most unexpected of all the things that happen to a man."*

The underlying basis of ageism is the dread and fear of growing older, becoming ill and dependent, and approaching death. People are afraid, and that leads to profound ambivalence. The young dread aging, and the old envy youth. Behind ageism is corrosive narcissism, the inability to accept our fate, for indeed we are all in love with our youthful selves, as is reflected in the yearning behind the expression "salad days."

Although undoubtedly universal, ageism in the United States is probably fueled by the worship of youth in a still-young country dominated by the myth of the unending frontier. In 1965, the Who, a British rock group, sang, "I hope I die before I get old," while in America "you never say die." Hollywood veils older actresses with gauzy lens filters. Moreover, age carries less authority.

The powerful imagery of the birth and adoration of the infant Jesus, and the journey of the Magi to see the Christ child, describes a birth of hope. How this contrasts with the final years of life! Children are seen as the future; older people, the past. Grimm's fairy tales depict gnarled and evil old women cursing innocent and beautiful youths with spells and afflictions.

Denial is a close cousin of ageism; in effect, it eliminates aging from consciousness.

One of the striking facts of human life is the intensity with which people avoid aging. Narcissistic preoccupation with our own aging and demise and perhaps, according to Freud, the inability of the unconscious to accept death make it difficult for society as a whole to deal with the challenges of aging. Note our gallows humor at birthdays, the money we spend on cosmetic surgery, and the popularity of anti-aging medicine. This was not always the case. In Europe in generations past, young men in high positions wore wigs they had powdered white in an attempt to appear older and, by implication, wiser. Today, men flock to cosmetic surgeons and colorists to preserve the illusion of youth.

. . .

ELDER ABUSE

Elder abuse is a widespread phenomenon that affects older adults who live in rich and poor nations alike. In the United States alone it is believed that as many as 1.2 million older adults are physically abused or neglected each year. Elder abuse takes many forms, including physical, emotional, financial, and sexual abuse—often by family members. It may involve neglect, such as the failure to provide food, shelter, clothing, medical care, and personal hygiene, as well as narcotic overmedication.

In 2004, UN Secretary General Kofi Annan released a report on the abuse of older persons that mentioned practices such as the ostracism of older women, which occurs in some societies when they are used as scapegoats for natural disasters, epidemics, or other catastrophes. The report stated: "Women have been ostracized, tortured, maimed or even killed if they failed to flee the community."

The World Health Organization (WHO) reported that 36 percent of nursing home staff in the U.S. reported having witnessed at least one incident of physical abuse of an older patient in the previous year, and 10 percent admitted having committed at least one act of physical abuse themselves. This represents sexism as well as ageism, for about 75 percent of nursing home residents are women. Other statistics are equally alarming:

- 1 million to 3 million Americans sixty-five and older have been injured, exploited, or otherwise mistreated by someone on whom they depend for care or protection.
- Estimates of the frequency of elder abuse range from 2 percent to 10 percent.
- Only one out of six incidents of elder abuse, neglect, exploitation, and self-neglect is brought to the attention of authorities.
- Only twenty-one states report that they maintain an elder abuse registry/database on perpetrators of substantiated cases, and less than half of states maintain a central abuse registry.
- It is estimated that each year five million older Americans are victims of financial exploitation, but only 4 percent of cases are reported. Many of these cases involve the unauthorized use of older person's assets and the transferring of power of attorney for an older person's assets without written consent.
- Of the nearly $1 billion National Institute on Aging budget, only $1.7 million goes to NIA elder abuse and neglect research funding.

AGEISM IN HEALTH-CARE SETTINGS

Ageism can be invoked by aesthetic revulsion. Especially when weakened by disease, older persons can be disheveled, unwashed, and appear ugly and decaying. Some older persons "let themselves go" and unwittingly add fuel to the fire. Sphincters loosen, depositing stains and smells. Ear and nose hairs grow more quickly in older bodies, as does the cartilage, causing the nose and ears to enlarge. Some profound and common disorders of old age—mobility problems, dementia, and incontinence—are unattractive and provoke a negative response.

When older men or women are malodorous, scabrous, or disturbing in dress and language, they can scare, disgust, and discomfort younger people. Such older persons become untouchable. (Touch is powerful and therapeutic. Some older persons living alone have not been touched for years.)

Medical schools unwittingly promote the virus of ageism. Fresh out of college, young students are confronted with aging and death and their own personal anxieties about both. They are left to their own devices to insulate themselves from anxiety and pain about disease, disability, disfigurement, and dying. A cadaver that requires dissection is usually the first older person medical students encounter, and they are not ordinarily provided with effective group or individual counseling, either at the time of dissection or later, upon the death of their first patient.

Defense mechanisms like gallows humor, cynicism, denial, the invention of negative language, and facetiousness are common. Long hours in medical training lead to angry exhaustion and feelings of being "put upon."

It was in medical school that I first become conscious of the medical profession's prejudice toward age. For the first time I heard such insulting epithets as "crock," which was used to describe middle-aged women and older patients who were labeled hypochondriacal because they had no apparent organic basis for their complaints, as well as having many symptoms, and "GOMER" (Get Out of My Emergency Room).

The hidden curriculum in medical schools undermines student's idealism and can compromise their education. For example, in some studies up to thirty-five percent of doctors erroneously consider an increase in blood pressure to be a normal process of aging. In physical diagnosis courses, medical students meet older people who are stripped of their individuality and seen as archives or museums of pathology, rather than as human beings. Men and women in their eighties are particularly valuable in these sessions because they often have a plethora of symptoms and conditions about which the student must learn.

In addition, few medical school graduates will practice geriatrics, and practicing physicians often do not invest the same amount of time dealing with older patients. Medicare expenditures per capita steadily decline as people grow older. In fact, a UCLA study reported that, as people enter their forties, physicians spend less time with them per encounter. Logically, it should be the reverse since medical problems tend to increase as we grow older, and the ramifications are sobering. Sixty percent of adults over sixty-five do not receive recommended preventive services, and 40 percent do not receive vaccines for flu and pneumonia. They receive even less preventive care for high blood pressure and cholesterol.

Some doctors question why they should even bother treating certain problems of the aged; after all, the patients are old. Is it worth treating them? Their problems are irreversible, unexciting, and unprofitable. Their lives are over.

Between 1955 and 1966, Morris Rocklin, a volunteer in the NIMH Human Aging Study, was studied until he turned 101 years of age. Rocklin complained about his painful right knee to his physician, who said, "What do you expect at your age?" To this typical statement by a physician, Rocklin replied indignantly, "So why doesn't my left leg hurt?" The symmetry of the human body offers a good test of the realities of medical ageism. Rocklin's oft-quoted response has been used by many geriatricians to educate medical students on the topic of ageism.

NURSING HOMES: AGEIST SCANDAL

Nursing homes are licensed by the states and must meet federal standards to participate in Medicaid or Medicare. About 95 percent of the nation's sixteen thousand nursing homes (which house 1.5 million men and women) participate in those programs. According to a government study conducted in 2002, nine of ten nursing homes in the United States lack adequate staff, and nurse's aides provide 90 percent of the care. In most nursing homes, the report said, a patient needs an average of 4.1 hours of care each day—2.8 hours from nurse's aides and 1.3 hours from registered nurses or licensed practical nurses.

In 2000, over 91 percent of nursing homes had nurse aide staffing levels that fell below the thresholds identified as minimally necessary to provide the needed care. In response, the Department of Health and Human Services concluded that "it is not currently feasible" for the federal government to require that homes achieve a minimum ratio of nursing staff to patients. Nursing homes would have to hire 77,000 to 137,000 registered nurses, 22,000 to 27,000 licensed practical nurses, and 181,000 to 310,000 nurse's aides. This would take $7.6 billion a year, an 8 percent increase over current spending. The solution given by the Bush administration was to encourage nursing homes to adopt better management techniques so nurse's aides can achieve high productivity and, ultimately, to rely on market forces.

AGE-BASED HEALTH-CARE RATIONING

Medical ageism is prevalent in preventive tests for cancer and treatment of a variety of illnesses, some of them life-threatening. For example:

- Only 10 percent of people sixty-five and over receive appropriate screening tests for bone density, colorectal and prostate cancer, and glaucoma. This despite the fact that the average age of colorectal cancer patients is seventy, that more than 70 percent of prostate cancer is diagnosed in men over sixty-five, and that people over sixty are six times more likely to suffer from glaucoma.
- Chemotherapy is underused in the treatment of breast cancer patients over sixty-five, even though for many of these patients it may improve survival.
- In a cost-cutting effort to reduce supposedly unnecessary medical tests in 1998, the American Cancer Society and government health agencies determined that if an older woman had no abnormalities in a Pap smear for three years in a row, she could be tested less often. Yet over 25 percent of cases of cervical cancer occur in women over sixty-five!
- The pelvic examination is often deferred because many doctors, especially men, do not like to do it. (In both men and women, the rectal examination may meet a similar fate.)
- Although deaths due to ischemic heart disease disproportionately affect persons over sixty-five (85 percent in the United States and 87 percent in France), few national comparisons focus on older people. For example, WHO's MONICA Project—the important international longitudinal study that monitors cross-national trends in cardiovascular disease—focuses on death before sixty-five.
- A patient under the age of seventy-five who is admitted with a heart attack is six times more likely to receive blood clot-dissolving drugs such as streptokinase than a patient over seventy-five, even though data indicate the value of streptokinase in improving the chances for survival of older patients.
- Advanced surgery for Parkinson's disease is less available to older persons.

Unless older people are knowledgeable or have strong advocates, even the more affluent members of our society experience age-determined limits in medical care. Parenthetically, when malpractice suits are won, older persons usually receive lower monetary awards.

. . .

119

Aging with Disabilities

Ageism and More

Debra J. Sheets

People who are old and who also have disabilities—a growing proportion of the population—find themselves in "double jeopardy" of experiencing prejudice and discrimination, which often leads to difficulty gaining access to needed healthcare and social services. . . .

With older Americans living longer and healthier lives, recent trends suggest that disability is declining and possibly becoming less severe. Still, the combination of large numbers of baby boomers and the increased prevalence of disability accompanying age means that the size of the population with disability will grow rapidly in the next decade. Currently, 32 million people (12.5 percent) living in our communities have a sensory, mental, physical, or other disability that impairs their ability to take care of themselves; more than one in three (38 percent) is age 65 or older. Self-care disability affects 6.7 million people; adults age 65 and older constitute nearly one-half (3.1 million) of this group.

While population aging has received considerable attention, the aging of the "disability population" has gone largely without comment. In the past, people with disabilities often did not survive even into middle age because of complications related to their disability. Now, for the first time in history, an estimated one of every 100 older Americans is aging with a long-term disability such as spinal cord injury, cerebral palsy, multiple sclerosis, post-polio, and intellectual or developmental disabilities. Fifty years ago, the average life expectancy of an individual with spinal cord injury was less than three years after the accident occurred. Today 40 percent of all survivors of such injury are 45 years of age and older, and more than one-half of the estimated 600,000 to one million polio survivors are now age 55 and older. Approximately 526,000 Americans age 60 or older are aging with intellectual or developmental disabilities. Other groups aging with disability include 200,000 people with spinal cord injuries and 600,000 with cerebral palsy.

. . . Many of those with long-term disabilities are experiencing unanticipated health problems (e.g., fatigue, pain) and functional declines (e.g., muscle weakness, mobility limitations) as they reach midlife. These secondary health conditions are related to the effects of aging superimposed on the primary disability. The conditions have been described as "premature aging" because they occur about fifteen to twenty years earlier than would be the case with normal aging. A related problem is that people aging with disabilities may face early and forced retirement as they become physically unable to continue working. In such cases, they often have not had time to plan for how they will address typical retirement issues such as housing, health insurance, transportation, income, and caregiving. Yet they remain too young to qualify for the age-based service system as they shift out of the disability service system, with its strong vocational focus. The resulting gap in services poses a threat to independence and quality of life for people aging with disability.

. . .

TOWARD A SHARED AGENDA TO COMBAT PREJUDICE

The aging and disability service systems have historically developed in parallel but separate tracks, particularly because of different funding sources, despite often overlapping concerns about issues such as affordable housing, public transportation, access to healthcare, long-term-care needs, and economic stability. In the early 1980s, aging and disability advocates began discussing the need to work together to pursue a unified policy agenda that would reflect shared concerns about these issues. In the 1990s several modest attempts to develop a unified agenda were undertaken but to little effect. Efforts between the aging and disability service systems ultimately stalled over disagreements that reflected differences in philosophical perspectives, the definition of problems, and what counted as a solution.

. . .

Recently, economic and political pressures have prompted about two-thirds of all states to consolidate and integrate aging and disability services into a single agency serving both groups—older adults and people with disabilities. Regardless, some advocates remain pessimistic about overcoming the difficulties that keep the aging and disability systems from meaningful collaboration around a shared agenda. However, others are more optimistic and point to a number of state- and local-level initiatives that involve cross-network collaborations and may reflect a coalescing around issues that include improving consumer choice and the quality of longterm care. How this will play out remains to be seen, but there are some promising forces furthering efforts to bring the two service spheres together.

Improvements in the service systems will do much to counter the effects of ageism on older people aging with disabilities. Advocacy efforts by these two groups working together must counter prejudice against elders and those with disability by providing those aging with disability opportunities to maintain their competence, image, and sense of worth within our society. Agencies must replace problem-based approaches with a strengths-based paradigm that focuses on ensuring inclusion and participation in the broader society. In addition, both systems must endorse the self-determination of people aging with disability by adopting a shared focus on consumer choice and the empowerment of individuals to reach their potential. Neither age nor disability should be viewed as a special concern; they should be recognized as issues that are in the interests of our society as a whole.

. . .

120

Black Elderly

Center on Aging Studies, University of Missouri—Kansas City

- *In 1985 approximately 14% of the population, 65 and over, were people of color.* By 2020, 21% are projected to be people of color, and by 2050 this percent is anticipated to increase to 33%. These numbers translate into increasing numbers of black elderly adults in our society. However, despite growing numbers of black elderly adults, most of the programs and services provided to elders of color continue to be based on research and perceptions regarding the majority population. The result is a general lack of ethnic-and culture-specific knowledge.

- *Approximately 33% of black elderly live in poverty.* Black elderly males experience a decline in their longevity. Many black elderly regard themselves as "unretired-retired," since they generally continue to work after retirement. Black elderly retirement is frequently related to subsequent physical or mental disability. Black elderly females who have declining health are frequently sole heads of households, and thus responsible for children or grandchildren. Black elderly underutilize public health services and tend to use emergency room services. Many do not have a regular personal physician, and generally experience problems in accessing all health care systems. In rural areas, nearly one-half of black elderly live at or below the poverty level.

- *Black male elders generally have less personal post-retirement resources and are more dependent on Social Security and Supplemental Security Income.* More than twice as many black males as white males, over the age of 65, are divorced or separated. It is always important to remember that there is cultural diversity within each ethnic group, including differences in values, traditions, educational levels, socioeconomic status, and lifestyles.

. . .

- *Due to life-long patterns of socioeconomic disadvantages (e.g., income, education, access to health care, etc.), and prejudicial treatment, many black elderly don't respond well to service providers of a different race.* In some cases, the elder person may demonstrate a complete lack of trust in the medical and/or mental health system. This can potentially result in fewer attempts to procure care, and low compliance with prescribed interventions. Blacks tend to be institutionalized for mental health reasons more often than whites; their admission to psychiatric institutions are also less likely to be voluntary. In addition, racial and ethnic minorities tend to receive less mental health treatment and are more likely to receive lower quality treatment.

- *Health conditions:* More than half of black elderly in America are in poor health. They also tend to experience higher rates of multiple chronic illnesses than the rest of the population. Hypertension, obesity, and diabetes, in particular, surface as three major diseases which are often found to be related to each other. Left untreated, any one of these diseases can progress into more severe health complications such as stroke, blindness, loss of an extremity, impaired mobility, kidney failure, or heart disease. These three diseases are often associated with a lifetime of poor dietary habits, limited exercise, behavioral responses to discrimination, socioeconomic factors (such as persistent poverty), and poor coping or problem-solving skills—some of which may include the use of sugar, food, alcohol, or drugs, in excess, as a means of minimizing emotional pain and escaping the harsh realities of life. In turn, decreased self-image, self-worth, feelings of helplessness, hopelessness, and frustration often accompany these conditions. Another possible problem is noncompliance with medication instructions and schedules. This problem is often the result of fixed incomes which may not always cover ongoing medication costs. . . .

- *Cancer is found to be a critical problem for black elderly Americans.* For example, as compared to white Americans, black Americans experience significantly higher rates of several types of cancer, with death rates three times higher for esophageal cancer and twice the mortality rate from stomach cancer. In addition, the death rate from lung cancer is 45% higher in black males compared to white males. Black females are also two to three times more likely to die from cervical or uterine cancer than white females.

- *Concerning dementia, research has shown that black females may be at increased risk of multi-infarct dementia due to a higher incidence of obesity and hypertension.*

The potential for black males to experience alcoholic dementia before age 50 is also increased due to early age onset of drinking and heavier patterns of consumption. Although the frequency of dementing illness is at least as frequent in the black American community as it is in the general population, black elderly may have lower rates of the Alzheimer's type of dementia. Because of a lack of resources, inefficient doctor-patient relationship, and/or lack of research data applicable to dementias in the black elderly, there is an above-average potential for misdiagnoses.

- *For black Americans, in particular, family is of primary importance.* Family networks provide the main source of needed assistance later in life for many black elderly. In fact, when black elderly live with their children, the possibility of them being institutionalized for disabilities decreases. In general, black elderly do not participate in social or recreational activities that are outside the realm of their individual cultural traditions, backgrounds, or experiences. However, they tend to utilize a more diverse pool of helpers, including both extended family and friends. This network, and its influence, must, in turn, be respected and utilized by outside caregivers and service providers. Increased spirituality, faith in God, and increased participation in religious activities and institutions can also play an important role in providing support for black elderly. Religious beliefs provide a resource for coping with the unexpected or losses (which naturally increase with age). The church may also serve as a focal point of supportive networks for emotional and material aid.

- *Developing a caregiving relationship:* For someone outside the family to establish and develop a caregiving relationship with a black elder may require special attention and sensitivity to the elder's unique ethnic and cultural experience, history, and family relationships. At a minimum, the service provider must make efforts toward building a trusting relationship—remembering that non-responsiveness or resistance on the part of the elder may represent a means of evaluating providers and their ability to work with the elder effectively. A big step in the right direction is achieved if the provider can meet elders where they are—which means helping the elder determine what will work best, rather than what the provider believes will be best for the elder.

121

Regardless of What You Were Taught to Believe

There Is Nothing Wrong with You: For Teens

Cheri Huber

. . .

CH: What do you wish adults understood about people your age?

B: I think they understand, because they were our age and they wanted to do exactly what we want to do. But for some reason they don't want us to do what they did. Even though their lives turned out fine, even though they have perfectly fine lives, they don't want us to follow them.

CH: So, do you feel like you know what happened with your parents, and they just won't cop to it?

Q: Sure. They say, "I did that but you shouldn't do it because it's bad. Even though I did it, you shouldn't do it. You should learn from my experience."

T: But we don't want to learn from someone else's experience. We want to have our own experience and learn from that. What happened to them doesn't mean anything to me. I want to find out for myself.

F: They think because they did something we're going to do it, too.

CH: So, adults keep bringing up the same stuff over and over and maybe you wouldn't even be thinking about it if they didn't keep bringing it up.

F: They keep accusing us of planning things that we're not even thinking about.

S: Sometimes they tell us too much. My parents have told me stuff I didn't want to hear like about where and when I was conceived and things they did when they were young. It's weird.

. . .

B: They don't let you talk back. Their idea of a conversation is interrogation. They say something and you try to say something back and they don't want to hear it. They say, "We want to talk to you about this." But they don't want you to say anything to them about it.

V: They won't let you question them and they won't explain their reasons. They won't ever tell you why.

CH: So do you often find yourself in a place of not understanding why they're doing what they're doing or demanding what they're demanding?

Group: YES!

CH: So what you're saying is that adults, even though they say they want to talk to you, aren't interested in having a conversation. Adults don't realize what conversation is. There isn't much of the one person says something then the other person replies.

V: Yeah, they want to preach.

G: They think a conversation revolves around their opinion and nothing else.

CH: And they're assuming you understand a lot of things you really don't understand?

Group: Yeah.

V: Like when my mom wants to talk to me, she never wants to talk to me on a personal level. She calls me out of my room and asks me "who ate the peanut butter?" And she yells at me like it's my fault. I did eat the peanut butter. I'm the one in the house who likes peanut butter. She always yells at me when she talks to me. It's always like whatever it is is my fault. I never know if she's accusing me of something or if that's just the way she talks to me. But when I want to talk to her about something important she's, like, okay, whatever. But when it's not serious and she wants to talk to me, she gets mad. I can't remember the last actual conversation I had with my mom.

CH: Is that what it feels like, that you're really different from your parents?

Group: Not really.

T: I'm apparently just like my mom. We all turn into our parents and its horrible!

. . .

CH: So, what do you want to tell adults? What should adults know?

—LISTEN. Basically that's it. It would be really nice if people listened to you when you have something to say.

—We need support, some praise, some acknowledgment of the good stuff we do.

—Be open to the stuff that's important to us even if its not important to them—not necessarily condone it, but don't say don't do it. Like wanting to be with our friends all the time. My parents may think it's a waste of time, but it's what I want to do and it beats sitting around the house on my butt. So, ok, you think it's a waste of time, but it's what I want to do, so don't give me a hard time about it.

VOICES

—Don't worry so much about who we hang out with. They just assume that if you're with certain people you're going to be just like those people. They think we have no will power, if someone suggests something or offers us something, we're going to go along with it automatically. They don't see us as individuals, they see us as who we're with.

—We have good morals, we can make good choices.

—We don't mean any harm. We just want to have fun. We're trying to learn new things.

—Trust us. Talk to us. Get to know us. And trust us.

—You want us to act like adults, treat us with the same respect you give to adults.

—If you want us to respect you, respect us.

CH: In other words, if the teaching is going to be successful, parents have to model what they want you to be.

—Teachers too. The best teachers I've had are the ones who treated us as actual people. I listened to them and excelled in their classes. But the teachers who hate us, the ones who are there for the summers off, I was exactly the opposite. We will be what adults expect us to be.

—You can't just tell us no. Give us a reason. We don't see what you see. We don't understand. You need to explain things to us.

—Don't say, "Because I'm the parent." If you don't have a good reason, if you can't explain it to me, I'm not going to do what you want.

—Adults want to know why. We have to give reasons. Give us the respect you want from us and explain to us your reasons. Tell us why we should do what you want us to do.

—"Because I said so," is not good enough. It makes me *have* to do the opposite!

—Adults have had a lot of experience we haven't had. Give us the benefit of that experience by explaining what they're thinking, how they see things.

—Give us all the information we need and support us in making a decision.

—Get to know who we are as individuals and support us.

—Don't constantly refer to the past and hold the past against us.

—We're not all alike. We're similar, but we are individuals.

—Support but don't push.

—We're not always going to be children.

—We have a lot of emotions inside. Sometimes we don't know what's best for us.

—We're not as bad as you think. You were our age once. Give us a break.

—Respect and support our relationships instead of just being freaked out about whether we're having sex.

—We're people, too.

—Going to your room and closing the door is normal!

—It doesn't matter what you see or hear on the outside, it's what's inside that counts.

—All teenagers want to have fun. Don't hold us back. Don't live your life through ours.

—We need privacy and we need attention.

. . .

122

Elder Liberation Draft Policy Statement

Marge Larabee

INTRODUCTION

Everyone is a particular age. Age is universal. One's age is a factor in the life of every person in every country, in every culture. We also deal with change and oppression at any age. However, age is of special importance to elders. We have lived long. In dealing with age oppression in our own lives, we elders also support each person of whatever age, especially young people, whatever country, whatever culture, to move outside the ageist oppression. Elders can be allies for successful aging at any age.

Like people of any age, we elders are: zestful, intelligent, fun-loving, powerful, creative, flexible, sexy human beings. We focus, in present time, on the steps we are now taking and will take in the short-term to accomplish our long range goals. We have a future.

. . .

We expect to be seen as unique individuals whose accomplishments and thinking are accepted on their own merit. Whether we choose traditional roles, and/or to "contemplate, reflect and guide," our actions are as valuable as production in the workplace. Any role we select rationally is appropriate for us.

In the world today there are increasing numbers of elders, more and more of whom continue to function as alert human beings as they chronologically reach eighty-five and older. We are a powerful political force. We plan on taking charge of our own activities and policies.

We have a vision and perspective on history and the way things can and should be now.

We have coped with much change and can apply what we have learned from those experiences.

We have gained better knowledge about how to keep ourselves well and functioning.

We are alive and lively and ready to break all stereotypes.

We will take time to spell out our oppression only to make clear what we need to do to liberate ourselves and others effectively and completely. Our focus will be on present time reality.

CHANGING SOCIAL PERSPECTIVES ON AGING AND AGEISM

When our society was based on agriculture, old age and experience were obvious assets for the group's survival. We turned to older persons for their wisdom and insights. These were relevant and essential. Landowners and others with economic and political power were often old people. Reverence for old age was based, in large part, on this reality. In most societies there is a strong correlation between the economic situation and the status of elders.

Dating from industrialization, western society has given old age a bad name. Rapidly evolving technologies have lessened the value of the knowledge and experience of older adults. In general, older persons have been considered obsolete. Older persons are seen as limiting the opportunities of newly trained young people and are expected to retire. The older people's skills, general wisdom and knowhow, gained from years of experience, are lost.

Knowledge and experience of age is changing. There is an increasing gap between chronological age and biological (functioning) age. A person can live seventy chronological years and still function as a forty year old. Yet many parts of our society, especially the work place, treat the elder stereotypically, in terms of the chronological seventy years, instead of the functioning age of forty years.

Society has lagged in addressing both the changing needs of elders who are functioning well, living longer, living healthier lives, and those caught in mental and physical patterns. The latter would benefit from a perception of them as persons *with* problems instead of *as* "problems."

A "youth" culture predominates at the expense of appreciating older adults' values and contributions. Myths and stereotypes about older persons are widespread. Elders are pictured as uninvolved, dependent, non-contributing. The growing numbers of individuals who contradict these stereotypes are considered the "exception" and "remarkable" instead of representative of what old age can really be like.

. . .

[A]geism is the invalidation and discrimination against older persons because of old age, or factors accompanying age, that have little to do with the person's worth, intelligence, or capabilities.

The resulting incorrect attitudes toward the older person are played out in our society. They condition people to think and act in terms of stereotypes and prejudice. The individual elder is affected by these social and cultural attitudes and values and internalizes them. We not only suffer from the external oppression but from the oppressive ideas and stereotypes that become internalized.

. . .

It is ageism whenever older persons are victimized, ignored or segregated, are flattered by being told they are different from other older persons, are not encouraged to take complete pride in themselves and live their lives fully.

. . . [A]geism, like other oppressions, supports the basic oppression of economic inequality and injustice (classism) by setting up antagonisms between different groups to keep them from acting together against injustice. This "divide and conquer" tactic has existed in each class society, from slavery through feudalism, and now under capitalism.

. . .

RETIREMENT

The institutionalized promotion of "retirement" goes along with the emphasis on young people. Industry moves older workers out of the labor force to make room for younger workers. "Retirement" was invented to enforce this replacement. Retirement is justified as necessary for our economy to function profitably. Retirement pits young against old in competition for security and esteem in an economy of (professed) scarcity. Incessant, insidious repetition fosters attitudes that elders have little to offer and can no longer participate in significant work and that any attempt to do so will limit the opportunities for younger people (similar arguments are made to discourage bringing women, people of color, or immigrants into the work force).

Older workers are encouraged to see retirement as a "reward" for years of effort. Retirement years are supposed to be "Golden Years." The facts are different: for many people, retirement is a time of enforced idleness, isolation, loss of self-esteem, and living on a dwindling or absent income.

Gradually, the convention that older persons cannot keep up the pace has been established. It is now widely believed that they cannot be productive, contributing members of society.

LIVING SITUATIONS

In the past it wasn't unusual for elders to live in an extended family in which they were known and had a place, and to which they contributed their wisdom and experience.

Today urbanization and increased geographic mobility have been factors in the breakdown of the extended family unit. As a result elders in nuclear families or alternative living situations experience increased invisibility and isolation.

Eighty-percent of the care of old people is provided by an informal network of family and friends, mostly women. This usually means wives, daughters and daughters-in-law. Many of these women are themselves elders, and they avoid institutionalizing their loved ones at great cost.

We need to examine the difficult role of caregiver. We need to find ways to offer a variety of services that will give help and support to this role.

HEALTH CARE

Limitation, deterioration and decline have erroneously been attributed solely to old age. Such decline may accompany old age, but it is actually separate and often reversible. The medical profession is slow to adopt a restoring or preventive approach to elders' health care. Because elders' health problems are often discussed as due to old age they are looked at as a questionable place to put time, money and resource. The disease process, the aging process and chronological aging must be viewed separately. When something goes wrong physically we cannot *assume* it's because of age.

RESEARCH ON ELDERS

Research on elders tends to be biased by ageist assumptions. Some studies focus on healthy people, others on sick people. No studies have been done of elders who systematically discharge and re-evaluate. As a result, the research findings have been limited or biased, or both. They have not given us a true picture of the wide range of ways in which elders age.

OLD AGE OPPRESSION AND OTHER OPPRESSIONS

The oppression of ageism intersects with and intensifies other oppressions. Sexism and old-ageism merge blatantly around the artificial standards of beauty for women and the value of women based on their reproductive functions. Older men suffer from stereotypical expectations of work performance and maintaining an ideal virility.

Elders also face intensified classism, racism, and homophobia.

INTERNALIZED . . . AGEISM

What does . . . ageism look like from the inside?

- As elders we often devalue our own work.
- We often feel and act inadequate. We act competitive and aggressive or else we withdraw.
- We sometimes criticize each other, settle for less, and have difficulty rejoicing in our achievements.
- We may feel intense irritation toward other elders and try to separate ourselves from them.
- We act as though we believe the stereotypes and forget how brave, smart and good-looking we are.
- We are flattered to be thought younger; we long to be youthful.
- We are grateful to be "included" by younger people.
- We give up on our future and our dreams.
- We don't feel we have much to say.
- We confuse growing older, aging and ill health.
- In some cases, we deny that old-ageism is real.

HOW WE INTERNALIZE . . . AGEISM

Denying old age leads to ignoring, overlooking, minimizing old age oppression. We think to ourselves: "It isn't really a very important oppression." The reality is that old-ageism is important to everybody and affects everybody, throughout their lives.

When young, we internalize stereotypes of disabled, old, sick and dying people. When we think of "old" we call to mind images of an old aunt, grandfather or neighbor we once knew. If they were sick, disabled or dying, these early memories remain as internalized stereotypes of "old." Then we have the same feeling responses to "old" now as we did then (either positive or negative). These feeling responses, in turn, affect how we see the changes in our own bodies.

. . .

MOVING OUT OF THE OPPRESSION

Begin to act. Create good directions and commitments for yourself. Build support groups around you. Put your plans into action.

STEPS

- Elders and non-elders need to have confident, high expectations of elders. Recognize that we are always learning, growing, and developing, that we have not completed our lives, our contributions, our accomplishments. See elders as able to make changes, to live through many more beginnings. Remember that there are feelings, griefs, fears to be worked through at any age. It is incorrect to assume that elders' distresses are more intractable because we have lived longer.
- Elders, let's do what's important in our lives, live whatever way we need to live, and not neglect this because we are older.
- Let's live a "no limits" life, be increasingly mindful that we are in charge of ourselves physically and emotionally. Let's take as a basic assumption that a person with no distress would age slowly, if at all.
- Remember that we are our own best allies.
  . . .
- Enlist the support of non-elders as allies; develop a long list and call on them frequently. Other age groups, especially young persons, have challenges in common with elders.
- Find ways to celebrate and call attention to successful aging. Delight in and make festive every birthday. Take it as an opportunity to share what is good and positive about aging.
- Take initiative and leadership to challenge . . . ageism.
- In whatever group you are a part of, find ways to honor and show respect for older persons, call forth their abilities and talents, and interrupt any ageist practices and behaviors.
- Make yourself available as a speaker on liberation from . . . ageism.
- Develop and take responsibility for a personal health plan.
- When something goes wrong physically, don't assume it's because of age.
- Confront . . . fears about aging, sickness and death.
  . . .
- Enrich your life and theirs by sharing it with people of several different generations.
  . . .
- Know the laws pertaining to older persons and lobby to establish non-ageist policies on employment, housing, healthcare, etc.
- Focus on friendships with older persons across race, gender, class differences.
- Encourage all older persons to be fully proud of themselves, including being proud of their age.
- Work cooperatively to rid ourselves of all oppressions, including old-ageism. None of us is free until we all are free.
- Develop your own strategies for ending old-ageism, and share them!
- Organize with other elders to take leadership for our liberation and the liberation of all other sections of the population. We can lead everything, and from such a position our interests can receive the attention and emphasis they deserve.
- Form alliances with all other oppressed groups, . . . to support each others' programs. To offer alliances to other liberation groups and request their support is to multiply our effectiveness and our confidence immediately.
  . . .

V O I C E S

123

People of Color over Fifty

Dottie Curry

Aging has less stigma in communities of color. There is more respect for age and experience. A lot of the respect for elders is left over from our traditional cultures.

Though grandparents and other older adults are respected and loved within their families, they suffer more from the inhuman treatment of society towards elder citizens than members of the dominant culture. Because of the tradition of segregation and reduced access to opportunities, older people of color are less likely to have good health care, adequate housing and good nutrition. Consequently older people have a lower quality of life and a shortened life span.

Because of the poverty and violence in inner cities, older women in our communities are often taking care of grandchildren or other young people left by the death of the young people's parents. The extended family concept is a good one, but there is very rarely enough money to take care of these children properly. A lot of times the older people are on public assistance for the elderly while at the same time receiving aid for dependent children.

. . . Most of the time, just as with every other issue with people of color, the aging issue is buried under the issues connected with racism, so if there is some difficulty, old-ageism is not looked at. We need for other elders to step outside their fear and encourage older people of color to . . . work on this very important issue. We need younger people to act as our allies and . . . [talk with us about] our internalized oppression (the internalized racism and the internalized ageism).

We need for people . . . to understand that the problems facing all people, and especially people of color, are multiplied when we become elders. This is especially true in such cities as Austin, Texas and Atlanta, Georgia, where the median age is twenty-five. Since people of color have been traditionally denied some jobs (they are currently phasing people over forty out of certain jobs), the employment situation for people of color over fifty is pretty grim.

Older people of color have a lot to offer: we are an asset to any group. Our contribution to the history of this country is immense. We need a chance to share this with the . . . world.

124

Adultism

Paul Kivel

Why do young people do poorly in school? Why do young people use drugs, or hang out on street corners, or get pregnant? A common answer to these questions is that many teens have low self-esteem, generally defined as a poor sense of one's worth or ability: a lack of confidence. Professional literature about adolescents, social service priorities, and funding trends all emphasize programs which build self-esteem.

IS THE PROBLEM LOW SELF-ESTEEM?

When I think back to my years as a teenager I notice how much I wanted to do and how little power I had to do it. I wanted to go places I couldn't; I wanted to try to do things I wasn't supposed to. I wanted to affect and change my classes, my community, my neighborhood, and I wasn't able to. I never had the money, wheels, friends, influence, or credibility to make a difference.

There were lots of promises from adults. If you study hard, work hard, stay clean, stay safe, don't have sex, don't drink or smoke, don't mess up, adults promised you a life filled with power and privileges. But the promise of power 10 or 20 years in the future was not inviting nor convincing. In the meantime, few adults listened to me, or allowed me to participate, or trusted me, or noticed me and my friends and fellow students.

Now, of course, when adults systematically don't notice you, listen to you, trust you or allow you to participate in making meaningful decisions, your sense of self-worth deteriorates. When they grade you continually on your academic performance your concept of your value can hinge on it too. If on top of this they belittle you, punish you arbitrarily, yell at you, put you down, beat you, or molest you, your self-esteem can plummet. And racism, sexism, heterosexism, and other forms of oppression directed at you can eliminate your self-esteem altogether.

OPPRESSION: THE ISSUE IS POWER

Our problem as young people was not low self-esteem. Rather, we had no power over our lives. Without power to protect ourselves, we were constantly restricted, disrespected, and abused by adults. At home, at school, in stores, at work, on the sports field, on the streets—adults had the authority to decide how we should dress, how we should talk, where we could be, who we could be with, and who we couldn't. They decided our future, through grades, discipline, records, arrests, report cards, evaluations, allowances, and/or the lack or neglect of all of the above.

Teens face the same lack of power today. Adults make promises to them; adolescence is a time of promise, of open futures, of the possibility of meaningful education, fully-remunerated work, and healthy relationships. The reality is a broken promise: limited education, high un- and underemployment, unplanned families, dysfunctional relationships, and an epidemic of violence.

INTERNALIZED OPPRESSION

And teens are still blamed for failure. They are labeled trouble-makers, irresponsible, immature, apathetic, lazy, dishonest, underachievers, and stupid by adults. Adults define this failure as a personal problem for each teen, a failure of self-esteem, and teens end up blaming themselves or attacking each other. Teen violence—the teen-to-teen abuse that happens in gangs, in couples, or from the school bully; the self-abuse from drugs or alcohol; unwanted pregnancy, and suicide—all of these can be seen as forms of learned helplessness and hopelessness in teens, ways that, because of abuse from adults, they have learned to give up on themselves.

. . .

Clearly adultism is part of the daily experience of all young people. In reality, we have failed them. We discriminate against teens, keep them unemployed, vulnerable to abuse, exposed to violence and drugs and uninformed about health and reproductive issues. Then we blame them if they get strung out on drugs. We blame them if they get pregnant or get someone else pregnant. We blame them if they drop out of school, or get picked up for hanging out.

Beyond their powerlessness in an adult-defined world, then, actual abuse keeps teens from succeeding. Current national estimates are that one out of four girls and one out of six boys is sexually abused. The rates of physical, sexual, and emotional abuse and neglect toward young people are alarming; violence against children—which can range from throwing an object to using a weapon—occurs in 62% of American families every year. Past experiences of personal violence drastically limit a young person's ability to succeed in the future by fostering self-doubt, mistrust, withdrawal, and self-destructive behavior.

Teens also correctly perceive that if they are a person of color, a woman, gay or lesbian, disabled, or from a poorer family, their opportunities to achieve are severely limited. For example, girls face lower expectations and sexual harassment. Black and Latino males face higher rates of institutional discipline, suspensions and arrests. Gay and lesbian teens have to deal with physical and verbal attacks and intimidation. Teens learn to blame themselves for this abuse as well.

When we only help them develop higher self-esteem we lie to teens. We lead them to believe that they are the problem and they are to blame. We mislead them into thinking that personal virtue, effort, perseverance and skill can completely change their lives. The reality is that many will fail. Their chances of surviving and succeeding are increased when they know what they are up against. Then they can work together, with us as allies, to change the odds.

ALLIANCE: WHAT DO YOUNG PEOPLE NEED FROM US?

BE AN ALLY

Teens need to see us as strong, reliable and completely on their side, knowing that we trust them, respect them, and will tell them the truth.

TELL THE TRUTH ABOUT POWER

Teens need us to tell them about how power is used and abused in this society—to be informed, clear, and firm about how racism, sexism, adultism, and the other "isms" work. We must be ready to share that information openly and in clear, direct language that does not fault them for lacking information.

TELL THE TRUTH ABOUT VIOLENCE

We also must help them identify the social violence directed at them because they are women, people of color, gay and lesbian, and/or poor, and young. Confirming this reality for them can help them to begin to take power to stop the violence.

SUPPORT HEALING

We need to let them know that it is not their fault that they were demanded, assaulted, or discriminated against, and that it happens to many of us. We need to pass on skills to them for avoiding further violence in their lives.

INTERRUPT ADULTISM

It is always appropriate to intervene supportively where young people's rights or due respect are being denied by adults.

INTERRUPT INTERNALIZED ADULTISM

It is always appropriate to intervene (supportively) against putdowns or devaluations one teen does to another, or a young person does to her/himself.

PROMOTE TRUE HISTORY

Young people need information about their struggles and achievements as young people so they can take pride in and build upon them. This directs them to think of themselves as a community responsible for one another's well-being.

BE A PARTNER

Teens need us to be willing to share the power and work with them.

MAKE MISTAKES OPENLY

Adults, of course, are never supposed to make mistakes. This can mean we never take the chance to reach that young person who is hardest to get to. Go ahead. Try anyway. And when you make a mistake, it's OK; just fix it, and try again.

DON'T DO IT ALONE

Take other adults with you, and train them to support you when your own issues come up, when you feel you've made a mistake, and so forth. The flip side of the mistreatment of teens is the isolation of adults. Getting support from other adults will help decrease the possibility of taking out your hurt on young people or trying to enlist support from them when they shouldn't have to be in a position to give it.

NEXT STEPS

TRUST THEM TO BE POWERFUL

It is about to be their world; they are strong, and have convictions and experience about what is right and what is wrong. Support and expect them to make their own decisions. Nothing will change until they do.

CELEBRATE THEIR SUCCESSES

Every day each teen makes dozens of choices to value their own thinking, relationships, preferences, desires, etc. Every teen finds ways to communicate that the oppression is hurting them, and every teen finds ways to express love even to those adults passing on the oppression. Every teen finds ways to get attention. These are all victories. They also often have to choose between limited options, and those choices are the exercise of will to minimize the oppression. They deserve adult allies who notice and point out these acts of self-determination, and celebrate them.

We can be strong and powerful adult allies to the young people we know if we can shift our emphasis from raising their self-esteem to increasing their power. That, in turn, will allow the exuberance, insight, and creativity of young people to contribute to bettering all our lives.

. . .

NEXT STEPS

125

Allies to Young People

Tips and Guidelines on How to Assist Young People to Organize

Jenny Sazama with help from teens in Boston

. . .

THINGS YOU CAN DO TO ASSIST YOUNG PEOPLE

Go to their space and their turf.

- Young people are so often asked to be a part of the adult world.
- Young people feel more empowered and groups build faster if work can be done on their terms and in a space where they feel comfortable.
- This is especially important when there are class and race differences. The unawareness of the "dominant" group is unintentional but strong. Safety needs to be built thoughtfully and carefully.

Build one-on-one relationships.

- This is a good way to get started in figuring out how to be an ally to young people. Choose one or two young people that you are interested in spending special time with. These may be young people that you notice are particularly sharp, or that you think would be good at bringing people together. There are things you are going to be able to accomplish one-on-one that are harder to do in a group.

Form an informal young people's advisory board for yourself.

- Get feedback from them. This will give you information about how to improve your work with young people continually. It will be an amazing growing experience for you, it will bring you closer to them, and it will help them feel that their thinking matters.

    . . .

Assist young people to rely on each other and to take themselves and each other seriously.

- Adults can not completely empower young people. They will not be truly powerful until they can rely on each other, trust each others' thinking and help each other. It's tempting to have the group center around us as adults, but our ultimate goal is for things to run well without us.
- Thoughtfully but firmly interrupt competition and put-downs. Society has told young people that they are not yet full humans and that their thinking is not valuable. They internalize these messages and then take them out on each other.
- Do group feedback. Ask people to give specific positive as well as growth/ improvement information to another member of the group, including you. They will learn the most from each other.

Expect to make lots of phone calls and personal contact.

- Because young people are so often told by society that they are not important, adult allies need to make lots of phone calls to personally remind people that meetings are important and that they are wanted.
- They may not call you back. Don't take it personally. Keep calling. Assume you are wanted.
- Remember that in most situations, young people are not taken seriously, and they are told that their struggles don't matter. When you call, you are talking to someone who probably doesn't feel valuable, and thus doesn't remember that the work that she does is valuable. You need to keep reminding her how important she is.

Don't cancel meetings or events.

- It's okay if only a few people show up for things you have planned. Go ahead with them anyway. If you can even get two or three people to get closer to each other or work together on a project, you've come that much closer to the goals of your group.
- Young people have a lot of inconsistency in their lives. It means a lot to them if you can show them that you will follow through with what you say.

    . . .

NEXT STEPS

Young people should be a central part of any organization, movement, church group, etc.

- It's necessary for the total health of any movement or organization for young people to be a central part of all facets of the organization. It's great to have a young person chair a youth committee, but also have her chair the outreach committee, or be in charge of the budget. If young people do not have the skills to take on these roles then train them. A young person's perspective is invaluable.
- Make sure that young people are general members to committees and boards, not just occasional representatives.
- Token representation is not helpful in the long term.

In meetings, ask young people to talk first. Never believe that they don't know.

- You may have to ask them to express their ideas at least ten times and you may have to ask in ten different ways.
- They may say they don't know or don't have an opinion. This is what we have all been told as young people many times before.
- They do have thoughts on almost any situation if given enough information, time to think and the expectation that of course they can think.

Ask young people what *they* think should be done in all situations.

- Discuss the goals of the group and how events reflect these goals, but resist the temptation to sway the group in the direction you think it should go.

Insist that young people are represented at every meeting, especially where young people are being discussed.

- It works better if there are at least two young people present.
- Meet with them ahead of time. Get them to share their thinking with you about the meeting topic. Remind them how important their thinking is and encourage them to speak during the meeting.

  . . .

Get young people leading quickly.

- It's great for us as adults to begin facilitating and leading meetings. The faster we can turn it over to young people, however, the faster it will grow.

  . . .

Appreciate yourself for the many important ways that you have been and continue to be a committed ally to young people.

NEXT STEPS

126

Hidden in Plain Sight

The Problem of Ageism in Public Schools

Gloria Graves Holmes

When those who have the power to name and to socially construct reality choose not to see you or hear you, whether you are dark-skinned, old, disabled, female or speak in a different accent or dialect than theirs, when someone with the authority of a teacher, say, describes the world and you are not in it, there is a moment of psychic disequilibrium, as if you looked into a mirror and saw nothing.

—Adrienne Rich

INTRODUCTION

. . . As a society, whether we like it or not, or are prepared for it or not, the young, and the "old" must coexist. They must see each other as part of the wholeness of human experience rather than from oppositional positions at the extremes of the age spectrum. A challenge to ageism means revising the images, and the underlying attitudes that allow us to equate "old age" with impotence and obsolescence, and difference from the idealized and socially acceptable "norm."

Ageism is partially an outgrowth of what Audre Lorde calls a mythical norm. She argues, "In America, this norm is usually defined as white, thin, male, young, heterosexual, Christian and financially secure. It is with this mythical norm that the trappings of power [and privilege] reside within society." Being able-bodied is also part of the mythical norm, and of course, any deviation from the "norm," mythical or otherwise, sows the seeds of discrimination and bias. In the case of older adults, the outcome is ageism.

It can be argued that ageism itself may be part of the normative order of American society, and "[a]s such it is passed from generation to generation through the process of socialization much like other cultural phenomena—love of country and church, motherhood, the success ethic, and so forth" (Levin and Levin, 1980, 85). Therefore, it is not surprising that the young and the old see each other's experiences through lenses clouded by pernicious ageist attitudes and related stereotypes, embedded in literary themes and characters, textbooks, media images, public policy, and cultural mores. Yet, aside from recognizing the term, ageism, defined by Robert Butler as "any attitude, action or institutional structure which subordinates a person or group because of age, or any assignment of roles in society purely on the basis of age," educators have done little to address or redress this form of bias that damages both the victim and the perpetrator in tangible and mutually reinforcing ways. Although ageism can be interpreted as bias against any age group, . . . I am defining it as a form of discrimination against older adults that has unique implications especially for young perpetrators. I want to dispel the idea that the subjects of aging and ageism are relevant only to old people, and demonstrate that aging and ageism have implications for individuals of all ages and for society at large.

In the twenty-first century, although we have the potential to live longer healthier lives, ageism in children and young people can erode that potential. Children and young people must be taught that (1) they have the power to influence their own longevity; (2) how and how well they take care of their bodies as children and throughout their life span is directly related to their future health and longevity; (3) ageism can lead to self-destructive and/or asocial behaviors; and (4) developing positive attitudes about aging and the aging process are essential first steps in challenging ageism.

Yes, we have the potential to live longer, healthier lives, but teachers have the responsibility to teach these life-changing lessons to their students. Whether or not children learn these lessons has far-reaching implications because the young are central to our perception of aging. They define the issues, "determine the status and position of the old person in the social order," and have the power to shape society's response to aging. Their social conditioning and their assumptions about old people will determine how the young define the issue of aging. When assumptions are based on misinformation and prejudice, teachers have a responsibility to interrupt ageist thinking, and correct any misguided notions.

. . .

Teachers can address these issues by adopting a *life span* approach to teaching and learning, which integrates a discussion of aging issues into all subject matter, demystifies aging, gives students a balanced view of older adults and aging, and contextualizes the aging process as part of the natural life cycle. In addition to providing a sociocultural and historical context for ageism, this chapter presents a rationale for bringing the discussion of ageism, the aging process, and a life span approach to teaching and learning into classrooms at all grade levels, and presents creative ideas and practical activities for teachers to use.

. . .

TEACHING ABOUT AGING: STEPS TO TAKE

As with any type of multicultural education, a life span approach to teaching and learning must begin with self-evaluation and reflection by teachers. Teachers must search for ageist biases within themselves before they can effectively integrate aging education into their subject matter. They must first understand, accept, and become comfortable with their own aging. The following process should be accompanied by appropriate staff development:

Self-reflection,
Integrate lifespan approach into existing curricula,
Provide materials that offer balanced insights about aging,
Focus on healthy living, healthy aging and the relationship between them,
Develop lessons that encourage critical thinking about the media's role in promoting ageism and poor lifestyle choices,
Incorporate ageism into multicultural/antibias initiatives
Develop partnerships with colleges/universities; share resources.

SAMPLE ACTIVITIES

These activities are excerpted from *Teaching About Aging: Enriching Lives Across the Lifespan*:

ELEMENTARY LEVEL

Language Arts and Social Studies

Have students list activities they can or cannot do now; examine the list for activities they can or cannot do when they grow older. Discuss growing older as a process of growth, development and change.

Math

Develop a timeline showing the ages of students and their siblings, parents or guardians, grandparents, and great-grandparents.

SECONDARY LEVEL

The Arts

Provide students with lists of long-lived artists, poets, and musicians, photographers, architects, dancers, or actors. Have students note the age at which important accomplishments were made. Include historical figures along with contemporary celebrities.

Language Arts

Compare older characters in popular fairy tales and nursery rhymes with contemporary cartoons and television programs.

Mathematics, Economics

Use age-related data, such as age demographics, changing life span, Social Security finances, to devise problems by which students simultaneously practice math skills and learn about aging.

Social Studies

Introduce and explore the topics of ageism (age prejudice) and gerontophobia (fear of aging) by gathering and analyzing advertisements, cartoons, comic strips, birthday cards, book illustrations, and common sayings.

CONCLUSION

> We should all be concerned about the future because we have to spend the rest of our lives there.
>
> (Charles Kettering, n.d.)

Children "learn" whether schools teach them or not. We tend to think of schools only as places that "teach" students. Yet, very often schools are in the business of "unteaching" students, of helping them "unlearn" values and reshaping their thinking; replacing misinformation or misguided notions with balanced perceptions and fact-based conclusions. Children are learning, every waking moment of every day, whether the "lessons" are formal or informal, acknowledged or unacknowledged. And the "teachers" are not just those who are paid to do the job in structured classroom settings. The negative lessons about what it means to be "old" are coming from TV, books, music, parents, and even teachers. Perhaps the worst kind of education we could provide students, according to Couper and Pratt,

> would be to teach them that their own future can be seen in the conditions of older people today . . . for better or worse, those who are now growing up and growing older will largely determine what it means to grow old in the years to come.

If schools do not systematically provide aging education that gives balanced views of the process, children will have little or no support to counter the misinformation that is swirling around them. Further, children will not acquire the attitudes and develop the skills that will enable them to live in a future that will be dominated by age/aging-related issues. If we do not teach students about aging, we are "teaching" students about aging. Although the lessons are subliminal, they may be the most affective.

127

What Allies of Elders Can Do

Patricia Markee

It feels like you can ignore ageism until you reach the age when it affects you, but in truth it affects you now. It has affected you ever since you were born. It will affect you much more deeply as you grow older, especially if you keep putting it off, denying reality: your age and the treatment you receive.

Although you must acknowledge this oppression now, you may not have to devote much time to it. You can simply select an elder to support. Remember that what we current elders don't figure out is going to land squarely on your shoulders to figure out (if you're lucky enough to become an elder). Supporting an elder against the oppression is an investment in your own future.

In addition to the above, we ask that our allies:

- Assume that we are potentially brilliant. Do not believe any stupid, slow, or bumbly pattern. These are the effects of distress, not aging.
- Assume that we have long, productive futures. Many elders over sixty-five do not have to work and have more discretionary time to be productive. We are not ready to die nor are we waiting to die. I have seen movies in which the old are expected to be the ones to sacrifice their lives. This colludes with the belief that we no longer have anything to contribute.
- Assume that we have not given up on life. Remember that we have seen several generations of young people pass through their teens, twenties, and thirties, and we have noticed that some things last and some things don't. We may not be interested in everything that comes along not because we are intellectually stagnant or afraid, but, because we may have chosen to place our energy into fewer but more lasting things.

- Assume that we are sexually attractive and that we have in front of us many more years of being sexual.
- Assume that everyone can learn from much of our experience; invite us to share our thinking . . . . Don't give up on us at the first sign of distress. Let's break the cycle of abandonment now.
- Assume that memory loss and physical and mental deterioration may be accumulated distress or ill health, not the process of aging.

    . . .

- Don't assume that you know anything about our physical capacities. We may have trouble sitting in a chair, or we may be able to play basketball.

    . . .

- Interrupt others when they assume we're just being critical. We have a right to speak up for our rights without being dismissed.
- Use the same criteria for us to become leaders as you do for others. Expect us to become leaders, in spite of our individual distress. Don't give up on us at the first sign of distress. . . . It's nice if we're "very alive for a fifty-year-old," spontaneous, can have fun, can tap dance at seventy-eight, or are learning to do cart-wheels. But we are more than a vehicle for contradicting your fears [about aging].
- When we have become effective leaders, remember that we are not the all-loving, all-knowing parent you always wanted. We are human beings like you, struggling to figure out our lives. We may have had the time to figure out a few more things, but we are not gods.

    . . .

- Judy Malinowski has discovered that one's assumptions about elders can best be uncovered by asking the questions, "What surprised you about old people?" Asking the question, "What don't you like about old people?" seems to produce only the response, "I love old people," as in "I love children, Afro-Americans, disabled people, etc."
- Pick an elder leader who is not being supported and support her or him. This is simply an investment in your own aging and you may learn a great deal. Besides, . . . it is the role of leaders from the non-target group; it is the role of white leaders to support people of color leaders; it is the role of owning-class and middle-class leadership to support working-class leadership; and it is the role of younger leaders to support elder leaders.

NEXT STEPS

SECTION 10

WORKING FOR SOCIAL JUSTICE
VISIONS AND STRATEGIES FOR CHANGE

Introduction

Ximena Zúñiga

It takes courage to interrogate yourself. It takes courage to look at the mirror and see past your reflection to who you really are when you take off the mask, when you're not performing the same old routines and social roles. It takes courage to ask—how did I become so well adjusted to injustice?
—Cornel West, *Hope on a Tightrope* (2008)

Change means growth, and growth can be painful. But we sharpen self-definition by exposing the self in work and struggle together with those whom we define as different from ourselves, although sharing the same goals.
—Audre Lorde, *Sister Outsider* (1984)

As a democratic relationship, dialogue is the opportunity available to me to open up to the thinking of others, and thereby not wither away in isolation.
—Paulo Freire, *Pedagogy of Hope* (1994)

We believe social justice is both a process and a goal. The goal of social justice is full and equal participation of all groups in a society that is mutually shaped to meet their needs. Social justice includes a vision of society in which the distribution of resources is equitable and all members are physically and psychologically secure . . . The process for attaining the goal of social justice, we believe, should also be democratic and participatory, inclusive and affirming of human agency and capacities for working collaboratively to create change.
—Lee Anne Bell, *Teaching for Diversity and Social Justice* (2007)

INTRODUCTION

Throughout this volume we have articulated the view that developing awareness and knowledge about the systemic and interlocking qualities of social oppression is a critical step we can take toward envisioning and working toward social justice. Our awareness and knowledge, as well as our identities, understandings, experiences, and emotions, shape our vision of what a more socially just world might look like and motivate us to work toward realizing those visions. That is why so much of this book focuses on describing and analyzing systems of privilege and oppression from different perspectives, how they manifest themselves, and how they impact people's lives. However, learning about social injustices can be overwhelming, especially if we don't believe there is anything we can do to change them. Both inside and outside of the classroom, we also need to find hope and acquire practical tools for creating change. Otherwise, our awareness and knowledge may simply become "a prescription for despair" (Tatum 1992, 24).

In this concluding section, we invite our readers to consider a vision for social justice and liberation that values critical consciousness, participation, connectedness, passion, bridge building across divides through dialogue and action, and alliances and coalitions for change, as pathways to individual and collective empowerment, equity, and safety and security for all social groups in society (Bell 2007; Zúñiga, Nagda, Chesler, and Cytron-Walker 2007). Such a vision requires an understanding of how various forms of privilege and oppression are connected at the psychological, interpersonal, intergroup, societal, and global levels.

As individuals, we may not be able to take actions against these injustices at all of these levels, but we can begin by learning about how we and others may participate in or be affected by injustices such as adultism and ageism, ethnoreligious oppression, racism, heterosexism, ableism, and so on, and by trying to change specific manifestations of oppression in our own spheres of influence (e.g., within ourselves, and in our interpersonal relationships with family, friends, and co-workers). In so doing, we learn more about how dynamics of exclusion, privilege, and oppression come into play in our personal and community lives, how different individuals and groups are affected similarly and differently by these dynamics, and how these issues connect to larger national and global issues and systems. At the same time, we also learn more about ourselves and develop the analytical, relational, and organizational skills needed to create change. Though, as Lorde reminds us, working for change can be painful, it can also be liberating as our individual actions may lead us to change hearts and minds, foster new connections across differences, and forge stronger ally relations and deeper forms of engagement with others. These kinds of actions provide us with tools to work within and build stronger coalitions to work for social justice and help us to develop a passion and a commitment for justice.

As our awareness, knowledge, commitments, passions, and skills grow, we may at some point choose to work in common causes or participate in collective actions that promote change. Creating pathways of personal and collective liberation, empowerment, and change calls for envisioning new possibilities, as well as understanding how change happens. For instance, we can envision new possibilities by educating ourselves and transforming different forms of privilege, discrimination, and oppression, as illustrated by several of the selections introduced early in this book (Katz, selection 65; Hehir, selection 110); becoming an ally (Evans and Washington, selection 86; Sazama, selection 125); engaging in dialogue across differences (Avayzian and Tatum, selection 23); or by joining organizations and creating coalitions to create change (Jeung, selection 59; Leondar-Wright, selection 41; Smith, selection 25). While change may begin with changes in consciousness, dialogue, participation in local, national and global social movements, and coalitional efforts to create change at school, work, or in the community may expand our spheres of influence and contribute to wider systemic change (see Harro, selection 7). Therefore, it is critical that we find ways to get ready—by reading, talking, and learning with and from people from all walks of life—young and old, urban and rural, privileged and disadvantaged—who have resisted and created change individually or in conjunction with others. This is important because, as Freire, Lorde, and West remind us, we need to find the courage to question and engage in dialogue, not only with ourselves, but with each other, in order to actualize our collective visions for a more inclusive and just democracy. Social action without vision, inspiration, courage, love, and hope can also be a prescription for despair. Hence, our individual *and* collective visions of a more just society are what will sustain us and move us to take action against social injustice.

In closing, it is important to acknowledge that individual and collective actions are powerful forces that inspire and move people and groups to transform society and actively contribute to the development of visions, knowledge, networks, organizations, and tools for creating and sustaining change over the long haul. This is partly why so many of the selections included in this section are from activist writers who have been actively engaged in civil rights movements, labor movements, feminist movements, lesbian, gay, bisexual and queer social movements, disability rights movements, and, more recently, women of color and youth organizing and immigration rights and anti-globalization movements. It is also important to recognize the strengths and limitations of our current visions. For instance, twentieth-century activists focused primarily on race/ethnicity, class, gender, sexuality, or intersecting issues, while emerging social movements of the twenty-first century are grappling more with new issues and intersections, such as immigration and international issues, interfaith issues and religious oppression, children's and youth rights, and transgender and queer issues. We do not know what the primary concerns of emerging and future activists will be, but we do know that they will bring new perspectives, new insights, and new tools for social change. We need both the wisdom and experience of older activists and the ideas and energy of young and emerging activists to create change. Together, we can build a world that is inclusive, democratic, and committed to human liberation and social justice.

READINGS IN THIS SECTION

The authors in our Contexts section outline conceptual frameworks for developing a vision for diversity and social justice and describe methods and practices that support the development of critical consciousness and actions and practices for social justice. In the first selection, Suzanne Pharr (selection 128) reminds us that "a truly democratic society is always in the process of redefining itself" and that struggles for liberation are an essential part of that process. She suggests that liberation requires transforming all forms of discrimination and barriers that keep large portions of the population from attaining economic and social justice, from participating fully in decisions affecting their lives, and from having the rights and responsibilities of living in a free society. In Pharr's view it is not enough to be aware of the historical and social context of oppression and its manifestations at the cultural, institutional and personal level. We need to have the ideological commitment to work for social justice; and a willingness to engage with our hearts, build and honor relationships across differences, hear other perspectives, lend support where there is pain and loss, develop individual and institutional integrity, and redefine and share power in our daily lives.

In the second selection, Barbara J. Love extends Freire's (1970, 1973) concept of liberatory consciousness for envisioning and creating change (selection 129). Love identifies four critical elements for developing such a consciousness: awareness, analysis, action, and accountability/ally-ship. In her view, the development of liberatory consciousness is a crucial step because it enables us to live our lives "in oppressive systems and institutions with awareness and intentionality, rather than on the basis of the socialization to which we have been subjected." It also enables us to remain hopeful, connected through ally relationships, and not give up to despair.

In the third selection, Patricia Hill Collins (selection 130) proposes that those who wish to engage in social justice actions with people different from themselves need to learn how to transcend barriers created by their own experiences with race, class, and gender oppression in order to build the types of coalitions essential for social change. Collins identifies three major challenges: recognizing that differing experiences with oppression create problems in relationships; learning how to build relationships and coalitions around common causes with people of different races, genders, and socioeconomic statuses; and developing the capacity for empathy for the experiences of individuals and groups different from ourselves. Probably the biggest challenge for people who want to work for social justice is in knowing where to begin to take responsibility for changing the systems that produce privilege and oppression. Allan G. Johnson (selection 131) identifies several approaches to help us think about "how to make ourselves part of the solution" as we transform ourselves, our schools, our workplaces, and our communities, and urges us to "make noise, be seen," because systems of oppression feed on silence. He also provides many examples of actions we can take and asks us to "dare to make people feel uncomfortable, beginning with yourself"—that is, to question ourselves and others, even if it is personally challenging or risky, and to "actively promote change in systems that are organized around privilege," beginning in our own spheres of influence.

The process of becoming evermore aware and confident in one's ability to make a difference involves a lifelong process of education, commitment, and empowerment. As Bobbie Harro suggests in "The Cycle of Liberation" (selection 7), this process requires education and building relationships with people "like you" and "different from you" in order to work for a more socially just future. Reading personal narratives and listening to personal stories from people actively involved in creating change is one of the ways we can begin to break the silence and learn from each other. The Voices section features two authors who have devoted their lives to promoting social justice in distinct but connected areas. Leonard Peltier (selection 132), a citizen of the Anishinabe and Dakota/Lakota Nations and Native American rights activist who has been incarcerated in a federal prison since 1976, offers a poignant statement about the imperative to "never cease in the fight for peace and equality for all people" as long as the work for social justice remains unfinished. Gloria E. Anzaldúa (selection 133), a visionary Chicana/woman of color feminist, *maestra*/scholar activist, discusses the concept of "allies," and what it takes "to help each other heal," using her own experiences as a Chicana, *mestiza*, Mexican, lesbian, activist, poet, and writer. She argues that it is very important when you are doing alliance work—bridge work, boundary work—to talk about who you are, where you come from, even at the risk of being challenged or being betrayed.

The selections in the concluding section, Next Steps, offer varied approaches, methods, and strategies that people working alone or together can use to organize, build alliances and dialogue across differences, and take actions toward building a more just society. Chip Smith (selection 134) outlines a thought-provoking approach to organizing for social justice starting with the premise that the systemic character of oppression becomes clearer as groups and organizations gain experience, resources, and influence. Drawing from his experience working against racism, sexism, and classism, Smith recommends the merging of social movements for national liberation, working-class power, and the ending of patriarchy. He proposes an approach that centers in self-determination, equity, and international solidarity. For instance, he invites organizers to "start where people are," develop critical understanding of complex issues, draw from social theory and embrace social justice values, increase ties among organizations, and build progressive social change organizations.

Andrea Ayvazian (selection 135) writes about the role of allies as agents for change. Allies are members of privileged groups, who take responsibility for challenging privilege and oppression and working for liberation and justice. Allies can also help reduce the violence that is pervasive in society, provide positive role models, particularly to young people, explore alternative pathways for creating change, and help pave the way toward the long haul. Ayvazian reminds us that being an ally is difficult and often lonely work. Therefore, like Susan Pharr, she asks that we take care of ourselves so we can persevere. Building alliances often requires engaging in difficult dialogues and bridging social identity-based conflicts to help develop and sustain ally relationships and social movement organizations. Ximena Zúñiga (selection 136) describes the intergroup dialogue approach aimed at bringing college students from different social identity groups together to examine controversial issues with the goal of consciousness-raising, bridging of differences and conflicts, and envisioning ways of creating greater equity and justice (Zúñiga,

Nagda, Chesler, and Cytron-Walker 2007). These semester-long dialogues enable participants to engage in facilitated and sustained processes of communication and critical reflection about hot topics across race/ethnicity, gender, sexuality, class, and other group differences, and explore individual and collective ways of taking action in one's spheres of influence.

From a social movement perspective, Elizabeth (Betita) Martinez (selection 137) underscores the importance of anticipating the challenges embedded in building alliances and the value of learning from our different and conflictual stories. Drawing from her women of color organizing experiences, she calls attention to what similar and different experiences of racism mean for different groups of women of color and how important it is to "act with integrity, speak with honesty, and reject any fear of our differences and conflicts." We conclude this section with an inspirational selection by Nicole McClelland and Kristina Rizga (selection 138) on youth activism. This report from the trenches is a powerful reminder that young people, and people from all walks of life, are actively involved in social struggle and building alliances to fight global warming, create equity in schools, combat racism, fill health-care needs after Katrina, seek labor rights for immigrant labor working in the fields, and work for peace and justice around the globe. These efforts are both inspirational and educational. As César Chávez, leader of the United Farm Workers Union, put it a long time ago, *Sí se puede, yes, we can*!

References

Bell, L. A. (2007). "Theoretical Foundations for Social Justice Education." In M. Adams, L. A. Bell, P. Griffin (eds), *Teaching for Diversity and Social Justice*, 2nd edition. New York: Routledge. pp. 1–14.

Freire, P. (1970). *Pedagogy of the Oppressed*. New York: Continuum.

Freire, P. (1973). *Education for Critical Consciousness*. New York: Continuum.

Freire, P. (1994). *Pedagogy of Hope*. New York: Continuum.

Lorde, A. (1984). *Sister Outsider*. Freedom, CA: Crossing Press.

Tatum, B. D. (1992). "Talking about Race, Learning about Racism: The Application of Racial Identity Development Theory in the Classroom." *Harvard Educational Review* 62 (1), 1–24.

West, C. (2008). *Hope on a Tightrope*. Carlsbad, CA: Smiley Books, Hay House.

Zúñiga, X., Nagda, B. A., Chesler, M., Cytron-Walker, A. (2007). *Intergroup Dialogue in High Education: Meaningful Learning about Social Justice*. ASHE-ERIC Higher Education Report Volume 32, Number 4. San Francisco: Jossey-Bass.

128

Reflections on Liberation

Suzanne Pharr

Liberation politics: seeking social and economic justice for all people; supporting inclusion, autonomy, choice, wholeness; building and honoring relationships; developing individual and institutional integrity, responsibility and accountability; redefining and sharing power.

These political times call for renewed dialogue about and commitment to the politics of liberation. Because a truly democratic society is always in the process of redefining itself, its evolution is fueled by struggles for liberation on the part of everyone wishing to participate in the development of the institutions and policies that govern our lives. Liberation requires a struggle against discrimination based on race, class, gender, sexual identity, ableism and age—those barriers which keep large portions of the population from having access to economic and social justice, from being able to participate fully in the decisions affecting our lives, from having a full share of both the rights and responsibilities of living in a free society.

. . .

This is the challenge for all of us. The work of liberation politics is to change hearts and minds, develop empathy with and sympathy for other people, and help each other discover how we are inextricably linked together for our common good and our survival on this planet.

Like power, liberation cannot be given; it must be created. Liberation politics requires

- helping individuals to fulfill their greatest potential by providing truthful information along with the tools and skills for using it, supporting their autonomy and self-government, and connecting them to life in community with others;
- fostering both individual freedom and mutual responsibility for others;
- recognizing that freedom demands people always be able to make their own choices about their lives;
- creating a politic of shared power rather than power-over;
- learning the non-violent skills of compromise and mediation in the sometimes difficult collective lives of family and community—in organizations, the workplace, and governing bodies;
- developing integrity in relationships through understanding that the same communal values—generosity and fairness, responsibility and freedom, forgiveness and atonement—must be maintained not just in personal relationships but in the workplace, social groups, and governing bodies;
- treating everyone as a valued whole person, not as someone to be used or controlled;
- maintaining civility in our relationships and being accountable for our behavior;
- seeing cultural differences as life-enhancing, as expanding possibilities;
- placing a broad definition of human rights at the center of our values: ensuring that every person has food, shelter, clothing, safety, education, health care, and a livable income.

. . .

We are seeking ways to bring people together to work on common causes across differences. If, indeed, all oppressions are connected, then it follows that the targets of this oppression are connected as well as their solution. This interconnection leads us to the idea of collaborative efforts to create democratic values, discourse and institutions.

We believe that we will succeed when we collectively create a vision that in practice offers a way of life so attractive that people will not be able to resist it. As progressive people across this country we are working to create a multi-issue, multi-racial and multi-cultural liberation movement; we are trying to redefine our work and bring more integrity to it; we are engaged in developing a clearer, more compelling vision, building stronger relationships among justice-seeking people, and including more people in the process of creating a democracy that works for all of us.

. . .

TRANSFORMATIONAL ORGANIZING AND BUILDING COMMUNITY

For whatever reasons, progressive people have not always talked a great deal about the strong moral convictions underlying why we do this work of social justice: *it is because we believe every person counts, has human dignity, and deserves respect, equality and justice.* This morality is the basis for our vision, and when we do our best vision-based organizing (as opposed to response-based or expediency-based), all our work flows from this basic belief.

Ours is a noble history. Because progressive people believe in the inclusion of everyone in the cause of justice and equality, we have struggled for civil rights for people of color, for women, for people with disabilities, and now for lesbians and gay men. We have worked to save the environment, to provide women autonomy and choice concerning our bodies, to end unjust wars, to end homelessness, hunger, and poverty, to create safe workplaces, decent wages and fair labor practices, to honor treaty rights, to eliminate HIV and improve health care, to eliminate biased crime and violence against women and children. We share broad principles of inclusion, fairness, and justice. We must not forget what provides the fire for our work, what connects us in the struggle for freedom and equality.

We are living in a time in which people are crying out for something to believe in, for a moral sense, for purpose, for answers that will bring some calm to the chaos they feel in their lives. As progressive people, we have not always offered up our vision of the world, our activities for justice, as a moral vision. When we have, as during the Civil Rights Movement, people working together for a common good have felt whole.

I believe it is our moral imperative to help each other make connections, to show how everyone is interrelated and belongs in community, or as it is currently expressed, "We all came on different ships but we're in the same boat now." It is at our peril if we do work that increases alienation and robs meaning from life. Today's expressions of violence, hatred, and bigotry are directly related to the level of alienation and disconnection felt by people. For our very survival, we must develop a sense of common humanity.

It may be that our most important political work is figuring out how to make the full human connection, how to engage our hearts as well as our minds, how to heal the injuries we have suffered, how to do organizing that transforms people as well as institutions. With these as goals, we need to re-think our strategies and tactics.

We have to think about our vision of change. Are we involved in a struggle for power that requires forces and resources on each side and a confrontational show-down in which only one side wins? If we are in a shoot-out, then the progressive side has already lost, for certainly there are more resources on the Right at this moment. In other cases where we can organize the most resources, such as the 1992 "No on 9" campaign in Oregon, what is the nature and permanency of the win? The anti-gay and lesbian constitutional amendment was defeated, but in general, people did not have a sense of ecstatic victory. I think there were two primary reasons: 1) the Right immediately announced its intention to take the fight to local rural communities and to build a string of victories in areas where it had developed support—indicating that this is indeed a long struggle for the hearts and souls of Oregonians; and 2) the campaign did not facilitate the building of lasting relationships, of communities, of progressive institutions—because it did not see itself as part of a movement. At the end, I believe people felt a war-like atmosphere had been created, but that the language and tactics of war had failed them. In the months that followed the election victory, people seemed fatigued, wary, often dispirited and in retreat. Rather than being transformed into new politics and relationships by their experience, they seemed battered by it.

Transformational Organizing. There is something to be learned when victory feels like defeat. Somehow, people did not emerge from the Oregon experience with a sense of vitality, of wholeness, of connection. Justice-seeking people must call into question our methods of organizing. Often we have thought that effective organizing is simply being able to move people as a group, sometimes through manipulation, to act in a particular way to achieve a goal. Too often the end has justified the means, and we have failed to follow Ghandi's belief that every step toward liberation must have liberation embedded within it. By concentrating on moving people to action, we have often failed to hear the voice of their spirit, their need for connection and wholeness—not for someday after the goal has been gained, but in the very process of gaining it.

I am not arguing that we should give up direct action, civil disobedience, issue campaigns, political education, confrontation, membership and voter drives, etc. We need to do these things and much more. I am suggesting that we re-think the meaning of social change and learn how to include the long-term work of transforming people as we work for social justice. We must re-define "winning." Our social change has to be more than amassing resources and shifting power from the hands of one group to another; we must seek a true shift in consciousness, one that forges vision, goals, and strategies from belief, not just from expediency, and allows us to become a strong political force.

The definition of transformational politics is fairly simple: it is political work that changes the hearts and minds of people, supports personal and group growth in ways that create healthy, whole people, organizations, and communities, and is based on a vision of a society where people—across lines of race, gender, class and sexuality—are supported by institutions and communities to live their best lives.

Among many possibilities, I want to suggest one way to do transformational work: through building community that is based on our moral vision.

Building Community, Making Connections. Where do we build community? Should it be geographic, consisting of everyone who lives in the same neighborhood? Based on identity, such as one's racial identity, sexual identity? Organizational or work identity? Where are the places that community happens?

It seems to me that community can be created in a vast number of places and ways. What is more important is the *how* of building community. To get to the how, we first have to define what community is. Community is people in any configuration (geographic, identity, etc.) bonded together over time through common interest and concern, through responsibility and accountability to one another, and at its best, through commitment, friendship and love.

To live in authentic community requires a deeper level of caring and interaction than many of us currently exhibit in our drive for individualism and self-fulfillment. That is, it calls for living with communal values. And we face a daunting challenge here because we all live in a culture that glorifies individualism. For example, what the Right calls "traditional family values" actually works against the often-quoted African proverb, "It takes a village to raise a child," which speaks to the communal value of the importance of every child in the life of the community, present and future. Such values point to very different solutions than those currently suggested for the problems of youth alienation, crime, and violence. Rather than increasing police forces and building more jails, with these shared values we would look toward more ways for the community as a whole to be responsible for and accountable to children. We would seek ways to support and nurture their lives. All of us would be teachers, parents and friends for every child.

Creating community requires seeing the whole, not just the parts, and understanding how they interrelate. However, the difficult part is learning how to honor the needs of the individual as well as those of the group, without denying the importance of either. It requires a balance between identity and freedom on the one hand and the collective good and public responsibility on the other. It requires ritual and celebration and collective ways to grieve and show anger; it requires a commitment to resolve conflict.

Most of all, it requires authenticity in relationships between and among whole people. This means that each of us has to be able to bring all of who we are to the relationship, neighbor to neighbor, friend to friend, worker to worker. Bringing all of who we are to community requires working across great differences in culture, in lifestyle, in belief. It demands that we look beyond our own lives to understand the lives of others. It demands that we interact with the lives of others. It requires understanding the connections among people's lives and then seeking comprehensive solutions to multi-issue, multifaceted problems. If we allow only certain parts of people to surface, and if we silence, reject or exclude basic pieces of their essential selves, then we begin designing systems of oppression. Community becomes based on power and non-consensual authority: those who have the most power and privilege dictate the community norms and their enforcement.

One of the goals of every political activity we engage in should be to move beyond superficial interactions to the building of relationships and community. Much of this work is simple, not difficult or complex; it merely requires redefining our values and how we spend our political time. For example, far too often I go to meetings, frequently held in sterile hotel conference rooms, where introductions are limited to people giving their names or, at best, what work they do. Building relationships—whether those of neighbor, friend, lover, work partner—requires that we ask *who are you?* In rural communities in the South and on American Indian reservations, people spend a lot of time talking about who their people are, how they are connected to people and place. Women activists in the housing projects in New Orleans get to know each other by telling their life lines, the major events that shaped them along the way. It is almost ritual for lesbians to get to know each other by telling their coming out stories—when and how they first experienced their lesbianism.

Building connection and relationship requires that we give it time, not just in meetings but in informal opportunities surrounding meetings, structured and unstructured. For instance, when I did political education on oppression issues within the battered women's movement, there was always a dramatic difference in the relationships that were built when we stayed in retreat centers or self-contained places away from distracting outside activities rather than in city hotels. So much of what happened in people's growth and understanding came from living, sleeping, and eating together in an atmosphere that encouraged interaction.

As a way to think about building community, we can ask ourselves these questions:

- In what settings with other people have I felt most whole? What is it that makes me feel known and accepted as who I am?
- What conditions make me most able to work well in partnership with other people? What makes me feel connected rather than alienated?
- What are communal values? What are the practices that support them?
- Where are the places where community is occurring? (For example, in care teams for people living with AIDS, in youth gangs, in certain churches or neighborhoods, in AA groups?) What are the characteristics of these communities?
- Who is being excluded from community? What barriers are there to participation?
- What are the qualities of an inclusive community as opposed to an exclusive community?
- What makes a community democratic?

Our communities are where our moral values are expressed. It is here that we are called upon to share our connection to others, our interdependence, our deepest belief in what it means to be part of the human condition, where people's lives touch one another, for good or for bad. It is here where the rhetoric of belief is forced into the reality of living. It is from this collection of people, holding within it smaller units called families, that we build and live democracy. Or, without care and nurturance, where we detach from one another and destroy our hope for survival.

POLITICAL INTEGRITY AND MULTI-ISSUE POLITICS

It is one thing for us to talk about liberation politics; it is of course another to live them. We lack political integrity when we demand liberation for one cause or one group of people and act out oppression or exploitation toward others. If we do not have an integrated analysis and a commitment to sharing power, it is easy to act out politics that simply reflect a hierarchy of domination.

In our social change organizations in particular we can find ourselves in this dangerous position: where we are demanding, for example, liberation from sexism but within the organization we act out racism, economic injustice, and homophobia. Each is reflected in who is allowed to lead, who makes the highest and lowest salaries, who is allowed to participate in the major decision-making, who decides how the resources are used. If the organization does not have a vision and a strategy that also include the elimination of racism, sexism, economic injustice, and homophobia (as well as oppressions relating to age, physical ability, etc.), then internal conflict is inevitable. People cannot single out just one oppression from their lives to bring to their work for liberation: they bring their whole selves.

Creating a multi-racial, multi-cultural, multi-issue vision of liberation is no easy task. It is much easier to stay within the framework of oppression where our women's organizations' leadership is primarily white, middle-class women, heterosexual or closeted lesbians; our civil rights organizations are male-dominated; our gay/lesbian/bi/transgender organizations are controlled by white gay men and/or white lesbians. And where the agendas for change reflect the values of those who dominate the leadership.

It is easier to talk about "diversity" than about shared power. Or to use a belief in identity politics to justify not including others in a vision for change. I do not believe in either diversity or identity politics as they are currently practiced.

First, diversity politics seem to focus on the necessity for having everyone (across gender, race, class, age, religion, physical ability) present and treated well in any given setting or organization. A core premise is that everyone is oppressed and all oppressions are equal. Since the publication of the report, "Workforce 2000," that predicted the U.S. workforce would be made up of 80% women and people of color by the year 2000, a veritable growth industry of "diversity consultants" has arisen to teach corporations how to "manage" diversity. With integration and productivity as goals, they focus on issues of sensitivity and inclusion—a human relations approach—with acceptance and comfort as high priorities. Popular images of diversity politics show people holding hands around America, singing "We Are the World." People are generally reassured that they do not have to give up anything when they diversify their workplace. They simply have to include other people and become more sensitive to differences.

Because the history of oppression is one of excluding, of silencing, of rendering people invisible, I have great appreciation for the part of diversity work that concentrates on making sure everyone is included. However, our diversity work fails if it does not deal with the power dynamics of difference and go straight to the heart of shifting the balance of power among individuals and within institutions. A danger of diversity politics lies in the possibility that it may become a tool of oppression by creating the illusion of participation when in fact there is no shared power. Having a presence within an organization or institution means very little if one does not have the power of decision-making, an adequate share of the resources, and participation in the development of the workplan or agenda. We as oppressed people must demand much more than acceptance. Tolerance, sympathy and understanding are not enough, though they soften the impact of oppression by making people feel better in the face of it. Our job is not just to soften blows but to make change, fundamental and far-reaching.

Identity politics, on the other hand, rather than trying to include everyone, brings together people who share a single common identity such as sexual orientation, gender, or race. Generally, it focuses on the elimination of a single oppression, the one that is based on the common identity; e.g., homophobia/heterosexism, sexism, racism. However, this can be a limited, hierarchical approach, reducing people of multiple identities to a single identity. Which identity should a lesbian of color choose as a priority—gender, race or sexual identity? And does choosing one necessitate leaving the other two at home? What do we say to bisexual or biracial people? Do we tell them to choose? Our multiple identities allow us to develop a politic that is broad in scope because it is grounded in a wide range of experiences.

There are positive aspects of organizing along identity lines: clarity of single focus in tactics and strategies, self-examination and education apart from the dominant culture, development of solidarity and group bonding. Creating organizations based on identity allows us to have visibility and collective power, to advance concerns that otherwise would never be recognized because of our marginalization within the dominant society.

However, identity politics often suffers from the failure to acknowledge that the same multiplicity of oppressions, a similar imbalance of power, exists within identity groups as within the larger society. People who group together on the basis of their sexual identity still find within these groups sexism and racism that have to be dealt with—or if gathering on the basis of race, there is still sexism and homophobia to be confronted. Whole, not partial, people come to identity groups, carrying several identities. Some of liberation movements' major barriers to building a unified and cohesive strategy, I believe, come from our refusal to work directly on the oppressions—those fundamental issues of power—within our own groups. A successful liberation movement cannot be built on the effort to liberate only a few or only a piece of who we are.

Diversity and identity politics are responses to oppression. In confronting oppressions we must always remember that they mean more than people just not being nice to one another. They are systemic, based in institutions and in general society, where one group of people is allowed to exert power and control over members of another group, denying them fundamental rights. Also, we must remember that oppressions are interconnected, operating in similar ways, and that many people experience more than one oppression.

. . .

The question, as ever, is what to do? I do not believe that either a diversity or identity politics approach will work unless they are changed to incorporate a multi-issue analysis and strategy that combine the politics of inclusion with shared power. But, one might say, it will spread us too thin if we try to work on everyone's issue, and ours will fall by the wayside. In our external work (doing women's anti-violence work, working against police brutality in people of color communities, seeking government funding for AIDS research), we do not have to work on "everybody's issue"—we can be focused. But how can we achieve true social change unless we look at all within our constituency who are affected by our particular issue? People who have AIDS are of every race, class, age, gender, geographic location, but when research and services are sought, it is women, people of color, poor people, who are most overlooked. The HIV virus rages on because those in power think that the people who contract it are dispensable. Are we to be like them? To understand why police brutality is so much more extreme in people of color communities than in white, we have to understand also why, even within these communities, it is even greater against poor people of color, women who are prostitutes, and gay men and lesbians of color. To leave any group out leaves a hole for everyone's freedoms and rights to fall through. It becomes an issue of "acceptable" and "unacceptable" people, deserving and undeserving of rights, legitimate and illegitimate, deserving of recognition as fully human or dismissable as something less.

Identity politics offers a strong, vital place for bonding, for developing political analysis. With each other we struggle to understand our relationship to a world that says that we are no more than our identity, and simultaneously denies there is oppression based on race or gender or sexual identity. Our challenge is to learn how to use the experiences of our many identities to forge an inclusive social change politic. The question that faces us is how to do multi-issue coalition building from an identity base. The hope for a multi-racial, multi-issue movement rests in large part on the answer to this question.

Our linkages can create a movement, and our divisions can destroy us. Each point of linkage is our strongest defense and also holds the most possibility for long-lasting social change.

If our organizations are not committed internally to the inclusion and shared power of all those who share our issue, how can we with any integrity demand inclusion and shared power in society at large? If women, lesbians and gay men are treated as people undeserving of equality within civil rights organizations, how can those organizations demand equality? If women of color and poor women are marginalized in women's rights organizations, how can those organizations argue that women as a class should be moved into full participation in the mainstream? If lesbian and gay organizations are not feminist and anti-racist in all their practices, what hope is there for the elimination of homophobia and heterosexism in a racist, sexist society? It is an issue of integrity.

In the larger social change community our failure to connect issues prevents us from being able to do strong coalition and alliance work with one another. Most frequently, coalitions and alliances are created to meet crisis issues which threaten all of us. Made up of groups that experience injustice, they should have common ground. They most frequently fall apart, I believe, because of failure in relationships. As in all human relationships, it is difficult to solve the issue of the moment without a history of trust, common struggle, and reciprocity. Homophobia, for example, has kept us "quiet" and invisible in our anti-racist work; racism has kept us "quiet" in our lesbian and gay work. We need to be visible in our work on all fronts. Working shoulder to shoulder on each other's issues enables us to get to know each other's humanity, to understand the broad sweep of issues, to build trust and solidarity.

Our separateness, by identity and by issue, prevents the building of a progressive movement. When we grasp the value and interconnectedness of our liberation issues, then we will at last be able to make true coalition and begin building a common agenda that eliminates oppression and brings forth a vision of diversity that shares both power and resources.

. . .

129

Developing a Liberatory Consciousness

Barbara J. Love

All members of society play a role in keeping a "dis-equal" system in place, whether the system works to their benefit or to their disadvantage. Through the socialization process, every member of society learns the attitudes, language, behaviors and skills that are necessary to function effectively in the existing society. This socialization prepares individuals to play roles of dominant or subordinate in systems of oppression.[1] For example, men are assigned the role of dominant and women are assigned the role of subordinate in the system of dis-equality based on gender. Whites are assigned to play the role of dominant and People of Color are assigned the role of subordinate in the system of dis-equality based on race. The socialization process of the society works to insure that each person learns what they need to know to behave in ways that contribute to the maintenance and perpetuation of the existing system, independent of their belief in its fairness or efficacy.

No single human can be charged with the creation of the oppressive systems in operation today. All humans now living have internalized the attitudes, understandings, and patterns of thoughts that allow them to function in and collaborate with these systems of oppression, whether they benefit from them or are placed at a disadvantage by them. The patterns of thought and behaviors that support and help to maintain racism, sexism, classism and other manifestations of oppression are not natural or inherent to any human. They are learned through this socialization process.

Many members of society, both those who benefit from oppression as well as those who are placed at disadvantage, want to work for social change to reduce inequity and bring about greater justice, yet continue to behave in ways that preserve and perpetuate the existing system. This happens because humans are products of their socialization and follow the habits of mind and thought that have been instilled in them. The institutions in which we live reward and reinforce behaviors that perpetuate existing systems and resist efforts toward change.

To be effective as a liberation worker—that is, one who is committed to changing systems and institutions characterized by oppression to create greater equity and social justice—a crucial step is the development of a liberatory consciousness. A liberatory consciousness enables humans to live their lives in oppressive systems and institutions with awareness and intentionality, rather than on the basis of the socialization to which they have been subjected. A liberatory consciousness enables humans to maintain an awareness of the dynamics of oppression characterizing society without giving in to despair and hopelessness about that condition, to maintain an awareness of the role played by each individual in the maintenance of the system without blaming them for the roles they play, and at the same time practice intentionality about changing the systems of oppression. A liberatory consciousness enables humans to live "outside" the patterns of thought and behavior learned through the socialization process that helps to perpetuate oppressive systems.

ELEMENTS OF A LIBERATORY CONSCIOUSNESS

The process for developing a liberatory consciousness has been discussed by many educators working for social change and social justice. Paulo Freire, the Brazilian educator, described it as developing critical consciousness. Carter G. Woodson described it as changing the "miseducation of the Negro." Michael Albert's humanist vision and bell hooks's feminist critical consciousness are examples of other ways that a liberatory consciousness has been discussed.

Four elements in developing a liberatory consciousness are described here. They include awareness, analysis, acting, and accountability/ally-ship. The labeling of these four components in the development of a liberatory consciousness is meant to serve as reminders in our daily living that the development and practice of a liberatory consciousness is neither mysterious nor difficult, static nor fixed, or something that some people have and others do not. It is to be continually practiced event by event, each time we are faced with a situation in which oppression or internalized oppression is evident. These labels remind us that every human can acquire the skill to become a liberation worker.

Awareness, the first part of the task, includes practicing awareness or noticing what is happening. The second part includes analyzing what is happening from a stance of awareness along with the possibilities for action. The third part of the task includes deciding on the basis of that analysis what needs to be done, and seeing to it that the action is accomplished. The fourth part may be the most troublesome part for it requires that individuals accept accountability to self and community for the consequences of the action that has been taken or not taken.

With a liberatory consciousness, every person gets a chance to theorize about issues of equity and social justice, to analyze events related to equity and social justice, and to act in responsible ways to transform the society.

AWARENESS

The awareness component of a liberatory consciousness involves developing the capacity to notice, to give our attention to our daily lives, our language, our behaviors, and even our thoughts. It means making the decision to live our lives from a waking position. It means giving up the numbness and dullness with which we have been lulled into going through life. For some, facing life with awareness may at first seem painful. One student, in a class examining oppression, declared with dismay, "You have taken the fun out of going to the movies. Now I can't watch stupid movies and laugh anymore." This student had observed that even while watching "stupid movies" certain attitudes were being instilled in his consciousness. He noticed that some of these were attitudes and ideas that he would reject if he were consciously paying attention.

Living with awareness means noticing what happens in the world around you. If a salesperson reaches around you to serve the person in line behind you, a liberatory consciousness means taking notice of this act rather than ignoring it, pretending that it did not happen, or thinking it is of little consequence. If disparaging remarks about people of a different group are made in your presence, awareness requires taking note that an event has occurred that effects the maintenance or elimination of oppression. It means noticing that the remark was made, and not pretending that the remark is harmless.

ANALYSIS

A liberatory consciousness requires every individual to not only notice what is going on in the world around her or him, but to think about it and theorize about it—that is, to get information and develop his or her own explanation for what is happening, why it is happening, and what needs to be done about it.

The analysis component of a liberatory consciousness includes the activity of thinking about what needs to be done in a given situation. Every human has the capacity to examine any situation in order to determine what seems to be true about that situation. Awareness coupled with analysis of that situation becomes the basis for determining whether change is required, and if it is, the nature of the change needed.

If what we observe to be true about a given situation seems consistent with our values of an equitable society, then the analysis will conclude that the situation is fine exactly as is. If, on the other hand, the observation leads to the conclusion that the situation is unjust, then a conclusion that the situation needs to be changed is reached.

Analysis will reveal a range of possible courses of action. Each possibility will be examined to determine what results are likely to be produced. Some possible activities will produce results that are consistent with our goals of justice and fairness while some will not. Analysis means considering the range of possible activities and the results that each of them is likely to produce.

ACTION

The action component of a liberatory consciousness proceeds from recognition that awareness and analysis alone are not enough. There can be no division between those who think and those who put thinking into action. The action component of a liberatory consciousness is based on the assumption that the participation of each of us in the liberation project provides the best possibility of gaining liberation for any of us.

The action component of a liberatory consciousness includes deciding what needs to be done, and then seeing to it that action is taken. Sometimes it means taking individual initiative to follow a course of action. Sometimes it means encouraging others to take action. Sometimes it means organizing and supporting other people to feel empowered to take the action that the situation requires. And sometimes, locating the resources that empower another person to act with agency is required. In still other cases, reminding others that they are right for the task, and that they know enough and are powerful enough to take on the challenge of seeing that the task is completed will be the action that is required. In any event, the liberatory consciousness requires each human to take some action in every situation when the opportunity to transform the society and move toward a more just world presents itself.

ACCOUNTABLE/ALLY-SHIP

The socialization to which we have been subjected results in our thinking and behaving in very role-specific ways. We have been socialized into roles of dominant and subordinant. One result is that our vision of possibilities for change is limited by our confinement in the roles to which we have been assigned. Many white people flounder in their efforts to extricate themselves from racist conditioning. They become stuck while working on racism because their socialization to the role of dominant provides very little opportunity to understand what life might be like outside that role. A Person of Color will often have a perspective or "window of understanding" that is unavailable to a white person because of the latter's socialization into whiteness. Left alone in their struggle, some individual white people do eventually figure the difficulty out; many do not. When a Person of Color chooses to share her or his "window of understanding," the growth and development of a white person, away from racist conditioning, can be significantly enhanced and quickened.

Similarly, a Person of Color can become stuck in patterns of internalized racism and left alone to struggle. A white person can hold a perspective that is outside the socialization into racial subordination that, when shared, boosts the efforts of a Person of Color to eliminate patterns of internalized racism. The same holds true for men addressing sexism and for women addressing internalized sexism, as well as for "owning-class" people, those raised poor, and working-class people who are concerned with classism.

People raised on one end of patterns of gender, race, and class subordination or domination can provide a different perspective for people raised on the other end. At the same time, people within role groups can assist other members of their own role group to recognize and eliminate those patterns of thought and behavior that originate in internalized subordination or domination. For example, women, People of Color, those raised poor, and working-class people can help each other better understand the ways that our automatic responses help to perpetuate and maintain our own oppression.

The accountability element of a liberatory consciousness is concerned with how we understand and manage this opportunity and possibility for perspective sharing and allyship in liberation work. Individuals engaged in liberation work can have confidence that, left to their own struggles, others will eventually figure out what they need to know to disentangle thought and behavior patterns from the internalized oppression, either internalized domination or internalized subordination. But working in connection and collaboration with each other, across and within "role" groups, we can make progress in ways that are not apparent when working in isolation and in separate communities.

In our liberation work, many of us have taken the position that is it is not the responsibility of members of the subordinant group to teach or help to educate members of the dominant group. This is a reasonable and essentially "righteous" position. Those people who bear the brunt of the oppression should not be required to also take responsibility for eliminating it. At the same time, it is self-evident that people in the subordinant group can take the lead in setting the world right. For one thing, if people in the dominant group had access to and were able to hold a perspective that allowed them to change systems and patterns of domination, they would have done so already. Members of the subordinant group can wait for members of the dominant group to recognize that their language or behavior is oppressive, or they can share their perspective in every place where it could make a difference, including in the lives of members of the dominant group. In the end, it is in their best interest to do so.

This does not mean that members of groups who have been socialized into roles of subordination should focus their attention outward on the dominant group, or that members of dominant groups should be focused on the subordinant group. It is to suggest that when the perspective of the other group can serve as the critical energy to move things forward, liberation will be hampered if we hold our thinking and perspectives back from each other. Concomitantly, it also suggests that individual members of dominant and subordinant groups offer their perspective to other members of their role group in the effort to move forward.

As liberation workers, it is axiomatic that we will make mistakes. Rather than self-condemnation or blame from others, it will be important to have the opportunity and the openness to hear an analysis from others that allows us to reevaluate problematic behaviors or positions. If a Black person notices another Black person acting out of internalized racism, a liberatory consciousness requires considering the usefulness of sharing a viewpoint that enables that person to explore the implications of internalized racism for their behavior. While we do not take responsibility for another's thinking or behavior, accountability means that we support each other to learn more about the ways that the internalized domination and internalized subordination manifests itself in our lives, and agree with each other that we will act to interrupt it.

Accepting accountability to self and community for the consequences of actions taken or not taken can be an elusive concept for a people steeped in the ideology of individualism. Multiplicities of experiences and points of view contribute to problematizing the concept of accountability as well. None of us can claim for ourselves the right to tell another that her analysis is retrogressive. Recent discussions of "political correctness" can also prove troubling in the effort to grasp the idea of accountability and make it a workable concept.

There will be no easy answers here. The significance of a liberatory consciousness is that we will always question, explore, and interrogate ourselves about possibilities for supporting the efforts of others to come to grips with our conditioning into oppression, and give each other a hand in moving outside of our assigned roles. The accountability element of a liberatory consciousness requires us to develop new agreements regarding our interactions with each other. As a beginning, we get to decide the extent to which we will make ourselves available to interrupt language and behavior patterns that, in our best analysis, originate in an internalization of the ideology of domination and subordination.

SUMMARY

In the end, institutions and systems respond to the initiatives of individuals and groups of individuals. Systems do not perpetuate themselves: they are perpetuated by the actions of people who act automatically on the basis of their socialization. If we all acted on the basis of values and beliefs of our own choosing, systems and institutions would show greater flexibility and propensity for change. As it now stands, most of us act on the basis of values and beliefs instilled in us through the socialization process, designed to prepare us to act in ways that insure the perpetuation of existing systems of oppression.

The development of a liberatory consciousness would allow us the opportunity to reclaim choice in our values and attitudes and consequently, in our response patterns. It would enable us to move from an automatic response system grounded in our socialization, to the capacity to act on a range of responses based on our own awareness, analysis and decision making, and the opportunities we have to learn from our colleagues and other who are themselves embarked on a journey to liberation.

Note

1 I prefer the spelling *subordinant* because: (1) *subordinant* is a noun; *subordinate* is an adjective, modifying the noun; (2) *subordinant* parallels *dominant*, but *subordinate* describes what is done to the *subordinants*; (3) if we were to parallel *subordinate*, then we would need to write *dominate*; and (4) using the modifying adjective to refer to groups of people seems to further objectify and reduce.

130

CONTEXT

Toward a New Vision

Race, Class, and Gender

Patricia Hill Collins

How can we transcend the barriers created by our experiences with race, class and gender oppression in order to build the types of coalitions essential for social change?

Reconceptualizing oppression and seeing the barriers created by race, class and gender as interlocking categories of analysis is a vital first step. But we must transcend these barriers by moving toward race, class and gender as categories of connection, by building relationships and coalitions that will bring about social change. What are some of the issues involved in doing this?

1. DIFFERENCES IN POWER AND PRIVILEGE

First, we must recognize that our differing experiences with oppression create problems in the relationships among us. Each of us lives within a system that vests us with varying levels of power and privilege. These differences in power, whether structured along axes of race, class, gender, age or sexual orientation, frame our relationships. African-American writer June Jordan describes her discomfort on a Caribbean vacation with Olive, the Black woman who cleaned her room:

> . . . even though both "Olive" and "I" live inside a conflict neither one of us created, and even though both of us therefore hurt inside that conflict, I may be one of the monsters she needs to eliminate from her universe and, in a sense, she may be one of the monsters in mine.

> (1985, 47)

Differences in power constrain our ability to connect with one another even when we think we are engaged in dialogue across differences. Let me give you an example. One year, the students in my course "Sociology of the Black Community" got into a heated discussion about the reasons for the upsurge of racial incidents on college campuses. Black students complained vehemently about the apathy and resistance they felt most White students expressed about examining their own racism. Mark, a White male student, found their comments particularly unsettling. After claiming that all the Black people he had ever known had expressed no such beliefs to him, he questioned how representative the viewpoints of his fellow students actually were. When pushed further, Mark revealed that he had participated in conversations over the years with the Black domestic worker employed by his family. Since she had never expressed such strong feelings about White racism, Mark was genuinely shocked by class discussions. Ask yourselves whether that domestic worker was in a position to speak freely. Would it have been wise for her to do so in a situation where the power between the two parties was so unequal?

In extreme cases, members of privileged groups can erase the very presence of the less privileged. When I first moved to Cincinnati, my family and I went on a picnic at a local park. Picnicking next to us was a family of White Appalachians. When I went to push my daughter on the swings, several of the children came over. They had missing, yellowed and broken teeth, they wore old clothing and their poverty was evident. I was shocked. Growing up in a large eastern city, I had never seen such awful poverty among Whites. The segregated neighborhoods in which I grew up made White poverty all but invisible. More importantly, the privileges attached to my newly acquired social class position allowed me to ignore and minimize the poverty among Whites that I did encounter. My reactions to those children made me realize how confining phrases such as "well, at least they're not Black" had become for me. In learning to grant human subjectivity to the Black victims of poverty, I had simultaneously learned to demand White victims of poverty. By applying categories of race to the objective conditions confronting me, I was quantifying and ranking oppressions and missing the very real suffering which, in fact, is the real issue.

One common pattern of relationships across differences in power is one that I label "voyeurism." From the perspective of the privileged, the lives of people of color, of the poor, and of women are interesting for their entertainment value. The privileged become voyeurs, passive onlookers who do not relate to the less powerful, but who are interested in seeing how the "different" live. Over the years, I have heard numerous African-American students complain about professors who never call on them except when a so-called Black issue is being discussed. The students' interest in discussing race or qualifications for doing so appear unimportant to the professor's efforts to use Black students' experiences as stories to make the material come alive for the White student audience. Asking Black students to perform on cue and provide a Black experience for their White classmates can be seen as voyeurism at its worst.

Members of subordinate groups do not willingly participate in such exchanges but often do so because members of dominant groups control the institutional and symbolic apparatuses of oppression. Racial/ethnic groups, women, and the poor have never had the luxury of being voyeurs of the lives of the privileged. Our ability to survive in hostile settings has hinged on our ability to learn intricate details about the behavior and world view of the powerful and adjust our behavior accordingly. I need only point to the difference in perception of those men and women in abusive relationships. Where men can view their girlfriends and wives as sex objects, helpmates and a collection of stereotyped categories of voyeurism—women must be attuned to every nuance of their partners' behavior. Are women "naturally" better in relating to people with more power than themselves, or have circumstances mandated that men and women develop different skills? Another pattern in relationships among people of unequal power concerns a different form of exploitation. In scholarly enterprises, relationships among students and teachers, among researchers and their subjects, and even among us as colleagues in teaching and scholarship can contain elements of academic colonialism. Years ago, a Black co-worker of mine in the Roxbury section of Boston described the academic colonialism he saw among the teachers and scholars in that African-American community:

> The people with notebooks from Harvard come around here and study us. They don't get to know us because they really don't want to and we don't want to let them. They see what they want to see, go back and write their books and get famous off of our problems.

Under academic colonialism, more powerful groups see their subordinates as people that they perceive as subordinate to them, not as entertainment as was the case in voyeurism, but as a resource to be benignly exploited for their own purposes.

The longstanding effort to "colorize" feminist theory by inserting the experiences of women of color represents at best, genuine efforts to reduce bias in women's studies. But at its worst colorization also contains elements of both voyeurism and academic colonialism. As a result of new technologies and perceived profitability, we can now watch black and white movie classics in color. While the tinted images we are offered may be more palatable to the modern viewer, we are still watching the same old movie that was offered to us before. Movie colorization adds little of substance—its contributions remain cosmetic. Similarly, women of color allegedly can teach White feminists nothing about feminism, but must confine ourselves to "colorizing" preexisting feminist theory. Rather than seeing women of color as fully human individuals, we are treated as the additive sum of our categories.

In the academy, patterns of relationships among those of unequal power such as voyeurism and academic colonialism foster reformist postures toward social change. While reformists may aim to make the movie more fun to watch by colorizing their scholarship and teaching via increased lip service to diversity, reformists typically insist on retaining their power to determine what is seen and by whom. In contrast, transformation involves rethinking these differences in power and privilege via dialogues among individuals from diverse groups.

Coming from a tradition where most relationships across difference are squarely rooted in relations of domination and subordination, we have much less experience relating to people as different but equal. The classroom is potentially one powerful and safe space where dialogues among individuals of unequal power relationships can occur. The relationship between Mark, the student in my class, and the domestic worker is typical of a whole series of relationships that people have when they relate across differences in power and privilege. The relationship among Mark and his classmates represents the power of the classroom to minimize those differences so that people of different levels of power can use race, class and gender as categories of analysis in order to generate meaningful dialogues. In this case, the classroom equalized racial difference so that Black students who normally felt silenced spoke out. White students like Mark, generally unaware of how they had been privileged by their whiteness, lost that privilege in the classroom and thus became open to genuine dialogue.

Reconceptualizing course syllabi represents a comparable process of determining which groups are privileged by our current research and pedagogical techniques and which groups are penalized. Reforming these existing techniques can be a critical first step in moving toward a transformed curriculum reflecting race, class and gender as interlocking categories of analysis. But while reform may be effective as a short term strategy, it is unlikely to bring about fundamental transformation in the long term. To me, social transformations, whether of college curricula or of the communities in which we live and work, require moving outside our areas of specialization and groups of interest in order to build coalitions across differences.

2. COALITIONS AROUND COMMON CAUSES

A second issue in building relationships and coalitions essential for social change concerns knowing the real reasons for coalition. Just what brings people together? One powerful catalyst fostering group solidarity is the presence of a common enemy. African-American, Hispanic, Asian-American, and women's studies all share the common intellectual heritage of challenging what passes for certified knowledge in the academy. But politically expedient relationships and coalitions like these are fragile because, as June Jordan points out:

C
O
N
T
E
X
T

It occurs to me that much organizational grief could be avoided if people understood that partnership in misery does not necessarily provide for partnership for change: When we get the monsters off our backs all of us may want to run in very different directions.

(1985, 47)

Sharing a common cause assists individuals and groups in maintaining relationships that transcend their differences. Building effective coalitions involves struggling to hear one another and developing empathy for each other's points of view. The coalitions that I have been involved in that lasted and that worked have been those where commitment to a specific issue mandated collaboration as the best strategy for addressing the issue at hand.

Several years ago, masters degree in hand, I chose to teach in an inner city, parochial school in danger of closing. The money was awful, the conditions were poor, but the need was great. In my job, I had to work with a range of individuals who, on the surface, had very little in common. We had White nuns, Black middle class graduate students, Blacks from the "community," some of whom had been incarcerated and/or were affiliated with a range of federal anti-poverty programs. Parents formed another part of this community, Harvard faculty another, and a few well-meaning White liberals from Colorado were sprinkled in for good measure.

As you might imagine, tension was high. Initially, our differences seemed insurmountable. But as time passed, we found a common bond that we each brought to the school. In spite of profound differences in our personal biographies, differences that in other settings would have hampered our ability to relate to one another, we found that we were all deeply committed to the education of Black children. By learning to value each other's commitment and by recognizing that we each had different skills that were essential to actualizing that commitment, we built an effective coalition around a common cause. Our school was successful, and the children we taught benefitted from the diversity we offered them.

I think that the process of curriculum transformation will require a process comparable to that of political organizing around common causes. None of us alone has a comprehensive vision of how race, class and gender operate as categories of analysis or how they might be used as categories of connection. Our personal biographies offer us partial views. Few of us can manage to study race, class and gender simultaneously. Instead, we each know more about some dimensions of this larger story and less about others. While we each may be committed to an inclusive, transformed curriculum, the task of building one is necessarily a collective effort. Just as the members of the school had special skills to offer to the task of building the school, we have areas of specialization and expertise, whether scholarly, theoretical, pedagogical or within areas of race, class or gender. We do not all have to do the same thing in the same way. Instead, we must support each other's efforts, realizing that they are all part of the larger enterprise of bringing about social change.

3. BUILDING EMPATHY

A third issue involved in building the types of relationships and coalitions essential for social change concerns the issue of individual accountability. Race, class and gender oppression form the structural backdrop against which we frame our relationship—these are the forces that encourage us to substitute voyeurism and academic colonialism for fully human relationships. But while we may not have created this situation, we are each responsible for making individual, personal choices concerning which elements of race, class and gender oppression we will accept and which we will work to change.

One essential component of this accountability involves developing empathy for the experiences of individuals and groups different than ourselves. Empathy begins with taking an interest in the facts of other people lives, both as individuals and as groups. If you care about me, you should want to know not only the details of my personal biography but a sense of how race, class and gender as categories of analysis created the institutional and symbolic backdrop for my personal biography. How can you hope to assess my character without knowing the details of the circumstances I face?

Moreover, by taking a theoretical stance that we have all been affected by race, class and gender as categories of analysis that have structured our treatment, we open up possibilities for using those same constructs as categories of connection in building empathy. For example, I have a good White woman friend with whom I share common interests and beliefs. But we know that our racial differences have provided us with different experiences. So we talk about them. We do not assume that because I am Black, race has only affected me and not her or that because I am a Black woman, race neutralizes the effect of gender in my life while accenting it in hers. We take those same categories of analysis that have created cleavages in our lives, in this case, categories of race and gender, and use them as categories of connection in building empathy for each other's experiences.

Finding common causes and building empathy is difficult, no matter which side of privilege we inhabit. Building empathy from the dominant side of privilege is difficult, simply because individuals from privileged backgrounds are not encouraged to do so. For example, in order for those of you who are White to develop empathy for the experiences of people of color, you must grapple with how your white skin has privileged you. This is difficult to do, because it not only entails the intellectual process of seeing how whiteness is elevated in institutions and symbols, but it also involves the often painful process of seeing how your whiteness has shaped your personal biography. Intellectual stances against the institutional and symbolic dimensions of racism are generally easier to maintain than sustained self-reflection about how racism has shaped all of our individual biographies. Were and are your fathers, uncles, and grandfathers really more capable than mine, or can their accomplishments be explained in part by the racism members of my family experienced? Did your mothers stand silently by and watch all this happen? More importantly, how have they passed on the benefits of their whiteness to you?

These are difficult questions, and I have tremendous respect for my colleagues and students who are trying to answer them. Since there is no compelling reason to examine the source and meaning of one's own privilege, I know that those who do so have freely chosen this stance. They are making conscious efforts to root out the piece of the oppressor planted within them. To me, they are entitled to the support of people of color in their efforts. Men who declare themselves feminists, members of the middle class who ally themselves with anti-poverty struggles, heterosexuals who support gays and lesbians, are all trying to grow, and their efforts place them far ahead of the majority who never think of engaging in such important struggles.

Building empathy from the subordinate side of privilege is also difficult, but for different reasons. Members of subordinate groups are understandably reluctant to abandon a basic mistrust of members of powerful groups because this basic mistrust has traditionally been central to their survival. As a Black woman, it would be foolish for me to assume that White women, or Black men, or White men or any other group with a history of exploiting African-American women have my best interests at heart. These groups enjoy varying amounts of privilege over me and therefore I must carefully watch them and be prepared for a relation of domination and subordination.

Like the privileged, members of subordinate groups must also work toward replacing judgments by category with new ways of thinking and acting. Refusing to do so stifles prospects for effective coalition and social change. Let me use another example from my own experiences. When I was an undergraduate, I had little time or patience for the theorizing of the privileged. My initial years at a private, elite institution were difficult, not because the coursework was challenging (it was, but that wasn't what distracted me) or because I had to work while my classmates lived on family allowances (I was used to work). The adjustment was difficult because I was surrounded by so many people who took their privilege for granted. Most of them felt entitled to their wealth. That astounded me.

I remember one incident of watching a White woman down the hall in my dormitory try to pick out which sweater to wear. The sweaters were piled up on her bed in all the colors of the rainbow, sweater after sweater. She asked my advice in a way that let me know that choosing a sweater was one of the most important decisions she had to make on a daily basis. Standing knee-deep in her sweaters, I realized how different our lives were. She did not have to worry about maintaining a solid academic average so that she could receive financial aid. Because she was in the majority, she was not treated as a representative of her race. She did not have to consider how her classroom comments or basic existence on campus contributed to the treatment her group would receive. Her allowance protected her from having to work, so she was free to spend her time studying, partying, or in her case, worrying about which sweater to wear. The degree of inequality in our lives and her unquestioned sense of entitlement concerning that inequality offended me. For a while, I categorized all affluent White women as being superficial, arrogant, overly concerned with material possessions, and part of my problem. But had I continued to classify people in this way, I would have missed out on making some very good friends whose discomfort with their inherited or acquired social class privileges pushed them to examine their position.

. . . As we go forth to the remaining activities of this workshop, and beyond this workshop, we might do well to consider Lorde's perspective:

> Each of us is called upon to take a stand. So in these days ahead, as we examine ourselves and each other, our works, our fears, our differences, our sisterhood and survivals, I urge you to tackle what is most difficult for us all, self-scrutiny of our complacencies, the idea that since each of us believes she is on the side of right, she need not examine her position.
>
> (1985)

I urge you to examine your position.

References

Lorde, Audre. (1985). "Sisterhood and Survival." Keynote address, conference on the Black Woman Writer and the Diaspora, Michigan State University.
Jordan, June. (1985). *On Call: Political Essays.* Boston: South End Press.

131

What Can We Do?

Allan G. Johnson

. . .

The problem of privilege and oppression is deep and wide, and to work with it we have to be able to see it clearly so that we can talk about it in useful ways. To do that, we have to reclaim some difficult language that names what's going on, language that has been so misused and maligned that it generates more heat than light. We can't just stop using words like *racism, sexism, ableism,* and *privilege,* however, because these are tools that focus our awareness on the problem and all the forms it takes. Once we can see and talk about what's going on, we can analyze how it works as a system. We can identify points of leverage where change can begin.

. . .

For several centuries, capitalism has provided the economic context for privilege and oppression. As such, it has been and continues to be a powerful force, especially in relation to class, gender, and race. Its effects are both direct and indirect. Historically, it was the engine that drove the development of modern racism. In a less direct way, it creates conditions of scarcity that set the stage for competition, fear, and antagonism directed across differences of race, ethnicity, and gender. Through the class differences that it creates, it also shapes people's experience of privilege and the lack of it. This is an example of the matrix of domination (or matrix of privilege) through which the various forms of difference and privilege interact and shape one another.

. . .

Although disadvantaged groups take the brunt of the trouble, privileged groups are also affected by it, partly because misery visited on others comes back to haunt those who benefit from it, especially in the form of defensiveness and fear. But trouble also affects privileged groups directly by limiting and shaping the lives of people who have privilege. The trouble also affects entire social systems, from families to corporations and schools to communities, societies, and global political and economic systems.

The greatest barrier to change is that dominant groups . . . don't see the trouble as *their* trouble, which means they don't feel obliged to do something about it. This happens for a variety of reasons—because they don't know the trouble exists in the first place, because they don't *have* to see it as their trouble, because they see it as a personal rather than a systemic problem, because they're reluctant to give up privilege, because they feel angry and deprived and closed to the idea that they have privilege, because they're blinded by prejudice, because they're afraid of what will happen if they acknowledge the reality of privilege and oppression.

. . .

[To] think about the trouble as everyone's responsibility—everybody's "hook"—and nobody's fault . . . is especially useful for members of privileged groups who have a hard time seeing themselves in relation to privilege without feeling guilty. It's easy to fall into this trap because people tend to use an individualistic model of the world that reduces everything to individual intentions and goodness or badness. A powerful and liberating alternative comes from the fact that we're always participating in something larger than ourselves, social systems. To understand privilege and oppression, we have to look at what we're participating in *and* how we participate . . . . This means we can be involved in a society's or organization's troubles without doing anything wrong and without being bad people.

Privilege is created and maintained through social systems that are dominated by, centered on, and identified with privileged groups. A racist society, for example, is white-dominated, white-centered, and white-identified. Since privilege is rooted primarily in systems—such as families, schools, and workplaces—change isn't simply a matter of changing people. The solution also has to include entire systems [that] . . . shape how people feel, think, and behave as individuals, how they see themselves and one another.

. . .

With this approach, we can begin to think about how to make ourselves part of the solution to the problem of privilege and oppression. . . .

It is in small and humble choices that privilege, oppression, and the movement toward something better actually happen.

. . . WHAT CAN WE DO?

. . .

ACKNOWLEDGE THAT PRIVILEGE AND OPPRESSION EXISTS

A key to the continued existence of every system of privilege is unawareness, because privilege contradicts so many basic human values that it invariably arouses opposition when people know about it. . . .

This is why most cultures of privilege mask the reality of oppression by denying its existence, trivializing it, calling it something else, blaming it on those most victimized by it, or diverting attention from it. Instead of treating oppression as a serious problem, we go to war or get embroiled in controversial "issues" such as capital gains tax cuts or "family values" or immigrant workers. There would be far more active opposition to white privilege, for example, if white people lived with an ongoing awareness of how it actually affects the everyday lives of those it oppresses as "not white." . . .

It's one thing to become aware and quite another to stay that way. The greatest challenge when we first become aware of a critical perspective on the world is simply to hang on to it. . . . In some ways, it's harder and more important to pay attention to systems of privilege than it is to people's behavior . . . . [F]or example, the structure of capitalism creates large social patterns of inequality, scarcity, and exploitation that have played and continue to play a major role in the perpetuation of various forms of privilege and oppression. It is probably wishful thinking to suppose we can end privilege without also changing a capitalist system of political economy that allows an elite to control the vast majority of wealth and income and leaves the rest of the population to fight over what's left. But such wishful thinking is, in fact, what we're encouraged to engage in most of the time—to cling to the idea that racism, for example, is just a problem with a few bad whites, rather than seeing how it is connected to a much larger matrix of privilege and oppression.

. . .

By itself, however, changing how we think won't be enough to solve the problem. Privilege will not simply go away as the result of a change in individual consciousness. Ultimately, we'll have to apply our understanding of how systems work to the job of changing systems themselves—economic, political, religious, educational, and familial. . . .

Maintaining a critical consciousness takes commitment and work. Awareness is something that either we maintain in the moment or we don't. And the only way to hang on to an awareness of privilege is to make that awareness an ongoing part of our lives.

PAY ATTENTION

Understanding how privilege and oppression operate and how you participate is where working for change begins. It's easy to have opinions, but it takes work to know what you're talking about. The simplest way to begin is to make reading about privilege part of your life. Unless you have the luxury of a personal teacher, you can't understand this issue without reading. Many people assume they already know what they need to know because it's part of everyday life. But they're usually wrong, because just as the last thing a fish would discover is water, the last thing people discover is society itself and something as pervasive as privilege.

We also have to be open to the idea that what we think we know is, if not wrong, so deeply shaped by systems of privilege that it misses most of the truth. This is why activists talk with one another and spend time reading one another's writing, because seeing things clearly is tricky. This is also why people who are critical of the status quo are so often self-critical as well—they know how complex and elusive the truth really is and what a challenge it is to work toward it. . . .

As you educate yourself, avoid reinventing the wheel. Many people have already done a lot of work that you can learn from. There's no way to get through it all, but you don't have to in order to develop a clear enough sense of how to act in meaningful and informed ways. . . . Men who feel there is no place for them in women's studies might start with books about patriarchy and gender inequality that are written by men. In the same way, whites can begin with writings on race privilege written by other whites. Sooner or later, however, dominant groups will need to turn to what people in subordinate groups have written, because they are the ones who have done most of the work of figuring out how privilege and oppression operate.

Reading is only the beginning. At some point you have to look at yourself and the world to see if you can identify what you're reading about. . . .

[T]aking responsibility means not waiting for others to tell you what to do, to point out what's going on, or to identify alternatives. If dominant groups are going to take their share of responsibility, it's up to them to listen, watch, ask, and listen again, to make it their business to find out for themselves. If they don't, they'll slide down the comfortable blindered path of privilege. And then they'll be *just* part of the problem and they *will* be blamed and they'll have it coming.

LEARN TO LISTEN

Attentive listening is especially difficult for members of dominant groups. If someone confronts you with your own behavior that supports privilege, . . . [d]on't tell them they're too sensitive or need a better sense of humor, and don't try to explain away what you did as something else than what they're telling you it was. Don't say you didn't mean it or that you were only kidding. Don't tell them what a champion of justice you are or how hurt you feel because of what they're telling you. Don't make jokes or try to be cute or charming, since only access to privilege can lead someone to believe these are acceptable responses to something as serious as privilege and oppression. Listen to what's being said. Take it seriously. Assume for the time being that it's true, because . . . it probably is. And then take responsibility to do something about it.

. . .

LITTLE RISKS: DO SOMETHING

. . .

When you *openly* change how you participate in a system, you do more than change your own behavior; you also change how the system happens. When you change how a system happens, you change the social environment that shapes other people's behavior, which, in turn, further changes how the system happens. And when you do that, you also help to change the consequences that come out of the dynamic relationship between systems and individuals, including patterns of privilege and oppression.

. . .

As you become more aware, questions will arise about what goes on at work, in the media, in families, in communities, in religious institutions, in government, on the street, and at school—in short, just about everywhere. The questions don't come all at once (for which we can be grateful), although they sometimes come in a rush that can feel overwhelming. If you remind yourself that it isn't up to you to do it all, however, you can see plenty of situations in which you can make a difference, sometimes in surprisingly simple ways. Consider the following possibilities.

Make noise, be seen. Stand up, volunteer, speak out, write letters, sign petitions, show up. Every oppressive system feeds on silence. Don't collude in it. Breaking the silence is especially important for dominant groups, because it undermines the assumption of solidarity that privilege depends on. If this feels too risky, practice being aware of how silence reflects your investment in solidarity with other dominant-group members. This can be a place to begin working on how you participate in making privilege and oppression happen: "Today I said nothing, colluded in silence, and this is how I benefited from it. Tomorrow I can try something different."

Find little ways to withdraw support from . . . [oppressive systems,] starting with yourself. It can be as simple as not laughing at a racist or heterosexist joke or saying you don't think it's funny, or writing a letter to your senator or representative or the editor of your newspaper, objecting to an instance of sexism in the media. When my local newspaper ran an article whose headline referred to sexual harassment as "earthy behavior," for example, I wrote a letter pointing out that harassment has nothing to do with being "earthy."

The key to withdrawing support is to interrupt the flow of business as usual. You can subvert the assumption that everyone's going along with the status quo by simply not going along. When you do this, you stop the flow, if only for a moment, but in that moment other people can notice and start to think and question. It's a perfect time to suggest the possibility of alternatives, such as humor that isn't at someone else's expense, or of ways to think about discrimination, harassment, and violence that do justice to the reality of what's going on and how it affects people.

. . .

Dare to make people feel uncomfortable, beginning with yourself. At the next local school board meeting, for example, you can ask why principals and other administrators are almost always white and male (unless your system is an exception that proves the rule), while the teachers they supervise and the lower-paid support staff are mostly women and people of color. Or look at the names and mascots used by local sports teams and see if they exploit the heritage and identity of Native Americans. If that's the case, ask principals and coaches and owners about it. Consider asking similar kinds of questions about privilege and difference in your place of worship, workplace, and local government.

It may seem that such actions don't amount to much, until you stop for a moment and feel your resistance to doing them—worrying, for example, about how easily you could make people uncomfortable, including yourself. If you take that resistance to action as a measure of power, then your potential to make a difference is plain to see. The potential for people to feel uncomfortable is a measure of the power for change inherent in such simple acts of not going along with the status quo.

Some will say it isn't "nice" to make people uncomfortable, but systems of privilege do a lot more than make people feel uncomfortable, and there isn't anything "nice" about allowing that to continue. Besides, discomfort is an unavoidable part of any meaningful process of change. You can't grow without being willing to challenge your assumptions and take yourself to the edge of your competencies, where you're bound to feel uncomfortable. If you can't tolerate ambiguity, uncertainty, and discomfort, then you'll never get beneath superficial appearances or learn or change anything of much value, including yourself.

. . .

Openly choose and model alternative paths. [Identifying] . . . alternatives and [following] . . . them openly so that other people can see what we're doing . . . creates tension in a system, which moves toward resolution . . . . We don't have to convince anyone of anything. As Gandhi put it, the work begins with us trying to be the change we want to see happen in the world. If you think this has no effect, watch how people react to the slightest departures from established paths and how much effort they expend trying to ignore or explain away or challenge those who choose alternative paths.

Actively promote change in how systems are organized around privilege. The possibilities here are almost endless, because social life is complicated and privilege is everywhere. You can, for example,

Speak out for equality in the workplace.

Promote awareness and training around issues of privilege.

Support equal pay and promotion practices for everyone.

Oppose the devaluing of women, people of color, and people with disabilities, and the work they do, from dead-end jobs to glass ceilings.

Support the well-being of mothers, children, and people with disabilities, and defend their right to control their bodies and their lives.

Don't support businesses that are inaccessible to people with disabilities, and tell them why you don't.

Don't support businesses that engage in unfair labor practices, including union-busting. Support the formation of unions. Although the U.S. labor movement has a long history of racism, sexism, and ableism, unions are currently one of the few organized efforts dedicated to protecting workers from the excesses of capitalism.

Become aware of how class divisions operate in social systems, from workplaces to schools, and how this results in the oppression of blue- and white-collar workers. Find out, for example, if staff at your college or university are paid a living wage, and speak up if they aren't. There is a great silence in this country around issues of class, in part because the dominant cultural ideology presents the United States as a classless society. Break the silence.

Oppose the increasing concentration of wealth and power in the United States and the global economy. The lower, working, and lower-middle classes are the last to benefit from economic upturns and the first to suffer from economic downturns. Press politicians and candidates for public office to take a stand on issues of class, starting with the acknowledgment that they exist.

. . .

When you witness someone else taking a risk—speaking out, calling attention to privilege and oppression—don't wait until later to tell them in private you're glad they did. Waiting until you're alone makes it safer for you but does the other person little good. Support is most needed when the risk is being taken, not later on, so don't wait. Make your support as visible and public as the courageous behavior that you're supporting.

Support the right of women and men to love whomever they choose. Raise awareness of homophobia and heterosexism. For example, ask school officials and teachers about what's happening to gay and lesbian students in local schools. If they don't know, ask them to find out, since it's a safe bet these students are being harassed, suppressed, and oppressed by others at one of the most vulnerable stages of life. When sexual orientation is discussed, whether in the media or among friends, raise questions about its relation to male privilege. Remember that it isn't necessary to have answers to questions in order to ask them.

Pay attention to how different forms of oppression interact with one another. There has been a great deal of struggle within women's movements, for example, about the relationship between male privilege and privilege in other forms, especially those based on race, social class, and sexual orientation. . . .

One way out of this conflict is to realize that male privilege isn't problematic just because it emphasizes *male* dominance but because it values and promotes dominance and control as ends in themselves. In that sense, all forms of oppression draw support from common roots, and whatever we do that calls attention to those roots undermines *all* forms of privilege. If working against male privilege is seen simply as enabling some women to get a bigger piece of the pie, then some women probably will "succeed" at the expense of others who are disadvantaged by race, class, sexual orientation, and disability status. . . . [I]f we identify the core problem as *any* society organized around principles of domination and privilege, then changing *that* requires us to pay attention to all the forms of privilege those principles promote. Whether we begin with race or gender or disability or class or the capitalist system, if we name the problem correctly we'll wind up going in the same general direction.

Work with other people. This is one of the most important principles of participating in change. From expanding consciousness to taking risks, working with people who support what you're trying to do makes all the difference in the world. . . .

Make contact. Connect to other people engaged in the same work. Do whatever reminds you that you're not alone in this.

It is especially important to form alliances across difference, . . . for whites to listen to people of color, for example—and to give credence to what people say about their own experience. This isn't easy to do, of course, since members of dominant groups may not like what they hear about their privilege from those who are most damaged by it. It is difficult to hear anger and not take it personally, but that is what allies have to be willing to do. It's also difficult for members of privileged groups to realize how mistrusted they are by subordinate groups and to not take that personally as well. . . .

In many ways, the biggest challenge for members of privileged groups is to work with one another on issues of privilege rather than trying to help members of subordinate groups. . . . For members of privileged groups to become allies, they must recall Frederick Douglass's words that "power concedes nothing without a demand" and add their weight to that demand. When dominant groups work against privilege, they do more than add their voices. They also make it more difficult for other members of dominant groups to dismiss calls for change as simply the actions of "special interest groups" trying to better their position.

. . .

Don't keep it to yourself. A corollary of looking for company is not to restrict your focus to the tight little circle of your own life. . . . At some point, taking responsibility means acting in a larger context, even if that means letting just one other person know what you're doing. It makes sense to start with yourself, but it's equally important not to end with yourself.

A good way to convert personal change into something larger is to join an organization dedicated to changing the systems that produce privilege and oppression. . . .

V
O
I
C
E
S

If all this sounds overwhelming, remember again that you don't have to deal with everything. You don't have to set yourself the impossible task of transforming society or even yourself. All you can do is what you can *manage* to do, secure in the knowledge that you're making it easier for other people—now and in the future—to see and do what *they* can do. So, rather than defeat yourself before you start, think small, humble, and doable rather than large, heroic, and impossible. Don't paralyze yourself with impossible expectations. . . .

Don't let other people set the standard for you. Start where you are and work from there. Make lists of all the things you could actually imagine *doing*—from reading another book about privilege to suggesting policy changes at school or work to protesting against capitalism to raising questions about who cleans the bathroom at home—and rank them from the most risky to the least. Start with the least risky and set reasonable goals ("What small risk for change will I take *today?*"). As you get more experienced at taking risks, you can move up your list. You can commit yourself to whatever the next steps are for you, the tolerable risks, the contributions that offer some way—however small it might seem—to help balance the scales. As long as you do something, it counts.

In the end, taking responsibility doesn't have to involve guilt and blame, letting someone off the hook, or being on the hook yourself. It simply means acknowledging an obligation to make a contribution to finding a way out of the trouble we're all in and to finding constructive ways to act on that obligation. You don't have to do anything dramatic or earth-shaking to help change happen. As powerful as systems of privilege are, they cannot stand the strain of lots of people doing something about it, beginning with the simplest act of naming the system out loud.

132

Prison Writings

My Life Is My Sundance

Leonard Peltier

Out of death comes life. Out of pain comes hope. This I have learned these long years of loss. Loss, but never despair. I have never lost hope or an absolute belief in the rightness of my cause, which is my People's survival.

I don't know how to save the world. I don't have the answers or The Answer. I hold no secret knowledge as to how to fix the mistakes of generations past and present. I only know that without compassion and respect for *all* of Earth's inhabitants, none of us will survive—nor will we deserve to.

The future, our mutual future, the future of all the peoples of humanity must be founded on respect. Let respect be both the catchword and the watchword of the new millennium we are now all entering together. Just as we want others to respect us, so we need to show respect to others.

We are in this together—the rich, the poor, the red, the white, the black, the brown, and the yellow. We are all one family of humankind. We share responsibility for our Mother the Earth and for all those who live and breathe upon her.

I believe our work will be unfinished until not one human being is hungry or battered, not a single person is forced to die in war, not one innocent languishes imprisoned, and no one is persecuted for his or her beliefs.

I believe in the good in humankind. I believe that the good can prevail, but only with great effort. And that effort is ours, each of ours, yours and mine.

We must be prepared for the danger that will surely come our way. Critics will attack us, try to distance us from each other and mock our sincerity. But if we are strong in our beliefs, we can reverse their assaults and grow even stronger in our commitments to Mother Earth, our struggles, and our future generations of children.

Never cease in the fight for peace, justice and equality for all people. Be persistent in all that you do and don't allow anyone to sway you from your conscience.

Sitting Bull said, "As individual fingers we can easily be broken, but all together we make a mighty fist."

The struggle is ours to win or lose.

V O I C E S

133

Allies

Gloria E. Anzaldúa

Becoming allies means helping each other heal. It can be hard to expose yourself and your wounds to a stranger who could be an ally or an enemy. But if you and I were to do good alliance work together, be good allies to each other, I would have to expose my wounds to you and you would have to expose your wounds to me and then we could start from a place of openness. During our alliance work, doors will close and we'll have to open them up again. People who engage in alliances and are working toward certain goals want to keep their personal feelings out of it, but you can't. You have to work out your personal problems while you are working out the problems of this particular community or this particular culture.

When you are doing alliance work it is very important to say who you are. For example, I am a Chicana, Mexicana, dyke, whatever. I come from a *campesina* background but I have now put one foot into middle-classness. I belong to the *inteligencia*, the intelligence class, the artistic class as an artist, and I am speaking today to you as all these people, but primarily as a Chicana or as a dyke, etc. You must situate yourself and tell what your stance is on particular things, so other allies know exactly where you are coming from. And they can later say, "Oh you say that you are talking from a working-class perspective but you have a house, you have a car, you have these privileges, you are a professor, or a salaried publisher, a privileged writer, etc." Allies might challenge some of your positions as a first step in finding out whether you are a real potential ally. Then you can get a sense of whether you can trust this person or not. And you go with your gut feeling. You go with how you feel, because sometimes they will say all the politically correct rhetoric, but you just know that they are trying to put one over on you.

I have edited three books, *This Bridge Called My Back*, *Haciendo Caras*, and *Signs: Theorizing Lesbian Experience*. In the first two books I consider anthologizing as my way of making alliances with women of color. In *Signs* it was more (or less) white women wanting to make alliances with lesbians of color. Many lesbians of color I asked to submit work didn't, because they didn't trust *Signs* because they know it to be elitist, esoteric and racist.

In the books that other people anthologize me in, some editors are very genuine and want to diversify their community. Then there are the anthologizers that call on me so that dykes of color will not call them and say, "You have one contributor of color and ninety white contributors, this is racist!" So they attempt to tokenize me, or they try to pull a fast one on their readers, by tokenizing in general. Some of my work is hard to assimilate and I consider assimilation in white culture like an amoeba trying to swallow me. But it is hard for them to assimilate me in that manner because of language and because of the way that I write. They can ignore some issues that I bring out, but because of my writing style, there are things they must confront. I don't write like a white person. I don't write like an academic or follow those rules. I break them.

If they can't assimilate my writing what they try and do is assimilate me, by tokenizing me. They bring me into their book, or into their conference, or into their alliance in a way that will acknowledge the easy stuff I raise, but ignore the more dangerous stuff. They try to do this to me all the time, so then I have to respond back, either on the phone or in a letter, and say, why? One anthology that asked for my work was called *Growing Up Latino*. Before I agreed to publish in it, I had this whole dialogue with one of the editors, and talked about naming the book Latino and not Chicano. I asked "How many Chicanos/Chicanas are in your book? How many are Latina and how do they identify themselves?" Once the magazine *New Chicano Writing* asked me to sit on their board. I called and voiced my objections to the editor before I agreed to join: I objected having Chica*no* writers but not Chica*na* in the title, and furthermore told them that the groundbreaking writing being done in the Chicano/Chicana community was by women. I also objected to their project only accepting work written in English. So the editor went home and thought about the issues and later called me and said, "I've changed the title of the magazine to New Chicana/Chicano writing, and people can write in Spanish, they can do bilingual, and they can do *Tex Mex*." Then I felt like the editor was open to me, and I agreed to be on their editorial board.

The biggest risk in forming alliances is betrayal. When you are betrayed you feel shitty. When I have been betrayed I have felt stupid, like why did I trust this person and allow this person to stab me in the back, it's all my fault, you know the victim syndrome. Betrayal, especially with Chicanas, betrayal is a big thing, because we were betrayed as women, as Indians, as a *minority* in this country, everything. We have been stabbed in the back by all of these various people. And betrayal makes you feel like less of a person, you feel shame, it reduces your self-esteem. It is politically deadening and dangerous, it's disempowering. When you lose your self-esteem you no longer trust yourself to make value judgments about other people, you lose confidence in yourself and your values. When a whole person is slowly destroyed, and this is what women of color are suffering from, their personhood is destroyed.

At first I felt really good belonging to the lesbian community, even though it was mostly white. It made me feel like where I had no home, I now had a new one. But after two or three or four years, I started looking at power, and who had power and who was trying to define for me what I was as a Chicana lesbian. I realized how my voice was silent and how my history was ignored and that drove me into looking at my roots, my queer roots in my own culture. I had to get a positive sense of being queer from my culture, not just from the white culture. Now I am in a place where I can look at both the white lesbian community and my own culture that is only beginning to have groups of lesbians organizing. *Ellas San Antonio* is a group of Chicana dykes, *Amigas y Que*, in Houston and Austin. But they were not in place when I was coming out. Chicana dyke organizations are just now coming into their power.

Now I look at my culture and white culture and the whole planet. I look at other nationalities and how they deal with their queer people, I'm getting a global perspective on being a queer person. And sometimes I feel very comfortable with a bunch of white dykes and other times I feel totally invisible, ignored. I feel that they only see the queer part of me. They don't see the Chicana part of me or the working class part of me. As long as I leave my class and culture outside the door when I enter a room full of white dykes I am okay, but if I bring in my race or class, then my role as educator starts.

I think that most white dykes really want a community that is diversified. And sometimes they want it so badly that they want to put everybody under this queer umbrella and say we are all in this together and we are all equal. But we are not equal. In their thirst and hunger for this diversity the issues of class and race are issues that they don't even want to examine, because they feel like they're divisive. So they are hungry for being politically correct and having women of color in their organizations, in their syllabi, and as performers, singers, writers and lovers. But a lot of times in order to bring us under the queer umbrella they will ignore or collapse the differences, not really deal with the issues. When it comes down to the numbers of who has power or *how many* dykes of color are getting in this anthology and how many don't—in terms of the real work, they fail. I mean the ideas are good, like the greater numbers/the greater strength kind of thing but they want us to leave our race and our class in the check room when we enter their space.

As a group, I think dykes are more progressively political than any other group because of feminism, and because of being (at least) doubly oppressed. Because they have been oppressed as dykes, I believe white lesbians are more apt to recognize the oppression of women of color. So they have a true wanting of multi-cultural groups. And there are always the false ones of course, there are always the ones that do want it to be white. But there is some honest motivation about wanting to be allies and in this they still have a lot of work to do. For example, one of the things they often don't contend with is the unconscious motivation of doing it out of guilt. But I am very hopeful and I think that I am one of the very few people. I think that most people of my age or younger have been burned out and disillusioned and feel like it's the pits right now. Much younger people than me have no hope, do not see alliances working, do not see white people reaching out or doing their work, and do not see the possibility of white people changing perspectives. Or allowing change to come into their lives, but I do.

134

Social Struggle

Chip Smith

. . . As people connect with others actively engaged in struggle—and reach out to new forces in creative ways—the movement grows. Organizations gain experience, resources, and influence. The systematic character of oppression becomes clearer. Social forces join together, work through differences, learn how to challenge for political power and carry through social transformation.

. . . Here we want to suggest an approach to organizing that over time will have the greatest chance of bringing into being a strategic front against white supremacy and racism.

STAY CENTERED ON SELF-DETERMINATION, AFFIRMATIVE ACTION, AND INTERNATIONALISM

Self-determination focuses attention on the central demand for political power by . . . oppressed . . . peoples. Without the fundamental democratic right to political power . . . the system of white supremacy and the racist ideas it generates in people's minds will continue. The struggles to end patriarchy and capitalism also involve questions of power—in personal relations through to the organized power of the working class to reshape society, with leadership centered among the oppressed. . . .

Affirmative action in its broadest sense is simply another way to talk about ending privilege. It emphasizes the historic roots of race and gender privilege and calls for proactive policies to set matters straight—affirmative action on the job, in the home, in popular culture, in the criminal justice system, in politics and throughout society. By orienting to the struggles of people of color at any particular moment, white organizers can distinguish the specific form the struggle is taking at the moment—be it for reparations, Katrina reconstruction, or immigration rights; or for an end to right-to-work laws or male violence.

Internationalism is a third bedrock perspective, because of the imperialist role of the United States in the world. This standpoint allows people to see clearly the underlying forces driving an issue like immigration, for example, or the war in Iraq, the "War against Drugs" in Colombia, and the "War on Terror" generally. It helps one be mindful of the material benefits—and associated racial and national prejudices—that come from living in a superpower in the Global North. Armed with this awareness, one can then—as a simple act of solidarity and with no special recognition due—turn that privilege around and target U.S. imperialism from the inside. The prescription to "Think globally, act locally" is sound—but it can be broadened to "Think globally, act globally," as well. . . .

START WHERE PEOPLE ARE AT

"Starting where people are at" is a truism of organizing—but it has two aspects. The first is the obvious call to listen to what people say without prejudgment and without pushing

NEXT STEPS

one's own views on others. In particular, for white people organizing among white work-ers, it means not leading with a rap on white privilege. The perspective of this book holds that white working class people are oppressed by capitalism. So the first step in organizing is to get a concrete feel for the ways people experience their lives and understand their situation. This listening aspect can help organizers appreciate both the problems people face and the ways they have to resolve them. Some individuals will be more active; others will be more passive—but observing all the while what is going on. And a few may be a source of issues themselves. By sorting out what the concerns are and who is dealing with them in what ways, an organizer can begin to get a sense of which folks to connect up with in a supportive way, and around which key issues.

The second aspect of this approach is less obvious. It comes down to being a true friend to folks you are working with. If the United States is white supremacist; if white folks are privileged simply by virtue of their skin color; and if this privilege has negative conse-quences for white people themselves, as well as for others—then there is an obligation to share this understanding and discuss it through with people. What makes the conversation possible is the underlying unity established by working together on issues of recognized importance. The overall learning process is two ways—but the main responsibility in con-necting with people is the organizer's.

   . . .

GO BROADER AND DEEPER

When engaging in struggle, the challenge often is to broaden the ranks of the forces fighting around an issue—take ending the war in Iraq, as one example. Two different approaches are possible for primarily white organizations in this situation: One amounts to activists' asking people of color to "come join our . . ." coalition, demonstration, or organization. As a way to entice a new constituency to take part in a demonstration, for example, the peace group might invite a speaker, include a slogan, or encourage an information table at their event. None of these steps is bad in itself, and the result can be a richer learning experience for the people who attend the demonstration. But the likelihood of large-scale participation by the new constituency is small at best.

A second approach is more long term in its outlook but carries with it the prospect of real unity of action in the future. Here the organizers identify issues of concern to the new constituency—perhaps by first bringing a speaker to the peace group's orga-nizational meeting. The second step is then to offer organizational support to one or several groups within the new constituency that are active—say, around police violence, domestic abuse, or LGBTQ rights. By actually following through on the commitment of support, the original peace group develops new ties with people in the community, learns the kinds of pressures people are experiencing in their lives, and in the course of joint activity gains some first-hand understanding of people's attitudes toward the war. Over time, these relationships generate a new, richer common language of resistance to oppression at home, as well as to the war. The peace folks bring their people out to dem-onstrations against police abuse. And when the next peace demonstration comes along, new community forces may now decide to be part of the planning process—helping to shape the event in a way that resonates with their community. By actively linking up in this way, primarily white organizations can transform their outlook and put their rela-tive privilege to work—through their personal connections and networks or fundraising skills—to oppose the concrete, material disadvantages being experienced by folks of color.

NEXT STEPS

DEVELOP CONSCIOUSNESS, THEORY, VALUES

People learn best from their own experience. People can hear all the arguments about why gay and lesbian folks are the same as everyone else and should enjoy the same rights. But until heterosexual folks meet and become friends with real human beings, the issue remains abstract. Personal relationships are critical—across the color line, among different oppressed nationality peoples, or with women in positions of leadership.

On becoming socially active, people are often open to new ideas as they search for ways to advance their issues. Engaging in struggle helps a person understand who holds power and what it takes to bring about a favorable result—what arguments work, in what settings, and with how many people mobilized to get the point across. No amount of discussion or study conveys a sense of popular power better than taking part in a campaign—win or lose. But people draw the clearest lessons through evaluating their collective experience together with others.

. . .

THE ROLE OF THEORY

. . . [T]heoretical work is essential to keep a movement on the path toward its goals, while adapting to changing circumstances.

Not paying attention to the deep structure of society and to long-term principles, by contrast, almost always leads people and organizations to conform to the system, even if they start out in militant opposition. . . . A community struggle around a school can turn into a platform for someone to run for city council—OK as far as it goes. But if that person's career becomes the goal instead of empowering the community, the campaign goes off track.

In general, campaigns can be summed up from three standpoints:

- What were the immediate benefits or losses from the struggle?
- To what extent did the broader popular movement gain strength?
- Were forces won to a deeper understanding of society, to the need for revolutionary organization, and to committing for the long haul?

A fourth criterion that overlaps the first two can be drawn out as well: Was there an advance in the battle for the minds of the broader public? Contesting the hegemony of ruling class ideas is critical to developing conditions where a mass movement can take hold and flourish.

By evaluating experience collectively along these dimensions, a movement deepens its theoretical understanding of the system and how to oppose it effectively. Also, individuals' summing up their personal experiences using these criteria can help people stay on course—by gaining insight into their strengths and weaknesses and clarifying how best to contribute to the struggle.

PHILOSOPHICAL OUTLOOK

Carrying the process of social activism and reflection more deeply can bring people to a philosophical outlook that embraces change and the power of ordinary people to transform the world. Seeing oneself in the flow of a constantly changing reality empowers people to relax into their role as change agents. Otherwise their activism can seem exceptional—passivity being the normal state—and required only by temporary difficulties in their lives. . . .

SOCIAL JUSTICE VALUES

The social justice movement embodies a set of values that can be brought to consciousness, validated, and taught to others. These values are secular in origin, emerging out of the concrete conditions of contemporary struggle. At the same time they overlap with the teachings of many religions, without requiring a specific accompanying belief system. Examples of such values are:

- *Solidarity:* realizing that "an injury to one is an injury to all"
- *Confidence in the power of ordinary people:* trusting grassroots people's ability to learn, struggle, and transform both the world and themselves
- *Openness and commitment to learning:* being skilled at listening, putting effort into study, and being willing to examine oneself and one's actions
- *Being active and useful:* being intentional about one's life; taking responsibility to understand the world and one's place in it, and to work to change things for the better
- *Courage:* being willing to take a stand and act on it—not only in relation to the dominant forces in society, but also in relation to ones family, friends, and comrades
- *Being all-sided:* striving to base judgments on the whole picture, while recognizing that all the information is usually not available
- *Commitment to shared effort:* rejecting privileges, and turning those that one must live with—like being white or male—to the advantage of the struggle
- *Being good at uniting:* seeing differences clearly while, at the same time, uniting wherever possible to broaden the movement and increase its impact
- *Reliability:* having one's words and actions be in accord with each other
- *Seeing clearly and acting appropriately:* being able to find one's bearings independently; making proper distinctions between who is a friend and who is not
- *Being principled, yet flexible:* knowing where one stands, while not being rigid
- *Valuing life:* having a sense of oneness with other people and the environment, and a commitment to their protection

. . .

Values should not be the exclusive property of the religious right, as they often seem to be today. The list above points to the powerful ethical system inherent in the revolutionary struggle to transform society. It also foreshadows the standards that are likely to guide behavior in the future—at least until people develop their moral outlook further under the new conditions of social liberation.

NURTURE THE STRATEGIC ALLIANCE WHERE YOU ARE

. . . While each movement has its own strategic configuration, priorities, and plan of action, the target is the same—a single, integral oppressive system that must be transformed . . . .

Being guided by such an awareness has implications for the way activists conduct their organizing work today. While engaging in a particular struggle, one can keep in mind the larger systemic reality of race, gender, and class oppression. By doing so, one can then look for intersections and ways to connect with other strategic forces. . . .

INCREASE TIES AMONG ORGANIZATIONS

. . . [T]here is much to learn to enable people in groups to function effectively together. The points made there about managing differences while uniting to carry out work applies also to groups of organizations—in the form of coalitions, federations, and fronts. In order for one group to join in united action with another, both groups have to first exist—so the first responsibility is to the health of one's own organization. But once this aspect is taken care of, it is good to find ways to link up with others. Organizations together can magnify each other's impact, deepen understanding of the issues, and learn important lessons on how to keep decision-making power at the base.

The dominant culture works overtime to keep people fragmented—focused solely on their own personal and small group issues. Part of building a movement, and then a movement of movements, is learning how to keep all the many relationships among individuals and organizations working in a positive way—handling differences, allowing space for independence and initiative, and maximizing impact in a way that is flexible and adaptive to changing circumstances.

. . .

In this spirit, initiatives are underway in the United States to "refound the left"—efforts aimed at bringing conscious movement forces into a formation that can contest for power. For our purposes, however, it is the overall outlook activists have in their organizing work that we want to stress. As people engage in social struggles, they can keep in mind the need to bring everything together in an organizational form that can contest for political, economic, and social power. Overcoming white supremacy and racism requires 1) an uncountable number of individual actions every day, 2) a multitude of organizations struggling around the issues that grassroots people deal with daily in their lives, and 3) a wealth of experience flowing out of the specific conditions in every community across the country. It also requires a revolutionary organization—party, alliance, front, or federation—that can concentrate people's vast experience and put it back out to them in a way that keeps the movement growing, struggling, learning, and moving forward together.

Movement activists can strive to embody and represent this outlook in their own lives and organizing work. In doing so, each person becomes a center of initiative. And the old Buddhist saying, "the universe in a grain of sand," becomes "the social justice movement in each individual."

And just as each individual is an integral whole made up of many parts, so too the social justice movement is the same—not just a collection of oppositional trends, tendencies, and competing initiatives, but a movement foreshadowing a different world, a new way of living together.

. . .

N
E
X
T

S
T
E
P
S

135

Interrupting the Cycle of Oppression

The Role of Allies as Agents of Change

Andrea Ayvazian

Many of us feel overwhelmed when we consider the many forms of systemic oppression that are so pervasive in American society today. We become immobilized, uncertain about what actions we can take to interrupt the cycles of oppression and violence that intrude on our everyday lives. One way to overcome this sense of immobilization is to assume the role of an ally. Learning about this role—one that each and every one of us is capable of assuming—can offer us new ways of behaving and a new source of hope. . . .

WHAT IS AN ALLY?

An ally is a member of a dominant group in our society who works to dismantle any form of oppression from which she or he receives the benefit. Allied behavior means taking personal responsibility for the changes we know are needed in our society, and so often ignore or leave to others to deal with. Allied behavior is intentional, overt, consistent activity that challenges prevailing patterns of oppression, makes privileges that are so often invisible visible, and facilitates the empowerment of persons targeted by oppression.

. . .

When we consider the different manifestations of systematic oppression and find ourselves in any of the categories where we are dominant—and therefore receive the unearned advantages that accrue to that position of advantage—we have the potential to be remarkably powerful agents of change as allies. Allies are whites who identify as anti-racists, men who work to dismantle sexism, able-bodied people who are active in the disability rights movement, Christians who combat anti-Semitism and other forms of religious prejudice. Allied behavior usually involves talking to other dominants about their behavior: whites confronting other whites on issues of racism, men organizing with other men to combat sexism, and so on. Allied behavior is clear action aimed at dismantling the oppression of others in areas where you yourself benefit—it is proactive, intentional, and often involves taking a risk.

To tether these principles to everyday reality, just think of the group Parents, Families and Friends of Lesbians and Gays (PFLAG) as the perfect example of allied behavior. PFLAG is an organization of (mainly) heterosexuals who organize support groups and engage in advocacy and education among other heterosexuals around issues of gay and lesbian liberation. PFLAG speakers can be heard in houses of worship, schools, and civic organizations discussing their own commitment to securing gay and lesbian civil rights. Because they are heterosexuals speaking (usually) to other heterosexuals, they often have a significant impact.

The anti-racism trainer Kenneth Jones, an African-American, refers to allied behavior as "being at my back." He has said to me, "Andrea. I know you are at my back on the issue

NEXT STEPS

of race equity—you're talking to white people who cannot hear me on this topic, you're out there raising these issues repeatedly, you're organizing with other whites to stand up to racism. And I'm at your back. I'm raising issues of gender equity with men, I am talking to men who cannot hear you, I've made a commitment to combat sexism."

REDUCING VIOLENCE

. . .

When I ponder the tremendous change a national network of allies can make in this country, I think not only of issues of equity and empowerment, but also of how our work could lead to diminishing levels of violence in our society. Let us consider for a moment the critical connection between oppression and violence on one hand, and the potential role of allied behavior in combating violence on the other.

A major source of violence in our society is the persistent inequity between dominant and targeted groups. Recall that oppression is kept in place by two factors:

1. Ideology, or the propagation of doctrines that purport to legitimize inequality; and
2. Violence (or the threat of violence) by the dominant group against the targeted group.

The violence associated with each form of systemic oppression noticeably decreases when allies (or dominants) rise up and shout a thunderous "No" to the perpetuation of these inequities. Because members of the dominant group are conferred with considerable social power and privilege, they carry significant authority when confronting perpetrators of violence in their own group—when whites deter other whites from using violence against people of color, when heterosexuals act to prevent gay bashing, and so on.

. . .

In our society, oppression and violence are woven together: one leads to the other, one justifies the other. Furthermore, members of the dominant group who are not perpetrators of violence often collude, through their silence and inactivity, with those who are. Allied behavior is an effective way of interrupting the cycle of violence by breaking the silence that reinforces the cycle, and by promoting a new set of behavior through modeling and mentoring.

PROVIDING POSITIVE ROLE MODELS

Not only does allied behavior contribute to an increase in equity and a decrease in violence, but allies provide positive role models that are sorely needed by today's young people. The role of ally offers young people who are white, male, and in other dominant categories a positive, proactive, and proud identity. Rather than feeling guilty, shameful, and immobilized as the "oppressor," whites and other dominants can assume the important and useful role of social change agent. There have been proud allies and change agents throughout the history of this nation, and there are many alive today who can inspire us with their important work.

. . .

I believe that it is difficult for young people to grow up and become something they have never heard of. It is hard for a girl to grow up and become a commercial airline pilot if it has never occurred to her that woman can and do fly jet planes. Similarly, it is hard for young people to grow up and fight racism if they have never met anyone who does.

And there *are* many remarkable role models whom we can claim with pride, and model ourselves after. People like Laura Haviland, who was a conductor on the Underground Railroad and performed unbelievably brave acts while the slavecatchers were right on her trail; Virginia Foster Durr, a southern belle raised with great wealth and privilege who, as an adult, tirelessly drove black workers to and from their jobs during the Montgomery bus boycott; the Rev. James Reeb, who went south during the Mississippi Freedom Summer of 1964 to organize and march; Hodding Carter, Jr., editor and publisher of a newspaper in the Mississippi Delta who used his paper to battle for racial equity and who took considerable heat for his actions. And more: the Grimke sisters, Lucretia Mott, William Lloyd Garrison, John Brown, Viola Liuzzo.

There are also many contemporary anti-racists like Morris Dees, who gave up a lucrative law practice to start the Southern Poverty Law Center and Klan Watch in Alabama and bring white supremacists to trial; Anne Braden, active for decades in the civil rights struggle in Kentucky; Rev. Joseph Bamdt, working within the religious community to make individual churches and entire denominations proclaim themselves as anti-racist institutions. And Peggy McIntosh, Judith Katz, and Myles Horton. And so many others. Why don't our young people know these names? If young people knew more about these dedicated allies, perhaps they would be inspired to engage in more anti-racist activities themselves.

CHOOSING OUR OWN ROLES

We also need to consider our role as allies. . . . In areas where we are dominant, is our struggle for equity and justice evident? When we think about our potential role as allies, we need to recall a Quaker expression: "Let our life be your teaching." The Quakers understand that our words carry only so much weight, that it is our actions, our daily behaviors, that tell the true story.

In my own life I struggle with what actions to take, how to make my beliefs and my behaviors congruent. One small step that has had interesting repercussions over the last decade is the fact that my partner (who is male) and I have chosen not to be legally married until gay and lesbian couples can be married and receive the same benefits and legal protection that married heterosexual couples enjoy. A small step, but it has allowed us to talk with folks at the YMCA about their definition of "family" when deciding who qualifies for their "family plan"; to challenge people at Amtrak about why some "family units" receive discounts when traveling together and others do not; and to raise questions in the religious community about who can receive formal sanction for their loving unions and who cannot. These are not earth-shattering steps in the larger picture, but we believe that small steps taken by thousands of people will eventually change the character of our communities.

. . .

PREPARING FOR THE LONG HAUL

Now I would be the first to admit that personally and professionally the role of ally is often exhausting. I know that it involves challenges—being an ally is difficult work, and it can

NEXT STEPS

often be lonely. We must remember to take care of ourselves along this journey, to sustain our energy and our zest for those ongoing challenges.

We must also remember that it is hard to go it alone: allies need allies. As with any other struggle in our lives, we need supportive people around us to help us to persevere. Other allies will help us take the small, daily steps that will, in time, alter the character of our communities. We know that allied behavior usually consists of small steps and unglamorous work. As Mother Teresa once said: "I don't do any great things. I do small things with great love."

Finally two additional points about us in our role as allies: First, we don't always see the results of our efforts. Sometimes we do, but often we touch and even change lives without ever knowing it. Consequently, we cannot measure our success in quantitative terms. Like waves upon the shore, we are altering the landscape—but exactly how, may be hard to discern.

. . .

Second, there is no such thing as a perfect ally. Perfection is not our goal. When I asked my colleague Kenneth Jones what stood out for him as the most important characteristic of a strong ally, he said simply: "being consistently conscious." He didn't say "never stumbling," or "never making mistakes." He said: "being consistently conscious." And so we do our best: taking risks, being smart, making errors, feeling foolish, doing what we believe is right, based on our best judgment at the time. We are imperfect, but we are steady. We are courageous but not faultless. As Lani Guinier said: "It is better to be vaguely right than precisely wrong." If we obsess about looking good instead of doing good, we will get caught in a spiral of ineffective action. Let's not get side-tracked or defeated because we are trying to be perfect.

. . .

Like most activists, I carry a dream inside me. . . . The dream is that we will create in this country a nonviolent army of allies that will challenge and break the cycle of oppression and usher in a new era of liberation, empowerment, and equity for persons historically targeted by systemic oppression. . . . May we move forward, claiming with pride our identities as allies, interrupting the cycle of oppression, and modeling a new way of behaving and believing.

136

Bridging Differences through Dialogue

Ximena Zúñiga

Building bridges between people from different social backgrounds becomes increasingly important as our society becomes more diverse and stratified. One way we can foster learning and understanding across differences is to bring college students together to talk and learn from each other, to find ways to comunicate, and to understand why it is not always easy to get along or to identify common ground. . . . This essay describes one promising approach for meeting this challenge, intergroup dialogue.

Intergroup dialogue is a face-to-face facilitated conversation between members of two or more social identity groups that strives to create new levels of understanding, relating, and action. The term social identity group refers to group affiliation based on a common status or history in society resulting from socially constructed group distinctions. Examples of groups that have participated in intergroup dialogues on college campuses include men and women; white people, biracial/multiracial people, and people of color; blacks, Latinos and Native Americans; lesbians, gay men, bisexual, and heterosexual people; people from working-, middle-, and upper-class socioeconomic backgrounds; and Christians, Muslims, and Jews. . . .

Intergroup dialogues encourage direct encounter and exchange about contentious issues, especially those associated with issues of social identity and social stratification. They invite students to actively explore the meanings of singular (as men or as women) or intersecting (as men of color or as white women) social identities and to examine the dynamics of privilege and oppression that shape relationships between social groups in our society. In addition, the dialogues build dispositions and skills for developing and maintaining relationships across differences and for taking action for equity and social justice.

. . .

Dialogue groups are co-led by trained facilitators who belong to the participating social identity groups. For example, a white student and a student of color would cofacilitate a cross-race dialogue. The programming strategies used to supervise and train dialogue facilitators vary across campuses. In some institutions, undergraduate students lead the groups after undergoing intensive training. In others, dialogue facilitators are professionals from counseling centers, student activities departments, human relations programs, or intergroup relations programs; or they are graduate students who have received specialized training in counseling, college student development, or social justice education as part of their programs of study. Regardless of the strategies used to train or supervise them, facilitators are expected to lead the dialogue process and to intervene when necessary. As discussed in a book chapter by Ruby Beale, Monita Thompson, and Mark Chesler entitled "Training Peer Facilitators for Intergroup Dialogue Leadership," efforts to prepare and support facilitators include the development of competencies in at least two areas: (1) knowledge and awareness about one's own and others' social identities and histories, and (2) small-group leadership skills, including the ability to lead difficult conversations and constructively explore conflicting needs or "hot" issues. A curricular guide and discussion questions to stimulate dialogue and reflection usually support the work of facilitators and student participants. . . .

WHAT IS THE INTERGROUP DIALOGUE APPROACH?

The intergroup dialogue approach combines experiential learning and dialogic bridge-building methods with critical analysis of socially constructed group differences and the systems of stratification that give rise to intergroup conflicts and social injustice. It explores the causes and effects of group differences through a social justice lens and draws from multidisciplinary perspectives on social identity groups, systems of inequality, and intergroup relations. This approach starts with the proposition that meaningful dialogue and learning across race and other social group boundaries requires an educational practice that intentionally builds upon three interconnected pedagogical processes: sustained communication, critical social awareness, and bridge building. . . .

Sustained Communication. Sustained face-to-face conversations encourage listening and questioning across lines of difference, which in turn fosters mutual understanding of similar and conflicting needs and perspectives. Such communication must be continued over an extended period to allow for the development of reciprocal, active, and committed communication. Dialogic methods and techniques such as the ones described by Helen Fox in *When Race Breaks Out* and Stephen Brookfield and Stephen Preskill in *Discussion as a Way of Teaching: Tools and Techniques for Democratic Classrooms* are helpful to support the development of dispositions and skills that enable participants to listen attentively to each other, talk openly and honestly, appreciate different perspectives, and ask "dumb" or "politically incorrect" questions.

For example, modeling techniques that demonstrate "sensitive intercultural interaction" or methods such as "paired listening," "talking circles," "fishbowls," "circle of voices," and more can encourage authentic voicing, and listening from the very beginning of a dialogue group. As facilitators encourage participants to ask questions and probe deeper, participants begin to take more risks and challenge each other's views more directly. In a white-biracial—multiracial—people of color dialogue, for example, the facilitators may decide to show a short segment from a film by Frances Reid entitled *Skin Deep* to encourage conversation about contentious issues related to race and racism on campus. After a short "free-write" to allow for personal time for thinking and feeling, the facilitators may structure a listening circle to encourage everyone to participate, and then ask, "What about this video feels familiar or surprising to you?" After everyone has responded, the facilitators may invite students to acknowledge what they heard, raise questions, and make comments. For example, after viewing a film like *Skin Deep*, questions about related issues will likely emerge, such as "special-interest floors in the residence halls," "the school's new affirmative action policy," or "examples of white privilege on campus." As David Schoem and his associates note in *Intergroup Dialogue: Deliberative Democracy in School, College, Community and Workplace*, trust in this type of group process only grows and is tested as students feel more free and confident to probe issues, challenge themselves and others, express anger, offer support, and raise difficult or controversial questions.

Critical Social Awareness. Spotlighting the political realities that lead to group differences can stimulate thoughtful conversations across race and other social group boundaries. Dialogue participants must develop both a shared vocabulary and a way to pinpoint the origins and impacts of group differences at the personal, interpersonal, and systemic level. The intergroup dialogue process allows participants to recognize, question, and analyze prevailing beliefs and behaviors that maintain systems of stratification and perpetuate estranged and oppressive relations between groups.

Active learning methods, such as the ones described in a book chapter by Ellen Junn entitled "Experiential Approaches to Enhancing Cultural Awareness" and in the selections in *Teaching for Diversity and Social Justice*, edited by Maurianne Adams, Lee Bell, and Pat Griffin, can gradually encourage intergroup dialogue participants to grapple with the differential impact of systems of privilege and oppression at the personal, community, and societal level. For instance, activities such as "privileged/targeted social identity timeline" or the "critical-incident exercise" take stock of students' experiences growing up as members of privileged (dominant status, more powerful) and targeted (subordinated status, less powerful) social groups. The "power shuffle" examines the impact of social group membership at the personal and community level. Simulation activities such as "star power" can help students recognize the impact of status differentials and power dynamics and make connections to everyday life. Through introspection, encounter, and critical analysis, active learning methods motivate students to become more aware of their own roles in interpersonal, group, and systemic conflicts. With the support of readings from various perspectives, students are encouraged to question their personal biases, to consider alternative perspectives toward a particular issue, and to situate each other's views and experiences in a larger social context.

An example of critical social awareness occurs in cross-race dialogues when the topic of "racial/ethnic separation and self-segregation" is explored. White students often perceive students of color as self-segregating on campus; yet to their surprise, students of color often see things the other way around. They think that white students are doing more of the self-segregation through their fraternities and sororities, intramural activities, study groups, living situations, and other campus activities. In the dialogue, the facilitators might challenge all students to consider what informs their perceptions of others' behaviors and encourage them to explore the interpersonal and institutional factors that may contribute to some of these dynamics. Facilitators ask questions, present relevant concepts or information, validate and acknowledge difficulties and challenges, question misinformation, and invite students to explore some of the reasons behind their perceptions. Such a discussion often sheds light on the extent to which the racial dynamics on campus create a hostile environment for students of color and contribute to their perceived need for "safe spaces." It also becomes apparent to white students that they actually are engaged in self-segregating behavior and that they need to take some responsibility for the campus climate.

Bridge Building. Critical and sustained conversation about issues of social identity and social stratification inevitably highlights conflicting perspectives across and within lines of difference. It also sheds light on the complex dynamics of connection and disconnection that result from estranged or oppressive relationships between members of social groups in the larger society. Such conflicts become valuable opportunities for students to engage in heart-to-heart conversations and discover together some of the underlying and multi-layered sources of tension and disconnection. The intergroup dialogue process begins to build bridges across differences when students can engage in difficult conversations, find value in each other's feelings or perspectives, establish areas of common concern, and be willing to work—separately or together—to counter some of the effects of social injustice.

For example, bridging may occur when a white male student acknowledges his own privileged status with increased self-awareness, openness, and sensitivity to the experience of others and is willing to take some responsibility for the racial climate on campus; or when a woman of color talks about how she experiences race and racism on campus, openly struggles to understand and appreciate some of the experiences of her white counterparts, and then explores ways of working with people from privileged groups to counter injustice.

The bridging process also engages participants in a journey that embraces new visions and possibilities for response. It offers support for exploring new ways of being, relating, and taking action with people across race and other group boundaries. As Patricia Hill Collins argues in "Toward a New Vision: Race, Class, and Gender as Categories of Analysis and Connection," transcending barriers requires that we recognize how our differing experiences with social oppression can compromise our relationships. When we develop empathy and accountability for the experiences of individuals and groups different from our own, everyone benefits. In the intergroup dialogues, these capacities are developed by cultivating a sense of co-responsibility and solidarity across and within lines of difference. Facilitators invite students to "walk the talk" in their personal, student, or work life and identify concrete ways of moving from dialogue to action outside the group. For instance, students may decide to take more courses focusing on racism or sexism, join an organization on campus that is dealing with some of the issues addressed in the dialogue, or become a resident assistant or a student leader to improve the racial or gender climate of their residence hall. By using educational and community practice methods such as the ones described by educators and community activists like John Anner in *Beyond Identity Politics* or http://www.thatway.org/dialogue, students can begin to identify possible actions and resources for working for change and coalition building. . . .

NEXT STEPS

137

Unite and Rebel!

Challenges and Strategies in Building Alliances

Elizabeth (Betita) Martínez

Women of color have come together against violence—and expanded the very meaning of the term—as never before in US history. In their organizing, scholarship, and advocacy work, initiated at the first Color of Violence Conference in 2000, INCITE! Women of Color Against Violence demonstrates the electrifying capacity of women of color to organize against that common enemy across racial and ethnic lines. As we engage this mission more broadly and deeply, we learn more about both the strengths and challenges that confront us in working together toward unity.

Sharing experiences of violence, in one form or another, provides the foundation for alliance-building between women of color. But, as the late and beloved Gloria Anzaldúa said in her book *Making Face, Making Soul/Haciendo Caras*, "Shared oppression by itself does not override the forces that keep us apart." In fact, white supremacy encourages the forces that divide us. "Divide and Conquer" has been a major strategy for maintaining white supremacy for centuries.

We see intensified efforts at division today, as changing demographics promise that whites will be a minority in this country relatively soon. Divisive tactics feature emphasis on job competition between the native-born and immigrants. We also hear the counterattack, accusing people of color of being "racist" toward each other or against whites. This tactic reminds us that we should understand racism to be an entire structure of power relations best called white supremacy. Communities of color rarely have structural power over each other (much less over white people) except in very limited situations such as on the job or in local political structures. At the same time, we can be prejudiced toward each other and act in racist-like ways. This does not mean we have the power to be racists, but such prejudice, such actions can be a serious barrier to alliance-building.

White supremacy not only encourages subtle and not so subtle expressions of racist-type attitudes between women of different colors. It also encourages internalized racist attitudes toward oneself as an individual, and toward one's own group. This too can undermine alliance-building, by fomenting a narrow nationalism intended to restore necessary self-respect in ways that can backfire against long-range, collective goals.

ANTICIPATING CHALLENGES

Working in a group of women that combines different racial or national origins, we should assume problems will develop and strategize how to address them. It helps to think about those problems as rooted in differences of class, race, color (and other physical characteristics), as well as nationality, culture, sexuality, and age. Disability is also an issue; failure to recognize it can generate a sense of apartness, of isolation and indifference. All of these "differences" are linked to historical experience. All are interconnected and cannot be discussed in isolation from each other.

Before looking at each area of difference and its specifics, let's reaffirm our goals. First, we want to build our united strength so as to help transform this society into one of justice and peace for all. We are all in it together, and transforming this society would be a precious achievement for us all. Is anything else more worthwhile?

Second, we should think in terms of building not only coalitions but also alliances. In a coalition, separate groups come together to address a common, usually immediate, single, problem or set of related problems. Coalitions are often necessary and even vital. They have potentially great immediate impact, and can pave the way for alliance-building.

Alliances should be broader in their focus, more profound, and more long-range, more lasting. The forces of white supremacy and imperialism are too strong for us to battle separately. Alliance can bring us together and give greater power to our resistant efforts over the years. Strong alliances make it possible for us to dream of someday seeing a global women of color movement to create a more just global society.

Finally, dealing with our differences and divisions cannot be left to casual concern or spontaneous resolution. It has to be one of our organizational priorities, a clear-cut part of program. That is the basic message of this article.

LEARNING OUR HERSTORIES

As we begin to examine the forces that obstruct alliance-building, we can see that ignorance and lack of understanding about our different communities greatly affect the influence of those forces. To combat the forces of division, we need to learn much more about the history of each community. Today, as Arab and Islamic people, as well as others of Middle Eastern/South Asian backgrounds have become the most recent, most visible victims of extreme racist oppression, we see yet another example of widespread ignorance. How much about the history and struggles of Arab, Islamic, Middle Eastern/South Asian communities is actually known by US-women of color not from these communities? How much is known about the long Palestinian struggle against US-supported Israeli expansion?

For women of color all over the world, the most common and destructive experiences of violence have come from war. In modern times, at least, war has consistently left more women and children dead than soldiers. Here in the United States, we find that women of color have been subjected to racist violence in both similar and different ways. If we look at their different herstories, we find that war is not uncommon.

. . .

STRATEGIES FOR ALLIANCE BUILDING

The similarities and differences in historical experiences of racism mean that women of color have different collective memories of violence, and, therefore, they may relate differently to each other without always realizing it or knowing why. Dissimilar sources of pain may keep us focused on what separates rather than unites. For example, an African American may associate state violence with her color while a Mexican/Latina will associate it with her language or accent.

NEXT STEPS

In addressing these and other challenges, each group of women of color could put together its own lists of do's and don't's based on real-life experiences; we each have different strategies to deal with the challenges, and to expand our strengths. Some will be very general and far-ranging, like the need to understand the different herstories and cultures of each racial group that have been discussed here. Yet, there are more specific rules and procedures centered on establishing mutual respect that can be drawn up.

For example, when a group of women goes to meet or work in a different setting from their own, be very aware of how the women in that unfamiliar setting do things: what are the spoken and unspoken rules, the protocols, the established values for human interchange. Don't be a know-it-all, but don't fail to share everything that might be helpful. Don't be in a hurry, too impatient to listen.

We also say, stick to dialogue. Don't give up, even if it becomes difficult. It's normal. There can be enormous resistance to speaking openly about one group's issues with another. And women are often especially afraid of hurting someone's feelings, stepping on toes, or sounding racist by bringing up feelings that might sound like stereotypes.

The Institute for MultiRacial Justice, whose mission is to help build alliances between peoples of color and combat conflicts, has experience with these barriers and inhibitions. One lesson has been the difficulty of having such dialogue in a large, public gathering. This was what happened at three forums with multicultural panelists in the late 1990s in the Bay Area. At the third session, the panelists included an African American journalist who came close to provoking real discussion when she described the feelings of some African Americans about bilingual education. She was not afraid of being provocative, which is often what we need most. But we often censor ourselves in public spaces. So the Institute tried smaller workshops as a way of facilitating dialogue. At one session, mixed-race participants expressed dissatisfaction with not having their own caucus like the race-specific people. This could be corrected.

What should we do, given the reluctance to speak openly? We must acknowledge our tendency toward silence around race and difference and work on solutions. Role-playing about some divisive issue can open people's eyes and generate discussion. Humor and a few provocative questions can loosen the grip of self-consciousness. It might help to set up a task force to undertake some specific project, like Black/Brown people working together to win more affordable housing.

Culture can also help generate communication and build bridges between different communities, as youth have shown with hip-hop, spoken word, and other forms of cultural expression. It can be a way for women to make fun of the differences or celebrate similarities, as the Latina Theater Lab did together with young Asian women actresses a few years ago in San Francisco. Cultural expression can liberate our alliance-building energy and talents.

Building an alliance comes most easily when it emerges organically from a conflict situation. After the so-called "Rodney King riots" in Los Angeles, as clashes continued between African Americans and Koreans, church leaders from San Francisco's Black community invited their members to meet and talk about the conflict with Koreans and other Asian Americans. Again it was a large public meeting without a collective, in-depth analysis of problems. Still, I felt encouraged that the discussion happened at all.

Let me add one last comment about an elusive problem related to building cross-racial respect and solidarity. There is a kind of spiritual violence that women working together for social justice sometimes inflict on one another. Those with more standing, influence, and power within a group dynamic can unthinkingly do violence to the spirit of someone with less power in the group. To deprecate or humiliate a sister out of competitiveness, or out of habits of domination that sometimes accompany leadership skills and intelligence, is to do a harmful violence to her spirit.

N E X T   S T E P S

This is an insidious kind of personal violence that must never be ignored, for when others say nothing, this second act of violence compounds the damage that's already been done. Silences can feed the cancer of unaddressed conflict, and this has destroyed more than one project, group, or organization. This is a matter of organizational integrity: we cannot righteously continue our struggle, any struggle, without facing it.

Women of color need to act with integrity, speak with honesty, and reject any fear of our differences and conflicts. To transform the goal of unity into a reason for denying conflict, as we sometimes do, is self-defeating. Today, as reactionary forces work to aggravate rather than diminish racism in this society, the times call for courage more than ever. Let us create a stubborn, imaginative, honest, powerful insurgency. Let us counter the enemy forces of divide and conquer with our strategy of unite and rebel!

138

Top 10 Youth Activism Victories in 2007

Nicole McClelland and Kristina Rizga

Anyone who laments that American young people are **apathetic, uninvolved** or **not sufficiently outraged** clearly isn't up on the news.

Luckily, though, we are. The past 12 months have been filled with many great youth organizing successes; some were covered extensively by mainstream media, and some went—sadly—unnoticed. From these extraordinary stories, Wiretap has culled a list of our favorite 10 youth victories of the year. They're not just the events you've heard about, like the hunger strikes at Harvard and Stanford, because the less-attended actions of low-income, low-profile youth groups can be equally triumphant. And they're not just acts of campus activism, either—because half of Americans between the ages of 18 and 25 are **not enrolled in college**. And though there are countless other examples of protest, cooperation, and informed dissent that went on and are still continuing around the country, here are 10 especially inspirational stories that went down this year. Congratulations to these and all other young people who took responsibility and took charge in 2007 to work hard both with their peers and with other groups, who put their energies into action for their communities, and for the world.

ENVIRONMENTAL ACTIVISM: STEPPING IT UP

It's time to go way beyond just switching light bulbs to fight global warming, and this year young people from all over the country proved their commitment to the planet. In February, nearly 600 student groups staged events during the Campus Climate Challenge **Week of Action**. But activists were just getting started, and college campuses were barely the starting point. On April 14, **Step It Up**—the brainchild of a group of young people and environmentalist and author **Bill McKibben**—brought people together at 1,400 locations nationwide demanding that Congress cut carbon emissions 80 percent by 2050. It was such a success that organizers kicked off Step It Up 2 just seven months later and got 14,000 messages sent to Congress and presidential candidates, 80 of whom sent statements or representatives or showed up at events. That same month, at **Power Shift 2007**, 5,500 young activists from across the country got together at the University of Maryland College Park to make Congress change its colors. Over four days in November, participants staged a rally on the Capitol and held more than 300 lobbying meetings to pressure congresspeople to provide more green jobs and greener policies for a greener, brighter, more sustainable future.

SHUTTING TOXIC THINGS DOWN

In a more local, but just as important, triumph for the environment, the members of **Youth United for Community Action**, an organization created and run by youths of color ages 13–30 in the Bay Area, became heroes of their neighborhood and role models for grassroots organizers nationwide when California granted their wish to shut down a hazardous-waste-handling company that had been plaguing the vicinity for more than four decades. YUCA worked to rid its community of Romic Environmental Technologies Corporation, which had been fined for multiple hazardous-waste violations by the California Department of Toxic Substances Control, for 16 years. Now that the state issued the order that Romic close most of its East Palo Alto operations, YUCA and its constituents **can breathe a little easier**—and much more safely.

PRESERVING COMMUNITY LAND AND CULTURE

In another major local victory for the environment, **Save the Peaks**, a coalition formed to protect the **San Francisco Peaks in Arizona**, won a court order that defended the sacred site. For years, the Arizona Snowbowl ski resort has operated on this traditionally holy ground, and in 2004 the US Forest Service approved the company's plans to expand—which included cutting down 74 acres of trees and using treated sewage water to make artificial snow. The plans posed a threat to the ecosystem, the health of surrounding communities, and the religious freedom of the 13 Native American Nations that hold the mountains hallowed. **The Youth of the Peaks** worked together with the coalition, protesting at the foot of the resort to let tourists know the issues surrounding the grounds they're playing on. In March, the 9th Circuit Court **ruled** that the expansion plans be stopped.

On October 17th, the court granted Arizona Snowbowl and the US Forest Service an appeal, which was heard on December 11th. Far from giving up, tribes and young activists in the coalition **attended the case,** and are encouraging others to **take action** as well while the community waits for a decision.

ELEMENTARY EDUCATION NATION

American schools are in deep trouble. More than half of black students in Illinois, Ohio, Michigan, New York, and Pennsylvania attend high schools in which the majority of students do not graduate. Nearly 40 percent of Latino students and 11 percent of white students drop out of high school.

Tired of waiting for politicians and philanthropists, who have pledged for decades to reform education, high school students worked diligently to improve their own schools in 2007. From **Urban Youth Collaborative** and **DRUM** in New York, to **Rethinkers** in New Orleans, to **Youth for Justice** in Los Angeles, youths across the country organized around everything from violence prevention to building eco-friendly, clean bathrooms. The **Detroit Summer Collective** is an especially innovative, all-volunteer-run program. In addition to making a **documentary** in 2007 that looks at the root causes and student-driven solutions to the high drop-out rates, the Collective is transforming the entire city of Detroit by teaching young people how to maintain organic gardens and sell produce to their communities, as well as organizing monthly **city pot lucks** that act as interracial and intergenerational town halls. A democracy can't thrive without informed citizens, and if the world's wealthiest and most powerful onc won't provide a decent K–12 education, these students will bring their communities together to do it.

HIGHER EDUCATION FOR THE MASSES, FOR REAL

Another crucial tool for social mobility in the United States is access to college. According to the **Public Policy Institute of California**, 42 percent of Asians and 40 percent of whites think that the vast majority of people who are qualified to go to college have the opportunity to do so. Why did 82 percent of Latinos and 75 percent of blacks say no? Probably in part because college tuition has been ever **increasing** and throwing **more students** into **debt**. Which is to why the passing of the **College Cost Reduction and Access Act**, the most significant tuition reform bill in 15 years, was an incredible achievement. Students nationwide brought the issue to the attention of both the media and their peers, and worked closely with politicians in swing districts. For two years, **PIRG** and **United States Student Association** have been mobilizing to get college affordability on the congressional agenda. PIRG's Raid on Student Aid campaign generated more than 10,000 phone calls, in addition to lobbying meetings and emails. The very fact that students were vital to getting the legislation passed shows how important they are for change, and now the Act will help generate even more students. Says PIRG's Luke Swarthout, "Without the work of students over the past two years, Congress probably wouldn't prioritize legislation like the College Affordability and Access Act."

Students in Maine scored two victories this year, when their state legislators voted **unanimously** to approve a citizen ballot initiative that will provide a tax credit to all graduates to offset their student loan repayment as long as they stay in Maine. **The League of Young Voters** worked with hundreds of volunteers to gather 73,000 signatures that helped get this unprecedented measure passed.

FREEING THE JENA 6

The day after a few courageous black students at Jena High School in Louisiana sat under a campus tree traditionally claimed by white students, two nooses were **dangling** from it. When white youths assaulted black students later that year, they were tried as juveniles and got away with a slap on the wrist. But when black students retaliated, the district attorney

N
E
X
T

S
T
E
P
S

tried the six 15- to 17-year-olds as adults and charged them with attempted second-degree murder, for which each potentially faced more than 20 years in prison.

A year later, despite mainstream media silence, this story burst into national prominence thanks to the most massive civil-rights-movement **mobilization** since the '60s when over 10,000 college students, activists, and hip-hop artists converged on Jena. Thousands of youths in Jena and **students** on campuses nationwide protested a case that epitomized a long-standing **history of unfair** sentencing of people of color in America. The US has the highest absolute, **per-capita**, and **juvenile rate** of incarceration in the world, with a **tenth of all black men** between ages 20 and 35 in jail or prison. The Jena 6 defense campaign mobilized millions of socially conscious youth, who represent the future leaders in the fight against the persistence of subtle and **not-so-subtle** racism in America. This massive, grassroots-driven campaign **helped overturn** the original sentences of the Jena 6, momentum that could be used to help thousands of other youths of color in America who were tried in the same, broken system to attain justice and re-enter their communities.

FILLING HEALTH CARE NEEDS, POST-KATRINA

In 2005, Shana Griffin and the other members of the New Orleans Women's Health and Justice Initiative thought it would be easy to raise money for a women's health clinic post-Katrina. The devastated city—with few cops, lots of strangers, staggering crime, and limited care—was far from an ideally safe environment for women. "But we got a reality check," she says; donations were far from pouring in. So the Initiative worked together with **INCITE**, a national activist organization of women of color against violence, many of whose members are under 30, meeting up four times a week. The women, who had no experience running a clinic, pooled and applied their applicable respective skills and secured and renovated a space, learned everything they could about the logistics of providing health care, put out calls for and coordinated volunteers, and raised funds. Just a year and a half after the idea was conceived, and "through hard work and sweat," on May 1, 2007, the New Orleans Women's Health Clinic opened. A group of paid staff and volunteers provides everything from prenatal care to reproductive health, sex health, and routine preventative health services four days a week. And the women who labored to provide the much-needed assistance to their peers are working hard to keep it that way.

FAIRER IMMIGRANT WAGES? LOVIN' IT

Two years of organizing and protesting **finally paid off** in April for the **Student/Farmworker Alliance**, which, in partnership with the immigrant-laborer-led **Coalition of Immokalee Workers**, finally achieved results from its long-standing boycott against McDonald's. The company agreed to pay an extra penny per pound to its tomato suppliers, nearly doubling the wages of the impoverished pickers in Florida. A month later, the parent company of Taco Bell, which struck a similar deal with the activists in 2005 after four years of their perseverance, announced that it would expand the agreement to its four other chains, including Pizza Hut and A&W.

Thanks to some long, tireless efforts, some of the country's biggest fast-food chains have improved their wage standards. But despite an amazingly successful year, the SFA and CIW aren't about to take a break now: They're still hard at work on getting **Burger King** to join the much-needed movement.

ANTI-WAR MOBILIZATION: JUST SAY "HELL NO"

First, the 29-year-old **Army Lt. Ehren Watada**—who was willing to serve in Afghanistan or any other conflict he didn't consider so morally and politically unconscionable—**refused** to deploy to Iraq; his actions subsequently **inspired** increasing numbers of soldiers to mobilize for an end of the war in Iraq. Then, on Friday, November 16th, the **Youth Against War and Racism** called for a high school walkout. More than 1,000 students from the Puget Sound area alone left their classes that morning to protest the war and a problem even closer to the students: military recruiters in schools. Participating in the **walkout** were more than 125 students from Foster High School in Tukwila district, Washington, where military recruiters prey on students, 71 percent of whom are from low-income families. When several Foster teachers who supported the protest were **threatened** with disciplinary action, **students rallied** to their support; ultimately, teachers weren't punished. Though many expect youths, especially low-income, to support and even fight in the war, they proved this year, **once again**, that they are not going to take it sitting down.

DON'T FORGET DARFUR

Three years after the United States classified the situation in Darfur, Sudan, as a genocide, students are still organizing to make sure the crucial cause **doesn't get ignored**. In April, two thousand white-clad activists played dead in Boston Commons for five minutes of silence. In December, thousands of students worldwide fasted to raise money to fight rape in the African region. **STAND**, a student anti-genocide coalition, helped organize those events and hundreds of others this year. Students have been **signing petitions, lobbying representatives**, staging events—anything to keep Darfur in the news. And the coverage has paid off. Companies have started divesting in ventures that support the government that allows the genocide to continue, and awareness is at an all-time high. As long as the violence rages, so will the activism. "The world has been slow to act to protect the people of Darfur," said STAND student director Scott Warren, "so students across the globe will be taking protection into their own hands."

Here's to anticipation for what a new generation of young activists will accomplish in 2008.

NEXT STEPS

Permission Acknowledgments

Ahmad, A. (2008). "Oral History of Adam Fattah." In L. Cristillo (ed.), *This is Where I Need to Be: Oral Histories of Muslim Youth in NYC*. New York: Student Initiative Press/CPET, Teachers College, Columbia University. pp. 27–30. Reprinted with permission of the Student Initiative Press.

Anzaldúa, G. (1994). "Allies." *Sinister Wisdom* (52), 47–52. Reprinted by permission of Anzaldúa Literary Trust.

Anzaldúa, G. (1999). *La Frontera: The New Mestiza*, 2nd edition. San Francisco: Aunt Lute Books. pp. 99–120. Selections of "La Conciencia de la Mestiza: Towards a New Consciousness." From *Borderlands/La Frontera: The New Mestiza*. Copyright © 1987, 1999, 2007 by Gloria Anzaldúa. Reprinted by permission of Aunt Lute Books.

Arminio, J. (2000). "Waking up White: What It Means to Accept Your Legacy, for Better or Worse." *About Campus* 5 (1), 29–30. Reprinted with permission of John Wiley & Sons, Inc.

Ashley and Deborah. (2007). "How to Curse in Sign Language." In J. Mooney (ed.), *The Short Bus: A Journey beyond Normal*. New York: Henry Holt. From pages 106–122, "How to Curse in Sign Language" from *The Short Bus: A Journey beyond Normal* by Jonathan Mooney. Copyright © 2007 by Jonathan Mooney. Reprinted by arrangement with Henry Holt and Company, LLC.

Aviles, Q. (2007). "My Tongue is Divided into Two." In R. Suarez, F. McCount, T. Miller (eds), *How I Learned English: 55 Accomplished Lessons in Language and Life*. Cambridge, MA: South End Press. pp. 175–181. By permission of the author.

Ayvazian, A. (2004). "Interrupting the Cycle of Oppression: The Role of Allies as Agents of Change." In P. S. Rothenberg (ed.), *Race, Class and Gender in the United States*, 6th edition. New York: Worth. pp. 598–604. By permission of the author.

Ayvazian, A., Tatum, B. D. (2004). "Women, Race and Racism: A Dialogue in Black and White." In J. V. Jordan, M. Walker, L. M. Hartling (eds), *The Complexity of Connection*. New York: The Guilford Press. pp. 147–163. Reprinted with permission of the publisher.

Bauer, M. (2008). "Migrant Tomato Workers Face Chronic Abuse." Southern Poverty Law Center. Available at http://www.splcenter.org/news/item.jsp?aid=308& printable=1. Reprinted by permission of SPLC and the author.

Bell, J. (1995). "Understanding Adultism: A Key to Developing Positive Youth-Adult Relationships." Available at http://www.freechild.org/bell.htm. Reprinted with permission of John Bell, Youth-Build USA.

Bell, L. A. (2007). "Theoretical Foundations for Social Justice Education." In M. Adams, L. A. Bell, P. Griffin (eds), *Teaching for Diversity and Social Justice*, 2nd edition. New York: Routledge. pp. 2–6. Permission to reprint granted by the editors.

Bernards, R. (2000). "Pioneers in Dialogue: Jews Building Bridges." In M. Adams, W. J. Blumenfeld, R. Castañeda, H. W. Hackman, M. L. Peters, X. Zúñiga (eds), *Readings for Diversity and Social Justice*. New York: Routledge. pp. 191–198. Reprinted with permission of the author.

Bernstein, A. (June 4, 2004). "Women's Pay: Why the Gap Remains a Chasm." *Business Week* (online). Reprinted by permission of the publisher.

Blumenfeld, W. J. (1992). "How Homophobia Hurts Everyone." In *Homophobia: How We All Pay the Price*. Boston: Beacon Press. pp. 1–12. Reprinted by permission of the author.

Blumenfeld, W. J. (2006). "Christian Privilege." *Equity and Excellence in Education* 39 (3), 195–210. Reproduced by permission of Taylor and Francis, Inc.

Bowen, G. (1998). "An Entire Rainbow of Possibilities." In L. Feinberg (ed.), *Trans Liberation: Beyond Pink or Blue*. Boston: Beacon Press. pp. 63–66. From *Trans Liberation* by Leslie Feinberg. Copyright © 1998 by Leslie Feinberg. Reprinted by permission of Beacon Press, Boston.

and Institutions. New York: Routledge. pp. 331–340. Reproduced by permission of Taylor and Francis/Routledge, Inc.

Deihl, M., Ochs, R. (2009). "Biphobia" (updated version). Original (1989/90) in *Empathy* 2 (1), 15–19. Reprinted by permission of the authors.

Dohrn, B. (2000). "'Look Out Kid, It's Something You Did': The Criminalization of Children." In *The Public Assault on America's Children: Poverty, Violence, and Juvenile Injustice*. New York: Teachers College Press. Reprinted with permission of the publisher.

Durkin, K. (2008). "Police Make Life Hell for Youth of Color." Available at http://www.workers.org/print.php. Copyright © 2008 Workers World. Verbatim copying and distribution of this entire article is permitted in any medium without royalty provided this notice is preserved.

Dyson, M. E. (2005). "Unnatural Disasters: Race and Poverty." In *Come Hell or High Water: Hurricane Katrina and the Color of Disaster*. New York: Basic Civitas Books. pp. 1–10, 142–145. From *Come Hell or High Water* by Michael Eric Dyson. Copyright © 2005 by Michael Eric Dyson. Reprinted by permission of CIVITAS, a member of Perseus Books Group.

Echo-Hawk, W. R. (1993). "Native American Religious Liberty: Five Hundred Years after Columbus." *American Indian Culture and Research Journal* 17 (3), 33–45. Reprinted from the *American Indian Culture and Research Journal*, volume 17, number 3, by permission of the American Indian Studies Center, UCLA. © 2008 Regents of the University of California.

Eck, D. (2001). *A New Religious America*: *How a "Christian Country" has Become the World's Most Religiously Diverse Nation*. San Francisco: HarperSanFrancisco. pp. 297–306, 316–320, and 320–328, as specified, from *A New Religious America* by Diana L. Eck. Copyright © 2001 by Diana L. Eck. Reprinted by permission HarperCollins Publishers.

Erevelles, N. (2006). "Disability in the New World Order." In INCITE! Women of Color against Violence (eds), *Color of Violence: The INCITE! Anthology*. Cambridge, MA: South End Press. pp. 25–31. Reprinted with permission of the publisher.

Evans, N. J., Washington, J. (2009). "Becoming an Ally: A New Examination" (updated version). Original (1991) in N. J. Evans. V. A. Wall (eds), *Beyond Tolerance: Gays, Lesbians, and Bisexuals on Campus*. Alexandria, VA: American College Personnel Association. pp. 195–204. Reprinted with permission from the American College Personnel Association (ACPA), One Dupont Circle, NW at the Center for Higher Education, Washington, D.C., 20036.

Fayad, M. (1994). "The Arab Woman and I." In J. Kadi (ed.), *Food for Our Grandmothers: Writings by Arab American and Arab Canadian Feminists*. Cambridge, MA: South End Press. pp. 170–172. Reprinted with permission of the publisher.

Fennell, J. (n.d.). *Girl Hate*. Unpublished manuscript. Reprinted with permission of the author.

Gansworth, E. (2003). "Identification Pleas." In M. Moore (ed.), *Genocide of the Mind*. New York: Thunder's Mouth Press/Nations Books. pp. 269–279. From *Genocide of the Mind* by MariJo Moore. Copyright © 2003 Amerinda. Reprinted by permission of Nation Books, a member of Perseus Books Group.

Garcia, J., Lardner, J., Zeldin, C. (2008). *Up to Our Eyeballs*. New York: The New Press. Copyright © 2008 by Demos: A Network for Ideas and Actions. Text originally appeared in *Up to Our Eyeballs* by Jose Garcia, James Lardner and Cindy Zeldin. Published by The New Press, 2008. Reprinted by permission of The New Press.

Giecek, T. S. with United for a Fair Economy. (2007). *Teaching Economics as If People Mattered: A High School Curriculum Guide to the New Economy*. Boston: United for a Fair Economy. Reprinted with permission of the publisher.

Gilbert, M. (2002). *The Routledge Atlas of the Holocaust*, 3rd edition. New York: Routledge. Reproduced by permission of Taylor and Francis/Routledge, Inc.

Gilbert, M. (2003). *The Routledge Atlas of Jewish History*, 6th edition. New York: Routledge. Reproduced by permission of Taylor and Francis/Routledge, Inc.

Gokhale, D. (2005). "The InterSEXion: A Vision for a Queer Progressive Agenda." *InterSEXion* (online journal). Available at http://intersexion.org/?q=node/1. Reprinted with permission of intersexion.org, an Online Queer Progressive Community. This essay was written by Deepali Gokhale, with valuable input from many conversations with members of the queer community in Atlanta, GA.

Goodman, E. (March 24, 2006). "Taking the Gay Insults Personally," *Boston Glove* (online). From *The Washington Post*, March 24, 2006. © 2006 *The Washington Post*. All rights reserved. Used by permission and protected by the Copyright Laws of the United States. The printing, copying, redistribution, or retransmission of the Material without express written permission is prohibited.

Jeung, R. (2007). "Faith-Based Multiethnic Tenant Organizing: The Oak Park Story." In P. Hondag-neu-Sotelo (ed.), *Religion and Social Justice for Immigrants*. New Brunswick, NJ: Rutgers University Press. pp. 59–72. Hondagneu-Sotelo, Pierrette, ed. *Religion and Social Justice for Immigrants*. Copyright © 2007 by Rutgers, The State University. Reprinted by permission of Rutgers University Press.

Johnson, A. G. (1997). "Patriarchy." In *The Gender Knot: Unraveling Our Patriarchal Legacy*. Philadelphia: Temple University Press. Material excerpted from "Patriarchy, the System: An It, Not a He, a Them, Or An Us" from *The Gender Knot: Unraveling Our Patriarchal Legacy* by Allan G. Johnson. pp. 75–79, 84–87, 89–92. Used by permission of Temple University Press. © 1997 by Allan G. Johnson. All rights reserved.

Johnson, A. G. (2006). "The Social Constructions of Difference," "What is Privilege," and "What Can We Do?" In *Privilege, Power, and Difference*, 2nd edition. New York: McGraw Hill. pp. 17–40, 125–153. Reprinted with permission of The McGraw-Hill Companies.

Jones, L. A. (2004). "As Much Love as You Can Muster." In S. Klein, J. Kemp (eds), *Reflections from a Different Journey: What Adults with Disabilities Wish All Parents Knew*. Blacklick, OH: McGraw-Hill Professional. pp. 179–183. Material reproduced with permission of The McGraw-Hill Companies.

Joshi, K. Y. (2006). "Religious Oppression" [author's revised version]. *New Roots in America's Sacred Ground*. New Brunswick, NJ: Rutgers University Press. pp. 118–144. Printed with permission of author and Rutgers University Press.

Katz, J. (2006). "Violence against Women Is a Men's Issue." In *The Macho Paradox*. Naperville, IL: Sourcebooks. pp. 5–18. Copyright © 2006 by Jackson Katz. Reprinted from the book *The Macho Paradox* with permission of its publisher, Sourcebooks.

Kaye/Kantrowitz, M. (1996). "Jews in the U.S.: Rising Costs of Whiteness." In X. Thompson, X. Tyagi (eds), *Names We Call Home*. New York: Routledge. pp. 121–137. Reproduced by permission of Taylor and Francis/Routledge, Inc.

Kimmel, M. S. (1994). "Masculinity as Homophobia: Fear, Shame and Silence in the Construction of Gender Identity." In H. Brod, M. Kaufman (eds), *Theorizing Masculinities*. Thousand Oaks, CA: Sage. pp. 119–141. Reprinted with permission of the publisher.

Kingsley, J. (2004). "What I'd Tell That Doctor." In S. Klein, J. Kemp (eds), *Reflections from a Different Journey: What Adults with Disabilities Wish All Parents Knew*. Blacklick, OH: McGraw-Hill Professional. pp. 13–14. Excerpt from "Who We Are" in *Count On Us: Growing Up with Down Syndrome*, copyright © 1994 by Jason Kingsley and Mitchell Levitz, reprinted by permission of Houghton Mifflin Harcourt Publishing Company.

Kirk, G., Okazawa-Rey, M. (2001). "Identities and Social Locations: Who Am I? Who Are My People?" In *Women's Lives: Multicultural Perspectives*, 2nd edition. New York: McGraw Hill. pp. 49–59. Reprinted with permission of The McGraw-Hill Companies.

Kivel, P. (1992). "Adultism." In A. Creighton with P. Kivel (ed.), *Helping Teens Stop Violence: A Practical Guide for Counselors, Educators, and Parents*. Alameda, CA: Hunter House. pp. 54–61. From "Adultism" by Paul Kivel. *Helping Teens Stop Violence* © 1990, 1992 by Allan Creighton, Battered Women's Alternatives, and Oakland Men's Project. To order, call (800) 266–5592, fax (510) 865–4295, or visit our website at www.hunterhouse.com. Reprinted by permission of the publisher.

LaDuke, W. (2005). "Introduction." In J. Baumgardner, A. Richards (eds), *Grassroots*. New York: Farrar, Straus, and Giroux. pp. xi–xv. "Introduction" by Winona LaDuke from *Grassroots: A Field Guide to Feminist Activism* by Jennifer Baumgardner and Amy Richards. Introduction copyright © by Winona LaDuke. Reprinted by permission of Farrar, Straus and Giroux, LLC.

Landesman, P. (January 25, 2004). "The Girls Next Door." *The New York Times* (online). From *The New York Times*, January 25, 2004. © 2004 *The New York Times*. All rights reserved. Used by permission and protected by the Copyright Laws of the United States. The printing, copying, redistribution, or retransmission of the material without express written permission is prohibited.

Larabee, M. (1993). "Elder Liberation Draft Policy Statement." *Older and Bolder* (5), 19–24. Copyright © 1993 Rational Island Publishers. Reprinted with permission of the publisher.

Leondar-Wright, B. (2005). *Class Matters: Cross-Class Alliance Building for Middle-Class Activists*. Gabriola, BC, Canada: New Society. Reprinted with permission of the publisher.

Lie, A. (2002). "Passing Realities." In J. Nestle, C. Howell, R. Wilchins (eds), *GenderQueer: Voices from beyond the Sexual Binary*. Los Angeles: Alyson Books. pp. 166–170. Reprinted with permission of the publisher.

Lippy, C. H. (2005). "Christian Nation or Pluralistic Culture: Religion in American Life." In J. A. Banks, C. A. M. Banks (eds), *Multicultural Education: Issues and Perspectives*, 5th edition. New York: Wiley. pp. 110–131. Copyright © 2005 John Wiley. Reproduced with permission of John Wiley & Sons, Inc.

Lipsitz, G. (1998). *The Possessive Investment in Whiteness: From Identity to Politics*. Philadelphia: Temple University Press. pp. 1–23. Materials excerpted from "The Possessive Investment in Whiteness" from *The Possessive Investment in Whiteness: From Identity to Politics* by George Lipsitz. Used by permission of Temple University Press. © 2006 by Temple University. All rights reserved.

Lorber, J. (1994). "'Night to His Day': The Social Construction of Gender." In *Paradoxes of Gender*. New Haven, CT: Yale University Press. pp. 13–36. Copyright © 1994 Yale University Press. Reprinted with permission of the publisher.

Love, B. J. (2000). "Developing a Liberatory Consciousness." In M. Adams, W. J. Blumenfeld, R. Castañeda, H. W. Hackman, M. L. Peters, X. Zúñiga (eds), *Readings for Diversity and Social Justice*. New York: Routledge. pp. 470–474. Permission of author.

Mantsios, G. (2007). "Class in America—2006." In P. Rothenberg (ed.), *Race, Class, and Gender in the United States: An Integrated Study*, 7th edition. New York: Worth. pp. 182–197. Reprinted with permission of the author.

Markee, P. (1993). "What Allies of Elders Can Do." *Older and Bolder* (5), 93–94. Copyright © 1993 Rational Island Publishers. Reprinted with permission of the publisher.

Martinez, E. (2006). "Unite and Rebel! Challenges and Strategies in Building Alliances." In INCITE! Women of Color against Violence (eds), *Color of Violence: The INCITE! Anthology*. Cambridge, MA: South End Press. pp. 191–195. Reprinted with permission of the publisher.

McClellan, N., Rizga, K. (2007). "Top 10 Youth Activism Victories in 2007." Available at http://www.wiretapmag.org/activism/43351/. Reprinted with permission from WiretapMag.org.

Meyerowitz, J. (2002). "Introduction." In *How Sex Changed: A History of Transsexuality in the United States*. Cambridge, MA: Harvard University Press. pp. 1–9. Reprinted by permission of the publisher from *How Sex Changed: A History of Transsexuality in the United States* by Joanne Meyerowitz, pp. 1–2, 4–9, Cambridge, Mass.: Harvard University Press, copyright © 2002 by the President and Fellows of Harvard College.

Morgan, R. (2007). "Connect: A Web of Words." In E. Ensler (ed.), *A Memory, a Monologue, a Rant and a Prayer*. New York: Villard. pp. 119–120. Reprinted by permission of the author.

Morgenson, G. (July 20, 2008). "The Debt Trap: Given a Shovel, Americans Dig Deeper into Debt." *The New York Times*. Available at http://www.nytimes.com/2008/07/20/business/20debt.html?pagewanted=print. From *The New York Times*, July 20, 2008. © 2008 *The New York Times*. All rights reserved. Used by permission and protected by the Copyright Laws of the United States. The printing, copying, redistribution, or retransmission of the material without express written permission is prohibited.

Nasir, N. S., Al-Amin, J. (2006). "Creating Identity-Safe Spaces on College Campuses for Muslim Students." *Change: The Magazine of Higher Learning*, March/April Special Issue, 23–27. Reprinted with permission of the Helen Dwight Reid Educational Foundation. Published by Heldref Publications, 1319 Eighteenth St., NW, Washington, D.C., 20036–1802. Copyright © 2006.

National Latina Institute for Reproductive Health. (2007). "National Statement on Healthcare For All." Available at http://www.raisingwomensvoices.net/PDF-docs/JumpstartLinkFiles/2bNLIRH HealthcareforAllstatement-FINAL-2.20.08.pdf. Reprinted with permission of National Latina Institute for Reproductive Health.

National Network for Immigrant and Refugee Rights. (2008). *Over-Raided, Under Siege: U.S. Immigration Laws and Enforcement Destroy the Rights of Immigrants*. By the Human Rights Immigrant Community Action Network, an initiative of the National Network for Immigrant and Refugee Rights. Retrieved February 14, 2008, from http://www.nnirr.org/resources/docs/UnderSiege_web2.pdf. Reprinted with permission of the author.

Null, G. (2000). "The Gulf War's Troubling Legacy." In P. Munson (ed.), *Stricken: Voices from the Hidden Epidemic of Chronic Fatigue Syndrome*, New York: Haworth Press. pp. 173–183. Permission of the author.

Oesterreich, H., Knight, M. (2008). "Facilitating Transitions to College for Students with Disabilities from Culturally and Linguistically Diverse Backgrounds." *Intervention in School and Clinic* 43 (5), 300–304. Reprinted with permission of the publisher.

Oliver, M. L., Shapiro, T. M. (2006). "Race, Wealth, and Equality." In *Black Wealth/White Wealth: A New Perspective on Racial Inequality*. New York: Routledge. pp. 11–33. Reproduced by permission of Taylor and Francis/Routledge, Inc.

Pelkey, L. (2001). "In the LD Bubble." In P. Rodis, A. Garrod, M. L. Boscardin (eds), *Learning Disabilities and Life Stories*. Boston: Allyn and Bacon. pp. 17–28. From Pano Rodis, Andre Garrod, and Mary Lynn Boscardin *Learning Disabilities and Life Stories,* 1/e. Published by Allyn and Bacon/Merrill Education, Boston, MA. Copyright © 2001 by Pearson Education. Reprinted by permission of the publisher.

Peltier, L. (1992). *My Life is My Sun Dance: Prison Writings*. New York: St. Martin's Griffin. Reprinted with permission of the publisher.

Peters, M., Castañeda, C., Hopkins, L., McCants, A. (2008). *Recognizing Ableist Beliefs and Practices and Taking Action as an Ally*. Unpublished manuscript. University of Massachusetts, Amherst, MA. Printed by permission of the authors.

Pharr, S. (1996). "Reflections on Liberation." In *In the Time of the Right*. Little Rock, AR: Chardon Press. pp. 87–122. By permission of the author.

Pliner, S. M., Johnson, J. R. (2004). "Historical, Theoretical and Foundational Principles of Universal Instructional Design in Higher Education." *Equity and Excellence in Education* 37 (2), 105–113. Reproduced by permission of Taylor and Francis, Inc.

Quindlen, A. (November 24, 2008). "The Loving Decision." *Newsweek* (online). Reprinted by permission of International Creative Management, Inc. Copyright © 2008 by Anna Quindlen for *Newsweek*.

Romero, M. (1992). *Maid in the U.S.A.* New York: Routledge. Reproduced by permission of Taylor and Francis/Routledge, Inc.

Root, M. P. P. (1996). *50 Experiences of Racially Mixed People*. Available at http://www.drmariaroot.com/doc/50Experiences.pdf. Reprinted with permission of the author.

Roppolo, K. (2003). "Symbolic Racism, History and Reality: The Real Problem with Indian Mascots." In M. Moore (ed.). *Genocide of the Mind*. New York: Thunder's Mouth Press/Nations Books. pp. 187–198. From *Genocide of the Mind* by MariJo Moore. Copyright © 2003 Amerinda. Reprinted by permission of Nation Books, a member of Perseus Books Group.

Russo, A., Spatz, M. (n.d.). *Stop the False Race/Gender Divide: A Call to Action*. Unpublished manuscript. Reprinted by permission of the authors.

Saint. (2005). "Why Can't Everybody Fear Me like That?" In Teachers College's Student Press Initiative (eds), *Killing the Sky: Oral Histories from Horizon Academy, Rikers Island*. New York: Student Press Initiative. By permission of the Student Press Initiative. www.publishspi.org.

Sazama, J. (1994). *Tips and Guidelines: For Allies to Young People*. Somerville, MA: Youth on Board. By permission of Youth on Board, 58 Day Street, Somerville, MA 02144, info@youthonboard.org, (p) 617–741–1242, (f) 617–623–4359.

Schlosser, L. Z. (2003). "Christian Privilege: Breaking a Sacred Taboo." *Journal of Multicultural Counseling and Development* 31, 195–210. Reprinted from *Journal of Multicultural Counseling and Development* 31, 195–210. © 2003 The American Counseling Association. Reprinted with permission. No further reproduction authorized without written permission from the American Counseling Association.

Schmidt, P. (September 28, 2007). "At the Elite Colleges—Dim White Kids." *The Boston Globe*. © 2007 The Globe Newspaper Company.

Semple, K. (October 16, 2008). "A Somali Influx Unsettles Latino Meatpackers." *The New York Times*, pp. A1, A21. From *The New York Times*, October 16, 2008. © 2008 *The New York Times*. All rights reserved. Used by permission and protected by the Copyright Laws of the United States. The printing, copying, redistribution, or retransmission of the material without express written permission is prohibited.

Serano, J. (2007). "Trans Woman Manifesto." In *Whipping Girl: A Transsexual Woman on Sexism and the Scapegoating of Femininity*. Emeryville, CA: Seal Press. pp. 11–20. From *Whipping Girl* by Julia Serano. Copyright © 2007 by Julia Serano. Reprinted by permission of Seal Press, a member of Perseus Books Group.

Sheets, D. J. (2005). "Aging with Disabilities: Ageism and More." *Generations* 29 (3), 37–41. Reprinted with permission from "Aging with Disabilities: Ageism and More," volume 29, issue 3, pages 37–41 (Fall). Copyright © 2005. American Society on Aging, San Francisco, California. www.asaging.org.

Smith, A. (2006). "Heteropatriarchy and the Three Pillars of White Supremacy: Rethinking Women of Color Organizing." In INCITE! (eds), *The Color of Violence: The INCITE! Anthology*. Cambridge, MA: South End Press. pp. 66–73. Reprinted with permission of the publisher.

Smith, C. (2007). "The Personal is Political." In *The Cost of Privilege*. Fayetteville, NC: Camino Press. pp. 374–382. Reprinted with permission of the author.

Solis y Martinez, D. E. (2008). "Mestiza/o Gender: Notes towards a Transformative Masculinity." In T. Hoppe (ed.), *Beyond Masculinity: Essays by Queer Men on Gender and Politics*. Available at http://www.beyondmasculinity.com/articles/martinez.php. Reprinted with permission of the author.

Spade, D. (2006). "Mutilating Gender." In S. Stryker, S. Whittle (eds), *The Transgender Studies Reader*. New York: Routledge/Taylor & Francis Group. pp. 315–332. Reproduced by permission of Taylor and Francis/Routledge, Inc.

Stryker, S. (2008). "Transgender Liberation." In *Transgender History*. Berkeley, CA: Seal Press/Perseus Books Group. pp. 59–75. From *Transgender History* by Susan Stryker. © 2008 Susan Stryker. Reprinted by permission of Seal Press, a member of Perseus Books Group.

Takaki, R. (1993). *A Different Mirror: A History of Multicultural America*. Boston: Little, Brown. pp. 1–17. From *A Different Mirror* by Ronald Takaki. Copyright © 1993 by Ronald Takaki. By permission of Little, Brown & Company.

Tatum, B. D. (1997). *Why Are All the Black Kids Sitting Together in the Cafeteria? And Other Conversations about Race*. New York: Basic Books. From *Why Are All the Black Kids Sitting Together in the Cafeteria?* By Beverly Daniel Tatum. Copyright © 1997 Beverly Daniel Tatum, Ph.D. Reprinted by permission of Basic Books, a member of Perseus Books Group.

Walker, A. (2007). "To Stop the Violence against Women." In E. Ensler (ed.), *A Memory, a Monologue, a Rant and a Prayer*. New York: Villard. pp. 173–175. Reprinted with permission of the publisher.

Wendell, S. (1996). "The Social Construction of Disability." In *The Rejected Body*. New York: Routledge. pp. 36–56. Reproduced by permission of Taylor and Francis/Routledge, Inc.

Williams, B. (2001). "What's Debt Got to Do with It?" In J. Goode, J. Maskovsky (eds), *The New Poverty Studies: The Ethnography of Power, Politics, and Impoverished People in the United States*. New York: New York University Press. pp. 79–101. Reprinted with permission of the publisher.

Williams, D. R. (2006). "From Pearl Harbor to 9/11: Lessons from the Internment of Japanese American Buddhists." In S. Prothero (ed.), *A Nation of Religions: The Politics of Pluralism in Multireligious America*. Durham: University of North Carolina Press. pp. 63–78. From *A Nation of Religions: The Politics of Pluralism in Multireligious America* by Stephen Prothero. Copyright © 2006 by the University of North Carolina Press. Used by permission of the publisher. www.uncpress.unc.edu.

Williams, P. (1997). "The Emperor's New Clothes." In *Seeing a Color Blind Future: The Paradox of Race*. New York: Noonday Press, Farrar, Strauss & Giroux. pp. 3–16. "The Emperor's New Clothes" from *Seeing a Color Blind Future: The Paradox of Race* by Patricia J. Williams. Copyright © 1997 by Patricia J. Williams. Reprinted by permission of Farrar, Straus and Giroux, LLC. "The Emperor's New Clothes" from *Seeing a Color Blind Future: The Paradox of Race*, copyright © 1997 by Patricia J. Williams. Reprinted by permission of Brandt & Hochman Literary Agents, Inc.

Wolanin, T. R. (2005). "Students with Disabilities: Financial Aid Policy Issues." *NASFFA Journal of Student Financial Aid* 35 (1), 17–26. Reprinted with permission of the publisher.

Yalowitz, B. (2003). "Billy Yalowitz." In C. Thompson, E. Shaefer (eds), *White Men Challenging Racism*. Durham, NC: Duke University Press. pp. 164–171. Copyright, 2003, Duke University Press. All rights reserved. Used by permission of the publisher.

Young, I. M. (1990). "Five Faces of Oppression." In *Justice and the Politics of Difference*. Princeton, NJ: Princeton University Press. pp. 39–65. Young, Iris M; *Justice and the Politics of Difference*. © 1990 Princeton University Press Reprinted by permission of Princeton University Press.

Zawam, H. (2008). "Oral History of Hagar Omran." In L. Cristillo (ed.), *This is Where I Need to Be: Oral Histories of Muslim Youth in NYC*. New York: Student Initiative Press/CPET, Teachers College, Columbia University. pp. 57–60. Reprinted with permission of the publisher.

Zúñiga, X. (2003). "Bridging Differences through Intergroup Dialogue." *About Campus* 7 (6), 8–16. Reprinted with permission of John Wiley & Sons, Inc.

About the Editors

Maurianne Adams is Professor of Education Emerita, Social Justice Education Concentration, School of Education at the University of Massachusetts Amherst. She teaches graduate foundations of social justice courses and consults internationally on faculty leadership, student development, and program implementation for social justice education. She co-edited and (co)wrote chapters for *Teaching for Diversity and Social Justice* (second edition, 2007) and its companion volume *Readings for Diversity and Social Justice* (2000). She co-edited *Strangers and Neighbors: Relations Between Blacks and Jews in the United States* (1999), edited *Promoting Diversity in the College Classroom* (1992), and has published numerous chapters and articles on social justice educational theory and pedagogy. She is editor of *Equity & Excellence in Education.*

Lee Anne Bell is Professor and Barbara Silver Horowitz Director of Education at Barnard College, Columbia University. Her recent writing describes the Storytelling Project, a model she developed with artists and educators for teaching about race and racism through storytelling and the arts. This project is described in articles in *Anthropology and Education Quarterly, Teachers College Record* and *Storytelling, Self and Society.* She is currently completing a book on the Storytelling Project titled *Storytelling for Social Justice.* She is co-editor and (co) author of chapters in *Teaching for Diversity and Social Justice* (second edition, 2007).

Warren J. Blumenfeld is Assistant Professor in the Department of Curriculum and Instruction at Iowa State University specializing in multicultural education and queer studies. His books include *Homophobia: How We All Pay the Price* (1992), *Looking at Gay and Lesbian Life* (1993), *Butler Matters: Judith Butler's Impact on Feminist and Queer Studies* (2005), and *Investigating Christian Privilege and Religious Oppression in the United States* (2009). He co-edited *Readings for Diversity and Social Justice* (2000).

Carmelita (Rosie) Castañeda is Assistant Professor, Department of Educational Studies, University of Wyoming in Laramie. She is author of *Teaching and Learning in Diverse Classrooms: Faculty Reflections on their Experiences and Pedagogical Practices of Teaching Diverse Students* (2002) and co-editor of *Readings for Diversity and Social Justice* (2000). She received the Latina leadership award, La Superación Latina (2007), given by Students for Campus and Community Chicana Awareness and La Radio Montañesa Voz de la Gente (KOCA) Bilingual Radio Station, Wyoming.

D. Chase James Catalano is a doctoral student in social justice education, University of Massachusetts Amherst. He is co-author of "Transgender Oppression Curriculum Design" for *Teaching for Diversity and Social Justice* (second edition, 2007). His research focuses on FtM issues in higher education, gender, and (trans)masculinity. He co-founded Transgender Issues Leadership Trainings (TILT) with Davey Shlasko, which provides higher education consulting for trans inclusion.

Keri DeJong is a doctoral student in social justice education, University of Massachusetts Amherst. She is an experienced intergroup dialogue facilitator, focusing on issues of race and ethnicity. She currently works in student affairs with young adults in higher education. Her doctoral research is focused on adultism, critical liberation theory, and intergroup dialogue.

Heather W. Hackman is Associate Professor in the Department of Human Relations and Multicultural Education at St Cloud State University and teaches courses in critical multicultural education, social justice education, race and racism in the United States, queer issues in the United States, and social change theory. She also trains nationally on issues of racism and white privilege in schools, sexism in education, and LGBT issues in P–12 settings. She co-edited *Readings for Diversity and Social Justice* (2000).

Larissa Hopkins is a doctoral student in social justice education, University of Massachusetts Amherst. Her research is focused on the social and academic experiences of low-income students at small elite liberal arts institutions. She works as a Learning Specialist and Consumer Manager at the Office of Disability Services at the University of Massachusetts, Amherst.

Khyati Y. Joshi is Associate Professor in the Sammartino School of Education at Fairleigh Dickinson University in Teaneck, New Jersey. She is author of *New Roots in America's Sacred Ground: Religion, Race, and Ethnicity in Indian America* (2006), which received the National Association for Multicultural Education's Philip C. Chinn Book Award in 2007. She co-edited *Understanding Religious Oppression and Christian Privilege* (2009) and *Asian Americans and the New South* (2009), and co-wrote "Religious Oppression Curriculum Design" in *Teaching for Diversity and Social Justice* (second edition, 2007). Dr. Joshi provides consultation and professional development for educational institutions on topics related to immigrants in schools, race in education, and religion and public schools.

Barbara J. Love is Associate Professor in the Social Justice Education Concentration at the University of Massachusetts Amherst. She consults internationally on organizational and individual empowerment and transformation, works with schools and school systems, and consults with college faculty and administration throughout the United States. She consults with organizations in North America, the Caribbean, Europe, and Africa on issues of diversity and inclusion. She co-wrote the chapter "Ageism and Adultism Curriculum Design" in *Teaching for Diversity and Social Justice* (second edition, 2007) and has written book chapters and articles on social justice pedagogy and critical race theory.

Madeline L. Peters is Director of Disability Services at the University of Massachusetts Amherst. She has been teaching, training, and consulting in diversity and human relations since 1986. Her research focuses on ableism and disability, learning disabilities and issues of double jeopardy. She co-wrote "Ableism Curriculum Design" for *Teaching for Diversity and Social Justice* (second edition, 2007), co-edited *Readings for Diversity and Social Justice* (2000), and as a disability advocate has won several lawsuits and one national lawsuit for the disabled.

Davey Shlasko is a trainer and consultant who teaches skills for building socially just communities and, particularly, for transgender liberation. Davey earned hir M.Ed. in Social Justice Education and is founder of Think Again Training and co-founder with Chase Catalano of Transgender Issues Leadership Trainings (/TILT/). Ze published "Queer (*v.*) pedagogy" in *Equity & Excellence in Education* (2005) and co-wrote "Transgender Oppression Curriculum Design" for *Teaching for Diversity and Social Justice* (second edition, 2007). Ze currently works with the Transgender Economic Empowerment Initiative in San Francisco.

Ximena Zúñiga is Associate Professor of Education, Social Justice Education Concentration, School of Education, University of Massachusetts Amherst. Her current activities include a four-year multi-institutional action research effort aimed at studying the impact of race and gender intergroup dialogues on college students. She is co-editor of *Multicultural Teaching in the University* (1993), *Readings for Diversity and Social Justice* (2000) and *Intergroup Dialogue in Higher Education: Meaningful Learning About Social Justice* (2007). Recent articles address racism, immigration and globalization issues in anti-racist education, reflective practice methods in preparing intergroup dialogue facilitators, and learning outcomes and engagement processes in intergroup dialogues. She also consults widely with faculty, student affairs and community leaders on social justice education and dialogic pedagogies and methods.